Read 91-113 ? Know Week 1 Reading
Read 91-114 & 120-137

522-79

661-684

West's Law School
Advisory Board

JESSE H. CHOPER
Professor of Law,
University of California, Berkeley

DAVID P. CURRIE
Professor of Law, University of Chicago

YALE KAMISAR
Professor of Law, University of San Diego
Professor of Law, University of Michigan

MARY KAY KANE
Professor of Law, Chancellor and Dean Emeritus,
University of California,
Hastings College of the Law

LARRY D. KRAMER
Dean and Professor of Law, Stanford Law School

WAYNE R. LaFAVE
Professor of Law, University of Illinois

JONATHAN R. MACEY
Professor of Law, Yale Law School

ARTHUR R. MILLER
Professor of Law, Harvard University

GRANT S. NELSON
Professor of Law,
University of California, Los Angeles

JAMES J. WHITE
Professor of Law, University of Michigan

LEGAL PROTECTION OF THE ENVIRONMENT

Second Edition

By

Craig N. Johnston
Professor
Lewis & Clark College

William F. Funk
Professor
Lewis & Clark College

Victor B. Flatt
A.L. O'Quinn Chair in Environmental Law Professor
University of Houston

AMERICAN CASEBOOK SERIES®

THOMSON
——★—— ™
WEST

Mat # 40605311

American Casebook Series and West Group are trademarks registered in the U.S. Patent and Trademark Office.

© West, a Thomson business, 2005
© 2007 Thomson/West
    610 Opperman Drive
    P.O. Box 64526
    St. Paul, MN 55164–0526
    1–800–328–9352

Printed in the United States of America

ISBN: 978–0–314–18125–1

TEXT IS PRINTED ON 10% POST
CONSUMER RECYCLED PAPER

To my wife, Jane, and children, Michael, Alison and Dan

To Judge James Oakes,
who first taught me environmental law

and

For Oscar

*

Preface

There is too much environmental law to be captured in any one book or course. Thus, every environmental law book must make choices about what to cover and what not to cover, what to emphasize and what not to emphasize. This book tries to cover the broad range of federal environmental law—the law that protects the environment.

It emphasizes a small number of federal statutes:

- the National Environmental Policy Act (NEPA), because it continues to play a major role in governing how federal agencies must act when they affect the environment, and it generates a significant amount of litigation brought by environmental groups;

- the Clean Water Act (CWA), the Clean Air Act (CAA), and the Resource Conservation and Recovery Act (RCRA), because they are the trinity of federal regulatory statutes that are intended to protect the water, the air, and the ground, respectively, from polluting activities;

- the Comprehensive Environmental Response, Compensation and Liability Act (CERCLA or Superfund), because it is a relatively unique remedial statute and one that has had massive impacts on the management of hazardous wastes; and

- the Endangered Species Act, because it is the most uncompromising federal environmental statute, has raised a number of problems in its implementation, and generates a large amount of litigation.

Most of these statutes have enforcement provisions by which governmental authorities or citizens can enforce the statutory or regulatory requirements on violators. This will be another area of emphasis.

This is a lot, so there must be things that are left out. Primarily what is left out is discussion of the theoretical and policy issues that underlie environmental statutes and their implementation in regulations. The authors are not averse to those issues, but the focus of this book is to portray the current status of environmental law. The introductory chapter will provide a short introduction to the primary theoretical and policy issues, but an in-depth appraisal we leave to an upper level course.

This book also limits its coverage of the constitutional, administrative, and common law aspects of environmental law as separate areas of study. Again, these are important, and the introductory chapter provides material on those subjects, but we leave fuller discussion of these matters to courses in constitutional law, administrative law, and torts.

Nevertheless, each of these subjects, and especially administrative law, can become inextricably intertwined with substantive environmental law, the practice of which almost invariably involves the work of administrative agencies. Consequently, in the course of the various chapters on different environmental law topics there will be some substantial exposure to these topics.

Acknowledgments

We would like to acknowledge Devra Davis, who has allowed us to use an excerpt from "When Smoke Ran Like Water." We would also like to acknowledge Chris Grady and Charles Irvine for their research assistance.

*

Summary of Contents

	Page
PREFACE	v
ACKNOWLEDGMENTS	vii
TABLE OF CASES	xxi

Chapter 1. Introduction **1**
   I. Introduction 1
  II. Some Perspectives on Environmental Law 2
 III. The Constitution and Environmental Law 35
 IV. Administrative Law Issues 79

Chapter 2. NEPA **91**
   I. Introduction to NEPA 91
  II. Overview of NEPA and the NEPA Process 92
 III. Is an EIS Required? 100
 IV. Is the EIS Adequate? 120
  V. State Environmental Policy Acts 133
 VI. The Effects of NEPA 134

Chapter 3. The Clean Water Act **138**
   I. Introduction 138
  II. Jurisdiction 139
 III. The Federal/State Relationship 159
 IV. Substantive Standards 171

Chapter 4. Clean Air Act **222**
   I. The Problem of Air Pollution 222
  II. The Clean Air Act—Overview 241
 III. The National Ambient Air Quality Standards ("NAAQS")
     Program 243
 IV. The Clean Air Act—Direct Controls on Sources 287
  V. The Clean Air Act—General Enforcement and Permits for
     Regulated Stationary Sources 358
 VI. The Clean Air Act—Mobile Sources 379
 VII. The Clean Air Act—Acid Deposition Control and the Use of
     Market Based Controls 388

Chapter 5. Resource Conservation and Recovery Act **393**
   I. Overview and Jurisdiction 393
  II. The Regulatory Program 412

Chapter 6. Regulatory Enforcement **426**
   I. Introduction 426

Page

  II. Investigations --- 426
 III. Enforcement Options -- 428
 IV. Federalism Issues in the Enforcement Context -------------------- 469
  V. Citizen Suits --- 475

Chapter 7. Comprehensive Environmental Response, Compensation and Liability Act ------------------------------- **522**
   I. Overview and Jurisdiction --- 522
  II. EPA Response-- 525
 III. Private Party Cost—Recovery and Contribution -------------------- 579

Chapter 8. Protection of Particular Natural Resources------- **601**
   I. The Endangered Species Act of 1973 -------------------------------- 601
  II. Protecting Wetlands --- 666
 III. The Surface Mining Control and Reclamation Act of 1977 ------- 725

Chapter 9. International Environmental Law ------------------- **748**
   I. Introduction --- 748
  II. An Overview of International Law ----------------------------------- 748
 III. The Emergence of International Environmental Law ------------- 755
 IV. Trade and the Environment-- 780

GLOSSARY OF ACRONYMS--- 817
INDEX --- 825

Table of Contents

_____

	Page
PREFACE	v
ACKNOWLEDGMENTS	vii
TABLE OF CASES	xxi
Chapter 1. Introduction	**1**
I. Introduction	1
II. Some Perspectives on Environmental Law	2
A. History of Environmental Law	2
B. Types of Regulations	6
C. Theoretical Issues	10
i. Public Goods	11
Notes and Comments	13
ii. Cost/Benefit Analysis	15
Notes and Comments	20
iii. Risk Analysis	20
Notes and Comments	23
iv. The Polluter Pays Principle	24
v. Sustainable Development	24
vi. The Precautionary Principle	26
vii. Environmental Ethics	30
Notes and Comments	32
viii. Environmental Justice	32
Notes and Comments	35
III. The Constitution and Environmental Law	35
A. Authority for Environmental Laws	35
Hodel v. Virginia Surface Mining and Reclamation Association, Inc.	39
Hodel v. Indiana	42
Notes and Comments	46
B. Constitutional Limitations on Environmental Laws	48
1. Tenth Amendment	48
2. The Eleventh Amendment	49
3. The Takings Clause	50
Notes and Comments	53
C. Constitutional Limitations on State Laws	54
1. The Supremacy Clause	54
2. The Dormant Commerce Clause	56
D. Constitutional Limitations on Bringing Lawsuits	58
Lujan v. Defenders of Wildlife	59
Notes and Comments	68
Massachusetts v. Environmental Protection Agency	69
Notes and Comments	78

Page

IV. Administrative Law Issues ---- 79
  A. Rulemaking ---- 79
  B. Adjudication ---- 80
  C. Presidential Oversight ---- 81
  D. Judicial Review ---- 82
    1. Obtaining Review ---- 82
      a. Preclusion of Review ---- 83
      b. APA Requirements for Review ---- 83
        i. Zone of Interests ---- 83
        ii. Finality ---- 84
        iii. Exhaustion of Administrative Remedies ---- 86
      c. Common Law Requirements for Review ---- 87
        i. Issue Exhaustion and Waiver ---- 87
        ii. Ripeness ---- 88
    2. The Scope of Judicial Review ---- 88

Chapter 2. NEPA ---- **91**
  I. Introduction to NEPA ---- 91
  II. Overview of NEPA and the NEPA Process ---- 92
    A. Process for Determining Whether an EIS Is Required ---- 93
      1. Statutory and Functional Equivalence Exemptions ---- 93
      2. Categorical Exclusions ---- 94
      3. Environmental Assessments ---- 98
    B. The EIS Process ---- 98
      1. Scoping ---- 99
      2. Notice and Publication ---- 99
    C. Enforcing NEPA's Requirements (an Introduction) ---- 99
  III. Is an EIS Required? ---- 100
    A. Is it a Major Action? ---- 100
      Kleppe v. Sierra Club American Electric Power System v. Sierra Club ---- 101
      Notes and Comments ---- 109
    B. Is it Federal? ---- 110
      Winnebago Tribe of Nebraska v. Ray ---- 110
      Notes and Comments ---- 113
    C. Does it Significantly Affect the Quality of the Human Environment ---- 113
      Grand Canyon Trust v. Federal Aviation Administration ---- 115
      Notes and Comments ---- 119
  IV. Is the EIS Adequate? ---- 120
    A. Environmental Effects ---- 120
      Robertson v. Methow Valley Citizens Council ---- 121
      Notes and Comments ---- 128
    B. Alternatives Consideration ---- 129
    C. Mitigation ---- 130
      Robertson v. Methow Valley Citizens Council ---- 130
      Notes and Comments ---- 132
  V. State Environmental Policy Acts ---- 133

Page

VI. The Effects of NEPA 134
  Notes and Comments 136

Chapter 3. The Clean Water Act **138**
  I. Introduction 138
  II. Jurisdiction 139
    A. Addition of a Pollutant 140
      Catskill Mountains Chapter of Trout Unlimited, Inc. v. City of New York 140
      Notes and Comments 143
    B. Navigable Waters 147
      Idaho Rural Council v. Bosma 148
      Notes and Comments 150
    C. Point Source 151
      United States v. Plaza Health Laboratories, Inc. 152
      Notes and Comments 157
  III. The Federal/State Relationship 159
    A. How States Become Authorized 159
      Natural Resources Defense Council, Inc. v. U.S. EPA 160
      Notes and Comments 164
    B. EPA Oversight 166
      Natural Resources Defense Council, Inc. v. U.S. EPA 167
      Notes and Comments 170
  IV. Substantive Standards 171
    A. Technology–Based Standards 171
      Weyerhaeuser Co. v. Costle 172
      Notes and Comments 180
    B. Water Quality–Based Requirements 187
      1. How Water Quality Standards Are Set 187
        Notes and Comments 190
      2. How Water Quality Standards Are Implemented for Point Sources 192
        Arkansas v. Oklahoma 193
        Notes and Comments 198
  V. Other Water Quality–Based Programs Under the CWA 201
    A. § 401 Certifications 201
      PUD No. 1 of Jefferson County v. Washington Dept. of Ecology 202
      Notes and Comments 209
    B. Sections 208 and 319 211
    C. The TMDL Program 212
      Pronsolino v. Nastri 214
      Notes and Comments 220

Chapter 4. Clean Air Act **222**
  I. The Problem of Air Pollution 222
  II. The Clean Air Act—Overview 241
  III. The National Ambient Air Quality Standards ("NAAQS") Program 243
    A. What Is a Criteria Pollutant? 243
      Massachusetts v. Environmental Protection Agency 243
      Notes and Comments 251

                                                                Page
III. The National Ambient Air Quality Standards ("NAAQS")
     Program—Continued
     B. How Is a National Ambient Air Quality Standard Estab-
        lished? 252
        Whitman v. American Trucking Associations, Inc. 262
        Notes and Comments 265
     C. How Are the National Ambient Air Quality Standards
        Met?—State Implementation Plans 266
        Notes and Comments 268
            1. What About the Transport of Criteria Pollutants? 269
               *Appalachian Power Company v. Environmental Protec-
               tion Agency* 269
               Notes and Comments 282
               Environmental Protection Agency 282
               Notes and Comments 284
     D. What Happens When the States Don't Meet the NAAQS—
        Non-compliance 285
        Notes and Comments 286
IV. The Clean Air Act—Direct Controls on Sources 287
     A. Introduction to Stationary Source Controls 287
     B. New Source Performance Standards 290
            1. Jurisdiction 290
               Wisconsin Electric Power Company v. Reilly 290
               Notes and Comments 298
            2. Performance Standard 299
               *Lignite Energy Council v. U.S. Environmental Protec-
               tion Agency* 299
               Questions and Notes 302
     C. New Source Review (Both Nonattainment New Source
        Review (NNSR) and Prevention of Significant Deteriora-
        tion (PSD)) 303
            1. Jurisdiction 304
               *Chevron, U.S.A., Inc. v. Natural Resources Defense
               Council, Inc.* 304
               Notes and Comments 310
               New York v. U.S. Environmental Protection Agency 313
               New York v. Environmental Protection Agency 328
               Notes and Comments 334
            2. Substantive Requirements 336
               a. Nonattainment New Source Review 336
               b. Prevention of Significant Deterioration 336
                  Notes and Comments 338
     D. National Emission Standards for Hazardous Air Pollutants 339
        *National Mining Ass'n v. United States Environmental Protection
        Agency* 339
        Notes and Comments 349
     E. The Visibility Program 351
        Utility Air Regulatory Group v. Environmental Protection Agency 352
        Notes and Comments 357
V. The Clean Air Act—General Enforcement and Permits for
   Regulated Stationary Sources 358
     A. What Is Required for a State Permit Program to Be
        Approved? 360

Page

V. The Clean Air Act—General Enforcement and Permits for
Regulated Stationary Sources—Continued
*Public Citizen, Inc. v. United States Environmental Protection
Agency* -- 360
Notes and Comments --- 366
B. EPA Oversight of Approved Programs ------------------ 367
*Alaska Department of Environmental Conservation v. Environ-
mental Protection Agency* --- 367
Notes and Comments --- 378
VI. The Clean Air Act—Mobile Sources ------------------------------ 379
Notes and Comments --- 388
VII. The Clean Air Act—Acid Deposition Control and the Use of
Market Based Controls --- 388
A. SO$_2$ Emission Limitation Program ------------------------- 390
B. NOx Emission Limitation Program --------------------------- 391
C. The Use of Market Based Trading Systems --------------- 392

Chapter 5. Resource Conservation and Recovery Act --------- 393
I. Overview and Jurisdiction -- 393
A. What Is a "Solid Waste"? ------------------------------------- 394
American Mining Congress v. U.S. EPA --------------------- 396
Notes and Comments --- 402
B. What Is a "Hazardous Waste"? ------------------------------- 408
Notes and Comments --- 410
II. The Regulatory Program --- 412
A. Generator Requirements --------------------------------------- 412
Notes and Comments --- 416
B. Requirements for Treatment, Storage and Disposal Facili-
ties (TSDs) -- 416
Notes and Comments --- 424

Chapter 6. Regulatory Enforcement ----------------------------- 426
I. Introduction -- 426
II. Investigations -- 426
III. Enforcement Options --- 428
A. EPA–Lead Civil Actions in Court ----------------------------- 429
Weinberger v. Romero–Barcelo --------------------------------- 429
Notes and Comments --- 435
United States v. The Municipal Authority of Union Township ------ 436
Notes and Comments --- 442
B. Administrative Enforcement ----------------------------------- 443
Southern Pines Associates v. United States --------------- 443
Notes and Comments --- 446
Notes and Comments --- 457
C. Criminal Enforcement -- 459
United States v. Weitzenhoff ------------------------------------ 459
Notes and Comments --- 467
IV. Federalism Issues in the Enforcement Context ----------------- 469
Harmon Industries, Inc. v. Browner --------------------------- 469
Notes and Comments --- 474
V. Citizen Suits -- 475
A. Notice --- 477

Page

V. Citizen Suits—Continued

B. Standing --- 477
Friends of the Earth v. Laidlaw Environmental Services ----------- 478
Notes and Comments --- 483
C. The Gwaltney Doctrine --------------------------------------- 487
Gwaltney of Smithfield, Ltd. v. Chesapeake Bay Foundation, Inc. 487
Notes and Comments --- 493
Friends of the Earth, Inc. v. Laidlaw Environmental Services ------ 497
Notes and Comments --- 503
D. The Effect of Prior Governmental Enforcement Actions ---- 505
E. Attorney Fees --- 508
Hensley v. Eckerhart --------------------------------------- 509
Buckhannon Board and Care Home, Inc. v. West Virginia Department of Health and Human Resources -------------------------------- 511
Notes and Comments --- 519

Chapter 7. Comprehensive Environmental Response, Compensation and Liability Act -------------------------------- 522
I. Overview and Jurisdiction --------------------------------------- 522
II. EPA Response-- 525
A. Liable Parties -- 526
1. Owner/Operator Liability ------------------------------- 527
a. Ownership Liability---------------------------------- 527
New York v. Shore Realty Corp. --------------------- 527
Notes and Comments-------------------------------- 528
b. Operator Liability --------------------------------- 531
United States v. Bestfoods--------------------------- 531
Notes and Comments-------------------------------- 537
2. Arrangers for Disposal or Treatment----------------- 541
United States v. Wade ------------------------------ 542
Notes and Comments-------------------------------- 544
B. Scope of Liability--- 547
United States v. Chem–Dyne Corp. ----------------------- 547
O'Neil v. Picillo-- 551
Notes and Comments--- 554
C. Defenses -- 556
Notes and Comments--- 561
A Note on the Brownfields Program------------------------- 563
D. A Quick Overview of the Cleanup Process----------------- 564
E. Settlement -- 568
United States v. Cannons Engineering Corp. -------------- 573
Notes and Comments--- 579
III. Private Party Cost—Recovery and Contribution -------------- 579
Cooper Industries, Inc. v. Aviall Services, Inc.----------------- 581
Atlantic Research Corp. v. United States ---------------------- 587
Notes and Comments--- 595

Chapter 8. Protection of Particular Natural Resources------- 601
I. The Endangered Species Act of 1973 --------------------------- 601
A. Outline of the Act--- 602
B. Section 4 --- 602
1. Listing -- 603
a. Endangered or Threatened------------------------ 603

Page

I. The Endangered Species Act of 1973—Continued
        Notes and Comments 604
        b. "A Significant Portion of its Range" 606
           Defenders of Wildlife v. Norton 606
           Notes and Comments 609
        c. "Species" Includes "Subspecies" 609
        d. "Species" Includes Distinct Population Segments 610
           National Association of Home Builders v. Norton 611
           Notes and Comments 617
     2. Critical Habitat 619
     3. Recovery 622
     4. The Procedures 622
        Notes and Comments 624
  C. Section 7 625
     1. The Affirmative Obligation 626
     2. The Procedural Requirements 627
        Thomas v. Peterson 629
        Lane County Audubon Society v. Jamison 633
        Newton County Wildlife Association v. Rogers 637
        Questions and Comments 639
     3. The Substantive Requirements 640
        Gifford Pinchot Task Force v. United States Fish & Wildlife Service 641
        Notes and Comments 644
     4. Exemptions 646
        Notes and Comments 647
        Problem 648
  D. Section 9 648
    Babbitt v. Sweet Home Chapter of Communities for a Great Oregon 649
    Notes and Questions 661
  E. Section 10 663
  F. Section 11 665
    Problem 665

II. Protecting Wetlands 666
  A. Section 404 of the Clean Water Act 667
     1. What Waters are Covered? 668
        United States v. Riverside Bayview Homes, Inc. 669
        Notes and Comments 673
        Solid Waste Agency of Northern Cook County v. United States Army Corps of Engineers 673
        Notes and Comments 679
        Rapanos v. United States 681
        Notes and Comments 696
     2. What Activities are Covered? 698
        National Mining Association v. U.S. Army Corps of Engineers 699
        Notes and Comments 702
     3. Exceptions from the Permit Requirement 705
     4. The 404 Permit 706
        a. The 404(b)(1) Guidelines and the Public Interest Review 707

Page

II. Protecting Wetlands—Continued
           Fund for Animals, Inc. v. Rice ---- 710
           Notes and Comments ---- 716
      b. General Permits and Alternative Procedures --- 717
         i. Nationwide Permits ---- 717
         ii. Other General Permits and Letters of Permission ---- 720
           Notes and Comments ---- 721
  B. The Swampbuster Program ---- 723
III. The Surface Mining Control and Reclamation Act of 1977 ---- 725
  A. Background ---- 725
  B. SMCRA's Provisions ---- 729
    Notes and Comments ---- 731
  C. Issues ---- 732
    1. Federalism Issues ---- 732
      Haydo v. Amerikohl Mining, Inc. ---- 734
      Molinary v. Powell Mountain Coal Company ---- 737
      Notes and Comments ---- 741
    2. Mountaintop-removal/Valley Fill Mining ---- 741
      Notes and Comments ---- 745
    3. Enforcement Issues ---- 745

Chapter 9. International Environmental Law ---- **748**
I. Introduction ---- 748
II. An Overview of International Law ---- 748
  A. Hard Law ---- 749
    1. Treaties ---- 749
    2. Customary International Law ---- 750
    3. General Principles of Law Recognized by Civilized Nations ---- 751
  B. Soft Law ---- 751
  C. Enforcement of International Law ---- 752
    Notes and Questions ---- 753
III. The Emergence of International Environmental Law ---- 755
  A. Transboundary Air Pollution ---- 755
  B. UN Conference on the Human Environment—The "Stockholm Conference" ---- 756
  C. Between Stockholm and Rio ---- 757
  D. UN Conference on Environment and Development—"Rio Earth Summit" ---- 758
    Notes and Questions ---- 758
  E. Global Climate Change ---- 759
    1. Climate Change Overview (excerpted from Climate Change Information Kit published by UNEP and UNFCCC 2002) ---- 759
    2. Climate Change and International Environmental Law ---- 761
      a. The United Nations Framework Convention on Climate Change ---- 762
      b. Obligations under the UNFCCC ---- 762

Page

III. The Emergence of International Environmental Law—Continued

           c. The Kyoto Protocol ------------------------------- 763
           d. Obligations Under the Kyoto Protocol------------ 772
           e. Kyoto Protocol Compliance Mechanisms -------- 773
                i. Land Use, Land–Use Change, and Forestry 773
               ii. Clean Development Mechanism --------------- 775
             iii. Joint Implementation----------------------- 775
             iv. Emissions Trading------------------------- 776
           f. Kyoto Protocol Enforcement---------------------- 776
           Notes and Questions---------------------------------- 777
    F. Next Steps in International Climate Change Law and
        Policy --- 779
IV. Trade and the Environment----------------------------- 780
    A. The World Trade Organization----------------------- 782
        1. The WTO Dispute System ----------------------- 783
        2. "Like Products"------------------------------- 785
        Notes and Questions----------------------------- 786
        3. Health, Safety, and Environmental Exceptions to
            GATT Requirements----------------------------- 786
        Notes and Questions----------------------------- 789
        Notes and Questions----------------------------- 790
        Notes and Questions----------------------------- 794
        Notes and Questions----------------------------- 797
        4. The Effect of International Environmental Agreements on WTO Requirements ----------------------- 797
        5. The SPS and TBT Agreements ------------------ 799
        Notes and Questions---------------------------- 813

GLOSSARY OF ACRONYMS--- 817
INDEX --- 825

*

Table of Cases

The principal cases are in bold type. Cases cited or discussed in the text are roman type. References are to pages. Cases cited in principal cases and within other quoted materials are not included.

Abbott Laboratories v. Gardner, 387 U.S. 136, 87 S.Ct. 1507, 18 L.Ed.2d 681 (1967), 85, 88

Aceto Agr. Chemicals Corp., United States v., 872 F.2d 1373 (8th Cir.1989), 529, 546

Acker v. E.P.A., 290 F.3d 892 (7th Cir. 2002), 86

ACORN v. Edwards, 81 F.3d 1387 (5th Cir. 1996), 53

Adams Fruit Co., Inc. v. Barrett, 494 U.S. 638, 110 S.Ct. 1384, 108 L.Ed.2d 585 (1990), 540

Ailor v. City of Maynardville, Tennessee, 368 F.3d 587 (6th Cir.2004), 504

Air Brake Systems, Inc. v. Mineta, 357 F.3d 632 (6th Cir.2004), 86

Akzo Coatings, Inc. v. Aigner Corp., 30 F.3d 761 (7th Cir.1994), 590

Alabama Power Co. v. Costle, 636 F.2d 323, 204 U.S.App.D.C. 51 (D.C.Cir.1979), 144, 310

Alabama Rivers Alliance v. F.E.R.C., 325 F.3d 290, 355 U.S.App.D.C. 390 (D.C.Cir.2003), 210

Alabama–Tombigbee Rivers Coalition v. Department of Interior, 26 F.3d 1103 (11th Cir.1994), 603

Alabama, State of v. United States E.P.A., 911 F.2d 499 (11th Cir.1990), 94

Alaska Dept. of Environmental Conservation v. E.P.A., 540 U.S. 461, 124 S.Ct. 983, 157 L.Ed.2d 967 (2004), 86, **367,** 448

Alaska, Dept. of Environmental Conservation v. United States E.P.A., 244 F.3d 748 (9th Cir.2001), 448

Alcan Aluminum Corp., United States v., 315 F.3d 179 (2nd Cir.2003), 530, 556

Alcan Aluminum Corp., United States v., 892 F.Supp. 648 (M.D.Pa.1995), 556

Alcan Aluminum Corp., United States v., 990 F.2d 711 (2nd Cir.1993), 555

Alcan Aluminum Corp., United States v., 964 F.2d 252 (3rd Cir.1992), 525, 545, 555

Alexander v. Choate, 469 U.S. 287, 105 S.Ct. 712, 83 L.Ed.2d 661 (1985), 33

Alexander v. Sandoval, 532 U.S. 275, 121 S.Ct. 1511, 149 L.Ed.2d 517 (2001), 33

Allsteel, Inc. v. United States E.P.A., 25 F.3d 312 (6th Cir.1994), 86, 375, 446

Alsea Valley Alliance v. Evans, 161 F.Supp.2d 1154 (D.Or.2001), 603

American Forest and Paper Ass'n v. United States E.P.A., 137 F.3d 291 (5th Cir. 1998), 171

American Iron and Steel Institute v. E.P.A., 526 F.2d 1027 (3rd Cir.1975), 178

American Min. Congress v. U.S. E.P.A. (AMC II), 907 F.2d 1179, 285 U.S.App. D.C. 173 (D.C.Cir.1990), 404

American Min. Congress v. U.S. E.P.A. (AMC I), 824 F.2d 1177, 263 U.S.App. D.C. 197 (D.C.Cir.1987), **396**

American Paper Institute, Inc. v. U.S. E.P.A., 890 F.2d 869 (7th Cir.1989), 171

American Petroleum Institute v. U.S. E.P.A. (API II), 216 F.3d 50, 342 U.S.App.D.C. 159 (D.C.Cir.2000), 406

American Petroleum Institute v. U.S. E.P.A. (API I), 906 F.2d 729, 285 U.S.App.D.C. 35 (D.C.Cir.1990), 404

American Trucking Associations, Inc. v. E.P.A., 283 F.3d 355, 350 U.S.App.D.C. 254 (D.C.Cir.2002), 266

American Trucking Associations, Inc. v. United States E.P.A., 175 F.3d 1027, 336 U.S.App.D.C. 16 (D.C.Cir.1999), 265

American Wildlands v. Browner, 260 F.3d 1192 (10th Cir.2001), 192, 198

Amoco Production Co. v. Village of Gambell, AK, 480 U.S. 531, 107 S.Ct. 1396, 94 L.Ed.2d 542 (1987), 435

A & N Cleaners and Launderers, Inc., United States v., 854 F.Supp. 229 (S.D.N.Y. 1994), 561

A & N Cleaners and Launderers, Inc., United States v., 788 F.Supp. 1317 (S.D.N.Y. 1992), 561

Appalachian Power Co. v. E.P.A., 249 F.3d 1032, 346 U.S.App.D.C. 38 (D.C.Cir.2001), **269**

Appalachian Power Co. v. E.P.A., 208 F.3d 1015, 341 U.S.App.D.C. 46 (D.C.Cir. 2000), 86

Arizonans for Official English v. Arizona, 520 U.S. 43, 117 S.Ct. 1055, 137 L.Ed.2d 170 (1997), 495

Arkansas v. Oklahoma, 503 U.S. 91, 112 S.Ct. 1046, 117 L.Ed.2d 239 (1992), **193**

ASARCO Inc. v. Environmental Protection Agency, 578 F.2d 319, 188 U.S.App.D.C. 77 (D.C.Cir.1978), 310

Association of Battery Recyclers, Inc. v. United States E.P.A., 208 F.3d 1047, 341 U.S.App.D.C. 78 (D.C.Cir.2000), 402, 405

Association of California Water Agencies v. Evans, 386 F.3d 879 (9th Cir.2004), 520

Association of Pacific Fisheries v. E.P.A., 615 F.2d 794 (9th Cir.1980), 144, 181

Association to Protect Hammersley, Eld, and Totten Inlets v. Taylor Resources, Inc., 299 F.3d 1007 (9th Cir.2002), 145

Atlantic Research Corp. v. United States, 459 F.3d 827 (8th Cir.2006), **587**

Atlantic States Legal Foundation, Inc. v. Pan American Tanning Corp., 993 F.2d 1017 (2nd Cir.1993), 497

Atlantic States Legal Foundation, Inc. v. Stroh Die Casting Co., 116 F.3d 814 (7th Cir.1997), 495, 497

Atlantic States Legal Foundation, Inc. v. Tyson Foods, Inc., 897 F.2d 1128 (11th Cir.1990), 442, 497

Atlantic States Legal Foundation, Inc. v. United Musical Instruments, U.S.A., Inc., 61 F.3d 473 (6th Cir.1995), 496

Auer v. Robbins, 519 U.S. 452, 117 S.Ct. 905, 137 L.Ed.2d 79 (1997), 150, 220

Aviall Services, Inc. v. Cooper Industries, Inc., 312 F.3d 677 (5th Cir.2002), 595

Avoyelles Sportsmen's League, Inc. v. Marsh, 715 F.2d 897 (5th Cir.1983), 698

Babbitt v. Sweet Home Chapter of Communities for a Great Oregon, 515 U.S. 687, 115 S.Ct. 2407, 132 L.Ed.2d 597 (1995), 158, **649**

Baltimore Gas and Elec. Co. v. Natural Resources Defense Council, Inc., 462 U.S. 87, 103 S.Ct. 2246, 76 L.Ed.2d 437 (1983), 126

Bangor, City of v. Citizens Communications Co., 2004 WL 483201 (D.Me.2004), 561

BASF Wyandotte Corp. v. Costle, 598 F.2d 637 (1st Cir.1979), 181

Bates v. Dow Agrosciences LLC, 544 U.S. 431, 125 S.Ct. 1788, 161 L.Ed.2d 687 (2005), 55

Bedford Affiliates v. Sills, 156 F.3d 416 (2nd Cir.1998), 561, 596

Bell Petroleum Services, Inc., Matter of, 3 F.3d 889 (5th Cir.1993), 555

Bennett v. Spear, 520 U.S. 154, 117 S.Ct. 1154, 137 L.Ed.2d 281 (1997), 68, 84, 85, 90, 476

Bersani v. United States E.P.A., 850 F.2d 36 (2nd Cir.1988), 708

Bestfoods v. Aerojet–General Corp., 173 F.Supp.2d 729 (W.D.Mich.2001), 538

Bestfoods, United States v., 524 U.S. 51, 118 S.Ct. 1876, 141 L.Ed.2d 43 (1998), **531**

B.F. Goodrich v. Betkoski, 99 F.3d 505 (2nd Cir.1996), 540

Biodiversity Legal Foundation v. Babbitt, 943 F.Supp. 23 (D.D.C.1996), 605

Biodiversity Legal Foundation v. Badgley, 309 F.3d 1166 (9th Cir.2002), 624

Bliss, United States v., 667 F.Supp. 1298 (E.D.Mo.1987), 545

Blum v. Stenson, 465 U.S. 886, 104 S.Ct. 1541, 79 L.Ed.2d 891 (1984), 521

Boomer v. Atlantic Cement Co., 309 N.Y.S.2d 312, 257 N.E.2d 870 (N.Y. 1970), 4

Borden Ranch Partnership v. United States Army Corps of Engineers, 261 F.3d 810 (9th Cir.2001), 704

Bowles v. Seminole Rock & Sand Co., 325 U.S. 410, 65 S.Ct. 1215, 89 L.Ed. 1700 (1945), 90, 150

BP Exploration & Oil, Inc.(93–3310) v. United States E.P.A., 66 F.3d 784 (6th Cir.1995), 181

Brace, United States v., 41 F.3d 117 (3rd Cir.1994), 724

Bragg v. Robertson, 83 F.Supp.2d 713 (S.D.W.Va.2000), 743

Bragg v. Robertson, 72 F.Supp.2d 642 (S.D.W.Va.1999), 742, 743

Bragg v. West Virginia Coal Ass'n, 248 F.3d 275 (4th Cir.2001), 734, 743

Browning–Ferris Industries of Illinois, Inc. v. Ter Maat, 195 F.3d 953 (7th Cir. 1999), 539

Buckhannon Bd. and Care Home, Inc. v. West Virginia Dept. of Health and Human Resources, 532 U.S. 598, 121 S.Ct. 1835, 149 L.Ed.2d 855 (2001), **511**

Burlington, City of v. Dague, 505 U.S. 557, 112 S.Ct. 2638, 120 L.Ed.2d 449 (1992), 521

C & A Carbone, Inc. v. Town of Clarkstown, N.Y., 511 U.S. 383, 114 S.Ct. 1677, 128 L.Ed.2d 399 (1994), 58

Calvert Cliffs' Coordinating Committee, Inc. v. United States Atomic Energy Commission, 449 F.2d 1109, 146 U.S.App.D.C. 33 (D.C.Cir.1971), 91

Cannon v. University of Chicago, 441 U.S. 677, 99 S.Ct. 1946, 60 L.Ed.2d 560 (1979), 33

Cannons Engineering Corp., United States v., 899 F.2d 79 (1st Cir.1990), **573**

Cannons Engineering Corp., United States v., 720 F.Supp. 1027 (D.Mass.1989), 575

Carson–Truckee Water Conservancy Dist. v. Clark, 741 F.2d 257 (9th Cir.1984), 626

Carter–Jones Lumber Co. v. Dixie Distributing Co., 166 F.3d 840 (6th Cir.1999), 541

Catellus Development Corp. v. United States, 34 F.3d 748 (9th Cir.1994), 546

Catron County Bd. of Com'rs, New Mexico v. United States Fish & Wildlife Service, 75 F.3d 1429 (10th Cir.1996), 625

Catskill Mountains Chapter of Trout Unlimited, Inc. v. City of New York (Catskill II), 451 F.3d 77 (2nd Cir.2006), 146

Catskill Mountains Chapter of Trout Unlimited, Inc. v. City of New York (Catskill I), 273 F.3d 481 (2nd Cir.2001), **140**

CDMG Realty Co., United States v., 96 F.3d 706 (3rd Cir.1996), 530

Center for Biological Diversity v. Badgley, 2001 WL 844399 (D.Or.2001), 605

Center for Biological Diversity v. Norton, 240 F.Supp.2d 1090 (D.Ariz.2003), 620

Center for Biological Diversity v. Norton, 262 F.3d 1077 (10th Cir.2001), 520

Center for Biological Diversity v. Rumsfeld, 198 F.Supp.2d 1139 (D.Ariz.2002), 645

Centerior Service Co. v. Acme Scrap Iron & Metal Corp., 153 F.3d 344 (6th Cir.1998), 590

Central Valley Chrysler–Jeep v. Witherspoon, 456 F.Supp.2d 1160 (E.D.Cal.2006), 55

Chem–Dyne Corp., United States v., 572 F.Supp. 802 (S.D.Ohio 1983), 529, **547**

Chemical Mfrs. Ass'n v. Natural Resources Defense Council, Inc., 470 U.S. 116, 105 S.Ct. 1102, 84 L.Ed.2d 90 (1985), 182, 184

Chemical Waste Management, Inc. v. Hunt, 504 U.S. 334, 112 S.Ct. 2009, 119 L.Ed.2d 121 (1992), 57

Chemical Waste Management, Inc. v. U.S. E.P.A., 976 F.2d 2, 298 U.S.App.D.C. 54 (D.C.Cir.1992), 425

Chemical Waste Management, Inc. v. U.S. E.P.A., 869 F.2d 1526, 276 U.S.App.D.C. 207 (D.C.Cir.1989), 410

Chesapeake Bay Foundation, Inc. v. Gwaltney of Smithfield, Ltd., 890 F.2d 690 (4th Cir.1989), 495, 497

Chesapeake Bay Foundation, Inc. v. Gwaltney of Smithfield, Ltd., 844 F.2d 170 (4th Cir.1988), 495

Chester Residents Concerned for Quality Living v. Seif, 132 F.3d 925 (3rd Cir.1997), 33

Chevron Pipe Line Co., United States v., 437 F.Supp.2d 605 (N.D.Tex.2006), 697

Chevron U.S.A., Inc. v. Natural Resources Defense Council, Inc., 467 U.S. 837, 104 S.Ct. 2778, 81 L.Ed.2d 694 (1984), 56, 89, **304,** 322

Chicago, City of v. Environmental Defense Fund, 511 U.S. 328, 114 S.Ct. 1588, 128 L.Ed.2d 302 (1994), 410

Christensen v. Harris County, 529 U.S. 576, 120 S.Ct. 1655, 146 L.Ed.2d 621 (2000), 141

Christiansburg Garment Co. v. Equal Employment Opportunity Commission, 434 U.S. 412, 98 S.Ct. 694, 54 L.Ed.2d 648 (1978), 519

Cipollone v. Liggett Group, Inc., 505 U.S. 504, 112 S.Ct. 2608, 120 L.Ed.2d 407 (1992), 54

Citizens Coal Council v. Norton, 330 F.3d 478, 356 U.S.App.D.C. 214 (D.C.Cir.2003), 732

Citizens for a Better Environment v. Steel Co., 90 F.3d 1237 (7th Cir.1996), 496

Citizens for a Better Environment–California v. Union Oil Co. of California, 83 F.3d 1111 (9th Cir.1996), 508

Citizens to Preserve Overton Park, Inc. v. Volpe, 401 U.S. 402, 91 S.Ct. 814, 28 L.Ed.2d 136 (1971), 89

City of (see name of city)

Colorado & Eastern R. Co., United States v., 50 F.3d 1530 (10th Cir.1995), 590

Comfort Lake Ass'n, Inc. v. Dresel Contracting, Inc., 138 F.3d 351 (8th Cir.1998), 497

Como–Falcon Coalition, Inc. v. United States Dept. of Labor, 465 F.Supp. 850 (D.Minn.1978), 121

Concerned Area Residents for Environment v. Southview Farm, 34 F.3d 114 (2nd Cir.1994), 157

Consolidated Edison Co. of New York, Inc. v. UGI Utilities, Inc., 423 F.3d 90 (2nd Cir.2005), 598

Cooper Industries, Inc. v. Aviall Services, Inc., 543 U.S. 157, 125 S.Ct. 577, 160 L.Ed.2d 548 (2004), **581**

CPC Intern., Inc. v. Aerojet–General Corp., 777 F.Supp. 549 (W.D.Mich.1991), 535

Darby, United States v., 312 U.S. 100, 312 U.S. 657, 61 S.Ct. 451, 85 L.Ed. 609 (1941), 37

Deaton, United States v., 209 F.3d 331 (4th Cir.2000), 703

Defenders of Wildlife v. Administrator, E.P.A., 882 F.2d 1294 (8th Cir.1989), 662

Defenders of Wildlife v. Babbitt, 1999 WL 33537981 (S.D.Cal.1999), 605

Defenders of Wildlife v. Kempthorne, 2006 WL 2844232 (D.D.C.2006), 640

Defenders of Wildlife v. Norton, 258 F.3d 1136 (9th Cir.2001), **606**

Defenders of Wildlife v. United States Environmental Protection Agency, 420 F.3d 946 (9th Cir.2005), 645

Department of Transp. v. Public Citizen, 541 U.S. 752, 124 S.Ct. 2204, 159 L.Ed.2d 60 (2004), 94

DiBiase Salem Realty Trust, United States v., 1993 WL 729662 (D.Mass.1993), 561

Dioxin/Organochlorine Center v. Clarke, 57 F.3d 1517 (9th Cir.1995), 198

Dolan v. City of Tigard, 512 U.S. 374, 114 S.Ct. 2309, 129 L.Ed.2d 304 (1994), 52

Donahey v. Bogle, 129 F.3d 838 (6th Cir. 1997), 540

Donovan v. Dewey, 452 U.S. 594, 101 S.Ct. 2534, 69 L.Ed.2d 262 (1981), 427

Douglas County v. Babbitt, 48 F.3d 1495 (9th Cir.1995), 625

Drummond v. United States, 324 U.S. 316, 65 S.Ct. 659, 89 L.Ed. 969 (1945), 475

Dubois v. Thomas, 820 F.2d 943 (8th Cir. 1987), 428

Eastern Enterprises v. Apfel, 524 U.S. 498, 118 S.Ct. 2131, 141 L.Ed.2d 451 (1998), 530

Edward Hines Lumber Co. v. Vulcan Materials Co., 861 F.2d 155 (7th Cir.1988), 529

E. I. du Pont de Nemours & Co. v. Train, 430 U.S. 112, 97 S.Ct. 965, 51 L.Ed.2d 204 (1977), 172

E.I. DuPont De Nemours and Co. v. United States, 460 F.3d 515 (3rd Cir.2006), 598

Environmental Defense v. Duke Energy Corp., ___ U.S. ___, 127 S.Ct. 1423, ___ L.Ed.2d ___ (2007), 335

Environmental Protection Agency v. California ex rel. State Water Resources Control Bd., 426 U.S. 200, 96 S.Ct. 2022, 48 L.Ed.2d 578 (1976), 180

E.P.A. v. National Crushed Stone Ass'n, 449 U.S. 64, 101 S.Ct. 295, 66 L.Ed.2d 268 (1980), 181

Evans, United States v., 2006 WL 2221629 (M.D.Fla.2006), 697

Ex parte (see name of party)

Federal Election Com'n v. Akins, 524 U.S. 11, 118 S.Ct. 1777, 141 L.Ed.2d 10 (1998), 68

Fleet Factors Corp., United States v., 901 F.2d 1550 (11th Cir.1990), 541

Florida Power & Light Co. v. Allis Chalmers Corp., 893 F.2d 1313 (11th Cir. 1990), 529, 546

Fogerty v. Fantasy, Inc., 510 U.S. 517, 114 S.Ct. 1023, 127 L.Ed.2d 455 (1994), 519

Fort Gratiot Sanitary Landfill, Inc. v. Michigan Dept. of Natural Resources, 504 U.S. 353, 112 S.Ct. 2019, 119 L.Ed.2d 139 (1992), 57

Foster v. United States, 922 F.Supp. 642 (D.D.C.1996), 562

Franklin v. Massachusetts, 505 U.S. 788, 112 S.Ct. 2767, 120 L.Ed.2d 636 (1992), 85

Franklin County Convention Facilities Authority v. American Premier Underwriters, Inc., 240 F.3d 534 (6th Cir.2001), 561

Friends of Earth, Inc. v. Laidlaw Environmental Services (TOC), Inc., 149 F.3d 303 (4th Cir.1998), 497

Friends of Milwaukee's Rivers v. Milwaukee Metropolitan Sewerage Dist., 382 F.3d 743 (7th Cir.2004), 508

Friends of the Earth, Inc. v. Gaston Copper Recycling Corp., 204 F.3d 149 (4th Cir. 2000), 484

Friends of the Earth, Inc. v. Gaston Copper Recycling Corp., 179 F.3d 107 (4th Cir. 1999), 485

Friends of the Earth, Inc. v. Laidlaw Environmental Services (TOC), Inc., 528 U.S. 167, 120 S.Ct. 693, 145 L.Ed.2d 610 (2000), 68, 476, **478, 497**

Friends of the Earth, Inc. v. Laidlaw Environmental Services (TOC), Inc., 890 F.Supp. 470 (D.S.C.1995), 507

Friends of the Earth, Inc. v. United States Army Corps of Engineers, 109 F.Supp.2d 30 (D.D.C.2000), 113, 133

Friends of the Payette v. Horseshoe Bend Hydroelectric Co., 988 F.2d 989 (9th Cir. 1993), 717

Friends of Wild Swan, Inc. v. United States Fish and Wildlife Service, 945 F.Supp. 1388 (D.Or.1996), 605

Fund for Animals, Inc. v. Rice, 85 F.3d 535 (11th Cir.1996), **710**

Garcia v. San Antonio Metropolitan Transit Authority, 469 U.S. 528, 105 S.Ct. 1005, 83 L.Ed.2d 1016 (1985), 48

GDF Realty Investments, Ltd. v. Norton, 326 F.3d 622 (5th Cir.2003), 47

Georgia, State of v. Tennessee Copper Co., 206 U.S. 230, 27 S.Ct. 618, 51 L.Ed. 1038 (1907), 4

Gerber v. Norton, 294 F.3d 173, 352 U.S.App.D.C. 375 (D.C.Cir.2002), 664

Gerke Excavating, Inc., United States v., 464 F.3d 723 (7th Cir.2006), 696

Gibbs v. Babbitt, 214 F.3d 483 (4th Cir. 2000), 48

Gifford Pinchot Task Force v. United States Fish and Wildlife Service, 378 F.3d 1059 (9th Cir.2004), 641, **641**

Goe Engineering Co., Inc. v. Physicians Formula Cosmetics, Inc., 1997 WL 889278 (C.D.Cal.1997), 561, 562

Grand Canyon Trust v. F.A.A., 290 F.3d 339, 351 U.S.App.D.C. 253 (D.C.Cir. 2002), **115**

Greater Yellowstone Coalition v. Flowers, 359 F.3d 1257 (10th Cir.2004), 120

Guardians Ass'n v. Civil Service Com'n of City of New York, 463 U.S. 582, 103 S.Ct. 3221, 77 L.Ed.2d 866 (1983), 33

Gwaltney of Smithfield, Ltd. v. Chesapeake Bay Foundation, Inc., 484 U.S. 49, 108 S.Ct. 376, 98 L.Ed.2d 306 (1987), **487**

Hallstrom v. Tillamook County, 493 U.S. 20, 110 S.Ct. 304, 107 L.Ed.2d 237 (1989), 477

Hanly v. Kleindienst, 471 F.2d 823 (2nd Cir.1972), 114, 119

Hans v. Louisiana, 134 U.S. 1, 10 S.Ct. 504, 33 L.Ed. 842 (1890), 49

Harmon Industries, Inc. v. Browner, 191 F.3d 894 (8th Cir.1999), **469**

Haydo v. Amerikohl Min., Inc., 830 F.2d 494 (3rd Cir.1987), **734**

Hazardous Waste Treatment Council v. United States E.P.A., 886 F.2d 355, 280 U.S.App.D.C. 338 (D.C.Cir.1989), 425

Headwaters, Inc. v. Talent Irrigation Dist., 243 F.3d 526 (9th Cir.2001), 144

Heckler v. Chaney, 470 U.S. 821, 105 S.Ct. 1649, 84 L.Ed.2d 714 (1985), 428

Hensley v. Eckerhart, 461 U.S. 424, 103 S.Ct. 1933, 76 L.Ed.2d 40 (1983), 508, **509**

Hodel v. Indiana, 452 U.S. 314, 101 S.Ct. 2376, 69 L.Ed.2d 40 (1981), **42**

Hodel v. Virginia Surface Min. and Reclamation Ass'n, Inc., 452 U.S. 264, 101 S.Ct. 2352, 69 L.Ed.2d 1 (1981), **39,** 48

Hunt v. Washington State Apple Advertising Com'n, 432 U.S. 333, 97 S.Ct. 2434, 53 L.Ed.2d 383 (1977), 59

Idaho Rural Council v. Bosma, 143 F.Supp.2d 1169 (D.Idaho 2001), **148**

ILCO, Inc., United States v., 996 F.2d 1126 (11th Cir.1993), 405

James City County, Va. v. E.P.A., 12 F.3d 1330 (4th Cir.1993), 707

Johnson v. Director, Office of Workers' Compensation Programs, 183 F.3d 1169 (9th Cir.1999), 88

Johnson, United States v., 467 F.3d 56 (1st Cir.2006), 697

Kaiser Aetna v. United States, 444 U.S. 164, 100 S.Ct. 383, 62 L.Ed.2d 332 (1979), 51

Kalamazoo River Study Group v. Rockwell Intern., 3 F.Supp.2d 799 (W.D.Mich. 1998), 561

Kayser–Roth Corp., United States v., 272 F.3d 89 (1st Cir.2001), 538

Kelley v. E.P.A., 15 F.3d 1100, 304 U.S.App. D.C. 369 (D.C.Cir.1994), 540

Kennecott v. United States E.P.A., 780 F.2d 445 (4th Cir.1985), 182

Kentuckians for Commonwealth Inc. v. Rivenburgh, 317 F.3d 425 (4th Cir.2003), 668, 742, 743

Kerr–McGee Chemical Corp. v. Lefton Iron & Metal Co., 14 F.3d 321 (7th Cir.1994), 561

Kimbell Foods, Inc., United States v., 440 U.S. 715, 99 S.Ct. 1448, 59 L.Ed.2d 711 (1979), 554

Klamath Siskiyou Wildlands Center v. Boody, 468 F.3d 549 (9th Cir.2006), 110

Kleppe v. New Mexico, 426 U.S. 529, 96 S.Ct. 2285, 49 L.Ed.2d 34 (1976), 36

Kleppe v. Sierra Club, 427 U.S. 390, 96 S.Ct. 2718, 49 L.Ed.2d 576 (1976), **101,** 126

Lane County Audubon Soc. v. Jamison, 958 F.2d 290 (9th Cir.1992), **633**

Lansford–Coaldale Joint Water Authority v. Tonolli Corp., 4 F.3d 1209 (3rd Cir. 1993), 540

League of Wilderness Defenders v. Forsgren, 309 F.3d 1181 (9th Cir.2002), 159

Lefebvre v. Central Maine Power Co., 7 F.Supp.2d 64 (D.Me.1998), 561

Leslie Salt Co. v. United States, 55 F.3d 1388 (9th Cir.1995), 442

Lignite Energy Council v. United States E.P.A., 198 F.3d 930, 339 U.S.App.D.C. 183 (D.C.Cir.1999), **299**

Lloyd A. Fry Roofing Co. v. United States Environmental Protection Agency, 554 F.2d 885 (8th Cir.1977), 447

Locke, United States v., 529 U.S. 89, 120 S.Ct. 1135, 146 L.Ed.2d 69 (2000), 56

Loggerhead Turtle v. County Council of Volusia County, Fla., 307 F.3d 1318 (11th Cir.2002), 520

Loggerhead Turtle v. County Council of Volusia County, Fla., 148 F.3d 1231 (11th Cir.1998), 662

Lopez, United States v., 514 U.S. 549, 115 S.Ct. 1624, 131 L.Ed.2d 626 (1995), 38

Louisiana–Pacific Corp. v. Asarco, Inc., 909 F.2d 1260 (9th Cir.1990), 540

LTV Steel Co., Inc., United States v., 118 F.Supp.2d 827 (N.D.Ohio 2000), 475

Lucas v. South Carolina Coastal Council, 505 U.S. 1003, 112 S.Ct. 2886, 120 L.Ed.2d 798 (1992), 51

Lujan v. Defenders of Wildlife, 504 U.S. 555, 112 S.Ct. 2130, 119 L.Ed.2d 351 (1992), **59,** 477

Lujan v. National Wildlife Federation, 497 U.S. 871, 110 S.Ct. 3177, 111 L.Ed.2d 695 (1990), 68, 84

Maine v. Taylor, 477 U.S. 131, 106 S.Ct. 2440, 91 L.Ed.2d 110 (1986), 57

Mall Properties, Inc. v. Marsh, 672 F.Supp. 561 (D.Mass.1987), 710

Mango, United States v., 199 F.3d 85 (2nd Cir.1999), 447

Marbled Murrelet v. Babbitt, 182 F.3d 1091 (9th Cir.1999), 519

Marbled Murrelet v. Babbitt, 83 F.3d 1060 (9th Cir.1996), 661

Marks v. United States, 430 U.S. 188, 97 S.Ct. 990, 51 L.Ed.2d 260 (1977), 696

Markwardt v. City of Guthrie, 18 Okla. 32, 90 P. 26 (Okla.Terr.1907), 3

Marsh v. Oregon Natural Resources Council, 490 U.S. 360, 109 S.Ct. 1851, 104 L.Ed.2d 377 (1989), 92, 110

Marshall v. Barlow's, Inc., 436 U.S. 307, 98 S.Ct. 1816, 56 L.Ed.2d 305 (1978), 427

Martin v. Reynolds Metals Co., 221 Or. 86, 342 P.2d 790 (Or.1959), 4

Massachusetts v. E.P.A., __ U.S. __, 127 S.Ct. 1438, __ L.Ed.2d __ (2007), **69, 243,** 388

Matter of (see name of party)

McKittrick, United States v., 142 F.3d 1170 (9th Cir.1998), 665

Mead Corp., United States v., 533 U.S. 218, 121 S.Ct. 2164, 150 L.Ed.2d 292 (2001), 89, 141

Mesquite, City of v. Aladdin's Castle, Inc., 455 U.S. 283, 102 S.Ct. 1070, 71 L.Ed.2d 152 (1982), 499

Methow Valley Citizens Council v. Regional Forester, 833 F.2d 810 (9th Cir.1987), 129

Metropolitan Water Reclamation Dist. of Greater Chicago v. North American Galvanizing & Coatings, Inc., 473 F.3d 824 (7th Cir.2007), 598

Michigan v. United States E.P.A., 213 F.3d 663, 341 U.S.App.D.C. 306 (D.C.Cir. 2000), 275

Michigan, State of v. Thomas, 805 F.2d 176 (6th Cir.1986), 82

Miller v. Schoene, 276 U.S. 272, 48 S.Ct. 246, 72 L.Ed. 568 (1928), 53

Mississippi Commission on Natural Resources v. Costle, 625 F.2d 1269 (5th Cir.1980), 189

Mississippi River Revival, Inc. v. City of Minneapolis, Minn., 319 F.3d 1013 (8th Cir.2003), 504

Missouri, State of v. Holland, 252 U.S. 416, 40 S.Ct. 382, 64 L.Ed. 641 (1920), 37

Molinary v. Powell Mountain Coal Co., Inc., 125 F.3d 231 (4th Cir.1997), **737,** 741

Monsanto Co., United States v., 858 F.2d 160 (4th Cir.1988), 530, 545

Montana v. United States, 440 U.S. 147, 99 S.Ct. 970, 59 L.Ed.2d 210 (1979), 475

Morrison, United States v., 529 U.S. 598, 120 S.Ct. 1740, 146 L.Ed.2d 658 (2000), 38

Motor Vehicle Mfrs. Ass'n of United States, Inc. v. New York State Dept. of Environmental Conservation, 17 F.3d 521 (2nd Cir.1994), 388

Municipal Authority of Union Tp., United States v., 150 F.3d 259 (3rd Cir.1998), **436**

National Ass'n of Home Builders v. Babbitt, 130 F.3d 1041, 327 U.S.App.D.C. 248 (D.C.Cir.1997), 47

National Ass'n of Home Builders v. Norton, 340 F.3d 835 (9th Cir.2003), **611**

National Ass'n of Metal Finishers v. E.P.A., 719 F.2d 624 (3rd Cir.1983), 181, 186

National Credit Union Admin. v. First Nat. Bank & Trust Co., 522 U.S. 479, 118 S.Ct. 927, 140 L.Ed.2d 1 (1998), 84

National Min. Ass'n v. United States Army Corps of Engineers, 145 F.3d 1399, 330 U.S.App.D.C. 329 (D.C.Cir. 1998), **699**

National Min. Ass'n v. United States E.P.A., 59 F.3d 1351, 313 U.S.App.D.C. 363 (D.C.Cir.1995), **339**

National Min. Ass'n v. U.S. Dept. of Interior, 70 F.3d 1345, 315 U.S.App.D.C. 133 (D.C.Cir.1995), 734, 741, 747

National Solid Wastes Management Ass'n v. Alabama Dept. of Environmental Management, 910 F.2d 713 (11th Cir.1990), 57

National Wildlife Federation v. Coleman, 529 F.2d 359 (5th Cir.1976), 641

National Wildlife Federation v. E.P.A., 286 F.3d 554, 351 U.S.App.D.C. 42 (D.C.Cir. 2002), 87, 182

National Wildlife Federation v. Gorsuch, 693 F.2d 156, 224 U.S.App.D.C. 41 (D.C.Cir.1982), 138, 145

National Wildlife Federation v. Lujan, 950 F.2d 765, 292 U.S.App.D.C. 356 (D.C.Cir.1991), 731

National Wildlife Federation v. National Marine Fisheries Service, 254 F.Supp.2d 1196 (D.Or.2003), 645

Natural Resources Defense Council v. California Dept. of Transp., 96 F.3d 420 (9th Cir.1996), 741

Natural Resources Defense Council v. United States Dept. of the Interior, 113 F.3d 1121 (9th Cir.1997), 622

Natural Resources Defense Council, Inc. v. Costle, 568 F.2d 1369, 186 U.S.App.D.C. 147 (D.C.Cir.1977), 143

Natural Resources Defense Council, Inc. v. Texaco Refining and Marketing, Inc., 2 F.3d 493 (3rd Cir.1993), 497

Natural Resources Defense Council, Inc. v. Train, 545 F.2d 320 (2nd Cir.1976), 251

Natural Resources Defense Council, Inc. v. Train, 6 Envtl. L. Rep. 20588 (D.D.C. 1976), 185

Natural Resources Defense Council, Inc. v. United States E.P.A., 16 F.3d 1395 (4th Cir.1993), 190

Natural Resources Defense Council, Inc. v. United States E.P.A., 966 F.2d 1292 (9th Cir.1992), 144

Natural Resources Defense Council, Inc. v. United States E.P.A., 863 F.2d 1420 (9th Cir.1988), 183

Natural Resources Defense Council, Inc. v. United States E.P.A., 859 F.2d 156, 273 U.S.App.D.C. 180 (D.C.Cir. 1988), **160, 167**

Natural Resources Defense Council, Inc. v. United States E.P.A., 824 F.2d 1146, 263 U.S.App.D.C. 166 (D.C.Cir.1987), 339

Natural Resources Defense Council, Inc. v. United States E.P.A., 822 F.2d 104, 261 U.S.App.D.C. 372 (D.C.Cir.1987), 183

Nevada Land Action Ass'n v. United States Forest Service, 8 F.3d 713 (9th Cir. 1993), 84

New Castle County v. Halliburton NUS Corp., 111 F.3d 1116 (3rd Cir.1997), 598

New Mexico Cattle Growers Ass'n v. United States Fish and Wildlife Service, 248 F.3d 1277 (10th Cir.2001), 622

Newton County Wildlife Ass'n v. Rogers, 141 F.3d 803 (8th Cir.1998), **637**

New York v. Burger, 482 U.S. 691, 107 S.Ct. 2636, 96 L.Ed.2d 601 (1987), 427

New York v. E.P.A., 443 F.3d 880, 370 U.S.App.D.C. 239 (D.C.Cir.2006), **328**

New York v. United States, 505 U.S. 144, 112 S.Ct. 2408, 120 L.Ed.2d 120 (1992), 49

New York v. United States E.P.A., 413 F.3d 3, 367 U.S.App.D.C. 3 (D.C.Cir. 2005), **313**

Nollan v. California Coastal Com'n, 483 U.S. 825, 107 S.Ct. 3141, 97 L.Ed.2d 677 (1987), 52

North Carolina, State of v. F.E.R.C., 112 F.3d 1175, 324 U.S.App.D.C. 209 (D.C.Cir.1997), 210

North and South Rivers Watershed Ass'n, Inc. v. Town of Scituate, 949 F.2d 552 (1st Cir.1991), 508

Northernaire Plating Co., United States v., 670 F.Supp. 742 (W.D.Mich.1987), 525, 561

Northern California River Watch v. City of Healdsburg, 457 F.3d 1023 (9th Cir. 2006), 697

Northern Spotted Owl v. Hodel, 716 F.Supp. 479 (W.D.Wash.1988), 604

Northwest Environmental Advocates v. City of Portland, 56 F.3d 979 (9th Cir.1995), 193

Norton v. Southern Utah Wilderness Alliance, 542 U.S. 55, 124 S.Ct. 2373, 159 L.Ed.2d 137 (2004), 85, 109

No Spray Coalition, Inc. v. City of New York, 351 F.3d 602 (2nd Cir.2003), 144

Nuclear Energy Institute, Inc. v. Environmental Protection Agency, 373 F.3d 1251, 362 U.S.App.D.C. 204 (D.C.Cir. 2004), 604

Nurad, Inc. v. William E. Hooper & Sons Co., 966 F.2d 837 (4th Cir.1992), 530

New York, State of v. General Elec. Co., 592 F.Supp. 291 (N.D.N.Y.1984), 525, 546

New York, State of v. Lashins Arcade Co., 91 F.3d 353 (2nd Cir.1996), 561

New York, State of v. Shore Realty Corp., 759 F.2d 1032 (2nd Cir.1985), 525, **527**

Oakland Cannabis Buyers' Co-op., United States v., 532 U.S. 483, 121 S.Ct. 1711, 149 L.Ed.2d 722 (2001), 435

Oconomowoc Lake, Village of v. Dayton Hudson Corp., 24 F.3d 962 (7th Cir. 1994), 150

Ohio Forestry Ass'n, Inc. v. Sierra Club, 523 U.S. 726, 118 S.Ct. 1665, 140 L.Ed.2d 921 (1998), 88

Ohio Valley Environmental Coalition v. Horinko, 279 F.Supp.2d 732 (S.D.W.Va. 2003), 189

OHM Remediation Services v. Evans Cooperage Co., Inc., 116 F.3d 1574 (5th Cir. 1997), 597

Oil, Chemical and Atomic Workers Intern. Union, AFL–CIO v. Department of Energy, 288 F.3d 452, 351 U.S.App.D.C. 199 (D.C.Cir.2002), 520

Olin Corp., United States v., 107 F.3d 1506 (11th Cir.1997), 47, 530

150 Acres of Land, United States v., 204 F.3d 698 (6th Cir.2000), 561, 562

O'Neil v. Picillo, 883 F.2d 176 (1st Cir. 1989), **551**

Oregon Natural Desert Ass'n v. Dombeck, 172 F.3d 1092 (9th Cir.1998), 209

Oregon Natural Resource Council v. Turner, 863 F.Supp. 1277 (D.Or.1994), 622

Oregon Natural Resources Council v. Daley, 6 F.Supp.2d 1139 (D.Or.1998), 605

Oregon Waste Systems, Inc. v. Department of Environmental Quality of State of Or., 511 U.S. 93, 114 S.Ct. 1345, 128 L.Ed.2d 13 (1994), 57

Overholt, United States v., 307 F.3d 1231 (10th Cir.2002), 468

Owen Elec. Steel Co. of South Carolina, Inc. v. Browner, 37 F.3d 146 (4th Cir.1994), 405

Pacific Coast Federation of Fishermen's Ass'n, Inc. v. National Marine Fisheries Service, 265 F.3d 1028 (9th Cir.2001), 641

Pacific Hide & Fur Depot, Inc., United States v., 716 F.Supp. 1341 (D.Idaho 1989), 562

Pacific Legal Foundation v. Andrus, 657 F.2d 829 (6th Cir.1981), 625

Pakootas v. Teck Cominco Metals, Ltd., 452 F.3d 1066 (9th Cir.2006), 756

Palazzolo v. Rhode Island, 533 U.S. 606, 121 S.Ct. 2448, 150 L.Ed.2d 592 (2001), 53

Penn Cent. Transp. Co. v. City of New York, 438 U.S. 104, 98 S.Ct. 2646, 57 L.Ed.2d 631 (1978), 51

Pennsylvania v. Union Gas Co., 491 U.S. 1, 109 S.Ct. 2273, 105 L.Ed.2d 1 (1989), 50

Pennsylvania Coal Co. v. Mahon, 260 U.S. 393, 43 S.Ct. 158, 67 L.Ed. 322 (1922), 50

Pennsylvania, Dept. of Environmental Resources v. E.P.A., 618 F.2d 991 (3rd Cir.1980), 183

Pennsylvania Federation of Sportsmen's Clubs, Inc. v. Hess, 297 F.3d 310 (3rd Cir.2002), 741

Pennsylvania Urban Development Corp. v. Golen, 708 F.Supp. 669 (E.D.Pa.1989), 597

Philadelphia, City of v. New Jersey, 437 U.S. 617, 98 S.Ct. 2531, 57 L.Ed.2d 475 (1978), 57

Pinal Creek Group v. Newmont Min. Corp., 118 F.3d 1298 (9th Cir.1997), 590

Platt v. City of Waterbury, 72 Conn. 531, 45 A. 154 (Conn.1900), 3

Plaza Health Laboratories, Inc., United States v., 3 F.3d 643 (2nd Cir.1993), **152**

PMC, Inc. v. Sherwin–Williams Co., 151 F.3d 610 (7th Cir.1998), 598

Pneumo Abex Corp. v. High Point, Thomasville and Denton R. Co., 142 F.3d 769 (4th Cir.1998), 546, 590

Power Engineering Co., United States v., 303 F.3d 1232 (10th Cir.2002), 475

Printz v. United States, 521 U.S. 898, 117 S.Ct. 2365, 138 L.Ed.2d 914 (1997), 49

Pronsolino v. Nastri, 291 F.3d 1123 (9th Cir.2002), **214**

Public Citizen, Inc. v. United States E.P.A., 343 F.3d 449 (5th Cir.2003), **360**

Public Interest Research Group of New Jersey, Inc. v. Hercules, Inc., 50 F.3d 1239 (3rd Cir.1995), 477

Public Interest Research Group of New Jersey, Inc. v. Magnesium Elektron, Inc., 123 F.3d 111 (3rd Cir.1997), 483

Public Interest Research Group of New Jersey, Inc. v. Powell Duffryn Terminals Inc., 913 F.2d 64 (3rd Cir.1990), 442, 484

Public Interest Research Group of New Jersey, Inc. v. Windall, 51 F.3d 1179 (3rd Cir.1995), 521

PUD No. 1 of Jefferson County v. Washington Dept. of Ecology, 511 U.S. 700, 114 S.Ct. 1900, 128 L.Ed.2d 716 (1994), 190, **202**

Puerto Rico Campers' Ass'n. v. Puerto Rico Aqueduct and Sewer Authority, 219 F.Supp.2d 201 (D.Puerto Rico 2002), 504

Pyramid Lake Paiute Tribe of Indians v. United States Dept. of Navy, 898 F.2d 1410 (9th Cir.1990), 626

Rancho Viejo, LLC v. Norton, 323 F.3d 1062, 355 U.S.App.D.C. 303 (D.C.Cir. 2003), 47

Rapanos v. United States, ___ U.S. ___, 126 S.Ct. 2208, 165 L.Ed.2d 159 (2006), 147, **681**

Reading Co., Matter of, 115 F.3d 1111 (3rd Cir.1997), 598

Redwing Carriers, Inc. v. Saraland Apartments, 94 F.3d 1489 (11th Cir.1996), 541, 590

Reeves, Inc. v. Stake, 447 U.S. 429, 100 S.Ct. 2271, 65 L.Ed.2d 244 (1980), 58

Reilly Tar & Chemical Corp., United States v., 606 F.Supp. 412 (D.Minn.1985), 447

Riley v. St. Luke's Episcopal Hosp., 252 F.3d 749 (5th Cir.2001), 504

Riverside Bayview Homes, Inc., United States v., 474 U.S. 121, 106 S.Ct. 455, 88 L.Ed.2d 419 (1985), 147, **669**

Robertson v. Methow Valley Citizens Council, 490 U.S. 332, 109 S.Ct. 1835, 104 L.Ed.2d 351 (1989), **121, 130**

Rock Island, Ill., City of, United States v., 182 F.Supp.2d 690 (C.D.Ill.2001), 475

Rohm and Haas Co., United States v., 790 F.Supp. 1255 (E.D.Pa.1992), 562

Ruckelshaus v. Sierra Club, 463 U.S. 680, 103 S.Ct. 3274, 77 L.Ed.2d 938 (1983), 519

Rumpke of Indiana, Inc. v. Cummins Engine Co., Inc., 107 F.3d 1235 (7th Cir. 1997), 597

Safe Air for Everyone v. Meyer, 373 F.3d 1035 (9th Cir.2004), 406

San Francisco BayKeeper, Inc. v. Tosco Corp., 309 F.3d 1153 (9th Cir.2002), 477, 504

Save Our Community v. United States E.P.A., 971 F.2d 1155 (5th Cir.1992), 698

Save the Bay, Inc. v. Administrator of Environmental Protection Agency, 556 F.2d 1282 (5th Cir.1977), 171

Scott v. City of Hammond, Ind., 741 F.2d 992 (7th Cir.1984), 213

S.D. Warren Co. v. Maine Bd. of Environmental Protection, ___ U.S. ___, 126 S.Ct. 1843, 164 L.Ed.2d 625 (2006), 145, 209

Selkirk Conservation Alliance v. Forsgren, 336 F.3d 944 (9th Cir.2003), 645

Seminole Tribe of Florida v. Florida, 517 U.S. 44, 116 S.Ct. 1114, 134 L.Ed.2d 252 (1996), 50

Serafini, United States v., 706 F.Supp. 346 (M.D.Pa.1988), 562

Shell Oil Co. v. E.P.A., 950 F.2d 741, 292 U.S.App.D.C. 332 (D.C.Cir.1991), 90, 411

Sierra Club v. City of Little Rock, 351 F.3d 840 (8th Cir.2003), 520

Sierra Club v. E.P.A., 322 F.3d 718, 355 U.S.App.D.C. 258 (D.C.Cir.2003), 520

Sierra Club v. Glickman, 156 F.3d 606 (5th Cir.1998), 626

Sierra Club v. Marsh, 816 F.2d 1376 (9th Cir.1987), 639

Sierra Club v. Morton, 405 U.S. 727, 92 S.Ct. 1361, 31 L.Ed.2d 636 (1972), 59

Sierra Club v. United States Army Corps of Engineers, 295 F.3d 1209 (11th Cir. 2002), 639

Sierra Club v. United States Fish and Wildlife Service, 245 F.3d 434 (5th Cir.2001), 622

Sierra Club v. Whitman, 268 F.3d 898 (9th Cir.2001), 428

Skidmore v. Swift & Co., 323 U.S. 134, 65 S.Ct. 161, 89 L.Ed. 124 (1944), 89, 141

Solar Turbines Inc. v. Seif, 879 F.2d 1073 (3rd Cir.1989), 376

Solid Waste Agency of Northern Cook County v. United States Army Corps of Engineers, 531 U.S. 159, 121 S.Ct. 675, 148 L.Ed.2d 576 (2001), 46, 147, **673**

South Dakota v. Dole, 483 U.S. 203, 107 S.Ct. 2793, 97 L.Ed.2d 171 (1987), 36

Southern Pines Associates by Goldmeier v. United States, 912 F.2d 713 (4th Cir.1990), **443**

South Florida Water Management Dist. v. Miccosukee Tribe of Indians, 541 U.S. 95, 124 S.Ct. 1537, 158 L.Ed.2d 264 (2004), 145, 698

Southwest Center for Biological Diversity v. Babbitt, 939 F.Supp. 49 (D.D.C.1996), 605

Speach, United States v., 968 F.2d 795 (9th Cir.1992), 468

Spirit of Sage Council v. Norton, 294 F.Supp.2d 67 (D.D.C.2003), 664

Sporhase v. Nebraska, ex rel. Douglas, 458 U.S. 941, 102 S.Ct. 3456, 73 L.Ed.2d 1254 (1982), 57

Staples v. United States, 511 U.S. 600, 114 S.Ct. 1793, 128 L.Ed.2d 608 (1994), 468

State of (see name of state)

Steel Co. v. Citizens for a Better Environment, 523 U.S. 83, 118 S.Ct. 1003, 140 L.Ed.2d 210 (1998), 68, 496

Strahan v. Coxe, 127 F.3d 155 (1st Cir. 1997), 662

Student Public Interest Research Group of New Jersey, Inc. v. Fritzsche, Dodge & Olcott, Inc., 759 F.2d 1131 (3rd Cir. 1985), 506

Sun Co., Inc. (R&M) v. Browning–Ferris, Inc., 124 F.3d 1187 (10th Cir.1997), 598

Supporters to Oppose Pollution, Inc. v. Heritage Group, 973 F.2d 1320 (7th Cir. 1992), 507

Susquehanna Fertilizer Co. v. Malone, 73 Md. 268, 20 A. 900 (Md.1890), 3

Sylvester v. United States Army Corps of Engineers, 882 F.2d 407 (9th Cir.1989), 708

Tahoe–Sierra Preservation Council, Inc. v. Tahoe Regional Planning Agency, 535 U.S. 302, 122 S.Ct. 1465, 152 L.Ed.2d 517 (2002), 51

Taylor, United States v., 1993 WL 760996 (W.D.Mich.1993), 562

Tennessee Valley Authority v. Hill, 437 U.S. 153, 98 S.Ct. 2279, 57 L.Ed.2d 117 (1978), 601

Tennessee Valley Authority v. Whitman, 336 F.3d 1236 (11th Cir.2003), 447

Texans United for a Safe Economy Educ. Fund v. Crown Cent. Petroleum Corp., 207 F.3d 789 (5th Cir.2000), 506

Thomas v. Peterson, 753 F.2d 754 (9th Cir.1985), **629**

Thompson/Center Arms Co., United States v., 504 U.S. 505, 112 S.Ct. 2102, 119 L.Ed.2d 308 (1992), 158

3M Co. (Minnesota Min. and Mfg.) v. Browner, 17 F.3d 1453, 305 U.S.App. D.C. 100 (D.C.Cir.1994), 458

TIC Inv. Corp., United States v., 68 F.3d 1082 (8th Cir.1995), 546

Train v. Colorado Public Interest Research Group, Inc., 426 U.S. 1, 96 S.Ct. 1938, 48 L.Ed.2d 434 (1976), 143

Train v. Natural Resources Defense Council, Inc., 421 U.S. 60, 95 S.Ct. 1470, 43 L.Ed.2d 731 (1975), 266

Trustees for Alaska v. E.P.A., 749 F.2d 549 (9th Cir.1984), 193

Umatilla Waterquality Protective Ass'n, Inc. v. Smith Frozen Foods, Inc., 962 F.Supp. 1312 (D.Or.1997), 149

Union Elec. Co. v. E.P.A., 427 U.S. 246, 96 S.Ct. 2518, 49 L.Ed.2d 474 (1976), 269

Union of Needletrades, Indus. and Textile Employees, AFL–CIO, CLC v. United States I.N.S., 336 F.3d 200 (2nd Cir. 2003), 520

United Haulers Ass'n, Inc. v. Oneida–Herkimer Solid Waste Management Authority, 261 F.3d 245 (2nd Cir.2001), 58

United States v. _____ (see opposing party)

USA Recycling, Inc. v. Town of Babylon, 66 F.3d 1272 (2nd Cir.1995), 58

Usery v. Turner Elkhorn Mining Co., 428 U.S. 1, 96 S.Ct. 2882, 49 L.Ed.2d 752 (1976), 530

Utility Air Regulatory Group v. E.P.A., 471 F.3d 1333, 374 U.S.App.D.C. 85 (D.C.Cir.2006), **352**

Village of (see name of village)

Wade, United States v., 577 F.Supp. 1326 (E.D.Pa.1983), **542**

Ward, United States v., 618 F.Supp. 884 (E.D.N.C.1985), 525, 545

Washington Toxic Coalition v. EPA, No. 01-132C (W.D.Wash. July 2, 2002), 639

Washington Toxics Coalition v. United States Dept. of Interior, Fish and Wildlife Service, 457 F.Supp.2d 1158 (W.D.Wash.2006), 640

Washington Wilderness Coalition v. Hecla Min. Co., 870 F.Supp. 983 (E.D.Wash. 1994), 148

Weinberger v. Romero–Barcelo, 456 U.S. 305, 102 S.Ct. 1798, 72 L.Ed.2d 91 (1982), **429**

Weitzenhoff, United States v., 35 F.3d 1275 (9th Cir.1993), **459**

Western Properties Service Corp. v. Shell Oil Co., 358 F.3d 678 (9th Cir.2004), 597

West Virginia Coal Ass'n v. Reilly, 728 F.Supp. 1276 (S.D.W.Va.1989), 742

Weyerhaeuser Co. v. Costle, 590 F.2d 1011, 191 U.S.App.D.C. 309 (D.C.Cir. 1978), **172**

Whitman v. American Trucking Associations, 531 U.S. 457, 121 S.Ct. 903, 149 L.Ed.2d 1 (2001), 6, **262**

Whitmore v. Arkansas, 495 U.S. 149, 110 S.Ct. 1717, 109 L.Ed.2d 135 (1990), 500

Wichita, Kansas, City of v. Trustees of APCO Oil Corp. Liquidating Trust, 306 F.Supp.2d 1040 (D.Kan.2003), 538

Wickard v. Filburn, 317 U.S. 111, 63 S.Ct. 82, 87 L.Ed. 122 (1942), 37

Willson v. Black–Bird Creek Marsh Co., 27 U.S. 245, 7 L.Ed. 412 (1829), 666

Wilshire Westwood Associates v. Atlantic Richfield Corp., 881 F.2d 801 (9th Cir. 1989), 524

Wilson, United States v., 133 F.3d 251 (4th Cir.1997), 680, 699

Winnebago Tribe of Nebraska v. Ray, 621 F.2d 269 (8th Cir.1980), **110**

Wisconsin Elec. Power Co. v. Reilly, 893 F.2d 901 (7th Cir.1990), **290,** 331

Wyoming Farm Bureau Federation v. Babbitt, 199 F.3d 1224 (10th Cir.2000), 665

Young, Ex parte, 209 U.S. 123, 28 S.Ct. 441, 52 L.Ed. 714 (1908), 50, 741

LEGAL PROTECTION OF THE ENVIRONMENT
Second Edition

*

Chapter 1

INTRODUCTION

I. INTRODUCTION

Environmental Law is law designed to protect the environment, and the plants and animals that rely on it, including us. In the scale of things, however, the law is a puny instrument to protect the environment. The environment is affected by so much that is not subject to human law. Nature itself alters the environment. A volcano erupts causing massive environmental effects, sometimes even worldwide. A hurricane visits devastation on a wide region.

Environmental degradation through human action is not just a modern phenomenon. Humans have been altering the environment since prehistoric times. Historians today believe that the inhabitants of Easter Island, who erected the great stone statues, essentially destroyed their civilization through overgrazing. John Fenley and Paul Bahn, THE ENIGMAS OF EASTER ISLAND: ISLAND ON THE EDGE (2003). The desert of what is now Iraq was once the fertile crescent that gave birth to the earliest human civilizations but which was destroyed through water diversions and non-sustainable farming practices. Jared Diamond, GUNS, GERMS, AND STEEL (1997). Population density and civilization combine to place great stresses on natural resources both as a source of food, fiber, and minerals and as a repository for human-generated waste. Sometimes the harm to the environment may make life more difficult or less attractive for humans; sometimes the harm is more direct, causing disease or injury to humans.

Civilization also brings law, and one response to human-caused environmental harm is law designed to reduce or eliminate such harm. For law to be effective, however, it must exist within a regime that values and enforces law. In the United States "the rule of law" is an important public value, but even here the "law" sometimes seems to be subordinate to other values reflecting the exigencies of the time. In developing nations, law may be only a marginal concern. In the worldwide community, one may well ask whether international law is law at all.

1

II. SOME PERSPECTIVES ON ENVIRONMENTAL LAW

A. History of Environmental Law

There are two enduring threads in environmental law over the past two or three centuries. One focuses on protecting the environment in its natural state, whether for moral, esthetic, economic, or recreational purposes. The other focuses on protecting the health of humans, animals, and plants from the polluting effects of human activity.

The first thread itself has two distinguishable lines. From Thoreau's Walden, an 1854 paean to the natural world and the simple life, to John Muir's founding of the Sierra Club in 1892, the call of nature as a source of inspiration and spiritual awakening found many adherents, whom we today call Preservationists. Preservationism was responsible for the original creation of the national parks and various reserved federal lands. Today, Preservationism is reflected in the Wilderness Act, the Endangered Species Act, and the National Historic Preservation Act, among other laws. The counter to Preservationism was Conservationism, and its leading figure was Gifford Pinchot, the father of the United States Forest Service. The theme of Conservationism, in Pinchot's words, was "the greatest good of the greatest number in the long run." In his day, Conservationism strove to limit the use and development of federal natural resources so that they would not destroy the system that created and maintained them. Today we know this as sustainable development. While both Preservationism and Conservationism are "environmental," the two can conflict precisely because the one stresses non-use values and the other embraces use values.

[margin handwritten note: Preservationism]

[margin handwritten note: Conservatism]

Both Preservationism and Conservationism focused on federal (and to a lesser extent state) lands, both because private lands were more likely already developed and because the regulation of private lands by limiting development was viewed as raising constitutional difficulties. Until the second half of the Twentieth Century, however, most federal lands were not protected by any environmental laws or considerations. National Parks, then and now, constituted a relatively small amount of federal land. Rather, federal policy generally favored the development of "unused" public lands for homesteading, grazing, mining, and timbering. This policy is perhaps epitomized by the 1872 General Mining Act, still in effect today, that allows unreserved federal lands to be used for "hard rock" mining without any environmental controls and without having to pay any royalties to the federal government. Thus, both Preservationism and Conservationism were environmental counterweights to the development-without-restriction mentality of the past, and the widespread adoption of environmental laws to protect public lands is of very recent vintage.

Between the two movements, Conservationism was, as might be imagined, the more successful. Preservationism succeeded in those areas in which development was not generally perceived as likely or profitable. For example, wilderness areas principally were established in timber-poor, steep-slope areas where forestry, grazing, and mining appeared unwarranted. Although today the conflicts between the Endangered Species Act and development are obvious, they were not obvious at the time of its passage. Then, it was thought that the major threat to endangered species was hunting. Holly Doremus, *Adaptive Management, the Endangered Species Act, and the Institutional Challenges of "New Age" Environmental Protection*, 41 Washburn L.J. 50, 57 (2001). Where development or use was possible, Conservationism was the preferred environmental solution because it promised protection of the environment but economic use at the same time. For example, the Federal Land Policy and Management Act (FLPMA), which generally governs public lands, establishes a policy of multiple use and sustained yield that is to be accomplished through systematic planning. The National Forest Management Act likewise requires planning for the various National Forests so that they may support not only timber harvesting and grazing but also recreation and wildlife habitat. Even the National Parks, in which traditional economic development and use, such as silviculture, mining, and grazing, are prohibited, are today governed more by Conservationism ideals as the Parks become recreational venues for tourists.

As opposed to environmentalism, pollution control has a long history. Urbanization and the Industrial Revolution both had environmental impacts that were hard to miss. However, just as the impacts were generally felt locally, the solutions were local in nature. For example, smoke control ordinances were passed by cities in the 19th Century, so that by the turn of the century most large American cities had such ordinances. Similarly, the first water pollution problem related to the need to provide safe water for drinking, washing, and cooking, and in the 19th Century large American cities created municipal water supply systems. This development made flush toilets feasible, but it naturally led to the second water pollution problem: disposing of the wastes and waste water in a safe manner, which resulted in the building of sewer systems. These at least transported the wastes from the streets and yards of the cities to the rivers, lakes, and oceans. Unfortunately, these fresh water sources were usually the very sources from which municipalities obtained their drinking water. Health problems could be avoided, however, by treating drinking water through filtration and chlorination, thus reducing the incentive to treat the waste water itself.

State common law actions were also used to address pollution issues. Usually commercial interests adversely affected by air or water pollution in sufficient degrees to justify litigation brought nuisance actions for both air and water pollution. For example, in *Platt v. City of Waterbury*, 72 Conn. 531, 45 A. 154 (1900), the owners of a mill sued because the city disposed of sewage waste into the river making it unfit for the mill's purposes. The court found a nuisance and entered an injunction that within three years the city would have to remove the sewage from its waste water. In *Markwardt v. City of Guthrie*, 18 Okla. 32, 90 P. 26 (1907), a farmer sued a city for polluting a stream that he used for irrigating his crops and watering his livestock. The court held that such pollution can be a nuisance. Similarly, in *Susquehanna Fertilizer Co. v.*

Malone, 73 Md. 268, 20 A. 900 (1890), the owner of a hotel and rental properties brought suit against a nearby fertilizer company because the air emissions harmed his business; the court found that there was a nuisance. Later, plaintiffs also brought suits involving air pollution as trespass claims. *See, e.g., Martin v. Reynolds Metals Co.*, 221 Or. 86, 342 P.2d 790 (1959) (aluminum plant air emissions that poisoned cattle on plaintiff's land, making it unfit for raising livestock, deemed a trespass).

While air emissions especially could extend over greater distances, even crossing state and national boundaries, this did not mean that common law solutions, originally developed for local problems in state courts, could not still be applicable. For example, in *Georgia v. Tennessee Copper Co.*, 206 U.S. 230, 27 S.Ct. 618, 51 L.Ed. 1038 (1907), Georgia sued in the United States Supreme Court to enjoin the discharge of sulphur dioxide in Tennessee that became sulphuric acid in the atmosphere resulting in "wholesale destruction of forests, orchards, and crops" in Georgia. The Supreme Court found a public nuisance and enjoined the defendants from discharging the emissions. *See also Trail Smelter Case (United States v. Canada)*, Arbitral Tribunal, 1941, 3 UN Rep. Int'l Arb. Awards (1941) (an international tribunal citing American common law cases rendered a judgment that the smelter in Canada must modify its operations to reduce substantially its emissions of sulphur dioxide that were adversely affecting the environment in the United States).

There were, however, a number of shortcomings with common law solutions. The cost and difficulty of litigation, especially before the widespread use of class actions, made lawsuits for pollution infeasible unless the pollution caused serious economic harm to someone with enough resources to bring a case against a major industrial (or municipal) polluter. Unless a particular polluter was especially egregious, there could be a difficulty of proof as to the source of the pollution causing the injury. Even when the proof was there, the nature of the appropriate remedy was difficult. Courts struggled with the idea of closing down a major industrial facility when the cost of closing it down dwarfed the financial costs of the pollution injury. *See, e.g., Boomer v. Atlantic Cement Co.*, 26 N.Y.2d 219, 309 N.Y.S.2d 312, 257 N.E.2d 870 (1970) (refusing to enjoin unconditionally the operation of a cement company; instead conditioning an injunction on the payment of damages to plaintiffs for past and future injuries). Finally, these common law remedies all acted as "after-the-fact" remedies; they might act to stop or compensate for injuries once suffered, but they were not available to stop the injury from occurring in the first place.

Nonetheless, common law actions continue to play an important role in both environmental regulation and health and safety regulation. The general elimination of asbestos from the economy was not a result of state or federal regulation but the result of the dogged persistence of a small number of lawyers who first established in court the health effects of exposure to asbestos and the organized attempts by the asbestos industry to deny and cover up those effects. While tobacco products have certainly not been eliminated from the economy and federal and state regulation both play a role reducing their sales, the effect of lawsuits establishing product liability on tobacco companies for the harm caused by cigarettes has had perhaps the biggest impact on sales. From John Travolta in Civil Action to Julia Roberts in Erin Brockovic, the popular media have portrayed some of the effects of toxic tort litigation brought under traditional common law tort theories.

Some conservative think tanks have suggested that private enforcement of common law rights should substitute for government regulatory programs. *See generally* Terry Anderson and Donald Leal, Free Market Environmentalism, Rev. Ed. (2001). When presented with the history of tort law's inadequacies, in particular with respect to air and water pollution, these organizations respond that the failure in these areas arises out of the lack of a property rights system for these media, which they maintain is the basis of effective tort law remedies. Therefore, they argue for the creation of property rights in air, water, and public resources, such as national forests, grazing lands, and even national parks. Others have suggested that these suggestions are unrealistic. *See, e.g.,* William Funk, *Free Market Environmentalism: Wonder Drug or Snake Oil?*, 15 Harv. J.L. Pub. Pol'y 511 (1992).

At the same time, other conservative think tanks have suggested that existing tort law has resulted in regulation by litigation, and they believe this is the worst form of regulation. *See, e.g.,* Kip Viscusi, Robert Hahn, and Robert Litan, Regulation Through Litigation (2002).

Whatever the ultimate result of this debate over the use of common law remedies as a substitute for government regulation, in the 1960s the consensus clearly was that the common law was not adequate. The year 1970 was a watershed in environmental law. On January 1, President Nixon signed into law the National Environmental Policy Act; on April 22, the nation celebrated the first Earth Day, a day of mass demonstrations in the nation's largest cities and its capital, and teach-ins at thousands of high schools and university campuses; the Environmental Protection Agency, the National Oceanic and Atmospheric Administration, and the Council on Environmental Quality all were created; and on the last day of the year, the Clean Air Act became law. The following years likewise saw a cascade of new environmental laws. The Federal Water Pollution Control Act, which we now call the Clean Water Act, was passed in 1972. In 1973 Congress passed the Endangered Species Act. In 1976, the Resource Conservation and Recovery Act, aimed primarily at controlling the disposal of hazardous wastes, became law; in 1977, the Surface Mining and Reclamation Act was adopted to regulate the effects of surface coal mining; and in 1980 the Comprehensive Environmental Response, Compensation and Liability Act was passed to clean up what had been the largely unregulated disposal of hazardous wastes on the land before 1976. The era of federal responsibility for and attention to the environment had arrived.

B. Types of Regulations

Government can regulate its own and private conduct in a variety of ways, and it can sometimes promote protection of the environment without "regulation" at all. Across the range of environmental laws, there is a broad array of regulatory methodologies.

Command-and-Control regulations are regulations that direct people to do certain specific things or prohibit them from doing certain specific things. Thus, the Clean Air Act's requirement for EPA to set maximum pollution emission limits on factories for certain types of pollutants results in command-and-control regulations applicable to those factories. Command-and-control regulations can take a variety of forms. For example, a pollution limit might be set on a **health-based** standard; that is, the emission standard is set on the basis of achieving a certain level of public health. Most of the early toxic pollutant regulatory requirements were supposed to be based on health concerns. Moreover, EPA is to set the primary National Ambient Air Quality Standards under the Clean Air Act at a level "requisite to protect the public health" "with an adequate margin of safety." 42 U.S.C. § 7409(b)(1). Such an approach ignores the costs involved in achieving this standard. *See Whitman v. American Trucking Ass'ns*, 531 U.S. 457, 121 S.Ct. 903, 149 L.Ed.2d 1 (2001).

This approach can be contrasted to the **technology-based** or **feasibility-limited** approaches. Under these approaches the regulation is set based upon what industry or a subset of industry can achieve in light of the present state of technology or of the economic abilities of the industry. Here the focus is more on costs rather than the health or environmental benefits of the regulation. For example, under the Clean Water Act, the general requirement for factories discharging toxic materials is that they use the "best available technology economically achievable." 33 U.S.C. § 1311(b)(2)(A). Similarly, new sources of pollution under the Clean Water Act must use "the best available demonstrated control technology." 33 U.S.C. § 1316(1). Perhaps what industry can attain under these approaches does not protect public health or the environment very well, or perhaps what industry can attain is greater than necessary to protect the public health or the environment. Technically, these standards ignore health and environmental considerations, although as we will see later, they may be motivated by health considerations. Under the Occupational Safety and Health Act, workers are to be protected from toxic materials so that "to the extent feasible, ... no employee will suffer material impairment of health or functional capacity...." 29 U.S.C. § 655(b)(5). Here, health concerns are not ignored, but health benefits are trumped by feasibility considerations. In this context, "feasibility" relates to the economic ability of an industry to continue in existence. In other words, a standard is not feasible if it would put an industry out of business. This does not mean that the standard might not put an individual company out of business.

Yet another approach is to set the requirement based upon a **balance of the benefits against the costs**. This can be done implicitly by prohibiting *unreasonable* risks to the health or environment, such as in the Federal Insecticide, Fungicide and Rodenticide Act's permitting requirement for pesticides, *see* 7 U.S.C. § 136a(c)(5)(C) & (D), or it can be done explicitly by requiring a cost-benefit analysis. For example, the Safe Drinking Water Act, after requiring that Maximum Contaminant Levels for drinking water be set "as close . . . as is feasible" to the level that will result in no anticipated adverse effects on health, 42 U.S.C. § 300g–1(b)(4) then authorizes EPA to reduce that protection to a level that "maximizes health risk reduction benefits at a cost that is justified by the benefits." 42 U.S.C. § 300g–1(b)(6)(A).

However the standard is derived, command-and-control regulations can specify that standard as either a **design standard** or as a **performance standard**. For example, an agency might specify a particular kind of equipment in a regulation, because the agency has determined that that type of equipment will achieve the performance required. This would be a design standard. Alternatively, the agency could specify in the regulation only the outcome required, such as a certain amount of pollution per hour, without specifying how that outcome is to be achieved. This is a performance standard. Especially when the statute requires either a technology basis or feasibility basis for the regulation, an agency will need to determine that a particular type of equipment does in fact exist and will in fact achieve a certain result in order for the standard to be feasible. At that point, the agency could merely specify that equipment as the regulatory requirement or set as the performance standard what that equipment actually achieves. There are benefits and detriments to each approach.

[margin handwriting: design standard / performance standard]

Performance standards provide the regulated entity more freedom in how to achieve the desired outcome, and concomitantly maximize economic efficiency by providing incentives to achieve the desired outcome at a lower cost than the particular means identified by the agency. Design standards, however, provide regulated entities enhanced certainty as to how to comply and usually make enforcement easier. Traditionally, environmental statutes did not specify whether regulations should be expressed as design standards or performance standards, but some more recent statutes, consistent with increased interest in enhancing regulatory efficiency, have specified the use of performance standards. *See*, *e.g.*, 42 U.S.C. § 300g–1(b)(4)(E)(Safe Drinking Water Act).

Most of the first generation of environmental laws utilized the command-and-control regulatory methodology. More recently, there is increasing interest in so-called "**second generation**" strategies. These have in common a desire to make environmental protection more efficient—achieving the same results at lower cost—and to create incentives for improving environmental enforcement beyond what the law may require. One form of second generation strategies involves **market-based** regulations, particularly what are known as "cap-and-trade" regulations. Market-based regulations refer to regulations that allow certain market concepts to operate within a more general regulatory environment in order to achieve greater efficiencies. Best-known are the cap-and-trade provisions of the Acid Rain Program of the Clean Air Act. 42 U.S.C. §§ 7651 et.seq. Under this program, rather than set limits for pollutants emitted at particular facilities, there is a nationwide "cap" on the amount of emissions of sulfur dioxide from coal-fired power plants, which is lower than the historical emissions. Facilities must have an allowance for each ton emitted and the number of allowances are set based upon the cap. The idea is that individual facilities may either reduce their emissions so that the allowances issued to them are sufficient to cover their emissions, or they may purchase allowances from other emitters, who do not need them because they have reduced their emissions below the amount for which they have allowances. Thus, those facilities that can reduce their emissions least expensively will do so, while those for whom it is more expensive will not. The result is, in theory, the most efficient reduction in emissions. Moreover, such a program can also create a spur to investment in environmental protection, because facilities that achieve reductions greater than required are able to sell their excess allowances to other facilities that may need them. Overall, the Acid Rain Program is considered a substantial success. *See, e.g.,* EPA, Acid Rain Program 2001 Progress Report (2002).

As a result of its success, there is an increasing tendency to use cap-and-trade and other trading systems in other situations. Whether they are appropriate in certain situations is, however, hotly debated. That is, when it does not matter where the pollutant is emitted, such as with greenhouse gases and to a large degree with precursors of acid rain, trading between different emitters, so long as the total emitted is reduced, may be efficient without adverse consequences. If, though, the pollutant emitted has locally undesirable effects, as is usually the case with particulates, smog precursors, and toxic pollutants, then allowing some facilities actually to increase their emissions, because elsewhere they will be decreased, can create local "hot spots." Thus, even if overall emissions are reduced, they may actually be increased in particular places, helping some people at the expense of others. *See generally* Jonathan Remy Nash and Richard L. Revesz, *Markets and Geography: Designing Marketable Permit Schemes to Control Local and Regional Pollutants,* 28 Ecology L.Q. 569 (2001). Moreover, depending upon the particulars of the cap-and-trade program, there may be substantial difficulties in enforcement. *See* Victor Flatt, *The Enron Story and Environmental Policy,* 33 Env. L.Rep. 10485, 10492 (2003).

Another form of second generation regulation involves individually tailored permits for facilities that address all their environmental impacts holistically, rather than trying to regulate each separate medium separately—air under the Clean Air Act, water under the Clean Water Act, etc. On the national level, EPA's Project XL (meaning "excel") is best known. It attempted to negotiate wide ranging permits that would also encourage efficiencies by having companies propose how they could maximize their environmental protection, perhaps trading greater than required protections in one area for reduced protections in another, where the sum was greater than otherwise would be obtained. Unlike the Acid Rain Program, Project XL is generally considered to have been a failure, and it has been discontinued. *See, e.g.*, Rena I. Steinzor, *Reinventing Environmental Regulation: The Dangerous Journey from Command to Self–Control*, 22 Harv. Envtl. L. Rev. 103 (1998). It was characterized by extremely high transaction costs—that is, the time and resources necessary for the companies to prove their case to EPA and for EPA to assure itself that the proposal would indeed be worthwhile—that made it impractical to use on a widespread basis. Another second generation initiative is to encourage companies to institute Environmental Management Systems (EMS), which hold the promise of liberating environmental performance from being considered a barrier to a company maximizing its profits to being viewed as one of the ways by which to measure a company's success. So far the track record for EMS's is mixed with both limited evidence that companies are adopting them or that their adoption in fact improves environmental performance. *See generally* Cary Coglianese and Jennifer Nash, ed., Regulating from the Inside: Can Environmental Management Systems Achieve Policy Goals? (2001).

Yet another form of environmental regulation is through publicizing environmental information. This can be used to reward good performers and tar bad performers. EPA's Toxic Release Inventory, which publishes nationwide data about toxic releases to the environment, is the best known example of this type of regulation. *See* www.epa.gov/tri/. Companies that are reported to be the largest toxic polluters, whether nationally or locally, find themselves under some public and political pressure to clean up their act. California's Proposition 65 prohibits businesses from knowingly exposing persons to a chemical known to cause cancer or reproductive toxicity without first giving a warning. As a result businesses are required to post signs advising persons of their possible exposure to carcinogens. At least in theory, this is supposed to create an incentive for businesses to reduce their use of carcinogenic substances so that they will not lose business from customers repelled by their signs.

Whatever the effects of these second generation strategies, no one seriously imagines that they can replace command-and-control regulations entirely. Pragmatists see a role for them to the extent that they are helpful, but these strategies are no magic bullet.

In a federal system such as the United States, all of the above techniques of regulation could be used by states on their own or by the federal government. As discussed earlier, federal regulation is a relatively recent phenomenon, but it has effectively come to occupy the field. That is, while states are generally allowed to provide for *greater* environmental protection (as described below under pre-emption) than the federal government, for the most part they have not exceeded the federal requirements. Nevertheless, the role of states in environmental law remains central. This is due to the form that most of the major federal environmental laws take, which is known as **cooperative federalism**.

Under the cooperative federalism model, states administer the federal laws on a day-to-day basis under the general supervision of a federal agency, usually EPA. For example, under the Clean Air Act, the Act establishes the basic requirements that states must follow in order to administer the federal law, and EPA reviews and approves the state program to ensure that it meets the Act's requirements. As will be discussed later, the federal government cannot require states to administer these programs, but the federal government can attempt to induce states to participate by, for example, providing money to pay the cost of administering the program. If a state refuses to administer the program or if a state does not comply with the requirements of the program it has agreed to administer, then EPA is supposed to establish and administer a federal program for the state. States may see an advantage in administering the federal program, besides other inducements, simply because it means that the state, rather than the federal government will make the discretionary decisions within the federally mandated framework. Because there remains a large area for the exercise of discretion in the day-to-day administration, this relieves the state of being totally at the mercy of an omni-present federal agency. Under the cooperative federalism model, EPA oversees the performance of states, has the authority to disapprove certain of the state decisions, and generally retains a back-up enforcement authority to enforce the federal requirements in the state against polluters—at least in theory. In practice, the monitoring of states and the use of back-up enforcement authority is substantially burdened by resource limitations.

C. Theoretical Issues

It may seem obvious that when we perceive human-caused environmental harms we respond by passing laws to address those harms. It is well to recognize, however, that humans cause environmental harms not because we affirmatively want to harm the environment, but because there is some activity that appears to be valuable to those causing the harm.

Sometimes the harm to the environment caused by the otherwise valuable human activity may not be obvious. For example, who would have imagined that aerosol sprays in deodorant cans (as well as other uses of chlorofluorocarbons) could destroy the ozone layer, potentially paving the way for worldwide environmental disaster, or that lead put in gasoline to avoid engine knock could be a potential airborne poison? In these cases, establishing that an activity does harm the environment is the first step. This may not be easy, however, and there may be disputes over the causes of harm and the extent of the harm. There are those today who question the existence or extent of global warming and whether it is induced by human behavior, despite the overwhelming consensus of the scientific community that human activity is causing global warming.

Sometimes the harm to the environment is obvious, but the value of the activity to those engaged in it is much greater than the harm suffered by them. Maybe others suffer greater harms, but they are not the ones involved in the harming activity. For example, a factory may emit air pollutants as part of its industrial process, but the factory is engaged in making a profit for its owners, paying taxes to the local government, and providing wages to its employees. It views itself, and is viewed by many others, as engaging in a valuable activity. But how valuable is it? The persons downwind who suffer from the smell, particles, or poison from the emissions may not view the activity's value in the same light. Their focus is on their harm. But how great is their harm? Those who suffer the harm might like the activity stopped, but stopping the activity might mean forgoing an overall benefit to the community.

Economists, in particular, have in recent years been studying these issues with the asserted goal of improving environmental laws. That is, economic theory may help elucidate the incentives for why persons harm the environment, and it may help to inform us as to the best ways to overcome those incentives at the least cost to society.

i. Public Goods

One focus of economists has been on the public goods problem; that is, when resources are publicly owned, but all can use them, those resources tend to be overused. The environmental problems associated with public goods were described in a classic article by Garrett Hardin.

THE TRAGEDY OF THE COMMONS
Garrett Hardin.
Science 162 (1968).

The tragedy of the commons develops in this way. Picture a pasture open to all. It is to be expected that each herdsman will try to keep as many cattle as possible on the commons. Such an arrangement may work reasonably satisfactorily for centuries because tribal wars, poaching, and disease keep the numbers of both man and beast well below the carrying capacity of the land. Finally, however, comes the day of reckoning, that is, the day when the long-desired goal of social stability becomes a reality. At this point, the inherent logic of the commons remorselessly generates tragedy.

As a rational being, each herdsman seeks to maximize his gain. Explicitly or implicitly, more or less consciously, he asks, "What is the utility to me of adding one more animal to my herd?" This utility has one negative and one positive component.

1. The positive component is a function of the increment of one animal. Since the herdsman receives all the proceeds from the sale of the additional animal, the positive utility is nearly + 1.

2. The negative component is a function of the additional overgrazing created by one more animal. Since, however, the effects of overgraz-

ing are shared by all the herdsmen, the negative utility for any particular decision-making herdsman is only a fraction of −1.

TRAGEDY

Adding together the component partial utilities, the rational herdsman concludes that the only sensible course for him to pursue is to add another animal to his herd. And another.... But this is the conclusion reached by each and every rational herdsman sharing a commons. Therein is the tragedy. Each man is locked into a system that compels him to increase his herd without limit—in a world that is limited. Ruin is the destination toward which all men rush, each pursuing his own best interest in a society that believes in the freedom of the commons. Freedom in a commons brings ruin to all.

Some would say that this is a platitude. Would that it were! In a sense, it was learned thousands of years ago, but natural selection favors the forces of psychological denial. The individual benefits as an individual from his ability to deny the truth even though society as a whole, of which he is a part, suffers. Education can counteract the natural tendency to do the wrong thing, but the inexorable succession of generations requires that the basis for this knowledge be constantly refreshed....

In an approximate way, the logic of the commons has been understood for a long time, perhaps since the discovery of agriculture or the invention of private property in real estate. But it is understood mostly only in special cases which are not sufficiently generalized. Even at this late date, cattlemen leasing national land on the Western ranges demonstrate no more than an ambivalent understanding, in constantly pressuring federal authorities to increase the head count to the point where overgrazing produces erosion and weed-dominance. Likewise, the oceans of the world continue to suffer from the survival of the philosophy of the commons. Maritime nations still respond automatically to the shibboleth of the "freedom of the seas." Professing to believe in the "inexhaustible resources of the oceans," they bring species after species of fish and whales closer to extinction.

The National Parks present another instance of the working out of the tragedy of the commons. At present, they are open to all, without limit. The parks themselves are limited in extent—there is only one Yosemite Valley—whereas population seems to grow without limit. The values that visitors seek in the parks are steadily eroded. Plainly, we must soon cease to treat the parks as commons or they will be of no value to anyone.

What shall we do? We have several options. We might sell them off as private property. We might keep them as public property, but allocate the right to enter them. The allocation might be on the basis of wealth, by the use of an auction system. It might be on the basis of merit, as defined by some agreed-upon standards. It might be by lottery. Or it might be on a first-come, first-served basis, administered to long queues. These, I think, are all objectionable. But we must choose—or acquiesce in the destruction of the commons that we call our National Parks.

POLLUTION

In a reverse way, the tragedy of the commons reappears in problems of pollution. Here it is not a question of taking something out of the commons, but of putting something in—sewage, or chemical, radioactive, and heat wastes into water; noxious and dangerous fumes into the air; and distracting and unpleasant advertising signs into the line of sight. The calculations of utility are much the same as before. The rational man finds that his share of the cost of the wastes he discharges into the commons is less than the cost of purifying his wastes before releasing them. Since this is true for everyone, we are locked into a system of "fouling our own nest," so long as we behave only as independent, rational, free enterprisers.

The tragedy of the commons as a food basket is averted by private property, or something formally like it. But the air and waters surrounding us cannot readily be fenced, and so the tragedy of the commons as a cesspool must be prevented by different means, by coercive laws or taxing devices that make it cheaper for the polluter to treat his pollutants than to discharge them untreated. We have not progressed as far with the solution of this problem as we have with the first. Indeed, our particular concept of private property, which deters us from exhausting the positive resources of the earth, favors pollution. The owner of a factory on the bank of a stream—whose property extends to the middle of the stream—often has difficulty seeing why it is not his natural right to muddy the waters flowing past his door. The law, always behind the times, requires elaborate stitching and fitting to adapt it to this newly perceived aspect of the commons. . . .

Notes and Comments

1. As Hardin indicates, one solution to a common resource problem is privatizing the resource. But even when the resource is one that commonly is privately held, such as land, there still are questions as to how to privatize the resource. The federal government gave away public lands to homesteaders in prior centuries. Those who demonstrated the desire to live on and farm the land were given the land. Many would consider the homesteading experiment a success from an economic and cultural perspective, but when Native American reservations were turned from common property into individual allotments, starting in 1887, the result was a disaster, which led to the repeal of that program in 1934.

2. The 1872 General Mining Act was another form of privatization. It was much like the idea of homesteading, except rather than give land to persons willing to live and farm it, this act gave land to persons who found "valuable minerals" on public land and were willing to develop it. Yet, this program is generally considered to be an environmental disaster, with the landowner solely concerned with maximizing his profit from mining and having no concern for the environment. The tragedy of the commons may have been averted, but this privatization destroys the resource even more surely than the commons described by Hardin. Why do you suppose that is?

Might it be the difference between a productive resource and an extractive resource?

3. Another way to privatize land, or resources on land, is simply to offer the public resource to the highest bidder. Timber sales and oil leases on public land are offered on this basis. Few believe that such "privatization" is likely to further environmental considerations, but these too could be characterized as extractive activities, not productive activities. Public grazing lands are also leased to ranchers for grazing cattle and sheep, but this privatized use of the lands has not resulted in the ranchers treating the lands in a sustainable manner. Why does this type of privatization not overcome the tragedy of the commons? Is it simply because the rancher does not own the land? As a practical matter, grazing permits for particular lands are almost invariably held by the same rancher indefinitely and are often considered rights that transfer with the rancher's own property.

4. Hardin's argument, based on economic concepts, which he says some might characterize as a platitude, can itself be challenged. In light of empirical research showing that traditional farming commons in fact were not overgrazed, other economist/lawyers have evolved a theory that cooperation with common goods can be as efficient as the free market with private goods in certain circumstances. *See*, *e.g.*, Robert C. Ellickson, ORDER WITHOUT LAW: HOW NEIGHBORS SETTLE DISPUTES (1991). What might be those certain circumstances—repeat players, close-knit societies, small groups? Are those circumstances transferable to larger political fields?

5. "Free Market Environmentalists" today argue in favor of privatizing federal forest and grazing lands, by selling them outright to the highest bidder, as a way of furthering environmental protection. They cite to Hardin's article for support of their position. What do you think? You might ask whether privately owned forest lands and privately owned grazing lands have fared better environmentally than public lands.

6. Hardin likens the National Parks to commons in that they are publicly owned and open to all, with the result that they are overused and in danger of being destroyed. National Parks too could be sold off to the highest bidder, perhaps to the Disney corporation, which could then run them like a theme park. Presumably, the new owner would run the Parks on a sustainable basis, making necessary investments and limiting use to the carrying capacity of the Parks. How do you suppose such an owner would do that? Would that be better than their present situation?

7. As Hardin notes, many of the commons today are not land-based and hence are not easily subjected to private ownership; you cannot fence air and water, and fisheries are not so easily reduced to ownership. Nevertheless, there are "water rights" that are a form of property, and regulatory experiments are being made in trying to address overfishing through assignment of fishing rights that could be bought and sold like other property, and theoretically would lead those having the rights not to overfish and destroy the value of their right.

8. Nevertheless, Hardin expected that "coercive laws or taxing devices" would be necessary where privatization was not a solution. Coercive laws generally mean government laws and regulations imposing limitations on what people can do and providing for punishments if people do not

comply with those limitations. Indeed, that is what most environmental law consists of.

ii.   Cost/Benefit Analysis

Since the beginning of the modern environmental movement, there has been a companion movement to improve the quality of governmental regulations by having government regulators explicitly consider the costs and the benefits of their regulations and to consider alternative regulatory mechanisms to maximize the net benefit of regulations. Although the practice originated with President Nixon, who created EPA and signed NEPA and the Clean Air Act into law, President Carter was the first to institutionalize a regularized practice requiring agencies to assess significant regulations in terms of their costs and benefits and to identify the least burdensome alternative. President Reagan enlarged and expanded this requirement and placed responsibility for overseeing agencies' compliance in the Office of Information and Regulatory Affairs (OIRA) in the Office of Management and Budget (OMB). When President Clinton was elected 12 years later, he, in essence, continued the same requirements, and the second President Bush has continued the Clinton executive order imposing the requirements for agency cost-benefit analysis and OMB review. In other words, over the past 20 years the idea that agencies should engage in cost-benefit analyses has become a bi-partisan concept, even if its application may have differed between administrations.

According to the various executive orders, cost-benefit analyses should assess all costs and benefits of available regulatory alternatives, including the alternative of not regulating. Costs and benefits are to include both those that are quantifiable (to the maximum extent feasible) and those that are qualitative or non-quantifiable. Then, to the extent permissible by law, the agency should choose the alternative that maximizes the net benefits to society.

The following selection describes the process of cost-benefit analysis and the arguments made by those who support its use.

ECONOMICS, EQUITY, AND THE ENVIRONMENT
Stephen M. Johnson (2004).

II.   COST-BENEFIT ANALYSIS PROCESS

The first step that an agency must take when preparing a cost-benefit analysis is to establish a baseline for the analysis by assessing what the world would look like without the proposed regulation. When the agency conducts the cost-benefit analysis, it will compare the costs and benefits of the proposed regulation (and other alternatives to that regulation) to that baseline. If more than one baseline is reasonable, and the analysis of costs and benefits will vary greatly depending on the selection of the baseline, the agency should calculate costs and benefits of the proposed rule against each of the reasonable baselines.

Once the agency has identified the baseline for analysis, it must calculate the *costs* of the proposed regulation (and alternatives). The "opportunity costs" of a proposed regulation should include the regulated community's compliance costs, the government's administrative costs for implementing the regulation, as well as other costs. The costs also include the costs of benefits that are foregone if the government adopts the regulation. Thus, the cost of banning a product includes the foregone net benefit of that product, taking into account any mitigation effects from substitutes for the product. Since the agency will be attempting to predict costs and outcomes that may or may not occur in the future, the agency should use probability estimates to assign a weight to costs or outcomes, depending on their likelihood.

The agency should also attempt to quantify the *benefits* of the regulation (and alternatives) in monetary terms, if possible, and use probability estimates to assign weights to the benefits, depending on their likelihood. In some cases, environmental regulations provide benefits that can be readily measured. For instance, when a regulation prevents damage to natural resources, it may be possible to measure the "use values" of those resources because there is a direct or indirect market for the resources. If the regulation prevents the destruction of thousands of fish in a commercial fishing region, the market value of the fish in the region can be directly measured. Similarly, while the market value of recreational fishing, hiking, or camping ... cannot be directly measured, their value is reflected in the prices of related goods that are directly traded in the market. Through the "revealed preference" method, economists can calculate the value of the recreational uses of those natural resources by examining the amount of money that was spent on fishing, hiking, and camping equipment, licensee travel to the region, and other goods and services related to the recreational use of the resources.

While market values can be directly or indirectly calculated for the "use values" of natural resources, it is much more difficult to calculate the monetary value of the "non-use values" ("passive use values") of natural resources, or the monetary value of many of the other benefits of environmental regulation because there is no market for many of those benefits. For instance, environmental regulations may reduce the potential number of cancer deaths, reduce the number of cases of asthma, prevent further pollution of a low-income community, protect endangered species, protect the peace and tranquility of a natural area, or provide a wide variety of other benefits. Since there is no market value for these benefits, agencies create artificial prices for the benefits by calculating what people would be "willing to pay" for the benefits, or "willing to accept" to give up the benefits.

There are two different methods that agencies normally use to calculate "willingness-to-pay" or "willingness-to-accept." The "hedonic price method" attempts to infer values for benefits from market behavior that can measured. For instance, the difference between the wages that are paid to persons who work in dangerous jobs and those who do

[margin handwritten note: hedonic method]

not is often used to determine the amount of money that a worker would accept to face an increased risk of harm. That value is then used to determine the value of lives saved by regulations. The other method that agencies commonly use to determine "willingness-to-pay" or "willingness-to-accept" is "contingent valuation." In this approach, a cross-section of the population that would be affected by a proposed government action is surveyed to determine how much they would be willing to pay for benefits that would be impacted by the government's action. Agencies have used hedonic pricing and contingent valuation to establish the value of human life (ranging from $1.5 million to almost $6 million), the value of an episode of acute bronchitis ($45), an emergency visit to the hospital for asthma ($9,000), a single episode of shortness of breath ($5.30), protection of grey wolves ($8 billion), and preservation of bald eagles (more than $25 billion), as well as many other benefits.

[handwritten margin note: Contingent Valuation]

While agencies have used hedonic pricing and contingent valuation to estimate values for a wide variety of benefits that are not directly or indirectly traded in the market, some benefits cannot be quantified in monetary terms. Nevertheless, agencies are required to identify, in cost-benefit analyses, the benefits that cannot be quantified. It is not clear, however, how the agency should weigh those benefits in the analysis.

When agencies calculate the costs and benefits of proposed regulations in cost-benefit analysis, they are examining costs and benefits that occur at different times. While costs are often incurred at the time that the regulation will be implemented, or shortly thereafter, to provide benefits that occur in the future, some costs might not arise until the future. Accordingly, as part of the cost-benefit analysis process, agencies *discount* future costs and benefits to present value for purposes of analysis. The discount rate is often an interest rate taken from financial markets, and OMB guidance recommends the use of a 7% discount rate. Thus, if a $1,000 cost will be incurred in 10 years, the present value of the cost, when discounted at a rate of 7%, will be $500.

* * *

III. ADVANTAGES OF COST-BENEFIT ANALYSIS

Supporters of cost-benefit analysis advocate the broader use of the process on several grounds. The primary argument in favor of cost-benefit analysis is an efficiency argument. When the government uses cost-benefit analysis to make decisions, supporters argue, the government will only impose costs on society when the benefits outweigh or justify the costs. Without cost-benefit analysis, supporters argue, the government has imposed restrictions on businesses that can cost billions of dollars for each life that they save. The billions of dollars that is spent to save one life, they argue, could be spent to save many more lives and provide many more benefits if the government utilized cost-benefit analysis. For instance, Professors Sunstein and Hahn argue that "better allocations of health care expenditures could save, each year, 60,200 additional lives at no additional cost...." Since there are limited resources that can be spent to protect human health and the environment, supporters argue, those resources should be used in the most efficient manner.

Supporters of cost-benefit analysis also criticize the high cost of regulations designed without cost-benefit analysis on the grounds that such regulations increase prices, reduce wages, and increase unemployment and poverty. Thus, they argue, regulation designed to protect health and the environment actually harms health.

Cost-benefit analysis advocates also contend that the process is more objective and transparent than the current regulatory process. Since the agency has to follow specific procedures and make decisions according to a readily identifiable standard, the agency is less likely to make arbitrary decisions or to make decisions that benefit politically favored groups. Similarly, supporters of cost-benefit analysis argue that the process makes agency decisionmaking transparent because it requires the agency to reveal all of its assumptions and uncertainties in language that the public, rather than merely toxicologists and biologists, can understand.

Defenders of cost-benefit analysis also argue that it is not merely an antiregulatory tool, and may even be used to support regulatory efforts by agencies. Professor Sunstein argues, for instance, that cost-benefit analysis has helped spur the removal of lead from gasoline and the elimination of chlorofluorocarbons (CFCs), and demonstrated that it was appropriate for EPA to reduce the acceptable level of arsenic in drinking water from 50 parts per billion. Similarly, a recent OMB report concluded that the health and social benefits of enforcing CAA regulations between 1992 and 2002 were five to seven times greater than the costs of complying with the rules.

Despite the bipartisan acceptance and arguments above in support of cost-benefit analysis, there is a rising critique of cost-benefit analysis from both practical and philosophical perspectives. Practically, studies have shown that the cost estimates for federal regulations, almost always based upon industry-supplied data, are invariably too high. *See* Frank Ackerman & Lisa Heinzerling, PRICELESS 37–39 (2004). This has the effect of suggesting that stricter regulations are less cost-effective than they actually are.

Numerous complaints have been raised regarding the methodology for valuing human life, or more accurately the benefits of regulations that reduce the risk of premature death. Many commentators have criticized the value assigned to a human life derived from studies of wage levels in risky industries, suggesting that the value is too low, because those studies do not adequately account for the lack of information about relative risks and the lack of job choices practically available to workers in these industries; they do not control for individuals' different attitudes toward risk, suggesting workers who choose riskier jobs do not place as great a premium on risk as the normal population; and they do not account for the difference between persons' willingness to accept and persons' willingness to pay, which numerous studies have found but which economists tend to discount. *See Id.*, at 75–81. And there are commentators who argue that the value of life assigned is too high because usually the premature death that is avoided is someone of advanced age and poor health—those most likely to be susceptible to environmental risks—who would only live for a few more years anyway. These commentators suggest a shift to valuing life-years, rather than simple life. A proposal by OIRA to use life-years, rather than the value of a whole life, which would reduce the monetary benefits of regulations that protect older persons, was withdrawn after a strong lobbying campaign by the American Association of Retired Persons. *See* Resources for the Future, Under Fire, EPA Drops the "Senior Death Discount," Tuesday, May 13, 2003, http://www.rff.org/rff/News/Coverage/2003/May/Under–Fire–EPA-drops-the-Senior–Death–Discount.cfm (visited on July 2, 2004).

Professors Ackerman and Heinzerling have suggested that what is really being measured by the so-called valuation of life is the value that people may perceive in living with reduced risk. That is, it is a benefit to live day-to-day feeling less afraid. This is a real value, but it is a different value than the value of a life itself. *See* Frank Ackerman & Lisa Heinzerling, *Pricing the Priceless: Cost–Benefit Analysis of Environmental Protection*, 150 U. Pa. L. Rev. 1553, 1564–1565 (2002).

Sometimes the difficulties in measuring costs or benefits results in simply not monetizing certain costs and benefits, but this too can create practical problems. For example, in 2002 the Bush administration's OMB reported to Congress that a Clinton administration initiated forest plan would impose $184 million in costs but only $219,000 in benefits. The costs reflected the value of the timber that would not be cut under the Clinton plan; the benefits would be costs the Forest Service would avoid by not having to build roads to get the timber out. In other words, OMB did not recognize *any* benefit in the non-monetized value of preserving uncut forest for habitat, recreation, and future generations. *See* PRICELESS, *supra*, at 6–7. And this is not an isolated example. *See, e.g.*, Richard W. Parker, *Grading the Government*, 70 U. Chi. L. Rev. 1345 (2003).

Beyond the practical objections to cost-benefit analysis as it is currently employed, there is also a significant philosophical objection to the attempt to monetize values that may not be appropriately monetized. For example, there are several commentators who argue that it is simply inappropriate to assign a value to human life. To bolster their argument they provide some examples where the valuation of human life simply seems improper. One noted example involves a study done by a famous Harvard cost-benefit proponent that concluded that government should subsidize smoking because the costs saved by government in pensions and health care resulting from premature deaths offset the value of the lives lost. Another example involved an attempt to value the costs and benefits of mitigating global warming. Using traditional valuation methods, lives in poor countries were only worth $100,000, while lives in rich countries were valued at $1.5 million. In other words, every American was worth 15 persons from Bangla Desh. *See* PRICELESS, *supra*, at 72–74.

The concept of discounting future costs and benefits also comes in for philosophical criticism when used for non-market values. For example, using OMB's preferred 7% discount rate, if the effect of a government required expenditure today is to prevent an unnecessary death in ten years, then it is not "cost effective" to impose any cost that is more than half of what a human life is worth. That is, lives in the future are discounted, as are other future benefits for the environment. Preserving nature for our children and our children's children generally does not pass the cost-benefit test.

Notes and Comments

1. The above discussion only scratches the surface of the debate over cost-benefit analysis. It is perhaps ironic that while environmentalists usually are critical of cost-benefit analyses, for the reasons described above, the basic analytical framework for cost-benefit analysis is identical to the decision structure mandated by the National Environmental Policy Act, fervently supported by environmentalists. As you will see later in this book, NEPA requires agencies to engage in an alternatives analysis for actions that may significantly affect the environment. That is, the agency compares what the effects of its proposed action and the reasonable alternatives would have on the environment in order to assess which alternative would achieve the desired result with the least adverse effect on the environment. Do you think environmentalists are not being consistent, or is there a principled basis for distinguishing between the environmental analysis and cost-benefit analysis?

2. It seems that many of the problems identified with cost-benefit analysis involve the difficulties or inappropriateness with trying to monetize certain values. Inasmuch as every executive order requiring cost-benefit analysis has only required quantification, as opposed to monetization, and then only to the extent feasible, why has there been such an attempt to assign dollar values to non-market and non-use values? One suggestion is that absent monetization, one would be comparing apples and oranges. Is it really so difficult to compare apples and oranges?

iii. Risk Analysis

Risk analysis is closely related to cost-benefit analysis and is a necessary prerequisite to it in the health and safety arena. Risk analysis is comprised of two parts: risk assessment and risk management. The former is supposed to determine what risk exists; the latter is supposed to decide what should be done about that risk. It is in the second step that cost-benefit comes into play. Once the risk assessment has determined the number of likely premature deaths from exposure to some chemical, the risk management decisionmaking process can determine how many premature deaths are acceptable. The following is a description of risk assessment.

RISK AND THE ENVIRONMENT: IMPROVING REGULATORY DECISION MAKING

A Report of the Carnegie Commission on Science,
Technology, and Government 76–78 (1993).

Risk assessment is a composite of established disciplines, including toxicology, biostatistics, epidemiology, economics, and demography. The goals of risk assessment are to characterize the nature of the adverse effects and to produce quantitative estimates of one or both of the following fundamental quantities: (1) the *probability* that an individual (a hypothetical or identified person) will suffer disease or death as a result of a specified exposure to a pollutant or pollutants; and (2) the *consequences* of such an exposure to an entire population (i.e., the number of cases of disease or death). . . .

The regulatory process is generally thought to encompass two elements, risk assessment and risk management. The distinction between these two components is important, though controversial. Risk assessment is usually conceived as the "Objective" part of the process, and risk management the subjective part. In risk assessment the analyst decides how big the problem is, while in risk management political decision makers decide what to do about the problem. The "conventional wisdom" (which some believe needs rethinking) stresses that risk management must not influence the processes and assumptions made in risk assessment, so the two functions must be kept conceptually and administratively separate.

Numerical estimates derived from risk assessment serve as inputs to several very different kinds of decisions, including (1) "acceptable risk" determinations (wherein action is taken if the risk exceeds some "bright line;" which can be zero); (2) "cost-benefit" determinations, where the risks reduced by a proposed action are translated into benefits (e.g., lives saved, life-years extended), expressed in dollar amounts, and compared to the estimated costs of implementing the action and some rule of thumb regarding how much cost it is wise to incur to achieve a given level of benefit (e.g., $10 million to save one additional life); and (3) "cost-effectiveness" determinations, where the action that maximizes the amount of risk reduction (not necessarily expressed in dollar terms) per unit cost is favored.

Since at least 1983 (with the publication of the National Research Council's "Redbook"), the dominant paradigm for risk assessment has been a sequential, four-step process:

- *Hazard identification*—in which a qualitative determination is made of what kinds of adverse health or ecological effects a substance can cause. Typically, agencies have focused on cancer as the effect that drives further analysis and regulation. So, for example, a typical hazard identification for vinyl chloride released from industrial facilities would involve the collection and critical analysis of short-term test-tube assays (for mutagenicity, etc.), of long-term animal assays (typically two-year rodent carcinogenicity tests), and of human epidemiologic data—either cohort studies (in which populations exposed to vinyl chloride are followed to assess whether their rates of any disease were significantly greater than those of unexposed or less-exposed populations) or case-control studies (which focus on victims of a particular disease to see whether they were significantly more likely to have been exposed to vinyl chloride than similar but disease-free individuals).

- *Exposure assessment*—in which a determination is made of the amounts of a substance to which a hypothetical person (usually the "maximally exposed individual") and/or the total population are exposed. To return to the vinyl chloride example, this part of risk assessment would bring to bear techniques of emissions characterization (how much vinyl chloride leaves the plant in a given time?), fate-and-transport analysis (how is the chemical dispersed in the atmosphere and transformed into other compounds?), uptake analysis (how much air do people breathe, both outdoors and indoors?), and demographic analysis (how many hours per day do people spend in various locations near the plant, and how long do they reside in one locale before moving away?).

- *Dose-response assessment*—in which an estimate is made of the probability or extent of injury at the exposure levels determined above, by quantifying the "potency" of the chemical in question. For vinyl chloride again, scientists would determine its carcinogenic potency by fitting the animal bioassay data (number of tumors produced at different exposure levels) to a mathematical model (usually one that is linear at low doses), and then transforming the resultant potency estimate for rodents into a human potency estimate through the use of a "scaling factor" (usually, a ratio of the body surface areas of the two species). Additionally, human epidemiologic data could be used to validate or supplant the animal-based potency estimate.

- *Risk characterization*—in which the results of the above steps are integrated to describe the nature of the adverse effects and the strength of the evidence and to present one or more "risk numbers." For example, EPA might say, "This vinyl chloride plant is estimated to produce up to 3 excess cases of liver cancer every 70 years among the 100,000 people living within 1 mile of the facility" or "the maximally exposed individual faces an excess lifetime liver cancer risk of 5.4×10^{-4}."

Risk assessment is essentially a tool for extrapolating from scientific data to a risk number. The tool is made up of a host of assumptions, which are an admixture of science and policy. Sometimes either science or policy predominates, but it is often difficult to get a broad consensus that this is so.

A view among some in industry and elsewhere is that risk assessment systematically overestimates risk and frightens the public: as they see it, the typical risk assessment takes a trivial emission source, pretends that people are pressed up against the fenceline of the source 24 hours a day for 70 years, gauges the toxicity of the pollutant released by exposing ultrasensitive rodents to huge doses in the laboratory, and then uses the most "conservative" dose-response model to estimate a risk to humans at the low ambient exposures of interest. The view of some in environmental and public interest groups, and elsewhere, is that risk assessment may often inherently underestimate the true magnitude of the problem, by ignoring complicating but salient factors, including synergies among exposures, vast variations in susceptibility among humans, and unusual exposure pathways (e.g., inhalation of steam in showers containing volatilized chemicals from contaminated water).

Because the science underlying most risk assessment assumptions is inconclusive, arguments over whether or not an assumption is scientifically valid often distill down to debates about whether it is better to err on the side of "false positives" (if there is an error, it will more likely be a false indication of danger) or "false negatives" (if there is an error, it will more likely be a false indication of safety). Those who might be harmed by the substance being assessed will generally favor false positives; those who would gain from the substance will generally favor false negatives.

Notes and Comments

1.　As the selection suggests, risk assessment is usually described as an objective process, in the sense that scientists, rather than policy makers, are in charge of the process. However, as the selection also indicates, risk assessment requires those involved in the process to make a number of assumptions, and these assumptions are not themselves objective. They reflect what those utilizing them believe is appropriate to the circumstances. This often means that important, qualitative decisions are being made in a manner that is not very transparent. Concern about how these decisions are made is one of the reasons for an increased demand for peer review of scientific determinations that affect regulatory decisions. *See, e.g.*, Office of Management and Budget, Final Information Quality Bulletin for Peer Review, 70 Fed. Reg. 2664 (January 14, 2005).

2.　An important part of risk assessments is establishing the dose/response relationship between the substance and the affected entity. Usually this is reflected as a dose/response curve, showing that at higher exposures (doses) the greater the response (e.g., the likelihood that cancer develops). For many toxic substances there is a threshhold level, a level at which a substance that is harmful at some levels of exposure is no longer harmful. For example, iodine is a poison that can kill you, but a lack of any iodine in your system will result in health problems. For some substances, scientists can run tests that result in a "no observable effect level" (NOEL), sometimes phrased as "no observable adverse effect level" (NOAEL), that provides the basis for a threshhold level. For carcinogens, however, generally there is no established NOEL or NOAEL. Instead, it is assumed that at very low levels of exposure one's risk of cancer diminishes but never disappears. Moreover, it is further assumed that there is a linear (straight-line) relationship between exposure and contracting cancer. That is, if exposure is reduced by a factor of ten, then one's risk of contracting cancer is reduced by a factor of ten. These assumptions can then result in a finding that a very small exposure to a substance will still pose some risk of causing cancer, perhaps one in 10 million. But if a population of 280 million people were subject to this small exposure, this would suggest 28 persons would die from the exposure. This conclusion, however, would be driven by *assumptions*. A different assumption, for example, that at this exposure level there is *no* increased risk of cancer, would lead to a conclusion that no one would die from this exposure. While still a different assumption, that at this level the dose/response is higher, could lead to the conclusion that 100 persons might die from this exposure. None of these conclusions might be provable or disprovable. And one might be as reasonable as another, but each reflects an attitude of what position one should take in the absence of information.

iv.   The Polluter Pays Principle

Earlier, in discussing the economic concept of public goods, it was noted that when people can use the commons, they do not bear the full cost of the harm they do to the commons. One theory of environmental laws is that they should impose the full cost of the pollution on the polluter. Then, the polluter receives the right price signals with respect to that pollution. Moreover, the notion that the polluter should pay for the harm it creates resonates even with non-economists.

Polluters can be made to pay in various ways. In theory, taxes could be levied on polluters calibrated to the cost of their pollution, but there are both technical difficulties in making that calibration and political difficulties in imposing taxes at all. Simply requiring polluters to spend money on pollution control equipment is a form of making them pay for their pollution. The Comprehensive Environmental Response, Compensation, and Liability Act (also known as Superfund) imposes a tort-like form of liability on persons whose hazardous substances are released to the environment.

v.   Sustainable Development

The idea of sustainable development is a mantra of the modern environmental movement, and the term has been used particularly to describe the goals of international environmental law. It was enshrined in the Declaration of Principles of the United Nations Conference on Environment and Development (UNCED) in 1992. There is, however, no agreed upon definition. Nevertheless, a common description is "development that meets the needs of the present without compromising the ability of future generations to meet their own needs." World Commission on Environment and Development, Our Common Future 8 (1987). The devil, however, is in the details. No one is in favor of unsustainable development.

The difficulty is for the most part in determining what is sustainable, especially for non-renewable resources. In a sense, no use of a non-renewable resource is sustainable forever. By definition, the resource is finite. However, ever since Malthus, predictions of non-renewable resource depletion have turned out to be erroneous. For example, predictions that petroleum supplies would be used up by various dates have been notably in error. In the United States, the federal government predicted in the 1930s that domestic reserves would be exhausted in less than 15 years. In 1951 the government adjusted its prediction and said that domestic reserves would be exhausted by 1965. Julian Simon, *The Ultimate Resource 2* (1996). In 1970, a famous study entitled *Limits to Growth*, produced by a number of scientists under the name of the Club of Rome, predicted that oil resources would be exhausted by 1992. Donella Meadows, et. al., *Limits to Growth* (1972). In 1987, Anne and Paul Ehrlich, scientists famous (or infamous) for their writings on the coming environmental crisis, predicted a worldwide oil crisis in the 1990s. Anne Ehrlich & Paul Ehrlich, *Earth* (1987). Today, the predictions continue with a recent issue of National Geographic publicizing the predictions of "some experts" that oil production is about to decline at any moment, or in 10 years, or in 35 years. Tim Appenzeller, *The End of Cheap Oil*, National Geographic 84, 90 (June 2004).

Others, however, read the data differently. Bjorn Lomborg, a Danish environmental officer who has become notorious for his conclusions that the environment is improving without regard to government environmental efforts, reported in 2001 that world oil reserves compared to annual production was higher than at any time prior to 1985. Bjorn Lomborg, *The Skeptical Environmentalist* 125 (2001). Moreover, he argued that the prophets of doom failed to recognize that throughout history, as a resource appeared to become more scarce, price signals motivated greater exploration for new discoveries, greater efficiencies in the use of the resource, as well as the development of substitutes for the now higher priced resource. If petroleum becomes too expensive, we will develop fuel cells. "Optimists," such as Lomborg, take comfort in the history of resource utilization, which seems to support their conclusion. In a famous showdown between "optimist" Julian Simon and "pessimist" Paul Ehrlich, Ehrlich bet Simon that the price of five mineral commodities would be higher in 1990 than in 1980. In fact, all five commodities were cheaper in 1990. *See* Lomborg, *supra*, at 136.

Nevertheless, even pessimists recognize that resources will not disappear; they will just become more expensive as the demand increases relative to the supply, and at a certain level the price might become prohibitive. To the extent that our way of life depends on the resources remaining relatively inexpensive, a significant price increase might jeopardize our way of life. The pessimists argue that we should take preventive measures today to avoid their predicted catastrophic effects of such price increases. If two-dollar a gallon gasoline seems expensive, imagine what $15 a gallon gasoline would do to our way of life. It is better to adopt practices today that will soften the blow that is bound to come, they say. And those practices are to reduce materialism, consumerism, and the never ending quest for growth. Not surprisingly, critics of materialism see sustainability as the hope for the future, while business and development interests see "sustainability" as a code word for opposing growth.

Sustainability perhaps has more meaning with respect to renewable resources, because it is here, especially with regard to worldwide fisheries and timber practices in much of the world that we find ready examples of non-sustainable practices. Even Lomborg concedes that there is overfishing of wild stocks and unsustainable deforestation in developing countries. Recognition of the problem, however, is only the beginning. Particularly in the developing world, suggestions by richer nations that resources should only be used sustainably are not taken kindly. In poorer nations the first demand is for basic necessities and then for some material goods, and this may place a higher priority on present-day needs than on those of future generations.

vi. The Precautionary Principle

Like sustainable development, the Precautionary Principle has become a fundamental principle of modern environmentalism, and it too is reflected in international legal documents, such as the 1992 Declaration of Principles by the United Nations Conference on Environment and Development. Again, however, there is no agreed upon definition of the principle, and the application of the principle in practice depends upon its definition. A generally liberal academic had the following to say about the principle.

CASS R. SUNSTEIN, THE PARALYZING PRINCIPLE

Regulation 32 (Winter 2002–2003).

All over the world, there is increasing interest in a simple idea for the regulation of risk: the Precautionary Principle. Simply put, the principle counsels that we should avoid steps that will create a risk of harm; until safety is established through clear evidence, we should be cautious. In a catchphrase: Better safe than sorry.

In ordinary life, pleas of this kind seem quite sensible. People buy smoke alarms and insurance. They wear seatbelts and motorcycle helmets, even if they are unlikely to be involved in an accident. Should rational regulators not follow the same approach as well? Many people believe so.

In many ways, the Precautionary Principle seems quite sensible, even appealing. To justify regulation, a certainty of harm should not be required; a risk, even a low one, may well be enough. It makes sense to expend resources to prevent a small chance of complete disaster; consider the high costs, pecuniary and otherwise, that are spent to reduce the risk of terrorist attack. On reasonable assumptions, the costs are worth incurring even if the probability of harm—in individual cases or even in the aggregate—is relatively low.

The Precautionary Principle might well be seen as a plea for a kind of regulatory insurance. Certainly the principle might do some real-world good, spurring us to attend to neglected problems. Nonetheless, the principle cannot be fully defended in those ways, simply because risks are on all sides of social situations. Any effort to be universally precautionary will be paralyzing, forbidding every imaginable step, including no step at all.

The Precautionary Principle enjoys widespread international support. But what does the principle mean or require? There are numerous definitions, and they are not all compatible with one another. We can imagine a continuum of understandings. At one extreme are weak versions to which no reasonable person could object; at the other extreme are strong versions that would appear to call for a fundamental rethinking of regulatory policy.

The most cautious and weak versions suggest, quite sensibly, that a lack of decisive evidence of harm should not be a ground for refusing to regulate. Regulation might be justified even if we cannot establish an incontrovertible connection between, say, low-level exposures to certain carcinogens and adverse effects on human health. Thus, the 1992 Rio Declaration states, "Where there are threats of serious or irreversible damage, lack of full scientific certainty shall not be used as a reason for postponing cost-effective measures to prevent environmental degradation."

The weak versions of the Precautionary Principle are unobjectionable and important. Every day, people take steps (and incur costs) to avoid hazards that are far from certain. We do not walk in moderately dangerous areas at night; we exercise; we buy smoke detectors; we buckle our seatbelts; we might even avoid fatty foods. Because the weak versions are sensible, I will not discuss them here. Instead, I will understand the principle in a strong way, to suggest that regulation is required whenever there is a possible risk to health, safety, or the environment, even if the supporting evidence is speculative and even if the economic costs of regulation are high. To avoid palpable absurdity, the idea of "possible risk" will be understood to require a certain threshold of scientific plausibility. To support regulation, no one thinks that it is enough if someone, somewhere, urges that a risk is worth taking seriously. But under the Precautionary Principle as I shall understand it, the threshold burden is minimal, and once it is met, there is something like a presumption in favor of stringent regulatory controls.

In 1982, the United Nations World Charter for Nature apparently gave the first international recognition to the strong version of the principle, suggesting that when "potential adverse effects are not fully understood, the activities should not proceed." The widely publicized Wingspread Declaration, from a meeting of environmentalists in 1998, is another example of the strong version:

When an activity raises threats of harm to human health or the environment, precautionary measures should be taken even if some cause and effect relationships are not established scientifically. In this context the proponent of the activity, rather than the public, should bear the burden of proof.

Unlike the weak version of the Precautionary Principle, the strong version is not limited to threats of serious or irreversible damage and reverses the burden of proof.

Belief in the strong version of the Precautionary Principle is not limited to any particular group. All over the world, the idea has been a staple of regulatory policy for several decades. In the United States, both Congress and the federal courts, without using the term explicitly, have built in a notion of precaution in some important cases, allowing or requiring regulation on the basis of conservative assumptions. The Precautionary Principle has played a significant role in international documents, to the point where it has become ubiquitous.

The most serious problem with the Precautionary Principle is that it offers no guidance—not that it is wrong, but that it forbids all courses of action, including inaction. To understand that point, it will be useful to anchor the discussion in some concrete problems:

* * *

- Genetic modification of food has become a widespread practice. But the risks involved are not known with precision. Some people fear that genetic modification will result in serious ecological harm and large risks to human health. Other people claim that genetic modification will have significant health benefits.

- Scientists are hardly in full accord about the dangers associated with global warming, but there is general agreement that global warming is occurring. It is possible that global warming will produce, by 2100, a mean temperature increase of 4.5 degrees C; that it will result in well over $5 trillion in annual monetized costs; and that it will also produce a significant number of deaths from malaria. The Kyoto Protocol would require most industrialized nations to reduce greenhouse gas emissions to between 92 and 94 percent of 1990 levels in an effort to reduce the degree of warming. Such reductions would impose substantial costs.

- Many people fear nuclear power on the ground that nuclear power plants raise various health and safety issues, including some possibility of catastrophe. But if a nation does not rely on nuclear power, it is likely to rely on fossil fuels, and in particular on coal-fired power plants. Such plants create risks of their own, including risks associated with global warming. China, for example, has relied on nuclear energy as a way of reducing greenhouse gases and other air pollution problems.

- There is a possible conflict between the protection of marine mammals and military exercises. The U.S. Navy, for example, engages in many such exercises, and it is possible that marine mammals are threatened as a result. Military activities in the oceans might well cause significant harm, but a decision to suspend those activities might also endanger military preparedness.

In those cases, what guidance does the Precautionary Principle provide? It is tempting to say that the principle calls for strong controls on ... genetic engineering of food, greenhouse gases, threats to marine mammals, and nuclear power. In all of those cases, there is a possibility of serious harms, and no authoritative scientific evidence suggests that the possibility is close to zero.

If the burden of proof is on the proponent of the activity or processes in question, the Precautionary Principle would seem to impose a burden of proof that cannot be met. Put to one side the question of whether the principle, so understood, is sensible; let us ask a more fundamental question: Is more stringent regulation really compelled by the Precautionary Principle?

The answer is that it is not. In most of the cases above, it should be easy to see that in its own way, stringent regulation would actually run afoul of the Precautionary Principle. The simplest reason is that such regulation might well deprive society of significant benefits, and for that reason produce risks and even deaths that would otherwise not occur. In some cases, regulation eliminates the "opportunity benefits" of a process or activity, and thus causes preventable deaths. If that is so, regulation is hardly precautionary.

The most familiar cases involve the "drug lag" produced by a highly precautionary approach to the introduction of new medicines and drugs into the market. If a government takes such an approach, it might protect people, in a precautionary way, against harms from inadequately tested drugs. But it will also prevent people from receiving potential benefits from those drugs. Is it "precautionary" to require extensive premarketing testing, or to do the opposite?

Or consider the case of genetic modification of food. Many people believe that a failure to allow genetic modification might well result in numerous deaths, and a small probability of many more. The reason is that genetic modification holds out the promise of producing food that is both cheaper and healthier, which would have large benefits in developing countries. Now the point is not that genetic modification will definitely have those benefits, or that the benefits of genetic modification outweigh the risks. The point is only that if the Precautionary Principle is taken literally, it is offended by regulation as well as by nonregulation.

Sometimes regulation would violate the Precautionary Principle because it would give rise to substitute risks in the form of hazards that materialize, or are increased, as a result of regulation. Consider nuclear power. It is reasonable to think that in light of current options, a ban on nuclear power will increase dependence on fossil fuels that contribute to global warming. If so, such a ban would seem to run afoul of the Precautionary Principle. Or consider the Environmental Protection

Agency's effort to ban asbestos, a ban that might well seem justified or even compelled by the principle. The difficulty, from the standpoint of that very principle, is that substitutes for asbestos also carry risks. Or return to possible risks to marine mammals from the U.S. Navy. Some people are concerned that efforts to eliminate those risks will endanger military preparedness, if only because of the rise of new administrative barriers to training exercises. In those circumstances, what is the appropriate approach, according to the Precautionary Principle?

vii.   Environmental Ethics

For the most part, our discussion has centered on protecting the environment for the benefit of humankind. Whether the issue is risk regulation or sustainable development, the focus is on how to benefit people. Even within this framework there are clearly ethical issues. One of these is described as intergenerational equity. The idea is simple: that one generation should neither hoard to itself all the benefits nor impose on later generations all the costs. You can see how the sustainable development idea relates to this ethical concern. Another ethical issue is captured by the expression: environmental justice. It is described in more detail below, but in short it is concerned with avoiding the imposition of environmental harms disproportionately on the poor or on minority populations.

Beyond the human concern, however, is another issue–whether the environment should be protected not for our utilitarian concerns but for a broader ethical principle. Probably the best known statement of this principle was made in the following work.

A SAND COUNTY ALMANAC
Aldo Leopold 201–204 (1949).

The Land Ethic

When god-like Odysseus returned from the wars in Troy, he hanged all on one rope a dozen slave-girls of his household whom be suspected of misbehavior during his absence.

This hanging involved no question of propriety. The girls were property. The disposal of property was then, as now, a matter of expediency, not of right and wrong.

Concepts of right and wrong were not lacking from Odysseus' Greece: witness the fidelity of his wife through the long years before at last his black-prowed galleys clove the wine-dark seas for home. The ethical structure of that day covered wives, but had not yet been extended to human chattels. During the three thousand years which have since elapsed, ethical criteria have been extended to many fields of conduct, with corresponding shrinkages in those judged by expediency only . . . .

The first ethics dealt with the relation between individuals; the Mosaic Decalogue is an example. Later accretions dealt with the relation between the individual and society. The Golden rule tries to integrate the individual to society; democracy to integrate social organization to the individual.

There is as yet no ethic dealing with man's relation to land and to the animals and plants which grow upon it. Land, like Odysseus' slave-girls, is still property. The land relation is still strictly economic, entailing privileges but not obligations.

The extension of ethics to this third element in human environment is, if I read the evidence correctly, an evolutionary possibility and an ecological necessity. It is the third step in a sequence. The first two have already been taken. Individual thinkers since the days of Ezekiel and Isaiah have asserted that the despoliation of land is not only inexpedient but wrong. Society, however, has not yet affirmed their belief. . . .

An ethic may be regarded as a mode of guidance for meeting ecological situations so new or intricate, or involving such deferred reactions, that the path of social expediency is not discernible to the average individual. Animal instincts are modes of guidance for the individual in meeting such situations. Ethics are possibly a kind of community instinct in-the-making.

All ethics so far evolved rest upon a single premise: that the individual is a member of a community of interdependent parts. His instincts prompt him to compete for his place in that community, but his ethics prompt him also to co-operate (perhaps in order that there may be a place to compete for).

The land ethic simply enlarges the boundaries of the community to include soils, waters, plants, and animals, or collectively: the land.

This sounds simple: do we not already sing our love for and obligation to the land of the free and the home of the brave? Yes, but just what and whom do we love? Certainly not the soil, which we are sending helter-skelter downriver. Certainly not the waters, which we assume have no function except to turn turbines, float barges, and carry off sewage. Certainly not the plants, of which we exterminate whole communities without batting an eye. Certainly not the animals, of which we have already extirpated many of the largest and most beautiful species. A land ethic of course cannot prevent the alteration, management, and use of these "resources", but it does affirm their right to continued existence, and, at least in spots, their continued existence in a natural state.

In short, a land ethic changes the role of *Homo sapiens* from conqueror of the land-community to plain member and citizen of it. It implies respect for his fellow-members, and also respect for the community as such.

In human history, we have learned (I hope) that the conqueror role is eventually self-defeating. Why? Because it is implicit in such a role that the conqueror knows, *ex cathedra,* just what makes the community clock tick, and just what and who is valuable, and what and who is worthless, in community life. It always turns out that he knows neither, and this is why his conquests eventually defeat themselves.

Notes and Comments

1. Leopold's thesis, that we should consider plants and animals—in short, nature—to be part of the same community that includes humankind, has a potential alternative conclusion to the one Leopold draws. That is, if humankind is part of nature, then whatever we do is "natural." If we destroy plants and animals, it is no more unethical than if a volcano, asteroid, or earthquake destroyed plants and animals. Or are ethical considerations uniquely human? If so, does that suggest an unbridgeable gap between humans and the rest of nature?

2. Leopold's ethical challenge is conspicuously agnostic. For those more religiously inclined, there can be a different ethical perspective. Historically, the focus has been on Genesis's reference to man having "dominion over the fish of the sea, and over the birds of the air, and over the cattle, and over all the earth, and over every creeping thing that creeps upon the earth." Genesis 1:26. This suggested that nature was man's for the taking; that it was there for man's benefit. More recently, scholars have argued that the Bible instead teaches that God enjoined man to be responsible for the environment; that God has made man the steward of the environment, responsible to God for the faithful execution of that duty. *See, e.g.*, John Copeland Nagle, *Playing Noah*, 82 U. MINN. L. REV. 1171 (1998); Chuck D. Barlow, *Why the Christian Right Must Protect the Environment: Theocentricity in the Political Workplace*, 23 B.C. ENVTL. AFF. L. REV. 781 (1996).

viii. Environmental Justice

As indicated above, the term "environmental justice" is used most often to describe concern with environmental harms being visited disproportionately on the poor and minority groups. In the 1980s a General Accounting Office report and a report by the Commission for Racial Justice of the United Church of Christ both found that the location of hazardous waste facilities were disproportionately found in black and Hispanic communities. These studies were then subjected to a number of criticisms. For example, the definition of a black or minority community was determined by the percentage of the population of the particular "community" exceeding the national average percentage of black or Hispanic residents. Thus, Staten Island, the "whitest" of the New York City boroughs, and the site of the largest solid waste site, was determined to be a minority community because 20% of its population is minority. Another criticism was that the studies did not show that the waste facilities were placed into existing minority communities, as opposed to the communities becoming minority communities through inmigration. *See, e.g.*, Vicki Been, *Locally Undesirable Land Uses in Minority Neighborhoods: Disproportionate Siting or Market Dynamics?*, 103 Yale L.J. 1383 (1994).

Notwithstanding the criticisms, there can be little question that poor people are more likely to suffer environmental harms than richer persons, just as they suffer worse housing, education, medical treatment, etc. And to the extent that the poor are disproportionately made up of minorities, minorities likewise will disproportionately bear the brunt of environmental problems. Moreover, to the extent that the political process can be used by affected persons to fight LULUs (locally unwanted land uses), those with the least political clout are the most likely to be the victims of LULU siting. Phrased as "environmental injustice" or "environmental racism," interest groups could perhaps hope to galvanize minority communities to use environmental laws and the political process to improve their situation.

For a while, a combination of environmental laws and Title VI of the Civil Rights Act of 1964 seemed like they might provide a handle to attack siting decisions that disproportionately affected minority communities. Title VI prohibits discrimination based on race, color, or national origin in any program receiving federal funds, and state agencies implementing the Clean Air Act, Clean Water Act, and other environmental statutes invariably receive federal funds to administer these laws under the cooperative federalism model. A person subject to discrimination under one of these programs can sue to enjoin the discrimination. That is, enforcement is not limited to the federal government enforcing the Act either through an injunction or withdrawing federal funds. *See Cannon v. University of Chicago*, 441 U.S. 677, 99 S.Ct. 1946, 60 L.Ed.2d 560 (1979). However, the Supreme Court has held that Title VI itself only prohibits *intentional* racial discrimination; it does not forbid disproportionate impacts. *See Alexander v. Choate*, 469 U.S. 287, 105 S.Ct. 712, 83 L.Ed.2d 661 (1985). Rarely, if ever, is the claim made that state officials have intentionally discriminated on the basis of race. Even if the suspicion is there, the proof is not. Rather, the claim is that the state official's decision has a disparate impact. Thus, at this point, Title VI provides little help.

There is, however, some authority for the idea that agencies can adopt regulations implementing Title VI that can go beyond prohibiting merely what the act itself prohibits. *See Guardians Assn. v. Civil Service Comm'n of New York City*, 463 U.S. 582, 103 S.Ct. 3221, 77 L.Ed.2d 866 (1983) (five justices in three separate opinions so indicated, but none of the opinions was joined by a majority of the Court). And indeed, agencies, including the EPA, have adopted regulations implementing Title VI that effectively prohibit discriminatory effects in its funded programs, even if the effect is unintentional. Consequently, minority persons who believed state environmental agencies' actions had the effect of disproportionately affecting them brought a number of suits alleging violations of EPA's regulations. *See, e.g., Chester Residents Concerned for Quality Living v. Seif*, 132 F.3d 925 (3d Cir. 1997), judgment vacated and case remanded, 524 U.S. 974, 119 S.Ct. 22, 141 L.Ed.2d 783 (1998) (mem.). In *Alexander v. Sandoval*, 532 U.S. 275, 121 S.Ct. 1511, 149 L.Ed.2d 517 (2001), however, the Supreme Court ruled that, while there is a private right of action directly under Title VI, there is no private right of action under an agency's Title VI regulations; these may be enforced only by the agency. Consequently, private suits under federal law trying to stop action receiving federal funds because of disparate effects on minority populations no longer may be brought.

While *Alexander v. Sandoval* did not directly rule on whether agencies may adopt regulations under Title VI that prohibit discriminatory effects without an intent to discriminate, the majority opinion stated that a finding of such a power would be "in considerable tension" with earlier decided cases. Nevertheless, that power is currently presumed to exist, and the agency regulations remain in effect, so that agencies may themselves enforce against discriminatory effects in programs they fund. Consequently, minority groups have filed Title VI complaints with EPA, requesting EPA to take enforcement action (or to deny approval to a particular state action because of the alleged discriminatory effects of the proposed state action). These have been notably unsuccessful. As of December 1, 2004, of the 118 complaints where action is completed, EPA has not found a single violation. *See* http://epa. gov/civilrights/docs/t6stdec012004.pdf (last visited on 2/23/2005). Perhaps not coincidentally, EPA's draft guidance on investigating administrative complaints published in June 2000 has never been finalized.

In 1994 President Clinton issued Executive Order 12898, Federal Actions to Address Environmental Justice in Minority Populations and Low–Income Populations. It continues in effect. The order required agencies to adopt an environmental justice strategy that identifies and addresses disproportionately high and adverse effects on minority and low-income populations. In addition, it requires agencies to conduct their programs in a manner that ensures such programs do not have the effect of excluding persons from the benefits of the programs because of their race, color, or national origin. Nevertheless, unlike Title VI, the executive order creates no private rights whatsoever and states that it is solely to improve the internal management of the executive branch. Consequently, like the regulatory reform executive orders discussed earlier in this chapter, courts will not consider whether agencies violate their requirements under the order.

This order has also had little to no effect on agencies' actions. Indeed, in 2004, the EPA Inspector General issued a scathing report on EPA's implementation of the order. In particular, it criticized the agency for not defining what a disproportionately high impact is or what is a minority or low-income community. The agency's response takes issue with the IG's report and suggests that the IG has misinterpreted the executive order:

> [T]he recommended OIG approach appears to be predicated on an intuitively reasonable but faulty interpretation of Executive Order 12898. The OIG recommended approach is premised on the commonly held notion, drawn from the Environmental Justice Movement's emergence from the Civil Rights Movement, that environmental justice can be achieved merely by identifying disproportionately high minority and low-income communities, and designating them as forming a "protected class." This approach

fails to recognize that the Nation's environmental laws do not recognize race, ethnicity, or income as protected classes. To the contrary, those environmental laws are designed to address human health and environmental effects for all communities.

Memorandum, Agency Response to Recommendations Provided in the OIG Evaluation Report (June 7, 2004) (http://www.epa.gov/compliance/ resources/publications/ej/ej_annual_project_reports.html, visited on July 8, 2004). In other words, EPA promotes environmental justice by assuring that all communities are protected, so there is no need to focus on minority and low-income groups.

Notes and Comments

1. It is easy to find fault with EPA's performance under either Title VI or Executive Order 12898. First, there is no specific funding for its environmental justice work. Probably more important, the task of determining who is responsible when poor and minority populations do not seem to benefit equally with others in America is, to say the least, daunting. And finally, why should we expect EPA to be any better in solving inequality with respect to environmental benefits than the rest of society is in solving inequality generally in America, especially when no environmental law provides them any particular tool? This seemingly hopeless job led some to criticize the Executive Order in the beginning as simply a political ploy to appeal to certain interest groups. *See, e.g.*, David Schoenbrod, *Environmental "Injustice" Is About Politics, Not Racism*, Wall St. J., Feb. 23, 1994, p. A21.

2. Nonetheless, even if the environmental justice movement has found the law an inhospitable partner, it is not without some successes in the political sphere. There are a number of cases where permits or siting permission have been denied, not on their face because of environmental justice issues, but because of the publicity and problems identified by an opposition movement motivated by environmental justice concerns. *See, e.g.*, Robert Holden and Tad Bartlett, *Leaving Communities Behind: the Evolving World of Environmental Justice*, 51 La. Bar J. 94 (August/September 2003)(telling the story of the proposed Shintech facility in Louisiana).

III.   THE CONSTITUTION AND ENVIRONMENTAL LAW

A.   Authority for Environmental Laws

As you have probably already learned in Constitutional Law, if not in high school, federal laws must find a basis in the Constitution. Unlike states, which have the inherent power to make all laws not prohibited by the Constitution, the federal government must be able to point to some constitutional provision as authority for laws passed by Congress. And there is no grant of authority in the Constitution for Congress to protect the environment. There are, however, a number of constitutional provisions that can provide a basis for environmental laws: the Commerce Clause, the Spending Clause, the Property Clause, and the Necessary and Proper Clause.

Probably the least problematic of these is the Property Clause, Article IV, Section 3, cl. 2: "The Congress shall have power to dispose of and make all needful rules and regulations respecting the territory or other property belonging to the United States." Not only is the textual authorization broad, but the Supreme Court has also read it broadly. *See Kleppe v. New Mexico*, 426 U.S. 529, 96 S.Ct. 2285, 49 L.Ed.2d 34 (1976) (upholding the Wild Free–Roaming Horses and Burros Act and concluding that Congress has "complete power" over federal lands). Consequently, any federal law regarding what happens on United States' property stands on strong constitutional foundations. Examples would include the National Forest Management Act, 16 U.S.C. §§ 1601 *et seq.*, and the Federal Land Policy and Management Act, 43 U.S.C. §§ 1701 *et seq.*, that govern the uses of lands owned by the federal government and managed by, respectively, the United States Forest Service and the Bureau of Land Management. Another example would be the provision of the Endangered Species Act that makes it unlawful to maliciously damage or destroy any endangered plant on lands under federal jurisdiction, 16 U.S.C. § 1538(a)(2)(B).

The Spending Clause is also broad. Article I, Section 8, cl. 1 provides that "Congress shall have the power to lay and collect taxes ... to pay the debts and provide for the common defence and general welfare of the United States." In other words, Congress can spend money for any purpose that furthers the general welfare of the United States. As yet, no court has found any expenditure not included within that authorization.

An important aspect of the spending power, however, is the ability to place conditions on expenditures. For example, states receive substantial sums of money from the federal government for the purpose of building highways, but there can be conditions on states receiving those funds beyond the simple requirement that they be used for building highways. One condition is that they cannot use those funds to build a highway through a park unless there is no feasible and prudent alternative route and plans minimize the adverse environmental impact on the park. 23 U.S.C. § 138. A condition of a different type is that the state will lose a portion of its highway funds if it does not maintain an adequate state implementation plan under the Clean Air Act. 42 U.S.C. § 7509(b)(1). In other words, a state may be induced to take certain actions it would not otherwise do by offering it money on the condition that it take those actions. There is a limit to such inducement, however. In *South Dakota v. Dole*, 483 U.S. 203, 107 S.Ct. 2793, 97 L.Ed.2d 171 (1987), the Supreme Court said that in order for a condition to be constitutional, (a) the condition itself must further the general welfare—but that, of course, is a very broad concept; (b) the condition must be unambiguous—the state must be on clear notice that by accepting the funds it is agreeing to the condition; (c) the condition must be related in some way to the reason the funds are being given to the state—in *Dole* the condition that states impose a minimum drinking age of 21 in order to receive all their federal highway funds was related because a higher drinking age meant less highway deaths; (d) the condition may not require the state to violate any constitutional provision; and (e) the condition must not be unduly coercive—in *Dole* the failure to impose the minimum drinking age would only result in the loss of a fairly small percentage of the state's highway funds and hence was not too coercive. Although these limitations on conditional spending can raise questions— especially with regard to the degree of necessary relationship between the condition and the federal spending and the point at which inducement becomes prohibited coercion—the courts have not invalidated any spending conditions in more than a half century.

The Necessary and Proper Clause together with the Treaty Clause can also provide a basis for congressional action. The Treaty Clause, Article II, Section 2, Cl. 2, states that the President makes treaties with the advice and consent of the Senate; the Necessary and Proper Clause, Article I, Section 8, Cl. 18, states that Congress can make all laws necessary and proper "for carrying into execution ... all other powers vested by this Constitution in the Government of the United States, or in any Department or Officer thereof." In *Missouri v. Holland*, 252 U.S. 416, 40 S.Ct. 382, 64 L.Ed. 641 (1920), the Supreme Court upheld the Migratory Bird Treaty Act against a challenge that it was beyond Congress's powers. Earlier lower court opinions had found such an act beyond Congress's Commerce Clause powers, but then the United States entered into a treaty with Canada to protect migratory birds. The Court said that Congress could enact legislation to carry into execution the United States' duties under that treaty, even absent any other constitutional basis for the legislation.

Undoubtedly, the Commerce Clause is the most important source of authority for environmental laws—it is the articulated basis for the Clean Air Act, the Clean Water Act, and the various laws dealing with hazardous wastes and substances. The history of the interpretation of the Commerce Clause reflects periods of expansive interpretation followed by more restrictive interpretation. The restrictive approach of the Supreme Court at the beginning of the New Deal in the early 1930s gave way to the "modern" approach by the 1940s. This modern approach is exemplified by the cases of *United States v. Darby*, 312 U.S. 100, 61 S.Ct. 451, 85 L.Ed. 609 (1941), and *Wickard v. Filburn*, 317 U.S. 111, 63 S.Ct. 82, 87 L.Ed. 122 (1942). In those cases, the Court held that the Commerce Clause authorized Congress to regulate (a) the channels of interstate commerce—meaning Congress could regulate the means by which commerce is carried interstate, such as highways, rail lines, airspace, navigable waters, the and the broadcast spectrum; (b) the instrumentalities of interstate commerce—meaning what crosses state lines as part of commerce; and (c) activities that have a substantial effect on interstate commerce. Moreover, in order to determine whether activities would have a substantial effect on interstate commerce, Congress is allowed to aggregate a large number of small activities. Thus, in *Wickard*, Congress could regulate a farmer's production of 239 bushels of wheat in excess of the allowed amount, because if Congress could not regulate that farmer's small amount, it would not be able to regulate all other farmers' small amounts, which in aggregate would amount to such a substantial amount of wheat that it would have a meaningful effect on the interstate market in wheat.

For more than a half century, after the adoption of the modern approach, no federal statute was found unconstitutional as beyond Congress's Commerce Clause power. Some believed that meaningful limits on federal power under the Commerce Clause had ceased to exist. In recent Supreme Court cases, however, the Court has established that there is a limit. In *United States v. Lopez*, 514 U.S. 549, 115 S.Ct. 1624, 131 L.Ed.2d 626 (1995), the Court found unconstitutional the Gun Free School Zones Act, which made it a federal crime to possess a firearm within 500 feet of a school. And *United States v. Morrison*, 529 U.S. 598, 120 S.Ct. 1740, 146 L.Ed.2d 658 (2000), held unconstitutional the Violence Against Women Act's provisions authorizing civil suits against persons who commit acts of violence motivated by gender. In these, what-might-be-called, "post-modern" cases, the Court did not change the tests it had established in *Darby* and *Wickard*; indeed, it reaffirmed them, but it did clarify how activities might have a substantial effect on interstate commerce and, in particular, when activities with small impacts could be aggregated to reach a substantial effect.

In *Lopez*, the government argued that guns in schools would impact the quality of education; the lessened quality of education would affect national skills and productivity, resulting in a substantial effect on interstate commerce. In *Morrison*, it argued that gender-motivated violence affected medical bills, insurance costs, and persons' willingness to travel in interstate commerce. The Court rejected aggregation in these contexts. It noted that all the earlier cases had involved regulation of economic activity, and it suggested that the modern cases recognized the reality of a national economic marketplace, so that as a practical matter even local economic activities would invariably be linked directly to that national economy, thereby authorizing federal regulation. However, in *Lopez* and *Morrison* the Court said that the local activities were not economic or commercial in nature and were simply local criminal activity traditionally dealt with by state law. To allow aggregation of all the direct and indirect effects of local criminal activity, in order to show substantial effect on interstate commerce, would effectively remove any limit on federal legislative authority and would create a general, federal police power. This would be inconsistent with the constitutional design.

The question for us is how this case law affects environmental law. The constitutional authority for only one environmental law has been decided by the Supreme Court, and that was before the post-modern Commerce Clause cases. In 1981 the Supreme Court decided a pair of cases challenging various provisions of the Surface Mining Control and Reclamation Act, 30 U.S.C. §§ 1201 *et seq.*

HODEL v. VIRGINIA SURFACE MINING AND RECLAMATION ASSOCIATION, INC.

Supreme Court of the United States, 1981.
452 U.S. 264, 101 S.Ct. 2352, 69 L.Ed.2d 1.

JUSTICE MARSHALL delivered the opinion of the Court.

These cases arise out of a pre-enforcement challenge to the constitutionality of the Surface Mining Control and Reclamation Act of 1977 (Surface Mining Act or Act).... In these appeals, we consider whether Congress, in adopting the Act, exceeded its powers under the Commerce Clause of the Constitution.... We conclude that in the context of a facial challenge, the Surface Mining Act does not suffer from any of these alleged constitutional defects, and we uphold the Act as constitutional.

I

A

The Surface Mining Act is a comprehensive statute designed to "establish a nationwide program to protect society and the environment from the adverse effects of surface coal mining operations." * * * Section 501 establishes a two-stage program for the regulation of surface coal mining: an initial, or interim regulatory phase, and a subsequent, permanent phase. The interim program mandates immediate promulgation and federal enforcement of some of the Act's environmental protection performance standards, complemented by continuing state regulation. Under the permanent phase, a regulatory program is to be adopted for each State, mandating compliance with the full panoply of federal performance standards, with enforcement responsibility lying with either the State or Federal Government.

Section 501(a) directs the Secretary to promulgate regulations establishing an interim regulatory program during which mine operators will be required to comply with some of the Act's performance standards, as specified by § 502(c). Included among those selected standards are requirements governing: (a) restoration of land after mining to its prior condition; (b) restoration of land to its approximate original contour; (c) segregation and preservation of topsoil; (d) minimization of disturbance to the hydrologic balance; (e) construction of coal mine waste piles used as dams and embankments; (f) revegetation of mined areas; and (g) spoil disposal....

Section 501(b) directs the Secretary to promulgate regulations establishing a permanent regulatory program incorporating all the Act's performance standards....

B

On October 23, 1978, the Virginia Surface Mining and Reclamation Association, Inc., an association of coal producers engaged in surface coal mining operations in Virginia, 63 of its member coal companies, and 4 individuals [*sic*] landowners filed suit in Federal District Court seeking declaratory and injunctive relief against various provisions of the Act. . . .

II

On cross-appeal, appellees argue that the District Court erred in rejecting their challenge to the Act as beyond the scope of congressional power under the Commerce Clause. They insist that the Act's principal goal is regulating the use of private lands within the borders of the States and not, as the District Court found, regulating the interstate commerce effects of surface coal mining. Consequently, appellees contend that the ultimate issue presented is "whether land as such is subject to regulation under the Commerce Clause, i. e. whether land can be regarded as 'in commerce.'" In urging us to answer "no" to this question, appellees emphasize that the Court has recognized that land-use regulation is within the inherent police powers of the States and their political subdivisions, and argue that Congress may regulate land use only insofar as the Property Clause grants it control over federal lands.

We do not accept either appellees' framing of the question or the answer they would have us supply. The task of a court that is asked to determine whether a particular exercise of congressional power is valid under the Commerce Clause is relatively narrow. The court must defer to a congressional finding that a regulated activity affects interstate commerce, if there is any rational basis for such a finding. This established, the only remaining question for judicial inquiry is whether "the means chosen by [Congress] must be reasonably adapted to the end permitted by the Constitution." The judicial task is at an end once the court determines that Congress acted rationally in adopting a particular regulatory scheme. . . .

Thus, when Congress has determined that an activity affects interstate commerce, the courts need inquire only whether the finding is rational. Here, the District Court properly deferred to Congress' express findings, set out in the Act itself, about the effects of surface coal mining on interstate commerce. Section 101(c) recites the congressional finding that

> "many surface mining operations result in disturbances of surface areas that burden and adversely affect commerce and the public welfare by destroying or diminishing the utility of land for commercial, industrial, residential, recreational, agricultural, and forestry purposes, by causing erosion and landslides, by contributing to floods, by polluting the water, by destroying fish and wildlife habitats, by impairing natural beauty, by damaging the property of citizens, by creating hazards dangerous to life and property by degrading the quality of life in local communities, and by counteract-

ing governmental programs and efforts to conserve soil, water, and other natural resources."

The legislative record provides ample support for these statutory findings.... In light of the evidence available to Congress and the detailed consideration that the legislation received, we cannot say that Congress did not have a rational basis for concluding that surface coal mining has substantial effects on interstate commerce....

The denomination of an activity as a "local" or "intrastate" activity does not resolve the question whether Congress may regulate it under the Commerce Clause. As previously noted, the commerce power "extends to those activities intrastate which so affect interstate commerce, or the exertion of the power of Congress over it, as to make regulation of them appropriate means to the attainment of a legitimate end, the effective execution of the granted power to regulate interstate commerce." This Court has long held that Congress may regulate the conditions under which goods shipped in interstate commerce are produced where the "local" activity of producing these goods itself affects interstate commerce. Appellees do not dispute that coal is a commodity that moves in interstate commerce. Here, Congress rationally determined that regulation of surface coal mining is necessary to protect interstate commerce from adverse effects that may result from that activity. This congressional finding is sufficient to sustain the Act as a valid exercise of Congress' power under the Commerce Clause.

Moreover, the Act responds to a congressional finding that nationwide "surface mining and reclamation standards are essential in order to insure that competition in interstate commerce among sellers of coal produced in different States will not be used to undermine the ability of the several States to improve and maintain adequate standards on coal mining operations within their borders." The prevention of this sort of destructive interstate competition is a traditional role for congressional action under the Commerce Clause. In *United States v. Darby*, the Court used a similar rationale to sustain the imposition of federal minimum wage and maximum hour regulations on a manufacturer of goods shipped in interstate commerce. The Court explained that the statute implemented Congress' view that "interstate commerce should not be made the instrument of competition in the distribution of goods produced under substandard labor conditions, which competition is injurious to the commerce and to the states from and to which the commerce flows." The same rationale applies here to support the conclusion that the Surface Mining Act is within the authority granted to Congress by the Commerce Clause.

Finally, we agree with the lower federal courts that have uniformly found the power conferred by the Commerce Clause broad enough to permit congressional regulation of activities causing air or water pollution, or other environmental hazards that may have effects in more than one State....

In sum, we conclude that the District Court properly rejected appellees' Commerce Clause challenge to the Act. . . .

HODEL v. INDIANA

Supreme Court of the United States, 1981.
452 U.S. 314, 101 S.Ct. 2376, 69 L.Ed.2d 40.

JUSTICE MARSHALL delivered the opinion of the Court.

This appeal, like *Hodel v. Virginia Surface Mining & Reclamation Assn., Inc.*, also decided today, involves a broad constitutional challenge to numerous important provisions of the Surface Mining Control and Reclamation Act of 1977. Many of the specific provisions attacked in this case, however, differ from the "steep-slope" provisions that were the primary focus of the challenge in *Virginia Surface Mining*. The United States District Court for the Southern District of Indiana ruled that the provisions of the Act challenged here are unconstitutional and permanently enjoined their enforcement. We noted probable jurisdiction, and we now reverse.

I

A

. . . Several of the challenged sections of the Act are known collectively as the "prime farmland" provisions. These sections establish special requirements for surface mining operations conducted on land that both qualifies as prime farmland under a definition promulgated by the Secretary of Agriculture and has historically been used as cropland. . . . A permit for surface coal mining on such lands may be granted only if the mine operator can demonstrate its "technological capability to restore such mined area, within a reasonable time, to equivalent or higher levels of yield as nonmined prime farmland in the surrounding area under equivalent levels of management. . . ." The operator must also show that it can "meet the soil reconstruction standards" for prime farmland. . . . Furthermore, § 519(c)(2) provides that upon its completion of mining activities on prime farmland, a mine operator can have its performance bond released only on a showing that soil productivity "has returned to equivalent levels of yield as nonmined land of the same soil type in the surrounding area under equivalent management practices. . . ."

Also challenged here are some of the Act's more general provisions that are applicable throughout the country. These include § 515(b)(3), which requires restoration of mined land to its approximate original contour, and the directive in § 515(b)(5) that surface mine operators remove topsoil separately during mining activities and preserve it for use during reclamation if it is not to be replaced immediately on the backfill area of the mining cut. Section 508 requires applicants for surface coal mining permits to submit proposed reclamation plans specifying the intended postmining use of the land and the method by which that use will be achieved. In addition, §§ 522(a), (c), (d) require States wishing to assume permanent regulatory authority over surface coal mining to establish an administrative procedure for determining whether particular lands are unsuitable for some or all kinds of surface mining. Section 522(e) proscribes mining activity within 100 feet of roadways and cemeteries or within 300 feet of public buildings, schools, churches, public parks, or occupied dwellings. Finally, the Act's procedures for collecting proposed civil penalties contained in § 518(c) are also drawn into question here. . . .

II

The District Court gave two rationales for its decision on the Commerce Clause issue. The court first held that the six "prime farmland" provisions are beyond congressional power to regulate interstate commerce because they are "directed at facets of surface coal mining which have no substantial and adverse effect on interstate commerce." . . .

With respect to the other 15 substantive provisions which apply to surface mining generally, the District Court reasoned that the only possible adverse effects on interstate commerce justifying congressional action are air and water pollution and determined that these effects are adequately addressed by other provisions of the Act. The court therefore concluded that these 15 provisions as well as the 6 prime farmland provisions "are not directed at the alleviation of water or air pollution, to the extent that there are [any] such effects, and are not means reasonably and plainly adapted to [the legitimate end of] removing any substantial and adverse effect on interstate commerce." We find both of the District Court's rationales untenable. . . .

In our view, Congress was entitled to find that the protection of prime farmland is a federal interest that may be addressed through Commerce Clause legislation. . . . More important, the court below incorrectly assumed that the relevant inquiry under the rational-basis test is the volume of commerce actually affected by the regulated activity. This Court held in *NLRB v. Fainblatt*, 306 U.S. 601, 606, 59 S.Ct. 668, 671, 83 L.Ed. 1014 (1939), that "[t]he power of Congress to regulate interstate commerce is plenary and extends to all such commerce be it great or small." The pertinent inquiry therefore is not how much commerce is involved but whether Congress could rationally conclude that the regulated activity affects interstate commerce.

Against this background, we have little difficulty in concluding that the congressional finding in this case satisfies the rational-basis test. The Senate considered information from the Interagency Report about the prime farmland acreage that might be affected by surface coal mining. . . .

In our judgment, the evidence summarized in the Reports mandates the conclusion that Congress had a rational basis for finding that surface coal mining on prime farmland affects interstate commerce in agricultural products. As we explained in *Stafford v. Wallace*, 258 U.S. 495, 521, 42 S.Ct. 397, 403, 66 L.Ed. 735 (1922):

> Whatever amounts to more or less constant practice, and threatens to obstruct or unduly to burden the freedom of interstate commerce is within the regulatory power of Congress under the commerce clause, and it is primarily for Congress to consider and decide the fact of danger and meet it. This court will certainly not substitute its judgment for that of Congress unless the relation of the subject to interstate commerce and its effect upon it are clearly non-existent.

The court below improperly substituted its judgment for the congressional determination.

We also conclude that the court below erred in holding that the prime farmland and 15 other substantive provisions challenged by appellees are not reasonably related to the legitimate goal of protecting interstate commerce from adverse effects attributable to surface coal mining. The court incorrectly assumed that the Act's goals are limited to preventing air and water pollution. As we noted in *Hodel v. Virginia Surface Mining & Reclamation Assn., Inc.*, Congress was also concerned about preserving the productive capacity of mined lands and protecting the public from health and safety hazards that may result from surface coal mining. All the provisions invalidated by the court below are reasonably calculated to further these legitimate goals.

For example, the approximate-original-contour requirement in § 515(b)(5) is designed to avoid the environmental and other harm that may result from unreclaimed or improperly restored mining cuts. . . .

Congress adopted the Surface Mining Act in order to ensure that production of coal for interstate commerce would not be at the expense of agriculture, the environment, or public health and safety, injury to any of which interests would have deleterious effects on interstate commerce. Moreover, as noted in *Hodel v. Virginia Surface Mining & Reclamation Assn., Inc.*, the Act reflects the congressional goal of protecting mine operators in States adhering to high performance and reclamation standards from disadvantageous competition with operators in States with less rigorous regulatory programs. The statutory provisions invalidated by the District Court advance these legitimate goals, and we conclude that Congress acted reasonably in adopting the regulatory scheme contained in the Act.[1] * * *

Justice REHNQUIST, concurring in the judgment in both *Hodel v. Virginia Surface Mining and Reclamation Assn., Inc.* and *Hodel v. Indiana.*

---

1. Appellees contend that a number of the specific provisions challenged in this case cannot be shown to be related to the congressional goal of preventing adverse effects on interstate commerce. This claim, even if correct, is beside the point. A complex regulatory program such as established by the Act can survive a Commerce Clause challenge without a showing that every single facet of the program is independently and directly related to a valid congressional goal. It is enough that the challenged provisions are an integral part of the regulatory program and that the regulatory scheme when considered as a whole satisfies this test.

* * * It would be a mistake to conclude that Congress' power to regulate pursuant to the Commerce Clause is unlimited. Some activities may be so private or local in nature that they simply may not be *in* commerce. Nor is it sufficient that the person or activity reached have *some* nexus with interstate commerce. Our cases have consistently held that the regulated activity must have a *substantial* effect on interstate commerce. Moreover, simply because Congress may conclude that a particular activity substantially affects interstate commerce does not necessarily make it so. Congress' findings must be supported by a "rational basis" and are reviewable by the courts. In short, unlike the reserved police powers of the States, which are plenary unless challenged as violating some specific provision of the Constitution, the connection with interstate commerce is itself a jurisdictional prerequisite for any substantive legislation by Congress under the Commerce Clause.

In many ways, the Court's opinions in these cases are consistent with that approach. In both the *Virginia* and *Indiana* cases, the Court exhaustively analyzes Congress' articulated justifications for the exercise of its power under the Commerce Clause and concludes that Congress' detailed factual findings as to the effect of surface mining on interstate commerce are sufficient to justify the exercise of that power. Though there can be no doubt that Congress in regulating surface mining has stretched its authority to the "nth degree," our prior precedents compel me to agree with the Court's conclusion. I therefore concur in the judgments of the Court.

There is, however, a troublesome difference between what the Court does and what it says. In both cases, the Court asserts that regulation will be upheld if Congress had a rational basis for finding that the regulated activity affects interstate commerce.... In my view, the Court misstates the test. As noted above, it has long been established that the commerce power does not reach activity which merely "affects" interstate commerce. There must instead be a showing that regulated activity has a *substantial effect* on that commerce....

In sum, my difficulty with some of the recent Commerce Clause jurisprudence is that the Court often seems to forget that legislation enacted by Congress is subject to two different kinds of challenge, while that enacted by the States is subject to only one kind of challenge. Neither Congress nor the States may act in a manner prohibited by any provision of the Constitution. Congress must show that the activity it seeks to regulate has a substantial effect on interstate commerce. It is my uncertainty as to whether the Court intends to broaden, by some of its language, this test that leads me to concur only in the judgments.

THE CHIEF JUSTICE [Burger], concurring in both cases.

I agree largely with what Justice REHNQUIST has said about ... the gradual case-by-case expansion of the reach of the Commerce Clause.

I agree fully with his view that we often seem to forget the doctrine that laws enacted by Congress under the Commerce Clause must be based on a substantial effect on interstate commerce. However, I join the

Court's opinions in these cases ... because in them the Court acknowledges and reaffirms that doctrine.

* * *

Notes and Comments

1. The opinions for the Court in both *Lopez* and *Morrison* were authored by then Chief Justice Rehnquist. In *Lopez* he took care to enshrine the point in his concurrence in the two *Hodels* that there must be a *substantial* effect on commerce in order to justify federal regulation under the third doctrinal test, not just *some* effect. In *Morrison* he made clear that congressional findings that an activity has a substantial effect on commerce are subject to serious judicial review and are not presumed valid. Both these points modify slightly the Court's earlier discussion in the *Hodels* but would not change the outcomes. More broadly, however, Rehnquist as Chief Justice writing for the Court in *Lopez* and *Morrison* also brought home his earlier statement as an Associate Justice that "some activities may be so private or local in nature that they simply may not be *in* commerce." Do *Lopez* and *Morrison* raise any question about the continued applicability of the two *Hodels* or whether the theory underlying them would be applied to uphold other environmental laws?

2. In a recent Supreme Court environmental case this concern with federal regulation of local activities under the Commerce Clause led the Court, in another opinion by Chief Justice Rehnquist, to interpret the Clean Water Act narrowly to avoid the constitutional question whether the Act more broadly interpreted would exceed Congress's power under the Commerce Clause. *See Solid Waste Agency of Northern Cook County v. U.S. Army Corps of Engineers*, 531 U.S. 159, 121 S.Ct. 675, 148 L.Ed.2d 576 (2001).

3. There are, of course, a number of environmental laws that regulate economic activity in ways that the *Lopez* and *Morrison* Courts would find fully within the traditional realm of federal regulation. For example, the Federal Insecticide, Fungicide, and Rodenticide Act, 7 U.S.C. §§ 136 *et seq.*, regulates the sale and use of pesticides; the Toxic Substances Control Act, 15 U.S.C. §§ 2601 *et seq.*, regulates the manufacture, sale, and disposal of chemicals that present an unreasonable risk of injury to health or the environment. The mobile source provisions of the Clean Air Act, 42 U.S.C. §§ 7521–7590, regulate what pollution controls new motor vehicles must have in order to be sold. In other words, these laws are directed at economic activity, albeit for the purpose of protecting the environment and public health and safety.

4. The Clean Water Act can probably avoid this line of cases altogether, because by its terms the CWA applies to "waters of the United States," which the Supreme Court has now interpreted to mean either navigable waters or waters somehow connected to or affecting those navigable waters. Navigable waters are themselves channels of interstate commerce and so can be regulated and protected without any showing of a substantial effect on interstate commerce. *But see* William Funk, *The Court, the Clean Water Act, and the Constitution:* SWANCC *and Beyond*, 31 ELR 10741 (2001)(arguing that because the CWA's purposes and effects do not involve protection of navigation or commerce by water, neither the navigability of the waters nor

the cases upholding federal regulation of waters as channels of interstate commerce should be relevant to the constitutionality of the CWA).

5. There are a number of post-*Lopez* or *Morrison* cases from the courts of appeals in which persons challenged the constitutionality of various environmental laws. *None* of those challenges has yet been successful. For example, in *United States v. Olin Corp.*, 107 F.3d 1506 (11th Cir. 1997), Olin challenged the constitutionality of the Comprehensive Environmental Response, Compensation and Liability Act, which makes persons liable for the clean up of hazardous substances that have been released to the environment. Olin argued that the disposal of hazardous substances at its site was not economic activity and the release did not affect interstate commerce. The Eleventh Circuit applied *Lopez* and found that the disposal of hazardous substances by companies on their sites was an economic activity and that, even if Olin's release itself did not affect interstate commerce, there was ample evidence that releases of hazardous substances in the aggregate did affect interstate commerce.

6. The Endangered Species Act has probably raised the most constitutional questions. Certain aspects of the ESA are clearly within Congress's power. For example, a major portion of the ESA's protections involves federal actions themselves or private actions on federal lands. Neither would raise a serious constitutional issue. Moreover, some of the ESA protections are undoubtedly authorized by the Commerce Clause. For example, the ESA regulates the importation of endangered species or their parts. Also, the ESA protects some species which are commercial in nature, such as salmon. The particular cases that may present problems involve protections on private lands of wildlife that has no commercial value. As of this writing, however, no cases involving such wildlife have held the Act unconstitutional as applied to them. In *Rancho Viejo, LLC v. Norton*, 323 F.3d 1062 (D.C. Cir. 2003), the court upheld the constitutionality of the ESA with respect to its protection of the Arroyo Southwestern Toad, a toad that lives only in California. In *GDF Realty Investments, Ltd. v. Norton*, 326 F.3d 622 (5th Cir. 2003), the court upheld the Act as applied to four spiders and two beetles that only live underground in two counties in Texas. In *National Ass'n of Home Builders v. Babbitt*, 130 F.3d 1041 (D.C. Cir. 1997), the court upheld the Act as applied to the Delhi Sands Flower–Loving Fly, that only lives in two counties in California. While these three cases all found the protection of these exotic species within the Commerce Clause power of Congress, they did not agree on how the Clause authorized this protection. For example, the *Rancho Viejo* court rested its analysis on the fact that the activity threatening the toad, and precluded by the ESA, was itself activity affecting interstate commerce— a residential housing development. The *GDF Realty* court, however, expressly rejected such a basis for its decision, finding instead that the ESA was an economic regulatory scheme because it protects biodiversity generally, and the total destruction of biodiversity would have a substantial effect on interstate commerce. Even if the destruction of a particular, non-commercial species would only have a de minimis effect on interstate commerce, to allow it to avoid regulation would enable the wholesale destruction of biodiversity one species at a time. In the *National Ass'n of Home Builders* case, there was no majority opinion, with one judge using an analysis similar to the *GDF Realty* court, one judge using an analysis similar to the *Rancho Viejo*

court, and one judge dissenting, arguing that the ESA could not constitutionally protect the Delhi Sands Flower–Loving Fly. *See also Gibbs v. Babbitt*, 214 F.3d 483 (4th Cir. 2000)(upholding ESA as applied to red wolves on the basis that taking wolves was itself an economic activity because, invariably, the taking was done to protect farmers' property and, alternatively, on the basis that Congress can protect an endangered species in order to return its numbers to a place where harvest of that species would have economic value).

B. Constitutional Limitations on Environmental Laws

Even if a matter is otherwise within the power of Congress to make law, there may be constitutional limitations on the exercise of that power. There are three constitutional limitations particularly applicable to environmental law: the Tenth Amendment, the Eleventh Amendment, and the Takings Clause of the Fifth Amendment.

1. Tenth Amendment

The Tenth Amendment reserves those powers not delegated to the United States to the States and to the people. The judicial construction of the Tenth Amendment, like much of the Constitution, has varied over time, sometimes providing real constraints on congressional action and at other times providing virtually no restriction. A Tenth Amendment issue has arisen in two distinct circumstances: one is where the federal law interferes with the way a state would like to regulate something, and the claim is that interference with a traditional state prerogative violates the Tenth Amendment; the other is where the federal law directly regulates a state or an entity of a state. In the former context, the Court has been fairly consistent in denying Tenth Amendment claims, holding that so long as Congress is acting within its Article I powers, the fact that it interferes with a historical state prerogative does not violate the Tenth Amendment. *See, e.g., Hodel v. Virginia Surface Mining and Reclamation Ass'n*, 452 U.S. 264, 101 S.Ct. 2352, 69 L.Ed.2d 1 (1981)(in a portion of the opinion edited from version earlier in this chapter). Thus, in these kinds of cases, the decision as to whether something is within Congress's constitutional power ends the analysis.

The second circumstance itself has two dimensions: (1) when the federal law regulates everyone who engages in certain activities, and a state or state entity happens to be one of those persons; and (2) when the federal law requires a state or state entity to act essentially as an agent of the federal government to carry out federal policy. The former situation is governed by the case of *Garcia v. San Antonio Metropolitan Transit Authority*, 469 U.S. 528, 105 S.Ct. 1005, 83 L.Ed.2d 1016 (1985). *Garcia* involved a federal law mandating minimum wages and overtime pay to any employee and whether those requirements could be enforced with respect to a municipal bus system. The Court held in this context that the Tenth Amendment was essentially tautological and had no independent force restricting laws otherwise within Congress's Commerce Clause power. In other words, the constitutional test is the same as when Congress regulates private entities. Therefore, federal laws may regulate states to the extent that they or their subdivsions engage in actions that have a substantial effect on interstate commerce. For example, federal laws might require state buildings to meet federal energy conservation requirements or prohibit state workers from harming federal endangered species.

The latter situation, however, when the federal law requires a state to act as an agent of the federal government to carry out federal policy, is governed by a different case: *New York v. United States*, 505 U.S. 144, 112 S.Ct. 2408, 120 L.Ed.2d 120 (1992). In this case, the Court found one part of the federal Low–Level Radioactive Waste Policy Amendments Act unconstitutional in light of the Tenth Amendment. That part effectively required states to adopt legislation to administer a federal program, or as the Court put it: the law commandeered the states to act as agencies of the federal government. That is, something may be subject to federal regulation under the Commerce Clause because of its substantial effect on interstate commerce, but the federal government may not accomplish that regulation simply by directing the states to adopt and administer the regulatory scheme on behalf of the federal government. A subsequent case, *Printz v. United States*, 521 U.S. 898, 117 S.Ct. 2365, 138 L.Ed.2d 914 (1997), made clear that the same prohibition exists when Congress attempts to commandeer state or local executive officials as well as when it commandeers state legislatures. In *New York*, nevertheless, the Court reaffirmed the constitutionality of the cooperative federalism model used by most environmental statutes, where the federal government provides that states may regulate the environment if their state plans are approved by EPA, but states are not required to so regulate. If they fail to adopt state plans that meet federal standards, then EPA adopts a federal plan that regulates the environment in the state in place of the state doing it. Thus, the state's decision to regulate according to the federal framework is voluntary and not required. Moreover, the court reiterated the ability of the federal government to provide funds to the states upon the condition that the states undertake certain activities. Again, however, because the state can refuse the funds (and thereby the conditions), the state's decision to regulate according to a federal framework is voluntary and not required.

2. The Eleventh Amendment

The Eleventh Amendment, passed to overrule an early Supreme Court decision that subjected a state to a suit in federal court brought by a citizen of another state, has been interpreted since 1890 generally to prohibit private suits against states in federal court. *See Hans v. Louisiana*, 134 U.S. 1, 10 S.Ct. 504, 33 L.Ed. 842 (1890). Despite its limited wording, the amendment was perceived as a constitutional recognition of state sovereign immunity from private law suits; it does not bar suits brought by the federal government against a state. While the Court has held that Congress can override that immunity under the powers granted to Congress in the Civil War Amendments, it was not clear whether

Congress could likewise overcome a state's sovereign immunity from private suits under its Article I powers. In 1989, a person sued Pennsylvania under the federal Comprehensive Environmental Response, Compensation and Liability Act for the costs of a hazardous waste cleanup, and the Supreme Court in a divided opinion held that CERCLA, enacted under Congress's Commerce Clause authority, could abrogate state sovereign immunity. *See Pennsylvania v. Union Gas Co.*, 491 U.S. 1, 109 S.Ct. 2273, 105 L.Ed.2d 1 (1989). However, seven years later the Court overruled *Union Gas* and held that Congress cannot abrogate state sovereign immunity under its Article I powers. *Seminole Tribe of Florida v. Florida*, 517 U.S. 44, 116 S.Ct. 1114, 134 L.Ed.2d 252 (1996). Thus, environmental statutes cannot generally authorize private suits, such as citizen suits or suits for compensation, like in CERCLA, against unconsenting states.

There is one major loophole around this prohibition. Early on, in *Ex parte Young*, 209 U.S. 123, 28 S.Ct. 441, 52 L.Ed. 714 (1908), the Court held that it did not violate state sovereign immunity for a private person to sue a state officer for injunctive relief, alleging the officer was violating the Constitution. This has subsequently been extended to suits alleging the state officer is violating federal law. Accordingly, if a state agency were polluting illegally under federal law, a person could sue the state official who heads the agency under a federal citizen suit provision for an injunction to stop the unlawful polluting.

As indicated earlier, state sovereign immunity does not bar EPA or the U.S. Department of Justice from suing states. Moreover, state sovereign immunity does not extend to local governments, so persons can generally sue municipalities and various forms of local government under citizen suit provisions.

3. The Takings Clause

The Fifth Amendment provides, among other things, that private property may not be taken for a public use without just compensation. This clause impacts environmental legislation because many environmental laws restrict what persons may do with their private property. They may not be able to develop their property in the ways they might wish because to do so would run afoul of one or more environmental laws. The issue then is whether that restriction on the use of their property "takes" their property. If an environmental law does "take" their property, the government must pay "just compensation"; the law is not enjoined as unconstitutional.

In a famous case, Justice Oliver Wendell Holmes declared that if a governmental regulation goes "too far," it will constitute a taking. *See Pennsylvania Coal Co. v. Mahon*, 260 U.S. 393, 43 S.Ct. 158, 67 L.Ed. 322 (1922). The question, of course, is how far is "too far." Over the years, the Court has developed a couple of *per se* tests; that is, if the circumstances fit these tests, then the regulation is a taking. If, however, neither of these circumstances apply, then the Court has directed that courts use one of two *ad hoc* tests, each of which balances a number of factors to determine whether the regulation goes too far and is a taking.

One *per se* test is whether the government regulation authorizes the physical possession or permanent physical invasion of a person's property. For example, in *Kaiser Aetna v. United States*, 444 U.S. 164, 100 S.Ct. 383, 62 L.Ed.2d 332 (1979), the Court found that requiring Kaiser Aetna to open its marina to the public amounted to a taking. Another *per se* test asks whether the government regulation has totally deprived the landowner of all value in the land. If so, it is a taking. This might occur where a restriction to protect the environment precludes the landowner from developing the land in any way. *See Lucas v. South Carolina Coastal Council*, 505 U.S. 1003, 112 S.Ct. 2886, 120 L.Ed.2d 798 (1992).

The more common situation, especially in environmental law applications, is a restriction on the development of some portion of a person's land, such as a prohibition on filling a wetland or developing an area that is habitat for an endangered species. One question that arises in this situation is whether the restriction on a portion of a person's land should be viewed as a total deprivation of economic value of that portion of the land, and therefore a *per se* taking of that portion of the land, or whether it should be viewed as only a partial deprivation of the value of the entire parcel. The Supreme Court has seemed consistently to answer this question to say that one must judge the deprivation in light of the entire parcel, not just the affected portion of the parcel, in determining whether there has been a total deprivation triggering a *per se* taking. *See, e.g., Tahoe–Sierra Preservation Council, Inc. v. Tahoe Regional Planning Agency*, 535 U.S. 302, 122 S.Ct. 1465, 152 L.Ed.2d 517 (2002).

Absent the physical possession or invasion of property or the total deprivation of economic value of the property, courts are to use a multifactored approach to determining whether a government restriction constitutes a taking. *Penn Central Transp. Co. v. City of New York*, 438 U.S. 104, 98 S.Ct. 2646, 57 L.Ed.2d 631 (1978), is the case generally cited for identifying those factors to be considered when a regulation generally restricts the use of property. The overall concern is to assure that the regulation does not force some people alone to bear burdens which, in all fairness and justice, should be borne by the public as a whole. Thus, the court is to consider the economic impact of the regulation, the extent to which the regulation has interfered with reasonable investment backed expectations, and the nature and character of the government action. An important consideration is whether the regulation provides a ''reciprocity of advantage,'' a term that refers to the effects of a regulation, like zoning, that applies to all and both benefits and restricts at the same time.

When a government regulation does not just restrict the use of property but also imposes a condition on its use, there is an additional or alternative *ad hoc* test to be applied to the condition. This is common in local land use planning contexts, but it can also occur under federal environmental laws, such as regulations under the Clean Water Act requiring persons who wish to fill waters of the United States to obtain a permit conditioned on the person engaging in various mitigation activities. The Court has said that such conditions, or regulatory exactions, must meet two requirements to avoid being a taking. First, there must be an "essential nexus" between the legitimate state interest justifying the restriction and the effects of the condition. That is, the effect of the condition must further the state interest for imposing the restriction. For example, in *Nollan v. California Coastal Comm'n*, 483 U.S. 825, 107 S.Ct. 3141, 97 L.Ed.2d 677 (1987), California failed this test when it required beachfront property owners to provide an easement to the public across their beach as a condition of obtaining a building permit. The Court found no connection between the state interest in requiring a building permit and the creation of an easement for the public to walk on the beach. The second requirement for conditions is that there must be a "rough proportionality" between the impacts of the condition on the private property owner and the furtherance of the legitimate state interest. For example, in *Dolan v. City of Tigard*, 512 U.S. 374, 114 S.Ct. 2309, 129 L.Ed.2d 304 (1994), Tigard had required a hardware store to donate a portion of its property as a "greenway" for a floodplain to counter the effects of increased runoff from the proposed development and for a bike path to mitigate the effects of increased traffic that would be generated by the proposed development. The Court held that neither of these conditions were roughly proportionate. First, there was no basis for requiring the owner to deed some of its property to the city for flood control purposes, when merely preserving that portion of the property in an undeveloped state would fully serve the flood control purposes. Second, there was no evidence that the amount of increased traffic to be generated by the development bore any relation to what effect the bike path would have in terms of reducing traffic.

Under either the *Penn Central* or the *Dolan* tests, courts must apply rather malleable concepts to particular situations. As a result, the outcome of cases using these tests are sometimes difficult to predict and may turn more on the particular facts and the proclivities of the particular judges than a "rule of law" might find ideal. Probably what drives the outcome in these cases more than the phrasing of the test is the assignment of the burden of proof. A person seeking to establish a taking under the *Penn Central* test has the burden of proof to establish that a taking has occurred. Under the *Dolan* test, while the plaintiff land owner still has the overall burden of proof, the government has the burden of proof with regard to the essential nexus and rough proportionality of the condition. Thus, plaintiffs tend to fare better under the *Dolan* test than the *Penn Central* test.

It has long been understood that a property owner has no right to use property in a manner that creates either a private or public nuisance. Consequently, any government regulation that bars a person from creating a nuisance, no matter how great an impact that might have on the person's property, would not deprive the person of any property *right*, so no compensation would be due. A question arises whether, if a legislature enacts a law barring something that courts have not recognized as a nuisance but which the legislature believes is "nuisance-like," such a law would be viewed as comparable to a nuisance and therefore could avoid a takings claim. An earlier Supreme Court decision, *Miller v. Schoene*, 276 U.S. 272, 48 S.Ct. 246, 72 L.Ed. 568 (1928), suggested that it could, but the more recent *Lucas* case seemed to take a harder line on the ability of legislatures to define "new" nuisances.

Underlying the nuisance exception and the "reasonable investment backed expectations" factor in the *Penn Central* test is the concept of background principles of property law. That is, when a person obtains property, the person takes that property subject to the background principles of property law—such as the principle that no one has the right to create a nuisance. But does this mean that all existing statutory and regulatory provisions are part of the background principles when a person obtains property? If you buy property knowing that the Clean Water Act restricts the filling of waters of the United States, can you later sue for just compensation if it turns out that you cannot fill the waters on your property that you must fill in order to develop the property? A recent Supreme Court case, *Palazzolo v. Rhode Island*, 533 U.S. 606, 121 S.Ct. 2448, 150 L.Ed.2d 592 (2001), overturned a Rhode Island Supreme Court decision that a law in existence when a person obtains property necessarily becomes part of the background principles under which the person takes the property. Such a rule, the Court said, would divest the owner at the time the regulation came into existence of the ability to transfer the interest possessed prior to the regulation. Instead, the prior existence of the regulation would be considered in the weighing of the *Penn Central* factors, in particular in considering the extent of the person's *reasonable* investment backed expectations.

If a person believes that the federal government has "taken" his property, his suit for compensation generally must be filed in the United States Court of Federal Claims, which has exclusive jurisdiction over suits for just compensation if the amount involved exceeds $10,000. 28 U.S.C. § 1491. Appeals from this court go to the United States Court of Appeals for the Federal Circuit, a court of appeals with nationwide jurisdiction. Thus, generally speaking, federal district courts and the geographic courts of appeals do not play significant roles in the development of Takings law, whereas the Federal Circuit's decisions are of special importance.

Notes and Comments

1. While the Tenth Amendment imposes a limitation on the tools the federal government may use to effect its regulatory ends, most persons do not consider the restrictions to impose significant burdens. Most federal environmental statutes that involve states follow the cooperative federalism model approved by the Court, or involve the conditional use of federal funds, also approved by the Court. Nevertheless, there may be some statutes that were drafted before or in ignorance of *New York v. United States* that run afoul of it. For example, in *ACORN v. Edwards*, 81 F.3d 1387 (5th Cir.

1996), the court found one subsection of the Safe Drinking Water Act unconstitutional under *New York*. That subsection required each state to establish a program to assist school districts in testing for, and remedying, lead contamination in drinking water from coolers under their jurisdiction. Can you see why that would raise problems under *New York v. United States*?

2. Environmentalists normally want to interpret the Takings Clause narrowly, so that it has minimal effect. They fear that if government action that protects the environment results in having to pay just compensation, government will be less willing to take action that protects the environment. Of course, if a law requires a government agency to take certain action to protect the environment, the fact that such action might require payment of just compensation to a private landowner would provide no legal excuse for not taking that action. Moreover, at the federal level, normally the agency doing the regulation would not be financially responsible for payment of the just compensation; a different federal appropriation would be involved. Nevertheless, to the extent that environmentally protective actions might result in large numbers of awards of just compensation, there obviously would be political ramifications to those actions. To date, however, the number of awards under the Takings Clause has been minimal, occurring almost entirely in connection with restrictions on the filling of wetlands.

3. One could argue that the failure to pay just compensation liberally might result in a backlash against environmental regulations that impact private persons' use of their property. If landowners actually could receive compensation for environmentally protective action, they might be much more willing to take it. The Clean Water Act's regulation of wetlands and the Endangered Species Act's restrictions have been especially controversial precisely because they have so often seemed to thwart traditional development or resource utilization to the economic detriment of landowners.

C. Constitutional Limitations on State Laws

While states do not need to find authority in the U.S. Constitution to make laws to protect the environment, the Constitution does place limitations on what states may do. For example, the Takings Clause, discussed above as a limitation on federal action, applies to state action through the Fourteenth Amendment, using the same tests described above.

1. The Supremacy Clause

The Supremacy Clause declares that federal laws are the supreme law of the land, so that federal laws may preempt states from protecting their own environment in ways they believe proper. There are said to be three different types of preemption: (1) express preemption, where a statute expressly precludes a state from regulating; (2) implied preemption, where a federal statute so fills the field as to imply that there is no room for further state regulation (sometimes called "field preemption"); and (3) conflict preemption, where a state law stands as an obstacle to the fulfilling the purpose of the federal law. *See, e.g., Cipollone v. Liggett Group, Inc.*, 505 U.S. 504, 112 S.Ct. 2608, 120 L.Ed.2d 407 (1992). Most of the basic environmental laws, however, do not create an exclusive federal regime. Usually they explicitly allow states to provide greater protection than mandated by federal laws. Nevertheless, there are exceptions.

An example is the Clean Air Act's requirements for pollution controls on automobiles. In order to ensure that auto manufacturers are not made subject to differing requirements in each of the various states, the Clean Air Act makes the federal pollution requirement the exclusive requirement, generally precluding states from adopting their own requirements. 42 U.S.C. § 7543(a). At the time the Act was passed in 1970, however, California had already imposed a requirement on cars sold in California, and southern California's air was particularly bad, so the Clean Air Act made an exception for California, requiring EPA to waive the preclusion provision if the state standard was as least as strict as the federal standard and it was needed to "meet compelling and extraordinary conditions." 42 U.S.C. § 7543(b). Later, this exception was broadened, so that other states with areas not meeting all the National Ambient Air Quality Standards could impose identical requirements as those approved for California. 42 U.S.C. § 7507. As a result, now car manufacturers essentially must produce two different kinds of cars, one that meets California's standards for sale in California and the other states that have adopted them, and one for the rest of the nation. Even non-environmental statutes may preempt some state environmental statutes. For example, an attempt by California to regulate greenhouse gas emissions from automobiles was challenged by automobile dealers claiming that such regulation was preempted by the federal Energy Policy and Conservation Act, which sets the Corporate Average Fuel Economy (CAFÉ) standards for automobiles. At this point, this issue is working its way through the lower courts. *See Central Valley Chrysler–Jeep v. Witherspoon*, 456 F.Supp.2d 1160 (E.D. Cal. 2006).

Another example of a federal law that explicitly preempts state law is the Federal Insecticide, Fungicide, and Rodenticide Act's labeling provisions. In order to protect persons who might be exposed to pesticides, FIFRA allows EPA to regulate the labels and directions for pesticides. FIFRA then says that states "shall not impose or continue in effect any requirements for labeling or packaging in addition to or different from those required under this chapter." Thus, manufacturers are subject only to a uniform national requirement for labeling and packaging.

Despite these clear statements of preemption, questions still may arise under these provisions as to whether the effects of state law result in a "requirement in addition to or different from" the federal standard. A recurring question has been whether Congress intended to preclude tort actions for negligence or strict liability when it writes preclusion provisions like the one in FIFRA. In *Cipollone v. Liggett Group, Inc.*, the Court addressed a similar preemption provision governing cigarette labeling and held that common law actions were preempted. However, in *Bates v. Dow Agrosciences, LLC*, 544 U.S. 431, 125 S.Ct. 1788, 161

L.Ed.2d 687 (2005), the Supreme Court distinguished *Cipollone*. The Court reiterated *Cipollone's* fundamental conclusion that the term "requirements" could include common-law duties as well as positive law duties, such as those imposed by state statutes and regulations. The Court acknowledged, however, that, if the common-law duties merely required persons to comply with federal law, they would not impose a requirement "in addition or different from" the federal requirement; they would merely create a different remedy. Moreover, common-law duties relating to the design, testing, or manufacture of the product or relating to express warranties would not be requirements for "labeling or packaging." With respect to the plaintiffs' common-law failure-to-warn and fraud claims, which would implicate labeling or packaging, the Court remanded the case to the court of appeals to determine if the state's common-law duties were "equivalent" to the federal prohibition on "false and misleading" statements and not inconsistent with any agency regulations giving content to the federal prohibition.

Determining field preemption is particularly difficult, because it involves a judicial inference of Congress's intent that must be derived from an overall sense of a statute. Where the matter involved is one traditionally regulated by the states, rather than the federal government, there is a presumption against field preemption, but ultimately the question is what Congress's purpose was. *See, e.g., United States v. Locke*, 529 U.S. 89, 120 S.Ct. 1135, 146 L.Ed.2d 69 (2000)(federal statutes governing requirements for ship construction and safe operation pre-empted field so that Washington could not require particular operating procedures by tankers in Puget Sound to protect against oil spills).

Another issue that can arise in preemption cases is the extent to which courts should defer to federal agency views on the preemptive effect of the agency's regulations. Sometimes these views are actually included in regulatory language, and the agency claims its views are entitled to strong deference under *Chevron, U.S.A., Inc. v. Natural Resources Defense Council*, 467 U.S. 837, 104 S.Ct. 2778, 81 L.Ed.2d 694 (1984). More commonly, the agency expresses its views in the preamble to a regulation or in an amicus brief in a court. Justice Breyer, in particular, has indicated his belief that courts should give substantial weight to an agency's view on preemption, but the case law is not yet clear on the subject.

2. The Dormant Commerce Clause

The constitutional doctrine of the Dormant Commerce Clause is complicated, if only because there is no textual basis for it. The original justification, that the grant of power to regulate commerce among the states to the federal government operated to withdraw any state power to regulate commerce among the states, has been rejected, but the doctrine nevertheless lives on. At its most basic level it precludes states from discriminating against interstate commerce in favor of their own commerce or from discriminating against out-of-state interests in commerce. Thus, for example, Nebraska could not forbid the export out of state of its ground water. *Sporhase v. Nebraska, ex rel. Douglas*, 458 U.S. 941, 102 S.Ct. 3456, 73 L.Ed.2d 1254 (1982). Similarly, New Jersey could not prohibit the importation of solid waste into the state. *City of Philadelphia v. New Jersey*, 437 U.S. 617, 98 S.Ct. 2531, 57 L.Ed.2d 475 (1978). Such discrimination is permissible only if there is no other way of achieving a legitimate state purpose. *See Maine v. Taylor,* 477 U.S. 131, 106 S.Ct. 2440, 91 L.Ed.2d 110 (1986)(upholding ban on the importation of baitfish because of inability to separate baitfish with parasites from other baitfish). It is not a legitimate state purpose merely to protect in-state economic interests. Moreover, "a State may not accord its own inhabitants a preferred right of access over consumers in other States to natural resources located within its borders." *City of Philadelphia*, 437 U.S. at 627. If a state statute regulates in-state and out-of-state interests equally, the fact that out-of-state interests may be disproportionately affected does not itself create a violation of the Dormant Commerce Clause, although if the disproportionate effect is significant, courts are to weigh the legitimate state interests furthered by the regulation against the costs to interstate commerce. If the latter clearly outweigh the former, the regulation would be found in violation of the Dormant Commerce Clause.

In the environmental area, there have been recurring problems related to states and localities' attempts to regulate the transportation and disposal of solid and hazardous waste. In *City of Philadelphia* the Court said that states could not ban the importation of solid waste. In *National Solid Wastes Management Ass'n v. Alabama Dept. of Envtl. Mgmt.*, 910 F.2d 713 (11th Cir. 1990), the Eleventh Circuit reached the same conclusion with respect to hazardous waste. In *Chemical Waste Management, Inc. v. Hunt*, 504 U.S. 334, 112 S.Ct. 2009, 119 L.Ed.2d 121 (1992), the Supreme Court overturned Alabama's response to the Eleventh Circuit decision, a surcharge imposed on in-state disposal of hazardous waste generated in other states that was higher than the charge imposed on disposal of the same waste generated in state. Oregon attempted to get around the *Hunt* decision by justifying its higher charge for the disposal of out-of-state solid waste than for in-state waste on the basis that in-state waste producers already had to pay taxes and other charges to the state. Thus, the claim was that the higher out-of-state charge was merely compensatory. The Court did not accept this claim and rejected the charge. *Oregon Waste Systems, Inc. v. Department of Envtl. Quality of the State of Or.*, 511 U.S. 93, 114 S.Ct. 1345, 128 L.Ed.2d 13 (1994). In *Fort Gratiot Sanitary Landfill, Inc. v. Michigan Dept. of Natural Resources*, 504 U.S. 353, 112 S.Ct. 2019, 119 L.Ed.2d 139 (1992), the Court found that a county ban on disposal of out-of-county solid waste, even though it applied not only to out-of-state waste but also to in-state waste from outside the county, violated the Dormant Commerce Clause.

Some states and localities have responded to solid waste problems by supporting the construction of waste recycling centers, separating out recyclables and thereby reducing the total volume of solid waste. The problem is that these facilities are expensive, and many localities have attempted to subsidize them by enacting "flow control ordinances," laws that require all local solid waste to be brought to the local recycling center at which there is a "tipping fee" for the waste disposed of there. This creates a legal monopoly enabling the recycling center to charge an inflated price, thereby enabling recovery of the high cost of its construction and operation. Absent such a legal monopoly, the wastes would simply be brought to commercial waste disposal sites, because typically they charge less than the recycling centers. These laws have also been challenged under the Dormant Commerce Clause, and in *C & A Carbone, Inc. v. Town of Clarkstown*, 511 U.S. 383, 114 S.Ct. 1677, 128 L.Ed.2d 399 (1994), the Supreme Court held that the town's flow control ordinance discriminated against interstate commerce and therefore was unconstitutional. It discriminated against interstate commerce in two ways: first, it restricted persons from sending waste out of state for disposal at lower cost and, second, it raised the cost of out-of-state waste sent into the locality (because it would then have to be sent to the high-cost recycling center).

There are a large number of lower court cases involving Dormant Commerce Clause challenges to flow control ordinances and other local attempts to manage solid waste problems. Some seem to apply *Carbone* in a straightforward and liberal manner and therefore tend to find the local actions unconstitutional. Others read it narrowly to find distinguishing circumstances that will enable the state or local law to pass muster. For example, because localities have historically collected solid waste and garbage for their residents as a government service, some courts have been willing to let local governments monopolize the solid waste collection industry, including running the recycling centers without violating the Dormant Commerce Clause. *See, e.g., United Haulers Ass'n, Inc. v. Oneida–Herkimer Solid Waste Management Authority*, 261 F.3d 245 (2d Cir. 2001); *USA Recycling, Inc. v. Town of Babylon*, 66 F.3d 1272 (2d Cir. 1995). Localities are in the best position when they actually own the facility that discriminates, as opposed to acting as a government regulator. Supreme Court precedent provides an exception to the Dormant Commerce Clause restrictions when a state or locality acts as a market participant rather than a market regulator. *See, e.g., Reeves, Inc. v. Stake*, 447 U.S. 429, 100 S.Ct. 2271, 65 L.Ed.2d 244 (1980). Thus, if a state or locality itself operates a landfill or recycling facility, it may as a market participant discriminate against out-of-state waste. Of course, if it acts merely as a market participant, it will not be able to require by law that everyone bring their waste to its facility, precisely what was required in *Carbone* in order to make the facility financially viable.

D. Constitutional Limitations on Bringing Lawsuits

In courses on Constitutional Law, you learn that Article III of the Constitution limits the jurisdiction of federal courts to "cases and controversies." Thus, in order for a federal court to hear a case, the case must meet the various tests that have been established in judicial decisions for determining whether it is a "case or controversy" within the meaning of Article III. One of the most important tests is whether a plaintiff has "standing" to bring a case. In order to have standing, a plaintiff must have suffered, or be about to suffer, injury caused by an allegedly unlawful action, and a court must be able to grant relief to redress or avoid the injury.

Many of the important recent standing cases have arisen in an environmental law context. A watershed case was *Sierra Club v. Morton*, 405 U.S. 727, 92 S.Ct. 1361, 31 L.Ed.2d 636 (1972). In that case, the Sierra Club brought a case against the Secretaries of Interior and Agriculture, alleging that their proposed approval of the development of a ski resort in the Sequoia National Forest adjacent to the Sequoia National Park would violate several environmental laws. The initial question before the Court, however, was whether the Sierra Club was entitled to obtain judicial review of the federal agencies' actions. While the Sierra Club was obviously interested in and concerned about development activities in wild areas in California, the Court held that such interest and concern were not sufficient to establish "standing"; the Sierra Club must suffer actual injury. However, the Court said, aesthetic or recreational injury would suffice. That is, if a member of the Sierra Club liked to walk in the woods where the development was scheduled to take place, the creation of a ski resort in place of a wild scenic area might injure the member's aesthetic or recreational experience. This would suffice to establish constitutional injury for purposes of standing.*

Subsequent to *Sierra Club v. Morton*, there have been a number of cases testing the limits of what kinds of injury will suffice for standing in environmental lawsuits. One of the most significant of these cases was *Lujan v. Defenders of Wildlife*.

LUJAN v. DEFENDERS OF WILDLIFE

Supreme Court of the United States, 1992.
504 U.S. 555, 112 S.Ct. 2130, 119 L.Ed.2d 351.

JUSTICE SCALIA delivered the opinion of the Court with respect to Parts I, II, III–A, and IV, and an opinion with respect to Part III–B in which the CHIEF JUSTICE, JUSTICE WHITE, and JUSTICE THOMAS join.

This case involves a challenge to a rule promulgated by the Secretary of the Interior interpreting § 7 of the Endangered Species Act of

---

* Public interest and environmental groups can bring lawsuits on behalf of one or more of their members under the doctrine of "representational" standing. Under this doctrine, an association can sue in its own name on behalf of its members if: (1) one of its members would have standing to bring the action, (2) the lawsuit relates to the purposes of the organization, and (3) neither the claim asserted nor the relief requested requires the participation of individual members (which in practical terms means the action is not for damages, but is for declaratory or injunctive relief). *See Hunt v. Washington State Apple Advertising Comm'n*, 432 U.S. 333, 97 S.Ct. 2434, 53 L.Ed.2d 383 (1977). Thus, much public interest and environmental litigation requires these groups to find members who actually would suffer the injury requisite for standing.

1973 (ESA), in such fashion as to render it applicable only to actions within the United States or on the high seas. The preliminary issue, and the only one we reach, is whether the respondents here, plaintiffs below, have standing to seek judicial review of the rule.

I

[The ESA, which is administered jointly by the Secretaries of Interior and Commerce, provides in § 7(a) that Federal agencies must consult with either the Secretary of Interior or Commerce before undertaking actions that might jeopardize the continued existence of any endangered species or threatened species. In 1978, the Fish and Wildlife Service (FWS) and the National Marine Fisheries Service (NMFS), on behalf of the Secretary of the Interior and the Secretary of Commerce respectively, promulgated a joint regulation stating that this obligation extends to Federal actions taken in foreign nations. In 1986, however, these agencies issued a revised regulation, reinterpreting the ESA, to limit the consultation obligation to Federal actions taken in the United States or on the high seas. Shortly thereafter, respondents, organizations dedicated to wildlife conservation causes, filed this action against the Secretary of the Interior, seeking a declaratory judgment that the new regulation is in error as to the geographic scope of this requirement of the ESA and an injunction requiring the Secretary to promulgate a new regulation restoring the initial interpretation. The District Court granted the Secretary's motion to dismiss for lack of standing, and the Eighth Circuit reversed.]

II

While the Constitution of the United States divides all power conferred upon the Federal Government into "legislative Powers," Art. I, § 1, "[t]he executive Power," Art. II, § 1, and "[t]he judicial Power," Art. III, § 1, it does not attempt to define those terms. To be sure, it limits the jurisdiction of federal courts to "Cases" and "Controversies," but an executive inquiry can bear the name "case" (the Hoffa case) and a legislative dispute can bear the name "controversy" (the Smoot–Hawley controversy). Obviously, then, the Constitution's central mechanism of separation of powers depends largely upon common understanding of what activities are appropriate to legislatures, to executives, and to courts. . . . One of those landmarks, setting apart the "Cases" and "Controversies" that are of the justiciable sort referred to in Article III . . . is the doctrine of standing. Though some of its elements express merely prudential considerations that are part of judicial self-government, the core component of standing is an essential and unchanging part of the case-or-controversy requirement of Article III.

Over the years, our cases have established that the irreducible constitutional minimum of standing contains three elements: First, the plaintiff must have suffered an "injury in fact"—an invasion of a legally-protected interest which is (a) concrete and particularized[2] and (b) "actual or imminent, not 'conjectural' or 'hypothetical.'" Second, there must be a causal connection between the injury and the conduct complained of—the injury has to be "fairly ... trace[able] to the challenged action of the defendant, and not ... th[e] result [of] the independent action of some third party not before the court." Third, it must be "likely," as opposed to merely "speculative," that the injury will be "redressed by a favorable decision."

The party invoking federal jurisdiction bears the burden of establishing these elements. Since they are not mere pleading requirements but rather an indispensable part of the plaintiff's case, each element must be supported in the same way as any other matter on which the plaintiff bears the burden of proof, *i.e.*, with the manner and degree of evidence required at the successive stages of the litigation. . . .

When the suit is one challenging the legality of government action or inaction, the nature and extent of facts that must be averred (at the summary judgment stage) or proved (at the trial stage) in order to establish standing depends considerably upon whether the plaintiff is himself an object of the action (or forgone action) at issue. If he is, there is ordinarily little question that the action or inaction has caused him injury, and that a judgment preventing or requiring the action will redress it. When, however, as in this case, a plaintiff's asserted injury arises from the government's allegedly unlawful regulation (or lack of regulation) of someone else, much more is needed. In that circumstance, causation and redressability ordinarily hinge on the response of the regulated (or regulable) third party to the government action or inaction—and perhaps on the response of others as well. The existence of one or more of the essential elements of standing "depends on the unfettered choices made by independent actors not before the courts and whose exercise of broad and legitimate discretion the courts cannot presume either to control or to predict," and it becomes the burden of the plaintiff to adduce facts showing that those choices have been or will be made in such manner as to produce causation and permit redressability of injury. . . .

III

We think the Court of Appeals failed to apply the foregoing principles in denying the Secretary's motion for summary judgment. Respondents had not made the requisite demonstration of (at least) injury and redressability.

A

Respondents' claim to injury is that the lack of consultation with respect to certain funded activities abroad "increas[es] the rate of

---

2. By particularized, we mean that the injury must affect the plaintiff in a personal and individual way.

extinction of endangered and threatened species." Of course, the desire to use or observe an animal species, even for purely aesthetic purposes, is undeniably a cognizable interest for purpose of standing. "But the 'injury in fact' test requires more than an injury to a cognizable interest. It requires that the party seeking review be himself among the injured." To survive the Secretary's summary judgment motion, respondents had to submit affidavits or other evidence showing, through specific facts, not only that listed species were in fact being threatened by funded activities abroad, but also that one or more of respondents' members would thereby be "directly" affected apart from their " 'special interest' in th[e] subject."

With respect to this aspect of the case, the Court of Appeals focused on the affidavits of two Defenders' members—Joyce Kelly and Amy Skilbred. Ms. Kelly stated that she traveled to Egypt in 1986 and "observed the traditional habitat of the endangered Nile crocodile there and intend[s] to do so again, and hope[s] to observe the crocodile directly," and that she "will suffer harm in fact as a result of [the] American . . . role . . . in overseeing the rehabilitation of the Aswan High Dam on the Nile . . . and [in] develop[ing] . . . Egypt's . . . Master Water Plan." Ms. Skilbred averred that she traveled to Sri Lanka in 1981 and "observed th[e] habitat" of "endangered species such as the Asian elephant and the leopard" at what is now the site of the Mahaweli Project funded by the Agency for International Development (AID), although she "was unable to see any of the endangered species;" "this development project," she continued, "will seriously reduce endangered, threatened, and endemic species habitat including areas that I visited . . . [, which] may severely shorten the future of these species;" that threat, she concluded, harmed her because she "intend[s] to return to Sri Lanka in the future and hope[s] to be more fortunate in spotting at least the endangered elephant and leopard." When Ms. Skilbred was asked at a subsequent deposition if and when she had any plans to return to Sri Lanka, she reiterated that "I intend to go back to Sri Lanka," but confessed that she had no current plans. . . .

We shall assume for the sake of argument that these affidavits contain facts showing that certain agency-funded projects threaten listed species—though that is questionable. They plainly contain no facts, however, showing how damage to the species will produce "imminent" injury to Mses. Kelly and Skilbred. That the women "had visited" the areas of the projects before the projects commenced proves nothing. As we have said in a related context, " '[p]ast exposure to illegal conduct does not in itself show a present case or controversy regarding injunctive relief . . . if unaccompanied by any continuing, present adverse effects.' " And the affiants' profession of an "inten[t]" to return to the places they had visited before—where they will presumably, this time, be deprived of the opportunity to observe animals of the endangered species—is simply not enough. Such "some day" intentions—without any description of concrete plans, or indeed even any specification of when the some day will be—do not support a finding of the "actual or imminent" injury that our cases require.

Besides relying upon the Kelly and Skilbred affidavits, respondents propose a series of novel standing theories. The first, inelegantly styled "ecosystem nexus," proposes that any person who uses any part of a "contiguous ecosystem" adversely affected by a funded activity has standing even if the activity is located a great distance away. This approach, as the Court of Appeals correctly observed, is inconsistent with our opinion in [*Lujan* v.] *National Wildlife Federation*, [497 U.S. 871, 110 S.Ct. 3177 (1990),] which held that a plaintiff claiming injury from environmental damage must use the area affected by the challenged activity and not an area roughly "in the vicinity" of it. . . .

Respondents' other theories are called, alas, the "animal nexus" approach, whereby anyone who has an interest in studying or seeing the endangered animals anywhere on the globe has standing; and the "vocational nexus" approach, under which anyone with a professional interest in such animals can sue. Under these theories, anyone who goes to see Asian elephants in the Bronx Zoo, and anyone who is a keeper of Asian elephants in the Bronx Zoo, has standing to sue because the Director of AID did not consult with the Secretary regarding the AID-funded project in Sri Lanka. This is beyond all reason. . . . It is clear that the person who observes or works with a particular animal threatened by a federal decision is facing perceptible harm, since the very subject of his interest will no longer exist. It is even plausible—though it goes to the outermost limit of plausibility—to think that a person who observes or works with animals of a particular species in the very area of the world where that species is threatened by a federal decision is facing such harm, since some animals that might have been the subject of his interest will no longer exist. It goes beyond the limit, however, and into pure speculation and fantasy, to say that anyone who observes or works with an endangered species, anywhere in the world, is appreciably harmed by a single project affecting some portion of that species with which he has no more specific connection.

B.

Besides failing to show injury, respondents failed to demonstrate redressability. . . . Since the agencies funding the projects were not parties to the case, the District Court could accord relief only against the Secretary: He could be ordered to revise his regulation to require consultation for foreign projects. But this would not remedy respondents' alleged injury unless the funding agencies were bound by the Secretary's regulation, which is very much an open question. . . .

A further impediment to redressability is the fact that the agencies generally supply only a fraction of the funding for a foreign project. AID, for example, has provided less than 10% of the funding for the Mahaweli Project. Respondents have produced nothing to indicate that the projects they have named will either be suspended, or do less harm to listed species, if that fraction is eliminated.... [I]t is entirely conjectural whether the nonagency activity that affects respondents will be altered or affected by the agency activity they seek to achieve. There is no standing.

IV

The Court of Appeals found that respondents had standing for an additional reason: because they had suffered a "procedural injury." The so-called "citizen-suit" provision of the ESA provides, in pertinent part, that "any person may commence a civil suit on his own behalf (A) to enjoin any person, including the United States and any other governmental instrumentality or agency ... who is alleged to be in violation of any provision of this chapter." The court held that, because § 7(a) requires interagency consultation, the citizen-suit provision creates a "procedural righ[t]" to consultation in all "persons"—so that *anyone* can file suit in federal court to challenge the Secretary's (or presumably any other official's) failure to follow the assertedly correct consultative procedure, notwithstanding their inability to allege any discrete injury flowing from that failure. To understand the remarkable nature of this holding one must be clear about what it does not rest upon: This is not a case where plaintiffs are seeking to enforce a procedural requirement the disregard of which could impair a separate concrete interest of theirs (*e.g.*, the procedural requirement for a hearing prior to denial of their license application, or the procedural requirement for an environmental impact statement before a federal facility is constructed next door to them).[7] ... Rather, the court held that the injury-in-fact requirement had been satisfied by congressional conferral upon all persons of an abstract, self-contained, noninstrumental "right" to have the Executive observe the procedures required by law. We reject this view.[8]

---

7. There is this much truth to the assertion that "procedural rights" are special: The person who has been accorded a procedural right to protect his concrete interests can assert that right without meeting all the normal standards for redressability and immediacy. Thus, under our case-law, one living adjacent to the site for proposed construction of a federally licensed dam has standing to challenge the licensing agency's failure to prepare an Environmental Impact Statement, even though he cannot establish with any certainty that the Statement will cause the license to be withheld or altered, and even though the dam will not be completed for many years. (That is why we do not rely, in the present case, upon the Government's argument that, *even if* the other agencies were obliged to consult with the Secretary, they might not have followed his advice.) What respondents' "procedural rights" argument seeks, however, is quite different from this: standing for persons who have no concrete interests affected—

persons who live (and propose to live) at the other end of the country from the dam.

8. ... We do *not* hold that an individual cannot enforce procedural rights; he assuredly can, so long as the procedures in question are designed to protect some threatened concrete interest of his that is the ultimate basis of his standing. The dissent, however, asserts that there exist "classes of procedural duties ... so enmeshed with the prevention of a substantive, concrete harm that an individual plaintiff may be able to demonstrate a sufficient likelihood of injury just through the breach of that procedural duty." If we understand this correctly, it means that the government's violation of a certain (undescribed) class of procedural duty satisfies the concrete-injury requirement by itself, without any showing that the procedural violation endangers a concrete interest of the plaintiff (apart from his interest in having the procedure observed). We cannot agree. The dissent is unable to cite a single case in which we actually found standing

We have consistently held that a plaintiff raising only a generally available grievance about government—claiming only harm to his and every citizen's interest in proper application of the Constitution and laws, and seeking relief that no more directly and tangibly benefits him than it does the public at large—does not state an Article III case or controversy....

To be sure, our generalized-grievance cases have typically involved Government violation of procedures assertedly ordained by the Constitution rather than the Congress. But there is absolutely no basis for making the Article III inquiry turn on the source of the asserted right. Whether the courts were to act on their own, or at the invitation of Congress, in ignoring the concrete injury requirement described in our cases, they would be discarding a principle fundamental to the separate and distinct constitutional role of the Third Branch—one of the essential elements that identifies those "Cases" and "Controversies" that are the business of the courts rather than of the political branches. "The province of the court," as Chief Justice Marshall said in *Marbury v. Madison*, "is, solely, to decide on the rights of individuals." Vindicating the *public* interest (including the public interest in government observance of the Constitution and laws) is the function of Congress and the Chief Executive. The question presented here is whether the public interest in proper administration of the laws (specifically, in agencies' observance of a particular, statutorily prescribed procedure) can be converted into an individual right by a statute that denominates it as such, and that permits all citizens (or, for that matter, a subclass of citizens who suffer no distinctive concrete harm) to sue. If the concrete injury requirement has the separation-of-powers significance we have always said, the answer must be obvious: To permit Congress to convert the undifferentiated public interest in executive officers' compliance with the law into an "individual right" vindicable in the courts is to permit Congress to transfer from the President to the courts the Chief Executive's most important constitutional duty, to "take Care that the Laws be faithfully executed," Art. II, § 3....

Nothing in this contradicts the principle that "[t]he ... injury required by Art. III may exist solely by virtue of 'statutes creating legal rights, the invasion of which creates standing.' " [But the cases in which this was said] involved Congress's elevating to the status of legally cognizable injuries concrete, *de facto* injuries that were previously inadequate in law (namely, injury to an individual's personal interest in living in a racially integrated community and injury to a company's interest in marketing its product free from competition.) As we said in *Sierra Club v. Morton*, "[Statutory] broadening [of] the categories of injury that may be alleged in support of standing is a different matter from abandoning the requirement that the party seeking review must himself have suf-

solely on the basis of a "procedural right" unconnected to the plaintiff's own concrete harm....

fered an injury." [I]t is clear that in suits against the government, at least, the concrete injury requirement must remain.

JUSTICE KENNEDY, with whom JUSTICE SOUTER joins, concurring in part and concurring in the judgment.

... While it may seem trivial to require that Mses. Kelly and Skilbred acquire airline tickets to the project sites or announce a date certain upon which they will return, this is not a case where it is reasonable to assume that the affiants will be using the sites on a regular basis, nor do the affiants claim to have visited the sites since the projects commenced. With respect to the Court's discussion of respondents' "ecosystem nexus," "animal nexus," and "vocational nexus" theories, I agree that on this record respondents' showing is insufficient to establish standing on any of these bases. I am not willing to foreclose the possibility, however, that in different circumstances a nexus theory similar to those proffered here might support a claim to standing. ...

I also join Part IV of the Court's opinion with the following observations. As government programs and policies become more complex and far-reaching, we must be sensitive to the articulation of new rights of action that do not have clear analogs in our common-law tradition. Modern litigation has progressed far from the paradigm of Marbury suing Madison to get his commission, or Ogden seeking an injunction to halt Gibbons' steamboat operations. In my view, Congress has the power to define injuries and articulate chains of causation that will give rise to a case or controversy where none existed before, and I do not read the Court's opinion to suggest a contrary view. In exercising this power, however, Congress must at the very least identify the injury it seeks to vindicate and relate the injury to the class of persons entitled to bring suit. The citizen-suit provision of the Endangered Species Act does not meet these minimal requirements, because while the statute purports to confer a right on "any person ... to enjoin ... the United States and any other governmental instrumentality or agency ... who is alleged to be in violation of any provision of this chapter," it does not of its own force establish that there is an injury in "any person" by virtue of any "violation."

The Court's holding that there is an outer limit to the power of Congress to confer rights of action is a direct and necessary consequence of the case and controversy limitations found in Article III. I agree that it would exceed those limitations if, at the behest of Congress and in the absence of any showing of concrete injury, we were to entertain citizen-suits to vindicate the public's nonconcrete interest in the proper administration of the laws. While it does not matter how many persons have been injured by the challenged action, the party bringing suit must show that the action injures him in a concrete and personal way. This requirement is not just an empty formality. It preserves the vitality of the adversarial process by assuring both that the parties before the court have an actual, as opposed to professed, stake in the outcome, and that "the legal questions presented ... will be resolved, not in the rarefied atmosphere of a debating society, but in a concrete factual context conducive to a realistic appreciation of the consequences of judicial action." In addition, the requirement of concrete injury confines the Judicial Branch to its proper, limited role in the constitutional framework of government. . . .

JUSTICE STEVENS, concurring in the judgment.

Because I am not persuaded that Congress intended the consultation requirement in § 7(a)(2) of the ESA, to apply to activities in foreign countries, I concur in the judgment of reversal. I do not, however, agree with the Court's conclusion that respondents lack standing because the threatened injury to their interest in protecting the environment and studying endangered species is not "imminent." Nor do I agree with the plurality's additional conclusion that respondents' injury is not "redressable" in this litigation.

In my opinion a person who has visited the critical habitat of an endangered species, has a professional interest in preserving the species and its habitat, and intends to revisit them in the future has standing to challenge agency action that threatens their destruction. Congress has found that a wide variety of endangered species of fish, wildlife, and plants are of "aesthetic, ecological, educational, historical, recreational, and scientific value to the Nation and its people." Given that finding, we have no license to demean the importance of the interest that particular individuals may have in observing any species or its habitat, whether those individuals are motivated by aesthetic enjoyment, an interest in professional research, or an economic interest in preservation of the species. . . .

The Court nevertheless concludes that respondents have not suffered "injury in fact" because they have not shown that the harm to the endangered species will produce "imminent" injury to them. I disagree. An injury to an individual's interest in studying or enjoying a species and its natural habitat occurs when someone (whether it be the government or a private party) takes action that harms that species and habitat. In my judgment, therefore, the "imminence" of such an injury should be measured by the timing and likelihood of the threatened environmental harm, rather than by the time that might elapse between the present and the time when the individuals would visit the area if no such injury should occur. . . .

Although I believe that respondents have standing, I nevertheless concur in the judgment of reversal because I am persuaded that the Government is correct in its submission that § 7(a)(2) does not apply to activities in foreign countries. . . .

JUSTICE BLACKMUN, with whom JUSTICE O'CONNOR joins, dissenting.

I part company with the Court in this case in two respects. First, I believe that respondents have raised genuine issues of fact—sufficient to survive summary judgment—both as to injury and as to redressability. Second, I question the Court's breadth of language in rejecting standing for "procedural" injuries. I fear the Court seeks to impose fresh limitations on the constitutional authority of Congress to allow citizen-suits in the federal courts for injuries deemed "procedural" in nature. I dissent.

Notes and Comments

1. The Court recognized that the citizen suit provision of the Endangered Species Act authorizes a lawsuit by "any person" to challenge action by any person violating the Act. How was it then that the Court held that Defenders of Wildlife could not bring the lawsuit? What does this say about persons later bringing lawsuits under the ESA's citizen suit provision?

2. What if the defendant's allegedly unlawful action is the failure to file some report with a federal agency that is required by some environmental law? For example, persons with a National Pollution Discharge Elimination System (NPDES) permit under the Clean Water Act generally are required to file monthly Discharge Monitoring Reports (DMRs). What if the polluter fails to file the reports? Or, under the Emergency Planning and Community Right-to-Know Act, companies that discharge toxic materials into the environment are required to file an annual report as to the amount and nature of those discharges. These reports are then collated and published by EPA as the Toxics Release Inventory (TRI)(www.epa.gov/tri/). Could an environmental group sue a company that failed to file its required report? What would be its injury? While there is no Supreme Court case answering this direct question, the Supreme Court did answer a similar question in *Federal Election Com'n v. Akins*, 524 U.S. 11, 118 S.Ct. 1777, 141 L.Ed.2d 10 (1998). In that case, a group failed to file an allegedly required campaign finance report with the FEC. An organization that tracked campaign finances and reported the information to its members sued the FEC to require the report to be filed. Over Justice Scalia's dissent (joined by Justices O'Connor and Thomas), the Court held that the plaintiff had suffered a particularized injury, rather than a generalized grievance, in not being able to access what would be important publicly available information.

3. The Court for a number of years seemingly was hostile to environmentalists, denying standing in other environmental cases besides *Defenders. See Lujan v. National Wildlife Federation*, 497 U.S. 871, 110 S.Ct. 3177, 111 L.Ed.2d 695 (1990)(lack of injury); *Steel Co. v. Citizens for a Better Environment*, 523 U.S. 83, 118 S.Ct. 1003, 140 L.Ed.2d 210 (1998)(lack of redressability). *Cf., Bennett v. Spear*, 520 U.S. 154, 117 S.Ct. 1154, 137 L.Ed.2d 281 (1997)(finding standing for "anti-environmentalists"). More recently, however, the cases have been more favorable for plaintiffs. *See Friends of the Earth, Inc. v. Laidlaw Environmental Services (TOC), Inc.*, 528 U.S. 167, 120 S.Ct. 693, 145 L.Ed.2d 610 (2000)(finding injury to plaintiffs from defendants' pollution without having to show that the pollution actually harmed the environment and finding a civil penalty adequate redressability), which will be dealt with in more detail in the later section of the book dealing with citizen suits. Most recently, the Court found standing in the following case.

MASSACHUSETTS v. ENVIRONMENTAL PROTECTION AGENCY

Supreme Court of the United States, 2007.
___ U.S. ___, 127 S.Ct. 1438, ___ L.Ed.2d ___.

JUSTICE STEVENS delivered the opinion of the Court.

[C]alling global warming "the most pressing environmental challenge of our time," a group of States, local governments, and private organizations, alleged in a petition for certiorari that the Environmental Protection Agency (EPA) has abdicated its responsibility under the Clean Air Act [by failing] to regulate the emissions of four greenhouse gases, including carbon dioxide [emitted by automobiles]. . . .

In response, EPA, supported by 10 intervening States and six trade associations, correctly argued that we may not address [the merits of the case] unless at least one petitioner has standing to invoke our jurisdiction under Article III of the Constitution. . . .

IV

Article III of the Constitution limits federal-court jurisdiction to "Cases" and "Controversies." Those two words confine "the business of federal courts to questions presented in an adversary context and in a form historically viewed as capable of resolution through the judicial process." *Flast v. Cohen,* 392 U.S. 83 (1968). . . .

The parties' dispute turns on the proper construction of a congressional statute, a question eminently suitable to resolution in federal court. Congress has moreover authorized this type of challenge to EPA action. See 42 U.S.C. § 7607(b)(1). That authorization is of critical importance to the standing inquiry: "Congress has the power to define injuries and articulate chains of causation that will give rise to a case or controversy where none existed before." *Lujan v. Defenders of Wildlife,* 504 U.S. 555, 580 (Kennedy, J., concurring in part and concurring in judgment). "In exercising this power, however, Congress must at the very least identify the injury it seeks to vindicate and relate the injury to the class of persons entitled to bring suit." *Ibid.* We will not, therefore, "entertain citizen suits to vindicate the public's nonconcrete interest in the proper administration of the laws." *Id.,* at 581.

EPA maintains that because greenhouse gas emissions inflict widespread harm, the doctrine of standing presents an insuperable jurisdictional obstacle. We do not agree. At bottom, "the gist of the question of standing" is whether petitioners have "such a personal stake in the outcome of the controversy as to assure that concrete adverseness which sharpens the presentation of issues upon which the court so largely depends for illumination." *Baker v. Carr,* 369 U.S. 186, 204 (1962). As Justice KENNEDY explained in his *Lujan* concurrence:

"While it does not matter how many persons have been injured by the challenged action, the party bringing suit must show that the action injures him in a concrete and personal way. This requirement is not just an empty formality. It preserves the vitality of the adversarial process by assuring both that the parties before the court have an actual, as opposed to professed, stake in the outcome, and that the legal questions presented ... will be resolved, not in the rarified atmosphere of a debating society, but in a concrete factual context conducive to a realistic appreciation of the consequences of judicial action." 504 U.S., at 581 (internal quotation marks omitted).

To ensure the proper adversarial presentation, *Lujan* holds that a litigant must demonstrate that it has suffered a concrete and particularized injury that is either actual or imminent, that the injury is fairly traceable to the defendant, and that it is likely that a favorable decision will redress that injury. However, a litigant to whom Congress has "accorded a procedural right to protect his concrete interests," *id.*, at 572, n. 7—here, the right to challenge agency action unlawfully withheld, § 7607(b)(1)—"can assert that right without meeting all the normal standards for redressability and immediacy," *ibid*. When a litigant is vested with a procedural right, that litigant has standing if there is some possibility that the requested relief will prompt the injury-causing party to reconsider the decision that allegedly harmed the litigant. *Ibid.*

Only one of the petitioners needs to have standing to permit us to consider the petition for review. We stress here, as did Judge Tatel below, the special position and interest of Massachusetts. It is of considerable relevance that the party seeking review here is a sovereign State and not, as it was in *Lujan,* a private individual.

Well before the creation of the modern administrative state, we recognized that States are not normal litigants for the purposes of invoking federal jurisdiction. As Justice Holmes explained in *Georgia v. Tennessee Copper Co.,* 206 U.S. 230, 237 (1907), a case in which Georgia sought to protect its citizens from air pollution originating outside its borders:

> "The case has been argued largely as if it were one between two private parties; but it is not. The very elements that would be relied upon in a suit between fellow-citizens as a ground for equitable relief are wanting here. The State owns very little of the territory alleged to be affected, and the damage to it capable of estimate in money, possibly, at least, is small. This is a suit by a State for an injury to it in its capacity of *quasi*-sovereign. In that capacity the State has an interest independent of and behind the titles of its citizens, in all the earth and air within its domain. It has the last word as to whether its mountains shall be stripped of their forests and its inhabitants shall breathe pure air."

Just as Georgia's "independent interest ... in all the earth and air within its domain" supported federal jurisdiction a century ago, so too does Massachusetts' well-founded desire to preserve its sovereign territory today. That Massachusetts does in fact own a great deal of the "territory alleged to be affected" only reinforces the conclusion that its stake in the outcome of this case is sufficiently concrete to warrant the exercise of federal judicial power.

When a State enters the Union, it surrenders certain sovereign prerogatives. Massachusetts cannot invade Rhode Island to force reductions in greenhouse gas emissions, it cannot negotiate an emissions treaty with China or India, and in some circumstances the exercise of its police powers to reduce in-state motor-vehicle emissions might well be pre-empted.

These sovereign prerogatives are now lodged in the Federal Government, and Congress has ordered EPA to protect Massachusetts (among others) by prescribing standards applicable to the "emission of any air pollutant from any class or classes of new motor vehicle engines, which in [the Administrator's] judgment cause, or contribute to, air pollution which may reasonably be anticipated to endanger public health or welfare." 42 U.S.C. § 7521(a)(1). Congress has moreover recognized a concomitant procedural right to challenge the rejection of its rulemaking petition as arbitrary and capricious. § 7607(b)(1). Given that procedural right and Massachusetts' stake in protecting its quasi-sovereign interests, the Commonwealth is entitled to special solicitude in our standing analysis.

With that in mind, it is clear that petitioners' submissions as they pertain to Massachusetts have satisfied the most demanding standards of the adversarial process. EPA's steadfast refusal to regulate greenhouse gas emissions presents a risk of harm to Massachusetts that is both "actual" and "imminent." *Lujan,* 504 U.S., at 560 (internal quotation marks omitted). There is, moreover, a "substantial likelihood that the judicial relief requested" will prompt EPA to take steps to reduce that risk. *Duke Power Co. v. Carolina Environmental Study Group, Inc.,* 438 U.S. 59, 79 (1978).

The Injury

The harms associated with climate change are serious and well recognized. Indeed, the National Research Council Report itself—which EPA regards as an "objective and independent assessment of the relevant science,"—identifies a number of environmental changes that have already inflicted significant harms, including "the global retreat of mountain glaciers, reduction in snow-cover extent, the earlier spring melting of rivers and lakes, [and] the accelerated rate of rise of sea levels during the 20th century relative to the past few thousand years...."

Petitioners allege that this only hints at the environmental damage yet to come. According to the climate scientist Michael MacCracken, "qualified scientific experts involved in climate change research" have reached a "strong consensus" that global warming threatens (among other things) a precipitate rise in sea levels by the end of the century, "severe and irreversible changes to natural ecosystems," a "significant reduction in water storage in winter snowpack in mountainous regions with direct and important economic consequences," and an increase in the spread of disease. He also observes that rising ocean temperatures may contribute to the ferocity of hurricanes.

That these climate-change risks are "widely shared" does not minimize Massachusetts' interest in the outcome of this litigation. See *Federal Election Comm'n v. Akins,* 524 U.S. 11, 24 (1998) ("[W]here a harm is concrete, though widely shared, the Court has found 'injury in fact' "). According to petitioners' unchallenged affidavits, global sea levels rose somewhere between 10 and 20 centimeters over the 20th century as a result of global warming. These rising seas have already begun to swallow Massachusetts' coastal land. Because the Commonwealth "owns a substantial portion of the state's coastal property," it has alleged a particularized injury in its capacity as a landowner. The severity of that injury will only increase over the course of the next century: If sea levels continue to rise as predicted, one Massachusetts official believes that a significant fraction of coastal property will be "either permanently lost through inundation or temporarily lost through periodic storm surge and flooding events." Remediation costs alone, petitioners allege, could run well into the hundreds of millions of dollars.

Causation

EPA does not dispute the existence of a causal connection between man-made greenhouse gas emissions and global warming. At a minimum, therefore, EPA's refusal to regulate such emissions "contributes" to Massachusetts' injuries.

EPA nevertheless maintains that its decision not to regulate greenhouse gas emissions from new motor vehicles contributes so insignificantly to petitioners' injuries that the agency cannot be haled into federal court to answer for them. For the same reason, EPA does not believe that any realistic possibility exists that the relief petitioners seek would mitigate global climate change and remedy their injuries. That is especially so because predicted increases in greenhouse gas emissions from developing nations, particularly China and India, are likely to offset any marginal domestic decrease.

But EPA overstates its case. Its argument rests on the erroneous assumption that a small incremental step, because it is incremental, can never be attacked in a federal judicial forum. Yet accepting that premise would doom most challenges to regulatory action. Agencies, like legislatures, do not generally resolve massive problems in one fell regulatory swoop. They instead whittle away at them over time, refining their preferred approach as circumstances change and as they develop a more-nuanced understanding of how best to proceed. That a first step might be tentative does not by itself support the notion that federal courts lack jurisdiction to determine whether that step conforms to law.

And reducing domestic automobile emissions is hardly a tentative step. Even leaving aside the other greenhouse gases, the United States transportation sector emits an enormous quantity of carbon dioxide into the atmosphere—according to the MacCracken affidavit, more than 1.7 billion metric tons in 1999 alone. That accounts for more than 6% of worldwide carbon dioxide emissions. To put this in perspective: Considering just emissions from the transportation sector, which represent less than one-third of this country's total carbon dioxide emissions, the United States would still rank as the third-largest emitter of carbon dioxide in the world, outpaced only by the European Union and China. Judged by any standard, U.S. motor-vehicle emissions make a meaningful contribution to greenhouse gas concentrations and hence, according to petitioners, to global warming.

The Remedy

While it may be true that regulating motor-vehicle emissions will not by itself *reverse* global warming, it by no means follows that we lack jurisdiction to decide whether EPA has a duty to take steps to *slow* or *reduce* it. See also *Larson v. Valente*, 456 U.S. 228, 244, n. 15 (1982) ("[A] plaintiff satisfies the redressability requirement when he shows that a favorable decision will relieve a discrete injury to himself. He need not show that a favorable decision will relieve his *every* injury"). Because of the enormity of the potential consequences associated with man-made climate change, the fact that the effectiveness of a remedy might be delayed during the (relatively short) time it takes for a new motor-vehicle fleet to replace an older one is essentially irrelevant.[23] Nor is it dispositive that developing countries such as China and India are poised to increase greenhouse gas emissions substantially over the next century: A reduction in domestic emissions would slow the pace of global emissions increases, no matter what happens elsewhere.

We moreover attach considerable significance to EPA's "agree[ment] with the President that 'we must address the issue of global climate change,' " and to EPA's ardent support for various voluntary emission-reduction programs. As Judge Tatel observed in dissent below, "EPA would presumably not bother with such efforts if it thought emissions reductions would have no discernable impact on future global warming."

In sum—at least according to petitioners' uncontested affidavits—the rise in sea levels associated with global warming has already harmed and will continue to harm Massachusetts. The risk of catastrophic harm, though remote, is nevertheless real. That risk would be reduced to some extent if petitioners received the relief they seek. We therefore hold that petitioners have standing to challenge the EPA's denial of their rulemaking petition. [The Court then went on to rule on the merits in plaintiffs' favor.]

---

23. See also *Mountain States Legal Foundation v. Glickman*, 92 F.3d 1228, 1234 (C.A.D.C.1996) ("The more drastic the injury that government action makes more likely, the lesser the increment in probability to establish standing"); *Village of Elk Grove Village v. Evans*, 997 F.2d 328, 329 (C.A.7 1993) ("[E]ven a small probability of injury is sufficient to create a case or controversy-to take a suit out of the category of the hypothetical-provided of course that the relief sought would, if granted, reduce the probability").

CHIEF JUSTICE ROBERTS, with whom JUSTICE SCALIA, JUSTICE THOMAS, and JUSTICE ALITO join, dissenting.

Global warming may be a "crisis," even "the most pressing environmental problem of our time." Indeed, it may ultimately affect nearly everyone on the planet in some potentially adverse way, and it may be that governments have done too little to address it. It is not a problem, however, that has escaped the attention of policymakers in the Executive and Legislative Branches of our Government, who continue to consider regulatory, legislative, and treaty-based means of addressing global climate change.

Apparently dissatisfied with the pace of progress on this issue in the elected branches, petitioners have come to the courts claiming broad-ranging injury, and attempting to tie that injury to the Government's alleged failure to comply with a rather narrow statutory provision. I would reject these challenges as nonjusticiable. Such a conclusion involves no judgment on whether global warming exists, what causes it, or the extent of the problem. Nor does it render petitioners without recourse. This Court's standing jurisprudence simply recognizes that redress of grievances of the sort at issue here "is the function of Congress and the Chief Executive," not the federal courts. *Lujan v. Defenders of Wildlife,* 504 U.S. 555, 576 (1992). I would vacate the judgment below and remand for dismissal of the petitions for review.

I

Article III, § 2, of the Constitution limits the federal judicial power to the adjudication of "Cases" and "Controversies." "If a dispute is not a proper case or controversy, the courts have no business deciding it, or expounding the law in the course of doing so." *DaimlerChrysler Corp. v. Cuno,* 126 S.Ct. 1854, 1860–1861 (2006). "Standing to sue is part of the common understanding of what it takes to make a justiciable case," *Steel Co. v. Citizens for Better Environment,* 523 U.S. 83, 102 (1998), and has been described as "an essential and unchanging part of the case-or-controversy requirement of Article III," *Defenders of Wildlife, supra,* at 560.

Our modern framework for addressing standing is familiar: "A plaintiff must allege personal injury fairly traceable to the defendant's allegedly unlawful conduct and likely to be redressed by the requested relief." *DaimlerChrysler, supra,* at 1861. Applying that standard here, petitioners bear the burden of alleging an injury that is fairly traceable to the Environmental Protection Agency's failure to promulgate new motor vehicle greenhouse gas emission standards, and that is likely to be redressed by the prospective issuance of such standards.

Before determining whether petitioners can meet this familiar test, however, the Court changes the rules. It asserts that "States are not normal litigants for the purposes of invoking federal jurisdiction," and that given "Massachusetts' stake in protecting its quasi-sovereign interests, the Commonwealth is entitled to *special solicitude* in our standing analysis."

Relaxing Article III standing requirements because asserted injuries are pressed by a State, however, has no basis in our jurisprudence, and support for any such "special solicitude" is conspicuously absent from the Court's opinion. The general judicial review provision cited by the Court, 42 U.S.C. § 7607(b)(1), affords States no special rights or status.... Under the law on which petitioners rely, Congress treated public and private litigants exactly the same.

Nor does the case law cited by the Court provide any support for the notion that Article III somehow implicitly treats public and private litigants differently. The Court has to go back a full century in an attempt to justify its novel standing rule, but even there it comes up short. The Court's analysis hinges on *Georgia v. Tennessee Copper Co.,* 206 U.S. 230 (1907)—a case that did indeed draw a distinction between a State and private litigants, but solely with respect to available remedies. The case had nothing to do with Article III standing....

In contrast to the present case, there was no question in *Tennessee Copper* about Article III injury. There was certainly no suggestion that the State could show standing where the private parties could not; there was no dispute, after all, that the private landowners had "an action at law." *Tennessee Copper* has since stood for nothing more than a State's right, in an original jurisdiction action, to sue in a representative capacity as *parens patriae*. Nothing about a State's ability to sue in that capacity dilutes the bedrock requirement of showing injury, causation, and redressability to satisfy Article III....

A claim of *parens patriae* standing is distinct from an allegation of direct injury. Far from being a substitute for Article III injury, *parens patriae* actions raise an additional hurdle for a state litigant: the articulation of a "quasi-sovereign interest" "*apart* from the interests of particular private parties." Just as an association suing on behalf of its members must show not only that it represents the members but that at least one satisfies Article III requirements, so too a State asserting quasi-sovereign interests as *parens patriae* must still show that its citizens satisfy Article III. Focusing on Massachusetts's interests as quasi-sovereign makes the required showing here harder, not easier. The Court, in effect, takes what has always been regarded as a *necessary* condition for *parens patriae* standing—a quasi-sovereign interest—and converts it into a *sufficient* showing for purposes of Article III....

All of this presumably explains why petitioners never cited *Tennessee Copper* in their briefs before this Court or the D.C. Circuit. It presumably explains why not one of the legion of *amici* supporting petitioners ever cited the case. And it presumably explains why not one of the three judges writing below ever cited the case either.

II

It is not at all clear how the Court's "special solicitude" for Massachusetts plays out in the standing analysis, except as an implicit concession that petitioners cannot establish standing on traditional terms. But the status of Massachusetts as a State cannot compensate for petitioners' failure to demonstrate injury in fact, causation, and redressability.

When the Court actually applies the three-part test, it focuses . . . on the State's asserted loss of coastal land as the injury in fact. If petitioners rely on loss of land as the Article III injury, however, they must ground the rest of the standing analysis in that specific injury. That alleged injury must be "concrete and particularized," and "distinct and palpable." Central to this concept of "particularized" injury is the requirement that a plaintiff be affected in a "personal and individual way" and seek relief that "directly and tangibly benefits him" in a manner distinct from its impact on "the public at large." Without "particularized injury, there can be no confidence of 'a real need to exercise the power of judicial review' or that relief can be framed 'no broader than required by the precise facts to which the court's ruling would be applied.' "

The very concept of global warming seems inconsistent with this particularization requirement. Global warming is a phenomenon "harmful to humanity at large," and the redress petitioners seek is focused no more on them than on the public generally—it is literally to change the atmosphere around the world.

If petitioners' particularized injury is loss of coastal land, it is also that injury that must be "actual or imminent, not conjectural or hypothetical," "real and immediate," and "certainly impending."

As to "actual" injury, the Court observes that "global sea levels rose somewhere between 10 and 20 centimeters over the 20th century as a result of global warming" and that "[t]hese rising seas have already begun to swallow Massachusetts' coastal land." But none of petitioners' declarations supports that connection. . . .

The Court's attempts to identify "imminent" or "certainly impending" loss of Massachusetts coastal land fares no better. One of petitioners' declarants predicts global warming will cause sea level to rise by 20 to 70 centimeters *by the year 2100.* [A]ccepting a century-long time horizon and a series of compounded estimates renders requirements of imminence and immediacy utterly toothless. "Allegations of possible future injury do not satisfy the requirements of Art. III. A threatened injury must be *certainly impending* to constitute injury in fact."

III

Petitioners' reliance on Massachusetts's loss of coastal land as their injury in fact for standing purposes creates insurmountable problems for them with respect to causation and redressability. To establish standing, petitioners must show a causal connection between that specific injury and the lack of new motor vehicle greenhouse gas emission standards, and that the promulgation of such standards would likely redress that injury. As is often the case, the questions of causation and redressability overlap. And importantly, when a party is challenging the Government's allegedly unlawful regulation, or lack of regulation, of a third party, satisfying the causation and redressability requirements becomes "substantially more difficult."

Petitioners view the relationship between their injuries and EPA's failure to promulgate new motor vehicle greenhouse gas emission standards as simple and direct: Domestic motor vehicles emit carbon dioxide and other greenhouse gases. Worldwide emissions of greenhouse gases contribute to global warming and therefore also to petitioners' alleged injuries. Without the new vehicle standards, greenhouse gas emissions—and therefore global warming and its attendant harms—have been higher than they otherwise would have been; once EPA changes course, the trend will be reversed.

The Court ignores the complexities of global warming, and does so by now disregarding the "particularized" injury it relied on in step one, and using the dire nature of global warming itself as a bootstrap for finding causation and redressability. First, it is important to recognize the extent of the emissions at issue here. Because local greenhouse gas emissions disperse throughout the atmosphere and remain there for anywhere from 50 to 200 years, it is global emissions data that are relevant. According to one of petitioners' declarations, domestic motor vehicles contribute about 6 percent of global carbon dioxide emissions and 4 percent of global greenhouse gas emissions. The amount of global emissions at issue here is smaller still; § 202(a)(1) of the Clean Air Act covers only *new* motor vehicles and *new* motor vehicle engines, so petitioners' desired emission standards might reduce only a fraction of 4 percent of global emissions.

This gets us only to the relevant greenhouse gas emissions; linking them to global warming and ultimately to petitioners' alleged injuries next requires consideration of further complexities. As EPA explained in its denial of petitioners' request for rulemaking,

> "predicting future climate change necessarily involves a complex web of economic and physical factors including: our ability to predict future global anthropogenic emissions of [greenhouse gases] and aerosols; the fate of these emissions once they enter the atmosphere (e.g., what percentage are absorbed by vegetation or are taken up by the oceans); the impact of those emissions that remain in the atmosphere on the radiative properties of the atmosphere; changes in critically important climate feedbacks (e.g., changes in cloud cover and ocean circulation); changes in temperature characteristics (e.g., average temperatures, shifts in daytime and evening temperatures); changes in other climatic parameters (e.g., shifts in precipitation, storms); and ultimately the impact of such changes on human health and welfare (e.g., increases or decreases in agricultural productivity, human health impacts)."

Petitioners are never able to trace their alleged injuries back through this complex web to the fractional amount of global emissions that might have been limited with EPA standards. In light of the bit-part domestic new motor vehicle greenhouse gas emissions have played in what petitioners describe as a 150–year global phenomenon, and the myriad additional factors bearing on petitioners' alleged injury—the loss of Massachusetts coastal land-the connection is far too speculative to establish causation.

IV

Redressability is even more problematic. To the tenuous link between petitioners' alleged injury and the indeterminate fractional domestic emissions at issue here, add the fact that petitioners cannot meaningfully predict what will come of the 80 percent of global greenhouse gas emissions that originate outside the United States. As the Court acknowledges, "developing countries such as China and India are poised to increase greenhouse gas emissions substantially over the next century," so the domestic emissions at issue here may become an increasingly marginal portion of global emissions, and any decreases produced by petitioners' desired standards are likely to be overwhelmed many times over by emissions increases elsewhere in the world. . . .

No matter, the Court reasons, because *any* decrease in domestic emissions will "slow the pace of global emissions increases, no matter what happens elsewhere." Every little bit helps, so Massachusetts can sue over any little bit.

The Court's sleight-of-hand is in failing to link up the different elements of the three-part standing test. What must be *likely* to be redressed is the particular injury in fact. The injury the Court looks to is the asserted loss of land. The Court contends that regulating domestic motor vehicle emissions will reduce carbon dioxide in the atmosphere, *and therefore* redress Massachusetts's injury. But even if regulation *does* reduce emissions—to some indeterminate degree, given events elsewhere in the world—the Court never explains why that makes it *likely* that the injury in fact—the loss of land—will be redressed. Schoolchildren know that a kingdom might be lost "all for the want of a horseshoe nail," but "likely" redressability is a different matter. The realities make it pure conjecture to suppose that EPA regulation of new automobile emissions will *likely* prevent the loss of Massachusetts coastal land. . . .

[JUSTICE SCALIA authored a dissent on the merits which CHIEF JUSTICE ROBERTS and JUSTICES ALITO and THOMAS joined.]

Notes and Comments

1. The five-four decision in *Defenders* has now become a 5–4 decision in the other direction in *Massachusetts v. EPA*. Chief Justice Rehnquist and Justice O'Connor, who provided votes toward the majority in *Defenders*, have been replaced by Chief Justice Roberts and Justice Alito, who reflect the same leaning. What has changed is Justice Kennedy from a concurring justice in finding no standing in *Defenders* to a vote for standing in *Massachusetts v. EPA*. Note how Justice Stevens' majority opinion highlights Justice Kennedy's concurrence in *Defenders* as support for finding standing.

2. Justice Stevens' opinion begins by stressing, first, that the Clean Air Act has a provision granting judicial review for final agency actions under that Act (here the denial of the petition for rulemaking), *see* 42 U.S.C. 7607(b), and second, that this was a case brought by a state, rather than a private litigant. How were these important to the conclusion that Massachusetts had standing? Didn't Justice Stevens demonstrate (at least to the majority's satisfaction) that Massachusetts was suffering an immediate, particularized harm caused by EPA's failure to act and that its action would at least remedy that harm—the normal standard for assessing standing?

3. Ultimately, whom do you find more persuasive on the law in *Massachusetts v. EPA*—Justice Stevens or Chief Justice Roberts?

IV. ADMINISTRATIVE LAW ISSUES

If you have already taken an administrative law course, this section of the chapter is just review. If you have not taken an administrative law course, this section is just an introduction to a subject that is a necessary one for anyone serious about environmental law. Administrative law is the law that governs agencies. Environmental law is law administered by agencies to protect the environment, so the law that governs agencies in administering environmental laws is essential not only to those in the agencies but also to those outside the agencies who wish to influence or challenge agency action.

A. Rulemaking

Normally, when Congress (or a state legislature) passes a law, it authorizes or requires an agency to administer the law. This is true of an environmental law like the Clean Air Act, for instance, that requires the Environmental Protection Agency to do certain things, or the National Forest Management Act that requires the Forest Service to manage national forests in certain ways. Usually this means that Congress requires or authorizes an agency to adopt **rules*** by which the statutory requirements will be implemented. For example, the Clean Air Act, among other things, requires EPA to adopt standards setting the minimum acceptable quality for the outdoor air with respect to pollutants that may adversely affect human health or the environment. Consequently, EPA has adopted a rule to protect human health with respect to carbon monoxide that allows no more than 9 parts per million (or 10 micrograms per cubic meter) in the air averaged over an eight-hour period. Similarly, the National Forest Management Act requires the Forest Service to adopt land and resource management plans for each national forest, and the Forest Service has adopted rules specifying what must be contained in those management plans.

The process by which these regulations are adopted is called **rulemaking**. The Administrative Procedure Act, 5 U.S.C. §§ 551 et seq., specifies certain procedures which agencies must follow as a general

---

* The term "rule" and the term "regulation" mean the same thing, and they can be used interchangeably.

matter when they engage in rulemaking. *See* 5 U.S.C. § 553. The general procedures required by the APA are often supplemented or replaced by more specific procedural requirements in the particular statutes being implemented or in other statutes. For example, the Clean Air Act contains specific procedures supplementing the APA's provisions. *See* 42 U.S.C. § 7607(d). In addition, the Regulatory Flexibility Act imposes special requirements when regulations, especially those of EPA or the Occupational Safety and Health Administration, impact small businesses, organizations or governmental units. *See* 5 U.S.C. §§ 601 et seq. Nevertheless, the normal procedure required for rulemaking is that:

- An agency must provide the public notice in the Federal Register of its intent to engage in rulemaking; the Federal Register is a daily publication of the federal government, but today notice is additionally provided through publication on the internet.

- The agency must provide the public an opportunity to comment on the agency's proposed rulemaking; the opportunity to comment in writing is always provided; often the public is also given the opportunity to comment orally at a hearing before agency officials.

- The agency must provide the public with adequate information about the proposed rulemaking to allow for the public comment to be meaningful; normally this means that the agency publishes an actual proposed rule as well as information explaining what the rule does and why; in addition, factual information that is the basis for the rule must be made available to the public.

- The agency must consider the public comments, and when it issues its final rule, it must respond to the significant comments made.

An agency's failure to follow these procedural requirements, for example, by not providing adequate notice of what it proposes to do, may lead to a court setting aside the rule, if a person challenges it.

In addition to the procedural requirements imposed by statute, which generally are subject to judicial review, there are other procedural requirements imposed on federal agencies by presidential executive orders, most importantly E.O. 12866.

Rulemaking that may have a significant effect on the human environment is also subject to the National Environmental Policy Act, which imposes its own procedural requirements. As you will see later, NEPA's requirements are not limited to rulemaking; they apply to any federal action that may have a significant impact. And as you will see, NEPA's requirements are themselves modeled after the procedural requirements for notice-and-comment rulemaking.

B. Adjudication

Adjudication is the agency equivalent of judicial trials. Most agencies conduct adjudication in various contexts. For example, EPA can assess money penalties against persons who violate the Clean Air Act by bringing a case against them before an Administrative Law Judge. *See* 42 U.S.C. § 7413(d). An ALJ is technically an employee of the agency, but ALJs have special personnel protections to provide them a certain amount of independence from agency policymakers and enforcement officers. Sometimes the adjudications are before other agency employees who do not have even the special protections afforded ALJs. For example, EPA can assess money penalties of less than $25,000 under the Clean Water Act in an adjudication before an adjudicator other than an ALJ.

When an ALJ is the adjudicator, the APA's adjudication procedures are used, and they typically mirror those of a court trial. When an ALJ is not the adjudicator, the APA's procedures are not used. These proceedings tend to be more informal, and persons may not necessarily have the right to call witnesses or cross examine witnesses.

A common type of non-penalty adjudication involves permit applications. For example, under several environmental statutes persons must obtain permits before they are allowed to emit pollution. Normally the adjudication of a permit application does not involve ALJs and often is done only through written submissions. It is unlike penalty proceedings in that the agency acts only as an adjudicator, not as a party participant. Occasionally, however, a public interest group may intervene in the proceeding to oppose the permit application.

In administrative adjudication, after the ALJ or other adjudicator makes a decision, the losing party typically may appeal the decision to the head of the agency, or in the case of the EPA, to the Environmental Appeals Board, which has the power to review the initial decision de novo. The person who loses on the administrative appeal, other than the agency, may then normally seek judicial review of the agency decision. Where the agency enforcement officers brought an enforcement action that was denied on administrative appeal, they may not seek judicial review; the administrative appellate decision is the decision of the *agency* and therefore binds its enforcement officers.

C. Presidential Oversight

As mentioned earlier, beginning with President Nixon, presidents have increasingly moved to strengthen their oversight of agency regulatory activities, in particular with health, safety, and environmental regulations. The current methodology of this oversight was created by President Reagan and has undergone little formal change over the years and different administrations. Under what is now Executive Order 12866, agencies must prepare an annual plan of their regulatory objectives and priorities and a list of all their planned significant regulatory activities for the year. The Office of Information and Regulatory Affairs (OIRA) in the Office of Management and Budget reviews the list for consistency with the President's priorities and policies, and informs the agency of any inconsistency.

Probably more importantly, the Order also imposes several requirements on agencies, other than independent regulatory agencies, with respect to "significant regulatory actions," which are defined as an action leading to a rulemaking that would have an effect of $100 million on the economy or would otherwise have a substantial effect on a number of listed values including the environment. The requirements include a mandate that, before proposed rules are proposed or final rules are adopted, agencies must submit the document and supporting cost-benefit analyses to OIRA for its review and comment. While OIRA does not have the authority actually to rewrite or veto the rules proposed by agencies, it does have a lot of power to influence agency outcomes, at least to the extent that Presidents want to support OIRA. OIRA also can influence agency actions pursuant to its authority under the Paperwork Reduction Act, 44 U.S.C. §§ 3501 *et seq.*, and under the Information Quality Act, 44 U.S.C. § 3516 note, both of which enable OIRA to impose further requirements on agency rulemakings and other actions.

One of the important differences between procedures imposed on agencies by the President through OIRA, as compared to procedures required by the APA or other statute, is that judicial review of the agencies' compliance is precluded. Each of the Executive Orders has specifically stated that they are an exercise of the internal management of the executive branch and are not intended to create any rights or benefits enforceable at law. Courts have respected this limitation and refused to review agency action under the orders. *See, e.g., State of Michigan v. Thomas*, 805 F.2d 176 (6th Cir. 1986).

Generally, OIRA has exercised its authority so as to be a brake on agency environmental rulemaking, and consequently its activities are viewed as detrimental by environmental groups and positive by business groups.

D. Judicial Review

Some environmental statutes have specific provisions governing judicial review of agency actions under the statute. *See, e.g.,* 42 U.S.C § 7607 (Clean Air Act). Others do not. When a statute does not itself provide for judicial review, a person may be able to obtain judicial review under the Administrative Procedure Act. Under the APA, courts may review agency actions to determine if they are contrary to statute, are arbitrary and capricious or an abuse of discretion, were adopted without complying with all procedural requirements, or, if the action was either formal rulemaking or adjudication, it was not supported by substantial evidence. 5 U.S.C. § 706(2). In addition, courts may review agency inaction in certain circumstances and compel agency action unlawfully withheld or unreasonably delayed. 5 U.S.C. § 706(1).

1. Obtaining Review

There are many hurdles to obtaining judicial review under the APA, even though the Supreme Court has said that there is a "presumption" of review of agency actions. Unless a plaintiff can overcome these hurdles, unlawful agency action may escape review. You have already met a constitutional requirement for review—standing. The APA contains several of its own, and the Court has imposed others as a matter of common law decisionmaking.

a. Preclusion of Review

The APA specifically precludes judicial review under the APA in two circumstances—when a statute precludes review and to the extent that the agency action was committed to agency discretion by law. In the environmental field there are not many statutes that preclude review under the APA, unless those statutes substitute their own review provisions. Moreover, there are few environmental statutes that commit agency decisionmaking to the agency's discretion. That is, the statutes constrain the agencies' discretion by indicating what factors should guide or govern the agencies' decisionmaking. However, an agency's decision whether or not to engage in enforcement actions against alleged violators is generally held to be inherently committed to agency discretion as prosecutorial discretion.

b. APA Requirements for Review

i. Zone of Interests

The APA provides that a person may obtain review under the APA only if a person suffers a "legal wrong" or is "adversely affected or aggrieved within the meaning of a relevant statute." 5 U.S.C. § 702. This is known as the "zone of interests" requirement.

If a person suffers "legal wrong" because of agency action, they are within the zone of interest of whatever law has been violated. A simple example is an agency action that limits a person's liberty or property interests. For instance, if the Corps of Engineers precludes a person from filling wetlands on his property under the Clean Water Act, and the person believes the agency action is unlawful under the CWA, then the person is said to suffer legal wrong under the CWA, and he can obtain judicial review of that action. However, if the Corps had granted a permit to a person to fill wetlands on his property, and an environmental organization believes that the permit violates the CWA, neither that organization nor its members suffers a legal wrong. Their liberty and property are not affected. Their interests may be adversely affected, but this implicates the second phrase in Section 702, not the first.

If a person does not suffer legal wrong because of an agency action, a person seeking judicial review of the action under the APA must be able to identify a statute that "arguably" protects the interest that the person is seeking to protect in bringing the lawsuit. For example, the environmental group upset about the filling of wetlands would need to show that their interest that is adversely affected—their interest in protecting the environment—is one that is arguably intended to be protected by the CWA. Normally, that is not difficult, but there are instances where there may be a problem. For instance, a group of ranchers tried to sue under the APA, asserting that the U.S. Forest Service had violated the National Environmental Policy Act (which does not have a judicial review provision) in adopting a Land and Resource Management Plan. In order to determine whether the ranchers could sue under the APA, however, the court first had to decide whether the interest they sought to protect—continued cattle grazing on U.S. Forest Service land—was an interest intended to be protected under NEPA. The court held that it was not. Rather, it said, "The purpose of NEPA is to protect the environment, not the economic interests of those adversely affected by agency decisions." *Nevada Land Action Ass'n v. U.S. Forest Service*, 8 F.3d 713 (9th Cir. 1993). Thus, even though the U.S. Forest Service may have violated NEPA, and the ranchers may have been harmed by the Plan, the ranchers were not able to obtain judicial review of the Plan, because they were not in the zone of interests protected by NEPA.

In determining the zone of interests, courts are to look to the particular provision involved in the case, not the statute generally. For example, in *Bennett v. Spear*, 520 U.S. 154, 117 S.Ct. 1154, 137 L.Ed.2d 281 (1997), where ranchers argued that the Fish & Wildlife Service had violated the Endangered Species Act, it was clear that the intent of the ESA generally was not to protect the interests of cattle grazing. However, the Court found that the ranchers were within the zone of interests of the particular ESA provision they alleged was violated, a requirement that the agency's decision reflect "the best scientific and commercial data available." This provision, the Court said, served not only "the ESA's overall goal of species preservation" but also the "avoid[ance of] needless economic dislocation produced by agency officials zealously but unintelligently pursuing their environmental objectives." It was the latter that was the interest claimed by the ranchers.

In any case, the zone of interests test is not intended to be especially rigorous, and the Supreme Court has emphasized that the plaintiff's interest need only be "arguably" within the zone of interests of the statute involved. *See, e.g., National Credit Union Admin. v. First Nat'l Bank & Trust Co.*, 522 U.S. 479, 118 S.Ct. 927, 140 L.Ed.2d 1 (1998). Thus, only where the interests of the plaintiff seem to have virtually no basis in the statutory provision involved is a court likely to find its claims outside the zone of interests.

ii. Finality

Only "final agency actions" are subject to judicial review under the APA. 5 U.S.C. § 704. In order for there to be a "final agency action," there must first be agency action. The APA defines "agency action" to "include[] the whole or a part of an agency rule, order, license, sanction, relief, or the equivalent thereof, or failure to act." 5 U.S.C. § 551(13). The Supreme Court has held that agency "programs" are not the type of discrete activities that are required for something to be an agency action within the meaning of the APA. *See Lujan v. National Wildlife Federation*, 497 U.S. 871, 110 S.Ct. 3177, 111 L.Ed.2d 695 (1990) ("land withdrawal review program" not itself subject to review, because it is not the product of an agency action, as opposed to particular actions that might occur under the program).

Norton v. Southern Utah Wilderness Alliance, 542 U.S. 55, 124 S.Ct. 2373, 159 L.Ed.2d 137 (2004), addressed what constitutes a "failure to act," such that the agency's failure to act might be final agency action subject to judicial review. There environmental groups claimed that the Bureau of Land Management had failed to protect wilderness study areas from destruction by off-road vehicles in violation of both its statutory mandate and its own land use plans. The Supreme Court said that this was in essence a challenge to the adequacy of the BLM's management of the wilderness study areas, and as such was not a challenge to the failure to take a particular, legally required discrete action. Only the failure to take one of the listed actions under the definition of "agency action" could qualify as a "failure to act" that would be subject to judicial review.

The purpose of the finality requirement in the term "final agency action" is to assure that agency proceedings are not interrupted by attempts to seek judicial review before the agency makes its final decision and that judicial review is based upon the authoritative agency decision, rather than some tentative determination. To carry out this purpose the Supreme Court has articulated a two-part test: "First, the action must mark the 'consummation' of the agency's decisionmaking process,—it must not be of a merely tentative or interlocutory nature. And second, the action must be one by which 'rights or obligations have been determined,' or from which 'legal consequences will flow.' " *Bennett v. Spear*, 520 U.S. 154, 178, 117 S.Ct. 1154, 1168, 137 L.Ed.2d 281 (1997). The second part of this test has also been phrased as requiring an impact that "is sufficiently direct and immediate" and has a "direct effect on ... day-to-day business.... The core question is whether the agency has completed its decisionmaking process, and whether the result of that process is one that will directly affect the parties." *Franklin v. Massachusetts*, 505 U.S. 788, 796–97, 112 S.Ct. 2767, 2773, 120 L.Ed.2d 636 (1992) (quoting from *Abbott Laboratories v. Gardner*, 387 U.S. 136, 152, 87 S.Ct. 1507, 1517, 18 L.Ed.2d 681 (1967)) This latter phraseology would appear to find "final" agency action when there is a real practical effect, even if the effect is not a legal one.

The distinction between a practical effect and a legal one can make a difference in at least two different situations. First, agencies often issue interpretive documents, opinion letters, guidance manuals, etc., intended to provide guidance to the public and direction to subunits in the agency. These documents, while technically "rules" under the APA, do not have legal force; they are merely advisory. They can, nevertheless, have tremendous practical effect. For example, the guidance may state that persons are deemed in violation of the law unless they take certain action that might be very expensive. Persons subject to that guidance, who believe it misinterprets the law, often would like to obtain judicial review. If, however, an action must have "legal consequences" or "determine rights or obligations,'' this guidance may not be final agency action. If an action need only have real, practical consequences, then the guidance probably would be final agency action. Thus, if an action must have legal consequences in order to be reviewable, the person faced with the guidance must choose whether to conform to what he believes is not a lawful interpretation of the law or to willfully violate the agency's guidance. The lower courts have not acted consistently in this situation. Sometimes they find a legal effect is required; sometimes they find a practical effect is sufficient. *See, e.g., Air Brake Systems, Inc. v. Mineta*, 357 F.3d 632 (6th Cir. 2004)(holding an interpretation letter non-final because of a lack of legal consequences); *Appalachian Power Co. v. EPA*, 208 F.3d 1015 (D.C. Cir. 2000)(holding a guidance document final because of its practical effects).

The second situation where a difference between a practical and legal effect is important in determining whether agency action is final and therefore reviewable commonly occurs in EPA enforcement. EPA believes that someone is violating one of the environmental laws that it enforces, so it issues a compliance order—an order directing the person to stop violating the law. The person receiving the order believes the order is unlawful. If the order has legal effect, it is clearly final agency action, but it may not be if it only has practical effect. EPA has successfully argued in a number of cases that its compliance orders do not have independent legal effect, because they merely restate the person's underlying legal duty. Again, the courts have not been totally consistent in deciding whether this is final agency action. *Compare, e.g., Acker v. EPA*, 290 F.3d 892 (7th Cir. 2002) (order that identified past violations and directed company to comply with law in the future not final action) *with Allsteel, Inc. v. EPA*, 25 F.3d 312, 315 (6th Cir. 1994)(holding an order to stop construction imposed legal obligations beyond those of the statute). Recently, however, the Supreme Court in dictum suggested that such orders should be final agency action. *Alaska Dept. of Environmental Conservation v. EPA*, 540 U.S. 461, 124 S.Ct. 983, 157 L.Ed.2d 967 (2004)(stressing the ''practical and legal consequences (lost costs and vulnerability to penalties)'' of EPA's order).

iii. Exhaustion of Administrative Remedies

Like the finality requirement, the doctrine of exhaustion is intended to keep courts from reviewing agency action until the agency has had a full opportunity to hear and consider a case and to correct its own errors. Originally this was a common law limitation on judicial review, and it continues to exist in non-APA cases. In cases brought under the APA, however, 5 U.S.C. § 704 creates a statutory exhaustion standard for determining whether an agency action is final. That is, an action is not final if a statute requires someone to exhaust their administrative remedies before obtaining judicial review, or if an agency by rule requires persons to exhaust their administrative remedies before going to court and the agency suspends its action pending the administrative review. For example, if an ALJ assesses an administrative penalty against a person in an EPA administrative enforcement action, the person may not immediately seek review of that decision in court, if EPA has required by rule that the person must first appeal to the Environmental Appeals Board and that the person need not pay the penalty until the appeal is finally decided.

Under common law exhaustion, a person must exhaust his administrative remedies whether or not the agency so requires by rule or suspends its action pending review, but there are also a number of exceptions to the general requirement to exhaust. An interesting question, not yet resolved by the courts, is whether those exceptions continue to apply under the APA when an agency requires exhaustion by rule.

c. Common Law Requirements for Review

Although the Administrative Procedure Act purports to state all the requirements for obtaining judicial review of agency action, the Supreme Court has accepted some common law limitations on judicial review as continuing to apply in APA cases, even though those limitations do not appear in the APA.

i. *Issue Exhaustion and Waiver*

Closely related to exhaustion doctrine in terms of their purpose and origin are the two closely related, if not overlapping, common law doctrines of issue exhaustion and waiver. Issue exhaustion requires that in order for a person to obtain judicial consideration of a particular legal claim, the person must have raised the issue before the agency. For example, a person might argue before an ALJ in an EPA enforcement action that the water he allegedly polluted was not water protected by the Clean Water Act, and losing there he might argue that point on appeal to the EPA Environmental Appeals Board. If he loses there, he could seek judicial review of that issue in court, but at this point he could not also argue that he did not actually pollute the water, because he had not argued that before the agency. This is similar to the judicial practice of not allowing persons to argue on appeal issues they did not raise in the initial trial.

The concept of waiver is similar but it has applied more often with regard to judicial review of rules, rather than judicial review of adjudications, where exhaustion issues usually apply. Courts have increasingly been willing to deny a person judicial review of certain issues in any agency rule, or to deny review of the rule altogether, if the person had not exercised their right to comment on the proposed rule during the rulemaking proceeding, or had not raised the issue to the agency that it was now raising to the court. Sometimes this requirement is specified by statute, *see, e.g.,* 42 U.S.C. § 7607(d)(7)(B)(requiring objections to a rule under the Clean Air Act to be raised before the agency as a prerequisite for judicial review). Other times, courts require it as a matter of common law in APA cases. *See, e.g., National Wildlife Federation v. EPA,* 286 F.3d 554, 562 (D.C. Cir. 2002). But *see* William Funk, Exhaustion of Administrative Remedies—New Dimensions Since *Darby*, 18 Pace Env.

L. Rev. 1 (2000)(criticizing trend). If the plaintiff can show "exceptional circumstances" justifying review notwithstanding the general policy of allowing agencies the opportunity to consider issues in the first instance, courts may then allow review. *See, e.g., Johnson v. Director, Office of Workers' Compensation Programs*, 183 F.3d 1169 (9th Cir. 1999)(finding exceptional circumstances where the agency had already considered and decided the issue in an earlier setting).

ii. Ripeness

The most important common law limitation on obtaining judicial review is the ripeness doctrine. It overlaps with the doctrines of finality and exhaustion in that it is intended to assure that courts do not become involved in agency activities until it is appropriate. The case of *Abbott Laboratories v. Gardner*, 387 U.S. 136, 148, 87 S.Ct. 1507, 1515, 18 L.Ed.2d 681 (1967), provided the Supreme Court's classic statement of the rule: "The problem is best seen in a twofold aspect, requiring us to evaluate both the fitness of the issues for judicial decision and the hardship to the parties of withholding court consideration." More recently, in an environmental case, *Ohio Forestry Ass'n v. Sierra Club*, 523 U.S. 726, 733, 118 S.Ct. 1665, 1670, 140 L.Ed.2d 921 (1998), the Court reiterated the test with a slight variation: "we must consider: (1) whether delayed review would cause hardship to the plaintiffs; (2) whether judicial intervention would inappropriately interfere with further administrative action; and (3) whether the courts would benefit from further factual development of the issues presented." However stated, the test involves a balancing of the plaintiff's interest in obtaining review at this time against the court's and the agency's interests in awaiting review in a different context. In *Ohio Forestry*, for example, the plaintiffs challenged a provision in a forest plan that allegedly would allow the Forest Service to make timber sales involving clear cuts in inappropriate cases. The Court said this was not ripe for review, because it was not clear that any timber sales allowing such cuts would actually occur, because the agency might not allow clear cuts in the inappropriate circumstances, and, moreover, even if the Forest Service did make such a timber sale, the plaintiffs could then challenge the particular timber sale, so there was no hardship to plaintiff in waiting for an actual timber sale involving a clear cut.

2. The Scope of Judicial Review

Once a court determines to hear a case, the question becomes the nature of that review. The Administrative Procedure Act specifies a number of bases upon which a court should invalidate agency action, 5 U.S.C. § 706. In environmental cases, the most frequent bases argued are that the agency action was: arbitrary and capricious, contrary to statute or rule, or adopted without following all the required procedures.

For an agency action to be "arbitrary and capricious" in essence means that the agency did not act reasonably in light of its statutory authority and all the information the agency had before it. The court assesses the agency's explanation for the action and the factual basis the agency provides for the action. The court is supposed to be deferential to the agency's decision in light of the agency's expertise and the fact that Congress has delegated the decisionmaking to the agency, not the courts. Nonetheless, many agency actions are set aside because the court simply does not believe the agency's action makes sense in light of all the information the agency had. This type of review stems from the seminal case of *Citizens to Preserve Overton Park v. Volpe*, 401 U.S. 402, 91 S.Ct. 814, 28 L.Ed.2d 136 (1971), in which the Court held that the Secretary of Transportation's decision to authorize a highway through a park without any explanation, when the statute required avoidance of parks to the extent feasible and prudent, could not be found to be reasonable.

Sometimes a court will not set aside the agency action but merely remand it to the agency for a better explanation. In these cases, the plaintiff may only obtain delay in the agency action, rather than setting it aside forever.

Agencies have no inherent authority, so they must look to some statute for the authority for what they do. Invariably there are disputes over the meaning of their statutory authorities or limitations. When agencies interpret the statutes they administer or the regulations they promulgate, the Supreme Court has established some tests for how courts are to view those interpretations. First, to the extent that the court, using traditional methods of statutory construction, believes the meaning of the statute or regulation is clear, that is the end of the issue—the court simply announces its interpretation without regard to the agency's interpretation. Second, to the extent that the statute is ambiguous, and the agency's interpretation has the force of law (as, for example, a regulation would have), a court is to defer to any reasonable agency interpretation. *See United States v. Mead Corp.*, 533 U.S. 218, 121 S.Ct. 2164, 150 L.Ed.2d 292 (2001); *Chevron, U.S.A., Inc. v. NRDC*, 467 U.S. 837, 104 S.Ct. 2778, 81 L.Ed.2d 694 (1984). Third, if the statute is ambiguous, and the agency's interpretation does not have the force of law (as an interpretive rule or policy statement would not), then a court is not to defer to the agency's interpretation, but it is to consider that interpretation in light of "the thoroughness evident in its consideration, the validity of its reasoning, its consistency with earlier and later pronouncements, and all those factors which give it the power to persuade, if lacking the power to control." *Skidmore v. Swift & Co.*, 323 U.S. 134, 65 S.Ct. 161, 89 L.Ed. 124 (1944). Sometimes, the deference commanded by *Chevron* is called "strong deference" and the respect suggested by *Skidmore* is called "weak deference." Many law review pages have been devoted to the distinctions between these two levels of review, and some have suggested that the alleged difference is more myth than reality, with courts invoking *Chevron* when they agree with the agency's interpretation and invoking *Skidmore* when they disagree. Whatever the truth of this debate, there is no question that lawyers expend a great deal of effort trying to convince courts that *Chevron* or *Skidmore* applies, depending upon which degree of deference aids their client. Usually this means that the agency is asserting *Chevron* should apply, so that the agency will receive maximum deference, whereas the private person challenging the agency's interpretation would rather have *Skidmore* apply. Which applies turns on whether the agency interpretation has the "force of law." The Supreme Court has made clear that legislative regulations, adopted after notice and comment, and formal adjudications under the APA both have the force of law. It has also said that informal guidance documents do not. However, the Court has eschewed drawing bright lines in this area, so there is considerable question as to what other agency interpretations have the force of law commanding *Chevron* deference. Finally, if the agency is interpreting its own regulation, to the extent it is not clear on its face, courts are to uphold the agency interpretation unless it is clearly erroneous. *Bowles v. Seminole Rock & Sand Co.* 325 U.S. 410, 65 S.Ct. 1215, 89 L.Ed. 1700 (1945). This is strong deference, whether or not the interpretation has the force of law.

The failure of an agency to comply with the procedural requirements for its action normally results in the invalidation of the agency action. If, for example, the agency does not provide adequate notice and comment before adopting a regulation, the regulation will likely be set aside. *See, e.g., Shell Oil Co. v. EPA*, 950 F.2d 741 (D.C. Cir. 1991)(holding so-called "mixture and derived from" rule invalid for not giving adequate notice of the issue). Moreover, challenges to agency action under the National Environmental Policy Act invariably involve a claim that the agency has failed to comply with the procedural requirements of NEPA, usually by not making the required Environmental Impact Statement. Similarly, challenges under the Endangered Species Act often involve a claim that an agency has not complied with the procedural requirement of Section 7 of the Act to consult with the Fish and Wildlife Service or NOAA Fisheries. *See, e.g., Bennett v. Spear*, 520 U.S. 154, 117 S.Ct. 1154, 137 L.Ed.2d 281 (1997).

Chapter 2

NEPA

I. INTRODUCTION TO NEPA

"[A]ll agencies of the Federal Government shall . . . include in every recommendation or report on proposals for . . . major federal actions significantly affecting the quality of the human environment, a detailed statement . . . on the environmental impact of the proposed action." 42 U.S.C. § 4332 (2)(C)(i).

With these simple words, the U.S. Congress, with President Nixon's signature, ushered in the modern era of environmental law in 1969. Although the National Environmental Policy Act (or "NEPA") may have evolved into something different than was originally foreseen, it represented the collective concern over mounting environmental problems and an attempt to try to address those problems legislatively. It is conceptually distinct from pollution-control laws such as the Clean Air Act, the Clean Water Act, and RCRA, because it does not seek to control the discharge of pollution per se; instead, it focuses on the environmental degradation that can result as a by-product of the actions of federal agencies, and those private activities which they can control or permit. Even with respect to these governmental actions (including permitting decisions), NEPA does not force federal agencies to select the most environmentally-friendly option. Rather, as the D.C. Circuit recognized in *Calvert Cliffs' Coordinating Committee, Inc. v. U.S. Atomic Energy Commission*, 449 F.2d 1109, 1112 (D.C. Cir. 1971), it merely requires them to consider the impact of their actions on the environment:

> Congress did not establish environmental protection as an exclusive goal; rather, it desired a reordering of priorities, so that environmental costs and benefits will assume their proper place along with other considerations.

Still, NEPA's impact on government action and the shape of our world has been far-reaching, and it has served as a model for both other federal laws and other environmental assessment laws the world over. The flexibility and breadth of such laws allow decisionmakers to examine environmental impacts in whatever form they arise. As such, NEPA and other NEPA-type laws contribute to far more informed decisionmaking.

[handwritten margin note: Do NOT need most environmentally friendly option just consider impact on environment]

91

At the same time, they can also lead to problems related to their very breadth.

NEPA's ultimate effects are debated to this day, with many arguing that it simply gives "Not in my Back Yard" types ("NIMBYs") an opportunity to stop or slow down important projects, at great cost to the government and society; while others argue that it gives a voice to environmental values that were not considered before and has changed our world for the betterment of humanity and the surrounding environment. As you read this chapter, and learn more about NEPA and its process, try to determine which camp you think is most correct.

II. OVERVIEW OF NEPA AND THE NEPA PROCESS

NEPA does several things. As the *Calvert Cliffs'* court also recognized, "Section 101 sets forth the Act's basic substantive policy: that the federal government 'use all practicable means and measures' to protect environmental values." 449 F.2d at 1112. Section 101(b) specifically gives all federal agencies the authority to consider environmental impacts and to alter their actions to account for the environment and environmental impacts. Students of administrative law will note the importance of this provision since federal agencies can only do or consider what Congress has directed. This provision allows federal agencies, which were generally created with one or a few specific purposes, such as building federal office buildings (GAO), leasing land for mineral exploration and extraction (BLM), harvesting of trees (Forest Service), or constructing dams (U.S. Army Corps of Engineers), to temper these goals with appropriate environmental consideration.

Additionally, § 202 creates the Council on Environmental Quality, or CEQ, which is to both coordinate the NEPA activities of other federal agencies and also promulgate regulations for NEPA implementation generally. The CEQ has been less active than was initially anticipated but still serves the important function of addressing questions of general NEPA implementation and coordination of NEPA requirements between agencies. Indeed, as the Supreme Court noted in *Marsh v. Oregon Natural Res. Council,* 490 U.S. 360, 372, 109 S.Ct. 1851, 1858, 104 L.Ed.2d 377 (1989), because the CEQ is the primary federal agency charged with implementing NEPA's requirements, its regulations "are entitled to substantial deference." The CEQ's regulations, as well as those of individual implementing agencies, can be found at http://ceq.eh.doe.gov/nepa/nepanet.htm.

But by far the most important feature of NEPA, and one that received scant debate at the time of passage, is § 102(2)(C), a procedural provision that requires all agencies to list environmental impacts of any federal action that significantly affects the quality of the human environment. The document prepared pursuant to this provision is known as an Environmental Impact Statement (EIS). The documentation an agency generates in determining whether an EIS is required, and in generating the EIS if mandated, in turn creates an administrative record the courts and others can use to determine whether the agency has fulfilled its NEPA obligations.

The *Calvert Cliffs'* court summarized the goals of the NEPA process as follows:

> The sort of consideration of environmental values which NEPA compels is clarified in Section 102(2)(A) and (B). In general, all agencies must use a "systematic, interdisciplinary, approach" to environmental planning and evaluation in decisionmaking which may have an impact on man's environment. In order to include all possible environmental factors in the decisional equation, agencies must identify and develop methods and procedures . . . which will insure that presently unquantified environmental amenities and values may be given appropriate consideration in decisionmaking along with economic and technical considerations.

NEPA process

449 F.2d at 1113.

Presumably, a consideration of the environmental impacts of a project also strengthens the information on environmental costs needed to do an analysis of the desirability of the project over all. Additionally, because the public is invited to participate, this creates an opportunity for public input on projects and, for better or worse, expands the time line for moving forward.

Federal actions (which will be explained more, *infra*) include federally sponsored projects, projects that are federally funded, and private projects that require federal approval or the granting of a federal permit in order to be completed.

The procedural requirement of Section 102(2)(c) gives rise to what is known as the NEPA process. This process includes the actions necessary to determine whether NEPA applies, the determination of whether an EIS is required, and the preparation of the EIS itself.

A. Process for Determining Whether an EIS Is Required

1. Statutory and Functional Equivalence Exemptions

The NEPA process usually begins with the agency making a determination of whether the procedural requirements of NEPA are even applicable to the action under consideration. By operation of other statutes, NEPA may not be applicable to certain actions. In 2003, for example, the Healthy Forests Initiative exempted certain significant logging projects from the NEPA process. 16 U.S.C. § 6513(c) (2004). Additionally, NEPA doesn't apply if its application is made impossible by other circumstances, such as in situations in which the relevant agency lacks discretion to consider the environmental impacts. For example, Congress might require a federal agency to take a particular action, such as building an office building in a particular style and in a particular place, which precludes the agency from considering any other options. The Supreme Court explained the logic of this implied exception in

Department of Transportation v. Public Citizen, 541 U.S. 752, 124 S.Ct. 2204, 2215, 159 L.Ed.2d 60 (2004):

> ... [I]nherent in NEPA and its implementing regulations is a "rule of reason," which ensures that agencies determine whether and to what extent to prepare an EIS based on the usefulness of any new potential information to the decisionmaking process. Where the preparation of an EIS would serve "no purpose" in light of NEPA's regulatory scheme as a whole, no rule of reason worthy of that title would require an agency to prepare an EIS.

Additionally, some courts have recognized a "functional equivalence" doctrine pursuant to which they have determined that if compliance with a different statute would be the same as NEPA review, then a separate process is not required. Most prominently, courts have applied this doctrine in the context of statutes enforced by EPA, with the courts routinely finding that EPA need not comply with NEPA despite the absence of any express statutory exemption. See, e.g., *Alabama v. U.S. EPA*, 911 F.2d 499 (11th Cir. 1990) (RCRA permitting).

2. Categorical Exclusions

Assuming that NEPA is not inapplicable for one of these reasons, the relevant "action agency" (that is, the agency proposing to undertake the action at issue) must determine whether an EIS is required. In practice, the first step in this process is a preliminary analysis to determine whether significant impacts on the environment are likely to occur from a government action, and thus whether a document must be prepared to list and analyze those impacts and consider action alternatives. 40 C.F.R. § 1501.3. This in turn depends on the meaning of these terms as defined by agency practice and case law over time. Some applicability decisions are obvious; others, less so.

Many agencies may make categorical determinations that certain actions they take, particularly repetitive and/or routine actions, will never rise to the level of an action that will significantly affect the quality of the human environment. 40 C.F.R. § 1508.4; see also 23 C.F.R. § 771.115. These actions therefore will never trigger the EIS requirement. Id. These are known as "categorical exclusions." 40 C.F.R. § 1508.4. An agency usually adopts these categorical exclusions through the notice and comment process. For many agencies, these categorical exclusions form the majority of agency actions.

CATEGORICAL EXCLUSIONS FROM NEPA–FEDERAL HIGHWAY ADMINISTRATION

23 C.F.R. § 771.119.

§ 771.117 Categorical exclusions.

(a) Categorical exclusions (CEs) are actions which meet the definition contained in 40 CFR § 1508.4, and, based on past experience with similar actions, do not involve significant environmental impacts. They are actions which: do not induce significant impacts to planned growth or land use for the area, do not require the relocation of significant numbers of people; do not have a significant impact on any natural, cultural, recreational, historic or other resource; do not involve significant air, noise, or water quality impacts; do not have significant impacts on travel patterns; and do not otherwise, either individually or cumulatively, have any significant environmental impacts.

(b) Any action which normally would be classified as a CE but could involve unusual circumstances will require the Administration, in cooperation with the applicant, to conduct appropriate environmental studies to determine if the CE classification is proper. Such unusual circumstances include:

(1) Significant environmental impacts;

(2) Substantial controversy on environmental grounds;

(3) Significant impact on properties protected by § 4(f) of the DOT Act or section 106 of the National Historic Preservation Act; or

(4) Inconsistencies with any Federal, State, or local law, requirement or administrative determination relating to the environmental aspects of the action.

(c) The following actions meet the criteria for CEs in the CEQ regulation (§ 1508.4) and § 771.117(a) of this regulation and normally do not require any further NEPA approvals by the Administration:

(1) Activities which do not involve or lead directly to construction, such as planning and technical studies; grants for training and research programs; research activities as defined in 23 U.S.C. § 307; approval of a unified work program and any findings required in the planning process pursuant to 23 U.S.C. § 134; approval of statewide programs under 23 CFR part 630; approval of project concepts under 23 CFR part 476; engineering to define the elements of a proposed action or alternatives so that social, economic, and environmental effects can be assessed; and Federal-aid system revisions which establish classes of highways on the Federal-aid highway system.

(2) Approval of utility installations along or across a transportation facility.

(3) Construction of bicycle and pedestrian lanes, paths, and facilities.

(4) Activities included in the State's "highway safety plan" under 23 U.S.C. § 402.

(5) Transfer of Federal lands pursuant to 23 U.S.C. § 317 when the subsequent action is not an FHWA action.

(6) The installation of noise barriers or alterations to existing publicly owned buildings to provide for noise reduction.

(7) Landscaping.

(8) Installation of fencing, signs, pavement markings, small passenger shelters, traffic signals, and railroad warning devices where no substantial land acquisition or traffic disruption will occur.

(9) Emergency repairs under 23 U.S.C. § 125.

(10) Acquisition of scenic easements.

(11) Determination of payback under 23 CFR part 480 for property previously acquired with Federal-aid participation.

(12) Improvements to existing rest areas and truck weigh stations.

(13) Ridesharing activities.

(14) Bus and rail car rehabilitation.

(15) Alterations to facilities or vehicles in order to make them accessible for elderly and handicapped persons.

(16) Program administration, technical assistance activities, and operating assistance to transit authorities to continue existing service or increase service to meet routine changes in demand.

(17) The purchase of vehicles by the applicant where the use of these vehicles can be accommodated by existing facilities or by new facilities which themselves are within a CE.

(18) Track and railbed maintenance and improvements when carried out within the existing right-of-way.

(19) Purchase and installation of operating or maintenance equipment to be located within the transit facility and with no significant impacts off the site.

(20) Promulgation of rules, regulations, and directives.

(d) Additional actions which meet the criteria for a CE in the CEQ regulations (40 CFR § 1508.4) and paragraph (a) of this section may be designated as CEs only after Administration approval. The applicant shall submit documentation which demonstrates that the specific conditions or criteria for these CEs are satisfied and that significant environmental effects will not result. Examples of such actions include but are not limited to:

(1) Modernization of a highway by resurfacing, restoration, rehabilitation, reconstruction, adding shoulders, or adding auxiliary lanes (e.g., parking, weaving, turning, climbing).

(2) Highway safety or traffic operations improvement projects including the installation of ramp metering control devices and lighting.

(3) Bridge rehabilitation, reconstruction or replacement or the construction of grade separation to replace existing at-grade railroad crossings.

(4) Transportation corridor fringe parking facilities.

(5) Construction of new truck weigh stations or rest areas.

(6) Approvals for disposal of excess right-of-way or for joint or limited use of right-of-way, where the proposed use does not have significant adverse impacts.

(7) Approvals for changes in access control.

(8) Construction of new bus storage and maintenance facilities in areas used predominantly for industrial or transportation purposes where such construction is not inconsistent with existing zoning and located on or near a street with adequate capacity to handle anticipated bus and support vehicle traffic.

(9) Rehabilitation or reconstruction of existing rail and bus buildings and ancillary facilities where only minor amounts of additional land are required and there is not a substantial increase in the number of users.

(10) Construction of bus transfer facilities (an open area consisting of passenger shelters, boarding areas, kiosks and related street improvements) when located in a commercial area or other high activity center in which there is adequate street capacity for projected bus traffic.

(11) Construction of rail storage and maintenance facilities in areas used predominantly for industrial or transportation purposes where such construction is not inconsistent with existing zoning and where there is no significant noise impact on the surrounding community.

(12) Acquisition of land for hardship or protective purposes; advance land acquisition loans under section 3(b) of the UMT Act. Hardship acquisition is early acquisition of property by the applicant at the property owner's request to alleviate particular hardship to the owner, in contrast to others, because of an inability to sell his property. This is justified when the property owner can document on the basis of health, safety or financial reasons that remaining in the property poses an undue hardship compared to others. Hardship and protective buying will be permitted only for a particular parcel or a limited number of parcels. These types of land acquisition qualify for a CE only where the acquisition will not limit the evaluation of alternatives, including shifts in alignment for planned construction projects, which may be required in the NEPA process. No project development on such land may proceed until the NEPA process has been completed.

(e) Where a pattern emerges of granting CE status for a particular type of action, the Administration will initiate rulemaking proposing to add this type of action to the list of categorical exclusions in paragraph (c) or (d) of this section, as appropriate.

[52 FR 32660, Aug. 28, 1987; 53 FR 11066, Apr. 5, 1988]

As can be seen from the list of categorical exclusions for the Federal Highway Administration, many of the activities do seem truly minor. Nevertheless, the procedural requirements of NEPA are always in effect for agency actions, unless precluded by law, and it is possible that certain actions that appear to meet the definition of categorical exclusions in reality might be an action that would have a significant affect on the quality of the human environment. If this is the case, the listing of an activity as a categorical exclusion is no defense for failure to prepare an EIS. This is recognized in the FHA categorical exclusion list in Part B, infra.

3. Environmental Assessments

For actions that are not routine, but where it is not obvious whether the action taken will result in a significant impact on the environment, an agency may often prepare what is known as an environmental assessment to assist in the applicability decision. The environmental assessment, or EA, analyzes the possibility of significant environmental impacts. 40 C.F.R. §§ 1501.3 and 1508.9. An agency may have its own rules guiding the process of preparing an EA. In general, however, an EA will include both a "mini" environmental analysis and a formal determination (with documentary support) regarding the potential for significant effects.

If the action agency determines through the EA process that, although the action has not been exempted from NEPA, it will have no significant impacts on the human environment, it issues a "finding of no significant impact" or a FONSI. 40 C.F.R. § 1508.13. The EA provides evidence of a critical procedural step in the process and also provides the basis for judicial review of any resulting FONSI.

At the EA stage, an agency may alter the action with required mitigation to reduce the environmental impacts to a level below "significant." Looked at differently, the agency is merely proposing a different action that would not trigger the EIS requirement. If an agency takes this action, it will produce what is known as a "mitigated FONSI," or a finding of no significant impact given the proposed mitigation.

B. The EIS Process

If the proposal is to go forward and the agency has determined that it is not excluded from NEPA, when significant environmental impacts are present, the agency must prepare an EIS. At this point an agency may also make a determination as to the jurisdiction of other agencies. It is possible that one project may require the action of more than one agency. Though the requirements of NEPA are always applicable to each agency's own action, it is possible for the agencies to coordinate their activities regarding EIS preparation, in order to avoid duplication. Usually one agency will take the lead, and is called the "lead agency."

1. Scoping

To begin the EIS process, the agency issues a "notice of intent" and determines the proper scope of impacts to be considered and the level of action alternatives that are to be explored. 40 C.F.R. §§ 1501.7 and 1508.22. This process is important because it determines not only the breadth of the environmental impacts to be analyzed, but also the presumed extent and reach of the project and its connections with other actions. An environmental impact statement must provide sufficient information for a decision maker to consider the environmental impacts of a project; and it must also examine alternatives to the action and mitigation measures that can be taken to limit the environmental impacts. 40 C.F.R. §§ 1502.14–.16. It is at this stage that other agencies and the public may be invited to assist the agency in determining the environmental impacts that may occur as well as alternatives and mitigation. This input into the process may be referred to as "scoping." 40 C.F.R. § 1501.7.

2. Notice and Publication

After the scope of the impact statement is determined, the agency prepares the "draft environmental impact statement" or DEIS, which is published in the Federal Register. 40 C.F.R. §§ 1502.9(a), 1503.1, and 1506.6. The agency is then to consider any comments submitted in response to the DEIS by either the public or any other agencies, and to incorporate them into the "final environmental impact statement" or FEIS, which is also published in the Federal Register. 40 C.F.R. §§ 1502.9(b), 1503.1, 1506.6. The agency must consider the FEIS before it takes action on a project. Occasionally, because of the discovery of new information or because of a realization that the FEIS is inadequate, an agency, of its own accord or under court order, may prepare a "supplementary environmental impact statement" or SEIS. 40 C.F.R. § 1502.9 (c). All environmental impact statements, together with comments and responses, are filed with both EPA and the CEQ. 40 C.F.R., § 1506.9. An agency cannot take any action requiring the preparation of an EIS until at least 90 days after the publication of the DEIS in the Federal Register and 30 days after the publication of the FEIS in the Federal Register. 40 C.F.R. §§ 1506.1 and 1506.10.

C. Enforcing NEPA's Requirements (an Introduction)

Citizens may enforce these NEPA procedures through lawsuits under the Administrative Procedures Act (or APA). 5 U.S.C. § 551 et seq. The plaintiff must allege that the government action was undertaken without the observance of the procedures that are required of NEPA. Typically these challenges fall into a few camps: 1) the agency didn't follow normal procedure in either documenting or analyzing the issue; 2) the agency did not prepare an EIS when it should have, an allegation that there was a significant impact on the human environment of a major federal action; or 3) the EIS itself was not adequate, in other words did not follow statutory requirements. As we will see below, however, the Supreme Court has deemed NEPA to be procedural, not substantive: an agency need only consider these environmental values; it need not select the "best" action for the environment.

The consideration of environmental impacts is the method by which environmental protection was to be a made part of the mandate of every federal agency. Congress hoped to influence decision making of federal agencies by forcing them to analyze and publicize information about the environmental effects of actions.

Analysis of NEPA's procedural requirements reveals several questions for a federal agency: is there an action? Is it federal? Does it affect the quality of the human environment? What impacts are there? What alternatives should be considered? What mitigation? Most of the remaining parts of the chapter explore these questions.

III. IS AN EIS REQUIRED?

As noted, *supra*, an EIS is to be prepared when there is a major federal action that will significantly affect the quality of the human environment. Assuming that the action is not outside the scope of NEPA by force of law or because it is a categorical exclusion, how is this determination made? In considering whether an action rises to the level of requiring an EIS, the agency must determine whether it is a major action, that is federal, and whether it will significantly affect the quality of the human environment. Sometimes this is obvious; sometimes less so. An agency may prepare an environmental assessment or other documentation to record its deliberations on these issues. But however the determination is presented procedurally, the agency must still find the answer to three questions.

A. Is it a Major Action?

Section 102(2)(C) specifies that the EIS be included in "every recommendation or report or proposals for legislation and other major Federal actions significantly affecting the quality of the human environment" that are performed by a federal agency. The requirement that an EIS attach to proposals for legislation has been undercut by a CEQ regulation that states that the EIS requirement is not to attach to appropriations requests, the most common legislative proposal of a federal agency. 40 C.F.R. § 1508.17. Instead, most of the controversy on NEPA application is in the second part that applies to "other major Federal actions."

Under NEPA, the term "action" has a fairly broad definition. Action is defined as anything carried out, funded, or approved by a federal agency. This last category especially can have a broad impact on the private sector if they must receive permits or leases from a federal agency, since that would constitute an approval by the agency. There are however, some gray areas. What about agency decisions *not* to take an action? Informal agency activities? Decisions not necessarily categorized as a proposal? Over time, court cases have helped to clarify when an agency activity is an "action" for purposes of NEPA, and when it is not. After reading the following case, see if you can discern a working test for this determination.

KLEPPE v. SIERRA CLUB AMERICAN ELECTRIC POWER SYSTEM v. SIERRA CLUB

Supreme Court of the United States, 1976.
427 U.S. 390, 96 S.Ct. 2718, 49 L.Ed.2d 576.

Mr. Justice POWELL delivered the opinion of the Court.

Section 102(2)(C) of [NEPA] requires that all federal agencies include a detailed statement of environmental consequences known as an environmental impact statement "in every recommendation or report on proposals for legislation and other major Federal actions significantly affecting the quality of the human environment."

I

Respondents, several organizations concerned with the environment, brought this suit in July 1973.... The defendants in the suit, petitioners here, were the officials of the Department [of Interior] and other federal agencies responsible for issuing coal leases, approving mining plans, granting rights-of-way, and taking the other actions necessary to enable private companies and public utilities to develop coal reserves on land owned or controlled by the Federal Government. Citing widespread interest in the reserves of a region identified as the "Northern Great Plains region," and an alleged threat from coal-related operations to their members' enjoyment of the region's environment, respondents claimed that the federal officials could not allow further development without preparing a "comprehensive environmental impact statement" under § 102(2)(C) on the entire region. They sought declaratory and injunctive relief.

[margin note: DoI granting coal mining rights]

[margin note: Resp say need EIS]

II

The record and the opinions of the courts below contain extensive facts about coal development and the geographic area involved in this suit. The facts that we consider essential, however, can be stated briefly.

The Northern Great Plains region identified in respondents' complaint encompasses portions of four States: northeastern Wyoming, eastern Montana, western North Dakota, and western South Dakota. There is no dispute about its richness in coal, nor about the waxing interest in developing that coal, nor about the crucial role the federal petitioners will play due to the significant percentage of the coal to which they control access. The Department has initiated, in this decade, three studies in areas either inclusive of or included within this region. The North Central Power Study was addressed to the potential for coordinated development of electric power in an area encompassing all or part of 15 States in the North Central United States....

III

major issue

The major issue remains the one with which the suit began: whether NEPA requires petitioners to prepare an environmental impact statement on the entire Northern Great Plains region.

... [Section] 102(2)(C) requires an impact statement "in every recommendation or report on proposals for legislation and other major Federal actions significantly affecting the quality of the human environment." Since no one has suggested that petitioners have proposed legislation on respondents' region, the controlling phrase in this section of the Act, for this case, is "major Federal actions." Respondents can prevail only is there has been a report or recommendation on a proposal for major federal action with respect to the Northern Great Plains region. Our statement of the relevant facts shows there has been none; instead, all proposals are for actions of either local or national scope.

case turns on maj. fed. action

local actions

The local actions are the decisions by the various petitioners to issue a lease, approve a mining plan, issue a right-of-way permit, or take other action to allow private activity at some point within the region identified by respondents. Several Courts of Appeals have held that an impact statement must be included in the report or recommendation on a proposal for such action if the private activity to be permitted is one "significantly affecting the quality of the human environment" within the meaning of § 102(2)(C). The petitioners do not dispute this requirement in this case, and indeed have prepared impact statements on several proposed actions of this type in the Northern Great Plains during the course of this litigation. Similarly, the federal petitioners agreed at oral argument that § 102(2)(C) required the Coal Programmatic EIS that was prepared in tandem with the new national coal-leasing program and included as part of the final report on the proposal for adoption of that program. Their admission is well made, for the new leasing program is a coherent plan of national scope, and its adoption surely has significant environmental consequences.

But there is no evidence in the record of an action or a proposal for an action of regional scope. The District Court, in fact, expressly found that there was no existing or proposed plan or program on the part of the Federal Government for the regional development of the area described in respondents' complaint. It found also that the three studies initiated by the Department in areas either included within or inclusive of respondents' region that is, the Montana–Wyoming Aqueducts Study, the North Central Power Study, and the NGPRP were not parts of any plan or program to develop or encourage development of the Northern Great Plains. That court found no evidence that the individual coal development projects undertaken or proposed by private industry and public utilities in that part of the country are integrated into a plan or otherwise interrelated. These findings were not disturbed by the Court of Appeals, and they remain fully supported by the record in this Court.

Quite apart from the fact that the statutory language requires an impact statement only in the event of a proposed action, respondents' desire for a regional environmental impact statement cannot be met for practical reasons. In the absence of a proposal for a regional plan of development, there is nothing that could be the subject of the analysis envisioned by the statute for an impact statement. Section 102(2)(C) requires that an impact statement contain, in essence a detailed statement of the expected adverse environmental consequences of an action, the resource commitments involved in it, and the alternatives to it. Absent an overall plan for regional development, it is impossible to predict the level of coal-related activity that will occur in the region identified by respondents, and thus impossible to analyze the environmental consequences and the resource commitments involved in, and the alternatives to, such activity. A regional plan would define fairly precisely the scope and limits of the proposed development of the region. Where no such plan exists, any attempt to produce an impact statement would be little more than a study along the lines of the NGPRP, containing estimates of potential development and attendant environmental consequences. There would be no factual predicate for the production of an environmental impact statement of the type envisioned by NEPA.

IV

A

The Court of Appeals, in reversing the District Court, did not find that there was a regional plan or program for development of the Northern Great Plains region. It accepted all of the District Court's findings of fact, but concluded nevertheless that the petitioners "contemplated" a regional plan or program, The court thought that the North Central Power Study, the Montana–Wyoming Aqueducts Study, and the NGPRP all constituted "attempts to control development" by individual companies on a regional scale. It also concluded that the interim report of the NGPRP, then expected to be released at any time, would provide the petitioners with the information needed to formulate the regional plan they had been "contemplating." The Court therefore remanded with instructions to the petitioners to inform the District Court of their role in the further development of the region within 30 days after the NGPRP interim report issued; if they decided to control that development, an impact statement would be required.

We conclude that the Court of Appeals erred in both its factual assumptions and its interpretation of NEPA. We think the court was mistaken in concluding, on the record before it, that the petitioners were "contemplating" a regional development plan or program. It considered the several studies undertaken by the petitioners to represent attempts to control development on a regional scale. This conclusion was based on a finding by the District Court that those studies, as well as the new national coal-leasing policy, were "attempts to control development by individual companies in a manner consistent with the policies and procedures of the National Environmental Policy Act of 1969." But in context, that finding meant only that the named studies were efforts to gain background environmental information for subsequent application in the decisionmaking with respect to individual coal-related projects. This is the sense in which the District Court spoke of controlling development consistently with NEPA. Indeed, in the same paragraph containing the language relied upon by the Court of Appeals, the District Court expressly found that the studies were not part of a plan or program to develop or encourage development.

Moreover, at the time the Court of Appeals ruled there was no indication in the record that the NGPRP was aimed toward a regional plan or program, and subsequent events have shown that this was not its purpose. The interim report of the study, issued shortly after the Court of Appeals ruled, described the effects of several possible rates of coal development but stated in its preface that the alternatives "are for study and comparison only; they do not represent specific plans or proposals." All parties agreed in this Court that there still exists no proposal for a regional plan or program of development.

Even had the record justified a finding that a regional program was contemplated by the petitioners, the legal conclusion drawn by the Court of Appeals cannot be squared with the Act. The court recognized that the mere "contemplation" of certain action is not sufficient to require an impact statement. But it believed the statute nevertheless empowers a court to require the preparation of an impact statement to begin at some point prior to the formal recommendation or report on a proposal. The Court of Appeals accordingly devised its own four-part "balancing" test for determining when during the contemplation of a plan or other type of federal action, an agency must begin a statement. The factors to be considered were identified as the likelihood and imminence of the program's coming to fruition, the extent to which information is available on the effects of implementing the expected program and on alternatives thereto, the extent to which irretrievable commitments are being made and options precluded "as refinement of the proposal progresses," and the severity of the environmental effects should the action be implemented.

The Court of Appeals thought that as to two of these factors the availability of information on the effects of any regional development program, and the severity of those effects the time already was "ripe" for an impact statement. It deemed the record unclear, however, as to the likelihood of the petitioners' actually producing a plan to control the development, and surmised that irretrievable commitments were being avoided because petitioners had ceased approving most coal-related projects while the NGPRP study was underway. The court also thought that the imminent release of the NGPRP interim report would provide the officials with sufficient information to define their role in development of the region, and it believed that as soon as the NGPRP was completed the petitioners would begin approving individual projects in the region, thus permitting irrevocable commitments of resources. It was for this reason that the court in its remand required the petitioners to report to the District Court their decision on the federal role with respect to the

Northern Great Plains as a region within 30 days after issuance of the NGPRP report.

The Court's reasoning and action find no support in the language or legislative history of NEPA. The statute clearly states when an impact statement is required, and mentions nothing about a balancing of factors. Rather, as we noted last Term, under the first sentence of § 102(2)(C) the moment at which an agency must have a final statement ready "is the time at which it makes a recommendation or report on a *proposal* for federal action." *Aberdeen & Rockfish R. C. v. SCRAP*, 422 U.S. 289, 320 (1975) (*SCRAP II*) (emphasis in original). The procedural duty imposed upon agencies by this section is quite precise, and the role of the courts in enforcing that duty is similarly precise. A court has no authority to depart from the statutory language and, by a balancing of court-devised factors, determine a point during the germination process of a potential proposal at which an impact statement should be prepared. Such an assertion of judicial authority would leave the agencies uncertain as to their procedural duties under NEPA, would invite judicial involvement in the day-to-day decisionmaking process of the agencies, and would invite litigation. As the contemplation of a project and the accompanying study thereof do not necessarily result in a proposal for major federal action, it may be assumed that the balancing process devised by the Court of Appeals also would result in the preparation of a good many unnecessary impact statements.

V

Our discussion thus far has been addressed primarily to the decision of the Court of Appeals. It remains, however, to consider the contention now urged by respondents. They have not attempted to support the Court of Appeals' decision. Instead, respondents renew an argument they appear to have made to the Court of Appeals, but which that court did not reach. Respondents insist that, even without a comprehensive federal plan for the development of the Northern Great Plains, a "regional" impact statement nevertheless is required on all coal-related projects in the region because they are intimately related.

There are two ways to view this contention. First, it amounts to an attack on the sufficiency of the impact statements already prepared by the petitioners on the coal-related projects that they have approved or stand ready to approve. As such, we cannot consider it in this proceeding, for the case was not brought as a challenge to a particular impact statement and there is no impact statement in the record. It also is possible to view the respondents' argument as an attack upon the decision of the petitioners not to prepare one comprehensive impact statement on all proposed projects in the region. This contention properly is before us, for the petitioners have made it clear they do not intend to prepare such a statement.

We begin by stating our general agreement with respondents' basic premise that § 102(2)(C) may require a comprehensive impact statement in certain situations where several proposed actions are pending at the same time. NEPA announced a national policy of environmental protection and placed a responsibility upon the Federal Government to further specific environmental goals by "all practicable means, consistent with other essential considerations of national policy." § 101(b), 42 U.S.C. § 4331(b). Section 102(2)(C) is one of the "action-forcing" provisions intended as a directive to "all agencies to assure consideration of the environmental impact of their actions in decisionmaking." Conference Report on NEPA, 115 Cong.Rec. 40416 (1969). By requiring an impact statement Congress intended to assure such consideration during the development of a proposal or as in this case during the formulation of a position on a proposal submitted by private parties. A comprehensive impact statement may be necessary in some cases for an agency to meet this duty. Thus, when several proposals for coal-related actions that will have cumulative or synergistic environmental impact upon a region are pending concurrently before an agency, their environmental consequences must be considered together. Only through comprehensive consideration of pending proposals can the agency evaluate different courses of action.

Agreement to this extent with respondents' premise, however, does not require acceptance of their conclusion that all proposed coal-related actions in the Northern Great Plains region are so "related" as to require their analysis in a single comprehensive impact statement.

Respondents conceded at oral argument that to prevail they must show that petitioners have acted arbitrarily in refusing to prepare one comprehensive statement on this entire region, and we agree. The determination of the region, if any, with respect to which a comprehensive statement is necessary requires the weighing of a number of relevant factors, including the extent of the interrelationship among proposed actions and practical considerations of feasibility. Resolving these issues requires a high level of technical expertise and is properly left to the informed discretion of the responsible federal agencies. Cf. SCRAP II, 422 U.S., at 325–326. Absent a showing of arbitrary action, we must assume that the agencies have exercised this discretion appropriately. Respondents have made no showing to the contrary.

Respondents' basic argument is that one comprehensive statement on the Northern Great Plains is required because all coal-related activity in that region is "programmatically," "geographically," and "environmentally" related. Both the alleged "programmatic" relationship and the alleged "geographic" relationship resolve, ultimately, into an argument that the region is proper for a comprehensive impact statement because the petitioners themselves have approached environmental study in this area on a regional basis. Respondents point primarily to the NGPRP, which they claim and petitioners deny focused on the region described in the complaint. The precise region of the NGPRP is unimportant, for its irrelevance to the delineation of an appropriate area for analysis in a comprehensive impact statement has been well stated by the Secretary:

"Resource studies (like the NGPRP) are one of many analytical tools employed by the Department to inform itself as to general resource availability, resource need and general environmental considerations so that it can intelligently determine the scope of environmental analysis and review specific actions it may take. Simply put, resource studies are a prelude to informed agency planning, and provide the data base on which the Department may decide to take specific actions for which impact statements are prepared. The scope of environmental impact statements seldom coincide with that of a given resource study, since the statements evolve from specific proposals for federal action while the studies simply provide an educational backdrop." Affidavit of Oct. 28, 1975, App. 191.

As for the alleged "environmental" relationship, respondents contend that the coal-related projects "will produce a wide variety of cumulative environmental impacts" throughout the Northern Great Plains region. They described them as follows: Diminished availability of water, air and water pollution, increases in population and industrial densities, and perhaps even climatic changes. Cumulative environmental impacts are, indeed, what require a comprehensive impact statement. But determination of the extent and effect of these factors, and particularly identification of the geographic area within which they may occur, is a task assigned to the special competency of the appropriate agencies. Petitioners dispute respondents' contentions that the interrelationship of environmental impacts is regionwide, and, as respondents' own submissions indicate, petitioners appear to have determined that the appropriate scope of comprehensive statements should be based on basins, drainage areas, and other factors. We cannot say that petitioners' choices are arbitrary. Even if environmental interrelationships could be shown conclusively to extend across basins and drainage areas, practical considerations of feasibility might well necessitate restricting the scope of comprehensive statements.

In sum, respondents' contention as to the relationships between all proposed coal-related projects in the Northern Great Plains region does not require that petitioners prepare one comprehensive impact statement covering all before proceeding to approve specific pending applications. As we already have determined that there exists no proposal for regionwide action that could require a regional impact statement, the judgment of the Court of Appeals must be reversed, and the judgment of the District Court reinstated and affirmed. The case is remanded for proceedings consistent with this opinion.

Mr. Justice MARSHALL, with whom Mr. Justice BRENNAN joins, concurring in part and dissenting in part.

While I agree with much of the Court's opinion, I must dissent from Part IV, which holds that the federal courts may not remedy violations of [NEPA] no matter how blatant until it is too late for an adequate remedy to be formulated. As the Court today recognizes, NEPA contemplates agency consideration of environmental factors throughout the decisionmaking process. Since NEPA's enactment, however, litigation has been brought primarily at the end of that process challenging agency decisions to act made without adequate environmental impact statements or without any statements at all. In such situations, the courts have had to content themselves with the largely unsatisfactory remedy of enjoining the proposed federal action and ordering the preparation of an adequate impact statement. This remedy is insufficient because, except by deterrence, it does nothing to further early consideration of environmental factors. And, as with all after-the-fact remedies, a remand for preparation of an impact statement after the basic decision to act has been made invites *post hoc* rationalizations, rather than the candid and balanced environmental assessments envisioned by NEPA. Moreover, the remedy is wasteful of resources and time, causing fully developed plans for action to be laid aside while an impact statement is prepared.

Nonetheless, until this lawsuit, such belated remedies were all the federal courts had had the opportunity to impose under NEPA. In this case, confronted with a situation in which, according to respondents' allegations, federal agencies were violating NEPA prior to their basic decision to act, the Court of Appeals ... seized the opportunity to devise a different and effective remedy. It recognized a narrow class of cases essentially those where both the likelihood of eventual agency action and the danger posed by nonpreparation of an environmental impact statement were great in which it would allow judicial intervention prior to the time at which an impact statement must be ready. The Court today loses sight of the inadequacy of other remedies and the narrowness of the category constructed by the Court of Appeals, and construes NEPA so as to preclude a court from ever intervening prior to a formal agency proposal. This decision, which unnecessarily limits the ability of the federal courts to effectuate the intent of NEPA, is mandated neither by the statute nor by the various equitable considerations upon which the Court relies.

I

The premises of the Court of Appeals' approach are not novel and indeed are reaffirmed by the Court today. Under § 102(2)(C) of NEPA, "the moment at which an agency must have a final (environmtal [sic] impact) statement ready 'is the time at which it makes a recommendation or report on a Proposal for federal action.' " Ante, at 2728, quoting Aberdeen & Rockfish R. Co. v. SCRAP, 422 U.S. 289, 320 (1975) (first emphasis added). Preparation of an impact statement, particularly on a complicated project, takes a considerable amount of time. Necessarily, if the statement is to be completed by the time the agency makes its formal proposal to act, preparation must begin substantially before the proposal must be ready. In this litigation, for instance, the federal petitioners assert that a statement on the region in which respondents are interested would take more than three years to complete. Accordingly, since it would violate NEPA for the Government to propose a plan for regional development of the Northern Great Plains without an accompanying environmental impact statement, if the Government contemplates making such a proposal at any time in the next three years it should already be working on its impact statement.

But an early start on the statement is more than a procedural necessity. Early consideration of environmental consequences through production of an environmental impact statement is the whole point of NEPA, as the Court recognizes. The legislative history of NEPA demonstrates that "(b)y requiring an impact statement Congress intended to assure (environmental) consideration During the development of a proposal...." Ante, at 2730 (emphasis added). Compliance with this duty allows the decisionmaker to take environmental factors into account when he is making decisions, at a time when he has an open mind and is more like to be receptive to such considerations. Thus, the final impact statement itself is but "the tip of an iceberg, the visible evidence of an underlying planning and decisionmaking process that is usually unnoticed by the public." Sixth Annual Report, Council on Environmental Quality 628 (1975).

Because an early start in preparing an impact statement is necessary if an agency is to comply with NEPA, there comes a time when an agency that fails to begin preparation of a statement on a contemplated project is violating the law. It is this fact, which is not disputed by the Court today, that was recognized by the Court of Appeals and that formed the basis of its remedy.

Notes and Comments

1.   Why is a regional impact statement important to the petitioners in this case? Would consideration of environmental impacts of individual leases capture all of the impacts that might occur if every piece of federal land with coal in the region is leased?

2.   Does the Court seem to indicate that there is "no federal action" for purposes of NEPA unless the federal agency charged with implementing NEPA believes there to be an "action?" What role does the Court's standard of review of the agency's actions play in such a case?

3.   Justice Marshall disagrees with the majority's opinion to the extent that it does not allow the NEPA process to apply until the agency has taken some formal action. Is this a fair reading of the majority opinion? Does this turn NEPA into an opportunity for *post hoc* rationalization?

4.   When should an idea become a "proposal" for purposes of NEPA? When the CEQ promulgated its NEPA regulations in 1977 (after *Kleppe*), it defined the term "proposal" as something that "exists at that stage in the development of an action when an agency subject to the Act has a goal and is actively preparing to make a decision on one or more alternative means of accomplishing that goal and the effects can be meaningfully evaluated." 40 C.F.R. § 1508.23. What impact, if any, should this have on the *Kleppe* analysis? If there is a "proposal" within the meaning of this definition, but no final agency decision, would there be a reviewable "agency action" within the meaning of § 706 of the APA? See *Norton v. Southern Utah Wilderness Alliance*, 542 U.S. 55, 124 S.Ct. 2373, 159 L.Ed.2d 137 (2004).

5. What if an agency alters its proposal? Is that a "new" federal action which requires the application of NEPA? The Supreme Court noted that this will sometimes be the case in *Marsh v. Oregon Natural Res. Council*, 490 U.S. 360, 374, 109 S.Ct. 1851, 104 L.Ed.2d 377 (1989). More recently, in *Klamath Siskiyou Wildlands v. Boody*, 468 F.3d 549 (9th Cir. 2006), the Ninth Circuit weighed in on this issue in the following terms:

> ... 40 C.F.R. § 1502.9(c)(1) requires a NEPA analysis if there are "significant new circumstances or information relevant to environmental concerns and bearing on the proposed action or its impacts." ...

> ... Given BLM's decision to dramatically change the vole's Survey and Manage designation ..., coupled with its argument that the [prior] decisions were based on a pool of data 80% of which was not available when the [earlier EIS] was created, [these] decisions and their impact can be nothing short of "significant."

468 F.3d at 561.

B. Is it Federal?

Any action "potentially subject to federal control or responsibility" is considered a federal action for purposes of NEPA. 40 C.F.R. § 1508.18. This can include federally controlled projects, federally funded projects, and federally permitted projects. Although this may seem straightforward in many ways, the way the federal control interacts with the project is critical to determining if an EIS is required. For instance, if a federal action includes the granting of a wetland fill permit under § 404 of the Clean Water Act, is the "fill" alone to be examined to determine whether this is a major federal action that will "significantly affect the quality of the human environment," or should the entire project made possible by the fill be examined? This "scope of review" or "small handle" problem refers to the level of federal involvement in a larger private project. In some cases, agencies may have their own views or guidelines concerning the "scope" of the project that should be considered "federal" for purposes of triggering the EIS requirement. One of the most thorough examinations of this issue is the following case:

WINNEBAGO TRIBE OF NEBRASKA v. RAY

United States Court of Appeals, Eighth Circuit, 1980.
621 F.2d 269.

BRIGHT, Circuit Judge.

Winnebago Tribe of Nebraska (the Tribe) appeals an order of the district court denying its request for a permanent injunction to bar construction of a proposed power line running from Raun, Iowa, to Hoskins, Nebraska. The Tribe claims the district court erred in holding that the issuance of a permit to cross the Missouri River by the Army Corps of Engineers (Corps) was not a "major federal action" within the meaning of [NEPA].

I. BACKGROUND.

Appellee Nebraska Public Power District (NPPD) began planning construction of a 345 KV transmission line from Raun, Iowa, to Hoskins, Nebraska, in 1975. The proposed line would cross the Missouri River 150 feet south of an Omaha Public Power District (OPPD) line and run through the Winnebago Indian Reservation. In the fall of 1977, NPPD informed the Tribe and the Bureau of Indian Affairs of its intent.

On July 13, 1978, appellee Iowa Public Service Company (IPS), a joint venturer with NPPD in this project, applied to the Corps for a permit to cross the Missouri River, as required by 33 U.S.C. § 403 (1976) (hereinafter section 10). Before granting the permit, the Corps prepared an environmental effect assessment on the impact of the river-crossing portion of the line (approximately 1.25 miles out of 67 miles). The assessment concluded that an environmental impact statement was not required because "(t)here are no significant environmental impacts associated with this project." The assessment did not mention any possible adverse effect on bald eagles, a protected species. The Corps granted the section 10 permit on January 10, 1979.

On April 30, 1979, the Tribe filed the present suit alleging noncompliance with NEPA and seeking to enjoin construction pending compliance.... The trial court ruled that the assessment properly considered only the river-crossing portion of the line, because the scope of the federal permit was limited to this area and the federal government was not funding the project....

II. ANALYSIS

Section 102(2)(C) of NEPA requires that the relevant federal agency prepare an EIS for "major federal actions significantly affecting the quality of the human environment." ...

The Tribe claims that the administrative record is deficient in three respects: (1) it ignores sixty-five miles of the sixty-seven mile transmission line; (2) it does not consider certain viable alternatives; and (3) it does not contemplate potential harm to bald eagles. We deal with these claims in the order presented.

A. Failure to Consider the Entire Project.

The Tribe alleges that the administrative record should have considered environmental impacts posed by the entire transmission line, rather than just the river-crossing portion. Appellant's claim presents two related issues: (a) whether the Corps wields such control and responsibility over the entire project that nonfederal segments must be included in the assessment; and (b) assuming limited federal involvement, whether the Corps nevertheless must consider the impacts of nonfederal segments as secondary effects of the proposed action.

The Tribe notes initially that the power line will not be constructed without the section 10 permit. In light of "but for" veto power, the Tribe argues, the Corps wields sufficient control over the entire project to require project-wide environmental analysis. Factual or veto control, however, must be distinguished from legal control or "enablement." See *NAACP v. Medical Center, Inc.*, 584 F.2d 619 (3d Cir. 1978) (*Medical Center*).

In "enablement" cases federal action is a legal condition precedent to accomplishment of an entire nonfederal project. *Medical Center*, 584 F.2d at 632–33. Thus, for example, the federal statute at issue in *Greene County Planning Board v. FPC*, 455 F.2d 412 (2d Cir.), cert. denied, 409 U.S. 849 (1972), required the Federal Power Commission to assure that the entire project was "best adapted" to a comprehensive environmental plan before licensing construction of a power line. See also *Cady v. Morton*, 527 F.2d 786 (9th Cir. 1975) (the federal grant of Indian coal leases was the legal condition precedent for the strip mining project); *Davis v. Morton*, 469 F.2d 593 (10th Cir. 1972) (ninety-nine year lease of Indian lands was legal condition precedent to entire development project). The statute at issue in this case is far narrower and cannot be construed as a grant of legal control over the entire project.

The court in *Medical Center* identified three factors helpful in determining whether "but for" or factual control requires project-wide analysis: (1) the degree of discretion exercised by the agency over the federal portion of the project; (2) whether the federal government has given any direct financial aid to the project; and (3) whether "the overall federal involvement with the project (is) sufficient to turn essentially private action into federal action." Id. at 629. In *Medical Center*, the agency had little or no discretion, there was no direct federal aid, and the court found the federal involvement insufficient.

In the present suit, while the Corps has broad discretion to consider environmental impacts, that discretion must be exercised within the scope of the agency's authority. As noted above, the Corps' jurisdiction under section 10 extends only to areas in and affecting navigable waters. As the Third Circuit observed in *United States v. Stoeco Homes, Inc.*, 498 F.2d 597, 607 (3d Cir. 1974):

> The federal environmental protection statutes did not ... by their terms enlarge the jurisdiction of the Army Corps of Engineers under the Rivers and Harbors Appropriation Act of 1899. If there is no such jurisdiction environmental protection is still a matter primarily of state concern.

The factors remaining for consideration under *Medical Center* are the presence of direct federal funding and the degree of federal involvement. There has been no direct or even indirect federal funding for this project. As for federal involvement, the fact that part of the line will cross the Winnebago Reservation does not suffice to turn this essentially private action into federal action. Federal law allows the state to condemn this land for any public purpose in the same manner as land owned in fee. 25 U.S.C. § 357 (1976). Thus, we conclude that the Corps did not have sufficient control and responsibility to require it to study the entire project.

The Tribe also notes that an agency must consider secondary or indirect impacts in determining whether there are any significant impacts upon the environment. See 40 C.F.R. § 1500.6(b) (1978). Appellant argues that the administrative record does not reflect consideration of a secondary effect of granting the permit namely, building the remainder of the line. If, however, appellant's position were correct, then an EIS for a properly segmented portion of highway would have to consider impacts of subsequent segments as well. A careful reading of the [CEQ] Guidelines, 40 C.F.R. § 1500.8(a)(3)(ii)(1978),[1] leads us to reject appellant's contention as erroneous. Completion of the nonfederal aspects of this single project does not constitute a secondary or indirect effect of the federal action.

Notes and Comments

1. What role does the agency's own construction of the Act play in the determination of the scope of the project?

2. Would the outcome of this case have been different if there had been two river crossings? Three?

3. Is it dispositive to simply consider whether the project as a whole can go forward in substantially the same form without the federal permit? In such a case, would the environmental impacts of the federal action be major if the action could substantially occur without any federal involvement?

4. In *Friends of the Earth v. U.S. Army Corps*, 109 F.Supp.2d 30 (D.D.C. 2000), the court found that the Corps permitting of casinos in Mississippi coastal water required a consideration of all upland impacts because the entire casino was "federal." The court noted that the Corps own regulations, issued after *Winnebago,* required the Corps to consider all impacts if the "environmental consequences of the larger project are essentially products of the Corps permit action." Id. at 40. In distinguishing *Winnebago* the court stated that "here, by contrast [to *Winnebago*], the agency's jurisdiction encompasses the heart of the development projects—the permitting of the floating casinos themselves." Id.

C. Does it Significantly Affect the Quality of the Human Environment

Once the scope of the "federal action" is ascertained, it must be determined whether it is one that "significantly affects the quality of the human environment." In some ways, this is similar to the question

---

1. 40 C.F.R. § 1500.8(a)(3)(ii) provides in part:

(ii) Secondary or indirect, as well as primary or direct, consequences for the environment should be included in the analysis. Many major Federal actions, in particular those that involve the construction or licensing of infrastructure investments (e.g., highways, airports, sewer systems, water resource projects, etc.), stimulate or induce secondary effects in the form of associated invest- ments and changed patterns of social and economic activities. Such secondary effects, through their impacts on existing community facilities and activities, through inducing new facilities and activities, or through changes in natural conditions, may often be even more substantial than the primary effects of the original action itself. For example, the effects of the proposed action on population and growth may be among the more significant secondary effects.

concerning which part of the action is federal, only here the question is expanded to whether the "federal" part of the action is one that will have a significant effect. In implementing regulations, the term "significant" is to be defined in context. 40 C.F.R. § 1508.27. The intensity of the impact will be judged relative to the context and the total input is also to be considered. This regulatory provision echoes similar determinations in case law. In adopting this construct, the CEQ was responding to and embracing logic the Second Circuit previously had set forth in *Hanly v. Kleindienst,* 471 F.2d 823, 830–31 (2d Cir. 1972):

> In the absence of any Congressional or administrative interpretation of the term, we are persuaded that in deciding whether a major federal action will "significantly" affect the quality of the human environment the agency in charge, although vested with broad discretion, should normally be required to review the proposed action in the light of at least two relevant factors: (1) the extent to which the action will cause adverse environmental effects in excess of those created by existing uses in the area affected by it, and (2) the absolute quantitative adverse environmental effects of the action itself, including the cumulative harm that results from its contribution to existing adverse conditions or uses in the affected area. Where conduct conforms to existing uses, its adverse consequences will usually be less significant than when it represents a radical change. Absent some showing that an entire neighborhood is in the process of redevelopment, its existing environment, though frequently below an ideal standard, represents a norm that cannot be ignored. For instance, one more highway in an area honeycombed with roads usually has less of an adverse impact than if it were constructed through a roadless public park.

> Although the existing environment of the area which is the site of a major federal action constitutes one criterion to be considered, it must be recognized that even a slight increase in adverse conditions that form an existing environmental milieu may sometimes threaten harm that is significant. One more factory polluting air and water in an area zoned for industrial use may represent the straw that breaks the back of the environmental camel. Hence the absolute, as well as comparative, effects of a major federal action must be considered.

Recall that the EIS requirement only attaches to "major federal actions that significantly affect the quality of the human environment." In such a case, why is it important that the agency consider effects of multiple, inter-related actions? Cumulative impacts? It should be noted that when inter-related and/or cumulative impacts of piecemeal actions are considered individually, the incremental changes taken by an agency may not rise to the level of a major federal action. This issue is explored in the following case:

GRAND CANYON TRUST v. FEDERAL AVIATION ADMINISTRATION

United States Court of Appeals, District of Columbia Circuit, 2002.
290 F.3d 339. As Amended Aug. 27, 2002.

Opinion for the Court filed by Circuit Judge ROGERS.

ROGERS, Circuit Judge:

The Grand Canyon Trust petitions for review of the decision of the Federal Aviation Administration ("FAA") approving the federal actions necessary to allow the city of St. George, Utah, to construct a replacement airport near Zion National Park. The Trust challenges the adequacy of the FAA's environmental assessment under § 102(2)(C) of [NEPA], and the FAA's conclusion that there would be no significant environmental impacts from the project necessitating preparation of an environmental impact statement under NEPA. Focusing on the noise impacts on the Park, the Trust principally contends that the FAA failed adequately to consider the cumulative impact on the natural quiet of the Park and instead addressed only the incremental impact of the replacement airport. We grant the petition.

I

In 1995, the FAA began working with the City of St. George, Utah, to determine the feasibility of continuing use of the existing airport as compared to development of a new airport at a new site. A growing retirement community and projected air-traffic demand was outstripping the capacity of the existing airport, which could not be expanded due to geographic constraints. Three sites in addition to a no-action alternative were examined. In response to comments on a draft environmental assessment, the FAA conducted a Supplemental Noise Analysis on the potential noise impacts of the replacement airport on Zion National Park ("the Park"). The Park is located approximately 25 miles northeast of St. George and the preferred replacement airport alternative.

The FAA concluded that the noise impacts on the Park from the replacement airport would be negligible and insignificant. On January 30, 2001, the FAA approved the final environmental assessment, concluding that an environmental impact statement was unnecessary, and issued the record of decision, setting forth actions, determinations, and approvals that will allow St. George to construct the replacement airport. It is the determination underlying this record of decision, that the proposed action will not significantly affect the environment of the Park, that the Trust challenges.

II

The essential disagreement between the parties is whether the FAA was required in its environmental assessment to address more than the incremental impact of the replacement airport as compared to the existing airport. NEPA requires federal agencies to prepare an environmental impact statement ("EIS") for "every . . . major Federal action significantly affecting the quality of the human environment." 42 U.S.C. § 4332(2)(C). An environmental assessment ("EA") is made for the purpose of determining whether an EIS is required. *See* 40 C.F.R. § 1508.9. "If *any* 'significant' environmental impacts might result from the proposed agency action then an EIS must be prepared *before* agency action is taken." *Sierra Club v. Peterson,* 717 F.2d 1409, 1415 (D.C.Cir. 1983).

An agency decision that an EIS is not required may be overturned "only if it was arbitrary, capricious or an abuse of discretion." *Sierra Club v. United States Dep't of Transportation,* 753 F.2d 120, 126 (D.C.Cir.1985). Under the long-established standard in this circuit, the court reviews an agency's finding of no significant impact to determine whether:

> First, the agency [has] accurately identified the relevant environmental concern. Second, once the agency has identified the problem it must have taken a 'hard look' at the problem in preparing the EA. Third, if a finding of no significant impact is made, the agency must be able to make a convincing case for its finding. Last, if the agency does find an impact of true significance, preparation of an EIS can be avoided only if the agency finds that the changes or safeguards in the project sufficiently reduce the impact to a minimum.

Id. at 127.

The Trust does not dispute that the FAA properly defined the relevant environmental concern of noise impacts from aircraft on the Park. Rather, the Trust contends that the FAA cannot be said to have taken a "hard look" at the problem when it considered only the incremental impacts of the replacement airport and not the total noise impact that will result from the relocated airport. The Trust notes that the EA does not address the cumulative impact in light of other air flights over the Park, air tours in or near the Park, and reasonably foreseeable future aircraft activity and airport expansions that will contribute to the cumulative noise impact on the Park. Indeed, the EA's statement on cumulative impact is, in full: "There are no known factors that could result in cumulative impacts as a result of the proposed St. George Replacement Airport." Further, the Trust notes, the FAA's Supplemental Noise Analysis disregards cumulative impacts. The FAA responds that it adequately considered the cumulative impact when it compared noise impacts associated with the replacement airport with the no-action alternative of continued use of the existing airport. It rejects the Trust's position that it was required in an EA to compare the project to an environmental baseline of natural quiet and to consider the total impact of aircraft noise on the Park.

The issue dividing the parties is settled by regulations promulgated by the [CEQ] to implement NEPA and by case law applying those regulations. "The CEQ regulations, which . . . are entitled to substantial deference, impose a duty on all federal agencies." *Marsh v. Oregon Natural Res. Council,* 490 U.S. 360, 372 (1989) (citations omitted). The CEQ regulations define each term within NEPA's requirement of an EIS for "every . . . major Federal action[ ] significantly affecting the quality of the human environment." 42 U.S.C. § 4332(2)(C); 40 C.F.R. § 1502.3. The term "significantly" is defined as those actions "with individually insignificant but cumulatively significant impacts. Significance exists if it is reasonable to anticipate a cumulatively significant impact on the environment." 40 C.F.R. § 1508.27(b)(7). "Cumulative impact," in turn, is defined as:

> the impact on the environment which results from the incremental impact of the action when added to other past, present, and reasonably foreseeable future actions regardless of what agency (Federal or non-Federal) or person undertakes such other actions. Cumulative impacts can result from individually minor but collectively significant actions taking place over a period of time.

40 C.F.R. § 1508.7. Although federal agencies have discretion to decide whether a proposed action "is significant enough to warrant preparation of an EIS," the court owes no deference to the FAA's interpretation of NEPA or the CEQ regulations because NEPA is addressed to all federal agencies and Congress did not entrust administration of NEPA to the FAA alone. *Citizens Against Rails-to-Trails v. Surface Transportation Board,* 267 F.3d 1144, 1150 (D.C.Cir.2001).

The courts, in reviewing whether a federal agency has acted arbitrarily and capriciously in finding no significant environmental impact, have given effect to the plain language of the regulations. While the factual settings differ in some respects from the instant case, the consistent position in the case law is that, depending on the environmental concern at issue, the agency's EA must give a realistic evaluation of the total impacts and cannot isolate a proposed project, viewing it in a vacuum. For example, in *Coalition on Sensible Transportation v. Dole,* 826 F.2d 60 (D.C.Cir.1987), this court stated that the CEQ regulations on cumulative impact "provide a distinct meaning to the concept" separate and apart from the notion of improper segmentation of agency action. *Id.* at 70. Noting that the regulatory definition of cumulative impact specifies that the " 'incremental impact of the action' [at issue]" must be considered " 'when added to other past, present, and reasonably foreseeable future actions,' " *id.* (quoting 40 C.F.R. § 1508.7), the court observed that, consistent with the regulation and purpose of NEPA, "[i]t makes sense to consider the 'incremental impact' of a project for possible cumulative effects by incorporating the effects of other projects into the background 'data base' of the project at issue." *Id.* at 70–71. The point, the court stated, was to provide in the EA "sufficient [information] to alert interested members of the public to any arguable cumulative impacts involving [ ] other projects." *Id.* at 71. . . .

The FAA, in finding that the St. George replacement airport would have no significant impact on the environment of the Park, concluded that "there is little discernable increased noise intrusion to the Park" from the proposed replacement airport as compared to the existing airport, and that "the increase in noise levels that would result from the development of a replacement airport is negligible [because] aircraft traffic will increase even if the replacement airport is not constructed." The FAA's analysis appears principally in a Supplemental Noise Analysis attached to the EA, and proceeds on the basis of a comparison of the noise impacts from predicted air traffic at the existing airport and predicted air traffic at the larger replacement airport. . . .

The FAA's noise analysis in the EA, including the Supplemental Noise Analysis, may, in fact, be a splendid incremental analysis, but it fails to address what is crucial if the EA is to serve its function. While, as the FAA stresses, the EA is not intended to be a lengthy document, *see* 40 C.F.R. § 1508.9(a)(1), it must at a minimum address the considerations relevant to determining whether an EIS is required. NEPA regulations require that an agency consider cumulative impacts and the FAA's EA fails to address the total noise impact that will result from the replacement airport. . . . Comments on the draft EA called the FAA's attention to the need to consider mitigation measures in view of the results of the study of noise-annoyance to persons in the Park; the EA does not respond and provides no analysis of the 2% to 9% or the 4% to 15% level of annoyance shown in the NPS study. Yet, as the FAA was aware, the NPS had identified Zion National Park as among the nine national parks of "highest priority" for attention to noise impact on their natural quiet from overflights. Comments also expressed concern about the total impacts of noise on the Park and on Park visitors, yet the EA contains no analysis of the impact of 54 daily flights in 2008 and 69 in 2018 associated with St. George.

The analysis in the EA, in other words, cannot treat the identified environmental concern in a vacuum, as an incremental approach attempts. Although the replacement airport may contribute only a 2% increase to the amount of overflights near or over the Park, there is no way to determine from the FAA's analysis in the EA whether, deferring to the FAA's expert calculations, a 2% increase, in addition to other noise impacts on the Park, will "significantly affect" the quality of the human environment in the Park. At no point does the FAA's EA aggregate the noise impacts on the Park. The analysis in the EA does not address the accumulated, or total, incremental impacts of various man-made noises, such as the 250 daily aircraft flights near or over the Park that originate at, or have as their destination, airports other than that in St. George. Neither does the EA consider in any manner the air tours near and over the Park originating from the St. George airport. Nor does the EA address the impact, much less the cumulative impact, of noise in the Park as a result of other activities, such as the planned expansions of other regional airports that have flights near or over the Park. Without analyzing the total noise impact on the Park as a result of the construction of the replacement airport, the FAA is not in a position to determine whether the additional noise that is projected to come from the expansion of the St. George airport facility at a new location would cause a significant environmental impact on the Park and, thus, to require preparation of an EIS.

Accordingly, we grant the petition without reaching the Trust's contention that an EIS is required because the project is "highly controversial," 40 C.F.R. § 1508.27(b)(4). We remand the case because the record is insufficient for the court to determine whether an EIS is required. On remand, the FAA must evaluate the cumulative impact of noise pollution on the Park as a result of construction of the proposed replacement airport in light of air traffic near and over the Park, from whatever airport, air tours near or in the Park, and the acoustical data collected by NPS in the Park in 1995 and 1998 mentioned in comments on the draft EA.

Notes and Comments

1. Should an agency be required to prepare an environmental impact statement because a project is "highly controversial?" What would be the benefit of such a requirement? If an agency did always prepare an EIS for projects that were "highly controversial" would they then avoid the type of preliminary litigation which invariably accompanies a decision not to prepare an impact statement for highly controversial projects? Would this save time and effort in the long run?

2. The *Grand Canyon* court applied *Hanly's* "straw that broke the camel's back" reasoning in determining whether the project's impacts would significantly affect the quality of the human environment. What impact will information about total noise in Zion National Park have on the decision to allow construction of a replacement airport for St. George, Utah? Particularly if the total noise after construction would only be 2% greater? Might it matter if the 2% increase is concentrated in a particular time period? Geographic area? Can we know this information without a more detailed environmental analysis?

3. The CEQ guidelines determining whether an action "significantly affects the quality of the human environment" are in agreement with early case law implementing NEPA. Recall that *Hanly v. Kleindienst*, 471 F.2d 823, 830 (2d Cir. 1972), addressed "significantly" this way:

> . . . [W]e are persuaded that in deciding whether a major federal action will "significantly" affect the quality of the human environment the agency in charge . . . should normally be required to review the proposed action in the light of . . . (1) the extent to which the action will cause adverse environmental harm in excess of those created by existing uses in the area affected by it, and (2) the absolute quantitative adverse environmental effects of the action itself.

Is the holding in *Grand Canyon* consistent with *Hanly*?

4. As mentioned in the overview at the beginning of this chapter, a project proponent may propose mitigation measures as a way of reducing the project's impacts below the "significance" threshold. Thus, one can mitigate one's way out of the EIS requirement by generating what is known as a "mitigated FONSI." It should be noted, however, that the CEQ takes the

position that any such proposed mitigation measures must be made legally enforceable (e.g., through a binding permit requirement) in order to support a FONSI. See, e.g., Forty Most Asked Questions Concerning CEQ's National Environmental Policy Act Regulations, 46 Fed. Reg. 18028, 18038 (1981); see also *Greater Yellowstone Coalition v. Flowers*, 359 F.3d 1257, 1276–77 (10th Cir. 2004) (and cases cited therein).

IV. IS THE EIS ADEQUATE?

If it is determined that an EIS must be prepared, the focus shifts to what the EIS should contain. Both Section 102(2)(c) of NEPA and the CEQ regulations at 40 C.F.R., part 1502 specify what the EIS is to contain.

The EIS is to include a cover sheet, summary, table of contents, a statement of the purpose and need for the proposed action, a description of the proposed action and alternatives to the proposed action. It must also include a description of the affected environment, a description of the environmental consequences of each proposed and alternative action, and a description of the means to mitigate identified consequences. Each of the substantive requirements is necessary for a true "consideration" of environmental effects to occur. By requiring a comparison of environmental effects and ease of mitigation of the proposal and other alternative scenarios, the EIS allows the decision maker to know exactly what is gained and lost by the proposal.

A. Environmental Effects

Since complex proposals may have many effects, the determination of the "environmental consequences" of an action is no easy task. According to the statute, the agency must consider direct and indirect effects and cumulative effects as well. Environmental impacts include impacts that are ecological, aesthetic, historical, cultural, economic, and social. 40 C.F.R. § 1508.8(b). One early NEPA case summarized the breadth of these impacts under NEPA:

The environmental concerns courts have expressed in these cases may be classified into four somewhat overlapping categories. The first regards what might be termed health and public safety. Courts have examined a project's potential effect on the quality of air and water, the noise level of the community, and the capacity of existing or proposed sewage and solid waste facilities. Relevant as well is whether the project will affect the local crime rate, present fire dangers, or otherwise unduly tap police and fire forces in the community. The second category involves consideration of the project's impact on social services, such as the availability of schools, hospitals, businesses, commuter facilities, and parking. Apart from its impact on a community's services, a project may alter the character of the area in which it locates—the third category. Conformance to local zoning ordinances, harmonization with proximate land uses, and a blending with the aesthetics of the area are concerns relevant to this category. The final category involves consideration of the project's impact on the community's development policy. Relocation of a federal facility from a downtown to a suburban location, for example, might contribute to urban blight and decay. Neighborhood stability and growth are values which have been found to be cognizable under NEPA.

Como–Falcon Coalition, Inc. v. United States Dept. Labor, 465 F.Supp. 850, 859 (D. Minn. 1978), *aff'd and modified*, 609 F.2d 342 (8th Cir. 1979), *cert. denied*, 446 U.S. 936, 100 S.Ct. 2154, 64 L.Ed.2d 789 (1980).

The EIS has also become the preferred context within which agencies are to consider environmental justice issues. The CEQ has published a guidance document to assist agencies in incorporating environmental justice considerations in their NEPA documents.

Because the considered effects can be so broad, once an EIS is required, agencies tend to make them over-inclusive rather than under-inclusive. The failure to consider any environmental impact may render the EIS deficient under NEPA. To assist in the determination of impacts and other considerations, agencies are to engage in a process called "scoping." 40 C.F.R. § 1507.3(c). The so-called "lead agency" (the agency that is to take the lead in preparation of the EIS if more than one agency is involved) is to invite comment on the scope of effects to be considered from any affected Federal, State, or local agency, and any affected Indian tribe. 40 C.F.R. § 1501 *et seq.* Any other interested persons may contribute as well. The scoping announcement is in the Federal Register, and an agency may, but is not required to, have a scoping hearing. 40 C.F.R. § 1501.7. Generally, the scoping process will result in a determination of the extent of actions to be considered, the range of alternatives to be analyzed, and of course, the environmental effects that are to be examined.

Sometimes not all environmental impacts can be determined ahead of time. Is an EIS inadequate if it fails to identify environmental impacts that cannot yet be determined? Even if it is not legally inadequate, can the agency make an informed decision? The following case addresses these questions.

ROBERTSON v. METHOW VALLEY CITIZENS COUNCIL

Supreme Court of the United States, 1989.
490 U.S. 332, 109 S.Ct. 1835, 104 L.Ed.2d 351.

Justice STEVENS delivered the opinion of the Court.

I

The Forest Service is authorized by statute to manage the national forests for "outdoor recreation, range, timber, watershed, and wildlife and fish purposes." 16 U.S.C. § 528. Pursuant to that authorization, the Forest Service has issued "special use" permits for the operation of approximately 170 Alpine and Nordic ski areas on federal lands.

The Forest Service permit process involves three separate stages. The Forest Service first examines the general environmental and financial feasibility of a proposed project and decides whether to issue a special use permit. Because that decision is a "major Federal action" within the meaning of NEPA, it must be preceded by the preparation of an [EIS]. If the Service decides to issue a permit, it then proceeds to select a developer, formulate the basic terms of the arrangement with the selected party, and issue the permit. The special use permit does not, however, give the developer the right to begin construction. In a final stage of review, the Service evaluates the permittee's "master plan" for development, construction, and operation of the project. Construction may begin only after an additional environmental analysis (although it is not clear that a second EIS need always be prepared) and final approval of the developer's master plan. This case arises out of the Forest Service's decision to issue a special use permit authorizing the development of a major destination Alpine ski resort at Sandy Butte in the North Cascade Mountains.

Sandy Butte is a 6,000–foot mountain located in the Okanogan National Forest in Okanogan County, Washington. At present Sandy Butte, like the Methow Valley it overlooks, is an unspoiled, sparsely populated area that the District Court characterized as "pristine." In 1968, Congress established the North Cascades National Park and directed the Secretaries of the Interior and Agriculture to agree on the designation of areas within, and adjacent to, the park for public uses, including ski areas. A 1970 study conducted by the Forest Service pursuant to this congressional directive identified Sandy Butte as having the highest potential of any site in the State of Washington for development as a major downhill ski resort.

In 1978, Methow Recreation, Inc. (MRI), applied for a special use permit to develop and operate its proposed "Early Winters Ski Resort" on Sandy Butte and an 1,165–acre parcel of land it had acquired adjacent to the National Forest. The proposed development would make use of approximately 3,900 acres of Sandy Butte; would entice visitors to travel long distances to stay at the resort for several days at a time; and would stimulate extensive commercial and residential growth in the vicinity to accommodate both vacationers and staff.

In response to MRI's application, the Forest Service, in cooperation with state and county officials, prepared an EIS known as the Early Winters Alpine Winter Sports Study (Early Winters Study or Study). The stated purpose of the EIS was "to provide the information required to evaluate the potential for skiing at Early Winters" and "to assist in making a decision whether to issue a Special Use Permit for downhill skiing on all or a portion of approximately 3900 acres of National Forest System land." A draft of the Study was completed and circulated in 1982, but release of the final EIS was delayed as Congress considered including Sandy Butte in a proposed wilderness area. When the Washington State Wilderness Act of 1984 was passed, however, Sandy Butte was excluded from the wilderness designation, and the EIS was released.

The Early Winters Study is a printed document containing almost 150 pages of text and 12 appendices. It evaluated five alternative levels of development of Sandy Butte that might be authorized, the lowest being a "no action" alternative and the highest being development of a 16–lift ski area able to accommodate 10,500 skiers at one time. The Study considered the effect of each level of development on water resources, soil, wildlife, air quality, vegetation, and visual quality, as well as land use and transportation in the Methow Valley, probable demographic shifts, the economic market for skiing and other summer and winter recreational activities in the Valley, and the energy requirements for the ski area and related developments. The Study's discussion of possible impacts was not limited to on-site effects, but also, as required by [CEQ] regulations, see 40 CFR § 1502.16(b), addressed "off-site impacts that each alternative might have on community facilities, socioeconomic and other environmental conditions in the Upper Methow Valley." As to off-site effects, the Study explained that "due to the uncertainty of where other public and private lands may become developed," it is difficult to evaluate off-site impacts, and thus the document's analysis is necessarily "not site-specific . . . ."

The effects of the proposed development on air quality and wildlife received particular attention in the Study. In the chapter on "Environmental Consequences," the first subject discussed is air quality. As is true of other subjects, the discussion included an analysis of cumulative impacts over several years resulting from actions on other lands as well as from the development of Sandy Butte itself. The Study concluded that although the construction, maintenance, and operation of the proposed ski area "will not have a measurable effect on existing or future air quality," the off-site development of private land under all five alternatives—including the "no action" alternative—"will have a significant effect on air quality during severe meteorological inversion periods." The burning of wood for space heat, the Study explained, would constitute the primary cause of diminished air quality, and the damage would increase incrementally with each of the successive levels of proposed development. The Study cautioned that without efforts to mitigate these effects, even under the "no action" alternative, the increase in automobile, fireplace, and wood stove use would reduce air quality below state standards, but added that "[t]he numerous mitigation measures discussed" in the Study "will greatly reduce the impacts presented by the model."

In its discussion of adverse effects on area wildlife, the EIS concluded that no endangered or threatened species would be affected by the proposed development and that the only impact on sensitive species was the probable loss of a pair of spotted owls and their progeny. With regard to other wildlife, the Study considered the impact on 75 different indigenous species and predicted that within a decade after development vegetational change and increased human activity would lead to a decrease in population for 31 species, while causing an increase in population for another 24 species on Sandy Butte. Two species, the pine marten and nesting goshawk, would be eliminated altogether from the area of development.

In a comment in response to the draft EIS, the Washington Department of Game voiced a special concern about potential losses to the State's largest migratory deer herd, which uses the Methow Valley as a critical winter range and as its migration route. The state agency estimated that the total population of mule deer in the area most likely to be affected was "better than 30,000 animals" and that "the ultimate impact on the Methow deer herd could exceed a 50 percent reduction in numbers." The agency asserted that "Okanogan County residents place a great deal of importance on the area's deer herd." In addition, it explained that hunters had "harvested" 3,247 deer in the Methow Valley area in 1981, and that, since in 1980 hunters on average spent $1,980 for each deer killed in Washington, they had contributed over $6 million to the State's economy in 1981. Because the deer harvest is apparently proportional to the size of the herd, the state agency predicted that "Washington business can expect to lose over $3 million annually from reduced recreational opportunity." The Forest Service's own analysis of the impact on the deer herd was more modest. It first concluded that the actual operation of the ski hill would have only a "minor" direct impact on the herd, but then recognized that the off-site effect of the development "would noticeably reduce numbers of deer in the Methow [Valley] with any alternative." Although its estimate indicated a possible 15 percent decrease in the size of the herd, it summarized the State's contrary view in the text of the EIS, and stressed that off-site effects are difficult to estimate due to uncertainty concerning private development.

Ultimately, the Early Winters Study recommended the issuance of a permit for development at the second highest level considered—a 16–lift ski area able to accommodate 8,200 skiers at one time. On July 5, 1984, the Regional Forester decided to issue a special use permit as recommended by the Study. In his decision, the Regional Forester found that no major adverse effects would result directly from the federal action, but that secondary effects could include a degradation of existing air quality and a reduction of mule deer winter range. He therefore directed the supervisor of the Okanogan National Forest, both independently and in cooperation with local officials, to identify and implement certain mitigating measures.

Four organizations (respondents) opposing the decision to issue a permit appealed the Regional Forester's decision to the Chief of the Forest Service. After a hearing, he affirmed the Regional Forester's decision. Stressing that the decision, which simply approved the general concept of issuing a 30–year special use permit for development of Sandy Butte, did not authorize construction of a particular ski area and, in fact, did not even act on MRI specific permit application, he concluded that the EIS's discussion of mitigation was "adequate for this stage in the review process."

Thereafter, respondents brought this action under the [APA], 5 U.S.C. §§ 701–706, to obtain judicial review of the Forest Service's decision. Their principal claim was that the Early Winters Study did not satisfy the requirements of NEPA. With the consent of the parties, the case was assigned to a United States Magistrate. After a trial, the Magistrate filed a comprehensive written opinion and concluded that the EIS was adequate. Specifically, he found that the EIS had adequately disclosed the adverse impacts on the mule deer herd and on air quality and that there was no duty to prepare a "worst case analysis" because the relevant information essential to a reasoned decision was available. In concluding that the discussion of off-site, or secondary, impacts was adequate, the Magistrate stressed that courts apply a "rule of reason" in evaluating the adequacy of an EIS and "take the uncertainty and speculation involved with secondary impacts into account in passing on the adequacy of the discussion of secondary impacts."

Concluding that the Early Winters Study was inadequate as a matter of law, the Court of Appeals reversed. *Methow Valley Citizens Council v. Regional Forester*, 833 F.2d 810 (CA9 1987). The court held that ... if the agency had difficulty obtaining adequate information to make a reasoned assessment of the environmental impact on the herd, it had a duty to make a so-called "worst case analysis." Such an analysis is " 'formulated on the basis of available information, using reasonable projections of the worst possible consequences of a proposed action.' *Save our Ecosystems* [*v. Clark*,] 747 F.2d [1240], at 1244–45 (CA9 1984) (quoting 46 Fed.Reg. 18032 (1981))."

II

Section 101 of NEPA declares a broad national commitment to protecting and promoting environmental quality. To ensure that this commitment is "infused into the ongoing programs and actions of the Federal Government, the act also establishes some important 'action-forcing' procedures." 115 Cong.Rec. 40416 (remarks of Sen. Jackson). Section 102 thus, among other measures "directs that, to the fullest extent possible ... all agencies of the Federal Government shall—'

* * *

"(C) include in every recommendation or report on proposals for legislation and other major Federal actions significantly affecting the quality of the human environment, a detailed statement by the responsible official on—

"(i) the environmental impact of the proposed action,

"(ii) any adverse environmental effects which cannot be avoided should the proposal be implemented,

"(iii) alternatives to the proposed action,

"(iv) the relationship between local short-term uses of man's environment and the maintenance and enhancement of long-term productivity, and "(v) any irreversible and irretrievable commitments of resources which would be involved in the proposed action should it be implemented." 42 U.S.C. § 4332.

The statutory requirement that a federal agency contemplating a major action prepare such an environmental impact statement serves NEPA's "action-forcing" purpose in two important respects. It ensures that the agency, in reaching its decision, will have available, and will carefully consider, detailed information concerning significant environmental impacts; it also guarantees that the relevant information will be made available to the larger audience that may also play a role in both the decisionmaking process and the implementation of that decision.

Simply by focusing the agency's attention on the environmental consequences of a proposed project, NEPA ensures that important effects will not be overlooked or underestimated only to be discovered after resources have been committed or the die otherwise cast. Moreover, the strong precatory language of § 101 of the Act and the requirement that agencies prepare detailed impact statements inevitably bring pressure to bear on agencies "to respond to the needs of environmental quality." 115 Cong.Rec. 40425 (1969) (remarks of Sen. Muskie).

Publication of an EIS, both in draft and final form, also serves a larger informational role. It gives the public the assurance that the agency "has indeed considered environmental concerns in its decisionmaking process," [*Baltimore Gas & Electric Co. v. NRDC*, 462 U.S. 87, 97 (1983)], and, perhaps more significantly, provides a springboard for public comment. Thus, in this case the final draft of the Early Winters Study reflects not only the work of the Forest Service itself, but also the critical views of the Washington State Department of Game, the Methow Valley Citizens Council, and Friends of the Earth, as well as many others, to whom copies of the draft Study were circulated. Moreover, with respect to a development such as Sandy Butte, where the adverse effects on air quality and the mule deer herd are primarily attributable to predicted off-site development that will be subject to regulation by other governmental bodies, the EIS serves the function of offering those bodies adequate notice of the expected consequences and the opportunity to plan and implement corrective measures in a timely manner.

The sweeping policy goals announced in § 101 of NEPA are thus realized through a set of "action-forcing" procedures that require that agencies take a " 'hard look' at environmental consequences," [*Kleppe v. Sierra Club*, 427 U.S., 390, 410, n. 21 (1976)], and that provide for broad dissemination of relevant environmental information. Although these procedures are almost certain to affect the agency's substantive decision, it is now well settled that NEPA itself does not mandate particular results, but simply prescribes the necessary process. See *Strycker's Bay Neighborhood Council, Inc. v. Karlen*, 444 U.S. 223, 227–228 (1980) *(per curiam)*; *Vermont Yankee Nuclear Power Corp. v. Natural Resources Defense Council, Inc.*, 435 U.S. 519, 558 (1978). If the adverse environmental effects of the proposed action are adequately identified and evaluated, the agency is not constrained by NEPA from deciding that other values outweigh the environmental costs. See *ibid.; Strycker's Bay, supra,* 444 U.S., at 227–228; *Kleppe, supra,* 427 U.S., at 410, n. 21. In this case, for example, it would not have violated NEPA if the Forest Service, after complying with the Act's procedural prerequisites, had decided that the benefits to be derived from downhill skiing at Sandy Butte justified the issuance of a special use permit, notwithstanding the loss of 15 percent, 50 percent, or even 100 percent of the mule deer herd. Other statutes may impose substantive environmental obligations on federal agencies, but NEPA merely prohibits uninformed—rather than unwise—agency action.

III

The Court of Appeals also concluded that the Forest Service had an obligation to make a "worst case analysis" if it could not make a reasoned assessment of the impact of the Early Winters project on the mule deer herd. Such a "worst case analysis" was required at one time by CEQ regulations, but those regulations have since been amended. Moreover, although the prior regulations may well have expressed a permissible application of NEPA, the Act itself does not mandate that uncertainty in predicting environmental harms be addressed exclusively in this manner. Accordingly, we conclude that the Court of Appeals also erred in requiring the "worst case" study.

In 1977, President Carter directed that CEQ promulgate binding regulations implementing the procedural provisions of NEPA. Pursuant to this Presidential order, CEQ promulgated implementing regulations. Under § 1502.22 of these regulations—a provision which became known as the "worst case requirement"—CEQ provided that if certain information relevant to the agency's evaluation of the proposed action is either unavailable or too costly to obtain, the agency must include in the EIS a "worst case analysis and an indication of the probability or improbability of its occurrence." 40 CFR § 1502.22 (1985). In 1986, however, CEQ replaced the "worst case" requirement with a requirement that federal agencies, in the face of unavailable information concerning a reasonably foreseeable significant environmental consequence, prepare "a summary of existing credible scientific evidence which is relevant to evaluating the . . . adverse impacts" and prepare an "evaluation of such impacts based upon theoretical approaches or research methods generally accepted in the scientific community." 40 CFR § 1502.22(b) (1987). The amended regulation thus "retains the duty to describe the consequences of a remote, but potentially severe impact, but grounds the duty in evaluation of scientific opinion rather than in the framework of a conjectural worst case analysis.' " 50 Fed.Reg. 32237 (1985).

The Court of Appeals recognized that the "worst case analysis" regulation has been superseded, yet held that "[t]his rescission . . . does not nullify the requirement . . . since the regulation was merely a codification of prior NEPA case law." 833 F.2d, at 817, n. 11. This conclusion, however, is erroneous in a number of respects. Most notably, review of NEPA case law reveals that the regulation, in fact, was not a codification of prior judicial decisions. The cases cited by the Court of Appeals ultimately rely on the Fifth Circuit's decision in *Sierra Club v. Sigler,* 695 F.2d 957 (1983). *Sigler,* however, simply recognized that the "worst case analysis" regulation codified the "judicially created princip[e]" that an EIS must "consider the probabilities of the occurrence of any environmental effects it discusses." *Id.,* at 970–971. As CEQ recognized at the time it superseded the regulation, case law prior to the adoption of the "worst case analysis" provision did require agencies to describe environmental impacts even in the face of substantial uncertainty, but did not require that this obligation necessarily be met through the mechanism of a "worst case analysis." See 51 Fed.Reg. 15625 (1986). CEQ's abandonment of the "worst case analysis" provision, therefore, is not inconsistent with any previously established judicial interpretation of the statute.

Notes and Comments

1. *Methow Valley* represents the Supreme Court's most definitive statement on the procedure-versus-substance debate under NEPA. On what basis does the Court conclude that NEPA is purely procedural? Does this conclusion seem consistent with the hortatory language in §§ 101 and 102? If NEPA were read to include substantive mandates, how would courts apply them? Consider, for example, a situation in which the Forest Service is proposing to go forward with a timber sale. How would a court enforce § 101(b)'s mandate that the Service use "all practicable means, consistent with other essential considerations of national policy ... to the end that the Nation may [among other things] (1) fulfill the responsibilities of each generation as trustee of the environment for succeeding generations; [and] (2) assure for all Americans safe, healthful, productive, and esthetically and culturally pleasing surroundings?"

2. Prior to the Supreme Court's procedure-versus-substance decisions that culminated in *Methow Valley,* most Circuits had determined that NEPA might allow for at least limited substantive review under the arbitrary and capricious standard. *Calvert Cliffs'* was typical of these decisions. In that case, the D.C. Circuit spoke of this possibility in the following terms:

> The reviewing courts probably cannot reverse a substantive decision on its merits, under Section 101, unless it be shown that the actual balance of costs and benefits that was struck was arbitrary or clearly gave insufficient weight to environmental values. But if the decision was reached procedurally without individualized consideration and balancing of environmental factors—conducted fully and in good faith—it is the responsibility of the courts to reverse.

449 F.2d at 1112. Does this line of analysis survive *Methow Valley*? What if the underlying statute pursuant to which the agency is acting contains a decision criterion that is broad enough to include a broad range of environmental factors? For example, as we will see in Chapter 8, the Corps of Engineers reads § 404 of the Clean Water Act as giving it the authority to deny dredge and fill permits under that section whenever it deems a particular project to be against the public interest. See 33 C.F.R. § 320.4(a).

If it does, might § 404 provide a wholly adequate basis unto itself for ensuring that the Corps appropriately accounts for any information it may have generated through its NEPA processes in making any final permitting decisions?

3. Can an agency adequately consider environmental impacts in the absence of a worst case scenario? Would the requirement of a worst case scenario improve the agency's ability to consider the environmental impacts? If so, should it not be included?

4. After this case, could a worst case analysis ever be required in an EIS?

B. Alternatives Consideration

The inclusion and analysis of alternatives to the proposed action is also a critical part of the EIS. Reasonable alternatives are to be considered, and an agency must always analyze a "no-action" alternative. The breadth of the alternatives to be considered can certainly affect the desirability of the proposed action. For instance, in the *Methow* case, *supra*, what kind of alternatives should be considered with respect to the proposed ski resort? In its alternatives analysis, is the forest service to examine only alternatives regarding the size of the proposed ski resort? The possibility of expanding ski resorts in other areas? Examine all possible recreational activities, such as bowling? Read the following from the Court of Appeals decision in *Methow Valley Citizens Council v. Regional Forester*, 833 F.2d 810, 815 (9th Cir. 1987), *rev'd in part*, 490 U.S. 332, 109 S.Ct. 1835, 104 L.Ed.2d 351 (1989) (although the Ninth Circuit's decision was reversed in part, its discussion of alternatives analysis stands):

To be adequate, an environmental impact statement must consider every reasonable alternative. *Friends of Endangered Species v. Jantzen*, 760 F.2d 976, 988 (9th Cir.1985); *California v. Block*, 690 F.2d at 766–67; *Adler v. Lewis*, 675 F.2d 1085, 1097 (9th Cir.1982) ("this court has held the alternatives discussion to be subject to 'reasonableness.'"); *Save Lake Washington v. Frank*, 641 F.2d 1330, 1334 (9th Cir.1981); *Lange v. Brinegar*, 625 F.2d 812, 818 (9th Cir.1980) ("The discussion of alternatives in an E.I.S. statement is subject to a construction of reasonableness."). An EIS is rendered inadequate by the existence of a viable but unexamined alternative. *Citizens for a Better Henderson*, 768 F.2d at 1057 (citations omitted). Furthermore, even if an alternative requires "legislative action", this fact "does not automatically justify excluding it from an EIS." *City of Angoon v. Hodel*, 803 F.2d 1016, 1021 (9th Cir.1986) (footnote omitted), *cert. denied*, 484 U.S. 870 (1987). Thus, the range of alternatives considered must be sufficient to permit a reasoned choice. *Life of the Land v. Brinegar*, 485 F.2d 460, 472 (9th Cir. 1973), *cert. denied*, 416 U.S. 961 (1974).

Here the Forest Service's purpose—to provide a "winter sports opportunity"—is broadly framed in terms of service to the public benefit. It is not, *by its own terms*, tied to a specific parcel of land.

There appears no tenable reason for the Forest Service to be wedded exclusively to the development of Sandy Butte. Thus it should have appeared obvious that investigation was warranted to determine whether the development of winter sports opportunities could be pursued at alternative sites.

Appellants have offered evidence suggesting that other sites may be well suited for the type of recreational development envisioned by the Forest Service. Unlike Sandy Butte, the sites discussed by the appellants are not adjacent to land owned by defendant MRI, but under the directive given to the Forest Service in its manual, that fact does not preclude consideration of other reasonable alternatives. Moreover, since we find it reasonable to assume that expansion of existing ski areas would have less environmental impact than would the construction of an entirely new ski area, while possibly achieving a comparable net increase in the total capacity of skiers served, such alternatives might have been appropriate for investigation.

This court, however, would not require that the Forest Service explore an unreasonably broad range of alternatives. Rather, the range "need not extend beyond those [alternatives] reasonably related to the purposes of the project." *Trout Unlimited,* 509 F.2d at 1286 (citations omitted). Thus, the Forest Service should more clearly articulate its goal, specifically identifying the market and geographic pool of skiers targeted. This will provide a clear standard by which it can determine which alternatives are appropriate for investigation and consideration in its EIS. In its present state, the EIS's discussion of alternatives to the proposed action is inadequate as a matter of law.

C. Mitigation

An EIS must also discuss how the proposed environmental impacts can be mitigated. The consideration of mitigation measures, particularly their ease and costs, assists in analyzing what the real environmental impacts of an action are. In *Methow Valley,* the Supreme Court indicated that the level of specificity required for mitigation measures would depend on the scope of the project itself. Larger projects or programmatic undertakings may identify more generic mitigation, while more specifically tailored proposals would require the inclusion of more specific mitigation measures. Importantly, the Supreme Court made clear in *Methow Valley* that mitigation measures do not have to be completely specified or identified at the time an action is taken.

ROBERTSON v. METHOW VALLEY CITIZENS COUNCIL

Supreme Court of the United States, 1989.
490 U.S. 332, 109 S.Ct. 1835, 104 L.Ed.2d 351.

[For more detailed facts, reread the case excerpt, *supra*].

In its discussion of air-quality mitigation measures, the EIS identified actions that could be taken by the county government to mitigate the adverse effects of development, as well as those that the Forest Service itself could implement at the construction stage of the project. The Study suggested that Okanogan County develop an air quality management plan, requiring weatherization of new buildings, limiting the number of wood stoves and fireplaces, and adopting monitoring and enforcement measures. In addition, the Study suggested that the Forest Service require that the master plan include procedures to control dust and to comply with smoke management practices.

The court [of appeals] held that the Forest Service could not rely on " 'the implementation of mitigation measures' " [with respect to] the EIS' treatment of air quality. Since the EIS made it clear that commercial development in the Methow Valley will result in violations of state air-quality standards unless effective mitigation measures are put in place by the local governments and the private developer, the Court of Appeals concluded that the Forest Service had an affirmative duty to "develop the necessary mitigation measures *before* the permit is granted." *Id.,* at 819 (emphasis in original) (footnote omitted). The court held that this duty was imposed by both the Forest Service's own regulations and § 102 of NEPA. *Ibid.* It read the statute as imposing a substantive requirement that "action be taken to mitigate the adverse effects of major federal actions." *Ibid.* [internal quotations omitted]. For this reason, it concluded that "an EIS must include a thorough discussion of measures to mitigate the adverse environmental impacts of a proposed action." 833 F.2d, at 819. The Court of Appeals concluded by quoting this paragraph from an opinion it had just announced:

> "The importance of the mitigation plan cannot be overestimated. It is a determinative factor in evaluating the adequacy of an environmental impact statement. Without a complete mitigation plan, the decisionmaker is unable to make an informed judgment as to the environmental impact of the project—one of the main purposes of an environmental impact statement." *Id.,* at 820 (quoting *Oregon Natural Resources Council v. Marsh,* 832 F.2d 1489, 1493 (CA9 1987), rev'd, 490 U.S. 360 (1988).

To be sure, one important ingredient of an EIS is the discussion of steps that can be taken to mitigate adverse environmental consequences. The requirement that an EIS contain a detailed discussion of possible mitigation measures flows both from the language of the Act and, more expressly, from CEQ's implementing regulations. Implicit in NEPA's demand that an agency prepare a detailed statement on "any adverse environmental effects which cannot be avoided should the proposal be implemented," 42 U.S.C. § 4332(C)(ii), is an understanding that the EIS will discuss the extent to which adverse effects can be avoided. More generally, omission of a reasonably complete discussion of possible mitigation measures would undermine the "action-forcing" function of NEPA. Without such a discussion, neither the agency nor other interested groups and individuals can properly evaluate the severity of the adverse effects. An adverse effect that can be fully remedied by, for example, an inconsequential public expenditure is certainly not as serious as a similar effect that can only be modestly ameliorated through the commitment of vast public and private resources. Recognizing the importance of such a discussion in guaranteeing that the agency has taken a "hard look" at the environmental consequences of proposed federal action, CEQ regulations require that the agency discuss possible mitigation measures in defining the scope of the EIS, 40 CFR § 1508.25(b) (1987), in discussing alternatives to the proposed action, § 1502.14(f), and consequences of that action, § 1502.16(h), and in explaining its ultimate decision, § 1505.2(c).

There is a fundamental distinction, however, between a requirement that mitigation be discussed in sufficient detail to ensure that environmental consequences have been fairly evaluated, on the one hand, and a substantive requirement that a complete mitigation plan be actually formulated and adopted, on the other. In this case, the off-site effects on air quality and on the mule deer herd cannot be mitigated unless nonfederal government agencies take appropriate action. Since it is those state and local governmental bodies that have jurisdiction over the area in which the adverse effects need be addressed and since they have the authority to mitigate them, it would be incongruous to conclude that the Forest Service has no power to act until the local agencies have reached a final conclusion on what mitigating measure they consider necessary. Even more significantly, it would be inconsistent with NEPA's reliance on procedural mechanisms—as opposed to substantive, result-based standards—to demand the presence of a fully developed plan that will mitigate environmental harm before an agency can act. Cf. *Baltimore Gas & Electric Co.,* 462 U.S., at 100 ("NEPA does not require agencies to adopt any particular internal decisionmaking structure").

We thus conclude that the Court of Appeals erred, first, in assuming that "NEPA requires that 'action be taken to mitigate the adverse effects of major federal actions,'" 833 F.2d, at 819 (quoting *Stop H–3 Assn. v. Brinegar,* 389 F.Supp., at 1111), and, second, in finding that this substantive requirement entails the further duty to include in every EIS "a detailed explanation of specific measures which *will* be employed to mitigate the adverse impacts of a proposed action," 833 F.2d, at 819 (emphasis supplied).

Notes and Comments

1. Is this aspect of *Methow Valley* any more than an outgrowth of the Supreme Court's view that NEPA imposes only procedural requirements? Would it have made any difference in this case if the Forest Service had possessed the full authority to mitigate any adverse effects?

2. *Methow Valley* stands for the proposition that NEPA does not *compel* agencies to implement mitigation measures at the EIS stage. But might it *authorize* them to? Does NEPA enlarge an agency's decision-making power in any way?

3. Earlier, we discussed how a project proponent may rely on mitigation to avoid doing an EIS at all. As we saw, in that context the CEQ takes the position that any such proposed mitigation measures must be made

legally enforceable, through a permit condition or other similar arrangement, if they are to provide the basis for a FONSI. Note, however, that at the EIS stage, such mitigation may be unnecessary. Imagine, for example, a casino project that is to be situated entirely within the waters of the United States. If, as in *Friends of the Earth v. U.S. Army Corps*, 109 F.Supp.2d 30 (D.D.C. 2000), the Corps determines the project to be "federalized" in its entirety, the developer would need to consider all of the project's effects, including its upland traffic impacts, in determining whether an EIS is required. If it wants to mitigate those effects in order to support a FONSI, it would need to agree to enforceable mitigation requirements (perhaps traffic lights or even shuttle buses). If, on the other hand, it were willing to do an EIS, it is by no means clear that the developer would ever have to agree to any similar mitigation requirements. Can you imagine situations in which such developers would agree to such conditions at the EA stage even though they might not be required to implement such measures after an EIS?

V. STATE ENVIRONMENTAL POLICY ACTS

By its terms, NEPA only applies to the actions of federal agencies. Activities controlled by other governmental entities or by private parties that do not require federal action will not be encompassed by NEPA. Recognizing this as a gap in environmental protection, many states have implemented similar acts at the state level. Though many state statutes bear some variation of the name "state environmental policy act," their operations may be wildly divergent. Because of this divergence, there is not really even agreement on which states have the so-called "little NEPAs," with one law review article claiming that there were 25 such statutes and another suggesting that there were only sixteen. Cole, et al., *Prospects for Health Impact Assessments in the United States* ..., 29 J.Health Pol., Policy, and Law 1153, 1162 (2004); Cliff Rechtschaffen, *Advancing Environmental Justice Norms*, 37 U.C. Davis L. Rev. 95, 120 (2003).

The States of Minnesota, Washington, New York, and California are often described as having the strongest State environmental policy acts, though other States have stringent requirements as well. Cole, *supra*, at 1162. As one commentator has noted, some State environmental policy acts may be more restrictive than NEPA because they often require more procedures of mandate certain actions based on findings of significant environmental impacts:

> The California Environmental Quality Act (CEQA), for example, provides that "[e]ach public agency shall mitigate or avoid the significant effects on the environment of projects that it carries out or approves whenever it is feasible to do so." The law does not absolutely prohibit government agencies from taking actions that have significant effects on the environment. Instead, it provides that "[i]f economic, social, or other conditions make it infeasible to mitigate one or more significant effects on the environment of a

project, the project may nonetheless be carried out or approved at the discretion of a public agency if the project is otherwise permissible under applicable laws and regulations." Similarly, the New York State Environmental Quality Review Act (SEQRA) requires government agencies, "to the maximum extent practicable," to minimize or avoid environmental impacts, taking into consideration social, economic, and other considerations. These substantive limitations are similar to the limitations imposed on the EPA and the U.S. Army Corps of Engineers when those agencies review applications for permits to develop wetlands under the Clean Water Act.

Minnesota's environmental review law goes even further and provides that [n]o state action significantly affecting the quality of the environment shall be allowed, nor shall any permit for natural resources management and development be granted, where such action or permit has caused or is likely to cause pollution, impairment, or destruction of the air, water, land or other natural resources located within the state, so long as there is a feasible and prudent alternative consistent with the reasonable requirements of the public health, safety, and welfare.

Washington takes a more moderate approach. The Washington State Environmental Protection Act broadly allows, but does not require, government agencies to deny or condition the approval of a project based on the environmental impacts of the project.

Stephen Johnson, *NEPA and SEPAs in the Quest for Environmental Justice*, 30 Loy. L.A. L. Rev. 565, 598 (1997).

Though other states may have some form of an environmental policy act, many are extremely limited. For example, the state of Georgia's environmental policy act does not apply to permitting and therefore doesn't reach many actions that can affect the environment. Ga. Code Ann. 12–16–3.

VI. THE EFFECTS OF NEPA

As can be seen in the foregoing discussion, the procedures required to implement the NEPA can be cumbersome and time-consuming. In an effort to avoid successful court challenges, many agencies "throw in the kitchen sink," providing long and detailed analyses of any possible environmental effects. Some believe that this does not promote the purposes of NEPA, since the crush of information may make it difficult for agencies and the public to really focus in on the most important problems. *See generally*, Bradley Karkkainen, Toward a Smarter NEPA: Monitoring and Managing Government's Environmental Performance, 102 Colum. L. Rev. 903, 904 (2002). Given the state of the EISs, many have raised the question whether the NEPA is worth all of this delay and cost. Do we thus have "too much" environmental analysis? One of the authors of this textbook has argued that the problem may be that we have too little; that, in particular, by failing to consider the environment as broadly as necessary to include such issues as risk allocation and environmental philosophy, agencies often run into opposition which is harder to understand and address:

46 Hastings Law Journal 85

November, 1994

THE HUMAN ENVIRONMENT OF THE MIND: CORRECTING NEPA IMPLEMENTATION BY TREATING ENVIRONMENTAL PHILOSOPHY AND ENVIRONMENTAL RISK ALLOCATION AS ENVIRONMENTAL VALUES UNDER NEPA

Victor B. Flatt

* * *

The real cause of the gap in environmental understanding between those who conduct a cost benefit analysis using environmental impacts from the NEPA process and those who oppose the project on environmental grounds is that NEPA has not been routinely construed broadly enough to allow for a consideration of all of the environmental impacts that concern society. Specifically, NEPA has not been construed as requiring consideration of environmental risk allocation and values associated with risk aversion, nor has it been construed as requiring an analysis of the value derived from holding and supporting a certain environmental philosophy.

When certain impacts on environmental values, such as environmental risk allocation and environmental philosophy, are not routinely considered under NEPA. but are of concern to society as a whole, this initial cost-efficient determination of project feasibility is lost with respect to these impacts. Allowing consideration of environmental risk allocation and environmental philosophical values would make NEPA more efficient. As one commentator stated with respect to the PANE Courts refusal to consider psychological distress. "[t]his consideration would ... allow the public to inform the agency of the public's willingness to accept a particular risk." Michael A. Christofe, Note, Psychological Distress Under NEPA, 19 Val. U. L. Rev. 899, 923 (1985).

Without consideration of these values, there will be projects which may have effects on environmental philosophy or risk allocation values, that will proceed against a wall of public opposition that may ultimately derail them. However, because these values are not presently considered or even acknowledged under NEPA, the opposition based on these values will not be well articulated, leaving a proponent of a project unsure of how to proceed to successfully address environmental concerns and complete the project. The opposition may take the form of a different environmental concern that a project proponent will address with massive expenditures for mitigation only to find that this was not the real concern at all, thus, leading to economic waste. Moreover, the proponents of the project may never spend resources to address or mitigate the real environmental concern; consequently, the opposition will remain stalwart.

If the opposition is finally successful in stopping a project, economic waste has occurred in gauging the depths of opposition that should have stopped a project before it even started. NEPA has been criticized for allowing too much delay to consider environmental problems, but many of these 'problems' mask concern about environmental risk allocation or an impact on environmental philosophy.

Even if there is little public opposition, as long as there is any legal challenge to a project, the project could be derailed and economic waste may occur, if environmental risk allocation or environmental philosophical values are affected. It is easy to suppose that some judges, like the general public, appreciate the value of environmental philosophy and risk allocation and may through NEPA delay, prohibit, or seem hostile to a project for these reasons. Since these values have not been explicitly recognized and considered under NEPA, the basis of the judicial action may not be expressed forthrightly. Just as in cases of general opposition to government actions, this 'hidden' or 'masked' judicial opposition prevents a project's proponent from addressing or considering the true environmental costs, leading to frustration and expense in NEPA litigation. It also incurs an indirect cost to the judiciary in terms of loss of institutional respect. Directly acknowledging these values will help restore that institutional trust.

If environmental risk allocation and environmental philosophy were explicitly considered under NEPA, then they could be addressed at low cost. The proponents of an action would have a clearer understanding of what values would be affected by a project and whether the project as presented or modified is viable, without the initial expenditure of large sums of money to address phantom environmental concerns. Even if environmental philosophical concerns or risk allocation values were not immediately clear, they would come into focus early in the project, allowing proper mitigation or abandonment of the project at a far lower cost than now exists.

Environmental risk allocation and environmental philosophy are the only major environmental values not to be considered under NEPA. Though values other than environmental ones may be at play in time use of NEPA, as these values are incorporated into the NEPA decision-making process, the use of NEPA merely as a delay tactic will decline. This will bring NEPA procedure more in line with its legislative intent and will make the NEPA process more cost-effective.

Notes and Comments

1. NEPA has lately been the subject of much attention. In 2002, the Bush administration undertook a review of NEPA and the NEPA process to analyze its strengths and weaknesses. That report stressed that agencies should try sharing information better (perhaps through the use of technolo-

gy); that there should be more mechanisms for collaboration; and that the CEQ could do more to strengthen effective NEPA compliance among some agencies, particularly with respect to determining categorical exclusions and Environmental Assessments. NEPA Task Force Report to the Council on Environmental Quality, *Modernizing NEPA Implementation*, http://ceq.eh. doe.gov/ntf/report/index.html. In 2005, a bi-partisan Congressional committee performed its own extensive review of NEPA. Its preliminary finding was that NEPA is a powerful and important law; its main suggestion was that many frequently-litigated terms, such as "major federal action, should be more clearly defined in the statute."

2. Although the criticism of NEPA has grown in recent years, and although NEPA's operation has been suspended for certain activities (such as leasing by the Forestry Department), NEPA remains an important aspect of federal actions, and through permitting, to private activities. The agency or lawyer ignores its application at great risk. In complying with NEPA, procedure is critically important, and, experience generally shows that a willingness to compromise on the proposal or action can go a long way towards forestalling delay and expense.

Chapter 3

THE CLEAN WATER ACT

THE NPDES PROGRAM

I. INTRODUCTION

The modern Clean Water Act ("CWA") assumed its current shape with the passage of the Federal Water Pollution Control Act of 1972, 33 U.S.C. § 1251 *et seq.*, Pub. L. 92–500 ("FWPCA"). In Section 101 of the new law, Congress announced that the statute's objective is to "restore and maintain the chemical, physical, and biological integrity of the Nation's waters." 33 U.S.C. § 1251(a). It further proclaimed several ambitious goals, including: (a) achieving by 1983, wherever attainable, a level of water quality that protects fish and wildlife and provides for recreation in and on the water (this is the so-called "fishable/swimmable" goal); and (b) eliminating, by 1985, all discharges of pollutants into the navigable waters. Id.

As we will see, we have fallen far short of these goals. Indeed, the statute never really contemplated that they would be met. As Judge Wald has pointed out,

> . . . [I]t is one thing for Congress to announce a grand goal, and quite another for it to mandate full implementation of that goal. Read as a whole, the Clean Water Act shows not only Congress' determined effort to clean up our polluted lakes and rivers, but also its practical recognition of the economic, technological, and political limits on total elimination of all pollution from all sources.

National Wildlife Federation v. Gorsuch, 693 F.2d 156, 178 (D.C. Cir. 1982). While the CWA aspires to the achievement of water quality standards that will meet its fishable/swimmable aspirations, its regulatory gaps have virtually ensured that this has not and will not come to pass for many of our waters. And as to the "no discharges" goal, the CWA simply contains no mandates that have ever, or are ever likely to, lead to the achievement of that objective.

Do not be dismayed, however. As distinguished an observer as Professor Oliver Houck has lauded the CWA as possibly our most successful environmental statute. Houck, TMDLs IV: The Final Frontier,

138

29 Envt. L. Rep. 10469 (Aug. 1999). Despite our growing population and economy, our Nation's waters are, generally speaking, significantly cleaner than they were when the FWPCA was first passed in 1972. Id. Undoubtedly, the CWA deserves credit for this.

We begin our detailed study of the CWA with the National Pollutant Discharge Elimination System ("NPDES") program, which is the major mechanism through which the statute seeks to control water pollution. In a nutshell, the CWA contemplates that those who discharge pollutants into our waterways will be regulated under a permit system that imposes both technology and, where necessary, water quality-based requirements. In theory, the technology-based requirements ensure that discharger will attain aggressive levels of pollutant-reduction that are uniform within each category of dischargers. The water quality-based requirements serve as a safety-net pursuant to which more aggressive controls will be required in situations in which the technology-based requirements may not result in the desired level of stream quality.

Before we focus on the substantive standards of the NPDES program, however, we consider some important preliminary matters: jurisdiction and the federal/state relationship.

II. JURISDICTION

Section 301(a) is the jurisdictional trigger for both the NPDES program under § 402 and the "dredge and fill" program under § 404 of the Act (this latter program is also known as the "wetlands" program, despite the fact that its scope transcends wetlands). Section 301(a) prohibits the "discharge of any pollutant" except as in conformance with several other sections of the Act, including §§ 402 and 404. In turn, Section 402 allows either EPA or the relevant State (depending upon whether the State is authorized to implement the program) to issue NPDES permits containing the relevant substantive requirements. (Likewise, Section 404 allows either the Corps of Engineers or—less often—the relevant State to issue permits for discharges of "dredged or fill material." We will consider this program in chapter 8, below.)

Section 502 defines the key statutory terms. Most significantly, Section 502(12) defines the term "discharge of a pollutant" to include "any addition of any pollutant to navigable waters from any point source." Thus it can be seen that there are three key elements of NPDES (and § 404) jurisdiction: there must be (1) an addition of a pollutant to (2) navigable waters (3) from a point source. If any one of these elements is missing, there is no NPDES (or § 404) jurisdiction. At the same time, note that if these three elements are present, no discharge can occur except as in compliance with the statutory sections listed in § 301(a). At least on the face of the statute, there is no de minimis exception. All discharges of pollutants are forbidden in the absence of a required permit.

In the NPDES world, classic examples of regulated dischargers include industrial facilities and sewage treatment plants that discharge contaminated wastewater into our rivers through outfall pipes. In these and other similar situations, there is typically little or no doubt as to whether the Act's jurisdictional elements are satisfied. As will be seen below, however, there has been much litigation defining the boundaries of these jurisdictional terms, and many important issues remain unresolved. As such, our focus will be on the uncertain boundaries of NPDES jurisdiction. At the same time, however, the reader should not lose sight of the fact that in many cases the existence of these elements is a foregone conclusion.

A. Addition of a Pollutant

While the phrase "addition of a pollutant" is not defined under the statute, Section 502(6) states that "the term 'pollutant' means dredged spoil, solid waste, incinerator residue, sewage, garbage, sewage sludge, munitions, chemical wastes, biological materials, radioactive materials, heat, wrecked or discarded equipment, rock, sand, cellar dirt and industrial, municipal, and agricultural waste discharged into water...." 33 U.S.C. § 1362(6). While this definition is framed as an exclusive one ("the term 'pollutant' means ..."), the breadth of some of its terms (e.g., "industrial, municipal and agricultural waste") results in there usually being little doubt as to whether pollutants are present in any offending discharges. As will be seen below, however, the question whether a particular point source is adding a pollutant has given rise to repeated litigation, often in the context of either dams or diversion projects that transfer water from one waterway to another. Consider the following case:

CATSKILL MOUNTAINS CHAPTER OF TROUT UNLIMITED, INC. v. CITY OF NEW YORK

United States Court of Appeals, Second Circuit, 2001.
273 F.3d 481, *reconsid. den.*, 451 F.3d 77 (2006).

WALKER, JR., Chief Judge:

Since before World War II, New York City has operated Schoharie Dam and Reservoir in the Catskill Mountains, to provide drinking water for New York City. Water is diverted south from the Schoharie Reservoir ("the Reservoir") through the Shandaken Tunnel ("the Tunnel") for several miles and released into Esopus Creek ("the Creek"), which in turn empties into Ashokan Reservoir. The transfer of water from the Reservoir to Esopus Creek and Ashokan Reservoir facilitates its delivery to New York City for use as drinking water.

Absent the tunnel, water leaving the Reservoir would flow north in Schoharie Creek, join the Mohawk River, and flow into the Hudson River. Water from Esopus Creek, on the other hand, makes its way southeast to the Hudson by way of Ashokan Reservoir. Schoharie Reservoir and Esopus Creek are hydrologically connected only insofar as both are tributaries of the Hudson. Under natural conditions, water from the Schoharie Reservoir would never reach Esopus Creek.

On March 31, 2000, [Catskill Mountains Chapter of Trout Unlimited, Inc. and other environmental groups ("Catskill")] filed a complaint ... alleging that the City, as owner and operator of the Schoharie Reservoir and Shandaken Tunnel, was in violation of 33 U.S.C. § 1311(a), which prohibits "the discharge of any pollutant" unless those discharges are conducted in accordance with a duly issued discharge permit. Catskill alleged that the Tunnel discharges pollutants in the form of "suspended solids," "turbidity," and heat into Esopus Creek. They alleged that the suspended solids and turbidity are the result of earth-disturbing activities within the Reservoir's watershed that produce fine, red-clay sediments in the Reservoir. They further alleged that the discharges cause the Creek to violate state water quality standards for turbidity and temperature. Esopus Creek, Catskill contended, is naturally clearer and cooler than the water entering it from the Tunnel and supports "one of the premier trout fishing streams in the Catskill Region."

As we have noted, the CWA prohibits, unless otherwise allowed by permit, "the discharge of any pollutant," 33 U.S.C. § 1311(a), which the Act defines to mean "any addition of any pollutant to navigable waters from any point source," 33 U.S.C. § 1362(12). The statute does not define "addition." The City argues that the release of water from Schoharie Reservoir into Esopus Creek is not an "addition," citing *National Wildlife Federation v. Gorsuch,* 693 F.2d 156 (D.C.Cir.1982), and *National Wildlife Federation v. Consumers Power Co.,* 862 F.2d 580 (6th Cir.1988), both of which accorded substantial deference to the EPA's position that the CWA's discharge permit requirement does not apply to discharges from dams. Catskill counters that the *Gorsuch* and *Consumers Power* courts accorded unjustified deference to the EPA's interpretation of "addition," that the cases are distinguishable on their facts, and that the City's conduct here qualifies as an "addition" under the plain meaning of that word. . . .

[The court first noted that the *Gorsuch* and *Consumers Power* courts' determinations that EPA's interpretation of "addition" was entitled to *Chevron* deference had been undermined by the Supreme Court's more recent opinions in *Christensen v. Harris County,* 529 U.S. 576 (2000) ("*Christensen*"), and *United States v. Mead Corp.,* 533 U.S. 218 (2001) ("*Mead*"). The court noted that *Christensen,* in particular, stands for the proposition that interpretations announced in informal policy statements—which was the only context in which EPA had spoken here—do not have the force of law and, thus, do not merit *Chevron* deference. As a consequence, the court determined that EPA's interpretation of "addition" was entitled to only *Skidmore* deference, meaning that the court would follow it only to the extent that it found it persuasive. *Skidmore v. Swift & Co.,* 323 U.S. 134, 140 (1944).]

The EPA's position, upheld by the *Gorsuch* and *Consumers Power* courts, is that for there to be an "addition," a "point source must *introduce* the pollutant into navigable water from the outside world." *Gorsuch,* 693 F.2d at 165 [(emphasis in original)]. We agree with this view provided that "outside world" is construed as any place outside the particular water body to which pollutants are introduced. Given that understanding of "addition," the transfer of water containing pollutants from one body of water to another, distinct body of water is plainly an addition and thus a "discharge" that demands an NPDES permit.

Both *Gorsuch* and *Consumers Power* essentially involved the recirculation of water, without anything added "from the outside world." Such recirculation, they concluded, could not be an "addition." In *Gorsuch,* water was released from a reservoir through a dam to the stream below. Plaintiffs complained that such a release amounted to a regulated discharge under the Act, requiring a permit. The reservoir above the dam and the stream below, at least arguably, were sufficiently the "same" water that the release might not be considered an "addition"; nothing was introduced to the water that was not, in some sense, already there. See 693 F.2d at 74–75.

In *Consumers Power,* the defendant had withdrawn water from Lake Michigan, along with some surprised fish, for hydroelectric power generation. The water and fish were then returned to the Lake after passing through hydroelectric generators, which puréed some of the fish. The court found that returning the fish to the Lake, albeit in a different form, was not an "addition" because the fish had already been there. *See* 862 F.2d at 586. Indeed, the court concluded that "[t]he water which passes through the [defendant's hydropower works] never loses its status as water of the United States." *Id.* at 589. The navigable water was recirculated, but nothing was added. The Sixth Circuit therefore also concluded that the releases from the defendant's hydropower works were not "introduced from the outside world." *See id.* at 586. . . .

The *Gorsuch* and *Consumers Power* decisions comport with the plain meaning of "addition," assuming that the water from which the discharges came is the same as that to which they go. If one takes a ladle of soup from a pot, lifts it above the pot, and pours it back into the pot, one has not "added" soup or anything else to the pot (beyond, perhaps, a *de minimis* quantity of airborne dust that fell into the ladle). In requiring a permit for such a "discharge," the EPA might as easily require a permit for Niagra Falls (sic).

The present case, however, strains past the breaking point the assumption of "sameness" made by the *Gorsuch* and *Consumers Power* courts. Here, water is artificially diverted from its natural course and travels several miles from the Reservoir through Shandaken Tunnel to Esopus Creek, a body of water utterly unrelated in any relevant sense to the Schoharie Reservoir and its watershed. No one can reasonably argue that the water in the Reservoir and the Esopus are in any sense the "same," such that "addition" of one to the other is a logical impossibility. When the water and the suspended sediment therein passes from the Tunnel into the Creek, an "addition" of a "pollutant" from a "point source" has been made to a "navigable water," and the terms of the statute are satisfied.

Given the ordinary meaning of the CWA's text ..., we cannot accept the *Gorsuch* and *Consumers Power* courts' understanding of "addition," at least insofar as it implies acceptance of ... a "singular entity" theory of navigable waters, in which an addition to one water body is deemed an addition to all of the waters of the United States.... Such a theory would mean that movement of water from one discrete water body to another would not be an addition even if it involved a transfer of water from a water body contaminated with myriad pollutants to a pristine water body containing few or no pollutants. Such an interpretation is inconsistent with the ordinary meaning of the word "addition."

* * *

Notes and Comments

1. The CWA is typical of most environmental statutes in that it is subject to two different numbering systems. Every section of the CWA has two section numbers: its Clean Water Act section number, which is based on the section numbers Congress used when it passed the Federal Water Pollution Control Act of 1972, and the U.S.C. section numbers assigned when that law was inserted into the United States Code. In this book, we will primarily use the CWA section numbers (e.g. § 301 of the CWA) instead of the U.S.C. section numbers (e.g., 33 U.S.C. § 1311). The vast majority of practitioners, and most courts, do the same. Having said that, however, we note that the *Catskill I* court and several other of the early decisions in this book use the U.S.C. section numbers. While this may cause some confusion at first, the student will quickly become adept at using both systems.

2. What were the pollutants at issue in *Catskill I*? Heat is on the statutory list, but what about "suspended solids" and "turbidity"? If the real pollutant at issue is a "fine, red-clay sediment," does that qualify? The definition includes rock and sand. Should it be read to therefore also include clay and other forms of dirt (beyond "cellar dirt")?

3. Section 501(a) of the CWA gives EPA the power to issue such regulations as it deems necessary to carry out its functions under the statute. Pursuant to this authority, EPA has promulgated its own definitions of the terms "pollutant" and "point source." See 40 C.F.R. § 122.2 (we will address the "navigable waters" construct below). EPA's definitions track, but are not identical to, those in the statute. For example, EPA's regulatory definition of "pollutant" varies from the statutory definition only in that it adds "filter backwash" and excludes radioactive materials that are regulated under the Atomic Energy Act. Are these revisions reasonable interpretations of the statutory definitions, or simply alterations thereof? Relying on some legislative history that was precisely on point, in *Train v. Colorado Public Interest Research Group*, 426 U.S. 1, 25, 96 S.Ct. 1938, 48 L.Ed.2d 434 (1976), the Supreme Court found that EPA acted properly in concluding the radioactive materials exclusion was consistent with the statutory definition. To the extent that any of the regulatory definitions constitute changes, however, they beg the question of whether EPA has the authority to make them. See also 40 C.F.R. § 122.3(a) (exempting discharges incidental to the normal operation of a vessel). In *Natural Resources Defense Council, Inc. v. Costle*, 568 F.2d 1369 (D.C. Cir. 1977) ("*NRDC v. Costle*"), EPA argued that

it could exempt agricultural point sources from the scope of the NPDES program, despite the fact that, at the time, there was no statutory basis for such an exemption. (EPA did not argue that it was interpreting any statutory language). The D.C. Circuit squarely rejected EPA's position, finding that "[t]he wording of the statute, legislative history, and precedents are clear: the EPA Administrator does not have the authority to exempt categories of point sources from the permit requirements of § 402." 568 F.2d at 1377. In a subsequent Clean Air Act case, however, the same D.C. Circuit seemed to limit *NRDC v. Costle*, holding that EPA has the implied authority to create de minimis exceptions to the permitting requirements under that statute. *Alabama Power Co. v. Costle*, 636 F.2d 323, 360 (D.C. Cir. 1979). In *Natural Resources Defense Council, Inc. v. U.S. EPA*, 966 F.2d 1292, 1306 (9th Cir. 1992), the Ninth Circuit allowed for the possibility of such a showing under the CWA, but found that it EPA had not met the de minimis standard in that case.

4. It is worth reiterating that the definition of "pollutant" contains no regulatory thresholds or de minimis exceptions. While *Alabama Power* may stand for the proposition that EPA has the implied authority to create de minimis exclusions, EPA does not appear to have ever invoked this potential authority. Thus, as it currently stands every addition of pollutants is covered under the Act, regardless of quantity or concentration, assuming the other jurisdictional requirements also are met.

5. One context in which the presence of a statutory pollutant is increasingly being litigated relates to the application of pesticides or herbicides to waterways for purposes of bug or weed control. In one case, the City of New York was applying pesticides to control the spread of the West Nile Virus. *No Spray Coalition, Inc. v. City of New York*, 351 F.3d 602 (2d Cir. 2003). In another, an irrigation district in Oregon was applying an herbicide to control the growth of weeds in its irrigation canals. *Headwaters, Inc. v. Talent Irrigation District*, 243 F.3d 526 (9th Cir. 2001). Are these types of materials "pollutants" within the meaning of the CWA? Interestingly, in the wake of *Headwaters*, which held that the CWA applied (the *No Spray* court remanded the issue to the lower court), EPA issued an "interim guidance" indicating its view that the application of pesticides and/or herbicides in accordance with the Federal Insecticide, Fungicide, and Rodenticide Act, 7 U.S.C. § 136 *et seq.* (FIFRA), does not require an NPDES permit. See 68 Fed. Reg. 48385 (2003). The primary basis for EPA's conclusion is that when these materials are applied in accordance with FIFRA, they are not "chemical wastes" because they are being applied for their intended purpose. *Id.* at 48388. How does EPA's interpretation change the framework for judicial review? Is it persuasive, within the meaning of *Skidmore*? If materials that are being applied for their intended purpose cannot qualify as "chemical waste," should it matter whether they are applied in accordance with FIFRA, given that (a) FIFRA was passed after the FWPCA in 1972 (by three days), and (b) neither statute refers to the other?

6. Another issue concerning the definition of "pollutant" involves what is meant by the phrase "biological materials." Clearly, this term encompasses, for example, the fish remains that fish processors generate as waste materials. See, e.g., *Association of Pacific Fisheries v. EPA*, 615 F.2d 794 (9th Cir. 1980). But what about living mussels introduced into a waterway to

promote mussel harvesting? See *Association to Protect Hammersley, Eld and Totten Inlets v. Taylor Resources, Inc.*, 299 F.3d 1007, 1016 (9th Cir. 2002) ("*APHETI*") (concluding that "[i]t would be anomalous to conclude that living shellfish sought to be *protected* under the Act are, at the same time, 'pollutants' the discharge of which may be *proscribed* by the Act"); but see *Consumers Power*, 862 F.2d at 585 ("under the CWA, live fish would be just as much a pollutant as a mixture of live and dead fish"). If you agree with *APHETI*, should this same logic apply to the invasive species contained in the ballast water discharges of trans-oceanic shippers? Does the CWA distinguish between these two scenarios?

7. Were you convinced by the *Catskill I* court's distinction between *Gorsuch* and *Consumers Power*, on the one hand, and the situation before it? One of the pollutants at issue in *Gorsuch* was sediment. Although these sediments would have moved downstream even absent the dam, the dam worsened their impact on water quality because they were discharged in short spikes rather than gradually making their way downstream. *National Wildlife Federation v. Gorsuch*, 693 F.2d 156, 164 (D.C. Cir. 1982). Should the adversity of this non-natural impact result in a determination that a pollutant has been added? As we will see in chapter 8, this same issue comes up in the context of determining whether "fallback" (e.g., the soil that falls off of excavation equipment when one is engaged in earth-moving within a wetland) should be deemed to trigger the application of § 404 jurisdiction. As suggested by the *Catskill I* court's ladle analogy, the *Gorsuch* court's approach may continue to predominate in the NPDES realm even in the post-*Christensen/Mead* era. In *South Florida Water Management District v. Miccosukee Tribe of Indians*, 541 U.S. 95, 124 S.Ct. 1537, 1545, 158 L.Ed.2d 264 (2004) ("*Miccosukee*"), the plaintiff Tribe conceded that pumping polluted water within the same water body could not constitute the addition of a pollutant. Relying on this concession, the Supreme Court remanded the case for, among other things, further factual development on the question whether the relevant waters were "meaningfully distinct." 541 U.S. at 112. In so doing, the Court indicated that a finding that they were not would result in a determination that the defendant did not require a permit. Id. If you were representing the Tribe, would you have made the same concession? What is the effect of the Court's having acted as if this concession might be outcome determinative upon remand? In *S.D. Warren Co. v. Maine Board of Environmental Protection*, ___ U.S. ___, 126 S.Ct. 1843, 164 L.Ed.2d 625 (2006), the Court returned to this subject with the following bit of dictum:

> ... Before *Miccosukee*, one could have argued that transferring polluted water from a canal to a connected impoundment constituted an "addition." *Miccosukee* is at odds with that construction of the statute, but it says nothing about [the issue that would be relevant to this case:] whether the transfer of polluted water from the canal to the impoundment constitutes a "discharge."

Id. at 1850 n.6 (note that, as we will discuss below, the issue in *S.D. Warren* involved whether the release at issue constituted a "discharge" under § 502(16), not whether it was a "discharge of a pollutant" under § 502(12)). Where does all of this leave us on the movement-within-a-waterway question?

8. What about the other prong of the *Catskill I* court's distinction? Do you agree that an interpretation that would allow water to be transferred from a very contaminated waterway into a pristine one would be "inconsistent with the ordinary meaning of the word 'addition?'" In *Miccosukee*, the Government weighed in on this issue more heavily than ever before, arguing in favor of what it now terms the "unitary waters" theory. As explained by the Court:

> The "unitary waters" argument focuses on the Act's definition of a pollutant discharge as any addition of any pollutant to navigable waters from any point source. § 1362(12). The Government contends that the absence of the word "any" prior to the phrase "navigable waters" in § 1362(12) signals Congress' understanding that NPDES permits would not be required for pollution caused by the engineered transfer of one "navigable water" into another....

541 U.S. at 106, 124 S.Ct. at 1543–1544. The Government also noted that requiring permits in the context of engineered diversions might affect thousands of water diversions, particularly in the western States. Id. at 108, 124 S.Ct. at 1544–45. Despite these arguments, the Court declined to rule on the issue, noting that neither the water district nor the Government had raised the issue either before the Court of Appeals or in their briefs respecting the petition for certiorari. Id. at 109, 124 S.Ct. at 1545. The Court thus remanded this issue to the Eleventh Circuit, together with the factual issue (referenced in note 7, above) of whether the two waterways in that case were in fact separate. Id. at 109 and 112, 124 S.Ct. at 1545 and 1547.

9. Since *Miccosukee*, there have been two further developments on the movement-from-one-waterway-to-another issue. First, EPA issued a proposed rule in which it announced its position that inter-basin water transfers are exempt from NPDES requirements. 71 Fed. Reg. 32887 (June 7, 2006). Interestingly, it did so without ever once either mentioning the "unitary waters" theory or referencing the statutory dynamics upon which it was based. Rather, its legal justification was a much more holistic one, based on the idea that Congress simply did not intend to regulate these types of transfers. And second, the Second Circuit reaffirmed its holding in *Catskill*, noting that neither *Miccosukee* nor a prior [2005] version of EPA's new administrative interpretation gave it any cause to doubt its earlier conclusion. *Catskill Mountains Chapter of Trout Unlimited, Inc.*, 451 F.3d 77 (2d Cir. 2006) (*Catskill II*). Do you agree? If you were sitting on the Eleventh Circuit upon remand, would you be persuaded by the Government's arguments regarding the "unitary waters" theory? How much deference would EPA's current interpretation be due? If EPA were to promulgate a legislative rule implementing its view, would you defer under *Chevron*?

10. In both *Miccosukee* and *Catskill I*, the defendants also argued that, in order for there to be an "addition" from "point source," the point source must create the pollutant, not just be a conduit through which the pollutant enters the relevant waters. Both courts squarely rejected this argument. In *Miccosukee*, for example, the Supreme Court noted that the definition of "point source" includes "conveyance[s]," concluding that this "makes plain that a point source need be the original source of the pollutant; it need only convey the pollutant to the 'navigable waters.'" 541 U.S. at 105, 124 S.Ct. at

1543; see also *Catskill I*, 273 F.3d at 493 (noting that even in the prototypical industrial setting, it is the pipe that is the point source, not the factory itself).

B.　Navigable Waters

Section 502(7) defines the term "navigable waters" to mean "the waters of the United States." In the absence of further statutory edification, EPA stepped into the breach by defining "waters of the United States" to mean:

(a) All waters which are currently used, were used in the past, or may be susceptible to use in interstate or foreign commerce, including all waters which are subject to the ebb and flow of the tide;

(b) All interstate waters, including interstate "wetlands;"

(c) All other waters such as intrastate lakes, rivers, streams (including intermittent streams), mudflats, sandflats, "wetlands," sloughs, prairie potholes, wet meadows, playa lakes, or natural ponds the use, degradation, or destruction of which would affect or could affect interstate or foreign commerce . . . ;

(d) All impoundments of waters otherwise defined as waters of the United States under this definition;

(e) Tributaries of waters identified in paragraphs (a) through (d) of this definition;

(f) The territorial sea; and

(g) "Wetlands" adjacent to waters (other than waters that are themselves wetlands) identified in paragraphs (a) through (f) of this definition.

Waste treatment systems, including treatment ponds or lagoons designed to meet the requirements of CWA . . . are not waters of the United States. . . .

40 C.F.R. § 122.2.

This rule, together with the Corps' equivalent rule at 33 C.F.R. § 328.3, has been subject to frequent litigation, including trips to the Supreme Court in *United States v. Riverside Bayview Homes, Inc.*, 474 U.S. 121, 106 S.Ct. 455, 88 L.Ed.2d 419 (1985) ("*Riverside Bayview*") (wetlands adjacent to truly navigable waters are "navigable waters"), *Solid Waste Agency of Northern Cook County v. U.S. Army Corps of Engineers*, 531 U.S. 159, 121 S.Ct. 675, 148 L.Ed.2d 576 (2001) ("*SWANCC*") (isolated ponds are not, at least where their only nexus to interstate commerce is based on the presence of migratory birds), and *Rapanos v. United States*, 126 S.Ct. 2208, 165 L.Ed.2d 159 (2006) (dealing with wetlands adjacent to non-navigable tributaries). We leave much of this discussion for our study of the "wetlands" program in chapter 8, because it is in that context that the outer bounds of the statutory waters have most often been tested. As an introductory matter, however, it is important to make to at least mention that if a particular aquatic area is not a "navigable water" for purposes of the wetlands program, then neither will it be a "navigable water" for purposes of NPDES jurisdiction; that is, if a wetland or body of surface water may be filled with fill material, so also may it be a repository for sewage or industrial effluent. This is so because, again, the jurisdictional terms under §§ 402 and 404 are the same: an addition of a pollutant to the navigable waters, from a point source. It all comes from Section 301, which is the jurisdictional underpinning of both permit programs.

Another "navigable waters" issue that comes up frequently in the NPDES realm involves discharges into groundwater that has a hydrologic connection to a nearby surface water. Consider the following decision:

IDAHO RURAL COUNCIL v. BOSMA

United States District Court, D. Idaho, 2001.
143 F.Supp.2d 1169.

WINMILL, Chief Judge.

In 1994, the Defendants ("Bosmas") established a substantial dairy operation ("Grand View Dairy" or "the dairy") in an area near Bliss, Idaho, which is directly upgradient from farms operated by the Butler and Walker families. The Butlers and the Walkers are members of Plaintiff Idaho Rural Council ("IRC"), an Idaho non-profit corporation with approximately 500 members throughout Idaho.

[Among other allegations, IRC alleged that wastewater from several of the dairy's holding ponds and an irrigation pond seeped into the groundwater and thereby into nearby springs. The dairy disputed whether, even if true, this constituted a violation of the CWA.]

... The courts which have considered the issue generally agree that waters of the United States do not include isolated, nontributory groundwater, and that discharges of pollutants into such groundwater are not subject to CWA regulation. The courts are split, however, on the issue of whether the discharge of pollutants into groundwater which find their way into and affect the waters of the United States are subject to CWA regulation. ...

One view is that Congress intended to regulate the discharge of any pollutants that could affect surface waters of the United States, whether it reaches the surface water directly or through groundwater. The rationale supporting this conclusion is simple and persuasive: "since the goal of the CWA is to protect the quality of surface waters, any pollutant which enters such waters, whether directly or through groundwater, is subject to regulation by NPDES permit." [*Washington Wilderness Coalition v. Hecla Mining Co.*, 870 F.Supp. 983, 990 (E.D.Wa.1994)]. Stated even more simply, whether pollution is introduced by a visible, aboveground conduit or enters the surface water through the aquifer matters little to the fish, waterfowl, and recreational users which are affected by the degradation of our nation's rivers and streams.

On the other hand, the Court is mindful of other decisions concluding that the CWA does not regulate the discharge of pollutants into any groundwaters, even where it ultimately affects the surface water. Those courts reach this conclusion based largely upon the legislative history of the CWA. They point out that Congress, in other provisions of the CWA, clearly included groundwater when they intended to do so, and that Congress considered "ground waters" to be a category of waters distinct from "navigable waters." [*Umatilla Waterquality Protective Assoc., Inc. v. Smith Frozen Foods, Inc.*, 962 F.Supp. 1312, 1318 (D.Or.1997)]. They also rely upon the legislative history of the CWA, which indicates that Congress specifically chose not to regulate groundwater, largely because "the jurisdiction regarding groundwaters is so complex and varied from State to State." *Id.* (quoting from S.Rep. No. 414, 92d Cong., 1st Sess. 73 (1971)), U.S.Code Cong. & Admin. News 1972, pp. 3668, 3749. Finally, they attach significance to the fact that the "EPA has offered no formal or consistent interpretation of the CWA that would subject discharges to groundwater to the NPDES permitting requirement." *Id.*

The Court agrees that this interpretive history establishes that Congress, in enacting the [CWA], concluded that it would not attempt the general regulation of discharges to groundwater. However, Congress's decision not to comprehensively regulate groundwater as part of the CWA, does not require the conclusion that Congress intended to exempt ground water from all regulation—particularly under circumstances where the introduction of pollutants into the groundwater adversely affects the adjoining surface waters. In short, the interpretive history of the CWA only supports the unremarkable proposition with which all courts agree—that the CWA does not regulate "isolated/nontributary groundwater" which has no affect on surface water. It does not suggest that Congress intended to exclude from regulation discharges into hydrologically connected groundwater which adversely affect surface water.

For these reasons, the Court finds that the CWA extends federal jurisdiction over groundwater that is hydrologically connected to surface waters that are themselves waters of the United States. This does not mean, however, that the plaintiff's burden is light. As Judge Van Sickle explained in *Washington Wilderness Coalition*:

> Plaintiffs must still demonstrate that pollutants from a point source affect surface waters of the United States. It is not sufficient to allege groundwater pollution, and then to assert a general hydrological connection between all waters. Rather, pollutants must be traced from their source to surface waters, in order to come within the purview of the CWA.

Id. Whether IRC can make this showing remains to be seen. However, the Court finds, for purposes of the Bosma's summary judgment motion, that the CWA regulates discharges from the Grand View Dairy into the groundwater where there exists a hydrological connection with [nearby springs], and such discharges can be traced from their source to those springs. . . .

Notes and Comments

1. Why weren't the holding and irrigation ponds "waters of the United States" themselves? Does this seem like a reasonable result? Are there any drawbacks to this approach?

2. The parties in *Bosma* agreed that the dairy was a point source. This may have been due to the fact that the statutory definition of "point source" specifically includes "concentrated animal feeding operation[s]" ("CAFOs"). See CWA § 502(14).

3. The most surprising aspect of the groundwater issue is how unsettled it is. Were you persuaded by the *Bosma* court's analysis? Does EPA's definition of "waters of the United States" speak to this issue? If not, should its silence be dispositive? Or does it simply leave in place an ambiguity that EPA can then resolve through administrative interpretation? If EPA were to amend its rule to specifically include hydrologically-linked groundwater, would that interpretation pass muster under *Chevron*? Is the statutory definition of "navigable waters" ambiguous in this regard? Can it reasonably be interpreted to encompass these groundwaters? In *Riverside Bayview*, which we will consider at length below, the Supreme Court—in a *Chevron* analysis—relied on the hydrologic link between adjacent wetlands and their nearby surface waters in upholding the Corps' assertion of jurisdiction over those adjacent wetlands. Does that suggest that the Court would do likewise in this context? *Cf. Village of Oconomowoc Lake v. Dayton Hudson Corp.*, 24 F.3d 962, 966 (7th Cir. 1994), *cert. denied*, 513 U.S. 930, 115 S.Ct. 322, 130 L.Ed.2d 282 (1994) (disagreeing with the *Bosma* result, but noting that "[b]y amending its regulations, EPA could pose a harder question").

4. If one reads EPA's definition of "water of the United States" as being ambiguous on this point, keep in mind that any EPA interpretation of that regulation (if initially offered as other than a litigating position) would be controlling unless it were plainly erroneous or inconsistent with the regulation. *Auer v. Robbins*, 519 U.S. 452, 461, 117 S.Ct. 905, 137 L.Ed.2d 79 (1997); *Bowles v. Seminole Rock & Sand Co.*, 325 U.S. 410, 414, 65 S.Ct. 1215, 89 L.Ed. 1700 (1945). This doctrine—which is alternately referred to as *Seminole Rock* or *Auer* deference—raises two immediate questions in this context: (1) has EPA ever opined on this issue in a fashion that should give rise to deference; and (2) if it has done so, was it interpreting the statute or, alternatively, was it interpreting its regulation. On the first point, EPA spoke at length on the issue of whether discharges to hydrologically-linked groundwaters should be jurisdictional in the preamble to its proposed new CAFO rules in 2001. 66 Fed. Reg. 2960 (2001). There, EPA said that it was "restating that the Agency interprets the [CWA] to apply to discharges of pollutants from a point source via ground water that has a direct hydrologic connection to surface water." Id. at 3015. It further offered an extensive "legal basis" for its interpretation, and noted at least five prior instances in which it had offered consistent interpretations. Id. at 3015–3018. In the final

rule, however, EPA distanced itself from this interpretation, eliminating its proposed control program and stating that "[n]othing in this rule shall be construed to expand, diminish, or otherwise affect the jurisdiction of the [CWA] over discharges to surface water via groundwater that has a direct hydrologic connection to surface water." 68 Fed. Reg. 7176, 7216–7217 (2003). Where does this leave us?

5. On the second point raised in the prior note, it is worth at least noting an oddity inherent in the juxtaposition of the various deference doctrines. If the court were to determine that the position advanced in EPA's proposed rule were a reasonable interpretation of an ambiguous rule, it would apply the relatively strong deference contemplated under *Seminole Rock* (although there would then also be a question as to whether the regulation, as interpreted, was consistent with the statute—which would pose a *Chevron* issue). Alternatively, if the court concluded that EPA were interpreting the statute, it would at best be entitled to the much weaker *Skidmore* deference. In other words, if an agency speaks informally, it will get a higher form of deference if it can argue that it is interpreting its own rule, rather than the statute. Justice Scalia, who believes that even informal pronouncements should get *Chevron* deference, bemoaned this dynamic in his dissent in *Mead*:

> . . . [T]he majority's approach will have a perverse effect on the rules that do emerge, given the principle (which the Court leaves untouched today) that judges must defer to reasonable agency interpretations of their own rules. Agencies will now have high incentive to rush out barebones, ambiguous rules construing statutory ambiguities, which they can then in turn further clarify through informal rulings entitled to judicial respect.

533 U.S. at 246 (citations omitted).

6. The *Bosma* court followed *Washington Wilderness Coalition* in requiring the plaintiffs to demonstrate that the defendants' pollutants had in fact migrated through the groundwater into the nearby surface waters. Does this requirement seem appropriate? What if the plaintiffs could demonstrate that some of the defendants' pollutants would inevitably make their way into the surface waters, even if it might take years? Can you argue that even less should be required?

C. Point Source

The requirement that the discharge be from a "point source" has historically been the most important jurisdictional dividing line under the CWA. As discussed in the case below, Congress sought to distinguish between discrete conveyances of pollutants, which were to be governed under the NPDES program, and contaminated runoff, which was to be addressed under the largely non-regulatory rubric of § 209 (later supplemented by § 319). In effectuating this framework, Congress defined the term "point source" to mean "any discernible, confined and discrete conveyance, including but not limited to any pipe, ditch, channel, tunnel, conduit, well, discrete fissure, container, rolling stock, concentrated animal feeding operation, or vessel or other floating craft, from which pollutants are or may be discharged." 33 U.S.C. § 1362(14). Note that while this definition requires a discrete conveyance, the list of examples set forth is framed non-exclusively ("including but not limited to . . ."). In its implementing rules, EPA maintains the non-exclusive orientation and adds only one further example ("landfill leachate collection system[s]") to the list. 40 C.F.R. § 122.2.

Not surprisingly, the indeterminate nature of these definitions has led to litigation over sources of pollution that are not on these lists. For example, should earth-moving equipment (e.g., bulldozers, backhoes and plows) qualify as a point source? If not, Section 404 will be rendered inapplicable to most wetland-destroying activities. What about sumps or surface impoundments that overflow during periods of heavy rain? While the following case arises in an unusual factual context, the majority and dissenting opinions highlight the tensions that arise in confronting these issues:

UNITED STATES v. PLAZA HEALTH LABORATORIES, INC.

United States Court of Appeals, Second Circuit, 1993.
3 F.3d 643.

PRATT, Circuit Judge:

[Geronimo Villegas was co-owner and vice president of Plaza Health Laboratories, Inc., a blood-testing laboratory in Brooklyn, New York. At least twice between April and September 1988, Villegas took containers of numerous vials of human blood from his business to his condominium in Edgewater, New Jersey. Once there, Villegas either put the containers in the river or, on one occasion, placed them at low tide within a crevice that separated the condominium complex from the river. This crevice was below the high-water line.

In May of that year, a group of eighth graders on a field trip discovered numerous glass vials containing human blood along the shore. Some of the vials had washed up on the shore; many were still in the water. Some were cracked, although most remained sealed with stoppers in solid-plastic containers or ziplock bags. That afternoon, New York City workers recovered approximately 70 vials from the area. Four months later, a maintenance worker at Villegas's condominium discovered a plastic container holding blood vials wedged between rocks in the bulkhead. New Jersey authorities retrieved numerous blood vials from the bulkhead later that day. Ten of the retrieved vials contained blood infected with the hepatitis-B virus. All of the vials recovered were eventually traced to Plaza Health Laboratories.

After being convicted of knowingly discharging pollutants from a "point source" without a permit under the CWA, Villegas appealed, arguing that the definition of "point source" does not include discharges that result from the individual acts of human beings.]

Human beings are not among the enumerated items that may be a "point source". Although by its terms the definition of "point source" is nonexclusive, the words used to define the term and the examples given ("pipe, ditch, channel, tunnel, conduit, well, discrete fissure", etc.) evoke images of physical structures and instrumentalities that systematically act as a means of conveying pollutants from an industrial source to navigable waterways.

In addition, if every discharge involving humans were to be considered a "discharge from a point source", the statute's lengthy definition of "point source" would have been unnecessary. It is elemental that congress does not add unnecessary words to statutes. Had congress intended to punish any human being who polluted navigational waters, it could readily have said: "any person who places pollutants in navigable waters without a permit is guilty of a crime."

The [CWA] generally targets industrial and municipal sources of pollutants, as is evident from a perusal of its many sections. Consistent with this focus, the term "point source" is used throughout the statute, but invariably in sentences referencing industrial or municipal discharges.

This emphasis was sensible, as "[i]ndustrial and municipal point sources were the worst and most obvious offenders of surface water quality. They were also the easiest to address because their loadings emerge from a discrete point such as the end of a pipe." David Letson, Point/Nonpoint Source Pollution Reduction Trading: An Interpretive Survey, 32 Nat.Resources J. 219, 221 (1992).

Finally on this point, we assume that congress did not intend the awkward meaning that would result if we were to read "human being" into the definition of "point source". Section 1362(12)(A) defines "discharge of a pollutant" as "any addition of any pollutant to navigable waters from any point source". Enhanced by this definition, § 1311(a) reads in effect "the addition of any pollutant to navigable waters from any point source by any person shall be unlawful". But were a human being to be included within the definition of "point source", the prohibition would then read: "the addition of any pollutant to navigable waters from any person by any person shall be unlawful", and this simply makes no sense. As the statute stands today, the term "point source" is comprehensible only if it is held to the context of industrial and municipal discharges.

The legislative history of the CWA ... confirms the act's focus on industrial polluters. Congress required NPDES permits of those who discharge from a "point source". The term "point source" ... was intended to function as a means of identifying industrial polluters—generally a difficult task because pollutants quickly disperse throughout the subject waters. The senate report for the 1972 amendments explains:

> In order to further clarify the scope of the regulatory procedures in the Act the Committee had added a definition of point source to distinguish between control requirements where there are specific confined conveyances, such as pipes, and control requirements which are imposed to control runoff. The control of pollutants from

runoff is applied pursuant to section 209 and the authority resides in the State or other local agency.

S.Rep. No. 92–414, reprinted in 1972 U.S.C.C.A.N. 3668, 3744.

We find no suggestion either in the act itself or in the history of its passage that congress intended the CWA to impose criminal liability on an individual for the myriad, random acts of human waste disposal, for example, a passerby who flings a candy wrapper into the Hudson River, or a urinating swimmer. . . .

[T]he cases that have interpreted "point source" have done so in civil-penalty or licensing settings, where greater flexibility of interpretation to further remedial legislative purposes is permitted, and the rule of lenity does not protect a defendant against statutory ambiguities. *See, e.g., Avoyelles Sportsmen's League, Inc. v. Marsh*, 715 F.2d 897, 922 (5th Cir.1983) ("point source" includes bulldozing equipment that discharged dredged materials onto wetland).

In sum, . . . § 1362(14) of the CWA does not expressly recognize a human being as a "point source"; nor does the act make structural sense when one incorporates a human being into that definition. The legislative history of the act adds no light to the muddy depths of this issue, and cases urging a broad interpretation of the definition in the civil-penalty context do not persuade us to do so here, where congress has imposed heavy criminal sanctions. . . .

We accordingly conclude that the term "point source" as applied to a human being is at best ambiguous.

In criminal prosecutions the rule of lenity requires that ambiguities in the statute be resolved in the defendant's favor. In other words, we cannot add to the statute what congress did not provide. . . .

Since the government's reading of the statute in this case founders on our inability to discern the "obvious intention of the legislature" to include a human being as a "point source", we conclude that the criminal provisions of the CWA did not clearly proscribe Villegas's conduct and did not accord him fair warning of the sanctions the law placed on that conduct. Under the rule of lenity, therefore, the prosecutions against him must be dismissed.

OAKES, Circuit Judge, dissenting:

I begin with the obvious, in hopes that it will illuminate the less obvious: the classic point source is something like a pipe. This is . . . because pipes and similar conduits are needed to carry large quantities of waste water, which represents a large proportion of the point source pollution problem. . . . Because not all pollutants are liquids, however, the statute and the cases make clear that means of conveying solid wastes to be dumped in navigable waters are also point sources. *See, e.g.,* 33 U.S.C. § 1362(14) ("rolling stock," or railroad cars, listed as an example of a point source); *Avoyelles Sportsmen's League, Inc. v. Marsh,* 715 F.2d 897, 922 (5th Cir.1983) (backhoes and bulldozers used to gather fill and deposit it on wetlands are point sources).

What I take from this look at classic point sources is that, at the least, an organized means of channeling and conveying industrial waste in quantity to navigable waters is a "discernible, confined and discrete conveyance." The case law is in accord: courts have deemed a broad range of means of depositing pollutants in the country's navigable waters to be point sources. See, e.g., *Rybachek v. EPA*, 904 F.2d 1276 (9th Cir.1990) (placer mining; sluice box from which discharge water is redeposited in stream is point source, despite provisions protecting some mining activities); *Sierra Club v. Abston Constr. Co.*, 620 F.2d 41, 45 (5th Cir.1980) (spill of contaminated runoff from strip mine, if collected or channeled by the operator, is point source discharge); *United States v. Earth Sciences, Inc.*, 599 F.2d 368, 374 (10th Cir.1979) (same)....

In short, the term "point source" has been broadly construed to apply to a wide range of polluting techniques, so long as the pollutants involved are not just humanmade, but reach the navigable waters by human effort or by leaking from a clear point at which waste water was collected by human effort....

Nonetheless, the term "point source" sets significant definitional limits on the reach of the [CWA]. Fifty percent or more of all water pollution is thought to come from nonpoint sources. S.Rep. 99–50, 99th Cong., 1st Sess. 8 (1985). So, to further refine the definition of "point source," I consider what it is that the Act does not cover: nonpoint source discharges.[1]

Nonpoint source pollution is, generally, runoff: salt from roads, agricultural chemicals from farmlands, oil from parking lots, and other substances washed by rain, in diffuse patterns, over the land and into navigable waters. The sources are many, difficult to identify and difficult to control. Indeed, an effort to greatly reduce nonpoint source pollution could require radical changes in land use patterns which Congress evidently was unwilling to mandate without further study. The structure of the statute—which regulates point source pollution closely, while leaving nonpoint source regulation to the states under the Section 208 program—indicates that the term "point source" was included in the definition of discharge so as to ensure that nonpoint source pollution would not be covered. Instead, Congress chose to regulate first that which could easily be regulated: direct discharges by identifiable parties, or point sources.

This rationale for regulating point and nonpoint sources differently ... helps define what fits within each category. Thus, Professor Rodgers has suggested, "[t]he statutory 'discernible, confined and discrete conveyance' ... can be understood as singling out those candidates suitable for control-at-the-source." 2 Rodgers, Environmental Law: Air and Water § 4.10 at 150 (1986). And, as Professor Rodgers notes, "[c]ase law confirms the controllability theory, adding to it a responsibility component, so that 'point sources' are understood both as sources that can be

---

1. The cases and commentators all seem to assume that all water pollution is either point source pollution or nonpoint source pollution.

cleaned up and as sources where fairness suggests the named parties should do the cleaning." *Id.*

... Villegas did not dispose of the materials on land, where they could be washed into water as nonpoint source pollution. Rather, he carried them, from his firm's laboratory, in his car, to his apartment complex, where he placed them in a bulkhead below the high tide line. I do not think it is necessary to determine whether it was Mr. Villegas himself who was the point source, or whether it was his car, the vials, or the bulkhead: in a sense, the entire stream of Mr. Villegas' activity functioned as a "discrete conveyance" or point source. The point is that the source of the pollution was clear, and would have been easy to control ...

Villegas' method may have been an unusual one for a corporate officer, but it would undermine the statute ... to regard as "ambiguous" a Congressional failure to list an unusual method of disposing of waste. I doubt that Congress would have regarded an army of men and women throwing industrial waste from trucks into a stream as exempt from the statute ... A different reading would encourage corporations perfectly capable of abiding by the [CWA's] requirements to ask their employees to stand between the company trucks and the sea, thereby transforming point source pollution (dumping from trucks) into nonpoint source pollution (dumping by hand)....

My colleagues also suggest that the statute is sufficiently ambiguous that the rule of lenity requires resolving the ambiguity in Villegas' favor. However, ... I do not think the [CWA] is ambiguous with respect to an individual physically disposing of medical wastes, in quantity, directly into navigable waters, by means of a controllable, discrete conveyance and course of action. As the Supreme Court has noted,

> [b]ecause the meaning of language is inherently contextual, we have declined to deem a statute 'ambiguous' for purposes of lenity merely because it was possible to articulate a construction more narrow than that urged by the Government.... Instead we have always reserved lenity for those situations in which a reasonable doubt persists about a statute's intended scope even after resort to 'the language and structure, legislative history, and motivating policies' of the statute.

Moskal v. United States, 498 U.S. 103, 108 (1990).

.... I think it plain enough that Congress intended the statute to bar corporate officers from disposing of corporate waste into navigable waters by hand as well as by pipe. Further, ... this is not a case in which the defendant had no fair warning that his actions were illegal. No compliance attorney here could have struggled with the difficulty of deciding whether this was activity for which a permit should be sought, as might be the case in a factory dealing with runoff that arguably was channeled and thereby transformed from nonpoint to point source pollution; rather, an attorney asked to advise Villegas whether his activity was permissible might say that there was as yet no case law indicating that such activity was point source pollution under the [CWA], but that such a view was certainly consistent with the Act and that the behavior would almost certainly be proscribed by that Act or some other.

Notes and Comments

1. Mr. Villegas did not dispute whether the blood vials were "pollutants" under the CWA. Would you have conceded this issue?

2. What exactly is the holding in *Plaza Health*? Would the court's approach allow individual homeowners to discharge sewage into rivers through pipes or ditches without fear of liability under the CWA? Would it, as Judge Oakes seemed to be concerned, allow industrial employees to discharge dioxin by the handful (presumably wearing gloves)? If not, how can this situation be distinguished from that of Mr. Villegas? Could a private individual discharge handfuls of paint thinner without fear of liability? If you think she can't do this under the CWA, what would you do about the litterer who tosses a gum wrapper off a bridge? Does the CWA distinguish between these two situations? If either both or neither of these individuals must be deemed to have committed a felony under the statute, how would that affect your analysis?

3. In *Earth Sciences* (cited by the dissent in *Plaza Health*), the defendant maintained several sumps (lined excavations) on the banks of a creek in Colorado to capture runoff from its mining activities. These sumps overflowed during a period of unusually high snow melt, spilling leachate into the creek. The court found that the sumps qualified as point sources despite the absence of a ditch or other conveyance between the sumps and the adjoining creek:

> Despite the large capacity (168,000 gallons for the reserve sump) we view this operation as a closed circulating system to serve the gold extraction process with no discharge. When it fails because of flaws in the construction or inadequate size to handle the fluids utilized, with resulting discharge, whether from a fissure in the dirt berm or overflow of a wall, the escape of liquid from the confined system is from a point source. Although the source of the excess liquid is rainfall or snow melt, this is not the kind of general runoff considered to be from nonpoint sources under the [CWA].

599 F.2d at 374. Similarly, in *Concerned Area Residents for the Environment v. Southview Farm*, 34 F.3d 114, 118 (1994) ("*Southview Farms*"), the Second Circuit held that an irrigation system qualified as a point source where it sprayed liquid manure onto a field in such quantities that the manure directly flowed into a stream. Do you agree with these analyses? If not, would you find jurisdiction in a situation in which a sewage treatment plant cut off its pipe such that its effluent landed a foot before the river bank, from which it then immediately flowed into the river? If you agree with *Earth Sciences* and *Southview Farms*, would you also find jurisdiction in a situation in which a golf course applies partially-treated sewage effluent to its fairways, with the result being that some of the pollutants are later carried into streams when it rains? What should be the operative principle in these types of cases?

4. In *Plaza Health*, the Second Circuit distinguished the cases the government had cited (including *Earth Sciences*) at least in part based on the fact that those earlier cases had arisen in a civil setting. Similarly in *Southview Farms*, Judge Oakes (now writing for a unanimous panel) distinguished *Plaza Health* as having been a criminal case which thus triggered the rule of lenity. 34 F.3d at 118. These distinctions may be too facile. In *United States v. Thompson/Center Arms Co.*, 504 U.S. 505, 112 S.Ct. 2102, 119 L.Ed.2d 308 (1992), a plurality of the Supreme Court applied the rule of lenity in a civil case involving a gun tax. Writing for the plurality, Justice Souter responded to the dissent's argument to the contrary in the following terms:

> Justice Stevens contends that lenity should not be applied because this is a "tax statute," rather than a "criminal statute." But this tax statute has criminal applications, and we know of no other basis for determining when the essential nature of a statute is "criminal." Surely, Justice Stevens cannot mean to suggest that in order for the rule of lenity to apply, the statute must be contained in the Criminal Code. Justice Stevens further suggests that lenity is inappropriate because we construe the statute today " 'in a civil setting,' " rather than a "criminal prosecution." The rule of lenity, however, is a rule of statutory construction whose purpose is to help give authoritative meaning to statutory language. It is not a rule of administration calling for courts to refrain in criminal cases from applying statutory language that would have been held to apply if challenged in civil litigation.

504 U.S. at 517 n.10. Many lower courts have applied lenity in the context of civil penalty actions. This, of course, raises the question whether there is sufficient ambiguity to give rise to lenity concerns in situations like those present in *Earth Sciences* and *Southview Farms* (or, in any Circuit other than the Second, even *Plaza Health*-type situations). How would you resolve these issues?

5. In *Babbitt v. Sweet Home Chapter of Communities for a Great Oregon*, 515 U.S. 687, 703–704 n.18, 115 S.Ct. 2407, 132 L.Ed.2d 597 (1995), the Supreme Court made clear that agencies can eliminate lenity concerns by promulgating rules that resolve statutory ambiguities. Should EPA revise its regulatory definition of "point source" to address the issues posed in some or all of these cases? If EPA were to do revise its definition to indicate that humans may qualify as point sources, would that solve the *"Plaza Health* problem" (assuming you think the result in that case is problematic)?

6. In response to *NRDC v. Costle* (discussed in the notes following *Catskill*, above), Congress amended the definition of "point source" to specifically exclude "agricultural stormwater discharges and return flows from irrigated agriculture." 33 U.S.C. § 1362(14). In *Southview Farms*, the Second Circuit deemed these exemptions inapplicable in that case because (1) even those discharges that occurred on rainy days were not the result of (but merely coincided with) the rainfall; and (2) the spraying of the manure was at volumes that were well beyond the agronomic rates that could be beneficial to crop production. 34 F.3d at 120–123.

7. In *League of Wilderness Defenders v. Forsgren*, 309 F.3d 1181 (9th Cir. 2002), the court found that the aerial application of insecticides from a plane satisfied the "point source" requirement.

III. THE FEDERAL/STATE RELATIONSHIP

When Congress revamped its approach to pollution control in the early 1970s, it had a decision to make: Should it turn these new programs entirely over to the newly-created EPA, or should it give the States the option of staying involved in significant ways. Congress chose the latter option, setting up a federal/state model that has come to be known as "cooperative federalism." Although Congress first created this model when it passed the Clean Air Act in 1970, we will address it in the most depth here in our discussion of the NPDES program, and will then only touch on some differences that apply under the Clean Air Act and the Resource Conservation and Recovery Act (RCRA) when we turn our attention to those statutes.

One of the express policies of the CWA is to "recognize, preserve, and protect the primary responsibilities of States to prevent, reduce, and eliminate pollution...." 33 U.S.C. § 1251(b). Congress implemented this policy in two main ways. First, it empowered the States to assume primary responsibility for the day-to-day implementation of the NPDES program. 33 U.S.C. § 1342(b). And second, it reserved to the States the primary role in establishing water quality standards. 33 U.S.C. § 1313. We will address the second of these roles when we consider the water quality-based mandates of the Act. Presently, we will consider how EPA and the States work together in implementing the NPDES program.

Taking part in this scheme of "cooperative federalism" is optional on the part of the States. If a particular State chooses not to do so, EPA will administer the program within that jurisdiction. Currently, 45 of the 50 States are authorized to administer most elements of the NPDES program. http://cfpub2.epa.gov/npdes/statestats.cfm. The District of Columbia and U.S. territories such as Puerto Rico and Guam also are eligible to seek authorization status, see 33 U.S.C. § 1362(3), although only the Territory of the Virgin Islands is currently authorized. Additionally, Section 518(e) authorizes EPA to treat Indian tribes as States for NPDES purposes if they demonstrate the ability to carry out the program.

There are two steps to understanding how the cooperative federalism scheme works. First, assuming a given State opts to participate, one must understand what the State must do to become "authorized" to implement the NPDES program. And second, one must learn how EPA exercises oversight authority in authorized States.

A. How States Become Authorized

Section 402(b) establishes the minimum requirements a State must meet if it chooses to become "authorized" as the primary implementer of the NPDES program within its boundaries. Under this provision, EPA

ref. State most
meet

must approve a given State's application for authorization if it finds that it meets the relevant requirements. These include the ability to issue permits that will meet the same substantive standards that would apply if EPA were acting as the permit-issuer. 33 U.S.C. § 1342(b)(1). They also include requirements relating to the State's investigatory powers, the involvement of both the public and EPA in State permit-issuance processes, and the State's ability to bring enforcement actions. 33 U.S.C. § 1342(b)(2), (3) and (7). It should be noted these requirements constitute federal "floors," not federal "ceilings;" that is, the States are free to go beyond these minimum requirements in any respects. Indeed, Section 510 of the CWA sets forth an express non-preemption clause, indicating that, except as expressly provided, nothing in the Act should be read as limiting the States' ability to adopt or enforce more stringent standards.

Section 304(i) specifically charged EPA with writing rules fleshing out § 402(b)'s authorization requirements. EPA has done so in 40 C.F.R. Part 123. These rules track the statutory requirements by requiring the States to issue permits containing the same technology-and water quality-based requirements as would apply if EPA were issuing the permits. 40 C.F.R. § 123.25(15). Additionally, they set minimum requirements State must meet regarding public involvement in the permit issuance process and, to a lesser extent, the enforcement realm. 40 C.F.R. §§ 123.25(27)-(32) and 123.27(d), respectively. And third, EPA requires the States to have both civil and criminal enforcement powers, although it does not require these powers to be equivalent to those which it possesses under the CWA. 40 C.F.R. § 123.27.

Certain aspects of these rules were challenged in the following case:

NATURAL RESOURCES DEFENSE COUNCIL, INC. v. U.S. EPA

United States Court of Appeals, District of Columbia Circuit, 1988.
859 F.2d 156.

Before ROBINSON, STARR and WILLIAMS, Circuit Judges.

PER CURIAM:

Because of Congress's desire to "recognize, preserve, and protect the primary responsibilities and rights of States to prevent, reduce, and to eliminate pollution," 33 U.S.C. § 1251(b), the CWA provides for state assumption of the NPDES permit program. Id. § 1342(b). It specifies some prerequisites to states' assuming permitting responsibilities, id., authorizes the Administrator to supplement them, id. §§ 1361(a), 1314(i)(2), and requires him to approve a state's application once satisfied that these standards have been met, id. § 1342(b)....

1. *Regulatory Uniformity and State Autonomy.* Petitioners challenge two regulations implementing the Act's provisions on state assumption of the permit program. Citizens for a Better Environment (CBE) attacks the standards for minimum public participation at the state level. NRDC complains of the absence of state authority to impose

a given maximum penalty. Both protests rest on the assumption that congressional emphasis on uniformity was directed to procedural as well as substantive standards, and that as a result federal requirements respecting public participation and penalties must be mirrored on the state level.

Uniformity is indeed a recurrent theme in the Act, a direct manifestation of concern that the permit program be standardized to avoid the "industrial equivalent of forum shopping" and the creation of "pollution havens" by migration of dischargers to areas having lower pollution standards. The desired uniformity, however, is spoken of almost exclusively in relation to effluent limitations. Moreover, Congress' quest for homogeneity is in tension with its independent emphasis on state autonomy, which . . . is enshrined in the Act as the basic policy to "recognize, preserve, and protect the primary responsibilities and rights of States," and is the very foundation of the permit program. . . .

In fashioning its guidelines on both participation and penalties, EPA endeavored to reconcile the competing objectives of regulatory uniformity and state autonomy by establishing a floor for citizen participation and state enforcement authority, while ensuring that states have the maximum possible independence. We are fully mindful of the rule that an agency is entitled to special deference when it harmonizes competing policies. . . . *Chevron U.S.A. v. NRDC*, 467 U.S. 837, 845 (1984). . . .

2. *Public Participation.* CBE assails on two grounds EPA's regulations specifying the minimum level of public participation that states must afford. CBE first claims that the regulations are inadequate because they do not include all of the protections built into the federal permit program. Alternatively, it contends that they fail to provide any meaningful right.

The requirement of public participation in efforts to control water pollution is established in the congressional declaration of policy and goals of the Act:

> Public participation in the development, revision, and enforcement of any regulation, standard, effluent limitation, plan, or program established by the Administrator or any State under this chapter shall be provided for, encouraged, and assisted by the Administrator and the States. The Administrator, in cooperation with the States, shall develop and publish regulations specifying minimum guidelines for public participation in such processes.[27]

The statutory text does not, however, elaborate on the extent of public participation contemplated by Congress. The legislative history of the Act repeatedly echoes the desire "that its provisions be administered and enforced in a fishbowl-like atmosphere." CBE asserts that in Section

---

27. 33 U.S.C. § 1251(e). Section 1342(b)(3), (7) makes this requirement a prerequisite for state assumption of the permit program.

1365, which governs citizen suits, Congress spelled out the elements of the public participation envisioned. . . .[30]

As CBE insists, Congress considered the citizen suit provision to be of dual importance, serving both as a method of prodding the agency, and as a backup means of enforcing the Act. On the other hand, Congress also expressed reservations about potential abuses of citizen suits. . . . Nowhere in either the Act or its legislative history is there any express statement that the provisions of Section 1365 extend to states, nor do we find persuasive any equivocal intimation in that direction. It would have been very easy for Congress to say so if that was what it had in mind. . . .

Finally, we note that EPA maintains that "[n]othing in the Act or its legislative history indicates that Congress intended that states be required to provide identical rights to those Congress specified for citizens in Federal court." Because we have found that Congress has not directly addressed the precise question at issue, and determined that "the agency's answer is based on a permissible construction of the statute, we defer to EPA's reading." [Citing *Chevron*]. We therefore hold that state-level citizen suits are not commanded by the Act, and find no impropriety in the Administrator's failure to require state programs to afford them.

CBE asks that, should we decide that state public participation specifications need not match the federal requirements, we hold that the present regulations are incapable of producing meaningful public involvement. We decline this invitation. The pertinent regulations read:

> Any state administering a program shall provide for public participation in the State enforcement process by providing either: (1) Authority which allows intervention as of right in any civil or administrative action . . . by any citizen having an interest which is or may be adversely affected; or (2) Assurance that the State agency or enforcement authority will: (i) Investigate and provide written responses to all citizen complaints . . . ; (ii) Not oppose intervention by any citizen when permissive intervention may be authorized by statute, rule, or regulation; and (iii) Publish notice of and provide at least 30 days for public comment on any proposed settlement of a State enforcement action.

40 C.F.R. § 123.27(d) (1987).

We might be somewhat more hospitable to CBE's claim, especially with regard to the second option, were it not for two statements by EPA in interpreting the regulations. First, in promulgating the regulations

---

30. As characterized by CBE, the participation requisite at the state level would allow citizens to "(1) initiate an enforcement action against polluters in state court; (2) intervene as of right in any enforcement action brought by the state; (3) initiate an action in state court against an enforcement agency for failure to perform a nondiscretionary duty; and (4) recover litigation costs for participating in enforcement." Compare 33 U.S.C. § 1365 (1982). CBE demands as well access to information and judicial review of state-issued permits.

and again in its brief before this court, the agency indicated that the first option—provision of intervention as of right—called for state intervention rights similar to those accorded by the federal rules. . . .

More importantly, however, EPA asserted at oral argument that the second option, to the extent that it is based on a state's agreement not to oppose permissive intervention, will not be available in states that do not provide some means of intervention. This interpretation is critical to our decision to uphold the agency. Were the second option open where permissive intervention is impossible, public participation would be limited to that flowing from the state's agreement to respond to citizen complaints and to entertain citizen comments on proposed settlements of state enforcement actions—rights dismissed by the Seventh Circuit as "no more than a legalistic articulation of a common courtesy and hardly . . . satisfaction of the EPA's statutory duty to issue regulations promoting public participation in state enforcement." *Citizens for a Better Environment v. EPA*, 596 F.2d 720, 726 (7th Cir. 1979).

With this caveat, however, we conclude that the regulations, as interpreted, provide meaningful and adequate opportunity for public participation consistent with the statutory mandate. . . .

3. *Maximum Penalties*. Section 1319 . . . . specifies the penalties assessable on the federal level. . . . Civil penalties for permit violations are "not to exceed $25,000 per day for each violation." 33 U.S.C. § 1319(d).

States are required to have "adequate authority" "[t]o abate violations of the permit or the permit program, including civil and criminal penalties and other ways and means of enforcement." § 1342(b)(7). The Administrator was charged with the responsibility of fashioning guidelines defining the minimum enforcement provisions deemed adequate. Pursuant to this mandate, the Administrator promulgated the regulations here in question, which require state authority

> [t]o assess or sue to recover in court civil penalties and to seek criminal remedies, including fines, as follows: (i) Civil penalties . . . shall be assessable in at least the amount of $5,000 a day for each violation. . . .

40 C.F.R. § 123.27(3).

Petitioner NRDC contends that these regulations are invalid because they do not compel the states to provide authority to levy the maximum penalties assessable in federal enforcement programs.

Throughout its consideration of the Act, Congress reiterated the important role penalties play in enforcement of water pollution standards, and emphasized the need for substantial penalties, for example:

> [S]anctions under existing law have not been sufficient to encourage compliance. . . . Therefore, the Committee proposes to increase significantly the penalties. . . . [I]f the timetables established throughout the Act are to be met, the threat of sanction must be real, and enforcement provisions must be swift and direct.

In this articulation of congressional purpose, coupled with the congressional expectation that states would bear the primary enforcement burdens of the Act, NRDC would find a mandate for state ability and willingness to assess the federally required maximum penalties.

This challenge by NRDC exposes the same logical infirmity flawing the attack leveled by CBE. It presumes an unexpressed congressional intent that state requirements must mirror the federal ones, a presumption inconsistent with the elements of the statutory scheme limiting operation of the provisions to enforcement efforts at the national level and explicitly empowering the Administrator to set the prerequisites for state plans. Nothing in the Act or its legislative history supports a reduction of the Administrator's discretion to activity purely ministerial, ... and the Administrator's conclusion to the contrary is eminently reasonable.

The rationale EPA offers for its disinclination to adopt the statutory maxima also buttresses this conclusion. The proposed regulations would have required the states to exert enforcement authority virtually identical with the federal, including the same levels of minimum and maximum fines. In final structure, however, the regulations, changed largely in response to state comments, reflect the balancing of uniformity and state autonomy contemplated by the Act:

> The Agency has determined that it is necessary to set specific minimum levels of fines and penalties which States must have the authority to recover in order to ensure effective State enforcement programs. Without such minimum levels, EPA would often be forced to take its own enforcement action in approved States because the State action imposed inadequate penalties. Such EPA action, while available as a backup, is not intended to be relied upon as the prime enforcement mechanism in approved States. Accordingly, the Agency has set minimum levels of fines and penalties. However, it has reduced the levels below those available to EPA based on the large volumes of comments from states requesting such relief.

We will not disturb this reasonable accommodation of manifestly competing interests, and consequently we uphold the agency's penalty regulations.

Notes and Comments

1. Section 402(b) compels EPA to approve State programs meeting the minimum requirements established therein. Additionally, as previously mentioned, Section 510 expressly preserves the ability of the States to establish more stringent standards if they so choose. In accordance with these provisions, EPA's authorization regulations confirm that they do not preclude States from adopting or enforcing more stringent requirements or from operating a program with a broader scope of coverage. 40 C.F.R. § 123.1(i). EPA will never disapprove a State program because it is too strict. Indeed, it

lacks the power to do so. If a State program has a broader scope of coverage than required (if, for example, a State requires permits for runoff from nonpoint sources), EPA views those broader requirements as being effective solely as a matter of State law. 40 C.F.R. § 123.1(i)(2).

2. What was the distinction that the *NRDC* court drew between effluent limitations, on the one hand, and the public participation and enforcement matters raised by CBE and NRDC, on the other? Reread § 402(b). Is there a statutory basis for this distinction? What policy reasons might Congress have had for requiring uniformity in the former realm but not in the others? In support of its argument that state-level citizen suits were required, CBE cited §§ 101(e), 402(b)(3) and (7), and 505. Do you agree with the court's conclusions regarding the effect of these provisions? If EPA had compelled the States to provide for state-level citizen suits as a precondition to authorization, would either the States or Industry have been able to resist this requirement?

3. Exactly what public participation rights did EPA require States seeking authorization to provide citizens in the enforcement process? Does this mandate seem reasonable in light of the policy directives in § 101(e)? What is the effect of requiring States not to oppose motions for permissive intervention? Was the court justified in relying on the explanatory statement EPA made at oral argument? What did the court suggest it would have done if EPA had only mandated that States respond to citizen complaints and entertain citizen comments on proposed settlements? Do you agree with the court's suggestion on this point?

4. Strangely, the *NRDC* court never mentioned that citizens have a federal cause of action against alleged violators under § 505(a)(1), even in authorized States. Does the availability of this federal cause of action change your view regarding the significance of EPA's having declined to compel the States to provide for state-level citizen suits?

5. As we will see in chapter 6, EPA has an array of administrative, civil judicial and criminal enforcement options available to it under § 309 of the CWA. These authorities apply even in authorized States. See 33 U.S.C. § 1342(i). Despite this ongoing federal authority, and in line with § 402(b)(7), EPA has required States to have both civil and criminal penalty authorities as a precondition to receiving authorization. As indicated by that portion of the *NRDC* decision addressing civil penalties, EPA has not required the States to have equivalent penalty authorities. Nor has it required the States to have any administrative enforcement powers; that is, EPA does not mandate that States have the power to compel compliance and/or impose fines without having to go the court. As seen in 40 C.F.R. § 123.37(3), EPA requires the States to have *either* the right to assess penalties or to seek them in court.

6. What does it mean to require that civil penalties be "assessable in at least the amount of $5,000 a day?" Why was NRDC dissatisfied with this requirement? Why were its arguments unavailing? What explanation did EPA offer for declining to require more? Were you persuaded? Do you agree that EPA's explanation at least passes *Chevron* muster? How should the fact that EPA retains enforcement authority in authorized States factor into this analysis?

B. EPA Oversight

Upon authorization, the relevant State takes the lead role in the day-to-day implementation of the NPDES program. It issues the permits, receives the dischargers' monitoring reports (known as "discharge monitoring reports" or "DMRs"), undertakes most inspections and, in the event of noncompliance, initiates most enforcement actions.

This is not to say, however, that EPA becomes inert after approving a given State's program. Instead, EPA shifts into an oversight mode. This oversight has some aspects that are discharger-specific and others that are more programmatic. With respect to specific dischargers, section 402(d)(1) specifically requires each State to transmit to EPA a copy of each permit application, and to provide EPA with a copy of any draft permit. Section 402(d)(2) precludes the State from issuing the permit if within 90 days EPA objects to it as being "outside the guidelines and requirements of the [Act]." Thus, EPA can effectively "veto" State permits. EPA also has an ongoing role in overseeing compliance matters. The State must keep EPA abreast of any instances of noncompliance. 40 C.F.R. § 123.45. Additionally, EPA retains its full investigatory powers under § 308 and its full enforcement powers under § 309. See, e.g., 33 U.S.C. § 1342(i). Accordingly, while EPA tends to defer to the States on most enforcement matters, this is largely a matter of EPA self-restraint. It has the statutory ability to step in and take the enforcement lead in particular cases if it so chooses.

On a more programmatic level, EPA can and does review how the State is implementing its program. This includes but transcends patterns that may be evident in how the State handles numerous permitting or enforcement matters. Additionally, for example, EPA will want to ensure that the State has an appropriate inspection strategy. It will also want to ensure that the State does not alter its program such that it no longer meets the authorization requirements. EPA has the ability to revoke State authorization if it finds that the State program, or the State's administration thereof, no longer meets the relevant requirements. 33 U.S.C. § 1342(c)(3).

We will now consider a second excerpt from the *NRDC* case. This excerpt addresses the scope of the power that EPA reserved to itself to veto State permits. As we will see, EPA has essentially reserved the ability to second-guess any and all decisions made by the States in issuing permits. One might wonder why EPA views this prerogative as being so important. The answer inheres in both the nature of the decisions that are made by permit-issuers, and the legal effect of those decisions, once made. While many of the decisions made in issuing a particular permit are straightforward (e.g., imposing the appropriate technology-based requirements in situations in which EPA has previously established the standards for that industry through rulemaking), others are much more judgmental. These include, for example, setting the appropriate water quality-based requirements (see 40 C.F.R. § 122.44(d)) and establishing the appropriate frequency for the monitoring and reporting requirements (see 40 C.F.R. § 122.44(i)). Less commonly (but as discussed in the following case), they can also include setting the appropriate technology-based limits in situations in which EPA has not previously set them.

The importance of these decisions (and thus, in EPA's view, of its oversight) is due to § 402(k), which creates what is referred to as a "permit shield." To paraphrase, that provision indicates that, for most purposes, compliance with an NPDES permit is deemed to be compliance with the CWA; the permit is conclusively presumed to contain all of the relevant requirements imposed under the Act. Even if the CWA or EPA's regulations otherwise contemplate that a discharger should be subject to additional or more stringent requirements, those requirements will be inapplicable if they are omitted or weakened in the discharger's permit. This, obviously, underscores the importance of ensuring that the permit "gets it right."

In this context, consider the following excerpts from the *NRDC* opinion:

NATURAL RESOURCES DEFENSE COUNCIL, INC. v. U.S. EPA

United States Court of Appeals, District of Columbia Circuit, 1988.
859 F.2d 156.

Before ROBINSON, STARR and WILLIAMS, Circuit Judges.

PER CURIAM:

[EPA promulgated 40 C.F.R. § 123.44(c), specifying six types of permit defects that would justify the exercise of its veto power. Industry challenged two of these, including subsection 6, in which EPA asserted its authority to veto a proposed permit if, in the absence of formally promulgated effluent limitations, the proposed permit fails in EPA's judgment to comport with the Act or regulations promulgated thereunder.]

In Industry's view, the sole basis for rejecting a proposed permit by virtue of improper effluent limits is if those limits are set pursuant to formally promulgated effluent limitations guidelines under section 1314(b). That section requires EPA to promulgate, pursuant to formal notice-and-comment rulemaking, guidelines ... to be used in setting effluent limits in particular permits....

Industry argues that these § 1314(b) guidelines are the "guidelines and requirements" referred to in § 1342(d). The agency may not, in Industry's view, reject permits based on noncompliance with effluent guidelines unless those limitations are set pursuant to § 1314, ...

Although it is consistent with some fragments of the statutory language, Industry's interpretation ultimately proves too much, and thus must be rejected as inconsistent with the structure of the Act. Section 1342(a)(1) requires EPA, in approving permits in the absence of formally promulgated effluent limitations guidelines, to exercise its best professional judgment (BPJ) as to proper effluent limits. When issuing permits according to its BPJ, EPA is required to adhere to the technology-based standards set out in § 1311(b). This is so despite the fact that EPA has not yet rigorously defined these standards through notice-and-comment rulemaking.

States issuing permits pursuant to § 1342(b) stand in the shoes of the agency, and thus must similarly pay heed to § 1311(b)'s technology-based standards when exercising their BPJ. Thus, notwithstanding Industry's contrary assertions, States are required to compel adherence to the Act's technology-based standards regardless of whether EPA has specified their content pursuant to § 1314(b). Accordingly, EPA contends that it may veto state permits that, in its estimation, fail to comply with § 1311's dictates.

In response, Industry asserts that even if a State must use its best professional judgment to comply with the § 1311(b) standards, its substantive decisions as to what constitutes BAT, BPT, et al., are subject to EPA veto only if inconsistent with nationally promulgated guidelines. In other words, EPA's interpretation of what § 1311(b) requires becomes an independent requirement of the Act only when determined pursuant to § 1314(b). Industry argues that its interpretation preserves Congress' intentional balance of federalism and uniformity: While state-issued permits must comply with formally promulgated national guidelines, in the absence of such guidelines ad hoc federal judgments cannot trump their ad hoc state counterparts. Under a contrary view, Industry contends, EPA would be able to roam freely, unconstrained by standards and at liberty to reject state-issued permits.

The battle lines are thus sharply drawn. Unfortunately, the express terms of § 1342(d) do not provide a ready answer to the interpretive question before us. The crucial language, "guidelines and requirements," fails conclusively to support either side's view. . . .

Industry's reading of the legislative history focuses broadly on Congress' intent that States play the primary role in administering the Act. As to that general proposition there can be no reasonable doubt. But the general, pro-federalism thrust of the statutory regime does not manifest itself in the legislative history in helpfully specific ways as to the issue at hand: whether in the absence of formally promulgated effluent limitations guidelines, EPA can veto state permits on the basis of inadequate effluent limits. . . .

As to the scope of the veto authority, it is ultimately unhelpful to fall back to general principles of federalism, for those principles, however important to our polity, do not answer the specific question at hand. Contrary to Industry's unflattering characterizations, EPA's oversight of state permits is not ad hoc, nor is the agency's discretion unfettered. The requirement articulated in section 1342(a)(1) that the factors listed in sections 1311 and 1314 be considered operates as a significant check on the agency's discretion.

In sum, the Act envisions a significant role for the States in its administration, but nothing in the legislative history indicates Congress' intent on the issue at hand. Contrary to Industry's assertions, EPA's discretion is constrained under the Act; so long as the agency exercises its veto power "judiciously," the veto regulations are not at odds with Congress' view of abiding principles of federalism. And it goes without saying that we are not confronted, in this global challenge to EPA's regulations, with a specific action by federal authorities that is seen by Industry as riding roughshod over the felt interests of a particular State. Finally, we cannot but observe that Industry is in the odd role of seeking to carry on a reverse sort of parens patriae role, attending to the interests of the several States, when the States themselves have not seen fit (at least in litigation) to call the veto regulation into question. Like Congress itself, the States have been silent on the point.

Next, we consider the structure of the Act. Industry points out that the Act is premised on shared state and federal authority, and that the veto regulations, in authorizing ad hoc federal rejection of state permits, gut this carefully crafted structure. . . .

But, again, the fact that the structure of the Act envisions that States will play a primary role under the Act does not mean that the agency's veto regulations go beyond what the statute permits. For, as we have seen, the Act undeniably provides some veto authority; the question is how much (or by what standard the authority is to be exercised). Industry can point to nothing in the Act that would reasonably lend itself to delimiting the bounds of the veto authority. . . . Absent such a showing, relying on the pro-federalism bent of the Act's structure does not, for reasons already stated, get us very far in resolving a highly specific question of statutory interpretation. Moreover, the veto regulations are not, as Industry would have it, "totally at odds with the principles of federalism embodied in the statute." Congress could not have intended, as Industry prefers, in all cases for state judgments about the proper conditions for permits to take precedence; the very presence of veto authority over individual permits belies this rather hard view of federalism principles.

EPA, on the other hand, mounts what seem to us more persuasive arguments based on the statute's structure. First, nowhere in the Act is there an indication that Congress intended that promulgation of . . . effluent limitations guidelines would be a precondition for vetoing state permits. . . .

In addition, EPA argues that Industry's position may lead to results that would violate the Act. . . . Under Industry's view, . . . until EPA has promulgated national guidelines setting forth its view of § 1311(b)'s technology-based requirements, the agency is powerless to supplant a state permitting authority's judgment of whether a particular permit meets the technology-based standards. From this, as EPA emphasizes, States would be able (under Industry's view) to approve permits that plainly violate section 1311(a)—the Act's bedrock prohibition of pollutant discharges—and the federal authority must nonetheless stand help-lessly aside, awaiting the uncertain coming of national effluent limita-tions guidelines. Cf. S. Beckett, Waiting for Godot.

This is the sort of situation (although admittedly stated in the extreme) that the Act's veto provision . . . was designed to address. EPA persuasively argues that . . . section 1342(d)'s veto authority provides considerable evidence that Congress intended federal minima (even if crafted on the basis of BPJ) to take precedence. In short, the several States are to be centrally involved in the Act's administration, but their involvement is to be in the achievement of federal goals. By virtue of Congress' policy decision to allow EPA to approve federal permits based on the Administrator's best professional judgment, it is consonant with that policy to allow a similar power with respect to vetoing state permits. Rejection of a state permit in the latter situation represents no more an ad hoc judgment than approval of a federal permit in the former.

[The court went on to conclude that, at a minimum, EPA's interpre-tation of its veto authority was reasonable and, thus, to be upheld under *Chevron*.]

Notes and Comments

1. Section 402(a)(1) itself does not use the term "best professional judgment." Instead, it requires EPA, when issuing permits before the relevant national standards have been set, to impose such conditions as it "determines are necessary to carry out the provisions of the [Act]." In its implementing regulations, EPA interpreted this as requiring a case-by-case determination pursuant to which the permit issuer is to try to anticipate what the national standards will be when they emerge. 40 C.F.R. § 125.3(c)(2). Elsewhere, EPA denominates this a "best professional judg-ment" (or "BPJ") determination. See, e.g., 40 C.F.R. § 125.3(a)(2)(i)(B). Elsewhere still, it requires authorized States to undertake this analysis when issuing permits. See 40 C.F.R. §§ 122.44(a)(1) and 123.25(a)(15).

2. Do you agree that section 402(d)(2) is unclear at to whether EPA may veto permits when it disagrees with a State's BPJ determination? If so, why didn't the court resolve the ambiguity by resort to the pro-federalism policies expressed in § 101(b)? What did the court mean when it said that Industry's argument "prove[d] too much?" Do you agree? Might there have been countervailing environmental benefits if the court had accepted Indus-try's position?

3. Might the court have viewed the issue in *NRDC* differently if the States had been the ones challenging EPA's regulations? Should Industry even have had standing to raise this challenge?

4. While section 402(d) empowers EPA to veto State permits, it does not on its face compel EPA to veto even blatantly deficient permits. Section 402(e) goes so far as to allow EPA to waive its review authority with respect to categories of point sources. See also 40 C.F.R § 123.24(d). As alluded to in *NRDC* (with the citation omitted), the legislative history suggests that Congress intended EPA to use its veto authority "judiciously." Should courts be able to review EPA decisions regarding whether to veto state permits?

When thinking about this question, keep in mind what happens after EPA's decision. If EPA declines to veto, the State then makes a final decision on the permit, which would then be subject to challenge (by either citizens and/or the applicant) in State court. EPA requires the States, as a precondition to authorization, to provide such a right of review. 40 C.F.R. § 123.30. If EPA vetoes a State permit, on the other hand, the State has the option either of revising the permit to meet EPA's objection or of having the permit issuance decision revert to EPA. See 33 U.S.C. § 1342(d)(4). How should these dynamics affect the availability of federal review regarding EPA's veto decisions? Compare *Save the Bay, Inc. v. Administrator of EPA*, 556 F.2d 1282 (5th Cir. 1977) (denying review in the federal Courts of Appeal regarding EPA's decision not to veto a State-issued permit, but suggesting that district court review might be available in at least some situations), and *American Paper Institute, Inc. v. U.S. EPA*, 890 F.2d 869 (7th Cir. 1989) (denying Court of Appeals review of an EPA veto where the State ultimately issued a permit meeting EPA's concerns). Is State court review adequate in these contexts? Is EPA's decision whether to veto a "final agency action?" If EPA's decision not to veto a State permit may be reviewable in some cases, by what standards would that decision be judged?

5.   As mentioned in the prior note, EPA requires the States to allow for judicial review of their permitting decisions as a precondition to authorization. While this requirement was not challenged in *NRDC*, its legality may be open to question. In *American Forest and Paper Ass'n v. U.S. EPA*, 137 F.3d 291 (5th Cir. 1998), the Fifth Circuit held that EPA cannot impose authorization requirements beyond those contemplated in § 402(b). It rejected EPA's argument that Section 304(i) allows it to supplement those requirements. Id. at 297–298. Read these two provisions. Do you agree with the Fifth Circuit? If so, do you find any basis in § 402(b) for the judicial review requirement contained in 40 C.F.R. § 123.30?

IV. SUBSTANTIVE STANDARDS

Sections 402(a) requires EPA, when it issues NPDES permits, to ensure that they comply with specified sections of the Act, including §§ 301, 306 and 307. As contemplated in § 402(b), EPA's regulations require authorized States to do the same. See 40 C.F.R. §§ 122.44 and 123.25. Sections 301, 306 and 307 establish a series of technology-based requirements applicable to various categories of dischargers. Additionally, Section 301(b)(1)(C) requires permit issuers to establish more stringent requirements where necessary to ensure compliance with water quality standards. Seen in this light, the statute is best viewed as taking a technology-first approach; that is, it relies on technology-based standards as a first resort in trying to achieve the statute's water quality goals. It does not entirely forsake a water quality-based approach, however. Instead, it relegates this approach to backup status, to be used when technology-based standards may not by themselves achieve compliance with water quality standards.

A. Technology–Based Standards

The CWA imposes different technology-based standards on different types of dischargers. Industrial dischargers who discharge directly into our nation's waters (referred to as "direct dischargers") are subject to one set of requirements. We will focus primarily on these standards below. Sewage treatment plants (generally referred to as "publicly owned treatment works" or "POTWs") are subject to another set of standards. See 33 U.S.C. § 1311(b)(1)(B). Industrial dischargers who discharge into sewage treatment systems (referred to as "pretreaters") are subject to yet a third set of standards. See 33 U.S.C. § 1317(b) and (c).

(margin note: Old discharger Standards)

Within the realm of direct dischargers, the CWA distinguishes between existing and new dischargers. For existing dischargers, the CWA established a phased approach pursuant to which dischargers were first required to install the best practicable control technology ("BPT") by 1977, 33 U.S.C. § 1311(b)(1), and then, generally speaking, the best available control technology that is economically achievable ("BAT") by 1983. Congress twice extended the timeline by which BAT had to be achieved, eventually settling on 1989 as the final deadline. See 33 U.S.C. § 1311(b)(2). New dischargers, by contrast, have to comply with what is, at least in theory, an even more demanding technology-based standard, the "best available demonstrated control technology" ("BADT"), which is sometimes alternatively referred to as the "new source performance standard" ("NSPS"). See 33 U.S.C. § 1316(a) and (b).

(margin note: New discharger standards)

The CWA was ambiguous on the question of who was supposed to set some of these standards. Section 304(b) clearly contemplated that EPA would establish "effluent limitation guidelines" that would inform the establishment of the actual effluent limitations. It did not clearly indicate, however, who would set the actual limitations that applied to individual dischargers. Instead, Section 301(b) merely indicated that the relevant standards were to "be achieved." This begged the question whether the States were bound to apply uniform standards established by EPA on an industry-by-industry basis, or, alternatively, whether they (the States) were in charge of setting the actual effluent limitations, with EPA's guidelines to serve as a mere reference point in their analysis. Resolving a split in the Circuits, the Supreme Court resolved this issue in *E.I. du Pont v. Train*, 430 U.S. 112, 97 S.Ct. 965, 51 L.Ed.2d 204 (1977), holding that EPA has the power to set industry-by-industry effluent limitations.

Although the following case addresses the BPT requirements that have now been displaced by BAT requirements for most pollutants, we include it because it contains one of the best discussions of some of the fundamental issues involved in the establishment of technology-based standards:

WEYERHAEUSER CO. v. COSTLE

United States Court of Appeals, Dist. of Columbia Circuit, 1978.
590 F.2d 1011.

McGOWAN, Circuit Judge:

To make paper from trees is an old art; to do it without water pollution is a new science. In papermaking, logs or wooden chips must be ground up or "cooked" in one of several processes until only cellulose pulp is left. The pulp is bleached and made into various types and grades of paper. The cooking solutions and wash water that are left contain a variety of chemicals produced during "cooking" and other processes, including acids and large quantities of dissolved cellulose-breakdown products. Indeed, in some pulping processes, more of the wood is discarded in the waste water than is used to make paper. EPA has selected three parameters for measuring the pollutant content of the industry's effluent, all of which have been used extensively in this and other industries' measurements: total suspended solids (TSS), biochemical oxygen demand (BOD), and pH. TSS reflects the total amount of solids in solution, while BOD reflects the amount of biodegradable material in solution, and pH measures the acidity of the solution.

EPA has divided this segment of the industry into 16 subcategories, and further subdivided it into 66 subdivisions, for the purposes of its rulemaking effort.... [O]f the 16 subcategories in the whole industry, only three the three that use some form of the "sulfite process" have evoked particularized challenges. The reaction of sulfite mill operators stems from the limitations' greater economic impact on them. That impact in turn results from the fact that the sulfite process creates one of the highest pollution loads of any industrial process, and certainly the highest within the pulping industry....

Some of the paper mills that must meet the effluent limitations under review discharge their effluents into the Pacific Ocean. Petitioners contend that the ocean can dilute or naturally treat effluent, and that EPA must take this capacity of the ocean ("receiving water capacity") into account in a variety of ways.[40] They urge what they term "common sense," *i.e.*, that because the amounts of pollutant involved are small in comparison to bodies of water as vast as Puget Sound or the Pacific Ocean, they should not have to spend heavily on treatment equipment, or to increase their energy requirements and sludge levels, in order to treat wastes that the ocean could dilute or absorb.[41]

40. Some petitioners contend that EPA should have taken receiving water capacity into account in setting pollutant parameters. They argue that the Agency should not have considered BOD as such a parameter because the ocean has so much dissolved oxygen that wastes with high BOD have negligible impact and that it should not have considered pH as a parameter because ocean salts buffer waste acidity. Other petitioners contend that EPA should have taken receiving water capacity into account in subcategorization. They argue that ocean-discharging plants are in a wholly different stance from other plants and should be in a separate subcategory. It is also urged that EPA should be forced to give variances for ocean-discharging plants. Finally, the argument for taking receiving water capacity into account is sometimes couched in terms of an environmental balancing test: since there is no environmental "credit" for preventing discharges that the oceans could treat, and there is an environmental "debit" for the air pollution and sludge disposal problems incident to treatment, the balance should tilt in favor of ocean-discharging plants. We regard all the contentions as equivalent in their crucial component that Congress intended to let EPA take receiving water capacity into account.

41. Apart from this simple "common sense" version of the argument, there is a

EPA's secondary response to this claim was that pollution is far from harmless, even when disposed of in the largest bodies of water. As congressional testimony indicated, the Great Lakes, Puget Sound, and even areas of the Atlantic Ocean have been seriously injured by water pollution.... In the main, however, EPA simply asserted that the issue of receiving water capacity could not be raised in setting effluent limitations because Congress had ruled it out....

The earliest version of the [FWPCA] was passed in 1948 and amended five times before 1972. Throughout that 24 year period, Congress attempted to use receiving water quality as a basis for setting pollution standards. At the end of that period, Congress realized not only that its water pollution efforts until then had failed, but also that reliance on receiving water capacity as a crucial test for permissible pollution levels had contributed greatly to that failure. *EPA v. State Water Resources Control Board*, 426 U.S. 200, 202 (1976).

Based on this experience, Congress adopted a new approach in 1972. Under the Act, "a discharger's performance is ... measured against strict technology-based effluent limitations specified levels of treatment to which it must conform, rather than against limitations derived from water quality standards to which it and other polluters must collectively conform." *Id.* at 204–05.

This new approach reflected developing views on practicality and rights. Congress concluded that water pollution seriously harmed the environment, and that although the cost of control would be heavy, the nation would benefit from controlling that pollution. Yet scientific uncertainties made it difficult to assess the benefits to particular bodies of receiving water. Even if the federal government eventually could succeed at the task at which had failed for 24 years and thus could determine benefits and devise water quality standards, Congress concluded that the requisite further delay was too long for the nation to wait.

Moreover, by eliminating the issue of the capacity of particular bodies of receiving water, Congress made nationwide uniformity in effluent regulation possible. Congress considered uniformity vital to free the states from the temptation of relaxing local limitations in order to woo or keep industrial facilities. In addition, national uniformity made pollution clean-up possible without engaging in the divisive task of favoring some regions of the country over others.

More fundamentally, the new approach implemented changing views as to the relative rights of the public and of industrial polluters.

---

more sophisticated economic version called the "optimal pollution" theory. This economic theory contends that there is a level or type of pollution that, while technologically capable of being controlled, is uneconomic to treat because the benefit from treatment is small and the cost of treatment is large. *See generally* W. Baxter, People or Penguins: The Case for Optimal Pollution (1974). These economic theories are premised on a view that we have both adequate information about the effects of pollution to set an optimal test, and adequate political and administrative flexibility to keep polluters at that level once we allow any pollution to go untreated. As discussed in this section, it appears that Congress doubted these premises.

Hitherto, the right of the polluter was pre-eminent, unless the damage caused by pollution could be proven. Henceforth, the right of the public to a clean environment would be pre-eminent, unless pollution treatment was impractical or unachievable. The Senate Committee declared that "(t)he use of any river, lake, stream or ocean as a waste treatment system is unacceptable" regardless of the measurable impact of the waste on the body of water in question. Legislative History at 1425 (Senate Report). The Conference Report stated that the Act "specifically bans pollution dilution as an alternative to waste treatment." *Id.* at 284. This new view of relative rights was based in part on the hard-nosed assessment of our scientific ignorance: "we know so little about the ultimate consequences of injection of new matter into water that (the Act requires) a presumption of pollution ..." *Id.* at 1332 (remarks of Sen. Buckley). It also was based on the widely shared conviction that the nation's quality of life depended on its natural bounty, and that it was worth incurring heavy cost to preserve that bounty for future generations.

The Act reflects the new approach in a number of provisions.... [I]ts goal was *zero* discharge of pollutants by 1985, section 101(a), *not* discharges at acceptable or tolerable levels for receiving water.... In only one limited instance, thermal pollution, is receiving water capacity to be considered in relaxing standards, and the section allowing such consideration was drafted as a clear exception. Section 316(a). Otherwise, receiving water quality was to be considered only in setting "*more stringent*" standards than effluent limitations otherwise would prescribe. Section 301(b)(1)(C) of the Act (emphasis added).

The Act was passed with an expectation of "mid-course corrections," Legislative History, at 175 (statement of Sen. Muskie), and in 1977 Congress amended the Act, although generally holding to the same tack set five years earlier. Notably, during those five years, representatives of the paper industry had appeared before Congress and urged it to change the Act and to incorporate receiving water capacity as a consideration. Nonetheless, Congress was satisfied with this element of the statutory scheme. Except for a provision specifically aimed at discharges from "publicly owned treatment plants," section 301(h) of the Act, it resolved in the recent amendments to continue regulating discharges into all receiving waters alike.[49]

Our experience with litigation under the Act, and particularly with this case, emphasized the weight of Congress' policies. Even without receiving water capacity as an issue to delay it, EPA was late in promulgating these regulations. We have wrestled with the problem of

---

49. Further support for this interpretation may be found in section 304 of the Act. This provision requires EPA in setting limitations to balance cost and "effluent reduction benefits." Although the section specifies other factors to be considered as well, none relates to the effect of regulation on the treated or receiving waters. The phrase "effluent reduction benefits" avoids any suggestion that receiving water quality is an issue. Effluent reduction occurs whenever less effluent is discharged, i.e., whenever a plant treats its wastes before discharge, and the same degree of reduction occurs whether the discharge is into a small stream or the Pacific Ocean.

weighing technological imponderables and can understand the greater difficulties that would have arisen if the receiving water issues involving even greater imponderables had also been involved. . . .

TI's balancing argument

Petitioners also challenge EPA's manner of assessing two factors that all parties agree must be considered: cost and non-water quality environmental impacts. They contend that the Agency should have more carefully balanced costs versus the effluent reduction benefits of the regulations, and that it should have also balanced those benefits against the non-water quality environmental impacts to arrive at a "net" environmental benefit conclusion. Petitioners base their arguments on certain comments made by the Conferees for the Act, and on the fact that the Act lists non-water quality environmental impacts as a factor the Agency must "take into account."

In order to discuss petitioners' challenges, we must first identify the relevant statutory standard. Section 304(b)(1)(B) of the Act identifies the factors bearing on [BPT] in two groups. First, the factors shall

Factors that must be incl.

include consideration of the total cost of application of technology in relation to the effluent reduction benefits to be achieved from such application.

and second, they

other factors to consider

shall also take into account the age of equipment and facilities involved, the process employed, the engineering aspects of the application of various types of control techniques, process changes, non-water quality environmental impact (including energy requirements), and such other factors as the Administrator deems appropriate(.)

The first group consists of two factors that EPA must compare: total cost versus effluent reduction benefits. We shall call these the "comparison factors." The other group is a list of many factors that EPA must "take into account:" age, process, engineering aspects, process changes, environmental impacts (including energy), and any others EPA deems appropriate. We shall call these the "consideration factors." Notably, section 304(b)(2)(B) of the Act, which delineates the factors relevant to setting [BAT], tracks the [BPT] provision before us except in one regard: in the [BAT] section. All factors, including costs and benefits, are consideration factors, and no factors are separated out for comparison.

Cong mandated a limited balancing test

Based on our examination of the statutory language and the legislative history, we conclude that Congress mandated a particular structure and weight for the [BPT] comparison factors, that is to say, a "limited" balancing test.[52] In contrast, Congress did not mandate any particular

---

52. Senator Muskie described the "limited" balancing test:

The modification of subsection 304(b)(1) is intended to clarify what is meant by the term "practicable". *The balancing test between total cost and effluent reduction benefits* is intended to limit the appli-

cation of technology only where the additional degree of effluent reduction is *wholly out of proportion* to the costs of achieving such marginal level of reduction for any class or category of sources. Legislative History, at 170 (emphasis added).

structure or weight for the many consideration factors. Rather, it left EPA with discretion to decide how to account for the consideration factors, and how much weight to give each factor. [Therefore,] we conclude that, on the one hand, we should examine EPA's treatment of cost and benefit under the [BPT] standard to assure that the Agency complied with Congress' "limited" balancing directive. On the other hand, our scrutiny of the Agency's treatment of the several consideration factors seeks to assure that the Agency informed itself as to their magnitude, and reached its own express and considered conclusion about their bearing. More particularly, we do not believe that EPA is required to use any specific structure such as a balancing test in assessing the consideration factors, nor do we believe that EPA is required to give each consideration factor any specific weight.

Our conclusions are based initially on the section's wording and apparent logic. By singling out two factors (the comparison factors) for separate treatment, and by requiring that they be considered "in relation to" each other, Congress elevated them to a level of greater attention and rigor. Moreover, the comparison factors are a closed set of two, making it possible to have a definite structure and weight in considering them and preventing extraneous factors from intruding on the balance.

By contrast, the statute directs the Agency only to "take into account" the consideration factors, without prescribing any structure for EPA's deliberations. As to this latter group of factors, the section cannot logically be interpreted to impose on EPA a specific structure of consideration or set of weights because it gave EPA authority to "upset" any such structure by exercising its discretion to add new factors to the mix.... So long as EPA pays some attention to the congressionally specified factors, the section on its face lets EPA relate the various factors as it deems necessary.

Consequently, we must review the comparison factors to determine if EPA weighed them through the "limited" balancing test as intended by Congress. On the other hand, we may review the consideration factors only to determine if EPA was fully aware of them and reached its own express conclusions about them. Since the two type of factors are separate, we divide our discussion accordingly.

Petitioners ... challenge the [cost-benefit] analysis for the sulfite sector, contending that EPA used an "overall" instead of an "incremental" method of balancing, and that its figures on the cost of [BPT] for the dissolving sulfite subcategory were underestimates....

... [EPA] assessed the costs of internal and external effluent treatment measures, not only for the industry, but also for each subcate-

Costs

gory. This included a separate cost assessment for the sulfite subcategories. An economic analysis was prepared to determine the impact of the costs on the industry. It found that the industry as a whole would readily absorb the cost of compliance with [BPT], estimated at $1.6 billion. Out of 270 mills employing 120,000 people, eight mills would likely be closed and 1800 people laid off. The Agency noted that the impact on the three heavily polluting sulfite subcategories would be the greatest. Of less than 30 sulfite mills, three would probably close, resulting in 550 people being laid off.

Benefits

Against these costs, EPA balanced the main effluent reduction benefit: overall 5,000 fewer tons per day of BOD discharged into the nation's waters. EPA refined this balance by calculating the cost per pound of BOD removed for each subcategory. Although sulfite mills must make large investments in waste treatment facilities, the cost-benefit balance is favorable for the limitations on these mills, because of the large volume of waste they produce and thus the greater treatment efficiency.

Π's say need to do c/b @ each increment

Petitioners' first contention is that EPA not only should have calculated the overall cost-benefit balance, but also should have made an "incremental" calculation of that balance. More precisely, they contend that EPA must undertake to measure the costs and benefits of each additional increment of waste treatment control, from bare minimum up to complete pollution removal.... [T]hey point to Senator Muskie's description of cost-benefit balancing, which suggests a focus on the "additional degree" or "marginal" amount of effluent reduction....

... While EPA has no discretion to avoid cost-benefit balancing for its [BPT] standards, it does have some discretion to decide how it will perform the cost-benefit balancing task. "(E)ven with [BPT], the cost of compliance was not a factor to be given primary importance," [*American Iron & Steel Inst. v. EPA*, 526 F.2d 1027, 1051 (3d Cir. 1975)], and, as such, cost need not be balanced against benefits with pinpoint precision.

doing increments would take too lng

A requirement that EPA perform the elaborate task of calculating incremental balances would bog the Agency down in burdensome proceedings on a relatively subsidiary task. Hence, the Agency need not on its own undertake more than a net cost-benefit balancing to fulfill its obligation under section 304.

EPA does have to look @ incremental analysis if industry does it

However, when an incremental analysis has been performed by industry and submitted to EPA, it is worthy of scrutiny by the Agency, for it may "avoid the risk of hidden imbalances between cost and benefit." *Id.* at 1076 n. 19 (Adams, J., concurring). If such a "hidden imbalance" were revealed here, and if the Agency had ignored it, we might remand for further consideration. But in this case the incremental analysis proffered by industry showed that the last and most expensive increment of BOD treated in sulfite mills cost less than $.15 per pound of BOD removed, which is below the average cost of treatment in most of the industry's subcategories. We would be reluctant to find that EPA had ignored a "hidden imbalance" when the most unfavorable incremental cost-benefit balance that is challenged falls well within the range of averages for the industry as a whole. . . .

B.

"(N)on-water quality environmental impact(s) (including energy requirements)" are among the "consideration factors" listed in section 304, and are the sole factors of that kind on which petitioners premise a challenge to the limitations. . . . [T]he Act does not specify a particular structure for EPA's treatment of the consideration factors but instead leaves the Agency with discretion in deciding how they will be "taken into account." In exercising that discretion, it is clear that EPA devoted considerable attention to assessing environmental impact and adequately set forth its conclusions with respect thereto. Most crucially, . . . EPA developed estimates of the new energy demands for the industry as a whole about 2.4% of the industry's total energy use and for each industry subcategory. For the sulfite subcategories, with their higher waste loads requiring greater waste treatment, the figure was an 18% increase in energy demand. EPA also developed estimates of the sludge disposal problem, which is the reverse side of effluent reduction benefit, because the waste that is removed from effluent must be disposed of as sludge. We are consequently convinced that EPA took adequately into account the environmental impacts of its regulations.

Petitioners assert, however, that we must impose on EPA a further and special requirement to engage in environmental balancing. They cite allegedly dramatic examples of negative environmental impacts from the air pollution and sludge disposal incident to waste treatment, and contend that EPA failed to give these enough "weight" in the balance. . . .

Congress' intent in passing this legislation was obviously not to minimize the importance of protecting the environment . . . Rather, Congress was resolved to rely on EPA's own internal structure and personnel attitudes to ensure that the net result of all of its programs would be a substantially enhanced natural environment. . . .

That Section 304 requires EPA to "take into account" non-water quality environmental impacts, therefore, reflects several concerns apart from a fear that the Agency will have an inadequate commitment to protection of the air and land. Perhaps most important, if these factors were not listed, EPA arguably would have no authority to temper its effluent regulations when its own conclusion was that such tempering was needed to protect the land and air. While committing the Agency to lead a comprehensive attack on water pollution, Congress did not intend that attack to prevent the Agency from realizing its other environmental goals. . . .

Thus, since Congress intended EPA's internal structure to protect the non-water environment, the judicial function is completed when we have assured ourselves that EPA expressly considered the probable environmental impacts of its regulations. As we have noted, EPA fully

investigated the environmental impacts, and thereby fulfilled this aspect
of its statutorily mandated duty.

Notes and Comments

1.   As the D.C. Circuit suggests, one of the reasons Congress moved to a
technology-first approach in 1972 was the perceived failure of earlier water
quality-based approaches. The Supreme Court characterized this shift in the
following terms:

> . . . [T]he Amendments are aimed at achieving maximum "effluent
> limitations" on "point sources". . . . Such direct restrictions on discharg-
> es facilitate enforcement by making it unnecessary to work backward
> from an overpolluted body of water to determine which point sources are
> responsible and which must be abated.

EPA v. California ex rel State Water Resources Control Board, 426 U.S. 200,
204, 96 S.Ct. 2022, 2024, 48 L.Ed.2d 578 (1976). What other justifications
does the D.C. Circuit cite for the shift? Taken together, are these arguments
persuasive? Professor Houck has cited the action-forcing nature of this
approach as a principal reason for the CWA's success. See, e.g., Houck,
Recent Developments Under the Clean Water Act NPDES Program (Feb. 5,
1991).

William Pedersen levels at least three attacks on technology-based
approaches. First, he argues that, "by imposing the same requirements on
similar plants everywhere they run the risk of regulating too little to meet
water quality goals in some areas and more than necessary in others."
Pedersen, Turning the Tide on Water Quality, 15 Ecology L.Q. 69, 82 (1988).
In the latter instance, he maintains, the result is requirements that are
"strict beyond any rational link to environmental improvements." Id. at 83.
Pedersen also argues that technology-based requirements are inefficient
because they do not rationally allocate the costs of reaching the desired level
of pollutant-reduction:

> . . . Only rarely will the costs of restricting pollutant X in industry A to
> a specified level–as calculated by rulemaking immersed in the details of
> determining the proper technology-based controls for that industry—
> equal the costs of restricting pollutant X to the level specified by a
> similarly parochial rulemaking for industry B. Whenever these costs
> differ, the efficiency of pollution control for a given body of water will
> suffer to the extent that the overall reduction target could be met by
> substituting low-cost reductions at a plant in one industry for high-cost
> reductions at a plant in another.

Id. And third, Pedersen laments what he perceives as the illogic of an
approach that requires EPA to learn so much about so many categories of
industry:

> EPA has implemented "uniform" effluent standards since 1972, issuing
> separate technology-based control requirements for each of 500 different
> industries. Each guideline has required a major and expensive rulemak-
> ing. Most of the effort was spent on exploring, for EPA's education,
> details of the costs and achievable reductions for various technologies in
> the industry under consideration at the time the guideline was being

developed. That knowledge had only short-term value; it quickly became outdated with economic changes and the advance of technology. Moreover, the process demanded that EPA develop expertise in an impossibly wide variety of fields, duplicating knowledge already acquired by the industries involved. EPA's resources would have produced for more permanent social return had they been invested in expanding our understanding of the effects both of discharges on water quality and of water quality on health and welfare.

Id. at 85 (footnotes omitted). On balance, how would you evaluate the advantages and disadvantages of technology-based approaches?

2. What was the statutory basis for the D.C. Circuit's conclusion that EPA need not take receiving water capacity into account? Did the mills have any statutory language supporting their positions? What were their positions, precisely? Was this a case in which the statutory language permitted only one reading, or was there any room for interpretive leeway under *Chevron*? Put another way, if EPA had chosen to subcategorize based on receiving water capacity, might the court have upheld that position?

3. The D.C. Circuit's analysis of the "comparison factors" and the "consideration factors," and their relative roles in the establishment of BPT and BAT has been embraced by other Circuits. See, e.g., *National Ass'n of Metal Finishers v. EPA*, 719 F.2d 624, 664 (3d Cir. 1983) ("*NAMF*") (in determining BPT, EPA must compare costs and benefits at least to the extent of applying the "wholly disproportionate" test); *Association of Pacific Fisheries v. EPA*, 615 F.2d 794, 805 and 817–818 (9th Cir. 1980) ("*Pacific Fisheries*") (applying the "wholly disproportionate" test to BPT, but indicating that EPA need not compare costs and benefits in determining BAT), and *BP Exploration & Oil, Inc. v. U.S. EPA*, 66 F.3d 784, 796, *reh'g den.* (6th Cir. 1995) ("*BP Exploration*") (EPA has discretion to determine how much weight to give the BAT factors, because they are all consideration factors). In *NAMF*, the court did determine that EPA was required to do an incremental analysis in applying the "wholly disproportionate" test. 719 F.2d at 664; but see *BASF Wyandotte Corp. v. Costle*, 598 F.2d 637, 656 (1st Cir. 1979) (agreeing fully with *Weyerhaueser* on this score).

4. Note that the D.C. Circuit upheld EPA's BPT determination in *Weyerhaueser* despite EPA's concession that it might result in the closure of 3 out of 30 sulfite mills. This is consistent with *EPA v. National Crushed Stone Ass'n*, 449 U.S. 64, 83, 101 S.Ct. 295, 307, 66 L.Ed.2d 268 (1980), in which the Supreme Court concluded that "Congress anticipated that [BPT] would cause economic hardship and plant closings." In *NAMF*, the court upheld EPA's BPT determination despite the Agency's projection that it would result in the closing of 20% of the electroplating job shops, with a corresponding loss of 10,000 jobs. 719 F.2d at 663.

5. In theory, BPT should have little ongoing significance. By 1989 existing sources were to move to BAT for toxics and so-called "non-conventional" pollutants (such as ammonia, phosphorus, iron, and color), see 33 U.S.C. § 1311(b)(2)(A), (C), (D) and (F), and to a lesser second-level standard—best conventional technology ("BCT")—for so-called "conventional pollutants" (such as BOD, pH, and suspended solids), see 33 U.S.C. § 1311(b)(2)(A). In practice, however, EPA often sets BCT at the same level

as BPT. See, e.g., 63 Fed. Reg. 18504, 18534–18536 (for the bleached pulp industry). Thus BPT, in effect, lives on, at least for conventional pollutants.

6. Again, the acronym "BAT" is shorthand for the "best available technology" that is "economically achievable." 33 U.S.C. § 1311(b)(2)(A). Perhaps obviously, BAT is more demanding than BPT. In *Kennecott v. U.S. EPA*, 780 F.2d 445 (4th Cir. 1985), the court described the difference between the two standards in the following terms:

> ... EPA defines BPT as "the average of the best existing performance by plants of various sizes, ages and unit processes within each industrial category or subcategory. This average is not based upon a broad range of plants within an industrial category or subcategory, but is based upon performance levels achieved by exemplary plants." *EPA v. Nat'l Crushed Stone Ass'n,* 449 U.S. 64, 76 n. 15, 101 S.Ct. 295, 303 n. 15, 66 L.Ed.2d 268 (1980), quoting 39 Fed.Reg. 6580 (1974).

> In the second stage, Congress directed EPA to set an even more stringent standard, basing effluent limitations on [BAT]. [BAT] reflects the intention of Congress to use the latest scientific research and technology in setting effluent limits, pushing industries toward the goal of zero discharge as quickly as possible. In setting BAT, EPA uses not the average plant, but the optimally operating plant, the pilot plant which acts as a beacon to show what is possible.

780 F.2d at 448; see also *Chemical Manuf. Ass'n v. NRDC*, 470 U.S. 116, 155, 105 S.Ct. 1102, 1123, 84 L.Ed.2d 90 (1985) (Marshall, J., dissenting).

7. Section 304(b)(2) essentially establishes a two-step procedure for establishing BAT. First, § 304(b)(2)(A) requires EPA to identify "the degree of effluent reduction attainable through the application of the best control measures and practices achievable." And second, § 304(b)(2)(B) requires EPA, in determining the "best measure and practices available," to "take into account the age of the equipment and facilities involved, the process employed, the engineering aspects of the application of various types of control techniques, process changes, the cost of achieving such effluent reduction, non-water quality environmental impact (including energy requirements), and such other factors as [EPA] deems appropriate." Consistent with these provisions, the courts have required EPA to demonstrate that the relevant technology is both technologically available and economically achievable for the industry as a whole (although not for each individual plant). See, e.g., *Pacific Fisheries*, 615 F.2d at 816–820. As indicated in *Weyerhaueser*, however, the factors in § 304(b)(2)(B) track the BPT factors, but they are all "consideration factors." What does "economically achievable" for the industry mean? Presumably, EPA can impose standards here that cause just as many closures as its BPT standards (subject to the availability of the § 301(c) variance, discussed in n.11 below). But must it? See *National Wildlife Federation v. EPA*, 286 F.3d 554, 564–565 (D.C. Cir. 2002) (EPA did not act arbitrarily and capriciously in determining that a technology was not economically achievable where it would result in four plant closures, lost shipments of $1.3 billion, and 4,800 lost jobs). Under what circumstances, if any, should EPA be able to settle for less than the "best" technology (here referring solely to technology's ability to remove pollutants) that meets both of the above requirements (i.e., it is technologi-

cally available and economically achievable)? Does the fact that EPA can consider non-water quality impacts and "such other factors as [it] deems appropriate" suggest that it has the discretion to select something less than the "best" (again, just technologically speaking) technology? If so, how much? Compare *BP Exploration*, 66 F.3d at 796 ("the CWA's requirement that EPA choose the 'best' technology does not mean the chosen technology must be the best pollutant removal"), and *NRDC v. U.S. EPA*, 863 F.2d 1420, 1426 (9th Cir. 1988) ("[t]he legislative history of the Act supports our conclusion that EPA should not delay requiring technologically feasible limitations as BAT in order to wait for precise cost figures").

8. As mentioned new sources are required to meet an even higher standard: the "best available demonstrated control technology" ("BADT"), sometimes alternatively referred to as the "new source performance standard" ("NSPS"). 33 U.S.C. § 1316(a)(1). The statute defines the term "new source" to encompass any source, the construction of which is commenced after the date of the proposal of any new source standards for that industrial category. 33 U.S.C. § 1316(a)(2). EPA's rules do three interesting things. First, they define the term "source" to include "building[s]," "structure[s]" and "installations," thus indicating that an existing facility may sometimes be treated as a new source to the extent that, for example, new buildings with discharge points are being added. 40 C.F.R. § 122.2. Second, they establish criteria governing the circumstances under which this should be so. 40 C.F.R. § 122.29(b)(1). And third, they clarify that a source that commences construction while a proposed new source standard is pending will no longer be treated as a new source if EPA fails to adopt a final standard within 120 days of the proposal. Id.; see also 33 U.S.C. § 306(a)(1) and (b)(1)(B). On the last of these points, compare *NRDC v. U.S. EPA*, 822 F.2d 104, 112–114 (D.C. Cir. 1987), and *Pennsylvania Dept. of Environmental Res. v. EPA*, 618 F.2d 991, 999 (3d Cir. 1980).

9. As to the BADT standard itself, Section 306(a)(1) authorizes EPA to select a zero discharge standard "where practicable." Beyond that, Section 306(b)(1)(B) merely requires EPA to "take into consideration the cost of achieving such effluent reduction, and any non-water quality environmental impact and energy requirements." Even though the phraseology of this latter subsection is not fundamentally different from that fleshing out the BAT standard in § 304(b)(1)(B), EPA often finds that new sources, collectively, can afford to incorporate higher levels of technology. Can you venture a guess as to why this might be so?

10. EPA generally does not set "design standards," requiring the use of particular technologies. Instead, it sets "performance standards," determining how much pollutant-reduction the relevant technologies would achieve and requiring the dischargers to achieve those levels however they see fit. See, e.g., *Pacific Fisheries*, 615 F.2d at 814. Additionally, it should be noted that, for each individual discharger, the permit issuer (whether EPA or the State) translates EPA's effluent limitation guidelines into specific permit conditions, adjusting for variables such as water usage and rates of production.

11. The CWA provides a few limited relief valves from the above-described technology-based schemes. See, e.g., 33 U.S.C. § 301(c), (g) and

(n). The two most significant of these are probably the "fundamentally different factors" ("FDF") variance in § 301(n) and what we will call the "affordability variance" in § 301(c). To best understand the FDF variance, one must consider how technology-based standards are set. In setting these standards, EPA (or its contractor) studies the types of plants in each relevant industry, develops a "model plant," and then uses that model plant as a reference point in determining what levels of pollutant reduction a given level of control technology would achieve, and how much it would cost the industry to incorporate that technology. However, not every plant in that industry will resemble the model plant EPA uses in its analysis. If the differences are great, a given plant may have to expend much more money than EPA anticipated to incorporate the relevant technology (e.g., to buy more land to have room for the surface impoundments that EPA factored in to its wastewater treatment assumptions), or may even be unable to do so (e.g., if the neighbors won't sell the land). The Supreme Court further explained this logic in *Chemical Manuf. Ass'n v. NRDC*, 470 U.S. 116, 105 S.Ct. 1102, 84 L.Ed.2d 90 (1985):

> ... An FDF variance does not excuse compliance with a correct requirement, but instead represents an acknowledgment that not all relevant factors were taken sufficiently into account in framing that requirement originally, and that those relevant factors, properly considered, would have justified—indeed, required—the creation of a subcategory for the discharger in question. As we have recognized, the FDF variance is a laudable corrective mechanism, "an acknowledgement (sic) that the uniform ... limitation was set without reference to the full range of current practices, to which the Administrator was to refer." *EPA v. National Crushed Stone Assn.*, 449 U.S. 64, 77–78 (1980). It is, essentially, not an exception to the standard-setting process, but rather a more fine-tuned application of it.

Id. at 130, 105 S.Ct. at 1110. EPA first developed the FDF variance without express statutory authorization. Do you agree with its logic? After the Supreme Court essentially blessed EPA's variance in a series of opinions (including *National Crushed Stone* and *Chemical Manuf.*), Congress codified it in the Water Quality Act Amendments of 1987. See 33 U.S.C. § 1311(n). At the same time, Congress placed some interesting restrictions on its use. Take a careful look at § 301(n). What do you think of the limits contained therein? What, in particular, do you think of the effect of § 301(n)(6), which indicates that the discharger must comply with the nationally-uniform effluent limitations while its request for an FDF variance is pending?

12. Section 301(c) essentially creates a temporary variance that applies if an existing source cannot afford the upgrade from BPT to BAT. The Supreme Court explained this variance in *National Crushed Stone*:

> A § 301(c) variance ... creates for a particular point source a BAT standard that represents for it the same sort of economic and technological commitment as the general BAT standard creates for the class. As with the general BAT standard, the variance assumes that [BPT] has been met by the point source and that the modification represents a commitment of the maximum resources economically possible to the

ultimate goal of eliminating all polluting discharges. No one who can afford the best available technology can secure a variance.

Id. at 74–75, 101 S.Ct. at 302. Thus, while it is clear that the imposition of BPT can result in plant closings, the imposition of BAT should not. EPA can set the standard at levels that would otherwise put plants out of business, but individual facilities can avoid this effect by showing that they: (1) have made the maximum use of technology within their economic capability, and (2) have made "reasonable further progress" in going beyond BPT. 33 U.S.C. § 1311(c), *National Crushed Stone*, 449 U.S. at 75, 101 S.Ct. at 303.

13. Both the FDF and § 301(c) variances are only available to existing sources. Do you understand why this might be the case? Additionally, section 301(*l*) precludes the availability of the § 301(c) variance (but not the FDF variance) if a given source discharges toxics regulated under § 307(a)(1).

14. As mentioned, sources that discharge toxics are subject to BAT or BADT for existing and new sources, respectively. It is worth noting, however, this constitutes a change from the 1972 version of the statute. Originally, § 307 contemplated that EPA would establish health-based standards for toxic pollutants, which were to be both cost-and technology oblivious. EPA found this mandate difficult to implement, however, and made little progress with respect thereto. Ultimately, environmentalists sued EPA and the lawsuit resulted in what became known as the "Flannery decree" (named after the district court judge who signed it), under which the environmentalists, EPA and the industrial intervenors all basically agreed to jettison the health-based approach in favor of the by-then-familiar technology-based approach. See *Natural Resources Defense Council v. Train*, 6 Envtl. L. Rep. 20588 (D.D.C. 1976). Can you imagine why each of the three groups might each have been interested in such a settlement? Congress essentially codified this Decree when it revisited § 307 in the 1977 Amendments. Although § 307(a)(2) retains the possibility that EPA may set more stringent health-based standards where appropriate (as did the Flannery decree), EPA has not initiated any new rulemakings under this authority since 1977.

15. One of the great, unspoken weaknesses of the CWA is that there are no clear requirements for EPA to update the technology-based standards for each industry as technology improves. Instead, the statute appears to vest EPA with wide, perhaps even unfettered, discretion in this regard. See, e.g, 33 U.S.C. §§ 304(b) (requiring EPA to update its effluent limitation guidelines for BPT and BAT "if appropriate") and 306(b)(1)(B) (requiring EPA to update its NSPS standards "from time to time"). Compare 42 U.S.C. § 7412 (d)(6) (requiring EPA to update its technology-based standards for air toxics at least every 8 years). As a result, many of EPA's technology-based standards under the CWA have become stale over time.

A Brief Note on the Requirements for Other Categories of Dischargers

As alluded to earlier, the CWA has other control programs relating to different categories of dischargers. Two of the most prominent of these are the programs relating to publicly owned treatment works ("POTWs") and those industrial dischargers who discharge not directly into the nation's waters, but rather into POTW systems (alternately referred to as "pretreaters" or "indirect dischargers").

Section 301(b)(1)(B) requires POTWs to meet effluent limitations based on "secondary treatment." This actually requires a two-step process, involving both "primary" and "secondary" treatment. EPA has described these processes in laymen's terms as follows:

Primary treatment

> [In primary treatment,] screens and sedimentation tanks are used to remove most materials that float or will settle. Primary treatment removes about 30 percent of carbonaceous biochemical oxygen demand from domestic sewage.

Secondary treatment

> [Secondary treatment relies on bacteria to consume] the organic parts of the waste. It is accomplished by bringing together waste, bacteria, and oxygen in trickling filters or in the activated sludge process. This treatment removes floating and settleable solids and about 90 percent of the oxygen-demanding substances and suspended solids. Disinfection is the final stage of secondary treatment.

See http://environment.about.com/cs/glossary/a/glossary_index.htm. EPA has established numeric standards for secondary treatment at 40 C.F.R. § 133.102.

Under the 1972 version of the CWA, POTWs were required to eventually move to a higher degree of treatment referred to as "tertiary treatment." Congress, however, repealed this requirement in 1981. It should be noted, however, that some States require tertiary treatment as a matter of State law. It should also be noted that, like direct industrial dischargers, POTWs are subject to the edicts of § 301(b)(1)(C) in that their permits must contain more stringent requirements (i.e., more stringent than secondary treatment) where necessary to meet water quality standards.

Pretreaters are governed under § 307(b) through (e). In general, these provisions require EPA to subject pretreaters to technology-based requirements that are analogous to those which would apply if they were discharging directly into the waterways: the pretreatment standards for existing sources are to be akin to BAT, and the pretreatment standards for new sources are to be comparable to BADT. See, e.g., *National Ass'n of Metal Finishers v. EPA*, 719 F.2d 624, 633 and 644 (3d Cir. 1983). There are several differences, however, between the pretreatment and NPDES programs. First, pretreaters are not required to have NPDES permits. Instead, they are deemed not to be "discharg[ing] ... pollutants," within the meaning of § 301(a), because their discharges, at least as a preliminary matter, are into POTW systems instead of the nation's waters. See 40 C.F.R. § 122.2 (definition of "discharge of a pollutant"). Because they do not receive permits, pretreaters are regulated directly under the pretreatment standards: Section 307(d) simply states that it shall be unlawful for any pretreater to operate in violation of any such standard.

Second, the pretreatment program has some twists that are not present in the NPDES realm. One of these imposes two additional prohibitions (beyond the need to comply with the categorical standards): specifically, it prohibits pretreaters from discharging any pollutants that will either "pass through" the POTW or "interfere" with its operation. 33 U.S.C. § 1317(b); see also 40 C.F.R. § 403.5. The first of these prohibitions is most relevant for those pretreaters who are in an industry with respect to which EPA has not yet set categorical standards. The second, perhaps obviously, is intended to ensure that the pretreater doesn't discharge anything that will interfere with the POTW's ability to do its primary job, which is to treat sewage.

The other twist worth mentioning is potential availability of what are called "removal credits." The basic idea here that a pretreater should be able to able to have its own treatment requirements relaxed if it can convince the POTW to remove some of its pollutants for it. See 33 U.S.C. § 1317(b), and 40 C.F.R. § 403.7. Under this framework, for example, ten pretreaters who discharge into the same POTW system might band together to convince the POTW to incorporate an additional treatment technology so that they may all be subject to reduced requirements. Indeed, they may even pay for the POTW's upgrade. In this manner, they may be able to take advantage of some economies of scale. The soft underbelly of the removal credits program, however, is that the POTW's sewage sludge may thereby become contaminated with heavy metals or other toxic substances. As a result of this threat, EPA has developed sewage sludge standards that POTWs must meet if they are to take part in the removal credits program. See 40 C.F.R. Part 503.

Last, and perhaps most significantly, the primary regulatory overseer under the pretreatment program is neither EPA nor the States, but rather the local POTWs. See, e.g., 40 C.F.R. § 403.8(f). In general, pretreaters are thus subject to subject to less-demanding monitoring requirements, fewer inspections, and less significant penalties where violations occur.

The pretreatment program is often criticized. See, e.g., Houck, Ending the War: A Strategy to Save America's Coastal Zone, 47 Md. L. Rev. 358 (1988). At the same time, there does not seem to be any likelihood of significant change any time soon.

B. Water Quality–Based Requirements

1. How Water Quality Standards Are Set

The CWA's statutory provisions addressing the establishment of water quality standards are straightforward but bare bones. Section 303(c) requires the States to develop such standards, and notes that they are to consist of both the designated uses of the waters and the water quality criteria necessary to protect those uses. It further requires that "[s]uch standards shall be established taking into account [the waters'] use and value for public water supplies, propagation of fish and wildlife, recreational purposes, and agricultural, industrial and other purposes, also taking into consideration their use and value for navigation." Section 303(c) also requires the States to review their water quality standards at least every three years to see if they need revision, and to submit any proposed revisions to EPA.

EPA has three authorities that are relevant to the standard-setting process. First, Section 304(a) tasks EPA with developing "criteria for water quality accurately reflecting the latest scientific knowledge" regarding adverse effects of pollutants. These criteria serve as guidance to the States for the standards-setting process. Second, EPA has an oversight role which requires it to review any State standards or any revisions to those standards. 33 U.S.C. § 1313(c)(1)-(3). If EPA finds that any such standards do not meet the requirements of the Act, Section 303(c)(3) indicates that EPA is to specify the deficiencies and give the relevant State an opportunity to cure them. If the State fails to do so, Section 303(c)(4) provides that EPA is to promulgate a federal water quality standard for that water body. And third, as previously mentioned, Section 501 gives EPA the authority "to prescribe such regulations as are necessary to carry out [its] functions under this chapter."

The last relevant statutory provisions are the Act's goal and policy statements in Section 101. As mentioned at the beginning of this chapter, § 101(a) establishes that the primary objective of the Act is "to restore and maintain the chemical, physical, and biological integrity of the Nation's waters." And Section 101(a)(2) provides that, pending the complete cessation of all polluting discharges, it is "the national goal that wherever attainable, an interim goal of water quality which provides for the protection and propagation of fish, shellfish and wildlife and provides for recreation in and on the water shall be achieved by July 1, 1983."

Relying on § 501, EPA has written regulations fleshing out how it will judge State standard submissions. These regulations have several key components. First, they essentially require the States to designate for each water all of the uses specified in § 101(a)(2) (i.e., "fishable/swimmable") that qualify as either "existing uses" or that are "attainable" in that waterway. They do this by: (a) requiring the States to conduct a "use attainability analysis" (UAA) if they designate or have designated uses that do not include all of the uses specified in § 101(a)(2); and (b) precluding the States from removing any "existing use," which is defined as any use which has been attained in the relevant water body at any point since 1975. See 40 C.F.R. §§ 131.3(e) and 131.10(g), (h) and (j). In effect, the UAA requirement creates a rebuttable presumption that all of the § 101(a)(2) uses are attainable in all waters unless the State demonstrates otherwise. In order to justify leaving a § 101(a)(2) use off the list, the State must show both that it is not an "existing use" and that it meets one of several other narrow requirements, e.g., that imposing controls more stringent than the statute's technology-based requirements would result in substantial and widespread economic and economic and social impact. 40 C.F.R. § 131.10(g)

Second, EPA's regulations reiterate the CWA's command that the States adopt criteria to protect the designated uses. They elaborate on the nature of this requirement as follows:

> Such criteria must be based on sound scientific rationale and must contain sufficient parameters or constituents to protect the designated use. For waters with multiple use designations, the criteria shall support the most sensitive use.

40 C.F.R. § 131.11(a). Consistent with § 304(a), EPA has developed a series of suggested water quality criteria to assist the States in the standards-setting process. Its latest efforts in this regard are reflected in a document referred to as EPA's "Gold Book" of suggested criteria. EPA, Quality Criteria for Water (1986). While these criteria are not binding on the States, EPA may require the States to justify any less stringent criteria. *Mississippi Commission on Natural Resources v. Costle*, 625 F.2d 1269 (1980) (*"Mississippi Commission"*).

It may help the student to think of the designated uses and the criteria set to protect them, collectively, as "traditional" water quality standards. Together, they should in theory result in standards that protect many aquatic uses. One problem with this approach, however, is that States tend to be very general in their specification of "designated uses." Beyond alluding to the general goals of § 101, EPA's Water Quality Handbook states only that "States should designate aquatic life uses that appropriately address biological integrity." As a result, States often designate uses with a fairly broad brush (e.g., designating a particular stream as "fishable"), which may or may not result in the establishment of criteria that are protective of all species of flora and fauna in a particular aquatic ecosystem.

Partly in response to this concern, EPA requires the States to augment the level of protection afforded by traditional water quality standards by adopting what is referred to as an "antidegradation" policy. See 40 C.F.R. § 131.12(a)(1)-(3). The court in *Ohio Valley Environmental Coalition v. Horinko*, 279 F.Supp.2d 732 (S.D.W.V. 2003) (*"Horinko"*), recently provided an excellent summation of these provisions and their effect:

> ... These three provisions establish what are commonly referred to as three "tiers" of antidegradation protection. Tier 1 applies to all waters, and requires that existing water uses be protected. 40 C.F.R. § 131.12(a)(1). Tier 2 applies to high quality waters, defined as waters "[w]here the quality of the waters exceed levels necessary to support propagation of fish, shellfish, and wildlife and recreation in and on the water." *Id.* § 131.12(a)(2). In Tier 2 waters, water *quality* (as opposed to uses) "shall be maintained and protected" unless the State finds, after a process of public participation, "that allowing lower water quality is necessary to accommodate important economic or social development in the area in which the waters are

located." *Id.* This process of public participation and a finding of economic or social necessity is known as Tier 2 review. Tier 3 applies to high quality waters that "constitute an outstanding National resource, such as waters of National and State parks and wildlife refuges and waters of exceptional recreational or ecological significance." *Id.* § 131.12(a)(3). In Tier 3 waters, "water quality shall be maintained and protected," with no exception for economic or social necessity. *Id. . . .*

Id. at 740 (emphasis in original).

Notes and Comments

1.   As we will see, EPA sets nationally-applicable air quality standards under the Clean Air Act. Why do you think Congress chose to have the States set the relevant standards on a water-body by water-body basis under the CWA? Why do you think that Congress chose the two-pronged approach of designating uses and then setting criteria to protect those uses? Why didn't Congress just require the States to set standards according to the most-demanding uses such as, for example, drinking water consumption?

2.   Again, EPA can reject a State's standards if it finds that they do not meet the requirements of the Act. 33 U.S.C. § 1313(c)(3); see also *Mississippi Commission*, 625 F.2d at 1278 (upholding EPA's decision to reject a Mississippi standard). This is not to say, however, that EPA will invariably reject State standards that are significantly less protective than EPA's suggested criteria. In *NRDC v. EPA*, 16 F.3d 1395 (4th Cir. 1993), for example, the court upheld EPA's decision to approve Maryland and Virginia's dioxin standards despite the fact that they allowed dioxin concentrations nearly 1,000 times greater than EPA's suggested criteria. The court found that EPA did not act arbitrarily and capriciously in determining that, despite this disparity, the standards were scientifically defensible and protective of beneficial uses. Id. at 1405–1406.

3.   Traditionally, States often have adopted narrative criteria in lieu of numeric ones. Common narrative criteria have included such statements as "no toxic pollutants in toxic amounts" and "no aesthetically displeasing conditions." In 1987, Congress limited this practice by requiring that the States adopt numerical criteria for toxic pollutants, where available. See 33 U.S.C. § 1313(c)(2)(B).

4.   Although Section 303(c) speaks of water quality standards consisting of both designated uses and the criteria necessary to protect them, the Supreme Court has held that, at least in some situations, a designated use may be treated as a fully effective water quality standard, even if the relevant State has not set a criterion to protect it from a given risk. *PUD No. 1 of Jefferson County v. Washington Dept. of Ecology*, 511 U.S. 700, 713–718, 114 S.Ct. 1900, 1910–1912, 128 L.Ed.2d 716 (1994) ("*PUD No. 1*"). We will return to this issue when we consider this case, below.

5.   Another problem posed by traditional water quality standards is that, even in situations in which the States may divide water bodies such as rivers into segments (usually by river mile), they tend to treat such segments as homogeneous ecosystems, instead of as complex systems they are, setting

a single criterion for each pollutant for that segment. While such a criterion may make sense for the middle of the water column, it may make little sense for any associated wetlands. It also may ignore other issues such as, for example, temperature stratification or the accumulation of some pollutants (e.g., heavy metals or dioxin) in river sediments. With prompting by EPA, some States have begun to address some of these concerns. It has proven to be a slow process, however, and EPA has been reluctant to push very hard.

6. In 1983, EPA acknowledged that there was no explicit requirement for an antidegradation policy in the CWA. It indicated its view, however, that the policy "is consistent with the spirit, intent, and goals of the Act, especially the clause" . . . restore and *maintain* the chemical, physical and biological integrity of the Nation's waters (§ 101(a). . . . EPA, Questions and Answers on Antidegradation, p. 1 (1983) ("Questions and Answers") (emphasis in original), available at www.epa.gov/waterscience/ library/wqstandards/antidegqa.pdf. Congress embraced this policy in 1987, specifically requiring that at least certain water-quality based effluent limitations conform with it. See 33 U.S.C. § 1313(d)(4)(B); see also *PUD No. 1*, 511 U.S. at 705, 114 S.Ct. at 1905–1906.

7. As alluded to above, one purpose of the antidegradation policy is to fill in gaps that may be present under the "traditional" water quality standards. Tier 1 does this by requiring the States to protect all "existing uses" regardless of whether they are reflected in the relevant water quality standards. EPA explains in the Questions and Answers document:

> No activity is allowable under the antidegradation policy which would partially or completely eliminate any existing use whether or not that use is designated in a State's water quality standards. . . . Species that are in the water body and which are consistent with the designated use (i.e., not aberrational) must be protected, even if not prevalent in number or importance. Nor can activity be allowed which would render the species unfit for maintaining the use. Water quality should be such that it results in no mortality and no significant growth or reproductive impairment of resident species. . . . An existing aquatic community composed entirely of invertebrates and plants, such as may be found in a pristine alpine stream, should still be protected whether or not such stream supports a fishery. . . .

Questions and Answers, p. 3. What is the regulatory significance of this guidance document?

8. As indicated in *Horinko*, Tiers 2 and 3 provide higher levels of protection for those water bodies that are cleaner than necessary to protect existing uses. The basic idea is to keep pristine waters pristine. As a policy matter, does this requirement make sense? Why are we interested in protecting water quality independent of any desire to protect the "uses" of those waters, broadly defined to include the health of all resident species, flora and fauna? Can one argue that we should be directing new growth to these areas, where there is excess assimilative capacity?

9. There are many unresolved questions regarding the effect of the antidegradation policy in certain contexts. These include, for example: (1) How does it apply in situations in which a water body supported a use in 1975 (again, a use will be deemed to be an "existing use" if it existed on or

after that date), but where the use was impaired at that time? Does the state have to provide the use with full protection, or only the level to which it was protected in 1975?; (2) How does the policy apply to existing pollutant loadings from individual plants that have remained unchanged, but where the uses may now be impaired by, for example, the combined effect of that load and those from other sources that may or may not be more difficult to control?; and (3) How does it apply, more generally, to loadings from nonpoint sources (e.g. sediment in stormwater runoff)? On this last point, compare Questions and Answers, at p. 6, with *American Wildlands v. Browner*, 260 F.3d 1192 (10th Cir. 2001).

2. How Water Quality Standards Are Implemented for Point Sources

Section 301(b)(1)(c) of the CWA indicates that permits must ensure compliance with water quality standards. EPA has three separate regulatory provisions implementing this requirement. First, 40 C.F.R. § 122.4(d) precludes the issuance of any permit "when the imposition of conditions cannot ensure compliance with the applicable water quality requirements of all affected States." Second, 40 C.F.R. § 122.4(i) specifically precludes the issuance of permits to new sources if their discharges will cause or contribute to water quality standard violations. It further requires these would-be sources to make specific showings, as a precondition to receiving a permit, if the relevant water body already exceeds a standard, and if the State has performed what is called a "pollutant loads allocation" for the relevant pollutant. See 40 C.F.R. § 122.4(i). And finally, 40 C.F.R. § 122.44(d) requires permit issuers to determine whether any permit applicant's discharge "will cause, have the reasonable potential to cause, or contribute to an excursion above any State water quality standard, including State narrative criteria for water quality." If so, the permit must include conditions ensuring compliance with those standards. Id.

Permit issuers, including both the States and EPA, implement these requirements with varying degrees of rigor. In best-case situations, they will essentially undertake what is called "total maximum daily load" ("TMDL") analysis, whether or not they do so under the formal auspices of the TMDL program. Since the TMDL program transcends point source discharges, we reserve full consideration of it for a few more pages. For present purposes, it is sufficient to note that, in performing this type of analysis, the permit issuer will first determine how much of the particular pollutant the relevant water body can assimilate on a daily basis without violating the relevant standard. Narrowly speaking, this is the actual TMDL. More broadly speaking, however, the TMDL analysis moves on to consider all of the inputs (both point and nonpoint) of the relevant pollutant into that water body. The permit issuer will then divide up the maximum daily load among all of these sources, in theory determining each source's "fair share" of a compliant load. Since many States have no effective regulatory programs relating to non-point sources, and EPA has none, in many cases the State must essentially assume all known nonpoint source loads as a given, and divide up the rest of the rest of the available allotment among the point source contributors.

As one might imagine, however, this is a resource-intensive process. Indeed, laying the scientific groundwork for establishing a TMDL for even a single pollutant on a single river may in some cases cost hundreds of thousands of dollars. Not surprisingly, many permit issuers are loath to engage in that kind of analysis in the context of individual permit applications. As a result, they tend to take one of two potential short-cuts. First, some permit issuers analyze the impacts of the applicant's proposed discharge in isolation in determining its impact on water quality; that is, they model the impact of the applicant's discharge on water quality standards, without taking into account other sources of the same pollutant. Perhaps obviously, such an approach does not serve the regulatory prohibition on discharges that *contribute* to violations of water quality standards. Second, some permit issuers rely on narrative prohibitions to the exclusion of numeric requirements (although some also use them to supplement such requirements). A typical permit condition of this type might simply state that "no wastes shall be discharged ... which will violate [water quality standards]." See, e.g., *Northwest Environmental Advocates v. City of Portland*, 56 F.3d 979, 985 (9th Cir. 1995), *reh'g den.*, 74 F.3d 945, *cert. den.* 518 U.S. 1018, 116 S.Ct. 2550, 135 L.Ed.2d 1069 (1996) (*"City of Portland"*).

There is scant case law regarding the legal propriety of these shortcuts. The Ninth Circuit has issued two opinions touching on these matters. First, in *Trustees for Alaska v. Environmental Protection Agency*, 749 F.2d 549, 557 (9th Cir. 1984), it held that regulators have an obligation to establish numeric water quality-based permit conditions, where feasible. And second, in *City of Portland*, it held that citizens may enforce narrative permit conditions of the type described above in citizen suits under § 505. 56 F.3d at 986–990.

The following Supreme Court opinion addresses the effect of § 301(b)(1)(C) on dischargers in upstream States in situations in which their discharges may pose water quality concerns in downstream States:

ARKANSAS v. OKLAHOMA

Supreme Court of the United States, 1992.
503 U.S. 91, 112 S.Ct. 1046, 117 L.Ed.2d 239.

Justice STEVENS delivered the opinion of the Court.

In 1985, the City of Fayetteville, Arkansas, applied to the EPA, seeking [an NPDES] permit for the City's new sewage treatment plant.... [EPA issued] a permit authorizing the plant to discharge up to half of its effluent ... into an unnamed stream in northwestern Arkansas. That flow passes through a series of three creeks for about 17 miles, and then enters the Illinois River at a point 22 miles upstream from the Arkansas–Oklahoma border.

Respondents challenged this permit before the EPA, alleging, inter alia, that the discharge violated the Oklahoma water quality standards.

Those standards provide that "no degradation [of water quality] shall be allowed" in the upper Illinois River, including the portion of the River immediately downstream from the state line.

Following a hearing, the [ALJ] concluded that the Oklahoma standards would not be implicated unless the contested discharge had "something more than a mere *de minimis* impact" on the State's waters. He found that the discharge would not have an "undue impact" on Oklahoma's waters and, accordingly, affirmed the issuance of the permit.

On a petition for review, the EPA's Chief Judicial Officer ["CJO"] first ruled that [§ 301(b)(1)(c)] "requires an NPDES permit to impose any effluent limitations necessary to comply with applicable state water quality standards." He then held that the Act and EPA regulations offered greater protection for the downstream State than the ALJ's "undue impact" standard suggested. He explained the proper standard as follows:

> "[A] mere theoretical impairment of Oklahoma's water quality standards—i.e., an infinitesimal impairment predicted through modeling but not expected to be actually detectable or measurable—should not by itself block the issuance of the permit. In this case, the permit should be upheld if the record shows by a preponderance of the evidence that the authorized discharges would not cause an actual *detectable* violation of Oklahoma's water quality standards." (Emphasis in original).

On remand, the ALJ made detailed findings of fact and concluded that the City had satisfied the standard set forth by the [CJO]. Specifically, the ALJ found that there would be no detectable violation of any of the components of Oklahoma's water quality standards. The [CJO] sustained the issuance of the permit.

Both the petitioners (collectively Arkansas) and the respondents in this litigation sought judicial review. Arkansas argued that the [CWA] did not require an Arkansas point source to comply with Oklahoma's water quality standards. Oklahoma challenged the EPA's determination that the Fayetteville discharge would not produce a detectable violation of the Oklahoma standards.

The Court of Appeals did not accept either of these arguments. The court agreed with the EPA that the statute required compliance with Oklahoma's water quality standards, and did not disagree with the Agency's determination that the discharges from the Fayetteville plant would not produce a detectable violation of those standards. Nevertheless, relying on a theory that neither party had advanced, the Court of Appeals reversed the Agency's issuance of the Fayetteville permit. The court first ruled that the statute requires that "where a proposed source would discharge effluents that would contribute to conditions currently constituting a violation of applicable water quality standards, such [a] proposed source may not be permitted." Then the court found that the Illinois River in Oklahoma was "already degraded," that the Fayetteville effluent would reach the Illinois River in Oklahoma, and that that effluent could "be expected to contribute to the ongoing deterioration of the scenic [Illinois R]iver" in Oklahoma even though it would not detectably affect the River's water quality.

IV

The parties have argued three analytically distinct questions concerning the interpretation of the [CWA]. First, does the Act require the EPA, in crafting and issuing a permit to a point source in one State, to apply the water quality standards of downstream States? Second, even if the Act does not require as much, does the Agency have the statutory authority to mandate such compliance? Third, does the Act provide, as the Court of Appeals held, that once a body of water fails to meet water quality standards no discharge that yields effluent that reach the degraded waters will be permitted?

In this case, it is neither necessary nor prudent for us to resolve the first of these questions. In issuing the Fayetteville permit, the EPA assumed it was obligated by both the Act and its own regulations to ensure that the Fayetteville discharge would not violate Oklahoma's standards. As we discuss below, this assumption was permissible and reasonable and therefore there is no need for us to address whether the Act requires as much. . . .

Our decision not to determine at this time the scope of the Agency's statutory *obligations* does not affect our resolution of the second question, which concerns the Agency's statutory *authority*. Even if the [CWA] does not require the Fayetteville discharge to comply with Oklahoma's water quality standards, the statute clearly does not limit the EPA's authority to mandate such compliance.

Since 1973, EPA regulations have provided that an NPDES permit shall not be issued "[w]hen the imposition of conditions cannot ensure compliance with the applicable water quality requirements of all affected States." 40 CFR § 122.4(d); *see also* 40 CFR § 122.44(d) (1991). Those regulations—relied upon by the EPA in the issuance of the Fayetteville permit—constitute a reasonable exercise of the Agency's statutory authority.

Congress has vested in the Administrator broad discretion to establish conditions for NPDES permits. Section 402(a)(2) provides that for EPA-issued permits "[t]he Administrator shall prescribe conditions for such permits to assure compliance with the requirements of [§ 402(a)(1)] and *such other requirements as he deems appropriate.*" 33 U.S.C. § 1342(a)(2) (emphasis supplied). Similarly, Congress preserved for the Administrator broad authority to oversee state permit programs: "No permit shall issue . . . if the Administrator . . . objects in writing to the issuance of such permit as being outside the guidelines and requirements of this chapter." 33 U.S.C. § 1342(d)(2).

The regulations relied on by the EPA were a perfectly reasonable exercise of the Agency's statutory discretion. The application of state water quality standards in the interstate context is wholly consistent with the Act's broad purpose, "to restore and maintain the chemical, physical, and biological integrity of the Nation's waters." 33 U.S.C. § 1251(a). Moreover, ... § 301(b)(1)(C) expressly identifies the achievement of state water quality standards as one of the Act's central objectives. The Agency's regulations conditioning NPDES permits are a well-tailored means of achieving this goal.

V

The Court of Appeals construed the [CWA] to prohibit any discharge of effluent that would reach waters already in violation of existing water quality standards. We find nothing in the Act to support this reading.

Although the Act contains several provisions directing compliance with state water quality standards, see, e.g., 33 U.S.C. § 1311(b)(1)(c), the parties have pointed to nothing that mandates a complete ban on discharges into a waterway that is in violation of those standards. The statute does, however, contain provisions designed to remedy existing water quality violations and to allocate the burden of reducing undesirable discharges between existing sources and new sources. *See, e.g.,* 33 U.S.C. § 1313(d). Thus, rather than establishing the categorical ban announced by the Court of Appeals—which might frustrate the construction of new plants that would improve existing conditions—the [CWA] vests in the EPA and the States broad authority to develop long-range, area-wide programs to alleviate and eliminate existing pollution. See 33 U.S.C. § 1288(b)(2).

To the extent that the Court of Appeals relied on its interpretation of the Act to reverse the EPA's permitting decision, that reliance was misplaced.

VI

The Court of Appeals also concluded that the EPA's issuance of the Fayetteville permit was arbitrary and capricious because the Agency misinterpreted Oklahoma's water quality standards. The primary difference between the court's and the Agency's interpretation of the standards derives from the court's construction of the Act. Contrary to the EPA's interpretation of the Oklahoma standards, the Court of Appeals read those standards as containing the same categorical ban on new discharges that the court had found in the [CWA]. Although we do not believe the text of the Oklahoma standards supports the court's reading ..., we reject it for a more fundamental reason—namely, that the Court of Appeals exceeded the legitimate scope of judicial review of an agency adjudication....

As discussed above, EPA regulations require an NPDES permit to comply "with the applicable water quality requirements of all affected States." 40 CFR § 122.4(d). This regulation effectively incorporates into federal law those state law standards the Agency reasonably determines to be "applicable." In such a situation, then, state water quality standards—promulgated by the States with substantial guidance from the

EPA and approved by the Agency—are part of the federal law of water pollution control.

Two features of the body of law governing water pollution support this conclusion. First, we have long recognized that interstate water pollution is controlled by federal law. Recognizing that the system of federally approved state standards as applied in the interstate context constitutes federal law is wholly consistent with this principle. Second, treating state standards in interstate controversies as federal law accords with the Act's purpose of authorizing the EPA to create and manage a uniform system of interstate water pollution regulation.

Because we recognize that, at least insofar as they affect the issuance of a permit in another State, the Oklahoma standards have a federal character, the EPA's reasonable, consistently held interpretation of those standards is entitled to substantial deference. In this case, the [CJO] ruled that the Oklahoma standards—which require that there be "no degradation" of the upper Illinois River—would only be violated if the discharge effected an "actually detectable or measurable" change in water quality.

This interpretation of the Oklahoma standards is certainly reasonable and consistent with the purposes and principles of the [CWA]. As the [CJO] noted, "unless there is some method for measuring compliance, there is no way to ensure compliance." Moreover, this interpretation of the Oklahoma standards makes eminent sense in the interstate context: if every discharge that had some theoretical impact on a downstream State were interpreted as "degrading" the downstream waters, downstream States might wield an effective veto over upstream discharges.

The EPA's application of those standards in this case was also sound. On remand, the ALJ scrutinized the record and made explicit factual findings regarding four primary measures of water quality under the Oklahoma standards: eutrophication, aesthetics, dissolved oxygen, and metals. In each case, the ALJ found that the Fayetteville discharge would not lead to a detectable change in water quality. He therefore concluded that the Fayetteville discharge would not violate the Oklahoma water quality standards. Because we agree with the [CJO] that these findings are supported by substantial evidence, we conclude that the Court of Appeals should have affirmed both the EPA's construction of the regulations and the issuance of the Fayetteville permit. . . .

In sum, the Court of Appeals made a policy choice that it was not authorized to make. Arguably, as that court suggested, it might be wise to prohibit any discharge into the Illinois River, even if that discharge would have no adverse impact on water quality. But it was surely not arbitrary for the EPA to conclude—given the benefits to the River from the increased flow of relatively clean water and the benefits achieved in Arkansas by allowing the new plant to operate as designed—that allowing the discharge would be even wiser. It is not our role, or that of the

Court of Appeals, to decide which policy choice is the better one, for it is clear that Congress has entrusted such decisions to [EPA].

Notes and Comments

1. As mentioned above, we will put off detailed consideration of the TMDL program for a few more pages because it transcends point sources. It is worth noting, however, that in 1987 Congress prioritized in § 304(*l*) what is essentially a mini-TMDL program for toxic pollutants. Under that provision, States were required to identify the stream segments within their boundaries that were not meeting toxics-related water quality standards, to identify the point sources contributing to those problems, and to develop "individual control strateg[ies]" for those sources which would result in the achievement of those standards within three years. 33 U.S.C. § 1314(*l*). While conceptually identical to the TMDL program, Section 304(*l*) differs in that (a) it relates only to point sources, and (b) it has aggressive statutory deadlines. For a good example of a case involving the § 304(*l*) program at work, see *Dioxin/Organochlorine Center v. Clarke*, 57 F.3d 1517 (9th Cir. 1995).

2. EPA allows the States to establish what are referred to as "mixing zones" in their water quality standards. 40 C.F.R. § 131.13. These are best viewed as implementation devices designed to allow for the consideration of a water body's assimilative capacity in determining whether a particular discharge will cause or contribute to violations of water quality standards. The Tenth Circuit further explained this concept in *American Wildlands v. Browner*, 260 F.3d 1192 (10th Cir. 2001):

> ... Mixing zones are "areas where an effluent discharge undergoes initial dilution and are extended to cover the secondary mixing in the ambient water body. A mixing zone is an allocated impact zone where acute and chronic water quality criteria can be exceeded as long as a number of protections are maintained." EPA, Water Quality Standards Handbook § 5.1.1, at 5–5 (2d ed.1994). The protections that must be maintained include the absence of "toxic conditions to aquatic life," "objectionable deposits," "floating debris," "objectionable color, odor, taste, or turbidity," and substances resulting in "a dominance of nuisance species." Id. at 5–5 to 5–6. Mixing zones are allowable as a practical necessity because "[i]t is not always necessary to meet all water quality criteria within the discharge pipe to protect the integrity of the water body as a whole. Sometimes it is appropriate to allow for ambient concentrations above the criteria in small areas near outfalls." Id. § 5.1, at 5–1.

Id. at 1195. Typically, mixing zones are quite small (e.g. a radius of 100 feet). Some States have been known to abuse this concept, however, by establishing mixing zones that encompass long reaches of entire streams.

3. As also mentioned above, in the *City of Portland* case the Ninth Circuit held that citizens can enforce narrative water quality-based permit conditions. In responding to Portland's argument that these conditions are too vague to be enforceable, the court pointed out that:

> The plain language of CWA § 505 authorizes citizens to enforce *all* permit conditions. That section provides: "[A]ny citizen may commence

a civil action ... (1) against any person ... who is alleged to be in violation of (A) an effluent standard or limitation under [the Clean Water Act]...." 33 U.S.C. § 1365(a)(1)(A). An effluent standard or limitation includes "(2) an effluent limitation or other limitation under section 1311 ... *or* (6) a permit or condition thereof...." 33 U.S.C. § 1365(f)(2), (f)(6) (emphasis added). This language clearly contemplates citizen suits to enforce "a permit or condition thereof." Portland holds [an NPDES permit], and the water quality standards are conditions of its permit.

56 F.3d at 986 (emphasis in original). The court further reasoned that:

... Congress recognized that water quality standards "often cannot be translated into effluent limitations...." For example, certain water quality standards cannot be expressed quantitatively, such as those that apply in this case to bacterial pollution, aesthetic conditions, and objectionable matter (scum, oily sleek, foul odors, and floating solids)....

By interpreting § 505 to exclude citizen suit enforcement of water quality standards that are not translated into quantitative limitations, Portland would have us immunize the entire body of qualitative regulations from an important enforcement tool. Such a result would be especially troubling in this case, because no effluent limitations cover the discharges from Portland's combined sewer overflows ("CSOs").

Id. at 989.

In dissent, Judge Kleinfeld bemoaned the illogic of allowing citizens to enforce narrative conditions:

Water quality standards are a useful device for government enforcement authorities ..., because they provide standards for effluent limitations and goals toward which enforcement should be aimed. They are too uncertain and amorphous, however, for use against specific polluters. Suppose, hypothetically, that a water quality standard allows for 100 units of a pollutant, upstream and non-point source polluters discharge 50 units, and the downstream discharger is permitted to discharge 50 units. If the upstream and non-point source polluters increase their discharge to 80 units, it does not automatically follow that the downstream discharger should be limited to 20. The burdens of so severe a limitation may exceed the burdens of the extra pollution, or enforcement efforts might more appropriately be directed at the other polluters. In the case at bar, the majority concedes that the social costs of filling the streets and basements of Portland with sewage, or spending between a half billion and $1.2 billion dollars on renovation, are the practical alternatives to tolerating violations of the water quality standards. A public authority might rationally decide that filling the streets and basements with sewage is worse than polluting the river with it, and that the citizens of Portland need several years to raise and spend the money necessary to avoid running the sewage into the streets, the basements, and the river.

Id. at 992. Is this lament primarily about the enforceability of narrative conditions or the wisdom of allowing citizens to pursue enforcement in situations in which governmental entities have chosen not to proceed? To the extent that it is the former, can it be squared with the language of § 505(f)(6)? See also CWA § 309(d) (allowing EPA to pursue penalties for any violation of permit conditions). To the extent that it is the latter, can it be squared with the very existence of citizen suits?

What are the real world implications of *City of Portland*? If you were representing a discharger, might the court's decision encourage you to seek numeric water quality-based permit conditions? Why or why not?

4. Reread § 301(b)(1)(C). Do you agree with the Supreme Court that it can reasonably be interpreted as requiring compliance with the water quality standards of downstream States? What water quality standard was at issue in *Arkansas v. Oklahoma*? What was the Illinois' actual status (in terms of pollution)? Note that merely listing a river as a "Tier 3" water does not by itself guarantee that river will never become degraded. Note also that the fact that the Illinois became degraded (presumably after it was designated as a Tier 3 water) did not prevent it from being entitled to that heightened degree of protection.

5. Would EPA's regulation have required compliance with the Oklahoma standard even if that standard had been much more stringent than anything contemplated in EPA's criteria (e.g., if it contained a narrative prohibition on any discharges of treated or untreated human waste)? In *International Paper Co. v. Ouellette*, the Supreme Court had held that, while § 510 preserves State common law claims, it only does so to the extent that those claims are based on the common law of the State in which the discharge occurs. It held that the plaintiffs in that case could not apply Vermont common law to a New York facility's discharges into Lake Champlain. 479 U.S. 481, 495–496, 107 S.Ct. 805, 813–814. In reaching this conclusion, the Court reasoned that "[i]f a New York source were liable for violations of Vermont law, that law could effectively override both the permit requirements and the policy choices made by the source State." Id. at 495, 107 S.Ct. at 813. Read § 510. Do you agree with the result in *Ouellette*? Can you square the outcome in that case with the result in Part IV of *Arkansas v. Oklahoma*?

6. What do you make of the discussion in Part V of the Court's opinion? How do you square it with § 301(b)(1)(C), as interpreted by 40 C.F.R. § 122.4(i)? Was this a situation in which the Court likely was simply unaware of EPA's regulation (which it did not cite)? Does the Court's analysis effectively overrule that provision? Remember that EPA was the permit issuer in *Arkansas v. Oklahoma* (Arkansas was unauthorized at the time). How do you think EPA would square its permit issuance with § 122.4(i)?

7. Why, in Part VI, did the Court determine that EPA' interpretation of the Oklahoma antidegradation policy was entitled to deference? Do you think the Court would have applied the same deference with respect to an Oklahoma discharger? Imagine, for example, a different situation in which EPA is reading a State's ambiguous water quality standard more strictly than the State is. If EPA vetoed a permit that the State proposed to issue to an in-state discharger, and the dispute rose all the way to the Supreme Court, to whose interpretation of the relevant standard do you think the Court would defer, if anyone's?

8. What did you think of EPA's interpretation of the Oklahoma standard in *Arkansas v. Oklahoma*? If we know for certain (through modeling) that some of the pollution will get down to Oklahoma, won't it "contribute" to a violation of Oklahoma's non-degradation provision? Did EPA, with the Supreme Court's blessing, essentially create a de minimis exception to the antidegradation policy? Is such an exception necessary? Is it at least reasonable? Do you think the same approach would or should apply to numeric water quality standards? How would such an approach apply to a pollutant like dioxin, where the water quality standards of several States (and EPA's suggested criterion) are set at 0.013 parts per quadrillion, which is nearly 1,000 times below the level of detection?

9. What is the take-away principle from *Arkansas v. Oklahoma*? Is it clear that new or expanded discharges are prohibited if: (a) the river already violates the water quality standard for a given pollutant; and (b) the new or increased load will result in detectable increases of that pollutant? Can you argue that the holding in the case is limited to interstate scenarios; i.e, that even non-detectable additions may be prohibited if the discharger is discharging directly into the waters that already violate water quality standards?

V. OTHER WATER QUALITY–BASED PROGRAMS UNDER THE CWA

We now turn our attention to four different aspects of the CWA that are designed to address water quality concerns, but which transcend the NPDES program. As we will see, the first and the last of these, Sections 401 and 303(d), overlap with the NPDES program in at least some of their applications. By contrast, the other two, §§ 208 and 319, address only nonpoint sources. Given their non-regulatory nature, we will treat them together and our consideration of them will be quite brief.

A. § 401 Certifications

Section 401(a) of the CWA requires any applicant for a Federal license or permit, if its activity will result in a discharge into the navigable waters, to provide the licensing or permitting authority with a certification from the State in which the discharge originates that the discharge will comply with several requirements of the CWA, most notably the water quality standard requirements under § 303. This provision has the effect of keeping the States in the forefront, vis-a-vis water quality concerns, even if they are unauthorized and hence are not issuing the relevant NPDES permits. Moreover, the § 401 certification requirement transcends the NPDES world, applying, for example, to § 404 permits issued by the Corps of Engineers under the wetlands program and licenses issued by the Federal Energy Regulatory Commission ("FERC") under the Federal Power Act, 16 U.S.C. § 791 et seq.

Consider the following decision:

PUD NO. 1 OF JEFFERSON COUNTY v. WASHINGTON DEPT. OF ECOLOGY

Supreme Court of the United States, 1994.
511 U.S. 700, 114 S.Ct. 1900, 128 L.Ed.2d 716.

JUSTICE O'CONNOR delivered the opinion of the Court.

Petitioners, [a city and a local utility district], propose to build the Elkhorn Hydroelectric Project on the Dosewallips River. If constructed as presently planned, the facility would be located just outside the Olympic National Park on federally owned land within the Olympic National Forest. The project would divert water from a 1.2–mile reach of the River (the bypass reach), run the water through turbines to generate electricity and then return the water to the River below the bypass reach.... [Because this project requires a FERC license, and because it] may result in discharges into the Dosewallips River, petitioners are ... required to obtain State certification of the project pursuant to § 401 of the CWA.

The water flow in the bypass reach, which is currently undiminished by appropriation, ranges seasonally between 149 and 738 cubic feet per second (cfs). The Dosewallips supports two species of salmon, Coho and Chinook, as well as Steelhead trout. As originally proposed, the project was to include a diversion dam which would completely block the river and channel approximately 75% of the River's water into a tunnel alongside the streambed. About 25% of the water would remain in the bypass reach, but would be returned to the original riverbed through sluice gates or a fish ladder. Depending on the season, this would leave a residual minimum flow of between 65 and 155 cfs in the River. Respondent undertook a study to determine the minimum stream flows necessary to protect the salmon and steelhead fisheries in the bypass reach. On June 11, 1986, respondent issued a § 401 water quality certification imposing a variety of conditions on the project, including a minimum stream-flow requirement of between 100 and 200 cfs depending on the season.

[After preliminary appeals in both the State administrative and judicial systems, the case reached the Washington Supreme Court. There, the court held that the State's antidegradation provisions] require the imposition of minimum stream flows. The court also found that § 401(d), which allows States to impose conditions based upon several enumerated sections of the CWA and "any other appropriate requirement of State law," authorized the stream flow condition....

The principal dispute in this case concerns whether the minimum stream flow requirement that the State imposed on the Elkhorn project is a permissible condition of a § 401 certification under the CWA. To resolve this dispute we must first determine the scope of the State's authority under § 401. We must then determine whether the limitation at issue here, the requirement that petitioners maintain minimum stream flows, falls within the scope of that authority.

. . . Petitioners concede that, at a minimum, the project will result in two possible discharges-the release of dredged and fill material during the construction of the project, and the discharge of water at the end of the tailrace after the water has been used to generate electricity. Petitioners contend, however, that the minimum stream flow requirement imposed by the State was unrelated to these specific discharges. . . .

If § 401 consisted solely of subsection (a), which refers to a state certification that a "discharge" will comply with certain provisions of the Act, petitioners' assessment of the scope of the State's certification authority would have considerable force. Section 401, however, also contains subsection (d), which expands the State's authority to impose conditions on the certification of a project. Section 401(d) provides that any certification shall set forth "any effluent limitations and other limitations . . . necessary to assure that any applicant" will comply with various provisions of the Act and appropriate state law requirements. The language of this subsection contradicts petitioners' claim that the State may only impose water quality limitations specifically tied to a "discharge." The text refers to the compliance of the applicant, not the discharge. Section 401(d) thus allows the State to impose "other limitations" on the project in general to assure compliance with various provisions of the CWA and with "any other appropriate requirement of State law." Although the dissent asserts that this interpretation of § 401(d) renders § 401(a)(1) superfluous, we see no such anomaly. Section 401(a)(1) identifies the category of activities subject to certification namely those with discharges. And § 401(d) is most reasonably read as authorizing additional conditions and limitations on the activity as a whole once the threshold condition, the existence of a discharge, is satisfied.

Our view of the statute is consistent with EPA's regulations implementing § 401. The regulations expressly interpret § 401 as requiring the State to find that "there is a reasonable assurance that the activity will be conducted in a manner which will not violate applicable water quality standards." 40 CFR § 121.2(a)(3) (1992). EPA's conclusion that activities-not merely discharges-must comply with state water quality standards is a reasonable interpretation of § 401, and is entitled to deference.

Although § 401(d) authorizes the State to place restrictions on the activity as a whole, that authority is not unbounded. The State can only ensure that the project complies with "any applicable effluent limitations and other limitations, under [33 U.S.C. §§ 1311, 1312]" or certain other provisions of the Act, "and with any other appropriate requirement of State law." 33 U.S.C. § 1341(d). The State asserts that the minimum stream flow requirement was imposed to ensure compliance with the state water quality standards adopted pursuant to § 303 of the CWA.

We agree with the State that ensuring compliance with § 303 is a proper function of the § 401 certification. Although § 303 is not one of the statutory provisions listed in § 401(d), the statute allows states to impose limitations to ensure compliance with § 301 of the Act. Section 301 in turn incorporates § 303 by reference. *See* 33 U.S.C. § 1311(b)(1)(C). As a consequence, state water quality standards adopted pursuant to § 303 are among the "other limitations" with which a State may ensure compliance through the § 401 certification process. This interpretation is consistent with EPA's view of the statute. *See* 40 CFR § 121.2(a)(3) (1992). Moreover, limitations to assure compliance with state water quality standards are also permitted by § 401(d)'s reference to "any other appropriate requirement of State law." We do not speculate on what additional state laws, if any, might be incorporated by this language. But at a minimum, limitations imposed pursuant to state water quality standards adopted pursuant to § 303 are "appropriate" requirements of state law....

Having concluded that, pursuant to § 401, States may condition certification upon any limitations necessary to ensure compliance with state water quality standards or any other "appropriate requirement of State law," we consider whether the minimum flow condition is such a limitation. Under § 303, state water quality standards must "consist of the designated uses of the navigable waters involved and the water quality criteria for such waters based upon such uses." In imposing the minimum stream flow requirement, the State determined that construction and operation of the project as planned would be inconsistent with one of the designated uses of Class AA water, namely "[s]almonid [and other fish] migration, rearing, spawning, and harvesting...."

Petitioners assert, however, that § 303 requires the State to protect designated uses solely through implementation of specific "criteria." According to petitioners, the State may not require them to operate their dam in a manner consistent with a designated "use"; instead, say petitioners, under § 303 the State may only require that the project comply with specific numerical "criteria."

We disagree with petitioners' interpretation of the language of § 303(c)(2)(A). Under the statute, a water quality standard must "consist of the designated uses of the navigable waters involved and the water quality criteria for such waters based upon such uses." 33 U.S.C. § 1313(c)(2)(A). The text makes it plain that water quality standards contain two components. We think the language of § 303 is most naturally read to require that a project be consistent with both components, namely the designated use and the water quality criteria. Accordingly, under the literal terms of the statute, a project that does not comply with a designated use of the water does not comply with the applicable water quality standards.

Consequently, pursuant to § 401(d) the State may require that a permit applicant comply with both the designated uses and the water quality criteria of the state standards. In granting certification pursuant to § 401(d), the State "shall set forth any . . . limitations . . . necessary to assure that [the applicant] will comply with any . . . limitations under [§ 303] . . . and with any other appropriate requirement of State law." A certification requirement that an applicant operate the project consistently with state water quality standards—i.e., consistently with the designated uses of the water body and the water quality criteria—is both a "limitation" to assure "compliance with . . . limitations" imposed under § 303, and an "appropriate" requirement of State law.

EPA has not interpreted § 303 to require the States to protect designated uses exclusively through enforcement of numerical criteria. In its regulations governing state water quality standards, EPA defines criteria as "elements of State water quality standards expressed as constituent concentrations, levels, or narrative statements, representing a quality of water that supports a particular use." § 40 CFR 131.3(b) (1992)(emphasis added). The regulations further provide that "[w]hen criteria are met, water quality will generally protect the designated use." Ibid. Thus, the EPA regulations implicitly recognize that in some circumstances, criteria alone are insufficient to protect a designated use.

Petitioners also appear to argue that use requirements are too open-ended, and that the Act only contemplates enforcement of the more specific and objective "criteria." But this argument is belied by the open-ended nature of the criteria themselves. As the Solicitor General points out, even "criteria" are often expressed in broad, narrative terms, such as " 'there shall be no discharge of toxic pollutants in toxic amounts.' " Brief for United States 18. In fact, under the CWA, only one class of criteria, those governing "toxic pollutants listed pursuant to section 1317(a)(1)" need be rendered in numerical form. *See* 33 U.S.C. § 1313(c)(2)(B); 40 CFR § 131.11(b)(2) (1992).

Washington's Class AA water quality standards are typical in that they contain several open-ended criteria which, like the use designation of the River as a fishery, must be translated into specific limitations for individual projects. For example, the standards state that "[t]oxic, radioactive, or deleterious material concentrations shall be less than those which may affect public health, the natural aquatic environment, or the desirability of the water for any use." Similarly, the state standards specify that "[a]esthetic values shall not be impaired by the presence of materials or their effects, excluding those of natural origin, which offend the senses of sight, smell, touch, or taste." We think petitioners' attempt to distinguish between uses and criteria loses much of its force in light of the fact that the Act permits enforcement of broad, narrative criteria based on, for example, "aesthetics."

Petitioners further argue that enforcement of water quality standards through use designations renders the water quality criteria component of the standards irrelevant. We see no anomaly, however, in the State's reliance on both use designations and criteria to protect water quality. The specific numerical limitations embodied in the criteria are a convenient enforcement mechanism for identifying minimum water conditions which will generally achieve the requisite water quality. And, in most circumstances, satisfying the criteria will, as EPA recognizes, be sufficient to maintain the designated use. *See* 40 CFR § 131.3(b). Water quality standards, however, apply to an entire class of water, a class which contains numerous individual water bodies.... While enforcement of criteria will in general protect the uses of these diverse waters, a complementary requirement that activities also comport with designated uses enables the States to ensure that each activity—even if not foreseen by the criteria—will be consistent with the specific uses and attributes of a particular body of water.

Under petitioners' interpretation of the statute, however, if a particular criterion, such as turbidity, were missing from the list contained in an individual state water quality standard, or even if an existing turbidity criterion were insufficient to protect a particular species of fish in a particular river, the State would nonetheless be forced to allow activities inconsistent with the existing or designated uses. We think petitioners' reading leads to an unreasonable interpretation of the Act. The criteria components of state water quality standards attempt to identify, for all the water bodies in a given class, water quality requirements generally sufficient to protect designated uses. These criteria, however, cannot reasonably be expected to anticipate all the water quality issues arising from every activity which can affect the State's hundreds of individual water bodies. Requiring the States to enforce only the criteria component of their water quality standards would in essence require the States to study to a level of great specificity each individual surface water to ensure that the criteria applicable to that water are sufficiently detailed and individualized to fully protect the water's designated uses. Given that there is no textual support for imposing this requirement, we are loath to attribute to Congress an intent to impose this heavy regulatory burden on the States.

The State also justified its minimum stream flow as necessary to implement the "antidegradation policy" of § 303....

... The State of Washington's antidegradation policy ... provides that "[e]xisting beneficial uses shall be maintained and protected and no further degradation which would interfere with or become injurious to existing beneficial uses will be allowed." The State concluded that the reduced streamflows would have just the effect prohibited by this policy. The Solicitor General, representing EPA, asserts, and we agree, that the State's minimum stream flow condition is a proper application of the state and federal antidegradation regulations, as it ensures that an "existing instream water us[e]" will be "maintained and protected."

Petitioners also assert more generally that the CWA is only concerned with water "quality," and does not allow the regulation of water "quantity." This is an artificial distinction. In many cases, water quantity is closely related to water quality; a sufficient lowering of the water quantity in a body of water could destroy all of its designated uses, be it for drinking water, recreation, navigation or, as here, as a fishery....

JUSTICE THOMAS, with whom JUSTICE SCALIA joins, dissenting.

... [A] State's authority under § 401(a)(1) is limited to certifying that "any discharge" that "may result" from "any activity," such as petitioners' proposed hydroelectric project, will "comply" with the enumerated provisions of the CWA; if the discharge will fail to comply, the State may "den[y]" the certification. . . . [33 U.S.C. § 1341(a)(1)].

The minimum stream flow condition imposed by respondents in this case has no relation to any possible "discharge" that might "result" from petitioners' proposed project. The term "discharge" is not defined in the CWA, but its plain and ordinary meaning suggests "a flowing or issuing out," or "something that is emitted." Webster's Ninth New Collegiate Dictionary 360 (1991). Cf. 33 U.S.C. § 1362(16) ("The term 'discharge' when used without qualification includes a discharge of a pollutant, and a discharge of pollutants"). A minimum stream flow requirement, by contrast, is a limitation on the amount of water the project can take in or divert from the river. That is, a minimum stream flow requirement is a limitation on intake-the opposite of discharge. . . .

The Court remarks that this reading of § 401(a)(1) would have "considerable force" were it not for what the Court understands to be the expansive terms of § 401(d). . . . According to the Court, the fact that § 401(d) refers to an "applicant," rather than a "discharge," complying with various provisions of the Act "contradicts petitioners' claim that the State may only impose water quality limitations specifically tied to a 'discharge. . . .'"

While the Court's interpretation seems plausible at first glance, it ultimately must fail. If ... § 401(d) permits States to impose conditions unrelated to discharges in § 401 certifications, Congress' careful focus on discharges in § 401(a)(1)—the provision that describes the scope and function of the certification process—was wasted effort. The power to set conditions that are unrelated to discharges is, of course, nothing but a conditional power to deny certification for reasons unrelated to discharges. Permitting States to impose conditions unrelated to discharges, then, effectively eliminates the constraints of § 401(a)(1).

Subsections 401(a)(1) and (d) can easily be reconciled to avoid this problem. . . . [Section] 401(a)(1) limits a State's authority in the certification process to addressing concerns related to discharges and to ensuring that any discharge resulting from a project will comply with specified provisions of the Act. It is reasonable to infer that the conditions a State is permitted to impose on certification must relate to the very purpose the certification process is designed to serve. Thus, while § 401(d) permits a State to place conditions on a certification to ensure compliance of the "applicant," those conditions must still be related to discharges. In my view, this interpretation best harmonizes the subsections of § 401. Indeed, any broader interpretation of § 401(d) would permit that subsection to swallow § 401(a)(1).

The text of § 401(d) similarly suggests that the conditions it authorizes must be related to discharges. The Court attaches critical weight to the fact that § 401(d) speaks of the compliance of an "applicant," but that reference, in and of itself, says little about the nature of the conditions that may be imposed under § 401(d). Rather, because § 401(d) conditions can be imposed only to ensure compliance with specified provisions of law—that is, with "applicable effluent limitations and other limitations, under section 1311 or 1312 of this title, standard[s] of performance under section 1316 of this title, ... prohibition[s], effluent standard[s], or pretreatment standard[s] under section 1317 of this title, [or] ... any other appropriate requirement[s] of State law"—one should logically turn to those provisions for guidance in determining the nature, scope, and purpose of § 401(d) conditions. Each of the four identified CWA provisions describes discharge-related limitations . . . . .

The final term on the list—"appropriate requirement[s] of State law"—appears to be more general in scope. Because this reference follows a list of more limited provisions that specifically address discharges, however, the principle ejusdem generis would suggest that the general reference to "appropriate" requirements of state law is most reasonably construed to extend only to provisions that, like the other provisions in the list, impose discharge-related restrictions. . . .

The Court adopts its expansive reading of § 401(d) based at least in part upon deference to [EPA's "conclusion"] that § 401(d) is not limited to requirements relating to discharges. . . .

. . . [T]he regulation to which the Court defers is hardly a definitive construction of the scope of § 401(d). On the contrary, the EPA's position on the question whether conditions under § 401(d) must be related to discharges is far from clear. Indeed, the only EPA regulation that specifically addresses the "conditions" that may appear in § 401 certifications speaks exclusively in terms of limiting discharges. According to the EPA, a § 401 certification shall contain "[a] statement of any conditions which the certifying agency deems necessary or desirable with respect to the discharge of the activity." 40 CFR § 121.2(a)(4) (1993). In my view, § 121.2(a)(4) should ... give the Court pause before it resorts to *Chevron* deference in this case.

. . . As an alternative to their argument that § 401(d) conditions must be discharge-related, petitioners assert that the state court erred when it sustained the stream flow condition under the "use" component of the State's water quality standards without reference to the corresponding "water quality criteria" contained in those standards. . . .

. . . A water quality standard promulgated pursuant to § 303 must "consist of the designated uses of the navigable waters involved and the water quality criteria for such waters based upon such uses." The Court asserts that this language "is most naturally read to require that a project be consistent with both components, namely the designated use and the water quality criteria. . . ."

The Court's reading strikes me as contrary to common sense. It is difficult to see how compliance with a "use" of a body of water could be enforced without reference to the corresponding criteria....

The problematic consequences of decoupling "uses" and "criteria" become clear once the Court's interpretation of § 303 is read in the context of § 401. In the Court's view, a State may condition the § 401 certification "upon any limitations necessary to ensure compliance" with the "uses of the water body." Under the Court's interpretation, then, state environmental agencies may pursue, through § 401, their water goals in any way they choose; the conditions imposed on certifications need not relate to discharges, nor to water quality criteria, nor to any objective or quantifiable standard, so long as they tend to make the water more suitable for the uses the State has chosen. In short, once a State is allowed to impose conditions on § 401 certifications to protect "uses" in the abstract, § 401(d) is limitless.

... [W]hile respondents in this case focused only on the "use" of the Dosewallips River as a fish habitat, this particular river has a number of other "[c]haracteristic uses," including "[r]ecreation (primary contact recreation, sport fishing, boating, and aesthetic enjoyment)." Under the Court's interpretation, respondents could have imposed any number of conditions related to recreation, including conditions that have little relation to water quality. In *Town of Summersville*, 60 FERC P 61,291, p. 61,990 (1992), for instance, the state agency required the applicant to "construct ... access roads and paths, low water stepping stone bridges, ... a boat launching facility ..., and a residence and storage building." These conditions presumably would be sustained under the [Court's approach]. In the end, it is difficult to conceive of a condition that would fall outside a State's § 401(d) authority under the Court's approach.

Notes and Comments

1. The jurisdictional trigger under § 401(a) is a "discharge" into the navigable waters. As Justice Thomas points out in his dissent, § 502(16) states that "the term 'discharge' when used without qualification includes a discharge of a pollutant, and a discharge of pollutants." This is the only definition in all of § 502 that uses the term "includes" instead of "means" in its prefatory clause. What were the relevant discharges in *PUD No. 1*? What, if anything, should the term "discharge" include beyond point source additions of pollutants to the navigable waters? Should it include, as the Court appeared to assume in *PUD No. 1*, discharges of clean water from dams? The Supreme Court returned to this issue in *S.D. Warren Co. v. Maine Dept. of Environmental Protection*, 126 S.Ct. 1843, 164 L.Ed.2d 625 (2006), unanimously determining that it does. In so holding, the Court relied on (as had Justice Thomas in his dissent in *PUD No. 1*) a dictionary definition of "discharge" as involving a " 'flowing or issuing out.' " 126 S.Ct. at 1847–1848 (quoting from Webster's New International Dictionary 742 (2d ed. 1949)). Should the term "discharge" also include stormwater runoff that contains nonpoint pollution? In *Oregon Natural Desert Ass'n v. Dombeck*, 172 F.3d 1092 (9th Cir. 1998), the Ninth Circuit reasoned as follows in concluding that it does not:

The terminology employed throughout the [CWA] cuts against ONDA's argument that the term "discharge" includes nonpoint source pollution like runoff from grazing. Neither the phrase "nonpoint source discharge" nor the phrase "discharge from a nonpoint source" appears in the Act. Rather, the word "discharge" is used consistently to refer to the release of effluent from a point source. By contrast, the term "runoff" describes pollution flowing from nonpoint sources. The term runoff is used throughout [§ 208], describing urban wastewater plans, and [§ 304(f)], providing guidelines for identification of nonpoint sources of pollution. Section [401] contains no reference to runoff.

172 F.3d at 1098. Are you persuaded?

2.   FERC licenses have terms of up to 50 years. See, e.g., 16 U.S.C. § 799. It seems clear that relicensing at the end of such a term triggers the § 401 certification requirement. See 18 C.F.R. § 4.38(f)(7)(iii). Amendments during the life of such licenses have proven trickier. In *North Carolina v. FERC*, 112 F.3d 1175 (D.C. Cir. 1997), a divided D.C. Circuit held that an operator was not required to go through § 401 certification where it was seeking an amendment for the construction of an intake structure that would facilitate the withdrawal of 60 million gallons of water per day from a lake. Although the dam discharged water through its turbines, the court held that a "decrease in the volume of water passing through the dam turbines cannot be considered a 'discharge' as that term is defined in the CWA." 112 F.3d at 1188. Judge Wald dissented, arguing that "if a State must consent before a new discharge is introduced into its waters, then a change in that discharge must require new consent." 112 F.3d at 1196. In *Alabama Rivers Alliance v. FERC*, 325 F.3d 290 (D.C. Cir. 2003), by contrast, the same D.C. Circuit held that certification was required where a licensee sought an amendment to upgrade its turbine generators, and where the new generators would have increased the flow of oxygen-deprived water.

3.   Turning now to *PUD No. 1*, were you persuaded by the majority's analysis with respect to the interplay between § 401(a) and (d)? What were the strongest elements of the majority's analysis? What were those of the dissent? Given the closeness of the issues in this case, many observers thought the outcome would hinge upon whose side the Government took. Ultimately, the Government sided with the State of Washington. Do you agree that this was a situation in which *Chevron* deference was appropriate?

4.   Assuming that § 401 only relates to point source discharges, and in light of *PUD No. 1*, we may now see that § 401 adds four significant elements to the control that States otherwise possess under the NPDES program:

— It applies in some situations in which neither the NPDES program nor the § 404 program apply; i.e., where there is a discharge that does not involve an addition of pollutants (as in most FERC-licensing scenarios);

— It ensures that unauthorized States will have the opportunity to protect their water quality in situations in which EPA is issuing NPDES permits;

— It gives the States (here, all of them) a similar oversight role in the context of § 404 permits; and

— In all of the above situations, it empowers the States to address not only the impact of the discharge, but also any water quality impacts associated with the rest of the applicant's activity.

It should be noted, however, that § 401 only *empowers* the States to protect their water quality interests, it does not *require* them to do so. Section 401(a) specifically provides that States will be deemed to have waived their § 401 prerogative if they do not take action upon a certification request "within a reasonable period of time (which shall not exceed one year)." EPA's regulations further flesh out this dynamic by (a) allowing States to affirmatively waive before the expiration of this period, and (b) giving the licensing or permitting agencies the authority to specify the default waiver period which, EPA indicates, should generally be 6 months. 40 C.F.R. § 121.16.

5. Section 401(d) specifically provides that any conditions established through the § 401 process shall become conditions of the relevant Federal license or permit. Any arguments about the merits of any decisions made by the States in the § 401 process may be raised only in State court.

6. Did you agree with the Court's analysis regarding the State's ability to establish conditions regarding compliance with the designated use? What did you think of the dissent's objections on this front? Note that the Washington Supreme Court had relied primarily on the State's antidegradation standards, whereas Justice O'Connor's opinion seems to treat them as a secondary ground supporting the Court's result. Does it make a difference which way one analyzes this issue? More broadly speaking, what are the implications of the Court's treatment of the second issue? How might it apply, for example, in the wetlands context?

B. Sections 208 and 319

The CWA contains two programs—besides the TMDL program—that encourage the States to address areawide water quality planning in a manner that addresses nonpoint pollution. The first of these, § 208, was created in 1972; the second, § 319, was enacted in 1987, in response to the perceived failure of § 208. Professor Robert Adler has provided a nice description of the basic structure and weaknesses of these programs:

> Section 208 required ... identification of various categories of nonpoint source pollution, and development of "procedures and methods" to control those sources "to the extent feasible"—known typically as "best management practices" or "BMPs." Section 208, however, included no specific requirement to match the controls selected or implemented under the plan with what was necessary to attain or maintain [water quality standards ("WQS")], as determined through TMDLs or otherwise. Moreover, the requirement that BMPs be "feasible" suggests a technology-based rather than water quality-based approach to BMP selection. In other words, while requiring general nonpoint-source pollution control practices,

the law included no numeric, water quality-based effluent limitations for nonpoint sources.

In 1987, Congress added a new program to address nonpoint source pollution (section 319). While requiring new lists of waters impaired by nonpoint sources of pollution, and new statewide plans to redress that pollution, section 319 adds little rigor to the Act's nonpoint source controls. The provision includes a general requirement that states develop new programs on a watershed-specific basis "to the maximum extent practicable." This requirement suggests the need for states to focus on specific water quality problems, including WQS violations, in individual watersheds. Aside from this vague admonition, however, section 319 did little to remedy the lack of a precise requirement for states to match specific management practices with the degree of control necessary (in combination with new and existing controls on point sources) to meet WQS. Moreover, although section 319 authorizes EPA to conduct listing and assessment if a state fails to do so, like section 208, it contains no express authority for EPA to prepare or implement a nonpoint source pollution control program if a state's program is nonexistent or inadequate.

Adler, Integrated Approaches to Water Pollution: Lessons from the Clean Air Act, 23 Harv. Envtl. L. Rev. 203, 227 (1999) (footnotes omitted).

While some States have utilized the federal dollars available under these programs to develop innovative nonpoint source control programs, the lack of any real federal teeth has limited the effectiveness of Sections 208 and 319. In essence, all EPA can do in the face of State inaction is to deny States the monies that would otherwise be available to implement these programs, and to undertake a modest amount of planning (but no implementation) itself under § 319.

C. The TMDL Program

On its face, Section 303(d)(1)(A) of the CWA requires the States to identify those waters for which BPT and secondary treatment are not stringent enough to achieve compliance with water quality standards. It also dictates that they "shall establish a priority ranking for such waters, taking into account the severity of the pollution and the uses to be made of such waters." This ranking sets the stage for the development of TMDLs, the establishment of which is addressed primarily in § 303(d)(1)(C). Under that provision, the States are required to establish, in accordance with their priority ranking, TMDLs for those pollutants identified by EPA as being suitable for such calculation. It further instructs that the "load shall be established at a level necessary to implement the applicable standards ... with seasonal variations and a margin of safety which takes into account any lack of knowledge concerning the relationship between effluent limitations and water quality." Not surprisingly, the States must submit these ranking lists and TMDLs to EPA for its approval. 33 U.S.C. § 1313(d)(2). If EPA disapproves a submittal, Section 303(d)(2) requires it to establish its own ranking and TMDLs within 30 days.

Despite the fact that § 303(d) has been in place since 1972, the TMDL program is still in its infancy. For many years, both the States and EPA essentially ignored its edicts. Then, in 1984, a citizens group was successful in establishing that EPA has a mandatory duty to take action even in situations in which a State (in that case, Indiana) had never submitted any TMDLs. In *Scott v. City of Hammond*, 741 F.2d 992, 998 (7th Cir. 1984), the Seventh Circuit indicated its willingness to treat Indiana's non-submittal as being the "constructive submission" of no TMDLs. Thus, the court determined, EPA had a non-discretionary duty under § 303(d)(2) to either approve or disapprove that implied determination. Id.

Shortly after *Hammond* was decided, EPA promulgated rules clarifying in somewhat more detail its view as to how the TMDL program should work. Importantly, it defined the term "total maximum daily load" to mean the sum of what it refers to as "wasteload allocations" for point sources, and "load allocations" for nonpoint sources. 40 C.F.R. § 130.2. In this way, EPA made clear that a TMDL is more than just an overall determination of the amount of the relevant pollutant that the relevant water body can assimilate without violating the relevant water quality standard; instead, it also involves an allocation of that gross amount among all known point and nonpoint sources. Additionally, EPA slightly narrowed the circumstances in which TMDLs are required by expanding the list of other requirements that can be utilized to render TMDLs unnecessary; whereas (as mentioned above) the statutory language focuses solely on BPT and secondary treatment, EPA's regulations indicate that TMDLs are unnecessary if compliance with water quality standards can be achieved through resort to any of the CWA's technology-based requirements, any more stringent State or local standards, and/or any other pollution control requirements, such as BMPs. 40 C.F.R. § 130.7(b)(1). Thus, in EPA's view, the TMDL program is to be utilized as a last resort if other regulatory approaches have failed to achieve compliance with water quality standards. At the same time, however, EPA's regulations require the States to demonstrate "good cause" for leaving any waters not meeting standards (referred to as "water quality limited segments") off the list. 40 C.F.R. § 130.7(b)(6)(iv).

These developments led at first to a trickle and eventually to a cascade of *Hammond*-type citizen suits in other states. In turn, most of these cases have resulted in either consent decrees or court orders establishing schedules pursuant to which either the States or EPA are developing either priority rankings or TMDLs.

Although nothing in § 303(d) establishes any enforceable requirements vis-a-vis nonpoint sources, the TMDL program is more threatening to those sources than §§ 208 and 319 in part because the very nature of the TMDL process encourages the States, in addressing situations in which the impairment is due to both point and nonpoint sources, to establish a "fair share" for each contributor, whether point or nonpoint. In turn, this dynamic encourages the States to develop mechanisms for ensuring that the nonpoint sources will not exceed their load allocations. Additionally, if the TMDL program applies to waters that are impaired entirely by nonpoint sources, the only way States can make progress is by developing mechanisms to ensure that nonpoint sources will abide by their loads.

In this last regard, consider the following case:

PRONSOLINO v. NASTRI

United States Court of Appeals, Ninth Circuit, 2002.
291 F.3d 1123.

BERZON, Circuit Judge.

* * *

In 1992, California submitted to the EPA a list of waters pursuant to § 303(d)(1)(A). Pursuant to § 303(d)(2), the EPA disapproved California's 1992 list because it omitted seventeen water segments that did not meet the water quality standards set by California for those segments. Sixteen of the seventeen water segments, including the Garcia River, were impaired only by nonpoint sources of pollution. After California rejected an opportunity to amend its § 303(d)(1) list to include the seventeen sub-standard segments, the EPA, again acting pursuant to § 303(d)(2), established a new § 303(d)(1) list for California, including those segments on it. California retained the seventeen segments on its 1994, 1996, and 1998 § 303(d)(1) lists.

California did not, however, establish TMDLs for the segments added by the EPA. Environmental and fishermen's groups sued the EPA in 1995 to require the EPA to establish TMDLs for the seventeen segments, and in a March 1997 consent decree the EPA agreed to do so. According to the terms of the consent decree, the EPA set March 18, 1998, as the deadline for the establishment of a TMDL for the Garcia River. When California missed the deadline despite having initiated public comment on a draft TMDL and having prepared a draft implementation plan, the EPA established a TMDL for the Garcia River. . . .

The Garcia River TMDL for sediment is 552 tons per square mile per year, a sixty percent reduction from historical loadings. The TMDL allocates portions of the total yearly load among the following categories of nonpoint source pollution: a) "mass wasting" associated with roads; b) "mass wasting" associated with timber-harvesting; c) erosion related to road surfaces; and d) erosion related to road and skid trail crossings.

In 1960, appellants Betty and Guido Pronsolino purchased approximately 800 acres of heavily logged timber land in the Garcia River watershed. In 1998, after re-growth of the forest, the Pronsolinos applied for a harvesting permit from the California Department of Forestry ("Forestry").

In order to comply with the Garcia River TMDL, Forestry and/or the state's Regional Water Quality Control Board required, among other things, that the Pronsolinos' harvesting permit provide for mitigation of 90% of controllable road-related sediment run-off and contain prohibitions on removing certain trees and on harvesting from mid-October until May 1. The Pronsolinos' forester estimates that the large tree restriction will cost the Pronsolinos $750,000.

To get permit Pro's had to do things that would cost 750k

Larry Mailliard, a member of the Mendocino County Farm Bureau, submitted a draft harvesting permit on February 4, 1998, for a portion of his property in the Garcia River watershed. Forestry granted a final version of the permit after incorporation of a 60.3% reduction of sediment loading, a requirement included to comply with the Garcia River TMDL. Mr. Mailliard's forester estimates that the additional restrictions imposed to comply with the Garcia River TMDL will cost Mr. Mailliard $10,602,000.

M had same deal as Pros. Cost him 10.6 mil

Section 303(d)(1)(A) requires listing and calculation of TMDLs for "those waters within [the state's] boundaries for which the effluent limitations required by section [301(b)(1)(A)] and section [301(b)(1)(B)] of this title *are not stringent enough to implement any water quality standard* applicable to such waters." § 303(d) (emphasis added). The precise statutory question before us is whether, as the Pronsolinos maintain, the term "not stringent enough to implement ... water quality standard[s]" as used in § 303(d)(1)(A) must be interpreted to mean *both* that application of effluent limitations will not achieve water quality standards *and* that the waters at issue are subject to effluent limitations. As only waters with point source pollution are subject to effluent limitations, such an interpretation would exclude from the § 303(d)(1) listing and TMDL requirements waters impaired only by nonpoint sources of pollution.

Issue in My case

The EPA ... interprets "not stringent enough to implement ... water quality standard[s]" to mean "not adequate" or "not sufficient ... to implement any water quality standard," and does not read the statute as implicitly containing a limitation to waters initially covered by effluent limitations. According to the EPA, if the use of effluent limitations will not implement applicable water quality standards, the water falls within § 303(d)(1)(A) regardless of whether it is point or nonpoint sources, or a combination of the two, that continue to pollute the water.

EPA says does not have to be covered by effluent limitation

Whether or not the appellants' suggested interpretation is entirely implausible, it is at least considerably weaker than the EPA's competing construction. The Pronsolinos' version necessarily relies upon: (1) understanding "stringent enough" to mean "strict enough" rather than "thorough going enough" or "adequate" or "sufficient"; and (2) reading the phrase "not stringent enough" in isolation, rather than with reference to the stated goal of implementing "any water quality standard applicable to such waters." Where the answer to the question "not stringent enough for what?" is "to implement any [applicable] water quality standard," the meaning of "stringent" should be determined by looking forward to the broad goal to be attained, not backwards at the inadequate effluent limitations. One might comment, for example, about a teacher that her standards requiring good spelling were not stringent enough to assure good writing, as her students still used bad grammar and poor logic. Based on the language of the contested phrase alone, then, the more sensible conclusion is that the § 303(d)(1) list must contain any waters for which the particular effluent limitations will not be adequate to attain the statute's water quality goals.

Placing the phrase in its statutory context supports this conclusion. Section 303(d) begins with the requirement that each state "identify those waters within its boundaries...." § 303(d)(1)(A). So the statute's starting point for the listing project is a compilation of each and every navigable water within the state. Then, only those waters that will attain water quality standards after application of the new point source technology are excluded from the § 303(d)(1) list, leaving all those waters for which that technology will not "implement any water quality standard applicable to such waters." § 303(d)(1)(A). The alternative construction, in contrast, would begin with a subset of all the state's waterways, those that have point sources subject to effluent limitations, and would result in a list containing only a subset of that subset—those waters as to which the applicable effluent limitations are not adequate to attain water quality standards.

The Pronsolinos' contention to the contrary notwithstanding, no such odd reading of the statute is necessary in order to give meaning to the phrase "for which the effluent limitations required by section [301(b)(1)(A)] and section [301(b)(1)(B)] ... are not stringent enough." The EPA interprets § 303(d)(1)(A) to require the identification of any waters not meeting water quality standards only if specified effluent limitations would not achieve those standards. 40 C.F.R. § 130.2(j). If the pertinent effluent limitations would, if implemented, achieve the water quality standards but are not in place yet, there need be no listing and no TMDL calculation. *Id.*

So construed, the meaning of the statute is different than it would be were the language recast to state only that "Each State shall identify those waters within its boundaries ... [not meeting] any water quality standard applicable to such waters." Under the EPA's construction, the reference to effluent limitations reflects Congress' intent that the EPA focus initially on implementing effluent limitations and only later avert its attention to water quality standards. *See e.g.,* 1 *Legislative History* 171 ("The Administrator should assign secondary priority to [§ 303] to the extent limited manpower and funding may require a choice between a water quality standards process and early and effective implementation of the effluent limitation-permit program." (statement of Sen. Muskie, principal author of the CWA and the Chair of the Senate's Public Works Committee)).

Nothing in § 303(d)(1)(A) distinguishes the treatment of point sources and nonpoint sources as such; the only reference is to the "effluent limitations required by" § 301(b)(1). So if the effluent limitations required by § 301(b)(1) are "as a matter of law" "not stringent enough" to achieve the applicable water quality standards for waters impaired by point sources not subject to those requirements, then they are also "not stringent enough" to achieve applicable water quality standards for other waters not subject to those requirements, in this instance because they are impacted only by nonpoint sources. . . .

The Pronsolinos' objection to this view of § 303(d) . . . is, in essence, that the CWA as a whole distinguishes between the regulatory schemes applicable to point and non-point sources, so we must assume such a distinction in applying §§ 303(d)(1)(A) and (C). We would hesitate in any case to read into a discrete statutory provision something that is not there because it is contained elsewhere in the statute. But here, the premise is wrong: There is no such general division throughout the CWA.

Point sources are treated differently from nonpoint sources for many purposes under the statute, but not all. In particular, there is no such distinction with regard to the basic purpose for which the § 303(d) list and TMDLs are compiled, the eventual attainment of state-defined water quality standards. Water quality standards reflect a state's designated *uses* for a water body and do not depend in any way upon the source of pollution. *See* § 303(a)-(c).

Nor is there any other basis for inferring from the structure of the Act an implicit limitation in §§ 303(d)(1)(A) and (C). The statutory subsection requiring water quality segment identification and TMDLs, § 303(d), appears in the section entitled "Water Quality Standards and Implementation Plans," not in the immediately preceding section, CWA § 302, entitled "Water Quality Related Effluent Limitations." So the section heading does not suggest any limitation to waters subject to effluent limitations.

Additionally, § 303(d) follows the subsections setting forth the requirements for water quality standards, § 303(a)-(c)—which, as noted above, apply without regard to the source of pollution—and precedes the "continuing planning process" subsection, § 303(e), which applies broadly as well. Thus, § 303(d) is structurally part of a set of provisions governing an interrelated goal-setting, information-gathering, and planning process that, unlike many other aspects of the CWA, applies without regard to the source of pollution.

True, there are, as the Pronsolinos point out, two sections of the statute as amended, § 208 and § 319, that set requirements exclusively for nonpoint sources of pollution. But the structural inference we are asked to draw from those specialized sections—that no *other* provisions of the Act set requirements for waters polluted by nonpoint sources— simply does not follow. Absent some irreconcilable contradiction between the requirements contained in §§ 208 and 319, on the one hand, and the listing and TMDL requirements of § 303(d), on the other, both apply.

There is no such contradiction. Section 208 provides for federal grants to encourage the development of state "areawide waste treatment management plans" for areas with substantial water quality problems, § 208(a), (f), and requires that those plans include a process for identifying and controlling nonpoint source pollution "to the extent feasible." § 208(b)(2)(F). Section 319, added to the CWA in 1987, directs states to adopt "nonpoint source management programs"; provides grants for nonpoint source pollution reduction; and requires states to submit a report to the EPA that "identifies those navigable waters within the State which, without additional action to control nonpoint sources of pollution, cannot reasonably be expected to attain or maintain applicable water quality standards or the goals and requirements of this chapter." § 319(a)(1)(A). This report must also describe state programs for reducing nonpoint source pollution and the process "to reduce, to the maximum extent practicable, the level of pollution" resulting from particular categories of nonpoint source pollution. § 319(a)(1)(C), (D).

The CWA is replete with multiple listing and planning requirements applicable to the same waterways (quite confusingly so, indeed), so no inference can be drawn from the overlap alone. Nor are we willing to draw the more discrete inference that the § 303(d) listing and TMDL requirements cannot apply to nonpoint source pollutants because the planning requirements imposed by § 208 and § 319 are qualified ones— "to the extent feasible" and "to the maximum extent practicable"— while the § 303(d) requirements are unbending. For one thing, the water quality standards set under § 303 are functional and may permit more pollution than it is "feasible" or "practicable" to eliminate, depending upon the intended use of a particular waterway. For another, with or without TMDLs, the § 303(e) plans for attaining water quality standards must, without qualification, account for elimination of nonpoint source pollution to the extent necessary to meet those standards. § 303(e)(3)(F).

The various reporting requirements that apply to nonpoint source pollution are no more impermissibly redundant than are the planning requirements. Congress specifically provided that in preparing the § 319 report, states may rely on information from § 303(e), which incorporates the TMDLs. § 319(a)(2). Moreover, states must produce a § 319 report only once, but must update the § 303(d)(1) list periodically. § 319; § 303(d)(2). Also, the § 319 report requires the identification of a plan to reduce nonpoint source pollution, without regard to the attainment of water quality standards, while the plans generated using the § 303(d)(1) lists and TMDLs are guided by the goal of achieving those standards. § 319; § 303(d), (e).

Essentially, § 319 encourages the states to institute an approach to the elimination of nonpoint source pollution similar to the federally-mandated effluent controls contained in the CWA, while § 303 encompasses a water quality based approach applicable to all sources of water pollution. As various sections of the Act encourage different, and complementary, state schemes for cleaning up nonpoint source pollution in the nation's waterways, there is no basis for reading any of those sections—including § 303(d)—out of the statute.

There is one final aspect of the Act's structure that bears consideration because it supports the EPA's interpretation of § 303(d): The list required by § 303(d)(1)(A) requires that waters be listed if they are impaired by a combination of point sources and nonpoint sources; the language admits of no other reading. Section 303(d)(1)(C), in turn, directs that TMDLs "shall be established at a level necessary *to implement* the applicable water quality standards...." *Id.* (emphasis added). So, at least in blended waters, TMDLs must be calculated with regard to nonpoint sources of pollution; otherwise, it would be impossible "to implement the applicable water quality standards," which do not differentiate sources of pollution....

Nothing in the statutory structure—or purpose—suggests that Congress meant to distinguish, as to § 303(d)(1) lists and TMDLs, between waters with one insignificant point source and substantial nonpoint source pollution and waters with only nonpoint source pollution. Such a distinction would, for no apparent reason, require the states or the EPA to monitor waters to determine whether a point source had been added or removed, and to adjust the § 303(d)(1) list and establish TMDLs accordingly. There is no statutory basis for concluding that Congress intended such an irrational regime.

Looking at the statute as a whole, we conclude that the EPA's interpretation of § 303(d) is not only entirely reasonable but considerably more convincing than the one offered by the plaintiffs in this case.

The Pronsolinos finally contend that, by establishing TMDLs for waters impaired only by nonpoint source pollution, the EPA has upset the balance of federal-state control established in the CWA by intruding into the states' traditional control over land use. That is not the case.

The Garcia River TMDL identifies the maximum load of pollutants that can enter the Garcia River from certain broad categories of nonpoint sources if the river is to attain water quality standards. It does not specify the load of pollutants that may be received from particular parcels of land or describe what measures the state should take to implement the TMDL. Instead, the TMDL expressly recognizes that "implementation and monitoring" "are state responsibilities" and notes that, for this reason, the EPA did not include implementation or monitoring plans within the TMDL.

Moreover, § 303(e) requires—separately from the § 303(d)(1) listing and TMDL requirements—that each state include in its continuing planning process "adequate implementation, including schedules of compliance, for revised or new water quality standards" "for all navigable waters within such State." § 303(e)(3). The Garcia River TMDL thus serves as an informational tool for the creation of the state's implementation plan, independently—and explicitly—required by Congress.

California chose both *if* and *how* it would implement the Garcia River TMDL. States must implement TMDLs only to the extent that they seek to avoid losing federal grant money; there is no pertinent statutory provision otherwise requiring implementation of § 303 plans or providing for their enforcement.

Finally, it is worth noting that the arguments that the Pronsolinos raise here would apply equally to nonpoint source pollution controls for blended waters. Yet, as discussed above, Congress definitely required that the states or the EPA establish TMDLs for all pollutants in waters on § 303(d)(1) lists, including blended waters.

For all the reasons we have surveyed, the CWA is best read to include in the § 303(d)(1) listing and TMDLs requirements waters impaired only by nonpoint sources of pollution. Moreover, to the extent the statute is ambiguous—which is not very much—the substantial deference we owe the EPA's interpretation, under either *Chevron* or *Skidmore,* requires that we uphold the agency's more than reasonable interpretation. We therefore hold that the EPA did not exceed its statutory authority in identifying the Garcia River pursuant to § 303(d)(1)(A) and establishing the Garcia River TMDL, even though the river is polluted only by nonpoint sources of pollution.

Notes and Comments

1. The Ninth Circuit began its discussion with an extensive analysis (which we have edited out) regarding the level of deference it owed to EPA's interpretation that § 303(d) applies regardless of whether there are any point sources on the relevant river segment. While EPA's TMDL regulations never explicitly address this point, the court noted that they "focus on the attainment of water quality standards, whatever the source of any pollution." 291 F.3d at 1132. As one example of this focus, the court cited EPA's definition of a TMDL as the "sum of the individual [wasteload allocations] for point sources and [load allocations] for nonpoint sources and natural background." 40 C.F.R. s 130.2(i). The court noted that "[n]o reason appears why, under this TMDL definition, the amount of either point source loads or nonpoint source loads cannot be zero." 291 F.3d at 1132. The court also noted that EPA had issued at least two directives interpreting its rules as requiring TMDLs for waterbodies impaired solely by nonpoint sources. Id. at 1132–1133. Citing *Auer v. Robbins*, 519 U.S. 452, 461, 117 S.Ct. 905, 137 L.Ed.2d 79 (1997) for the proposition that EPA's interpretation of its own rules was "controlling unless plainly erroneous or inconsistent with the regulation" (which we have elsewhere termed "*Seminole Rock* deference"), the court then appeared to conclude that EPA's regulations, as so understood, were entitled to *Chevron* deference. 291 F.3d at 1133. Interestingly, however (as reflected in the last paragraph of the opinion), the court then waffled, suggesting that EPA's interpretation was at least entitled to *Skidmore* deference. Id. at 1133 and 1134–1135. Which of these standards of deference do you think was appropriate?

2. Putting aside issues of deference, were you persuaded by the court's interpretation of the "not stringent enough" formulation? Was the court's teaching-standards analogy a good one? What did you think of the Pronsoli-

nos' structural arguments? Were you satisfied by the court's response to those arguments? And finally, what did you make of the Prosolinos' federalism argument? As we will see when we address *SWANCC* (in chapter 8, below), this is an argument that generated some traction in that case.

3. Note the quote from Senator Muskie in the *Pronsolino* opinion, which may at least partially explain EPA's extreme slowness in implementing the TMDL program. How much attention should agencies pay to Congressional admonitions such as this one, in situations where, as here, those admonitions are in no way reflected in the statutes themselves?

4. In July 2000, EPA published a much more extensive set of TMDL rules that, among other things, expressly required TMDLs for waters polluted solely by nonpoint sources. 65 Fed.Reg. 43586 (July 13, 2000). Additionally, these new rules would have established time lines for the listing of waterways, the implementation of measures to implement the TMDLs, and the ultimate attainment of water quality standards. Id. They also would have required the States to develop implementation plans (including any necessary enforcement mechanisms) capable of providing "reasonable assurance" that their scheme would unfold as contemplated. Id. In the end, however, these rules never took effect. In 2001, the Bush Administration put them on hold until 2003. 66 Fed.Reg. 53044 (Oct. 18, 2001). And in 2003, it announced that it was withdrawing them altogether. 68 Fed.Reg. 13608 (March 19, 2003). While EPA simultaneously announced that it was still looking into the possibility of regulatory updates, most observers are not holding their breath.

Chapter 4

CLEAN AIR ACT

I. THE PROBLEM OF AIR POLLUTION

The following is an excerpt of chapter 1 from When Smoke Flows Like Water, by Devra Davis:

> Donora, Pennsylvania, was the kind of place where an adventurous three-year-old like my brother Marty could wander five miles away from home and never really be lost. He made front page headlines both times, "Runaway Marty Does It Again!" read the second one, but each time, somebody brought him back up the steep hills, around the curvy slag-lined, coal-paved roads, back to our house.
>
> All of us children roamed free. Behind my house was a barren stretch of caked, light brown earth the size of two football fields. At its edge, the smooth dusty ground sloped down, at an angle perfect for sliding, to some black ditches with iridescent pools of oily water at the bottom. After a few hours of playing with my friends in the fantastic cracks and crevices of this field, I usually found myself half a mile down the road, at my beloved grandmother Bubbe Pearl's house. She was always home, and her bedroom was perfumed with the smell of chicken soup.
>
> Nestled into the hillside inside a sharp horseshoe bend in the Monongahela River, Donora had sprung up around its metalworks and steel industry. In 1900, William Donner began building an iron mill alongside the fast-moving river, and enough immigrants showed up for jobs that the town was officially incorporated a year later. By midcentury it featured a church or two on most corners, an intense Little League system, and one of the best high-school football teams in the Valley. The main street ran for two blocks with no traffic light and was anchored at one end by the Fraternal Order of Eagles, the Masons, the Polish Falcons, the Sons of Croatia, and a bowling alley. An ice cream cone with two big scoops cost a nickel at Weiss' Drug Store, and at Niccolanco's, a single penny could buy a child's fortune in sugar: 5 Tootsie Rolls, 3 red-hot jawbreakers, or 10 of the smaller gumballs.

Nobody needed a clock. Dinner times, school recesses, and PTA meetings were announced by the shrieking mill whistles. When there was a fire, long blasts from the mill would signal what precinct of town the fire was in. Short blasts would indicate the street number. Any time a fire whistle went off, anyone who could stopped whatever he was doing to go help. The firemen were all volunteers.

Everybody in Donora either worked for "the world's largest nail mill," as the sign atop the factory gate announced, or worked to feed, clothe, fuel or take care of those who did.

* * *

Donora was a simple town, not pretty in any conventional sense, with cobblestone streets that snaked up and down hills so steep they had stairs instead of sidewalks. It was a young place, full of working people, few of them over 60—the sort of place where weeks would pass and nobody would die.

* * *

In the 1950s, the mills began to shut down, and Donora became a place to leave. Nobody spoke about what was happening. My family moved to Pittsburgh when I was ready to begin high school, searching, like half the town's families, for better opportunities. One day I came home from my college classes, dropped my books in the hall, and said to my mother, "Mom, was there *another* place called Donora?" I had never heard much discussion about where we came from. Now it had grabbed my attention in an unsettling way.

My mother had just put a kettle on to boil. "Why do you ask?" she said.

"Well there are several Allentowns, several Websters, a couple of Eagles. There's Pittsburg, Kansas, and Pittsburgh, Pennsylvania. So maybe there are a few Donoras?"

She moved into the kitchen and sat down on the bench next to the built-in white table. I followed her in, took a big breath, and continued to press. "I read in a book at school that in a town with the *same* name as ours, there was pollution. Was Donora polluted? Or was there *another* Donora?" I could not imagine that what I'd read had anything to do with where I'd grown up. I had never heard about our town being anything other than a wonderful place. I had never heard of pollution. The word sounded dirty, something to be ashamed of.

The whistle of the teakettle interrupted, and my mother got up to take the pot off the stove. At first I thought she was going to tell me about someplace else, another Donora somewhere. I was pretty sure of that, but then I could tell she was hesitating. Slowly she poured the steaming water into a small blue cup, dunking the tea bag in briefly. Without even asking if I wanted any, with a nod that commanded me to join her, she poured another blue cup of water, passed the same tea bag into it, and handed it to me. We sat across from each other with steaming teacups on the table between us. She sighed and finally replied, 'Nobody knew from pollution then. That was just the way it was. We didn't think much about it.

"Remember all that grime we had on the cars, how we had to drive with the headlights on at three in the afternoon? How the sun didn't shine for days at a time? Remember how women always had their curtains hanging out to dry every week? A lot of us gave up on curtains altogether. Venetian blinds were better, because they could be wiped down. My mother's house had 36 windows and we were always washing them. By the time we got to the last one, the first was already soiled. They were never really clean." I had expected an explanation, but what she gave me was a reminiscence.

There in the sunny kitchen of our big house, ten years and thirty miles away from our old town, it felt like we were on another planet. Outside I could see the sunlight on the green grass. Bubbe Pearl had never made it out of Donora. She had once been famous for her strength the first woman in the Valley to hand-crank a Model T Ford. A legendary driver, she frequently drove the nine hours to Atlantic City with her five children beside her, long before there was a Pennsylvania Turnpike. Nobody ever passed her. But when I was growing up she kept her bed in her dining room because she could not make it up the stairs to a bedroom. She could never be more than a few steps away from an oxygen tank. Traveling beauticians regularly attended to her and to dozens of other women who were too sick to walk up and down the hills to the beauty parlor. When I was very young, I simply assumed that all blue-haired grannies stayed in bed, tethered to oxygen tanks.

"But they say people got really sick in Donora. Did people get sick?"

"Well, we used to say, That's not coal dust, that's gold dust. As long as the mills were working, the town was in business. That's what kept your Zadde and your father employed. Nobody was going to ask if it made a few people ill. People had to eat."

I shot her the kind of skeptical look that daughters have been giving mothers since time immemorial. "Look, today they might call it pollution," she sighed. "Back then it was just a living."

So Donora was famous, but no one ever talked about it. We lapsed into silence.

* * *

Every child in Donora knew how to make steel. You needed limestone, coal and iron ore. A pamphlet handed out at one of the Donora Steel & Wire Works' annual Open Houses explained that a normal day's operation required 45 carloads of iron ore, 40 cars of coke, 6 of limestone, and 6 of miscellaneous materials. Each day the plant burned as much coal as all the homes in Pittsburgh.

These ingredients regularly arrived via massive coal-fired barges snaking up the Monongahela River. Along the Donora side of the river, we could watch the barges rising through the intricate system of locks. Huge metal gates would open, the giant vessel would slowly move inside as if being swallowed by some gigantic whale, and then the gates would bellow with the crunching, creaking, groaning sounds of metal on metal as they majestically swept shut. The captain would tie up to the side of the lock with oily, blackened hawsers as thick as my leg, crossing them at bow and stern. The lockmaster and barge captain would wave a thumbs-up, and hundreds of thousands of gallons of muddy river water would surge into the lock. Then, with a movement that never ceased to amaze us, the ship would gradually inch upward, as though lifted by some phantom force, until it could float out the other side and continue its journey to the mills.

Other supplies came on long freight trains that ran along the river and right through the center of the string of furnaces, rolling mills and smelters. Still others came right out of the ground nearby. Cliffs of limestone were regularly sliced away with huge shovels, draglines and half-tracks. Family mines, some in people's backyards, yielded Appalachian coal from some of the richest seams in the world.

More than anything else, coal was essential to keeping Donora alive. It heated our homes and fired the massive furnaces and ovens of the mills. Mountainous piles of coal at the mills meant the town was in business. In addition to needing coal for the furnaces, steel making depended on a derivative of coal called coke. Coke was essentially coal with the greasy impurities baked out at hellish temperatures. The pure carbon that remained determined whether what came out of the blast furnace was iron or steel.

As a blacksmith hammers a piece of wrought iron to shape it, he must keep it hot so that it remains soft. In charcoal-fired forges like those in Donora, carbon solids and carbon monoxide remain in contact with the iron surface at relatively high temperatures. The hammered surface combines with small amounts of carbon (the iron is carburized) to create a new alloy. When it contains just one part per thousand of carbon, iron is not ordinary iron any more; it becomes steel. This small trace of carbon distributed throughout the dense mass of iron makes it stronger, so that it will take a better edge, build a stronger bridge, or support a taller building than almost any other material humans know how to make.

A coke oven was a pretty simple affair, a gigantic beehive about the size of a one-car garage, built in honeycomb fashion out of fired bricks. Coal was shoveled in and heated to intense temperatures; coke came out. The gases and smoke that are baked out of the coal are supposed to remain in the oven, but they do not. Seductively sweet aromatic hydrocarbons fill the air and ground nearby.

A commercial coking operation required a string of about eighteen ovens, called a battery. Like a great shark that has to keep moving to stay alive, a coke battery had to run all the time, at temperatures above 2,000 degrees Fahrenheit. The ovens had to be blocked shut to assure a constant, even temperature. If they ever cooled, they could not be restarted. This meant that once the oven was fired, hardy souls with a good tolerance for heat had to carefully stack bricks together over the opening. Folks who worked the ovens tended to be young.

* * *

By 1950, however, the mill in Donora had converted entirely to more modern blast furnaces. The center of the blast furnace is called the "dead man" because it is absolutely devoid of air: metal formed in this zone will have no bubbles to weaken it. The limestone served as a kind of sponge, to soak up the impurities. When cooked to the right point, the limestone and impurities floated to the top where they could be skimmed off as slag, leaving the heavier stuff that ultimately became steel to sink to the bottom.

On summer evenings, my family and I would sit in lawn chairs behind our house and watch the fiery spray and sparks coming off the blast furnace as it was topped off. Sluice gates from the furnace channeled the steaming, molten slag into waiting gondola cars shaped like giant teacups. The train was hauled, still smoking, to the dump, where the slag was poured off between the surrounding bluffs. The remaining white-hot liquid steel moved slowly on tracks to where it was poured from huge ladles into five-ton molds to make ingots. An ingot was about four men long and two men wide, red, hot, heavy and forbidding. They were then shipped on slow wheels to the rolling mill, where they went through gigantic rolling pins for stretching, soaking, coating, blooming, heat-treating and galvanizing, to produce the essentials of industrial life.

A few years before I was born, a steelworker fell into the ladle being used to draw off the molten brew, just as the furnace was being tapped. They said he'd been drinking, though how this was proved is beyond me. Not a single body part was recovered. They buried the bucket outside, near the blast furnace.

I loved the spectacular, sprawling fire that lit up the sky for miles. The night sky, glowing with molten metal from the furnaces, was a fiercely hypnotic sight. My cousin Mark remembers that people on their way to Pittsburgh would stop their cars on the other side of the river just to watch.

* * *

The greatest enemy of steel, oddly enough, is air. Oxygen is constantly trying to bind with metals like iron, to create that permanent orange layer better known as rust. Iron had to be painted with a film that contained metals like cadmium or lead to keep out the air. Even steel eventually succumbed to rusting unless it was galvanized. Once the ingots had been milled, stretched, rolled, or cut into sheets, slabs, girders or fences, they could be given a galvanic shield to protect them against air. This essentially meant plunging the steel into a bath of molten zinc at about 850 degrees. The zinc would bond to the surface of the steel, forming a series of layered zinc-iron alloys. When done properly, these alloy layers last for three or four decades.

During the violent work slowdowns and protests before World War I that gave rise to the big steelworkers union, Donora remained staunchly anti-union. (In 1919, it would be the only town to oppose the Homestead strike.) For being the consummate company town, Donora was rewarded with a zinc plant. The new zinc works was built in 1915 as one of the world's largest facilities; it stretched for forty acres along the river and was out of date the moment it opened. Its massive, horizontal coal-fired furnaces were already giving way to electrically powered plants that were less smoky and that did not create such quantities of toxic zinc fumes. The plant's smokestacks, moreover, were less than 150 feet tall, too short to propel their contents above the 600–foot hills around them. In 1933, after the plant had been firing for less than two decades, a Pennsylvania historian reported that bones from some old Indian graves had washed out of the hillside downwind of the zinc plant. What was coming out of the smokestacks had killed all the grass so that the dead could not stay buried.

**Figure 1.1: Topological map of Donora mill
area, with plumes from zinc mill**

Working zinc was like coking, only worse. The zinc furnaces were so hot that you could see heat rising from them for miles, in rivers of distorted light like fun-house mirrors. At its peak, the Donora Zinc Works employed about 1500 men, who enjoyed an average workday of just three hours and yet received the highest wages in town, this in an era before unions had entered the plants. There was some difference of opinion about why this was. The workers themselves used to say it was because they were so efficient that they could fill the ovens in three hours with as much raw material as could be processed in an entire day. An historian of the town's pollution, Lynn Snyder, maintains that zinc workers worked a three-hour day because nobody could have tolerated more time than that in front of the red-hot furnaces. As soon as the furnaces were filled with the materials from which zinc would be cooked out, the workers were allowed to leave.

Most of the plant's employees had emigrated from parts of Spain where their families had produced zinc workers for generations. They did not mix much with the rest of the townsfolk. One fellow who had worked in a zinc plant commented to me, "I was the only one in the workforce who could read or speak English. Most of the workers were under 25. Few of them lasted very long." He described for me his last day in the plant: "Five guys had gone before me to shovel out the finished zinc. Each one of them keeled over, real sick, kinda pale, and nearly passed out. I was the sixth one in. I couldn't take it either. I left. Spent a week in bed and never returned." Not many ever made it to the age of 30 as zinc workers.

Zinc is one of those elements that the body needs in very small doses in certain forms, but that is poisonous in larger amounts and other forms. When bound with sugars in microdoses, zinc probably fights colds by killing rhinoviruses. But when combined with gases of sulfur, carbon, fluoride or nitrogen, zinc can be exceptionally dangerous. And it was not the only poison rising from those ovens. The smelting of zinc and the making of steel both use lots of flurospar, a rock made of crystals of fluoride tied with calcium. During smelting, fluorspar creates a penetratingly and corrosively toxic fluoride gas which can eat the gloss off light bulbs, etch normal glass, and scar the teeth of children. One investigator found that mottled teeth, characteristic of fluoride poisoning, was common among young people in the Valley. My father had teeth like that, spotted no matter what he did. We figured he simply hadn't brushed enough as a kid.

Fumes from the mills, coke ovens, coal stoves, and zinc furnaces were often trapped in the Valley by the surrounding hills. They gave us spectacularly beautiful sunsets and plenty of barren dirt fields to play on.

* * *

On calm, cloudless, dry nights, the air gives up its heat to the surrounding hillsides, and growing denser as it cools, flows downhill like water. Usually, the temperature within any column of air is cooler the higher you get. Where there are valleys, the colder air from the hills can create an inversion layer that keeps warmer air from rising. Hot air balloons fly because hot air is lighter than cold air. But when an inversion happens, balloons cannot fly, smoke cannot rise, and fumes, hot when released, cool and sink back to the ground, unable to dissipate.

October 26th, 1948, brought a massive, still blanket of cold air over the entire Monongahela Valley. All the gases from Donora's mills, its furnaces and stoves, were unable to rise above the hilltops and began to fill the homes and streets of the town with a blinding fog of coal, coke and metal fumes. At first, cars and trucks tried to creep along with their headlights lit, but by midday, traffic came to a standstill as drivers could no longer see the street. "I could not even see my hand at the end of my arm," recalls Vince Graziano, then a strapping young steelworker. "I actually could not find my way home. I got lost that day."

Later, Berton Roueche, *The New Yorker*'s distinguished medical writer, described it this way:

> The fog closed over Donora on the morning of Tuesday, October 26th. The weather was raw, cloudy, and dead calm, and it stayed that way as the fog piled up all that day and the next. By Thursday, it had stiffened adhesively into a motionless clot of smoke. That afternoon, it was just possible to see across the street. Except for the stacks, the mills had vanished. The air began to have a sickening smell, almost a taste.

Arnold Hirsh, a World War II veteran then just beginning his half-century as the town's leading attorney, watched the gathering fog from his Main Street office. "The air looked yellow, never like that before. Nothing moved. I went over to Seventh Street and stood at the corner of McKean, looking down towards the river, and you could just barely see the railroad tracks. Right there on the tracks was a coal-burning engine puffing away. It issued a big blast of black smoke that went up about six feet in the air and stopped cold. It just hung there, with no place to go, in air that did not move."

The sturdy people of Donora were not perturbed. On Friday afternoon, the town's annual Halloween parade took place under a spooky haze. Children's costumes appeared and disappeared in the mist as the parade moved the two blocks down Main Street. My mother remembers it as a ghastly sight, but it fit the occasion. "Of course we all went," she told me later. "This fog was heavy, but there was only one Halloween every year. Only this time we could not see much." People could barely see their own feet. Within days, nearly half the town would fall ill.

Donora did not abandon its routines easily. The high-school football team, the Dragons, practiced kickoffs in preparation for the next day's home game against their great rivals, the Monongahela Wildcats. Jimmy Russell, the head coach, had to yell "Kick!" so that the receiving team would know the ball was in the air. He had no idea that some players had taken advantage of the fog and left early.

The football game between Donora and Monongahela went off as scheduled. The entire town turned out for pep rallies and parades, with strutting drum majorettes leading the black-and-orange-uniformed marching band. The spectators often lost sight of the ball and could only guess from the referees' whistles when to cheer. When Donora's star tight end, Stanley Sawa, was ordered by the public address system in midgame to "Go home! Go home now!" some in the stands thought it was a prank.

Still in his uniform, with his helmet in his hands, Sawa raced up and down the hills to his family's home at the bottom of 5th Street. Fifth Street was one of the many streets that were so steep they had stairs instead of sidewalks, where nobody ever tried to park a car because the brake would not hold. He dashed into the house.

"What's going on?" he huffed. "Why'd you make me leave the game?"

"It's your dad," a neighbor told him.

"What are you talking about?" Sawa demanded. "Where is he?"

"In there, with the doctor," came the reply. "It doesn't look good."

The elder Sawa, who earned his living lifting massive loads of coke and iron ore, had been brought home from the mill, short of breath, dizzy, thinking he only needed to lie down. By the time Stanley arrived home his father had already died.

Monongahela won the game, 27 to 7. Spectators leaving the field quickly learned that by 10:00 that morning, nine people had died. Within 24 hours the number would be up to eighteen.

Arnold Hirsh had tried to attend the game. "My brother Wallace and I decided we would walk up the Fifth Street steps. We had just gotten out of the service. He had been a lieutenant in the Navy, and I had been an infantry officer. We were both in as good shape as you could be. When we finally got to the top of those steps on our way to the game, we simply could not take another step. We did not say another word to each other. We could barely talk. We turned and headed straight home."

When they got there, they found their mother in distress. "My mother, who had not been well for years, just could not catch her breath," Hirsh recalled. Donora had eight doctors at the time, all of whom made regular house calls. This time, however, no one would come. "I called Doc Rongaus and he said that he just could not make it. He said, the whole town is sick. Even healthy fellas are dropping. Get your mother the hell out of town!" The Hirshes drove into the Allegheny Mountains, away from the fog. Arnold's mother had come to Donora in 1920 as a healthy teenage bride. Both of her parents, who lived elsewhere, survived to almost 100. By the time her two children were grown, she was an invalid with a weak heart and serious breathing difficulties. She died two years after the smog, having barely reached her fifties.

Doc Rongaus gave the same advice to anyone who would listen: Leave if you can. The firemen of Donora went from door to door delivering whiffs of oxygen from tanks to those who were stranded. One of the firemen, John Volk, remembered borrowing oxygen canisters from the Monongahela, Monessen and Charleroi fire departments. "There never was such a fog. You couldn't see your hand in front of your face, day or night. Hell, even inside the station the air was blue. I drove on the left side of the street with my head out the window, steering by scraping the curb."

When I visited him recently at an old age home, Doc Rongaus told me that folks who made it to Palmer Park seemed to recover. The park sat high on a hill and was one of the few green places near the town, probably because fumes from the mills did not regularly sweep over it. "My brother and I hauled women and children in horse-drawn wagons up to the park. Soon as we got them above the smog, they would get much better." Church ladies from nearby towns provided food and blankets to the involuntary campers.

Others shut themselves in. "I had an elderly aunt and uncle," Arnold Hirsh recalls, "who lived on the corner of Fourth and McKean, named Myerson. My aunt looked out the window and figured out that this was something pretty bad. She closed her doors and kept them closed. They had no problem at all. They just stayed inside for five days."

The folks who ran the mills stuck to their routine. The whistles that kept the daily rhythms of the town shrieked on schedule, and the shifts that kept the plants running 24 hours a day did not cease. Although many people whispered that the mills had put something strange into the air, the superintendent of the zinc works, Michael Neale, knew that his mill was doing nothing unusual. That weekend, the enormous volume of telephone calls created a five-hour wait before frantic relatives could speak to local residents. Roger Blough, then Chief Counsel of American Steel and Wire and later its CEO, finally reached Neale at 3:00 Sunday morning to tell him to "dead fire" the furnaces, without zinc ore. A zinc furnace, like a coke oven, cannot be allowed to stop; once cooled, it can never be restarted. Dead firing would protect the equipment while reducing the plant's emissions. Resentful of the interference and unconvinced there was a problem, Neale only complied after a group of company-hired chemists arrived at six that morning, some hours after he had received the order to reduce operations. He described this action as a gesture of concern for the community, not an admission of responsibility for the smog. As he later told the press, "the zinc works has operated for 32 years with no problem."

It was Walter Winchell, with that voice that resonated importance and certainty, who made Donora famous. "Good evening, America!" he said in his national radio broadcast that Saturday night. "The small, hard-working steel town of Donora, Pennsylvania is in mourning tonight, as they recover from a catastrophe. People dropped dead from a thick killer fog that sickened much of the town. Folks are investigating what has hit the area." But, he had already given the answer many would come to accept: it was a "killer fog," a freak of the weather, ultimately an act of G-d.

By the time the fog began to ebb that Sunday, the local funeral home had run out of caskets. Still, the Pittsburgh Post Gazette reported, "the citizenry maintained an attitude of outward calm which was surprising to observe. Here and there on the streets the youngsters continued their games of touch football and rode their bikes." Rains early on the morning of November 1 washed the skies of whatever had hit the town. By November 2, the zinc mill was once again running at full steam. The same work ethic that had kept the football team practicing, the marching band playing, and the cheerleaders cheering also kept the town from delaying getting back to work.

Photographs taken from same point at same time of day showing comparison of atmospheric pollution on different days.

Figure 1.2: Photos taken from the same point at the same time of day, showing comparison of pollution on different days

* * *

The day after the funerals, Dr. Joseph Shilen, a county medical official, filed a report with the Pennsylvania Secretary of Health recommending that the zinc works be reopened. The incident, he wrote, was unlikely to recur. Asked to investigate the smog, John J. Blumfield, Deputy Head of Industrial Hygiene for the Public Health Service, refused to do so, calling it "a one-time atmospheric freak."

What happened in Donora was not freakish, nor was it the first time that winds and weather combined with industrial fumes to kill so many that the deaths could hardly be counted. Neither Donorans nor many others knew that in 1930, in the Meuse Valley of Belgium, dozens of people had died within days in a smoky fog. Here too, the exact count was never tallied. Like Donora, the city of Liege sat on a series of steep hills around a river valley, surrounded by metal mills and smelters. The conditions were similar: heavy fogs, lots of fumes from the mills, and workers who depended absolutely on the mills to feed their families.

Some experts who studied the Liege disaster in 1936 warned of the consequences if a similar catastrophe were to befall a larger city. Given the size and age distribution of Liege's population, they calculated that if the same conditions ever hit London, over 4,000 would die in a single week. Nobody listened.

One Belgian investigator painstakingly demonstrated that fluoride gases were the likely cause of the devastation. Sulfur, he pointed out, in heavy doses leaves distinct marks on the linings of the lungs, but fluoride gases do not. They pass right into the bloodstream and attack the heart and other organs, without marring the nasal passages, throat or lungs. The lungs of those who died in Liege were clean. Nobody noticed.

* * *

For Donora, as for Liege, the important questions never got asked. Information critical to figuring out what went on remained hidden, sometimes in full view. As a result, the right things never got counted.

After the smog, a brief campaign erupted against the zinc mill, led by folks outside of Donora. Abe Celapino, a prosperous farmer and restaurant owner from across the bridge in Webster, whose cows and chickens had died, joined forces with the Monessen Daily Independent in calling for the mill to be relocated to a desert area. The editor-in-chief remarked that this might soon be unnecessary: the mill was creating its own desert area where it stood. Dr. Bill Rongaus, the only member of the Borough Council at the time who was not employed by the mills, pointed out that the zinc mill was likely to account for the sudden sickness. "There was fog in Monessen, too," he told the Donora Board of Health, "but it didn't kill people there the way this did. There's something in the air here that isn't found anywhere else." Celapino alleged that Michael Duda, a zinc worker and Borough Council member, had told him late one night in Celapino's restaurant, "I've got a darn good job and I'm going to keep it. I don't care what it kills."

In the month that followed, calls for major studies of the town were rebuffed by people who did not want to know the answer, and others who feared what it would ultimately mean for the town's workforce.

It was revealed that the town council and the Chamber of Commerce had requested advice from the Pennsylvania Department of Forests and Waters the previous March. A reply from Deputy Forester James Cornely was read to a community hearing just after the smog had cleared: "It is my belief that Donora could demand that smoke filters could be placed in the smoke stacks of the zinc plant; and if done in the right manner with the suggestions of a possible usable precipitate or residue being produced, the result might be satisfactory."

This was an early suggestion for what later became standard industry practice. The escaping fumes contained valuable metals and other materials that could be trapped and reused, netting the mills more money and the town less pollution. But the mill operators in Donora had no interest in such a device.

* * *

A Philadelphia chemist brought in to study the problem, Philip Sadtler, speculated that the toxin came directly from the mills. Within months of the disaster, he reported in *Chemical and Engineering News,* the journal of the American Chemical Society, that he had found over 1000 parts per million of fluoride in an air conditioning unit from Donora. Blood taken from those who died showed 12 to 25 times the normal levels of fluoride.

Their lungs, Doc Rongaus recalled some fifty years later, looked fine at autopsy. A report issued by the State of Pennsylvania corroborates his memory, especially in its description of the person identified as Case P:

> The evidence discloses that the larynx, trachea and bronchi of the first order were little affected. Apparently, the irritating agent was carried into the lung and exerted its primary effect upon the terminal bronchi, the bronchioles and the pulmonary parenchyma. However, the agent must have had a low irritating capacity since none of the cases exhibited a degree of hemorrhage, oedema, or necrotizing process commonly associated with the inhalation of lethal irritating substances. Analogy might be made here with certain war gases. Phosgene, for example, has little effect upon the upper respiratory tract. The finer bronchi and lungs undergo intense oedema and congestion during the acute phase of the poisoning.

In other words, the body's upper breathing system was not disturbed by whatever was in the air in Donora. Whatever killed these people slipped deeply and directly into the body, making a bloody swollen mess of the lower lungs, much like phosgene, a nerve gas used in World Wars I and II.

But the source of the poison was never identified. The lethal smog of Donora spawned an entire new academic profession, focusing on the study of humans exposed to polluted air. The Public Health Service was charged with analyzing, assessing, measuring and confirming what had happened. Donora was investigated to death not because so many studies were done but because the absence of definitive evidence of air pollution's harmfulness was taken as evidence of its safety.

The few investigators who warned that all this was not merely bad weather were dismissed. About a year after the inconclusive Public Health Service report was issued, a remarkably candid critique appeared in *Science* magazine, on January 20, 1950. Clarence A. Mills, a physician from the University of Cincinnati, had been trying for years to generate support for studying the conditions of the Monongahela Valley. He wrote that just two years before the disaster, there had been no interest in such research.

He asked, "Just what did their year's work, with a staff of 25 investigators show?"

The answer was pitifully little.

> The most valuable part of their year's work analysis of poison output from the steel and zinc plant stacks remains unused and unevaluated in their written reports. They spent months analyzing the valley air for poisons, but failed to calculate the concentrations probably present during the killing smog a year ago, when an inversion blanket clamped a lid down over the valley's unfortunate people. Had they made such calculation, they would have found that even one day's accumulation of the very irritating red oxides of nitrogen from the acid plant stacks would have caused concentrations almost as high as had been set as the maximum allowable for safety of factory workers exposed only for an 8-hour work day. At the end of 4 days of last year's blanketing smog, concentrations reached were probably more than four times higher than the 10 milligrams per cubic meter of air listed as the upper limits of safety! And the Donora people breathed the poisoned air not 8 hours a day but for 4 whole days.

Mills noted the eerie and tragic parallels between Donora and Liege, where nearly identical conditions created lethal brews involving low lying mill towns, zinc and steel fumes. And he challenged the claim that the Public Health Service had opened up a new field of inquiry, charging them with ignoring years of work by others.

> Let us hope that the Donora tragedy may prove such an object lesson in air pollution dangers that no industrial plant will feel safe in the future in pouring aloft dangerous amounts of poisonous materials. Let us hope that the Donora disaster will awaken people everywhere to the dangers they face from pollution of the air they must breathe to live. These 20 suffered only briefly, but many of the 6000 made ill that night will face continuing difficulties in breathing for the remainder of their lives. Herein lies the greater health danger from polluted air continuing

damage to the respiratory system through years of nonkilling exposure.

It has a strange ring to it, "years of nonkilling exposure."

* * *

The first medical experts into Donora after the smog conducted all the proper clinical tests on the twenty who died right away. Following traditional approaches, they looked into each of the vital organs and all the other tissues that could be stained and assembled. They looked at each slide, each x-ray one at a time, and never put them all together. No measurements were made of pollution in Donora until two months after the fatal smog had ended. As Mills noted, no effort was made to reconstruct what had gone on during the episode itself. Worse, the experts never looked at the survivors. If they had, they would have learned that in the month after the smog lifted, at least fifty extra people had died.

The notion of "extra" deaths may seem strange. As my mother says, you only get one chance to die. But epidemiologists can, and routinely do, predict the number of people who should die in any given population in any given time period, and thus can tell if a group of deaths is occurring that should not. These statistical patterns of dying are human lives with the tears removed, the literal bodies of evidence. In Donora, one of every three people got very sick during the weeklong smog. Even a decade later, the town's death rate was much higher than in surrounding towns. But no attempt was made to link these deaths to the smog, or to air quality in general.

* * *

Figure 1.3: Map of the Donora Deaths

It was not merely a sudden bad break of weather. It was foggy then, but the Valley is foggy in fall today, and the fogs will continue for as long as warmer river water emits vapor into colder air. What killed the people in Donora was what many suspected but could never prove. Most of the deaths occurred in the parts of town that sat just under the plume that spewed within a half-mile circle of the zinc mill.

* * *

Donora is a different place now. After the big strikes in the fifties, the massive, inefficient mills shut down, leaving the town to cope with deteriorating schools and a crumbling tax base. Many of the men, unwilling to give up the homes they had so painstakingly built (or unable to sell them) began commuting 60 or even 100 miles a day to take jobs in other towns. The Monongahela, ever a poisonous brown, began to flow blue. "First they tore down the big plants," one resident recalls. "Then they built a McDonald's and no one came. So they boarded that up and built a parking lot. Now nobody parks there either." Main Street now has a single traffic light, a second one having been converted back to a four-way stop sign to save on maintenance. The former Hotel Donora, once home to dozens of bachelor millworkers and a temporary morgue during the smog, is a martial arts training center and occasional rooming house.

* * *

In 1998, just about the time of the 50th anniversary of the disaster, an earnest high-school student named Justin Shawley got a monument set up. The State Historical and Museum Commission erected a five foot square bronze plaque near the center of the former steel mill as a memorial to those who died. To mark the occasion, residents and local and State officials held a service at Our Lady of the Valley Catholic Church, one of Donora's few remaining houses of worship. The plaque says:

The 1948 Donora Smog

> *Major Federal clean air laws became a legacy of this environmental disaster that focused national attention on air pollution. In late October of 1948, a heavy fog blanketed this valley, and as the days passed, the fog became a thick, acrid smog that left about 20 people dead and thousands ill. Not until October 31 did the Donora Zinc Works shut down its furnaces, just hours before rain finally dispersed the smog.*

It is a touching monument. The fifty people who died in the month following the smog are nowhere counted. The thousands who died over the following decade are nowhere counted. And there is no counting of the thousands whom Clarence Mills called the "non-killed" all those who went on to suffer in various poorly understood ways. Standing there by the ruins of the old mill, I thought I understood, just a little, what Sol Filler must have felt on revisiting Tereisenstadt: These people are well intentioned. They are trying to commemorate, to remember, to atone. But they are not trying hard enough.

Every single one of Bubbe Pearl's five children developed heart problems. None of their illnesses would ever be tied to where they grew up. They are not listed on any memorial to Donora's dead. My dazzling, athletic Uncle Len dropped dead at age 50 on a handball court in Southern California, years and miles away from the Monongahela River Valley. But he carried Donora with him in his heart, and in other body tissues as well. By the time my mother reached the same age, a decade later, coronary artery bypass operations were available to keep her alive. She needed three of them. Aunt Gert required only two.

Bubbe Pearl's tombstone sits in the lovely Jewish cemetery with its spectacular view of the river valley. When I was born she was still a fierce driver, but by the time my brother arrived, a year and half later, she had become an invalid. She did not die during the smog of 1948 either but only some two dozen heart attacks later. The attacks were so common that they became almost a ritual. The room would go quiet, and my mother, the baby of the family, would steady her own mother by the arm and steer her to the bed. The heavy, mottled-green, steel oxygen tank would be wheeled over, the valve turned on, and the gas mask pulled over Bubbe's nose and mouth. Her skin often matched the blue-white color of her hair.

Aunt Gert, the oldest sister, always had to leave the room, unable to stand by helplessly while her mother fought for air. Sometimes Bubbe would shriek "Oy vey!" But usually there was silence, and sighing. We would all wait for Dr. Levin. Dr. Levin always came, always calm, always sure. His arrival meant that everything would be all right.

The night she finally died, he did not come. I could not stop crying. I had seen her nearly die so many times, I was sure it was a mistake.

The story of Donora, Pennsylvania vividly illustrates the multiple, complex issues that we face with air pollution. Like other forms of environmental pollution that are covered in this book, air pollution may be invisible, but can also be deadly. It can kill immediately, or over a longer time. It can be made up of gases inherently poisonous to the human body, or it can consist of gases that are naturally occurring but that in large quantities pose danger. It can scar the lungs and scar the countryside.

Most importantly, it is not an intentionally created product, but instead a by-product of modern development, in this case, combustion of fossil fuels and the production of useful products made possible by such combustion. Since the exploitation of energy fuels economic expansion, it is also the story of jobs and livelihoods.

Though we know much more about the causes and effects of air pollution now than at the time of the Donora "killer fog," the basic issues of air pollution have not changed. We still grapple with acutely toxic air pollutants, and most of our major metropolitan areas contain levels of common pollutants that are considered unhealthy. Our major causes of air pollution still come from combustion byproducts, and there is still discussion about the trade-off of clean air and jobs.

What is different today is that we have chosen as a society to address these problems directly through the Clean Air Act ("CAA"). The practice of environmental law that deals with air pollution is very much the story of the implementation and administration of this act. The Act has been amended several times, but importantly, one basic policy choice made originally in the 1970 version of the Act has remained constant— that is that all inhabitants of the United States should ideally be able to breathe clean air and not suffer health impairments due to air pollution. Though this still remains normatively true, it is also true that we still have unhealthful air pollution and political disagreements over the proper way to control air pollution. Like most of environmental law, the real complexities of air pollution control are in the administration of the law and not so much the law itself. It is at the agency level where decisions about safe levels of exposure, measurement and prediction about pollution, and the technology that is necessary to control it are made. It is also in this arena where some of the basic questions about the future of the CAA, and how closely it will hew to its original goals, are being debated. Therefore this chapter will deal extensively with the implementation of the law and the process that is used in that implementation. The practice of Environmental Law requires knowing whether the agency charged with administering the law is following the law substantively, and implementing it under the correct procedures. Before we can understand whether the agencies are in fact administering the CAA correctly, we must first understand the basics of the law itself.

II. THE CLEAN AIR ACT—OVERVIEW

The Clean Air Act of 1970 was a very ambitious environmental law that arose out of an increasing consciousness regarding air pollution, its harms, and causes, and an increasingly affluent society that sought to provide decent standards of living, including health protection, to all of its citizens.

The 1970 Act had three major parts. One part required the Administrator (of what soon became EPA) to set health based standards for all common ubiquitous pollutants, commonly referred to as the criteria pollutants. 42 U.S.C. §§ 7408 and 7409. These originally included nitrogen oxides, sulfur oxides, particulate matter, volatile organic compounds, carbon monoxide, and ozone. In small quantities, most of these pollutants are not harmful, and indeed some are necessary compounds in our atmosphere. However, in the amounts produced by our modern industrial society, with its heavy dependence on the combustion of fossil fuels, of which these compounds are byproducts, these air pollutants can cause immediate and chronic health problems.

The second major part of the 1970 Act dealt with how these health based standards were to be reached and enforced. The answer, then as now, was that the States were to establish State Implementation Plans, or SIPS, which provided the regulatory controls necessary to establish and maintain these health based standards promulgated by the Administrator. 42 U.S.C. § 7410.

Finally the Act sought to intervene directly in pollution control by establishing technology or process standards for the control of pollution at its source. This in turn was divided into sections dealing with both stationary, industrial sources, such as power plants, 42 U.S.C. § 7411, and mobile sources, such as automobiles and trucks. 42 U.S.C. § 7521.

In response to concerns that a uniform national standard failed to adequately protect areas of the country that had particularly pristine air, in 1977 Congress amended the CAA to prevent the deterioration of the air quality in these areas. 42 U.S.C. § 7470. This program, aptly named the Prevention of Significant Deterioration (or PSD) program, divided the country into three classes of air quality and then limited the amount of pollution that could be added to these areas in order to maintain that level. 42 U.S.C. §§ 7471–7473. In particular, national parks were to be set at the highest (or Class I) level. 42 U.S.C. § 7472. These limits were to be enforced by doing preconstruction review of any major sources to ensure that the air pollution increment would not be exceeded. 42 U.S.C. § 7475.

Congress last significantly amended the CAA in 1990. At that time, it was clear that many of the nation's urban areas had failed to meet the national ambient air quality standards EPA had set, particularly that for ground level ozone. The 1990 Act sought to impose compliance by mandating very particular requirements in those areas that failed to implement the standards. For ozone, these requirements were set based upon the severity of the problem. 42 U.S.C. § 7511.

The 1990 amendments also created a program for establishing and trading increments of sulfur dioxide. Called the Acid Rain Trading provisions, this program was the most ambitious use of market trading devices for pollution control up until that time. 42 U.S.C. § 7651b.

The 1990 Amendments also created a permitting program, similar to that of the Clean Water Act, which required the permitting of all major sources of air pollution. The permitting system also required that the ultimate permitting agency harmonize all the CAA requirements applicable to one source. 42 U.S.C. § 7661a(5).

Making sense of all of the CAA's requirements simultaneously has been a challenge for administrative agencies, the regulated community, and the affected public. Sources of air pollution often must comply with requirements imposed under a number of different CAA programs, many of which overlap in their application to particular pollutants. Though the permitting program has been of some assistance in harmonizing the myriad requirements for sources of air pollution, the state and federal executive branch agencies that administer the various parts of the law have various philosophies of enforcement that make consistent application of requirements and ongoing improvement of air quality elusive. It is here where the real action under the CAA occurs. To practice or understand air pollution control requires an examination of how the agencies have administered and will administer the various parts of the CAA. We will explore these parts of the Act in turn.

As you read about the agency actions, challenges to those actions, and court rulings on the legality of those actions, keep in mind that agencies may have wide deference in how to administer certain laws, and that deference is directly related to the flexibility the legislation has granted them. Thus, pay attention not only to your own interpretation of a statute, but also to whether the EPA's interpretation is within the bounds of discretion committed to it under the Act. If it is, and the agency has followed proper procedure, it is that interpretation that becomes the hard and fast requirement. If not, the implementation must be challenged or negotiated until a legal status is reached. Remember also that requirements based on administrative action can be changed without changing the legislation as long as the interpretation is validly within the agency's discretion and proper procedure has been followed.

III. THE NATIONAL AMBIENT AIR QUALITY STANDARDS ("NAAQS") PROGRAM

A. What Is a Criteria Pollutant?

The linchpin of the 1970 Amendments was the National Ambient Air Quality Standards (NAAQS) program. From the outset, this program has focused on State efforts either to attain or maintain the desired level of air quality for what are referred to as "criteria pollutants." Section 108 deals with the designation of criteria pollutants. Section 108(a)(1) requires EPA to designate "each air pollutant—

(A) emissions of which, in his judgment, cause or contribute to air pollution which may reasonably be anticipated to endanger public health or welfare;

(B) the presence of which in the ambient air results from numerous or diverse mobile or stationary sources; and

(C) for which air quality criteria had not been issued before December 31, 1970, but for which he plans to issue air quality criteria under this section."

42 U.S.C. § 7408(a)(1).

The Supreme Court has not addressed § 108(a)(1) directly. As this edition went to press, however, the Court considered the effect of § 202(a)(1) of the CAA, which has language very similar to that in § 108(a)(1)(A). Consider the following case:

MASSACHUSETTS v. ENVIRONMENTAL PROTECTION AGENCY

Supreme Court of the United States, 2007.
—— U.S. ——, 127 S.Ct. 1438, —— L.Ed.2d ——.

JUSTICE STEVENS delivered the opinion of the Court.

[We previously considered the standing component of this case in Chapter 1.]

VI

On the merits, the first question is whether § 202(a)(1) of the [CAA] authorizes EPA to regulate greenhouse gas emissions from new motor vehicles in the event that it forms a "judgment" that such emissions contribute to climate change. We have little trouble concluding that it does. In relevant part, § 202(a)(1) provides that EPA "shall by regulation prescribe ... standards applicable to the emission of any air pollutant from any class or classes of new motor vehicles or new motor vehicle engines, which in [the Administrator's] judgment cause, or contribute to, air pollution which may reasonably be anticipated to endanger public health or welfare." 42 U.S.C. § 7521(a)(1). Because EPA believes that Congress did not intend it to regulate substances that contribute to climate change, the agency maintains that carbon dioxide is not an "air pollutant" within the meaning of the provision.

The statutory text forecloses EPA's reading. The [CAA's] sweeping definition of "air pollutant" includes "*any* air pollution agent or combination of such agents, including *any* physical, chemical ... substance or matter which is emitted into or otherwise enters the ambient air.... ." § 7602(g) (emphasis added). On its face, the definition embraces all airborne compounds of whatever stripe, and underscores that intent through the repeated use of the word "any." Carbon dioxide, methane, nitrous oxide, and hydrofluorocarbons are without a doubt "physical [and] chemical ... substance[s] which [are] emitted into ... the ambient air." The statute is unambiguous.[26]

Rather than relying on statutory text, EPA invokes postenactment congressional actions and deliberations it views as tantamount to a congressional command to refrain from regulating greenhouse gas emissions. Even if such postenactment legislative history could shed light on the meaning of an otherwise-unambiguous statute, EPA never identifies any action remotely suggesting that Congress meant to curtail its power to treat greenhouse gases as air pollutants. That subsequent Congresses have eschewed enacting binding emissions limitations to combat global warming tells us nothing about what Congress meant when it amended § 202(a)(1) in 1970 and 1977. And unlike EPA, we have no difficulty reconciling Congress' various efforts to promote interagency collaboration and research to better understand climate change with the agency's pre-existing mandate to regulate "any air pollutant" that may endanger the public welfare. See 42 U.S.C. § 7601(a)(1). Collaboration and research do not conflict with any thoughtful regulatory effort; they complement it.

EPA finally argues that it cannot regulate carbon dioxide emissions from motor vehicles because doing so would require it to tighten mileage standards, a job (according to EPA) that Congress has assigned to DOT. But that DOT sets mileage standards in no way licenses EPA to shirk its

---

26. In dissent, Justice SCALIA maintains that because greenhouse gases permeate the world's atmosphere rather than a limited area near the earth's surface, EPA's exclusion of greenhouse gases from the category of air pollution "agent[s]" is entitled to deference under *Chevron U.S.A. Inc. v. Natural Resources Defense Council, Inc.,* 467 U.S. 837 (1984). EPA's distinction, however, finds no support in the text of the statute, which uses the phrase "the ambient air" without distinguishing between atmospheric layers. Moreover, it is a plainly unreasonable reading of a sweeping statutory provision designed to capture "*any* phys-

ical, chemical ... substance or matter which is emitted into or otherwise enters the ambient air." 42 U.S.C. § 7602(g). Justice SCALIA does not (and cannot) explain why Congress would define "air pollutant" so carefully and so broadly, yet confer on EPA the authority to narrow that definition whenever expedient by asserting that a particular substance is not an "agent." At any rate, no party to this dispute contests that greenhouse gases both "ente[r] the ambient air" and tend to warm the atmosphere. They are therefore unquestionably "agent[s]" of air pollution.

environmental responsibilities. EPA has been charged with protecting the public's "health" and "welfare," 42 U.S.C. § 7521(a)(1), a statutory obligation wholly independent of DOT's mandate to promote energy efficiency. The two obligations may overlap, but there is no reason to think the two agencies cannot both administer their obligations and yet avoid inconsistency.

While the Congresses that drafted § 202(a)(1) might not have appreciated the possibility that burning fossil fuels could lead to global warming, they did understand that without regulatory flexibility, changing circumstances and scientific developments would soon render the [CAA] obsolete. The broad language of § 202(a)(1) reflects an intentional effort to confer the flexibility necessary to forestall such obsolescence. Because greenhouse gases fit well within the [CAA's] capacious definition of "air pollutant," we hold that EPA has the statutory authority to regulate the emission of such gases from new motor vehicles.

VII

The alternative basis for EPA's decision—that even if it does have statutory authority to regulate greenhouse gases, it would be unwise to do so at this time—rests on reasoning divorced from the statutory text. While the statute does condition the exercise of EPA's authority on its formation of a "judgment," 42 U.S.C. § 7521(a)(1), that judgment must relate to whether an air pollutant "cause[s], or contribute[s] to, air pollution which may reasonably be anticipated to endanger public health or welfare," *ibid*. Put another way, the use of the word "judgment" is not a roving license to ignore the statutory text. It is but a direction to exercise discretion within defined statutory limits.

If EPA makes a finding of endangerment, the [CAA] requires the agency to regulate emissions of the deleterious pollutant from new motor vehicles. *Ibid*. EPA no doubt has significant latitude as to the manner, timing, content, and coordination of its regulations with those of other agencies. But once EPA has responded to a petition for rulemaking, its reasons for action or inaction must conform to the authorizing statute. Under the clear terms of the [CAA], EPA can avoid taking further action only if it determines that greenhouse gases do not contribute to climate change or if it provides some reasonable explanation as to why it cannot or will not exercise its discretion to determine whether they do. *Ibid*. To the extent that this constrains agency discretion to pursue other priorities of the Administrator or the President, this is the congressional design.

EPA has refused to comply with this clear statutory command. Instead, it has offered a laundry list of reasons not to regulate. For example, EPA said that a number of voluntary executive branch programs already provide an effective response to the threat of global warming, that regulating greenhouse gases might impair the President's ability to negotiate with "key developing nations" to reduce emissions, and that curtailing motor-vehicle emissions would reflect "an inefficient, piecemeal approach to address the climate change issue."

Although we have neither the expertise nor the authority to evaluate these policy judgments, it is evident they have nothing to do with whether greenhouse gas emissions contribute to climate change. Still less do they amount to a reasoned justification for declining to form a scientific judgment. . . .

Nor can EPA avoid its statutory obligation by noting the uncertainty surrounding various features of climate change and concluding that it would therefore be better not to regulate at this time. If the scientific uncertainty is so profound that it precludes EPA from making a reasoned judgment as to whether greenhouse gases contribute to global warming, EPA must say so. That EPA would prefer not to regulate greenhouse gases because of some residual uncertainty—which, contrary to Justice SCALIA's apparent belief, is in fact all that it said, see 68 Fed.Reg. 52929 ("We do not believe . . . that it would be either effective or appropriate for EPA *to establish [greenhouse gas] standards for motor vehicles* at this time" (emphasis added))—is irrelevant. The statutory question is whether sufficient information exists to make an endangerment finding.

In short, EPA has offered no reasoned explanation for its refusal to decide whether greenhouse gases cause or contribute to climate change. Its action was therefore "arbitrary, capricious, . . . or otherwise not in accordance with law." 42 U.S.C. § 7607(d)(9)(A). We need not and do not reach the question whether on remand EPA must make an endangerment finding, or whether policy concerns can inform EPA's actions in the event that it makes such a finding. We hold only that EPA must ground its reasons for action or inaction in the statute.

JUSTICE SCALIA, with whom THE CHIEF JUSTICE, JUSTICE THOMAS, and JUSTICE ALITO join, dissenting.

I

A

The provision of law at the heart of this case is § 202(a)(1) of the [CAA], which provides that the Administrator of [EPA] "shall by regulation prescribe . . . standards applicable to the emission of any air pollutant from any class or classes of new motor vehicles or new motor vehicle engines, which *in his judgment* cause, or contribute to, air pollution which may reasonably be anticipated to endanger public health or welfare." 42 U.S.C. § 7521(a)(1) (emphasis added). As the Court recognizes, the statute "condition[s] the exercise of EPA's authority on its formation of a 'judgment.' " There is no dispute that the Administrator has made no such judgment in this case.

The question thus arises: Does anything *require* the Administrator to make a "judgment" whenever a petition for rulemaking is filed? Without citation of the statute or any other authority, the Court says yes. Why is that so? When Congress wishes to make private action force an agency's hand, it knows how to do so. Where does the CAA say that the EPA Administrator is required to come to a decision on this question whenever a rulemaking petition is filed? The Court points to no such provision because none exists.

Instead, the Court invents a multiple-choice question that the EPA Administrator must answer when a petition for rulemaking is filed. The Administrator must exercise his judgment in one of three ways: (a) by concluding that the pollutant *does* cause, or contribute to, air pollution that endangers public welfare (in which case EPA is required to regulate); (b) by concluding that the pollutant *does not* cause, or contribute to, air pollution that endangers public welfare (in which case EPA is *not* required to regulate); or (c) by "provid[ing] some reasonable explanation as to why it cannot or will not exercise its discretion to determine whether" greenhouse gases endanger public welfare (in which case EPA is *not* required to regulate).

I am willing to assume, for the sake of argument, that the Administrator's discretion in this regard is not entirely unbounded—that if he has no reasonable basis for deferring judgment he must grasp the nettle at once. The Court, however, with no basis in text or precedent, rejects all of EPA's stated "policy judgments" as not "amount[ing] to a reasoned justification," effectively narrowing the universe of potential reasonable bases to a single one: Judgment can be delayed *only* if the Administrator concludes that "the scientific uncertainty is [too] profound." The Administrator is precluded from concluding *for other reasons* "that it would . . . be better not to regulate at this time." . . .

The Court dismisses [EPA's policy rationales] as "rest[ing] on reasoning divorced from the statutory text." "While the statute does condition the exercise of EPA's authority on its formation of a 'judgment,' . . . that judgment must relate to whether an air pollutant 'cause[s], or contribute[s] to, air pollution which may reasonably be anticipated to endanger public health or welfare.' " True but irrelevant. When the Administrator *makes* a judgment whether to regulate greenhouse gases, that judgment must relate to whether they are air pollutants that "cause, or contribute to, air pollution which may reasonably be anticipated to endanger public health or welfare." 42 U.S.C. § 7521(a)(1). But the statute says *nothing at all* about the reasons for which the Administrator may *defer* making a judgment—the permissible reasons for deciding not to grapple with the issue at the present time. Thus, the various "policy" rationales that the Court criticizes are not "divorced from the statutory text," except in the sense that the statutory text is silent, as texts are often silent about permissible reasons for the exercise of agency discretion. The reasons the EPA gave are surely considerations executive agencies *regularly* take into account (and *ought* to take into account) when deciding whether to consider entering a new field: the impact such entry would have on other Executive Branch programs and on foreign policy. There is no basis in law for the Court's imposed limitation. . . .

B

Even on the Court's own terms, however, the same conclusion follows. As mentioned above, the Court gives EPA the option of determining that the science is too uncertain to allow it to form a "judgment" as to whether greenhouse gases endanger public welfare. Attached to this option (on what basis is unclear) is an essay requirement: "If," the Court says, "the scientific uncertainty is so profound that it precludes EPA from making a reasoned judgment as to whether greenhouse gases contribute to global warming, EPA must say so." But EPA *has* said precisely that—and at great length, based on information contained in a 2001 report by the National Research Council (NRC) entitled Climate Change Science: An Analysis of Some Key Questions ...

II

A

Even before reaching its discussion of the word "judgment," the Court makes another significant error when it concludes that "§ 202(a)(1) of the [CAA] *authorizes* EPA to regulate greenhouse gas emissions from new motor vehicles in the event that it forms a 'judgment' that such emissions contribute to climate change." ([E]mphasis added). For such authorization, the Court relies on what it calls "the Clean Air Act's capacious definition of 'air pollutant.' "

"Air pollutant" is defined by the Act as "any air pollution agent or combination of such agents, including any physical, chemical, ... substance or matter which is emitted into or otherwise enters the ambient air." 42 U.S.C. § 7602(g). The Court is correct that "[c]arbon dioxide, methane, nitrous oxide, and hydrofluorocarbons" fit within the second half of that definition: They are "physical, chemical, ... substance[s] or matter which [are] emitted into or otherwise ente[r] the ambient air." But the Court mistakenly believes this to be the end of the analysis. In order to be an "air pollutant" under the Act's definition, the "substance or matter [being] emitted into ... the ambient air" must also meet the *first* half of the definition—namely, it must be an "air pollution agent or combination of such agents." The Court simply pretends this half of the definition does not exist.

The Court's analysis faithfully follows the argument advanced by petitioners, which focuses on the word "including" in the statutory definition of "air pollutant." As that argument goes, anything that *follows* the word "including" must necessarily be a subset of whatever *precedes* it. Thus, if greenhouse gases qualify under the phrase following the word "including," they must qualify under the phrase preceding it. Since greenhouse gases come within the capacious phrase "any physical, chemical, ... substance or matter which is emitted into or otherwise enters the ambient air," they must also be "air pollution agent[s] or combination[s] of such agents," and therefore meet the definition of "air pollutant[s]."

That is certainly one possible interpretation of the statutory definition. The word "including" can indeed indicate that what follows will be an "illustrative" sampling of the general category that precedes the word. Often, however, the examples standing alone are broader than the general category, and must be viewed as limited in light of that category. The Government provides a helpful (and unanswered) example: "The phrase 'any American automobile, including any truck or minivan,' would not naturally be construed to encompass a foreign-manufactured [truck or] minivan." Brief for Federal Respondent 34. The general principle enunciated—that the speaker is talking about *American* automobiles—carries forward to the illustrative examples (trucks and minivans), and limits them accordingly, even though in isolation they are broader. Congress often uses the word "including" in this manner. In 28 U.S.C. § 1782(a), for example, it refers to "a proceeding in a foreign or international tribunal, including criminal investigations conducted before formal accusation." Certainly this provision would not encompass criminal investigations underway in a *domestic* tribunal.

In short, the word "including" does not require the Court's ... result. It is perfectly reasonable to view the definition of "air pollutant" in its entirety: An air pollutant *can* be "any physical, chemical, ... substance or matter which is emitted into or otherwise enters the ambient air," but only if it retains the general characteristic of being an "air pollution agent or combination of such agents." This is precisely the conclusion EPA reached: "[A] substance does not meet the CAA definition of 'air pollutant' simply because it is a 'physical, chemical, ... substance or matter which is emitted into or otherwise enters the ambient air.' It must also be an 'air pollution agent.'" 68 Fed.Reg. 52929, n. 3. Once again, in the face of textual ambiguity, the Court's application of *Chevron* deference to EPA's interpretation of the word "including" is nowhere to be found.[2] Evidently, the Court defers only to those reasonable interpretations that it favors.

B

Using (as we ought to) EPA's interpretation of the definition of "air pollutant," we must next determine whether greenhouse gases are "agent[s]" of "air pollution." If so, the statute would authorize regulation; if not, EPA would lack authority.

Unlike "air pollutants," the term "air pollution" is not itself defined by the CAA; thus, once again we must accept EPA's interpretation of that ambiguous term, provided its interpretation is a "permissible construction of the statute." *Chevron*, 467 U.S., at 843. In this case, the petition for rulemaking asked EPA for "regulation of [greenhouse gas]

---

2. Not only is EPA's interpretation reasonable, it is far more plausible than the Court's alternative. As the Court correctly points out, "all airborne compounds of whatever stripe" would qualify as "physical, chemical, ... substance[s] or matter which [are] emitted into or otherwise ente[r] the ambient air," 42 U.S.C. § 7602(g). It follows that *everything* airborne, from Frisbees to flatulence, qualifies as an "air pollutant." This reading of the statute defies common sense.

emissions from motor vehicles to reduce the risk of global climate change." 68 Fed.Reg. 52925. Thus, in deciding whether it had authority to regulate, EPA had to determine whether the concentration of greenhouse gases assertedly responsible for "global climate change" qualifies as "air pollution." EPA began with the commonsense observation that the "[p]roblems associated with atmospheric concentrations of CO_2," *id.,* at 52927, bear little resemblance to what would naturally be termed "air pollution":

> EPA's prior use of the CAA's general regulatory provisions provides an important context. Since the inception of the Act, EPA has used these provisions to address air pollution problems that occur primarily at ground level or near the surface of the earth. For example, national ambient air quality standards (NAAQS) established under CAA section 109 address concentrations of substances in the ambient air and the related public health and welfare problems. This has meant setting NAAQS for concentrations of ozone, carbon monoxide, particulate matter and other substances in the air near the surface of the earth, not higher in the atmosphere.... CO_2, by contrast, is fairly consistent in concentration throughout the world's atmosphere up to approximately the lower stratosphere. *Id.,* at 52926–52927.

In other words, regulating the buildup of CO_2 and other greenhouse gases in the upper reaches of the atmosphere, which is alleged to be causing global climate change, is not akin to regulating the concentration of some substance that is *polluting* the *air*.

We need look no further than the dictionary for confirmation that this interpretation of "air pollution" is eminently reasonable. The definition of "pollute," of course, is "[t]o make or render impure or unclean." Webster's New International Dictionary 1910 (2d ed.1949). And the first three definitions of "air" are as follows: (1) "[t]he invisible, odorless, and tasteless mixture of gases which surrounds the earth"; (2) "[t]he body of the earth's atmosphere; esp., the part of it near the earth, as distinguished from the upper rarefied part"; (3) "[a] portion of air or of the air considered with respect to physical characteristics or as affecting the senses." *Id.,* at 54. EPA's conception of "air pollution"—focusing on impurities in the "ambient air" "at ground level or near the surface of the earth"—is perfectly consistent with the natural meaning of that term.

In the end, EPA concluded that since "CAA authorization to regulate is generally based on a finding that an air pollutant causes or contributes to air pollution," 68 Fed.Reg. 52928, the concentrations of CO_2 and other greenhouse gases allegedly affecting the global climate are beyond the scope of CAA's authorization to regulate. "[T]he term 'air pollution' as used in the regulatory provisions cannot be interpreted to encompass global climate change." *Ibid.* Once again, the Court utterly fails to explain why this interpretation is incorrect, let alone so unreasonable as to be unworthy of *Chevron* deference.

* * *

The Court's alarm over global warming may or may not be justified, but it ought not distort the outcome of this litigation. This is a straightforward administrative-law case, in which Congress has passed a malleable statute giving broad discretion, not to us but to an executive agency. No matter how important the underlying policy issues at stake, this Court has no business substituting its own desired outcome for the reasoned judgment of the responsible agency.

Notes and Comments

1. At the time the 1970 CAA was passed, several pollutants were already identified as meeting the § 108(a)(1) standard. These included sulfur oxides, particulates, carbon monoxide, hydrocarbons and photochemical oxidants. Since then, EPA has replaced photochemical oxidants with ozone and has removed hydrocarbons from the list. Additionally, EPA has added two other substances—nitrogen oxide, as a result of a specific statutory command in § 108(c), and lead, which it added as a result of a citizen suit; see *Natural Resources Defense Council, Inc. v. Train*, 545 F.2d 320 (2d Cir. 1976).

2. The § 202(a)(1) language at issue in *Massachusetts* is structurally identical to the language in § 108(a)(1)(A), requiring the Administrator to address those air pollutants emitted by cars which "in his judgment cause, or contribute to, air pollution which may reasonably be anticipated to endanger public health or welfare." 42 U.S.C. § 7521(a)(1). Section 202(a)(1) does not, however, have language paralleling § 108(a)(1)(B) and (C). Reread those subsections. How much flexibility do they give EPA? Significantly, in *NRDC v. Train*, the Second Circuit rejected EPA's argument that § 108(a)(1)(C) gives it an independent basis for declining to designate pollutants that meet the requirements of § 108(a)(1)(A) and (B), noting that Congress' plan of achieving the desired level of air quality "would become an exercise in futility if the Administrator could avoid listing pollutants simply by choosing not to issue air quality criteria." 545 F.2d at 327. Do you agree with the Second Circuit's analysis?

3. Do you agree with the Supreme Court's analysis in *Massachusetts* on the "air pollutant" question? Is the statute clear enough to preclude any application of *Chevron*? What did you think of the majority's analysis on the question whether EPA was required to make a finding under § 202(a)(1)? In the future, could EPA avoid this problem by declining to respond to any petitions like that filed by Massachusetts? If someone were to file a petition regarding, to borrow Justice Scalia's phrase (in fn. 2), either frisbees or flatulence, would EPA be compelled to respond on the merits?

4. On the "finding" issue, Massachusetts and the other petitioners could have made one of three arguments: most aggressively, they could have argued that EPA is required to regulate greenhouse gases because they meet the endangerment test; alternatively, they could have argued that EPA is required to make a finding as to whether the relevant gases meet the test;

or, least aggressively, they could merely have argued that EPA is required to decide whether to make a finding, and to make this decision based upon permissible grounds. Which did they make? Which did the majority embrace? Do you understand why this might be so?

Chemical Reaction of Fossil Fuel Combustion

CxHy (such as propane $-C_3H_8$) $+ O_2$ in the presence of Sulfur (S) impurities

Nitrogen (N) in the air

$= CO_2 + H_2O + CO$ (from incomplete combustion of carbon) $+ NO_2 + SOx + CxHy$ (remaining organic compounds from incomplete combustion of fuel) $+$ particulates (relatively large pieces of carbon that did not combust) $+$ energy

CO, NO_2, SOx, organic compounds, and particulates have all been designated as criteria pollutants. Ozone or photochemical oxidants, are formed from the reaction of Nitrogen Oxides with volatile organic compounds in the presence of sunlight and heat. In addition, when gasoline was leaded, the burning of gasoline also produced lead.

A more difficult question than what constitutes a criteria pollutant, is what level of that pollutant can be considered "safe."

B. How Is a National Ambient Air Quality Standard Established?

Once criteria pollutants are determined, Section 109 requires the Administrator to determine what ambient level of these pollutants will ensure the safety of the public. The process of setting allowable ambient pollution levels requires studying health effects of air pollution, which is not a precise science. A general discussion of the health effects of the criteria pollutants follows:

The Clean Air Problem

Health effects

Ozone

Roughly one out of every three people in the United States is at a higher risk of experiencing problems from ground-level ozone.

- One group at high risk is active children because they often spend a large part of the summer playing outdoors.

- People of all ages who are active outdoors are at increased risk because, during physical activity, ozone penetrates deeper into the parts of the lungs that are more vulnerable to injury.

- People with respiratory diseases, including asthma, that make their lungs more vulnerable to ozone may experience health effects earlier and at lower ozone levels than other people.

- Though scientists don't yet know why, some healthy people are unusually sensitive to ozone. They may experience health effects at more moderate levels of outdoor exertion or at lower ozone levels than the average person.

- Ozone can irritate the respiratory system, causing coughing, throat irritation, and/or an uncomfortable sensation in the chest.

- Ozone can reduce lung function and make it more difficult to breathe deeply and vigorously. Breathing may become more rapid and shallow than normal. This may limit a person's ability to engage in vigorous activities.

- Ozone can aggravate asthma. When ozone levels are high, more people with asthma have attacks that require a doctor's attention or use of medication. One reason this happens is that ozone makes people more sensitive to allergens such as pets, pollen, and dust mites, which are common triggers of asthma attacks.

- Ozone can increase susceptibility to respiratory infections.

- Ozone can inflame and damage the lining of the lungs. Within a few days, the damaged cells are shed and replaced—much like the skin peels after a sunburn. Studies suggest that if this type of inflammation happens repeatedly over a long time period (months, years, a lifetime), lung tissue may become permanently scarred, resulting in permanent loss of lung function and a lower quality of life.

Particle Pollution (Particulates)

Particles smaller than 10 micrometers in diameter can cause or aggravate a number of health problems and have been linked with illnesses and deaths from heart or lung diseases. These effects have been associated with both short-term exposures (usually over a 24–hour period, but possibly as short as one hour) and long-term exposures (years).

- Sensitive groups for particle pollution include people with heart or lung disease, older adults (who may have undiagnosed heart or lung disease), and children.

- People with heart or lung diseases—such as congestive heart failure, coronary artery disease, asthma, or chronic obstructive pulmonary disease—and older adults are more likely to visit emergency rooms, be admitted to hospitals, or in some cases, even die. When exposed to particle pollution, people with heart disease may experience chest pain, palpitations, shortness of breath, and fatigue. Particle pollution has also been associated with cardiac arrhythmias and heart attacks.

- When exposed to particles, people with existing lung disease may not be able to breathe as deeply or vigorously as they normally would. They may experience symptoms such as coughing and shortness of breath. Healthy people also may experience these effects, although they are unlikely to experience more serious effects.

- Particle pollution also can increase susceptibility to respiratory infections and can aggravate existing respiratory diseases, such as asthma and chronic bronchitis, causing more use of medication and more doctor visits.

Carbon Monoxide (CO)

Carbon monoxide enters the bloodstream through the lungs and binds to hemoglobin, the substance in blood that carries oxygen to cells. It actually reduces the amount of oxygen reaching the body's organs and tissues.

- People with cardiovascular disease, such as angina, are most at risk. They may experience chest pain and other cardiovascular symptoms if they are exposed to carbon monoxide, particularly while exercising.

- People with marginal or compromised cardiovascular and respiratory systems (for example, individuals with congestive heart failure, cerebrovascular disease, anemia, chronic obstructive lung disease), and possibly young infants and fetuses, also may be at greater risk from carbon monoxide pollution.

- In healthy individuals, exposure to higher levels of carbon monoxide can affect mental alertness and vision.

Sulfur Dioxide (SO$_2$)

Sulfur dioxide is an irritant gas that is removed by the nasal passages. Moderate activity levels that trigger mouth breathing, such as a brisk walk, are needed for sulfur dioxide to cause health effects.

- People with asthma who are physically active outdoors are most likely to experience the health effects of sulfur dioxide. The main effect, even with brief exposure, is a narrowing of the airways (called bronchoconstriction). This may cause wheezing, chest tightness, and shortness of breath. Symptoms increase as sulfur dioxide levels and/or breathing rates increase. When exposure to sulfur dioxide ceases, lung function typically returns to normal within an hour.

- At very high levels, sulfur dioxide may cause wheezing, chest tightness, and shortness of breath even in healthy people who do not have asthma.

- Long-term exposure to sulfur dioxide can cause respiratory illness, alter the lung's defense mechanisms, and aggravate existing cardiovascular disease. People with cardiovascular disease or chronic lung disease, as well as children and older adults, may be most susceptible to these effects.

(Source: EPA Brochure—Air Quality Index: A Guide to Air Quality and Your Health, EPA–454/K–03–002, August 2003.)

JOURNAL OF TOXICOLOGY: CLINICAL TOXICOLOGY
COPYRIGHT 2002 GALE GROUP INC.
ALL RIGHTS RESERVED.
COPYRIGHT 2002 MARCEL DEKKER, INC.

Saturday, June 1, 2002 ISSN: 0731–3810; Volume 40; Issue 4.

* * *

FACTORS RELATED TO TOXIC EXPOSURE SEVERITY

Air pollutants are gaseous or in the form of particle suspension. Exposures are difficult to assess and to characterize because a mixture of pollutants is often involved. Epidemiological data indicate the association of acid aerosol levels with mortality and respiratory symptoms in children. The affect of this specific pollutant is not clear. The role of other pollutants such as ozone, nitrogen oxides, sulfur oxides, and fine particles produced by the same sources may also be significant.

The main factors influencing penetration and retention within the respiratory tract are solubility, particle size, concentration, reactivity of the pollutant, and pattern of ventilation.

Solubility

Gases that are highly soluble in water, like sulfur dioxide (SO_2), are almost totally extracted by the nose and pharynx, whereas the less soluble gases like nitrogen dioxide (NO_2), ozone, or nonsoluble gases like CO are less removed by the upper respiratory tract and penetrate deeper into the lung. Exercise, by increasing minute ventilation, increases the total quantity reaching the deep lung. Moderate to heavy exercise may also increase penetration of soluble gases in the deep lung, bypassing the nasal passage when oral breathing is used.

Particle Size

Particles, liquid droplets or solid particles, remain in suspension (aerosol). Among other factors related to child airway anatomy and rate of ventilation, the penetration of particles depends on their size. Particles larger than 10 μm (micrometers) are filtered by the nose and nasopharynx and cleared within hours. Particles of less than 10 μm are deposited on the tracheo bronchial tree. Particles of 1–2 μm may reach the alveoli. Particles of less than 0.5 μm are carried by gases to alveoli and impacted on the alveolar surfaces. They are cleared from the deep lung by macrophages within days or months.

Pollution by respirable particles is assessed through PM10, defined as particulate matter with an aerodynamic diameter equal, or less than a nominal 10 μm. This parameter is used for ambient air quality surveillance.

Reactivity, Mechanisms of Action

The mechanisms by which inhaled gases and particles injure the lung are diverse and still not fully understood.

Oxidant Gases

Oxidant gases, like ozone, NO_2 and SO_2 cause inflammation of the respiratory tract and deep lung. Studies have investigated the putative mechanisms underlying the effects of NO_2, SO_2, ozone, and respirable particles. They suggest that exposure to these agents may lead to perturbation of the airway epithelium and the release of pro-inflammatory mediators from epithelial cells, which then activate inflammatory cells, such as eosinophils.

Organic Compounds

Organic compounds absorbed onto particles may also cause inflammation and act as initiators of cancer. Several epidemiological studies have demonstrated a clear association between episodes of outdoor air pollution and impaired lung function and infection of the lower and upper respiratory tracts.

Pattern of Ventilation

The amount of pollutants reaching the respiratory tract and the deep lung is directly related to the minute ventilation. A child's ventilation pattern differs from that of an adult, with a higher rate and tidal volume relative to weight. This may explain in part the special vulnerability of child to respiratory pollutants. Such a vulnerability to pollutants is much increased for asthmatic children and adolescents. It has been suggested that children with bronchial hyperresponsiveness and raised serum concentrations of total IgE are more vulnerable to the effects of air pollution, although they are not necessarily identified as such because they do not present with chronic respiratory symptoms.

Different studies conducted in Seattle area hospitals suggest that health effects among asthmatic children resulting from short-term changes in air pollution levels are an important public health problem. A London study reports a most significant association between consultations for childhood asthma and NO_2 levels in the outdoor air and between other lower respiratory disease consultations (bronchitis) and SO_2 levels.

POLLUTANTS OF SPECIAL CONCERN IN CHILDREN

Children are exposed to numerous air pollutants both outdoors and indoors. The concentration of many pollutants has been found to be greater indoors than outdoors. This is of special concern because children (especially infants and young children) spend most of their time indoors. Because of the large number of agents, we will not review every hazardous air contaminant, but will focus on the main outdoor and indoor nonbiological air pollutants for children.

As airborne lead has decreased with the extended use of unleaded gasoline throughout the world, the main outdoor pollutants of concern in children remain ozone, CO, NO_2, SO_2, and particles.

Aside from the numerous volatile or semi-volatile substances used in the household, the indoor air pollution resulting from combustion and biomass burning related to heating and cooking is of special concern and represents a major public health challenge in developing countries. It is estimated that approximately 50% of the world population and up to 90% of rural households in developing countries still rely on unprocessed biomass fuels in the form of wood, dung, and crop residues for heating and cooking. These are too often burnt indoors in open fires or poorly functioning stoves. The most important pollutants from combustion of domestic origin are particles (small particles less than 10 μm in diameter and particularly less than 2.5 μm), CO, nitrogen oxides, and sulfur oxides (principally from coal). To a lesser extent, formaldehyde (gas stoves, space heaters) and polyclic organic matter including benzo[a]pyrene (open fire) are other indoor air pollutants.

Ozone

Origin

Ozone comes from motor vehicle and industry emissions as a product of the reaction of certain sunlight radiations on nitrogen oxides and hydrocarbons. The highest levels are formed in the afternoon during the summer, a time when children are often playing outdoors.

Health Effects in Children

The clinical effects observed in children are acute or subacute and result in persistent manifestations as cough, upper respiratory tract irritation, pain on inspiration, airway inflammation, increased bronchial permeability, and decrements in pulmonary function.

These respiratory symptoms may be associated with headache, nausea, malaise, and difficulties to sustain exercise for vigorously exercising children.

Many studies suggest that moderate levels of ozone may affect lungs in healthy school children and in asthmatic children. Whereas admission rates for persons of all ages, including the elderly, increase following summertime ozone exposure, children less than two years old were observed to be at greater risk. In a cohort of 846 asthmatic children aged 4–9 years, Mortimer et al. reported children who had had a low birth weight or a premature birth showed the greatest responses to ozone. Moreover, it has been reported that decreased peak flow persists for more than one week and that repeated exposures may result in persistent airway hyperresponsiveness.

Long-term consequences of chronic exposure to ozone are not clearly established, but animal and epidemiological studies suggest long-term health effects. Some experimental animal and clinical toxicological evidence suggests ozone exposure acts synergistically with other pollutants and aeroallergens.

Airborne Particles, Sulfur Oxides, and Acid Aerosols

Origin

Particles, sulfur oxides and acid aerosols are a complex group of distinct pollutants that have common sources and usually vary in concentration.

The sulfur oxides come from the combustion of fuels as coal and petroleum. The composition of airborne particles is complex and variable, coming from numerous, natural and manmade sources, including the same combustion sources. Those include industrial and agricultural smoke, engine and car exhausts, and home heating fumes. Particles, sulfur oxides, and nitrogen oxides contribute to the formation of acid aerosols in the atmosphere. While increasing smoke stack heights may have lowered local ambient levels, the residence time of sulfur oxides and particles in the air have been increased, thereby promoting transformation to various particulate sulfate compounds, including acidic sulfates. These sulfate particles constitute a large fraction of the total mass of smaller particles (< 3 μm in aerodynamic diameter).

Health Effects in Children

Epidemiological studies have consistently provided evidence of their adverse health effects. Clinical manifestations include acute respiratory symptoms, asthma, bronchitis, chronic cough, and chest illness. Particulates and SO_2 are implicated in acute morbidity and mortality. The toxicity of particulate matter depends on its chemical composition, which, for example, may include toxins like trace metals or hydrocarbons, and the size of particles, which determines the location of their deposit within the respiratory tract.

Daily fluctuations in PM10 levels (30–150 μg/m^3) have been shown to be related to acute respiratory hospital admissions in children, to school and kindergarten absences, to a decrement in peak flow rates in normal children, and to increased medication use in children with asthma.

Acid aerosols have been said to be the most important toxic component of PM10 toxicity. In a recent chamber exposure study, children with allergies or asthma show a positive association between symptoms and acid dose. The role of acid aerosols in respiratory toxicity attributable to particulates, however, has also been challenged.

Controversies surrounding such investigatory results have been explained partly by the relationship between toxic exposure and symptoms may be difficult to analyze, and also because asthmatics can manage their symptoms and pulmonary function with medication, thus blurring the relationship between toxic exposure and hospitalization rate.

It has been reported that health effects display a time lag, with weak same-day effects and stronger cumulative effects of air pollution on asthmatic children for both peak expiratory flow and symptoms. Epidemiological studies suggest a positive association between respiratory morbidity and mortality with particulate matter that has a diameter [less than or equal to] 10 μm. Within the broader toxicological understanding of particulate matter, toxicity in asthmatic children has not yet been clearly established.

Nitrogen Oxides

Origin

Nitrogen oxides come from the combustion of fuels such as coal and petroleum. They are emitted outdoors, but also predominantly indoors, and particularly in those houses without flues for gas appliances.

Health Effects in Children

In the past, the epidemiological evidence for toxic effects of nitrogen oxides were considered inconclusive partly because of methodological problems. More recently evidence has been reported that NO_2 is associated with an increase in respiratory symptoms among the general population, particularly in children. Studies in asthmatic children have shown an airway hyperresponsiveness to NO_2 in a homelike environment. In children under 14 years of age, significant associations were demonstrated between daily personal exposure to NO_2 levels readily available in the domestic setting and chest tightness on the same day, breathlessness on exertion with a one-day lag, daytime and nighttime asthma attacks on the same day and with a one-day lag time. Part of the discrepancy between the early and recent studies may be related to the fact that, in children, short-term peak levels of exposure are important to consider in relation to adverse respiratory effects associated with NO_2 exposure.

Carbon Monoxide

Origin

Carbon monoxide is a tasteless, odorless, colorless, nonirritating gas produced by the incomplete combustion of organic material. It is also produced endogenously in man. It is one of many ubiquitous contaminants of both outdoor and indoor environments. Outdoors CO is a result of emissions from transportation sources, primarily from motor vehicles and combustion gases. The indoor sources include unvented or defective gas, coal, wood and fuel stoves, fire places, kerosene space heaters, water heaters, barbecues, car exhaust from attached garage, and cigarette smoke. CO is probably the most insidious and dangerous indoor air pollutant, and is responsible for poisoning with high mortality rates and sequelae. Carbon monoxide is of special concern for children because it may be found in certain conditions in highly toxic amounts in the indoor air where children spend most of their time.

Health Effects in Children

Carbon monoxide is a major public health problem both in developed and developing countries. It is responsible for a significant percentage of all poisoning deaths.

The frequency of health problems associated with sublethal levels of CO is difficult to quantify. Not all cases of acute or subacute CO poisoning are reported or diagnosed, and complete up-to-date data are difficult to obtain in most developed countries, even more in developing countries. It has been estimated that over 40,000 emergency department visits occurred annually for acute CO poisoning in the United States. Children are frequently poisoned in homes or in the back of a car. In a study concerning 4902 patients hospitalized for CO poisoning, children under 15 years of age represented 23%. Moreover, 6% of these CO-poisoned patients were pregnant women, raising the problem of fetal intoxication.

Acute and Subacute Clinical Effects in Children

The symptoms of CO poisoning in adults are described well in the literature. Several series have shown that the clinical presentation of adults and older children are similar. It includes headache, nausea, vomiting, visual disturbances, dizziness, weakness, confusion, ataxia, syncope, seizures, lethargy, coma, and death.

Unfortunately, little information exists regarding CO poisoning in infants and small children. Many of the early manifestations of CO poisoning, such as headache, nausea, and blurred vision are difficult or impossible to observe in an infant.

We have performed a two-year prospective study comparing clinical manifestations and outcome in 140 children, aged newborn–14 years, and 774 adults with CO poisoning. Results showed that clinical manifestations in children differed from those in adults. Symptoms like headache, nausea, and coma were less frequent, whereas loss of consciousness, convulsions, and lethargy were more frequent in children than in adults. Neurological examination also showed differences, with fewer abnormal plantar responses and more flaccidity in children than in adults.

Long–Term Manifestations

Moderate to severe CO poisoning is known to be responsible for long-term manifestations and delayed neurological sequelae. These manifestations have also been described in children. It is difficult to determine the incidence of delayed neurological manifestations in a pediatric population particularly because some frequent manifestations like memory impairment are difficult to detect in an infant and may be overlooked. Several series have reported various rates of incidence. These long-term manifestations have been reported to be less frequent in children than in adults. The most frequently reported symptoms involve the so-called high cortical functions like memory impairment, personality alterations, signs of parietal dysfunction, and more rarely motor symptoms (hemiplegia, akinesia). Temporary cortical blindness and involuntary movements have also been reported. Further studies are needed to determine the long-term consequences of CO poisoning in children.

Fetus Intoxication

Experimental and clinical studies have demonstrated the toxic effects of CO exposure on the fetus during all stages of gestation. Fetal hypoxia is more pronounced than maternal tissue hypoxia, and the severity of fetal intoxication cannot be assessed solely by the maternal state. These effects include teratogenesis, neurological dysfunction, decreased birth weight, and increased risk of fetal death. Even at 40w CO concentration, some evidence has been reported concerning the contribution of CO to the association of ambient air pollution with reduced birth weight.

In our center, we surveyed all women intoxicated by CO during pregnancy. We found a four-fold increase in the relative risk of fetal death. In this series, where every woman was treated with hyperbaric oxygen, no increase in prematurity, fetal hypotrophy, or malformation rate could be detected compared with the general population. Long-term prospective surveillance of these children has been implemented in order to assess the neurological deterioration if it occurs later during child development.

CONCLUSION

Various factors related to age, physiologic maturity, and exposure patterns make children potentially more susceptible than adults to the adverse effects of air pollution. Besides acute manifestations, exposure during childhood may have long lasting effects and requires special follow-up.

Our own experience acquired through studies of CO exposure taught us how toxic manifestations may be different in children compared to adults. Special attention has to be given to the unique physiology and other qualities of the child in order to properly evaluate the clinical consequences of their toxic exposures. Such considerations emphasize the key roles of poison centers, clinical toxicologists, and pediatricians working in collaboration towards the identification, assessment, and surveillance of toxic risks from air pollution for children health and development.

* * *

Based on these findings and others like them, the EPA had the following ambient levels established for these pollutants as of 2004:

Criteria Air Pollutants	Allowable Exposure Primary standard*	CFR Section
Sulfur Dioxide	Annual: 0.030 ppm 24–hour: 0.14 ppm	40 CFR § 50.4 (a) 40 CFR § 50.4 (b)
Sulfur Dioxide	3–hour: 0.5 ppm * (secondary standard)	40 CFR § 50.5 (a)
Particulate Matter 10	Annual: 50 µg/m3 24–hour: 150 µg/m3	40 CFR § 50.6 (b) 40 CFR § 50.6 (a)
Particulate Matter 2.5	Annual: 15 µg/m3 24–hour: 65 µg/m3	40 CFR § 50.7 (a)(1) 40 CFR § 50.7 (a)(1)
Carbon Monoxide	8–hour: 9 ppm 1–hour: 35 ppm	40 CFR § 50.8 (a)(1) 40 CFR § 50.8 (a)(2)
Ozone	8–hour: .08 ppm 1–hour: 12 ppm	40 CFR § 50.10 (a) 40 CFR § 50.9 (a)

Criteria Air Pollutants	Allowable Exposure Primary standard*	CFR Section
Nitrogen Dioxide	Annual: 0.053 ppm	40 CFR § 50.11 (a)
Lead	Calendar Quarter: 1.5 Sg/m3	40 CFR § 50.12

Given the nature of these criteria pollutants, the various effects they can cause, and the different "at risk" populations, how does EPA actually establish a "safe" level under Sec. 109? What factors can it consider? What evidence can it use? How much deference is given to its air quality modeling? How does this alter the legal strategies of parties who will be affected by the establishment of these standards? The following case answers some of these questions.

WHITMAN v. AMERICAN TRUCKING ASSOCIATIONS, INC.

Supreme Court of the United States, 2001.
531 U.S. 457, 121 S.Ct. 903, 149 L.Ed.2d 1.

Justice SCALIA delivered the opinion of the Court:

Section 109(a) of the CAA requires the Administrator of the EPA to promulgate NAAQS for each air pollutant for which "air quality criteria" have been issued under § 108. Once a NAAQS has been promulgated, the Administrator must review the standard (and the criteria on which it is based) "at five-year intervals" and make "such revisions ... as may be appropriate." CAA § 109(d)(1). These cases arose when, on July 18, 1997, the Administrator revised the NAAQS for particulate matter and ozone. See NAAQS for Particulate Matter, 40 CFR § 50.7 (1999); NAAQS for Ozone, 40 CFR §§ 50.9, 50.10 (1999).

In *Lead Industries Assn., Inc. v. EPA*, [647 F.2d 1130, 1148 (D.C. Cir. 1980)], the District of Columbia Circuit held that "economic considerations [may] play no part in the promulgation of ambient air quality standards under Section 109" of the CAA. In the present cases, the court adhered to that holding, 175 F.3d, at 1040–1041, as it had done on many other occasions. Respondents argue that these decisions are incorrect. We disagree ...

Section 109(b)(1) instructs the EPA to set primary ambient air quality standards "the attainment and maintenance of which ... are requisite to protect the public health" with "an adequate margin of safety." Were it not for the hundreds of pages of briefing respondents have submitted on the issue, one would have thought it fairly clear that this text does not permit the EPA to consider costs in setting the standards. The language, as one scholar has noted, "is absolute." D. Currie, Air Pollution: Federal Law and Analysis 4–15 (1981). The EPA, "based on" the information about health effects contained in the technical "criteria" documents compiled under § 108(a)(2) is to identify the maximum airborne concentration of a pollutant that the public health can tolerate, decrease the concentration to provide an "adequate" margin of safety, and set the standard at that level. Nowhere are the costs of achieving such a standard made part of that initial calculation.

Against this most natural of readings, respondents make a lengthy, spirited, but ultimately unsuccessful attack. They begin with the object of § 109(b)(1)' s focus, the "public health." When the term first appeared in federal clean air legislation—in the Act of July 14, 1955, which expressed "recognition of the dangers to the public health" from air pollution—its ordinary meaning was "[t]he health of the community." Webster's New International Dictionary 2005 (2d ed.1950). Respondents argue, however, that § 109(b)(1), as added by the Clean Air Amendments of 1970, meant to use the term's secondary meaning: "[t]he ways and means of conserving the health of the members of a community, as by preventive medicine, organized care of the sick, etc." *Ibid.* Words that can have more than one meaning are given content, however, by their surroundings, and in the context of § 109(b)(1) this second definition makes no sense. Congress could not have meant to instruct the Administrator to set NAAQS at a level "requisite to protect" "the art and science dealing with the protection and improvement of community health." Webster's Third New International Dictionary 1836 (1981). We therefore revert to the primary definition of the term: the health of the public.

Even so, respondents argue, many more factors than air pollution affect public health. In particular, the economic cost of implementing a very stringent standard might produce health losses sufficient to offset the health gains achieved in cleaning the air—for example, by closing down whole industries and thereby impoverishing the workers and consumers dependent upon those industries. That is unquestionably true, and Congress was unquestionably aware of it. Thus, Congress had commissioned in the Air Quality Act of 1967 (1967 Act) "a detailed estimate of the cost of carrying out the provisions of this Act; a comprehensive study of the cost of program implementation by affected units of government; and a comprehensive study of the economic impact of air quality standards on the Nation's industries, communities, and other contributing sources of pollution." § 2, 81 Stat.505. The 1970 Congress, armed with the results of this study, not only anticipated that compliance costs could injure the public health, but provided for that precise exigency. Section 110(f)(1) of the CAA permitted the Administrator to waive the compliance deadline for stationary sources if, inter alia, sufficient control measures were simply unavailable and "the continued operation of such sources is *essential . . . to the public health* or welfare." 84 Stat. 1683 (emphasis added). Other provisions explicitly permitted or required economic costs to be taken into account in implementing the air quality standards. Section111(b)(1)(B), for example, commanded the Administrator to set "standards of performance" for certain new sources of emissions that as specified in § 111(a)(1) were to "reflec[t] the degree of emission limitation achievable through the application of the best system of emission reduction which (taking into account the cost of achieving such reduction) the Administrator determines has been adequately demonstrated." Section 202(a)(2) prescribed that emissions standards for automobiles could take effect only "after such period as the Administrator finds necessary to permit the development and application of the requisite technology, giving appropriate consideration to the cost of compliance within such period."

Subsequent amendments to the CAA have added many more provisions directing, in explicit language, that the Administrator consider costs in performing various duties. See, e.g., 42 U.S.C. § 7545(k)(1) (reformulate gasoline to "require the greatest reduction in emissions . . . taking into consideration the cost of achieving such emissions reductions"); § 7547(a)(3) (emission reduction for nonroad vehicles to be set "giving appropriate consideration to the cost" of the standards). We have therefore refused to find implicit in ambiguous sections of the CAA an authorization to consider costs that has elsewhere, and so often, been expressly granted. See *Union Elec. Co. v. EPA*, 427 U.S. 246, 257, and n. 5 (1976).

[Respondents' next argument] is that § 109(b)(1)'s terms "adequate margin" and "requisite" leave room to pad health effects with cost concerns. Just as we found it "highly unlikely that Congress would leave the determination of whether an industry will be entirely, or even substantially, rate-regulated to agency discretion—and even more unlikely that it would achieve that through such a subtle device as permission to 'modify' rate-filing requirements," *MCI Telecommunications Corp. v. American Telephone & Telegraph Co.*, [512 U.S. 218, 231 (1994)], so also we find it implausible that Congress would give to the EPA through these modest words the power to determine whether implementation costs should moderate national air quality standards.

The same defect inheres in respondents' next two arguments: that while the Administrator's judgment about what is requisite to protect the public health must be "based on [the] criteria" documents developed under § 108(a)(2), see § 109(b)(1), it need not be based solely on those criteria; and that those criteria themselves, while they must include "effects on public health or welfare which may be expected from the presence of such pollutant in the ambient air," are not necessarily limited to those effects. Even if we were to concede those premises, we still would not conclude that one of the unenumerated factors that the agency can consider in developing and applying the criteria is cost of implementation. That factor is both so indirectly related to public health and so full of potential for canceling the conclusions drawn from direct health effects that it would surely have been expressly mentioned in §§ 108 and 109 had Congress meant it to be considered. Yet while those provisions describe in detail how the health effects of pollutants in the ambient air are to be calculated and given effect, see § 108(a)(2), they say not a word about costs.

. . . The text of § 109(b), interpreted in its statutory and historical context and with appreciation for its importance to the CAA as a whole, unambiguously bars cost considerations from the NAAQS-setting process, and thus ends the matter for us as well as the EPA.[4] . . .

We agree with the Solicitor General that the text of § 109(b)(1) of the CAA at a minimum requires that "[f]or a discrete set of pollutants and based on published air quality criteria that reflect the latest scientific knowledge, [the] EPA must establish uniform national standards at a level that is requisite to protect public health from the adverse effects of the pollutant in the ambient air." Tr. of Oral Arg. in No. 99–1257, p. 5. Requisite, in turn, "mean[s] sufficient, but not more than necessary." Id., at 7.

Notes and Comments

1. One of the two regulatory changes at issue in *American Trucking* involved EPA's effort to revise the ozone standard from a one-hour-average standard of 0.12 to an eight-hour-average standard of 0.08 ppm. The lower court characterized EPA's justification of this change in the following terms:

> . . . EPA's explanations for its decisions amount to assertions that a less stringent standard would allow the relevant pollutant to inflict a greater quantum of harm on public health, and that a more stringent standard would result in less harm. Such arguments only support the intuitive proposition that more pollution will not benefit public health, not that keeping pollution at or below any particular level is "requisite" or not requisite to "protect the public health" with an "adequate margin of safety," the formula set out by § 109(b)(1).

Consider EPA's defense of the 0.08 ppm level of the ozone NAAQS. EPA explains that its choice is superior to . . . 0.09 ppm, because more people are exposed to more serious effects at 0.09 than at 0.08. In defending the decision not to go down to 0.07, EPA never contradicts the intuitive proposition . . . that reducing the standard to that level would bring about comparable changes. Instead, it gives three other reasons. The principal substantive one is based on the criteria just discussed:

> The most certain O_3-related effects, while judged to be adverse, are transient and reversible (particularly at O_3 exposures below 0.08 ppm), and the more serious effects with greater immediate and potential long-term impacts on health are less certain, both as to the percentage of individuals exposed to various concentrations who are likely to experience such effects and as to the long-term medical significance of these effects.

In other words, effects are less certain and less severe at lower levels of exposure. This seems to be nothing more than a statement that lower exposure levels are associated with lower risk to public health. . . .

American Trucking Ass'n v. U.S. EPA, 175 F.3d 1027, 1035, *reh'g den. in pert. part*, 195 F.3d 4 (1999). Based on this analysis, the D.C. Circuit had

---

4. Respondents' speculation that the EPA is secretly considering the costs of attainment without telling anyone is irrelevant to our interpretive inquiry. If such an allegation could be proved, it would be grounds for vacating the NAAQS, because the Administrator had not followed the law. It would not, however, be grounds for this Court's changing the law.

concluded that, as interpreted by EPA, the § 109(b)(1) standard ("requisite to protect the public health") violated the nondelegation doctrine. Id. at 1038. In a portion of the opinion not reprinted above, the Supreme Court reversed, finding that "[t]he scope of discretion § 109(b)(1) allows is in fact well within the outer limits of our nondelegation precendents." 531 U.S. at 474, 121 S.Ct. at 913.

On remand, the same three-judge panel that had issued the above-quoted opinion back in 1999 (although Judge Tatel had dissented) unanimously determined that EPA's analysis passed muster under the arbitrary and capricious standard of review. *American Trucking Ass'n v. EPA*, 283 F.3d 355 (D.C. Cir. 2002).

Do you understand why the same concerns that led two members of the original panel to find nondelegation problems did not later cause them to conclude that the 0.08 ppm standard was arbitrary and capricious? What do these opinions teach us about the "requisite to protect the public health" standard? What if a new Administration wanted to move the standard to either 0.09 or 0.07 ppm? How would you evaluate the prospects of any challenge to such a move? Of how much help is the last paragraph from the excerpted portion of the Supreme Court's opinion?

2. As mentioned in *American Trucking*, § 109(d)(1) requires EPA to revisit the NAAQS standards every five years to determine if the same standards should still govern in the face of new evidence. This allows standards to be revisited not only based on scientific understanding, but provides a chance for political influences as well. After *American Trucking*, how sure are you that cost will never play a role in the setting of these standards? Does footnote 4 adequately address the concern that EPA may be taking cost in account sub rosa?

3. Much concern has recently been expressed about the NAAQS for particulates, with special attention to small particulates. New evidence may continue to alter this standard for some time to come.

C. How Are the National Ambient Air Quality Standards Met?—State Implementation Plans

When Congress passed the CAA in 1970, it left the primary responsibility for enforcing the NAAQS to each State. Each State was to ensure that all criteria air pollutants were controlled at levels below the NAAQS throughout the entire State. Section 110 charged the States with creating plans to implement these standards—the State Implementation Plans (SIPs)—and EPA with approving them. The Supreme Court summarized both the historical backdrop and the basics of this scheme in *Train v. Natural Resources Defense Council, Inc.*, 421 U.S. 60, 95 S.Ct. 1470, 43 L.Ed.2d 731 (1975):

Congress initially responded to the problem of air pollution by offering encouragement and assistance to the States. In 1955 the Surgeon General was authorized to study the problem of air pollution, to support research, training, and demonstration projects, and to provide technical assistance to state and local governments attempting to abate pollution. In 1960 Congress directed the Surgeon

General to focus his attention on the health hazards resulting from motor vehicle emissions. The Clean Air Act of 1963 authorized federal authorities to expand their research efforts, to make grants to state air pollution control agencies, and also to intervene directly to abate interstate pollution in limited circumstances. Amendments in 1965 and in 1966 broadened federal authority to control motor vehicle emissions and to make grants to state pollution control agencies.

The focus shifted somewhat in the Air Quality Act of 1967. It reiterated the premise of the earlier Clean Air Act 'that the prevention and control of air pollution at its source is the primary responsibility of States and local governments.' Its provisions, however, increased the federal role in the prevention of air pollution, by according federal authorities certain powers of supervision and enforcement. But the States generally retained wide latitude to determine both the air quality standards which they would meet and the period of time in which they would do so.

The response of the States to these manifestations of increasing congressional concern with air pollution was disappointing. Even by 1970, state planning and implementation under the Air Quality Act of 1967 had made little progress. Congress reacted by taking a stick to the States in the form of the Clean Air Amendments of 1970, enacted on December 31 of that year. These Amendments sharply increased federal authority and responsibility in the continuing effort to combat air pollution. Nonetheless, the Amendments explicitly preserved the principle: 'Each State shall have the primary responsibility for assuring air quality within the entire geographic area comprising such State....' § 107(a). The difference under the Amendments was that the States were no longer given any choice as to whether they would meet this responsibility. For the first time they were required to attain air quality of specified standards, and to do so within a specified period of time.

Within nine months after the Agency's promulgation of primary and secondary air quality standards, each of the 50 States was required to submit to the Agency a plan designed to implement and maintain such standards within its boundaries. § 110(a)(1) of the Clean Air Act. The Agency was in turn required to approve each State's plan within four months of the deadline for submission, if it had been adopted after public hearings and if it satisfied eight general conditions set forth in§ 110(a). Probably the principal of these conditions, and the heart of the 1970 Amendments, is that the plan provide for the attainment of the national primary ambient air quality standards in the particular State 'as expeditiously as practicable but . . . in no case later than three years from the date of approval of such plan.' § 110(a)(2)(A). In providing for such attainment, a State's plan must include 'emission limitations, schedules, and timetables for compliance with such limitations'; it must also contain such other measures as may be necessary to insure both timely attainment and subsequent maintenance of national ambient air standards. § 110(a)(2)(B).

We believe that the foregoing analysis of the structure and legislative history of the Clean Air Amendments shows that Congress intended to impose national ambient air standards to be attained within a specific period of time.... We also believe that Congress, consistent with its declaration that '(e)ach State shall have the primary responsibility for assuring air quality' within its boundaries, § 107(a), left to the States considerable latitude in determining specifically how the standards would be met. This discretion includes the continuing authority to revise choices about the mix of emission limitations....

421 U.S. at 63–87, 95 S.Ct. at 1474–1485.

Notes and Comments

1. The SIP is best viewed as the State's blueprint for how it will either attain or maintain compliance with the NAAQS. Compliance with the NAAQS is not measured on a State-wide basis. Instead, each State has been broken down into a number of "air quality control regions" (which we sometimes alternatively refer to as "air-sheds"), for the purpose of measuring compliance at a more local level. See 42 U.S.C. § 7407(b) and (c). Each air quality control region is then designated as being either in attainment, in nonattainment, or as unclassifiable for each of the relevant NAAQS. See 42 U.S.C. § 7407(d). Thus, the planning under § 110(a)(1) occurs on an air-shed-by-air-shed basis and, within each air-shed, on a pollutant-by-pollutant basis. It is also worth noting that the air quality control regions may sometimes overlap State boundaries. In those cases, the affected States work together in developing the relevant plan. As one example of how this can work, in Oregon the Portland/Vancouver air-shed (which includes Vancouver, WA) historically has suffered periods of nonattainment for carbon monoxide and ozone (though it is currently in attainment for both), while it has always been in attainment for the other criteria pollutants. The Medford /Ashland air-shed, by contrast, historically has had nonattainment problems solely for particulate matter, though it recently achieved attainment even for that. See 71 Fed. Reg. 35153 (June 19, 2006).

2. As we will see below, the CAA has evolved to the point where it now imposes many mandatory controls on sources (such as those imposed under §§ 111 (New Source Performance Standards ("NSPS")) and 112 (National Emission Standards for Hazardous Air Pollutants ("NESPHAPs")) which erode, at least some extent, the "considerable latitude" to which the Supreme Court referred in *Train v. NRDC*. However, these requirements are only minima. The States are free to impose more stringent requirements as part of their SIP strategies. Moreover, the SIP picks up many sources that are left uncovered by these more prescriptive sections. For example, sources that predated the 1970 CAA amendments, and which therefore may not qualify as "new sources" subject to NSPS, are often regulated solely as a matter of State discretion through the SIP process (at least with respect to those emissions which don't trigger NESHAPs). The SIP would also be the place where the State might identify some more creative solutions, such as the creation of car-pooling programs or the imposition of controls on wood-

stoves or activities such as leaf-or field-burning. Beyond the control strategies, § 110(a)(2) also requires that the SIP include systems to monitor and analyze air-quality data, as well as a system to enforce the substantive elements of the plan.

3. In *Union Electric Co. v. EPA*, 427 U.S. 246, 96 S.Ct. 2518, 49 L.Ed.2d 474 (1976), the Supreme Court upheld EPA's position that it is powerless to reject a SIP so long as EPA is convinced the State's strategy will work. In that case, the petitioners argued that EPA was required to reject Missouri's plan because it imposed requirements on them that allegedly were economically and technologically infeasible. In agreeing with EPA, the Court held that "the State has virtually absolute power in allocating emissions limitations so long as the national standards are met." 427 U.S. at 267, 96 S.Ct. at 2530.

4. In reality, SIPs are dynamic processes. States are constantly modifying their SIPs to reflect changing conditions (e.g., to account for emissions by new businesses). Additionally, § 110(k)(5) gives EPA the power to require a State to revise its SIP whenever it finds that a SIP is "substantially inadequate" to attain or maintain compliance with the NAAQS. Once a SIP revision submittal is complete, EPA has 12 months to either approve or disapprove it. 42 U.S.C. § 7410(k)(2). If EPA disapproves a SIP submission, it must promulgate a federal implementation plan (FIP) within two years unless the State corrects the deficiency. 42 U.S.C. § 7410(c)(1).

1. What About the Transport of Criteria Pollutants?

In designing their SIPS, States are required not only to ensure the attainment of the NAAQS in their own States, but also that in-state air pollution sources do not "contribute significantly to nonattainment in, or interfere with maintenance by, any other State with respect to any such national.... ambient air quality standard." 42 U.S.C. § 7410(a)(2)(D)(i)(I). Such a requirement is logical in a federalized system, but how is it to be measured or enforced? Two parts of the CAA address this question. Section 126 requires EPA to take action against sources in other States that contribute to the degradation of another State's SIP. Additionally, in 1990 Congress added sections 176A and 184, which authorize the EPA to set up a multi-state transport region to deal with the cumulative effects of transport. 42 U.S.C. §§ 7506a and 7511c. Both methods have their drawbacks; as the following case illustrates, both methods depend on vigorous enforcement by EPA, due to the great deference the agency's findings receive.

APPALACHIAN POWER COMPANY v. ENVIRONMENTAL PROTECTION AGENCY

United States Court of Appeals, District of Columbia Circuit, 2001.
249 F.3d 1032.

Before: WILLIAMS, GINSBURG, and SENTELLE, Circuit Judges
PER CURIAM:

A. *Statutory Framework*

Under the [CAA], the EPA promulgates [NAAQS] for criteria air pollutants, including tropospheric ozone. *See* 42 U.S.C. § 7409. The EPA then designates those areas of the United States that fail to meet the various NAAQS. 42 U.S.C. § 7407(d). States, in turn, are required to adopt [SIPs] providing for the attainment of the NAAQS. 42 U.S.C. § 7410. The SIPs are submitted to the EPA for approval, and may be revised at the EPA's insistence if found to be inadequate to ensure maintenance of the NAAQS or public health. States that fail to comply with these requirements are subject to various sanctions and the imposition of a Federal Implementation Plan ("FIP"). 42 U.S.C. § 7509.

Much air pollution is a local or regional problem. Some pollution, however, is caused or augmented by emissions from other states. Emissions from "upwind" regions may pollute "downwind" regions. Several provisions of the CAA are designed to address such transboundary air pollution. In particular, section 110(a)(2)(D)(i)(I) of the Act requires states to prohibit emissions within the state in amounts that will "contribute significantly to nonattainment in, or interfere with maintenance by, any other State" of the NAAQS.

CAA section 126 provides a mechanism whereby downwind states may petition the EPA to directly regulate upwind sources of pollution. Under section 126(b), a downwind state "may petition the Administrator for a finding that any major source or group of stationary sources emits or would emit any air pollutant in violation" of CAA section 110(a)(2)(D). Once the EPA makes a section 126(b) finding, section 126(c) provides that:

> it shall be a violation of this section and the applicable implementation plan in such State—
>
> (1) for any major proposed new (or modified) source with respect to which a finding has been made under subsection (b) of this section to be constructed or to operate in violation [of this section or section 110], or
>
> (2) for any major existing source to operate more than three months after such finding has been made with respect to it.

The Administrator may allow the continued operation of existing sources beyond three months provided such sources comply with emission limitations and compliance schedules provided by the Administrator which "bring about compliance ... as expeditiously as practicable, but in no case later than three years after the date of such finding."

At issue in this case is the extent of the EPA's authority to make findings and directly regulate sources in upwind states under section 126, and whether the EPA's section 126 rule was arbitrary and capricious or contrary to law.

B. The NOx SIP Call

In October 1998, the EPA issued a final rule calling upon [22] states[1] and the District of Columbia to revise their ozone SIPs to address interstate air pollution (aka "interstate transport"). *See* Finding of Significant Contribution and Rulemaking for Certain States in the Ozone Transport Assessment Group Region for Purposes of Reducing Regional Transport of Ozone, 63 Fed. Reg. 57,356 (1998) ("*NOx SIP Call*"). Concluding that upwind states contribute significantly to ozone nonattainment problems in downwind states, the EPA required each jurisdiction to promulgate a new SIP to reduce NOx emissions. This "NOx SIP call" required states to reduce NOx emissions by the amount that could be accomplished by emission controls capable of reducing emissions at a cost of $2,000 or less per ton. Under the rule, revised SIPs were due by September 30, 1999, and SIP provisions covering stationary sources had to be implemented by May 1, 2003. Failure to submit an adequate NOx SIP by the deadline would result in implementation of a FIP by the EPA. In other words, if the states do not submit a plan for meeting their CAA obligations, the EPA will impose one of its own.

C.   *The Original Section 126 Rule–Conditional Findings*

In August 1997, eight states submitted petitions requesting that the EPA find that stationary sources in upwind states contribute significantly to downwind air pollution. Specifically, the petitioning states sought findings pursuant to CAA section 126(b), that specified sources or categories thereof are the source of NOx emissions that contribute significantly to ozone nonattainment in the petitioning states in violation of CAA section 110(a)(2)(D). Each petition further sought to have the EPA implement direct federal regulation of stationary sources in upwind states, primarily electric generating facilities and fossil-fuel fired industrial boilers and turbines. Because the section 126 petitions raised many of the same issues as the NOx SIP call, and would require comparable emission reductions, the EPA coordinated its response to the section 126 petitions with the NOx SIP call rulemaking.

In a final rule published on May 25, 1999, the EPA determined that NOx emissions in twelve states and the District of Columbia contribute significantly to nonattainment of the one-hour ozone NAAQS in Connecticut, Massachusetts, New York, and Pennsylvania. 64 Fed. Reg. 28,250 (May 25, 1999) ("*May 1999 Rule*"). The twelve states are Delaware, Indiana, Kentucky, Maryland, Michigan, New Jersey, New York, North Carolina, Ohio, Pennsylvania, Virginia, and West Virginia.

Rather than make section 126 findings at that time, however, the EPA determined that it was appropriate to postpone such findings pending the resolution of the NOx SIP call process. Accordingly, the EPA issued a rule providing that the findings would automatically be deemed made with regard to sources from a given state should that state fail to comply with a NOx SIP call deadline. The EPA based this decision on

---

1. The states are Alabama, Connecticut, Delaware, Georgia, Illinois, Indiana, Kentucky, Maryland, Massachusetts, Michigan, Missouri, New Jersey, New York, North Carolina, Ohio, Pennsylvania, Rhode Island, South Carolina, Tennessee, Virginia, West Virginia, and Wisconsin.

the judgment that full compliance with the NOx SIP call would obviate the need for section 126 findings. Once made, the section 126 findings would require covered sources to come into compliance no later than May 1, 2003. Sources that failed to comply by that date would be required to cease operations.

D. Revised Section 126 Rule–Final Findings

Subsequent to the completion of the section 126 rulemaking, this court issued two orders which caused the EPA to change course. First, ... this court remanded the EPA's proposed revisions to the ozone NAAQS. *American Trucking Ass'ns v. EPA,* 175 F.3d 1027, *reh'g granted in part and denied in part,* 195 F.3d 4 (D.C.Cir.1999), *rev'd in part sub nom. Whitman v. American Trucking Ass'ns,* 531 U.S. 457 (2001). Second, this court issued an order staying the NOx SIP call deadline.

In response to these orders, the EPA revised the section 126 rule. 65 Fed. Reg. 2674 (Jan. 18, 2000) (*"Jan. 2000 Rule"*). In particular, the EPA made the requested findings of significant contributions, granting the relevant portions of the section 126 petitions and delinking the section 126 findings from compliance with the NOx SIP call. The EPA explained that it was "implementing the requirements of section 126 of the CAA in the absence of any currently effective requirement for upwind States to address the interstate pollution transport problems themselves." *Id.* at 2683. Instead, the EPA's new rule contained a provision to withdraw the relevant findings upon approval of a NOx SIP in accordance with the October 1998 NOx SIP call.

As with the NOx SIP call, the EPA considered both NOx emissions and the cost of control in determining which sources contribute significantly to downwind ozone nonattainment. Based upon its analysis of the cost of emissions controls, the EPA concluded that measures which can reduce NOx emissions for $2,000 or less per ton are highly cost-effective. The EPA then divided NOx emission sources into various categories and determined the level of emission reduction that would be highly cost-effective for each category.

The section 126 rule also established an emission allowance "cap and trade" program, known as the Federal NOx Budget Trading Program. Under this program, ... regulated sources are allocated tradeable NOx emission allowances and are prohibited from emitting more NOx than the amount of allowances held. If a facility emits more than its initial allowance allocation, it must purchase additional allowances from another facility, reduce its emissions, or cease operations.

To determine the initial allocations, the EPA established a NOx emission cap for each upwind state. Each state's cap is based upon expected emission reductions from highly cost-effective controls in that state as of 2007. Ninety-five percent of each state's cap is allocated proportionally among existing sources based upon each facility's heat input. Five percent of the cap is set aside for future, as-yet-unproposed sources. These initial allocations will apply for the 2003–07 time period.

The EPA will issue revised allocations for the 2008–12 time period, and every five years thereafter.

Since the issuance of the final section 126 rule, this Court has ruled on various challenges to the EPA's NOx SIP call. In *Michigan v. EPA*, 213 F.3d 663 (D.C.Cir.2000), we upheld the SIP call in most respects, remanding portions of the rule to the EPA. Of greatest relevance to these proceedings, we upheld the EPA's analyses of interstate transport of NOx emissions and its use of cost-effectiveness criteria in determining which upwind sources "contribute significantly" to nonattainment in downwind states. Subsequently, we entered an order amending the deadline for full implementation of NOx SIP revisions from May 1, 2003 to May 31, 2004.

After the EPA published the final section 126 rule in January 2000, numerous groups petitioned this Court for review. Among the petitioners are a group of upwind states from the midwestern and southeastern United States ("MW & SE State Petitioners"); utilities and other operators of electric generating facilities ("Non–State Petitioners"); companies that operate non-electric generating/industrial facilities ("Non–EGU Petitioners"); and several individual companies that have facility–specific concerns ("Facility–Specific Petitioners"). A group of northeastern states ("NE State Petitioners") also petitioned for review alleging that the EPA's rule did not go far enough in controlling upwind NOx emissions. The northeastern states otherwise intervened in support of the EPA, as did a group of environmental organizations. The various petitions for review were consolidated into this case.

II. COMMON AND GENERAL ISSUES

A. Scrivener's Error

The Clean Air Act Amendments of 1990 eliminated a subsection of § 110 of the [CAA], causing § 110(a)(2)(E) to be renumbered as § 110(a)(2)(D). The Amendments correspondingly updated several references to § 110(a)(2)(E)(i) that had appeared in § 126 of the [CAA], but changed them to read "section 110(a)(2)(D)(ii)." The 1990 Amendments thus not only substituted "(D)" for "(E)" in § 126, as necessitated by the renumbering, but also substituted "(ii)" for "(i)." The EPA, which contends that the Congress amended § 126 only in order to update the cross-references so as to preserve the ststus quo ante, claims that this substitution of "(ii)" for "(i)" was "inadvertent[]." The agency therefore construes § 126 as if this "inadvertence" had not occurred, i.e., as if that section referred to § 110(a)(2)(D)(i). The Non-State Petitioners, by contrast, argue that § 126 should be read as written, that is, to refer to § 110(a)(2)(D)(ii).

Section 126 gives a state the right to petition the EPA to find "that any major source or group of stationary sources [in another state] emits or would emit any air pollutant in violation of the prohibition of" a subsection of § 110(a)(2)(D), the subsection here at issue. 42 U.S.C. § 7426(b). As we have noted, the ability of such a source or group of sources to operate is severely constrained once such a finding is made. 42 U.S.C. § 7426(c). The constraints in § 126(c) are triggered by the "prohibition" in whichever subsection of § 110(a)(2)(D) it is that § 126 cross-references. Section 110(a)(2)(D) provides that a [SIP] must

(D) contain adequate provisions—

(i) prohibiting ... any source or other type of emissions activity within the State from emitting any air pollutant in amounts which will—

(I) contribute significantly to nonattainment in, or interfere with maintenance by, any other State with respect [to the NAAQS] or

(II) interfere with [various other] measures.

(ii) insuring compliance with the applicable requirements of sections 7426 [CAA § 126] and 7415 [CAA § 115] of this title (relating to interstate and international pollution abatement).

42 U.S.C. § 7410(a)(2)(D). Thus, prior to the 1990 Amendments, § 126 provided an avenue by which a state could compel the EPA to enforce emissions limitations upon a neighboring state the emissions from which contributed to its own nonattainment of the NAAQS. The EPA argues that § 126 should still be read to have this effect, notwithstanding the substitution of "(ii)" for "(i)" therein.

According to the petitioners' reading, the 1990 amendment of §§ 126(b) and (c) gave each state the right to compel enforcement against another state that fails to provide notice of new sources and took away their right to compel enforcement against a state that actually pollutes the complaining state's air. Even were we to assume that such a counterintuitive switch from substantive to procedural compliance could plausibly reflect congressional policy, the petitioners' reading would still be flawed. Section 126(b) permits a state to petition the EPA to find that "any major source or group of stationary sources emits or would emit any air pollutant in violation of the prohibition of section 7410(a)(2)(D)(ii)." The notice requirement of § 126(a), to which the petitioners claim this reference ultimately points, binds states only to warn their neighbors of proposed new and modified sources; it does not restrict the behavior of sources or groups of sources, whose "violation" of § 110(a)(2)(D) is the predicate for a § 126(b) finding.

B. *The NOx SIP Call and § 126*

The Administrator ... must require a state to revise its SIP "as necessary" whenever she finds such a plan "substantially inadequate to ... comply" with various requirements of the Act, including the requirement that the plan "contain adequate provisions" to prevent sources within a state from contributing significantly to any other state's nonattainment or nonmaintenance of the NAAQS. *Id.* § 7410(a)(2)(D)(i)(I), 7410(k)(5). Pursuant to this authority, in October 1998 the EPA issued a request for SIP revisions, or a "SIP call," that required 22 states and the District of Columbia to revise their SIPs in order to mitigate the interstate transport of ozone. This court upheld the essential elements of the NOx SIP call in March 2000, although we remanded the rule for further proceedings with regard to three states and to certain types of sources. [*Michigan v. EPA*, 213 F.3d 663, 695 (D.C.Cir. 2000)].

In August 1997, during the preparation of the NOx SIP call, eight states petitioned the EPA to find, pursuant to CAA § 126(b), that "major stationary sources or groups of sources" in specified states were contributing to the petitioning states' failure to meet the NAAQS for ozone. In the first of the two rules challenged here, the EPA announced that because it was "operating on basically the same set of facts" in making determinations under § 126 as it had when it issued the NOx SIP call—that is, facts showing that upwind sources contributed to downwind nonattainment of the NAAQS—it would eschew making formal findings under § 126. 64 Fed. Reg. at 28,274/3, 28,275/2. Instead, the agency made the "affirmative technical determination" that sources in upwind states were contributing to nonattainment in downwind states, and provided that a formal finding to that effect under § 126 would be deemed to be made for such sources in a state if by May 1, 2000, EPA has not either (a) approved a state's SIP revision to comply with the NOx SIP call or (b) promulgated implementation plan provisions meeting the [CAA] section 110(a)(2)(D)(i) requirements.

Id. at 28,275/2.

The EPA used this "automatic trigger mechanism," 65 Fed. Reg. at 2679/1, as part of a "coordinated approach" to the SIP call and the § 126 petitions, 64 Fed. Reg. at 28,275/3: § 126 findings would be withheld until the conclusion of the SIP call, but would be entered automatically should a state's response to the SIP call be either unsatisfactory or untimely. May 1, 2000 was chosen as the date for triggering the § 126 finding because § 126(c) allows the EPA to permit sources found to contribute to another state's nonattainment to continue to operate for no more than three years after the date of such a finding. For findings made on May 1, 2000, the three-year clock would expire on May 1, 2003—the same date by which states were required to have implemented controls over sources of interstate ozone under the original NOx SIP call.

The petitioners' primary argument . . . is that Title I of the [CAA] is animated by a commitment to "cooperative federalism" under which the EPA is to determine what level of air quality is required but must defer in the first instance to the judgments of the states regarding how to achieve that level. This principle, according to the petitioners, requires that a SIP call inviting states to respond to the problem of interstate transport be the preferred remedy, while direct federal regulation of sources, as authorized by § 126, must be a last resort reserved for cases in which states cannot or do not meet their SIP obligation.

The petitioners contend that the delay in the NOx SIP call deadline, because it did not affect the "Congress' clear preference" for state implementation decisions, should not have altered the EPA's determination that the SIP call takes precedence over § 126.... The EPA, which considers [§§ 110 and 126] to be "independent statutory tools to address the problem of interstate pollution transport" that the EPA may deploy either singly or in tandem, 65 Fed. Reg. at 2680/1, reasonably construes both provisions.

The EPA's view accords with the position of the Second Circuit which, in *Connecticut v. EPA,* was presented with the converse of the question before us: Do §§ 110 and 126 require the EPA to postpone its approval of SIP revisions pending its final action upon petitions for findings under § 126(b)? [656 F.2d 902, 906–08 (2d Cir. 1981)]. Although the *Connecticut* court suggested that § 126(b) appears to have been primarily designed as a means for resolving interstate pollution disputes in situations where an SIP is not being revised, *id.* at 907—a dictum in some tension with the EPA's view that § 126 is "independent" of the SIP revision process—the Second Circuit's point was only that the EPA need not, upon receipt of a § 126 petition, suspend the SIP revision process. The court therefore concluded, properly we think, that "[a]s the substantive inquiry for decision is the same in both [§ 110 and § 126] proceedings, an argument that one proceeding must be completed as a prerequisite to a final decision in the other makes no sense." *Id.* at 907; *see also id.* at 908 n. 4 (quoting statement of H.R. Rep. No. 95–249, at 331, *reprinted in* 4 a Legislative History of the Clean Air Act Amendments of 1977, at 2798 (1978), that "the § 126(b) process is designed to provide an 'entirely alternative method and basis for preventing and abating interstate pollution' ") (emphasis omitted).

C. Significant Contribution

Non–State Petitioners challenge the methodology by which EPA reached its findings of "significant contribution" to nonattainment of the "1–hour" ozone rule under § 126. EPA started with the two-step method that it had used in issuing the SIP call and that we upheld in *Michigan v. EPA,* 213 F.3d 663, 674–80 (D.C.Cir.2000). As we explained there, EPA first performed computer modeling to determine whether a state's manmade NOx emissions perceptibly hindered a downwind state's attainment. For any state exceeding EPA's threshold criteria, EPA then defined as "significant" those emissions that could be eliminated through application of "highly cost-effective" controls, namely measures costing no more than $2,000 per ton of NOx removed. *Id.* Similarly, EPA relied here on the statewide threshold findings made in the SIP call and then applied the same cost-effectiveness criterion to determine which sources to include.

As discussed above, both the SIP call and the § 126 rulemaking are directly linked to the requirement under § 110(a)(2)(D)(i) that SIPs contain provisions prohibiting "any source or other type of emissions activity within the State from emitting any air pollutant in amounts which will ... contribute significantly to nonattainment...." § 110(a)(2)(D)(I). But the necessary determinations are different in at least two material respects. First, whereas the SIP call exercise yielded a total amount of NOx cutback for each state, which the state was then free to achieve however it might, here the mandate applies directly to sources. Second, whereas § 110(a)(2)(D)'s broad reference to "any source or other type of emissions activity" supported SIP call findings based on aggregate emissions from within each regulated state, § 126 demands that the significant contribution come from a "major source or group of *stationary* sources." 42 U.S.C. § 7426(b) (emphasis added).

The Non–State Petitioners argue that this latter distinction renders EPA's reliance on the SIP call findings inadequate; the findings based on *all* emissions can't determine whether stationary source emissions are sufficient. Instead of using those findings, petitioners argue, EPA needed first to make the more rigorous finding that the specified stationary sources within a given state *independently* met its threshold test for effect on downwind nonattainment.

Petitioners find support for their view of the statute in *Michigan,* where we said that the first step in EPA's § 110(a)(2)(D)(i) finding must show a *"measurable contribution"* to downwind nonattainment. 213 F.3d at 683–84. Here, EPA did not purport to satisfy such a standard on the basis of the covered stationary sources alone. Rather, it conceded, "[i]t is conceivable that modeling only the emissions from the section 126 sources would result in smaller ambient impacts downwind [compared to total man-made emissions], and.... those smaller impacts, if analyzed on the basis of the metrics and thresholds developed for State-wide [total man-made] emissions, may not exceed those thresholds." 64 Fed. Reg. at 28,283/1.

EPA defended its approach both as a recognition of the fact that the ozone problem is due to the *accumulation* of emissions and as a sensible reconciliation of § 110(a)(2)(D)(i) and § 126. On the need for some aggregation, of course, there can be no quarrel. Congress's use of the phrase "group of ... sources" plainly reflected a decision to act against sources whose emissions, while harmless individually, could become harmful when combined with others. And, given the relevant statutory provisions, it was reasonable for EPA to link its stationary source findings to the significance of a state's *total* NOx emissions. By speaking of stationary sources that emit pollutants "in violation of the prohibition of [§ 110(a)(2)(D)(i)]," Congress clearly hinged the meaning of § 126 on that of § 110(a)(2)(D)(i). EPA reasoned that if it treated any state's entire manmade emissions as the controlling aggregate for both purposes and found a "significant contribution," "then the State's section 126 sources *may be* subject to SIP controls." *Id.* at 28,282/3 (emphasis added). In other words, a source can be subject to § 126 controls only if it is at least *at risk* of being subject to SIP controls. The effect, of course, is to displace the discretion the state would enjoy in the SIP process under § 110(a)(2)(D)(i). But this displacement of state power seems not materially greater than is inherent in EPA's interpretation of § 126, which we uphold vis-à-vis the objections petitioners raised in their initial briefs. EPA's current reading, to be sure, may not be the only possible or even the most compelling view of § 126. Perhaps the EPA could reasonably read it as petitioners would, and require that stationary sources as a whole independently satisfy some "meaningful contribution" test before they may be subject to § 126 findings. But given § 126's silence on what it means for a stationary source to violate § 110(a)(2)(D)(i), EPA's approach is at least reasonable, and therefore entitled to deference under *Chevron*.

In the present case Non–State Petitioners do not dispute that emissions from affected § 126 sources actually contribute to total man-made NOx emissions that, at the statewide aggregate level, meet the EPA criteria upheld in *Michigan*. The process here does not involve sweeping up individual sources that might well not be part of the problem at all. The concern that drove our discussion in *Michigan* is inapplicable.

D. *Emission Limitation Determinations*

In order to allocate NOx emission allowances to individual sources, the EPA made state-by-state emission projections for 2007. The EPA based each state's NOx emission budget on projected 2007 heat input (or "utilization") for electric generating units ("EGUs") and projected 2007 emissions for non-electric generating, industrial facilities ("non-EGUs"). The projections were developed with computer models working off of "baseline" emissions and heat input data from 1995 and 1996. . . .

The MW & SE Petitioners contend that the EPA's emissions growth projections were arbitrary and capricious because they relied upon a computer model—the [Integrated Planning Model] "IPM"—that under-estimated growth rates for electric power generation in some upwind states. Several states, including North Carolina, submitted comments to the EPA arguing that they projected significantly greater growth in electric power generation than that predicted by the IPM.

Rather than address the specific complaints of each commenting state, the EPA defended its reliance upon the IPM on three broad grounds. First, all state NOx budget growth rates should be based upon the same methodology to ensure consistency in the NOx cap's application. Second, the IPM "has received extensive comment, review, and revision over the past several years" during the NOx SIP call and other proceedings. Third, the IPM "provides a reasonable forecast of State growth rates because it carefully takes into account the most important determinants of electricity generation growth that are facing the power industry today."

Given the highly deferential standard of review applied to such questions, and the EPA's clear authority to rely upon computer models in place of inconsistent, incomplete, or unreliable empirical data, the Agency's decision to rely upon the IPM, rather than the projections offered by individual states, was not arbitrary and capricious. In the EPA's judgment, the IPM offered a more comprehensive and consistent means of allocating emission allowances than sorting through the various state-specific projections. That the EPA's projections depend, in large part, on economic projections, rather than environmental factors, makes little difference. "[I]t is within the scope of the agency's expertise to make such a prediction about the market it regulates, and a reasonable prediction deserves our deference notwithstanding that there might also be another reasonable view." *Environmental Action, Inc. v. FERC,* 939 F.2d 1057, 1064 (D.C.Cir.1991). MW & SE State Petitioners may believe their projections are superior to the EPA's—and they may even be correct—but they have not proved their case.

E.　Regulation of "Future" Sources

The section 126 rule establishes a NOx budget for each upwind state found to contribute significantly to nonattainment in the petitioning states. Ninety-five percent of this budget is allocated in the form of NOx emission allowances to existing sources. Five percent of each state's budget is set aside for future sources. In this fashion, the rule caps emissions on existing and proposed sources, as well as sources to be proposed and built in the future.

MW & SE State Petitioners challenge the EPA's authority to impose the NOx cap limits to future, as-yet-unproposed stationary sources under section 126. Petitioners argue that the statute does not authorize the EPA to regulate future sources, and that the EPA's contrary interpretation of section 126 is unreasonable. We disagree.

We review the EPA's interpretation under the two-part analysis established in *Chevron U.S.A. Inc. v. Natural Resources Defense Council, Inc.,* 467 U.S. 837 (1984). "First, always," we must consider "whether Congress has directly spoken to the precise question at issue." An affirmative answer "is the end of the matter; for the court, as well as the agency, must give effect to the unambiguously expressed intent of Congress." *Id.* at 842–43. If, on the other hand, "the statute is silent or ambiguous with respect to the specific issue," we must uphold "a reasonable interpretation made by the administrator of an agency." *Id.* at 843, 844.

Under section 126(b) a downwind state "may petition the Administrator for a finding that any major source or group of stationary sources emits or would emit any air pollutant" in an amount which contributes significantly to nonattainment in the petitioning state. Once the EPA makes a section 126(b) finding, section 126(c) provides that:

> it shall be a violation of this section and the applicable implementation plan in such State—
>
> (1) for any major proposed new (or modified) source with respect to which a finding has been made under subsection (b) of this section to be constructed or to operate in violation [of this section or section 110], or
>
> (2) for any major existing source to operate more than three months after such finding has been made with respect to it.

The Administrator may allow the continued operation of existing sources beyond three months provided such sources comply with emission reductions provided by the Administrator to "bring about compliance . . . as expeditiously as practicable, but in no case later than three years after the date of such finding." *Id.*

Petitioners argue that the EPA's interpretation fails at the first step of *Chevron,* contending that section 126(c) authorizes the EPA to regulate existing and proposed sources but not future sources that are not as yet proposed. In petitioners' view, the enumeration of two classes of sources that may be controlled—"major existing sources" and "proposed new (or modified) sources"—precludes the EPA's authority over a third class of sources—"future as-yet-unproposed" sources. *Expressio unius est exclusio alterius.* Petitioners argue that irrespective of whether the EPA can make findings with regard to future, as-yet-unproposed sources, it is not empowered to prohibit their construction or limit their emissions under section 126(c).

We reject petitioners' contention that the statute unambiguously reflects congressional intent to limit the EPA to the two categories defined by petitioners. Section 126 is at least subject to the interpretation that Congress intended to authorize the regulation of emissions from future sources. Under section 126(b), the EPA may find that "any major source or group of stationary sources emits *or would emit*" pollution in violation of section 110. The inclusion of the future conditional phrase "would emit" arguably contemplates the EPA's intervention to prevent future emissions that would contribute significantly to nonattainment in downwind states. Similarly, as the EPA argues, section 126(c) explicitly bars the construction or operation of "any major new proposed sources." By barring the *construction* of those sources, the statute clearly contemplates the imposition of controls on at least some facilities that do not yet exist. These provisions, taken together, may not compel the regulation of future sources under section 126, but they do not unambiguously forbid it. At the least, they introduce sufficient ambiguity into the statutory scheme to prevent resolution of this issue under *Chevron* step one.

In the absence of an unambiguous expression of congressional intent in the plain language of the statute, we advance to the second step of the *Chevron* analysis to determine whether the EPA's interpretation of section 126 is a reasonable one. We conclude that it is. Prior to 1990, section 126(b) only authorized EPA findings that "a major source emits or would emit any air pollutant" which contributes significantly to nonattainment in a downwind state. The 1990 Clean Air Act Amendments expanded the scope of this provision by allowing EPA findings with regard to "any major source *or group of stationary sources.*" Similarly, the EPA notes that the cross-referenced provision of the act, section 110(a)(2)(D)([i]) prohibits "type [s] of emissions activity" that contribute significantly. 42 U.S.C. § 7410(a)(2)(D)(I). Like section 126, section 110 confers authority based upon the kind of activity in question. It does not impose any temporal limit.

The statutory language allows the EPA to regulate facilities in upwind states as a class or category, e.g. all coal-fired power plants in North Carolina. If such facilities, as a class, contribute significantly to nonattainment in northeastern states, this is as true for as-yet-unbuilt plants as it is for existing ones. Therefore, the EPA argues, it is reasonable to include future sources in the "group of stationary sources" found to contribute significantly to downwind nonattainment under section 126(b). Indeed, it would be irrational to enable the EPA to make findings that a group of sources in an upwind state contribute to downwind nonattainment, but then preclude the EPA from regulating new sources that contribute to that same pollution. As the EPA explained in its Response to Comments:

> Once EPA has determined that the emissions from the existing sources in an upwind State already make a significant contribution to one or more petitioning downwind States, any additional emissions from a new source in that upwind State would also constitute a portion of that significant contribution, unless the emissions from that new source are limited to the level of highly effective controls.

The EPA's construction of section 126 avoids this result.

The language of section 126(c) does not make the EPA's interpretation an unreasonable one. Petitioners note that section 126(c) specifically identifies two classes of sources—"major existing sources" and "proposed new (or modified) sources"—and makes no mention of future, as-yet-unproposed sources. What petitioners ignore is that section 126(c), by its terms, defines what constitutes a violation of section 126. For a facility to violate the law, by definition it must either exist or be proposed. Future, as-yet-unproposed sources are not mentioned because unproposed, unbuilt facilities cannot themselves be in violation of anything. At the time they become subject to the section 126(c) limitation, however, they will either be an "existing" or "proposed new" source. That is to say, section 126(c) has no direct effect on plants that have yet to be proposed for the precise reason that they have not yet been proposed. This does not mean, however, that facilities proposed after the promulgation of the EPA's findings are exempt from section 126(c). Once they are proposed, they become part of the regulated class.

Perhaps it would be reasonable for the EPA to interpret the statute as urged by petitioners. Section 126 is arguably a stop-gap provision designed to protect downwind states from upwind pollution by empowering the federal government to take direct action against those specific upwind facilities which cause downwind harm. From a structural standpoint, this interpretation may seem intuitive: States regulate all emitters; the EPA only regulates those emitters shown to contribute significantly to downwind nonattainment despite the existence of a SIP. Yet however rational this alternative interpretation of the Clean Air Act may be, under *Chevron* step two, the EPA's interpretation controls so long as it is based upon a permissible construction of the statute. As we conclude that the EPA adopted a reasonable interpretation of section 126's somewhat ambiguous provisions, its interpretation is upheld.

Notes and Comments

1. As noted in the case, the very real problems with transport, particularly of ozone forming chemicals, led to more specific measures to control them in the 1990 amendments. Nevertheless as the case also indicates, great uncertainty about tracing sources makes specific actions difficult under section 126, which is why the EPA tried to work more for a global solution. What happens when there is no effective control of out-of-State sources? What if, because of out-of-State pollution, a State has to enact stricter standards to meet the NAAQS? The effective failure of the EPA to regionally control ozone forming chemicals dealt setbacks to several States.

ENVIRONMENTAL PROTECTION AGENCY

66 Federal Register 7904 (Jan. 26, 2001).

Adequacy Status of the Atlanta, GA, Submitted Ozone Attainment State Implementation Plan for Transportation Conformity Purposes; Withdrawal of Adequacy Finding

SUMMARY: EPA has decided to withdraw our finding of adequacy for the motor vehicle emissions budgets in the Atlanta, Georgia, ozone attainment SIP submitted on October 28, 1999. We are withdrawing our adequacy finding for several reasons. The United States Court of Appeals for the District of Columbia circuit decided on August 30,2000, that the implementation of the Nitrogen Oxides (NOX) State Implementation Plan (SIP) Call rule could not be required before May 31, 2004. The emission levels in the Atlanta attainment SIP motor vehicle emissions budget for NOX were based in part on the assumption that transport of ozone recursors into Atlanta from upwind states would be addressed by May 2003 pursuant to EPA's NOX SIP Call. Further, the Georgia Environmental Protection Division (EPD)recently requested that EPA withdraw its adequacy determination of the Atlanta ozone attainment SIP motor vehicle emissions budgets. The notice of the adequacy determination that is being withdrawn was made on February 15, 2000, in a letter to the State and was published in the Federal Register on February 28, 2000.

SUPPLEMENTARY INFORMATION:

Background

On February 15, 2000, EPA Region 4 sent a letter to the Georgia Environmental Protection Division stating that the motor vehicle emissions budgets for nitrogen oxides (NOX) and volatile organic compounds (VOCs) in the October 28, 1999, Atlanta ozone attainment SIP for 2003 were adequate for the purpose of transportation conformity. EPA published a notice in the Federal Register on February 28, 2000, [65 FR 10490] announcing that we had made an adequacy determination for the motor vehicle emissions budgets in Atlanta's attainment SIP. This finding was also announced on EPA's conformity website, http://www. epa.gov/oms/traq.

Transportation conformity is required by section 176(c) of the Clean Air Act. EPA's conformity rule requires that transportation plans, programs, and projects conform to SIPs and establishes the criteria and procedures for determining whether or not they do conform. Conformity to a SIP means that transportation activities will not produce new air quality violations, worsen existing violations, or delay timely attainment of the national ambient air quality standards.

EPA described the process for determining the adequacy of submitted SIP budgets in guidance (May 14, 1999, memo titled "Conformity Guidance on Implementation of March 2, 1999, Conformity Court Decision"). This guidance was used in making the adequacy determination on the motor vehicle emissions budgets contained in the attainment demonstration for Atlanta. The criteria by which EPA determines whether a SIP's motor vehicle emission budgets are adequate for conformity purpose are outlined in 40 CFR 93.118(e)(4). An adequacy review is separate from EPA's SIP completeness review, and it also should not be used to prejudge EPA's ultimate action to approve or disapprove the SIP. The SIP could later be disapproved for reasons unrelated to transportation conformity even though the budgets had been deemed adequate.

* * *

EPA believes that a consequence of the D.C. Circuit's order delaying the implementation date of the NOX SIP Call rule is that the budget submitted by Georgia can no longer be considered adequate for purposes of transportation conformity. This belief is based on the fact that the attainment demonstration relied on the expected reductions from the NOX SIP call in 2003, where as those reductions can not now be assumed prior to 2004.

Furthermore, on December 21, 2000, Georgia sent a letter withdrawing the motor vehicle emission budgets contained in the October28, 1999, SIP submittal and asked that EPA not undertake any further consideration of these budgets until the State concludes the work necessary to submit a revised budget. The revised budget is expected to be based on the results of the recent study of vehicle speeds data, updated vehicle registration data, and modeling information relevant to the estimation of current and future motor vehicle emissions developed since submission of the previous budget. Based on these changes of fact and law, the parties filed a joint motion to the 11th Circuit to hold further proceedings on review of the adequacy determination in abeyance and for permission for EPA to withdraw the finding of adequacy. All parties in those proceedings have agreed that because it is not appropriate for the transportation agencies to rely upon the currently submitted budget for the purpose of making transportation conformity determinations, the stay entered by the Court on July 19, 2000,should remain in effect pending EPA's completion of the withdrawal action. On January 12, 2001, the court granted EPA the motion to withdraw the adequacy determination.

Consequently, EPA has decided to withdraw the February 15 adequacy determination. Even though adequacy determinations are not considered rulemaking subject to procedural requirements of the Administrative Procedures Act, EPA's policy is to provide a notice and comment period on adequacy determinations. However, we are not providing opportunity for comment on this withdrawal notice for two reasons. EPA is taking this action without prior notice and comment because adequacy determinations are not considered rulemaking subject to the procedural requirements of the Administrative Procedures Act. In addition, EPA does not believe further notice through EPA's conformity website is necessary in advance, since as a result of the stay issued by the court, the conformity determination made by USDOT on July 25, 2000, did not rely on the motor vehicle emission budgets submitted in the attainment SIP. Therefore, although EPA had found these budgets to be adequate, they were never used for transportation conformity purposes.Further, because of the delay in the NOX SIP Call implementation date, it is clear that the budgets can no longer be considered adequate, and Georgia has requested that EPA withdraw the adequacy determination. Consequently, further public comment would be unnecessary and not in the public interest. In this action, EPA is also withdrawing all statements and comments previously made in relation to its earlier determination of the adequacy of the budgets for transportation conformity purposes. The substance of the budgets and any revisions to them will be further reviewed by EPA as part of its final decision to approve or disapprove the 1–hour ozone attainment demonstration SIP for the Atlanta nonattainment area. This SIP was initially submitted to EPA on October 28, 1999, and was supplemented on January 31, 2000, and July 31, 2000. EPA will consider all of these submissions as well as all comments timely submitted as we decide whether to approve or disapprove the SIP.

Notes and Comments

1. Why was Georgia's SIP approval withdrawn? Is this "fair" to the State of Georgia? What can it do about out-of-state emissions?

2. In 2005, EPA issued by far its most dramatic SIP Call to date. In the so-called Clean Air Interstate Rule ("CAIR"), EPA found that 28 eastern States and the District of Columbia contribute significantly to nonattainment of the NAAQS for fine particulates and ozone in downwind states. 70 Fed. Reg. 25162, et seq. (2005). CAIR focuses on SOx and NOx as the

pollutants of concern (both contribute to formation of fine particles and NOx contributes to the formation of ground-level ozone). CAIR encourages, but does not require, the States to opt into a ''cap and trade'' system addressing power plants. If a given State declines to participate in this system, it is required to develop its own system for meeting its emissions budget. Id. Not surprisingly, various (primarily industrial) interest groups are currently challenging CAIR. If it survives these challenges, it will be interesting to see the extent to which it reduces out-of-state spillover. It seems clear at this stage that in many areas of the country the NAAQS program cannot work without effective controls addressing out-of-State pollution.

D.   What Happens When the States Don't Meet the NAAQS— Non-compliance

As noted in *Train v. NRDC*, supra, the States were not very successful at addressing air pollution before the passage of the 1970 CAA amendments. Unfortunately, though direct controls on pollution sources had some salutary effect on the situation, the State role in ensuring that the NAAQS be obtained through their SIPs did not work as expected after the 1970 Act either. Nevertheless, EPA has only rarely stepped in to establish a FIP.

Over time, Congress has amended the CAA to include increasingly stringent requirements and guidelines for States that have not met the NAAQS in the air quality control regions under their control. The Clean Air Act amendments of 1977 included particular requirements for States that had as yet failed to meet the NAAQS, including the requirement to impose both ''reasonably available control technology'' (''RACT'') on existing sources in nonattainment areas, 42 U.S.C. § 7502(c)(1), and the much more aggressive ''lowest achievable emission rate'' (''LAER'') on major new sources. 42 U.S.C. § 7503(a)(2). Additionally, as we will see, States must compel major new sources to procure offsetting emission reductions from other sources. Though there was some improvement in the 1980s, significant problems remained. Moreover, certain efforts to control pollution, such as severe restrictions on driving, were not politically palatable. Due to the continuing problems of the non-compliant areas, the 1990 Amendments sought to curtail the discretion of States even further by requiring that specific elements be included in areas that had failed to reach attainment. In particular, the requirements were specific to ozone non-attainment areas, carbon monoxide non-attainment areas, and particulate matter non-attainment areas. See 42 U.S.C. §§ 7511, 7512, and 7513. For ozone, these requirements addressed the magnitude of the problem in particular areas by dividing the non-attainment regions into categories with more stringent requirements for the areas with the greatest nonattainment problems as shown in Table 1 below.

TABLE 1

Area class	Design value*	Primary standard attainment date**
Marginal	0.121 up to 0.138	3 years after November 15, 1990
Moderate	0.138 up to 0.160	6 years after November 15, 1990
Serious	0.160 up to 0.180	9 years after November 15, 1990
Severe	0.180 up to 0.280	15 years after November 15, 1990
Extreme	0.280 and above	20 years after November 15, 1990

* The design value is measured in parts per million (ppm).
** The primary standard attainment date is measured from November 15, 1990.

Each area was also required to make progress reports and show actual progress and the ability to reach attainment in the time period specified.

In many ways, the 1990 amendments were more realistic about the problem and the timetable required for solutions. For instance, the Los Angeles air quality control region, considered to be the worst non-attainment area for ozone and characterized as "extreme" non-attainment at the time of the 1990 amendments, was required to adopt very stringent requirements on sources in the area. These included high offsets for new sources, special fuel requirements, and the ability to directly control traffic flow. 42 U.S.C. § 7511a (e). However, attainment of the standard was not required until 2010. 42 U.S.C. § 7511.

In addition, the 1990 amendments set forth possible sanctions for failing to meet the requirements of these non-attainment timetables. 42 U.S.C. § 7509. Importantly, these included the possibility of cutting highway funds to an area if the area failed to stay on timetable. 42 U.S.C. § 7509 (b)(1). Additionally, § 176(c)(1)(B) generally prohibits federal agencies providing federal assistance or issuing permits for projects that would cause or contribute to non-attainment.

Notes and Comments

1. As these dates have approached there has been a flurry of litigation about whether the States are in fact on track to meet their requirements through their SIPs, and what should be done if they do not. Despite some progress, environmental groups still do not believe that some States have made the choices necessary to come into compliance. And many criticize the EPA for approving plans that some complain are inadequate and thus fail to

satisfy the demonstration of progress and the ultimate satisfaction of the standard. Because of the discretion given an agency in approving plans that are based on sometimes conflicting assumptions or studies, it is true that the EPA could be quite generous with its assumptions regarding the States' ability to reach the required goals in the required time period. Sanctions were assessed against the State of Georgia for failing to provide a method to bring the Atlanta area into compliance, but no other area has yet faced the sanction of loss of federal highway dollars for road expansion. The hard choices required for cities to comply have even encouraged several congresspersons to propose statutory exemptions. These are emblematic of the concerns that healthful levels may never be achieved.

2. The increasingly specific deadlines and onerous sanctions Congress has used in trying to promote compliance with the NAAQS pose an additional policy issue regarding the extent to which they eliminate the advantage of regulatory flexibility. As noted in the chapter on the role of administrative law in the environmental process, Congress generally sets overall goals but leaves implementation to the agencies on the theory that they can more quickly change standards in response to new realities in either the understanding of the problem or the potential solutions thereto. This contrasts sharply with the heavy-handed approach reflected in the 1990 amendments. Given the incredibly difficult task cities such as Los Angeles face in trying to meet the NAAQS, do you think it's appropriate for Congress to play such a prescriptive role?

IV. THE CLEAN AIR ACT—DIRECT CONTROLS ON SOURCES

A. Introduction to Stationary Source Controls

Unlike the standard setting and implementation of the ambient air quality standards discussed above, direct controls on sources take a different tack for controlling air pollution. Instead of relying on States to determine the best way to reach ambient levels of air quality, source controls require the specific installation of equipment or process changes on the sources themselves. Though there are many arguments about the efficiency of such an approach, it has the virtue of certainty. In general, once the equipment or process is in place, it is easier to monitor and any benefits are measurable. With other plans which may use various methods for lowering pollution loading it may not be clear whether the plan's components are being enforced or are effective. Indeed, the enforceability and measurability of direct controls on sources marks an important innovation in the 1970 Act.

The CAA's first direct stationary-source controls appeared in 1970 in the form of § 111's New Source Performance Standards. In 1977, Congress added stationary-source controls to prevent the deterioration of air quality in pristine areas and to assist in remedying nonattainment problems. Later still, the 1990 amendments imposed technology-based requirements on most sources of hazardous pollutants.

In many ways, the CAA's direct stationary-source controls are similar to the kinds of BAT/BADT standards that we already have seen under the CWA (although the NSPS requirements pre-dated them). As we will see below, however, in some contexts there are significant differences.

Sample Emissions Standards in Statute:

§ 111(e) and (a)(1)—New Source Performance Standards (NSPS) (all new and modified sources)

> After the effective date of any standards of performance promulgated under this section, it shall be unlawful for any owner or operator of any new source to operate such source in violation of any standard of performance applicable to such source.

> The term "standard of performance" means a standard for emissions of air pollutants which reflects the degree of emission limitation achievable through the application of the best system of emission reduction which (taking into account the cost of achieving such reduction and any nonair quality health and environmental impact and energy requirements) the Administrator determines has been adequately demonstrated.

§ 112(d)—Maximum Achievable Control Technology (MACT) (sources of hazardous air pollutants under the National Emission Standards for Hazardous Air Pollutants (NESHAPs) program)

> **(2)** Emission standards promulgated under this subsection and applicable to new or existing sources of hazardous air pollutants shall require the maximum degree of reduction in emissions of hazardous air pollutants subject to this section . . . that the Administrator . . . determines is achievable for new or existing sources.

> **(3)** [The degree of reduction for new sources shall not be less than the emission control achieved in practice by best controlled similar sources. Emission standards for existing sources may not be less stringent than the average emission rate for the best performing 12% of existing sources or, in some cases, the average emission achieved by the best performing five sources.]

§§ 165(a)(4) and 169(3)—Best Available Control Technology (BACT) (major new sources and modifications in attainment areas under the PSD program)

> [New and modified major emitting facilities] shall be "subject to the best available control technology for each pollutant subject to regulation under this chapter emitted from, or which results from, such facility."

> "Best available control technology" means an emission limitation based on the maximum degree of reduction of each pollutant . . . which the permitting authority, on a case-by-case basis, taking into account energy, environmental, and economic impacts and other costs, determines is achievable . . . through application of production processes and available methods, systems, and techniques . . . .

§ 169A(b)(2)(A) and (g)(2)—Best Available Retrofit Technology (BART) (existing sources contributing to visibility degradation)

[States are charged with determining BART for existing major stationary sources that emit pollutants which "may reasonably be anticipated to cause or contribute to" visibility impairment.

Subsection (g)(2) lists the factors the States are to consider when determining BART: the costs of compliance, the energy and nonair quality environmental impact of compliance, any existing pollution control technology in use at the source, the remaining useful life of the source, and the anticipated improvement in visibility from use of such technology.]

§ 172(c)(1)—Reasonably Available Control Technology (RACT) (existing sources in nonattainment areas)

Such plan provisions shall provide for the implementation of all reasonably available measures as expeditiously as practicable (including such reductions in emissions from existing sources, in the area as may be obtained through the adoption, at a minimum, of reasonably available control technology) and shall provide for attainment of the national primary ambient quality standards.

§§ 173(a)(2) and 171(3)—Lowest Achievable Emission Rate (LAER) (major new sources and modifications in nonattainment areas, under what is called the Nonattainment New Source Review (NNSR) program)

Where this program applies, permits to construct and operate may only be issued if the proposed source is required to comply with the lowest achievable emission rate.

For a given source, the "lowest achievable emission rate" is the rate of emission which reflects (A) the most stringent emission limitation in that SIP for such class of source unless owner demonstrates that such limitations are not achievable, or (B) the most stringent emission limitation achieved in practice by such class of source, whichever is most stringent.

On their face, the differences between these requirements are subtle. One thing they all have in common, though, is that, where they apply, they may serve to restrict the otherwise unfettered discretion that States would possess in developing their SIP control strategies.

One of the most vexing problems facing those who seek to master the Clean Air Act involves developing understandings both of when each of these requirements applies and of how these various requirements interrelate with each other. This complexity is compounded by the fact that the underlying programs often overlap in their coverage of emission streams or the pollutants contained therein. For example, many hazardous air pollutants (such as benzene and toluene) are also ozone precursors. Thus, new sources that emit significant quantities of these pollutants may be subject to both the NESHAPs program and either the PSD or NNSR program (which of the latter two might apply would depend on the attainment status of the relevant air quality control region). In such cases, the relevant facility would need to identify the most stringent requirement that applies to its emission of the relevant pollutant, for that would be controlling; to put it another way, the most stringent requirement would "trump" any lesser requirements that might otherwise have applied.

In the following pages, we will provide an introduction to five of the most significant stationary source control programs under the CAA: New Source Performance Standards (NSPS), Nonattainment New Source Review (NNSR), Prevention of Significant Deterioration (PSD), National Emission Standards for Hazardous Air Pollutants (NESHAPs), and the Visibility program. As we will see, while these programs have significant differences, they also often have elements in common. Indeed, the NNSR and PSD programs have enough in common that they are often collectively referred to as "New Source Review" (NSR), and will for the most part be treated together below.

B. New Source Performance Standards

1. Jurisdiction

The NSPS program is a technology-based program that applies to new and modified sources irrespective of the attainment status of the air quality control region in which the source is located. In this respect, the NSPS program operates independently of the NAAQS program (although the controls it requires will obviously factor into a State's SIP-planning process).

The following case addresses which modifications will trigger the NSPS requirements:

WISCONSIN ELECTRIC POWER COMPANY v. REILLY

United States Court of Appeals, Seventh Circuit, 1990.
893 F.2d 901.

CUDAHY, Circuit Judge.

... In section 111 of the [CAA], Congress required the EPA to promulgate [NSPS] in order to regulate the emission of air pollutants from new sources. These standards addressed hourly rates of emission and, in addition to new sources, applied to modifications of existing facilities that created new or increased pollution. Indeed, section 111(a)(2) of the Act stated that NSPS would apply

> to any stationary source, the construction *or modification* of which is commenced after the publication of regulations (or, if earlier, proposed regulations) prescribing a standard of performance under this section which will be applicable to such source.

42 U.S.C. § 7411(a)(2) (emphasis supplied). Congress then defined "modification" as

> *any physical change* in, or change in the method of operation of, a stationary source *which increases the amount of any air pollutant*

emitted by such source or which results in the emission of any air pollutant not previously emitted.

42 U.S.C. § 7411(a)(4) (emphasis supplied).

From this framework, the EPA promulgated regulations for [the NSPS program]. In this case, its regulations concerning modifications are central. The EPA defines "modification" in substantially the same terms used by Congress:

> [A]ny physical or operational change to an existing facility which results in an increase in the emission rate to the atmosphere of any pollutant to which a standard applies shall be considered a modification within the meaning of section 111 [42 U.S.C. § 7411] of the Act.

40 C.F.R. § 60.14(a). To determine whether a physical change constitutes a modification for purposes of NSPS, the EPA must determine whether the change increases the facility's hourly rate of emission. 40 C.F.R. § 60.14. . . .

Even at first blush, the potential reach of these modification provisions is apparent: the most trivial activities—the replacement of leaky pipes, for example—may trigger the modification provisions if the change results in an increase in the emissions of a facility. As a result, the EPA promulgated specific exceptions to the modification provisions:

> The following shall not, by themselves, be considered modifications under this part:
>
> (1) Maintenance, repair, and replacement which the Administrator determines to be routine for a source category . . .
>
> (2) An increase in production rate of an existing facility, if that increase can be accomplished without a capital expenditure on that facility.
>
> (3) An increase in the hours of operation. . . .

40 C.F.R. § 60.14(e).

WEPCO's Port Washington electric power plant is located on Lake Michigan north of Milwaukee, Wisconsin. The plant consists of five coal-fired steam generating units that were placed in operation between 1935 and 1950. Each generating unit has a design capacity of 80 megawatts, but the recent performance of some of the units has declined due to age-related deterioration of the physical plant.

WEPCO . . . conducted a Plant Availability Study in 1983 to examine and assess the condition of the power plant. As a result of the Study, WEPCO concluded "that extensive renovation of the five units and the plant common facilities is needed if operation of the plant is to be continued." Letter from Thomas J. Cassidy, Executive Vice President of WEPCO, to Jacqueline K. Reynolds, Secretary to the Public Service Commission of Wisconsin, at 2 (July 8, 1987) [Cassidy Letter]. The Study noted that the air heaters on the first four units had deteriorated severely, while the rear steam drums in units 2 through 5 had experienced serious cracking.[1] Air heater deterioration prevented units 1 and 4 from operating at full capacity, while the potential for steam drum blowout required a reduction in pressure (and output) in units 2 and 3. The possibility of catastrophic failure (steam drum blowout) in unit 5 was so great that WEPCO shut down the unit completely.

As a result of this Study, WEPCO submitted a proposed replacement program (which it termed a "life extension" project) to the Wisconsin Public Service Commission for its approval, as required by state law. WEPCO explained in its proposal that "[r]enovation is necessary to allow the Port Washington units to operate beyond their currently planned retirement dates of 1992 (units 1 and 2) and 1999 (units 3, 4 and 5) . . . [and that renovation would render the plant] capable of generating at its designed capability until year 2010. . . ." Cassidy Letter at 1–2. Among the renovations required were repair and replacement of the turbine-generators, boilers, mechanical and electrical auxiliaries and the common plant support facilities. After preliminary review of the program, the Public Service Commission consulted the Wisconsin Department of Natural Resources, [which in turn consulted EPA, to determine whether the renovation triggered any regulatory requirements].

EPA staff members conferred with WEPCO representatives between March and September 1988 to gain additional information regarding the proposed repair and replacement project. On September 9, 1988, EPA Acting Assistant Administrator Don R. Clay issued a memorandum in which he preliminarily concluded that the project would subject the plant to both NSPS and PSD requirements.

. . . Alleging that the EPA has misconstrued both the [CAA] and its own regulations, WEPCO appeals the EPA's final determination. . . .

A. The Underlying Statutory Framework

. . . We must first consider whether WEPCO's Port Washington replacement program constitutes a modification under the terms of the controlling statute. Section 7411(a)(4) defines modification as "any physical change . . . which increases the amount of any air pollutant emitted. . . ." Both parts of this definition—any physical change and an increase in emissions—must be satisfied before a replacement will be considered a "modification."

1. Physical Change

Certainly, under the plain terms of the Act, WEPCO's replacement program constitutes a "physical change." WEPCO proposes to replace rear steam drums on units 2, 3, 4 and 5; each of these steam drums measures 60 feet in length, 50.5 inches in diameter and 5.25 inches in thickness. In addition, WEPCO plans to replace another major component, the air heaters, in units 1–4. To implement this four-year program, WEPCO will need to make the replacements by taking the units succes-

---

1. Air heaters preheat combustion air to improve the efficiency of the steam generat- ing units. Steam drums separate saturated steam from water within the boiler.

sively out of service for nine-month periods. Id. These steps clearly amount to a "physical change" in the Port Washington plant.

WEPCO does not dispute that its steam drum and air heater replacements will result in an altered plant. But WEPCO does assert that Congress did not intend for simple equipment replacement to constitute a physical change for purposes of the [CAA's] modification provisions:

> The plain meaning of "modify" is "to change or alter" [Webster's New World Dictionary] or "to make basic or fundamental changes in." [Webster's Ninth New Collegiate Dictionary] Reflecting the plain meaning of this term, Congress provided that a facility (1) must undergo a physical or operational "change" before it is evaluated under the modification provision.... Thus, under the plain meaning of the Act, a unit should not be deemed "modified" as a result of replacement of equipment with equipment similar to that replaced. As in the case of Port Washington, such like-kind replacement does not "change or alter" the design or nature of the facility. Rather, it merely allows the facility to operate again as it had before the specific equipment deteriorated.

Petitioner's Brief at 32–33.

Chevron instructs us to rely more on congressional direction and on agency construction (pursuant to congressional delegation) than on glosses found in the dictionary. What WEPCO calls "plain" is anything but plain and takes the definition far beyond the words enacted by Congress. [*Chevron U.S.A., Inc. v. Natural Resources Defense Council, Inc.*, 467 U.S. 837, 843–45 (1984)]. Thus, whether the replacement of air heaters and steam drums is a "basic or fundamental change" in the Port Washington plant is irrelevant for our purposes, given Congress's directions on the subject: "The term 'modification' means *any* physical change...." 42 U.S.C. § 7411(a)(4) (emphasis supplied). We follow Congress's definition of "modification"—not Webster's—when interpreting this term within the context of the [CAA].

Nor can we find any support in the relevant case law for the narrow constructions of "modification" and "physical change" offered by WEP-CO. The Supreme Court reported in *Chevron* that Senator Muskie, one of the principal supporters of the Clean Air Act, remarked: "A source ... is subject to all the nonattainment requirements as a modified source if it makes *any physical change* which increases the amount of any air pollutant...." 467 U.S. at 853 (emphasis supplied). And other courts considering the modification provisions of NSPS and PSD have assumed that "any physical change" means precisely that. *See, e.g., National–Southwire Aluminum Co. v. EPA*, 838 F.2d 835 (6th Cir.), cert. denied, 488 U.S. 955 (1988) (turning off pollution control equipment constitutes "physical change" and modification); *Alabama Power Co. v. Costle*, 636 F.2d 323, 400 (D.C.Cir.1979) ("[T]he term 'modification' is nowhere limited to physical changes exceeding a certain magnitude."); *ASARCO Inc. v. EPA*, 578 F.2d 319, 322 (D.C.Cir.1978) (NSPS applies to any stationary source that is "physically or operationally changed in such a way that its emission of any air pollutant increases.").

Further, to adopt WEPCO's definition of "physical change" would open vistas of indefinite immunity from the provisions of NSPS and PSD. Were we to hold that the replacement of major generating station systems—including steam drums and air heaters—does not constitute a physical change (and is therefore not a modification), the application of NSPS and PSD to important facilities might be postponed into the indefinite future. There is no reason to believe that such a result was intended by Congress. The Clean Air Act Amendments were enacted to "speed up, expand, and intensify the war against air pollution in the United States with a view to assuring that the air we breathe throughout the Nation is wholesome once again." H.R.Rep. No. 91–1146, 91st Cong., 2d Sess. 1, 1, reprinted in 1970 U.S.Code Cong. & Admin.News 5356, 5356....

2. Increase in Emissions

The controversy involving WEPCO's alleged increase in emissions primarily concerns the regulations, not the statute: WEPCO argues that the EPA's *regulatory* method of measuring emissions is arbitrary and capricious. From a statutory standpoint, however, the modification provisions of the Clean Air Act Amendments are activated once a physical change is coupled with an "increase [ ] [in] the amount of any air pollutant emitted." 42 U.S.C. § 7411(a)(4). In the case before us, WEPCO does not dispute that its replacement program—intended to enable its deteriorated generators to operate at full capacity—will cause its emissions to increase from their current operating levels. The question for resolution, however, is whether the EPA properly construed its regulations by comparing actual emission rates with so-called "baseline" rates to determine the increase in emissions for [NSPS purposes]. We will discuss this subject later; but for purposes of the statutory requirement, we simply observe that the rejuvenated Port Washington plant will produce more emissions after the completion of the renovation project than the operating deteriorated plant produced shortly before the project was undertaken.

B. The EPA's Regulations

Although we have determined that WEPCO's repair and replacement program satisfies the modification provisions of the [CAA], this is not the end of our inquiry. WEPCO's attack focuses primarily on EPA regulations, which in a number of respects are narrower than the statute....

1. Physical Change and the "Routine" Exception

EPA regulations define "modification" as "any physical or operational change to an existing facility which results in an increase in the emission rate to the atmosphere of any pollutant to which a standard applies." 40 C.F.R. § 60.14(a). To a major degree, this definition parallels 42 U.S.C. section 7411(a)(2), and it is unnecessary to repeat the analysis already applied to the statute. However, the EPA has ... used its regulations to exempt a number of activities from the broader definition. The exemption that may be relevant here is accomplished by the following language:

The following shall not, by themselves, be considered modifications under this part:

(1) Maintenance, repair, and replacement which the Administrator determines to be routine for a source category....

340 C.F.R. § 60.14(e).

WEPCO relies on this language to argue that, even if its repair and replacement program amounts to a physical change, it was specifically exempted by the regulations.

... [W]e accord substantial deference to an agency's interpretation of its own regulations, especially with respect to technical and complex matters. In this connection, to determine whether proposed work at a facility is routine, "EPA makes a case-by-case determination by weighing the nature, extent, purpose, frequency, and cost of the work, as well as other relevant factors, to arrive at a common-sense finding." Clay Memorandum at 3. The EPA considered all these factors in determining that the Port Washington project was not routine; first, the EPA observed that the nature and extent of the project was substantial: WEPCO proposed to replace sixty-foot steam drums (in units 2, 3, 4 and 5) and air heaters (in units 1, 2, 3 and 4) during successive nine-month outages at each unit. Id. at 4. Certainly, the magnitude of the project (as well as the down-time required to implement it) suggests that it is more than routine.

Further, the EPA points to WEPCO's admission in its application that "[work items] falling into the category of repetitive maintenance that are normally performed during scheduled equipment outages ... are not included in this application." Cassidy Letter at 1. This admission suggests that WEPCO at first blush did not regard the repair and replacement project as ordinary or routine.

In addition, the EPA noted that far from being routine, the Port Washington project apparently was unprecedented: "WEPCO did not identify, and EPA did not find, even a single instance of renovation work at any electric utility generating station that approached the Port Washington life extension project in nature, scope or extent." Respondent's Brief at 44. We surmise, although the record is silent, that the "case of first impression" character of the project may reflect historical practice in the electric utility industry of replacing old plants (at the expiration of their useful lives) with new plants, employing improved technologies and achieving improved efficiencies. This was the typical practice, rather than the mere extension of life of existing plants through massive like-kind replacements.

The purpose, frequency and cost of the work also support the EPA's decision here. WEPCO admits that the plans for extensive renovation "represent a life extension of the units from their planned retirement dates," Cassidy Letter at 2–3, and it recognizes that "the renovation work items included in this application are those that would normally occur only once or twice during a unit's expected life cycle." Id. at 1. Indeed, WEPCO reported that it had never previously replaced a steam drum or "header" of comparable size at any of its coal-fired electrical generating facilities. Further, the Port Washington renovation project will cost at least $70.5 million. These factors suggest that the project is not routine.

. . . WEPCO [argues] that because any replacement project will presumably extend the life of a facility, the EPA's reliance on life extension as a factor in denying the "routine" nature of a project is overbroad. Although perhaps persuasive on its face, WEPCO's analysis is ultimately wide of the mark. While it is certainly true that the repair of deteriorated equipment will contribute to the useful life of any facility, it does not necessarily follow that the repairs in question would extend the life expectancy of the facility. The need for some repairs along the line is a given in determining in the first instance the life expectancy of a plant. WEPCO cannot seriously argue that its units' planned retirement dates of 1992 (units 1 and 2) and 1999 (units 3, 4 and 5) did not take into account at least minor equipment repairs and replacements. And WEPCO concedes that the Port Washington program will extend the life expectancy of the plant until 2010. The EPA concluded that the proposed project will increase the life expectancy of the Port Washington facility, and this conclusion was a factor in the finding that the work was not routine. These determinations were not arbitrary and capricious.

2. Increases in Emissions

. . . [T]he EPA's NSPS program is concerned primarily with increases in emission rates, expressed in kilograms per hour of discharged pollutants. 40 C.F.R. § 60.14. The EPA compares the hourly emissions of the unit at its current maximum capacity to its potential emissions at maximum capacity after the change. In this calculation, the agency disregards the unit's maximum design capacity; this factor often sheds little light on the unit's actual current capacity to produce emissions.[5]

The EPA applied these procedures in examining the generating units at Port Washington. The EPA asked WEPCO to submit figures for the actual operations and emissions of each unit at the Port Washington plant for the years 1978 to 1987; the EPA then relied upon the 1987 figures to calculate the emissions baseline against which post-replacement emissions could be compared. WEPCO, however, challenged the EPA's acceptance of these preliminary baseline figures, arguing that units 1, 2, 3 and 4 were capable of operating at higher rates of production than those calculated by the EPA based upon the 1987

---

5. Of course, if the unit is currently operating at maximum design capacity, there will be no difference between the measure of emissions at maximum design capacity and at current maximum capacity. Since the units at Port Washington were operating well below maximum design capacity (and unit 5 was completely shut down), that is not the case here.

figures. WEPCO conducted five ten-hour tests at each unit to determine its maximum capacity. Upon reviewing the test results, the EPA agreed that units 2 and 3 could be operated at their design capacities, and it revised the baseline levels for these units. The agency concluded that because there would be no increase in production or emissions, NSPS would not apply to these units following the renovation project. Nonetheless, the EPA refused to alter the baseline levels for units 1 and 4, noting that WEPCO's tests had not been conducted pursuant to the test protocol as required by the regulations and the Wisconsin State Implementation Plan (units 1 and 4 exceeded certain maximum allowable emission limits). Comparing these1987 baseline levels to the maximum capacity of the plant after renovation, the EPA concluded that the renovation project would be subject to the provisions of NSPS.

WEPCO asks us to overturn the EPA's final ruling that the Port Washington project triggers NSPS. Specifically, WEPCO argues that, by using 1987 figures in determining the emissions baseline, the EPA failed to apply its own regulations: WEPCO asserts that these figures "reflected voluntary decisions by WEPC[O] regarding safety considerations (e.g., the 'zero' rate for Unit 5) and an electricity demand which did not require operation of the units at higher capacities." WEPCO also posits that the EPA's refusal to compare representative pre-renovation emissions with actual post-renovation emissions is contrary to EPA regulations and amounts to an abuse of agency discretion.[6]

WEPCO's first assertion is easily dismissed. The EPA's choice of the 1987 figures was based entirely upon WEPCO's own data. And, when WEPCO complained that its own data did not reflect WEPCO's pre-renovation capabilities, the EPA permitted WEPCO to conduct new tests that eventually resulted in the revision of the baselines for units 2 and 3.

WEPCO's second charge is far more substantial. WEPCO argues that NSPS regulations require the EPA to use a "representative" year in determining a baseline rate of emissions. The EPA disputes this claim, arguing that "[a]s to NSPS, there is no 'representative emissions' concept.... Rather ... the baseline emission rates for units 1–5 are determined by hourly maximum capacity just prior to the renovations."[7] Thomas Letter at 5.

---

6. As a preliminary matter, we note that WEPCO has not asked us to review the propriety of the NSPS regulations themselves. Indeed, we have no jurisdiction to conduct such an inquiry: 42 U.S.C. § 7607(b)(1) reserves such questions for [D.C. Circuit]. In this case, WEPCO simply requests that we consider whether the EPA properly applied these regulations to the Port Washington generating units. We have jurisdiction to undertake such an inquiry.

7. The regulations themselves provide, in part:

(a) ... any physical or operational change to an existing facility which re-

sults in an increase in the emission rate to the atmosphere of any pollutant to which a standard applies shall be considered a modification....

(b) Emission rate shall be expressed as kg/hr of any pollutant discharged into the atmosphere for which a standard is applicable. [The regulation goes on to specify in detail how the emission rates are to be determined, including a statement that tests should be "conducted under such conditions as the Administrator shall specify to the owner or operator based on representative performance of the facility."]

40 C.F.R. § 60.14 (1988).

WEPCO's interpretation of the regulations, at first blush, seems sensible: since the regulations require that the manual emission tests and continuous monitoring systems be based upon the "representative performance" of the facility, the emission factor test approach must also be based upon "representative performance." 40 C.F.R. § 60.14.[8] Otherwise, the tests might reach inconsistent results, making the rate of emissions entirely dependent upon the type of test used by the facility. Hence, argues WEPCO, the EPA must examine the emission rates during a representative period, not 1987.

WEPCO's analysis, however, relies upon a flawed premise. WEPCO assumes that the phrase "representative performance of the facility" suggests that the EPA must choose a representative year. Read in context, however, the phrase refers generally to all the conditions of the test, not specifically to its timing:

> Tests shall be conducted under such conditions as the Administrator shall specify to the owner or operator based on representative performance of the facility. At least three valid test runs must be conducted before and at least three after the physical or operational change. All operating parameters which may affect emissions must be held constant to the maximum feasible degree for all test runs.

40 C.F.R. § 60.14(b)(2). Compare 40 C.F.R. § 52.21(b)(21)(ii) (PSD program) ("The Administrator shall allow the use of a different time period upon a determination that it is more representative of normal source operation."). Put simply, section 60.14 ensures that the operator will not doctor testing conditions to produce favorable emission results. The EPA's explanation of its regulations, which of course is given deference, supports this interpretation: "According to the proposed regulation, each set of emission tests (using manual tests or continuous monitors) conducted before and after a physical or operational change would consist of at least three runs, *and would be conducted under representative operating conditions*." 39 Fed.Reg. 36946, 36947 (1974) (emphasis supplied). WEPCO has not argued that it conducted its own tests under unrepresentative conditions, nor has it challenged any other part of the test protocol. And WEPCO does not claim that the tests were conducted during a period of operations that substantially differed from the normal operations of the deteriorated Port Washington plant. Further, the fact that the EPA permitted WEPCO to conduct additional emissions tests on the units (during which, presumably, WEPCO could maintain representative operating conditions) undermines WEPCO's assertion that the regulations were applied arbitrarily or capriciously.

Notes and Comments

1. Can repairs ever be "routine repair and maintenance" if they prolong the useful life of the facility? Could the court have ruled solely on

---

8. The emission factor test is the only technique that can predict emission rates after renovations. Because the determination at issue here must be made before the renovations are undertaken, the EPA relied on this test in evaluating the Port Washington project.

that ground in *WEPCo*? Is this an ambiguity in the statute subject to *Chevron* deference?

2. If the sole criteria for determining whether a "modification" occurs that subjects a source to NSPS is whether there is any increase in emissions, what is the baseline from which increases are to be measured?

3. While § 111 is focused almost exclusively on new sources and modifications, § 111(d) transcends that realm by tasking EPA with writing regulations pursuant to which the States would in turn set standards for at least some existing sources. See 42 U.S.C. § 7411(d). These provisions have been invoked sparingly.

2. Performance Standard

LIGNITE ENERGY COUNCIL v. U.S. ENVIRONMENTAL PROTECTION AGENCY

United States Court of Appeals, District of Columbia Circuit, 1999.
198 F.3d 930.

Before: EDWARDS, Chief Judge, SILBERMAN and HENDERSON, Circuit Judges.

PER CURIAM:

Fossil-fuel fired steam generating units ("boilers") emit nitrogen oxides (NOx), air pollutants that can cause deleterious health effects and contribute to the formation of acid rain. Section 111 of the [CAA] requires EPA to establish performance standards for the emission of NOx from newly constructed boilers; these "new source performance standards" are to be set at a level that

> reflects the degree of emission limitation achievable through the application of the best system of emission reduction which (taking into account the cost of achieving such reduction and any nonair quality health and environmental impact and energy requirements) the Administrator determines has been adequately demonstrated.

42 U.S.C. § 7411(a)(1). In its 1990 Clean Air Act Amendments Congress specifically directed EPA to exercise its [§] 111 authority and establish new NOx standards that incorporate "improvements in methods for the reduction of emissions of oxides of nitrogen." 42 U.S.C. § 7651f(c)(1).

In response to these statutory mandates, EPA promulgated a rule lowering its NOx new source performance standards to .15 lb/MMBtu (pounds of NOx emitted per million BTU burned) for utility boilers[1] and

---

1. To be precise, the emission standard for utility boilers is an output-based standard of 1.6 pounds of NOx emitted per megawatt-hour of electricity generated. However, as this output-based standard was intended by EPA to correlate with a .15 lb/MMBtu input-based standard, we refer to its input-based equivalent for simplicity's sake throughout this opinion. We reject petitioners' argument that EPA's decision to shift to an output-based standard for utility boilers unfairly "penalizes" the use of low-energy coals, like lignite; it would seem just as easy to argue that an input-based standard "penalizes" high-energy fuels.

.20 lb/MMBtu for industrial boilers. These standards reflect the level of NOx emissions achievable by what EPA considers to be the "best demonstrated system" of emissions reduction: the use of selective catalytic reduction (SCR) in combination with combustion control technologies.[2] Petitioners' central claim is that EPA selected SCR as the basis for its NOx standards without properly balancing the factors that § 111 requires it to "take into account." Because § 111 does not set forth the weight that be should assigned to each of these factors, we have granted the agency a great degree of discretion in balancing them; EPA's choice will be sustained unless the environmental or economic costs of using the technology are exorbitant.

Petitioners argue that SCR is not the "best demonstrated system" under § 111 because the incremental cost of reducing NOx emissions is considerably higher with SCR than with combustion controls. Recent improvements in combustion controls will enable many boilers to attain emissions levels close to EPA's SCR-based standards; accordingly, petitioners assert that EPA should have based its standards on these less expensive technologies. However, in light of EPA's unchallenged findings showing that the new standards will only modestly increase the cost of producing electricity in newly constructed boilers, we do not think that EPA exceeded its considerable discretion under § 111. Moreover, petitioners' argument stressing the comparable environmental merits of advanced combustion controls is to a certain extent self-defeating, since the [NSPS] set by EPA are not technology-forcing, and continuing advances in combustion control technologies will reduce the amount of NOx reduction that must be captured by the more expensive SCR technology.

It was also within EPA's discretion to issue uniform standards for all utility boilers, rather than adhering to its past practice of setting a range of standards based on boiler and fuel type. Petitioners recognize that EPA is not required by law to subcategorize—section 111 merely states that "the Administrator *may* distinguish among classes, types, and sizes within categories of new sources," 42 U.S.C. § 7411(b)(2) (emphasis added)—but argue that it was arbitrary and capricious for EPA to decline to do so. EPA explains that its change to uniform standards is justified by SCR's performance characteristics: Unlike the technologies on which past [NSPS] were based, flue gas treatment technologies like SCR limit NOx emissions after combustion, and the effectiveness of SCR is thus far less dependent upon boiler design or fuel type. Petitioners respond that there are reasons to expect SCR to perform less adequately on boilers burning high-sulfur coals, but EPA collected continuous emissions monitoring data on two high-sulfur coal-

---

2. SCR is a "flue gas treatment technology"; it reduces NOx after combustion by injecting ammonia into the flue gas in the presence of a catalyst, breaking down NOx and producing nitrogen and water. In setting past standards, EPA had focused solely on combustion control technologies, which instead reduce NOx by suppressing its formation during the combustion process.

fired utility boilers that showed that the .15 lb/MMBtu standard was achievable, and supplemented this study with similar evidence from foreign utility boilers. EPA also considered petitioners' concerns about the impact of alkaline metals on the performance of the catalyst used in the SCR process, and concluded that such "catalyst poisoning" is not a significant problem in coal-fired boilers. Mindful of the high degree of deference we must show to EPA's scientific judgment, we accept these determinations and sustain EPA's uniform standard for utility boilers.

Petitioners offer a broader challenge to EPA's .20 lb/MMBtu standard for industrial boilers, claiming that SCR is not "adequately demonstrated" for any coal-fired industrial boilers. EPA was unable to collect emissions data for the application of SCR to these boilers, but this absence of data is not surprising for a new technology like SCR, nor does it in and of itself defeat EPA's standard. Because it applies only to new sources, we have recognized that section 111 "looks toward what may fairly be projected for the regulated future, rather than the state of the art at present." *Portland Cement Ass'n v. Ruckelshaus,* 486 F.2d 375, 391 (D.C.Cir.1973). Of course, where data are unavailable, EPA may not base its determination that a technology is adequately demonstrated or that a standard is achievable on mere speculation or conjecture, but EPA may compensate for a shortage of data through the use of other qualitative methods, including the reasonable extrapolation of a technology's performance in other industries. *See, e.g., Weyerhaeuser Co. v. Costle,* 590 F.2d 1011, 1054 n. 70 (D.C.Cir.1978).

EPA has done precisely that here, concluding from its study of utility boilers that SCR is "adequately demonstrated" and the .20 lb/MMBtu standard is "achievable" for coal-fired industrial boilers as well. Utility and industrial boilers are similar in design and both categories of boilers can attain similar levels of NOx emissions reduction through combustion controls, which means that SCR will be required to capture comparable quantities of NOx for both boiler types. While petitioners argue that SCR is less likely to be effective on industrial boilers because they have widely fluctuating load cycles, EPA has shown that SCR can be successfully applied to coal-fired utility boilers under a "wide range of operating conditions" including those analogous to the load cycles of industrial boilers. 63 Fed.Reg. at 49,444. We think that it was reasonable for EPA to extrapolate from its studies of utility boilers in setting an SCR-based [NSPS] for coal-fired industrial boilers.

We also sustain EPA's application of the .20 lb/MMBtu standard to combination boilers, which simultaneously combust a mixture of fuels. The preexisting NOx emissions standards established a range of values for combustion boilers that varied by fuel type: while combination boilers burning natural gas with non-coal solid fuels (*e.g.,* wood) were subject to a .30 lb/MMBtu standard, the performance standards for combination boilers combusting coal with oil or natural gas were determined based upon the proportion of the boiler's total heat input provided by each fuel. It is difficult to understand petitioners' objection to the application of the industrial boiler standard to boilers burning natural gas and wood. A reduction of that standard from .30 to .20 lb/MMBtu is perfectly reasonable in light of the significant advances in NOx emissions technology since 1986; indeed, EPA studies show that wood-fired boilers can reach emissions levels far lower than .20 lb/MMBtu through the application of flue gas treatment technologies. And our conclusion that the .20 lb/MMBtu standard is achievable for boilers burning only coal necessarily defeats petitioners' objection that the industrial boiler standard is unreasonable as applied to combination boilers burning coal simultaneously with other fuels with *lower* NOx emissions characteristics.

Petitioners' final objection is to EPA's valuation of steam energy produced by "cogeneration facilities." EPA's adoption of an output-based standard for utility boilers raised the question of how to calculate the energy produced by these units, which generate thermal steam energy in addition to electrical energy. Steam energy produced by cogeneration facilities is exported for several different industrial uses; however, because of inefficiencies in transporting and converting steam, only a fraction of steam energy produced by cogeneration facilities is actually used in the industrial process. EPA resolved this problem by assigning a 50% credit for steam energy when determining a cogeneration unit's output. Petitioners describe this credit as an arbitrary and capricious "discounting" of steam energy's value, but it just as easily could be called a subsidy: The maximum efficiency for the conversion of steam to electrical energy is only 38%, and EPA's final rule justifies the 50% credit on the ground that it will *encourage* cogeneration. In light of the difficulties that would attend calculating the useful energy of steam heat produced by cogeneration facilities on a unit-by-unit basis, we conclude that EPA's resolution of this issue was acceptable.

Questions and Notes

1.   What did you think of the court's analysis in this case? Under what circumstances should EPA be required to subcategorize for different types of sources? Do you agree that the .20 lb/MMBtu standard was adequately demonstrated?

2.   Note that the court cites the *Weyerhaeuser* case for the proposition that EPA may in come cases extrapolate from a technology's performance in other industries. This serves to underscore the similarity between the analyses EPA is to engage in when setting technology-based standards under the CWA and CAA.

3.   In 2005, EPA issued a controversial set of regulations known as the "Clean Air Mercury Rule," governing coal-fired power plants. 70 Fed. Reg. 28606, et. seq. (2005). Among other things, this rule embodies a radical rethinking of the range of potential approaches to standard setting under § 111(a). Specifically, it embodies a "cap and trade" component similar to that featured in the "acid rain" program, which we will consider below. Under the mercury rule, if the States opt in, they are to allocate their initial State-wide allowances to individual plants; the plants are then free to trade their allowances among each other a national basis. Id. at 28624. Interestingly, only existing facilities to be regulated under § 111(d) receive the full

benefits of this cap and trade approach; new sources regulated under § 111(b) must still meet a traditional technology-based NSPS standard even under the new rule. Id. at 28616. Still, however, EPA's approach to facilities regulated under § 111(d) is noteworthy because that subsection uses the same language, "standard[] of performance," as is used in § 111(b). Indeed, EPA's legal justification for its action interprets the statutory definition of that phrase in § 111(a), and thus could just as easily apply to new sources. Id. at 28616–17. Do you think a "cap and trade" approach makes sense in the mercury context? Do you agree that § 111(a) can be interpreted to allow one? If it can, does this mean that EPA has the freedom to use a "cap and trade" approach in other technology-based settings? As one might expect, the new mercury rule is currently being challenged. It remains to be seen whether it will survive review by the D.C. Circuit.

C.　New Source Review (Both Nonattainment New Source Review (NNSR) and Prevention of Significant Deterioration (PSD))

The story of the Clean Air Act, like that of all of our environmental laws, involves the continuing evolution of administrative standards and enforcement. Although the CAA has gone through significant revisions since its inception, the main focus on setting the concentrations of air pollution to safe levels and protecting human health has not changed. What has changed is the way this is to be implemented. As noted in the introductory chapter on the role of administrative law, there can be huge differences in cost, methods, and effects depending upon how the implementation of a law occurs.

The NSPS program that we just considered imposes technology-based requirements on all qualifying new and modified sources, irrespective of the attainment status of the relevant air-shed for the pollutants to be emitted. In 1977, Congress codified two new programs applicable to new and modified "major" sources, nonattainment new source review (NNSR) and the Prevention of Significant Deterioration (PSD) program. These programs, which collectively are often referred to as "NSR," impose similar (but by no means identical) requirements on qualifying sources. Not surprisingly, the NNSR program applies if the relevant source is in a nonattainment area for the pollutants it will emit, and the PSD program will apply if the area is in attainment.

The story of NSR and how and when it applies to existing sources is one of the most complicated and interesting stories of regulatory evolution, and it is still being written as this book goes to press. As you read this section, note the interplay of policy decisions made by Congress and the president in the passage of this part of the law and then the policy decisions inherent in the executive control of the implementation of this law. Also note the importance of the administrative process to what we call environmental law.

As we will see, the requirements that apply under both the NNSR and PSD programs are quite strict (and expensive). As such, sources going through changes have even greater incentives to avoid having those changes be deemed to be triggering "modifications" for purposes of NSR than they would if only the potential application of NSPS were at stake.

In the end, the story of the NSR illustrates very well that any real impacts in actual air pollution reduction depend greatly on how the public and stakeholders engage in the administrative process. If you do not learn this anywhere else in the book, it is important to know that environmental victories and thus environmental law itself is rarely about cases, but more about the inputs and outputs of the administrative process.

1. Jurisdiction

For new sources, the question whether NSR applies is relatively straightforward. In the NNSR context, the question is whether the source will emit or have the potential to emit more than 100 tons per year of any pollutant. See 42 U.S.C. §§ 7502(c)(5) and 7602(j). In the PSD context, the question is the same for sources in 28 listed categories of industry; the relevant threshold changes to 250 tons per year for other, unspecified sources. See 42 U.S.C. §§ 7475(a)(1) and 7479(1).

The issue is much more complicated for existing sources that are going through modifications. The question whether a "modification" has occurred for NSR purposes has much in common with the analysis of that same issue in the NSPS context (indeed, the *WEPCo* case had a significant PSD component in addition to the NSPS discussion upon which we focused). This is particularly unsurprising given that, as we will see, both of the NSR programs expressly incorporate the NSPS definition of the term "modification" itself. EPA has drawn some important distinctions in how it applies this statutory concept in these various contexts. First, EPA defines the term "source" differently in the NSR context than it does under NSPS. As we also will see, this has major implications in determining whether the NSR programs apply. Additionally, in recent years EPA promulgated two significant rules changing its approach to defining which modifications would trigger NSR (neither of these rules were intended to apply in the NSPS context).

We begin with the famous *Chevron* case:

CHEVRON, U.S.A., INC. v. NATURAL RESOURCES DEFENSE COUNCIL, INC.

Supreme Court of the United States, 1984.
467 U.S. 837, 104 S.Ct. 2778, 81 L.Ed.2d 694.

Justice STEVENS delivered the opinion of the Court.

In the Clean Air Act Amendments of 1977, Congress enacted certain requirements applicable to States that had not achieved the national air quality standards established by the [EPA] pursuant to earlier legislation. The amended [CAA] required these "nonattainment" States to establish a permit program regulating "new or modified major stationary sources" of air pollution. Generally, a permit may not be issued for a new or modified major stationary source unless several stringent conditions are met. The EPA regulation promulgated to implement this permit requirement allows a State to adopt a plantwide definition of the term "stationary source."[2] Under this definition, an existing plant that contains several pollution-emitting devices may install or modify one piece of equipment without meeting the permit conditions if the alteration will not increase the total emissions from the plant. The question presented by these cases is whether EPA's decision to allow States to treat all of the pollution-emitting devices within the same industrial grouping as though they were encased within a single "bubble" is based on a reasonable construction of the statutory term "stationary source."

The EPA regulations containing the plantwide definition of the term stationary source were promulgated on October 14, 1981. 46 Fed.Reg. 50766. Respondents filed a timely petition for review ... pursuant to 42 U.S.C. § 7607(b)(1).[4] The Court of Appeals set aside the regulations.

The court observed that the relevant part of the amended [CAA] "does not explicitly define what Congress envisioned as a 'stationary source, to which the permit program ... should apply,'" and further stated that the precise issue was not "squarely addressed in the legislative history." In light of its conclusion that the legislative history bearing on the question was "at best contradictory," it reasoned that "the purposes of the nonattainment program should guide our decision here." Based on two of its precedents concerning the applicability of the bubble concept to certain [CAA] programs,[6] the court stated that the bubble concept was "mandatory" in programs designed merely to maintain existing air quality, but held that it was "inappropriate" in programs enacted to improve air quality. Since the purpose of the permit program—its "raison d'être," in the court's view—was to improve air quality, the court held that the bubble concept was inapplicable in these cases under its prior precedents. It therefore set aside the regulations embodying the bubble concept as contrary to law. We granted certiorari to review that judgment ..., and we now reverse.

[We omit the main portion of the deference discussion for which this case is most famous. The Court concluded that discussion as follows:]

In light of these well-settled principles it is clear that the Court of Appeals misconceived the nature of its role in reviewing the regulations at issue. Once it determined, after its own examination of the legislation, that Congress did not actually have an intent regarding the applicability

---

2. "(i) 'Stationary source' means any building, structure, facility, or installation which emits or may emit any air pollutant subject to regulation under the Act.

"(ii) 'Building, structure, facility, or installation' means all of the pollutant-emitting activities which belong to the same industrial grouping, are located on one or more contiguous or adjacent properties, and are under the control of the same person (or persons under common control) except the activities of any vessel." 40 CFR § § 51.18(j)(1)(i) and (ii) (1983).

4. Petitioners, Chevron U.S.A. Inc. [and others] were granted leave to intervene and argue in support of the regulation.

6. *Alabama Power Co. v. Costle*, 636 F.2d 323 (D.C. Cir. 1979); *ASARCO Inc. v. EPA*, 578 F.2d 319 (D.C. Cir. 1978).

of the bubble concept to the permit program, the question before it was not whether in its view the concept is "inappropriate" in the general context of a program designed to improve air quality, but whether the Administrator's view that it is appropriate in the context of this particular program is a reasonable one. Based on the examination of the legislation and its history which follows, we agree with the Court of Appeals that Congress did not have a specific intention on the applicability of the bubble concept in these cases, and conclude that the EPA's use of that concept here is a reasonable policy choice for the agency to make.

[Since 1970, § 111(a)(3) has defined the term "stationary source," for purposes of the NSPS program, to mean "any building, structure, facility, or installation which emits or may emit any air pollutant." When Congress created the NNSR program in 1977, it made it applicable to new or modified "major stationary source[s]." 42 U.S.C. § 7502(c)(5).]

The 1977 Amendments contain no specific reference to the "bubble concept." Nor do they contain a specific definition of the term "stationary source," though they did not disturb the definition of "stationary source" contained in § 111(a)(3), applicable by the terms of the Act to the NSPS program. Section 302(j), however, defines the term "major stationary source" as follows:

"(j) Except as otherwise expressly provided, the terms 'major stationary source' and 'major emitting facility' mean any stationary facility or source of air pollutants which directly emits, or has the potential to emit, one hundred tons per year or more of any air pollutant (including any major emitting facility or source of fugitive emissions of any such pollutant, as determined by rule by the Administrator)."

The legislative history of the portion of the 1977 Amendments dealing with nonattainment areas does not contain any specific comment on the "bubble concept" or the question whether a plantwide definition of a stationary source is permissible under the permit program. It does, however, plainly disclose that in the permit program Congress sought to accommodate the conflict between the economic interest in permitting capital improvements to continue and the environmental interest in improving air quality. . . .

. . . [P]rior to the 1977 Amendments, the EPA had adhered to a plantwide definition of the term "source" under a NSPS program. After adoption of the 1977 Amendments, proposals for a plantwide definition were considered in at least three formal proceedings.

In January 1979, the EPA considered the question whether [it should apply a plantwide definition of source under both the PSD and NNSR programs. In the resulting proposal,] the EPA, in effect, provided a bifurcated answer to that question. In those areas that did not have a revised SIP in effect by July 1979, the EPA rejected the plantwide definition; on the other hand, it expressly concluded that the plantwide approach would be permissible in certain circumstances if authorized by an approved SIP.

Significantly, the EPA expressly noted that the word "source" might be given a plantwide definition for some purposes and a narrower definition for other purposes. It wrote:

"Source means any building structure, facility, or installation which emits or may emit any regulated pollutant. 'Building, structure, facility or installation' means plant in PSD areas and in nonattainment areas except where the growth prohibitions would apply or where no adequate SIP exists or is being carried out." [44 Fed. Reg. at 51925 (1979)].[28]

The EPA's summary of its proposed Ruling discloses a flexible rather than rigid definition of the term "source" to implement various policies and programs:

"In summary, EPA is proposing two different ways to define source for different kinds of NSR programs:

"(1) For PSD and complete Part D SIPs, review would apply only to plants, with an unrestricted plant-wide bubble.

"(2) For the offset ruling, restrictions on construction, and incomplete Part D SIPs, review would apply to both plants and individual pieces of process equipment, causing the plant-wide bubble not to apply for new and modified major pieces of equipment.

"In addition, for the restrictions on construction, EPA is proposing to define 'major modification' so as to prohibit the bubble entirely . . . ." Id., at 51934.

In August 1980, however, the EPA adopted a regulation that, in essence, applied the basic reasoning of the Court of Appeals in these cases. The EPA took particular note of the two then-recent Court of Appeals decisions, which had created the bright-line rule that the "bubble concept" should be employed in a program designed to maintain air quality but not in one designed to enhance air quality. Relying heavily on those cases, EPA adopted a dual definition of "source" for nonattainment areas that required a permit whenever a change in either the entire plant, or one of its components, would result in a significant increase in emissions even if the increase was completely offset by reductions elsewhere in the plant. The EPA expressed the opinion that this interpretation was "more consistent with congressional intent" than the plantwide definition because it "would bring in more sources or modifications for review," 45 Fed.Reg. 52697 (1980), but its primary legal analysis was predicated on the two Court of Appeals decisions.

In 1981 a new administration took office and initiated a "Government-wide reexamination of regulatory burdens and complexities." 46 Fed.Reg. 16281. In the context of that review, the EPA reevaluated the various arguments that had been advanced in connection with the

---

28. In its explanation of why the use of the "bubble concept" was especially appropriate in preventing significant deterioration (PSD) in clean air areas, the EPA stated: "In addition, application of the bubble on a plant-wide basis encourages voluntary upgrading of equipment, and growth in productive capacity." Id., at 51932.

proper definition of the term "source" and concluded that the term should be given the same definition in both nonattainment areas and PSD areas.

In explaining its conclusion, the EPA first noted that the definitional issue was not squarely addressed in either the statute or its legislative history and therefore that the issue involved an agency "judgment as how to best carry out the Act." Ibid. It then set forth several reasons for concluding that the plantwide definition was more appropriate. It pointed out that the dual definition "can act as a disincentive to new investment and modernization by discouraging modifications to existing facilities" and "can actually retard progress in air pollution control by discouraging replacement of older, dirtier processes or pieces of equipment with new, cleaner ones." Ibid. Moreover, the new definition "would simplify EPA's rules by using the same definition of 'source' for PSD, nonattainment new source review and the construction moratorium. This reduces confusion and inconsistency." Ibid. Finally, the agency explained that additional requirements that remained in place would accomplish the fundamental purposes of achieving attainment with NAAQS's as expeditiously as possible.

The definition of the term "stationary source" in § 111(a)(3) refers to "any building, structure, facility, or installation" which emits air pollution. This definition is applicable only to the NSPS program by the express terms of the statute; the text of the statute does not make this definition applicable to the permit program. Petitioners therefore maintain that there is no statutory language even relevant to ascertaining the meaning of stationary source in the permit program aside from § 302(j), which defines the term "major stationary source." We disagree....

The definition in § 302(j) tells us what the word "major" means—a source must emit at least 100 tons of pollution to qualify—but it sheds virtually no light on the meaning of the term "stationary source." It does equate a source with a facility—a "major emitting facility" and a "major stationary source" are synonymous under § 302(j). The ordinary meaning of the term "facility" is some collection of integrated elements which has been designed and constructed to achieve some purpose. Moreover, it is certainly no affront to common English usage to take a reference to a major facility or a major source to connote an entire plant as opposed to its constituent parts. Basically, however, the language of § 302(j) simply does not compel any given interpretation of the term "source."

Respondents recognize that, and hence point to § 111(a)(3). Although the definition in that section is not literally applicable to the permit program, it sheds as much light on the meaning of the word "source" as anything in the statute. As respondents point out, use of the words "building, structure, facility, or installation," as the definition of source, could be read to impose the permit conditions on an individual building that is a part of a plant. A "word may have a character of its own not to be submerged by its association." *Russell Motor Car Co. v.*

United States, 261 U.S. 514, 519 (1923). On the other hand, the meaning of a word must be ascertained in the context of achieving particular objectives, and the words associated with it may indicate that the true meaning of the series is to convey a common idea. The language may reasonably be interpreted to impose the requirement on any discrete, but integrated, operation which pollutes. This gives meaning to all of the terms—a single building, not part of a larger operation, would be covered if it emits more than 100 tons of pollution, as would any facility, structure, or installation. Indeed, the language itself implies a "bubble concept" of sorts: each enumerated item would seem to be treated as if it were encased in a bubble. While respondents insist that each of these terms must be given a discrete meaning, they also argue that § 111(a)(3) defines "source" as that term is used in § 302(j). The latter section, however, equates a source with a facility, whereas the former defines "source" as a facility, among other items.

We are not persuaded that parsing of general terms in the text of the statute will reveal an actual intent of Congress. We know full well that this language is not dispositive; the terms are overlapping and the language is not precisely directed to the question of the applicability of a given term in the context of a larger operation. To the extent any congressional "intent" can be discerned from this language, it would appear that the listing of overlapping, illustrative terms was intended to enlarge, rather than to confine, the scope of the agency's power to regulate particular sources in order to effectuate the policies of the Act.

In addition, respondents argue that the legislative history and policies of the Act foreclose the plantwide definition, and that the EPA's interpretation is not entitled to deference because it represents a sharp break with prior interpretations of the Act.

Based on our examination of the legislative history, we agree with the Court of Appeals that it is unilluminating.... Respondents' argument based on the legislative history relies heavily on Senator Muskie's observation that a new source is subject to the LAER requirement. But the full statement is ambiguous and like the text of § 173 itself, this comment does not tell us what a new source is, much less that it is to have an inflexible definition. We find that the legislative history as a whole is silent on the precise issue before us....

Our review of the EPA's varying interpretations of the word "source"—both before and after the 1977 Amendments—convinces us that the agency primarily responsible for administering this important legislation has consistently interpreted it flexibly—not in a sterile textual vacuum, but in the context of implementing policy decisions in a technical and complex arena. The fact that the agency has from time to time changed its interpretation of the term "source" does not, as respondents argue, lead us to conclude that no deference should be accorded the agency's interpretation of the statute. An initial agency interpretation is not instantly carved in stone. On the contrary, the agency, to engage in informed rulemaking, must consider varying interpretations and the wisdom of its policy on a continuing basis. Moreover, the fact that the agency has adopted different definitions in different contexts adds force to the argument that the definition itself is flexible, particularly since Congress has never indicated any disapproval of a flexible reading of the statute.

Significantly, it was not the agency in 1980, but rather the Court of Appeals that read the statute inflexibly to command a plantwide definition for programs designed to maintain clean air and to forbid such a definition for programs designed to improve air quality. The distinction the court drew may well be a sensible one, but our labored review of the problem has surely disclosed that it is not a distinction that Congress ever articulated itself, or one that the EPA found in the statute before the courts began to review the legislative work product. We conclude that it was the Court of Appeals, rather than Congress or any of the decisionmakers who are authorized by Congress to administer this legislation, that was primarily responsible for the 1980 position taken by the agency.

The arguments over policy that are advanced in the parties' briefs create the impression that respondents are now waging in a judicial forum a specific policy battle which they ultimately lost in the agency and in the 32 jurisdictions opting for the "bubble concept," but one which was never waged in the Congress. Such policy arguments are more properly addressed to legislators or administrators, not to judges.

We hold that the EPA's definition of the term "source" is a permissible construction of the statute which seeks to accommodate progress in reducing air pollution with economic growth. . . .

Notes and Comments

1. Although the *Chevron* Court mentions that EPA at one time adhered to the "bubble policy" even under NSPS, the D.C. Circuit rejected this approach in *ASARCO, Inc. v. EPA*, 578 F.2d 319 (D.C. Cir. 1978). EPA subsequently modified its regulatory definition to comport with the court's opinion. This revision still applies under NSPS, meaning that bubbling is unavailable under that program. See 40 C.F.R. § 60.2. Can you imagine why one might rationally distinguish between NSPS and the NSR programs with respect to the potential availability of bubbles? Having said that, does *Chevron* suggest that EPA might now be able to incorporate bubbling into NSPS if it so chooses?

2. As mentioned in *Chevron*, § 302(j) contemplates that EPA must, at least in some cases, specifically determine through a rulemaking that fugitive emissions should be counted in order to consider them in determining what constitutes a "major stationary source." As we will see when we consider the *National Mining Ass'n* case below, in *Alabama Power Co. v. Costle*, 636 F.2d 323 (D.C. Cir. 1979), the D.C. Circuit read this provision as applying not just to NNSR, but also PSD. Further, it deemed it to preclude any consideration of fugitives—which EPA defines to mean "those emissions which could not reasonably pass through a stack, chimney, vent or other functionally equivalent opening," 40 C.F.R. § 51.165(a)(1)(ix))—absent such

a rulemaking. EPA has acquiesced in this holding, and has promulgated rules allowing for the consideration of fugitives in 27 industries. 40 C.F.R. §§ 51.165(a)(1)(iv)(C) (NNSR) and 52.21(b)(1)(iii) (PSD). If a source is not in one of these categories, its fugitive emissions are not counted in the NSR analysis.

3. Is the "bubble" concept consistent with phasing out heavily polluting sources over time? Does it allow an increase in efficiency which prolongs the life of a plant in such a way that it contravenes the purposes of the CAA? Is the statute ambiguous, thus allowing the agency to go either way? Could EPA now decide to abandon the "bubble" concept and analyze each source separately for purposes of NSR? Though "bubbling" is controversial, Congress did not statutorily alter the process in the 1990 CAA Amendments. Does this indicate the "wisdom" of *Chevron* deference?

4. Do you see why industry might favor the "bubble" concept and why others may oppose it? Note the diagram of the plant below with 2 smokestacks. Assume the plants with both smokestacks need repair and major changes to work at all, and that, because they have been becoming less efficient with age, upgrading would increase pollution. If each smokestack was considered a "source" under the statute, an increase in emissions of one upgraded smokestack, even if the other smokestack emission decreased dramatically, would trigger new source review, requiring pollution control equipment at great expense. This requires the plant to pay a lot of money for pollution control equipment or allow the plant to eventually cease operation altogether. Upgrading one smokestack of the factory would cost a great deal, even if overall emissions did not increase because of the phaseout of the second smokestack.

With "bubbling", the plant can do the same thing, but at no cost, because the total considered is the total of both smokestacks under one "bubble." But also notice that this "bubbled" factory would produce more pollution than the "unbubbled" factory, because the first factory would have triggered the imposition of pollution control devices which would have cut emissions overall drastically.

WITHOUT BUBBLE

Poll'n potential before alteration
Smokestack #1   SS #2
100 tons   100 tons

After alteration
     SS#1   SS #2
    195 tons   5 tons

WITH BUBBLE:

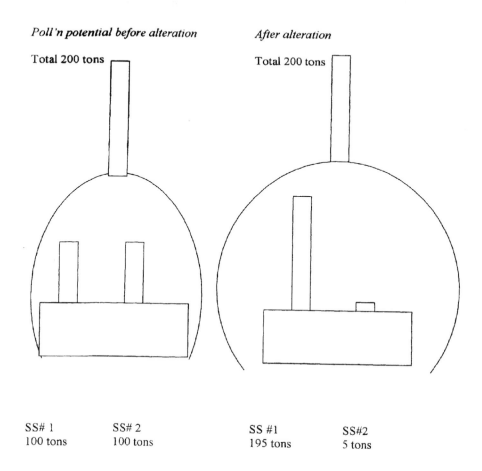

Poll'n potential before alteration   *After alteration*

Total 200 tons   Total 200 tons

SS# 1	SS# 2	SS #1	SS#2
100 tons	100 tons	195 tons	5 tons

As mentioned above, EPA recently promulgated two new rules addressing how "modification[s]" are treated under NSR. The following cases involve challenges to these rules:

NEW YORK v. U.S. ENVIRONMENTAL PROTECTION AGENCY

United States Court of Appeals, District of Columbia Circuit, 2005.
413 F.3d 3, reh'g den. 431 F.3d 801 (2005).

Before: ROGERS and TATEL, Circuit Judges, and WILLIAMS, Senior Circuit Judge.

PER CURIAM.

In 1977, Congress amended the [CAA] to strengthen the safeguards that protect the nation's air quality. Among other things, these amendments directed that major stationary sources undertaking modifications must obtain preconstruction permits, as must major new sources, through a process known as "New Source Review" ("NSR"). According to a preexisting definition referenced in the 1977 amendments, a source undertakes a modification when "any physical change . . . or change in the method of operation . . . which increases the amount of any air pollutant emitted by such source" occurs. 42 U.S.C. § 7411(a)(4). The [EPA] has interpreted this rather terse definition in numerous rules, including ones issued in 1980, 1992, and most recently in 2002.

Industry, government, and environmental petitioners now challenge this 2002 rule, which departs sharply from prior rules in several significant respects. Roughly speaking, industry petitioners argue that the 2002 rule interprets "modification" too broadly, while government and environmental petitioners argue that the rule's interpretation is too narrow. . . .

I. BACKGROUND

[When Congress codified the NSR programs (NNSR and PSD) in 1977, it incorporated by reference the definition of "modification" it had enacted in 1970 for purposes of the NSPS program.] Seeking to understand what the 1977 Congress meant by modification—the central issue in this case—we thus begin with the 1970 CAA amendments and their implementing regulations.

[Section 111(a)(4) of the CAA, which originally had relevance only to the NSPS program, defines the term "modification" to include]:

any physical change in, or change in the method of operation of, a stationary source which increases the amount of any air pollutant emitted by such source or which results in the emission of any air pollutant not previously emitted.

42 U.S.C. § 7411(a)(4). This definition requires *both* a change—whether physical or operational—*and* a resulting increase in emissions of a pollutant.

EPA's 1975 NSPS regulation . . . elaborated upon this statutory definition, doing so in provisions whose meaning the parties debate today. One part of the 1975 regulation provided that " '[m]odification' means any physical change in, or change in the method of operation of, an existing facility which increases the amount of any air pollutant (to which a standard applies) emitted into the atmosphere by that facility." Using somewhat different terms, another part of the 1975 regulation stated that "any physical or operational change to an existing facility which results in an increase in the emission rate to the atmosphere of any pollutant to which a standard applies shall be considered a modification within the meaning . . . of the Act," with "[e]mission rate . . . expressed as kg/hr of any pollutant discharged into the atmosphere." Yet neither the 1975 regulation nor its preamble explained why EPA found it necessary to offer these two separate glosses on "modification."

[In 1977, Congress made both of the new NSR programs applicable to both new and modified sources. In both contexts, Congress defined the term modification by reference to the NSPS definition. See, id. § 7479(2)(C) and 7501(4).] In sum, the 1977 amendments carved out a significant difference between existing sources on the one hand and new or modified sources on the other. The former faced no NSR obligations— in the common phrase, they were "grandfathered"—while the latter were subject to strict standards. . . .

EPA promulgated an NSR regulation in 1978. The 1978 regulation defined a major "modification" as a "physical change, change in the method of operation of, or addition to a stationary source which increases the potential emission rate of any air pollutant regulated under the act." The phrase "potential emission rate," though new to EPA regulations relating to "modification," went unchallenged during ensuing litigation over other aspects of the 1978 regulation. That litigation culminated in this circuit's *Alabama Power Co. v. Costle* decision, issued initially as a brief opinion, 606 F.2d 1068 (D.C.Cir.1979), that was superceded six months later by a much longer one, 636 F.2d 323 (D.C.Cir. 1979).

In the period between the two *Alabama Power* opinions, EPA proposed a new NSR regulation. The proposed definition of modification continued focusing on potential emissions rates rather than actual emissions. After the issuance of the revised *Alabama Power* opinion, however, EPA changed its definition of modification. The final 1980 rule defined the term as follows: " '[m]ajor modification' means any physical change in or change in the method of operation of a major stationary source that would result in a *significant net emissions increase* of any pollutant subject to regulation under the Act." 45 Fed.Reg. 52,676, 52,735 (Aug. 7, 1980) (emphasis added). The regulation defined "[n]et emissions increase" as "any increase in actual emissions from a particular physical change or change in method of operation" that occurred after taking into account, through a process known as "netting," "any other increases and decreases in actual emissions at the source that are contemporaneous with the particular change and are otherwise creditable." *Id.* at 52,736. The regulation then defined "actual emissions" as follows:

> (ii) In general, actual emissions as of a particular date shall equal the average rate, in tons per year, at which the unit actually emitted the pollutant during a two-year period which proceeds the particular date and which is representative of normal source operation. The Administrator shall allow the use of a different time period upon a determination that it is more representative of normal source operation. Actual emissions shall be calculated using the unit's actual operating hours, production rates, and types of materials processed, stored, or combusted during the selected time period.

> (iii) The Administrator may presume that source-specific allowable emissions for the unit are equivalent to the actual emissions of the unit.

(iv) For any emissions unit which has not begun normal operations on the particular date, actual emissions shall equal the potential to emit of the unit on that date.

Id. at 52,737. In contrast to the proposed regulation's approach, this regulation emphasized "actual emissions." Justifying the shift, EPA explained in the regulation's preamble that while the initial *Alabama Power* decision had used the phrase "potential to emit," the later opinion used language that, "like the [statutory] definition, suggest[ed] changes in actual emissions," and that EPA had followed suit. *Id.* at 52,700. Finally, the 1980 regulation provided that "[a] physical change or change in the method of operation shall not include . . . an increase in the hours of operation or in the production rate." *Id.* at 52,735–36.

Several parties petitioned this court for review of the 1980 rule, but we stayed that challenge because of ongoing settlement discussions with EPA. Ultimately, EPA and the parties entered into an agreement providing that the agency would undertake a new rulemaking and that if the new rule failed to meet certain conditions, the parties could revive their stayed petitions.

In the proceedings before us today, industry petitioners and EPA dispute what the 1980 rule meant. Both agree that for a source to undertake a modification, it must first make a physical or operational change other than an increase in the hours of operation. They disagree over how to measure an "increase" in emitted pollutants once a change has occurred. According to industry petitioners, the 1980 regulation provided that an emissions "increase" occurs only if the maximum hourly emissions rate goes up as a result of the physical or operational change. According to EPA, however, an increase occurs under the 1980 regulations if, after netting, a source's past annual emissions (typically measured by averaging out the two "baseline" years prior to the change) are less than future annual emissions (measured by calculating the source's potential to emit after the change). EPA proffered this interpretation, which quickly became known as the "actual-to-potential" test, in proceedings leading up to *Puerto Rican Cement Co. v. EPA*, 889 F.2d 292 (1st Cir.1989), and *Wisconsin Electric Power Co. v. Reilly*, 893 F.2d 901 (7th Cir.1990) (*"WEPCo"*). . . .

Puerto Rican Cement's facts illustrate the practical difference between industry's and EPA's interpretations. In that case, a factory sought to make a physical change: it would replace old cement kilns that operated 60% of the time with a new kiln that would emit fewer pollutants per hour. "If operated to achieve about the same level of production [as the old ones], the new kiln will pollute far less than the older kilns; but, if the Company operates the new kiln at significantly higher production levels, it will emit more pollutants than did the older kilns." 889 F.2d at 293. Under the actual-to-potential test, the company "increased" its emissions after the change, making it subject to NSR: operated at full potential, the new kiln would emit more pollutants than the old kilns had emitted when actually in operation. Under the interpretation urged by industry petitioners, however, the company had not undergone an "increase" in emissions—and thus would not trigger NSR—since the new kiln would have a lower hourly emissions rate than the old ones. Siding with EPA, the First Circuit agreed that the company had to obtain an NSR permit to make the intended change. *Id.* at 296–99.

WEPCo, which is important because of EPA's response to it, addressed whether EPA could apply the actual-to-potential test to utility plants undergoing extensive renovations. The petitioner argued that given the particular nature of the utility market, it was unfair to compare a utility's past actual emissions with its future potential emissions. Instead, the petitioner argued—and the Seventh Circuit agreed—that EPA should measure future emissions by projecting future actual emissions rather than by assuming, as it had done under the actual-to-potential test, that the source would operate at full capacity in the future. 893 F.2d at 916–18.

The Seventh Circuit decided *WEPCo* shortly before Congress enacted the 1990 amendments to the CAA. In those amendments, Congress added several programs—distinct from NSR—aimed at further securing good air quality through regulating existing sources[, including those relating to acid rain and regional haze]. Though it also made some changes related to NSR, Congress ultimately neither addressed the issues raised in *WEPCo,* nor revisited its statutory definition of modification, instead leaving it up to EPA to respond to that decision.

EPA dealt with *WEPCo* by issuing a 1992 rule that changed the test utilities used for measuring emissions increases. Under the new test, known as the "actual-to-projected-actual test," utilities would determine whether they had post-change increases in emissions—and thus whether they needed NSR permits—by comparing actual emissions before the change to their projections of actual post-change emissions.

Various petitioners challenged the 1992 rule, but once again we stayed the proceedings as EPA began a new rulemaking process. This new process went slowly. EPA issued a proposed rule in 1996, [but took no final action until 2002]. In the meantime, EPA began investigating numerous sources for noncompliance with the existing NSR program. It ended up bringing complaints against thirty-two utilities in ten states.

In 2002, EPA issued a new final rule to "reduce burden, maximize operating flexibility, improve environmental quality, provide additional certainty, and promote administrative efficiency." 67 Fed.Reg. at 80,189. This rule departed from the prior rules in several significant respects relevant to this litigation. First, it adopted the actual-to-projected-actual test for all existing sources. 40 C.F.R. § 52.21(a)(2)(iv)(c) (2004), though leaving sources the option to continue using the actual-to-potential test if they preferred, 40 C.F.R. § 52.21(b)(41)(ii)(d). Second, it altered the method for measuring past actual emissions. Under the 1980 rule, sources determined past actual emissions by averaging their annual emissions during the two years immediately prior to the change, though they could use either different, more representative periods or source-specific allowable emissions levels, if they could convince the permitting authorities. In contrast, under the 2002 rule, sources other than electric utilities determine past actual emissions by averaging annual emissions of *any* two consecutive years during the ten years prior to the change. 40 C.F.R. § 52.21(b)(48)(ii)). EPA determined that this change eliminated the need for case-specific alternatives. [67 Fed.Reg. at 80,200]. Adopting a statement from the 1992 rule's preamble, the 2002 rule also set a five-year lookback period for electric utilities. 40 C.F.R. § 52.21(b)(48)(i)). [Additionally], the rule provided that sources that saw no reasonable possibility that post-change emissions would prove higher than past actual emissions need keep no records of actual post-change emissions. 40 C.F.R. § 52.21(r)(6)). . . .

Numerous petitioners now challenge the 2002 rule. Industry petitioners object to the actual-to-projected-actual test, arguing that the CAA requires EPA to compare past potential emissions with future potential emissions (i.e., use a "potential-to-potential" test). . . . Between them, government and environmental petitioners challenge virtually all aspects of the 2002 rule, including the use of a ten-year lookback period for selecting the two-year baseline . . . [and] the recordkeeping standards. . . .

II. Industry Challenges

. . . [I]ndustry petitioners attack the 2002 rule's definition of "modification" for NSR purposes on the ground that it unlawfully differs from its definition for NSPS purposes. While the NSPS regulatory definition of modification allegedly focuses on the hourly rate of emissions, the NSR definition focuses on net emissions increases measured in tons per year. *Compare* 40 C.F.R. § 60.14 (NSPS), *with id.* § 52.21(b)(2)(ii) (NSR). Industry claims that this divergence is unlawful because Congress intended to adopt for NSR purposes the NSPS regulatory definition in existence at the time of the 1977 amendments. We are not convinced.

Industry rests its claim that modification must have the same regulatory meaning for NSR as prevailed for NSPS in 1977 on the fact that Congress, by a cross-reference, used the same language in both statutory contexts. Thus, the NNSR portion of the Act provided:

> The terms "modifications" and "modified" mean the same as the term "modification" as used in section 7411(a)(4) of this title.

42 U.S.C. § 7501(4). Similarly, the PSD portion of the statute provides that "construction" includes "the modification (as defined in section 7411(a) of this title) of any source or facility." *Id.* § 7479(2)(C). So far as appears, then, these incorporations by reference are the equivalent of Congress's having simply repeated in the NSR context the definitional language used before in the NSPS context.

We have (naturally) required indications in the statutory language or history to infer that Congress intended to incorporate into a statute a preexisting regulatory definition. Industry suggests there is "abundant indication" of such intent, pointing to Congress's having said that modification (in the NNSR portion of the statute) has the meaning of the same word *"as used in"* the NSPS portion of the statute. It also cites a conference committee report that explains agreement to cover modification as well as construction in Part C of the Act (PSD) (a point apparently originally excluded unintentionally) by saying that construction is being defined "to conform to *usage* in other parts of the Act." *See* 123 CONG. REC. 32,253 (Nov. 1, 1977) (emphasis added). But the phrases "usage" and "used in" refer not to regulatory usage, but only to usage in the statute itself. They tell us no more than if Congress had used a little more ink and repeated the NSPS definitions verbatim. Elsewhere in the Act, moreover, Congress did incorporate regulatory provisions expressly by reference. *See, e.g.,* Pub.L. No. 95–95, § 129(a)(1) (1977) ("the interpretative regulation of the Administrator of the Environmental Protection Agency published in 41 Federal Register 55524 . . . shall apply. . . ."); 42 U.S.C. § 7502 note. Congress's failure to use such an express incorporation of prior regulations for "modification" cuts against the proposed inference.

Industry petitioners also invoke *Bragdon v. Abbott,* 524 U.S. 624, 632 (1998), for the proposition that when Congress repeats a well-established term, it implies that Congress intended the term to be construed in accordance with preexisting regulatory interpretations. But that proposition does industry little good here, as the regulatory definitions in the NSPS and PSD programs already differed at the time of the 1977 amendments.

In fact, the NSPS regulations adopted in 1975 and in force at the time of the 1977 CAA amendments themselves used two different (and possibly inconsistent) definitions of modification. Section 60.2(h) defined modification to include "any physical change in, or change in the method of operation of, an existing facility which increases the amount of any air pollutant (to which a standard applies) emitted into the atmosphere by that facility." But 40 C.F.R. § 60.14(a) provided that "any physical or operational change to an existing facility which results in an increase in the emissions rate to the atmosphere of any pollutant to which a standard applies shall be considered a modification," and § 60.14(b) specified that the emissions rate should be expressed in "kg/hr of any pollutant discharged into the atmosphere." Industry's briefs, curiously, mention only § 60.14, never § 60.2(h). Given the two quite differently worded regulatory definitions of "modification" *within* the NSPS program at the time of the 1977 amendments, it would take a rather pointed indication from Congress to support the idea that it expressly adopted one of them for NSR. No such indication exists. We express no opinion as to whether Congress intended to require that EPA use identical regulatory definitions of modification across the NSPS and NSR programs. *Cf. United States v. Duke Energy Corp.,* [411 F.3d 539, 546–51 (4th Cir. 2005)]. That argument was not made by industry petitioners in their opening brief and is therefore waived . . .

[Turning to the next issue, t]he previous rules allowed state SIPs to provide for calculation of baseline emissions by using a unit's "source-specific allowable emissions" as the unit's actual emissions. Petitioner Newmont challenges the elimination of this provision in the 2002 rule, arguing that EPA's decision lacks adequate reasoning and violates the statute.

EPA's reasoning was simple enough—that the baseline is intended to be an indicator of emissions associated with utilization "actually achieved." Otherwise changes increasing emissions beyond historic levels would avoid NSR. Newmont makes the counterargument that EPA's decision imposes a foolhardy "use it or lose it" regime in which sources are encouraged to continue emitting at high levels to avoid losing the "right" to emit. A closer approximation is that the rule imposes a "use it for twenty-four months in ten years or lose it" regime, in which "lose it" entails an obligation to comply with review procedures for modifications at the source. In any event, such choices are for EPA to make so long as the agency engages in reasoned decision-making. Although EPA never expressly addressed this possibly perverse incentive, its resolute focus on the significance of changes in "actual" emissions suggests that it found the risk of firms' strategic use of emissions ceilings relatively minor when compared with the benefits of catching actual increases and subjecting them to NSR.

III. Baseline Emissions

The NSR provisions of the CAA require "new and modified major stationary sources" of air pollution to obtain preconstruction permits and to install pollution control technology in order to protect and enhance air quality. 42 U.S.C. §§ 7475, 7502, 7503. An existing source triggers NSR when it makes a "modification," defined as:

> any physical change in, or change in the method of operation of, a stationary source which increases the amount of any air pollutant emitted by such source or which results in the emission of any air pollutant not previously emitted.

Id. § 7411(a)(4). To determine whether a change "increases" emissions, the source must first calculate its baseline level of "actual emissions." The 1980 rule defined "actual emissions" as "the average rate, in tons per year, at which the unit actually emitted the pollutant during a two-year period which precedes the [change] and which is representative of normal source operation." 45 Fed.Reg. at 52,737.... While EPA historically used the two-year period immediately preceding the change to calculate baseline actual emissions, "in some cases" it allowed use of "an earlier period." 67 Fed.Reg. at 80,188.

The 2002 rule reinterprets the term "increases" by adopting a new method for calculating baseline actual emissions. For sources other than electric utilities, "baseline actual emissions" are defined as "the average rate, in tons per year, at which the emissions unit actually emitted the pollutant during any consecutive 24–month period selected by the [source] within the 10–year period immediately preceding [the change]." 40 C.F.R. § 52.21(b)(48)(ii). A source must adjust its baseline downward to reflect any legally enforceable emissions limitations that have been imposed since the baseline period, and it may not use a more "representative" baseline period outside the ten-year "lookback period." A source may use a different baseline period for each regulated pollutant. 40 C.F.R. § 52.21(b)(48)(ii)(d). The 2002 rule also codifies the presumption established in the 1992 rule that for an electric utility, "any 2 consecutive years within the 5 years prior to the proposed change is representative of normal source operations." 40 C.F.R. § 52.21(b)(48)(i).

Government and environmental petitioners ... contend that the ten-year lookback period reflects an impermissible interpretation of the statutory term "increases" because it allows sources to increase their emissions beyond their most recent levels without triggering NSR....

While the CAA defines a "modification" as any physical or operational change that "increases" emissions, it is silent on how to calculate such "increases" in emissions. 42 U.S.C. § 7411(a)(4). According to government petitioners, the lack of a statutory definition does not render the term "increases" ambiguous, but merely compels the court to give the term its "ordinary meaning." *See Engine Mfrs. Ass'n v. S. Coast Air Quality Mgmt. Dist.,* 541 U.S. 246 (2004). Relying on two "real world" analogies, government petitioners contend that the ordinary meaning of "increases" requires the baseline to be calculated from a period immediately preceding the change. They maintain, for example, that in determining whether a high-pressure weather system "increases" the local temperature, the relevant baseline is the temperature immediately preceding the arrival of the weather system, not the temperature five or ten years ago. Similarly, in determining whether a new engine "increases" the value of a car, the relevant baseline is the value of the car immediately preceding the replacement of the engine, not the value of the car five or ten years ago when the engine was in perfect condition.

EPA maintains that its choice of the ten-year lookback period is entitled to deference under *Chevron* Step 2 because it is based on a permissible construction of the ambiguous term "increases." EPA disputes the validity of government petitioners' analogies, pointing out, for example, that if the weather system arrives in the evening, it is inappropriate to compare the nighttime temperature immediately following the arrival of the system to the daytime temperature immediately preceding the arrival of the system. The important point is that the period immediately preceding a change may not be analogous to the period following the change and thus may not yield a meaningful comparison for the purpose of determining whether the change "increases" emissions. Hence, government petitioners' reliance on the "ordinary meaning" of "increases" fails to address a practical reality. Indeed, during oral argument, counsel for government petitioners agreed that the provision in the 1980 rule for use of a "more representative" period not immediately preceding the change is consistent with the statutory language because some flexibility is needed to account for anomalous disruptions in operations. It follows that the statutory term "increases" does not plainly and unambiguously require the baseline period to immediately precede the change. Rather, the statute is silent or ambiguous on how to calculate baseline emissions, and the issue is whether the ten-year lookback period is based on a permissible interpretation of the statute under *Chevron* Step 2.

Under *Chevron* Step 2, a court must defer to the agency's interpretation of the ambiguous statutory term if it "represents a reasonable accommodation of conflicting policies that were committed to the agency's care by the statute." [*Chevron U.S.A., Inc. v. NRDC*, 467 U.S. 837, 845 (1984)]. In particular, the agency's interpretation is entitled to deference when "the regulatory scheme is technical and complex, the agency considered the matter in a detailed and reasoned fashion, and the decision involves reconciling conflicting policies." *Id.* at 865.

There can be no doubt that EPA is entitled to balance environmental concerns with economic and administrative concerns, at least to a point. The Supreme Court recognized in *Chevron* that, in enacting the NSR program, "Congress sought to accommodate the conflict between the economic interest in permitting capital improvements to continue and the environmental interest in improving air quality," *id.* at 851, and delegated the responsibility of balancing those interests to EPA. Different interpretations of the term "increases" may have different environmental and economic consequences, and in administering the NSR program and filling in the gaps left by Congress, EPA has the authority to choose an interpretation that balances those consequences. In so doing, the Supreme Court has instructed, EPA may "properly rely upon the incumbent administration's view of wise policy to inform its judgments." *Id.* at 865. Furthermore, as there is no question that the NSR program is technical and complex, EPA may properly rely on its extensive experience and expertise in administering the program. Based on what EPA describes in its brief as more than twenty years of experience with the NSR program under the 1980 rule and more than "ten years of review, analysis, and communications with stakeholders," EPA responded to industry complaints that the 1980 rule was "too complex and burdensome" and adopted the ten-year lookback period as part of an effort to simplify and streamline the NSR program without sacrificing air quality.

It is EPA's position that the ten-year lookback period is based on a permissible interpretation of the CAA because it "fulfills the statutory goal of balancing economic growth with the need to protect air quality." According to EPA, the ten-year lookback period promotes economic growth and administrative efficiency by affording sources the flexibility to respond rapidly to market changes, focusing limited regulatory resources on changes most likely to harm the environment, and eliminating conflicts over whether a proposed baseline period is "more representative of normal source operations." At the same time, EPA believes that the ten-year lookback period protects air quality by eliminating the regulatory disincentive to make physical or operational changes that improve efficiency and reduce emissions rates. We conclude that EPA supports these conclusions with "detailed and reasoned" analysis based on its experience and expertise.

In explaining the benefits of the ten-year lookback period, EPA appropriately refers to the problems experienced under the 1980 rule. EPA notes that under the 1980 rule, establishing a representative baseline period other than the two-year period immediately preceding the change was "complex and time-consuming" and often involved "disputed judgment calls." EPA further notes that under the 1980 rule, sources experiencing periods of low production faced the unwelcome choice of either "surrendering capacity" by capping emissions at unrepresentative low levels or incurring the time and expense of securing NSR permits "for even small, non-excluded changes to a portion of the plant." According to industry comments on the ten-year lookback period, this dilemma discourages sources from making economically efficient and environmentally beneficial changes during periods of low production. Similarly, . . . government petitioner New Jersey explained in comments on the ten-year lookback period that the 1980 rule "results in a baseline that decreases each time production decreases. In other words, if economic downturn temporarily slows production at a facility for a few years, the facility's baseline actually decreases and the facility loses operational flexibility. It also discourages facilities from voluntarily implementing pollution prevention measures." Letter from Catherine Cowan, Assistant Comm'r, N.J. Dep't of Envtl. Protection, to EPA (Dec. 4, 1996). EPA confirms that one "common complaint" about the 1980 rule is that sources have "limited ability to consider the operational fluctuations associated with normal business cycles when establishing baseline actual emissions unless [the] reviewing authority agrees that another period is 'more representative of normal source operation.' " 67 Fed.Reg. at 80,191–92.

In response to these concerns, EPA commissioned a study of the business cycles of nine major emitting industries, including charcoal production, carbon black manufacturing, Portland cement manufacturing, lime manufacturing, iron and steel manufacturing, primary copper smelting, primary aluminum production, primary zinc and lead smelting, and secondary metal production. The study examined industry output data from 1982 to 1994 and measured each industry's business cycle from peak to peak and from trough to trough. Peak-to-peak cycles ranged from three to six years, and trough-to-trough cycles ranged from three to eight years.

Government and environmental petitioners contend that the business cycle study does not support EPA's choice of a ten-year lookback period because none of the industries in the study had business cycles longer than eight years, and the study did not consider whether emissions vary with business cycles. However, petitioners ignore the study's conclusions that "business cycles differ markedly by industry" and that "a minimum of ten years of data is recommended to capture an entire industry cycle." Moreover, while the study did not track emissions, it did track output, which generally correlates with emissions. Hence, the business cycle study supports EPA's conclusion that a ten-year lookback period "is a fair and representative time frame for encompassing a source's normal business cycle." 67 Fed.Reg. at 80,200. . . . [G]overnment and environmental petitioners provide no basis for the court to determine whether a particular time frame is reasonable under the CAA. Absent such an explanation, the court must defer to EPA's policy choice because it is supported by the business cycle study and not "manifestly contrary to the statute." *Chevron,* 467 U.S. at 844.

Environmental petitioners further contend that the ten-year lookback period does not ensure a representative baseline because it allows sources with shorter business cycles to choose among two or three peaks, not just the most recent one. . . .

EPA recognizes that "business cycles differ markedly by industry." . . . But in an effort to promote operational flexibility and administrative efficiency, EPA chose to apply a fixed ten-year lookback period to all sources in order to lend "clarity and certainty to the process" and to avoid the administrative burden of determining "representative" baselines on a case-by-case basis. This policy choice, which reconciles conflicting interests in accuracy and efficiency, based on years of regulatory experience, is entitled to deference under *Chevron* Step 2, for petitioners fail to demonstrate that EPA's choice is impermissible under the CAA.

. . . [E]nvironmental petitioners [also] contend that the ten-year lookback period violates this court's interpretation of the CAA in *Alabama Power,* 636 F.2d 323. Under *Alabama Power* and the 1980 rule, a physical or operational change constitutes a "modification" subject to NSR only if it results in a *net* increase in emissions; thus, a source making a change that increases emissions from one unit can "net out" of NSR based on a "contemporaneous" change that decreases emissions from another unit. *See id.* at 401–02. The court stated in *Alabama Power* that EPA has "discretion, within reason, to define which changes are contemporaneous," 636 F.2d at 402, and the 1980 rule defines "contemporaneous" as within a five-year period, 40 C.F.R. § 52.21(b)(3)(ii). The 2002 rule retains this definition of "contemporaneous" but allows a source to use a ten-year lookback period to calculate baseline emissions when determining whether an offsetting change decreases emissions. *See* 67 Fed.Reg. at 80,197. For example, to determine whether a change made in 2005 will trigger NSR, a source may use baseline emissions from 1995 and 1996 to calculate the emissions increase caused by the 2005 change; it may then choose an offsetting change made in 2000 and use baseline emissions from 1990 to 1991 to calculate the emissions decrease caused by the 2000 change in order to determine whether that decrease offsets the increase caused by the 2005 change.

Rather than challenge the five-year contemporaneity period as such, environmental petitioners contend that the ten-year lookback period combined with the five-year contemporaneity period allows a source to avoid NSR based on a fifteen-year-old decrease in emissions, thereby violating the contemporaneity requirement of *Alabama Power.* An emissions increase caused by a change made in 2005, for example, can be offset by an emissions decrease that relies on a baseline from 1990. But as EPA points out, it is only the baseline of the emissions decrease that is fifteen years old, not the change that causes the decrease, which must still occur within five years of the change that causes the increase. *Alabama Power* requires only that "any offset *changes* claimed by industry must be substantially contemporaneous," not that the baselines must be substantially contemporaneous. 636 F.2d at 402 (emphasis added). Therefore, environmental petitioners fail to demonstrate that the ten-year lookback period violates the contemporaneity requirement of *Alabama Power.*

In enacting the NSR program, Congress did not specify how to calculate "increases" in emissions, leaving EPA to fill in that gap while balancing the economic and environmental goals of the statute. Based on its experience with the NSR program and its examination of the relevant data, EPA determined that a ten-year lookback period would alleviate the problems experienced under the 1980 rule and advance the economic and environmental goals of the CAA. Because we conclude that petitioners fail to demonstrate that EPA's policy determination is impermissible, we defer to EPA's statutory interpretation under *Chevron* Step 2....

IV. METHODOLOGY AND ENFORCEABILITY

Shifting from the baseline to the other half of the actual-to-projected-actual emissions calculation, we consider government and environmental petitioners' [challenge to the "reasonable possibility" trigger for the rule's recordkeeping and reporting requirements.]

Sources making physical or operational changes under the 2002 rule need not keep records unless they meet three criteria. First, sources must choose to project post-change emissions, instead of using the actual-to-potential test. 40 C.F.R. § 52.21(r)(6)). Second, under the actual-to-projected-actual test, sources must determine they will not trigger NSR by significantly increasing their emissions. *Id.* Third, sources must nonetheless believe that there is a "reasonable possibility that [the] project . . . may result in a significant emissions increase." *Id.* Sources satisfying all three criteria must record the following information about the change:

(a) A description of the project;

(b) Identification of the emissions unit(s) whose emissions of a regulated NSR pollutant could be affected by the project; and

(c) A description of the applicability test used to determine that the project is not a major modification for any regulated NSR pollutant, including the baseline actual emissions, the projected actual emissions, the amount of emissions excluded under [the demand growth exclusion] and an explanation for why such amount was excluded, and any netting calculations, if applicable.

Id. Additionally, sources meeting the three standards must, for each unit involved in the change, track post-change emissions and, depending on the nature of the change, retain the data for five or ten years. 40 C.F.R. § 52.21(r)(6)(iii)). Significant increases as compared to the baseline must be reported to sources' reviewing authorities, 40 C.F.R. § 52.21(r)(6)(v)), who presumably would require such sources to undergo NSR.

By contrast, sources believing that no reasonable possibility of a significant emissions increase exists need keep no records at all—neither the data on which they based their projections nor records of actual emissions going forward. 40 C.F.R. § 52.21(r)(6)). Government petitioners argue that by allowing sources to decide whether to keep records relating to a particular change, EPA has rendered the actual-to-projected-actual methodology unenforceable. How, they ask, will EPA ensure that sources are not escaping NSR if they are allowed to destroy the data crucial to that determination?

Insisting that no enforceability problem exists, EPA argues that the 2002 rule *increases* recordkeeping requirements for non-utilities. Although it is technically correct that non-utilities were subject to less stringent recordkeeping requirements pre–2002, EPA's position ignores the major differences between the current and former methods. Prior to 2002, sources other than utilities evaluated post-change emissions under the more onerous actual-to-potential test, which presumed that sources would operate at their maximum post-change potential to emit. Given that assumption, sources' actual post-change emissions could not, by definition, exceed their potential-to-emit, making records of these actual emissions unnecessary for the purpose of ascertaining whether post-change emissions increased beyond expectations. Moreover, to avoid NSR, which is easily triggered under the actual-to-potential test, sources could opt to establish an enforceable emissions cap based on projected post-change actual emissions. Thus, under the pre–2002 regime, non-utilities either accepted the rigors of the actual-to-potential test, eliminating the need for recordkeeping, or subjected their actual emissions to monitoring by state permitting authorities.

The flaw in EPA's position is further underscored by comparing the recordkeeping requirements of the pre–2002 actual-to-projected-actual emissions methodology—applicable only to utilities—to the current version. Previously, utilities whose projections included no significant emissions increase had to supply permitting authorities with a minimum of five years of data to verify the projections' accuracy. Under the 2002 rule, by contrast, so long as sources foresee no "reasonable possibility" that changes may cause significant emissions increases, they have no obligation to retain the data underlying their projections, let alone send that information to permitting authorities. 40 C.F.R. § 52.21(r)(6)).

Of course, one might wonder why sources with no "reasonable possibility" of significantly increased emissions should keep records at all. If EPA actually knew which sources had no "reasonable possibility" of triggering NSR, these sources would obviously have no need to keep records. The problem is that EPA has failed to explain how, absent recordkeeping, it will be able to determine whether sources have accurately concluded that they have no "reasonable possibility" of significantly increased emissions. We recognize that less burdensome requirements may well be appropriate for sources with little likelihood of triggering NSR, but EPA needs to explain how its recordkeeping and reporting requirements allow it to identify such sources.

EPA argues that "[t]here will be many cases where there will be a reasonable possibility that a significant increase will occur, and the 2002 rule imposes new recordkeeping requirements in those circumstances." Although this is certainly true, and although it is also true that sources failing to "maintain records in that situation ... will have violated the recordkeeping requirements of the NSR Rule," EPA misses the point. As petitioners emphasize, the rule allows sources that take advantage of the "reasonable possibility" standard to avoid recordkeeping altogether, thus thwarting EPA's ability to enforce the NSR provisions.

According to EPA, "the existence of vigorous enforcement demonstrates that EPA is willing and able to enforce its rules and that facilities have an incentive to be accurate in how they determine whether NSR applies." To be sure, the record reveals a willingness to act against NSR violators, but EPA never explains how it can continue such enforcement efforts with respect to sources which, believing no reasonable possibility of a significant emissions increase exists, keep no data by which the agency could prove an NSR transgression. Acknowledging as much in its response to comments about the demand growth exclusion, EPA noted that it is "very important that the source retain a record of all information available to support its initial claim" to an exclusion because "[t]his information may be required by the reviewing authority."

At oral argument, EPA counsel asserted that under the reasonable possibility standard, enforcement authorities could conduct inspections and request information. Although conceding that nothing in the record addressed how authorities could access data through these mechanisms once a source had failed to keep records, counsel maintained that the methodology is enforceable simply because such actions are "inherent" in EPA's enforcement authority. EPA certainly has such inherent enforcement authority, but even inherent authority depends on evidence.

Because EPA has failed to explain how it can ensure NSR compliance without the relevant data, we will remand for it either to provide an acceptable explanation for its "reasonable possibility" standard or to devise an appropriately supported alternative.

NEW YORK v. ENVIRONMENTAL PROTECTION AGENCY

United States Court of Appeals, District of Columbia Circuit, 2006.
443 F.3d 880.

ROGERS, Circuit Judge.

In *New York v. EPA*, 413 F.3d 3 (D.C.Cir.2005) (*"New York I"*), the court addressed the first of two rules promulgated by [EPA] providing ways for stationary sources of air pollution to avoid triggering [NSR]. The court upheld in part and vacated in part the first rule. We now address the second rule, the Equipment Replacement Provision ("ERP"), which amends the Routine Maintenance, Repair, and Replacement Exclusion ("RMRR") from NSR requirements. Under section 111(a)(4) of the [CAA], sources that undergo "any physical change" that increases emissions are required to undergo the NSR permitting process. The exclusion has historically provided that routine maintenance, repair, and replacement do not constitute changes triggering NSR. The ERP both defined and expanded that exclusion. EPA explained:

> [The] rule states categorically that the replacement of components with identical or functionally equivalent components that do not exceed 20% of the replacement value of the process unit and does not change its basic design parameters is not a change and is within the RMRR exclusion.

68 Fed.Reg. 61,248, 61,270 (Oct. 27, 2003). Hence, the ERP would allow sources to avoid NSR when replacing equipment under the twenty-percent cap notwithstanding a resulting increase in emissions. The court stayed the effective date of the ERP on December 24, 2003. We now vacate the ERP because it is contrary to the plain language of section 111(a)(4) of the Act.

The [CAA] requires new and modified sources of pollution to undergo NSR, a permitting process that imposes specific pollution control requirements depending upon the geographic location of the source. Section 111(a)(4) of the Act describes when a source is to be considered "modified":

> The term "modification" means *any physical change* in, or change in the method of operation of, a stationary source which increases the amount of any air pollutant emitted by such source or which results in the emission of any air pollutant not previously emitted. (Emphasis added).

Since the inception of NSR, RMRR has been excluded from the definition of "modification." Heretofore, EPA applied the RMRR exclusion through "a case-by-case determination by weighing the nature, extent, purpose, frequency, and cost of the work as well as other factors to arrive at a common sense finding." 67 Fed.Reg. 80,290, 80,292–93 (Dec. 31, 2002). Consistent with *Alabama Power Co. v. Costle*, 636 F.2d 323 (D.C.Cir.

1979), which recognized EPA's discretion to exempt from NSR "some emission increases on grounds of *de minimis* or administrative necessity," *id.* at 400, EPA has for over two decades defined the RMRR exclusion as limited to "*de minimis* circumstances." 68 Fed.Reg. at 61,272. The ERP provides a bright-line rule and expands the traditional scope of the RMRR by exempting certain equipment replacements from NSR. *See, e.g.,* 40 C.F.R. § 52.21(cc)(2005).[29]

The government and environmental petitioners contend that the ERP is contrary to the plain text of the Act because the statutory definition of "modification" applies unambiguously to any physical change that increases emissions, necessarily including the emission-increasing equipment replacements excused from NSR by the rule. They maintain that the word "any," when given its natural meaning, requires that the phrase "physical change" be read broadly, such that EPA's attempt to read "physical change" narrowly would relegate the word "any" to an insignificant role.

In evaluating the petitioners' contention, we proceed under the familiar two-part test of *Chevron,* 467 U.S. 837 (1984). If "Congress has directly spoken to the precise question at issue . . . that is the end of the matter; for the court, as well as the agency, must give effect to the unambiguously expressed intent of Congress." *Id.* at 842–43. Only if the statute is silent or ambiguous do we defer to the agency's interpretation, asking "whether [it] is based on a permissible construction of the statute." *Id.* at 843. "If a court, employing traditional tools of statutory construction, ascertains that Congress had an intention on the precise question at issue, that intention is the law and must be given effect." *Id.* at 843 n. 9.

The petitioners and EPA agree that the phrase "physical change" is susceptible to multiple meanings, each citing dictionary definitions. However, "the sort of ambiguity giving rise to *Chevron* deference is a creature not of definitional possibilities, but of statutory context." [Citation omitted]. As the parties point out, the ordinary meaning of "physical change" includes activities that "make different in some particular," "make over to a radically different form," or "replace with another or others of the same kind or class." WEBSTER'S THIRD NEW INTERNATIONAL DICTIONARY 373 (1981).... The parties agree that in "[r]eal-world, common-sense usage," "physical change" includes equipment replacements. They further agree that the ERP would excuse from

---

29. The ERP provides:

Without regard to other considerations, routine maintenance, repair and replacement includes, but is not limited to, the replacement of any component of a process unit with an identical or functionally equivalent component(s), and maintenance and repair activities that are part of the replacement activity, provided that all of the requirements in paragraphs (cc)(1) through (cc)(3)of this section are met. 40 C.F.R.

§ 52.21(cc). Paragraph (cc)(1) establishes that the fixed capital cost of the replacement component cannot exceed twenty percent of the replacement value of the process unit. Paragraph (cc)(2) states that the replacement cannot change the basic design parameters of the process unit. Paragraph (cc)(3) requires that the replacement activity not cause the process unit to exceed any independent, legally enforceable emission limitation....

NSR requirements certain emission-increasing activities that EPA has historically considered to be "physical changes."

The parties' essential disagreement, then, centers on the effect of Congress's decision in defining "modification" to insert the word "any" before "physical change." According to the petitioners, the word "any" means that the phrase "physical change" covers any activity at a source that could be considered a physical change that increases emissions. According to EPA, "any" does nothing to resolve ambiguity in the phrase it modifies. EPA maintains that because "physical change" is "susceptible to multiple meanings," [68 Fed. Reg.] at 61,271, "identifying activities that are 'changes' for NSR purposes ... requires an exercise of Agency expertise," "the classic situation in which an agency is accorded deference under *Chevron*," *id.* at 61,272. Under this approach, once EPA has identified an activity as a "physical change," the word "any" requires that the activity be subject to NSR. We conclude that the differences between the parties' interpretations of the role of the word "any" are resolved by recognizing that "[r]ead naturally, the word 'any' has an expansive meaning, that is, 'one or some indiscriminately of whatever kind,'" *United States v. Gonzales,* 520 U.S. 1, 5 (1997), and that courts must give effect to each word of a statute. Because Congress used the word "any," EPA must apply NSR whenever a source conducts an emission-increasing activity that fits within one of the ordinary meanings of "physical change."

In a series of cases, the Supreme Court has drawn upon the word "any" to give the word it modifies an "expansive meaning" when there is "no reason to contravene the clause's obvious meaning." [Citation omitted]. Indeed, the Court has read the word "any" to signal expansive reach when construing the Clean Air Act. In *Harrison v. PPG Industries, Inc.,* 446 U.S. 578 (1980), the Court resolved a jurisdictional dispute under section 307(b)(1) by interpreting the phrase "any other final action," which the Court "discern[ed to have] no uncertainty." *Id.* at 588. The Court never suggested that the term "final action" was itself devoid of multiple meanings depending on the context, but rather stated that when Congress amended the Act in 1977, "it expanded its ambit to include not simply 'other final action,' but rather '*any* other final action.'" *Id.* at 589. "[I]n the absence of legislative history to the contrary," the Court held that the statutory phrase "must be construed to mean exactly what it says, namely, *any other* final action." *Id.*

Although EPA is correct that the meaning of "any" can differ depending upon the statutory setting, *see Nixon v. Missouri Mun. League,* 541 U.S. 125, 132 (2004), the context of the Clean Air Act warrants no departure from the word's customary effect. Unlike *Nixon,* the question of statutory interpretation here does not arise in a setting in which the Supreme Court has required heightened standards of clarity to avoid upsetting fundamental policies. EPA points to no "strange and indeterminate results" that would emerge from adopting the natural meaning of "any" in section 111(a)(4) of the Act. Given Congress's goal in adopting the 1977 amendments of establishing a balance between economic and environmental interests, it is hardly "farfetched," *Nixon,* 541 U.S. at 138, for Congress to have intended NSR to apply to any type of physical change that increases emissions. In this context, there is no reason the usual tools of statutory construction should not apply and hence no reason why "any" should not mean "any." Indeed, EPA's interpretation would produce a "strange," if not an "indeterminate," result: a law intended to limit increases in air pollution would allow sources operating below applicable emission limits to increase significantly the pollution they emit without government review.

Even without specific reliance on the effect of "any," this court has construed the definition of "modification" broadly. In *Alabama Power,* the court explained that "the term 'modification' [in section 111(a)(4)] is nowhere limited to physical changes exceeding a certain magnitude." 636 F.2d at 400. Although the legislative history indicated that one Senator intended the term to apply only to "major expansion program[s]," *id.* at 400 n. 47, the court observed that "the language of the statute clearly did not enact such limit into law," *id.* at 400. The court further observed that "[i]mplementation of the statute's definition of 'modification' will undoubtedly prove inconvenient and costly to affected industries; but the clear language of the statute unavoidably imposes these costs except for *de minimis* increases." *Id .* ... Likewise, the Seventh Circuit concluded in *WEPCo* that the purposes of the 1977 amendments to the Act required an expansive reading of the plain language of section 111(a)(4). [*See Wisconsin Elec. Power Co. v. Reilly,* 893 F.2d 901, 908–10 (7th Cir. 1990)].

... EPA's approach to interpreting "physical change" ... contravenes several rules of statutory interpretation. EPA's position is that the word "any" does not affect the expansiveness of the phrase "physical change"; it only means that, once the agency defines "change" as broadly or as narrowly as it deems appropriate, everything in the agency-defined category is subject to NSR. To begin, that reading, contrary to "a cardinal principle of statutory construction," would make Congress's use of the word "any" "insignificant" if not "superfluous." Reading the definition in this way makes the definition function as if the word "any" had been excised from section 111(a)(4); there is virtually no role for "any" to play. Additionally, the approaches of EPA and industry would require Congress to spell out all the applications covered by a definition before a court could conclude that Congress had directly spoken regarding a particular application, ignoring the fact that a definition, like a general rule, need not list everything it covers. EPA's approach would ostensibly require that the definition of "modification" include a phrase such as "regardless of size, cost, frequency, effect," or other distinguishing characteristic. Only in a Humpty Dumpty world would Congress be required to use superfluous words while an agency could ignore an expansive word that Congress did use. We decline to adopt such a worldview.

In contrast, the petitioners' approach, by adopting an expansive reading of the phrase "any physical change," gives natural effect to all the words used by Congress and reflects both their common meanings and Congress's purpose in enacting the 1970 and 1977 amendments. To improve pollution control programs in a manner consistent with the balance struck by Congress in 1977 between "the economic interest in permitting capital improvements to continue and the environmental interest in improving air quality," *Chevron,* 467 U.S. at 851, Congress defined the phrase "physical change" in terms of increases in emissions. After using the word "any" to indicate that "physical change" covered all such activities, and was not left to agency interpretation, Congress limited the scope of "any physical change" to changes that "increase [ ] the amount of any air pollutant emitted by such source or which result [ ] in the emission of any air pollutant not previously emitted." 42 U.S.C. § 7411(a)(4). Thus, only physical changes that do not result in emission increases are excused from NSR. Because Congress expressly included one limitation, the court must presume that Congress acted "intentionally and purposely" when it did not include others. So construed, each word in the phrase "any physical change" has a meaning consonant with congressional intent and the scope of the definitional phrase is limited only by Congress's determination that such changes be linked to emission increases.

The expansiveness of the petitioners' approach does not leave the definition of "any physical change" without limits. The modifier "any" cannot bring an activity that is never considered a "physical change" in ordinary usage within the ambit of NSR. But when Congress places the word "any" before a phrase with several common meanings, the statutory phrase encompasses each of those meanings; the agency may not pick and choose among them. EPA, through its historical practice and its words, has acknowledged that the equipment replacements covered by the ERP are "physical changes" under one of the ordinary meanings of the phrase. EPA may not choose to exclude that "[r]eal-world, common-sense usage of the word 'change.'" [68 Fed.Reg.] at 61,271. Moreover, a physical change is not the sole criterion for triggering NSR under the definition of "modification." The expansive meaning of "any physical change" is strictly limited by the requirement that the change increase emissions. *See* 42 U.S.C. § 7411(a)(4).

The fact that EPA, through the RMRR exclusion, has historically interpreted "any physical change" to exclude changes of trivial regulatory concern on a *de minimis* rationale, *see Alabama Power,* 636 F.2d at 360–61, does not demonstrate that the meaning of "physical change" is ambiguous. Rather, it reflects an agency's inherent power to overlook "trifling matters," *id.* at 360, a "principle [that] is a cousin of the doctrine that, notwithstanding the 'plain meaning' of a statute, a court must look beyond the words to the purpose of the act where its literal terms lead to 'absurd or futile results,' " *id.* at 360 n. 89 (citations omitted). As the Supreme Court has instructed, "the venerable maxim *de minimis non curat lex* ('the law cares not for trifles') is part of the established background of legal principles against which all enactments are adopted, and which all enactments (absent contrary indication) are deemed to accept." [Citation omitted]. Reliance on the *de minimis* doctrine invokes congressional intent that agencies diverge from the plain meaning of a statute only so far as is necessary to avoid its futile application. Thus, the court in *Alabama Power* acknowledged that "EPA does have discretion, in administering the statute's 'modification' provision, to exempt from PSD review some emission increases on grounds of *de minimis* or administrative necessity." 636 F.2d at 400. As applied, the court explained that *de minimis* standards served to alleviate "severe" administrative and economic burdens by lifting requirements on "minuscule" emission increases. *See id.* at 405. While the court today expresses no opinion regarding EPA's application of the *de minimis* exception, given the limits on the scope of the *de minimis* doctrine, EPA appropriately has not attempted to justify the ERP as an exercise of *de minimis* discretion. As EPA has disclaimed the assertion that its prior expansive interpretations of "any physical change" were "absurd or futile," it is in no position to claim that the ERP is necessary to avoid absurdity.

"Therefore, for EPA to avoid a literal interpretation at *Chevron* step one, it must show either that, as a matter of historical fact, Congress did not mean what it appears to have said, or that, as a matter of logic and statutory structure, it almost surely could not have meant it." *Engine Mfrs. Ass'n v. EPA*, 88 F.3d 1075, 1089 (D.C.Cir.1996). The discussion in *New York I* and *WEPCo* of Congress's basic goals in enacting the 1977 amendments—to intensify the war against air pollution, to establish a permit program that struck a balance between economic and environmental interests, and to stimulate technology to control pollution— demonstrate the futility of EPA's endeavor. EPA cannot show that historical fact prevents a broad reading of "any physical change" inasmuch as EPA for decades has interpreted that phrase to mean "virtually all changes, even trivial ones, ... generally interpret[ing] the [RMRR] exclusion as being limited to *de minimis* circumstances." 68 Fed.Reg. at 61,272.

As for logic, EPA cannot show any incoherence in Congress requiring NSR for equipment replacements that increase emissions while allowing replacements that do not increase emissions to avoid NSR. EPA acknowledges the reasonableness of its past expansive interpretation of "any physical change." ... Absent a showing that the policy demanded by the text borders on the irrational, EPA may not "avoid the Congressional intent clearly expressed in the text simply by asserting that its preferred approach would be better policy." *Engine Mfrs.*, 88 F.3d at 1089.

Likewise, EPA offers no reason to conclude that the structure of the Act supports the conclusion that "any physical change" does not mean what it says. EPA does not address the Act's structure except in defending the reasonableness of the ERP as a policy choice. In that context, EPA points to the Act's "many other systematic air programs," particularly "model market-based programs," as support for its view that economic and environmental interests can be effectively balanced while limiting the application of NSR to existing sources. Although EPA might prefer market-based methods of controlling pollution, Congress has chosen a different course with NSR.

Accordingly, we hold that the ERP violates section 111(a)(4) of the [CAA] in two respects. First, Congress's use of the word "any" in defining a "modification" means that all types of "physical changes" are covered. Although the phrase "physical change" is susceptible to multiple meanings, the word "any" makes clear that activities within each of the common meanings of the phrase are subject to NSR when the activity results in an emission increase. As Congress limited the broad meaning of "any physical change," directing that only changes that increase emissions will trigger NSR, no other limitation (other than to avoid absurd results) can be implied. The definition of "modification," therefore, does not include only physical changes that are costly or major. Second, Congress defined "modification" in terms of emission increases, but the ERP would allow equipment replacements resulting in non-*de minimis* emission increases to avoid NSR. Therefore, because it violates the Act, we vacate the ERP.

Notes and Comments

1. On their face, the statutory provisions relating to both NNSR and PSD appear to contemplate that the permitting requirements will apply to any modification of a major source. See §§ 172(c)(5) and 171(4) (NNSR), and 165(a) and 169(c) (PSD). As mentioned in *New York II* (and also in Chapter 3, *supra*), however, in *Alabama Power* the D.C. Circuit determined that EPA had the discretion to exempt *de minimis* increases from NSR review. EPA has relied on this authority to create, inter alia, volumetric thresholds for what constitutes a "major modification" triggering NSR review, see 40 C.F.R. §§ 51.165(a)(1)(v)(A) and (x)(A) (NNSR) and 52.21(b)(2)(i) and (23)(i) (PSD). If a modification does not qualify as "major" under these regulations, it is deemed to be *de minimis* and does not trigger NSR review. EPA has set identical thresholds for the pollutants that are covered under both programs. These thresholds are as follows:

Carbon monoxide: 100 tons per year (tpy)

Nitrogen oxides: 40 tpy

Sulfur dioxide: 40 tpy

Particulate matter:

    25 tpy of particulate matter emissions;

    15 tpy of PM_{10} emissions

Ozone: 40 tpy of volatile organic compounds or NO_x

Lead: 0.6 tpy

These thresholds were not challenged when promulgated. Note that, in *New York II*, the D.C. Circuit said it was expressing no opinion about them. Do you understand why the petitioners did not challenge them in that case? See 42 U.S.C. § 7607(b).

2.　As mentioned in *New York I*, in determining whether there is a "significant net emissions increase," and therefore a "major modification," EPA has moved to an approach that gives many sources the option of comparing their actual baseline emissions to their projected-actual future emissions. See, e.g., 40 C.F.R. § 52.21(a)(2)(iv)(c) (PSD). At one point, the *New York I* court characterizes Industry's main argument as being that EPA is required to use a "potential-to-potential" test rather than an "actual-to-projected-actual" test. We have edited out a portion of the decision where the court deemed unripe one aspect of Industry's attack on EPA's focus on actual versus potential past emissions, but the court deals with essentially the same argument in dealing with Newmont's challenge. Do you understand why Industry would prefer to focus on potential (or "allowable") past emissions, even if it meant that the comparison would be with potential future emissions? Do you agree with the policy choice EPA made in focusing on actual past emissions?

3.　Do you agree with EPA's decision to focus on tons per year, rather than hourly emission rates, in the NSR context? Do you agree with the court's conclusion that Congress did not codify EPA's regulatory definition of "modification" in 40 C.F.R. § 60.14(a) for NSR purposes when it referenced § 111(a) in both §§ 169(2)(C) (PSD) and 171(4) (NNSR)? As this book went to press, the Supreme Court addressed this issue in *Environmental Defense v. Duke Energy Corp.*, ___ U.S. ___, 127 S.Ct. 1423, ___ L.Ed.2d ___ (2007). The Court unanimously agreed with the D.C. Circuit that EPA's regulations contemplate an approach based on annual emission rates. *Id.* at 1434–1436. Interestingly, it declined to address whether any challenge as to whether this approach comports with the statute is time-barred under § 307(b) of the Act. *Id.* at 1346.

4.　Are you convinced by the *New York I* court's "lookback" analysis? Do you agree with the policy decisions that EPA made? Do you understand how ten-year lookback period works together with the five-year contemporaneity dynamics?

5.　As mentioned in *New York I*, EPA originally followed an actual-to-potential approach in its netting analysis under the 1980 regulations. In a portion of the *WEPCo* decision that we did not read, the Seventh Circuit rejected this approach for utilities, indicating that EPA should apply an actual-to-projected-actual approach. EPA acquiesced in this reading, revising its rules for utilities in 1992, while leaving in place the actual-to-potential approach for all other sources. Even in the actual-to-potential context, however, EPA had taken controls into account in determining a source's potential to emit (based upon a mandate from the D.C. Circuit in *Alabama Power*), so long as those controls were federally enforceable. See, EPA, Emissions Trading Policy Statement, 51 Fed. Reg. 43814, 43832 (1986). How does that approach differ from what EPA did with respect to enforceability in the 2002 rule? Do you agree with how the D.C. Circuit responded in *New York I*? In your view, does the projected-actual approach square with the potential-to-emit language in both §§ 169(1) and 302(j)? What options does EPA have in responding to *New York I*?

6.　Despite the fact that it is now somewhat outdated, the Emissions Trading Policy Statement (referred to in the prior note) is an outstanding source for learning about how EPA addresses netting, bubbling, offsetting (see below), and other related issues.

7. Do you agree with the court's analysis in *New York II*? Where does the court's decision leave both the regulated community and EPA?

2. Substantive Requirements

a. Nonattainment New Source Review

Assuming the NNSR threshold is triggered, § 173(a) requires a source to meet five requirements in order to receive the desired permit, the first two of which are much more important than the others. First, it must obtain offsetting emission reductions from other sources either in the same air quality control region or, under limited circumstances, in one that is nearby. 42 U.S.C. § 7503(a)(1) and (c). Second, the facility must meet the lowest achievable emission rate (LAER). 42 U.S.C. § 7503(a)(2). Third, it must demonstrate that any other major sources it operates in the State are in compliance with the relevant CAA requirements. 42 U.S.C. § 7503(a)(3). Fourth, EPA cannot have determined that the State is not adequately implementing its SIP for the relevant area. 42 U.S.C. § 7503(a)(4). And fifth, the permit issuer must determine that "benefits of the proposed source significantly outweigh the environmental and social costs" it would impose. 42 U.S.C. § 7503(a)(5).

Section 171(3) defines LAER as either:

(A) the most stringent emission limitation which is contained in the implementation plan of any State for such class or category of source, unless the owner or operator of the proposed source demonstrates that such limitations are not achievable, or

(B) the most stringent emission limitation which is achieved in practice by such class or category of source, whichever is more stringent.

The two most notable things about LAER, as compared to the other technology-based standards we have looked at thus far, are that (1) it is set on a case-by-case basis in the permit issuance process, as opposed to through a national rulemaking; and (2) affordability for the industry as a whole plays no role in its determination; if any source in the industry has achieved a given level of performance, LAER must be set at least at that level. The first point is noteworthy because it ensures that, if applied appropriately, LAER will be up-to-date in ways that other technology-based standards seldom are.

b. Prevention of Significant Deterioration

In the PSD context, § 165(a) imposes two main requirements. First, each source subject to this program must implement the best available control technology (BACT). 42 U.S.C. § 7475(a)(4). And second, it must demonstrate that its emissions will neither cause nor contribute to the violation of any "increment" under the PSD program. 42 U.S.C. § 7475(a)(3).

BACT is defined as "an emission limitation based on the maximum degree of [pollutant] reduction ... which the [state] permitting authority, on a case-by-case basis, taking into account energy, environmental, and economic impacts and other costs, determines is achievable for [the] facility." 42 U.S.C. § 7479(3). BACT is like LAER in that it is set on a case-by-case basis through the permit issuance process. Unlike in the context of LAER, here the permit issuer is to take cost into account. In 1989, EPA issued what it called its "top-down policy" indicating that permit issuers are to start with the assumption that BACT is equal to the very most aggressive known option (presumably LAER), and justify any reduction from that in light of the statutory factors. The extent to which EPA currently requires rigid adherence to this policy is unclear.

The increment idea addresses the same concern as the antidegradation policy under the CWA; that is, how do we prevent pristine areas from getting dirtier? Here there was a very real concern that the areas with the cleanest air would be adversely affected as industrial sources chose to move from already degraded industrial areas to pristine ones. To address this concern, the PSD program divides air quality control areas in attainment for each criteria pollutant into three classes. The class designation then determines how much additional pollution can ever be added to the ambient air in those air quality control regions. Class I areas are those that Congress concluded have, or should have, the most pristine air quality. These include all international parks and the larger national parks, national monuments and wilderness areas. 42 U.S.C. § 7472. All other attainment (or unclassifiable) areas were to originally be classified as Class II areas. 42 U.S.C. § 7472. This is done on a pollutant-by-pollutant basis, an area may be in attainment (and Class II) for one or more of the criteria pollutants but be in nonattainment for others. States may petition to reclassify Class II areas as Class III, which allows a greater increment of pollution. In no case can the national ambient air quality standard be exceeded for any criteria pollutant for which an area is already in attainment.

The increments allowed in each class under the PSD program are set out in the statute for sulfur dioxide and for particulates, and are created by regulation for the other criteria pollutants. See 42 U.S.C. § 7473. The increments for each class area for sulfur dioxide and particulates are as follows:

Class I

Pollutant	Max. allowable increase (mg/cubic meter)
Particulate Matter:	
Annual geometric mean	5
Twenty-four-hour maximum	10
Sulfur Dioxide:	
Annual arithmetic mean	2

Twenty-four-hour maximum	5
Three-hour maximum	25

Class II

Pollutant	Max. allowable increase (mg/cubic meter)
Particulate Matter:	
Annual geometric mean	19
Twenty-four-hour maximum	37
Sulfur Dioxide:	
Annual arithmetic mean	20
Twenty-four-hour maximum	91
Three-hour maximum	512

Class III

Pollutant	Max. allowable increase (mg/cubic meter)
Particulate Matter:	
Annual Geometric mean	37
Twenty-four-hour maximum	75
Sulfur Dioxide:	
Annual arithmetic mean	40
Twenty-four-hour maximum	182
Three-hour maximum	700

Notes and Comments

1. In the NNSR context, the State typically retains some discretion regarding the extent to which the offset requirement will be greater than 1 to 1. Most commonly, the States insist on a ratio of something like 1.1 to 1, or 1.2 to 1, which, in the latter context, for example would mean that the new source would pay someone else to reduce their emissions by 1.2 times the amount which the new source will add. Thus, the States not only are able to ensure that the new sources will not make the area's nonattainment problem worse, they can use them and the reductions they generate as part of a strategy of making "reasonable further progress" toward bringing the area back into attainment. See 42 U.S.C. § 7502(c)(2). As previously mentioned, the 1990 amendments impose mandatory offset ratios in some circumstances, in some instances as high as 1.5 to 1 (for extreme areas). See 42 U.S.C. § 7511a(e)(1).

2. There is no pre-set price for the required offsets. The free market controls. The sources of offsets may include one's competitors, other industries, or more creative possibilities such as old car buy-back programs. EPA does require that they be surplus (i.e., reductions not required by current law), enforceable, permanent, and quantifiable. See Emissions Trading Policy Statement, 51 Fed. Reg. at 83831–32. How would the negotiation dynamics be skewed if one were in the position of having to procure an offset from a competitor?

3. As you can see, the PSD cap means that the total amount of additional pollution ever allowed is limited. Who gets to allocate the limited amount of deterioration that is allowed under the increment system? Is the cap going to be stringently observed? How should we address the effect of pollution sources that don't undergo PSD review because they fall under the 100 ton or 250 ton thresholds? Could they use up the increment? Section 165(e)(2) contemplates that the PSD analysis is to include "continuous air quality monitoring data gathered [to determine the status of the relevant increments]." The States, however, have been lax about performing this monitoring, preferring (for budgetary reasons) to impose any required monitoring costs on permit applicants in the context of particular applications. In practice, this may result in either shoddy analysis or significant delay.

4. Does the increment system encourage major stationary sources to stake a claim for the increments as soon as possible? What happens if the required monitoring show that the increment in nearly exceeded, or if it is exceeded but the NAAQS is not? Should new sources be able to buy offsets from older sources?

D. National Emission Standards for Hazardous Air Pollutants

Although the criteria pollutants have received the most attention under the CAA, from the outset Congress also spread a wider regulatory net for toxic substances, here typically referred to as "hazardous air pollutants" (or "HAPs"). Here, as under the CWA, the original approach was health-based. Also as under the CWA, EPA found this scheme difficult to administer. See, e.g., *Natural Resource Defense Council v. U.S. EPA*, 824 F.2d 1146 (D.C.Cir. 1987). Indeed, by the late 1980s, EPA had moved forward with standards for only eight air toxics (asbestos, benzene, beryllium, coke oven emissions, inorganic arsenic, mercury, radionuclide, and vinyl chloride), and many of these regulatory efforts were prompted by litigation.

In 1989, EPA promulgated a new framework for establishing standards based upon a risk-based approach. 54 Fed Reg 38,044 (1989). Despite this effort, however, Congress weighed in aggressively in the 1990 CAA amendments, imposing a technology-based regime with both strict requirements and short timelines for compliance.

Consider the following decision:

NATIONAL MINING ASS'N v. UNITED STATES ENVIRONMENTAL PROTECTION AGENCY

United States Court of Appeals, District of Columbia Circuit, 1995.
59 F.3d 1351.

Before: SILBERMAN, GINSBURG, and RANDOLPH, Circuit Judges

PER CURIAM:

This is a petition for review of an order of [EPA] implementing the 1990 amendments to § 112 of the [CAA]. Petitioners are General Electric Company and four trade associations . . .

In 1990, as part of its comprehensive overhaul of the [CAA], Congress revised § 112 of the Act, which regulates emissions of hazardous air pollutants. Dissatisfied with EPA's health-based regulation of hazardous air pollutants under the 1970 program, Congress replaced this approach with a detailed, technology-based regulatory scheme. The 1990 amendments to § 112 establish an initial list, which EPA may periodically revise, of 189 hazardous air pollutants. 42 U.S.C. § 7412(b)(1)-(3). EPA must publish a list of "categories and subcategories" of "major sources" and certain "area sources" that emit these pollutants. 42 U.S.C. § 7412(c). For each listed "category or subcategory of major sources and area sources" of hazardous air pollutants, § 112(d) of the Act directs EPA to promulgate emission standards.

Under the Act, "major sources" of hazardous air pollutants are potentially subject to stricter regulatory control than are "area sources." For example, major sources must comply with technology-based emission standards requiring the maximum degree of reduction in emissions EPA deems achievable, often referred to as "maximum achievable control technology" or MACT standards. 42 U.S.C. § 7412(d)(1)-(2) . . . . .

[In 1994, EPA promulgated a rule establishing how it would implement these new requirements. 59 Fed.Reg. 12,408 (1994).]

Among other things, the general provisions rule implements § 112(a)(1)'s definition of "major source." The rule defines "major source" in terms nearly identical to those in § 112(a)(1):

> Major source means any stationary source or group of stationary sources located within a contiguous area and under common control that emits or has the potential to emit considering controls, in the aggregate, 10 tons per year or more of any hazardous air pollutant or 25 tons per year or more of any combination of hazardous air pollutants, unless the Administrator establishes a lesser quantity, or in the case of radionuclides, different criteria from those specified in this sentence.

40 C.F.R. § 63.2. A "stationary source" is "any building, structure, facility or installation which emits or may emit any air pollutant." Id. An "area source [is] any stationary source . . . that is not a major source." Id. . . .

Petitioners challenge three aspects of EPA's implementation of the definition of "major source." First, National Mining Association and American Forest and Paper Association (collectively referred to as [NMA]) and General Electric question EPA's requiring the aggregation of all hazardous air emissions within a plant site—instead of only those emissions from equipment in similar industrial categories—in a § 112 major source determination. Second, [NMA] challenges EPA's requiring the inclusion of "fugitive emissions" in a source's aggregate emissions in determining whether the source is major. Third, Chemical Manufacturers Association and American Petroleum Institute (collectively referred to as [CMA]) contend that EPA overstepped its regulatory authority by permitting a source to reduce its "potential to emit" only with "federally enforceable" emission controls and limitations.

A

General Electric and [NMA] have similar arguments against the final rule's implementation of § 112(a)(1). Both maintain that EPA may not, in determining whether a site is a major source, include emissions from all facilities on a contiguous plant site under common control. These petitioners assert that, for purposes of major source determinations, EPA may aggregate emissions from different facilities on a contiguous plant site under common control only when the facilities fall within a similar industrial classification. General Electric says EPA must aggregate emissions on a "source category" basis; [NMA] contends that EPA may combine emissions only if the emitting facilities fall within the same two-digit Standard Industrial Classification (SIC) Code.

In the preamble to the final rule, EPA made clear that in determining whether a source is major, emissions from all sources of hazardous air pollutants within a plant site must be aggregated, so long as the sources are geographically adjacent and under common control. 59 Fed.Reg. at 12,412. As a result, if the total annual emissions of hazardous air pollutants from a plant site exceed the designated thresholds, each source emitting pollutants at the site must comply with the stricter MACT emission standards applicable to sources under § 112(d)(2), and with other requirements applicable to major sources.

Petitioners read § 112(a)(1) more restrictively. In their view, EPA's approach will impermissibly regulate "minor facilities" that happen to be located at an industrial site with annual emissions of hazardous air pollutants that, in the aggregate, exceed the major source thresholds. They contend that EPA may require aggregation of emissions from sources only if those sources fall within a single source category— General Electric's argument, or the same two-digit SIC Code–[NMA's] contention. It follows, according to petitioners, that a source must comply with regulatory requirements applicable to major sources only if it belongs to some group of sources at an industrial site emitting, in the aggregate, more than the major source threshold. Under petitioners' theories, it is possible that only some of a site's sources would have to comply with the regulatory requirements applicable to major sources, including the stricter emission limitations of § 112(d)(2). Other sources of hazardous air pollutants would be regulated as area sources, possibly subject to less stringent emission standards or to none at all. 42 U.S.C. § 7412(c)(5).

EPA rejected petitioners' methods of implementing "major source." With respect to General Electric's source category definition, EPA acknowledged that "[m]ore than one source category on the EPA's source category list may be represented within a plant that is a major source" of hazardous air pollutants, as is the case for a large chemical manufacturing complex. 59 Fed.Reg. at 12,411. Congress intended, according to

EPA, "that all portions of a major source be subject to MACT [emission standards] regardless of the number of source categories into which the facility is divided." 59 Fed.Reg. at 12,411. "Thus, the EPA will set one or more MACT standards for a major source, and sources within that major source will be covered by the standard(s), regardless of whether, when standing alone, each one of those regulated sources would be major." Id. EPA also rejected the SIC Code approach to implementing "major source," advanced here by [NMA]. Because § 112(a)(1) does not refer to SIC Codes, EPA reasoned that Congress intended major sources of hazardous air pollutants to "encompass entire contiguous . . . plant sites without being subdivided according to industrial classifications." 59 Fed.Reg. at 12,412. A separation of emission sources by SIC Codes "would be an artificial division of sources that, in reality, all contribute to public exposure around a plant site." Id.

If § 112(a)(1) is viewed in isolation, EPA's reading of the provision is not simply consistent with the provision; it is nearly compelled by the statutory language. Section 112(a)(1) states that a "group of stationary sources" need meet only three conditions to be termed a "major source": (1) sources within the group must be "located within a contiguous area"; (2) they must be "under common control"; and (3) in the aggregate, they must emit or, considering controls, have the potential to emit 10 or more tons per year of a single hazardous air pollutant or 25 or more tons per year of any combination of hazardous air pollutants. Section 112(a)(1) says nothing about combining emissions only from sources within the same source categories or SIC Codes. In this respect, EPA's definition of "major source," set forth in the preamble to the final rule, is faithful to the language of § 112(a)(1).

Petitioners ask us to look beyond the language of § 112(a)(1). In the first of several loosely connected arguments, General Electric recites fragments from § 112's other provisions, including: (1) § 112(c)(1), which directs EPA to publish "a list of all categories and subcategories of major sources and area sources"; (2) § 112(d)(1), which directs EPA to establish emission standards "for each category or subcategory of major sources and area sources"; and (3) § 112(j)(2), which describes what an operator of a "major source in [a] category" must do if EPA does not promulgate an emission standard for that "category of major sources." From these portions of § 112, General Electric leaps to the conclusion that "major source must be defined 'with reference to' (and cannot be broader than) the source category defined by EPA for § 112 regulation."

General Electric's logic is hard to grasp. Rather than supporting General Electric, the provisions the company invokes, read in full and in context, tend to support EPA's implementation of "major source" without reference to source categories. Section 112 directs EPA to perform certain tasks on a category-wide basis—it is to identify categories of major and area sources of hazardous air pollutants (§ 112(c)(1)), and it must promulgate category-wide emission standards for these sources (§ 112(d)(2)). It by no means follows that because the statute in several provisions uses the terms "major source" and "category" in the same sentence—which is all General Electric's argument amounts to—EPA must read a source category restriction into § 112(a)(1)'s definition of "major source." Nor does § 112(c) somehow prohibit EPA from applying § 112(d)'s MACT emission limitations "to minor sources in a listed category of major sources without complying with the statutory requirements for listing area sources." See Brief for General Electric at 18. Section 112(c) simply requires the listing of all major sources and those area sources presenting adverse health or environmental effects. Neither § 112(c) nor § 112(d) says anything about EPA's including "minor sources" in a "listed category of major sources."

B

[NMA] also thinks EPA erred in deciding to count "fugitive emissions" of hazardous air pollutants in determining whether a "source" is a "major source," without first conducting a rulemaking pursuant to § 302(j). "Fugitive emissions" are defined in the final rule as:

> those emissions from a stationary source that could not reasonably pass through a stack, chimney, vent or other functionally equivalent opening. Under section 112 of the Act, all fugitive emissions are to be considered in determining whether a stationary source is a major source.

59 Fed.Reg. at 12,433 (to be codified at 40 C.F.R. § 63.2).

Section 302(j) of the Act, as interpreted in *Alabama Power v. Costle*, [636 F.2d 323, 369–70 (D.C.Cir. 1979)], requires EPA to conduct a separate rulemaking to achieve this result, so [NMA] contends. This provision states that, "[e]xcept as otherwise expressly provided," a "major stationary source" or "major emitting facility" is any stationary source of air pollutants that "directly emits, or has the potential to emit" at least 100 tons per year of any air pollutant, including "any major ... source of fugitive emissions ... as determined by rule by the Administrator." *Alabama Power* held that EPA could not, without rulemaking, include fugitive emissions of air pollutants in a facility's aggregate emissions for purposes of determining whether the facility was a "major emitting facility" within § 169(1). 636 F.2d at 368–70. For the [PSD], § 169(1) defines "major emitting facility" as any of 28 categories of sources that emit 100 or more tons per year of any air pollutant. For "any other source," the threshold is 250 or more tons per year. Id. Although § 169(1) did "expressly make a substantial modification in the 302(j) definition of 'major,'" it had "no 'express' provision modifying section 302(j)'s 'rule' requirement as to fugitive emissions." *Alabama Power*, 636 F.2d at 370. "Therefore under section 169(1) controlled in this respect by section 302(j), the calculation of the threshold quantity emissions may include fugitive emissions only as determined by rule by the Administrator." 636 F.2d at 370.

Finding this case indistinguishable from *Alabama Power*, [NMA] spins out the following argument: § 112(a)(1) defines "major source" in terms of a "stationary source or group of stationary sources"; a § 112 major source is thus, "by definition, a 'major stationary source,'" subject to the requirements of § 302(j); § 112(a)(1) does not expressly exempt a major source from § 302(j)'s fugitive emissions rulemaking requirement; therefore, EPA may not require a source to include fugitive emissions of hazardous air pollutants in the source's total emissions without a § 302(j) rulemaking.

[NMA's] argument is not very persuasive. *Alabama Power* was decided in the pre-*Chevron* age. Moreover, there is a notable difference between § 302(j) and § 112(a)(1). Section 302(j) speaks of sources that "directly" emit air pollutants, on the one hand, and fugitive emissions on the other, thus suggesting that emissions of the fugitive variety are not direct. By contrast, § 112(a)(1) does not contain the modifier "directly," and it does not mention fugitive emissions as a separate category of emissions. Furthermore, one cannot say that § 302(j) supplies "quantitative terms" for § 112(a)(1)'s definition of "major source," as it did for § 169(1), one of the provisions at issue in *Alabama Power*, 636 F.2d at 369. When it comes to hazardous air pollutants, the quantities—10 tons of any one kind per year or 25 tons of a combination—are specified in § 112(a)(1), not § 302(j), which has a 100–ton threshold.

While [NMA's] argument is thin, EPA's counterargument is hardly overwhelming. EPA thinks its best point is that § 112(a)(1) defines "major source" whereas § 302(j) defines "major stationary source" and "major emitting facility"; since the phrases are different so must be the meanings with respect to counting fugitive emissions. The problem with this argument is that at a critical juncture § 302(j) also uses the phrase "major source"—a "major stationary source" may include a "major . . . source of fugitive emissions" if EPA so decides in a rulemaking. And as the Association notes, other provisions of the Act unrelated to § 112 or § 302(j) refer to "major source" and "major stationary source" interchangeably. If EPA's point related to differences between major stationary sources and major mobile sources, the omission of "stationary" in § 112(a)(1) and its inclusion in § 302(j) might be significant, but that of course is not EPA's point.

EPA fares better when it tells us that title V of the Act explicitly draws a distinction between the nomenclature of § 112 and that of § 302, defining "major source" for permitting purposes as either a "major source as defined in section 7412 [§ 112]" or a "major stationary source as defined in section 7602 [§ 302] . . . or part D of subchapter I [nonattainment program]." 42 U.S.C. § 7661(2). And on EPA's side is the Senate committee report stating that the definition of "major source" in § 112 "will only apply in the context of this section and should not be confused with other meanings of the term 'major source' in parts C [PSD] or D (non-attainment) of the Act." S.REP. NO. 228, supra, at 150–51, U.S.Code Cong. & Admin.News 1990, at 3535–3536.

We conclude that EPA may require the inclusion of fugitive emissions in a site's aggregate emissions without conducting any special rulemaking, even if "major source" and "major stationary source" mean the same thing. Section 112(a)(1) expressly provides that a "major source" is any stationary source or group of stationary sources *"located within a contiguous area and under common control"* and emitting more than 10 tons per year of a single hazardous air pollutant or 25 tons per year of such pollutants combined. An emission may be fugitive, but it is still an emission from a stationary source. And so the italicized language certainly may be read as EPA reads it—that all emissions are to be counted in determining whether a source is major, subject only to the qualification that they emanate from a contiguous site under common control. So read, § 112(a)(1) satisfies § 302(j)'s "[e]xcept as otherwise expressly provided" clause such that fugitive emissions may be counted in a source's aggregate emissions without a special rulemaking.

C

As noted above, in determining whether a source is to be categorized as a "major source" of emissions (or by default an "area" source), EPA was directed by Congress to calculate the amount of hazardous air pollutants a stationary source "emits or has the potential to emit considering controls." [CAA] § 112(a)(1). In its final rule, EPA defined a source's "potential to emit" as its "maximum capacity . . . to emit a pollutant under its physical and operational design." 59 Fed.Reg. at 12,434. To comply with the statutory directive to "consider [] controls" while determining emissions capacities, the rule also provides:

> Any physical or operational limitation on the capacity of the stationary source to emit a pollutant, including air pollution control equipment and restrictions on hours of operation or on the type or amount or material combusted, stored, or processed, shall be treated as part of its design if the limitation or the effect it would have on emissions is federally enforceable.

Id. Under the rule, a control is deemed to be "federally enforceable" if it is "enforceable by the Administrator and citizens under the Act or . . . under other statutes administered by the Administrator." Id. at 12,433.

Petitioner [CMA] argues that this restrictive definition—which disregards emissions limitations imposed by state or local regulations not deemed "federally enforceable"—is contrary to the language of § 112(a)(1) of the Act. The government contends that since the word "controls" is not defined in the statute, it was open to EPA under *Chevron* to define the term, and it has done so reasonably. According to petitioners, even if *Chevron* Step II is to be reached—because the statute does not reveal a specific congressional intent—we should conclude that EPA's construction of "controls" is impermissible.

It is common ground that Congress meant the word "controls" to refer to governmental regulations and not, for instance, operational restrictions that an owner might voluntarily adopt. (We note, however, that the word could be read that broadly, which certainly supports the government's position that the term is not clear on its face.) Petitioners further conceded at oral argument—quite properly, we believe—that

Congress intended the term to stand for effective controls. EPA clearly is not obliged to take into account controls that are only chimeras and do not really restrain an operator from emitting pollution. Nevertheless, petitioners claim that EPA has imposed the federal enforceability requirement in pursuit of policy objectives unrelated to concerns about the effectiveness of controls imposed at the state and local level. EPA is accused of interpreting the statute so as to pressure states—through the ministrations of sources eager to have local controls counted in determining their capacity to emit under § 112—to seek EPA approval of state emissions policies. This objective, petitioners claim, is no part of § 112's requirement that controls be considered in determining whether a facility qualifies as a major source. It is an impermissible interpretation since it subordinates the effectiveness of controls to other considerations not approved by Congress.

Although it is the regulations implementing the 1990 amendments to the [CAA] which are directly before us, this dispute had its genesis at least a decade earlier. Following the passage of the Clean Air Act Amendments of 1977, the agency took the position that the phrase "potential to emit" as used in the definition of "major emitting facilities" excluded even emissions-reducing equipment, such as scrubbers, filters, and other technologies. We rejected that position in *Alabama Power*. See 636 F.2d at 353–55. In the wake of that case, EPA proposed a new definition of "potential to emit" that would have taken into account air pollution control equipment, but not operational restraints. The final regulations issued in 1980, however, adopted the position that capacity calculations could factor in operational restraints—but only if they were "federally enforceable." See 45 Fed.Reg. 52,676, 52,746 (1980). The regulations defined as "federally enforceable" those emissions restrictions that were "enforceable by the Administrator." Id. at 52,737. The requirement of federal enforceability was, EPA explained, "necessary, as a practical matter, to ensure that sources will perform the proper operation and maintenance for the control equipment." Id. at 52,688.

The 1980 rule was challenged in this court, but in a February 1982 settlement, EPA agreed to amend its position on federal enforceability. The proposal that followed would have taken into account emission limits "enforceable under federal, state or local law and discoverable by the Administrator and any other person." But by the time the final rule was issued, in 1989, the agency had apparently decided to abandon the terms of the settlement. The final regulations reverted to the former position of requiring federal enforceability as the sine qua non for crediting operational restraints. "Federal enforceability" was still defined to reach only those limitations "enforceable by the Administrator," but this term now included state constraints imposed under federally approved plans. See 54 Fed.Reg. 27,274, 27,285–86 (1989). New litigation followed but the cases were stayed (in our court) in anticipation of the 1990 amendments.

Congress thus acted in 1990 against a backdrop of over a decade of skirmishing between the agency and affected companies, during which the issue of whether and to what extent state and local controls were to be credited in calculating a source's "potential to emit" was very much in the forefront. In drafting § 112 Congress specifically directed EPA to consider controls in determining which producers should be classified as "major sources," but conspicuously did not limit controls to those that are federally enforceable. The government maintains that since Congress did not specify what kind of controls would qualify, EPA was free to answer that question. It permissibly did so by once again requiring that they had to be "federally enforceable," a term which, in EPA's final manifestation of the concept, applies to "all limitations and conditions that are enforceable by the Administrator and citizens under the Act or that are enforceable under other statutes administered by the Administrator." 54 Fed.Reg. at 12,433.

As we have noted, it is certainly permissible for EPA to have refused to take into account ineffective controls (indeed, it is likely that a contrary interpretation would be impermissible). But is it also open to EPA under the statute to refuse to consider controls on grounds other than their lack of effectiveness? To qualify as "federally enforceable," (as best we can determine) controls are required, in addition to being effective as a practical matter, to have been approved by EPA and integrated into the state implementation plan, or SIP, drawn up by each state to enforce substantive restrictions under the [CAA] and submitted to the Administrator for approval under § 110, 42 U.S.C. § 7410. Once included within the SIP, a state control becomes enforceable not only by the state which is its primary regulating authority, but also by the Administrator under § 113 of Act, and, in certain settings, by private citizens, who can bring suit for noncompliance with federal pollution control programs under § 304.

EPA has identified several state and local regulatory approaches through which states can impose restraints and have them deemed "federally enforceable." Constraints imposed upon a source under a state operating permit, for example, will be deemed "federally enforceable" if the state program has been approved as a "federally enforceable state operating permit program," or FESOPP, by EPA. A state permitting program cannot stand alone; it must be incorporated into the SIP, must impose upon sources a legal obligation to observe the permit constraints, must be enforceable as a practical matter—i.e., must be "effective"—must not be inconsistent with other requirements under the SIP or federal law, and must be issued pursuant to a public hearing process. Other approaches are available as well. General, as opposed to source-specific, permits can also be issued under a FESOPP, or under a state general permitting program similarly approved for inclusion within the SIP. And a state can impose constraints by general prohibitionary or exclusionary rules, so long as they are included within its SIP. Finally, the SIP could be amended to reflect special, source-specific limitations.

For each of these regulatory methods, however, EPA has proposed conditions for achieving "federal enforceability" that go beyond the mere effectiveness of particular constraint as a practical matter. Inclusion in the SIP, for example, is required in each instance even though EPA's own approach suggests that it is a consideration independent of and in addition to the need that a constraint be effective for it to count towards reductions. There may, moreover, be regulatory techniques in addition to those that EPA deems susceptible to "federal enforceability" that are equally effective, and yet which are foreclosed as mechanisms for reducing a source's capacity to emit as a result of EPA's approach.

What EPA has not explained is how its refusal to consider limitations other than those that are "federally enforceable" serves the statute's directive to "consider[ ] controls" when it results in a refusal to credit controls imposed by a state or locality even if they are unquestionably effective. Under EPA's regime, even a state program of unassailable effectiveness would not qualify in computing a source's capacity to emit unless it had been submitted not only for EPA approval, but also for inclusion in the SIP. In doing so, EPA would sacrifice a statutory objective in pursuit of ends that, at least as presented in argument to us, have not been justified, either in terms of § 112 or other provisions of the Act. EPA has not explained why it is essential that a control be included within a SIP. It is not apparent why a state's or locality's controls, when demonstrably effective, should not be credited in determining whether a source subject to those controls should be classified as a major or area source.

. . . EPA's core justifications for its federal enforceability policy are the need to avoid the administrative burden that EPA would have to bear were it obligated to evaluate the effectiveness of state and local controls and the desirability of uniformity in environmental enforcement. These, of course, are not illegitimate agency objectives. Administrative problems, in particular, can under certain circumstances inform an agency's construction of imprecise statutory language. Here, however, EPA would have us accept a rather strained interpretation of the statute based on what appears to be only its unwillingness to evaluate any state or local controls that are not federalized. If there is a closer fit between the notion of "federal enforceability" and § 112's concern with crediting effective controls it is not evident on this record.

As for national uniformity, the government contends that "one of Congress' driving concerns in amending the hazardous air pollutants provision in the Act in 1990 was to remedy the haphazard state of air toxic regulations. . . . The states' approaches to regulation varied widely," creating " 'a patchwork of differing standards' " (citing H.R.REP. NO. 490(I), 101st Cong., 2d Sess. 232 (1990)). Just so; but the amendments do create a national substantive standard, namely categories of sources (major and area) and corresponding technological compliance measures. By no means does that suggest that Congress necessarily intended for state emissions controls to be disregarded in determining whether a source is classified as "major" or "area" under that national standard. Nor did Congress mandate that EPA assume the administration and enforcement of all governmental efforts at emissions limits. If such administration and enforcement is necessary to ensure that controls are effective in the context of the extant regulatory environment, EPA has certainly not made that case and has not indicated how that consideration supports its claim that its interpretation of the statute is reasonable.

Notes and Comments

1. Why do we even need the NESHAPs program? Why do you think these concerns aren't adequately addressed under the NAAQS program? One answer might be that the NAAQS program has more of a broad-brush approach, focusing on pollutants that are more ubiquitous and measuring compliance at the air-shed level. Under the NESHAPs program, by contrast, the focus is on the particular toxics that are emitted by specific industries and we are concerned about even plant-specific exposures (as opposed to air-shed averages). See, e.g., 42 U.S.C. 7412(f)(2)(A) (reflecting a concern for "the maximum exposed individual" in some circumstances under § 112). Additionally, the plain reality is that, while the NAAQS program addresses some substances that are in fact toxic, in the late–1980s EPA still determined that more than 2.7 billion pounds of hazardous air pollutants were emitted annually in the United States.

2. As mentioned in *National Mining Ass'n* ("*NMA*"), Congress itself generated a list of 189 hazardous air pollutants (HAPs). It compiled this list from information furnished by companies in compliance with the Emergency Planning and Community Right to Know Act, 42 U.S.C. § 1100., et seq. The list is capable of either expanding or contracting, either at EPA's initiative or in response to petitions. The threshold for adding new HAPs to the list is quite low–under § 112(b)(3)(B), EPA must add a substance to the list in response to a petition if it finds that it "[is] known to cause or may reasonably be anticipated to cause adverse effects to human health or adverse environmental effects"—and the threshold for deleting HAPs is quite high—EPA must find that the substance "may not reasonably be anticipated" to cause the same effects (§ 112(b)(3)(C)). Perhaps surprisingly, in light of these dynamics, at the time of this writing the number of listed HAPs has shrunk by three since the list's initial creation. See 40 C.F.R. §§ 63.60–63.63.

3. Section 112(c)(1) gave EPA 12 months (until November 15, 1991) to publish a list of the sources, by category or subcategory, of the air pollutants. Under § 112(a), stationary sources are classified as "major" sources if they emit more than 10 tons per year of any HAP or 25 tons per year of any combination of HAPs; "area" sources include all other stationary sources that emit HAPs. Major sources are to be subject to MACT, as we will discuss below. With respect to area sources, however, EPA is to list a given category or subcategory only if it finds that it "presents a threat of adverse effects to human health or the environment ... warranting regulation under this section." 42 U.S.C. § 7412(c)(3). Only if EPA decides to list a particular category or subcategory does § 112(d)(5) then require it to set standards for the relevant sources based on "generally available control technologies" (GACT). Do you understand why Congress might have chosen to leave EPA with some discretion with respect to area sources?

4. *NMA* dealt with EPA's elaboration as to what constitutes a "major source." Were you convinced by the court's analysis of each of the presented issues? To what extent did EPA have interpretive leeway on the first two issues? To the extent that it had such leeway, do you think EPA made the right decisions as a matter of regulatory policy? On the enforceability issue, did you agree with the court's *Chevron* analysis?

5. Section 112(n)(1)(A) charges EPA with the discretion to determine whether it should regulate electric utility units under § 112. EPA was first to study the issue, and then to determine whether regulation under § 112 was "appropriate and necessary." 42 U.S.C. § 7412 (n)(1)(A). After first determining that it would regulate coal-and oil-fired utility units under § 112, in 2005 EPA reversed course, choosing instead to regulate these facilities under § 111 (as discussed in the NSPS section, above). See, e.g., 70 Fed. Reg. 28606, 28607–08 (preamble to the "Clean Air Mercury Rule"). Again, this approach is currently being challenged.

6. Section 112(d)(2) identifies MACT as the required standard for major sources. In reading that provision, note that it looks like a fairly standard technology-based formulation, with a clear indication that EPA is to take cost into account. Interestingly, however, § 112(d)(3) then sets minimum thresholds for what MACT must be; in so doing, it differentiates between new and existing sources. For new sources, MACT must be at least as stringent as the level of reduction "achieved in practice by the best controlled similar source." 42 U.S.C. § 7412(d)(3). For existing sources, MACT generally must reflect at least "the average emission limitation achieved by the best performing 12 percent of existing sources." 42 U.S.C. § 7412(d)(3)(A). If a given category has less than 30 sources, the existing source MACT must be at least as strict as the average level of control "achieved by the best performing 5 sources." 42 U.S.C. § 7412(d)(3)(B).

7. The MACT standards were to be set on a rolling schedule, with the final deadline having been in 2000. 42 U.S.C. § 7412(e). Under § 112(i)(5), existing sources could obtain a six-year extension of compliance with MACT if they achieved a 90% emission reduction from a 1987 baseline prior to proposal of the MACT standard. Why do you think Congress would have created this incentive for early-reducers?

8. With respect to modifications, § 112(g)(2) distinguishes between "modification[s]" and "reconstruction[s]." If a given change is only a "modification," as defined in § 112(a)(5), the source need only meet the MACT for existing sources. If it is a "reconstruction," as defined in 40 C.F.R. § 63.2, the source is treated as a new source. Interestingly, § 112(g)(1) allows sources to use the "bubble" concept to avoid having their changes be deemed to be modifications at all. This is a rare invocation of the bubble principle in what is otherwise a pure technology-based program. Moreover, Congress introduced an additional twist on the concept in this context: § 112(g)(1) allows parties to credit reductions in emissions of a different HAP if EPA deems that HAP to be more hazardous than the one the emissions of which will be increased.

9. Section 112(d)(6) requires EPA to review its MACT standards every 8 years and revise them as appropriate. Thus, as both new and existing sources apply MACT, the average of the best 12 percent will improve and, on

the next go-around, the MACT for existing sources will become more stringent. Given this "ratcheting" effect, what advice would you give a client if it was retrofitting its existing equipment to meet the MACT standards? Would it be worth trying to anticipate where MACT might be set eight years from now? If numerous existing sources try to play this game, what effect will that have on the standards to be set in later periodic reviews?

10. As under the CWA, when Congress moved to a technology-based approach for toxics under the CAA it did not eliminate the option of health-based protection if the technology-based controls prove inadequate to protect the public health. See 42 U.S.C. § 7412(f). Specifically, for each category of sources that emits known or suspected carcinogens, § 112(f)(2) imposes an ongoing duty on EPA to assess whether the MACT standard reduces "the lifetime excess cancer risks to the individual most exposed to emissions [from a source in that category] to less than one in one million." If not, the EPA is required to prepare standards addressing the residual risks created by emissions of the particular HAP.

E. The Visibility Program

The visibility requirements of the CAA are closely related to the PSD program. When Congress codified that program in 1977, it identified visibility as an "air quality related value[]" worthy of protection under the statute. 42 U.S.C. § 7475(d)(2)(B). In those same 1977 amendments, Congress created a separate set of requirements to protect visibility in the so-called "Class I areas" it had identified under the PSD program. As we will see, Section 169A leaves significant discretion in the States' hands, tasking them with adopting long term strategies, to be incorporated into their SIPs, to remedy any impairment of visibility in these Class I areas. It does, however, specifically require the States to identify and control certain major sources whose emissions cause or contribute to the visibility impairment. Moreover, it charged EPA with writing rules that would flesh out the statutory requirements.

EPA developed its regulations implementing the Visibility program in two stages. Phase I focused on "reasonably attributable" impairment, which the regulations defined to mean impairment "caused by the emission of air pollutants from one, or a small number of sources." 40 C.F.R. § 51.301. The second phase focused on "regional haze," defined to mean impairment "caused by the emission of air pollutants source located over a wide geographic area." Id. EPA prioritized the former because of the perceived heightened complexity involved in addressing regional haze. 45 Fed. Reg. 80,084, 80,086 (1980).

Substantively, the elements of the two phases eventually proved to be quite similar. In both contexts, the States were (are) to develop both general, long-term strategies, see 40 C.F.R. §§ 51.302(c)(2) and 51.308(d)(3), and in most cases to impose the "best available retrofit technology" ("BART") on certain major sources if those sources emit pollutants that "may reasonably be anticipated to cause or contribute" to impairment in a Class I area. 40 C.F.R. §§ 51.302(c)(4)(i) and 51.308(e)(1)(ii). See also 42 U.S.C. § 7491(b)(2).

The following case involves a challenge to the most recent iteration of the Regional Haze Rule:

UTILITY AIR REGULATORY GROUP v. ENVIRONMENTAL PROTECTION AGENCY

United States Court of Appeals, District of Columbia Circuit, 2006.
471 F.3d 1333.

WILLIAMS, Senior Circuit Judge.

In the eastern United States, the average visual range in most national parks and wilderness areas designated as Class I Federal areas, see 42 U.S.C. § 7472(a), is less than 30 kilometers, about 20 percent of what it would be under natural conditions. In order to address this problem, the [EPA] promulgated a Regional Haze Rule, 40 C.F.R. § 51.308 ["the Haze Rule"], pursuant to Section 169A of the [CAA]. The Haze Rule requires that under specified circumstances states impose best available retrofit technology ("BART") on any BART-eligible sources. The latter are a specific class of large stationary pollution sources that "were put in place between August 7, 1962 and August 7, 1977, and whose operations fall within one or more of 26 specifically listed source categories." 40 C.F.R. § 51.301. The regulation calls for imposition of BART if the source "may reasonably be anticipated to cause or contribute to any impairment of visibility in any mandatory Class I Federal area." 40 C.F.R. § 51.308(e)(1)(ii). The Haze Rule also permits states to reduce haze by alternate means, including a regional approach, so long as the alternative would be "better-than-BART"—i.e., would improve visibility more rapidly than under BART. 40 C.F.R. § 51.308(e)(2). Aspects of the Haze Rule have been before this court twice before, *Center for Energy and Economic Development v. E.P.A.,* 398 F.3d 653 (D.C.Cir.2005) ("*CEED*"); *American Corn Growers Ass'n v. E.P.A.,* 291 F.3d 1 (D.C.Cir.2002) ("*Corn Growers*")....

This case involves challenges from multiple groups, including the Center for Energy and Economic Development and the Utility Air Regulatory Group ("industry petitioners"), and the National Parks Conservation Association ("environmental petitioner"). In its brief, EPA succinctly summarizes the challenges: "Industry Petitioners generally challenge the rule as inappropriately requiring States to apply BART to too many sources, while the Environmental Petitioner argues that the rule improperly allows States to exempt too many sources from BART." Because we believe the Haze Rule is a reasonable interpretation of CAA § 169A, we affirm the rule against both sets of challenges.

As we explained in *Corn Growers,* § 169A(a)(1) of the [CAA] established a national goal of preventing and remedying existing visibility impairment at Class I areas, and CAA § 169A(b)(2) directs EPA to issue regulations requiring that states adopt measures—including BART—to make "reasonable progress" towards meeting this national goal.

As outlined in § 169A(b)(2)(A) and implemented by the Haze Rule, the BART process consists of two steps. First, in the "Attribution Step" ("Step I"), states must review each "BART-eligible source" within the state to determine whether any such source emits "any air pollutant which may reasonably be anticipated to cause or contribute to any impairment of visibility in any mandatory Class I Federal area;" sources that do so are "subject to BART." See 40 C.F.R. § 51.308(e)(1)(ii). An earlier preamble to the Haze Rule *required* states to "find that a BART-eligible source is 'reasonably anticipated to cause or contribute' to regional haze if it can be shown that the source emits pollutants within a geographic area from which pollutants can be emitted and transported downwind to a Class I area," an approach known as "collective contribution." 64 Fed.Reg. 35,714, 35,740/1 (1999). In *Corn Growers* we struck down such guidance as "inconsistent with the Act's provisions giving the *states* broad authority over BART determinations." 291 F.3d at 8 (emphasis added). In doing so, however, we did not foreclose the states themselves from deciding to take a collective approach in the Attribution Step, see *id.* at 18 (Garland, J., dissenting on other grounds), and the current rule identifies "collective contribution" as only one of at least three different approaches that a state may take in meeting its obligations under CAA § 169A(b)(2)(A). See 70 Fed.Reg. at 39,117/2. Under the current Haze Rule, a state can complete the Attribution Step by using collective attribution, by demonstrating that, cumulatively, none of its BART-eligible sources contributes to visibility impairment, or by analyzing each source's individual contribution. *Id.* States "may also use other reasonable approaches for analyzing the visibility impacts of an individual source or group of sources." 70 Fed.Reg. at 39,162/1.

The second step outlined in § 169A(b)(2)(A), the "Determination Step" ("Step II"), requires states to determine the particular technology that an individual source "subject to BART" must install. That determination requires consideration of five factors: "the cost of compliance, the energy and nonair quality environmental impacts of compliance, any existing pollution control technology in use at the source, the remaining useful life of the source, and the degree of improvement in visibility which may reasonably be anticipated to result from the use of such technology." 42 U.S.C. § 7491(g)(2); see also 40 C.F.R. § 51.308(e)(1)(ii). In *Corn Growers,* we held that these five factors "were meant to be considered together by the states," 291 F.3d at 6, but that EPA could not require the states to evaluate the improvement factor collectively while mandating that the other four factors be evaluated separately for each individual source. Compare *id.* at 8 with *id.* at 8–9.

BART is not, however, the sole means by which states can meet their obligations under the [CAA]. The Haze Rule also permits states

> to implement or require participation in an emissions trading program or other alternative measure rather than to require sources subject to BART to install, operate, and maintain BART. Such an emissions trading program or other alternative measure must

achieve greater reasonable progress than would be achieved through the installation and operation of BART.

40 C.F.R. § 51.308(e)(2). We affirmed the use of such "better than BART" approaches in *CEED*, though we objected to the particular program under review there. See *CEED,* 398 F.3d at 660. We said nothing about how better-than-BART might be measured.

After our *CEED* decision, EPA introduced the following test to evaluate whether a BART-alternative achieves "greater reasonable progress" than BART:

If the distribution of emissions is not substantially different than under BART, and the alternative measure results in greater emission reductions, then the alternative measure may be deemed to achieve greater reasonable progress. If the distribution of emissions is significantly different, the State must conduct dispersion modeling.... The modeling would demonstrate "greater reasonable progress" if both of the following two criteria are met:

(i) Visibility does not decline in any Class I area, and

(ii) There is an overall improvement in visibility, determined by comparing the average differences between BART and the alternative over all affected Class I areas.

40 C.F.R. § 51.308(e)(3).

On March 10, 2005, EPA issued the Clean Air Interstate Rule ("CAIR"), requiring reductions in emissions of sulfur dioxide and nitrogen oxides in 28 eastern states and the District of Columbia. 70 Fed.Reg. 25,162 (2005). CAIR imposes specified emissions reduction requirements on each affected state, and enables states to meet the requirements by means of cap-and-trade programs. 70 Fed.Reg. at 39,106/3. In conjunction with the introduction of CAIR, EPA amended the Haze Rule to add a new regulation—contested here—providing that "[a] State that opts to participate in the Clean Air Interstate Rule cap-and trade ... program ... need not require affected BART-eligible EGUs [electric generating units] to install, operate, and maintain BART." 40 C.F.R. § 51.308(e)(4).

In adopting the current version of § 51.308(e)(4), EPA provided analyses demonstrating that CAIR would achieve greater overall emission reductions than BART, and would make greater reasonable progress according to the two-pronged visibility test outlined in § 51.308(e)(3)—i.e., that CAIR would result in a greater aggregate visibility improvement (than BART) averaged over all Class I areas without reducing visibility at any individual area. In doing so, however, EPA also noted that the "determination that CAIR makes greater reasonable progress than BART for EGUs is not a determination that CAIR satisfies all reasonable progress requirements in CAIR affected States.... [A state] cannot assume that CAIR will satisfy all of its visibility-related obligations." 70 Fed.Reg. at 39,143/3. In particular, despite the rule changes reflecting CAIR, the EPA retained a regulation specifying that states must establish reasonable progress goals "[f]or *each* mandatory Class I

Federal area located within [a] State," and that such goals must "provide for an improvement in visibility for the most impaired days . . . and ensure no degradation in visibility for the least impaired days. . . ." 40 C.F.R. § 51.308(d)(1) (emphasis added).

Industry petitioners claim that the collective attribution process allows states virtually to skip the Attribution Step; "once a State finds that a single BART-eligible source in the State affects visibility in a Class I area, other BART-eligible sources in the State may be swept into the BART Determination process without any analysis as to their effect on visibility." This is true, but because the substance of the impact issue remains open in Step II, it is of little consequence. . . .

Industry petitioners' valid concern is that collective attribution will force sources to install BART even when such installations would serve no purpose whatsoever. But this fear is unwarranted. As EPA openly conceded at oral argument, if an individual source is found subject to BART in Step I because of collective attribution, that source can nonetheless challenge the necessity of installing BART in Step II—and have the impact issue resolved de novo. Recall that Step II involves the weighing of five factors, the last of which is the visibility impact of imposing BART. If that impact is *zero* because the source does not contribute to visibility impairment in the first place, then the source need not impose BART, regardless of the results dictated by the other four factors or the use of collective attribution in Step I. Counsel for EPA, commenting in oral argument on the passage in EPA's description of the BART determination process that industry found most alarming ("States, as a general matter, must require owners and operators of greater than 750 MW power plants to meet these BART emission limits," 70 Fed.Reg. at 39,131/3), repeatedly confirmed that a finding of zero impact at this stage would trump the four remaining factors and excuse the application of BART. We adopt counsel's interpretation as our own understanding of the interplay between Steps I and II of the Haze Rule and between the impact criterion and the other factors.

That individual sources found subject-to-BART under collective attribution can nonetheless challenge the necessity of installing BART at the Determination Step does not render collective attribution a meaningless exercise. By setting a low threshold above which sources "may reasonably be anticipated to cause or contribute to any impairment," CAA § 169A(b)(2)(A), collective attribution essentially places on a source itself the burden of demonstrating that it doesn't contribute to visibility impairment. At oral argument, counsel for industry disclaimed any legal quarrel with EPA's assignment of the burden. We find EPA's interpretation reasonable as against industry's challenges.

The environmental petitioner argues that EPA's substitution of CAIR for BART contravenes the language and structure of the [CAA] because it cannot guarantee "reasonable progress" at *all* Class I areas. This argument is predicated on a belief that the [CAA] requires that BART-alternatives such as CAIR "do better" than BART at each individual Class I area (as opposed to simply in the aggregate), and, evidently, on every type of day (best days, worst days, etc.).

. . . [We] squarely reject [the] claim that the [CAA] requires EPA to ensure that any BART-alternative improves visibility at least as much as BART at every Class I area and in all categories of days. The plain language of the Act imposes no such mandate, and EPA's refusal to read one in is reasonable.

As we said in *Corn Growers,* "[t]he statutory goal enunciated in [CAA] § 169A(a)(1) is quite clear: 'the prevention of any future, and the remedying of any existing, impairment of visibility.' " 291 F.3d at 10. In order to meet this goal, the [CAA] specifically calls for regulations to assure that "reasonable progress" is made by the states. 42 U.S.C. § 7491(a)(4). Because "reasonable progress" is nowhere defined in the Act itself, we review EPA's interpretation of the term under the standard framework of *Chevron U.S.A., Inc. v. Natural Resources Defense Council, Inc.,* 467 U.S. 837 (1984), and defer to the agency's interpretation so long as it is reasonable.

Recall that under the Haze Rule reasonable progress means that "[f]or *each* mandatory Class I Federal area . . . [states] must provide for an improvement in visibility for the *most impaired* days . . . and ensure no degradation in visibility for the least impaired days over the same period." 40 C.F.R. § 51.308(d)(1) (emphasis added). Moreover, unless there is some reasonable excuse, this progress must be sufficient to attain natural visibility conditions at every single Class I area by 2064. 40 C.F.R. § 51.308(d)(1)(ii). Indeed, EPA emphasized in its briefs that because "the regulatory scheme as a whole (and all the regulations promulgated pursuant to it) must be designed to achieve the goal [of reasonable progress] at *every* Class I area," (emphasis added), states must, if CAIR is substituted for BART and is not likely to achieve that goal, take "other measures as necessary to achieve reasonable progress goals including at *each* Class I area," (emphasis added). Thus, EPA not only agrees with petitioner that CAA § 169A(a)(1)'s declaration of a "national goal" that includes "the *remedying of any existing* [ ] *impairment* of visibility . . . [that] results from manmade air pollution" implies a need for ubiquitous improvement over time (emphasis added), but it has adopted regulations manifesting that goal.

Nonetheless, the [CAA] leaves wide discretion about how the goal is to be achieved. Notwithstanding the Act's discussion of BART in § 169A(b), we have already held in *CEED* that EPA may leave states free to implement BART-alternatives so long as those alternatives also ensure reasonable progress. 398 F.3d at 660. Moreover, nothing in § 169A(b)'s "reasonable progress" language requires at least as much improvement at each and every individual area as BART itself would achieve (much less improvement at each area at every instant); and EPA's requirement of some improvement at all areas on the worst days, coupled with no degradation at any area on the best days, 40 C.F.R. § 51.308(d)(1), appears a reasonable notion of reasonable progress. Finally, EPA allows use of a BART alternative only if it combines *aggregate* improvement (relative to BART) with universal, area-specific absence of degradation, 40 C.F.R. § 51.308(e)(3); on this metric CAIR-for-BART is far better than BART.

Notes and Comments

1. EPA's regulations define "visibility impairment" to mean "any humanly perceptible change in visibility (light extinction, visual range, contrast, coloration) from that which would have existed under natural conditions." 40 C.F.R. § 51.301.

2. Read together, subsections 169A(b)(2)(A) and 169A(g)(7) identify the "major stationary source[s]" subject to BART-analysis as those: (a) within 26 specified categories of industry; (b) which were built between 1962 and 1977; and (c) which have the potential to emit 250 tons or more of any pollutant. Why do you think Congress would have selected that time period? Oddly, the statutory definition does not specify the time period within which the potential emissions must be capable of occurring. Perhaps unsurprisingly, EPA interpreted this as involving potential yearly emissions. 40 C.F.R. § 51.301 (definition of "existing stationary facility").

3. In *Utility Air Regulatory Group*, the D.C. Circuit noted that it earlier had held in *Corn Growers* that EPA must leave the States with "broad authority over BART determinations" (here meaning the determination as to whether BART is required). Read § 169A(b)(2)(A). Do you see why the court reached that conclusion? The key sentence of the relevant provision in EPA's Phase I regulations reads as follows:

> The State must identify and analyze for BART each existing stationary facility which may reasonably be anticipated to cause or contribute to impairment . . . where the impairment is reasonably attributable to that existing stationary facility.

40 C.F.R. § 51.302(c)(4)(i). Does this provision clearly reserve to the States the contemplated discretion? If an implementing State disagreed with EPA regarding whether a given source met this standard, leading to EPA's rejection of the State's SIP submittal, how would you expect a court to resolve that disagreement in any resulting litigation? If you think this regulation does not reserve the contemplated State discretion, what would the regulation's status be, given that this aspect of it was not challenged upon issuance? See 42 U.S.C. § 7607(b). Alternatively, if the States do have the relevant discretion, as the *Corn Growers* and *Utility Air Regulatory Group* courts determined that they do at least in the regional haze context, does that mean that a given State can hide behind the scientific uncertainty of determining specific sources if it does not wish to address the visibility problem?

4. Do you agree with the *Utility Air Regulatory Group* court's analysis regarding the interplay between the "attribution" and "determination" steps, as they relate to individual facilities?

5. Both the statute and EPA's regulations generally charge the States with determining what BART is on a case-by-case basis, and then implementing it through the SIP-revision process. See 42 U.S.C. § 7491(b)(2)(A)

and 40 C.F.R. §§ 51.302(c)(4)(i) (in the reasonable attribution context) and 51.308(3) (in the context of regional haze). EPA, of course, gets to review these determinations, either at point of SIP-revision and/or at the Title V permit-review stage (see below). If EPA rejects a State's BART-determination, and litigation ensues, to whose decision, if anyone's, will the reviewing court owe deference?

6.   What do you think of the D.C. Circuit's response to the issue raised by the environmental petitioner? What is the effect of forgoing BART with respect to a source affecting a particular Class I area, due to CAIR-generated benefits experienced elsewhere? Is the fallback option of a general (i.e., not area-specific) "reasonable progress" requirement adequate? Read § 169A(b)(2), focusing on the relationship between the introductory clause and its underlying subsections (A) and (B). Here is the analysis of those provisions that the *Utility Air Regulatory Group* court referenced from same court's earlier decision in *CEED*:

> The Center asserts that § 169A(b)(2) can be read only one way. That is, each SIP's constituent measures must "includ[e]" BART. That [the BART-alternatives EPA has embraced here]—unlike § 169A—also applies to BART-*in* eligible sources is no answer, the Center insists, at least to the extent EPA applies the [alternative approaches] to BART-eligible ones. The Center also cites excerpts from the Clean Air Act's legislative history to suggest Congress did not intend to give EPA a choice on whether to include BART.
>
> EPA, by contrast, sees "at least two permissible interpretations" of § 169A(b)(2). One is the Center's. The other is that each SIP's "emission limits, schedules of compliance and other measures" must "include[e]" (sic) BART only "as may be necessary to make reasonable progress toward" national visibility goals. *Id.* (quoting 42 U.S.C. § 7491(b)(2)). If [the proposed] alternatives would achieve greater progress than BART, then BART would not be "necessary to make reasonable progress." . . .
>
> The Center never explains why EPA *must* detach the "inclu[sion]" of BART from the condition that it be "necessary to make reasonable progress" to national visibility goals. Nor can we discern a reason. . . .
> Thus the Center has shown neither that Congress's language precluded non-BART alternatives where BART wasn't "necessary to make reasonable progress," nor that EPA's reading is otherwise unreasonable.

398 F.3d at 659–660. The BART-alternatives EPA approved (and the court upheld) in *CEED* were designed to achieve better-than-BART results in the relevant "transport region." Id. at 656. Do you agree with the *Utility Air Regulatory Group* court that § 169A(b)(2) reasonably can be read to excuse the application of BART based on benefits generated in distant areas?

V.   THE CLEAN AIR ACT—GENERAL ENFORCEMENT AND PERMITS FOR REGULATED STATIONARY SOURCES

Like other environmental laws, the full implementation of the Clean Air Act may be difficult if not supported by adequate administration and enforcement. Like the CWA, the CAA relies on principles of cooperative federalism, in that the States and the federal government share responsibility for ensuring that it is properly implemented. As discussed, *supra*, the States are to implement the ambient air quality standards by creating the SIPs. As noted in that discussion, the States were not always effective in doing so. Moreover, despite the failure of the States to ensure the attainment of the NAAQS, the EPA did not readily exercise its authority to implement FIPs in their place, despite a requirement for it to do so.

Additionally, the States are often given the primary authority to implement the other parts of the Act, such as the PSD program. But what is to ensure that they do so effectively? The public? Section 304 does create a citizen-suit authority, but (as discussed in Chapter 6) these suits do not lie against States where they fail to adequately enforce. The federal government? As noted by one of the authors of this book,

> [W]ithout money, the threat of a true federal takeover largely disappeared, as the federal government could no longer afford the direct control of pollution compliance within most states.

> Federal supervision of state enforcement was not as fail-safe a scheme as its proponents initially believed. The laws and standards were still there and they might be enforced with much energy from citizens. But all the laws on earth do not amount to much if they are not enforced, or if the enforcement lacks teeth. With the credible threat of a federal takeover removed, the states could go back to, or continue, their race to the bottom. Yet this time, they did not race with the laxity of laws, but with the lack of zeal of enforcement of laws—a competition that is much more hidden and insidious, and one in which some states may not want to compete.

Victor Flatt, *A Dirty River Runs Through It* . . . , 25 B. C. Envtl. L. Rev. 1, 3 (1998).

This failure of enforcement, particularly at the State level, was one of the reasons that Congress created the specific hammers in the 1970 Clean Air Act. The EPA's oversight failure may have led to the more specific legislative requirements for ozone non-compliance in the 1990 amendments. The 1990 amendments also added a permit feature to assist in providing information which could help with enforcement.

In 1990, Congress promulgated Title V of the CAA. 42 U.S.C. §§ 7661–7661f. Title V establishes an overarching permit program for stationary sources. It requires all major stationary sources of air pollution to obtain permits incorporating CAA requirements and establishes procedures for federal authorization of State-run Title V permit programs. Title V permits do not impose additional requirements on sources but, to facilitate compliance, consolidate all applicable requirements in a single document. 42 U.S.C. § 7661a(a). The hope is that Title V will aid compliance by having all of the requirements in one place.

Congress decided that the States should run the Title V program much like they administer the NPDES program for water pollution sources. Section 502(d) governs how State programs were to be submitted, reviewed, and approved. As under the NPDES program, the ultimate default here is EPA administration of the program if the State failed to submit an approvable program, 42 U.S.C. § 7661a(d)(3), or if EPA determines that a State is not adequately administering and enforcing a program it had previously approved. 42 U.S.C. § 7661(a)(i)(1).

A. What Is Required for a State Permit Program to Be Approved?

The following case further explores the requirements of the Title V permit program and illustrates the difficulty in challenging the EPA's approval of a State program.

PUBLIC CITIZEN, INC. v. UNITED STATES ENVIRONMENTAL PROTECTION AGENCY

United States Court of Appeals, Fifth Circuit, 2003.
343 F.3d 449.

BARKSDALE, Circuit Judge:

In 1990, Congress enacted Title V for the CAA. Title V requires major stationary sources of air pollution, such as factories, to receive operating permits incorporating CAA requirements and establishes a procedure for federal authorization of state-run Title V permit programs. Title V permits do not impose additional requirements on sources but, to facilitate compliance, consolidate all applicable requirements in a single document. *See* 42 U.S.C. § 7661a(a).

Congress directed the EPA to promulgate regulations establishing the minimum elements for a Title V operating permit program. Those minimum elements were to include certain requirements identified in the CAA. *See* 42 U.S.C. § 7661a(b) (articulating ten minimum elements for state programs).

The CAA required each State to develop, and submit to the EPA for approval, an operating permit program that met the requirements of the Act and its regulations. 42 U.S.C. § 7661a(d)(1). Section 502(d)(1) of the CAA authorized the EPA to grant full approval to permit programs "to the extent" that the program met the CAA's requirements.

In the event a State was not eligible for full approval, but "substantially" met the minimum requirements, the CAA authorized the EPA to grant "interim approval". 42 U.S.C. § 7661a(g). On granting interim approval, the EPA had to identify deficiencies to be addressed before the program could receive full approval; the State was then required to revise and resubmit the program. *Id.* Interim approval could only last for two years and could not be renewed. *Id.*

Congress established firm deadlines for these processes. Pursuant to the statutory schedule: by November 1993, States were to submit proposed permit programs; by November 1994, the EPA had to either grant full or interim approval, or deny approval; by November 1995, the EPA was to take over state permit programs that did not meet federal requirements and had not been granted interim approval; and by November 1996, the EPA was to take over state permit programs that had been granted interim approval but did not qualify for full approval. In other words, compliant programs were to be operating no later than November 1996, six years after Title V became law. *See* 42 U.S.C. § 7661a(b), (d)(1), (d)(3), and (g).

If a program was not fully approved before the deadline, or if interim approval expired without the EPA's having granted full approval, the CAA mandated stiff sanctions, including exposure to financial penalties (*e.g.*, loss of highway funds). *See* 42 U.S.C. § 7661a(d)(2)(B) (incorporating § 7509(b)). Moreover, the EPA would be required to implement a federal Title V permitting program in that State, pursuant to EPA regulations. *See* 42 U.S.C. § 7661a(d)(3).

After the EPA approved a State's Title V permit program, the EPA was to maintain an oversight role. The CAA provides that, whenever the EPA makes a determination that a State is not adequately administering and enforcing its permit program in accordance with Title V, it shall provide a notice of deficiency (NOD) to the State. 42 U.S.C. § 7661a(i)(1). If the State does not correct the deficiency within 18 months, it faces sanctions and, eventually, EPA takeover of its program. 42 U.S.C. § 7661a(i)(2), (4).

The EPA issued regulations providing minimum requirements for state permit programs and, pursuant to those rules, began reviewing and authorizing state permit programs. It issued numerous interim approvals. Despite the statutory language that interim approval was to last only two years and could not be renewed, the EPA also extended those approvals for an additional ten months as the November 1996 deadline approached. It subsequently extended interim approval three times.

The EPA was sued for doing so. *Sierra Club v. EPA*, No. 00–1262 (D.C.Cir. 2000). As part of the settlement of that action, the EPA agreed: (1) to implement a federal permit program by 1 December 2001 in any State that did not have full approval; and (2) to take and respond by 1 December 2001 to public comments regarding deficiencies in state permit programs. *Id.* (Settlement Agreement). Regarding such public comments, it committed to respond on the merits to any claims of deficiency raised during the comment period and either issue an NOD or explain why it did not do so.

In 1993, Texas submitted its Title V program to the EPA for approval. In 1996, the EPA granted interim approval to Texas' program. The EPA identified numerous deficiencies in its approval notice that Texas was required to correct before it could obtain full approval. Subsequently, Texas submitted program revisions for the EPA's review.

Pursuant to the *Sierra Club* Settlement Agreement, the EPA published a Federal Register notice inviting public comments about Texas' program; Petitioners submitted comments in which they objected to full approval, based on their belief that Texas had not corrected all of the interim deficiencies and that additional deficiencies existed that had not been identified previously. The EPA determined, however, that Texas' revisions satisfactorily addressed the program deficiencies *identified during interim approval*; accordingly, it granted Texas full approval in December 2001.

Regarding the deficiencies *not identified by the time of interim approval,* the EPA concluded that newly identified deficiencies did not prohibit full approval. It stated it would respond to those alleged deficiencies in a separate, then concurrently pending administrative proceeding. In January 2002, based upon the EPA's review of the public comments, it issued an NOD that identified six deficiencies.

In February 2002, the EPA issued a response letter explaining its rationale for not issuing NODs for other deficiencies claimed by Petitioners. The response explained that the EPA agreed with Petitioners concerning some of the issues and was working with Texas to ensure its program was being implemented consistent with Title V; on other issues, it did not agree with Petitioners.

Petitioners first maintain the EPA, in December 2001, had no authority to grant Texas' permit program full approval without finding that the program met the requirements of Title V and its implementing regulations. They further maintain that the EPA acted arbitrarily and capriciously in granting full approval because Texas had not corrected all deficiencies identified at interim approval.

The first issue is a question of statutory interpretation governed by the *Chevron* standard. Under the EPA's interpretation of the statutory provisions governing interim and full approval, CAA § 502g (governing interim approval) provides an alternate path to full approval. Full approval would otherwise be governed by CAA § 502(d), and would not be permitted when the EPA determined (as it did) that the program did not meet all of Title V's requirements. According to the EPA, if a State is granted interim approval, then to receive full approval it need only remedy deficiencies identified by the EPA *at the time of interim approval.*

Petitioners dispute this interpretation, contending that, when the EPA is aware of deficiencies, it may not fully approve a program (regardless of whether it becomes aware of the deficiencies *before or after* interim approval). According to Petitioners: there is but one path to full approval, that provided by CAA § 502d; and only deficiency-free programs may be approved. Petitioners urge that the EPA's interpretation is contrary to the clear and unambiguous intent of Congress; and, in the alternative, that the approval was arbitrary and capricious because it contradicts EPA regulations and memoranda.

CAA § 502(d), relied upon by Petitioners, provides:

Not later than 3 years after November 15, 1990, the Governor of each State shall develop and submit to the Administrator a permit program under State or local law or under an interstate compact meeting the requirements of this subchapter ... Not later than 1 year after receiving a program, and after notice and opportunity for public comment, the Administrator shall approve or disapprove such program, in whole or in part. The Administrator may approve a program to the extent that the program meets the requirements of this chapter, including the regulations issued under subsection (b) of this section. If the program is disapproved, in whole or part, the Administrator shall notify the Governor of any revisions or modifications necessary to obtain approval. The Governor shall revise and resubmit the program for review under this section within 180 days after receiving notification.

CAA § 502(g), which governs interim approval, provides in part:

If a program (including a partial permit program) submitted under this subchapter substantially meets the requirements of this subchapter but is not fully approvable, the Administrator may by rule grant the program interim approval. In the notice of final rulemaking, the Administrator shall specify the changes that must be made before the program can receive full approval.

We agree with the Second Circuit that ambiguity exists in these provisions. *See New York Pub. Interest Research Group v. Whitman,* 321 F.3d 316, 328 (2nd Cir.2003)[:]

It arises because the text of § 502(g), governing interim approval, does not clearly describe the process by which a permit program that has received interim approval receives full approval. After making the changes specified at the time of interim approval, must the state resubmit its plan for evaluation under the standards set forth in § 502(d), which would require the EPA to examine the program's compliance with Title V? Or does a state's program automatically qualify for full approval when the state makes *"the* changes" specified at the time of interim approval?

Id. (emphasis added).

On fully approving Texas' program, the EPA acknowledged this ambiguity, finding an "apparent tension" between the requirement that it grant full approval only to programs that meet minimum requirements and the requirement that it grant full approval to any program that has corrected interim deficiencies. 66 Fed.Reg. at 63319.

Therefore, the EPA had to decide "whether Texas by virtue of correcting the deficiencies identified in the [interim approval was] eligible ... for full approval, or whether Texas *must also* correct any new or recently identified deficiencies as a prerequisite to receiving full approval". *Id.* at 63319–20 (emphasis added). The EPA concluded:

[T]he appropriate and more cohesive reading of the statute recognizes the EPA's authority to grant Texas full approval [where interim-approval deficiencies have been corrected] while working simultaneously with the state, in [the EPA's] oversight capacity, on any additional problems that were recently identified. To conclude otherwise would disrupt the current administration of the state program and cause further delay in Texas's ability to issue operating permits to major stationary sources.

Id. at 63320.

Because Congress did not unambiguously express its intent on this issue through the CAA, the EPA's interpretation is entitled to deference under *Chevron*. As a result, we must decide whether the EPA's interpretation is "based on a permissible construction of the [CAA]".

We hold that it is. First, CAA § 502(g) provides that, in the notice of final rulemaking granting interim approval, the EPA must "specify *the* changes that must be made before the program can receive full approval". (Emphasis added.) This suggests the interim-approval notice must identify all of the changes required for full approval, and the making of those specified changes (not all possible changes) triggers full approval.

Second, as the Second Circuit noted:

[T]he EPA's interpretation comports with the timetable established by Congress, if not adhered to by the EPA. Under § 502(g), interim approval expires after two years and is not renewable. Changes identified at the time of interim approval may require modifications of state statutes or regulations and, therefore, may be time consuming. *If a state were required, not only to make the changes identified at the start of interim approval but also to correct deficiencies arising during interim approval,* a state's efforts to receive full approval could be sabotaged by the identification of new deficiencies during or at the end of interim approval. Should these events occur it is doubtful whether the state could resubmit its plan for full approval since § 502(d) provides that any such submission must occur "[n]ot later than three years after November 15, 1990," 42 U.S.C. § 7661a(d)(1), and the statute does not otherwise authorize resubmission.

New York Pub. Interest Research Group, 321 F.3d at 329 (emphasis added).

Finally, the CAA provides a mechanism for correcting deficiencies in fully-approved programs—the NOD process. Like the Second Circuit, "[w]e question whether Congress would have armed the EPA with this arsenal if it believed that every deficiency would be corrected during the interim approval period". *Id.* at 329. Moreover, the NOD process also applies to programs that have been granted interim approval, providing a means to correct deficiencies not identified at the time of interim approval. Thus, Congress provided processes for making corrections to programs once they initially enter the approval process and are given at least interim approval.

Petitioners nonetheless contend that the EPA acted arbitrarily and capriciously in granting full approval to Texas because it had not corrected [] the deficiencies identified at interim approval. The EPA responds that it evaluated Texas' response to each deficiency and concluded that Texas had satisfactorily addressed the EPA's concerns.

... Petitioners point to Texas' Audit Privilege Act as an interim-approval-identified deficiency that had not been corrected. They maintain the Audit Privilege Act prevents Texas from having adequate authority to enforce its permit program.

Title V includes, as one of its minimum elements, the requirement that the State have adequate authority to assure that sources comply with all applicable requirements and to enforce permits. 42 U.S.C. § 7661a(b)(5); *see also* 40 C.F.R. § 70.11(c) (penalties must be "appropriate to the violation"). Texas, through its Audit Privilege Act, provides for certain immunities and privileges associated with information obtained through an environmental audit of a facility.

In the EPA's interim approval notice for Texas, it noted its concern that the Audit Privilege Act might prevent Texas from having adequate enforcement authority. 61 Fed.Reg. at 32697. The EPA stated that, to qualify for full approval, Texas would be required to demonstrate that the Audit Privilege Act did not limit Texas' ability to adequately enforce and administer the operating permit program. *Id.*

In response, Texas amended the Audit Privilege Act. According to the EPA, these amendments: (1) eliminated the application of immunity and privilege provisions to criminal actions; (2) eliminated the application of immunity where a violation results in a serious threat to health or the environment, or where the violator has obtained a substantial economic benefit that gives it a competitive advantage; (3) clarified that the law would not sanction individuals who report violations of environmental laws to government agencies; and (4) clarified that the privilege does not impair access to information required to be made available under federal or state law.

Petitioners concede that Texas has made these changes to its Audit Privilege Act since 1996, but insist that the law still: prevents Texas from having adequate enforcement authority; prevents it from being able to assess appropriate penalties; and improperly makes audit documents privileged. The EPA responds that it reasonably determined that limited immunity does not, *per se,* preclude States from possessing adequate enforcement authority.

Concerning the adequacy of Texas' enforcement authority, Petitioners insist the Audit Privilege Act prevents Texas from being able to recover civil penalties for each violation of the Act because it has granted certain immunities. On the other hand, the EPA determined the immunities provided by Texas' Audit Privilege Act did not deprive Texas of adequate enforcement authority. It reasoned the Act does not: limit Texas' ability to seek declaratory or injunctive relief for violations disclosed by an audit; affect Texas' ability to pursue criminal sanctions, if appropriate; or preclude actions seeking penalties for serious violations. This determination was not arbitrary and capricious.

Regarding the Audit Privilege Act's impact on Texas' ability to impose appropriate penalties, Title V and Part 70 require that Texas have authority to recover penalties of up to $10,000 per day in an amount "appropriate to the violation". 40 C.F.R. § 70.11; *see also* 42 U.S.C. § 7661a(b)(5)(E). The EPA has interpreted these provisions to require that state law allow for the consideration of the penalty factors identified in CAA § 113(e): the violator's compliance history; the economic benefit of noncompliance; and the seriousness of the violation.

Petitioners note minor semantic differences between the federal penalty factors and those allowed consideration under the Audit Privilege Act. For example, Texas must be able to penalize violations resulting in substantial economic benefit; Texas' Audit Privilege Act provides an exception to immunity for violations that "have resulted in a significant economic benefit which gives the violator a clear advantage over its business competitors". Tex.Rev.Civ. Stat. Art. 4447cc § 10(d)(5). Notwithstanding minor variations, the EPA reasonably determined that Texas' statutory language allowed it to consider the appropriate factors in imposing punishments.

Petitioners assert Texas' Audit Privilege Act impermissibly makes audit documents privileged. The EPA responds that Texas addressed this concern by adding a section to the Audit Privilege Act that restored the authority of the State's employees, "[n]otwithstanding the privilege established under this Act" to "review information that is required to be available under a specific state or federal law. . . ." Tex.Rev.Civ.Stat. art. 4447cc, § 9(b). The EPA determined this section restored Texas' authority to view any documents required to be collected, maintained, or reported under Title V, which it deemed sufficient to address the deficiency and for Texas to conduct both civil and criminal investigations. This assessment was not arbitrary or capricious.

Notes and Comments

1. Take a close look at § 502(a) of the CAA. It specifically lists, as among those who are required to obtain Title V permits, any source that is regulated under either § 111 (NSPS) or § 112 (NESHAPs), as well as sources required to have permits under either part C (PSD) or part D (NNSR) of subchapter I of the CAA. Additionally, it gives EPA the power to impose the permitting requirement on other stationary sources. EPA has exercised this power broadly at 40 C.F.R. § 70.3(a)(1), sweeping in, among others, any "major stationary source" under § 302(j). See also CAA § 501(2) and 40 C.F.R. § 70.2 (definitions of "major source" for purposes of Title V). This has the effect of capturing every major source covered under both the Visibility and acid rain programs. This is further borne out in EPA's regulatory definition of "applicable requirement," which picks up the Visibility and acid rain requirements in subsections (1) and (5), respectively (indeed, subsection (1) of the definition even picks up RACT, at least for major sources). See 40 C.F.R. § 70.2. Thus, for major sources the Title V permit becomes the repository of all relevant CAA requirements.

2. Was the Fifth Circuit correct in applying the *Chevron* protocol to the interpretations EPA advanced in approving the Texas Title V program? If so, do you agree with the court's application of that protocol?

3. We will address audit issues again in Chapter 6. The Texas law at issue in *Public Citizen* was an early example of the types of State laws that preceded EPA's efforts to adopt its own Audit Policy. Did you agree with EPA and the court's analysis regarding the extent to which it comported with Title V requirements?

B. EPA Oversight of Approved Programs

Even though the CAA, like most other pollution-control statutes, is based on a cooperative model under which the federal government delegates primary implementation authority to the States, the federal government still retains significant control. In addition to retaining the authority to revoke a State's program for failure to follow delegated criteria (which it has rarely exercised), EPA has also asserted that it has jurisdiction to both implement and enforce the Act, even if a State chooses not to act. Generally, the courts have been deferential to EPA's attempts to take direct action if EPA has been dissatisfied with the State action. Given the great difficulty and unlikelihood of EPA's directly taking over an entire program, this may be the only way to create a credible control on State discretion. The next case involves EPA's decision to take a direct action on a permit specifying a technology standard under the CAA.

In addition to addressing EPA's oversight authority, this case also provides a discussion of how the general CAA requirements may be assumed by the States, and the factual issues that continually arise in determining what standard meets the technological requirements of NSPS and PSD for stationary sources. As you read the facts of the case, think about what position you would have taken had you been Teck Cominco. Is it financially logical to try to have the PSD requirement be the less expensive of two options? How do you convince the permitting agency of that option? What about the oversight capability? Could a compromise have been reached with the EPA earlier? Could political pressure have been brought to bear on the agency? Is it easier to bring pressure on a state agency rather than a federal one?

ALASKA DEPARTMENT OF ENVIRONMENTAL CONSERVATION v. ENVIRONMENTAL PROTECTION AGENCY

Supreme Court of the United States, 2004.
540 U.S. 461, 124 S.Ct. 983, 157 L.Ed.2d 967.

Justice GINSBURG delivered the opinion of the Court.

This case concerns the authority of [EPA] to enforce the provisions of the [PSD] program. Under that program, no major air pollutant emitting facility may be constructed unless the facility is equipped with

[BACT]. BACT [means] "an emission limitation based on the maximum degree of [pollutant] reduction . . . which the permitting authority, on a case-by-case basis, taking into account energy, environmental, and economic impacts and other costs, determines is achievable for [the] facility. . . ." [42 U.S.C. § 7479(3)].

Regarding EPA oversight, the Act includes a general instruction and one geared specifically to the PSD program. The general prescription, § 113(a)(5) of the Act, authorizes EPA, when it finds that a State is not complying with a CAA requirement governing construction of a pollutant source, to issue an order prohibiting construction, to prescribe an administrative penalty, or to commence a civil action for injunctive relief. Directed specifically to the PSD program, CAA § 167 instructs EPA to "take such measures, including issuance of an order, or seeking injunctive relief, as necessary to prevent the construction" of a major pollutant emitting facility that does not conform to the PSD requirements of the Act.

In the case before us, "the permitting authority" under § 7479(3) is the State of Alaska, acting through Alaska's Department of Environmental Conservation (ADEC). The question presented is what role EPA has with respect to ADEC's BACT determinations. Specifically, may EPA act to block construction of a new major pollutant emitting facility permitted by ADEC when EPA finds ADEC's BACT determination unreasonable in light of the guides § 7479(3) prescribes? We hold that the Act confers that checking authority on EPA.

I

Congress enacted the [CAA] in response to "dissatisfaction with the progress of existing air pollution programs." *Union Elec. Co. v. EPA,* 427 U.S. 246, 249 (1976). The amendments aimed "to guarantee the prompt attainment and maintenance of specified air quality standards." *Ibid.* [Sections] 108(a) and 109(a) of the Act require EPA to publish lists of emissions that "cause or contribute to air pollution which may reasonably be anticipated to endanger public health or welfare," and to promulgate primary and secondary national ambient air quality standards (NAAQS) for such pollutants. . . . The Agency published initial NAAQS in 1971, and in 1985, NAAQS for the pollutant at issue in this case, nitrogen dioxide. 40 CFR § 50.11 (2002).

Section 165 of the Act installs a permitting requirement for any "major emitting facility," defined to include any source emitting more than 250 tons of nitrogen oxides per year, § 7479(1). No such facility may be constructed or modified unless a permit prescribing emission limitations has been issued for the facility. § 7475(a)(1). . . . Modifications to major emitting facilities that increase nitrogen oxide emissions in excess of 40 tons per year require a PSD permit. 40 CFR § 51.166(b)(23)(i) (2002).

The Act sets out preconditions for the issuance of PSD permits. *Inter alia,* no PSD permit may issue unless [the proposed facility is subject to BACT]. Under the federal Act, a limited class of sources must gain advance EPA approval for the BACT prescribed in the permit. 42 U.S.C. § 7475(a)(8).

Among measures EPA may take to ensure compliance with the PSD program, two have special relevance here. The first prescription, § 113(a)(5) of the Act, provides that "[w]henever, on the basis of any available information, [EPA] finds that a State is not acting in compliance with any requirement or prohibition of the chapter relating to the construction of new sources or the modification of existing sources," EPA may "issue an order prohibiting the construction or modification of any major stationary source in any area to which such requirement applies." The second measure, § 167 of the Act, trains on enforcement of the PSD program; it requires EPA to "take such measures, including issuance of an order, or seeking injunctive relief, as necessary to prevent the construction or modification of a major emitting facility which does not conform to the [PSD] requirements."

Teck Cominco Alaska, Inc. (Cominco), operates a zinc concentrate mine, the Red Dog Mine, in northwest Alaska approximately 100 miles north of the Arctic Circle and close to the native Alaskan villages of Kivalina and Noatak. The mine is the region's largest private employer. It supplies a quarter of the area's wage base....

In 1988, Cominco obtained authorization to operate the mine, a "major emitting facility" under the Act.... The mine's PSD permit authorized five 5,000 kilowatt Wartsila diesel electric generators, MG–1 through MG–5, subject to operating restrictions; two of the five generators were permitted to operate only in standby status. Petitioner Alaska Department of Environmental Conservation (ADEC) issued a second PSD permit in 1994 allowing addition of a sixth full-time generator (MG–6), removing standby status from MG–2, and imposing a new operational cap that allowed all but one generator to run full time.

In 1996, Cominco initiated a project, with funding from the State, to expand zinc production by 40%. Anticipating that the project would increase nitrogen oxide emissions by more than 40 tons per year, Cominco applied to ADEC for a PSD permit to allow, *inter alia,* increased electricity generation by its standby generator, MG–5. On March 3, 1999, ADEC preliminarily proposed as BACT for MG–5 the emission control technology known as selective catalytic reduction (SCR),[5] which reduces nitrogen oxide emissions by 90%. In response, Cominco amended its application to add a seventh generator, MG–17, and to propose as BACT an alternative control technology—Low NOx[6]—that achieves a 30% reduction in nitrogen oxide pollutants.

---

5. SCR requires injections of "ammonia or urea into the exhaust before the exhaust enters a catalyst bed made with vanadium, titanium, or platinum. The reduction reaction occurs when the flue gas passes over the catalyst bed where the NOx and ammonia combine to become nitrogen, oxygen, and water...."

6. In Low NOx, changes are made to a generator to improve fuel atomization and modify the combustion space to enhance the mixing of air and fuel.

On May 4, 1999, ADEC, in conjunction with Cominco's representative, issued a first draft PSD permit and preliminary technical analysis report that concluded Low NOx was BACT for MG–5 and MG–17. To determine BACT, ADEC employed EPA's recommended top-down methodology:

> "In brief, the top-down process provides that all available control technologies be ranked in descending order of control effectiveness. The PSD applicant first examines the most stringent—or 'top'—alternative. That alternative is established as BACT unless the applicant demonstrates, and the permitting authority in its informed judgment agrees, that technical considerations, or energy, environmental, or economic impacts justify a conclusion that the most stringent technology is not 'achievable' in that case. If the most stringent technology is eliminated in this fashion, then the next most stringent alternative is considered, and so on." EPA, New Source Review Workshop Manual B2 (Draft Oct. 1990) (hereinafter New Source Review Manual);[7]

Applying top-down methodology, ADEC first homed in on SCR as BACT for MG–5, and the new generator, MG17. "[W]ith an estimated reduction of 90%," ADEC stated, SCR "is the most stringent" technology. Finding SCR "technically and economically feasible," ADEC characterized as "overstated" Cominco's cost estimate of $5,643 per ton of nitrogen oxide removed by SCR. Using Cominco's data, ADEC reached a cost estimate running between $1,586 and $2,279 per ton. Costs in that range, ADEC observed, "are well within what ADEC and EPA conside[r] economically feasible." Responding to Cominco's comments on the preliminary permit, engineering staff in ADEC's Air Permits Program pointed out that, according to information Cominco provided to ADEC, "SCR has been installed on similar diesel-fired engines throughout the world."

Despite its staff's clear view "that SCR (the most effective individual technology) [was] technologically, environmentally, and economically feasible for the Red Dog power plant engines," ADEC endorsed the alternative proffered by Cominco. To achieve nitrogen oxide emission reductions commensurate with SCR's 90% impact, Cominco proposed fitting the new generator MG–17 and the six existing generators with Low NOx.[8] Cominco asserted that it could lower net emissions by 396 tons per year if it fitted all seven generators with Low NOx rather than fitting two (MG–5 and MG–17) with SCR and choosing one of them as the standby unit. Cominco's proposal hinged on the "assumption . . . that under typical operating conditions one or more engines will not be running due to maintenance of standby-generation capacity." If all seven

---

7. Nothing in the Act or its implementing regulations mandates top-down analysis. See 42 U.S.C. § 7479(3); 40 CFR § 52.21(j) (2002). EPA represents that permitting authorities "commonly" use top-down methodology.

8. Two generators already were fitted with a technology called Fuel Injection Timing Retard that results in a 20% to 30% reduction in nitrogen oxide emissions.

generators ran continuously, however, Cominco's alternative would increase emissions by 79 tons per year. Accepting Cominco's submission, ADEC stated that Cominco's Low NOx solution "achieve[d] a similar maximum NOx reduction as the most stringent controls; [could] potentially result in a greater NOx reduction; and is logistically and economically less onerous to Cominco."

On the final day of the public comment period, July 2, 1999, the United States Department of the Interior, National Parks Service (NPS), submitted comments to ADEC. NPS objected to the projected offset of new emissions from MG–5 and MG–17 against emissions from other existing generators that were not subject to BACT. Such an offset, NPS commented, "is neither allowed by BACT, nor achieves the degree of reduction that would result if all the generators that are subject to BACT were equipped with SCR." NPS further observed that the proposed production-increase project would remove operating restrictions that the 1994 PSD permit had placed on four of the existing generators—MG–1, MG–3, MG–4, and MG–5. Due to that alteration, NPS urged, those generators, too, became part of the production-expansion project and would be subject to the BACT requirement.

Following NPS' lead, EPA wrote to ADEC on July 29, 1999, commenting: "Although ADEC states in its analysis that [SCR], the most stringent level of control, is economically and technologically feasible, ADEC did not propose to require SCR.... [O]nce it is determined that an emission unit is subject to BACT, the PSD program does not allow the imposition of a limit that is less stringent than BACT." A permitting authority, EPA agreed with NPS, could not offset new emissions "by imposing new controls on other emission units" that were not subject to BACT. New emissions could be offset only against reduced emissions from sources covered by the same BACT authorization. EPA further agreed with NPS that, based on the existing information, BACT would be required for MG–1, MG–3, MG–4, and MG–5.

After receiving EPA comments, ADEC issued a second draft PSD permit and technical analysis report on September 1, 1999, again finding Low NOx to be BACT for MG–17. Abandoning the emissions-offsetting justification advanced in the May 4 draft permit, ADEC agreed with NPS and EPA that "emission reductions from sources that were not part of the permit action," here MG–1, MG–2, MG–3, MG–4, MG–5, and MG–6, could not be considered in determining BACT for MG–17.[9]

ADEC conceded that, lacking data from Cominco, it had made "no judgment ... as to the impact of ... [SCR] on the operation, profitability, and competitiveness of the Red Dog Mine." Contradicting its May

---

9. Rather than subject MG–1, MG–3, MG–4, and MG–5 to BACT, ADEC and Cominco "agreed to permit conditions that would require low NOx controls on MG–1, MG–3, MG–4, and MG–5, and emission limits that reflect the previous 'bubbled' limits. Under this approach, the permit would re- sult in no increase in actual or allowable emissions from any of these engines and the installation of BACT would not be necessary for these four units." *Id.,* at 149. EPA found no cause to question this ADEC–Cominco agreement. *Ibid.*

1999 conclusion that SCR was "technically and economically feasible," ADEC found in September 1999 that SCR imposed "a disproportionate cost" on the mine. ADEC concluded, on a "cursory review," that requiring SCR for a rural Alaska utility would lead to a 20% price increase, and that in comparison with other BACT technologies, SCR came at a "significantly higher" cost. No economic basis for a comparison between the mine and a rural utility appeared in ADEC's technical analysis.

EPA protested the revised permit. In a September 15, 1999, letter, the Agency stated: "Cominco has not adequately demonstrated any site-specific factors to support their claim that the installation of [SCR] is economically infeasible at the Red Dog Mine. Therefore, elimination of SCR as BACT based on cost-effectiveness grounds is not supported by the record and is clearly erroneous."

To justify the September 1, 1999, permit, EPA suggested, ADEC could "include an analysis of whether requiring Cominco to install and operate [SCR] would have any adverse economic impacts upon Cominco specifically." *Id.*, at 127. Stating that such an inquiry was unnecessary and expressing "concerns related to confidentiality," Cominco declined to submit financial data. *Id.*, at 134. In this regard, Cominco simply asserted, without detail, that the company's "overall debt remains quite high" despite continuing profits. *Id.*, at 134–135. Cominco also invoked the need for "[i]ndustrial development in rural Alaska." *Id.*, at 135.

On December 10, 1999, ADEC issued the final permit and technical analysis report. Once again, ADEC approved Low NOx as BACT for MG–17 "[t]o support Cominco's Red Dog Mine Production Rate Increase Project, and its contributions to the region." ADEC did not include the economic analysis EPA had suggested. Indeed, ADEC conceded again that it had made "no judgment . . . as to the impact of . . . [SCR's] cost on the operation, profitability, and competitiveness of the Red Dog Mine." Nonetheless, ADEC advanced, as cause for its decision, SCR's adverse effect on the mine's "unique and continuing impact on the economic diversity of th[e] region" and on the venture's "world competitiveness." ADEC did not explain how its inferences of adverse effects on the region's economy or the mine's "world competitiveness" could be made without financial information showing SCR's impact on the "operation, profitability, and competitiveness" of the mine. Instead, ADEC reiterated its rural Alaska utility analogy, and again compared SCR's cost to the costs of other, less stringent, control technologies.

The same day, December 10, 1999, EPA issued an order to ADEC, under §§ 113(a)(5) and 167 of the Act, prohibiting ADEC from issuing a PSD permit to Cominco "unless ADEC satisfactorily documents why SCR is not BACT for the Wartsila diesel generator [MG–17]." In the letter accompanying the order, the Agency stated that "ADEC's own analysis supports the determination that BACT is [SCR], and that ADEC's decision in the proposed permit therefore is both arbitrary and erroneous."

On February 8, 2000, EPA, again invoking its authority under § § 113(a)(5) and 167 of the Act, issued a second order, this time prohibiting Cominco from beginning "construction or modification activities at the Red Dog mine." A third order, issued on March 7, 2000, superseding and vacating the February 8 order, generally prohibited Cominco from acting on ADEC's December 10 PSD permit but allowed limited summer construction. On April 25, 2000, EPA withdrew its December 10 order. Once ADEC issued the permit, EPA explained, that order lacked utility. On July 16, 2003, ADEC granted Cominco a PSD permit to construct MG–17 with SCR as BACT. Under the July 16, 2003, permit, SCR ceases to be BACT "if and when the case currently pending before the Supreme Court of the United States of America is decided in favor of the State of Alaska."

III

Centrally at issue in this case is the question whether EPA's oversight role ... extends to ensuring that a state permitting authority's BACT determination is reasonable in light of the statutory guides. Sections 113(a)(5) and 167 lodge in the Agency encompassing supervisory responsibility over the construction and modification of pollutant emitting facilities in areas covered by the PSD program. 42 U.S.C. § § 7413(a)(5) and 7477. In notably capacious terms, Congress armed EPA with authority to issue orders stopping construction when "a State is not acting in compliance with any [CAA] requirement or prohibition ... relating to the construction of new sources or the modification of existing sources," § 7413(a)(5), or when "construction or modification of a major emitting facility ... does not conform to the requirements of [the PSD program]," § 7477.

The federal Act enumerates several "[p]reconstruction requirements" for the PSD program. § 7475. Absent these, "[n]o major emitting facility ... may be constructed." *Ibid.* One express preconstruction requirement is inclusion of a BACT determination in a facility's PSD permit. §§ 7475(a)(1) and (4).... [T]he Act defines BACT as "an emission limitation based on the maximum degree of reduction of [a] pollutant ... which the permitting authority, on a case-by-case basis, taking into account energy, environmental, and economic impacts and other costs, determines is achievable for [a] facility." § 7479(3). Under this formulation, the permitting authority, ADEC here, exercises primary or initial responsibility for identifying BACT in line with the Act's definition of that term.

All parties agree that one of the "many requirements in the PSD provisions that the EPA may enforce" is "that a [PSD] permit contain a BACT limitation." It is therefore undisputed that the Agency may issue an order to stop a facility's construction if a PSD permit contains no BACT designation.

EPA reads the Act's definition of BACT, together with CAA's explicit listing of BACT as a "[p]reconstruction requiremen[t]," to mandate not simply *a* BACT designation, but a determination of BACT faithful to the statute's definition. In keeping with the broad oversight role §§ 113(a)(5) and 167 vest in EPA, the Agency maintains, it may review permits to ensure that a State's BACT determination is reasonably moored to the Act's provisions. We hold, as elaborated below, that the Agency has rationally construed the Act's text and that EPA's construction warrants our respect and approbation.

BACT's statutory definition requires selection of an emission control technology that results in the "maximum" reduction of a pollutant "achievable for [a] facility" in view of "energy, environmental, and economic impacts, and other costs." 42 U.S.C. § 7479(3). This instruction, EPA submits, cabins state permitting authorities' discretion by granting only "authority to make *reasonable* BACT determinations," *i.e.,* decisions made with fidelity to the Act's purpose "to insure that economic growth will occur in a manner consistent with the preservation of existing clean air resources," 42 U.S.C. § 7470(3). Noting that state permitting authorities' statutory discretion is constrained by CAA's strong, normative terms "maximum" and "achievable," § 7479(3), EPA reads § § 113(a)(5) and 167 to empower the federal Agency to check a state agency's unreasonably lax BACT designation.

EPA stresses Congress' reason for enacting the PSD program—to prevent significant deterioration of air quality in clean-air areas within a State and in neighboring States. §§ 7470(3), (4). That aim, EPA urges, is unlikely to be realized absent an EPA surveillance role that extends to BACT determinations. The Agency notes in this regard a House Report observation:

> Without national guidelines for the prevention of significant deterioration a State deciding to protect its clean air resources will face a double threat. The prospect is very real that such a State would lose existing industrial plants to more permissive States. But additionally the State will likely become the target of "economic-environmental blackmail" from new industrial plants that will play one State off against another with threats to locate in whichever State adopts the most permissive pollution controls. H.R.Rep. No. 95–294, p. 134 (1977), U.S.Code Cong. & Admin.News 1977, 1077, 1213.

The House Report further observed that "a community that sets and enforces strict standards may still find its air polluted from sources in another community or another State." *Id.,* at 135, U.S.Code Cong. & Admin.News 1977, 1077, 1214. Federal agency surveillance of a State's BACT designation is needed, EPA asserts, to restrain the interjurisdictional pressures to which Congress was alert.

The CAA construction EPA advances in this litigation is reflected in interpretive guides the Agency has several times published. We "normally accord particular deference to an agency interpretation of 'longstanding' duration," *Barnhart v. Walton,* 535 U.S. 212, 220 (2002), recognizing that "well-reasoned views" of an expert administrator rest on " 'a body of experience and informed judgment to which courts and litigants may properly resort for guidance,' " *Bragdon v. Abbott,* 524 U.S. 624, 642 (1998).

ADEC argues that the statutory definition of BACT, § 7479(3), unambiguously assigns to "the permitting authority" alone determination of the control technology qualifying as "best available." Because the Act places responsibility for determining BACT with "the permitting authority," ADEC urges, CAA excludes federal Agency surveillance reaching the substance of the BACT decision. EPA's enforcement role, ADEC maintains, is restricted to the requirement "that the permit contain a BACT limitation."

Understandably, Congress entrusted state permitting authorities with initial responsibility to make BACT determinations "case-by-case." § 7479(3). A state agency, no doubt, is best positioned to adjust for local differences in raw materials or plant configurations, differences that might make a technology "unavailable" in a particular area. But the fact that the relevant statutory guides—"maximum" pollution reduction, considerations of energy, environmental, and economic impacts—may not yield a "single, objectively 'correct' BACT determination," surely does not signify that there can be no *unreasonable* determinations. Nor does Congress' sensitivity to site-specific factors necessarily imply a design to preclude in this context meaningful EPA oversight under §§ 113(a)(5) and 167. EPA claims no prerogative to designate the correct BACT; the Agency asserts only the authority to guard against unreasonable designations.

Under ADEC's interpretation, EPA properly inquires whether a BACT determination appears in a PSD permit, but not whether that BACT determination "was made on reasonable grounds properly supported on the record." Congress, however, vested EPA with explicit and sweeping authority to enforce CAA "requirements" relating to the construction and modification of sources under the PSD program, including BACT. We fail to see why Congress, having expressly endorsed an expansive surveillance role for EPA in two independent CAA provisions, would then implicitly preclude the Agency from verifying substantive compliance with the BACT provisions and, instead, limit EPA's superintendence to the insubstantial question whether the state permitting authority had uttered the key words "BACT."

We emphasize, however, that EPA's rendition of the Act's less than crystalline text leaves the "permitting authority" considerable leeway. The Agency acknowledges "the need to accord appropriate deference" to States' BACT designations, and disclaims any intention to " 'second guess' state decisions." Only when a state agency's BACT determination is "not based on a reasoned analysis" may EPA step in to ensure that the statutory requirements are honored.[14] EPA adhered to that limited

---

14. According to the Agency, "[i]t has proven to be relatively rare that a state agency has put EPA in the position of having to exercise [its] authority," noting that only two other reported judicial decisions concern EPA orders occasioned by States' faulty BACT determinations. [Citing *Allsteel, Inc. v. EPA,* 25 F.3d 312 (C.A.6 1994),

role here, explaining why ADEC's BACT determination was "arbitrary" and contrary to ADEC's own findings. EPA's limited but vital role in enforcing BACT is consistent with a scheme that "places primary responsibilities and authority with the States, backed by the Federal Government." S.Rep. No. 95–127, p. 29.

Nor do we find compelling ADEC's suggestion, reiterated by the dissent, that, if state courts are not the exclusive judicial arbiters, EPA would be free to invalidate a BACT determination "months, even years, after a permit has been issued." This case threatens no such development. It involves preconstruction orders issued by EPA, not postconstruction federal Agency directives. EPA itself regards it as "imperative" to act on a timely basis, recognizing that courts are "less likely to require new sources to accept more stringent permit conditions the farther planning and construction have progressed." In the one instance of untimely EPA action ADEC identifies, the federal courts declined to permit enforcement to proceed. See *United States v. AM General Corp.*, 34 F.3d 472, 475 (C.A.7 1994)EPA, we are confident, could not indulge in the inequitable conduct ADEC and the dissent hypothesize while the federal courts sit to review EPA's actions.

Justice KENNEDY, with whom THE CHIEF JUSTICE, Justice SCALIA, and Justice THOMAS join, dissenting.

The majority holds that, under the CAA, state agencies are vested with "initial responsibility for identifying BACT in line with the Act's definition of that term" and that EPA has a "broad oversight role" to ensure that a State's BACT determination is "reasonably moored to the Act's provisions." The statute, however, contemplates no such arrangement. It directs the "permitting authority"—here, [ADEC]—to "determine" what constitutes BACT. To "determine" is not simply to make an initial recommendation that can later be overturned. It is "[t]o decide or settle ... conclusively and authoritatively." American Heritage Dictionary 495 (4th ed.2000).

The BACT definition presumes that the permitting authority will exercise discretion. It presumes, in addition, that the BACT decision will accord full consideration to the statutory factors and other relevant and necessary criteria. Contrary to the majority's holding, the statute does not direct the State to find as BACT the technology that results in the "maximum reduction of a pollutant achievable for [a] facility" in the abstract. Indeed, for a State to do so without regard to the other mandatory criteria would be to ignore the words of the statute. The Act requires a more comprehensive judgment. It provides that the permitting authority must "tak[e] into account" a set of contextual consider-

---

and *Solar Turbines Inc. v. Seif,* 879 F.2d 1073 (C.A.3 1989)]. EPA's restrained and moderate use of its authority hardly supports the dissent's speculation that the federal Agency will "displac[e]" or "degrad[e]" state agencies or relegate them to the performance of "ministerial" functions. Nor has EPA ever asserted authority to override a state-court judgment. Preclusion principles, we note in this regard, unquestionably do apply against the United States, its agencies and officers. See, *e.g., Montana v. United States,* 440 U.S. 147 (1979).

ations—"energy, environmental, and economic impacts and other costs"—to identify the best control technology "on a case-by-case basis." 42 U.S.C. § 7479(3). The majority reaches its narrow view of the scope of the State's discretion only by wresting two adjectives, "maximum" and "achievable," out of context. In doing so, it ignores "the cardinal rule that a statute is to be read as a whole." *King v. St. Vincent's Hospital,* 502 U.S. 215, 221 (1991).

To be sure, §§ 113(a)(5) and 167 authorize EPA to enforce requirements of the Act. These provisions, however, do not limit the States' latitude and responsibility to balance all the statutory factors in making their discretionary judgments. If a State has complied with the Act's requirements, §§ 113(a)(5) and 167 are not implicated and can supply no separate basis for EPA to exercise a supervisory role over a State's discretionary decision. The Court of Appeals for the Ninth Circuit had it altogether backwards when it reasoned that, "because neither Section 113(a)(5) nor Section 167 contains any exemption for requirements that involve the state's exercise of discretion," EPA had the authority to issue orders countermanding the State's BACT determination. 298 F.3d 814, 820 (2002). The question is not whether the two sections contain any exemption. Rather, it is about the nature of the Act's requirements and whether EPA has the authority to set aside a BACT determination when no requirement of the Act was violated in the first place. In affirming the judgment of the Court of Appeals, the majority repeats the same analytical error. When the statute is read as a whole, it is clear that the CAA commits BACT determinations to the discretion of the relevant permitting authorities. Unless an objecting party, including EPA, prevails on judicial review, the determinations are conclusive.

Here the state agency, ADEC, recognized it was required to make a BACT determination. It issued two detailed reports in response to comments by interested parties and concluded that Low Nitrogen Oxide (NOx) was BACT. The requirement that the agency weigh the list of statutory factors, study all other relevant considerations, and decide the technology that can best reduce pollution within practical constraints was met in full. As even EPA acknowledged, ADEC "provid[ed] a detailed accounting of the process." This is not a case, then, where the state agency failed to have a BACT review procedure in place or altogether refused to apply the statute's formal requirements. EPA's only quarrel is with ADEC's substantive conclusion. In disagreeing with ADEC, EPA's sole contention, in the section of its order titled "Findings of *Fact,*" is that "SCR is BACT." In addition, EPA does not allege that using Low NOx would violate other CAA requirements, such as the [NAAQS], Alaska's [PSD] increments, or other applicable emission standards, see 42 U.S.C. § 7475(a)(3). On this state of the record there is no deviation from any statutory "requirement." As a result, EPA has no statutory basis to invoke the enforcement authority of §§ 113(a)(5) and 167.

When Congress intends to give EPA general supervisory authority, it says so in clear terms. In addition to requiring EPA's advance approval of BACT determinations in some instances, 42 U.S.C. § 7475(a)(8), the statute grants EPA powers to block the construction or operation of polluting sources in circumstances not at issue here, §§ 7426(b), (c)(1), 7410(a)(2)(D)(i).... No analogous language is used in the statutory definition of BACT.

EPA insists it needs oversight authority to prevent a "race to the bottom," where jurisdictions compete with each other to lower environmental standards to attract new industries and keep existing businesses within their borders. Whatever the merits of these arguments as a general matter, EPA's distrust of state agencies is inconsistent with the Act's clear mandate that States bear the primary role in controlling pollution and, here, the exclusive role in making BACT determinations. In "cho[osing] not to dictate a Federal response to balancing sometimes conflicting goals" at the expense of "[m]aximum flexibility and State discretion," H.R.Rep. No. 95–294, p. 146 (1977), U.S.Code Cong. & Admin.News 1977, 1077, 1225, Congress made the overriding judgment that States are more responsive to local conditions and can strike the right balance between preserving environmental quality and advancing competing objectives. By assigning certain functions to the States, Congress assumed they would have a stake in implementing the environmental objectives of the Act. At the same time, Congress charged EPA with setting ambient standards and enforcing emission limits, 42 U.S.C. § 7475(a)(3), to ensure that the Nation takes the necessary steps to reduce air pollution.

The presumption that state agencies are not to be trusted to do their part is unwarranted in another respect: EPA itself said so. As EPA concedes, States, by and large, take their statutory responsibility seriously, and EPA sees no reason to intervene in the vast majority of cases. In light of this concession, EPA and *amici* not only fail to overcome the established presumption that States act in good faith, but also admit that their fears about a race to the bottom bear little relation to the real-world experience under the statute.

Notes and Comments

1. Whose analysis do you find more compelling, the majority's or the dissent's? Is there any textual support in either of the relevant provision for the "reasoned analysis" compromise that EPA advocates and the majority embraces? Read § 113(a)(5). Who do you think Congress intended to be the recipient of any orders issued thereunder, the State or the facility?

2. Once a State has an approved Title V program, the PSD permitting requirements become subsumed in the Title V permit issuance process. See 42 U.S.C. § 7661a(a). In that context, EPA has powers like those we considered in the NPDES context—it can block the issuance of any permit that it finds does not conform to the relevant requirements. 42 U.S.C. § 7661d(b). How should this authority affect the dynamics the Court addressed in the *Alaska* case?

VI. THE CLEAN AIR ACT—MOBILE SOURCES

Many of the criteria pollutants come from the exhaust of cars, trucks, and other mobile sources. Unlike stationary sources, the regulation of pollution from mobile sources does not lend itself well to State control. Most automobiles are in a nationwide market and can be transported easily. Thus, the CAA amendments of 1970 proposed a federal solution that was to require significant reductions in mobile source pollution within 5 years. These deadlines were later amended, but the national requirements have remained. With one exception, these requirements are uniform. Because it was seen as having a more intractable problem with mobile source pollution and had already begun regulating these sources before the passage of the 1970 CAA amendments, California has been allowed to create additional controls.

In addition, mobile source control can also be seen as encompassing controls on the fuel that will be used in the sources. The 1990 Amendments created fuel standards that had to be adopted depending on the severity of the ozone or Carbon Monoxide non-compliance problem in an area.

Though mobile sources have indeed become less polluting per unit of energy emitted over the last thirty years, the sheer growth in the volume of sources and miles traveled threatens to swamp the gains that have been made. Though States could regulate mobile sources indirectly through zoning or other transportation demand management techniques, most control of mobile sources comes through this section of the Clean Air Act. The following excerpt provides an excellent account of mobile source controls and the issues involved therein. Although the environmental lawyer may not routinely deal with mobile source controls, with increased control on stationary sources, it is possible that the solution to truly clean air may only exist with reductions in mobile source emissions. Therefore, it is important to know the regulatory structure involved.

ENVIRONMENTAL LAWYER
FEBRUARY, 2000

Arnold W. Reitze, Jr.
[citations omitted].

ARTICLES

MOBILE SOURCE AIR POLLUTION CONTROL

The reduction of air pollution from mobile sources is a major goal of the Clean Air Act. The United States Environmental Protection Agency has interpreted the statute's requirements in thousands of pages of the Federal Register and through other guidance documents. Moreover, states regulate the use of vehicles and impose controls on their transportation systems to protect air quality. . . .

The major regulated pollutants from motor vehicles are carbon monoxide (CO), nitrogen oxides (NOx), hydrocarbons (HC) or volatile organic compounds (VOCs), which are a chemically reactive subset of HC, and particulate matter (PM10) from diesel engines. VOCs and NOx react in the presence of sunlight to produce photochemical oxidants. Photochemical oxidants, which include ozone and a myriad of less easily identifiable air pollutants, are commonly known as smog.

In 1997, transportation sources in the United States were responsible for a large percentage of the nations total emissions, including: 76.6% of the CO emissions; 49.2% of the NOx; 39.9% of the VOCs; 23.0% of the PM10, 13.3% of the lead; and 6.8% of the SO_2 emissions. From 1988 to 1997, CO emissions from transportation sources in the United States decreased by twenty-five percent, and VOCs decreased by twenty-eight percent. Nitrogen oxide emissions from highway vehicles decreased eight percent from 1988 to 1997.

Other substances emitted from motor vehicles may be regulated as hazardous air pollutants (HAPs). Motor vehicles are responsible for the release of approximately twenty-one percent of the nation's HAP, although the percentages contributed in each state ranges from as much as fifty-five percent in Hawaii to as low as ten percent in Alabama. EPA estimates that HAP emissions from mobile sources decreased about sixteen percent from 1993 to 1996, primarily because of the shift to the use of reformulated gasoline. For the thirty HAPs that pose the most significant health risk, EPA estimates that mobile sources contribute thirty-one percent in rural areas and forty-five percent in urban areas. In addition, motor vehicles are significant sources of stratospheric ozone-depleting substances because of the chemicals used in motor vehicle air conditioners.

Transportation sources also accounted for thirty-two percent of the United States carbon dioxide (CO_2) emissions from fossil fuel consumption in 1997. CO_2 is the leading cause of global warming. Each gallon of gasoline used by a motor vehicle results in the release of about twenty pounds of CO_2 (containing 5.47 pounds of carbon) into the atmosphere. Since 1984, CO_2 emissions from United States transportation sources have increased from 379.0 million metric tons (mmt) of carbon to 473.1 mmt in 1997. However, this tonnage increase represents just a 1.7% increase in the transportation share of the overall CO_2 emissions from total fossil fuel use over the same period of time. The worldwide contribution of emissions of global warming gases from motor vehicles is far more dramatic. Since 1950, the worldwide total of automobiles has increased from about 53 million to about 486 million in 1996, which has resulted in a decrease in the United States' percentage of the world's automobiles from 76.0% to 26.7%.

Today motor vehicles used in the United States emit significantly less pollution per mile traveled than the vehicles of the 1960s. As previously discussed, however, in 1997 transportation sources still accounted for over three-quarters of the CO, about two-fifths of the VOC, and about half of the NOx emissions in the United States. The improvements in emissions from mobile sources were made while annual vehicle miles traveled (VMT) increased. Since the 1970 CAA Amendments were enacted, annual VMT has increased from slightly under 1.100 trillion miles to 2.560 trillion miles in 1997. This increase in the use of motor vehicles helped nullify the reductions in exhaust emissions per VMT achieved through the use of air pollution controls. In addition, the increased size of the vehicle fleet reduced the overall effectiveness of evaporative controls. In 1970 there were 89.244 million automobiles and 14.211 million light trucks registered in the United States; in 1997 the number had increased to 129.749 million automobiles and 70.224 million light trucks.

These figures show that the mix of vehicles changed dramatically as sport utility vehicles (SUVs) and light-duty trucks (LDT) were used as substitutes for automobiles. In 1976 pickup trucks, vans and utility vehicles made up 19.8% of vehicle sales; that figure rose to 30.69% in 1998. The increased use of trucks and SUVs results in higher emissions and fuel efficiency that is significantly lower, than if consumers drove automobiles. The fuel economy of automobiles for the model year (MY) 1999 averages 28.3 miles per gallon (mpg), while MY 1999 LDT average 20.8 mpg. Fossil fuels used for transportation went from 8.38 quadrillion British Thermal Units or "quads" in 1950 to 16.04 quads in 1970 and then increased to 19.24 quads in 1977 and 21.80 quads in 1990. In 1998 the amount of fossil fuels used for transportation had climbed to 24.25 quads. This is an increase, for the 1988 to 1998 period, of 1.1% per year. Transportation used two-thirds of the petroleum consumed in the United States in 1998. The reason that air quality in the United States has modestly improved despite substantial increases in vehicle miles traveled and in the size of the vehicle fleet is due to the development of technologies that have significantly reduced emissions per vehicle mile traveled.

* * *

C. Exhaust Emissions

Exhaust emissions include unburned fuel and other HC, CO, and NOx. CO is a colorless, odorless, poisonous gas created from fuel combustion in an oxygen deficient environment resulting from an overly rich fuel mixture. The VOC component of HC and NOx are controlled primarily to prevent the formation of photochemical oxidants measured as ozone.In addition to their contribution to the creation of ozone, NOx react with water vapor to produce acid rain,and nitrous oxide is a greenhouse gas.

1. Control of Nitrogen Oxides From Motor Vehicles

Air is a mixture of gases, which is about seventy-eight percent nitrogen and about twenty-one percent oxygen by volume. Most NOx comes from the elemental nitrogen in the air which chemically reacts at high temperatures is used for combustion. When air is heated to over 1200–C (2192–F), nitrogen combines with oxygen to create nitric oxide, also called nitrogen oxide (NO). At temperatures above 1700–C (3092–F) the rate of NO formation increases significantly as shown by the following equation.

$N_2 + O_2 \_ 2\ NO$

Most of the nitrogen emissions from an internal combustion engine are in the form of NO. NO reacts instantly with oxygen at room temperature to form nitrogen dioxide (NO_2).

$2NO + O_2 \_ 2\ NO_2$

NO_2 is a criteria pollutant a pollutant controlled directly by the CAA. The NO_2 then reacts with many substances. It combines with water to produce nitric acid (HNO_3). It also reacts with ultraviolet light (hv) to produce ozone, as illustrated by the following chemical equations:

$NO_2 + hv \_ NO + O$

$O + O_2 \_ O_3 + M$

A major problem concerning the control of exhaust emissions is that, in general, increased air and combustion temperature decrease HC formation but increase NOx formation. The CO concentration in exhaust emissions is primarily a function of the air-to-fuel ratio. Increasing the supply of air decreases the supply of CO emissions. However, fuel rich mixtures and lower combustion temperatures will reduce NOx formation, but will increase CO and HC production. Thus, many vehicle manufacturers aim to reduce NOx formation during combustion and clean up the CO and HC emissions later in the vehicle's exhaust system. Nevertheless, it should be emphasized that the relationship between HC, CO, and NOx formation is complex. Excess air usually increases NOx formation and reduces HC, however, the chemistry of combustion at various air-to-fuel ratios is quite complex.

Control strategies for NOx can be grouped into two categories: combustion controls and post-combustion controls. The principal post-combustion NOx control used in automobiles is the reduction catalyst discussed below. In contrast, combustion controls are aimed at adjusting the parameters of the burning of fuel to minimize NOx production. These include:

Combustion Temperature. A decrease in temperature reduces

NOx formation, but also decreases engine efficiency. Thus, more fuel is needed to do the same amount of work;

Air-to-Fuel Ratio. A very rich or very lean mixture reduces NOx formation, but a rich mixture increases HC and CO production and wastes fuel. A lean mixture may result in reduced performance;

Engine Speed (RPM). An increase in engine speed (RPM) will decrease NOx emissions;

Ambient Air Temperature. As ambient temperature decreases the intake air temperature decreases leading to decreased combustion temperatures and, thus, lower NOx emissions;

Humidity. Increased humidity in the intake air lowers NOx emissions.

2. Air-to-Fuel Ratio

Maximizing combustion efficiency, from an air pollution perspective, requires that all fuel be burned, and if this is achieved, the byproducts will be limited to heat, CO_2, water vapor, and nitrogen. This stoichiometric combustion results in no criteria air pollutants being released. The equation for complete combustion will vary depending upon the mix of combustible HC in the fuel.

* * *

III. Introduction to Legal Controls on Mobile Source Air Pollution

The technology for the control of motor vehicle emissions was driven by the legal requirements imposed on new vehicles by California and subsequently by the federal government. These legal developments will be examined in the material that follows.

* * *

The 1970 CAA Amendments provided the basic approach used today. Specifically, under the 1970 CAA Amendments:

motor vehicle emissions were to be controlled primarily through improved technology mandated by the federal government for new vehicles (except for California); reduction of HC, CO, and NOx emissions from vehicles by ninety percent was targeted; and

the states could impose programs aimed at in-use vehicles to reduce the vehicle miles traveled or to keep in-use vehicles properly maintained.

In 1977, Congress again amended air pollution controls through the CAA Title II Amendments. The Title II Amendments:

postponed until MY 1980 the more stringent CO and HC standards;

relaxed the NOx emission standard from 0.4 gpm to 1 gpm for MY 1981 and thereafter;

allowed California to continue to have more stringent emissions standards, but nonattainment areas in other states could adopt California standards with EPA's approval;

modified the waiver for California to require the state's standards to be as protective of the public health and welfare as federal standards;

required inspection and maintenance ("I/M") programs in areas that are nonattainment for CO and O_3;

added warranty and tampering provisions;

relaxed the standards applicable to vehicles sold at high altitudes;

softened testing requirements for small manufacturers;

tightened provisions concerning fuel additives;

relaxed lead additive requirements for small refineries;

ordered the administrator of the EPA (the Administrator) to set standards for heavy duty vehicles and motorcycles;

allowed refueling requirements to be imposed; and

allowed other pollutants that endangered public health or welfare to be regulated.

The 1970 CAA Amendments gave EPA the authority and responsibility to establish programs to provide for a ninety percent reduction by MY 1975 of HC and CO emissions that were allowable on 1970 MY cars and a ninety percent reduction by MY 1976 of NOx that was emitted from 1971 MY cars. To reach these goals, EPA established federal emission standards of 0.41 gpm for HC; 3.4 gpm for CO; and 0.4 gpm NOx. However, the achievement of the emissions reduction goals was delayed by EPA and Congressional actions between 1973 and 1990.

First, in 1973 EPA granted a one year postponement. The following year Congress postponed the reduction goals until 1977 (1978 for NOx) under the Energy Supply and Environmental Coordination Act (ESECA). Then in 1975, EPA granted another one year postponement. Congress again delayed implementation in 1977 when it amended the 1970 CAA Amendments to set new standards for MY 1978 79, 1980 and 1981 and all vehicles thereafter. Finally, in 1990, Congress set new emission standards under the 1990 CAA Amendments.

Under section 202 of the 1970 CAA, MY 1970 emissions were the baseline for determining the allowable CO and HC emissions for vehicles manufactured during or after MY 1975. For vehicles of MY 1976 and thereafter, the baseline for NOx emissions was MY 1971. The 1990 CAA Amendments include language similar to the 1970 CAA Amendments and use MY 1970 as the CO and HC baseline. The following chart illustrates the emissions baselines for HC, NOx, and CO; the NOx reduction is specified in a gpm standard without reference to a baseline. Pre–1990 Federal Exhaust Standards for Gasoline–Powered Light Vehicles in grams per mile (gpm):

MY		Hydrocarbons	/Carbon Monoxide	/Nitrogen Oxides
1968	1969	N/A	N/A	no standard
1970	1971	2.2	23.0	no standard
1972		3.4	39.0	no standard
1973	1974	3.4	39.0	3.0
1975	1976	1.5	15.0	3.1
1977	1979	1.5	15.0	2.0
1980		0.41	7.0	2.0
1981	1993	0.41	3 .4	1.0

B. Synopsis of the 1990 Clean Air Act Mobile Source Control Provisions

The 1990 CAA Amendments revised and tripled the size of the mobile source provisions in the 1970 CAA. The most significant new provisions impose:

more stringent controls on conventional vehicles;

new controls on gasoline and diesel fuels to reduce air pollution emissions; a program to encourage the development of "clean-fuel" vehicles; and more controls on mobile sources such as nonroad vehicles, trains, ships, and mobile equipment. Various provisions in subchapter I of the 1970 CAA Amendments make the states responsible for the establishment and enforcement of emission control strategies applicable to in-use vehicles that are incorporated in their SIPs. Since 1977, most states and the District of Columbia have been required to develop I/M programs for their air quality control regions that have non-attainment status for automotive related pollutants. Based on 1997 data, about 52.6 million people in the United States reside in an area where an air quality standard is violated. Over 47 million people live where the ozone standard is exceeded, and 9.1 million live where the CO standard is violated. Thus, most Americans who live in urbanized areas are subject to I/M programs. These I/M programs increased in stringency under the 1990 CAA Amendments for areas with a serious ozone nonattainment status or a moderate CO nonattainment status and a design value greater than 12.7 parts per million (ppm). In addition, other transportation control strategies are to be used to develop a transportation control plan that is part of the SIP.

* * *

In the 1990 CAA Amendments the standards for light-duty vehicles (LDV) and LDT became more stringent. Standards also were to be promulgated for motorcycles, heavy-duty engines (HDE), offroad vehicles, and marine engines. Emissions standards for heavy-duty vehicle engines have been less stringent than for LDV, but the 1990 CAA Amendments aimed to reduce the disparity. Emission standards apply to vehicles and engines for their useful life.

More stringent controls on LDV and LDT included new tailpipe emission limitations, new requirements for limiting emissions during cold temperature operation, and new requirements concerning the control of evaporative losses, including losses during refueling. There also are requirements for vehicles to have onboard diagnostic (OBD) capabilities in order to ensure that CAA requirements are met during the prescribed vehicle's life and to ensure compliance with the new warranty requirements, as well as provisions for the control of emissions from alternatively fueled vehicles.

Under the warranty provisions of section 207(a) and (b) coverage of major components, including the catalytic converter, was increased to 8 years or 80,000 miles, but the coverage for other minor emission components was reduced to 2 years or 24,000 miles. The warranty provisions were the only environmental issue decided in the U.S. House of Representatives by a contested floor vote. The warranty provisions included in the final bill were derived from the Sikorski–Green Amendment, which represented a compromise between service station owners and environmentalists.

A new section, 202(l), created a program to control hazardous air pollutants emitted from motor vehicles. The statute directed EPA to produce a study on the need to control such emissions and the means and measures for control. The section directs the agency to focus on emissions that pose the greatest risk to human health or about which there are significant uncertainties. Benzene, formaldehyde, and 1,3–butadiene are specifically to be regulated under section 211(k)(10)(C), and section 112(b)(1). EPA was directed to regulate under section 202(l)(2) to control hazardous emissions from motor vehicles to the greatest degree achievable by May 15, 1995. Benzene and formaldehyde are the only pollutants required to be regulated under section 202(l)(2). Fuels can be regulated under section 211(c).

IV.   Emission Standards After the CAA Amendments of 1990

* * *

New standards also were established for two categories of LDT those over 6000 GVWR and those under 6000 pounds GVWR but over 3750 pounds loaded vehicle weight (LVW). Final regulations issued June 5, 1991, set the Tier I NOx standard at 1.0 gpm for light-duty diesels and included a 0.08 gpm PM standard for 5/50,000 vehicles and a 0.10 gpm PM standard for 10/100,000 vehicles.

By 1999 EPA was to determine the need, cost, and feasibility of Tier 2 standards for 2004 and later MY gasoline and diesel-fueled LDV and LDT of 3750 pounds LVW or less. Tier 2 standards will apply for the extended useful life of ten years or 100,000 miles, whichever occurs first. The statute requires the Administrator to study whether emissions can be reduced to 0.125 gpm for NMHC, 1.7 gpm for CO, and 0.2 gpm for NOx.

On April 28, 1998, EPA announced the release of a Draft Tier 2 Study. The draft study examined three issues: (1) the need for further emission reductions to attain the ambient air standards; (2) the technical feasibility of meeting more stringent standards by MY 2004; and (3) the cost-effectiveness of such further reductions. The draft study included evidence that a need existed for further emission reductions, and that more stringent emission standards are technologically feasible and cost effective.

* * *

EPA subsequently proposed "Tier 2 Motor Vehicle Emission Standards and Gasoline Sulfur Control Requirements" on May 13, 1999. The proposed rule would impose more stringent emission requirements on automobiles, pickup trucks, mini-vans, and SUVs that are operated on any fuel. The cost of meeting the Proposed Rule is projected to be less than $100 per automobile and less than $200 per light truck. The Rule is to be phased in between 2004 and 2007 for automobiles and light trucks, but emission requirements for heavy LDT would be phased in during 2008 and 2009. The new NOx standard is an average of 0.07 gpm, which is significantly more stringent than the existing 0.4 gpm standard for automobiles and the 0.7 gpm for light trucks. The automotive industry however, seems to be supporting the new standard as achievable. The petroleum industry, however, is critical of the proposed rule's sulfur reduction requirement for fuel because of its costs and because of its applicability to areas of the country that are in compliance.

The day after the proposed rule appeared in the Federal Register, the U.S. Court of Appeals for the District of Columbia Circuit struck down the new NAAQS for ozone and for PM. On June 30, 1999, after the opinion was issued, EPA promulgated a clarification of the proposed Tier 2 rule to explain that the D.C. Circuit's opinion concerning the NAAQS for ozone and PM did not change EPA's proposed requirements for the Tier 2 program.

On December 21, 1999, President Clinton announced the issuance of a final rule to reduce dramatically the emissions from SUVs, mini-vans, vans, and LDT by tightening tailpipe emissions and by imposing more stringent standards on the sulfur content of gasoline. All classes of passenger vehicles beginning in 2004 must meet an average standard of 0.07 gpm for NOx emissions.

Vehicles under 6000 pounds will be phased in between 2004 and 2007. For heavier vehicles, including the heaviest LDT over 6000 pounds, the standard in 2004 will not exceed 0.6 gpm, which is more than a sixty percent reduction from the current standard. These vehicles are required to further decrease emissions between 2004 and 2007 to 0.2 gpm. By 2008, half of the vehicles are required to meet the 0.07 gpm standard, with the remaining vehicles complying by 2009. The heaviest passenger vehicles weighing between 8500 and 10,000 pounds have until 2008 to comply and have additional options for compliance.

In 2004, gasoline manufacturers cannot exceed the cap of 300 ppm of sulfur and must maintain an annual corporate average sulfur level of 120 ppm. In 2005, the corporate average requirement drops to 90 ppm and the refinery average will be 30 ppm. In 2006, the cap falls to 80 ppm. Small refiners and some western states have less stringent time criteria, but must comply with the 30 ppm average and 80 ppm cap by 2007.

EPA estimates that, as a result of these rules, projected emissions reductions of NOx will be 1.2 million tons annually in 2010, 2 million tons per year (tpy) by 2020, and nearly 3 million tpy by 2030. EPA estimates these standards will cost industry $5.3 billion, but will yield health and environmental benefits valued at $25.2 billion. The consumer cost is less than $1000 per car, $200 per each LDT, and under two cents per gallon of gas.

Notes and Comments

1. Perhaps obviously, the Supreme Court's opinion in *Massachusetts v. Environmental Protection Agency*, ___ U.S. ___, 127 S.Ct. 1438, ___ L.Ed.2d ___ (2007), may have major implications for the future of the mobile source control program. As we have seen, the Court in *Massachusetts* held that EPA has a mandatory duty to decide whether there is enough scientific certainty to allow it to make an endangerment finding under the standard of § 202(a)(1).

2. The original Clean Air Act essentially prohibited states from regulating the emissions from new motor vehicles, limiting that regulation to the federal government. 42 U.S.C. § 7543(a). However, California was given the option of imposing its own controls on new motor vehicle emissions, because California had already had such controls and because of California's unique problems. Under current law, California must petition EPA for a waiver, which EPA must grant if it finds that California's controls in the aggregate will be as protective as the federal controls, unless EPA determines that finding is arbitrary and capricious, that the state controls are not necessary to meet "compelling and extraordinary conditions," or that the state controls or enforcement mechanisms are inconsistent with the intent of the federal statute governing mobile source controls. 42 U.S.C. § 7543(b). California currently operates under such a waiver. The 1977 amendments to the Clean Air Act authorized other states with non-attainment plans to adopt the California standards in lieu of the federal standards. 42 U.S.C. § 7507. In recent years, as the federal government has failed to increase the stringency for automobiles, several "blue" states have adopted the California Low Emission Vehicle (LEV) standards under this provision, in particular to attack greenhouse gas emissions. *See* http://www.greencarcongress.com/2006/06/oregon_formally.html (last visited on 3/21/07). Nevertheless, this is very controversial, and manufacturers routinely object to California waivers and other states' identical standards. *See, e.g., Motor Vehicle Mfrs. Ass'n of U.S., Inc. v. New York State Dept. of Environmental Conservation*, 17 F.3d 521 (2d Cir. 1994).

VII. THE CLEAN AIR ACT—ACID DEPOSITION CONTROL AND THE USE OF MARKET BASED CONTROLS

The problem of "acid rain" has been recognized for over thirty years. In both Europe and North America, the hydration of sulfur and nitrogen oxides created acids (sulfuric acid and nitric acid) that can then be deposited hundreds of mile from the source. This "acid rain" (though it is more likely dry deposition) can eat away at public monuments and buildings and can change the Ph of natural systems, killing both plants and animals. In North America, this problem was of particular concern to Canada, which believed that most of the acid production harming its environment originated in the United States.

In response to this problem, in 1980, Congress passed the Acid Precipitation Act, which mandated a 10–year scientific, technological and economic study to examine the relationship between combustion of fossil fuels and the creation of acids and other pollutants. The National Acid Precipitation Assessment Program (NAPAP) was established to coordinate this study. NAPAP concluded that Sulfur Dioxide (SO_2) and Nitrogen Dioxide (NOx) are precursors to the formation of ozone. Once released into the atmosphere they can travel several hundred miles during which time they are chemically altered into ambient acidic sulfates and nitrates. NAPAP's studies indicated that the damage caused by these acidic depositions is large; it adversely affects water, vegetation, humans and visibility. Because the pollutants can travel long distances, the NAPAP research demonstrated that it was critical to develop regional, even international, solutions to limit emissions of SO_2 and NOx into the atmosphere.

During the 1980's Canada continued to lobby the US government to develop an international approach to controlling these emissions. In 1991, Canada and the United States signed the Agreement on Air Quality in which both countries agreed on a "cap and trade" program.

In Canada, the federal government agreed to reduce, through provincial programs, SO_2 by 2.3 million tonnes and to establish a national cap on SO_2 emissions of 3.2 tonnes by the year 2000. Each province was assigned a specific limitation on SO_2 emissions, and the provinces were free to decide how to achieve the reduction needed to comply with the emission cap. Options included control options, process changes, changes in fuel source, energy conservation programs to reduce electric demand or back end control technologies such as controlling limits on sulfur content in heavy fuel oil. A central feature of the provincial program was "trading," in which the electric utilities were allocated a share of the "emission cap" and allowed to trade freely among their various power plants and generating plants within the province to meet their allocation.

In the United States, Congress met their commitments under the Agreement on Air Quality through the provisions of Title IV of the 1990 Clean Air Act. Rather than rely upon the States or specific source controls as they did in dealing with criteria pollutants, Congress adopted a national goal to reduce SO_2 emissions by 10 million tons below 1980 emission levels and reduce NOx by approximately 2 million tons below the 1980 levels. The regulatory scheme set out in Title IV is quite unique and reflected a radical departure for Congress. Rather than embroil Congress or the EPA in micromanaging how industry would comply, Congress translated the goal of "10 million ton reduction in SO_2 emissions" into a total cap that would be divided between each sulfur dioxide generating electric utility. Congress then set out a generous 20–year timetable for achieving this goal. Further, Congress gave the utilities a new tool by which to meet their targets, the trading of emissions.

A. SO$_2$ Emission Limitation Program

A "cap and trade" regulatory model is designed to give the regulated parties maximum flexibility in designing their solution to the limit established for them. This model had longed been hailed by economists for allowing the reduction of pollution at the lowest possible cost to the regulated industry. Environmental groups had long been suspicious of the theory, expressing concerns that it might be difficult to monitor, and that it would send the wrong message that it was "OK to pollute." The battle over the use of this emissions program was heated, but ultimately, its presence allowed the Republican Party and the first President Bush to agree to the 1990 Clean Air Act Amendments as a whole.

The adopted program works in the following way. Sources are all given an initial amount of pollutant that they can emit. They can reach this target in numerous ways. They are free to switch fuels, install control technology, change operations, replace facilities, retire facilities or trade their emission "credits or allowances" in order to ensure that their emissions, when accumulated, are within the allocation they received.

In Phase I, Congress identified the 110 electric utility plants that were thought to be the largest contributors to SO$_2$ and NOx emissions and allocated a specific number of "allowances" to them. 42 U.S.C. § 7651b. Each allowance was equivalent to 1 ton of SO$_2$ emissions. The number of allowances received was calculated on the basis of a baseline, which was calculated as the annual average quantity of British Thermal Units (Btus) produced in calendar years 1985, 1986 and 1987. 42 U.S.C. § 7651a(A). Then using this baseline, each unit was allowed to emit 2.5 pounds of SO$_2$ per British Thermal Unit (Btu) heat input. 2.5 lbs of emissions amounted to a significant reduction in the amount of SO$_2$ previously emitted by most of the utilities. By the end of 1995, each of these utilities was required to operate such that its emissions did not exceed the number of allowances it had been granted that year. In order to meet their cap, each utility was free to adopt a myriad of options as discussed above, including the right to purchase or sell emission allowances.

In Phase II, Congress required the EPA to allocate a specified number of allowances between the remaining 2,200 electric utility companies in the United States. The total number of allowances granted each year was determined based on the annual reduction in SO$_2$ emissions required to meet the stated goal of 10 million tons. Again, each allowance issued is equivalent to 1 ton of SO$_2$ emissions. Once granted, the utility is required to ensure that its emissions do not exceed its allowances. It can do this through a number of mechanisms including the purchase and sale of emission allowances.

New source emitters, i.e., new electric utility plants, were required to acquire allowances from the market in order to receive a permit to operate. In Phase II a certain number of allowances were set aside for new source emitters to purchase from the EPA. If additional allowances were required, the utility could go to the market and purchase them from other utilities.

The critical, and most innovative, element of this regulatory program was the creation of a market in pollution wherein "clean" utilities could make money selling excess allowances. The market was monitored through a permitting program. Each permit would specify the number of allowances a utility would be granted. 42 U.S.C. § 7651g. The application for a permit would detail how the utility would ensure that its emissions were within the allocated allowances. Failure to operate in compliance with the permit or the plan was punishable by significant penalties ($2,000 per ton in excess of allowed emissions); potential to require the utility to offset its SO_2 emissions by an equivalent amount in subsequent years; and an equivalent reduction in the allowances granted in subsequent years.

In order to accommodate new sources, Congress required the EPA to set aside 2.5% of emission allowances into a special allowance reserve and to offer them for sale at a price of $1,500.00. This sale was to be held on an annual basis. Congress also required the EPA to establish an annual auction. Specifically, in Phase I, the EPA was to set aside 150,000 tons per year and in Phase II this would be increased to 250,000 tons per year of SO_2 allowances for the auction. In addition to the allowances set aside by the EPA, utilities that had excess allowances were also free to submit them for sale at the auction. The auction was to be conducted on an annual basis. During the first few years the price received for credits was very low and there was very little trading activity. Since implementation of Phase II, however, trading activity has increased and the market is viable. In recent years, the price of an individual allowance has continued to rise, reflecting both the rise in demand for electric power, and the lowered total of emissions allowed.

B. NOx Emission Limitation Program

Both Canada and the United States agreed to limit the emissions of NOx in the Air Quality Agreement of 1991. The United States is obligated to reduce NOx emissions by approximately 2 million tons from 1980 levels. The emission reductions are expected to come from both stationary sources (electric utility plants) and mobile sources (motor vehicles). Unlike the regulatory program adopted for SO_2 emissions, the NOx emissions are controlled through a more traditional regulatory model under both Title IV(Acid Deposition) and Title II (Criteria Pollutants) of the Clean Air Act and a "cap and trade" program was not originally established.

Pursuant to Section 7651f, the EPA is required to establish the limitations for NOx emissions for two types of electric utility boilers: tangentially fired boilers are limited to 0.45/lb per mmBtu and (b) dry bottom wall-fired boilers are limited to 0.5lb/mmBtu. It is unlawful for either type of boiler to emit NOx in excess of these express limitations.

By 1997, the EPA was required to establish limits for other types of boilers. These limits are to be set based on the degree of reduction achievable through retrofit application of the best system of continuous emission reduction, taking into account (i) available technology, (ii) costs, (iii) energy and environmental impacts and (iv) a determination that the cost is comparable to the costs of NOx controls set by Congress in this section. 42 U.S.C. Sec. 7651f(d).

However, if a utility does not think that it will be able to meet the emission limits, it can apply for an "alternative emission limit," which is to be granted if the EPA determines that the unit cannot meet the applicable limitation using low NOx burner technology. Units are not required to install any additional control technology beyond low NOx burner technology in order to comply with the limits imposed.

In 2005, the EPA moved to implement general reductions over the Eastern United States because of the particular problems governing interstate movement of NOx, and subsequent effects on ozone levels within States.

C. The Use of Market Based Trading Systems

As noted above, the truly revolutionary part of the Acid Rain Program was its use of trading mechanisms to achieve its overall goals. By most counts, the program has been a success. It has reduced the amount of Sulfur Dioxide produced at a far lower cost than was initially believed. Although the acidification of natural systems had proved to be a harder problem to address than first believed, the reductions in Sulfur Dioxide have produced important collateral health benefits. Nevertheless, the success of the Sulfur Dioxide trading program is not necessarily a recipe for future programs. There are many unique parts of the program which may not be able to be replicated in other programs.

The future of the Clean Air Act may or may not revolve around the increasing use of market trading schemes and the abandonment of technology-based regimes. As we have seen, EPA has moved in that direction with both the Clean Air Interstate Rule and the Clean Air Mercury Rule. Beyond those contexts, the Bush Administration has pushed for a much broader usage of these principles in"Clear Skies Intiative." Under that initiative, the Administration would replace the new source performance standards and other technological controls with a much broader "cap and trade" program. How well-advised do you think such changes would be? Are other amendments to the CAA called for? What would you suggest?

Chapter 5

RESOURCE CONSERVATION
AND RECOVERY ACT

I. OVERVIEW AND JURISDICTION

We now turn our attention to the Resource Conservation and Recovery Act, more commonly known as "RCRA," 42 U.S.C. § 6901, et seq. RCRA took its basic statutory shape in 1976, when Congress converted what had previously been known as the Solid Waste Disposal Act into RCRA. Pub. L. No. 94–580, 90 Stat. 2795 (1976). From the outset, RCRA has had two major programs: Subtitle C, covering hazardous waste management; and Subtitle D, governing "solid waste" facilities that do not also handle hazardous waste. In 1984, Congress passed what to date has been its only set of comprehensive amendments to RCRA, the Hazardous and Solid Waste Amendments of 1984 ("HSWA"), Pub. L. No. 98–616, 98 Stat. 3224 (1984). Additionally, when Congress amended CERCLA in 1986, it simultaneously added a third major program to RCRA, Subtitle I, regulating those who store either petroleum or hazardous substances (other than hazardous waste) in underground storage tanks. Pub. L. No. 99–499, 100 Stat. 1615 (1986).

For purposes of this course, we will focus solely on Subtitle C, RCRA's hazardous waste provisions. Subtitle C governs those who generate, transport, or treat, store or dispose of hazardous waste. Although Congress created Subtitle C in 1976, it took EPA until May of 1980 to develop the regulations giving shape to the program. 45 Fed. Reg. 33119 (May 19, 1980). Hence, there was no effective hazardous waste regulatory program in place until that time.

Not surprisingly, the key jurisdictional trigger under Subtitle C is the term "hazardous waste." In order to understand which materials qualify as "hazardous wastes" under Subtitle C, students must familiarize themselves with the interrelationship between some key statutory and regulatory definitions. Section 1004(5) of RCRA defines the term "hazardous waste" as follows:

> The term "hazardous waste" means a solid waste, or combination of solid wastes, which because of its quantity, concentration, or physical, chemical, or infectious characteristics may—

[handwritten margin note: def. of hazardous waste]

393

def. of haz. waste cont'd

(A) cause, or significantly contribute to an increase in mortality or an increase in serious irreversible, or incapacitating reversible, illness; or

(B) pose a substantial present or potential hazard to human health or the environment when improperly treated, stored, transported, or disposed of, or otherwise managed.

42 U.S.C. § 6903(5).

The first thing to note about this definition is that, in order to qualify as a hazardous waste, a material must first qualify as a "solid waste." Thus, as Judge Kenneth Starr (of Monica Lewinski fame) pointed out in the *American Mining Congress* case below, the universe of "hazardous wastes" under RCRA is a subset of the universe of "solid wastes." This latter term is also defined, in § 1004(27), as follows:

Def. of solid waste

The term "solid waste" means any garbage, refuse, sludge from a waste treatment plant, water supply treatment plant, or air pollution control facility and other discarded material, including solid, liquid, semisolid, or contained gaseous material resulting from industrial, commercial, mining, and agricultural operations, and from community activities, but does not include solid or dissolved material in domestic sewage, or solid or dissolved materials in irrigation return flows or industrial discharges which are point sources subject to permits under section 1342 of Title 33, or source, special nuclear, or byproduct material as defined by the Atomic Energy Act of 1954, [42 U.S.C.A. § 2011 et seq.].

42 U.S.C. § 6903(27).

One could paraphrase the thrust of these two provisions as being that, subject to narrow exceptions, the term "hazardous waste" includes any discarded material that poses a substantial threat to human health or the environment when improperly managed. Seen in that light, the need for further regulatory explication is clear, particularly when one considers that Subtitle C contemplates a regulatory program backed up by both civil and criminal sanctions. In fact, Congress tasked EPA with establishing a more refined regulatory definition of those wastes which it deemed worthy of full-blown regulation under Subtitle C. See 42 U.S.C. § 6921. In this vein, EPA has promulgated complicated regulatory frameworks for determining both when materials qualify as "solid wastes" for purposes of Subtitle C, and when those same materials will also qualify as "hazardous wastes."

We will deal both of these constructs below. For now, it is important to understand that a material must meet the regulatory definitions of both of these terms in order be subject to the requirements of Subtitle C.

A. What Is a "Solid Waste"?

The first thing to note is that a "solid waste" does not have to be solid. This much is clear from the statutory definition, which includes liquids and even "contained gaseous materials." Due to this dynamic, many practitioners refer to this first element of the jurisdictional test as simply involving whether the material is a "waste," deeming the term "solid" to be of no regulatory consequence.

EPA's regulatory definition of "solid waste" focuses on when EPA deems materials to have been "discarded." As we will see in the following case, EPA historically has defined the term "discarded" in a way that asserts jurisdiction over materials EPA deems to have been either "abandoned" or "recycled" in environmentally problematic ways. Additionally, EPA has identified some materials that it deems to be "solid wastes" simply because they are "inherently waste-like." See 40 C.F.R. § 261.2(a)(2)(iii) and (d).

By far the most controversial—and complicated—issue in all of RCRA involves EPA's assertion of jurisdiction over materials that are destined for recycling. The basic tensions underlying this controversy are obvious. EPA has summarized its three historical arguments in favor of asserting jurisdiction in the following terms:

- The statute and the legislative history suggest that Congress expected EPA to regulate as wastes some materials that are destined for recycling.

- Many materials stored or transported prior to recycling present the same types of threats to human health and the environment as materials stored or transported prior to disposal. In fact, EPA found that recycling operations have accounted for a number of notorious damage incidents. For example, materials destined for recycling were involved in one-third of the first 60 filings under RCRA's imminent and substantial endangerment authority, and 20 of the first sites listed under CERCLA....

- Excluding all materials destined for recycling would allow materials to move in and out of the hazardous waste management system depending on what any person handling the material intended to do with it. This seems inconsistent with the mandate to track hazardous wastes and control them from "cradle to grave."

68 Fed.Reg. 61558, 61561–61562 (Oct. 28, 2003).

At the same time, subjecting certain types of recycling to regulation under Subtitle C may dramatically increase the cost of extracting further value from those materials. At the margin, it may encourage companies to buy new feedstock materials for their industrial processes rather than using recycled materials. At some level, of course, this undermines the "recovery" goal of the Resource, Conservation and *Recovery* Act (emphasis added).

How should EPA resolve this tension? How much flexibility does the statute allow it? The best way to understand these issues is by tracking their historical evolution. We begin with the following case, which (for reasons which will become clear) is referred to as *"AMC I"*:

AMERICAN MINING CONGRESS v. U.S. EPA

United States Court of Appeals, District of Columbia Circuit, 1987.
824 F.2d 1177.

STARR, Circuit Judge:

RCRA is a comprehensive environmental statute under which EPA is granted authority to regulate solid and hazardous wastes....

Congress' "overriding concern" in enacting RCRA was to establish the framework for a national system to insure the safe management of hazardous waste. H.R.Rep. No. 1491, 94th Cong., 2d Sess. 3 (1976), U.S.Code Cong. & Admin.News 1976, pp. 6238, 6240, 6241....

... [Under Subtitle C], EPA is directed to promulgate regulations establishing a comprehensive management system. [42 U.S.C. § 6921]. EPA's authority, however, extends only to the regulation of "hazardous waste." Because "hazardous waste" is defined as a subset of "solid waste," *id.* § 6903(5), the scope of EPA's jurisdiction is limited to those materials that constitute "solid waste." That pivotal term is defined by RCRA as

> any garbage, refuse, sludge from a waste treatment plant, water supply treatment plant, or air pollution control facility *and other discarded material*, including solid, liquid, semisolid or contained gaseous material, resulting from industrial, commercial, mining, and agricultural operations, and from community activities....

42 U.S.C. § 6903(27) (emphasis added). As will become evident, this case turns on the meaning of the phrase, "and other discarded material," contained in the statute's definitional provisions.

EPA's interpretation of "solid waste" has evolved over time. On May 19, 1980, EPA issued interim regulations defining "solid waste" to include a material that is "a manufacturing or mining by-product and sometimes is discarded." 45 Fed.Reg. 33,119 (1980). This definition contained two terms needing elucidation: "by-product" and "sometimes discarded." In its definition of "a manufacturing or mining by-product," EPA expressly *excluded* "an intermediate manufacturing or mining product which results from one of the steps in a manufacturing or mining process and is typically processed through the next step of the process within a short time." *Id.*

In 1983, the agency proposed narrowing amendments to the 1980 interim rule. 48 Fed.Reg. 14,472 (1983). The agency showed especial concern over *recycling* activities. In the preamble to the amendments, the agency observed that, in light of the interlocking statutory provisions and RCRA's legislative history, it was clear that "Congress indeed intended that materials being recycled or held for recycling can be wastes, and if hazardous, hazardous wastes." *Id.* at 14,473. The agency also asserted that "not only can materials destined for recycling or being

[handwritten margin notes:]
EPA to establish regs for hazardous waste

Def. of solid waste

issue in case

interim def. of solid waste

def. of "by-product" excludes intermediate manuf

EPA said that recycled material could be hazardous waste

recycled be solid and hazardous wastes, but the Agency clearly has the authority to regulate recycling activities as hazardous management." *Id.*

While asserting its interest in recycling activities (and materials being held for recycling), EPA's discussion left unclear whether the agency in fact believed its jurisdiction extended to materials recycled in an industry's on-going production processes, or only to materials disposed of and recycled as part of a waste management program. In its preamble, EPA stated that "the revised definition of solid waste sets out the Agency's view of its jurisdiction over the recycling of hazardous waste . . . Proposed section 261.6 then contains exemptions from regulations for those hazardous waste recycling activities that we do not think require regulation." *Id.* at 14,476. The amended regulatory description of "solid waste" itself, then, did not include materials "used or reused as effective substitutes for raw materials in processes using raw materials as principal feedstocks." *Id.* at 14,508. EPA explained the exclusion as follows:

> [These] materials are being used essentially as raw materials and so ordinarily are not appropriate candidates for regulatory control. Moreover, when these materials are used to manufacture new products, the processes generally are normal manufacturing operations. . . . The Agency is reluctant to read the statute as regulating actual manufacturing processes.

Id. at 14,488. This, then, seemed clear: EPA was drawing a line between discarding and ultimate recycling, on the one hand, and a continuous or ongoing manufacturing process with one-site "recycling," on the other. If the activity fell within the latter category, then the materials were not deemed to be "discarded."

After receiving extensive comments, EPA issued its final rule on January 4, 1985. 50 Fed.Reg. 614 (1985). Under the final rule, materials are considered "solid waste" if they are abandoned by being disposed of, burned, or incinerated; or stored, treated, or accumulated before or in lieu of those activities. In addition, certain recycling activities fall within EPA's definition. EPA determines whether a material is a RCRA solid waste when it is recycled by examining both the material or substance itself and the recycling activity involved. The final rule identifies five categories of "secondary materials" (spent materials, sludges, by-products, commercial chemical products, and scrap metal). These "secondary materials" constitute "solid waste" when they are disposed of; burned for energy recovery or used to produce a fuel; reclaimed; or accumulated speculatively. *Id.* at 618–19, 664.[1] Under the final rule, if a material

---

1. Under the final rule, a "use constituting disposal" is defined as direct placement on land of wastes or products containing or derived from wastes. A material is "accumulated speculatively" if it is accumulated prior to being recycled. If the accumulator can show that the materials feasibly can be recycled, and that during a one-year calendar period the amount of material recycled or transferred for recycling is 75% or more of the amount present at the beginning of the year, the materials are not considered solid wastes. A material is "reclaimed" if it is processed to recover a usable product, or if it is regenerated. *Id.*

[margin note: It is gold waste UNLESS directly reused]

constitutes "solid waste," it is subject to RCRA regulation *unless* it is directly reused as an ingredient or as an effective substitute for a commercial product, or is returned as a raw material substitute to its original manufacturing process.[2] *Id.* In the jargon of the trade, the latter category is known as the "closed-loop" exception. In either case, the material must not first be "reclaimed" (processed to recover a usable product or regenerated). *Id.* EPA exempts these activities "because they are like ordinary usage of commercial products." *Id.* at 619.

[margin note: AMC & API say that rules applied to in process mats. exceed EPA juris.]

Petitioners, American Mining Congress ("AMC") and American Petroleum Institute ("API"), challenge the scope of EPA's final rule. Relying upon the statutory definition of "solid waste," petitioners contend that EPA's authority under RCRA is limited to controlling materials that are *discarded* or *intended for discard*. They argue that EPA's reuse and recycle rules, as applied to inprocess secondary materials, regulate materials that have not been discarded, and therefore exceed EPA's jurisdiction.

To understand petitioners' claims, a passing familiarity with the nature of their industrial processes is required.

Petroleum refineries vary greatly both in respect of their products and their processes.... In general, the refining process starts by "distilling" crude oil into various hydrocarbon streams or "fractions." The "fractions" are then subjected to a number of processing steps. Various hydrocarbon materials derived from virtually all stages of processing are combined or blended in order to produce products such as gasoline, fuel oil, and lubricating oils. Any hydrocarbons that are not usable in a particular form or state are returned to an appropriate stage in the refining process so they can eventually be used. Likewise, the hydrocarbons and materials which escape from a refinery's production vessels are gathered and, by a complex retrieval system, returned to appropriate parts of the refining process. Under EPA's final rule, this reuse and recycling of materials is subject to regulation under RCRA.

In the mining industry, primary metals production involves the extraction of fractions of a percent of a metal from a complex mineralogical matrix (i.e., the natural material in which minerals are embedded). Extractive metallurgy proceeds incrementally. Rome was not built in a day, and all metal cannot be extracted in one fell swoop. In consequence, materials are reprocessed in order to remove as much of the pure metal as possible from the natural ore. Under EPA's final rule, this reprocessed ore and the metal derived from it constitute "solid waste." What is more, valuable metal-bearing and mineral-bearing dusts are often released in processing a particular metal. The mining facility typically

---

2. Specifically, the final rule excludes materials recycled by being: "(1) [u]sed or reused as ingredients in an industrial process to make a product, *provided the materials are not being reclaimed;* or (2) [u]sed or reused as effective substitutes for commercial products; or (3) [r]eturned to the original process from which they are generated, without first being reclaimed." *Id.* (emphasis added). In the third category, the material must be returned to the original manufacturing process as a substitute for raw material feedstock, and the process must use raw materials as principal feedstocks.

recaptures, recycles, and reuses these dusts, frequently in production processes different from the one from which the dusts were originally emitted. The challenged regulations encompass this reprocessing, to the mining industry's dismay.

Because the issue is one of statutory interpretation, the principles enunciated in *Chevron U.S.A., Inc. v. NRDC*, 467 U.S. 837 (1984), and its progeny guide our inquiry....

... Congress, it will be recalled, granted EPA power to regulate "solid waste." Congress specifically defined "solid waste" as "discarded material." EPA then defined "discarded material" to include materials destined for reuse in an industry's *ongoing* production processes. The challenge to EPA's jurisdictional reach is founded, again, on the proposition that in-process secondary materials are outside the bounds of EPA's lawful authority. Nothing has been *discarded*, the argument goes, and thus RCRA jurisdiction remains untriggered.

The first step in statutory interpretation is, of course, an analysis of the language itself.... Here, Congress defined "solid waste" as "discarded material." The ordinary, plain-English meaning of the word "discarded" is "disposed of," "thrown away" or "abandoned." Encompassing materials retained for immediate reuse within the scope of "discarded material" strains, to say the least, the everyday usage of that term.

... [Of course], a complete analysis of the statutory term "discarded" calls for more than resort to the ordinary, everyday meaning of the specific language at hand. For, "the sense in which [a term] is used in a statute must be determined by reference to the purpose of the particular legislation." *Burnet v. Chicago Portrait Co.*, 285 U.S. 1, 6 (1932)....

... RCRA was enacted in response to Congressional findings that the "rising tide of scrap, discarded, and waste materials" generated by consumers and increased industrial production had presented heavily populated urban communities with "serious financial, management, intergovernmental, and technical problems in the disposal of solid wastes." [42 U.S.C. § 6901(a)].... Also animating Congress were its findings that "disposal of solid and hazardouse [sic] waste" without careful planning and management presents a danger to human health and the environment; that methods to "separate usable materials from solid waste" should be employed; and that usable energy can be produced from solid waste. *Id.* § 6901(b), (c), (d).

The question we face, then, is whether, in light of the National Legislature's expressly stated objectives and the underlying problems that motivated it to enact RCRA in the first instance, Congress was using the term "discarded" in its ordinary sense—"disposed of" or "abandoned"—or whether Congress was using it in a much more open-ended way, so as to encompass materials no longer useful in their original capacity though destined for immediate reuse in another phase of the industry's ongoing production process.

[handwritten margin note: Ct. goes w/ plain meaning def. of disposal]

For the following reasons, we believe the former to be the case. RCRA was enacted, as the Congressional objectives and findings make clear, in an effort to help States deal with the ever-increasing problem of solid waste *disposal* by encouraging the search for and use of alternatives to existing methods of disposal (including recycling) and protecting health and the environment by regulating hazardous wastes. To fulfill these purposes, it seems clear that EPA need not regulate "spent" materials that are recycled and reused in an *ongoing* manufacturing or industrial process. These materials have not yet become part of the waste disposal problem; rather, *they are destined for beneficial reuse or recycling in a continuous process by the generating industry itself.*

The situation in this case thus stands in sharp contrast to that in *Riverside Bayview,* another post-*Chevron* case. There, the Corps of Engineers had defined "the waters of the United States" within the meaning of the Clean Water Act, 33 U.S.C. §§ 1311, 1362 (1972), to include "wetlands." Recognizing that it strained common sense to conclude that "Congress intended to abandon traditional notions of 'waters' and include in that term 'wetlands' as well," the Court performed a close and searching analysis of Congress' intent to determine if this counterintuitive result was nonetheless what Congress had in mind. *Id.* at 461–65. The Court based its holding (that the agency's expansive definition of "waters of the United States" was reasonable) on several factors: Congress' acquiescence in the agency's interpretation; provisions of the statute expressly including "wetlands" in the definition of "waters"; and, importantly, the danger that forbidding the Corps to regulate "wetlands" would defeat Congress' purpose since pollutants in "wetlands" water might well flow into "waters" that were indisputably jurisdictional. *Id.* at 465. Thus, due to the nature of the water system, the very evil that Congress sought to interdict—the befouling of the "waters of the United States"—would likely occur were the Corps of Engineers' jurisdiction to stop short of wetlands. *Riverside Bayview,* 106 S.Ct. at 463.

We are constrained to conclude that, in light of the language and structure of RCRA, the problems animating Congress to enact it, and the relevant portions of the legislative history, Congress clearly and unambiguously expressed its intent that "solid waste" (and therefore EPA's regulatory authority) be limited to materials that are "discarded" by virtue of being disposed of, abandoned, or thrown away. While we do not lightly overturn an agency's reading of its own statute, we are persuaded that by regulating in-process secondary materials, EPA has acted in contravention of Congress' intent. Accordingly, the petition for review is granted.

Mikva, Circuit Judge, dissenting:

. . . Congress had broad remedial objectives in mind when it enacted RCRA, most notably to "regulat[e] the treatment, storage, transportation, and disposal of hazardous wastes which have adverse effects on the environment." 42 U.S.C. § 6902(4). The disposal problem Congress was combatting encompassed more than just abandoned materials. RCRA makes this clear with its definition of the central statutory term "disposal":

> the discharge, deposit, injection, dumping, spilling, leaking, or placing of any solid waste or hazardous waste into or on any land or water so that such solid waste or hazardous waste or any constituent thereof may enter the environment or be emitted into the air or discharged into any waters, including ground waters.

42 U.S.C. § 6903(3). This definition clearly encompasses more than the everyday meaning of disposal, which is a "discarding or throwing away." *Webster's Third International Dictionary* 654 (2d ed. 1981). The definition is *functional*: waste is disposed under this provision if it is put into contact with land or water in such a way as to pose the risks to health and environment that animated Congress to pass RCRA. Whether the manufacturer subjectively intends to put the material to additional use is irrelevant to this definition, as indeed it should be, because the manufacturer's state of mind bears no necessary relation to the hazards of the industrial processes he employs.

Faithful to RCRA's functional approach, EPA reasonably concluded that regulation of certain in-process secondary materials was necessary to carry out its mandate. The materials at issue in this case can pose the same risks as abandoned wastes, whether or not the manufacturer intends eventually to put them to further beneficial use. As the agency explained, "[s]imply because a waste is likely to be recycled will not ensure that it will not be spilled or leaked before recycling occurs." The storage, transportation, and even recycling of in-process secondary materials can cause severe environmental harm. Indeed, the EPA documented environmental disasters caused by the handling or storage of such materials. It also pointed out the risk of damage from spills or leaks when certain in-process secondary materials are placed on land or in underground product storage.

Moreover, the agency's action is carefully aligned with Congress' functional approach to problems of waste disposal. The agency is not seeking to regulate all recycled materials. Rather, it has promulgated a complicated scheme of different categories so as to regulate materials only when they present the same types of environmental risks RCRA seeks to correct. EPA stressed that "to determine if a secondary material is a RCRA solid waste when recycled, one must examine both the material and the recycling activity involved. A consequence is that the same material can be a waste if it is recycled in certain ways, but would not be a waste if it is recycled in other ways." Thus, the agency has sought to regulate these materials only when they present the risks Congress was combatting in RCRA....

... EPA has interpreted solid waste in a manner that seems to expand the everyday usage of the word "discarded." Its conclusion, however, is fully supportable in light of the statutory scheme and legislative history of RCRA. The agency concluded that certain on-site recycled materials constitute an integral part of the waste disposal problem. This judgment is grounded in the EPA's technical expertise and is adequately supported by evidence in the record. The majority nevertheless reverses the agency because it believes that the materials at issue "have not yet become part of the waste disposal problem." This declaration is nothing more than a substitution of the majority's own conclusions for the sound technical judgment of the EPA. The EPA's interpretation is a reasonable construction of an ambiguous statutory provision and should be upheld. . . .

Notes and Comments

1. The D.C. Circuit is the only Circuit that can hear pre-enforcement challenges to EPA's RCRA rules. 42 U.S.C. § 6976(a)(1); see also *Association of Battery Recyclers, Inc. v. U.S. EPA*, 208 F.3d 1047, 1052 (D.C. Cir. 2000). Perhaps obviously, this dynamic serves to underscore the importance of its rulings; barring Supreme Court review, when the D.C. Circuit speaks its determinations typically will be the final word on these issues.

2. As indicated in *AMC I*, EPA asserted its general regulatory power over "secondary materials" when they are recycled by being (1) used in a manner constituting disposal; (2) burned for energy recovery; (3) reclaimed; or (4) accumulated speculatively. 40 C.F.R. § 261.2(c). Leaving aside reclamation for the moment, can you understand why EPA is concerned about the other three forms of recycling? Can you think of problematic examples of each?

3. EPA's regulations define "reclaimed" in the following manner:

> A material is "reclaimed" if it is processed to recover a usable product, or if it is regenerated. Examples are recovery of lead values from spent batteries and regeneration of spent solvents.

40 C.F.R. § 261.1(c)(4). Do you agree that the petroleum and mining materials in *AMC I* were being reclaimed? Were the practices at issue akin to the recovery of lead values from spent batteries?

4. It is worth noting that the *AMC I* court mischaracterized the "closed-loop" exclusion. EPA's regulations contain two distinct exceptions. First, as noted by the court, secondary materials generally avoid classification as "solid waste" if they are recycled by being reused as an ingredient or as an effective substitute for a commercial product, or are returned as raw material substitutes to the original process from which they were generated, without first being reclaimed. See 40 C.F.R. § 261.2(3). Beyond that, however, materials can still avoid regulation if they are reclaimed and returned to the original manufacturing process, so long as the reclamation process meets certain requirements, most notably that "[o]nly tank storage is involved, and the entire process through completion of reclamation is closed by being entirely connected with pipes or other comparable enclosed means of conveyance." 40 C.F.R. § 261.4(a)(8). It is this latter exception that is known as the "closed-loop" exclusion. Do you agree with EPA's decision to create these exceptions?

5. Did you agree with the court's *Chevron* analysis? At one level, the disagreement between the majority and Judge Mikva seems to hinge upon

whether the courts should defer to EPA's determination regarding whether a particular management scenario for secondary materials indicates that those materials have "become part of the waste disposal problem." Should they? Would that allow EPA too much license to distort the otherwise ordinary meaning of "discarded?"

6. How would you characterize the effect of *AMC I* on EPA's regulatory construct? Does it affect EPA's ability to regulate recycling outside of the reclamation context? How great is its effect within the reclamation context? Interestingly, in a portion of the opinion we have edited out, the court addressed a number of statutory provisions which EPA had argued indicated Congress's support for an expansive definition of "discarded." One of them, § 3014, deals with the circumstances under which EPA should treat used oil as a hazardous waste. The court distinguished the effect of this provision in the following terms:

> Section [3014] addresses "used oil" collected by and utilized in the "oil recycling industry." Oil recyclers typically collect discarded used oils, distill them, and sell the resulting material for use as fuel in boilers. Regulation of those activities is likewise consistent with an everyday reading of the term "discarded." It is only when EPA attempts to extend the scope of that provision to include the recycling of *undiscarded* oils at petroleum refineries that conflict occurs.

824 F.2d at 1187 n.14 (emphasis in original). Does this affect your reading of *AMC I*?

7. Shortly after the D.C. Circuit issued its opinion in *AMC I*, EPA issued a proposed rule responding to the court's decision. There, EPA characterized the effect of the court's decision as follows:

> The court's decision does not affect the Agency's authority to regulate as hazardous wastes those secondary materials recycled in ways where the recycling activity itself is characterized by discarding as defined by the court. That is, manufacturing processes (or other types of recycling) involving an element of discard which do not involve secondary materials passing through a continuous, on-going manufacturing process remain within the Agency's jurisdiction.

53 Fed.Reg. 519, 520 (Jan. 8, 1988). More specifically, EPA asserted that the court's holding had no effect on its ability to regulate recycling where the reuse constitutes disposal, or involves either burning for energy recovery or speculative accumulation. Id. at 521–523. Additionally, EPA stated its belief that it continued to have jurisdiction over many forms of reclamation. In particular, it asserted that it still had the authority to regulate the reclamation of spent materials (e.g., spent solvents), because in its view they are by definition no longer directly usable in on-going manufacturing processes. Id. at 522. With respect to sludges and byproducts, by contrast, EPA asserted that it would determine, on a case-by-case basis, whether they were being reutilized in an ongoing manufacturing process when it considered whether to "list" particular waste streams as hazardous waste. Id. at 523. It later articulated the factors it would consider in making these determinations in the following terms:

(a) Whether the sludge or by-product is typically recycled on an industry-wide basis; (b) whether the material is replacing a raw material and the degree to which it is similar in composition to the raw material; (c) the relation of the recovery practice to the principal activity of the facility; and (d) whether the secondary material is managed in a way designed to minimize loss, plus other relevant factors.

53 Fed.Reg. 33412, 35415 (Sept. 13, 1988).

8. For more than 10 years after *AMC I*, all of the case law in this area seemed to support EPA's narrow interpretation of the court's opinion and, consequently, its broad authority to assert regulatory jurisdiction over the recycling of secondary materials. Most notably, in *American Mining Congress v. U.S. EPA*, 907 F.2d 1179 (D.C. Cir. 1990) ("*AMC II*"), the D.C. Circuit addressed an industry challenge, based on *AMC I*, asserting that EPA could not regulate the petitioners' wastewater treatment sludge stored in surface impoundments, so long as they might at some point in the future reclaim some of the metals in the sludge. The court rejected the petitioners' plain meaning argument in the following terms:

> Petitioners read *AMC* too broadly. *AMC*'s holding concerned only materials that are "destined for *immediate reuse* in another phase of the industry's ongoing production process," and that "have not yet become part of the waste disposal problem." Nothing in *AMC* prevents the agency from treating as "discarded" the wastes at issue in this case, which are managed in land disposal units that *are* part of wastewater treatment systems, which have therefore become "part of the waste disposal problem," and which are *not* part of ongoing industrial processes. Indeed, [we have] explicitly rejected the very claim that petitioners assert in this case, namely, that under RCRA, potential reuse of a material prevents the agency from classifying it as "discarded."

907 F.2d at 1186 (emphasis in original). Turning to the reasonableness of EPA's interpretation, the court concluded its analysis as follows:

> ... In this case, the agency determined that material placed in wastewater treatment surface impoundments where it is "capable of posing a substantial present or potential hazard to human health or the environment when improperly treated, stored, transported or disposed of, or otherwise managed," 40 C.F.R. § 261.11(a)(3), by leaching into the ground, is "discarded material," and hence a "solid waste." As the agency notes, because of their propensity to leak hazardous materials into the environment, surface impoundments are a central focus of RCRA's regime. In addition, Congress made clear in the legislative history of RCRA its concern to regulate hazardous materials in surface impoundments. In light of this evidence, we conclude that the agency's interpretation of "discarded" is both reasonable and consistent with the statutory purposes of RCRA.

Id. at 1187.

9. The case to which the *AMC II* court referred in the last sentence of the first indented quote in the prior note was *American Petroleum Institute v. U.S. EPA*, 906 F.2d 729 (D.C. Cir. 1990) ("*API I*"). The relevant portion of that case involved an environmental attack on EPA's determination that it

lost regulatory jurisdiction over a certain waste stream (referred to as "K061" waste) once it was delivered to a metals reclamation facility. Relying on *AMC I*, EPA contended that regulating the reclamation process "would be like directly regulating the industrial production of zinc from ore." Id. at 740 n.15. The court squarely rejected this logic:

> [*AMC I*] is by no means dispositive of EPA's authority to regulate K061 slag. Unlike the materials in question in *AMC*, K061 is indisputably "discarded" *before* being subject to metals reclamation. Consequently, it *has* "become part of the waste disposal problem"; that is why EPA has the power to require that K061 be subject to mandatory metals reclamation. *See* 53 Fed.Reg. 11,752–53 (recognizing this point). Nor does anything in *AMC* require EPA to cease treating K061 as "solid waste" once it reaches the metals reclamation facility. K061 is delivered to the facility not as part of an "*ongoing* manufacturing or industrial process" within "the generating industry," but as part of a mandatory waste treatment plan prescribed by EPA. As such, the resulting slag appears to remain within the scope of the agency's authority as "sludge from a *waste treatment plant*." 42 U.S.C. § 6903(27)....

Id. at 741 (emphasis in original).

10. Can the two *AMC* opinions be harmonized? Recall that in *AMC I*, the court resolved the issue at Step 1 of the *Chevron* analysis. When taken together, do these two opinions make clear where the D.C. Circuit views the plain meaning of the term "discarded" as ending, and where EPA's power to resolve any residual ambiguity begins?

11. As mentioned in note 1 above, other courts can consider the legality of EPA's RCRA rules only in enforcement actions. As a result, other Circuits don't hear nearly as many of these cases. During the 1990s, however, those that did so routinely upheld EPA's authority to regulate the materials at issue. In *United States v. Ilco, Inc.*, 996 F.2d 1126 (11th Cir. 1993), for example, the Eleventh Circuit upheld EPA's authority to deem the lead components of spent batteries "solid waste," despite the fact that the defendant was going to reclaim them at its lead smelting facility. And in *Owen Electric Steel Co. v. Browner*, 37 F.3d 146 (4th Cir. 1994), the Fourth Circuit held that EPA could regulate the slag produced by a steel mill in a situation in which the mill "cured" the material on the ground for six months prior to selling it for use as road bed material. Quoting from *AMC I*, the court concluded that "the fundamental inquiry in determining whether a by-product has been 'discarded' is whether the by-product is *immediately* recycled for use in the same industry; if not, then the by-product is justifiably seen as 'part of the waste disposal problem.'" Id. at 150 (emphasis in original).

12. In 2000, the tide turned again. First, in *Association of Battery Recyclers, Inc. v. U.S. EPA*, 208 F.3d 1047 (D.C. Cir. 2000) ("*Battery Recyclers*"), the D.C. Circuit rejected a new protocol EPA had developed for determining whether certain secondary materials derived from mineral processing qualified as "solid waste." If the materials were to be recycled back into the manufacturing process, EPA's new rule had made their potential status as waste hinge upon the method of interim storage: If the materials were stored in tanks, containers, buildings, or on properly main-

tained pads, they would not be deemed wastes; alternatively, if they were stored in less environmentally sound ways, they would be deemed to be wastes. Id. at 1051. In a facial challenge, the D.C. Circuit rejected this approach, emphasizing that the length of the storage period was "of no consequence" according to the regulation. Most alarmingly, from EPA's perspective, the court harkened back to *AMC I* as the bellwether case within the Circuit. Moreover, it limited the "immediate reuse" language from that opinion by indicating that "immediate" in this context means "directly," not "at once." Id. at 1053. The court went on to distinguish *API I* as a case in which a waste was generated by one industry and reclaimed within another, id. at 1054, and *AMC II* as involving a situation in which it was unclear whether the materials would ever be reclaimed, id. at 1055.

13. In a second case from that year, the D.C. Circuit in *American Petroleum Institute v. U.S. EPA*, 216 F.3d 50 (D.C. Cir. 2000) ("*API II*"), considered whether certain oil-bearing wastes generated by the petroleum industry qualified as "solid waste" before they went through a CWA primary treatment system, even though that system would result in the recapture of some valuable oil. The court vacated EPA's determination that they did, finding EPA's conclusion that the wastewater treatment purpose predominated over the recycling purpose to be unsupported by the record. Id. at 57. Moreover, despite having previously noted that EPA should get deference on the question whether an industrial by-product is best characterized as discarded or an "in-process material," the court determined that EPA had not adequately explained why, even if the wastewater treatment purpose predominated, this would "compel the further conclusion that the wastewater has been discarded." Id. at 58.

14. In *Safe Air for Everyone v. Meyer*, 373 F.3d 1035 (9th Cir. 2004), the Ninth Circuit addressed the question whether bluegrass farmers who engage in the open burning of grass residues after harvest are burning "solid waste" for purposes of RCRA (the issue came up in the context of a citizen suit under § 7002(a)(1)(b), which requires only that the relevant material was a solid waste, not that it was a "hazardous waste" under Subtitle C). The court held that this practice did not involve either the treatment or disposal of agricultural waste, but rather the reuse of the residue in a continuous process of growing bluegrass. The crux of the court's analysis was as follows:

> . . . [T]here is no dispute that the Growers realize farming benefits from reusing grass residue in the process of open burning. Safe Air did not present testimony challenging the Growers' contentions that: (1) grass residue offers nutrients to bluegrass fields; (2) burnt grass residue ash resulting from open burning helps fertilize bluegrass fields; (3) open burning reduces the incidence of weed, fungi, and insect infestation in bluegrass fields; and (4) open burning blackens bluegrass fields, which contributes to creating optimal conditions for the next bluegrass harvest. Safe Air dismisses these indisputable benefits as "incidental," but our view is necessarily controlled by RCRA's statutory language suggesting that materials must be "discarded" to be considered solid waste. Because there is undisputed evidence that the Growers reuse the grass residue in a continuous farming process effectively designed to produce Kentucky bluegrass, there is no genuine issue of material fact as to

whether grass residue is "discarded material." It is not. The bluegrass residue is not discarded, abandoned, or given up, and it does not qualify as "solid waste" under RCRA, based on its statutory definition of "solid waste" as "discarded material."

Id. at 1044–1045. Do you agree?

15. In October of 2003, EPA proposed major revisions to its definition of "solid waste." 68 Fed.Reg. 61558 (Oct. 28, 2003). EPA already had withdrawn the specific rules the D.C. Circuit deemed invalid in *Battery Recyclers*. Despite having done so, however, it stated that it viewed *Battery Recyclers* "as creating an opportunity to re-examine its rules and interpretations and clarify whether they regulate certain materials that are not 'discarded.' " Id. at 61563. In short, the new proposal provides that "any material which is generated and reclaimed in a continuous process within the same industry . . . is not 'discarded' for purposes of Subtitle C, provided that the recycling process is 'legitimate.' " Id. If finalized, this new approach would go beyond any of the existing cases by allowing the reclamation to occur at other facilities, so long as they operate within the same industry. EPA explained its justification for this proposal in the following terms:

> . . . [P]rocesses and facilities that operate within the same industry are likely to use similar raw materials and process them in a similar manner. They are also likely to have expertise as to the types of secondary materials produced by their industry, their potential for recycling, and appropriate practices for managing such materials. For these practical reasons, EPA believes that the potential for environmental harm from de-regulating this type of recycling practice is likely to be relatively small compared to other types of recycling practices.

Id. at 61565. Moreover, the proposal would expand upon *Battery Recyclers* by defining the "continuous process" concept by reference to the "speculative accumulation" idea it already applies to secondary materials not requiring reclamation, see 40 C.F.R. § 261.2(c)(4); under this framework, the person accumulating the material must show that during a calendar year it recycled or transferred for recycling at least 75 percent of the material (by weight or volume) it had at the beginning of the year. Id. at 61576; see also 40 C.F.R. § 261.1(c)(8). Finally, EPA proposed a series of "legitimacy" criteria that it would use on a case-by-case basis to differentiate the permissible reclamation from what it views as "sham" recycling. The proposed criteria are as follows:

> 1. The secondary material to be recycled is managed as a valuable commodity. Where there is an analogous raw material, the secondary material should be managed in a manner consistent with the management of the raw material. Where there is no analogous raw material, the secondary material should be managed to minimize the potential for releases into the environment.

> 2. The secondary material provides a useful contribution to the recycling process or to a product of the recycling process and evaluating this criterion should include consideration of the economics of the recycling transaction. The recycling process itself may involve reclamation, or direct reuse without reclamation.

3.   The recycling process yields a valuable product or intermediate that is: (i) Sold to a third party; or (ii) Used by the recycler or the generator as an effective substitute for a commercial product or as a useful ingredient in an industrial process.

4.   The product of the recycling process: (i) Does not contain significant amounts of hazardous constituents that are not found in analogous products; and (ii) Does not contain significantly elevated levels of any hazardous constituents that are found in analogous products; and (iii) Does not exhibit a hazardous characteristic that analogous products do not exhibit.

Id. at 61583. Does this seem like an appropriate approach? Keeping in mind that this proposal has not been finalized, how would you advise industrial clients to proceed in light of the mixed messages provided in the case law to date? If you represented EPA, what types of cases would you recommend for either civil or criminal enforcement?

B.   What Is a "Hazardous Waste"?

If a given material qualifies as a "solid waste," the second step in determining whether Subtitle C applies is to determine whether it also qualifies as a "hazardous waste" within the regulatory meaning of that phrase. As mentioned above, Congress specifically contemplated that EPA would establish a regulatory construct for determining which wastes, within the broad statutory parameters of § 1004(5), were worthy of full-blown regulation under Subtitle C. 42 U.S.C. § 6921(a) and (b).

Section 3001(b) specifically contemplated that EPA would promulgate regulations "identifying the characteristics of hazardous waste, and listing particular hazardous wastes...." Consistent with this instruction, EPA created a two-pronged approach for determining which wastes are hazardous. 40 C.F.R. § 261.3(a). EPA listed certain waste streams as being per se hazardous. If a company generates one of these so-called "listed" wastes, it must treat it as a hazardous waste, regardless of the concentrations of any of the relevant contaminants in any particular batch of waste. Thus, for these wastes there is no need to test each batch; if they are on one of the lists, they are covered. Additionally, EPA identified four "characteristics" of hazardous waste: ignitability, corrosivity, reactivity and toxicity. These characteristics serve as a "catch-all" mechanism for waste streams that are not specifically listed; regardless of whether a particular waste stream is listed, it if exhibits one of these four characteristics it must be treated as a hazardous waste. For these waste streams, therefore, the generator must determine, on a case-by-case basis, whether a given batch of its waste exhibits one of the four characteristics. 40 C.F.R. § 262.11.

Broadly speaking, there are four categories of listed wastes. Some listed waste streams are industry-specific. These are denominated "K" series wastes, which means only that each waste stream is given a code number that begins with the letter "K" and is followed by three digits. They include, for example, wastewater treatment sludges from wood preserving processes that use creosote or pentachlorophenol (K001), and

K wastes

untreated process wastewater from the production of toxaphene (K098). Others are process specific, but involve industrial processes than transcend any one particular industry. These waste streams, which are known as "F" series wastes, include for example spent cyanide plating bath solutions from electroplating operations (F007).

In addition, there are two categories of chemical products which are deemed hazardous when they are discarded as commercial chemical products, off-specification by-products, or in soils or debris from the cleanup of any spills of either these products or by-products. "U" series wastes include such chemicals as mercury (U151) and methyl ethyl ketone (U159). "P" series wastes, which include such chemicals as dieldrin (P037) and sulfuric acid (P115), are considered acute hazardous wastes. The significance of their being deemed acutely hazardous lies in the effect it has on the amount a waste a given generator can generate without being considered a fully-regulated generator—a given entity will be deemed a fully-regulated generator if it generates more than 1 kilogram of acute hazardous waste per month. 40 C.F.R. § 261.5(e).

[handwritten margin note: U wastes / P wastes]

As mentioned, EPA has identified four "characteristics" which can render waste hazardous regardless of whether EPA has listed a particular waste stream: ignitability, corrosivity, reactivity and toxicity. For most liquids, the test of ignitability is whether the waste has a flash point of less than 60 C, using a specified test method. 40 C.F.R. §§ 261.21. For aqueous waste, the corrosivity test hinges on whether the material has a pH of less than or equal to 2 or greater than or equal to 12.5. 40 C.F.R. § 261.22(a). For reactivity, the standard test is whether the waste is normally unstable and readily undergoes violent change without detonating, whether it reacts violently with water or forms potentially explosive mixtures or generates toxic gases when mixed with water, or whether it is capable of detonation or explosive reaction under certain circumstances. 40 C.F.R. § 261.23.

[handwritten margin notes: Ignitability Test / corrosivity test / reactivity test]

EPA's toxicity characteristic attempts to determine whether toxic constituents may leach out of the relevant waste stream at harmful levels under typical landfill conditions. Perhaps obviously, this is due to the fact that if a given waste stream is deemed not to be hazardous waste, whoever generates it may send it to a standard municipal landfill. EPA has developed a test known as the "toxicity characteristic leachate procedure" (or "TCLP"), which is designed to mimic landfill conditions. If this test reveals that the toxic constituents would leach out at levels of concern under such conditions, the waste stream qualifies as a hazardous waste. The TCLP numbers (that is, the test results that trigger regulation) are generally 100 times the drinking water standards for the relevant constituents; for trichloroethylene, for example, the TCLP number is .5 mg/l, 40 C.F.R. § 261.24, whereas the "maximum concentration limit" under the Safe Drinking Water Act for that same chemical is .005 mg/l, 40 C.F.R § 141.61. This is due to the fact that EPA uses this "100 times" factor as a standard assumption as to how much dilution and attenuation would occur with respect to the relevant constituents be-

[handwritten margin note: TCLP (toxicity) Test]

tween the point at which it leaches from the waste at the landfill and the point at which it reaches a potential drinking water source.

Finally, it is worth noting that listed wastes (but not characteristic wastes) are subject to three expansive principles that dramatically increase the scope of RCRA's regulatory net. First, they are subject to the "mixture rule," which provides that the mixture of a listed waste and any other solid waste is by definition a hazardous waste. 40 C.F.R. § 261.3(b)(2). Second, the "derived from" rule provides, in effect, that any solid waste generated from the treatment, storage or disposal of a listed waste is still a hazardous waste. 40 C.F.R. § 261.3(c)(2) and (d)(1). And third, EPA interprets two of its existing rules as indicating that any soils, groundwater or debris which have been contaminated by listed wastes must be treated as hazardous waste. See 40 C.F.R. § 261.3(c)(1) and (d)(2). The D.C. Circuit upheld this interpretation, known as the "contained in policy," in *Chemical Waste Management v. U.S. EPA*, 869 F.2d 1526 (D.C. Cir. 1989).

Notes and Comments

1. From the outset of the regulatory program, EPA has excluded household waste from the definition of "hazardous waste." 40 C.F.R. § 261.4(b). In the preamble underlying this regulation, EPA made clear that this was a "waste stream" exclusion, meaning that the exclusion also applied to any non-household entities that might transport, treat, store and/or dispose of this waste. 45 Fed.Reg. 33099 (May 19, 1980). In HSWA, the 1984 Amendments to RCRA, Congress codified this exclusion in § 3001(i) of RCRA. The existence of this exclusion means that a homeowner can take the paint thinner from her basement and pour it out in her backyard without violating RCRA or, for that matter, any other federal law (we are not recommending this). Yet if an industrial entity did the same thing, it would in all likelihood be committing a felony under RCRA, see 42 U.S.C. § 6928(d)(2). Does this distinction make sense?

2. While § 3001(i) made clear that municipal solid waste incinerators would not be deemed to be treating, storing or disposing of hazardous wastes if they received and burned only household hazardous wastes, the question arose as to whether these same facilities would be deemed to have generated a hazardous waste if the ash they generated through their incineration processes failed the TCLP. The Supreme Court ultimately addressed this question in *City of Chicago v. Environmental Defense Fund*, 511 U.S. 328, 114 S.Ct. 1588, 128 L.Ed.2d 302 (1994), holding that § 3001(i) plainly limits the exclusion to the incinerators' handling of the household waste itself and does not extend it to any ash generated through the process of incineration. This holding has major implications for these municipal incinerators. Prior to bringing the litigation that resulted in the Supreme Court's decision, EDF had done studies which indicated that incinerator fly ash fails the TCLP 80 to 90 percent of the time, and that bottom ash does so 20 to 25 percent of the time. Moreover, these incinerators collectively generate more than 8 million tons of ash per year. Read § 3001(i) carefully. Do you agree with the Supreme Court's determination? Would it matter to you whether EPA had interpreted the relevant statutory language one way or the other? In 1995,

EPA moved to mitigate the effect of the Court's holding at least somewhat by expressly allowing these facilities to mix their fly ash and bottom ash together before performing the required waste determination. 60 Fed.Reg. 6666 (Feb. 3, 1995).

3. In *Shell Oil Co. v. EPA*, 950 F.2d 741 (D.C. Cir. 1991), the D.C. Circuit belatedly determined that EPA had provided inadequate notice and comment when it promulgated the mixture and derived-from rules in 1980. Concerned about the impacts of its ruling, however, the court suggested that EPA reenact the rules on an interim basis under the "good cause" exception to the notice and comment provisions of the APA, 5 U.S.C. § 553(b)(3)(B). EPA promptly did so. 57 Fed.Reg. 7628 (March 3, 1992). Congress later required EPA to revise the rule by 1994, but expressly provided that the interim rules would remain in effect until EPA acted. Pub. L. 102–389, 106 stat. 1571, 1602–3 (1992). To make a long story short, EPA has yet to act despite a court order requiring it to have done so by April 30, 2000. Pending such action, its "interim" rules remain in effect.

4. Although the derived-from rule provides that any wastes generated through the treatment of listed wastes are hazardous waste, it specifically recognizes the general proposition that any "materials that are reclaimed from solid wastes and that are used beneficially are not solid wastes and thus are not hazardous wastes...." 40 C.F.R. § 261.3(c)(2)(I).

5. Generators of non-listed waste streams do not need to test every single batch of waste for every characteristic. Instead, EPA's rules allow them to either test or apply their "knowledge of the hazard characteristic of the waste in light of the materials or the processes used." 40 C.F.R. § 262.11(c).

6. Many commentators have criticized EPA's regulatory definition of "hazardous waste." The mixture and derived-from rules have come under particular attack, with commentators alleging that they result in the over-regulation of materials posing little environmental risk. See, e.g., Pedersen, The Future of Federal Solid Waste Regulation, 16 Colum. J. Envtl. L. 109 (1991). Over the years, EPA has floated a variety of proposed methodologies to address these concerns. In 1992, for example, it suggested several potential approaches, three of which are worth highlighting. One approach, called the expanded characteristic option (or "ECHO"), would have expanded reliance on the TCLP by adding many new substances to the list that generators need to test for, with a corresponding decrease in the number of listed wastes. A second option would have identified concentration-based exit criteria at which listed wastes, if treated to the specified levels, would no longer be considered hazardous. And finally, a third option would have specified management practices that, if utilized, would have eliminated a given generator's need to manage a particular waste as hazardous. See generally, 57 Fed.Reg. 21450 (May 20, 1992). What do you think of these approaches? To date, EPA has yet to move forward with any of them. In the "contained-in" context, it does have a proposed rule pending that would conditionally exclude from the definition of hazardous waste disposable industrial wipes that are contaminated with hazardous solvents. 68 Fed.Reg. 65586 (Nov. 20, 2003).

II. THE REGULATORY PROGRAM

Subtitle C contains separate regulatory programs for those who generate, transport, and treat, store or dispose of hazardous waste. In EPA's regulations, the generator requirements are found in 40 C.F.R. Part 262, the transporter requirements in Part 263, and the treatment, storage and disposal ("TSD") requirements in Parts 264 and 265, as supplemented by the TSD permit requirements in Part 270.

In our discussion below, we will not try to provide comprehensive coverage of any of these programs. Instead, it is our aim to provide a brief overview of both the generator and TSD requirements, together with a problem in each area designed to (1) familiarize students with some of the basic issues that arise, and (2) provide them with some facility in working with the federal regulations. We will forgo any coverage of the transporter requirements, which are quite straightforward.

A. Generator Requirements

RCRA breaks generators of hazardous waste down into three categories, subject to widely varying degrees of regulation. In the highest category are the so-called "fully-regulated" generators. These generators, who will be the focus of our discussion below, are those who generate more than 1,000 kilograms of hazardous waste per month, or more than 1 kilogram of acute hazardous waste. See 40 C.F.R. §§ 262.34 and 261.5(f), respectively. In the 1980s, EPA estimated that these generators, while comprising only 2% of the generator universe, generate 99% of all hazardous waste. The next category down includes what EPA calls "small quantity generators" ("SQGs"), or those who generate between 100 and 1,000 kilograms of hazardous waste per month. SQGs are subject to a slightly relaxed set of requirements, as compared with the fully-regulated generators. For example, they can store their wastes for longer without qualifying as a TSD. 40 C.F.R. § 262.34(d). And finally, there are the so-called "conditionally-exempt generators" ("CEGs"). This category applies to those who generate less than 100 kilograms of hazardous waste per month (or less than 1 kilogram of acute hazardous waste). 40 C.F.R. § 261.5. To maintain the exemption, CEGs need only comply with a very limited set of requirements, including most notably never accumulating more than 1,000 kilograms at their facilities and sending their wastes to either hazardous waste facilities or approved solid waste facilities under Subtitle D. 40 C.F.R. § 261.5(g). Perhaps the best way to understand this favored treatment is to think of the CEGs as being more like households than they are like fully-regulated generators.

The threshold requirements stated in the above paragraph are aggregate totals, based on the total amount of all hazardous wastes that the particular generator generates at its entire facility each month. It should also be noted that one's generator status can vary from month-to-month depending on how much waste one generated during that particular month. Having said that, most generators decide that it is easiest to simply comply with the most demanding set of requirements to which they are commonly subject. For example, fully-regulated generators who store waste for any period of time are required to have "contingency plans," but small quantity generators who do the same are not. Compare 40 C.F.R. § 262.34(a)(4) and (d). Still, if a given generator hovers right around the 1,000 kg/month threshold from month to month, it would probably determine that it is in its best interest to keep its contingency plan in effect, even if it might not be required to do so during some particular months.

Turning more directly to the regulations that apply to fully-regulated generators, the first thing to note is that even these most-regulated generators are not required to have permits. Instead, they need only obtain what are referred to as "EPA identification numbers." 40 C.F.R. § 262.12. Because they don't have permits, RCRA generators are regulated directly under the relevant regulations, either 40 C.F.R. Part 262 or the State's equivalent regulations (in authorized States). This means that they need not go through the expensive process of acquiring a permit. It also means, however, that they lose the advantage of the so-called "permit shield." Compare 40 C.F.R. § 270.4.

There are five main requirements that apply to fully-regulated generators. First, like all generators (even CEGs), they must comply with the so-called "waste-determination" requirements; that is, they must determine whether a given waste stream is in fact hazardous waste. 40 C.F.R. § 262.11. Second, to the extent that they are going to store wastes on even a short-term basis, they must comply with the storage requirements set forth in 40 C.F.R. § 262.34 (which are the subject of our generator hypothetical, below). Third, when they send waste off-site, they must comply with the manifest and packaging requirements. See 40 C.F.R. Part 262, subpart B and § 262.30. Fourth, they must comply with certain record-keeping requirements. 40 C.F.R. Part 262, subpart D. And finally, they are subject to one additional requirement designed to implement RCRA's "land ban" program—they must identify the appropriate treatment standard that the waste is subject to under that program. See 40 C.F.R. § 268.7. (We will discuss the land ban program further below).

Reqs for full-reggen.

#1

#2

#3

#4

#5

With this background, consider the following hypothetical:

A RCRA Generator Hypothetical

West Aerospace, Inc. ("West") does business in the State of Confusion, an unauthorized state under RCRA. The company manufactures aircraft parts and wings, and engages in metal finishing attendant thereto. Its hazardous waste activity records indicate that it generates more than 4,000 pounds of various hazardous wastes per month, including several "listed" spent solvents (F001, F002, F003 and F005), a listed stream of spent cyanide plating bath solutions (F007), and several waste streams that fail the TCLP. These latter streams include several paint wastes, strippers and contaminated fuels.

Bonnie Lee, an EPA inspector, recently visited the facility and made several findings. With respect to personnel training, she noted that the West employee who supervised the drum storage area, Billy Sunday, told her that when he started seven month ago, his boss had simply told him that he would teach him what he needed to know on an as-needed basis. Sunday further stated that he had received minimal training as time went along, and that he was unaware as to whether the company had a written personnel training plan or any other training records.

Billy Sunday

Lee also identified several issues with respect to drum storage. First, she found three containers of listed spent solvents in the drum storage area with lids that were ajar. The "accumulation date" labels on the outside of these drums indicated that no waste had been added to them in more than three weeks. Second, Lee noted that the "accumulation date" label on one of these drums indicated that the first wastes had been added to it 105 days before the inspection. And third, she observed an open drum of paint-and-solvent-contaminated solids (cloths, rags, wipes, and debris) in a satellite accumulation area—the paint shop—that was not marked "hazardous waste" and did not have a marked accumulation date. The workers in the area conceded that some of these items had been used to clean up small spills of listed solvents.

3 lids ajar

1 drum 105 days old

open drum rags used to clean up waste

As a courtesy, Lee left a copy of her inspection report at the facility. West's president, August West, has come to you seeking help in understanding the nature and significance of these alleged deficiencies. Consider the following regulations in formulating your advice.

40 C.F.R. Part 262, Subpart C—Pre–Transport Requirements

§ 262.34   Accumulation Time.

(a) Except as provided in paragraphs (d), (e), and (f) of this section, a generator may accumulate hazardous waste on-site for 90 days or less without a permit or without having interim status, provided that:

(1) The waste is placed:

(i) In containers and the generator complies with subparts I, AA, BB and CC of 40 CFR part 265 . . .

(2) The date upon which each period of accumulation begins is clearly marked and visible for inspection on each container;

(3) While being accumulated on-site, each container and tank is labeled or marked clearly with the words, "Hazardous Waste"; and

(4) The generator complies with the requirements for owners or operators in subparts C and D in 40 CFR Part 265, with § 265.16, and with 40 CFR 268.7(a)(4).

(b) A generator who accumulates hazardous waste for more than 90 days is an operator of a storage facility and is subject to the requirements of 40 CFR Parts 264 and 265 and the permit requirements of 40

CFR Part 270 unless he has been granted an extension to the 90–day period. . . .

(c)(1) A generator may accumulate as much as 55 gallons of hazardous waste or one quart of acutely hazardous waste listed in § 261.33(e) in containers at or near any point of generation where wastes initially accumulate, which is under the control of the operator of the process generating the waste, without a permit or interim status and without complying with paragraph (a) of this section provided he:

(i) Complies with §§ 265.171, 265.172, and 265.173(a) of this chapter; and

(ii) Marks his containers either with the words "Hazardous Waste" or with other words that identify the contents of the containers.

(2) A generator who accumulates either hazardous waste or acutely hazardous waste listed in § 261.33(e) in excess of the amounts listed in paragraph (c)(1) of this section at or near any point of generation must, with respect to that amount of excess waste, comply within three days with paragraph (a) of this section or other applicable provisions of this chapter. During the three day period the generator must continue to comply with paragraphs (c)(1)(i)-(ii) of this section. The generator must mark the container holding the excess accumulation of hazardous waste with the date the excess amount began accumulating.

40 C.F.R. Part 265, Subpart B—General Facility Standards

§ 265.16   Personnel Training.

(a)(1) Facility personnel must successfully complete a program of classroom instruction or on-the-job training that teaches them to perform their duties in a way that ensures the facility's compliance with the requirements of this part. . . .

(2) This program must be directed by a person trained in hazardous waste management procedures, and must include instruction which teaches facility personnel hazardous waste management procedures . . . relevant to the positions in which they are employed.

(3) At a minimum, the training program must be designed to ensure that facility personnel are able to respond effectively to emergencies by familiarizing them with emergency procedures, emergency equipment, and emergency systems. . . .

(b) Facility personnel must successfully complete the program required in paragraph (a) of this section within six months after the effective date of these regulations or six months after the date of their employment or assignment to a facility, or to a new position at a facility, whichever is later. . . .

(c) Facility personnel must take part in an annual review of the initial training required in paragraph (a) of this section.

(d) The owner or operator must maintain the following documents and records at the facility:

(1) The job title for each position at the facility related to hazardous waste management, and the name of the employee filling each job;

(3) A written description of the type and amount of both introductory and continuing training that will be given to each person filling a position listed under paragraph (d)(1) of this section;

(4) Records that document that the training or job experience required under paragraphs (a), (b), and (c) of this section has been given to, and completed by, facility personnel.

(e) Training records on current personnel must be kept until closure of the facility. . . .

40 C.F.R. Part 265, Subpart I—Use and Management of Containers

§ 265.173 Management of containers.

(a) A container holding hazardous waste must always be closed during storage, except when it is necessary to add or remove waste.

(b) A container holding hazardous waste must not be opened, handled, or stored in a manner which may rupture the container or cause it to leak.

Notes and Comments

1. What violations can you be sure have been committed in the above hypothetical? Are there any potential violations with respect to which you would need further facts to make a final determination? Are the relevant regulations unclear regarding the regulatory significance of any of these facts? If so, what positions would you expect EPA to take, and what do you think its prospects for success would be?

2. It is worth noting that one can generate a waste in perhaps unexpected ways. The term "generator" is defined in 40 C.F.R. § 260.10 to mean "any person . . . whose act or process first produces hazardous waste identified or listed in part 261 of this chapter *or whose act first causes a hazardous waste to become subject to regulation.*" (Emphasis added). Moreover, 40 C.F.R. § 262.11 requires any "person who generates a solid waste" to "determine if that waste is a hazardous waste." EPA has long interpreted these regulations as requiring, for example, one who cleans up contaminated soil to determine whether those materials qualify as hazardous wastes, regardless of when the original release occurred. The theory is that, by cleaning up the soil, the relevant party is generating a solid waste, and thus must perform the waste determination to determine whether it is hazardous.

B. Requirements for Treatment, Storage and Disposal Facilities (TSDs)

Speaking generally, there are two types of TSDs under RCRA. Some facilities are in the business of treating, storing or disposing of other companies' hazardous waste. Think, for example, of Chemical Waste Management's hazardous waste disposal facility in Emelle, Alabama. Others, however, are simply manufacturing facilities that have determined that it is in their financial interest to engage in some TSD activities attendant to their manufacturing processes. For example, many manufacturers store waste for longer than the 90–day grace period allotted to fully-regulated generators. Some eventually may reclaim some or all of the waste themselves, or others may treat their waste through a Clean Water Act treatment system and discharge some portion of the waste stream through an NPDES permit.

One common requirement that applies to all TSDs is that they must apply for a permit under § 3005(b) of the statute. See also 40 C.F.R. Part 270. Not all TSDs have final permits, however. When Congress created the permit requirement, Congress recognized that it would take EPA a while to issue permits to every TSD. Accordingly, Congress created a "grandfathering" mechanism pursuant to which facilities that were already treating, storing or disposing of hazardous waste were granted "interim status" to keep engaging in these activities until such time as EPA processed their permit applications.

To this day, more than half of all TSDs are operating under "interim status." In 1984, Congress established deadlines by which EPA was required to process permit applications for various categories of TSDs, with the latest deadline expiring in 1992. 42 U.S.C. § 6925(c). This tactic failed, however, because all a given facility needed to do to retain interim status despite these deadlines was to apply for a final permit determination. Id. Hence, there was no real pressure on EPA to meet the deadlines. Moreover, since there has been a constant need for additional treatment capacity, and since new facilities cannot receive interim status, EPA has naturally tended to prioritize the issuance of permits to new facilities over the conversion of interim status facilities to fully-permitted status.

Beyond the permit requirement, EPA has two sets of regulations establishing the substantive standards for TSDs. The requirements for interim status facilities are found in 40 C.F.R. Part 265, and those for fully-permitted facilities are found in Part 264. The regulations are conceptually similar, though those for fully-permitted facilities are more stringent in some respects. In both contexts, there are some fairly generic standards that apply to all TSDs, such as personnel training, contingency planning, and record-keeping requirements. See, e.g., 40 C.F.R. Part 265, subparts B, C, D and E. Additionally, there are elaborate facility standard requirements for particular types of TSDs or TSD activities. These include specific standards for managing containers and for designing and operating specific types of units such as tank systems, surface impoundments, landfills and incinerators. See, e.g., 40 C.F.R. Part 265, subparts J, K, N and O.

Probably the most significant and expensive broadly applicable requirements in the TSD realm are those relating to groundwater monitoring, closure and post-closure, and financial responsibility. See, e.g., 40 C.F.R. Part 265, subparts F, G and H. We will use a second RCRA hypothetical to introduce the student to RCRA's groundwater monitoring and closure requirements:

A RCRA TSD Hypothetical

Environmental Management, Inc. ("EMI") operates a TSD in the State of Bliss (another "unauthorized" state), which includes a hazardous waste surface impoundment. West's facility has "interim status" under RCRA.

Because EMI's property is on an incline, Pearly Baker, its environmental compliance manager assumed that the company could meet the requirements of Section 265.91 by installing one well immediately up the hill from the impoundment and three immediately on the downhill side. For several years, all went well. EMI sampled for all appropriate parameters twice a year and reported all results to EPA. Because Baker never heard anything in response from EPA, she eventually stopped reporting the results and merely entered them in her operating record. Last year, EMI first detected significant amounts of total organic halogen in two of its downgradient wells. Because EMI had never had any problems in the past, Baker attributed these results to sampling error. In the next sampling round, six months later, all four of EMI's wells showed significant concentrations of both total organic halogen and total organic carbon. Although the wastes EMI puts in the impoundment could have caused these results, Baker assumed that, because the upgradient well was contaminated, the contamination must be coming from an off-site location. Again, she noted these facts in her operating record, but did not report them to EPA.

Last month, EMI's insurance company reviewed EMI's monitoring data and informed Baker that it would decline to renew EMI's RCRA-based policies. In response, EMI decided it would close the surface impoundment. EMI's closure plan contemplates that it will "clean close" the impoundment, under 40 C.F.R. § 265.228(a)(1), by letting all of the liquids it cannot discharge into the river evaporate during the dry season, and then sending any remaining sludge to In Your Back Yard, an approved hazardous waste incineration facility. The dry season is at least three months away and the evaporation process would take another three months.

Yesterday, an EPA inspector showed up at EMI's facility and learned all of the above facts. While the inspector was there, Baker gave him a copy of EMI's closure plan and indicated that EMI would commence closure upon approval of the plan. The inspector comes to you, EPA lawyer extraordinaire, and wants to know what violations have been committed and what other implications these facts have under the relevant regulations. What do you tell him?

40 C.F.R. Part 265, Subpart F—Ground–Water Monitoring

§ 265.90 Applicability.

(a) Within one year after the effective date of these regulations, the owner or operator of a surface impoundment, landfill, or land treatment facility which is used to manage hazardous waste must implement a ground-water monitoring program capable of determining the facility's impact on the quality of ground water in the uppermost aquifer underlying the facility. . . .

(b) . . . [T]he owner or operator must install, operate, and maintain a ground-water monitoring system which meets the requirements of § 265.91, and must comply with §§ 265.92–265.94. This ground-water monitoring program must be carried out during the active life of the facility, and for disposal facilities, during the post-closure care period as well.

§ 265.91 Ground–Water Monitoring System.

(a) A ground-water monitoring system must be capable of yielding ground-water samples for analysis and must consist of:

(1) Monitoring wells (at least one) installed hydraulically upgradient (i.e., in the direction of increasing static head) from the limit of the waste management area. Their number, locations, and depths must be sufficient to yield ground-water samples that are:

(i) Representative of background ground-water quality in the uppermost aquifer near the facility; and

(ii) Not affected by the facility; and

(2) Monitoring wells (at least three) installed hydraulically downgradient (i.e., in the direction of decreasing static head) at the limit of the waste management area. Their number, locations, and depths must ensure that they immediately detect any statistically significant amounts of hazardous waste or hazardous waste constituents that migrate from the waste management area to the uppermost aquifer.

§ 265.92 Sampling and Analysis.

(a) The owner or operator must obtain and analyze samples from the installed ground-water monitoring system. The owner or operator must develop and follow a ground-water sampling and analysis plan. . . .

(b) The owner or operator must determine the concentration or value of the following parameters in ground-water samples in accordance with paragraphs (c) and (d) of this section:

(3) Parameters used as indicators of ground-water contamination:

(i) pH

(ii) Specific Conductance

(iii) Total Organic Carbon

(iv) Total Organic Halogen

(c)(1) For all monitoring wells, the owner or operator must establish initial background concentrations or values of all parameters specified in paragraph (b) of this section. He must do this quarterly for one year.

(d) After the first year, all monitoring wells must be sampled and the samples analyzed with the following frequencies:

(2) Samples collected to indicate ground-water contamination must be obtained and analyzed for the parameters specified in paragraph (b)(3) of this section at least semi-annually.

§ 265.93   Preparation, Evaluation, and Response.

(b) For each indicator parameter specified in § 265.92(b)(3), the owner or operator must calculate the arithmetic mean and variance, based on at least four replicate measurements on each sample, for each well monitored in accordance with § 265.92(d)(2), and compare these results with its initial background arithmetic mean. The comparison must consider individually each of the wells in the monitoring system, and must use the Student's t-test at the 0.01 level of significance to determine statistically significant increases (and decreases, in the case of pH) over initial background.

(c)(1) If the comparisons for the upgradient wells made under paragraph (b) of this Section show a significant increase (or pH decrease), the owner or operator must submit this information in accordance with § 265.94(a)(2)(ii).

(2) If the comparisons for downgradient wells made under paragraph (b) of this Section show a significant increase (or pH decrease), the owner or operator must then immediately obtain additional ground-water samples from those downgradient wells where a significant difference was detected, split the samples in two, and obtain analyses of all additional samples to determine whether the significant difference was a result of laboratory error.

(d)(1) If the analyses performed under paragraph (c)(2) of this Section confirm the significant increase (or pH decrease), the owner or operator must provide written notice to the Regional Administrator—within seven days of the date of such confirmation—that the facility may be affecting ground-water quality.

(2) Within 15 days after the notification under paragraph (d)(1) of this Section, the owner or operator must develop and submit to the Regional Administrator a specific plan, based on the outline required under paragraph (a) of this Section and certified by a qualified geologist or geotechnical engineer, for a ground-water quality assessment program at the facility.

(3) The plan to be submitted under § 265.90(d)(1) or paragraph (d)(2) of this Section must specify:

(i) The number, location, and depth of wells;

(ii) Sampling and analytical methods for those hazardous wastes or hazardous waste constituents in the facility;

(iii) Evaluation procedures, including any use of previously-gathered ground-water quality information; and

(iv) A schedule of implementation.

(4) The owner or operator must implement the ground-water quality assessment plan which satisfies the requirements of paragraph (d)(3) of this Section, and, at a minimum, determine:

(i) The rate and extent of migration of the hazardous waste or hazardous waste constituents in the ground water; and

(ii) The concentrations of the hazardous waste or hazardous waste constituents in the ground water.

(5) The owner or operator must make his first determination under paragraph (d)(4) of this Section as soon as technically feasible, and, within 15 days after that determination, submit to the Regional Administrator a written report containing an assessment of the ground-water quality.

§ 265.94   Recordkeeping and Reporting.

(a) Unless the ground water is monitored to satisfy the requirements of § 265.93(d)(4), the owner or operator must:

(2) Report the following ground-water monitoring information to the Regional Administrator:

(ii) Annually: Concentrations or values of the parameters listed in § 265.92(b)(3) for each ground-water monitoring well, along with the required evaluations for these parameters under § 265.93(b). The owner or operator must separately identify any significant differences from initial background found in the upgradient wells, in accordance with § 265.93(c)(1). During the active life of the facility, this information must be submitted no later than March 1 following each calendar year.

40 C.F.R. Part 265, Subpart G—Closure and Post—Closure

§ 265.111   Closure Performance Standard.

The owner or operator must close the facility in a manner that:

(a) Minimizes the need for further maintenance, and

(b) Controls, minimizes or eliminates, to the extent necessary to protect human health and the environment, post-closure escape of hazardous waste, hazardous constituents, leachate, contaminated run-off, or hazardous waste decomposition products to the ground or surface waters or to the atmosphere, and

(c) Complies with the closure requirements of this subpart, including, but not limited to, the requirements of §§ 265.197, 265.228, 265.258, 265.280, 265.310, 265.351, 265.381, 265.404, and 264.1102.

§ 265.112   Closure Plan; Amendment of Plan.

(a) Written plan. By May 19, 1981, or by six months after the effective date of the rule that first subjects a facility to provisions of this section, the owner or operator of a hazardous waste management facility must have a written closure plan. Until final closure is completed and certified in accordance with § 265.115, a copy of the most current plan must be furnished to the Regional Administrator upon request, including request by mail. . . .

(b) Content of plan. The plan must identify steps necessary to perform partial and/or final closure of the facility at any point during its active life. The closure plan must include, at least:

(1) A description of how each hazardous waste management unit at the facility will be closed in accordance with § 265.111; and

(2) A description of how final closure of the facility will be conducted in accordance with § 265.111. The description must identify the maximum extent of the operation which will be unclosed during the active life of the facility; and

(3) An estimate of the maximum inventory of hazardous wastes ever on-site over the active life of the facility and a detailed description of the methods to be used during partial and final closure, including, but not limited to methods for removing, transporting, treating, storing or disposing of all hazardous waste, identification of and the type(s) of off-site hazardous waste management unit(s) to be used, if applicable; and

(4) A detailed description of the steps needed to remove or decontaminate all hazardous waste residues and contaminated containment system components, equipment, structures, and soils during partial and final closure including, but not limited to, procedures for cleaning equipment and removing contaminated soils, methods for sampling and testing surrounding soils, and criteria for determining the extent of decontamination necessary to satisfy the closure performance standard; and

(5) A detailed description of other activities necessary during the partial and final closure period to ensure that all partial closures and final closure satisfy the closure performance standards, including, but not limited to, ground-water monitoring, leachate collection, and run-on and run-off control; and

(6) A schedule for closure of each hazardous waste management unit and for final closure of the facility. The schedule must include, at a minimum, the total time required to close each hazardous waste management unit and the time required for intervening closure activities which will allow tracking of the progress of partial and final closure. . . .

(c) Amendment of plan. The owner or operator may amend the closure plan at any time prior to the notification of partial or final closure of the facility. . . .

(1) The owner or operator must amend the closure plan whenever:

(i) Changes in operating plans or facility design affect the closure plan, or

(ii) There is a change in the expected year of closure, if applicable, or

(iii) In conducting partial or final closure activities, unexpected events require a modification of the closure plan.

(2) The owner or operator must amend the closure plan at least 60 days prior to the proposed change in facility design or operation, or no later than 60 days after an unexpected event has occurred which has affected the closure plan.... These provisions also apply to owners or operators of surface impoundments ... who intended to remove all hazardous wastes at closure, but are required to close as landfills in accordance with § 265.310.

(d) Notification of partial closure and final closure.

(1) The owner or operator must submit the closure plan to the Regional Administrator at least 180 days prior to the date on which he expects to begin closure of the first surface impoundment ..., or final closure if it involves such a unit, whichever is earlier....

§ 265.113   Closure; Time Allowed for Closure.

(a) Within 90 days after receiving the final volume of hazardous wastes, or the final volume of nonhazardous wastes if the owner or operator complies with all applicable requirements in paragraphs (d) and (e) of this section, at a hazardous waste management unit or facility, or within 90 days after approval of the closure plan, whichever is later, the owner or operator must treat, remove from the unit or facility, or dispose of on-site, all hazardous wastes in accordance with the approved closure plan. The Regional Administrator may approve a longer period if the owner or operator demonstrates that:

(1)(i) The activities required to comply with this paragraph will, of necessity, take longer than 90 days to complete ... ; and

(2) He has taken and will continue to take all steps to prevent threats to human health and the environment from the unclosed but not operating hazardous waste management unit or facility, including compliance with all applicable interim status requirements.

40 C.F.R. Part 265, Subpart K—Surface Impoundments

§ 265.228   Closure and Post–Closure Care.

(a) At closure, the owner or operator must:

(1) Remove or decontaminate all waste residues, contaminated containment system components (liners, etc.), contaminated subsoils, and structures and equipment contaminated with waste and leachate, and manage them as hazardous waste unless § 261.3(d) of this chapter applies; or

(2) Close the impoundment and provide post-closure care for a landfill under Subpart G and § 265.310, including the following:

(i) Eliminate free liquids by removing liquid wastes or solidifying the remaining wastes and waste residues;

(ii) Stabilize remaining wastes to a bearing capacity sufficient to support the final cover; and

(iii) Cover the surface impoundment with a final cover designed and constructed to:

(A) Provide long-term minimization of the migration of liquids through the closed impoundment;

(B) Function with minimum maintenance;

(C) Promote drainage and minimize erosion or abrasion of the cover;

(D) Accommodate settling and subsidence so that the cover's integrity is maintained; and

(E) Have a permeability less than or equal to the permeability of any bottom liner system or natural subsoils present.

(b) In addition to the requirements of Subpart G, and § 265.310, during the post-closure care period, the owner or operator of a surface impoundment in which wastes, waste residues, or contaminated materials remain after closure in accordance with the provisions of paragraph (a)(2) of this section must:

(1) Maintain the integrity and effectiveness of the final cover, including making repairs to the cover as necessary to correct the effects of settling, subsidence, erosion, or other events;

(2) Maintain and monitor the leak detection system in accordance with §§ 265.221(c)(2)(iv) and (3) of this chapter and 265.226(b) and comply with all other applicable leak detection system requirements of this part;

(3) Maintain and monitor the ground-water monitoring system and comply with all other applicable requirements of Subpart F of this part; and

(4) Prevent run-on and run-off from eroding or otherwise damaging the final cover. . . .

Notes and Comments

1.   How would you respond to the questions posed by the EPA inspector? Can West still go through "clean closure?" If so, what would it entail? What are the implications of the requirement in 40 C.F.R. § 265.228 that the facility remove all contaminated subsoils?

2.   It should be noted that EPA has the tools to require cleanup of contamination like that presented in the hypothetical if it deems it warranted. For interim status facilities, EPA can order "corrective action" under § 3008(h) of RCRA. For fully-permitted facilities, corrective action require-

ments are addressed in the relevant permits. See 40 C.F.R. §§ 264.100 and 264.101.

3. Note that the groundwater monitoring requirements do not apply to all TSDs. Rather, they only apply to those TSDs that manage wastes in surface impoundments, landfills, or land treatment facilities. 40 C.F.R. § 265.90(a).

4. TSDs can close individual units without closing their entire facilities. 40 C.F.R. § 265.112(b)(1). In fact, a given TSD can close all of its TSD units without closing its entire facility. Over the years, many TSDs (particularly manufacturers) have chosen to "revert" to generator status by ceasing all of their TSD activities. Thus, the student should not necessarily equate "closing" with the shutting down of a plant. It often means that a particular company has simply chosen to change its operations to an extent that alters its regulatory status.

5. RCRA's financial responsibility requirements have two main components. First, all TSDs must meet certain "financial assurance" requirements designed to ensure that they will have the necessary resources to implement their closure and (if applicable) post-closure plans. See, e.g., 40 C.F.R. §§ 265.142–265.146. Perhaps obviously, the goal here is to minimize the possibility that these RCRA facilities will require cleanup under other programs such as CERCLA. As a result, facilities have to estimate their projected closure and post-closure costs. 40 C.F.R. §§ 265.142 and 265.144. They then have to either pass a financial test indicating that these funds will be available, or set aside the requisite funds in some sort of bankruptcy-proof mechanism. See, e.g., 40 C.F.R. §§ 265.143 and 265.145. The second component of the financial responsibility requirements is that facilities have insurance designed to protect their neighbors. All TSDs must have coverage for what are termed "sudden accidental occurrences." See, e.g., 40 C.F.R. § 265.147(a). Additionally, land disposal facilities must have coverage for "nonsudden" occurrences as well. 40 C.F.R. § 265.147(b).

6. In passing HSWA in 1984, Congress created what is commonly referred to as the "land ban" program. See 42 U.S.C. § 6924(b)–(n). This program restricts the land disposal of hazardous wastes by requiring that they first be treated in accordance with standards set by EPA. 42 U.S.C. § 6924(m). The details of this program are far too complicated to be treated in an overview course. It is worth noting, however, that the D.C. Circuit has upheld the linchpins of EPA's implementation strategy. First, in *Hazardous Waste Treatment Council v. U.S. EPA*, 886 F.2d 355 (D.C. Cir. 1989), it upheld EPA's authority to generally require the "best demonstrated available technology" ("BDAT") as the relevant treatment standard. And second, in *Chemical Waste Management, Inc. v. U.S. EPA*, 976 F.2d 2 (1992), it affirmed EPA's authority generally to require that characteristic wastes be treated to BDAT even though they no longer qualify as hazardous wastes once they no longer exhibit the relevant characteristic. EPA's "land ban" regulations are found at 40 C.F.R. Part 268.

Chapter 6

REGULATORY ENFORCEMENT

I. INTRODUCTION

As we have seen, the federal environmental statutes impose many binding legal requirements on regulated entities. Not surprisingly, these requirements are backed up by the threat of enforcement actions. Indeed, under most statutes the regulated entities operate under the supervision of three potential regulatory overseers. Using the Clean Water Act as an example, Section 309 gives the United States access to a broad range of enforcement powers, including the power to seek both civil and criminal sanctions. Section 402(i) indicates that these authorities apply even in authorized States. Additionally, as we have seen, Section 402(b)(7) requires States to provide their environmental agencies with similar powers as a precondition to authorization. And finally, Section 505 puts citizens on virtually the same footing as EPA, at least with respect to the ability to seek civil relief in court.

In the discussion below, we will focus primarily on the federal enforcement powers granted to EPA and citizens. While the precise contours of the State enforcement models may vary somewhat from what will be addressed below, the reader should rest assured that most of the principles discussed below will at least be relevant in State enforcement settings. Additionally, as the reader will soon see, we will focus primarily on the statutory dynamics of the Clean Water Act in our discussions in this chapter. This is due in significant part to the fact that there is much more enforcement case law under the CWA than there is under the other major command-and-control statutes. It will also serve to maintain some consistency in our discussions. Even more so in this context, however, the student should be assured that the relevant principles are more often than not directly applicable under the other statutes. While some differences will be noted, in most contexts the federal environmental laws have very similar statutory enforcement dynamics.

II. INVESTIGATIONS

The first step in any compliance oversight process involves compliance evaluation. Perhaps obviously, this requires access to the information necessary to evaluate a particular regulated entity's compliance status. Section 308 of the CWA provides a good example of the types of investigatory powers Congress typically vests in EPA. First, it gives EPA the power to compel point source operators to monitor their effluent, to maintain records, and to make such reports as EPA reasonably requires. 33 U.S.C. § 1318(a)(2)(A). Not surprisingly, EPA has established regulations on these fronts. The gist of these regulations is that permittees are required to monitor their discharges in accordance with specified protocols, and report the results of that monitoring monthly in what are called Discharge Monitoring Reports (or "DMRs"). See 40 C.F.R. § 122.41(j) and (l). Additionally, permittees must report all instances of noncompliance either within 24–hours (if they may endanger health or the environment) or, otherwise, at the time they submit their next DMRs, see 40 C.F.R. § 122.41(l)(6) and (7). They are also required to maintain copies of all relevant reports, including the underlying data, for at least three years. 40 C.F.R. § 122.41(j)(2). Permittees are subject to felony sanctions if they knowingly either fail to maintain or submit the required information, or if they submit false material statements. See 33 U.S.C. § 1319(c)(2) and (4).

Section 308 also gives EPA the power to inspect any premises in which an effluent source is located or in which any required records are maintained; it further expressly allows EPA to copy any relevant records, to inspect any monitoring equipment, and to sample any effluent. 33 U.S.C. § 1318(a)(2)(B). EPA's permit regulations elaborate on these requirements by compelling permittees to provide EPA (or an authorized State) with access to their facilities for any of the above purposes. Thus, the failure to do so constitutes a permit violation, subject to both civil and criminal enforcement.

Interestingly, EPA has never asserted the right to engage in warrantless inspections under any of the environmental statutes it administers. See, generally, *Donovan v. Dewey*, 452 U.S. 594, 101 S.Ct. 2534, 69 L.Ed.2d 262 (1981), and *New York v. Burger*, 482 U.S. 691, 107 S.Ct. 2636, 96 L.Ed.2d 601 (1987). As a practical matter, most regulated entities consent to EPA's inspections without requiring it to obtain a warrant. Even if a facility were to stand on its rights, the most that EPA would need to demonstrate to obtain a warrant for routine inspections would be something called "administrative probable cause." This requires only either one of two showings: (1) that EPA has "specific evidence of an existing violation," or (2) that "reasonable legislative or administrative standards for conducting an . . . inspection are satisfied with respect to a particular [facility]." *Marshall v. Barlow's, Inc.*, 436 U.S. 307, 320, 98 S.Ct. 1816, 1824, 56 L.Ed.2d 305 (1978) (internal quotations omitted). Moreover, EPA can obtain such warrants from the courts in ex parte proceedings (that is, without the facility-owner being present). Given these dynamics, do you understand why most regulated entities consent to EPA's inspections? Under what circumstances, if any, would there be a tactical advantage to insisting upon a warrant? What might be the drawbacks of such an approach?

III. ENFORCEMENT OPTIONS

Once EPA learns that a particular facility has violated one of its regulatory programs, it must first determine whether to enforce and, if so, how. The decision as to whether to enforce is not as simple as one might think. Environmental violations may range from the relatively trivial (e.g., a facility submits a full and accurate DMR, but submits it one day late) to the very serious (e.g., a facility discharges highly toxic wastes into a small river without a permit). EPA surely wants the discretion to forgo enforcement completely with respect to relatively minor violations, especially in situations in which a facility otherwise has demonstrated its commitment to environmental compliance. In other cases, EPA may want to let the States take the enforcement lead, even with respect to relatively serious violations, in the interest of promoting harmony in the "cooperative federalism" scheme.

Under the CWA, Section 309(a) on its face appears to require EPA, upon a finding of violation, to bring some action to compel compliance if it determines, after 30–days notice, that the State "has not commenced an appropriate enforcement action." It does this by stating that, in such circumstances, EPA "shall issue an order requiring [the alleged violator] to comply ... or shall bring a civil action [under § 309(b)]." 33 U.S.C. § 1319(a)(1); see also § 1319(a)(3) (seemingly compelling EPA to either issue an order or file a court action, regardless of what the State does). Despite these formulations, however, the courts have been virtually unanimous in determining that EPA does not have a mandatory duty to bring enforcement actions in such situations. See, e.g., *Dubois v. Thomas*, 820 F.2d 943 (8th Cir. 1987) ("*Dubois*"), and *Sierra Club v. Whitman*, 268 F.3d 898 (9th Cir. 2001). In so holding, the courts have relied on both (1) the fact that nothing in these provisions explicitly requires EPA to make any findings as to a particular facility's compliance status; and (2) the Supreme Court's opinion in *Heckler v. Chaney*, 470 U.S. 821, 105 S.Ct. 1649, 84 L.Ed.2d 714 (1985), in which the Court determined that the Food and Drug Administration had the discretion not to bring an enforcement action under the Federal Food, Drug and Cosmetic Act, 21 U.S.C. § 301, et seq., despite statutory language indicating that violators "shall be imprisoned." See, e.g., *Dubois*, 820 F.2d at 946–950.

In those cases in which EPA does choose to enforce, it chooses between three basic approaches. First, EPA is empowered to seek both injunctive relief and penalties through the initiation of civil actions in federal court. See, e.g., 33 U.S.C. § 1319(b) and (d). Alternatively, it can essentially seek the same forms of relief administratively. As mentioned above, Section 309(a) of the CWA gives EPA the power to issue administrative orders compelling violators to comply with the statute. See 33 U.S.C. § 1319(a)(3). Additionally, in 1987 Congress gave EPA the related power to impose administrative penalties under § 309(g). Collectively, these two authorities constitute EPA's second basic enforcement pathway. And third, in many (but not all) noncompliance situations, EPA has the option of pursuing criminal sanctions. In general, EPA may purse felony sanctions in situations in which regulated entities have committed "knowing" violations. See, e.g., 33 U.S.C. § 1319(c)(2). As we will see, these formulations pose the issue of exactly what the violator must "know" in order to be criminally accountable.

In the pages below, we consider all three of these enforcement pathways. We will also consider the extent which prior State enforcement action may limit EPA's options.

A.   EPA–Lead Civil Actions in Court

Not surprisingly, the environmental statutes give the Government the authority to seek judicial relief both compelling compliance and imposing penalties. Under the CWA, for example, Section 309(b) authorizes EPA, when faced with a violation, to seek either a permanent or temporary injunction. It also provides the court with "jurisdiction to restrain such violation and to require compliance." Additionally, Section 309(d) gives courts the authority to impose fines of up to $25,000 "per day for each violation" of the CWA. Despite this statutory language, the maximum fine for each violation has since been increased to $32,500 pursuant to the Federal Civil Penalties Inflation Adjustment Act, 28 U.S.C. § 2461 note. See 69 Fed.Reg. 7121 (Feb. 13, 2004).

On the injunctive relief front, one question that frequently arises relates to the degree of discretion the courts possess in fashioning relief under these provisions. Is the court, in any particular case, obligated to compel compliance even if such a decree might result in significant hardship to the defendant or others? If so, within what period of time must compliance be achieved? Consider the following case:

WEINBERGER v. ROMERO–BARCELO

Supreme Court of the United States, 1982.
456 U.S. 305, 102 S.Ct. 1798, 72 L.Ed.2d 91.

WHITE, Justice.

The issue in this case is whether the Federal Water Pollution Control Act ("FWPCA") requires a district court to enjoin immediately all discharges of pollutants that do not comply with the Act's permit requirements or whether the district court retains discretion to order other relief to achieve compliance. . . .

For many years, the Navy has used Vieques Island, a small island off the Puerto Rico coast, for weapons training. . . . During air-to-ground training, however, pilots sometimes miss land-based targets, and ordnance falls into the sea. That is, accidental bombings of the navigable waters and, occasionally, intentional bombings of water targets occur. . . .

In 1978, respondents, who include the Governor of Puerto Rico and residents of the island, sued to enjoin the Navy's operations on the island. . . .

As the District Court construed the FWPCA, the release of ordnance from aircraft or from ships into navigable waters is a discharge of pollutants, even though the EPA ... had not promulgated any regulations setting effluent levels or providing for the issuance of an NPDES permit for this category of pollutants. Recognizing that violations of the Act "must be cured," the District Court ordered the Navy to apply for an NPDES permit. It refused, however, to enjoin Navy operations pending consideration of the permit application. It explained that the Navy's "technical violations" were not causing any "appreciable harm" to the environment.[1] Moreover, because of the importance of the island as a training center, "the granting of the injunctive relief sought would cause grievous, and perhaps irreparable harm, not only to Defendant Navy, but to the general welfare of this Nation." The District Court concluded that an injunction was not necessary to ensure suitably prompt compliance by the Navy....

The Court of Appeals for the First Circuit vacated the District Court's order and remanded with instructions that the court order the Navy to cease the violation until it obtained a permit. Relying on *TVA v. Hill*, 437 U.S. 153 (1978), in which this Court held that an imminent violation of the Endangered Species Act required injunctive relief, the Court of Appeals concluded that the District Court erred in undertaking a traditional balancing of the parties' competing interests. "Whether or not the Navy's activities in fact harm the coastal waters, it has an absolute statutory obligation to stop any discharges of pollutants until the permit procedure has been followed and [EPA] ... has granted a permit...."

It goes without saying that an injunction is an equitable remedy. It "is not a remedy which issues as of course," *Harrisonville v. W.S. Dickey Clay Mfg. Co.*, 289 U.S. 334, 337–338 (1933), or "to restrain an act the injurious consequences of which are merely trifling." *Consolidated Canal Co. v. Mesa Canal Co.*, 177 U.S. 296, 302 (1900). The Court has repeatedly held that the basis for injunctive relief in the federal courts has always been irreparable injury and the inadequacy of legal remedies.

In exercising their sound discretion, courts of equity should pay particular regard for the public consequences in employing the extraordinary remedy of injunction. The grant of jurisdiction to ensure compliance with a statute hardly suggests an absolute duty to do so under any and all circumstances, and a federal judge sitting as chancellor is not mechanically obligated to grant an injunction for every violation of law.

... Of course, Congress may intervene and guide or control the exercise of the courts' discretion, but we do not lightly assume that Congress has intended to depart from established principles....

---

1. The District Court wrote: "In fact, if anything, these waters are as aesthetically acceptable as any to be found anywhere, and Plaintiff's witnesses unanimously testified as to their being the best fishing grounds in Vieques." "[I]f the truth be said, the control of large areas of Vieques [by the Navy] probably constitutes a positive factor in its over all ecology. The very fact that there are in the Navy zones modest numbers of various marine species which are practically nonexistent in the civilian sector of Vieques or in the main island of Puerto Rico, is an eloquent example of res ipsa loquitur."

In *TVA v. Hill*, we held that Congress had foreclosed the exercise of the usual discretion possessed by a court of equity. There, we thought that "[o]ne would be hard pressed to find a statutory provision whose terms were any plainer" than that before us. 437 U.S., at 173. The statute involved, the Endangered Species Act, required the District Court to enjoin completion of the Tellico Dam in order to preserve the snail darter, a species of perch. The purpose and language of the statute under consideration in *Hill*, not the bare fact of a statutory violation, compelled that conclusion. Section 7 of the Act requires federal agencies to "insure that actions authorized, funded, or carried out by them do not jeopardize the continued existence of [any] endangered species . . . or result in the destruction or modification of habitat of such species which is determined . . . to be critical." The statute thus contains a flat ban on the destruction of critical habitats.

It was conceded in *Hill* that completion of the dam would eliminate an endangered species by destroying its critical habitat. Refusal to enjoin the action would have ignored the [explicit provisions of the statute.] Congress, it appeared to us, had chosen the snail darter over the dam. . . . [O]nly an injunction could vindicate the objectives of the Act.

That is not the case here. An injunction is not the only means of ensuring compliance. The FWPCA itself, for example, provides for fines and criminal penalties. Respondents suggest that failure to enjoin the Navy will undermine the integrity of the permit process by allowing the statutory violation to continue. The integrity of the Nation's waters, however, not the permit process, is the purpose of the FWPCA. . . .

This purpose is to be achieved by compliance with the Act, including compliance with the permit requirements. Here, however, the discharge of ordnance had not polluted the waters, and, although the District Court declined to enjoin the discharges, it neither ignored the statutory violation nor undercut the purpose and function of the permit system. The court ordered the Navy to apply for a permit.[9] It temporarily, not permanently, allowed the Navy to continue its activities without a permit.

In *Hill*, we also noted that none of the limited "hardship exemptions" of the Endangered Species Act would "even remotely apply to the Tellico Project." 437 U.S., at 188. The prohibition of the FWPCA against discharge of pollutants, in contrast, can be overcome by the very permit the Navy was ordered to seek. The Senate Report to the 1972 Amendments explains that the permit program would be enacted because "the

---

9. The Navy applied for an NPDES permit in December 1979. In May 1981, the EPA issued a draft NPDES permit and a notice of intent to issue that permit. The FWPCA requires a certification of compliance with state water quality standards before the EPA may issue an NPDES permit. 33 U.S.C. § 1341(a). The Environmental Quality Board of the Commonwealth of Puerto Rico denied the Navy a water quali-

ty certificate in connection with this application for an NPDES in June 1981. In February 1982, the Environmental Quality Board denied the Navy's reconsideration request and announced it was adhering to its original ruling. In a letter dated April 9, 1982, the Solicitor General informed the Clerk of the Court that the Navy has filed an action challenging the denial of the water quality certificate.

Committee recognizes the impracticality of any effort to halt all pollution immediately." That the scheme as a whole contemplates the exercise of discretion and balancing of equities militates against the conclusion that Congress intended to deny courts their traditional equitable discretion in enforcing the statute.

Other aspects of the statutory scheme also suggest that Congress did not intend to deny courts the discretion to rely on remedies other than an immediate prohibitory injunction. Although the ultimate objective of the FWPCA is to eliminate all discharges of pollutants into the navigable waters by 1985, the statute sets forth a scheme of phased compliance. As enacted, it called for the achievement of [BPT by 1977] and [BAT by 1983]. This scheme of phased compliance further suggests that this is a statute in which Congress envisioned, rather than curtailed, the exercise of discretion.

The FWPCA directs the Administrator of the EPA to seek an injunction to restrain immediately discharges of pollutants he finds to be presenting "an imminent and substantial endangerment to the health of persons or to the welfare of persons." 33 U.S.C. § 1364(a). This rule of immediate cessation, however, is limited to the indicated class of violations. For other kinds of violations, the FWPCA authorizes the Administrator of the EPA "to commence a civil action for appropriate relief, including a permanent or temporary injunction, for any violation for which he is authorized to issue a compliance order...." 33 U.S.C. § 1319(b). The provision makes clear that Congress did not anticipate that all discharges would be immediately enjoined. Consistent with this view, the administrative practice has not been to request immediate cessation orders. "Rather, enforcement actions typically result, by consent or otherwise, in a remedial order setting out a detailed schedule of compliance designed to cure the identified violation of the Act." Brief for Petitioners 17. Here, again, the statutory scheme contemplates equitable consideration.

This Court explained in *Hecht Co. v. Bowles*, 321 U.S. 321 (1944), that a major departure from the long tradition of equity practice should not be lightly implied.... We do not read the FWPCA as foreclosing completely the exercise of the court's discretion. Rather than requiring a district court to issue an injunction for any and all statutory violations, the FWPCA permits the district court to order that relief it considers necessary to secure prompt compliance with the Act. That relief can include, but is not limited to, an order of immediate cessation.

The exercise of equitable discretion, which must include the ability to deny as well as grant injunctive relief, can fully protect the range of public interests at issue at this stage in the proceedings. The District Court did not face a situation in which a permit would very likely not issue, and the requirements and objective of the statute could therefore not be vindicated if discharges were permitted to continue. Should it become clear that no permit will be issued and that compliance with the

FWPCA will not be forthcoming, the statutory scheme and purpose would require the court to reconsider the balance it has struck.

STEVENS, Justice, dissenting.

. . . Because the [FWPCA] does not specifically command the federal courts to issue an injunction every time an unpermitted discharge of a pollutant occurs, the Court today is obviously correct in asserting that such injunctions should not issue "automatically" or "mechanically" in every case. It is nevertheless equally clear that by enacting the [FWPCA] Congress channeled the discretion of the federal judiciary much more narrowly than the Court's rather glib opinion suggests. Indeed, although there may well be situations in which the failure to obtain an NPDES permit would not require immediate cessation of all discharges, I am convinced that Congress has circumscribed the district courts' discretion on the question of remedy so narrowly that a general rule of immediate cessation must be applied in all but a narrow category of cases. . . .

Contrary to the impression created by the Court's opinion, the Court of Appeals did not hold that the District Court was under an absolute duty to require compliance with the FWPCA "under any and all circumstances," or that it was "mechanically obligated to grant an injunction for every violation of law." The only "absolute duty" that the Court of Appeals mentioned was the Navy's duty to obtain a permit before discharging pollutants into the waters off Vieques Island . . .

. . . The Court of Appeals' reasoning was correct in all respects. It recognized that the statute categorically prohibits discharges of pollutants without a permit. Unlike the Court, it recognized that the requested injunction was the only remedy that would bring the Navy into compliance with the statute on Congress' timetable. . . . The position of the Court of Appeals in effect was that the federal courts' equitable discretion is constrained by a strong presumption in favor of enforcing the law as Congress has written it. By reversing, the Court casts doubt on the validity of that position. This doubt is especially dangerous in the environmental area, where the temptations to delay compliance are already substantial.

The Court distinguishes *TVA v. Hill*, 437 U.S. 153, on the ground that the Endangered Species Act contained a "flat ban" on the destruction of critical habitats. But the statute involved in this case also contains a flat ban against discharges of pollutants into coastal waters without a permit. . . .

It is true that in *TVA v. Hill* there was no room for compromise between the federal project and the statutory objective to preserve an endangered species; either the snail darter or the completion of the Tellico Dam had to be sacrificed. In the FWPCA, the Court tells us, the congressional objective is to protect the integrity of the Nation's waters, not to protect the integrity of the permit process. Therefore, the Court continues, a federal court may compromise the process chosen by Congress to protect our waters as long as the court is content that the waters are not actually being harmed by the particular discharge of pollutants.

On analysis, however, this reasoning does not distinguish the two cases. Courts are in no better position to decide whether the permit process is necessary to achieve the objectives of the FWPCA than they are to decide whether the destruction of the snail darter is an acceptable cost of completing the Tellico Dam. Congress has made both decisions, and there is nothing in the respective statutes or legislative histories to suggest that Congress invited the federal courts to second-guess the former decision any more than the latter.

A disregard of the respective roles of the three branches of government also tarnishes the Court's other principal argument in favor of expansive equitable discretion in this area. The Court points out that Congress intended to halt water pollution gradually, not immediately, and that "the scheme as a whole contemplates the exercise of discretion and balancing of equities." In the Court's words, Congress enacted a "scheme of phased compliance." Equitable discretion in enforcing the statute, the Court states, is therefore consistent with the statutory scheme.

The Court's sophistry is premised on a gross misunderstanding of the statutory scheme. Naturally, in 1972 Congress did not expect dischargers to end pollution immediately. Rather, it entrusted to expert administrative agencies the task of establishing timetables by which dischargers could reach that ultimate goal. These timetables are determined by the agencies and included in the NPDES permits; the conditions in the permits constitute the terms by which compliance with the statute is measured. Quite obviously, then, the requirement that each discharger subject itself to the permit process is crucial to the operation of the "scheme of phased compliance." By requiring each discharger to obtain a permit before continuing its discharges of pollutants, Congress demonstrated an intolerance for delay in compliance with the statute. It is also obvious that the "exercise of discretion and balancing of equities" were tasks delegated by Congress to expert agencies, not to federal courts, yet the Court simply ignores the difference.

The decision in *TVA v. Hill* did not depend on any peculiar or unique statutory language. Nor did it rest on any special interest in snail darters. The decision reflected a profound respect for the law and the proper allocation of lawmaking responsibilities in our Government. There we refused to sit as a committee of review. Today the Court authorizes free-thinking federal judges to do just that. Instead of requiring adherence to carefully integrated statutory procedures that assign to nonjudicial decisionmakers the responsibilities for evaluating potential harm to our water supply as well as potential harm to our national security, the Court unnecessarily and casually substitutes the chancellor's clumsy foot for the rule of law.

Notes and Comments

1. The phraseology of § 309(b) (quoted in *Romero-Barcelo*) is similar to that in the equitable relief provisions of other federal environmental statutes. See, e.g., 42 U.S.C. §§ 6928(a)(1) (RCRA) and 7413(b) (CAA).

2. How would you characterize the Court's holding in *Romero-Barcelo*? How did the Court distinguish *TVA v. Hill*? How did Justice Stevens respond? What aspects of the CWA did the Court cite as being supportive of its result? Are they persuasive? Do you think the Court would have reached the same result if the Navy's discharges had been causing clear harm to the waters? What if there had simply been more doubt about whether a permit would issue? What approach did Justice Stevens advocate? Under the majority's approach, does the fact that Congress forbade permitless discharges merit any weight in the equitable balancing process? Should it?

3. In the later case of *Amoco Production Co. v. Village of Gambell*, 480 U.S. 531, 107 S.Ct. 1396, 94 L.Ed.2d 542 (1987), the Supreme Court, while denying a rule of automatic injunction under the Alaska National Interest Lands Conservation Act, did state that:

> . . . Environmental injury, by its nature, can seldom be adequately remedied by money damages and is often permanent or at least of long duration, *i.e.*, irreparable. If such injury is sufficiently likely, therefore, the balance of harms will usually favor the issuance of an injunction to protect the environment.

Id. at 545, 107 S.Ct. at 1404. Even more recently, in *United States v. Oakland Cannabis Buyers' Cooperative*, 532 U.S. 483, 121 S.Ct. 1711, 149 L.Ed.2d 722 (2001), the Supreme Court reversed a decision by the Ninth Circuit in which the latter court had held that the district court in that case had the discretion to decline to enjoin the Cooperative's ongoing distribution of marijuana in violation of the Controlled Substances Act:

> . . . [T]he mere fact that the District Court had discretion does not suggest that the District Court, when evaluating the motion to modify the injunction, could consider any and all factors that might relate to the public interest or the conveniences of the parties, including the medical needs of the Cooperative's patients. On the contrary, a court sitting in equity cannot ignore the judgment of Congress, deliberately expressed in legislation. A district court cannot, for example, override Congress' policy choice, articulated in a statute, as to what behavior should be prohibited. "Once Congress, exercising its delegated powers, has decided the order of priorities in a given area, it is . . . for the courts to enforce them when enforcement is sought." [*TVA v. Hill*], 437 U.S., at 194. Courts of equity cannot, in their discretion, reject the balance that Congress has struck in a statute. *Id.*, at 194–195. Their choice (unless there is statutory language to the contrary) is simply whether a particular means of enforcing the statute should be chosen over another permissible means; their choice is not whether enforcement is preferable to no enforcement at all. Consequently, when a court of equity exercises its discretion, it may not consider the advantages and disadvantages of nonenforcement of the statute, but only the advantages and disadvantages of "employing the extraordinary remedy of injunction," *Romero-Barcelo*, 456 U.S., at 311, over the other available methods of enforce-

ment. Cf. *id.*, at 316 (referring to "discretion to rely on remedies other than an immediate prohibitory injunction"). To the extent the district court considers the public interest and the conveniences of the parties, the court is limited to evaluating how such interest and conveniences are affected by the selection of an injunction over other enforcement mechanisms. . . .

Id. at 487–498, 121 S.Ct. at 1721–1722. How, if at all, should these cases affect the analysis under statutes such as the CWA?

Section 309(d) provides courts with a similar degree of discretion in the penalty imposition realm. First, it establishes the statutory range, which again, despite what § 309(d) says, should now be read as providing for penalties "not to exceed [$32,500] per day for each violation." See 69 Fed.Reg. 7121 (Feb. 13, 2004). Second, it dictates that, in determining the appropriate fine within that statutory range, the court shall consider

the seriousness of the violation or violations, the economic benefit (if any) resulting from the violation, any history of such violations, any good-faith efforts to comply with the applicable requirements, the economic impact of the penalty on the violator, and such other matters as justice may require.

33 U.S.C. § 1319(d).

How should courts apply these factors? Consider the following case, which, despite its formal name, is commonly referred to as *"Dean Dairy:"*

UNITED STATES v. THE MUNICIPAL AUTHORITY OF UNION TOWNSHIP

United States Court of Appeals, Third Circuit, 1998.
150 F.3d 259.

SLOVITER, Circuit Judge.

Appellant Dean Dairy Products, Inc., appeals the district court's imposition of a $4,031,000 civil penalty against it for Clean Water Act violations. Dean Dairy contends that the district court erred when it assessed the economic benefit Dean Dairy gained during the period of the Clean Water Act violations on the basis of Dean Dairy's "wrongful profits."

. . . Briefly stated, Dean Dairy, operating in Union Township, Belleville, Pennsylvania, is a wholly-owned subsidiary of Dean Foods, Inc., the country's largest milk processor. Since 1974 Dean Dairy's wastewater, a result of the production of sour cream, cottage cheese, yogurt and ice cream, has been discharged and treated by Union Township's [POTW]. . . .

Beginning in July 1989, Dean Dairy exceeded [its pretreatment limits]. Its wastewater, containing the impermissibly high levels of BOD and TSS, flowed from Union Township's POTW into the nearby Kishacoquillas Creek, which was damaged as a result. There is no dispute that because Dean Dairy issued monitoring reports to Union Township on a monthly basis, it had been aware of its violations since July 1989.

In 1994, the United States filed a civil enforcement action against Dean Dairy under the [CWA] for close to 1800 violations ... Following discovery, the United States moved for and was granted summary judgment on the issue of Dean Dairy's liability for the CWA violations. The action against the Municipal Authority of Union Township was settled and therefore the Authority is not a party to this appeal. Dean Dairy does not contest its liability for the violations. Its appeal is limited to the amount of the civil penalty imposed.

The district court found Dean Dairy liable for 1,754 violations ... between July 1989 and April 1994. It also found that Dean Dairy continued to violate [the relevant requirements] after the United States filed suit. Although Dean Dairy took certain steps to address the violations ... between 1991 and 1994, the district court found these efforts were belated and ineffective. It was only the construction of a $865,000 pretreatment system, which became operational in April 1995, that succeeded in reducing Dean Dairy's pollutants to permissible levels.

Important to the issue before us is that Dean Dairy considered various options to meet its permit obligations but, as the district court found, "it continued to produce at a volume which it recognized was very likely to generate [violations]. [Dean Dairy] chose not to reduce production volume because it viewed the concomitant reduction in earnings as too high a price to pay for compliance with the Clean Water Act."

Although the district court applied the six statutory factors a court must consider in assessing the appropriate penalty for a CWA violation, the appellant presents the case as if the court concentrated almost exclusively on the "economic benefit" factor. In fact, the district court made extensive findings of fact and issued conclusions of law on each of the six factors. The court noted that the history of Dean Diary's violations dated back to 1989, that the excessive discharges required the Pennsylvania Fish and Boat Commission to cease stocking fish in areas of the Kishacoquillas Creek, and that its two-year delay to take meaningful action to remedy the violations did "not speak highly of its good faith in this matter."

In connection with its evaluation of the economic benefit factor, ... the district court acknowledged that the parties had previously stipulated that Dean Dairy did not realize any economic benefit from delaying the capital investments necessary to achieve compliance.... This was due to the unusual fact that, by delaying the construction of the pretreatment plant, Dean Dairy was actually losing money because it was paying higher usage fees to the POTW for its increased volume. Thus, Dean Dairy did not reap an economic benefit by delaying the construction of the pretreatment plant. The court nevertheless found that Dean Dairy *did* realize an economic benefit during the period of the violations because it produced "at a volume above that which would have allowed it to operate within its IU permit."

In making the finding of economic benefit, the district court relied upon a document produced by Dean Dairy ... that outlined various options by which Dean Dairy could comply with its permit. The district court noted that Option #4 of that document indicated that Dean Dairy could drop PennMaid as a customer and thereby reduce the amount of wastewater generated. Dean Dairy recognized, however, that losing the revenues from PennMaid would result in a loss of earnings in the amount of $417,000 in fiscal year 1994.

In its opinion, the district court commented on [this information] as follows: "Production volume at [Dean Dairy] was higher in each year from 1989 to 1993 than it was in 1994, and, therefore, it is reasonable to believe that [Dean Dairy] gained at least $417,000 in earnings annually during the period of its violations. On this basis, the court concludes that between July 1989 and April 1994, [Dean Dairy] gained approximately $2,015,500 by violating its [pretreatment requirements]." The district court also determined that the figure should be doubled in order to provide a proper deterrent and punishment, and accordingly imposed a total penalty of $4,031,000.

Section 1319(d) of the [CWA] provides in pertinent part:

> Any person who violates ... this title, or any permit condition or limitation ... shall be subject to a civil penalty not to exceed $25,000 per day for each violation. In determining the amount of a civil penalty the court shall consider the seriousness of the violation or violations, the economic benefit (if any) resulting from the violation, any history of such violations, any good-faith efforts to comply with the applicable requirements, the economic impact of the penalty on the violator, and such other matters as justice may require.

The statute does not define the term "economic benefit" used in this section. It is apparent, however, that the goal of the economic benefit analysis is to prevent a violator from profiting from its wrongdoing. In *United States v. Smithfield Foods, Inc.*, 972 F.Supp. 338, 348 (E.D.Va.1997), the district court explained that "[c]ourts use economic benefit analysis to level the economic playing field and prevent violators from gaining an unfair competitive advantage."

A similar rationale was also given by [EPA], which emphasized that the reason for considering economic benefit to a violator in assessing a CWA penalty is to remove or neutralize the economic incentive to violate environmental regulations. In a 1990 Manual to its BEN computer program, established to assist in the calculation of civil CWA penalties, the EPA explained:

> An organization's decision to comply with environmental regulations usually implies a commitment of financial resources; both initially, in the form of a capital investment or one-time expenditure, and over time, in the form of annual, continuing expenses. These expenditures might result in better protection of public health or environmental quality; however, they are unlikely to yield any direct economic benefit (i.e., net gain) to the organization. If these financial resources were not used for compliance, they presumably would

be invested in projects with an expected direct economic benefit to the organization. This concept of alternative investment; that is, the amount the violator would normally expect to make by not investing in pollution control, is the basis for calculating the economic benefit of noncompliance.... EPA uses the Agency's penalty authority to remove or neutralize the economic incentive to violate environmental regulations. In the absence of enforcement and appropriate penalties, it is usually in the organization's best economic interest to delay the commitment of funds for compliance with environmental regulations and to avoid certain other associated costs, such as operating and maintenance expenses.

EPA BEN User's Manual I–6 (July 1990), *quoted in Friends of the Earth, Inc. v. Laidlaw Envtl. Servs. (TOC), Inc.*, 890 F.Supp. 470 (D.S.C.1995) ("*Laidlaw I* ").

Few published cases discuss the "economic benefit" factor of the Clean Water Act in any detail, and those that do are, in large part, district court opinions. In *Laidlaw*, the court described economic benefit as: "the after-tax present value of avoided or delayed expenditures on necessary pollution control measures." 890 F.Supp. at 481. The theory is that economic benefit "represents the opportunity a polluter had to earn a return on funds that should have been spent to purchase, operate, and maintain appropriate pollution control devices." *Id.*

This court has previously recognized that a violator's economic benefit under the Clean Water Act may not be capable of ready determination. In *Public Interest Research Group of New Jersey, Inc. v. Powell Duffryn Terminals Inc.*, 913 F.2d 64 (3d Cir.1990), we stated:

> Precise economic benefit to a polluter may be difficult to prove. The Senate Report accompanying the 1987 amendment that added the economic benefit factor to section 309(d) recognized that a reasonable approximation of economic benefit is sufficient to meet plaintiff's burden for this factor.... The determination of economic benefit or other factors will not require an elaborate or burdensome evidentiary showing. Reasonable approximations of economic benefit will suffice.

Id. at 80 (citation omitted).

Because of the difficulty of determining the appropriate penalty under the Clean Water Act, the court will accord the district court's award of a penalty wide discretion, even though it represents an approximation. This was emphasized by the Supreme Court when it said, more than a decade ago, "Congress [made the] assignment of the determination of the amount of civil penalties to trial judges.... Since Congress itself may fix the civil penalties, it may delegate that determination to trial judges. In this case, highly discretionary calculations that take into account multiple factors are necessary in order to set civil penalties under the Clean Water Act." *Tull v. United States*, 481 U.S. 412, 426–27 (1987).

Courts have applied different methods in determining the appropriate penalty for a Clean Water Act violation. Some courts have employed a "top down" approach in which the maximum possible penalty is first established, then reduced following an examination of the six "mitigating" factors. See, e.g., *Powell Duffryn,* 913 F.2d at 79.

Other courts have used a "bottom up" approach whereby the economic benefit a violator gained by noncompliance is established and adjusted upward or downward using the remaining five factors in § 1319(d). *See, e.g., Smithfield Foods,* 972 F.Supp. at 354. Because the statute does not prescribe either method, it appears that a court is free to use its discretion in choosing the appropriate method.

Had the district court in this case taken a "top-down" approach, it would have begun at the maximum penalty, which was approximately $45,825,000, based on the statutory penalty of $25,000 a day. Instead, the court applied the "bottom up" approach by determining Dean Dairy's economic benefit acquired through the Fairmont plant's production at a volume that resulted in more wastewater than permissible under its permit. These were knowing violations, as its own document demonstrated it was aware that if it had reduced its wastewater volume by reducing its production, it would have been in compliance with its IU permit. . . . [I]f Dean Dairy had reduced volume, it believed it would have lost PennMaid as a customer. Dean Dairy's own document prepared by Ron Crock, its controller, demonstrated that this loss of PennMaid would have had a negative impact of $417,000 per year. This was the basis on which the district court calculated Dean Dairy's economic benefit as $2,015,500, which when doubled, resulted in the penalty of $4,031,000. That penalty was barely 9% of the maximum statutory penalty to which Dean Dairy was subject.

It is not surprising that no published case has used this method of ascertaining a violator's economic benefit because it is the rare violator who actually loses money by delaying compliance with the law. Typically, a violator benefits economically by avoiding or delaying the construction of antipollution equipment that would have placed it in compliance with its permit. In *Smithfield Foods,* the court explained that, "[w]hen a company delays or avoids certain costs of capital and operations and maintenance necessary for compliance, the company is able to use those funds for other income-producing activities, such as investing that money in their own company." *Id.* at 349. Therefore, in that case, [the court found] "the avoided and/or delayed cost of compliance . . . to be both the best and the appropriate method to determine how much money defendants made on the funds they did not spend for compliance." *Id.* at 349.

This case is unusual because Dean Dairy's delay in constructing a pretreatment plant was not beneficial to its "bottom line"; in effect, Dean Dairy was actually penalizing itself in failing to promptly build the pretreatment plant. Our general assumption of the reasonable capitalist went awry with this company.

There are methods other than the delayed or avoided capital expenditure for ascertaining economic benefit.... It is significant that neither the statute nor the case law supports the contention that the cost-avoidance method is the *only* permissible method of determining the amount a polluter has gained from violating the law....

In contrast to the situation in *Smithfield Foods,* the "cost-avoided" method of determining economic benefit is not a method that fits the facts that were presented to the district court because Dean Dairy did not profit by delaying its construction of the pretreatment plant. But it clearly gained *other* economic benefits by failing to adopt the method that was readily available. The wastewater from the Fairmont plant is created by the required daily cleaning of its vats and other processing equipment. A reduction of production would reduce the wastewater. Thus, if Dean Dairy wanted to avoid the cost entailed by the purchase of new equipment, it had the option of reducing volume.

The approach adopted by the district court is not in conflict with the CWA or basic economic principles. A violator who chooses to continue to violate its permit while experimenting with less costly remedies necessarily subjects itself to the surrender via penalty of any economic benefit it acquired. The fact that the violator has also penalized itself by failing to implement cost-effective methods that would have put it into compliance with its permit and thereby saved it money is certainly no basis to mitigate its penalty.

Requiring a company to reduce the amount of pollution it creates to comply with its permit is not unreasonable. As the court in *Tyson Foods* stated: "There was one simple and straightforward way for Tyson to avoid paying civil penalties for violations of the Clean Water Act: After purchasing the plant, Tyson could have ceased operations until it was able to discharge pollutants without violating the requirements of its ... permit. Tyson chose not to do this and it must now bear the consequences of that decision." 897 F.2d at 1141–42. Similarly, Dean Dairy chose neither what proved to be the economically sensible option (building the pretreatment facility) nor the alternative option of reducing the amount of wastewater produced. Accordingly, it must bear the consequences.

We conclude that the district court's method of calculation of the penalty was within its discretion. We do not suggest that we have any dissatisfaction with the cost-avoided method of determining a violator's economic benefit in the usual case. However, under these unusual circumstances, we see no legally significant difference in measuring the economic benefit achieved by avoiding the costs of antipollution equipment, and the economic benefits achieved by failing to reduce the volume of pollution created. Both methods aim to recoup any benefits a violator gained by breaking the law and which gave the violator an advantage vis-a-vis its competitors. The penalty thus achieves the leveling of the playing field intended by Congress.

Notes and Comments

1. In *Tull*, the Supreme Court determined that the defendants in EPA civil judicial enforcement cases are entitled to request a jury trial on the issue of liability. At the same time, however, the Court concluded that Congress could constitutionally delegate to the court the responsibility to determine the appropriate penalty, assuming liability is found. 481 U.S. at 426–427. Given these dynamics, would you expect that many such defendants would seek a jury trial? Why or why not?

2. Does Section 309(d) require the courts to impose some penalty in every case in which liability is established? Interestingly, all three Circuits that have squarely addressed this question have concluded that it does, with only one of these decisions even drawing a dissenting opinion. See *Leslie Salt Co. v. United States*, 55 F.3d 1388 (9th Cir. 1995) (and cases cited therein). Reread § 309(d). Do you agree with this result? If so, what is the minimum fine a court could impose in response to a truly trivial violation?

3. As noted in the Third Circuit's opinion, the district court in *Dean Dairy* had taken pains to consider all of the § 309(d) factors before focusing in on the economic benefit as the key factor in its analysis. This was in accordance with other decisions indicating that district courts must at least consider all six of the statutory factors in their penalty analysis. See, e.g., *Atlantic States Legal Found., Inc. v. Tyson Foods, Inc.*, 897 F.2d 1128 (11th Cir. 1990).

4. The *Dean Dairy* court identifies at least two related rationales for recapturing the economic benefit from violators: (1) it puts the violator back on a level economic playing field with its competitors who did whatever was necessary to comply with the law; and (2) it removes the economic incentive to violate environmental standards. A third, still-related rationale might include the simple desire to recapture ill-gotten gains. Should courts be required to recapture the economic benefit in all cases in which it is clear that the defendant did indeed enjoy such a benefit? Does § 309(d) mandate that result? Even if it doesn't, should the Courts of Appeal be more inclined to find an abuse of discretion in situations in which a district court has imposed a penalty that does not fully recapture the economic benefit?

5. What did you think of the "lost profits" approach to quantifying the economic benefit? Were there any costs in *Dean Dairy* that the defendant should perhaps have been able to use to offset some of the economic benefit, as calculated? Should defendants be able to subtract whatever sums they pay their lawyers in their defense of enforcement actions from what would otherwise be their economic benefit?

6. How should courts take factors such as "good faith" and "the economic impact . . . on the violator" into account in assessing penalties? We will return to these questions when we address administrative enforcement.

7. Most of the pollution control statutes contain no statute-specific statute of limitations for civil penalty actions. As a result, the courts have looked to the default five year federal statute of limitations for penalty actions found in 28 U.S.C. § 2462. See, e.g., *Public Interest Research Group of New Jersey, Inc. v. Powell Duffryn Terminals Inc.*, 913 F.2d 64, 73–76 (3d Cir. 1990).

B. Administrative Enforcement

Congress often provides EPA with administrative enforcement mechanisms it may use as an alternative to going to court. As mentioned, for example, the Clean Water Act gives EPA the power to issue unilateral orders requiring the recipients (typically referred to as "respondents") to comply with the law. 33 U.S.C. § 1319(a)(3). Additionally, Section 309(g) provides EPA with the authority to impose administrative fines for violations of the Act.

These authorities are significant in two respects. First, they may provide EPA with the advantage of speed—it is much easier to generate prompt compliance if all you have to do is order someone to comply, without any required discovery, hearings, or other procedural constraints. Second, they leave more power in EPA's hands, as opposed to in those of the courts. In the administrative realm, for example, EPA gets to make it own decisions about what steps are required to bring a violator into compliance, and as to how long it should take the violator to undertake them. If the respondent complies with the order, that's that.

Some statutes, such as RCRA, specifically provide respondents with the right to request an administrative hearing before the compliance order becomes final. See 42 U.S.C. § 6928(b). Others, such as the CWA, provide for no such hearing and are silent as to whether such respondents may seek judicial review before deciding whether or not to comply. See 33 U.S.C. §§ 1319(a)(3) and 1369(b). The following case addresses the effect of this silence on the question whether the recipients of these orders are entitled to what is referred to as "preenforcement" review of those orders:

SOUTHERN PINES ASSOCIATES
v. UNITED STATES

United States Court of Appeals, Fourth Circuit, 1990.
912 F.2d 713.

Ervin, Chief Judge:

Southern Pines is a Virginia limited partnership which owns 293.41 acres of land located in Chesapeake, Virginia. VICO has a contract with Southern Pines and has been involved in clearing and building upon 40 acres of the property.

On May 23, 1989, [EPA] issued a "Findings of Violation and Order for Compliance" to Southern Pines, informing the company that it had violated section 301(a) of the Clean Water Act by discharging fill material into wetlands without a permit. The order instructed Southern Pines to (1) "cease and desist all filling activities in the wetlands" at the site; (2) "[c]ontact EPA within 5 working days" to discuss restoration of the areas; (3) implement a plan for restoration after EPA approval; and (4) submit written notice of intent to comply with the order. In a cover letter accompanying the order, EPA asked Southern Pines to provide information about the site for it to review in order to make a "final determination of the boundaries of the wetlands that fall under the jurisdiction of the Clean Water Act."

Upon receiving EPA's order, Southern Pines and VICO discontinued all work except logging which does not require a permit. . . .

On July 19, 1989, Southern Pines and VICO filed a complaint and a petition for a temporary restraining order. . . . They alleged that EPA's assertion of jurisdiction over the property created an actual controversy within the meaning of the Declaratory Judgment Act and argued that EPA lacks jurisdiction over the site because the wetlands on the property are not adjacent to any body of water.[1] The district court dismissed the case for lack of subject matter jurisdiction.

Southern Pines and VICO . . . argue that jurisdiction is proper under *Abbott Laboratories v. Gardner*, 387 U.S. 136 (1967), a case in which drug manufacturers challenged regulations promulgated by the Commissioner of Food and Drugs.

The Supreme Court held that judicial review was proper in *Abbott* because the Federal Food, Drug, and Cosmetic Act did not preclude review, and because the controversy was ripe for judicial resolution. However, the first question addressed by the Supreme Court in *Abbott* was whether "Congress by the Federal Food, Drug, and Cosmetic Act intended to forbid pre-enforcement review" of the regulation at issue in that case. The Court found that the statutory scheme did not preclude the action. The case before us today is distinguishable from *Abbott* because the statutory structure and history of the CWA provides clear and convincing evidence that Congress intended to exclude this type of action. We agree with the Seventh Circuit which recently held in *Hoffman Group, Inc. v. EPA*, 902 F.2d 567 (7th Cir.1990), that Congress "has impliedly precluded judicial review of a compliance order except in an enforcement proceeding."

In determining whether a statute precludes judicial review, we look not only to its language, but also to "the structure of the statutory scheme, its objectives, its legislative history, and the nature of the administrative action involved." *Block v. Community Nutrition Institute*, 467 U.S. 340, 345 (1984). The language, structure, objectives, and history of the CWA, persuade us that Congress intended to preclude judicial review.

The objective of the CWA is "to restore and maintain the chemical, physical, and biological integrity of the Nation's waters." 33 U.S.C. § 1251. To achieve this goal, the Act prohibits any discharge of dredge or fill materials into waters of the United States unless authorized by a permit issued by the Corps of Engineers pursuant to section 404 of the Act. 33 U.S.C. § 1311(a). Congress provided EPA with a choice of

---

1. The Act does not require Southern Pines to obtain a permit unless it is discharging fill materials into navigable waters. Navigable waters are "waters of the United States including the territorial seas." Waters of the United States include "wetlands adjacent to waters (other than waters that are themselves wetlands). . . . " 40 C.F.R. § 230.3(s)(7) (1988).

procedures for enforcing the Act. Section 309(a)(3) of the Act provides that when, on the basis of available information, the Administrator of EPA identifies a person in violation of the Act, the Administrator shall "either issue an order requiring such person to comply with [the Act], or he shall bring a civil action in accordance with subsection (b) of this section." In 1987, Congress added section 309(g) to the Act which provides that EPA may also assess administrative penalties against those who violate the Act or a permit issued under the Act. When EPA proceeds under section 309(g), the violator is entitled to a hearing before the agency, and the public is provided with an opportunity to comment. 33 U.S.C. § 1319(g)(2). Orders assessing administrative penalties are subject to judicial review. 33 U.S.C. § 1319(g)(8).

In this case, EPA issued a compliance order. A compliance order is a document served on the violator, setting forth the nature of the violation and specifying a time for compliance with the Act. 33 U.S.C. § 1319(a)(5)(A). If a violator fails to abide by that order, EPA may seek to enforce the order by bringing a suit in federal district court under section 309(b) of the Act. However, EPA need not issue a compliance order before bringing an action. The penalties for violating either the Act or a compliance order are the same. The court may issue an injunction to require compliance, and it may impose civil penalties of up to $25,000 per day for each violation of the Act, a permit, or a compliance order. 33 U.S.C. § 1319(d). The violator is subject to the same injunction and penalties whether or not EPA has issued a compliance order.[3]

The CWA is not the only environmental statute which allows EPA to issue pre-enforcement administrative orders. Both the Clean Air Act ("CAA"), 42 U.S.C. §§ 7401 et seq., and the Comprehensive Environmental Response, Compensation, and Liability Act (CERCLA), 42 U.S.C. §§ 9601 et seq., also provide for pre-enforcement agency action. The CAA, like the CWA, provides that EPA may issue a compliance order before bringing suit. Based upon the legislative history of the CAA, courts have found that Congress intended to preclude judicial review of compliance orders issued under the CAA. *See Union Electric Co. v. EPA*, 593 F.2d 299, 304 (8th Cir.), *cert. denied*, 444 U.S. 839; *Lloyd A. Fry Roofing Co. v. EPA*, 554 F.2d 885 (8th Cir.1977).

CERCLA allows the EPA to order that a site be cleaned up prior to bringing suit. 42 U.S.C. §§ 9604, 9606, 9607. Prior to 1986 courts held that pre-enforcement remedial actions taken by the EPA under CERCLA were not subject to judicial review because litigation would interfere with CERCLA's policy of prompt agency response. *See, e.g., Wagner Seed Co. v. Daggett*, 800 F.2d 310, 315 (2d Cir.1986). In 1986 Congress added a provision to CERCLA which specifically precludes federal jurisdiction over pre-enforcement remedial action. 42 U.S.C. § 9613(h).

---

3. Because the compliance order does not alter Southern Pines' and VICO's obligations under the Act, and EPA can bring a suit whether or not it issues an order, Southern Pines and VICO are not faced with any greater threat from EPA just because EPA seeks to negotiate a solution rather than to institute civil proceedings immediately.

The structure of these environmental statutes indicates that Congress intended to allow EPA to act to address environmental problems quickly and without becoming immediately entangled in litigation. The CWA is not only similar in structure to the CAA and CERCLA, but its enforcement provisions were modeled after the enforcement provisions of the CAA. Considering this legislative history, the structure of these statutes, the objectives of the CWA, and the nature of the administrative action involved, we are persuaded that Congress meant to preclude judicial review of compliance orders under the CWA just as it meant to preclude pre-enforcement review under the CAA and CERCLA.

Southern Pines and VICO argue that this case does not involve pre-enforcement review because the compliance order is an "enforcement procedure." They also claim that this case should be distinguished from *Hoffman* because they are not merely contesting the extent of EPA's jurisdiction but are claiming that EPA totally lacks jurisdiction.

Southern Pines' action seeks pre-enforcement review because EPA has not yet sought penalties for any violation of the Act or its order. The cases discussing pre-enforcement review under the CAA and CERCLA concern action taken prior to the initiation of judicial proceedings. *See, e.g., Lloyd A. Fry Roofing Co.*, 554 F.2d 885.

We are also unpersuaded by Southern Pines' and VICO's attempt to distinguish this case from *Hoffman*. Allowing the parties to challenge the existence of EPA's jurisdiction would delay the agency's response in the same manner as litigation contesting the extent of EPA's jurisdiction. Southern Pines and VICO can contest the existence of EPA's jurisdiction if and when EPA seeks to enforce the penalties provided by the Act....

Notes and Comments

1. Do you agree that the CWA "provides clear and convincing evidence" that Congress intended to preclude preenforcement review? What were the statutory bases for the court's conclusion? Are they compelling? The court asserts that Southern Pines was subject to the same enforcement threat regardless of whether EPA had issued the compliance order. In reaching this conclusion, the Fourth Circuit implicitly assumed two things: (1) that those who violate compliance orders are subject to the same potential fines they would face absent the issuance of the order (i.e., if EPA went straight to court); and (2) that these respondents may raise the same substantive defenses in contesting the alleged violations that they could have raised if EPA had simply gone straight to court. Review § 309(d) and (g)(1) of the CWA in considering the first of these assumptions. Do you agree with the Fourth Circuit? If Southern Pines continued its filling activities after receiving the order, would EPA have had a basis for arguing for either enhanced or additional fines for any continued filling activities? Did the order otherwise impose any obligations that could have led to separately finable offenses? Compare *Allsteel, Inc. v. U.S. EPA*, 25 F.3d 312, 315 (6th Cir. 1994).

2. With respect to the court's second assumption, the question is whether, for example, Southern Pines would have been able to raise its

argument that EPA lacked jurisdiction over the site as a defense in an action seeking penalties for its disregard of the order. If it could not, it clearly would have been disadvantaged by EPA's having selected the administrative order route. This is so because, if EPA had gone straight to court (i.e., without issuing an order first), it would have had the burden of demonstrating jurisdiction to establish that Southern Pines had in fact violated the statute. In assuming that Southern Pines could test the legality of the order in an action seeking penalties for the violation thereof, the Fourth Circuit was following the general presumption of reviewability, as set forth in the APA. 5 U.S.C. § 701(a)(1); see also *Lloyd A. Fry Roofing Co. v. U.S. EPA*, 554 F.2d 885, 891 (8th Cir. 1977) (denying preenforcement review under the CAA, but noting that the respondent would be able to raise the same arguments if and when EPA went to court to enforce the order), and *United States v. Mango*, 199 F.3d 85 (2d Cir. 1999) (allowing the defendant to challenge the legality of the relevant § 404 permit conditions in a criminal enforcement action for the violation thereof); cf. 33 U.S.C. § 1369(b)(2). Interestingly, however, in *Tennessee Valley Authority v. Whitman*, the Eleventh Circuit recently concluded that one who is alleged to have violated the requirements of a CAA order may not contest the legality of those requirements. 336 F.3d 1236, 1250, 1257 (11th Cir. 2003). Based on this conclusion, the court deemed the orders unconstitutional. Id. at 1260. What do you make of this approach?

3. The above notes raise questions about the legal effect of EPA's administrative orders. If we assume, though, that (a) these orders do "raise the stakes" in terms of the sanctions to which the respondents may be exposed, but that (b) the respondents will be able to contest the validity of these orders in any subsequent actions seeking penalties for the violation thereof, what are the policy dynamics hinging upon the availability of preenforcement review? What would the implications be for the Government (and the environment) if the recipients of these orders could forestall compliance by seeking judicial review in each and every case? On the other hand, what are the implications for companies like Southern Pines of denying preenforcement review? Absent such review, Southern Pines had two choices: It could either comply with the order or decline to do so. If Southern Pines had chosen to comply, when would it have had an opportunity to test EPA's assertion of jurisdiction? When considering this question, keep in mind that EPA's order not only required Southern Pines to cease all filling activities, but also ultimately to restore the areas that already had been filled. If, on the other hand, it had failed to comply, it may have faced the threat of increased penalties if EPA later established that the order was in fact lawful. Given this threat, a company in Southern Pines' position might decide to comply rather than risk this threat of penalties, even if it reasonably believed that the order was unlawful. From EPA's perspective, of course, this is part of the beauty of administrative orders: the respondents may decide to forgo their right to a day in court because of the increased sanctions they may bear if the are ultimately proven to be in the wrong. From the respondents' perspectives, this chilling of their due process rights may feel like a violation of those rights. On this latter point, see *United States v. Reilly Tar & Chemical Corp.*, 606 F.Supp. 412 (D.Minn. 1985).

4. In addition to raising preclusion arguments of the type seen in *Southern Pines*, the Government has sometimes argued that its administrative orders do not constitute final agency actions within the meaning of the APA. While this argument may have some ongoing viability in contexts in which EPA's orders merely restate statutory commands, the Supreme Court has rejected it in situations in which the orders impose new legal obligations. In *Alaska Dept. of Env. Conservation v. Environmental Protection Agency*, 540 U.S. 461, 124 S.Ct. 983, 998–999, 157 L.Ed.2d 967 (2004) (*Alaska*), the Court went out of its way to resolve this question despite the Government's decision not to contest this issue at the Supreme Court level:

> In this Court, EPA agrees with the Ninth Circuit's [determination that EPA's order was a final agency action]. We are satisfied that the Court of Appeals correctly applied the guides we set out in *Bennett v. Spear*, 520 U.S. 154, 177–178 (1997) (to be "final," agency action must "mark the 'consummation' of the agency's decisionmaking process," and must either determine "rights or obligations" or occasion "legal consequences" (internal quotation marks omitted)). As the Court of Appeals stated, EPA had "asserted its final position on the factual circumstances" underpinning the Agency's orders, [*Alaska v. U.S. EPA*, 244 F.3d 748, 750 (9th Cir. 2001)], and if EPA's orders survived judicial review, Cominco could not escape the practical and legal consequences (lost costs and vulnerability to penalties) of any ADEC-permitted construction Cominco endeavored, *ibid*.

5. Finally, it is worth noting the result in *Alaska* indicates that EPA's orders under the CAA are now reviewable on a preenforcement basis in all situations in which they impose legal obligations beyond those specifically set forth in the statute. This is due to the fact that Congress amended that statute's judicial review provision in 1977 to specifically provide for review of all final agency actions. 42 U.S.C. § 7607(b). Thus, the statutory preclusion and final agency action issues are now convergent under the CAA.

In addition to providing for administrative compliance orders, most environmental statutes give the Government the authority to impose administrative penalties. In this context, some statutes, such as RCRA, provide EPA with the authority to impose the same penalties that it could seek if it went to court; i.e., up to $25,000 per day for each violation, 42 U.S.C. § 6928(a)(3) (adjusted to $32,500 pursuant to the Federal Civil Penalties Inflation Adjustment Act, 28 U.S.C. § 2461 note). Under that approach, EPA may impose administrative fines limited only by the overall number of violations in a particular case. Indeed, EPA can and does assess administrative penalties in excess of $1,000,000 in situations in which it determines that a violator has committed a large number of serious violations. Not surprisingly, given the seriousness of these enforcement actions, EPA is at least required to provide the respondent with the ability to request a hearing before an administrative law judge (ALJ) before the order becomes final. See 42 U.S.C. § 6928(b) and 40 C.F.R. Part 22.

Under other statutes, such as the CWA, Congress has placed overall caps on the penalty amounts EPA can trigger without going to court. Under that statute, for example, the largest fine EPA can impose administratively is $125,000, 33 U.S.C. § 1319(g)(2)(B) (adjusted to $162,500). If it wants to assess a fine of more than that, it has to go to court.

The CWA is also reflective of a recent trend of tiering the amount of administrative process required to the penalty amount EPA seeks to impose. If it seeks to impose a fine of greater than $25,000 (adjusted to $32,500) in one action, EPA must provide an APA-type hearing under 40 C.F.R. Part 22. If it is willing to settle for less than that (and less than $10,000 per violation), an informal hearing before a "hearings officer" will suffice. See 33 U.S.C. § 1319(g)(2). This trend was further borne out in the 1990 amendments to the CAA, where Congress provided EPA with the authority to issue "field citations" in the amount of up to $5,000 (adjusted to $6,500), subject to a limited right of appeal as specified by EPA. 42 U.S.C. § 7413(d)(3). EPA has yet to write regulations implementing this program, however.

In the administrative penalty context, EPA (as opposed to a court) must determine the appropriate fine from within its statutory ranges. In general, the statutes require EPA to consider the same vague sorts of penalty factors that we saw in the judicial-penalties context. See, e.g., 33 U.S.C. § 1319(g)(3) and 42 U.S.C. § 6928(a)(3). Despite the imprecision in these criteria, EPA has an institutional interest in ensuring that like violations are treated in a similar fashion. Otherwise, sophisticated respondents would be able to research the fines paid in other cases and argue for a lowest-common-denominator approach. To further this objective, EPA has adopted "penalty policies" to guide its enforcement staff is determining the appropriate fines. Consider these excerpts from EPA's RCRA Civil Penalty Policy:

RCRA CIVIL PENALTY POLICY
Environmental Protection Agency, October 1990.
I. Summary of the Policy

The penalty calculation system established through EPA's RCRA Civil Penalty Policy consists of (1) determining a gravity-based penalty for a particular violation, from a penalty assessment matrix, (2) adding a "multi-day" component, as appropriate, to account for a violation's duration, (3) adjusting the sum of the gravity-based and multi-day components, up or down, for case specific circumstances, and (4) adding to this amount the appropriate economic benefit gained through non-compliance. More specifically, the Revised RCRA Civil Penalty Policy establishes the following penalty calculation methodology:

Penalty Amount = gravity-based component + multiday component + adjustments + economic benefit

* * *

Two factors are considered in determining the gravity-based penalty component:

- potential for harm; and
- extent of deviation from a statutory or regulatory requirement.

These two factors constitute the seriousness of a violation under RCRA, and have been incorporated into the following penalty matrix from which the gravity-based component will be chosen:

Matrix

Extent of Deviation From Requirement

Potential for Harm

	MAJOR	MODERATE	MINOR
MAJOR	$25,000 to 20,000	$19,999 to 15,000	$14,999 to 11,000
MODERATE	$10,999 to 8,000	$7,999 to 5,000	$4,999 to 3,000
MINOR	$2,999 to 1,500	$1,499 to 500	$499 to 100

The policy also explains how to factor into the calculation of the gravity component the presence of multiple and multi-day (continuing) violations. The policy provides that for days 2 through 180 of multi-day violations, multi-day penalties are mandatory, presumed, or discretionary, depending on the "potential for harm" and "extent of deviation" of the violations. For each day for which multi-day penalties are sought, the penalty amounts must be determined using the multi-day penalty matrix. The penalty amounts in the multi-day penalty matrix range from 5% to 20% (with a minimum of $100 per day) of the penalty amounts in the corresponding gravity-based matrix cells. Regions also retain discretion to impose multi-day penalties (1) of up to $25,000 per day, when appropriate under the circumstances, and (2) for days of violation after the first 180, as needed to achieve deterrence.

Where a company has derived significant savings or profits by its failure to comply with RCRA requirements, the amount of economic benefit from noncompliance gained by the violator will be calculated and added to the gravity-based penalty amount. The Agency has developed and made available to Agency personnel a computer model that can quickly and accurately calculate economic benefit—BEN.

After the appropriate gravity-based penalty amount (including the multi-day component) has been determined, it may be adjusted upward or downward to reflect particular circumstances surrounding the violation. Except in the unusual circumstances outlined in Section VIII the amount of any economic benefit enjoyed by the violator is not subject to adjustment. When adjusting the gravity-based penalty amount the following factors should be considered:

- good faith efforts to comply/lack of good faith (upward or downward adjustment);

- degree of willfulness and/or negligence (upward or downward adjustment);

- history of noncompliance (upward adjustment);

- ability to pay (downward adjustment);

- environmental projects to be undertaken by the violator (downward adjustment); and

- other unique factors, including but not limited to the risk and cost of litigation (upward or downward adjustment).

These factors (with the exception of (i) upward adjustment factors such as history of noncompliance, and (ii) the statutory downward adjustment factor reflecting a violator's good faith efforts to comply) should usually be considered after the penalty in the complaint has been proposed, i.e., during the settlement stage.

A detailed discussion of the policy follows. . . .

* * *

VI. Determination of Gravity-Based Penalty Amount

RCRA Section 3008(a)(3) states that the seriousness of a violation must be taken into account in assessing a penalty for the violation. The gravity-based component is a measure of the seriousness of a violation. The gravity-based penalty amount should be determined by examining two factors:

- potential for harm; and

- extent of deviation from a statutory or regulatory requirement.

A. Potential for Harm

The RCRA requirements were promulgated in order to prevent harm to human health and the environment. Thus, noncompliance with any RCRA requirement can result in a situation where there is a potential for harm to human health or the environment. Even violations such as recordkeeping violations create a risk of harm to the environment or human health by jeopardizing the integrity of the RCRA regulatory program. Accordingly, the assessment of the potential for harm resulting from a violation should be based on two factors:

- the risk of human or environmental exposure to hazardous waste and/or hazardous constituents that may be posed by noncompliance, and

- the adverse effect noncompliance may have on statutory or regulatory purposes or procedures for implementing the RCRA program.

1. Risk of Exposure

The risk of exposure presented by a given violation depends on both the likelihood that human or other environmental receptors may be exposed to hazardous waste and/or hazardous constituents and the degree of such potential exposure . . .

2. Harm to the RCRA Regulatory Program

There are some requirements of the RCRA program which, if violated, may not be likely to give rise directly or immediately to a significant risk of contamination. Nonetheless, all regulatory requirements are fundamental to the continued integrity of the RCRA program. Violations of such requirements may have serious implications and merit substantial penalties where the violation undermines the statutory or regulatory purposes or procedures for implementing the RCRA program. Some examples of this kind of regulatory harm include:

- failure to comply with financial assurance requirements
- failure to submit a timely/adequate Part B application
- failure to respond to a formal information request
- operating without a permit or interim status
- failure to prepare or maintain a manifest
- failure to install or conduct adequate groundwater monitoring.

* * *

B. Extent of Deviation From Requirements

The "extent of deviation" from RCRA and its regulatory requirements relates to the degree to which the violation renders inoperative the requirement violated. In any violative situation, a range of potential noncompliance with the subject requirement exists. In other words, a violator may be substantially in compliance with the provisions of the requirement or it may have totally disregarded the requirement (or a point in between). In determining the extent of the deviation, the following categories should be used:

- MAJOR: the violator deviates from requirements of the regulation or statute to such an extent that most (or important aspects) of the requirements are not met resulting in substantial noncompliance.

- MODERATE: the violator significantly deviates from the requirements of the regulation or statute but some of the requirements are implemented as intended.

- MINOR: the violator deviates somewhat from the regulatory or statutory requirements but most (or all important aspects) of the requirements are met.

* * *

VII. MULTIPLE AND MULTI-DAY PENALTIES

A. Penalties for Multiple Violations

In certain situations, EPA may find that a particular firm has violated several different RCRA requirements. A separate penalty should be sought in a complaint and obtained in settlement or litigation for each separate violation that results from an independent act (or failure to act) by the violator and is substantially distinguishable from any other charge in the complaint for which a penalty is to be assessed. A given charge is independent of, and substantially distinguishable from, any other charge when it requires an element of proof not needed by the others. In many cases, violations of different sections of the regulations constitute independent and substantially distinguishable violations....

It is also possible that different violations of the same section of the regulations could constitute independent and substantially distinguishable violations. For example, in the case of a firm which has open containers of hazardous waste in its storage area, 40 CFR § 265.173(a), and which also ruptured these or different hazardous waste containers while moving them on site, 40 CFR § 265.173(b), there are two independent acts. While the violations are both of the same regulatory section, each requires distinct elements of proof. In this situation, two counts with two separate penalties would be appropriate. For penalty purposes, each of the violations should be assessed separately and the amounts totalled.

Penalties for multiple violations also should be sought in litigation or obtained in settlement where one company has violated the same requirement in substantially different locations. An example of this type of violation is failure to clean up discharged hazardous waste during transportation, 40 CFR § 263.31. A transporter who did not clean up waste discharged in two separate locations during the same trip should be charged with two counts. In these situations the separate locations present separate and distinct risks to public health and the environment. Thus, separate penalty assessments are justified.

* * *

There are instances where a company's failure to satisfy one statutory or regulatory requirement either necessarily or generally leads to the violation of numerous other independent regulatory requirements.... In cases such as these where multiple violations result from a single initial transgression, assessment of a separate penalty for each distinguishable violation may produce a total penalty which is disproportionately high. Accordingly, in the specifically limited circumstances described, enforcement personnel have discretion to forego separate penalties for certain distinguishable violations, so long as the total penalty for all related violations is appropriate considering the gravity of the offense and sufficient to deter similar future behavior and recoup economic benefit.

B. Penalties for Multi-Day Violations

RCRA provides EPA with the authority to assess in administrative actions or seek in court civil penalties of up to $25,000 per day of noncompliance for each violation of a requirement of Subtitle C (or the regulations which implement that subtitle). This language explicitly authorizes the Agency to consider the duration of each violation as a factor in determining an appropriate total penalty amount. Accordingly, any penalty assessed should consist of a gravity-based component, economic benefit component, and to the extent that violations can be shown or presumed to have continued for more than one day, an appropriate multi-day component. The multi-day component should reflect the duration of the violation at issue, subject to the guidelines set forth in Section VII C., below.

* * *

C. Calculation of the Multi–Day Penalty

After the duration of the violation has been determined, the multi-day component of the total penalty is calculated, pursuant to the Multi–Day Matrix, as follows:

(1) Determine the gravity-based designations for the violation, e.g., major-major, moderate-minor, or minor-minor.

(2) Determine, for the specific violation, whether multi-day penalties are mandatory, presumed, or discretionary, as follows:

Mandatory multi-day penalties: Multi-day penalties are mandatory for days 2–180 of all violations with the following gravity-based designations: major-major, major-moderate, moderate-major.... Multi-day penalties for days 181+ are discretionary.

Presumption in favor of multi-day penalties: Multi-day penalties are presumed appropriate for days 2–180 of violations with the following gravity based designations: major-minor, moderate-moderate, minor-major. Therefore, multi-day penalties must be sought, unless case-specific facts overcoming the presumption for a particular violation are documented carefully in the case files. The presumption may be overcome for one or more days. Multi-day penalties for days 181+ are discretionary.

Discretionary multi-day penalties: Multi-day penalties are discretionary, generally, for all days of all violations with the following gravity-based designations: moderate-minor, minor-moderate, minor-minor.... The bases for decisions to impose or not impose any discretionary multi-day penalties must be documented in the case files.

(3) Locate the corresponding cell in the following Multi–Day Matrix. Multiply a dollar amount selected from the appropriate cell in the multi-day matrix (or, where appropriate, a larger dollar amount not to exceed $25,000) by the number of days the violation lasted.

MULTI–DAY MATRIX OF MINIMUM
DAILY PENALTIES (in dollars)

Extent of Deviation

Potential for Harm

	MAJOR	MODERATE	MINOR
MAJOR	$5,000 to 1,000	$4,000 to 750	$3,000 to 550
MODERATE	$2,200 to 400	$1,600 to 250	$1,000 to 150
MINOR	$600 to 100	$300 to 100	$100

The dollar figure to be multiplied by the number of days of violation will generally be selected from the range provided in the appropriate multi-day cell. The figure selected should not be less than the lowest number in the range provided....

VIII.   EFFECT OF ECONOMIC BENEFIT OF NONCOMPLIANCE

The Agency civil penalty policy mandates the recapture of any significant economic benefit of noncompliance that accrues to a violator. Enforcement personnel shall evaluate the economic benefit of noncompliance when penalties are calculated. A fundamental premise of the policy is that economic incentives for noncompliance are to be eliminated. If violators are allowed to profit by violating the law, there is little incentive to comply ... An economic benefit component should be calculated and added to the gravity-based penalty component when a violation results in "significant" economic benefit to the violator, as defined below.

It is generally the Agency's policy not to settle cases (i.e., the penalty amount) for an amount less than the economic benefit of noncompliance. However, the Agency civil penalty policy explicitly sets out three general [areas] where settling the total penalty amount for less than the economic benefit may be appropriate. The RCRA policy has added a fourth exception for cases where ability to pay is a factor. The four exceptions are:

- the economic benefit component consists of an insignificant amount (i.e., less than $2,500);

- there are compelling public concerns that would not be served by taking a case to trial;

- it is unlikely, based on the facts of the particular case as a whole, that EPA will be able to recover the economic benefit in litigation;

- the company has documented an inability to pay the total proposed penalty.

A. *Economic Benefit of Delayed Costs and Avoided Costs*

Compliance/enforcement personnel should examine two types of economic benefit from noncompliance in determining the economic benefit component:

- benefit from delayed costs; and
- benefit from avoided costs.

Delayed costs are expenditures which have been deferred by the violator's failure to comply with the requirements. The violator eventually will have to spend the money in order to achieve compliance. Delayed costs are the equivalent of capital costs . . .

Avoided costs are expenditures which are nullified by the violator's failure to comply. These costs will never be incurred. Avoided costs include the usual operating and maintenance costs which would include any annual periodic costs such as leasing monitoring equipment. . . .

* * *

IX. ADJUSTMENT FACTORS AND EFFECT OF SETTLEMENT

A. *Adjustment Factors*

* * *

The adjustment factors can increase, decrease or have no effect on the penalty amount obtained from the violator. Adjustments should generally be applied to the sum of the gravity-based and multi-day components of the penalty for a given violation. Note, however, that after all adjustment factors have been applied the resulting penalty shall not exceed the statutory maximum of $25,000 per day of violation. . . .

Application of the adjustment factors is cumulative, i.e., more than one factor may apply in a case. For example, if the base penalty derived from the gravity-based and multi-day matrices is $109,500, and upward adjustments of 10% will be made for both history of noncompliance and degree of willfulness and/or negligence, the total adjusted penalty would be $131,400 ($109,500 + 20%).

For any given factor (except ability to pay and litigative risk) enforcement personnel can, assuming proper documentation, adjust the sum of the gravity-based and multi-day penalty components for any given violation up or down (1) by as much as 25% of that sum in ordinary circumstances or (2) from 26% to 40% of that sum, in unusual circumstances. Downward adjustments based on inability to pay or litigative risk will vary in amount depending on the individual facts present in a given case and in certain circumstances may be applied to the economic benefit component.

However, if a penalty is to achieve deterrence, both the violator and the general public must be convinced that the penalty places the violator in a worse position than those who have complied in a timely fashion. Moreover, allowing a violator to benefit from noncompliance punishes those who have complied by placing them at a competitive disadvantage. For these reasons, the Agency should at a minimum, absent the special circumstances enumerated in section VIII, recover any significant economic benefits resulting from failure to comply with the law. If violators are allowed to settle for a penalty less than their economic benefit of noncompliance, the goal of deterrence is undermined. Except in extraordinary circumstances, which include cases where there are demonstrated limitations on a respondent's ability to pay or very significant litigative risks, the final adjusted penalty should also include a significant gravity-based component beyond the economic benefit component.

* * *

Notes and Comments

1. Note that EPA views its penalty policies as having relevance in both the judicial and administrative contexts. As it indicates in its introduction to the RCRA policy, in the judicial setting EPA may use the policy in framing its argument to the court as to the appropriate size of the penalty. While the court is not bound by the policy, it may find it a helpful way of analyzing penalty matters. Moreover, note that EPA indicates that it will use the policy as a benchmark for analyzing potential settlements in both judicial and administrative penalty cases.

2. Consider the following hypothetical:

Toymota, Inc., has a large manufacturing plant in the State of Bliss, an unauthorized State under RCRA. As part of its waste management activities, Toymota operates a hazardous waste surface impoundment and is thus regulated as a "TSD" (treatment, storage or disposal facility) under RCRA. Every year for the past ten years, it has purchased its required RCRA insurance from the same insurance company. Last year's policy expired on October 31. As it has done every year, Toymota applied for continuing coverage in June of last year. The insurance sales representative told Toymota's corporate vice-president that there should be no problem.

In August, Toymota applied for a loan to expand its production capacity. Because it was proposing to use its property as collateral for the loan, Toymota's lender asked it to hire a consultant to do an environmental assessment of the property. In late September, the consultant issued its report, indicating that some contamination had been found downgradient of the impoundment. Given how far the plume had migrated, the consultant surmised that the prior owner of the property likely had caused the contamination. The prior owner had used the impoundment during the pre-RCRA era.

On October 22, Toymota's insurance company informed it that it would not renew the required insurance. Since that time, Toymota has applied to more that 40 insurance companies seeking the necessary coverage. During a recent inspection, the VP told the EPA inspector about all of these events and indicated that she expected that the facility would obtain coverage within the next few weeks.

How should EPA respond? If it pursues an administrative penalty, what arguments will both sides make with regard to the appropriate penalty amount?

3. What do you think of EPA's effort to ensure consistent penalties? Is the policy likely to achieve this result? Do you think EPA could do better? If so, how? What do you think of the way in which EPA treats multi-day violations? What about the general manner in which it treats the adjustment factors? Do you agree that, in general, these factors should only be applied to the "gravity-based" portion of the fine? However you feel about that question, do you agree that the maximum adjustment, even in "unusual circumstances," for a factor such as "good faith efforts to comply" should be 40%?

4. In the interest of saving space, we have edited out the Penalty Policy's discussion of specific adjustment factors. There are, however, two points worth making about the "ability to pay" factor. First, EPA notes that this factor will result only in a downward adjustment; that is, EPA will never increase a company's fine over what the policy otherwise would contemplate because of that company's wealth. Do you agree with this approach? And second, EPA states that it "generally will not assess penalties that are clearly beyond the means of the violator." This latter point is subject to some express provisos: (1) the burden of demonstrating inability to pay is always on the respondent; (2) EPA will consider installment plans or delayed-payment schedules as a first resort before resorting to straight penalty reductions; and (3) EPA reserves the ability to impose fines that will put a company out of business where it has a long history of violations or where it is unable or refuses to correct the violations. Does this seem like an appropriate approach to these issues?

5. As mentioned, the recipients of administrative penalty orders commonly have the right to request at least some form of administrative hearing before the orders become final. See, e.g., 42 U.S.C. § 6928(b). Additionally, there is invariably a subsequent right of appeal to the courts, either under the environmental statute itself or under the APA. The courts review administratively-assessed penalties under the "abuse of discretion" standard of review. This standard is dictated either by the relevant environmental statute or by default under the APA. See, e.g., 33 U.S.C. § 1319(g)(8) and 5 U.S.C. § 706(2)(A).

6. The D.C. Circuit has determined that EPA's administrative penalty actions are subject to the same five-year statute of limitations (28 U.S.C. § 2462) that applies in the judicial realm. *3M Co. v. Browner*, 17 F.3d 1453 (D.C. Cir. 1994).

7. EPA has two other noteworthy policies that essentially act as addenda to its traditional penalty policies. First, EPA has created what it calls the "Final EPA Supplemental Environmental Projects Policy" (commonly known as the "SEP Policy"). 63 Fed. Reg. 24796 (May 1, 1998). Under this policy, EPA is willing to forgo portions of either judicial or administrative penalties if the relevant regulated entity agrees to perform environmentally beneficial projects that it is not otherwise legally required to perform. Not surprisingly, the SEP Policy has many conditions and caveats. Most notably, the environmental project that generates the reduc-

tion must have what EPA terms a "nexus" to the environmental concerns addressed by the requirements that were violated. Additionally, EPA insists that the violator must still pay a penalty reflecting at least the full economic benefit that it generated through its violative activities; this portion of the penalty cannot be mitigated by the SEP.

Second, EPA has developed what most people refer to as its "Audit Policy." 65 Fed. Reg. 19618 (April 11, 2000) (formally, if ponderously, entitled "Incentives for Self–Policing, Disclosure, Correction and Prevention of Violations"). Under this policy, EPA is willing to forgo penalties in situations in which regulated entities have voluntary programs in place to ferret out their own violations, where they do so, and where they notify EPA and promptly correct the problems. Perhaps obviously, the goal of the Audit Policy is to encourage regulatory self-policing in a world in which EPA and the States have limited inspection and enforcement resources. Here also, there are significant conditions and caveats. As under the SEP Policy, EPA will not waive the economic-benefit portion of the penalty; instead, only the gravity-based portion is in play. Additionally, the policy provides essentially no protection if corporate officials were either consciously involved in or willfully blind to the violations, or if the violation resulted in either serious environmental harm or an imminent and substantial endangerment. Outside of these situations, however, the Audit Policy contemplates broad penalty forgiveness if its conditions are met. Do you agree with EPA's decision to offer these incentives?

C. Criminal Enforcement

Most environmental statutes also provide the Government with the option of seeking criminal sanctions for at least some regulatory violations. Here again, the CWA is fairly typical of most pollution-control statutes. Section 309(c) establishes four categories of criminal violations: negligent violations, knowing violations, knowing endangerments, and knowing false statements. The first of these is a misdemeanor; the other three are felonies, with the most serious sanctions (fines of up to $250,000–or $1,000,000 for organizations—and jail terms of up to 15 years) for knowing endangerments.

By far the most significant legal issue in the area of environmental crimes relates to the mental state requirement for knowing violations: What does one have to know, for example, in order to be convicted of "knowingly" violating one's NPDES permit? Do you just have to know the basic facts: e.g., that you are discharging less-than-fully-treated wastewater through a pipe into a waterway? Or do you have to also be aware of the legal significance of these facts? Consider the following case:

UNITED STATES v. WEITZENHOFF
United States Court of Appeals, Ninth Circuit, 1994.
35 F.3d 1275.

FLETCHER, Circuit Judge:

In 1988 and 1989 [Michael] Weitzenhoff was the manager and [Thomas] Mariani the assistant manager of the East Honolulu Community Services Sewage Treatment Plant ("the plant"), located not far from Sandy Beach, a popular swimming and surfing beach on Oahu. The plant is designed to treat some 4 million gallons of residential wastewater each day by removing the solids and other harmful pollutants from the sewage so that the resulting effluent can be safely discharged into the ocean. The plant operates under a permit issued pursuant to the [NPDES program], which established the limits on the Total Suspended Solids ("TSS") and Biochemical Oxygen Demand ("BOD")—indicators of the solid and organic matter, respectively, in the effluent discharged at Sandy Beach. During the period in question, the permit limited the discharge of both the TSS and BOD to an average of 976 pounds per day over a 30–day period. It also imposed monitoring and sampling requirements on the plant's management.

permit reg.

[As part of its treatment process, the plant generated something called "waste activated sludge" ("WAS").] From March 1987 through March 1988, the excess WAS generated by the plant was hauled away to another treatment plant, the Sand Island Facility. In March 1988, certain improvements were made to the East Honolulu plant and the hauling was discontinued. Within a few weeks, however, the plant began experiencing a buildup of excess WAS. Rather than have the excess WAS hauled away as before, however, Weitzenhoff and Mariani instructed two employees at the plant to dispose of it on a regular basis by pumping it from the storage tanks directly into the outfall, that is, directly into the ocean. The WAS thereby bypassed the plant's effluent sampler so that the samples taken and reported to Hawaii's Department of Health ("DOH") and the EPA did not reflect its discharge.

excess WAS dumped into ocean

The evidence produced by the government at trial showed that WAS was discharged directly into the ocean from the plant on about 40 separate occasions from April 1988 to June 1989, resulting in some 436,000 pounds of pollutant solids being discharged into the ocean, and that the discharges violated the plant's 30–day average effluent limit under the permit for most of the months during which they occurred. Most of the WAS discharges occurred during the night, and none was reported to the DOH or EPA. DOH inspectors contacted the plant on several occasions in 1988 in response to complaints by lifeguards at Sandy Beach that sewage was being emitted from the outfall, but Weitzenhoff and Mariani repeatedly denied that there was any problem at the plant. In one letter responding to a DOH inquiry in October 1988, Mariani stated that "the debris that was reported could not have been from the East Honolulu Wastewater Treatment facility, as our records of effluent quality up to this time will substantiate." One of the plant employees who participated in the dumping operation testified that Weitzenhoff instructed him not to say anything about the discharges, because if they all stuck together and did not reveal anything, "they [couldn't] do anything to us."

Following an FBI investigation, Weitzenhoff and Mariani were charged in a thirty-one-count indictment with conspiracy and substantive violations of the [CWA]. At trial, Weitzenhoff and Mariani admitted having authorized the discharges, but claimed that their actions were justified under their interpretation of the NPDES permit. . . .

Section 1311(a) of the CWA prohibits the discharge of pollutants into navigable waters without an NPDES permit. Section 1319(c)(2) makes it a felony offense to "knowingly violate [ ] section 1311, 1312, 1316, 1317, 1318, 1321(b)(3), 1328, or 1345 . . ., or any permit condition or limitation implementing any of such sections in a permit issued under section 1342."

Prior to trial, the district court construed "knowingly" in section 1319(c)(2) as requiring only that Weitzenhoff and Mariani were aware that they were discharging the pollutants in question, not that they knew they were violating the terms of the statute or permit. According to appellants, the district court erred in its interpretation of the CWA and in instructing the jury that "the government is not required to prove that the defendant knew that his act or omissions were unlawful," as well as in rejecting their proposed instruction based on the defense that they mistakenly believed their conduct was authorized by the permit. Apparently, no court of appeals has confronted the issue raised by appellants.

As with certain other criminal statutes that employ the term "knowingly," it is not apparent from the face of the statute whether "knowingly" means a knowing violation of the law or simply knowing conduct that is violative of the law. We turn, then, to the legislative history of the provision at issue to ascertain what Congress intended.

In 1987, Congress substantially amended the CWA, elevating the penalties for violations of the Act. Increased penalties were considered necessary to deter would-be polluters. S.Rep. No. 50, 99th Cong., 1st Sess. 29 (1985). With the 1987 amendments, Congress substituted "knowingly" for the earlier intent requirement of "willfully" that appeared in the predecessor to section 1319(c)(2). The Senate report accompanying the legislation explains that the changes in the penalty provisions were to ensure that "[c]riminal liability shall . . . attach to any person who is not in compliance with all applicable Federal, State and local requirements and permits *and causes* a POTW [publicly owned treatment works] to violate any effluent limitation or condition in any permit issued to the treatment works." *Id.* (emphasis added). Similarly, the report accompanying the House version of the bill, which contained parallel provisions for enhancement of penalties, states that the proposed amendments were to "provide penalties for dischargers or individuals who knowingly or negligently violate *or cause the violation of* certain of the Act's requirements." H.R.Rep. No. 189, 99th Cong., 1st Sess. 29–30 (1985) (emphasis added). Because they speak in terms of "causing" a violation, the congressional explanations of the new penalty provisions strongly suggest that criminal sanctions are to be imposed on an individual who knowingly engages in conduct that results in a permit violation, regardless of whether the polluter is cognizant of the requirements or even the existence of the permit.

Our conclusion that "knowingly" does not refer to the legal violation is fortified by decisions interpreting analogous public welfare statutes. The leading case in this area is *United States v. International Minerals & Chem. Corp.*, 402 U.S. 558 (1971). In *International Minerals*, the Supreme Court construed a statute which made it a crime to "knowingly violate[ ] any ... regulation" promulgated by the ICC pursuant to 18 U.S.C. § 834(a), a provision authorizing the agency to formulate regulations for the safe transport of corrosive liquids. *Id.* at 559. The Court held that the term "knowingly" referred to the acts made criminal rather than a violation of the regulation, and that "regulation" was a shorthand designation for the specific acts or omissions contemplated by the act. *Id.* at 560–62. "[W]here ... dangerous or deleterious devices or products or obnoxious waste materials are involved, the probability of regulation is so great that anyone who is aware that he is in possession of them or dealing with them must be presumed to be aware of the regulation." *Id.* at 565.

This court followed *International Minerals* in *United States v. Hoflin*, 880 F.2d 1033 (9th Cir.1989), *cert. denied*, 493 U.S. 1083 (1990), when it held that knowledge of the absence of a permit is not an element of the offense defined by 42 U.S.C. § 6928(d)(2)(A), part of [RCRA]. *Id.* at 1039. "There can be little question that RCRA's purposes, like those of the Food and Drug Act, ' .... touch phases of the lives and health of people which, in the circumstances of modern industrialism, are largely beyond self-protection.' " *Id.* at 1038 (quoting *United States v. Dotterweich*, 320 U.S. 277, 280 (1943)). . . .

Appellants seek to rely on the Supreme Court's decision in *Liparota v. United States,* 471 U.S. 419 (1985), to support their alternative reading of the intent requirement. *Liparota* concerned 7 U.S.C. § 2024(b)(1), which provides that anyone who "knowingly uses, transfers, acquires, alters, or possesses [food stamp] coupons or authorization cards in any manner not authorized by [the statute] or regulations" is subject to a fine or imprisonment. *Id.* at 420. The Court, noting that the conduct at issue did not constitute a public welfare offense, distinguished the *International Minerals* line of cases and held that the government must prove the defendant knew that his acquisition or possession of food stamps was in a manner unauthorized by statute or regulations. *Id.* at 432–33.

Subsequent to the filing of the original opinion in this case, the Supreme Court decided two cases which Weitzenhoff contends call our analysis into question. *See Ratzlaf v. United States,* 114 S.Ct. 655 (1994); *Staples v. United States,* 114 S.Ct. 1793 (1994). We disagree.

The statute in *Ratzlaf* does not deal with a public welfare offense, but rather with violations of the banking statutes. The Court construed the term "willfully" in the anti-structuring provisions of the Bank Secrecy Act to require both that the defendant knew he was structuring transactions to avoid reporting requirements and that he knew his acts were unlawful. The Court recognized that the money structuring provisions are not directed at conduct which a reasonable person necessarily should know is subject to strict public regulation and that the structuring offense applied to all persons with more than $10,000, many of whom could be engaged in structuring for innocent reasons. *Ratzlaf*, 114 S.Ct. at 660–62. In contrast, parties such as Weitzenhoff are closely regulated and are discharging waste materials that affect public health. The *International Minerals* rationale requires that we impute to these parties knowledge of their operating permit. This was recognized by the Court in *Staples*.

why Ratzlaf does NOT work

The specific holding in *Staples* was that the government is required to prove that a defendant charged with possession of a machine gun knew that the weapon he possessed had the characteristics that brought it within the statutory definition of a machinegun. But the Court took pains to contrast the gun laws to other regulatory regimes, specifically those regulations that govern the handling of "obnoxious waste materials." *See Staples*, 114 S.Ct. at 1798. It noted that the mere innocent ownership of guns is not a public welfare offense. *Id.* 1804. The Court focussed on the long tradition of widespread gun ownership in this country and, recognizing that approximately 50% of American homes contain a firearm, *id.* at 1801, acknowledged that mere ownership of a gun is not sufficient to place people on notice that the act of owning an unregistered firearm is not innocent under the law.

Staples

Staples thus explicitly contrasted the mere possession of guns to public welfare offenses, which include statutes that regulate " 'dangerous or deleterious devices or products or obnoxious waste materials,' " *id.* at 1800, and confirmed the continued vitality of statutes covering public welfare offenses, which "regulate potentially harmful or injurious items" and place a defendant on notice that he is dealing with a device or a substance "that places him in 'responsible relation to a public danger.' " *Id.* "[I]n such cases Congress intended to place the burden on the defendant to ascertain at his peril whether [his conduct] comes within the inhibition of the statute." *Id.* at 1798 (citations and internal quotations omitted).

why Staples does NOT work

Unlike "[g]uns [which] in general are not 'deleterious devices or products or obnoxious waste materials,' *International Minerals, supra* [402 U.S.], at 565, that put their owners on notice that they stand 'in responsible relation to a public danger[,]' *Dotterweich*, 320 U.S. at 281," *Staples*, 114 S.Ct. at 1800, the dumping of sewage and other pollutants into our nation's waters is precisely the type of activity that puts the discharger on notice that his acts may pose a public danger. Like other public welfare offenses that regulate ... the disposal of hazardous wastes [and] the undocumented shipping of acids ...., the improper and excessive discharge of sewage causes cholera, hepatitis, and other serious illnesses, and can have serious repercussions for public health and welfare.[7]

The dumping itself is enof to put someone on notice

---

7. In *Staples*, the Court also noted that the penalty attached to a violation of a criminal statute in the past has been a relevant factor in determining whether the

The criminal provisions of the CWA are clearly designed to protect the public at large from the potentially dire consequences of water pollution, and as such fall within the category of public welfare legislation. *International Minerals* rather than *Liparota* controls the case at hand. The government did not need to prove that Weitzenhoff and Mariani knew that their acts violated the permit or the CWA.

KLEINFELD, Circuit Judge, with whom Circuit Judges REINHARDT, KOZINSKI, TROTT, and T.G. NELSON join, dissenting from the order rejecting the suggestion for rehearing en banc.

... In my view, this is a case of exceptional importance, for two reasons. First, it impairs a fundamental purpose of criminal justice, sorting out the innocent from the guilty before imposing punishment. Second, it does so in the context of the [CWA]. This statute has tremendous sweep. Most statutes permit anything except what is prohibited, but this one prohibits all regulated conduct involving waters and wetlands except what is permitted. 33 U.S.C. § 1311(a). Much more ordinary, innocent, productive activity is regulated by this law than people not versed in environmental law might imagine.

The harm our mistaken decision may do is not necessarily limited to [CWA] cases. Dilution of the traditional requirement of a criminal state of mind, and application of the criminal law to innocent conduct, reduces the moral authority of our system of criminal law. If we use prison to achieve social goals regardless of the moral innocence of those we incarcerate, then imprisonment loses its moral opprobrium and our criminal law becomes morally arbitrary.

As the panel opinion states the facts, these two defendants were literally "midnight dumpers." They managed a sewer plant and told their employees to dump 436,000 pounds of sewage into the ocean, mostly at night, fouling a nearby beach. Their conduct, as set out in the panel opinion, suggests that they must have known they were violating their [NPDES] permit. But we cannot decide the case on that basis, because the jury did not. The court instructed the jury that the government did not have to prove the defendants knew their conduct was unlawful, and refused to instruct the jury that a mistaken belief that the discharge was authorized by the permit would be a defense. Because of the way the jury was instructed, its verdict is consistent with the

statute defines a public welfare offense. The Court recognized that public welfare offenses originally involved statutes that provided only light penalties such as fines or short jail sentences, *see* 114 S.Ct. at 1802, but that modern statutes now punish public welfare offenses with much more significant terms of imprisonment. *E.g., International Minerals*, 402 U.S. 558 (ten years imprisonment if death or bodily injury results from violation); *United States v. Freed*, 401 U.S. 601, 609–10 (1971) (five years imprisonment for possession of unregistered gre-

nade); *Hoflin*, 880 F.2d 1033 (two years imprisonment for certain violations of RCRA). While the *Staples* opinion expresses concern with this evolution of enhanced punishments for public welfare offenses, it refrains from holding that public welfare offenses may not be punished as felonies. *Staples*, 114 S.Ct. at 1804 (stating that the early cases suggest that public welfare offenses might not extend to felonies, but noting that "[w]e need not adopt such a definitive rule of construction to decide this case").

proposition that the defendants honestly and reasonably believed that their NPDES permit authorized the discharges.

This proposition could be true. NPDES permits are often difficult to understand and obey. The EPA had licensed the defendants' plant to discharge 976 pounds of waste per day, or about 409,920 pounds over the fourteen months covered by the indictment, into the ocean. The wrongful conduct was not discharging waste into the ocean. That was socially desirable conduct by which the defendants protected the people of their city from sewage-borne disease and earned their pay. The wrongful conduct was violating the NPDES permit by discharging 26,000 more pounds of waste than the permit authorized during the fourteen months. Whether these defendants were innocent or not, in the sense of knowing that they were exceeding their permit limitation, the panel's holding will make innocence irrelevant in other permit violation cases where the defendants had no idea that they were exceeding permit limits. The only thing they have to know to be guilty is that they were dumping sewage into the ocean, yet that was a lawful activity expressly authorized by their federal permit.

The statute says "knowingly violate[s] . . . any permit condition or limitation." "Knowingly" is an adverb. It modifies the verb "violates." The object of the verb is "any permit condition or limitation." . . . Congress has distinguished those who knowingly violate permit conditions, and are thereby felons, from those who unknowingly violate permit conditions, so are not. The panel reads the statute as though it says "knowingly discharges pollutants." It does not. If we read the statute on the assumption that Congress used the English language in an ordinary way, the state of mind required is knowledge that one is violating a permit condition.

This approach has the virtue of attributing common sense and a rational purpose to Congress. It is one thing to defy a permit limitation, but quite another to violate it without realizing that one is violating it. Congress promulgated a parallel statute making it a misdemeanor "negligently" to violate a permit condition or limitation. 33 U.S.C. § 1319(c)(1)(A). If negligent violation is a misdemeanor, why would Congress want to make it a felony to violate the permit without negligence and without even knowing that the discharge exceeded the permit limit? That does not make any sense. It would deter people from working in sewer plants, instead of deterring people from violating permits. All dischargers acting lawfully pursuant to a permit know that they are discharging pollutants. The presence or absence of that knowledge, which is the only mental element determining guilt under the panel's decision, has no bearing on any conduct Congress could have meant to turn into a felony. The only knowledge which could have mattered to Congress, the only knowledge which distinguishes good conduct from bad, is knowledge that the discharge violates the permit. That is what the statute says, "knowingly violates," not "knowingly discharges." There is no sensible reason to doubt that Congress meant what it said and said what it meant.

The panel reaches its surprising result in surprising ways. First, it says that the statute is ambiguous.... As explained above, a grammatical and sensible reading of the statute leaves no room for ambiguity. But for the sake of discussion, suppose that the statute is ambiguous, as the panel says. Then the rule of lenity requires that the construction allowing the defendant more liberty rather than less be applied by the courts....

The panel ... tries to bolster its construction by categorizing the offense as a "public welfare offense," as though that justified more aggressive criminalization without a plain statutory command. This category is a modernized version of "malum prohibitum." Traditionally the criminal law distinguishes between malum in se, conduct wrong upon principles of natural moral law, and malum prohibitum, conduct not inherently immoral but wrong because prohibited by law. Black's Law Dictionary 1112 (4th ed. 1951). To put this in plain, modern terms, any normal person knows murder, rape and robbery are wrong, and they would be wrong even in a place with no sovereign and no law. Discharging 6% more pollutants than one's permit allows is wrong only because the law says so....

Staples reminds us that "offenses that require no *mens rea* generally are disfavored." 114 S.Ct. at 1797. *Mens rea* may be dispensed with in public welfare offenses, but the penalty is a "significant consideration in determining whether the statute should be construed as dispensing with *mens rea*." 114 S.Ct. at 1802.... If Congress makes a crime a felony, the felony categorization alone is a "factor tending to suggest that Congress did not intend to eliminate a *mens rea* requirement. In such a case, the usual presumption that a defendant must know the facts that make his conduct illegal should apply." 114 S.Ct. at 1804. In the case at bar, "the facts that make his conduct illegal" are the permit violations, not the discharges of pollutants. Discharge of pollutants was licensed by the federal government in the NPDES permit. Under *Staples*, it would be presumed, even if the law did not plainly say so, that the defendant would have to know that he was violating the permit in order to be guilty of the felony.

The panel cites *International Minerals* ... in support of its reading.... Because of the syntactically similar statute at issue in that case, it is the strongest authority for the panel's decision and raises the most serious question for my own analysis. It held that a shipper of sulfuric acid could be convicted of violating a statute applying to those who "knowingly violate[]" regulations governing shipments of corrosive liquids, regardless of whether he had knowledge of the regulations. *International Minerals* expressly limits its holding to "dangerous or deleterious devices or products or obnoxious waste materials." 402 U.S. at 565. The Court distinguished materials not obviously subject to regulation:

> Pencils, dental floss, paper clips may also be regulated. But they may be the type of products which might raise substantial due process questions if Congress did not require ... "*mens rea*" as to

each ingredient of the offense. But where, as here ..., dangerous or deleterious devices or products or obnoxious waste materials are involved, the probability of regulation is so great that anyone who is aware that he is in possession of them or dealing with them must be presumed to be aware of the regulation.

Id. at 564–65. *International Minerals* would have much persuasive force for *Weitzenhoff*, because of the grammatical similarity of the statute, if (1) the [CWA] limited pollutants to "dangerous or deleterious devices or products or obnoxious waste materials;" (2) the crime was only a misdemeanor; and (3) *Staples* had not come down this term. But all three of these conditions are contrary to fact. The pollutants to which the [CWA] felony statute applies include many in the "pencils, dental floss, paper clips" category. Hot water, rock, and sand are classified as "pollutants" by the Clean Water Act. *See* 33 U.S.C. § 1362(6). Discharging silt from a stream back into the same stream may amount to discharge of a pollutant. For that matter, so may skipping a stone into a lake. So may a cafeteria worker's pouring hot, stale coffee down the drain. Making these acts a misdemeanor is one thing, but a felony is quite another, as *Staples* teaches.

The panel, finally, asserts that as a matter of policy, the [CWA] crimes "are clearly designed to protect the public at large from the dire consequences of water pollution." That is true, but the panel does not explain how the public is to be protected by making felons of sewer workers who unknowingly violate their plants' permits.... Sewage workers perform essential work of great social value. Probably nothing has prevented more infant mortality, or freed more people from cholera, hepatitis, typhoid fever, and other disease, than the development in the last two centuries of municipal sewer systems. Sewage utility workers perform their difficult work in malodorous and dangerous environments. We have now imposed on these vitally important public servants a massive legal risk, unjustified by law or precedent, if they unknowingly violate their permit conditions.

Nor is the risk of prison limited to sewage plant workers. It applies to anyone who discharges pollutants pursuant to a permit, and unknowingly violates the permit. The panel suggests that criminalizing this innocent conduct will protect the public from water pollution. It is at least as likely that the increased criminal risk will raise the cost and reduce the availability of such lawful and essential public services as sewage disposal....

Notes and Comments

1. In his dissent from the denial of the rehearing *Weitzenhoff*, Judge Kleinfeld concedes that the defendants must have known that they were violating their permit. Do you understand why he still thought the conviction needed to be reversed? Given the high degree of likelihood that a jury would have found awareness of illegality in this case, why do you think the Government at trial opposed a jury instruction that would have required such a finding?

2. Congress, of course, can eliminate any doubt regarding the mental state requirements under a given statute by clearly specifying one standard or another. In some environmental contexts, for example, the courts have found that Congress has required awareness of illegality by using the term "willfully." See, e.g., *United States v. Overholt*, 307 F.3d 1231, 1245–1246 (10th Cir. 2002) (under the Safe Drinking Water Act). If Congress speaks clearly, that is the end of the matter, at least absent the potential due process problems alluded to in *International Minerals*. In *Weitzenhoff*, Judge Kleinfeld argues that the phase "knowingly violates" is clear. Do you agree? Can such a position be squared with *International Minerals*?

3. If Congress uses ambiguous phraseology (e.g., "knowingly violates," or, if you prefer, "knowingly discharges pollutants"), one way to resolve such ambiguities might be through resort to statutory structure. In a pair of decisions under RCRA, for example, the Ninth Circuit relied on such structural arguments in holding that, while the Government need not prove that those who disposed of hazardous waste were aware that they did not have a permit to do so, to convict transporters it must prove that they were aware of the receiving facility's lack of a permit. Compare *Hoflin*, 880 F.2d at 1038 (applying 42 U.S.C. § 3008(d)(2)(A)), and *United States v. Speach*, 968 F.2d 795 (9th Cir. 1992) (applying subsection (d)(1)). Assuming that we can read the phrase "knowingly violates" to be ambiguous, does the structure of § 309 of the CWA provide any help?

4. Another way to resolve ambiguity might be through the application of legislative history. What arguments of this type did the majority advance in *Weitzenhoff*? Were they persuasive?

5. As Judge Kleinfeld points out, discharging illegal amounts of pollution does not fit the classic definition of a "malum in se" offense; rather, it would be characterized as a "malum prohibitum" offense. In the "regulatory crimes" context, the Supreme Court has fashioned an interpretive protocol to help resolve ambiguities involving mental-state requirements: If the regulatory regime criminalizes what the Court characterizes as "public welfare offenses," such as in *International Minerals*, the Court's default assumption is that Congress did not intend to require the Government to prove awareness of illegality. On the other hand, if the regime criminalizes what the Court considers "innocent conduct," as in *Liparota*, *Ratzlaf*, and *Staples*, the Court's default assumption is that the statute requires proof that the defendant knew she was acting illegally. See generally *Staples v. United States*, 511 U.S. 600, 114 S.Ct. 1793, 128 L.Ed.2d 608 (1994). One commentator has described the circumstances in which the Court has applied these competing assumptions in the following terms:

> ... The Court assumes that Congress meant to adopt the common law notion that felony convictions require proof of mens rea. Given that regulatory crimes were not taken from the common law, the Court determines the mens rea requirement by fitting the statute into one of two categories and applying the interpretive approach developed for each. Some statutes fit into the category of "public welfare offenses" (PWOs). These statutes address uncommon conduct that seriously threatens the community's health or safety. For such statutes, the Court interprets the mens rea requirement to be awareness of facts that make

the conduct dangerous and uncommon. Such awareness is a kind of modern take on traditional mens rea: A person aware of engaging in a dangerous and uncommon activity is aware of wrongdoing if he or she does not take steps to determine the legally correct way of conducting the task. Non–PWO statutes regulate "innocent" conduct—that is, conduct that does not seriously threaten the community's health or safety, is common, or is both non-threatening and common. To ensure a mens rea requirement, the Court usually interprets these statutes to require proof that the defendant was aware the behavior was unauthorized by regulatory law in general. This is mens rea in the traditional sense because the person is aware of violating the law, even in a general sense, and it is morally wrong to violate legal authority knowingly.

Mandiberg, Fault Lines in the Clean Water Act: Criminal Enforcement, Continuing Violations, and Mental State, 33 Envt'l Law 173, 191–193 (2003) (footnotes omitted). Do you agree with the *Weitzenhoff* majority (and every other appellate court that has addressed the question) that the CWA is a proper context in which to apply the PWO doctrine? What legal objections does Judge Kleinfeld raise? What are his policy objections? Is it possible to apply one rule to defendants like Mr. Weitzenhoff and another to homeowners who may innocently add fill material to swampy areas without dreaming that the CWA might apply?

IV. FEDERALISM ISSUES IN THE ENFORCEMENT CONTEXT

We already have seen, in our discussion of the Clean Water Act, that States are required to have certain enforcement powers in order to become "authorized" to implement statutes such as the CWA, the CAA and RCRA. Despite that, however, it is clear that EPA retains the enforcement powers we have been addressing in this Chapter even in authorized States. Indeed, several of the relevant enforcement provisions specifically contemplate ongoing federal enforcement power, though they may condition its exercise in narrow ways, such as by requiring EPA to give authorized States advance notice and/or the opportunity to undertake an appropriate enforcement response. Compare 33 U.S.C. § 1319(a)(1), 42 U.S.C. § 6928(a)(2), and 42 U.S.C. § 7413(a)(1).

The more difficult issue involves EPA's ability to "overfile;" that is, to file a separate enforcement action relating to the same violations addressed by a State in situations in which either the State was unsuccessful or EPA deems its response to have been unsatisfactory. The following case is an example of the second of these two scenarios:

HARMON INDUSTRIES, INC. v. BROWNER

United States Court of Appeals, Eighth Circuit, 1999.
191 F.3d 894.

Hansen, Circuit Judge.

Harmon Industries operates a plant in Grain Valley, Missouri, which it utilizes to assemble circuit boards for railroad control and safety equipment. In November 1987, Harmon's personnel manager discovered that maintenance workers at Harmon routinely discarded volatile solvent residue behind Harmon's Grain Valley plant. This practice apparently began in 1973 and continued until November 1987. Harmon's management was unaware of its employees' practices until the personnel manager filed his report in November 1987. Following the report, Harmon ceased its disposal activities and voluntarily contacted the Missouri Department of Natural Resources (MDNR). The MDNR investigated and concluded that Harmon's past disposal practices did not pose a threat to either human health or the environment. The MDNR and Harmon created a plan whereby Harmon would clean up the disposal area. Harmon implemented the clean up plan. While Harmon was cooperating with the MDNR, the EPA initiated an administrative enforcement action against Harmon in which the federal agency sought $2,343,706 in penalties. Meanwhile, Harmon and the MDNR continued to establish a voluntary compliance plan. In harmonizing the details of the plan, Harmon asked the MDNR not to impose civil penalties. Harmon based its request in part on the fact that it voluntarily self-reported the environmental violations and cooperated fully with the MDNR.

On March 5, 1993, while the EPA's administrative enforcement action was pending, a Missouri state court judge approved a consent decree entered into by the MDNR and Harmon. In the decree, MDNR acknowledged full accord and satisfaction and released Harmon from any claim for monetary penalties. MDNR based its decision to release Harmon on the fact that the company promptly self-reported its violation and cooperated in all aspects of the investigation. After the filing of the consent decree, Harmon litigated the EPA claim before an administrative law judge (ALJ). The ALJ found that a civil penalty against Harmon was appropriate in this case. The ALJ rejected the EPA's request for a penalty in excess of $2 million but the ALJ did impose a civil fine of $586,716 against Harmon. A three-person Environmental Appeals Board panel affirmed the ALJ's monetary penalty. Harmon filed a complaint challenging the EPA's decision in federal district court on June 6, 1997. In its August 25, 1998, summary judgment order, the district court found that the EPA's decision to impose civil penalties violated [RCRA] and contravened principles of res judicata. The EPA appeals to this court.

[RCRA] permits states to apply to the EPA for authorization to administer and enforce a hazardous waste program. See 42 U.S.C. § 6926(b). If authorization is granted, the state's program then operates "in lieu of" the federal government's hazardous waste program. Id. The EPA authorization also allows states to issue and enforce permits for the treatment, storage, and disposal of hazardous wastes. Id. "Any action taken by a State under a hazardous waste program authorized under [the RCRA] [has] the same force and effect as action taken by the [EPA] under this subchapter." 42 U.S.C. § 6926(d). Once authorization is granted by the EPA, it cannot be rescinded unless the EPA finds that (1) the state program is not equivalent to the federal program, (2) the state program is not consistent with federal or state programs in other states, or (3) the state program is failing to provide adequate enforcement of compliance in accordance with the requirements of federal law. See 42 U.S.C. § 6926(b)....

Missouri, like many other states, is authorized to administer and enforce a hazardous waste program pursuant to the RCRA. Despite having authorized a state to act, the EPA frequently files its own enforcement actions against suspected environmental violators even after the commencement of a state-initiated enforcement action. The EPA's process of duplicating enforcement actions is known as overfiling. The permissibility of overfiling apparently is a question of first impression in the federal circuit courts....

The EPA contends that the district court's interpretation runs contrary to the plain language of the RCRA. Specifically, the EPA cites section 6928 of the RCRA, which states that:

(1) Except as provided in paragraph (2), whenever on the basis of any information the [EPA] determines that any person has violated or is in violation of any requirement of this subchapter, the [EPA] may issue an order assessing a civil penalty for any past or current violation, requiring compliance immediately or within a specified time period, or both, or the [EPA] may commence a civil action in the United States district court in the district in which the violation occurred for appropriate relief, including a temporary or permanent injunction.

(2) In the case of a violation of any requirement of [the RCRA] where such violation occurs in a State which is authorized to carry out a hazardous waste program under section 6926 of this title, the [EPA] shall give notice to the State in which such violation has occurred prior to issuing an order or commencing a civil action under this section.

42 U.S.C. § 6928(a)(1) and (2).

The EPA argues that the plain language of section 6928 allows the federal agency to initiate an enforcement action against an environmental violator even in states that have received authorization pursuant to the RCRA. The EPA contends that Harmon and the district court misinterpreted the phrases "in lieu of" and "same force and effect" as contained in the RCRA. According to the EPA, the phrase "in lieu of" refers to which regulations are to be enforced in an authorized state rather than who is responsible for enforcing the regulations. The EPA argues that the phrase "same force and effect" refers only to the effect of state issued permits. The EPA contends that the RCRA, taken as a whole, authorizes either the state or the EPA to enforce the state's regulations, which are in compliance with the regulations of the EPA. The only requirement, according to the EPA, is that the EPA notify the state in writing if it intends to initiate an enforcement action against an alleged violator.

An examination of the statute as a whole supports the district court's interpretation. The RCRA specifically allows states that have received authorization from the federal government to administer and enforce a program that operates "in lieu of" the EPA's regulatory program. 42 U.S.C. § 6926(b). While the EPA is correct that the "in lieu of" language refers to the program itself, the administration and enforcement of the program are inexorably intertwined.

The RCRA gives authority to the states to create and implement their own hazardous waste program. The plain "in lieu of" language contained in the RCRA reveals a congressional intent for an authorized state program to supplant the federal hazardous waste program in all respects including enforcement. Congressional intent is evinced within the authorization language of section 6926(b) of the RCRA. Specifically, the statute permits the EPA to repeal a state's authorization if the state's program "does not provide adequate enforcement of compliance with the requirements of" the RCRA. Id. This language indicates that Congress intended to grant states the primary role of enforcing their own hazardous waste program. Such an indication is not undermined, as the EPA suggests, by the language of section 6928. Again, section 6928(a)(1) allows the EPA to initiate enforcement actions against suspected environmental violators, except as provided in section 6928(a)(2). Section 6928(a)(2) permits the EPA to enforce the hazardous waste laws contained in the RCRA if the agency gives written notice to the state. Section 6928(a)(1) and (2), however, must be interpreted within the context of the entire Act. Harmonizing the section 6928(a)(1) and (2) language that allows the EPA to bring an enforcement action in certain circumstances with section 6926(b)'s provision that the EPA has the right to withdraw state authorization if the state's enforcement is inadequate manifests a congressional intent to give the EPA a secondary enforcement right in those cases where a state has been authorized to act that is triggered only after state authorization is rescinded or if the state fails to initiate an enforcement action. Rather than serving as an affirmative grant of federal enforcement power as the EPA suggests, we conclude that the notice requirement of section 6928(a)(2) reinforces the primacy of a state's enforcement rights under RCRA. Taken in the context of the statute as a whole, the notice requirement operates as a means to allow a state the first chance opportunity to initiate the statutorily-permitted enforcement action. If the state fails to initiate any action, then the EPA may institute its own action. Thus, the notice requirement is an indicator of the fact that Congress intended to give states, that are authorized to act, the lead role in enforcement under RCRA.

The "same force and effect" language of section 6926(d) provides additional support for the primacy of states' enforcement rights under the RCRA when the EPA has authorized a state to act in lieu of it. The EPA argues that the "same force and effect" language is limited to state permits because the words appear under a heading that reads: "Effect of State Permit." The EPA contends that the "same force and effect" language indicates only that state-issued permits will have the same force and effect as permits issued by the federal government. . . .

Regardless of the title or heading, the plain language of section 6926(d) states that "[a]ny action taken by a State under a hazardous waste program authorized under this section shall have the same force and effect as action taken by the [EPA] under this subchapter." 42 U.S.C. § 6926(d). In this context, the meaning of the text is plain and obvious. "Any action" under this provision broadly applies to any action authorized by the subchapter, and this language is not limited to the issuance of permits. The state authorization provision substitutes state action (not excluding enforcement action) for federal action. It would be incongruous to conclude that the RCRA authorizes states to implement and administer a hazardous waste program "in lieu of" the federal program where only the issuance of permits is accorded the same force and effect as an action taken by the federal government. Contrary to the EPA's assertions, the statute specifically provides that a "[s]tate is authorized to carry out [its hazardous waste program] in lieu of the Federal program . . . and to issue and enforce permits." 42 U.S.C. § 6926(b). Issuance and enforcement are two of the functions authorized as part of the state's hazardous waste enforcement program under the RCRA. Nothing in the statute suggests that the "same force and effect" language is limited to the issuance of permits but not their enforcement. . . .

Utilizing a sort of reverse plain language argument, the EPA contends that its approach is logically consistent with the framework of the RCRA. The EPA cites the statute's citizen suit provision for the proposition that limitations on a parties' right to act are expressly stated within the statute itself. Section 6972(b)(1)(B), provides that "if the [EPA] or State has commenced and is diligently prosecuting a civil or criminal action in a court of the United States or a State," then a private citizen suit is not permitted. Id. The EPA argues that if Congress had intended to limit the EPA's right to file an enforcement action, it would have expressly stated its intention as it did in the citizen suit context. We find the EPA's argument unpersuasive. . . . Section 6926 . . . contains express language that establishes the primacy of states' enforcement rights once the EPA has granted a state authorization. The mere fact that Congress did not choose to employ the exact same language as contained in an unrelated part of the act does not detract from the plain language used in the state authorization section. Again, Congress provided that the state's program should operate in lieu of the federal program and that the state action should operate with the same force and effect as action taken by the EPA. We find the language contained in the state authorization section of the Act to be as unambiguous as the citizen suit provision. . . .

Even assuming some ambiguity exists in the statutory language, the primacy of the states' enforcement rights, once the EPA has authorized a state to act, is illustrated further through the RCRA's legislative history. . . . The House Report states that although the "legislation permits the states to take the lead in the enforcement of the hazardous wastes [sic] laws[,] . . . the Administrator [of the EPA] is not prohibited from acting in those cases where the state fails to act, or from withdrawing approval of the state hazardous waste plan and implementing the federal hazardous waste program pursuant to . . . this act." [H.R.Rep. 1491, 94th Cong., 2nd Sess. 24, reprinted in 1976 U.S.C.C.A.N. 6262, 6269]. The House Report also states that the EPA, "after giving the appropriate notice to a state that is authorized to implement the state hazardous waste program, that violations of this Act are occurring and the state [is] failing to take action against such violations, is authorized to take appropriate action against those persons in such state not in compliance with the hazardous waste title." Id. at 6270. The House Report thus supports our interpretation of the statute—that the federal government's right to pursue an enforcement action under the RCRA attaches only when a state's authorization is revoked or when a state fails to initiate any enforcement action.

A contrary interpretation would result in two separate enforcement actions. Such an interpretation, as explained above, would derogate the RCRA's plain language and legislative history. Companies that reach an agreement through negotiations with a state authorized by the EPA to act in its place may find the agreement undermined by a later separate enforcement action by the EPA. While, generally speaking, two separate sovereigns can institute two separate enforcement actions, those actions can cause vastly different and potentially contradictory results. Such a potential schism runs afoul of the principles of comity and federalism so clearly embedded in the text and history of the RCRA. . . .

* * *

Notes and Comments

1. Note that, technically speaking, *Harmon* did not involve an "overfiling" situation, because EPA filed its administrative action before Missouri undertook any formal enforcement response. Should this fact have influenced the court's analysis?

2. What did you think of the court's effort to "harmonize" the relevant subsections in §§ 3006 and 3008 (§§ 6926 and 6928 in U.S.C.-speak)? Can § 3006(b) bear the weight the court gave it? On the other hand, what did you think of EPA's attempt to avoid the effect of § 3006(d)? What did you make of EPA's argument based on § 7002 (§ 6972)? Does it seem plausible that Congress would have authorized citizens to proceed in the face of non-diligent State enforcement, while at the same time precluding EPA from doing so? At the same time, however, doesn't the House Report tend to support the *Harmon* court's result?

3. While *Harmon* constituted a bombshell when it first was issued, its long-term significance is open to question. The United States has continued to press what it believes to be its authority to overfile in appropriate cases. In a subsequent RCRA case, the Tenth Circuit expressly rejected the *Harmon* analysis, concluding that "[n]othing in the text of the statute suggests that [withdrawal of authorization] in a prerequisite to EPA enforce-

ment or that it is the only remedy for inadequate enforcement." *United States v. Power Engineering Co.*, 303 F.3d 1232, 1238–1239 (10th Cir. 2002). Moreover, the "in lieu of" and "same force and effect" language the 8th Circuit relied on in *Harmon* is unique to RCRA. Both the Clean Water Act and the Clean Air Act, by contrast, appear to contain language that contemplates overfiling in at least some situations. See, e.g., 33 U.S.C. § 1319(g)(6)(A) (indicating narrow circumstances in which EPA may not overfile) and 42 U.S.C. § 7413(e) (stating that, in determining penalties, the court shall consider "payment by the violator of penalties previously assessed for the same violation"). Given these different statutory dynamics, it is perhaps unsurprising that what little post-*Harmon* case law there is tends to support EPA's ability to overfile under these other statutes. See, e.g., *United States v. LTV Steel Co., Inc.*, 118 F.Supp.2d 827 (N.D. Ohio 2000).

4. As a secondary basis for its decision (which we have edited out), the *Harmon* court found that EPA's action was barred by res judicata. In so holding, the 8th Circuit first noted that the Full Faith and Credit Act, 28 U.S.C. § 1738, required it to apply Missouri res judicata law to determine the preclusive effect to which the Missouri state court judgment was entitled. In performing the required "party identity" analysis, however, the court relied heavily on RCRA's "in lieu of" and "same force and effect" language in concluding that EPA is always in privity with authorized States when they act under RCRA. Other courts have rejected this approach, relying on *Drummond v. United States*, 324 U.S. 316, 318, 65 S.Ct. 659, 89 L.Ed. 969 (1945), and *Montana v. United States*, 440 U.S. 147, 154, 99 S.Ct. 970, 59 L.Ed.2d 210 (1979), for the proposition that the United States should not be bound by a prior judgment unless it had a "laboring oar" in the controversy. See, e.g., *Power Engineering*, 303 F.3d at 1240–1241.

5. Even if we assume that EPA has the power to overfile in most or all situations, that still leaves the question of the circumstances under which EPA should choose to exercise this authority. What policy dynamics did the *Harmon* court identify that might bear on this question? Did it seem like a complete list? In its guidance documents and its "Memoranda of Agreement" with the States, EPA generally does two things: first, it articulates what it believes to be its unfettered discretion in this area; but second, and most importantly, it states that it will only overfile in situations in which the relevant State has failed to take what it terms "timely and appropriate" action. See, e.g., *United States v. City of Rock Island, Ill.*, 182 F.Supp.2d 690, 693 (C.D. Ill. 2001). In practice, this means that overfiling is a relatively rare phenomenon. Did you agree with EPA's decision to overfile in *Harmon?* Interestingly, despite EPA's decision to overfile, it did not pursue to case to the point of seeking Supreme Court review of the Eight Circuit's decision. Can you think of why this might be so?

V. CITIZEN SUITS

One of Congress's most important innovations when it created the modern environmental statutes was the concept of citizen suits. The basic idea is very simple: if neither EPA nor the relevant State is enforcing the law appropriately, citizens can pursue alleged violators in federal court in their stead. Thus, it is often said that Congress has empowered these citizens to act as "private attorneys general," acting on the public's behalf. See, e.g., *Bennett v. Spear*, 520 U.S. 154, 165, 117 S.Ct. 1154, 137 L.Ed.2d 281 (1997).

It is important to note that in this section of the book we are distinguishing between actions under the citizen-suit provisions of the environmental laws, on the one hand, and challenges to environmental decisions under the Administrative Procedure Act. Assuming the elements of reviewability are present, citizens (and regulated entities) can use the APA to challenge a whole host governmental decisions made in the environmental context, such as those made in issuing rules, permits or administrative orders. Under the citizen suit provisions, by contrast, Congress typically has granted citizens two potential causes of action: one against regulated entities who are violating the relevant standards, and another against EPA where it has failed to perform a nondiscretionary duty. See, e.g., 33 U.S.C. § 1365(a)(1) and (2), respectively; see also *Bennett v. Spear*, 520 U.S. at 173–174, for a discussion of the difference between citizen suit and APA claims. Here, we will focus on one of these latter two causes of action—suits that citizens can bring under provisions such as § 505(a)(1) of the CWA against regulated entities who are alleged to be violating the applicable statutory or regulatory standards.

We begin by stressing the similarities between these citizen suits and EPA-lead civil judicial actions. If you read § 505(a) of the CWA, for example, you will see that, like EPA under § 309, citizens are entitled to seek both injunctive relief and penalties. In fact, Section 505(a) simply cross-references § 309(d) regarding the courts' authority to apply the appropriate fines. Thus, these suits can be seen as being very much like the EPA civil judicial-enforcement actions we considered at the beginning of this chapter: like EPA, citizens have to make their prima facie case by proving the relevant violations; once they do so, they are entitled to the same relief EPA would have been entitled to if it had brought the action. This, of course, is fully consistent with the notion that the citizens who bring these cases are fulfilling a quasi-public role—that of the private attorney general—rather than a purely private one. The nature of this undertaking is further underscored when one realizes that any penalties assessed in these actions are payable to the United States Treasury, not to the citizens themselves. See, e.g., *Friends of the Earth v. Laidlaw Environmental Services (TOC)*, 528 U.S. 167, 185, 120 S.Ct. 693, 145 L.Ed.2d 610 (2000).

Despite these similarities, however, there are five key differences between citizen suits and EPA enforcement actions. The first four of these constitute additional hurdles that citizens must overcome in order to successfully prosecute their actions. These include: (1) the need to provide notice to EPA, the State and the alleged violator prior to bringing suit; (2) the requirement that citizens demonstrate that they have standing; (3) the need to overcome what we will loosely refer to as the "*Gwaltney* doctrine;" and (4) the fact that their suits are more likely to be barred by prior governmental enforcement actions.

Perhaps surprisingly, the fifth difference constitutes an area in which citizen enforcers are treated better than the Government is when it brings regulatory enforcement actions. If citizens are successful in bringing their claims, they are entitled to an award of attorney fees, to be paid by the defendant. See, e.g., 33 U.S.C. § 1365(d). EPA, by contrast, must bear its own legal costs. Compare, e.g., 33 U.S.C. § 1319 (containing no provision comparable to § 505(d)).

[handwritten margin note: II5 → Atty's fees]

We will now consider all five of these differences, in varying degrees of detail. Keep in mind, however, that the similarities between governmental enforcement actions and citizen suits are in many ways more significant than the differences.

A. Notice

The environmental citizen suit provisions commonly require that the would-be plaintiff provide advance notice of its potential lawsuit to EPA, the State and the alleged violator, typically 60 days before filing suit. See, e.g., 33 U.S.C. § 1365(b)(1)(A). One idea behind these notice requirements is that it gives EPA and the State a window within which they may each decide whether to commence their own enforcement action, which in turn might render the citizen suit unnecessary.

[handwritten margin note: Notice]

The Supreme Court has determined that these notice requirements are jurisdictional, meaning that they cannot be waived and may be raised at any time during the relevant proceedings. Additionally, any suit filed without proper notice must be dismissed. *Hallstrom v. Tillamook County*, 493 U.S. 20, 110 S.Ct. 304, 107 L.Ed.2d 237 (1989).

As contemplated under the statutes, see, e.g., 33 U.S.C. § 1365(b), EPA has developed rules fleshing out the notice requirements for each of the relevant statutes. See, e.g., 40 C.F.R. Part 135 (rules for the CWA and the Safe Drinking Water Act). While recognizing that any defects are fatal, the courts have been fairly generous in construing these requirements. See, e.g., *Public Interest Research Group of New Jersey, Inc. v. Hercules, Inc.*, 50 F.3d 1239 (3d Cir. 1995), and *San Francisco BayKeeper, Inc. v. Tosco Corp.*, 309 F.3d 1153 (9th Cir. 2002).

B. Standing

We already have touched on standing issues in Chapter 1, including consideration of *Lujan v. Defenders of Wildlife*, 504 U.S. 555, 112 S.Ct. 2130, 119 L.Ed.2d 351 (1992) ("*Defenders*"). We here revisit these matters, with a particular focus on the injury and causation questions that are likely to arise in citizens suits. We reserve discussion of yet another standing issue—whether citizens have standing to seek penalties that are payable to the Treasury—until our discussion of the *Gwaltney* doctrine, below.

In *Defenders*, we saw that the plaintiffs' "some day" intentions (to use Justice Scalia's phrase) to revisit sites half-way around the world were insufficient to demonstrate the type of "imminent" injury necessary to satisfy Article III. What kinds of showing do plaintiffs have to make in situations in which they live near the offending discharge? Consider the following case:

FRIENDS OF THE EARTH v. LAIDLAW ENVIRONMENTAL SERVICES

Supreme Court of the United States, 2000.
528 U.S. 167, 120 S.Ct. 693, 145 L.Ed.2d 610.

Justice GINSBURG delivered the opinion of the Court.

In 1986, defendant-respondent Laidlaw Environmental Services (TOC), Inc., bought a hazardous waste incinerator facility in Roebuck, South Carolina, that included a wastewater treatment plant. Shortly after Laidlaw acquired the facility, the South Carolina Department of Health and Environmental Control (DHEC) ... granted Laidlaw an NPDES permit authorizing the company to discharge treated water into the North Tyger River. The permit ... placed limits on Laidlaw's discharge of several pollutants into the river, including ... mercury, an extremely toxic pollutant....

[From the outset, and despite several attempted technological fixes,] Laidlaw consistently failed to meet the permit's stringent 1.3 ppb (parts per billion) daily average limit on mercury discharges. The District Court later found that Laidlaw had violated the mercury limits on 489 occasions between 1987 and 1995.

On June 12, 1992, FOE filed this citizen suit against Laidlaw under § 505(a) of the [CWA], alleging noncompliance with the NPDES permit and seeking declaratory and injunctive relief and an award of civil penalties. Laidlaw moved for summary judgment on the ground that FOE had failed to present evidence demonstrating injury in fact, and therefore lacked Article III standing to bring the lawsuit.... After examining [the] evidence, the District Court denied Laidlaw's summary judgment motion, finding—albeit "by the very slimmest of margins"— that FOE had standing to bring the suit.

... The record indicates that after FOE initiated the suit, but before the District Court rendered judgment, Laidlaw violated the mercury discharge limitation in its permit 13 times.... The last recorded mercury discharge violation occurred in January 1995, long after the complaint was filed but about two years before judgment was rendered.

On January 22, 1997, the District Court issued its judgment. It found that Laidlaw had gained a total economic benefit of $1,092,581 as a result of its extended period of noncompliance with the mercury discharge limit in its permit. The court concluded, however, that a civil penalty of $405,800 was adequate in light of the guiding factors listed in 33 U.S.C. § 1319(d).... The court declined to grant FOE's request for injunctive relief, stating that an injunction was inappropriate because "Laidlaw has been in substantial compliance with all parameters in its NPDES permit since at least August 1992."

II

A

In *Lujan v. Defenders of Wildlife*, 504 U.S. 555, 560–561 (1992), we held that, to satisfy Article III's standing requirements, a plaintiff must show (1) it has suffered an "injury in fact" that is (a) concrete and particularized and (b) actual or imminent, not conjectural or hypothetical; (2) the injury is fairly traceable to the challenged action of the defendant; and (3) it is likely, as opposed to merely speculative, that the injury will be redressed by a favorable decision . . . .

Laidlaw contends first that FOE lacked standing from the outset even to seek injunctive relief, because the plaintiff organizations failed to show that any of their members had sustained or faced the threat of any "injury in fact" from Laidlaw's activities. In support of this contention Laidlaw points to the District Court's finding, made in the course of setting the penalty amount, that there had been "no demonstrated proof of harm to the environment" from Laidlaw's mercury discharge violations.

The relevant showing for purposes of Article III standing, however, is not injury to the environment but injury to the plaintiff. To insist upon the former rather than the latter as part of the standing inquiry (as the dissent in essence does) is to raise the standing hurdle higher than the necessary showing for success on the merits in an action alleging noncompliance with an NPDES permit. Focusing properly on injury to the plaintiff, the District Court found that FOE had demonstrated sufficient injury to establish standing. For example, FOE member Kenneth Lee Curtis averred in affidavits that he lived a half-mile from Laidlaw's facility; that he occasionally drove over the North Tyger River, and that it looked and smelled polluted; and that he would like to fish, camp, swim, and picnic in and near the river between 3 and 15 miles downstream from the facility, as he did when he was a teenager, but would not do so because he was concerned that the water was polluted by Laidlaw's discharges. Curtis reaffirmed these statements in extensive deposition testimony. For example, he testified that he would like to fish in the river at a specific spot he used as a boy, but that he would not do so now because of his concerns about Laidlaw's discharges.

Other members presented evidence to similar effect. CLEAN member Angela Patterson attested that she lived two miles from the facility; that before Laidlaw operated the facility, she picnicked, walked, birdwatched, and waded in and along the North Tyger River because of the natural beauty of the area; that she no longer engaged in these activities in or near the river because she was concerned about harmful effects from discharged pollutants; and that she and her husband would like to purchase a home near the river but did not intend to do so, in part because of Laidlaw's discharges. CLEAN member Judy Pruitt averred that she lived one-quarter mile from Laidlaw's facility and would like to fish, hike, and picnic along the North Tyger River, but has refrained from those activities because of the discharges. FOE member Linda

Moore attested that she lived 20 miles from Roebuck, and would use the North Tyger River south of Roebuck and the land surrounding it for recreational purposes were she not concerned that the water contained harmful pollutants. In her deposition, Moore testified at length that she would hike, picnic, camp, swim, boat, and drive near or in the river were it not for her concerns about illegal discharges. CLEAN member Gail Lee attested that her home, which is near Laidlaw's facility, had a lower value than similar homes located further from the facility, and that she believed the pollutant discharges accounted for some of the discrepancy. Sierra Club member Norman Sharp averred that he had canoed approximately 40 miles downstream of the Laidlaw facility and would like to canoe in the North Tyger River closer to Laidlaw's discharge point, but did not do so because he was concerned that the water contained harmful pollutants.

These sworn statements, as the District Court determined, adequately documented injury in fact. We have held that environmental plaintiffs adequately allege injury in fact when they aver that they use the affected area and are persons "for whom the aesthetic and recreational values of the area will be lessened" by the challenged activity. *Sierra Club v. Morton*, 405 U.S. 727, 735 (1972).

Our decision in *Lujan v. National Wildlife Federation*, 497 U.S. 871 (1990), is not to the contrary. In that case an environmental organization assailed the Bureau of Land Management's "land withdrawal review program," a program covering millions of acres, alleging that the program illegally opened up public lands to mining activities. The defendants moved for summary judgment, challenging the plaintiff organization's standing to initiate the action under the [APA]. We held that the plaintiff could not survive the summary judgment motion merely by offering "averments which state only that one of [the organization's] members uses unspecified portions of an immense tract of territory, on some portions of which mining activity has occurred or probably will occur by virtue of the governmental action." 497 U.S., at 889.

In contrast, the affidavits and testimony presented by FOE in this case assert that Laidlaw's discharges, and the affiant members' reasonable concerns about the effects of those discharges, directly affected those affiants' recreational, aesthetic, and economic interests. These submissions present dispositively more than the mere "general averments" and "conclusory allegations" found inadequate in *National Wildlife Federation*. Id., at 888. Nor can the affiants' conditional statements—that they would use the nearby North Tyger River for recreation if Laidlaw were not discharging pollutants into it—be equated with the speculative " 'some day' intentions" to visit endangered species halfway around the world that we held insufficient to show injury in fact in *Defenders of Wildlife*. 504 U.S., at 564.

Los Angeles v. Lyons, 461 U.S. 95 (1983), relied on by the dissent, does not weigh against standing in this case. In *Lyons*, we held that a plaintiff lacked standing to seek an injunction against the enforcement of a police chokehold policy because he could not credibly allege that he faced a realistic threat from the policy. 461 U.S., at 107, n. 7. In the footnote from *Lyons* cited by the dissent, we noted that "[t]he reasonableness of Lyons' fear is dependent upon the likelihood of a recurrence of the allegedly unlawful conduct," and that his "subjective apprehensions" that such a recurrence would even take place were not enough to support standing. Id., at 108, n. 8. Here, in contrast, it is undisputed that Laidlaw's unlawful conduct—discharging pollutants in excess of permit limits—was occurring at the time the complaint was filed. Under Lyons, then, the only "subjective" issue here is "[t]he reasonableness of [the] fear" that led the affiants to respond to that concededly ongoing conduct by refraining from use of the North Tyger River and surrounding areas. Unlike the dissent, we see nothing "improbable" about the proposition that a company's continuous and pervasive illegal discharges of pollutants into a river would cause nearby residents to curtail their recreational use of that waterway and would subject them to other economic and aesthetic harms. The proposition is entirely reasonable, the District Court found it was true in this case, and that is enough for injury in fact.

    Justice SCALIA, with whom Justice THOMAS joins, dissenting.

    Plaintiffs, as the parties invoking federal jurisdiction, have the burden of proof and persuasion as to the existence of standing. *Lujan v. Defenders of Wildlife*, 504 U.S. 555, 561 (1992) (hereinafter *Lujan*). The plaintiffs in this case fell far short of carrying their burden of demonstrating injury in fact. The Court cites affiants' testimony asserting that their enjoyment of the North Tyger River has been diminished due to "concern" that the water was polluted, and that they "believed" that Laidlaw's mercury exceedances had reduced the value of their homes. These averments alone cannot carry the plaintiffs' burden of demonstrating that they have suffered a "concrete and particularized" injury, *Lujan*, 504 U.S., at 560. General allegations of injury may suffice at the pleading stage, but at summary judgment plaintiffs must set forth "specific facts" to support their claims. Id., at 561. And where, as here, the case has proceeded to judgment, those specific facts must be " 'supported adequately by the evidence adduced at trial,' " *ibid*. In this case, the affidavits themselves are woefully short on "specific facts," and the vague allegations of injury they do make are undermined by the evidence adduced at trial.

    Typically, an environmental plaintiff claiming injury due to discharges in violation of the Clean Water Act argues that the discharges harm the environment, and that the harm to the environment injures him. This route to injury is barred in the present case, however, since the District Court concluded after considering all the evidence that there had been "no demonstrated proof of harm to the environment," that the "permit violations at issue in this citizen suit did not result in any health risk or environmental harm," that "[a]ll available data . . . fail to show that Laidlaw's actual discharges have resulted in harm to the North Tyger River," and that "the overall quality of the river exceeds levels necessary to support . . . recreation in and on the water."

The Court finds these conclusions unproblematic for standing, because "[t]he relevant showing for purposes of Article III standing ... is not injury to the environment but injury to the plaintiff." This statement is correct, as far as it goes. We have certainly held that a demonstration of harm to the environment is not enough to satisfy the injury-in-fact requirement unless the plaintiff can demonstrate how he personally was harmed. In the normal course, however, a lack of demonstrable harm to the environment will translate, as it plainly does here, into a lack of demonstrable harm to citizen plaintiffs. While it is perhaps possible that a plaintiff could be harmed even though the environment was not, such a plaintiff would have the burden of articulating and demonstrating the nature of that injury. Ongoing "concerns" about the environment are not enough, for "[i]t is the reality of the threat of repeated injury that is relevant to the standing inquiry, not the plaintiff's subjective apprehensions," *Los Angeles v. Lyons*, 461 U.S. 95, 107, n. 8. At the very least, in the present case, one would expect to see evidence supporting the affidavits' bald assertions regarding decreasing recreational usage and declining home values, as well as evidence for the improbable proposition that Laidlaw's violations, even though harmless to the environment, are somehow responsible for these effects. Plaintiffs here have made no attempt at such a showing, but rely entirely upon unsupported and unexplained affidavit allegations of "concern."

Indeed, every one of the affiants deposed by Laidlaw cast into doubt the (in any event inadequate) proposition that subjective "concerns" actually affected their conduct. Linda Moore, for example, said in her affidavit that she would use the affected waterways for recreation if it were not for her concern about pollution. Yet she testified in her deposition that she had been to the river only twice, once in 1980 (when she visited someone who lived by the river) and once after this suit was filed. Similarly, Kenneth Lee Curtis, who claimed he was injured by being deprived of recreational activity at the river, admitted that he had not been to the river since he was "a kid," and when asked whether the reason he stopped visiting the river was because of pollution, answered "no." As to Curtis's claim that the river "looke[d] and smell[ed] polluted," this condition, if present, was surely not caused by Laidlaw's discharges, which according to the District Court "did not result in any health risk or environmental harm." 956 F.Supp., at 602. The other affiants cited by the Court were not deposed, but their affidavits state either that they would use the river if it were not polluted or harmful (as the court subsequently found it is not), or said that the river looks polluted (which is also incompatible with the court's findings), ibid. These affiants have established nothing but "subjective apprehensions."

The Court is correct that the District Court explicitly found standing—albeit "by the very slimmest of margins," and as "an awfully close call." That cautious finding, however, was made in 1993, long before the court's 1997 conclusion that Laidlaw's discharges did not harm the environment. As we have previously recognized, an initial conclusion that plaintiffs have standing is subject to reexamination, particularly if later evidence proves inconsistent with that conclusion. Laidlaw challenged the existence of injury in fact on appeal to the Fourth Circuit, but that court did not reach the question. Thus no lower court has reviewed the injury-in-fact issue in light of the extensive studies that led the District Court to conclude that the environment was not harmed by Laidlaw's discharges.

Inexplicably, the Court is untroubled by this, but proceeds to find injury in fact in the most casual fashion, as though it is merely confirming a careful analysis made below. Although we have previously refused to find standing based on the "conclusory allegations of an affidavit" *Lujan v. National Wildlife Federation*, 497 U.S. 871, 888 (1990), the Court is content to do just that today. By accepting plaintiffs' vague, contradictory, and unsubstantiated allegations of "concern" about the environment as adequate to prove injury in fact, and accepting them even in the face of a finding that the environment was not demonstrably harmed, the Court makes the injury-in-fact requirement a sham. If there are permit violations, and a member of a plaintiff environmental organization lives near the offending plant, it would be difficult not to satisfy today's lenient standard.

Notes and Comments

1.   Justice Ginsburg was surprisingly non-specific about which injuries of which affiants provided the requisite standing. Several of the affiants indicated that they were forgoing activities such as hiking, picnicking and camping near the North Tyger River as a result of their concerns about the discharges. If the affiants had engaged in these activities, how would Laidlaw's discharges of mercury have adversely affected them? Does it matter whether they could see or smell the offending discharges? If they could not, should it be enough if they merely "knew" the pollutants were there? See *Public Interest Research Group of New Jersey, Inc. v. Magnesium Elektron, Inc.*, 123 F.3d 111, 121 (3d Cir. 1997) (a pre-*Laidlaw* case denying standing in this situation because "absent a showing of tangible injury to the River or its immediate surroundings, PIRG's members are no less 'concerned bystanders' than any other citizen who takes an interest in our environment"). Is *Magnesium Elektron* still good law in light of *Laidlaw*?

2.   Ms. Lee attested that she believed that Laidlaw's discharges had adversely affected her property value. Should courts accept these assertions at face value? Does *Laidlaw* stand for the proposition that they must do so?

3.   Perhaps the most Constitutionally-significant injuries in *Laidlaw* were those articulated by the affiants who said that they would like to fish, swim or wade in the River, but were afraid to do so in light of the defendant's discharges. What is the essence of the disagreement between the majority and the dissent with respect to these injuries? How should courts determine the reasonableness of the plaintiffs' concerns? Put another way, how much pollution should courts require to be present in water before they recognize that those who forgo swimming in it (or drinking it) have standing to complain? Is Justice Scalia right that, under the majority's approach, "[i]f there are permit violations, and a member of a plaintiff environmental

organization lives near the offending plant, it would be difficult not to satisfy today's lenient standard?"

4. *Laidlaw* appears to have been what we will call a "one polluter" case; there was no apparent contention that other sources of pollution may have been causing or contributing to the alleged harms being suffered by the plaintiff's affiants. When these allegations are present, they can pose interesting causation and redressability questions. If the plaintiff's alleged injury relates to seeing an oily sheen on the water, for example, how much proof should the courts require as to whether the defendant's oily discharges were in fact the source of the oil observed? If the defendant is one of a number of sources of the relevant oil, should the plaintiff be denied standing for want of redressability if it cannot show that the river will be observably less oily absent the defendant's discharges? In *Public Interest Research Group of New Jersey, Inc. v. Powell Duffryn Terminals Inc.*, 913 F.2d 64 (3d Cir. 1990), the Third Circuit concluded that all the plaintiff must show to demonstrate causation in multiple-polluter situations is that the defendant

> has 1) discharged some pollutant in concentrations greater than allowed by its permit 2) into a waterway in which the plaintiffs have an interest that is or may be adversely affected by the pollutant and that 3) this pollutant causes or contributes to the kinds of injuries alleged by the plaintiffs.

Id. at 72. With regard to redressability, the court found that "[p]laintiffs need not show that the waterway will be returned to pristine condition in order to establish the minimal requirements of Article III." Id. at 73. Do you agree with the Third Circuit on these fronts? Judge Aldisert concurred in *Powell-Duffryn*, but expressed his reservations in the following terms:

> Throughout my extensive preparation of this case including close attention at argument and discussion with my colleagues at conference, I was persuaded that the member/plaintiffs had failed to show an actual injury that was traceable to the permit violations. I am now willing to join my colleagues' view. But I feel somewhat like Lord Byron's fair maiden in Don Juan, c 1, dedication cxvii,
>
>> A little more she strove, and much repented, And whispering "I will ne'er consent"—consented.

Id. at 83.

The Gaston Copper Saga

The impact of *Laidlaw* can perhaps best be seen in the effect it had on the Fourth Circuit in *Friends of the Earth, Inc. v. Gaston Copper Recycling Corp.*, 204 F.3d 149 (4th Cir. 2000). In that case, the plaintiffs' best standing affiant, Mr. Shealy, testified that South Carolina officials had tested his lake the year before the lawsuit was filed and had found copper, zinc, nickel, iron and PCBs, all of which pollutants the defendant's smelting facility had discharged in the past. As a result, he testified that he was injured in three ways: (1) he reduced his consumption of the fish from the lake; (2) he restricted his grandchildren's access to the water; and (3) his property value had diminished because the lake was known to be polluted.

Before *Laidlaw* was decided, the panel majority at the Fourth Circuit level found that the plaintiffs had not demonstrated that they were injured because:

> ... [N]o evidence was presented that established that Shealy's lake ... [was] in fact adversely affected by pollution.... Indeed, there were no toxicity tests, or tests or studies of any kind, performed on waters from Shealy's lake.... Further, none of the members even testified that there was an observable negative impact on the waters that they used or on the surrounding ecosystem of such water. Their concerns were based on mere speculation as to the presence of pollution without any evidence to support their fears or establish the presence of pollutants in the allegedly affected waters.

179 F.3d 107, 113–114 (4th Cir. 1999).

Upon rehearing after *Laidlaw*, the *en banc* panel of the Fourth Circuit unanimously reversed course, determining that Mr. Shealy was "a classic example of an individual who has suffered an environmental injury in fact fairly traceable to a defendant's conduct." 204 F.3d at 155. The majority opinion at the *en banc* level was written by Chief Judge Wilkinson, who had dissented from the original panel opinion. Perhaps unsurprisingly (given the fact that he thought the panel was wrong in the first place), his opinion does not place much reliance on *Laidlaw*.

More interesting are the three concurring opinions. Judge Luttig, with Judge Niemeyer concurring, wrote that:

> I concur in the judgment of the court, but not in its opinion. Through no fault of this court, the Supreme Court's recent decision in [*Laidlaw*], has rendered much of the discussion in today's opinion not merely unnecessary, but affirmatively confusing. Rather than persist in the fiction (as we do in the court's opinion) that Laidlaw was part of the fabric of standing jurisprudence at the time of argument in this case, or worse (as we also do) that that decision was merely an unexceptional reaffirmation of the Court's previous precedents, I would simply reverse the district court's judgment on the specific reasoning of the Supreme Court in *Laidlaw* and say little else. The unfortunate implication left by the court's failure to address the significant change in environmental standing doctrine worked by the Supreme Court's recent decision in *Laidlaw* (and by the court's comfortable, but mistaken, assumption that the Supreme Court's decisions prior to Laidlaw themselves dictated the conclusion we reach today), is that the district court seriously erred in its application of the standing doctrine extant at the time that it ruled— which it did not.

Id. at 164–165. Judge Niemeyer also wrote separately:

> Before the Supreme Court's recent decision in [*Laidlaw*], I would have affirmed the district court in this case because the plaintiffs, who expressed only a subjective belief of injury, have not shown that they "personally [have] suffered some actual or threatened injury as a result of the putatively illegal conduct of the defendant and that the injury fairly can be traced to the challenged action." *Valley Forge Christian*

College v. Americans United for Separation of Church and State, Inc., 454 U.S. 464, 472 (1982). . . .

As my concurrence in Judge Luttig's opinion indicates, I believe that the decision in Laidlaw represents a sea change in constitutional standing principles, and in view of that decision I agree that we are now required to reverse.

Id. at 164. And finally, Judge Hamilton lamented that:

The Supreme Court's decision in [*Laidlaw*] has unnecessarily opened the standing floodgates, rendering our standing inquiry "a sham," (Scalia, J., dissenting). However, being bound by [*Laidlaw*]., I concur in the court's judgment reversing the district court's judgment and remanding the case for a determination as to whether Gaston Copper has discharged pollutants in excess of its permit limits.

Id. at 165.

The panel majority in *Gaston Copper* had also found that the plaintiffs had failed to demonstrate causation. Cobbling together the facts from the various opinions, one is left with the following:

1. Gaston Copper discharged into Lake Watson, which flowed into the Boggy Branch, which, in turn, was a tributary of Bull Swamp Creek, which eventually flowed into the North Fork of the Edisto River. The distance from Lake Watson to the North Fork of the Edisto River was at least 10 miles (and maybe as many as 16.5 miles).

2. Mr. Shealy's lake was four miles downstream from Watson Lake and was fed in part by Bull Swamp Creek; however, there were 31 ponds between Gaston Copper and Mr. Shealy's lake, and three other tributaries fed into Mr. Shealy's lake;

3. The South Carolina Department of Health and Environmental Control (DHEC) had identified the same heavy metals and PCBs in Mr. Shealy's lake as were contained in the plant's discharges. Apparently, none of the parties submitted evidence regarding the existence of other potential sources of these contaminants (or the lack thereof); and

4. In response to a question raised during the comment period for Gaston Copper's permit, DHEC had indicated the "runoff" from Gaston Copper's discharges would "go to Boggy Branch to Bull Swamp to the Edisto River." Unfortunately, none of the relevant opinions indicated whether Gaston Copper's pollutants would have had to travel through Mr. Shealy's lake to get to the Edisto River. The opinions do not preclude the possibility that, while the Bull Swamp Creek fed into Mr. Shealy's lake, it could have been a side channel that did not feed back into either the Creek or the Edisto River.

The *en banc* panel in *Gaston Copper* rejected the panel majority's causation analysis, finding traceability as a matter of law. 204 F.3d at 161–162. It did so, however, without any reference to *Laidlaw*, which is perhaps unsurprising given that *Laidlaw* did not address the causation element of the standing test. Interestingly, the two judges in the panel majority (Judges Hamilton and Williams) must have read *Laidlaw* as undermining their earlier analysis on this front as well, or they presumably would have dissented from the *en banc* result.

Do you agree that *Laidlaw* should have affected even the causation analysis in *Gaston Copper*? Do you think the plaintiffs put on enough evidence to support a finding of causation even if *Laidlaw* is deemed irrelevant?

C. The Gwaltney Doctrine

As the Supreme Court mentions in the first case below, there is little doubt that the Government can bring penalty actions with respect to violations to "wholly past" violations; that is, violations that have ceased prior to the commencement of the enforcement action. In the citizen suit context, however, the question whether citizens may bring or maintain actions after the violation has ceased can raise a host of issues regarding statutory interpretation, redressability and mootness. Because these issues are closely intertwined, we treat them together under the general rubric of the *Gwaltney* doctrine. We begin with the case that gives the doctrine its name:

GWALTNEY OF SMITHFIELD, LTD. v. CHESAPEAKE BAY FOUNDATION, INC.

Supreme Court of the United States, 1987.
484 U.S. 49, 108 S.Ct. 376, 98 L.Ed.2d 306.

Justice MARSHALL delivered the opinion of the Court.

In this case, we must decide whether § 505(a) of the Clean Water Act confers federal jurisdiction over citizen suits for wholly past violations.

... The holder of a federal NPDES permit is subject to enforcement action by the Administrator for failure to comply with the conditions of the permit. The Administrator's enforcement arsenal includes administrative, civil, and criminal sanctions. § 1319. The holder of a state NPDES permit is subject to both federal and state enforcement action for failure to comply. §§ 1319, 1342(b)(7). In the absence of federal or state enforcement, private citizens may commence civil actions against any person "alleged to be in violation of" the conditions of either a federal or state NPDES permit. § 1365(a)(1). If the citizen prevails in such an action, the court may order injunctive relief and/or impose civil penalties payable to the United States Treasury. § 1365(a).

The Commonwealth of Virginia established a federally approved state NPDES program administered by the Virginia State Water Control Board (Board). In 1974, the Board issued a NPDES permit to ITT–Gwaltney authorizing the discharge of seven pollutants from the company's meat-packing plant on the Pagan River in Smithfield, Virginia. The permit, which was reissued in 1979 and modified in 1980, established effluent limitations, monitoring requirements, and other conditions of discharge. In 1981, petitioner Gwaltney of Smithfield acquired the assets of ITT–Gwaltney and assumed obligations under the permit.

Between 1981 and 1984, petitioner repeatedly violated the conditions of the permit by exceeding effluent limitations on five of the seven pollutants covered. These violations are chronicled in the Discharge Monitoring Reports that the permit required petitioner to maintain. The most substantial of the violations concerned the pollutants fecal coliform, chlorine, and total Kjeldahl nitrogen (TKN). Between October 27, 1981, and August 30, 1984, petitioner violated its TKN limitation 87 times, its chlorine limitation 34 times, and its fecal coliform limitation 31 times. Petitioner installed new equipment to improve its chlorination system in March 1982, and its last reported chlorine violation occurred in October 1982. The new chlorination system also helped to control the discharge of fecal coliform, and the last recorded fecal coliform violation occurred in February 1984. Petitioner installed an upgraded wastewater treatment system in October 1983, and its last reported TKN violation occurred on May 15, 1984.

Respondents Chesapeake Bay Foundation and Natural Resources Defense Council ... sent notice in February 1984 to Gwaltney, the Administrator of EPA, and the Virginia State Water Control Board, indicating respondents' intention to commence a citizen suit under the Act based on petitioner's violations of its permit conditions. Respondents proceeded to file this suit in June 1984, alleging that petitioner "has violated ... [and] will continue to violate its NPDES permit." Respondents requested that the District Court provide declaratory and injunctive relief, impose civil penalties, and award attorney's fees and costs....

... Gwaltney moved in May 1985 for dismissal of the action for want of subject-matter jurisdiction under the Act. Gwaltney argued that the language of § 505(a), which permits private citizens to bring suit against any person "alleged to be in violation" of the Act, requires that a defendant be violating the Act at the time of suit. Gwaltney urged the District Court to adopt the analysis of the Fifth Circuit in *Hamker v. Diamond Shamrock Chemical Co.*, 756 F.2d 392 (1985), which held that "a complaint brought under [§ 505] must allege a violation occurring at the time the complaint is filed." *Id.*, at 395. Gwaltney contended that because its last recorded violation occurred several weeks before respondents filed their complaint, the District Court lacked subject-matter jurisdiction over respondents' action.

The District Court rejected Gwaltney's argument, concluding that § 505 authorizes citizens to bring enforcement actions on the basis of wholly past violations. The District Court found that "[t]he words 'to be in violation' may reasonably be read as comprehending unlawful conduct that occurred solely prior to the filing of the lawsuit as well as unlawful conduct that continues into the present." In the District Court's view, this construction of the statutory language was supported by the legislative history and the underlying policy goals of the Act. The District

Court held in the alternative that respondents satisfied the jurisdictional requirements of § 505 because their complaint alleged in good faith that Gwaltney was continuing to violate its permit at the time the suit was filed.

The Court of Appeals affirmed, expressly rejecting the Fifth Circuit's approach in *Hamker* and holding that § 505 "can be read to comprehend unlawful conduct that occurred only prior to the filing of a lawsuit as well as unlawful conduct that continues into the present." The Court of Appeals concluded that its reading of § 505 was consistent with the Act's structure, legislative history, and purpose. Although it observed that "[a] very sound argument can be made that [respondents'] allegations of continuing violations were made in good faith," the Court of Appeals declined to rule on the District Court's alternative holding, finding it unnecessary to the disposition of the case.

Subsequent to the issuance of the Fourth Circuit's opinion, the First Circuit also had occasion to construe § 505. It took a position different from that of either the Fourth or the Fifth Circuit, holding that jurisdiction lies under § 505 when "the citizen-plaintiff fairly alleges a continuing likelihood that the defendant, if not enjoined, will again proceed to violate the Act." *Pawtuxet Cove Marina, Inc. v. Ciba–Geigy Corp.*, 807 F.2d 1089, 1094 (1986). The First Circuit's approach precludes suit based on wholly past violations, but permits suit when there is a pattern of intermittent violations, even if there is no violation at the moment suit is filed. . . .

It is well settled that "the starting point for interpreting a statute is the language of the statute itself." *Consumer Product Safety Comm'n v. GTE Sylvania, Inc.*, 447 U.S. 102, 108 (1980). The Court of Appeals concluded that the "to be in violation" language of § 505 is ambiguous, whereas petitioner asserts that it plainly precludes the construction adopted below. We must agree with the Court of Appeals that § 505 is not a provision in which Congress' limpid prose puts an end to all dispute. But to acknowledge ambiguity is not to conclude that all interpretations are equally plausible. The most natural reading of "to be in violation" is a requirement that citizen-plaintiffs allege a state of either continuous or intermittent violation—that is, a reasonable likelihood that a past polluter will continue to pollute in the future. Congress could have phrased its requirement in language that looked to the past ("to have violated"), but it did not choose this readily available option.

Respondents urge that the choice of the phrase "to be in violation," rather than phrasing more clearly directed to the past, is a "careless accident," the result of a "debatable lapse of syntactical precision." But the prospective orientation of that phrase could not have escaped Congress' attention. Congress used identical language in the citizen suit provisions of several other environmental statutes that authorize only prospective relief. [Citing the Clean Air Act, RCRA, and TSCA]. Moreover, Congress has demonstrated in yet other statutory provisions that it knows how to avoid this prospective implication by using language that explicitly targets wholly past violations.[2]

Respondents seek to counter this reasoning by observing that Congress also used the phrase "is in violation" in § 309(a) of the Act, which authorizes the Administrator of EPA to issue compliance orders. That language is incorporated by reference in § 309(b), which authorizes the Administrator to bring civil enforcement actions. Because it is little questioned that the Administrator may bring enforcement actions to recover civil penalties for wholly past violations, respondents contend, the parallel language of § 309(a) and § 505(a) must mean that citizens, too, may maintain such actions.

Although this argument has some initial plausibility, it cannot withstand close scrutiny and comparison of the two statutory provisions. The Administrator's ability to seek civil penalties is not discussed in either § 309(a) or § 309(b); civil penalties are not mentioned until § 309(d), which does not contain the "is in violation" language. This Court recently has recognized that § 309(d) constitutes a separate grant of enforcement authority:

> "Section 1319 [§ 309] does not intertwine equitable relief with the imposition of civil penalties. Instead each kind of relief is separably authorized in a separate and distinct statutory provision. Subsection (b), providing injunctive relief, is independent of subsection (d), which provides only for civil penalties."

Tull v. United States, 481 U.S. 412, 425 (1987). In contrast, § 505 of the Act does not authorize civil penalties separately from injunctive relief; rather, the two forms of relief are referred to in the same subsection, even in the same sentence. The citizen suit provision suggests a connection between injunctive relief and civil penalties that is noticeably absent from the provision authorizing agency enforcement. A comparison of § 309 and § 505 thus supports rather than refutes our conclusion that citizens, unlike the Administrator, may seek civil penalties only in a suit brought to enjoin or otherwise abate an ongoing violation.

Our reading of the "to be in violation" language of § 505(a) is bolstered by the language and structure of the rest of the citizen suit provisions in § 505 of the Act. These provisions together make plain that the interest of the citizen-plaintiff is primarily forward-looking.

---

2. For example, [RCRA] was amended in 1984 to authorize citizen suits against any "past or present" generator, transporter, owner, or operator of a treatment, storage, or disposal facility "who has contributed or who is contributing" to the "past or present" handling, storage, treatment, transportation, or disposal of certain hazardous wastes. 42 U.S.C. § 6972(a)(1)(B) (1982 ed., Supp. III). Prior to 1984, [RCRA] contained language identical to that of § 505(a) of the Clean Water Act, authorizing citizen suits against any person "alleged to be in violation" of waste disposal permits or standards. 42 U.S.C. § 6972(a)(1). Even more on point, the most recent Clean Water Act amendments permit EPA to assess administrative penalties without judicial process on any person who "has violated" the provisions of the Act. Water Quality Act of 1987, § 314, Pub.L. 100–4, 101 Stat. 46.

One of the most striking indicia of the prospective orientation of the citizen suit is the pervasive use of the present tense throughout § 505. A citizen suit may be brought only for violation of a permit limitation "which is in effect" under the Act. 33 U.S.C. § 1365(f). Citizen-plaintiffs must give notice to the alleged violator, the Administrator of EPA, and the State in which the alleged violation "occurs." § 1365(b)(1)(A). A Governor of a State may sue as a citizen when the Administrator fails to enforce an effluent limitation "the violation of which is occurring in another State and is causing an adverse effect on the public health or welfare in his State." § 1365(h). The most telling use of the present tense is in the definition of "citizen" as "a person . . . having an interest which is or may be adversely affected" by the defendant's violations of the Act. § 1365(g). This definition makes plain what the undeviating use of the present tense strongly suggests: the harm sought to be addressed by the citizen suit lies in the present or the future, not in the past.

Any other conclusion would render incomprehensible § 505's notice provision, which requires citizens to give 60 days' notice of their intent to sue to the alleged violator as well as to the Administrator and the State. If the Administrator or the State commences enforcement action within that 60-day period, the citizen suit is barred, presumably because governmental action has rendered it unnecessary. It follows logically that the purpose of notice to the alleged violator is to give it an opportunity to bring itself into complete compliance with the Act and thus likewise render unnecessary a citizen suit. If we assume, as respondents urge, that citizen suits may target wholly past violations, the requirement of notice to the alleged violator becomes gratuitous. Indeed, respondents, in propounding their interpretation of the Act, can think of no reason for Congress to require such notice other than that "it seemed right" to inform an alleged violator that it was about to be sued.

Adopting respondents' interpretation of § 505's jurisdictional grant would create a second and even more disturbing anomaly. The bar on citizen suits when governmental enforcement action is under way suggests that the citizen suit is meant to supplement rather than to supplant governmental action. The legislative history of the Act reinforces this view of the role of the citizen suit. The Senate Report noted that "[t]he Committee intends the great volume of enforcement actions [to] be brought by the State," and that citizen suits are proper only "if the Federal, State, and local agencies fail to exercise their enforcement responsibility." S.Rep. No. 92–414, p. 64 (1971), *reprinted in* 2 A Legislative History of the Water Pollution Control Act Amendments of 1972, p. 1482 (1973) (hereinafter Leg.Hist.). Permitting citizen suits for wholly past violations of the Act could undermine the supplementary role envisioned for the citizen suit. This danger is best illustrated by an example. Suppose that the Administrator identified a violator of the Act and issued a compliance order under § 309(a). Suppose further that the Administrator agreed not to assess or otherwise seek civil penalties on the condition that the violator take some extreme corrective action, such as to install particularly effective but expensive machinery, that it

[handwritten margin note: Present tense in statute]

otherwise would not be obliged to take. If citizens could file suit, months or years later, in order to seek the civil penalties that the Administrator chose to forgo, then the Administrator's discretion to enforce the Act in the public interest would be curtailed considerably. The same might be said of the discretion of state enforcement authorities. Respondents' interpretation of the scope of the citizen suit would change the nature of the citizens' role from interstitial to potentially intrusive. We cannot agree that Congress intended such a result.

Our conclusion that § 505 does not permit citizen suits for wholly past violations does not necessarily dispose of this lawsuit, as both lower courts recognized. The District Court found persuasive the fact that "[respondents'] allegation in the complaint, that Gwaltney was continuing to violate its NPDES permit when plaintiffs filed suit[,] appears to have been made fully in good faith." On this basis, the District Court explicitly held, albeit in a footnote, that "even if Gwaltney were correct that a district court has no jurisdiction over citizen suits based entirely on unlawful conduct that occurred entirely in the past, the Court would still have jurisdiction here." The Court of Appeals acknowledged, also in a footnote, that "[a] very sound argument can be made that [respondents'] allegations of continuing violations were made in good faith," but expressly declined to rule on this alternative holding. Because we agree that § 505 confers jurisdiction over citizen suits when the citizen-plaintiffs make a good-faith allegation of continuous or intermittent violation, we remand the case to the Court of Appeals for further consideration.

Petitioner argues that citizen-plaintiffs must prove their allegations of ongoing noncompliance before jurisdiction attaches under § 505. We cannot agree. The statute does not require that a defendant "be in violation" of the Act at the commencement of suit; rather, the statute requires that a defendant be "alleged to be in violation." Petitioner's construction of the Act reads the word "alleged" out of § 505. As petitioner itself is quick to note in other contexts, there is no reason to believe that Congress' drafting of § 505 was sloppy or haphazard. We agree with the Solicitor General that "Congress's use of the phrase 'alleged to be in violation' reflects a conscious sensitivity to the practical difficulties of detecting and proving chronic episodic violations of environmental standards." Our acknowledgment that Congress intended a good-faith allegation to suffice for jurisdictional purposes, however, does not give litigants license to flood the courts with suits premised on baseless allegations. Rule 11 of the Federal Rules of Civil Procedure, which requires pleadings to be based on a good-faith belief, formed after reasonable inquiry, that they are "well grounded in fact," adequately protects defendants from frivolous allegations.

Petitioner contends that failure to require proof of allegations under § 505 would permit plaintiffs whose allegations of ongoing violation are reasonable but untrue to maintain suit in federal court even though they lack constitutional standing. Petitioner reasons that if a defendant is in complete compliance with the Act at the time of suit, plaintiffs have suffered no injury remediable by the citizen suit provisions of the Act. Petitioner, however, fails to recognize that our standing cases uniformly recognize that allegations of injury are sufficient to invoke the jurisdiction of a court. In *Warth v. Seldin*, 422 U.S. 490, 501 (1975), for example, we made clear that a suit will not be dismissed for lack of standing if there are sufficient "allegations of fact"—not proof—in the complaint or supporting affidavits. This is not to say, however, that such allegations may not be challenged. In *United States v. SCRAP*, 412 U.S. 669, 689 (1973), we noted that if the plaintiffs' "allegations [of standing] were in fact untrue, then the [defendants] should have moved for summary judgment on the standing issue and demonstrated to the District Court that the allegations were sham and raised no genuine issue of fact." If the defendant fails to make such a showing after the plaintiff offers evidence to support the allegation, the case proceeds to trial on the merits, where the plaintiff must prove the allegations in order to prevail. But the Constitution does not require that the plaintiff offer this proof as a threshold matter in order to invoke the District Court's jurisdiction.

Petitioner also worries that our construction of § 505 would permit citizen-plaintiffs, if their allegations of ongoing noncompliance become false at some later point in the litigation because the defendant begins to comply with the Act, to continue nonetheless to press their suit to conclusion. According to petitioner, such a result would contravene both the prospective purpose of the citizen suit provisions and the "case or controversy" requirement of Article III. Longstanding principles of mootness, however, prevent the maintenance of suit when " 'there is no reasonable expectation that the wrong will be repeated.' " *United States v. W.T. Grant Co.*, 345 U.S. 629, 633, (1953). In seeking to have a case dismissed as moot, however, the defendant's burden "is a heavy one." 345 U.S., at 633. The defendant must demonstrate that it is "absolutely clear that the allegedly wrongful behavior could not reasonably be expected to recur." *United States v. Phosphate Export Assn., Inc.*, 393 U.S. 199, 203 (1968). Mootness doctrine thus protects defendants from the maintenance of suit under the Clean Water Act based solely on violations wholly unconnected to any present or future wrongdoing, while it also protects plaintiffs from defendants who seek to evade sanction by predictable "protestations of repentance and reform." *United States v. Oregon State Medical Society*, 343 U.S. 326, 333 (1952).

Because the court below erroneously concluded that respondents could maintain an action based on wholly past violations of the Act, it declined to decide whether respondents' complaint contained a good-faith allegation of ongoing violation by petitioner. We therefore remand the case for consideration of this question. The judgment of the Court of Appeals is vacated, and the case is remanded for further proceedings consistent with this opinion.

Notes and Comments

1. How persuasive was the Court's statutory analysis in *Gwaltney*? Do you agree that any other reading would render incomprehensible § 505's

requirement that the plaintiff give notice to the alleged violator, in addition to the EPA and the state? Interestingly, the legislative histories of both § 505 and its predecessor provision in the Clean Air Act (§ 304) are silent as to why Congress required notice to the alleged violator. Are there any other possible explanations as to why Congress may have done so? In writing for the majority, Justice Marshall also relied in part on the fact that § 505(b)(1)(B) bars citizen suits when either EPA or the State undertakes diligent enforcement action. Does this bar support the Court's interpretation? In answering this question, keep in mind that "diligent prosecution" does not necessarily result in immediate compliance—there are some situations in which even aggressive enforcement actions will result in compliance schedules that may have yet to have run their course when a citizens group files its action. In such situations, shouldn't the bar apply? On the other hand, might not there be some situations in which a prior governmental enforcement action might be deemed to be non-diligent, even though the violation might be wholly past—such as, for example, a situation in which a State imposes no fine for several flagrant and serious (though wholly-past) hazardous waste disposal events? If these things are true, does this undermine the Court's conclusion that the presence of the bar sheds light on the "wholly past" violation issue? As we will see in our consideration of these bar provisions, below, Justice Marshall's paragraph on this dynamic in *Gwaltney* has had a significant effect on how some courts have interpreted those provisions.

2. Regardless of what one thinks of some of the issues raised in the previous note, the Supreme Court's holding in *Gwaltney* clearly reflects a defensible reading of § 505(a)(1) itself. The ultimate test the Court established has two parts. First, at the time of filing the plaintiff must make "a good faith allegation of continuous or intermittent violation." Second, so long as the plaintiff submits enough evidence to survive a motion for summary judgment, "the case proceeds to trial on the merits, where the plaintiff must prove the allegations to prevail." How does this differ from the test that the petitioner advanced? What is the practical effect of this distinction? How should a court determine whether the plaintiff's allegations were made in good faith?

3. The *Gwaltney* majority did not address with any specificity how plaintiffs should go about proving the required continuous or intermittent violations at trial. In his concurrence, Justice Scalia offered the following:

> . . . The phrase in § 505(a), "to be in violation," unlike the phrase "to be violating" or "to have committed a violation," suggests a state rather than an act—the opposite of a state of compliance. A good or lucky day is not a state of compliance. Nor is the dubious state in which a past effluent problem is not recurring at the moment but the cause of that problem has not been completely and clearly eradicated. When a company has violated an effluent standard or limitation, it remains, for purposes of § 505(a), "in violation" of that standard or limitation so long as it has not put in place remedial measures that clearly eliminate the cause of the violation. It does not suffice to defeat subject-matter jurisdiction that the success of the attempted remedies becomes clear months or even weeks after the suit is filed. Subject-matter jurisdiction "depends on the state of things at the time of the action brought"; if it

existed when the suit was brought, "subsequent events" cannot "ous[t]" the court of jurisdiction.

Thus, I think the question on remand should be whether petitioner had taken remedial steps that had clearly achieved the effect of curing all past violations by the time suit was brought....

484 U.S. at 69–70 (citations omitted). On remand, the Fourth Circuit determined that the plaintiffs could prevail by either "(1) by proving violations that continue on or after the date the complaint is filed, or (2) by adducing evidence from which a reasonable trier of fact could find a continuing likelihood of a recurrence in intermittent or sporadic violations." *Chesapeake Bay Found., Inc. v. Gwaltney of Smithfield, Ltd.*, 844 F.2d 170, 171–172 (4th Cir. 1988). This test has been universally embraced by other courts. See, e.g., *Atlantic States Legal Found., Inc. v. Stroh Die Casting Co.*, 116 F.3d 814, 825 (7th Cir. 1997).

4.   Most lower courts have concluded that they should analyze *Gwaltney* issues on a "parameter-by-parameter" basis; that is, they should recognize that a facility may have solved some problems but not others by the time the complaint is filed, and that should treat each problem separately for purposes of determining whether the relevant violations were in wholly past. In *Gwaltney*, for example, the Fourth Circuit ultimately determined that the company had solved its chlorine problems, but not its TKN problems, before the complaint was filed. Thus, the court determined that it should uphold that portion of the penalty relating to the TKN violations ($289,822), but reverse that portion relating to the chlorine issues ($995,500). *Chesapeake Bay Found., Inc. v. Gwaltney of Smithfield, Ltd.*, 890 F.2d 690, 687–698 (4th Cir. 1989). Do you agree that this is the proper mode of analysis?

In the penultimate paragraph of his majority opinion in *Gwaltney*, Justice Marshall noted that the petitioner raised Article III questions regarding the plaintiffs' ability to continue to press their lawsuit if the violations ceased. This contention invoked both redressability and mootness concerns. This is perhaps unsurprising given that, as noted in the continuation of *Laidlaw* below, the Supreme Court has often described the doctrine of mootness as "the doctrine of standing set in a time frame: The requisite personal interest that must exist at the commencement of the litigation (standing) must continue throughout its existence (mootness)." *Arizonans for Official English v. Arizona*, 520 U.S. 43, 68, n.22, 117 S.Ct. 1055, 137 L.Ed.2d 170 (1997). On the redressability front, the theory is that, at least in situations in which there is no ongoing violation, the plaintiffs receive no Constitutionally-cognizable benefit from penalties paid to the Treasury. While this might be a pure standing argument in situations in which the defendant eliminated the violations before the lawsuit was filed, it morphs into a mootness argument where the purported solution occurs during the pendency of the suit.

The petitioner in *Gwaltney* was apparently hedging its bets, arguing that it had solved all of its problems before the suit was filed, while at the same time raising concerns about whether the lawsuit should continue if it solved them during its pendency. Interestingly, even the first of these theories posed standing issues. Despite that, however, the majority addressed the effect of the allegedly wholly-past nature of the violations solely on statutory grounds. Indeed, the Court's only mention of standing is in its mootness discussion in the second-to-last paragraph.

The fact that the Supreme Court resolved the primary issue in *Gwaltney* solely on statutory grounds raised the question of whether Congress could "fix" the *Gwaltney* result by amending the citizen suit provisions to specifically authorize citizen actions with respect to wholly past violations. Indeed, Congress moved to do essentially that when it amended the Clean Air Act in 1990, allowing suits against those alleged "to have violated" the relevant CAA standards, at least in situations in which the violations were not one-time events. See 42 U.S.C. § 7004(a)(1). Before too long, however, the Supreme Court returned to "wholly past violation" issue in *Steel Co. v. Citizens for a Better Environment*, 523 U.S. 83, 118 S.Ct. 1003, 140 L.Ed.2d 210 (1998).

Steel Co. involved a situation in which the plaintiff, before filing suit, had sent the defendant a notice letter under the Emergency Planning and Community Right–To–Know Act of 1986, 42 U.S.C. § 11001 et seq. (EP-CRA). In its notice, the plaintiff alleged that Steel Co. had violated the statute for seven years by failing to submit the required chemical inventory forms. During the 60–day notice period, the defendant submitted all of the required forms, and, when the suit was filed, argued that the plaintiffs could not maintain an action for wholly past violations. Ultimately, the Seventh Circuit held that they could, determining that EPCRA's citizen-suit provision (42 U.S.C. § 11046) was worded sufficiently differently from § 505 of the CWA so as to call for a contrary result. *Citizens for a Better Environment v. Steel Co.*, 90 F.3d 1237 (7th Cir. 1996). This created a split in the Circuits. Compare *Atlantic States Legal Found., Inc. v. United Musical Instruments, U.S.A., Inc.*, 61 F.3d 473 (Sixth Cir. 1995) (deeming *Gwaltney* applicable).

When *Steel Co.* reached the Supreme Court, Justice Scalia, writing for the majority, did not even address the statutory question. Instead, he resolved the case on standing grounds, finding that, absent ongoing violations, penalties payable to the Treasury do not provide sufficient redressability to support standing under Article III. 523 U.S. at 107. In response to Justice Stevens' argument that the deterrent effect that penalties would have on Steel Co. should suffice, id. at 127 (dissenting), Justice Scalia responded as follows:

> Justice Stevens thinks it is enough that respondent will be gratified by seeing petitioner punished for its infractions and that the punishment will deter the risk of future harm.... Obviously, such a principle would make the redressability requirement vanish. By the mere bringing of his suit, every plaintiff demonstrates his belief that a favorable judgment will make him happier. But although a suitor may derive great comfort and joy from the fact that the United States Treasury is not cheated, that a wrongdoer gets his just deserts, or that the nation's laws are faithfully enforced, that psychic satisfaction is not an acceptable Article III remedy because it does not redress a cognizable Article III injury. Relief that does not remedy the injury suffered cannot bootstrap a plaintiff into federal court; that is the very essence of the redressability requirement.

Id. at 106–107.

Steel Co. essentially constitutionalized the *Gwaltney* doctrine; that is, it established that Article III precludes Congress from "solving" the "*Gwaltney* problem" simply by making clear its desire that citizen plaintiffs be able to pursue penalties payable to the Treasury for wholly-past violations. Additionally, the Court's view that penalties payable to the Treasury yield citizen plaintiffs only "psychic satisfaction" raised the question whether such citizens should ever be able seek this form of relief, even where there are ongoing violations.

At the same time that these issues were percolating, the Courts of Appeals were wrestling with the mootness issues posed by *Gwaltney*. How difficult would it be for a citizen-suit defendant to show that it was "absolutely clear that the allegedly wrongful behavior could not reasonably be expected to recur?" And what was the effect of such a showing, if made? Did it result in the mooting only of any claims for injunctive relief, or did it moot the entire case, including the claims for penalties for past violations (both pre-and post-complaint)?

Most court resolved these issues in ways that favored the plaintiffs, emphasizing the difficulty of establishing mootness in the "voluntary cessation" context, and limiting its effect when demonstrated to claims for injunctive relief. See, e.g., *Atlantic States Legal Foundation, Inc. v. Pan Am. Tanning Corp.*, 993 F.2d 1017, 1019–1021 (2d Cir. 1993); *Chesapeake Bay Foundation, Inc. v. Gwaltney of Smithfield, Ltd.*, 890 F.2d 690, 696–697 (4th Cir. 1989); *Atlantic States Legal Foundation, Inc. v. Stroh Die Casting Co.*, 116 F.3d 814, 820 and 822 (7th Cir.), *cert. denied*, 522 U.S. 981, 118 S.Ct. 442, 139 L.Ed.2d 379 (1997); *Natural Resources Defense Council v. Texaco Refining & Mktg., Inc.*, 2 F.3d 493, 502–504 (3d Cir. 1993) (on the penalty issue); and *Atlantic States Legal Foundation, Inc. v. Tyson Foods, Inc.*, 897 F.2d 1128, 1134–1137 (11th Cir. 1990) (same); compare *Comfort Lake Assn. v. Dresel Contracting, Inc.*, 138 F.3d 351, 356 (8th Cir. 1998) (agreeing with the above cases, but applying different rules where the case was mooted by regulatory enforcement actions).

The most discordant opinion was the Fourth Circuit's in *Friends of the Earth, Inc. v. Laidlaw Environmental Services (TOC), Inc.*, 149 F.3d 303 (4th Cir. 1998). There, the court relied on *Steel Co.* in finding the case to be moot because the lower court had denied the plaintiffs' claim for injunctive relief. The court reasoned that, if penalties were all that was at issue, they would provide no redress to the plaintiffs and thus could not provide a basis for ongoing jurisdiction in the case. *Id.* at 306–307.

This set the stage for the Supreme Court's consideration in *Laidlaw*, the injury portion of which we already have considered. We now present those portions of *Laidlaw* addressing the redressability and mootness issues:

FRIENDS OF THE EARTH, INC. v. LAIDLAW ENVIRONMENTAL SERVICES

Supreme Court of the United States, 2000.
528 U.S. 167, 120 S.Ct. 693, 145 L.Ed.2d 610.

Justice GINSBURG delivered the opinion of the Court.

Laidlaw argues next that even if FOE had standing to seek injunctive relief, it lacked standing to seek civil penalties. Here the asserted defect is not injury but redressability. Civil penalties offer no redress to private plaintiffs, Laidlaw argues, because they are paid to the government, and therefore a citizen plaintiff can never have standing to seek them.

Laidlaw is right to insist that a plaintiff must demonstrate standing separately for each form of relief sought. But it is wrong to maintain that citizen plaintiffs facing ongoing violations never have standing to seek civil penalties.

We have recognized on numerous occasions that "all civil penalties have some deterrent effect." *Hudson v. United States*, 522 U.S. 93, 102 (1997). More specifically, Congress has found that civil penalties in Clean Water Act cases do more than promote immediate compliance by limiting the defendant's economic incentive to delay its attainment of permit limits; they also deter future violations. This congressional determination warrants judicial attention and respect. "The legislative history of the Act reveals that Congress wanted the district court to consider the need for retribution and deterrence, in addition to restitution, when it imposed civil penalties. . . . [The district court may] seek to deter future violations by basing the penalty on its economic impact." *Tull v. United States*, 481 U.S. 412, 422–423 (1987).

It can scarcely be doubted that, for a plaintiff who is injured or faces the threat of future injury due to illegal conduct ongoing at the time of suit, a sanction that effectively abates that conduct and prevents its recurrence provides a form of redress. Civil penalties can fit that description. To the extent that they encourage defendants to discontinue current violations and deter them from committing future ones, they afford redress to citizen plaintiffs who are injured or threatened with injury as a consequence of ongoing unlawful conduct.

The dissent argues that it is the availability rather than the imposition of civil penalties that deters any particular polluter from continuing to pollute. This argument misses the mark in two ways. First, it overlooks the interdependence of the availability and the imposition; a threat has no deterrent value unless it is credible that it will be carried out. Second, it is reasonable for Congress to conclude that an actual award of civil penalties does in fact bring with it a significant quantum of deterrence over and above what is achieved by the mere prospect of such penalties. A would-be polluter may or may not be dissuaded by the existence of a remedy on the books, but a defendant once hit in its pocketbook will surely think twice before polluting again.

Laidlaw contends that the reasoning of our decision in *Steel Co.* directs the conclusion that citizen plaintiffs have no standing to seek civil penalties under the Act. We disagree. *Steel Co.* established that citizen suitors lack standing to seek civil penalties for violations that have abated by the time of suit. We specifically noted in that case that there was no allegation in the complaint of any continuing or imminent violation, and that no basis for such an allegation appeared to exist. In short, *Steel Co.* held that private plaintiffs, unlike the Federal Government, may not sue to assess penalties for wholly past violations, but our decision in that case did not reach the issue of standing to seek penalties for violations that are ongoing at the time of the complaint and that could continue into the future if undeterred.[4]

Satisfied that FOE had standing under Article III to bring this action, we turn to the question of mootness.

The only conceivable basis for a finding of mootness in this case is Laidlaw's voluntary conduct—either its achievement by August 1992 of substantial compliance with its NPDES permit or its more recent shutdown of the Roebuck facility. It is well settled that "a defendant's voluntary cessation of a challenged practice does not deprive a federal court of its power to determine the legality of the practice." [*City of Mesquite v. Aladdin's Castle*, 455 U.S. 283, 289 (1982)]. "[I]f it did, the courts would be compelled to leave '[t]he defendant . . . free to return to his old ways.' " Id., at 289, n. 10. In accordance with this principle, the standard we have announced for determining whether a case has been mooted by the defendant's voluntary conduct is stringent: "A case might become moot if subsequent events made it absolutely clear that the allegedly wrongful behavior could not reasonably be expected to recur." *United States v. Concentrated Phosphate Export Assn.*, 393 U.S. 199, 203 (1968). The "heavy burden of persua[ding]" the court that the challenged conduct cannot reasonably be expected to start up again lies with the party asserting mootness. Ibid.

The Court of Appeals justified its mootness disposition by reference to *Steel Co.*, which held that citizen plaintiffs lack standing to seek civil penalties for wholly past violations. In relying on *Steel Co.*, the Court of Appeals confused mootness with standing. The confusion is understandable, given this Court's repeated statements that the doctrine of mootness can be described as "the doctrine of standing set in a time frame: The requisite personal interest that must exist at the commencement of the litigation (standing) must continue throughout its existence (mootness)." *Arizonans for Official English*, 520 U.S., at 68, n. 22.

Careful reflection on the long-recognized exceptions to mootness, however, reveals that the description of mootness as "standing set in a time frame" is not comprehensive. As just noted, a defendant claiming that its voluntary compliance moots a case bears the formidable burden of showing that it is absolutely clear the allegedly wrongful behavior could not reasonably be expected to recur. By contrast, in a lawsuit

---

4. . . . [T]he dissent's . . . charge that citizen suits for civil penalties under the Act carry "grave implications for democratic governance" seems to us overdrawn. Certainly the federal Executive Branch does not share the dissent's view that such suits dissipate its authority to enforce the law. In fact, the Department of Justice has endorsed this citizen suit from the outset, submitting amicus briefs in support of FOE in the District Court, the Court of Appeals, and this Court. As we have already noted, the Federal Government retains the power to foreclose a citizen suit by undertaking its own action. 33 U.S.C. § 1365(b)(1)(B). And if the Executive Branch opposes a particular citizen suit, the statute allows the Administrator of the EPA to "intervene as a matter of right" and bring the Government's views to the attention of the court. § 1365(c)(2).

brought to force compliance, it is the plaintiff's burden to establish standing by demonstrating that, if unchecked by the litigation, the defendant's allegedly wrongful behavior will likely occur or continue, and that the "threatened injury [is] certainly impending." [*Whitmore v. Arkansas*, 495 U.S. 149, 158 (1990)]. Thus, in *Lyons*, as already noted, we held that a plaintiff lacked initial standing to seek an injunction against the enforcement of a police chokehold policy because he could not credibly allege that he faced a realistic threat arising from the policy. 461 U.S., at 105–110. Elsewhere in the opinion, however, we noted that a citywide moratorium on police chokeholds—an action that surely diminished the already slim likelihood that any particular individual would be choked by police—would not have mooted an otherwise valid claim for injunctive relief, because the moratorium by its terms was not permanent. Id., at 101. The plain lesson of these cases is that there are circumstances in which the prospect that a defendant will engage in (or resume) harmful conduct may be too speculative to support standing, but not too speculative to overcome mootness.

Laidlaw also asserts, in a supplemental suggestion of mootness, that the closure of its Roebuck facility, which took place after the Court of Appeals issued its decision, mooted the case. The facility closure, like Laidlaw's earlier achievement of substantial compliance with its permit requirements, might moot the case, but—we once more reiterate—only if one or the other of these events made it absolutely clear that Laidlaw's permit violations could not reasonably be expected to recur. The effect of both Laidlaw's compliance and the facility closure on the prospect of future violations is a disputed factual matter. FOE points out, for example—and Laidlaw does not appear to contest—that Laidlaw retains its NPDES permit. These issues have not been aired in the lower courts; they remain open for consideration on remand.

Justice STEVENS, concurring.

... [P]etitioners' claim for civil penalties would not be moot even if it were absolutely clear that respondent's violations could not reasonably be expected to recur because respondent achieved substantial compliance with its permit requirements after petitioners filed their complaint but before the District Court entered judgment. As the Courts of Appeals (other than the court below) have uniformly concluded, a polluter's voluntary post-complaint cessation of an alleged violation will not moot a citizen-suit claim for civil penalties even if it is sufficient to moot a related claim for injunctive or declaratory relief. [Citations]. This conclusion is consistent with the structure of the Clean Water Act, which attaches liability for civil penalties at the time a permit violation occurs. 33 U.S.C. § 1319(d) ("Any person who violates [certain provisions of the Act or certain permit conditions and limitations] shall be subject to a civil penalty ... ").....

Justice KENNEDY, concurring.

Difficult and fundamental questions are raised when we ask whether exactions of public fines by private litigants, and the delegation of

Executive power which might be inferable from the authorization, are permissible in view of the responsibilities committed to the Executive by Article II of the Constitution of the United States. The questions presented in the petition for certiorari did not identify these issues with particularity; and neither the Court of Appeals in deciding the case nor the parties in their briefing before this Court devoted specific attention to the subject. In my view these matters are best reserved for a later case. With this observation, I join the opinion of the Court.

Justice SCALIA, with whom Justice THOMAS joins, dissenting.

... Only last Term, we held that such penalties do not redress any injury a citizen plaintiff has suffered from past violations. *Steel Co.*, 523 U.S. 83, 106–107 (1998). The Court nonetheless finds the redressability requirement satisfied here, distinguishing *Steel Co.* on the ground that in this case the petitioners allege ongoing violations; payment of the penalties, it says, will remedy petitioners' injury by deterring future violations by Laidlaw. It holds that a penalty payable to the public "remedies" a threatened private harm, and suffices to sustain a private suit.

That holding has no precedent in our jurisprudence, and takes this Court beyond the "cases and controversies" that Article III of the Constitution has entrusted to its resolution. Even if it were appropriate, moreover, to allow Article III's remediation requirement to be satisfied by the indirect private consequences of a public penalty, those consequences are entirely too speculative in the present case. The new standing law that the Court makes—like all expansions of standing beyond the traditional constitutional limits—has grave implications for democratic governance....

The Court recognizes, of course, that to satisfy Article III, it must be "likely," as opposed to "merely speculative," that a favorable decision will redress plaintiffs' injury, [*Lujan*, 504 U.S. at 561].... It concludes, however, that in the present case "the civil penalties sought by FOE carried with them a deterrent effect" that satisfied the "likely [rather than] speculative" standard. Ibid. There is little in the Court's opinion to explain why it believes this is so.

The Court points out that we have previously said "all civil penalties have some deterrent effect." That is unquestionably true: As a general matter, polluters as a class are deterred from violating discharge limits by the availability of civil penalties. However, none of the cases the Court cites focused on the deterrent effect of a single imposition of penalties on a particular lawbreaker. Even less did they focus on the question whether that particularized deterrent effect (if any) was enough to redress the injury of a citizen plaintiff in the sense required by Article III. They all involved penalties pursued by the government, not by citizens.

If the Court had undertaken the necessary inquiry into whether significant deterrence of the plaintiffs' feared injury was "likely," it would have had to reason something like this: Strictly speaking, no polluter is deterred by a penalty for past pollution; he is deterred by the fear of a penalty for future pollution. That fear will be virtually nonexistent if the prospective polluter knows that all emissions violators are given a free pass; it will be substantial under an emissions program such as the federal scheme here, which is regularly and notoriously enforced; it will be even higher when a prospective polluter subject to such a regularly enforced program has, as here, been the object of public charges of pollution and a suit for injunction; and it will surely be near the top of the graph when, as here, the prospective polluter has already been subjected to state penalties for the past pollution. The deterrence on which the plaintiffs must rely for standing in the present case is the marginal increase in Laidlaw's fear of future penalties that will be achieved by adding federal penalties for Laidlaw's past conduct.

I cannot say for certain that this marginal increase is zero; but I can say for certain that it is entirely speculative whether it will make the difference between these plaintiffs' suffering injury in the future and these plaintiffs' going unharmed. In fact, the assertion that it will "likely" do so is entirely farfetched. . . .

Article II of the Constitution commits it to the President to "take Care that the Laws be faithfully executed," Art. II, § 3, and provides specific methods by which all persons exercising significant executive power are to be appointed, Art. II, § 2. As Justice Kennedy's concurrence correctly observes, the question of the conformity of this legislation with Article II has not been argued—and I, like the Court, do not address it. But Article III, no less than Article II, has consequences for the structure of our government, and it is worth noting the changes in that structure which today's decision allows.

By permitting citizens to pursue civil penalties payable to the Federal Treasury, the Act does not provide a mechanism for individual relief in any traditional sense, but turns over to private citizens the function of enforcing the law. A Clean Water Act plaintiff pursuing civil penalties acts as a self-appointed mini-EPA. Where, as is often the case, the plaintiff is a national association, it has significant discretion in choosing enforcement targets. Once the association is aware of a reported violation, it need not look long for an injured member, at least under the theory of injury the Court applies today. And once the target is chosen, the suit goes forward without meaningful public control.[2] The availability of civil penalties vastly disproportionate to the individual injury gives citizen plaintiffs massive bargaining power—which is often used to achieve settlements requiring the defendant to support environmental projects of the plaintiffs' choosing. Thus is a public fine diverted to a private interest.

---

2. The Court points out that the government is allowed to intervene in a citizen suit, but this power to "bring the Government's views to the attention of the court," is meager substitute for the power to decide whether prosecution will occur. Indeed, according the Chief Executive of the United States the ability to intervene does no more than place him on a par with John Q. Public, who can intervene—whether the government likes it or not—when the United States files suit. § 1365(b)(1)(B).

To be sure, the EPA may foreclose the citizen suit by itself bringing suit. 33 U.S.C. § 1365(b)(1)(B). This allows public authorities to avoid private enforcement only by accepting private direction as to when enforcement should be undertaken—which is no less constitutionally bizarre. Elected officials are entirely deprived of their discretion to decide that a given violation should not be the object of suit at all, or that the enforcement decision should be postponed.[3] This is the predictable and inevitable consequence of the Court's allowing the use of public remedies for private wrongs.

Notes and Comments

1.   As mentioned, *Steel Co.* makes clear that Congress cannot "solve" the *"Gwaltney* problem" simply by making clear its desire that citizen plaintiffs be able to pursue penalties payable to the Treasury for wholly-past violations. What if Congress provides the possibility of other forms of relief. In 1990, for example, Congress amended the Clean Air Act to specifically allow up to $100,000 of any penalty imposed in a CAA citizen suit to be diverted to "beneficial mitigation projects" (which are presumably similar to what EPA refers to as a "supplemental environmental project" in its SEP Policy). 42 U.S.C. § 7604(g)(2). Recall that Congress also amended the CAA to allow citizen suits for at least some wholly-past violations. See 42 U.S.C. § 7604(a)(1). Should the potential availability of these mitigation projects provide the required redressability? If so, should it also citizens to seek additional penalty amounts payable to the Treasury?

2.   Note the starkness of the argument Laidlaw was advancing regarding penalties. If it had succeeded in establishing that citizens cannot seek penalties payable to the Treasury even where there are ongoing violations, it may (subject to the potential qualifications in note 1, above) have been the death knell for citizen penalty actions.

3.   What did you make of the debate between Justice Ginsburg and Justice Scalia regarding whether the impact of penalties on a violator's future behavior should be an adequate basis for finding redressability? Do you agree that "a defendant once hit in its pocketbook will surely think twice before polluting again?" Or is it "entirely speculative" as to whether the actual imposition of fines for past violations (as distinct from the threat thereof for new violations) will make such a difference?

4.   In *Steel Co.*, eight Justices (all but Justice Stevens) concurred in the majority's redressability analysis. Two years later, with the composition of the Court unchanged, seven Justices (all but Justices Scalia and Thomas) concurred in the *Laidlaw* redressability analysis. Were you convinced by the distinction the *Laidlaw* Court drew between the two cases? Why is it that penalties provide sufficient redressability in situations in which there are

---

3. The Court observes that "the federal Executive Branch does not share the dissent's view that such suits dissipate its authority to enforce the law," since it has "endorsed this citizen suit from the outset." Of course, in doubtful cases a long and uninterrupted history of presidential acquiescence and approval can shed light upon the constitutional understanding. What we have here—acquiescence and approval by a single Administration—does not deserve passing mention.

ongoing violations, but not where, as in *Steel Co.*, the defendant brought itself into (temporary?) compliance by filing all of the required reports?

5. Do you understand the nature of the burden shifting the Court discusses in its mootness analysis? Note that the combined effect of *Gwaltney*, *Steel Co.* and *Laidlaw* places enormous significance on whether the defendant allegedly eliminates the root cause of the violations before or after the filing of the complaint. If its potentially curative actions were taken before filing, the plaintiff will bear the burden of showing that there is an ongoing violation. On the other hand, if it completes those same steps the day after filing, the defendant will bear the burden of showing that it is "absolutely clear that the allegedly wrongful behavior could not reasonably be expected to recur." Does this make sense?

6. Does *Laidlaw* shed any further light on the difficulty of making the required mootness showing? The post-*Laidlaw* case law suggests that the courts continue to consider this analysis as requiring a fact-specific inquiry, with the results being varied thus far. Compare *Puerto Rico Campers' Ass'n v. Puerto Rico Aqueduct & Sewer Auth.*, 219 F.Supp.2d 201 (D.P.R. 2002), and *San Francisco Baykeeper, Inc. v. Tosco Corp.*, 309 F.3d 1153 (9th Cir. 2002) (neither finding mootness), with *Ailor v. City of Maynardville, Tenn.*, 368 F.3d 587 (6th Cir. 2004), and *Mississippi River Revival, Inc. v. City of Minneapolis*, 319 F.3d 1013, 1016 (8th Cir. 2003) (both finding mootness).

7. What should the effect be if a defendant makes the required mootness demonstration? Thus far, the lower courts seem to be reading *Laidlaw* as indicating that such showings result in the mooting not only of claims for injunctive relief, but also of those for penalties. See, e.g., *Mississippi River Revival*, 319 F.3d at 1016. Do you agree? In answering this question, keep in mind that penalties were the only thing at issue in *Laidlaw*; that is, the plaintiffs had not appealed the district court's denial of their claim for injunctive relief. At the same time, consider the implications of allowing defendants to moot claims for penalties at any time during the course of the lawsuit. If they can do so, how much fear will prospective defendants have of citizen suits if they are confident that they can conclusively resolve their compliance problems during the pendency of any such suits? In such situations, would the plaintiffs at least be entitled to an award of attorney fees? We will address this question in our discussion of fee awards, below.

8. Justices Kennedy and Scalia both hinted at lurking Article II issues in their opinions in *Laidlaw*. As alluded to by Justice Scalia, these issues hinge on what are referred to as the "Take Care" and "Appointments" clauses in Article II. What did you think of Justice Scalia's points and Justice Ginsburg's responses in footnote 4 of the majority opinion? Cf. *Riley v. St. Luke's Episcopal Hospital*, 252 F.3d 749 (5th Cir. 2001) (rejecting an Article II challenge to the False Claims Act).

9. We close this section with a song that one of the authors wrote in response to the Court's opinion in *Laidlaw*, to be sung to the tune of Eric Clapton's "Layla" (originally recorded by Clapton's band Derek and the Dominos, on the album "Layla and Other Assorted Love Songs").

LAIDLAW

by Craig N. Johnston adapted from Layla
(by Eric Clapton and Jim Gordon)

What do we do when we get sued now
If the Court's not on our side?
If we can't rely on standing constraints
Do they expect us to comply?

Laidlaw! What are these non-use injuries?
Laidlaw! Based on subjectivity
Laidlaw! Antonin please ease our worried minds

Defenders gave us consolation
And *Steel Co.* made us paint the town
But like fools, we put our faith in you
You and C.T. got voted down

Laidlaw! What about these penalties?
Laidlaw! Where's the redressability?
Laidlaw! Antonin please ease our worried minds

Let's make the best of the situation
Article II's our last resort
Please don't say we'll never find a way
To keep these plaintiffs out of court

Laidlaw! What was it Sandra didn't see?
Laidlaw! Where were the Chief and Kennedy?
Laidlaw! Antonin please ease our worried minds

Laidlaw! We miss the old majority
Laidlaw! How can we pay these penalties?
Laidlaw! Antonin please ease our worried minds

D. The Effect of Prior Governmental Enforcement Actions

The environmental citizen suit provisions typically contain express provisions addressing the preclusive effect of prior governmental enforcement actions. These provisions tend to fall into one of two categories. Virtually all of the statutes have a provision precluding citizens from filing suit if either EPA or the State "has commenced" and "is diligently prosecuting" an action "in a court" to require compliance with the relevant standard. See, e.g., 33 U.S.C. § 1365(b)(1)(B), 42 U.S.C. § 6972(b)(1)(B), and 42 U.S.C. § 7604(b)(1)(B). Second, a few statutes, notably including the CWA, have an additional provision specifically governing the preclusive effect of administrative-penalty actions. See, e.g., 33 U.S.C. § 1319(g)(6).

Let us first address the more common preclusion provisions. Given that most statutes do not have separate provisions addressing the preclusive effect of administrative actions, as a threshold matter it becomes important to know whether such actions can every qualify as actions "in a court;" if not, administrative actions will never preclude citizen suits under those statutes. Despite the oddness of this result from a policy perspective (does it really make sense to allow for follow-up citizen suits in situations in which EPA may have imposed multi-million dollar administrative penalties under RCRA?), the vast majority of Circuits have determined that Congress meant what it said—i.e, that only judicial enforcement actions may give rise to the bar under these "in a court" formulations. See, e.g., *Texans United for a Safe Economy Education Fund v. Crown Central Petrol. Corp.*, 207 F.3d 789 (5th Cir. 2000) (and cased cited therein). Even the Third Circuit, which is the only Circuit that has diverged from the majority view, established a demanding "substantial equivalence" test that few administrative schemes would ever meet. See, e.g., *Student Public Interest Research Group of New Jersey, Inc. v. Fritsche, Dodge & Olcott, Inc.*, 759 F.2d 1131 (3d Cir. 1985).

In situations in which either EPA or the State either is pursuing or has completed a judicial enforcement action, the key question becomes whether the "diligence" standard has been met. Here also, the courts appear to be of two views. The district court's opinion in *Laidlaw* is indicative of the approach that most courts have taken. There, the court described its approach and its view the tensions inherent in its inquiry in the following terms:

> First, the citizen-plaintiffs bear the burden of proving that the state agency's prosecution was not diligent. This burden is a heavy one because diligence on the part of the enforcement agency is presumed. As several courts have recognized, "the state [enforcement] agency must be given great deference to proceed in a manner it considers in the best interests of all parties involved." *Arkansas Wildlife Fed'n v. ICI Americas Inc.*, 842 F.Supp. 1140, 1147 (E.D.Ark.1993), aff'd, 29 F.3d 376 (8th Cir.1994), cert. denied, 513 U.S. 1147.

Deference to governmental enforcement agencies is appropriate because the CWA delegates the primary enforcement responsibility to designated state and federal agencies. For example, the requirement in section 505(b)(1)(A) that a citizen must file a notice letter sixty days before bringing a private enforcement suit clearly was designed to give the governmental agencies the "first shot" at enforcement. As the Supreme Court stated in *Gwaltney*, "the citizen suit is meant to supplement rather than to supplant governmental action." 484 U.S. at 60. Appropriate limitations on citizen suits generally "allow for smoother operation of ordinary enforcement mechanisms" and encourage out-of-court settlements between agencies and polluters. *Connecticut Coastal Fishermen's Ass'n v. Remington Arms Co.*, 777 F.Supp. 173, 179, 186 (D.Conn.1991), aff'd in part, rev'd in part, 989 F.2d 1305 (2d Cir.1993).

On the other hand, Congress certainly intended to provide private citizens with significant opportunities to participate in the enforcement of the CWA. As the United States Court of Appeals for the Second Circuit stated, "Congress made clear that citizen groups are not to be treated as nuisances or troublemakers but rather as welcomed participants in the vindication of environmental interests." *Friends of the Earth v. Consolidated Rail Corp.*, 768 F.2d 57, 63 (2d Cir.1985). In addition to authorizing citizen suits under section 505, the CWA provides several opportunities for citizens to participate in governmental enforcement activities. Indeed, as noted previously, the last phrase of section 505(b)(1)(B) provides that if a citizen suit is barred by the EPA's or the state's diligent prosecution of a judicial action, "in any such action in a court of the United States any citizen may intervene as a matter of right." 33 U.S.C. § 1365(b)(1)(B).

Thus, the issue presently before the court involves a delicate balance between the Act's preference for governmental enforcement efforts and the recognized policy of allowing private citizens to participate in the enforcement process. Of course, the overriding concern is to assure vigorous enforcement of the CWA to achieve the stated goals of the Act.

890 F.Supp. 470, 486–487 (D.S.C. 1995). With these points in mind, the court went on to engage in a searching review of the record, ultimately determining that South Carolina's enforcement action did not constitute diligent enforcement despite the fact that it resulted in the imposition of a $100,000 penalty. In so finding, the court relied on the fact that the state: (a) began its enforcement action only at the violator's request (to preempt the citizen suit), (b) negotiated the consent decree in record time (to beat the expiration of the notice period), (c) made no effort to even calculate the defendant's economic benefit, although it clearly was substantially in excess of the penalty-amount; (d) waived penalties for future violations despite the fact that the decree lacked a definite date by which compliance would be achieved, and (e) allowed the citizen plaintiffs no effective opportunity to intervene before the consent decree was entered. Id.

The Seventh Circuit took a different approach in *Supporters to Oppose Pollution, Inc. v. The Heritage Group*, 973 F.2d 1320 (7th Cir. 1992) ("*Heritage Group*"). In writing for the majority, Judge Easterbrook, like the *Laidlaw* court, began by referring to Justice Marshall's "supplement" versus "supplant" discussion from *Gwaltney*. He went on, however, to draw a very different conclusion as to its implications for the "diligence" inquiry:

> . . . An Administrator unable to make concessions is unable to obtain them. A private plaintiff waiting in the wings then is the captain of the litigation. And it makes no difference that this person chooses to sue another party. . . .

> "Diligent" prosecution is all the statute requires. Although StOP wants a trial on the question whether the EPA's prosecution was

"diligent," such follow-up inquiries are appropriate only when the agency loses its suit and the private litigant insists that the agency had not tried hard enough. RCRA permits a follow-on private suit if the public suit was not prosecuted diligently. But if the agency prevails in all respects, that is the end; § 6972(b)(1)(B) does not authorize a collateral attack on the agency's strategy or tactics. . . .

Id. at 1324.

Which of these approaches do you think is correct? Cf. *Friends of Milwaukee's Rivers v. Milwaukee Metropolitan Sewerage District*, 382 F.3d 743 (7th Cir. 2004) (in which the Seventh Circuit, without expressly overruling *Heritage Group*, appears to embrace a more aggressive oversight role in evaluating diligence for purposes of analyzing privity in determining whether a citizen suit was barred by res judicata).

As mentioned, some statutes have specific provisions governing the preclusive effect of administrative-penalty actions. The most notable of these provisions, § 309(g)(6) of the CWA, is extremely complex and has given rise to a whole sub-universe of judicial opinions. While the issues are too numerous and complicated to deal with in an overview course, students at least should be aware that the area is a minefield and that the courts are badly split on many of the issues. Compare, e.g., *North & South Rivers Watershed Ass'n v. Scituate*, 949 F.2d 552 (1st Cir. 1991), with *Citizens for a Better Environment–California v. Union Oil Co. Of Calif.*, 83 F.3d 1111 (9th Cir. 1996).

E. Attorney Fees

The environmental citizen suit provisions, like many other statutes adopting the private-attorney-general model, provide for the award of attorney fees and costs to successful plaintiffs. These amounts are to be paid by the defendants. The intent, of course, is to promote citizen enforcement by enabling would-be plaintiffs to retain competent counsel.

The attorney fee aspects of these citizen-suit provisions have been the subject of much litigation. The Supreme Court's most extensive treatment of these issues was in *Hensley v. Eckerhart*, 461 U.S. 424, 103 S.Ct. 1933, 76 L.Ed.2d 40 (1983), a civil rights case. There, Justice Powell included in his majority opinion what is essentially a primer on both what it takes to qualify as a "prevailing party" and how fees should be calculated. We include this portion of the opinion, below. We also include the Court's much more recent opinion in the *Buckhannon* case. This latter case addresses the much more controversial question of whether a plaintiff should be deemed to have "prevailed" if its lawsuit prompts the defendant to come into compliance, but if the defendant does so during the pendency of the case in a way that renders the suit moot.

HENSLEY v. ECKERHART

Supreme Court of the United States, 1983.
461 U.S. 424, 103 S.Ct. 1933, 76 L.Ed.2d 40.

JUSTICE POWELL delivered the opinion of the Court:

A plaintiff must be a "prevailing party" to recover an attorney's fee under [42 U.S.C. § 1988]. The standard for making this threshold determination has been framed in various ways. A typical formulation is that "plaintiffs may be considered 'prevailing parties' for attorney's fees purposes if they succeed on any significant issue in litigation which achieves some of the benefit the parties sought in bringing suit." *Nadeau v. Helgemoe*, 581 F.2d 275, 278–279 (CA1 1978). This is a generous formulation that brings the plaintiff only across the statutory threshold. It remains for the district court to determine what fee is "reasonable."

The most useful starting point for determining the amount of a reasonable fee is the number of hours reasonably expended on the litigation multiplied by a reasonable hourly rate. This calculation provides an objective basis on which to make an initial estimate of the value of a lawyer's services. The party seeking an award of fees should submit evidence supporting the hours worked and rates claimed. Where the documentation of hours is inadequate, the district court may reduce the award accordingly.

The district court also should exclude from this initial fee calculation hours that were not "reasonably expended." S.Rep. No. 94–1011, p. 6 (1976). Cases may be overstaffed, and the skill and experience of lawyers vary widely. Counsel for the prevailing party should make a good faith effort to exclude from a fee request hours that are excessive, redundant, or otherwise unnecessary, just as a lawyer in private practice ethically is obligated to exclude such hours from his fee submission. "In the private sector, 'billing judgment' is an important component in fee setting. It is no less important here. Hours that are not properly billed to one's client also are not properly billed to one's *adversary* pursuant to statutory authority." *Copeland v. Marshall*, 641 F.2d 880, 891 (1980) (en banc).

The product of reasonable hours times a reasonable rate does not end the inquiry. There remain other considerations that may lead the district court to adjust the fee upward or downward, including the important factor of the "results obtained." This factor is particularly crucial where a plaintiff is deemed "prevailing" even though he succeeded on only some of his claims for relief. In this situation two questions must be addressed. First, did the plaintiff fail to prevail on claims that were unrelated to the claims on which he succeeded? Second, did the plaintiff achieve a level of success that makes the hours reasonably expended a satisfactory basis for making a fee award?

In some cases a plaintiff may present in one lawsuit distinctly different claims for relief that are based on different facts and legal theories. In such a suit, even where the claims are brought against the same defendants—often an institution and its officers, as in this case—counsel's work on one claim will be unrelated to his work on another claim. Accordingly, work on an unsuccessful claim cannot be deemed to have been "expended in pursuit of the ultimate result achieved." *Davis v. County of Los Angeles*, 8 E.P.D. P 9444 (CD Cal.1974). The congressional intent to limit awards to prevailing parties requires that these unrelated claims be treated as if they had been raised in separate lawsuits, and therefore no fee may be awarded for services on the unsuccessful claim.

It may well be that cases involving such unrelated claims are unlikely to arise with great frequency. Many civil rights cases will present only a single claim. In other cases the plaintiff's claims for relief will involve a common core of facts or will be based on related legal theories. Much of counsel's time will be devoted generally to the litigation as a whole, making it difficult to divide the hours expended on a claim-by-claim basis. Such a lawsuit cannot be viewed as a series of discrete claims. Instead the district court should focus on the significance of the overall relief obtained by the plaintiff in relation to the hours reasonably expended on the litigation.

Where a plaintiff has obtained excellent results, his attorney should recover a fully compensatory fee. Normally this will encompass all hours reasonably expended on the litigation, and indeed in some cases of exceptional success an enhanced award may be justified. In these circumstances the fee award should not be reduced simply because the plaintiff failed to prevail on every contention raised in the lawsuit. Litigants in good faith may raise alternative legal grounds for a desired outcome, and the court's rejection of or failure to reach certain grounds is not a sufficient reason for reducing a fee. The result is what matters.[11]

If, on the other hand, a plaintiff has achieved only partial or limited success, the product of hours reasonably expended on the litigation as a whole times a reasonable hourly rate may be an excessive amount. This will be true even where the plaintiff's claims were interrelated, nonfrivolous, and raised in good faith. Congress has not authorized an award of fees whenever it was reasonable for a plaintiff to bring a lawsuit or whenever conscientious counsel tried the case with devotion and skill. Again, the most critical factor is the degree of success obtained.

11. We agree with the District Court's rejection of "a mathematical approach comparing the total number of issues in the case with those actually prevailed upon." Such a ratio provides little aid in determining what is a reasonable fee in light of all the relevant factors. Nor is it necessarily significant that a prevailing plaintiff did not receive all the relief requested. For example, a plaintiff who failed to recover damages but obtained injunctive relief, or vice versa, may recover a fee award based on all hours reasonably expended if the relief obtained justified that expenditure of attorney time.

Application of this principle is particularly important in complex civil rights litigation involving numerous challenges to institutional practices or conditions. This type of litigation is lengthy and demands many hours of lawyers' services. Although the plaintiff often may succeed in identifying some unlawful practices or conditions, the range of possible success is vast. That the plaintiff is a "prevailing party" therefore may say little about whether the expenditure of counsel's time was reasonable in relation to the success achieved. In this case, for example, the District Court's award of fees based on 2,557 hours worked may have been reasonable in light of the substantial relief obtained. But had respondents prevailed on only one of their six general claims, . . . a fee award based on the claimed hours clearly would have been excessive.

There is no precise rule or formula for making these determinations. The district court may attempt to identify specific hours that should be eliminated, or it may simply reduce the award to account for the limited success. The court necessarily has discretion in making this equitable judgment. This discretion, however, must be exercised in light of the considerations we have identified.

A request for attorney's fees should not result in a second major litigation. Ideally, of course, litigants will settle the amount of a fee. Where settlement is not possible, the fee applicant bears the burden of establishing entitlement to an award and documenting the appropriate hours expended and hourly rates. The applicant should exercise "billing judgment" with respect to hours worked and should maintain billing time records in a manner that will enable a reviewing court to identify distinct claims.

We reemphasize that the district court has discretion in determining the amount of a fee award. This is appropriate in view of the district court's superior understanding of the litigation and the desirability of avoiding frequent appellate review of what essentially are factual matters. It remains important, however, for the district court to provide a concise but clear explanation of its reasons for the fee award. When an adjustment is requested on the basis of either the exceptional or limited nature of the relief obtained by the plaintiff, the district court should make clear that it has considered the relationship between the amount of the fee awarded and the results obtained.

BUCKHANNON BOARD AND CARE HOME, INC. v. WEST VIRGINIA DEPARTMENT OF HEALTH AND HUMAN RESOURCES

Supreme Court of the United States, 2001.
532 U.S. 598, 121 S.Ct. 1835, 149 L.Ed.2d 855.

CHIEF JUSTICE REHNQUIST delivered the opinion of the Court.

Numerous federal statutes allow courts to award attorney's fees and costs to the "prevailing party." The question presented here is whether this term includes a party that has failed to secure a judgment on the merits or a court-ordered consent decree, but has nonetheless achieved the desired result because the lawsuit brought about a voluntary change in the defendant's conduct. We hold that it does not.

Buckhannon Board and Care Home, Inc., which operates care homes that provide assisted living to their residents, failed an inspection by the West Virginia Office of the State Fire Marshal because some of the residents were incapable of "self-preservation" as defined under state law. On October 28, 1997, ... [Buckhannon and others (petitioners)] brought suit in the United States District Court for the Northern District of West Virginia against the State of West Virginia, two of its agencies, and 18 individuals (hereinafter respondents), seeking declaratory and injunctive relief that the "self-preservation" requirement violated the Fair Housing Amendments Act of 1988 (FHAA), 42 U. S. C. § 3601 et seq., and the Americans with Disabilities Act of 1990 (ADA), 42 U. S. C. § 12101 et seq.

... In 1998, the West Virginia Legislature enacted two bills eliminating the "self-preservation" requirement, and respondents moved to dismiss the case as moot. The District Court granted the motion, finding that the 1998 legislation had eliminated the allegedly offensive provisions and that there was no indication that the West Virginia Legislature would repeal the amendments.

Petitioners requested attorney's fees as the "prevailing party" under the FHAA, 42 U. S. C. § 3613(c)(2), and ADA, 42 U. S. C. § 12205. Petitioners argued that they were entitled to attorney's fees under the "catalyst theory," which posits that a plaintiff is a "prevailing party" if it achieves the desired result because the lawsuit brought about a voluntary change in the defendant's conduct. Although most Courts of Appeals recognize the "catalyst theory,"[3] the Court of Appeals for the Fourth Circuit rejected it in *S–1 and S–2 v. State Bd. of Ed. of N. C.*, 21 F. 3d 49, 51 (1994) (en banc). The District Court accordingly denied the motion and, for the same reason, the Court of Appeals affirmed....

In the United States, parties are ordinarily required to bear their own attorney's fees—the prevailing party is not entitled to collect from the loser. Under this "American Rule," we follow "a general practice of not awarding fees to a prevailing party absent explicit statutory authority." *Key Tronic Corp. v. United States*, 511 U. S. 809, 819 (1994). Congress, however, has authorized the award of attorney's fees to the "prevailing party" in numerous statutes in addition to those at issue here....[4]

---

3. See, e.g., Stanton v. Southern Berkshire Regional School Dist., 197 F. 3d 574, 577, n. 2 (CA1 1999); Marbley v. Bane, 57 F. 3d 224, 234 (CA2 1995); Baumgartner v. Harrisburg Housing Authority, 21 F. 3d 541, 546–550 (CA3 1994); Payne v. Board of Ed., 88 F. 3d 392, 397 (CA6 1996); Zinn v. Shalala, 35 F. 3d 273, 276 (CA7 1994); Little Rock School Dist. v. Pulaski Cty. School Dist., #1, 17 F. 3d 260, 263, n. 2 (CA8 1994); Kilgour v. Pasadena, 53 F. 3d 1007, 1010 (CA9 1995); Beard v. Teska, 31 F. 3d 942, 951–952 (CA10 1994); Morris v. West Palm Beach, 194 F. 3d 1203, 1207 (CA11 1999).

4. We have interpreted these fee-shifting provisions consistently, see *Hensley v. Eckerhart*, 461 U. S. 424, 433, n. 7 (1983),

In designating those parties eligible for an award of litigation costs, Congress employed the term "prevailing party," a legal term of art. Black's Law Dictionary 1145 (7th ed. 1999) defines "prevailing party" as "[a] party in whose favor a judgment is rendered, regardless of the amount of damages awarded <in certain cases, the court will award attorney's fees to the prevailing party>.—Also termed successful party." This view that a "prevailing party" is one who has been awarded some relief by the court can be distilled from our prior cases.[5]

In *Hanrahan v. Hampton*, 446 U. S. 754, 758 (1980), we reviewed the legislative history of § 1988 and found that "Congress intended to permit the interim award of counsel fees only when a party has prevailed on the merits of at least some of his claims." Our "[r]espect for ordinary language requires that a plaintiff receive at least some relief on the merits of his claim before he can be said to prevail." *Hewitt v. Helms*, 482 U. S. 755, 760 (1987). We have held that even an award of nominal damages suffices under this test. See *Farrar v. Hobby*, 506 U. S. 103 (1992).

In addition to judgments on the merits, we have held that settlement agreements enforced through a consent decree may serve as the basis for an award of attorney's fees. See *Maher v. Gagne*, 448 U. S. 122 (1980). Although a consent decree does not always include an admission of liability by the defendant, it nonetheless is a court-ordered "chang[e] [in] the legal relationship between [the plaintiff] and the defendant." *Texas State Teachers Assn. v. Garland Independent School Dist.*, 489 U. S. 782, 792 (1989). These decisions, taken together, establish that enforceable judgments on the merits and court-ordered consent decrees create the "material alteration of the legal relationship of the parties" necessary to permit an award of attorney's fees.

We think, however, the "catalyst theory" falls on the other side of the line from these examples. It allows an award where there is no judicially sanctioned change in the legal relationship of the parties. Even under a limited form of the "catalyst theory," a plaintiff could recover attorney's fees if it established that the "complaint had sufficient merit to withstand a motion to dismiss for lack of jurisdiction or failure to state a claim on which relief may be granted." Brief for United States as Amicus Curiae 27. This is not the type of legal merit that our prior decisions, based upon plain language and congressional intent, have found necessary. Indeed, we held in *Hewitt* that an interlocutory ruling that reverses a dismissal for failure to state a claim "is not the stuff of which legal victories are made." 482 U. S., at 760. A defendant's voluntary change in conduct, although perhaps accomplishing what the

and so approach the nearly identical provisions at issue here.

5. We have never had occasion to decide whether the term "prevailing party" allows an award of fees under the "catalyst theory" described above. Dicta in Hewitt v. Helms, 482 U. S. 755, 760 (1987), alluded to the possibility of attorney's fees where "vol-untary action by the defendant . . . affords the plaintiff all or some of the relief . . . sought," but we expressly reserved the question, see id., at 763 ("We need not decide the circumstances, if any, under which this 'catalyst' theory could justify a fee award") . . . .

plaintiff sought to achieve by the lawsuit, lacks the necessary judicial imprimatur on the change. Our precedents thus counsel against holding that the term "prevailing party" authorizes an award of attorney's fees without a corresponding alteration in the legal relationship of the parties.

The dissenters chide us for upsetting "long-prevailing Circuit precedent." But, as Justice Scalia points out in his concurrence, several Courts of Appeals have relied upon dicta in our prior cases in approving the "catalyst theory." Now that the issue is squarely presented, it behooves us to reconcile the plain language of the statutes with our prior holdings.... While urging an expansion of our precedents on this front, the dissenters would simultaneously abrogate the "merit" requirement of our prior cases and award attorney's fees where the plaintiff's claim "was at least colorable" and "not ... groundless." We cannot agree that the term "prevailing party" authorizes federal courts to award attorney's fees to a plaintiff who, by simply filing a nonfrivolous but nonetheless potentially meritless lawsuit (it will never be determined), has reached the "sought-after destination" without obtaining any judicial relief.

Petitioners nonetheless argue that the legislative history of the Civil Rights Attorney's Fees Awards Act supports a broad reading of "prevailing party" which includes the "catalyst theory." We doubt that legislative history could overcome what we think is the rather clear meaning of "prevailing party"—the term actually used in the statute. Since we resorted to such history in *Garland*, 489 U. S., at 790, *Maher*, 448 U. S., at 129, and *Hanrahan*, 446 U. S., at 756–757, however, we do likewise here.

The House Report to § 1988 states that [t]he phrase "prevailing party" is not intended to be limited to the victor only after entry of a final judgment following a full trial on the merits, H. R. Rep. No. 94–1558, p. 7 (1976), while the Senate Report explains that "parties may be considered to have prevailed when they vindicate rights through a consent judgment or without formally obtaining relief," S. Rep. No. 94–1011, p. 5 (1976). Petitioners argue that these Reports and their reference to a 1970 decision from the Court of Appeals for the Eighth Circuit, *Parham v. Southwestern Bell Telephone Co.*, 433 F. 2d 421 (1970), indicate Congress' intent to adopt the "catalyst theory."[9] We think the legislative history cited by petitioners is at best ambiguous as to the

---

9. Although the Court of Appeals in *Parham* awarded attorney's fees to the plaintiff because his 'lawsuit acted as a catalyst which prompted the [defendant] to take action ... seeking compliance with the requirements of Title VII,' 433 F. 2d, at 429–430, it did so only after finding that the defendant had acted unlawfully, see id., at 426 ("We hold as a matter of law that [plaintiff's evidence] established a violation of Title VII"). Thus, consistent with our holding in *Farrar*, *Parham* stands for the proposition that an enforceable judgment permits an award of attorney's fees. And ... the Court of Appeals in *Parham* ordered the District Court to "retain jurisdiction over the matter for a reasonable period of time to insure the continued implementation of the appellee's policy of equal employment opportunities." 433 F. 2d, at 429. Clearly *Parham* does not support a theory of fee shifting untethered to a material alteration in the legal relationship of the parties as defined by our precedents.

availability of the "catalyst theory" for awarding attorney's fees. Particularly in view of the "American Rule" that attorney's fees will not be awarded absent "explicit statutory authority," such legislative history is clearly insufficient to alter the accepted meaning of the statutory term. *Key Tronic,* 511 U. S., at 819.

Petitioners finally assert that the "catalyst theory" is necessary to prevent defendants from unilaterally mooting an action before judgment in an effort to avoid an award of attorney's fees. They also claim that the rejection of the 'catalyst theory' will deter plaintiffs with meritorious but expensive cases from bringing suit. We are skeptical of these assertions, which are entirely speculative and unsupported by any empirical evidence (e.g., whether the number of suits brought in the Fourth Circuit has declined, in relation to other Circuits, since the decision in *S–1 and S–2*).

Petitioners discount the disincentive that the "catalyst theory" may have upon a defendant's decision to voluntarily change its conduct, conduct that may not be illegal. "The defendants' potential liability for fees in this kind of litigation can be as significant as, and sometimes even more significant than, their potential liability on the merits," *Evans v. Jeff D.,* 475 U. S. 717, 734 (1986), and the possibility of being assessed attorney's fees may well deter a defendant from altering its conduct.

[Moreover,] it is not clear how often courts will find a case mooted: "It is well settled that a defendant's voluntary cessation of a challenged practice does not deprive a federal court of its power to determine the legality of the practice" unless it is "absolutely clear that the allegedly wrongful behavior could not reasonably be expected to recur." *Friends of Earth, Inc. v. Laidlaw Environmental Services (TOC), Inc.,* 528 U. S. 167, 189 (2000). If a case is not found to be moot, and the plaintiff later procures an enforceable judgment, the court may of course award attorney's fees. Given this possibility, a defendant has a strong incentive to enter a settlement agreement, where it can negotiate attorney's fees and costs.

JUSTICE SCALIA, with whom JUSTICE THOMAS joins, concurring.

The dissent distorts the term "prevailing party" beyond its normal meaning for policy reasons, but even those seem to me misguided. They rest upon the presumption that the catalyst theory applies when "the suit's merit led the defendant to abandon the fray, to switch rather than fight on, to accord plaintiff sooner rather than later the principal redress sought in the complaint." As the dissent would have it, by giving the term its normal meaning the Court today approves the practice of denying attorney's fees to a plaintiff with a proven claim of discrimination, simply because the very merit of his claim led the defendant to capitulate before judgment. That is not the case. To the contrary, the Court approves the result in *Parham v. Southwestern Bell Tel. Co.,* 433 F. 2d 421 (CA8 1970), where attorney's fees were awarded "after [a] finding that the defendant had acted unlawfully." What the dissent's stretching of the term produces is something more, and something far less reasonable: an award of attorney's fees when the merits of plaintiff's case remain unresolved—when, for all one knows, the defendant only "abandon[ed] the fray" because the cost of litigation—either financial or in terms of public relations—would be too great. In such a case, the plaintiff may have "prevailed" as Webster's defines that term— "gain[ed] victory by virtue of strength or superiority." But I doubt it was greater strength in financial resources, or superiority in media manipulation, rather than superiority in legal merit, that Congress intended to reward.

It could be argued, perhaps, that insofar as abstract justice is concerned, there is little to choose between the dissent's outcome and the Court's: If the former sometimes rewards the plaintiff with a phony claim (there is no way of knowing), the latter sometimes denies fees to the plaintiff with a solid case whose adversary slinks away on the eve of judgment. But it seems to me the evil of the former far outweighs the evil of the latter. There is all the difference in the world between a rule that denies the extraordinary boon of attorney's fees to some plaintiffs who are no less "deserving" of them than others who receive them, and a rule that causes the law to be the very instrument of wrong—exacting the payment of attorney's fees to the extortionist.

The dissent points out that petitioners' object in bringing their suit was not to obtain "a judge's approbation," but to "stop enforcement of a [West Virginia] rule." True enough. But not even the dissent claims that if a petitioner accumulated attorney's fees in preparing a threatened complaint, but never filed it prior to the defendant's voluntary cessation of its offending behavior, the wannabe-but-never-was plaintiff could recover fees; that would be countertextual, since the fee-shifting statutes require that there be an "action" or "proceeding," see 42 U. S. C. § 3613(d); § 1988(b)—which in legal parlance (though not in more general usage) means a lawsuit. Does that not leave achievement of the broad congressional purpose identified by the dissent just as unsatisfactorily incomplete as the failure to award fees when there is no decree? . . . My point is not that it would take no more twisting of language to produce prelitigation attorney's fees than to produce the decreeless attorney's fees that the dissent favors. My point is that the departure from normal usage that the dissent favors cannot be justified on the ground that it establishes a regime of logical even handedness. There must be a cutoff of seemingly equivalent entitlements to fees—either the failure to file suit in time or the failure to obtain a judgment in time. The term "prevailing party" suggests the latter rather than the former. One does not prevail in a suit that is never determined.

JUSTICE GINSBURG, with whom JUSTICE STEVENS, JUSTICE SOUTER, and JUSTICE BREYER join, dissenting.

Prior to 1994, every Federal Court of Appeals (except the Federal Circuit, which had not addressed the issue) concluded that plaintiffs . . . could obtain a fee award if their suit acted as a "catalyst" for the change they sought, even if they did not obtain a judgment or consent decree. The Courts of Appeals found it "clear that a party may be considered to have prevailed even when the legal action stops short of final ... judgment due to ... intervening mootness." Interpreting the term "prevailing party" in "a practical sense," federal courts across the country held that a party "prevails" for fee-shifting purposes when "its ends are accomplished as a result of the litigation."

In 1994, the Fourth Circuit en banc, dividing 6–to–5, broke ranks with its sister courts. The court declared that, in light of *Farrar v. Hobby*, 506 U. S. 103 (1992), a plaintiff could not become a "prevailing party" without "an enforceable judgment, consent decree, or settlement." *S–1 and S–2 v. State Bd. of Ed. of N. C.*, 21 F. 3d 49, 51 (1994). As the Court today acknowledges, the language on which the Fourth Circuit relied was dictum. . . .

After the Fourth Circuit's en banc ruling, nine Courts of Appeals reaffirmed their own consistently held interpretation of the term "prevail."

The array of federal court decisions applying the catalyst rule suggested three conditions necessary to a party's qualification as "prevailing" short of a favorable final judgment or consent decree. A plaintiff first had to show that the defendant provided "some of the benefit sought" by the lawsuit. Under most Circuits' precedents, a plaintiff had to demonstrate as well that the suit stated a genuine claim, i.e., one that was at least "colorable," not "frivolous, unreasonable, or groundless." Plaintiff finally had to establish that her suit was a "substantial" or "significant" cause of defendant's action providing relief. In some Circuits, to make this causation showing, plaintiff had to satisfy the trial court that the suit achieved results "by threat of victory," not "by dint of nuisance and threat of expense." One who crossed these three thresholds would be recognized as a "prevailing party" to whom the district court, "in its discretion," could award attorney's fees.

Developed over decades and in legions of federal-court decisions, the catalyst rule and these implementing standards deserve this Court's respect and approbation.

The Court today detects a "clear meaning" of the term prevailing party that has heretofore eluded the large majority of courts construing those words. "Prevailing party," today's opinion announces, means "one who has been awarded some relief by the court." The Court derives this "clear meaning" principally from Black's Law Dictionary, which defines a "prevailing party," in critical part, as one "in whose favor a judgment is rendered" (quoting Black's Law Dictionary 1145 (7th ed. 1999)).

One can entirely agree with Black's Law Dictionary that a party "in whose favor a judgment is rendered" prevails, and at the same time resist ... any implication that only such a party may prevail. In prior cases, we have not treated Black's Law Dictionary as preclusively definitive; instead, we have accorded statutory terms, including legal "term[s] of art," a contextual reading. Notably, this Court did not refer to Black's

Law Dictionary in *Maher v. Gagne*, 448 U. S. 122 (1980), which held that a consent decree could qualify a plaintiff as "prevailing." The Court explained:

> "The fact that [plaintiff] prevailed through a settlement rather than through litigation does not weaken her claim to fees. Nothing in the language of [42 U. S. C.] § 1988 conditions the District Court's power to award fees on full litigation of the issues or on a judicial determination that the plaintiff's rights have been violated." Id., at 129.

... In everyday use, "prevail" means "gain victory by virtue of strength or superiority: win mastery: triumph." Webster's Third New International Dictionary 1797 (1976). There are undoubtedly situations in which an individual's goal is to obtain approval of a judge, and in those situations, one cannot "prevail" short of a judge's formal declaration. In a piano competition or a figure skating contest, for example, the person who prevails is the person declared winner by the judges. However, where the ultimate goal is not an arbiter's approval, but a favorable alteration of actual circumstances, a formal declaration is not essential. Western democracies, for instance, "prevailed" in the Cold War even though the Soviet Union never formally surrendered. Among television viewers, John F. Kennedy "prevailed" in the first debate with Richard M. Nixon during the 1960 Presidential contest, even though moderator Howard K. Smith never declared a winner.

A lawsuit's ultimate purpose is to achieve actual relief from an opponent. Favorable judgment may be instrumental in gaining that relief. Generally, however, "the judicial decree is not the end but the means. At the end of the rainbow lies not a judgment, but some action (or cessation of action) by the defendant...." *Hewitt v. Helms*, 482 U. S. 755, 761 (1987)....

Under a fair reading of the FHAA and ADA provisions in point, I would hold that a party "prevails" in "a true and proper sense," when she achieves, by instituting litigation, the practical relief sought in her complaint. The Court misreads Congress, as I see it, by insisting that, invariably, relief must be displayed in a judgment, and correspondingly that a defendant's voluntary action never suffices....

Under the catalyst rule that held sway until today, plaintiffs who obtained the relief they sought through suit on genuine claims ordinarily qualified as "prevailing parties," so that courts had discretion to award them their costs and fees. Persons with limited resources were not impelled to "wage total law" in order to assure that their counsel fees would be paid. They could accept relief, in money or of another kind, voluntarily proffered by a defendant who sought to avoid a recorded decree. And they could rely on a judge then to determine, in her equitable discretion, whether counsel fees were warranted and, if so, in what amount.

The concurring opinion adds another argument against the catalyst rule: That opinion sees the rule as accommodating the "extortionist" who obtains relief because of "greater strength in financial resources, or superiority in media manipulation, rather than superiority in legal merit." This concern overlooks both the character of the rule and the judicial superintendence Congress ordered for all fee allowances. The catalyst rule was auxiliary to fee-shifting statutes whose primary purpose is "to promote the vigorous enforcement" of the civil rights laws. [*Christiansburg Garment Co. v. EEOC*, 434 U. S. 412, 422 (1978)]. To that end, courts deemed the conduct-altering catalyst that counted to be the substance of the case, not merely the plaintiff's atypically superior financial resources, media ties, or political clout. And Congress assigned responsibility for awarding fees not to automatons unable to recognize extortionists, but to judges expected and instructed to exercise "discretion." So viewed, the catalyst rule provided no berth for nuisance suits. . . .

Notes and Comments

1. In *Hensley*, the Court embraced the First Circuit's conclusion that "plaintiffs may be considered 'prevailing parties' for attorney's fee purposes if the succeed on any significant issue in litigation which achieves some of the benefit the parties sought in bringing suit." Interestingly, elsewhere in *Hensley* the Court cited *Christiansburg Garment Co. v. EEOC*, 434 U.S. 412, 421, 98 S.Ct. 694, 700, 54 L.Ed.2d 648 (1978) for the proposition that prevailing defendants are entitled to fee awards only "where the suit was vexatious, frivolous, or brought to harass or embarrass the defendant." *Hensley*, 461 U.S., at 429 n.2, 103 S.Ct., at 1937. While there is legislative history supporting this dichotomy, see *Christiansburg*, 434 U.S., at 420, 98 S.Ct., at 699–700, one must wonder whether this unequal treatment is supportable in statutory schemes that simply provide for fee awards to "prevailing parties." Cf. *Fogerty v. Fantasy, Inc.*, 510 U.S. 517, 525–539, 114 S.Ct. 1023, 127 L.Ed.2d 455 (1994) (Thomas, concurring).

2. Few if any environmental statutes use the same "prevailing party" formulations that were litigated in *Hensley* and *Buckhannon*. Instead, the environmental statutes tend to fall into two camps. Some, like the Clean Water Act and RCRA, provide for fee awards to any "prevailing or substantially prevailing party." 33 U.S.C. § 1365(d), 42 U.S.C. § 6772(a). Others, such as the Endangered Species Act and the Clean Air Act, don't use either the "prevailing party" or "substantially prevailing party" formulations. Instead, they authorize a fee awards "whenever the court determines such an award is appropriate." See 16 U.S.C. § 1540(g)(4), and 42 U.S.C. § 7604(d). Putting mootness issues aside for the moment, should the threshold requirements for awards be the same under these different formulations? In *Ruckelshaus v. Sierra Club*, 463 U.S. 680, 103 S.Ct. 3274, 77 L.Ed.2d 938 (1983), the Supreme Court has determined that, despite the CAA's "whenever appropriate" phraseology, courts cannot award fees to losing parties. See also *Marbled Murrelet v. Babbitt*, 182 F.3d 1091 (9th Cir. 1999) (deeming the *Christiansburg* test applicable to prevailing defendants under the ESA).

3. What did you think of the Supreme Court's statutory analysis in *Buckhannon*? Do you find the statutory language to be clear? Do you find

the legislative history to be ambiguous? What did you think of the policy arguments advanced by the various Justices?

4. How, if at all, should the different statutory formulations under statutes such as the CWA ("prevailing or substantially prevailing") or the CAA ("whenever appropriate") affect the application of *Buckhannon*? Thus far, the Circuit Courts have been unanimous in determining that *Buckhannon* applies under statutes that use the "substantially prevailing" formulation. See, e.g., *Sierra Club v. City of Little Rock*, 351 F.3d 840 (8th Cir. 2003) ("*Little Rock*") (assuming without discussion that *Buckhannon* applies under the CWA); see also *Oil, Chem. & Atomic Workers Int'l Union v. Department of Energy*, 288 F.3d 452, 455 (D.C. Cir. 2002), and *Union of Needletrades, Industrial and Textile Employees v. U.S. INS*, 336 F.3d 200, 207–210 (2d Cir. 2003) (both under the Freedom of Information Act, 5 U.S.C. § 552). At the same time, they have been similarly unanimous in concluding that they may still apply the catalyst theory under statutes with the "where appropriate" standard. See, e.g., *Sierra Club v. Environmental Protection Agency*, 322 F.3d 718 (D.C. Cir. 2003) (CAA), and *Association of Calif. Water Agencies v. Evans*, 386 F.3d 879 (9th Cir. 2004), and *Loggerhead Turtle v. County Council of Volusia County, Fla.*, 307 F.3d 1318 (11th Cir. 2002) (both under the ESA). Do you agree with these results?

5. Short of a consent decree, what, if anything, do you think should constitute a sufficient "judicial imprimatur" under *Buckhannon*? What if, for example, the court has endorsed the plaintiff's legal theories in denying the defendant's motion for summary judgment, but has reserved final judgment until it has a chance to review the defendant's discharge monitoring reports to determine the total number of violations? How much discretion does the court have to control whether or when it generates the necessary imprimatur? What if, when the defendant moves for a finding of mootness, the plaintiff asks the court to pass on whether violations have been committed and whether its lawsuit was the catalyst for the defendant's coming into compliance? Can the court pass on these questions at that point in time? If it can and does, would that be a sufficient imprimatur? See *Little Rock*, 351 F.3d 840 (denying fees for want of an imprimatur despite the fact that the lower court had found liability, without asking whether the plaintiff's lawsuit had triggered the defendant's compliance). If the court can do so, must it?

6. Even if courts may continue to apply the catalyst theory under statutes (such as the ESA) using the "where appropriate" test, the court still must find that the plaintiff's lawsuit led to the defendant's compliance. This is not always a foregone conclusion. Compare *Center for Biological Diversity v. Norton*, 262 F.3d 1077 (10th Cir. 2001), with *Association of Calif. Water Agencies v. Evans*, 386 F.3d 879 (9th Cir. 2004).

7. How will *Buckhannon* affect the decisions of plaintiffs' lawyers as to whether to take on particular citizen suits? How will it affect both plaintiffs' and defendants' incentives during the course of the lawsuits? Does it create any conflict of interest problems for plaintiffs' lawyers?

8. In later cases, the Supreme Court has established a "strong presumption" that what it refers to as the "lodestar" figure (that is, the product of reasonable hours times a reasonable rate) represents the "reason-

able" fee. See, e.g., *City of Burlington v. Dague*, 505 U.S. 557, 562, 112 S.Ct. 2638, 2641, 120 L.Ed.2d 449 (1992). It has also determined that these fees cannot be increased to account for the risk of failure in particular cases (so-called "contingency enhancements"). Id. at 566–567, 112 S.Ct., at 2643–2644. Under what circumstances should courts award prevailing plaintiffs less than the lodestar? See *Little Rock*, 351 F.3d 840.

9. If courts deem full fee awards appropriate, they generally determine the reasonable hourly rate by the prevailing market rates for lawyers of similar skill in the relevant community, regardless of whether the plaintiff is represented by private or nonprofit counsel. See, e.g., *Blum v. Stenson*, 465 U.S. 886, 895, 104 S.Ct. 1541, 79 L.Ed.2d 891 (1984), and *Public Interest Research Group of New Jersey, Inc. v. Windall*, 51 F.3d 1179 (3d Cir. 1995). Does this create the possibility of a windfall to the plaintiff in some situations?

Chapter 7

COMPREHENSIVE ENVIRONMENTAL RESPONSE, COMPENSATION AND LIABILITY ACT

I. OVERVIEW AND JURISDICTION

Congress first passed the Comprehensive Environmental Response, Compensation and Liability Act ("CERCLA") in 1980, 42 U.S.C. §§ 9601–9675, Pub. L. No. 96–510, 94 Stat. 2767 (1980), in response to the discovery of infamous sites such as Love Canal in Niagara Falls, New York, and the "Valley of the Drums" in Shepardsville, Kentucky. Since then, Congress has comprehensively amended CERCLA once, through the Superfund Amendments and Reauthorization Act ("SARA"), Pub. L. 99–499, 100 Stat. 1615 (1986). Additionally, it has tinkered with the statute on several occasions since, most notably through the Small Business Liability Relief and Brownsfields Revitalization Act ("Brownfields Amendments"), Pub. L. 107–118, Stat. 2356 (2002).

From its inception, CERCLA has had a very different cast than the other pollution-control statutes we have considered in this course. Unlike statutes such as the Clean Water Act and RCRA, it is not a traditional "command and control" statute. It imposes very few regulatory obligations. Instead, it is a remedial program, giving EPA and others the tools they need to address contamination and to impose liability for past actions associated with it, even if those actions were consistent with all then-existing laws and standards of care. While "command and control" programs are primarily forward looking, CERCLA is backward looking. It doesn't tell companies how they have to run their businesses to minimize the risk of contamination; instead, it merely imposes responsibility for such contamination should it occur.

CERCLA provides EPA with four basic options for responding to contamination problems. First, it may in investigate or clean up a site itself § 104 and then seek reimbursement from any potentially responsible parties ("PRPs") under § 107. If EPA chooses this option, it draws upon the Superfund ("Fund") to front load its investigatory and/or

option #1 under CERCLA

522

cleanup expenses. The amount of money in the Fund has varied over time, from a high-water mark of $8.5 billion in 1986 to an annual appropriation of $1.25 billion in 2005. Second, EPA may seek to compel any PRP (or group of PRPs) to conduct any necessary investigations or cleanup activities by initiating a judicial action seeking a court order under § 106. Third, it may issue one or more PRPs a unilateral order requiring them to conduct the same activities, also under § 106. And finally, it may negotiate a settlement with some or all of the PRPs under which they agree to undertake any necessary response actions. See 42 U.S.C. § 9622.

EPA tends to focus its attention on sites that are on what is referred to as the National Priorities List ("NPL"). Roughly speaking, this is a list of the most contaminated sites in the country, as determined by EPA. There were 1,245 sites on this list as of July 22, 2004. When EPA is drawing upon the Fund, it can only undertake full-blown "remedial actions," as distinct from short-term steps known as "removals," if the site is on NPL. 40 C.F.R. § 300.425(b); see also 42 U.S.C. § 101(23) and (24) (definitions of removal and remedial action). While EPA is not similarly restricted under its other response options, it seldom seeks the full range of CERCLA-type relief at non-NPL sites.

CERCLA also provides states, Indian tribes, and even private parties with the ability to seek cost recovery from PRPs for any costs incurred in the cleanup process (although, as will be seen, would-be private-party plaintiffs face some additional constraints). 42 U.S.C. § 9607(a)(4)(A) and (B). The vast majority of these non-EPA lead cleanups occur at sites that are not on the NPL. Additionally, § 113(f)(1) and (3) supplement the private-party cost-recovery authority by allowing PRPs to bring claims for contribution in certain situations in which they allege that they have paid more than their fair share of any necessary cleanup costs.

The basic elements of CERCLA jurisdiction consist of three requirements: (1) a release or substantial threat of a release; (2) of a hazardous substance; (3) from a facility. See §§ 104(a)(1), 106(a), and 107(a)(4). There are other elements that apply to CERCLA's enforcement mechanisms. If a CERCLA plaintiff is suing for cost-recovery, for example, it must show that it has expended funds on cleanup, and it must demonstrate that the defendants are liable under § 107. 42 U.S.C. § 9607(a). Alternatively, if EPA is ordering the PRPs to do the work, § 106 requires it to have determined that the site "may" present "an imminent and substantial endangerment to public health or welfare or the environment." 42 U.S.C. § 9606. But it is the breadth of CERCLA's three key jurisdictional terms that gives the statute its remarkable sway. If an otherwise-eligible plaintiff is confident that these elements are present, it will be confident that CERCLA provides it with a powerful tool to induce those responsible to either undertake, fund, or contribute to cleanup efforts.

CERCLA's most important jurisdictional element is established through its definition of the term "hazardous substance." Section

101(14) defines this term primarily through a process of incorporation, using both Congress's and EPA's prior efforts in classifying contaminants of concern under other environmental programs. Specifically, the realm of CERCLA hazardous substances is defined to include:

i. Any toxic pollutants or hazardous substances designated pursuant to the Clean Water Act;

ii. Any listed or characteristic hazardous wastes under RCRA;

iii. Any hazardous air pollutants under the Clean Air Act; and

iv. Any imminently hazardous chemical substances or mixtures with respect to which EPA has taken action under § 7 of the Toxic Substances Control Act.

Additionally, EPA can specifically designate any substance as a hazardous substance specifically for purposes of the CERCLA program. CERCLA § 102.

The entire list of hazardous substances is found at 40 C.F.R. Part 302, Table 302.4. In addition to contaminants such as trichloroethylene ("TCE") and dioxin, it includes substances as ubiquitous as lead, copper, chlorine, and fluorine. Additionally, neither the statutory definition nor EPA's list contains any quantity or concentration requirements. The presence of these substances in any amount or concentration will satisfy this jurisdictional element.

The only significant constraint in CERCLA's definition of "hazardous substance" inheres in what is known as the "petroleum exclusion." Specifically, Section 101(14) excludes "petroleum, including crude oil and any fraction thereof which is is not otherwise specifically listed or designated as a hazardous substance ..." from the ambit of the CERCLA program. This exclusion is not scientifically based; petroleum-based wastes frequently contain toxic constituents at levels that would qualify them as hazardous wastes under RCRA. Instead, the petroleum exclusion originated from the circumstances surrounding the enactment of CERCLA. At the time Congress was considering CERCLA, it also was considering a parallel oil spill bill (H.R. 85) that would have comprehensively addressed petroleum-based contamination. Releases of hazardous substances were to be addressed under one bill and releases of oil under the other. At the last minute, however, the Senate failed to move forward on H.R. 85, leaving the problem of land-based petroleum contamination unaddressed except in relatively rare instances where it poses an accompanying threat to the navigable waters.

The precise contours of the petroleum exclusion have been subject to considerable litigation. At least two general principles have emerged. On the one hand, there is consensus that petroleum will not lose its exempt status where hazardous substances such as benzene, ethylbenzene, toluene, and lead are added to it during the refining process. See, e.g., *Wilshire Westwood Assoc. v. Atlantic Richfield Corp.*, 881 F.2d 801 (9th Cir.1989). On the other hand, there is also agreement that the exclusion does not encompass oil which through use has become contaminated with other hazardous substances. See *United States v. Alcan Aluminum Corp.*, 964 F.2d 252 (3d Cir.1992).

CERCLA defines the term "release" to mean "any spilling, leaking, pumping, pouring, emitting, emptying, discharging, injecting, escaping, leaching, dumping, or disposing into the environment...." CERCLA § 101(22). Giving effect to the breadth of this language, the courts have determined that any uncontrolled movement of contaminants in the environment qualifies as a release. CERCLA also authorizes response and imposes liability for actions taken in response to "threatened release[s]." See §§ 104(a)(1), 106(a), and 107(a)(4). While undefined in the statute, the courts have indicated that a "threatened release" may be established by (1) evidence of the presence of hazardous substances at a facility; (2) together with evidence of the unwillingness of any party to assert control over the substances. *United States v. Northernaire Plating Co.*, 670 F.Supp. 742, 747 (W.D.Mich.1987), *aff'd sub nom. United States v. R.W. Meyer, Inc.*, 889 F.2d 1497, 1507 (6th Cir.1989), *cert. denied*, 494 U.S. 1057, 110 S.Ct. 1527, 108 L.Ed.2d 767 (1990); *see also New York v. Shore Realty Corp.*, 759 F.2d 1032, 1045 (2d Cir.1985)(a facility's lack of expertise in handling hazardous waste or its failure to comply with licensing requirements may, by itself, constitute a threatened release).

The final jurisdictional requirement common to all of CERCLA's options is that the release or threatened release be from a "facility." See §§ 106(a) and 107(a)(4). However, this term imposes almost no substantive limitation on the scope of the program. Section 101(9) defines it to include "any site or area where a hazardous substance has ... come to be located." In line with this definition, courts have recognized that this definition includes far more than what typically would be considered to be hazardous waste facilities. See, e.g., *United States v. Ward*, 618 F.Supp. 884, 895 (D.N.C.1985) (roadsides where hazardous waste had been dumped); and *New York v. General Electric Co.*, 592 F.Supp. 291 (N.D.N.Y.1984) (a dragstrip where PCB–contaminated oils had been applied as a dust suppressant). Moreover, the relevant "facility" need not correspond to or be coextensive with property boundaries. In some cases, it can be broader; in others, narrower.

II. EPA RESPONSE

As mentioned, EPA has four options in responding to the actual or threatened contamination when these jurisdictional elements are satisfied. It may: (1) investigate or clean up the site and then seek cost recovery; (2) commence a judicial abatement action; (3) issue a unilateral administrative order requiring investigation or cleanup; or (4) negotiate a settlement under which the PRPs agree to perform the necessary actions. In all four of these contexts, EPA's cleanup methodology is delimited by the National Contingency Plan ("NCP"), which Congress tasked EPA with creating in § 105 of CERCLA. See 40 C.F.R. §§ 300.400–300.440. The NCP serves as the blueprint for response, regardless of which of the four enforcement option EPA pursues, and regardless of who is to perform the relevant investigatory or cleanup activities.

Many students reasonably assume that EPA typically pursues the first of the above options; i.e., that it cleans up the relevant sites and then sues for cost recovery. In fact, this is not the case. While EPA often uses its § 104 authorities to begin its investigations and/or to implement some preliminary response measures, at most sites it relies on the PRPs to undertake the bulk of the necessary investigations and/or cleanup activities, albeit subject to EPA oversight. Typically, this happens pursuant to consent decrees, pursuant to which the PRPs "voluntarily" agree to take the lead on these required activities. In order to understand why the PRPs agree to do this (often at the cost of tens of millions of dollars), one must understand a bit about the leverage that EPA has in these settlement negotiations.

EPA's general enforcement strategy in the CERCLA context is to promote settlement by relying on its unilateral order authority in situations in which negotiations fail. See, e.g., EPA, Enforcement First for Remedial Action at Superfund Sites (Sept. 20, 2002), www.epa.gov/ compliance/resources/policies/cleanup/superfund/enffirst-mem.pdf. In order to understand why this strategy is so effective, one must understand the power of EPA's unilateral order authority. Again, § 106 gives EPA the power to issue unilateral orders compelling PRPs to implement any required investigations or cleanup activities. In order to do so, EPA need only determine that the basic statutory elements are present and that the site "may" present an "imminent and substantial endangerment." 42 U.S.C. § 9606(a). Moreover, the statute explicitly precludes the courts from reviewing the legality of these orders of a pre-enforcement basis. 42 U.S.C. § 9613(h). Further, § 107(c)(3) allows EPA to seek punitive damages of up to three times the cost of cleanup if the recipient of such an order fails to comply therewith and its noncompliance is deemed to be "without sufficient cause." Given the threat of these sanctions, it is hardly surprising that most PRPs choose to proceed via consent, rather than face the threat of receiving such an order.

As a prelude to negotiation, EPA of course must identify those parties it deems to be liable under § 107. Additionally, if it is seeking to impose joint and several liability, it must determine whether that doctrine applies given the facts of the particular case. As such, we now turn to those issues:

A. Liable Parties

The elements of liability under CERCLA are straightforward. In governmental enforcement actions, EPA (or the State or Indian tribe) must show three things in order to establish liability:

1. That there has been a release or threatened release of a hazardous substance from a facility;

2. That the government or other authorized party incurred response costs because of the release or threatened release; and

3. That the party being sued falls into one of the four classes of PRPs under § 107.

See CERCLA § 107(a).

Section 107 imposes liability on four classes of "persons." These include (1) the present owner and operator of the site; (2) anyone who owned or operated the site at a time when hazardous substances were disposed of there; (3) anyone who "arranged for disposal or treatment" of such substances at the site; and (4) any transporters who selected the site. In practice, the vast majority of PRPs will fit within one of three groups—the current owner or operator of the site, the company that contaminated the site or allowed the contamination to occur (owner/operator at the time of disposal), or the generators who arranged to have their materials disposed of at the site. Hence, our discussion will focus on owner/operator and generator liability.

1. Owner/Operator Liability

a. Ownership Liability

The combined effect of § 107(a)(1) and (2) is to impose strict liability on both the current owner of the contaminated site and anyone who owned it during any periods of prior disposal. The seminal "current owner" liability case is *New York v. Shore Realty Corp.*, 759 F.2d 1032 (2d Cir.1985):

NEW YORK v. SHORE REALTY CORP.

United States Court of Appeals, Second Circuit, 1985.
759 F.2d 1032.

OAKES, CIRCUIT JUDGE

[Shore Realty ("Shore") agreed to purchase a piece of property at which a hold-over tenant was storing approximately 700,000 gallons of hazardous chemicals in a group of above-and below-ground tanks. Upon learning of the potential for contamination, Shore sought a waiver from the State of New York regarding any potential liability it might incur as the purchaser of the property. Despite being denied this waiver, Shore took title "and obtained certain rights over against the tenants," whom it shortly evicted. Despite the prompt eviction, however, tenants had added nearly 90,000 gallons of chemicals to the tanks during Shore's ownership period.]

Shore argues that it is not covered by section 9607(a)(1) because it neither owned the site at the time of disposal nor caused the presence or the release of hazardous waste at the facility. While section 9607(a)(1) appears to cover Shore, Shore attempts to infuse ambiguity into the statutory scheme, claiming that section 9607(a)(1) could not have been intended to include all owners, because the word "owned" in section 9707(a)(2) would be unnecessary since an owner "at the time of disposal" would necessarily be included in section 9607(a)(1). Shore claims that

Congress intended that the scope of section 9607(a)(1) be no greater than that of section 9607(a)(2) and that both should be limited by the "at the time of disposal" language. By extension, Shore argues that both provisions should be interpreted as requiring a showing of causation. We agree with the State, however, that section 9607(a)(1) unequivocally imposes strict liability on the current owner of a facility from which there is a release or threat of release, without regard to causation.

Shore's claims of ambiguity are illusory; section 9607(a)'s structure is clear. Congress intended to cover different classes of persons differently. Section 9607(a)(1) applies to all current owners and operators, while section 9607(a)(2) primarily covers prior owners and operators. Moreover, section 9607(a)(2)'s scope is more limited than that of section 9607(a)(1). Prior owners and operators are liable only if they owned or operated the facility "at the time of disposal of any hazardous substance"; this limitation does not apply to current owners, like Shore. . . .

Shore's causation argument is also at odds with the structure of the statute. Interpreting section 9607(a)(1) as including a causation requirement makes superfluous the affirmative defenses provided in section 9607(b), each of which carves out from liability an exception based on causation. Without clear congressional command otherwise, we will not construe a statute in any way that makes some of its provisions surplusage. . . .

Our interpretation draws further support from the legislative history. Congress specifically rejected including a causation requirement in section 9607(a). The early House version imposed liability only upon "any person who caused or contributed to the release or threatened release." H.R. 7020, 96th Cong., 2d Sess. § 3071(a), 126 Cong. Rec. 26,779. The compromise version, to which the House later agreed, imposed liability on classes of persons without reference to whether they caused or contributed to the release or threatened release. . . .

Furthermore, as the State points out, accepting Shore's arguments would open a huge loophole in CERCLA's coverage. It is quite clear that if the current owner could avoid liability merely by having purchased the site after chemical dumping had ceased, waste sites certainly would be sold, following the cessation of dumping, to new owners who could avoid the liability otherwise required by CERCLA. Congress had well in mind that persons who dump or store hazardous waste sometimes cannot be located or may be deceased or judgment proof. . . . We will not interpret section 9607(a) in any way that apparently frustrates the statute's goals, in the absence of a specific congressional intention otherwise. . . .

Notes and Comments

1. Why do you think Shore framed its argument in terms of whether it fit within the scope of § 107(a)(1), instead of directly addressing the standard of liability issue?

2. CERCLA itself says little about the standard of liability it imposes. Section 101(32) merely indicates that the term "liability" under the statute

"shall be construed to be the standard of liability which obtains under [§ 311 of the Clean Water Act]." Interestingly, § 311 itself does not specify any standard of liability. This has not posed any serious problems, however. Numerous courts had previously interpreted that section as imposing strict liability. See *United States v. Chem–Dyne Corp.*, 572 F.Supp. 802, 805 (S.D. Ohio 1983) (and cases cited therein). In his testimony on the Senate floor, Senator Randolph, one of CERCLA's sponsors, indicated that Congress was aware of these decisions: "We have kept strict liability in the compromise, specifying the standard of liability under section 311 of the [CWA]; that is, strict liability." 126 Cong. Rec. S14,964 (daily ed. Nov. 24, 1980). As a result, the courts have been unanimous in determining that CERCLA imposes strict liability. *Shore Realty* is considered the seminal case in this regard. Indeed, it is the most frequently-cited CERCLA decision of all time.

3. It is one thing to hold that a statute imposes strict liability. It is another to determine that it imposes liability without respect to causation. Do you understand the distinction between the two? Were you persuaded by the *Shore Realty* court's causation analysis? Does it go beyond traditional notions of fairness to impose strict liability on the current owners of contaminated land regardless of whether they played any part in causing the relevant contamination? If so, is the new leap justified? Did you find satisfactory the *Shore Realty* court's justification that imposing strict liability was necessary to prevent a sale of the property to new owners who would "avoid the liability otherwise required by CERCLA?"

4. In the last paragraph you have from this excerpt from *Shore Realty*, the court emphasized that it would not interpret § 107 "in any way that apparently frustrate's the statute's goals, in the absence of a specific congressional intention otherwise." Many courts have expressed similar sentiments in interpreting CERCLA, noting, for example, that "a liberal judicial interpretation is consistent with CERCLA's 'overwhelmingly remedial' statutory scheme." *United States v. Aceto Agricultural Chemicals Corp.*, 872 F.2d 1373, 1380 (8th Cir. 1989); see also *Florida Power & Light Co. v. Allis Chalmers Corp.*, 893 F.2d 1313, 1317 (11th Cir. 1990). Other courts, such as the Seventh Circuit, have disagreed. In *Edward Hines Lumber Co. v. Vulcan Materials Co.*, 861 F.2d 155 (7th Cir. 1988), Judge Easterbrook responded to the invocation of this "remedial purpose" argument in the following terms:

> ... To the point that courts could achieve "more" of the legislative objectives by adding to the lists of those responsible, it is enough to respond that statutes have not only ends but also limits. Born of compromise, laws such as CERCLA and SARA do not pursue their ends to their logical limits. A court's job is to find and enforce stopping points no less than to implement other legislative choices.

861 F.2d at 157. Which approach do you think is correct? Why?

5. CERCLA liability is not only strict and causation-free, the courts unanimously have determined that it is also retroactive. They have reached this conclusion despite the fact that the statute contains no explicit statement regarding its retroactive application. In so holding, the courts have relied on the fact that: (1) Section 107(a)(2) imposes liability on those who owned contaminated properties at the time the disposal activities occurred; (2) Section 103(c) required those who owned certain sites where disposal had

occurred to notify EPA within 180 days after the CERCLA's passage, and penalized those who failed to do so by depriving them of any defenses to which they may otherwise have been entitled; and (3) CERCLA's legislative history indicates that one of CERCLA's central purposes is to impose the costs of cleanup on those who caused the relevant contamination. See *United States v. Olin Corp.*, 107 F.3d 1506 (11th Cir. 1997). Are you persuaded? The courts have been similarly unanimous in determining that the imposition of this retroactive liability is not unconstitutional. In the leading case of *United States v. Monsanto Co.*, 858 F.2d 160 (4th Cir. 1988), cert. denied, 490 U.S. 1106, 109 S.Ct. 3156, 104 L.Ed.2d 1019 (1989), the Fourth Circuit relied on the Supreme Court's earlier decision in *Usery v. Turner Elkhorn Mining Co.*, 428 U.S. 1, 96 S.Ct. 2882, 49 L.Ed.2d 752 (1976), in which the Court upheld the retroactive operation of the Black Lung Benefits Act of 1972. The *Monsanto* court further noted that:

> ... CERCLA does not exact punishment. Rather it creates a reimbursement obligation on any person judicially determined responsible for the costs of remedying hazardous conditions at a waste disposal facility. The restitution of cleanup costs was not intended to operate, nor does it operate in fact, as a criminal penalty or a punitive deterrent....

858 F.2d at 174–175. More recent decisions have held that this analysis survives the Supreme Court's more recent decision in *Eastern Enterprises v. Apfel*, 524 U.S. 498, 118 S.Ct. 2131, 141 L.Ed.2d 451 (1998). See, e.g., *United States v. Alcan Aluminum*, 315 F.3d 179, 188–190 (2d Cir. 2003) (and cases cited therein).

6. Since *Shore Realty*, Congress has established two significant, but still relatively narrow, defenses to current landowner liability. First, when it passed SARA in 1986, Congress created what is referred to as the "innocent landowner defense." See 42 U.S.C. § 9601(35)(A). Second, when Congress passed the Brownfields Amendments in 2002, it created the "prospective purchaser" exclusion, which shields some parties who knowingly purchase contaminated sites. 42 U.S.C. § 9607(r). We will discuss these provisions in more detail in subpart B.3 of this chapter, below.

7. Another interesting issue under § 107(a) involves the liability of so-called "interim owners." Imagine a situation in which A contaminated land and then sold it to B, who, without having added to the contamination, then sold the land to C, the current owner. A and C are clearly liable under § 107(a); but what about B? Most courts have held that such parties are not liable, determining that the passive migration of hazardous substances within soils and/or groundwater does not make parties like B owners "at the time of disposal" within the meaning of § 107(a)(2). See, e.g., *United States v. CDMG Realty Co.*, 96 F.3d 706 (3d Cir. 1996) (noting that while CERCLA's definition of "disposal"—which it incorporates from RCRA through reference—includes leaking, it does not include "leaching"); cf. *Nurad, Inc. v. William E. Hooper & Sons Co.*, 966 F.2d 837 (4th Cir.), cert. denied sub nom *Mumaw v. Nurad, Inc.*, 506 U.S. 940, 113 S.Ct. 377, 121 L.Ed.2d 288 (1992) (holding an interim owner liable where there was an ongoing leak from underground storage tank during its period of ownership).

b. Operator Liability

In addition to imposing liability on owners, § 107(a)(1) and (2) impose liability on both the current operator of the facility and anyone who operated the facility at the time of disposal. In many cases, these operators will be obvious: they will be the entities who are or were doing business on the property; to the extent that they are distinct from the owners, they will typically have been lessees.

More difficult questions arise, however, when one considers the extent to which entities such as parent corporations or individuals such as corporate officers or employees may qualify as "operators" under CERCLA. In these contexts, two separate questions can be raised: First, does the relevant entity or individual bear "direct" liability under the statute by virtue of being an "operator" in its own right; and second, is "piercing the corporate veil" appropriate such that the relevant entity or individual can be deemed to be derivatively liable for the sins of the relevant subsidiary or employer. Consider the following case:

UNITED STATES v. BESTFOODS

Supreme Court of the United States, 1998.
524 U.S. 51, 118 S.Ct. 1876, 141 L.Ed.2d 43.

JUSTICE SOUTER delivered the opinion of the Court.

In 1957, Ott Chemical Co. (Ott I) began manufacturing chemicals at a plant near Muskegon, Michigan, and its intentional and unintentional dumping of hazardous substances significantly polluted the soil and ground water at the site. In 1965, respondent CPC International Inc. incorporated a wholly owned subsidiary to buy Ott I's assets in exchange for CPC stock. The new company, also dubbed Ott Chemical Co. (Ott II), continued chemical manufacturing at the site, and continued to pollute its surroundings. CPC kept the managers of Ott I, including its founder, president, and principal shareholder, Arnold Ott, on board as officers of Ott II. Arnold Ott and several other Ott II officers and directors were also given positions at CPC, and they performed duties for both corporations.

In 1972, CPC sold Ott II to Story Chemical Company, which operated the Muskegon plant until its bankruptcy in 1977. Shortly thereafter, when respondent Michigan Department of Natural Resources (MDNR) examined the site for environmental damage, it found the land littered with thousands of leaking and even exploding drums of waste, and the soil and water saturated with noxious chemicals. MDNR sought a buyer for the property who would be willing to contribute toward its cleanup, and after extensive negotiations, respondent Aerojet–General Corp. arranged for transfer of the site from the Story bankruptcy trustee in 1977. Aerojet created a wholly owned California subsidiary, Cordova Chemical Company (Cordova/California), to purchase the property, and Cordova/California in turn created a wholly owned Michigan subsidiary,

Cordova Chemical Company of Michigan (Cordova/Michigan), which manufactured chemicals at the site until 1986.

By 1981, [EPA] had undertaken to see the site cleaned up, and its long-term remedial plan called for expenditures well into the tens of millions of dollars. To recover some of that money, the United States filed this action under § 107 in 1989, naming five defendants as responsible parties: CPC, Aerojet, Cordova/California, Cordova/Michigan, and Arnold Ott. (By that time, Ott I and Ott II were defunct.) . . .

[In the liability phase, the district court found CPC directly liable as an operator under § 107(a)(2), finding it "particularly telling that CPC selected Ott II's board of directors and populated its executive ranks with CPC officials, and that a CPC official, G.R.D. Williams, played a significant role in shaping Ott II's environmental compliance policy."

An en banc panel of the Sixth Circuit ultimately reversed on this point (7 judges to 6), holding that parent corporations could be liable as "operators" only where they essentially operate the facility either in the stead of their subsidiaries or as joint venturers alongside their subsidiaries. In either event, the en banc panel determined that their must be an abuse the corporate form to an extent that would give rise to piercing the corporate veil under traditional, state-law tests. Applying this analysis, the decided that under Michigan veil-piercing law CPC was not liable for controlling the actions of its subsidiaries, since the parent and subsidiary corporations maintained separate personalities and CPC did not utilize the subsidiary corporate form to perpetrate fraud or subvert justice.]

It is a general principle of corporate law deeply "ingrained in our economic and legal systems" that a parent corporation (so-called because of control through ownership of another corporation's stock) is not liable for the acts of its subsidiaries. Douglas & Shanks, Insulation from Liability Through Subsidiary Corporations, 39 Yale L. J. 193 (1929) (hereinafter Douglas) [and other citations]. Thus it is hornbook law that "the exercise of the 'control' which stock ownership gives to the stockholders . . . will not create liability beyond the assets of the subsidiary. That 'control' includes the election of directors, the making of by-laws . . . and the doing of all other acts incident to the legal status of stockholders. Nor will a duplication of some or all of the directors or executive officers be fatal." Douglas 196. Although this respect for corporate distinctions when the subsidiary is a polluter has been severely criticized in the literature, nothing in CERCLA purports to reject this bedrock principle, and against this venerable common-law backdrop, the congressional silence is audible. The Government has indeed made no claim that a corporate parent is liable as an owner or an operator under § 107 simply because its subsidiary is subject to liability for owning or operating a polluting facility.

But there is an equally fundamental principle of corporate law, applicable to the parent-subsidiary relationship as well as generally, that the corporate veil may be pierced and the shareholder held liable for the corporation's conduct when, inter alia, the corporate form would otherwise be misused to accomplish certain wrongful purposes, most notably fraud, on the shareholder's behalf. Nothing in CERCLA purports to rewrite this well-settled rule, either. CERCLA is thus like many another congressional enactment in giving no indication "that the entire corpus of state corporation law is to be replaced simply because a plaintiff's cause of action is based upon a federal statute," and the failure of the statute to speak to a matter as fundamental as the liability implications of corporate ownership demands application of the rule that "[i]n order to abrogate a common-law principle, the statute must speak directly to the question addressed by the common law." The Court of Appeals was accordingly correct in holding that when (but only when) the corporate veil may be pierced,[1] may a parent corporation be charged with derivative CERCLA liability for its subsidiary's actions.[2]

[handwritten margin note: when veil ca be pierced,]

If the act rested liability entirely on ownership of a polluting facility, this opinion might end here; but CERCLA liability may turn on operation as well as ownership, and nothing in the statute's terms bars a parent corporation from direct liability for its own actions in operating a facility owned by its subsidiary. As Justice (then-Professor) Douglas noted almost 70 years ago, derivative liability cases are to be distinguished from those in which "the alleged wrong can seemingly be traced to the parent through the conduit of its own personnel and management" and "the parent is directly a participant in the wrong complained of." Douglas 207, 208. In such instances, the parent is directly liable for its own actions. The fact that a corporate subsidiary happens to own a polluting facility operated by its parent does nothing, then, to displace the rule that the parent "corporation is [itself] responsible for the wrongs committed by its agents in the course of its business," *Mine Workers v. Coronado Coal Co.*, 259 U.S. 344, 395 (1922), and whereas the rules of veil-piercing limit derivative liability for the actions of another corporation, CERCLA's "operator" provision is concerned primarily with direct liability for one's own actions. It is this direct liability that is properly seen as being at issue here.

Under the plain language of the statute, any person who operates a polluting facility is directly liable for the costs of cleaning up the pollution. This is so regardless of whether that person is the facility's

---

1. There is significant disagreement among courts and commentators over whether, in enforcing CERCLA's indirect liability, courts should borrow state law, or instead apply a federal common law of veil piercing. [Citations]. Since none of the parties challenges the Sixth Circuit's holding that CPC and Aerojet incurred no derivative liability, the question is not presented in this case, and we do not address it further.

2. Some courts and commentators have suggested that this indirect, veil-piercing approach can subject a parent corporation to liability only as an owner, and not as an operator. See, e.g., *Lansford-Coaldale Joint Water Auth. v. Tonelli Corp.*, supra, at 1220; Oswald, Bifurcation of the Owner and Operator Analysis under CERCLA, 72 Wash. U. L. Q. 223, 281–282 (1994) (hereinafter Oswald). We think it is otherwise, however. If a subsidiary that operates, but does not own, a facility is so pervasively controlled by its parent for a sufficiently improper purpose to warrant veil piercing, the parent may be held derivatively liable for the subsidiary's acts as an operator.

owner, the owner's parent corporation or business partner, or even a saboteur who sneaks into the facility at night to discharge its poisons out of malice. If any such act of operating a corporate subsidiary's facility is done on behalf of a parent corporation, the existence of the parent-subsidiary relationship under state corporate law is simply irrelevant to the issue of direct liability.

This much is easy to say; the difficulty comes in defining actions sufficient to constitute direct parental "operation." Here of course we may again rue the uselessness of CERCLA's definition of a facility's "operator" as "any person ... operating" the facility, 42 U. S. C. § 9601(20)(A)(ii), which leaves us to do the best we can to give the term its "ordinary or natural meaning." In a mechanical sense, to "operate" ordinarily means "[t]o control the functioning of; run: operate a sewing machine." American Heritage Dictionary 1268 (3d ed. 1992); see also Webster's New International Dictionary 1707 (2d ed. 1958) ("to work; as, to operate a machine"). And in the organizational sense more obviously intended by CERCLA, the word ordinarily means "[t]o conduct the affairs of; manage: operate a business." American Heritage Dictionary, supra, at 1268; see also Webster's New International Dictionary, supra, at 1707 ("to manage"). So, under CERCLA, an operator is simply someone who directs the workings of, manages, or conducts the affairs of a facility. To sharpen the definition for purposes of CERCLA's concern with environmental contamination, an operator must manage, direct, or conduct operations specifically related to pollution, that is, operations having to do with the leakage or disposal of hazardous waste, or decisions about compliance with environmental regulations.

With this understanding, we are satisfied that the Court of Appeals correctly rejected the District Court's analysis of direct liability. But we also think that the appeals court erred in limiting direct liability under the statute to a parent's sole or joint venture operation, so as to eliminate any possible finding that CPC is liable as an operator on the facts of this case.

By emphasizing that "CPC is directly liable under section 107(a)(2) as an operator because CPC actively participated in and exerted significant control over Ott II's business and decision-making," the District Court applied the "actual control" test of whether the parent "actually operated the business of its subsidiary," as several Circuits have employed it.

The well-taken objection to the actual control test, however, is its fusion of direct and indirect liability; the test is administered by asking a question about the relationship between the two corporations (an issue going to indirect liability) instead of a question about the parent's interaction with the subsidiary's facility (the source of any direct liability). If, however, direct liability for the parent's operation of the facility is to be kept distinct from derivative liability for the subsidiary's own operation, the focus of the enquiry must necessarily be different under the two tests. "The question is not whether the parent operates the subsidiary, but rather whether it operates the facility, and that operation is evidenced by participation in the activities of the facility, not the subsidiary. Control of the subsidiary, if extensive enough, gives rise to indirect liability under piercing doctrine, not direct liability under the statutory language." Oswald 269. The District Court was therefore mistaken to rest its analysis on CPC's relationship with Ott II, premising liability on little more than "CPC's 100–percent ownership of Ott II" and "CPC's active participation in, and at times majority control over, Ott II's board of directors." [*CPC Int'l, Inc. v. Aerojet–General Corp.*, 777 F.Supp. 549, 572, 575 (W.D.Mich.1991)]. The analysis should instead have rested on the relationship between CPC and the Muskegon facility itself.

[handwritten: what analysis should have focused on.]

In addition to (and perhaps as a reflection of) the erroneous focus on the relationship between CPC and Ott II, even those findings of the District Court that might be taken to speak to the extent of CPC's activity at the facility itself are flawed, for the District Court wrongly assumed that the actions of the joint officers and directors are necessarily attributable to CPC. The District Court emphasized the facts that CPC placed its own high-level officials on Ott II's board of directors and in key management positions at Ott II, and that those individuals made major policy decisions and conducted day-to-day operations at the facility. . . .

In imposing direct liability on these grounds, the District Court failed to recognize that "it is entirely appropriate for directors of a parent corporation to serve as directors of its subsidiary, and that fact alone may not serve to expose the parent corporation to liability for its subsidiary's acts."

This recognition that the corporate personalities remain distinct has its corollary in the "well established principle [of corporate law] that directors and officers holding positions with a parent and its subsidiary can and do 'change hats' to represent the two corporations separately, despite their common ownership." Since courts generally presume "that the directors are wearing their 'subsidiary hats' and not their 'parent hats' when acting for the subsidiary," it cannot be enough to establish liability here that dual officers and directors made policy decisions and supervised activities at the facility. The Government would have to show that, despite the general presumption to the contrary, the officers and directors were acting in their capacities as CPC officers and directors, and not as Ott II officers and directors, when they committed those acts. . . . [13]

[handwritten: what Gov needs to show about d.r.]

---

13. We do not attempt to recite the ways in which the Government could show that dual officers or directors were in fact acting on behalf of the parent. Here, it is prudent to say only that the presumption that an act is taken on behalf of the corporation for whom the officer claims to act is strongest when the act is perfectly consistent with the norms of corporate behavior, but wanes as the distance from those accepted norms approaches the point of action by a dual officer plainly contrary to the interests of the subsidiary yet nonetheless advantageous to the parent.

In sum, the District Court's focus on the relationship between parent and subsidiary (rather than parent and facility), combined with its automatic attribution of the actions of dual officers and directors to the corporate parent, erroneously ... treated CERCLA as though it displaced or fundamentally altered common law standards of limited liability. [If such were the case, there] would in essence be a relaxed, CERCLA-specific rule of derivative liability that would banish traditional standards and expectations from the law of CERCLA liability. But, as we have said, such a rule does not arise from congressional silence, and CERCLA's silence is dispositive.

We accordingly agree with the Court of Appeals that a participation-and-control test looking to the parent's supervision over the subsidiary, especially one that assumes that dual officers always act on behalf of the parent, cannot be used to identify operation of a facility resulting in direct parental liability. Nonetheless, a return to the ordinary meaning of the word "operate" in the organizational sense will indicate why we think that the Sixth Circuit stopped short when it confined its examples of direct parental operation to exclusive or joint ventures, and declined to find at least the possibility of direct operation by CPC in this case.

In our enquiry into the meaning Congress presumably had in mind when it used the verb "to operate," we recognized that the statute obviously meant something more than mere mechanical activation of pumps and valves, and must be read to contemplate "operation" as including the exercise of direction over the facility's activities. The Court of Appeals recognized this by indicating that a parent can be held directly liable when the parent operates the facility in the stead of its subsidiary or alongside the subsidiary in some sort of a joint venture. We anticipated a further possibility above, however, when we observed that a dual officer or director might depart so far from the norms of parental influence exercised through dual officeholding as to serve the parent, even when ostensibly acting on behalf of the subsidiary in operating the facility. Yet another possibility, suggested by the facts of this case, is that an agent of the parent with no hat to wear but the parent's hat might manage or direct activities at the facility.

Identifying such an occurrence calls for line drawing yet again, since the acts of direct operation that give rise to parental liability must necessarily be distinguished from the interference that stems from the normal relationship between parent and subsidiary. Again norms of corporate behavior ... are crucial reference points. Just as we may look to such norms in identifying the limits of the presumption that a dual officeholder acts in his ostensible capacity, so here we may refer to them in distinguishing a parental officer's oversight of a subsidiary from such an officer's control over the operation of the subsidiary's facility. "[A]ctivities that involve the facility but which are consistent with the parent's investor status, such as monitoring of the subsidiary's performance, supervision of the subsidiary's finance and capital budget decisions, and articulation of general policies and procedures, should not give rise to direct liability." Oswald 282. The critical question is whether, in degree and detail, actions directed to the facility by an agent of the parent alone are eccentric under accepted norms of parental oversight of a subsidiary's facility.

There is, in fact, some evidence that CPC engaged in just this type and degree of activity at the Muskegon plant. The District Court's opinion speaks of an agent of CPC alone who played a conspicuous part in dealing with the toxic risks emanating from the operation of the plant. G.R.D. Williams worked only for CPC; he was not an employee, officer, or director of Ott II, and thus, his actions were of necessity taken only on behalf of CPC. The District Court found that "CPC became directly involved in environmental and regulatory matters through the work of . . . Williams, CPC's governmental and environmental affairs director. Williams . . . became heavily involved in environmental issues at Ott II." 777 F. Supp., at 561. He "actively participated in and exerted control over a variety of Ott II environmental matters," ibid., and he "issued directives regarding Ott II's responses to regulatory inquiries," id., at 575.

We think that these findings are enough to raise an issue of CPC's operation of the facility through Williams's actions, though we would draw no ultimate conclusion from these findings at this point. Not only would we be deciding in the first instance an issue on which the trial and appellate courts did not focus, but the very fact that the District Court did not see the case as we do suggests that there may be still more to be known about Williams's activities. Indeed, even as the factual findings stand, the trial court offered little in the way of concrete detail for its conclusions about Williams's role in Ott II's environmental affairs, and the parties vigorously dispute the extent of Williams's involvement. Prudence thus counsels us to remand, on the theory of direct operation set out here, for reevaluation of Williams's role, and of the role of any other CPC agent who might be said to have had a part in operating the Muskegon facility.

Notes and Comments

1. Under what circumstances did the Supreme Court determine that CPC might bear direct liability in *Bestfoods*? Did it require that CPC be found to have participated in the pollution-causing activities? That it was involved in environmental decision-making at the underlying facility? That it exercised a more general form of operational control over activities at the underlying facility? That it exercised some degree of operational supervision over Ott II in general (even if not with respect to the day-to-day activities at the relevant facility)? That it had the capacity to control either the operations or the environmental decisions at the underlying facility? Did you agree with the Court's approach? Why or why not?

2. If *Bestfoods* requires some degree of involvement in one of the above categories of activities, how much involvement is required? Is mere participation enough? Or does the parent's representative have to have issued directives or exercised decision-making authority? Why did the Supreme

Court determine that a remand was necessary? On remand, the lower court found these facts with respect to Mr. Williams:

> ... Williams was a lawyer who coordinated air and water pollution programs for CPC. From 1966 through 1972, he drafted or was copied on numerous CPC environmental documents. Beginning in 1966, he was involved with the Muskegon facility of Ott II, upon the recommendation of dual-director Harold Hellman.
>
> While Williams never visited the site, he consulted with Ott II officers concerning Ott II's responses to environmental agency surveys. In September 1966, he attended one meeting with the Michigan Water Resource Commission, together with Ott II officials. Prior to that meeting, Williams advised Ott II representatives not to tell the MWRC about the opinion of Ott II's engineering consultants that a biological treatment facility may be required in future. Williams generally advised Ott II to delay as much as possible the making of capital expenditures.
>
> The record reflects, however, that, despite Williams' recommendations, Ott II officials shared with the MWRC the recommendations of their engineering consultants shortly after the September meeting. The report was discussed at the November 10, 1966 meeting with the MWRC. Thereafter, on November 18, 1966, the Ott II board approved $375,000 for completion of the first phases of the engineering plan and so advised the MWRC, contrary to the recommendation of Williams, who sought to delay all expenditures until 1968. Since none of Ott II's engineers recommended biological treatment or additional incinerators or deep well in 1966, Ott's decision not to seek or approve funds for such treatment in 1966 cannot be viewed as being caused by Williams' advice.
>
> Taken together, the record reflects that while Williams may have advocated that Ott II delay implementation of waste treatment plans, his advice was rejected. Although delays in discharge compliance eventually occurred, and although the biological treatment facility was never built, those delays are not shown to have resulted from any influence Williams may have had on Ott II at the September 1966 meeting. Instead, they reflect the Ott II decision to connect to the county waste water treatment system, and the record contains no evidence that Williams was involved in that decision.

Bestfoods v. Aerojet–General Corp., 173 F.Supp.2d 729, 749 (W.D. Mich. 2001). Based on these findings, the court found the record "far too thin to conclude that Williams was responsible for any delays in compliance," *id.* at 750, and that "his limited involvement with the MWRC in 1966 is not consistent with the control of Ott II," *id.* The court went on to conclude that the government had not established that CPC's activities gave rise to "operator" status.

For purposes of comparison, in *United States v. Kayser–Roth Corp.*, 272 F.3d 89 (1st Cir. 2001), the First Circuit reaffirmed its finding of parent liability upon determining that the parent's representative "played a central role in decisions about environmental compliance" at the relevant facility. Id. at 104. And in *City of Wichita, Kansas v. Trustees of the APCO Oil Corp. Liquidating Trust*, 306 F.Supp.2d 1040, 1055 (D.Kan. 2003) (*City of Wichita*), the court found that "an operator ... must make the relevant decisions on a frequent, typically day-to-day basis." The court found this standard satisfied where there was uncontroverted testimony that the relevant corporate president was present at weekly management meetings at which environmental compliance issues were discussed, and that no decisions were made at those meetings without the president's approval. Id. at 1055–1056. Are these decisions consistent with each other? If not, which do you find to be more in line with *Bestfoods*?

3. Is the Supreme Court's discussion of operator liability relevant to entities other than parent corporations? In *City of Wichita*, the court assumed the *Bestfoods* approach also applies to individuals such as corporate officers. See also *Browning–Ferris Indus. of Illinois, Inc. v. Ter Maat*, 195 F.3d 953 (7th Cir. 1999) (accord). If *Bestfoods* indicates that corporate officers will only bear CERCLA liability if they involve themselves in environmental decision-making, does the Court's opinion bear the risk of encouraging these officers to delegate all such decisions to their underlings? Is this sound policy?

4. The issue of individual liability under CERCLA appears to have arisen mostly (perhaps solely) in the context of a closely-held corporations. Is CERCLA's text limited to imposing liability only upon officers or employees of closely-held firms? Are the policy justifications for imposing liability enhanced in this context? Why do you think there is little or no case law involving entities such as General Electric's vice-president in charge of environmental operations, its environmental compliance managers, or its environmental supervisors at each G.E. facility? At a pragmatic level, the most significant difference between these situations and those involving closely-held corporations is that, assuming liability, companies like G.E. are likely to be both willing and able to assume whatever share of liability they are deemed to be "responsible" for at any given site. But is there a legal difference? If you represented G.E.'s compliance manager, how would you assess his or her exposure under CERCLA for the liabilities G.E. has incurred based upon activities occurring during his or her tenure in that position? Would your assessment vary if bankruptcy of the corporation was a potential concern? Would in-house lawyers who give legal advice be immune from liability? What about outside counsel? Assume now that you represent EPA. Is there any reason, even outside the bankruptcy context, why you might want to sue some officers or mid-level managers from large corporations? If you did, might it discourage capable and environmentally-concerned individuals from accepting such positions? Is this enough of a reason not to do so?

5. What instructions did the Supreme Court provide for how lower courts should address the so-called "dual officer" problem, where the same individual might be an officer for both the parent corporation and its subsidiary? Is this approach satisfactory?

6. What application would the Supreme Court's approach to "operator" liability have, if any, with respect to someone who operated or is currently operating a completely non-polluting business on a contaminated site? Is there such thing as a business that never engages in environmental decision-making? Imagine, for example, that a bookstore leases a contaminated site. Assuming it played no role in causing the contamination, would it

qualify as a current "operator" under § 107(a)(1)? If not, does this suggest a problem with the Court's analysis? Alternatively, does the term "operator" itself provide a basis for distinguishing between some types of lessees and others with regard to the extent to which they may be subject to causation-free liability under § 107(a)(1)?

7. What if EPA had written a rule specifying the situations in which it felt that parent corporations and corporate officers or employees should bear "direct" operator liability under CERCLA? Is this a situation in which EPA's views would be entitled to deference? The D.C. Circuit addressed this question in *Kelley v. EPA*, 15 F.3d 1100 (D.C. Cir. 1994), in which the State of Michigan challenged EPA's authority to issue regulations purporting to govern the situations in which lenders would bear liability under CERCLA. The court determined that "Congress meant the judiciary, not EPA, to determine liability issues." It further explained that:

> ... "A precondition to deference under *Chevron* is a congressional delegation of administrative authority." [*Adams Fruit Co. v. Barrett*, 494 U.S. 638, 649 (1990)]. *Chevron*, which sets forth the reigning rationale for judicial deference to agency interpretation of statutes, is premised on the notion that Congress implicitly delegated to the agency the authority to reconcile reasonably statutory ambiguities or to fill reasonably statutory interstices. Where Congress does not give an agency authority to determine (usually formally) the interpretation of a statute in the first instance and instead gives the agency authority only to bring the question to a federal court as the "prosecutor," deference to the agency's interpretation is inappropriate. ...

Id. Interestingly, EPA did not seek Supreme Court review of the *Kelley* decision. Moreover, it does not appear to have written any rules since then interpreting CERCLA's liability provisions. Why do you think EPA has acquiesced (at least implicitly) in the *Kelley* result? Should EPA have the authority to promulgate legislative rules interpreting § 107? What other ambiguities in that section would EPA have been able to address through rulemaking if it had prevailed in *Kelley*? Would EPA be able to "correct" any adverse judicial opinions on an after-the-fact basis? In the mid–1990s, EPA sought a legislative "fix" regarding the scope of its rulemaking authority under CERCLA in the Superfund Reauthorization process. Some of the bills Congress considered in 1994 provided EPA with the authority that the D.C. Circuit found lacking in *Kelley*.

8. Before *Bestfoods* there was a split of sorts in the Circuits regarding whether courts should look to state or federal common law in resolving veil-piercing issues. Most courts had determined that they should apply principles of federal common law, see, e.g., *Lansford–Coaldale Joint Water Auth. v. Tonolli Corp.*, 4 F.3d 1209, 1221 (3d Cir. 1993) (in the context of parent liability), and *B.F. Goodrich v. Betkoski*, 99 F.3d 505, 519 (2d Cir. 1996), *cert. den. sub nom Zollo Drum Co., Inc. v. B.F. Goodrich Co.*, 524 U.S. 926, 118 S.Ct. 2318, 141 L.Ed.2d 694 (1998) and *Louisiana–Pacific Corp. v. Asarco, Inc.*, 909 F.2d 1260, 1263 (9th Cir. 1990) (both in the context of successor liability), but at least two Circuits had found that it would look to principles of state law, *Donahey v. Bogle*, 129 F.3d 838, 843 (6th Cir. 1997), *vacated on other grounds*, 524 U.S. 924, 118 S.Ct. 2317, 141 L.Ed.2d 692 (1998),

reinstated 16 Fed.Appx. 283 (6th Cir. 2000) (successor liability), and *Red-wing Carriers, Inc. v. Saraland Apartments*, 94 F.3d 1489, 1500–1502 (11th Cir. 1996) (limited partnership). What, if anything, did the Supreme Court indicate about this issue? How should lower courts react to the Court's opinion in this regard?

9. Note that, in footnote 10, the Court specifically recognized that veil-piercing may transcend the "ownership" liability realm. There, the court speaks (in *dicta*) to parent corporations that pervasively control subsidiaries that would only qualify as "operators" under CERCLA. Would the same logic apply to the parents of those subsidiaries that qualify as "arrangers for disposal" under § 107(a)(3)? See *Carter-Jones Lumber Co. v. Dixie Distributing Co.*, 166 F.3d 840, 846 (6th Cir. 1999). As the *Bestfoods* Court points out in context of operator liability, this is a different question than would be posed if we were asking whether the parent qualified as an "arranger" in its own right. Do you understand the distinction?

10. The issue of lender liability under CERCLA, mentioned in note 7 above, had a controversial life for some time, but has receded in the wake of legislative changes. From the outset, CERCLA's definition of definition of "owner or operator" has provided an exemption for those who own property to protect their security interests, so long as they refrain from "participat[ing] in the management" of those facilities. 42 U.S.C. § 9601(20). As originally drafted, however, the statute left key questions unresolved. Two issues in particular proved vexing: What types of lender oversight would be deemed to constitute the type of "participat[ion] in ... management" that voided the defense? And second, under what circumstances, if any, could a lender foreclose on its security interest without losing its statutory protection? Notably, in *United States v. Fleet Factors Corp.*, 901 F.2d 1550 (11th Cir. 1990), the Eleventh Circuit determined that lenders could incur liability "by participating in the financial management of a facility to a degree indicating a capacity to influence the corporation's treatment of hazardous wastes." *Id.* at 1557. It further opined that "a secured creditor will be liable if its involvement with the management of the facility is sufficiently broad to support the inference that it could affect hazardous waste disposal decisions if it so chose." *Id.* at 1558. This decision created a backlash, resulting first in EPA's efforts to back-pedal by writing a lender-friendly rule, which the D.C. Circuit then invalidated in *Kelley*. Ultimately, however, Congress essentially codified EPA's rule by passing the Asset Conservation, Lender Liability, and Deposit Insurance Protection Act of 1996 as a rider to the Omnibus Consolidated Appropriations Act. Pub. L. No. 104–208, §§ 2501–2505. Lenders will rarely face direct liability under these new provisions. See 42 U.S.C. § 9601(20)(E) and (F).

2. Arrangers for Disposal or Treatment

As previously mentioned, § 107(a)(3) imposes liability on those who "arranged for disposal or treatment" of any hazardous substances at the relevant facility. Most typically, this provision serves to impose liability on the so-called "generators" of the waste; that is, the companies that generated the particular substances that came to be located at the relevant site. The following case, while decided quite early in the

CERCLA era, contains what probably remains the best treatment to date of the elements of generator liability under § 107(a)(3):

UNITED STATES v. WADE

United States District Court, Eastern District of Pennsylvania, 1983.
577 F.Supp. 1326.

NEWCOMER, DISTRICT JUDGE

[This case involved the "Wade" site in Chester, Pennsylvania. In addition to suing the property owner and others, the government also sought cost-recovery from Apollo Metals, Inc., Congoleum Corporation, Gould, Inc. and Sandvik, Inc. ("generator defendants").]

The generator defendants . . . argue that the government has not and cannot establish the requisite causal relationship between their wastes and the costs incurred by the government in cleaning up the site.

In a nutshell, the generator defendants' causation argument is as follows. To establish liability under the Act the government must prove a link, or more specifically a causal nexus, between costs incurred in clean-up and a given generator's waste. The argument is based on traditional tort concepts of proximate causation. The generator defendants first argue that the government has no admissible evidence that their wastes were in fact disposed of at the Wade site. The government agrees that actual dumping of a defendant's waste at the Wade site is an element of its case but urges that its evidence on this issue is not only admissible but also dispositive.

[The court first determined that the issues regarding whether each generator's wastes in fact wound up at the Wade site would have to be resolved at trial.]

Even assuming the government proves that a given defendant's waste was in fact disposed of at the Wade site, the generator defendants argue it must also prove that a particular defendant's actual waste is presently at the site and has been the subject of a removal or remedial measure before that defendant can be held liable. In the alternative, the generator defendants argue that at a minimum the government must link its costs incurred to waste of the sort created by a generator before that generator may be held liable. This argument in part overlaps the defendants' argument pertaining to recoverable damages. Based on my reading of the Act, I must reject both causation requirements urged by the generator defendants.

The liability provision of CERCLA provides in relevant part as follows:

Notwithstanding any other provision or rule of law, and subject only to the defenses set forth in subsection (b) of this section— . . .

(3) Any person who by contract, agreement, or otherwise arranged for disposal or treatment or arranged with a transporter for transport for disposal or treatment of hazardous substances

owned or possessed by such person, by any other party or entity, at any facility owned or operated by another party or entity and containing *such* hazardous substances ... (4) ... from which there is a release, or a threatened release which causes the incurrence of response costs, of *a* hazardous substance, shall be liable for—

(A) All costs of removal or remedial action incurred by the United States Government or a state not inconsistent with the national contingency plan.

42 U.S.C. § 9607(a)(emphasis added). At one extreme the Act could be read to impose liability on certain parties who merely arrange for transport of their waste but never actually do so. I do not understand the government to urge such a construction and would reject it. I mention the possibility only to underscore the lack of precision with which the statute was drafted.

Part of the generator defendants' argument revolves around the use of the word "such" in referring to the "hazardous substances" contained at the dump site or "facility." It could be read to require that the facility contain a particular defendant's waste. On the other hand it could be read merely to require that hazardous substances like those found in a defendant's waste must be present at the site. The legislative history provides no enlightenment on this point. I believe that the less stringent requirement was the one intended by Congress.

The government's experts have admitted that scientific technique has not advanced to a point that the identity of the generator of a specific quantity of waste can be stated with certainty. All that can be said is that a site contains the same kind of hazardous substances as are found in a generator's waste. Thus, to require a plaintiff under CERCLA to "fingerprint" wastes is to eviscerate the statute. Given two possible constructions of a statute, one which renders it useless should be rejected. Generators are adequately protected by requiring a plaintiff to prove that a defendant's waste was disposed of at a site and that the substances that make the defendant's waste hazardous are also present at the site.

Besides eviscerating the statute the generator defendant's contention would lead to ludicrous results. For example, assuming wastes could be "fingerprinted," once all the hazardous substances in a generator's waste had migrated from the "facility" the generator could no longer be held liable. In fact, one generator makes this argument.

I turn now to the generator defendants' contention that the government must link its costs incurred to wastes of the sort created by them.

A reading of the literal language of the statute suggests that the generator defendants read too much into this portion of its causation requirement. Stripping away the excess language, the statute appears to impose liability on a generator who has (1) disposed of its hazardous substances (2) at a facility which now contains hazardous substances of the sort disposed of by the generator (3) if there is a release of that or some other type of hazardous substance (4) which causes the incurrence of response costs. Thus, the release which results in the incurrence of response costs and liability need only be of "*a*" hazardous substance and not necessarily one contained in the defendant's waste. The only required nexus between the defendant and the site is that the defendant have dumped his waste there and that the hazardous substances found in the defendant's waste are also found at the site. I base my disagreement with defendants' reading in part on the Act's use of "such" to modify "hazardous substance" in paragraph three and the switch to "a" in paragraph four.

Additional support for my reading may also be found in the legislative history of the Act. The original House Committee bill imposed liability on "any person who caused or contributed to the release." H.R. 7020, 96th Cong., 2d Sess., § 3071(a)(1), 126 Cong. Rec. at H9459 (daily ed. September 23, 1980). Although the committee bill was changed in several important respects by the full House, this language was also contained in the final House-passed version. Id. at H9479. This language clearly requires a causal nexus between a generator and the release causing the incurrence of response costs, and the House Committee understood it to do so[. Citing an early House Report]. The problem with the generator defendants' reliance on this report, however, is that the liability provision which was ultimately enacted bears no real resemblance to the House-passed bill to which the report refers. Instead, the legislation enacted specifies certain groups which will be held liable when a release of a hazardous substance causes the incurrence of clean-up costs. One of those groups is those who have disposed of hazardous substances at the site if hazardous substances of that sort are present at the site.

Deletion of the causation language contained in the House-passed bill and the Senate draft is not dispositive of the causation issue. Nevertheless, the substitution of the present language for the prior causation requirement evidences a legislative intent which is in accordance with my reading of the Act.

Notes and Comments

1. What did the *Wade* court mean when it required, as its first element of generator liability, that CERCLA plaintiffs establish that a given generator's wastes were in fact "disposed of" at the site? Do plaintiffs need to show that each generator's wastes were in fact dumped or otherwise disposed of onto the ground? Alternatively, may a given generator be held liable without any showing that its wastes were part of the release that triggered the need for cleanup? Or even that its wastes came into contact with any soils or groundwater? What if a generator can show that none of its drums ever leaked or otherwise caused any releases. Cf. CERCLA § 107(b)(3).

2. Restating its holding slightly, the *Wade* court essentially determined that CERCLA plaintiffs must establish four elements in order to impose liability on a given generator. They must show (1) that the relevant genera-

tor has arranged for the disposal or treatment of hazardous substances (2) at a facility which now contains hazardous substances of a type similar to those sent by the generator (3) and that there is a release or threatened release of that or some other type of hazardous substance (4) which causes the incurrence of response costs. Do you agree with the court's determination that CERCLA plaintiffs need not even establish that there are wastes like those of the generator in the release at issue? What is the effect of this ruling?

3. Is the *Wade* interpretation the most defensible reading of the statute, or was the court overly influenced by the difficulties of proof that would pertain under any other causation test? At least two appellate courts have agreed with the *Wade* causation analysis. *United States v. Monsanto*, 858 F.2d 160, 167–69 (4th Cir.1988), *cert. denied*, 490 U.S. 1106, 109 S.Ct. 3156, 104 L.Ed.2d 1019 (1989); *United States v. Alcan Aluminum Corp.*, 964 F.2d 252, 264–66 (3d Cir.1992). Should the standard change if science advances to the point where the government is able to "fingerprint" wastes with more precision?

4. What should be required before a given generator is found to have "arrange[d] for disposal . . . at any facility . . . containing such substances?" Should EPA be required to show that the defendant selected the relevant site? The courts universally have determined that a given generator need not have selected the relevant site in order to be held liable if its wastes wound up there. Can this result be squared with the statutory language? Why have the courts been so adamant on this point? See *United States v. Ward*, 618 F.Supp. 884, 895 (E.D.N.C.1985)("To [require a showing of such knowledge] would allow generators of hazardous waste to escape liability under CERCLA by closing their eyes to the method in which their wastes were disposed of"). Is this logic compelling?

5. At a minimum, *Wade* appears to require EPA to demonstrate that each particular generator's wastes in fact arrived at the relevant facility. What if hundreds of generators send their waste to one facility, which then sporadically commingles the wastes and redirects them to numerous other facilities? Will each of the original generators be jointly and severally liable for cleanup at all of the "remote" sites? Is there some preliminary showing EPA should be required to make regarding the likelihood of each particular generator's wastes having wound up at each remote site, as a precondition to imposing liability? See *United States v. Bliss*, 667 F.Supp. 1298 (E.D.Mo. 1987) (holding the generators liable for each remote site on the theory that at least trace amounts of their waste were likely in the mixtures delivered to each site). What if the wastes were not physically commingled, but the operator of the original facility distributed the wastes to the remote sites without keeping any records of whose wastes were going where? Should the same rule obtain?

6. How should the issue of "direct" liability for parent corporations and individuals play out in the context of "arranger" liability under § 107(a)(3)? In a pre-*Bestfoods* case, the Eighth Circuit determined that CERCLA imposes different liability tests regarding parent corporations in the "operator" and "arranger for disposal" contexts:

... The critical distinction between operator liability under [§ 107(a)(2)] and arranger liability under [§ 107(a)(3)], for purposes of this parent corporation liability analysis, is that subsection (a)(2) requires only that the person operate the facility where disposal occurs at the time of disposal; by contrast, subsection (a)(3) requires that the person arrange for the disposal, treatment, or transportation for disposal or treatment. Therefore, while a parent corporation need only have the authority to control, and exercise actual or substantial control, over the operations of its subsidiary in order to incur direct liability for the subsidiary's on-site disposal practices, we believe that, in order for a parent corporation to incur direct arranger liability for a subsidiary's off-site disposal practices, there must be some causal connection or nexus between the parent corporation's conduct and the subsidiary's arrangement for disposal, or the off-site disposal itself.

United States v. TIC Investment Corp., 68 F.3d 1082, 1091–92 (8th Cir.1995) Does this distinction make sense? Does it survive *Bestfoods*?

7. Under what circumstances, if any, should the sale of a hazardous substance, or of a material or product containing hazardous substances, be deemed to constitute an "arrange[ment] for disposal" under § 107(a)(3)? There seem to be two lines of cases in this area. First, there are cases in which a company sells something that has been through its primary intended use, but which may have residual value to someone else (e.g., a recycler). In these cases, the court have typically deemed these sales to be arrangements for disposal. See, e.g., *Catellus Development Corp. v. United States*, 34 F.3d 748 (9th Cir.1994) (defendant sold spent automotive batteries to a lead reclamation facility), and *New York v. General Electric Co.*, 592 F.Supp. 291 (N.D.N.Y.1984) (defendant sold contaminated waste oil to a drag strip for use as a dust suppressant). In 1999, Congress passed a rider exempting certain recycling transactions from the scope of § 107(a)(3). See 42 U.S.C. § 9627. Take a look at that provision. Does it strike an appropriate balance? See also *Pneumo Abex Corp. v. High Point, Thomasville and Denton Railroad Co.*, 142 F.3d 769 (4th Cir. 1998). The second line of cases involves situations in which someone sells a virgin product that they know will at some point release hazardous substances into the environment. The leading case here is *Florida Power & Light Co. v. Allis Chalmers Corp.*, 893 F.2d 1313 (11th Cir. 1990). While declining to establish a per se rule of non-liability, the Eleventh Circuit in that case found that the plaintiffs had "not met their burden of demonstrating that the transactions involved anything more than a mere sale" in a situation in which the defendants had sold transformers that one of the plaintiffs had used for 40 years before disposing of them. Id. at 1319. Are there situations in which the initial sale of a manufactured product should give rise to liability? What if a timber company sells railroad ties impregnated with pentachlorophenol, creosote and other hazardous substances, knowing that these substances are likely to leach out into the environment? Compare CERCLA § 107(i) (exempting the application of registered pesticides from CERCLA's liability scheme).

8. The Eighth Circuit issued perhaps the most far-reaching "arranger" liability case to date in *United States v. Aceto Agricultural Chemicals Corp.*, 872 F.2d 1373 (8th Cir. 1989). In that case, the court determined that EPA had stated a claim upon which relief could be granted when it sued six

pesticide manufacturers who had hired another company to formulate their technical grade pesticides into commercial grade pesticides. The court found it particularly relevant that the manufacturers retained title to the pesticides throughout the formulation process, and that the generation of waste was inherent in the process. It rejected the defendants' arguments that they hired the formulator to formulate, not to dispose, and that had no ability to control the formulator's operational or disposal activities. Do you agree with this result? Interestingly, almost as an afterthought, the Eight Circuit indicated that the district court had not erred in applying the common law "abnormally dangerous activities" doctrine as a basis for imposing vicarious liability on the manufacturers. Should this doctrine have any sway under CERCLA? If so, what are its implications?

B. Scope of Liability

We already have seen that the courts have interpreted CERCLA as imposing both strict and retroactive liability, despite the Act's silence on those points. We now turn to the scope of the liability CERCLA imposes. Here also, the statute is silent on its face. Despite this silence, however, the courts have had little difficulty in determining that CERCLA generally imposes joint and several liability, though it does not mandate its imposition in all cases. We begin our discussion of when and how the doctrine applies under CERCLA with the two leading cases in this area:

UNITED STATES v. CHEM–DYNE CORP.

United States District Court, Southern District of Ohio, 1983.
572 F.Supp. 802.

CARL B. RUBIN, Chief Judge.

. . . In order to expedite discovery and trial preparation, the defendants have moved for an early determination that they are not jointly and severally liable for the cleanup costs at Chem–Dyne.

The liability section lists the classes of persons potentially liable under the Act for the costs incurred by government removal or remedial action. In contrast to plaintiff's assertion that joint and several liability is clear from the express statutory language, the Court finds the language ambiguous with regard to the scope of liability. Consequently, in an attempt to discern the Congressional intent, the Court will review and weigh the legislative history of the Act.

As background, two different superfund bills proceeded simultaneously through the House and Senate. On November 24, 1980, the Senate made its final amendment to its bill, thereby eliminating the term strict, joint and several liability from its provisions. Subsequently, on December 3, 1980, the House struck the language in its bill and substituted the language of the Senate bill, which was later enacted. The defendants quote at length from Senator Helms' speech:

Retention of joint and several liability in S. 1480 received intense and well-deserved criticism from a number of sources, since it could impose financial responsibility for massive costs and damages awards on persons who contributed only minimally (if at all) to a release or injury. Joint and several liability for costs and damages was especially pernicious in S. 1480, not only because of the exceedingly broad categories of persons subject to liability and the wide array of damages available, but also because it was coupled with an industry-based fund. Those contributing to the fund will frequently be paying for conditions they had no responsibility in creating or even contributing to. To adopt a joint and several liability scheme on top of this would have been grossly unfair.

The drafters of the Stafford Randolph substitute have recognized this unfairness, and the lack of wisdom in eliminating any meaningful link between culpable conduct and financial responsibility. Consequently, all references to joint and several liability in the bill have been deleted . . .

It is very clear from the language of the Stafford Randolph substitute itself, from the legislative history, and from the liability provisions of section 311 of the Federal Water Pollution Control Act, that now the Stafford Randolph bill does not in and of itself create joint and several liability.

This view of statutory construction is at odds with the guidelines provided by the Supreme Court. Senator Helms was an opponent of the bill. Accordingly, his statements are entitled to little weight in construing the statute.

Senator Stafford, sponsor of the bill, succinctly noted that there was an elimination of the term joint and several liability as well as an elimination of the scope of liability. Senator Randolph, sponsor, explained the significance of these modifications:

> We have kept strict liability in the compromise, specifying the standard of liability under section 311 of the Clean Water Act, but we have deleted any reference to joint and several liability, relying on common law principles to determine when parties should be severally liable . . . The changes were made in recognition of the difficulty in prescribing in statutory terms liability standards which will be applicable in individual cases. The changes do not reflect a rejection of the standards in the earlier bill.

* * *

> It is intended that issues of liability not resolved by this act, if any, shall be governed by traditional and evolving principles of common law. An example is joint and several liability. Any reference to these terms has been deleted, and the liability of joint tortfeasors will be determined under common or previous statutory law.

[The court also quoted similar statements from Representatives Florio and Waxman.]

Statements of the legislation's sponsors are properly accorded substantial weight in interpreting the statute, although the remarks of a single legislator are not controlling. The fact that the term joint and several liability was deleted from a prior draft of the bill or that the term liability refers to the standard under 33 U.S.C. § 1321, in and of itself, is not dispositive of the scope of liability under CERCLA.... A reading of the entire legislative history in context reveals that the scope of liability and term joint and several liability were deleted to avoid a mandatory legislative standard applicable in all situations which might produce inequitable results in some cases. The deletion was not intended as a rejection of joint and several liability. Rather, the term was omitted in order to have the scope of liability determined under common law principles, where a court performing a case by case evaluation of the complex factual scenarios associated with multiple-generator waste sites will assess the propriety of applying joint and several liability on an individual basis.

Because the legislative history evinces the intent that the scope of liability under [§ 107] be determined from traditional and evolving principles of common law, the next issue becomes whether state or federal common law should be applied. In situations where, as here, there is a lack of an express statutory provision selecting state or federal law, the inevitable incompleteness presented by all legislation means that interstitial federal lawmaking is a basic responsibility of the federal courts. ...

State law as a rule of decision is not mandated under the *Erie* doctrine in this case because it falls within the exception provided for federal laws. 28 U.S.C. § 1652; *Erie v. Tompkins*, 304 U.S. 64, (1938). Although *Erie* eliminated the power of federal courts to create federal general common law, the power to fashion federal specialized common law remains untouched when it is "necessary to protect uniquely federal interests."

The improper disposal or release of hazardous substances is an enormous and complex problem of national magnitude involving uniquely federal interests. Typically, an abandoned waste site will consist of waste produced by companies in several states within the area or region. The pollution of land, groundwater, surface water and air as a consequence of this dumping presents potentially interstate problems. A driving force toward the development of CERCLA was the recognition that a response to this pervasive condition at the state level was generally inadequate.... Additionally, the superfund monies expended, for which the United States seeks reimbursement, are funded by general revenues and excise taxes. The degree to which the United States will be able to protect its financial interest in the trust fund is directly related to the scope of liability under CERCLA and is in no way dependent upon the laws of any state. When the United States derives its authority for reimbursement from the specific Act of Congress passed in the exercise of a constitutional function or power, its rights should also derive from federal common law. In conclusion, the rights, liabilities and responsibilities of the United States under [§ 107] are governed by a federal rule of decision.

The question now becomes whether the scope of liability should be interpreted according to the incorporated state law of the forum state or a federally created uniform law. This determination is a matter of judicial policy dependent upon a variety of considerations relevant to the nature of the specific governmental interests and to the effects upon them of applying state law. Federal programs that by their nature are and must be uniform in character throughout the nation necessitate the formulation of federal rules of decision. CERCLA is such a federal program. . . . A liability standard which varies in the different forum states would undermine the policies of the statute by encouraging illegal dumping in states with lax liability laws. There is no good reason why the United States' right to reimbursement should be subjected to the needless uncertainty and subsequent delay occasioned by diversified local disposition when this matter is appropriate for uniform national treatment.

[handwritten margin note: Do Not want liability to vary from state to state]

Finding, then, that the delineation of a uniform federal rule of decision is consistent with the legislative history and policies of CERCLA and finding further that no compelling local interests mandate the incorporation of state law, a determination of the content of the federal rule is the final step in the analysis. Federal statutes dealing with similar subject matter are a prime repository of federal policy on a subject and a starting point for ascertaining federal common law. Neither statutes nor decisions of a particular state can be conclusive when fashioning federal law.

Typically, as in this case, there will be numerous hazardous substance generators or transporters who have disposed of wastes at a particular site. The term joint and several liability was deleted from the express language of the statute in order to avoid its universal application to inappropriate circumstances. An examination of the common law reveals that when two or more persons acting independently caused a distinct or single harm for which there is a reasonable basis for division according to the contribution of each, each is subject to liability only for the portion of the total harm that he has himself caused. Restatement (Second) of Torts §§ 433A, 881 (1976). But where two or more persons cause a single and indivisible harm, each is subject to liability for the entire harm. Furthermore, where the conduct of two or more persons liable under [§ 107] has combined to violate the statute, and one or more of the defendants seeks to limit his liability on the ground that the entire harm is capable of apportionment, the burden of proof as to apportionment is upon each defendant. These rules clearly enumerate the analysis to be undertaken when applying [§ 107] and are most likely to advance the legislative policies and objectives of the Act.

The question of whether the defendants are jointly or severally liable for the clean-up costs turns on a fairly complex factual determination. Read in the light most favorable to the plaintiff, the following facts illustrate the nature of the problem. The Chem–Dyne facility contains a variety of hazardous waste from 289 generators or transporters, consisting of about 608,000 pounds of material. Some of the wastes have commingled but the identities of the sources of these wastes remain unascertained. The fact of the mixing of the wastes raises an issue as to the divisibility of the harm. Further, a dispute exists over which of the wastes have contaminated the ground water, the degree of their migration and concomitant health hazard. Finally, the volume of waste of a particular generator is not an accurate predictor of the risk associated with the waste because the toxicity or migratory potential of a particular hazardous substance generally varies independently with the volume of the waste.

Because there are genuine issues of material fact concerning the divisibility of the harm and any potential apportionment, the defendants are not entitled to judgment as a matter of law.

O'NEIL v. PICILLO

United States Court of Appeals, First Circuit, 1989.
883 F.2d 176, *cert. denied*, 493 U.S. 1071, 110
S.Ct. 1115, 107 L.Ed.2d 1022 (1990).

COFFIN, SENIOR CIRCUIT JUDGE

[In 1977, the Picillo family agreed to allow part of their pig farm in Coventry, Rhode Island to be used as a disposal site for drummed and bulk waste. Thousands of barrels of hazardous waste were dumped on the farm, culminating in a major fire caused by the improper storage of incompatible wastes. In 1979, the state and EPA jointly undertook to clean up the area. What they found, in the words of the district court, were massive trenches and pits "filled with free-flowing, multi-colored, pungent liquid wastes" and thousands of "dented and corroded drums containing a veritable potpourri of toxic fluids."

The State of Rhode Island sued to recover the cleanup costs it incurred between 1979 and 1982 and to hold the responsible parties liable for all future costs associated with the site. The state's complaint originally named thirty-five defendants, all but five of whom eventually entered into settlements totalling $5.8 million, the money to be shared by the state and EPA. After a month-long bench trial, the district court found three of the remaining five companies jointly and severally liable for all past costs not covered by the settlement agreements, as well as for all future cleanup costs. Two of the three generators held liable at trial, American Cyanamid and Rohm and Haas, appealed, contending that their contribution to the disaster was insubstantial and that it was, therefore, unfair to hold them jointly and severally liable for all of the state's past expenses not covered by settlements.]

It is by now well settled that Congress intended that the federal courts develop a uniform approach governing the use of joint and several liability in CERCLA actions. The rule adopted by the majority of courts,

*only apportioned
if harm is ÷*

and the one we adopt, is based on the Restatement (Second) of Torts: damages should be apportioned only if the defendant can demonstrate that the harm is divisible.

The practical effect of placing the burden on defendants has been that responsible parties rarely escape joint and several liability, courts regularly finding that where wastes of varying (and unknown) degrees of toxicity and migratory potential commingle, it simply is impossible to determine the amount of environmental harm caused by each party. It has not gone unnoticed that holding defendants jointly and severally liable in such situations may often result in defendants paying for more than their share of the harm. Nevertheless, courts have continued to impose joint and several liability on a regular basis, reasoning that where all of the contributing causes cannot fairly be traced, Congress intended for those proven at least partially culpable to bear the cost of the uncertainty.

In enacting [SARA], Congress had occasion to examine this case law. Rather than add a provision dealing explicitly with joint and several liability, it chose to leave the issue with the courts, to be resolved as it had been—on a case by case basis according to the predominant "divisibility" rule first enunciated by the *Chem–Dyne* court. Congress did, however, add two important provisions designed to mitigate the harshness of joint and several liability. First, the 1986 Amendments direct the

Amendment #1

EPA to offer early settlements to defendants who the Agency believes are responsible for only a small portion of the harm, so-called *de minimis* settlements. See § 122(g). Second, the Amendments provide for a statu-

Amendment #2

tory cause of action in contribution, codifying what most courts had concluded was implicit in the 1980 Act. See § 113(f)(1). Under this section, courts "may allocate response costs among liable parties using such equitable factors as the court determines are appropriate."

While a right of contribution undoubtedly softens the blow where parties cannot prove that the harm is divisible, it is not a complete panacea since it frequently will be difficult for defendants to locate a sufficient number of additional, solvent parties. Moreover, there are significant transaction costs involved in bringing other responsible parties to court. If it were possible to locate all responsible parties and to do so with little cost, the issue of joint and several liability obviously would be of only marginal significance. We, therefore, must examine carefully appellants' claim that they have met their burden of showing that the harm in this case is divisible.

*D's say b/g only surface
clean up, D's only
gave barrels cause tg.
out now much it
costs get rid of barrel*

Appellants begin by stressing that the state's past costs involved only surface cleanup. They then argue that because it was possible to determine how many barrels of waste they contributed to the site, it is also possible to determine what proportion of the state's removal expenses are attributable to each of them simply by estimating the cost of excavating a single barrel....

The state's removal efforts proceeded in four phases, each phase corresponding roughly to the cleanup of a different trench. The trenches were located in different areas of the site, but neither party has told us the distance between trenches. Appellants contend that it is possible to apportion the state's removal costs because there was evidence detailing (1) the total number of barrels excavated in each phase, (2) the number of barrels in each phase attributable to them, and (3) the total cost associated with each phase. In support of their argument, they point us to a few portions of the record, but for the most part are content to rest on statements in the district court's opinion. Specifically, appellants point to the following two sentences in the opinion: (1) "I find that [American Cyanamid] is responsible for ten drums of toxic hazardous material found at the site;" and (2) as to Rohm and Haas, "I accept the state's estimate [of 49 drums and 303 five-gallon pails]." Appellants then add, without opposition from the government, that the ten barrels of American Cyanamid waste discussed by the district court were found exclusively in Phase II, and that the 303 pails and 49 drums of Rohm and Haas waste mentioned by the court were found exclusively in Phase III. They conclude, therefore, that American Cyanamid should bear only a minute percentage of the $995,697.30 expended by the state during Phase II in excavating approximately 4,500 barrels and no share of the other phases, and that Rohm and Haas should be accountable for only a small portion of the $58,237 spent during Phase III in removing roughly 3,300 barrels and no share of the other phases. We disagree.

The district court's statements concerning the waste attributable to each appellant were based on the testimony of John Leo, an engineer hired by the state to oversee the cleanup. We have reviewed Mr. Leo's testimony carefully. Having done so, we think it inescapably clear that the district court did not mean to suggest that appellants had contributed only 49 and 10 barrels respectively, but rather, that those amounts were all that could be *positively attributed* to appellants.

Mr. Leo testified that out of the approximately 10,000 barrels that were excavated during the four phases, only "three to four hundred of the drums contained markings which could potentially be traced." This is not surprising considering that there had been an enormous fire at the site, that the barrels had been exposed to the elements for a number of years, and that a substantial amount of liquid waste had leaked and eaten away at the outsides of the barrels. Mr. Leo also testified that it was not simply the absence of legible markings that prevented the state from identifying the overwhelming majority of barrels, but also the danger involved in handling the barrels. Ironically, it was appellants themselves who, in an effort to induce Mr. Leo to lower his estimate of the number of barrels attributable to each defendant, elicited much of the testimony concerning the impossibility of accurately identifying all of the waste.

In light of the fact that most of the waste could not be identified, and that the appellants, and not the government, had the burden to account for all of this uncertainty, we think it plain that the district court did not err in holding them jointly and severally liable for the state's past removal costs. Perhaps in this situation the only way appellants could have demonstrated that they were limited contributors would have been to present specific evidence documenting the whereabouts of their waste at all times after it left their facilities. But far from doing so, appellants deny all knowledge of how their waste made its way to the site. Moreover, the government presented evidence that much of Rohm and Haas' waste found at the site came from its laboratory in Spring House, Pennsylvania and that during the relevant years, this lab generated over two thousand drums of waste, all of which were consigned to a single transporter. Under these circumstances, where Rohm and Haas was entrusting substantial amounts of waste to a single transporter who ultimately proved unreliable, we simply cannot conclude, absent evidence to the contrary, that only a handful of the 2,000 or more barrels reached the site.

Notes and Comments

1. Did you agree with the *Chem-Dyne* court's determination that CERCLA imposes joint and several liability in situations in which its application would be consistent with the common law? *Picillo* is typical of the post-*Chem-Dyne* case law in its assumption that this is the case.

2. Both the *Chem-Dyne* and *Picillo* courts determined that they develop uniform federal rules in determining whether joint and several liability applies in individual cases. Recall that in *Bestfoods* the Supreme Court, while declining to resolve the question, seemed skeptical as to whether the courts should apply federal rules of decision in analyzing questions of parent-corporation liability under CERCLA. In *United States v. Kimbell Foods, Inc.*, 440 U.S. 715, 99 S.Ct. 1448, 59 L.Ed.2d 711 (1979), the Court identified three factors courts should look to in resolving whether they should apply state or federal rules of decision in filling in the interstices of federal programs:

> (1) whether the federal program by its nature must be uniform, (2) whether application of state law would frustrate special objectives of the federal program, and (3) the extent to which application of a federal rule would disrupt commercial relationships predicated on state law.

Id. at 728–729. What rationales did the *Chem-Dyne* court determine supported the application of federal rules of decision in resolving issues relating to the imposition of joint and several liability? Were you persuaded? Are the dynamics different in the joint and several liability context than they might be in the context of piercing the corporate veil?

3. What test does the *Chem-Dyne* court apply for when joint and several liability should be imposed? Do you agree with this test? How is it likely to apply in most contexts? Why did the court impose joint and several liability regarding the removal costs in *Picillo*? To the extent that the court rested its indivisibility finding on the problems of proof posed by inadequate records regarding the generators of each drum, *Picillo* appears to be the only appellate decision in which a court has applied joint and several liability based upon indivisibility problems other than those posed through the commingling of waste. Why did the defendants bear the burden of accounting for the uncertainty regarding all unlabeled drums? Does this result make sense? Could EPA apply this same theory if a transporter distributed wastes

from numerous customers to various sites without keeping records of whose wastes went where?

4. EPA raised an alternative "averted harm" theory in *Picillo* based on the idea that even if it were possible to determine what proportion of the state's removal costs were attributable to the appellants, joint and several liability still would have been proper because the appellants' drums would have led to an indivisible harm had not the government intervened. The court expressed reservations about this theory, but chose not to directly address it in reaching its decision. Do you agree with the court's reservations? Why or why not?

5. Under what circumstances should PRPs be able to avoid joint and several liability under CERCLA? Section 433A(1) of the Restatement (Second) of Torts states that:

(1) Damages for harm are to be apportioned among two or more causes where

(a) there are distinct harms, or

(b) there is a reasonable basis for determining the contribution of each cause to a single harm.

The first of these scenarios is easy to apply. Assume, for example that a given site has two separate contaminated areas, with one containing PCB-contaminated soils, and the other solvent-based soil and groundwater contamination. If a given PRP could show that it sent only PCBs to the site, and that there are no PCB or PCB-derivatives in the second area, it would be able to establish divisibility as a matter of law.

6. Can you envision any circumstances in which the Restatement's second scenario might come into play? In *In the Matter of Bell Petroleum Services, Inc.*, 3 F.3d 889 (5th Cir. 1993), all of the parties (including EPA) seemed to assume that courts can apportion liability as a matter of law in situations in which multiple parties contribute known quantities of the same contaminant (in that case, chromium) to the same commingled mass. In that case, the dispute was over whether the relevant defendant had made an adequate showing with respect to the volumes discharged. The Fifth Circuit determined that it had, declaring that "evidence sufficient to permit a rough approximation is all that is required under the Restatement." Id. at 904 n. 19. Additionally, in two cases involving Alcan Aluminum Corp., the Second and Third Circuits determined that, in multi-waste cases, the government could not overcome apportionment arguments merely by demonstrating that the defendant's wastes have commingled with others and that the resulting mixture required investigation or remediation. *United States v. Alcan Aluminum Corp.*, 964 F.2d 252, 270 (3d Cir. 1992); *United States v. Alcan Aluminum Corp.*, 990 F.2d 711, 722 (2d Cir. 1993). In both cases, the courts remanded to the district court to give Alcan the opportunity to prove that its "emulsion did not or could not, *when mixed with other hazardous wastes,* contribute to the release and the resultant response costs...." 964 F.2d at 271 (emphasis in original); 990 F.2d at 722. The courts determined that, if Alcan could make this showing, it would not only result in apportionment, but in fact its apportionable share would be zero. Do you agree with these decisions, and with the assumption that EPA was willing to buy into in *Bell*

Petroleum? How much of a swath do they cut from the general rule of joint and several liability? We should perhaps note that Alcan was ultimately unable to make the showing required by the courts in either of the *Alcan* cases. See *United States v. Alcan Aluminum Corp.*, 892 F.Supp. 648, 655 (M.D.Pa. 1995); and *United States v. Alcan Aluminum Corp.*, 315 F.3d 179, 187 (2d Cir. 2003).

7. Where it applies, joint and several liability allows EPA, in theory, to sue any one of perhaps several hundred generators for the entire cost of cleanup at a given site. In its efforts to dismantle the joint and several liability scheme, industrial advocates frequently have raised the specter of EPA imposing the entire cost of cleanup at a given site upon a so-called "one-drum generator." In practice, however, EPA has been much more moderate, typically trying to negotiate settlements with all identified PRPs. Given the transaction costs and delays involved with CERCLA–scale multi-party negotiations, why do you think EPA has pursued this course?

8. In practice, EPA tends to use joint and several liability for at least three purposes. First, it uses the threat of joint and several liability as an inducement to settlement. Second, it frequently uses the doctrine to reallocate what are referred to as "orphan shares" (the liability shares, for example, of parties who cannot be located or who may be bankrupt or have dissolved) among the remaining solvent parties. And third, if negotiations break down and EPA is left in the position of either issuing a unilateral order or commencing a cost-recovery action, it may use joint and several liability as a means of limiting the number of PRPs to whom it will issue an order or against whom it will commence a law suit. Are all of these purposes appropriate? Are there others that you would add?

9. As noted by the *Picillo* court, the SARA amendments "soften[ed] the blow" of joint and several liability by providing an explicit contribution right in § 113(f). Do you share the court's perception that this right is only of limited benefit to PRPs that have been subjected to more than their proportionate share of liability? Why?

10. If EPA or, perhaps more accurately, the Department of Justice chooses to sue fewer than the full range of potential defendants in a multi-party case, should the named defendants be entitled to join any unnamed PRPs as third-party defendants? Would you expect EPA to resist such efforts? Why or why not?

C. Defenses

Section 107(b) of CERCLA establishes three narrow defenses to liability. Additionally, in passing the Brownfields Amendments, Congress added a series of new exclusions to liability to § 107 which function like defenses in that, generally speaking, they impose on defendants the burden of demonstrating that they qualify thereunder. CERCLA § 107(o), (p), (q) and (r). In this section, we provide a brief overview of the three most significant carve-outs from the CERCLA liability scheme: the "traditional" third-party defense under § 107(b)(3), the "innocent landowner defense" under that same section, and the "prospective purchaser exclusion" under § 107(r).

Section 107(b)(3) provides a "third-party" defense that applies if a party not in contractual privity with the person asserting the defense was the sole cause of the relevant release or threatened release and the resulting damages. Specifically, § 107(b)(3) requires that the party who caused the release or threatened release be neither an employee nor an agent of the defendant, nor "one whose act or omission occurs in connection with a contractual relationship, either directly or indirectly, with the defendant ... " Additionally, it requires that the defendant establish that:

> (a) he exercised due care with respect to the hazardous substance concerned, taking into consideration the characteristics of such hazardous substance, in light of all relevant facts and circumstances, and (b) he took precautions against foreseeable acts or omissions of any such third party and the consequences that could foreseeably result from such acts or omissions ...

[margin note: 3rd Party defense]

CERCLA § 107(b). In its "traditional" (and only pre-SARA) application, one who has status liability (e.g., the current owner of a site) may establish this defense if an unrelated third party caused the relevant release. This would be the case, for example, if the contamination was caused by a vandal or other "midnight dumper." It might also be the case if contamination from an upgradient parcel seeped down onto his or her property (although to this extent, § 107(b)(3) would now seem to overlap with the new defense in § 107(q)). In either event, the relevant party would also have to establish that it meets § 107(b)(3)'s "due care" requirements.

The innocent landowner defense is actually a subset of the § 107(b)(3) defense. As EPA has noted, before SARA was passed EPA "took the position that a real estate deed represented a contractual relationship within the meaning of § 107(b)(3), thus eliminating the availability of the third party defense for a landowner in the chain of title with a party who had caused or contributed to the release." EPA Guidance on Landowner Liability under Section 107(a)(1) of CERCLA, *De Minimis* Settlements under Section 122(g)(1)(B) of CERCLA, and Settlements with Prospective Purchasers of Contaminated Property, June 6, 1989, at p. 9–10 ("Innocent Landowner Guidance"). Congress appeared to confirm this interpretation in 1986, making explicit in § 101(35)(A) that deeds and other land contracts give rise to the type of "contractual relationship" that can defeat the § 107(b)(3) defense. At the same time, however, Congress created an exception to this general rule for those purchasers that, before acquiring title, diligently investigate the potential existence of contamination and find none, so long as, after having purchased the property, they act appropriately if and when they become aware that there was preexisting contamination. These so-called "innocent landowners" are deemed not to have had a "contractual relationship" with the person causing the release for purposes of § 107(b)(3). CERCLA § 101(35)(A)(I).

[margin note: innocent landowner exception]

The million dollar question in the innocent landowner context involves the degree of investigation that purchasers must have undertaken before they bought the relevant property. In this regard, § 101(35)(A)(i) requires the defendant to show that it "did not know and had no reason to know" of the relevant contamination. In order to demonstrate this, § 101(35)(B) requires it to establish that it made "all appropriate inquiry into the previous ownership and uses of the property consistent with good commercial or customary practice...." As originally passed, SARA required the court to take the following factors into account in determining whether "all appropriate inquiry" has been made:

1. Any specialized knowledge or experience on the part of the landowner;

2. The relationship of the purchase price to the value of the property if uncontaminated;

3. Commonly known or reasonably ascertainable information about the property;

4. The obviousness of the presence or likely presence of contamination on the property; and

5. The ability to detect such contamination by appropriate inspection.

See CERCLA Section 101(35)(B)(iv).

Over the years, these standards proved unacceptably vague. Neither EPA nor the courts developed clear guidelines for what constitutes "all appropriate inquiry" under differing factual circumstances. Absent this guidance, the private sector of necessity began to work out for itself what it thought was necessary to establish the defense. Soon, a series of industry practices emerged. In most transactions involving commercial or industrial property, the would-be purchaser would begin its analysis with what became known a "phase 1" site assessment. This typically consisted of a site visit and walk-around, interviews with past and present employees, title searches, file reviews at both the facility and the relevant regulatory agencies, and a review of aerial photographs, if available. This assessment was intended to determine the potential existence of contamination. If this inquiry didn't raise any "red flags," most would-be purchasers felt comfortable proceeding with the purchase. In 1997, the American Society for Testing and Materials ("ASTM") developed standardized guidelines for these "phase 1" assessments. See ASTM Standard E–1527–97, Standard Practices for Environmental Site Assessment: Phase 1 Site Assessment, Process.

When it passed the Brownfields Amendments in 2002, Congress returned to this issue, establishing a three-tiered scheme for resolving "all appropriate inquiry" questions. In short, Congress charged EPA with writing rules fleshing out these requirements, which will be binding upon the courts when issued with respect to investigations performed after that time. CERCLA § 101(35)(B)(iii). Congress did not intend, however, for these new rules to have retroactive effect. Instead, the revised § 101(35)(B) contemplates that the courts will continue to apply the original five factors set out in SARA to questions about the validity of any investigations performed before May 31, 1997. Additionally, Congress codified the ASTM standards as the appropriate measuring stick for pre-purchase investigations conducted between May 31, 1997, and the date when EPA promulgates the new standards. CERCLA Section 101(35)(B)(iv)(I) and (II). Thus, we now have the following framework:

1. For purchases before May 31, 1997, the courts are to apply the original five statutory factors, now set out in § 101(35)(B)(iv)(I);

2. For purchases between May 31, 1997, and the date when EPA promulgates its new rules, the courts are to apply the ASTM standards; and

3. Once EPA promulgates its rules, the courts are to apply them.

In the Brownfields Amendments, Congress also created the "prospective purchaser exclusion" to address another perceived flaw in the preexisting scheme. For the first 21 years of CERCLA's existence, those who purchased property knowing it was contaminated were strictly liable and, generally speaking, had no defenses. Perhaps obviously, the specter of this liability served to discourage investments in contaminated land. Oftentimes, would-be buyers walked away from deals at the first indication of potentially significant contamination issues, choosing to shift their development focus from previously-developed industrial properties (denominated "brownfields") to hitherto undeveloped land (denominated "greenfields"). Other developers simply set their sights on greenfields in the first place, choosing to avoid the headaches associated with even beginning to analyze the environmental risks at previously developed sites. At the macroscopic level, these dynamics served to stifle the redevelopment or urban, industrial areas, pushing new growth outside of the industrial core areas and, frequently, into the suburbs. In turn, this posed social justice issues, as industrial flight tended to take the associated jobs farther and farther from inner-city populations, leaving only scarred land at former industrial sites.

Beginning in late 1980s, EPA began to grapple with this problem by creating what were referred to as "prospective purchaser agreements" ("PPAs"). See Innocent Landowner Guidance. EPA moved even more aggressively in this direction in 1995, issuing a new Guidance on Settlements with Prospective Purchasers of Contaminated Property, together with a model agreement. 60 Fed.Reg. 34792 (1995) ("Prospective Purchaser Guidance"). Still, from the perspective of would-be purchasers, these relief valves were seen to be too limited. Most significantly, due to resource constraints EPA limited the availability of PPAs to facilities at which EPA action had been taken, was undergoing, or was anticipated to be taken. 60 Fed. Reg. at 34793. As EPA explained, this criterion was meant "to ensure that EPA [did] not become unnecessarily involved in purely private real estate transactions or expend its limited resources in negotiation which [were] unlikely to produce a sufficient benefit to the public." Id. While this was understandable from an Agency resources standpoint, it placed severe limitations on the availability of PPAs. As we have seen, the specter of CERCLA liability far transcends any list of sites at which EPA is or is likely to become involved. As previously mentioned, EPA tends to focus its attention on site that are or are likely to be on the NPL. Currently, just over 1,200 sites are on the NPL. See www.epa.gov/superfund. By contrast, the U.S. Conference of Mayors has estimated that there are more than 450,000 brownfield sites. S.Rep. No. 107–2, 107th Cong., 1st Sess., p.1 (March 12, 2001). Under EPA's then-existing approach, the benefits of the PPA program were simply unavailable if a particular site was not on EPA's radar screen.

In the Brownfields Amendments, Congress fundamentally altered the CERCLA liability scheme as it relates to prospective purchasers. In the new Section 107(r), Congress provided an exclusion for "bona fide prospective purchaser[s]." This exclusion is available only to those whose potential liability would be based solely on their ownership or operation. CERCLA § 107(r). Moreover, the term "bona fide prospective purchaser" is defined in a way that makes clear that the exclusion is prospective only; i.e. it only applies to those who acquired their interest in the relevant facility after the date of the Brownfields Amendments (January 11, 2002). CERCLA § 101(40). Additionally, the definition requires the owner to establish the following elements:

A. It must have acquired the property after "[a]ll disposal of hazardous substances;"

B. It must have satisfied the "all appropriate inquiry" standard before acquiring the property;

C. It must make all legally required notices with regard to the discovery or release of any hazardous substances;

D. It must exercise appropriate care with respect to any hazardous substances found, including taking reasonable steps to stop any continuing releases, prevent any threatened releases, and prevent or limit exposure to existing releases;

E. It must provide full cooperation, assistance and access to anyone authorized to conduct response actions;

F. It must be in compliance with any land use restrictions that are part of the response action, and it must not have impeded the effectiveness of any institutional controls;

G. It must have complied with all EPA information requests under § 104(e); and

H. It must not be potentially affiliated with anyone with is potentially liable (e.g., through a familial or corporate relationship).

Id. If these conditions are met, however, there is no longer any need for the owner to enter into a PPA. The relevant owner simply bears no liability under CERCLA. There is one caveat, however: Section 107(r)(2) allows EPA to impose a lien on the property to cover any unrecovered response costs if its cleanup increased the value of the property. The amount of the lien cannot exceed the increase in value attributable to the response. CERCLA § 107(r)(4)(A).

Notes and Comments

1. What kinds of contractual relationships should preclude the application of the traditional § 107(b)(3) defense? Should all land sale agreements do so? Should a landowner be deemed to have a disqualifying "indirect" contractual relationship with all prior owners in the chain of title. Compare *New York v. Lashins Arcade Co.*, 91 F.3d 353 (2d Cir. 1996), with *Lefebvre v. Central Maine Power Co.*, 7 F.Supp. 2d 64, 68 n.3 (D.Me. 1998), *Goe Eng'g Co. v. Physicians Formula Cosmetics*, 1997 WL 889278, at 10 n.7 (C.D.Cal. 1997), and *Bangor v. Citizens Communication Co.*, 2004 WL 483201 (D.Me. 2004); see also Johnston, Current Landowner Liability Under CERCLA: Restoring the Need for Due Diligence, 9 Fordham Env'l Law Journal 401 (1998). Should a lessor have a disqualifying relationship with all of its tenants, or all of its subtenants? See *Bedford Affiliates v. Sills*, 156 F.3d 416, 425 (2d Cir. 1998), *United States v. A & N Cleaners*, 788 F.Supp. 1317 (S.D.N.Y.1992), and *United States v. Northernaire Plating Co.*, 670 F.Supp. 742 (W.D.Mich. 1987). Even if lessors might otherwise be eligible for a § 107(b)(3) defense, what kinds of precautions should they be required to undertake to meet the requirements of § 107(b)(3) when they are aware that their sublessees are operating businesses like dry cleaning establishments? What if they are unaware to the types of businesses to which their lessees may be subleasing the properties? Should they have a duty to inform themselves of the nature of these businesses and their work practices? Should they be able to pass any such obligations on to their lessees by contract? See *United States v. A & N Cleaners and Launderers, Inc.*, 854 F.Supp. 229, 243–244 (S.D.N.Y. 1994).

2. What should the "due care" obligation entail when a property owner who otherwise has a valid defense under § 107(b)(3) becomes aware of contamination on his or her property? Should it be enough merely to contact either State authorities or EPA? Should it matter whether these authorities are actively responding to the relevant contamination? Compare *Kerr–McGee Chemical v. Lefton Iron & Metal Co.*, 14 F.3d 321 (7th Cir.1994); *New York v. Lashins Arcade Co.*, 91 F.3d 353 (2d Cir. 1996); *United States v. 150 Acres of Land*, 204 F.3d 698, 706 (6th Cir. 2000); *Franklin County Convention Facilities Auth. v. American Premier Underwriters, Inc.*, 240 F.3d 534, 548 (6th Cir. 2001); and *United States v. DiBiase Salem Realty Trust*, 1993 WL 729662 (D.Mass. 1993). It may be one thing to expect an otherwise non-liable landowner to remove some corroded drums, or to fence off a contaminated area. But is it reasonable to require such a landowner to undertake extensive removal or remedial measures? Do courts need to be leery about requiring landowners to act like liable parties in order to preserve their defenses? See *Kalamazoo River Study Group v. Rockwell International*, 3 F.Supp.2d 799, 807–807 (W.D.Mich. 1998), *rev'd on other grounds*, 228 F.3d 648 (6th Cir. 2000) (riparian landowners were not required to take affirmative actions to address contaminated sediments in the Kalamazoo River); see also EPA's Final Policy Toward Owners of Property Containing Contaminated Aquifers,

60 Fed. Reg. 34790, 34791 (1995) (stating EPA's view that if a landowner otherwise has a valid § 107(b)(3) defense, its failure to conduct groundwater monitoring or to install groundwater remediation systems should not, in the absence of exceptional circumstances, be deemed a failure to exercise "due care").

3. The innocent landowner defense (like the prospective purchaser defense) applies only to pre-existing contamination. CERCLA § 101(35)(A). If a particular case involves disposal during the owner's period of ownership, that owner must find comfort, if at all, in CERCLA's other defenses (e.g., the traditional § 107(b)(3) defense).

4. In the innocent landowner context, should the amount of money at issue in a given transaction be relevant to the degree of inquiry required? This factor could cut either way in different factual settings. Should someone buying a small business (e.g., an auto repair shop) be expected to spend up to 50% or more of the purchase price on environmental investigations? Will the market bear this degree of investigation? Should those who purchase such businesses effectively be rendered unable to establish an innocent landowner defense? At the other extreme, should a company undertaking a $100 million corporate acquisition be able to rely on a $5,000 "phase 1" site assessment even if that assessment reveals no evidence of contamination?

5. Should "no inquiry" ever constitute "all appropriate inquiry?" The Government has consistently argued that, at a minimum, a visual inspection should be required in order to establish the defense. See, e.g., Innocent Landowner Guidance, supra, at 12 n. 11. Several courts have rejected this absolutist position, requiring at a minimum some evidence regarding the customary due diligence practices under the circumstances. See *United States v. 150 Acres of Land*, 204 F.3d 698, 707 (6th Cir. 2000); *United States v. Serafini*, 706 F.Supp. 346, 353 (M.D.Pa.1988); and *United States v. Pacific Hide & Fur Depot*, 716 F.Supp. 1341, 1348–49 (D.Idaho 1989). Not surprisingly, however, in some contexts courts have deemed the lack any pre-purchase investigations to be fatal to any attempts to establish an innocent landowner defense. See, e.g., *Foster v. United States*, 922 F.Supp. 642, 655–56 (D.D.C. 1996) (finding the innocent landowner defense unavailable where the purchaser undertook no environmental investigation before buying the site in 1985); *United States v. Taylor*, 1993 WL 760996 (W.D.Mich.1993) (deeming the defense unavailable with respect to a purchase in 1986 where "[a]ny diligence would have revealed problems"); and *United States v. Rohm and Haas Co.*, 790 F.Supp. 1255, 1264 (E.D.Pa. 1992), *aff'd* 2 F.3d 1265 (3d Cir. 1993) (landowner did not meet test where it offered no evidence of having investigated the prior uses or previous ownership of the property). In one of the most defendant-friendly innocent landowner cases to date, the court in *Goe Engineering Co., Inc. v. Physicians Formula Cosmetics*, 1997 WL 889278 (C.D.Cal. 1997), found that the purchaser met the all appropriate inquiry standard where it had inspected the property prior to purchasing it in 1985, even though it apparently had undertaken no sampling despite having seen oil staining on the floor and some 50–gallon drums outside, and its having been aware of the fact that the prior owner had operated a machine shop using underground storage tanks (UST's) at the site. The court found that the plaintiffs had failed to offer "any legal or scientific authority for their contention that the presence of oil stains, barrels, or

UST's should put a purchaser on notice that the property may be contaminated with hazardous substances." Id. at 13.

6. Congress may have caught some landowners off guard by imposing the ASTM standards retroactively for the five year period between 1997 and 2002. During that period, many consulting firms looked to those standards for guidance, but may have deviated from them somewhat on the theory that what they were doing was still "appropriate" under the then-existing statutory standards. Many of those investigations may now be deemed to be defective as a matter of law according to the ASTM standards.

7. EPA issued proposed rules fleshing out the "all appropriate inquiry" requirements in August of 2004. 65 Fed.Reg. 52542 (Aug. 26, 2004).

A Note on the Brownfields Program

As we have seen, Congress provided targeted liability relief when it passed the Brownfields Amendments. At the same time, Congress sought to further promote the redevelopment of brownfield sites by creating a grant program primarily for the benefit of local governments, States and Indian tribes. This program has two key features. First, Congress authorized the appropriation of $50 million per year for each of the fiscal years 2002 through 2006, for a grant program, administered by EPA, to encourage States and Indian tribes to establish or enhance their response programs. CERCLA § 128. Second, Congress authorized the appropriation of $200 million per year for each of those same years for direct grants to local governments, States, Indian tribes and even non-profit groups, to be used inventory, characterize, assess and remediate brownfield sites. CERCLA § 104(k). The term "brownfield site" is defined broadly to mean any site at which actual or potential contamination may be complicating the expansion, redevelopment or reuse of the property, but is qualified by several exclusions, including actual or proposed NPL sites and other sites being addressed under either CERCLA or RCRA. CERCLA § 101(39).

To be eligible for State program grants, State or tribal programs must have either entered into a Memorandum of Agreement (MOA) with EPA or established a program containing the following elements: (1) a survey and inventory of brownfield sites; (2) oversight and enforcement authorities to ensure that response actions will be appropriate; (3) mechanisms and resources to provide meaningful opportunities for public participation; and (4) mechanisms for approval of cleanup plans, and a requirement for certification regarding the completion of any necessary response activities. CERCLA § 128(a)(1)(A) and (2). In addition to using these grants to establish or enhance their response programs, States and tribes can use them either (1) to capitalize revolving loan funds for brownfields remediation, or (2) to purchase insurance or develop other risk sharing mechanisms as a funding source for response actions. CERCLA § 128(a)(1)(B).

There are actually three types of brownfield-specific grants under § 104(k). First, EPA can award grants of up to $200,000 (or, in some cases, up to $350,000) per site to either States, tribes, or various local governmental authorities (collectively denominated "eligible entities") to inventory, characterize and assess brownfield sites. CERCLA § 104(k)(1), (2)(A) and (B), and (4)(A)(i). Second, EPA can provide grants of up to $200,000 to either

grant #1

grant # 2

grant # 3

eligible entities or non-profit organizations for the remediation of sites owned by those entities. CERCLA § 104(k)(3)(A)(ii). And third, EPA can award grants of up to $1 million to eligible entities for the purpose of capitalizing revolving loan funds, and can supplement these grants in later years. CERCLA § 104 (3)(A)(i) and (4)(A)(ii). In turn, eligible entities can use these funds to award loans to site owners or developers, or to award grants to either other eligible entities or non-profit organizations. CERCLA § 104(k)(3)(B)(i) and (ii). The statute also provides criteria to guide these granting decisions. See, CERCLA § 104(k)(3)(C) (relating to site remediation), (k)(4)(A)(ii) (relating to supplemental loan fund grants), and (k)(5)(C) (general criteria).

Three other aspects of the Brownfields Amendments are worth noting. First, the new Section 105(h) provides that, upon request of the States, EPA should generally defer listing certain sites, called "eligible response sites," on the NPL so long as the States are either conducting response actions or pursuing or overseeing private-party responses. "Eligible response sites" correlate generally, but not precisely, with brownfield sites; they specifically do not include sites that EPA has determined are eligible for placement on the NPL. See CERCLA § 101(41). Second, Congress sought to remove where possible a perceived impediment to brownfields redevelopment; i.e., the rigorousness of the NCP. In this vein, Section 104(k)(5)(A)(i)(II) limits EPA's ability to condition grants on compliance with the NCP to those situations where EPA determines that a particular requirement of the NCP is relevant and appropriate. Third, Section 128(b) now generally bars EPA from bringing an action under either § 106 or § 107 at an "eligible response site" if someone is conducting or has completed a response action under a State cleanup program. There are exceptions that apply when the State asks EPA to get involved, when EPA determines that the site may still present an imminent and substantial endangerment, or when new information indicates that the site still presents a threat. CERCLA § 128(b).

D. A Quick Overview of the Cleanup Process

The topic of CERCLA cleanups is quite complex. We will only treat it briefly here. Students should be aware that the discussion below is intended to provide only a brief overview and is in many ways oversimplified.

Statutorily, § 104(a)(1) authorizes EPA to act, consistent with the NCP, to provide for both removal and remedial actions. Section 121 establishes the applicable cleanup standards. EPA has integrated both of these provisions through the NCP, which is found at 40 C.F.R. §§ 300.400–300.440.

The NCP requires that CERCLA cleanup decisions be made through a prolonged process that includes several different steps and provides opportunities for involvement on behalf of both the affected state and local governments and the public generally. The procedure may include the following components:

1. The preliminary assessment and site investigation ("PA/SI");

2. The decision to implement removal action;

3.   The decision regarding whether the site merits placement on the NPL;

4.   The remedial investigation and feasibility study ("RI/FS"); and

5.   The issuance of a proposed plan, the provision of an opportunity for public comment, and the issuance of a record of decision ("ROD").

In short, the PA/SI has two primary purposes: (1) to determine the need for removal action; and (2) to generate the information necessary to determine whether the site warrants placement on the NPL. While both the statute and the NCP define the term "removal" broadly, CERCLA § 101(22) and 40 C.F.R. § 300.5, these measures are best conceptualized as short term steps that either stabilize releases, abate threatened releases, or mitigate near-term threats. 53 Fed.Reg. 51411 (Dec. 21, 1988). At the same time EPA is considering or implementing these actions, it is trying to determine whether the site warrants placement on the NPL. EPA evaluates sites for potential listing on the NPL based primarily on a ranking system known as the Hazard Ranking System ("HRS"). See 40 C.F.R. § 300.425(c); and 40 C.F.R. Part 300, Appendix A. EPA feeds data from observed or potential releases of hazardous substances into the HRS to derive a numeric score indicating EPA's preliminary assessment of the perceived risk associated with the site and comparing it with perceived risks at other sites. Currently, the magic number is 28.5; any site scoring higher than that number under the HRS qualifies for listing on the NPL. 55 Fed.Reg. 51,559 (Dec. 14, 1990).

The remedial investigation and feasibility study ("RI/FS") is at the heart of the CERCLA remedy selection process. As stated at 40 C.F.R. § 300.430(a)(2), the purpose of the RI/FS is "to assess site conditions and evaluate alternatives to the extent necessary to select a remedy." Conceptually, the two components of the RI/FS can be separated. The purpose of the remedial investigation is to gather sufficient data to characterize the conditions at the site for the purpose of developing and evaluating effective remedial alternatives. 40 C.F.R. § 300.430(d). The RI assesses the physical characteristics of the site, the nature and extent of the contamination, and the actual and potential pathways of exposure to the surrounding population. The feasibility study, by contrast, develops and analyzes alternatives for appropriate response. It is important to note, however, that in practice the RI and FS "are not sequential but rather concurrent processes." 55 Fed.Reg. 8712 (March 8, 1990). Thus, the very first step in the RI/FS process—the "scoping" stage—includes the identification of both "likely response scenarios and potentially applicable technologies ... that may address site problems" and "the type, quality, and quantity of data that will be collected during the RI/FS to support decisions regarding remedial response activities." 40 C.F.R. § 300.430(b).

Ultimately, the most important function of the RI/FS is to set the stage for remedy selection by zeroing in on a preferred alternative. To do this, the RI/FS must encompass both a risk assessment and a process for determining the desired level of risk reduction—this latter part being frequently referred to as the "how clean is clean" question. Both of these undertakings are both complex and controversial. On the latter front, the relevant provisions of § 121 establish at least five requirements that CERCLA remedial actions must meet:

1. They must attain a degree of cleanup that assures protection of human health and the environment (§ 121(b)(1));

2. With regard to hazardous substances that will remain after completion, they must, in most circumstances, meet all "applicable" and/or "relevant and appropriate" requirements under federal and state law ("ARARs") (§ 121(d)(2)) (these include, for example, Safe Drinking Water Act standards if the groundwater at the site is a potential source of drinking water);

3. They must utilize permanent solutions and alternative treatment technologies or resource recovery technologies to the maximum extent practicable (§ 121(b)(1));

4. They must provide for cost-effective response, taking into account the total long-and short-term costs of such actions (including operation and maintenance costs)(§ 121(a) and (b)(1)); and

5. They must be in accordance with the NCP to the extent practicable (§ 121(a)).

As if to underscore the Congressional desire for permanent remedies, § 121(b)(1) establishes two specific statutory preferences. First, it provides that remedies that emphasize "treatment which permanently and significantly reduces the volume, toxicity or mobility of the hazardous substances ... are to be preferred over remedial actions not involving such treatment." It further states that "[t]he offsite transport and disposal of hazardous substances or contaminated materials without such treatment should be the least favored alternative remedial action where practicable treatment technologies are available." CERCLA § 121(b).

SARA added two provisions addressing state and community involvement in the remedy-selection process. Section 121(f) required EPA to promulgate regulations "providing for substantial and meaningful involvement by each State in initiation, development, and selection of remedial actions to be undertaken in that State." Section 117 requires EPA both to "[p]rovide a reasonable opportunity for submission of written and oral comments and an opportunity for a public hearing at or near the facility at issue" regarding the contemplated remedy, and to respond "to each of the significant comments, criticisms, and new data submitted ... " CERCLA § 117(a) and (b).

EPA sought to implement these mandates, some of which (e.g., the preference for permanence versus the insistence on cost-effectiveness) appear to conflict with each other, in the 1990 NCP. It did this by establishing nine criteria according to which potential remedies are to be evaluated during both the FS alternatives analysis and the ultimate remedy-selection process. The criteria include:

1. Overall protection of human health and the environment;

2. Compliance with ARARs;

3. Long-term effectiveness and permanence;

4. Reduction of toxicity, mobility, or volume through treatment;

5. Short-term effectiveness;

6. Implementability;

7. Cost;

8. State acceptance; and

9. Community acceptance.

40 C.F.R. § 300.430(e)(9) and (f)(1).

These criteria are not given equal weight in the remedy-selection process. EPA has identified the first two criteria (protectiveness and ARAR–compliance) as "threshold criteria" that each alternative must meet in order to be eligible for selection, unless a specific ARAR is waived (see below). 40 C.F.R. § 300.430(f)(1)(i)(A). The next five criteria (long-term effectiveness and permanence; reduction of toxicity, mobility, and volume through treatment; short-term effectiveness; implementability; and cost) are deemed "primary balancing criteria" and are used to weigh major tradeoffs between alternative cleanup strategies. 40 C.F.R. § 300.430(f)(1)(i)(B); see also 53 Fed.Reg. 51428 (Dec. 21, 1988). Finally, the last two criteria, state and community acceptance, are referred to as "modifying criteria," primarily because the information necessary to fully consider them typically will not be complete until after the official public comment period. 40 C.F.R. § 300.430(f)(1)(i)(C); see also 55 Fed. Reg. 8730 (March 8, 1990).

We conclude our discussion of remedy selection with some brief consideration of how EPA defines "protectiveness" under this program. In the absence of ARARs specifying a more stringent result, EPA assesses protectiveness primarily in terms of toxicity and carcinogenicity. For systemic toxicants, EPA's regulations provide that "acceptable exposure levels shall represent concentration levels to which the human population, including sensitive subgroups, may be exposed without adverse effect ..." 40 C.F.R. § 300.430(e)(2)(i)(A)(1). For known or suspected carcinogens, EPA takes the view that the appropriate risk range for CERCLA sites is between "10^{-4}" to "10^{-6}," with the 10^{-6} level serving as the point of departure. 40 C.F.R. § 300.430(e)(2)(i)(A)(2). A 10^{-6} cancer risk indicates that if 1,000,000 people were exposed to the contamination over the course of a lifetime, using predetermined exposure and carcinogenicity assumptions, the exposure theoretically would result in one additional cancer case. The 10^{-4} risk level would indicate that, theoretically, 100 out of those same 1,000,000 people would develop cancer, again assuming certain levels of exposure and toxicity. In the preamble to the 1990 NCP, EPA explained the point of departure concept in the following terms:

> Where the aggregate risk of contaminants based on existing ARARs exceeds 10^{-4} or where remediation goals are not determined by ARARs, EPA uses 10^{-6} as a point of departure for establishing preliminary remediation goals. This means that a cumulative risk level of 10^{-6} is used as the starting point ... for determining the most appropriate risk level that alternatives should be designed to attain. The use of 10^{-6} expresses EPA's preference for remedial actions that result in risks at the more protective end of the risk range, but this does not reflect a presumption that the final remedial action should attain such a risk level. Factors related to exposure, uncertainty and technical limitations may justify modification of initial cleanup levels that are based on the 10^{-6} risk level. The ultimate decision on what level of protection will be appropriate depends on the selected remedy, which is based on the [nine remedy-section criteria].

55 Fed.Reg. 8718 (March 8, 1990); *see also Id.* at 8717.

E. Settlement

We conclude our discussion of EPA response with an overview of the approaches EPA uses to promote settlement under CERCLA. As mentioned at the outset, EPA long has exhibited a preference for resolving CERCLA cases through the negotiation of settlements under which PRPs perform the necessary investigatory and/or remedial activities. Congress embraced this approach when it passed SARA in 1986, creating a specific provision promoting and establishment guidelines for settlement. Section 122(a) urges EPA to enter into settlements whenever it determines that they are in the public interest and consistent with the NCP. If EPA decides not to pursue settlement in a particular case, the same section requires it to explain to the PRPs in writing why it has chosen to forsake such an approach. (Note, however, that any decision by EPA not to pursue settlement is not subject to judicial review.)

EPA usually begins the settlement process as quickly as it can once it has determined who might bear potential liability for a particular site. EPA notifies PRPs of their potential liability through what are known as "notice letters." EPA's policy is to send out notice letters to all or virtually all parties for whom there is sufficient evidence to make a preliminary determination of potential liability. EPA may begin informal negotiations with the PRPs as soon as they receive their notice letters. Often, EPA will hold a "PRP meeting" to explicitly begin the negotiation process. At some sites, there may be just a handful of PRPs; at others, these meetings can involve dozens or even hundreds of parties. Not surprisingly, in these cases EPA is reluctant to engage in negotiations with individual PRPs. Instead, it seeks to negotiate with the PRP community collectively, or at least with all of those PRPs who are willing to negotiate in good faith.

In multi-party cases, EPA's first order of business generally is to seek to reach agreement with the *de minimis* parties. Section 122(g) requires EPA to enter into settlements with *de minimis* PRPs as promptly as possible whenever such settlements are practicable and in the public interest. Section 122(g)(1)(A) defines the universe of *de minimis* generators as including those whose contribution to the site is minimal both in the amount and toxicity of the substances involved. In practice, EPA usually further defines this group as including any generator who sent less than 1% of the overall volume of waste to the site.

One of the clear Congressional goals underlying § 122(g) was to eliminate *de minimis* parties from CERCLA cases as quickly and with as much finality as possible. As a result, EPA provides *de minimis* settlors with a degree of finality that is unavailable to other parties. In order to understand the distinction here, it is necessary to have a broader understanding of how settlement works generally. EPA has two major "carrots" it can offer to PRPs as inducements to settlement. First, it can provide both major and *de minimis* parties with "covenants not to sue" warranting that the government will not, as a general matter, seek any further relief from the settling parties. CERCLA § 122(f) and (g)(2). Second, it can provide either group of parties with "contribution protection" protecting them from potential suits by other PRPs through which they otherwise might seek to impose further liability on the settling parties regarding the site at issue. CERCLA §§ 113(f)(2) and 122(g)(4) and (h)(4). At least under the first of these two inducements, the protection that EPA provides to *de minimis* settlors is more absolute. As will be discussed below, major party settlements generally contain "reopeners" allowing EPA to pursue settling PRPs anew if conditions that were unknown at the time of the settlement subsequently are discovered, if new information later reveals that the remedy was not protective of human health or the environment, or if, in an EPA–lead cleanup situation, there are significant cost overruns. *De minimis* settlements, by contrast, typically include none of these reopeners; instead, they tend to include a reopener covering only situations in which new information comes to light indicating that a given party should not have qualified for *de minimis* status in the first place.

In exchange for this enhanced degree of finality, EPA typically extracts from *de minimis* settlors what it refers to as a "premium" payment designed to account for the uncertainties that they are avoiding by being allowed to settle without the more broad types of reopeners. EPA notes that:

> ... The premium charged should be in addition to the *de minimis* party's *pro rata* share of the site response costs. The premium should be sufficient to compensate the Agency for the risks associated with: (1) Settling at a site where the future response action has not been chosen; (2) possible cost overruns for a remedy not yet selected and; (3) potential inability to recover response costs from other sources.

Early *De Minimis* Waste Settlement Guidance, 57 Fed.Reg. at 29318 (July 1, 1992).

Once the *de minimis* negotiations are far enough along, EPA turns its attention to the major parties. Here, the dynamics are much more complex. For one thing, there is much more money at stake. Additionally, if there are to be any battles as to what the appropriate remedy should be, this is where they typically play out. Moreover, it is here that EPA and the PRPs must sort through the difficult issues regarding which PRPs are to pay how much, an issue that can get complicated, for example, when trying to determine the appropriate shares of the major generators as compared to owner/operators. And finally, because EPA typically asks the major parties to perform the necessary investigatory and/or remedial activities, it is during these negotiations that the PRPs must determine (generally as a group) whether they are willing to sign a consent decree or, alternatively, whether they would prefer to run the risk of having EPA issue them a unilateral order.

Depending on where EPA is on the technical side of the case, EPA may offer the major parties the opportunity to perform the RI/FS. EPA views negotiations concerning the RI/FS differently from those regarding cleanup. While the Agency is interested in having PRPs conduct RI/FSs, it is not inclined to spend long periods of time negotiating these agreements. Accordingly, EPA requires that PRPs meet three conditions as a precondition to negotiations regarding who will perform the RI/FS: they must (1) organize quickly into a group representing enough parties to assume full responsibility for conducting the RI/FS; (2) agree to follow EPA's scope of work for the RI/FS (although some minor negotiation may be allowed); and (3) demonstrate to the Agency their capability of adequately carrying out the RI/FS. EPA, "Participation of Potentially Responsible Parties in Development of Remedial Investigations and Feasibility Studies Under CERCLA," dated May 20, 1984.

Regardless of whether EPA is negotiating regarding the RI/FS or the ultimate remedy, it has at its disposal a procedural device wherein, at its option, it can invoke a formalized framework imposing rigid time constraints on the negotiation process. Under this process, known as "special notice," EPA sends out what in most circumstances will be a second notice letter prior to the RI/FS ("RI/FS special notice") and a third notice letter prior to the initiation of the remedial action ("RD/RA special notice"). To the extent the information is available, these notices are to provide each PRP with the names and addresses of the other PRPs, the volume and nature of the substances contributed by each PRP, and a volumetric ranking. See CERCLA § 122(e)(1). Under § 122(e)(2), the PRPs receiving the notice letter then have 60 days to coordinate and make a proposal for either undertaking the cleanup or financing a governmental cleanup. EPA must abstain from commencing any response actions under § 104(a), any RI/FS activities under § 104(b), or an action under § 106 during this 60-day period. If EPA determines that the PRPs submit a "good faith offer" within the 60-day period, it shall not commence any RI/FS activities for 30 more days, or any cleanup activities under § 104(a) or enforcement actions under § 106 for 60 more days.

Perhaps obviously enough, these moratoria are intended to provide for periods of negotiation between EPA and the PRPs. EPA, however, cleverly has interpreted these moratoria not only as a "floor" on the necessary negotiation period, but also a "ceiling." That is, EPA interprets the 90–and 120–day timeframes as placing a cap on the period of its negotiations with the PRPs. The current Agency position is that if the relevant negotiations are not concluded within the relevant timeframe, EPA generally will exercise its option to issue a unilateral order under § 106. Thus EPA has transformed the special notice device into a tool that permits it to invoke rigid "drop dead" dates at a moment's notice during the negotiations, instilling a clear sense of urgency in the negotiations.

As mentioned, the primary benefits EPA can confer to encourage settlement are a covenant not to sue and contribution protection. See CERCLA §§ 122(f), 113(f), and 122(h)(4). As also mentioned, EPA insists upon broader reopeners here than in the *de minimis* context. One is statutorily based: § 122(f)(6) provides that, in most situations, any covenant not to sue for future liability must include a reopener allowing EPA to pursue the settling PRPs for conditions that were unknown at the time EPA certified that the remedial action was complete. Additionally, § 122(f)(6)(C) authorizes EPA to include in any reopener such other terms as it deems necessary to protect human health and the environment. EPA's current policy is to include a reopener covering all situations where new information reveals that the remedy is not protective of human health and the environment. In cost-recovery settlements, it also frequently imposes a reopener addressing the possibility of cost-over-runs.

The major-party negotiations frequently founder not upon fights between EPA and the PRPs, but on those between warring factions among the PRPs themselves. Interestingly, EPA is often a disinterested observer in exactly how these battles play out, being much more interested in simply whether they are resolved on a timely basis. What role should EPA play in resolving any of these questions? Interestingly, at many sites EPA in the end acts almost as a facilitator or mediator because there tends to be a collective assumption among EPA and the PRPs that EPA will be made whole; the only question is how much each PRP is going to have to pay. In fact, § 122(e)(3)(A) contemplates such a role in authorizing EPA to provide the PRPs with what is called a "nonbinding preliminary allocation of responsibility" (or—in acronym-speak—an "NBAR") allocating percentages of the total cost among the PRPs if it determines that such a step would expedite settlements and remedial action. While EPA seldom formally invokes the NBAR process, its very existence speaks to the odd neutral-party role that EPA frequently assumes in CERCLA negotiations.

A further significant question that PRPs may face in CERCLA negotiations involves whether to enter into a consent decree on EPA's terms or to risk the alternatives—either a unilateral order or an EPA–lead cleanup. In multi-party cases, the choice may not be available. If some subset of the PRPs are going to enter into a decree, the others may have to choose simply between signing on or being left out in the cold as non-settlors (whom EPA pejoratively refers to as "recalcitrants"). (The harshness of this dichotomy will be considered further below.) In other cases, however, the PRPs collectively may have the power to determine at least the method through which their poison will be administered. While settlement may offer the benefits of a covenants not to sue and contribution protection, it also has its costs. Most notable among these are the various one-sided provisions EPA insists upon including in its consent decrees. These include, for example, the accrual of stipulated penalties not only during periods of clear noncompliance, but also in situations where the respondents may have raised legitimate but ultimately unsuccessful arguments regarding the implementation of the decree during a dispute resolution process. See EPA's Revised Model RD/RA Consent Decree, 60 Fed.Reg. 38817 (July 28, 1995), at paragraphs 68 and 77.

How much liability, if any, should EPA reserve for non-settlors in the negotiation process? From one perspective, it can be argued that EPA should impose all remaining liabilities, after any *de minimis* settlements, on the settling major parties. Under this route, the government bears no further risk and the settling parties can file suit against the non-settlors for contribution. This approach does have some drawbacks, however. To the extent that it imposes on settling parties the transaction costs of pursuing the non-settlors, it tends to discourage proactive behavior (i.e., settling) on the part of those parties that would like to step forward and assume their cleanup obligations. Conversely, it tends to reward those who "lie in the weeds," by increasing the chance that they will never be sued—given the transaction costs, the settling PRPs may not find it to be in their best interest to pursue all non-settlors.

In the *Cannons* case (set forth below), EPA chose to tier its settlement offers in a way that would encourage early settlement and thus necessarily, given the combined effects of joint and several liability and contribution protection, impose any resulting shortfalls on the remaining non-settlors. See CERCLA § 113(f)(2) (settlement with one PRP "reduces the potential liability of the others by the amount of the settlement"). After raising approximately $13.5 million through the *de minimis* settlement, which was entered administratively, EPA negotiated a settlement with the major parties that resulted in their commitment to commit approximately $34 million to the past and future cleanup efforts, with appropriate reopeners. This, however, left 37 nonsettlors—all of whom were *de minimis* parties—exposed to almost $11 million in unresolved liability.

Prior to the finalization of the major party decree, many of the non-settling *de minimis* parties began to recognize that they might be left bearing disproportionate amounts of liability. They therefore sought to be included in the major-party settlement, agreeing to be bound by its terms including the various reopeners. EPA declined to allow them to participate in this decree. Why do you think EPA did so? After having been rebuffed in their efforts to join in the major-party settlement, these non-settlors then asked EPA if it would negotiate another *de minimis* settlement on the same terms as the first. EPA declined, but did put forward a second *de minimis* offer with an enhanced premium of 160%, thus allowing these generators to settle only if each agreed to pay 260% of its volumetric share of the total projected response costs. The first *de minimis* settlement had been based upon a premium of 60 percent. Thus, EPA's tiering methodology resulted in a penalty of 100% of the base volumetric share due to the nonsettlors' failure to have accepted its first *de minimis* proposal. Perhaps surprisingly, twelve *de minimis* parties accepted this offer, contributing an aggregate total of another $792,000 to the cleanup effort, but still leaving more than $10 million in liability for the non-settlors. When EPA moved to enter the decrees, the nonsettling parties objected to EPA's negotiating tactics. This litigation eventually resulted in the following First Circuit opinion:

UNITED STATES v. CANNONS ENGINEERING CORP.

United States Court of Appeals, First Circuit, 1990.
899 F.2d 79.

SELYA, CIRCUIT JUDGE.

Our starting point is well defined. [SARA] authorized a variety of types of settlements which the EPA may utilize in CERCLA actions, including consent decrees providing for PRPs to contribute to cleanup costs and/or to undertake response activities themselves. See 42 U.S.C. § 9622 (1987). SARA's legislative history makes pellucid that, when such consent decrees are forged, the trial court's review function is only to "satisfy itself that the settlement is reasonable, fair, and consistent with the purposes that CERCLA is intended to serve." H.R.Rep. No. 253, Pt. 3, 99th Cong., 1st Sess. 19 (1985), *reprinted in* 1986 U.S.Code Cong. & Admin.News 3038, 3042. Reasonableness, fairness, and fidelity to the statute are, therefore, the horses which district judges must ride.

That said, we are quick to concede that these three steeds are all mutable figures taking on different forms and shapes in different factual settings. Yet, the concepts' amorphous quality is no accident or quirk of fate. We believe that Congress intended, first, that the judiciary take a broad view of proposed settlements, leaving highly technical issues and relatively petty inequities to the discourse between parties; and second, that the district courts treat each case on its own merits, recognizing the wide range of potential problems and possible solutions. When a court considers approval of a consent decree in a CERCLA case, there can be no easy-to-apply check list of relevant factors.

We agree with the district court that fairness in the CERCLA settlement context has both procedural and substantive components. To measure procedural fairness, a court should ordinarily look to the negotiation process and attempt to gauge its candor, openness, and bargaining balance.

In this instance, the district court found the proposed decrees to possess the requisite procedural integrity and appellants have produced no persuasive reason to alter this finding. It is clear the district court believed that the government conducted negotiations forthrightly and in good faith, and the record is replete with indications to that effect. Most of appellants' contrary intimations are vapid and merit summary rejection. But their flagship argument—that the procedural integrity of the settlement was ruptured because appellants were neither allowed to join the [major party (MP)] decree nor informed in advance that they would be excluded—requires comment.

Appellants claim that they were relatively close to the 1% [volumetric contribution] cutoff point [for being treated as *de minimis* parties], and were thus arbitrarily excluded from the major party settlement, avails them naught. Congress intended to give the EPA broad discretion to structure classes of PRPs for settlement purposes. We cannot say that the government acted beyond the scope of that discretion in separating minor and major players in this instance, that is, in determining that generators who had sent less than 1% of the volume of hazardous waste to the Sites would comprise the [*de minimis* classification (DMC)] and those generators who were responsible for a greater percentage would be treated as major PRPs. While the dividing line was only one of many which the agency could have selected, it was well within the universe of plausibility. And it is true, if sometimes sad, that whenever and wherever government draws lines, some parties fall on what they may perceive as the "wrong" side. There was no cognizable unfairness in this respect. Moreover, having established separate categories for different PRPs, the agency had no obligation to let defendants flit from class to class, thus undermining the rationale and purpose for drawing lines in the first place.

Nor can we say that appellants were entitled to more advance warning of the EPA's negotiating strategy than they received. At the time de minimis PRPs were initially invited to participate in the administrative settlement, the EPA, by letter, informed all of them, including appellants, that:

> The government is anxious to achieve a high degree of participation in this de minimis settlement. Accordingly, the terms contained in this settlement offer are the most favorable terms that the government intends to make available to parties eligible for de minimis settlement in this case.

[*United States v. Cannons Engineering Corp.*, 720 F.Supp. 1027, 1033 (D.Mass.1989)]. Appellants knew, early on, that they were within the DMC and could spurn the EPA's proposal only at the risk of paying more at a later time. Although appellants may have assumed that they could ride on the coattails of the major parties and join whatever MP decree emerged—the government had, on other occasions, allowed such cafeteria-style settlements—the agency was neither asked for, nor did it give, any such assurance in this instance. As a matter of law, we do not believe that Congress meant to handcuff government negotiators in CERCLA cases by insisting that the EPA allow polluters to pick and choose which settlements they might prefer to join. And as a matter of equity, we think that if appellants were misled at all, it was by their own wishful thinking.

The district court found the consent decrees to have been the product of fair play. Given that the decrees were negotiated at arm's length among experienced counsel, that appellants . . . had an opportunity to participate in the negotiations and to join both the first and the second de minimis settlements, and that the agency operated in good faith, the finding of procedural fairness is eminently supportable.

Substantive fairness introduces into the equation concepts of corrective justice and accountability: a party should bear the cost of the harm for which it is legally responsible. The logic behind these concepts dictates that settlement terms must be based upon, and roughly correlated with, some acceptable measure of comparative fault, apportioning liability among the settling parties according to rational (if necessarily imprecise) estimates of how much harm each PRP has done.

Even accepting substantive fairness as linked to comparative fault, an important issue still remains as to how comparative fault is to be measured. There is no universally correct approach. It appears very clear to us that what constitutes the best measure of comparative fault at a particular Superfund site under particular factual circumstances should be left largely to the EPA's expertise. Whatever formula or scheme EPA advances for measuring comparative fault and allocating liability should be upheld so long as the agency supplies a plausible explanation for it, welding some reasonable linkage between the factors it includes in its formula or scheme and the proportionate shares of the settling PRPs. Put in slightly different terms, the chosen measure of comparative fault should be upheld unless it is arbitrary, capricious, and devoid of a rational basis.

Not only must the EPA be given leeway to construct the barometer of comparative fault, but the agency must also be accorded flexibility to diverge from an apportionment formula in order to address special factors not conducive to regimented treatment. While the list of possible variables is virtually limitless, two frequently encountered reasons warranting departure from strict formulaic comparability are the uncertainty of future events and the timing of particular settlement decisions. Common sense suggests that a PRP's assumption of open-ended risks may merit a discount on comparative fault, while obtaining a complete release from uncertain future liability may call for a premium. By the same token, the need to encourage (and suitably reward) early, cost-effective settlements and to account inter alia for anticipated savings in transaction costs inuring from celeritous settlement can affect the construct. Because we are confident that Congress intended EPA to have considerable flexibility in negotiating and structuring settlements, we think reviewing courts should permit the agency to depart from rigid adherence to formulae wherever the agency proffers a reasonable good-faith justification for departure.

We also believe that a district court should give the EPA's expertise the benefit of the doubt when weighing substantive fairness—particularly when the agency, and hence the court, has been confronted by ambiguous, incomplete, or inscrutable information. In settlement negotiations, particularly in the early phases of environmental litigation, precise data relevant to determining the total extent of harm caused and the role of each PRP is often unavailable. Yet, it would disserve a principal end of the statute—achievement of prompt settlement and a concomitant head start on response activities—to leave matters in limbo until more precise information was amassed. As long as the data the EPA uses to apportion liability for purposes of a consent decree falls along the broad spectrum of plausible approximations, judicial intrusion is unwarranted—regardless of whether the court would have opted to employ the same data in the same way.

In this instance, we agree with the court below that the consent decrees pass muster from a standpoint of substantive fairness. They adhere generally to principles of comparative fault according to a volumetric standard, determining the liability of each PRP according to volumetric contribution. And, to the extent they deviate from this formulaic approach, they do so on the basis of adequate justification. In particular, the premiums charged to de minimis PRPs in the administrative settlement, and the increased premium charged in the DMC decree, seem well warranted.

The argument that the EPA should have used relative toxicity as a determinant of proportionate liability for response costs, instead of a strictly volumetric ranking, is a stalking horse. Having selected a reasonable method of weighing comparative fault, the agency need not show that it is the best, or even the fairest, of all conceivable methods. The choice of the yardstick to be used for allocating liability must be left primarily to the expert discretion of the EPA, particularly when the PRPs involved are numerous and the situation is complex. We cannot reverse the court below for refusing to second-guess the agency on this score.

Appellants' next asseveration—that the decrees favor major party PRPs over their less culpable counterparts—is a gross distortion. While the DMC and MP decrees differ to some extent in application of the volumetric share formula, requiring lower initial contributions under the latter, the good-faith justification for this divergence is readily apparent. In return for the premium paid, de minimis PRPs can cash out, thus obtaining two important benefits: reduced transaction costs and absolute finality with respect to the monetization of their overall liability. The major PRPs, on the other hand, retain an open-ended risk anent their liability at three of the Sites, making any comparison of proportionate contributions a dubious proposition. At the very least, assumption of this unquantifiable future liability under the MP decree warranted some discount—and the tradeoff crafted by the government's negotiators seems reasonable. Indeed, the acceptance of the first and second DMC settlement offers by so many of the de minimis PRPs is itself an indication of substantive fairness toward the class to which appellants belong. On this record, the district court did not misuse its discretion in ruling that the decrees sufficiently tracked the parties' comparative fault.

The last point which merits discussion under this rubric involves the fact that the agency upped the ante as the game continued, that is, the premium assessed as part of the administrative settlement was increased substantially for purposes of the later DMC decree. Like the district court, we see no unfairness in this approach. For one thing, litigation is expensive—and having called the tune by their refusal to subscribe to the administrative settlement, we think it not unfair that appellants, thereafter, would have to pay the piper. For another thing, rewarding PRPs who settle sooner rather than later is completely consonant with CERCLA's makeup.

Although appellants berate escalating settlement offers as discriminating among similarly situated PRPs, we think that the government's use of such a technique is fair and serves to promote the explicit statutory goal of expediting remedial measures for hazardous waste sites. That the cost of purchasing peace may rise for a laglast is consistent with the method of the statute; indeed, if the government cannot offer such routine incentives, there will be little inducement on the part of any PRP to enter an administrative settlement. Of course, the extent of the differential must be reasonable and the graduation neither unconscionable nor unduly coercive, but these are familiar subjects for judicial review in a wide variety of analogous settings. We believe that the EPA is entitled to make use of a series of escalating settlement proposals in a CERCLA case and that ... the serial settlements employed in this instance were substantively fair.

In the SARA Amendments, Congress explicitly created a statutory framework that left nonsettlors at risk of bearing a disproportionate amount of liability. The statute immunizes settling parties from liability for contribution and provides that only the amount of the settlement—not the pro rata share attributable to the settling party—shall be subtracted from the liability of the nonsettlors.[5] This can prove to be a

---

5. The statute provides:
A person who has resolved its liability to the United States or a State in an administrative or judicially approved settlement

substantial benefit to settling PRPs—and a corresponding detriment to their more recalcitrant counterparts.

Although such immunity creates a palpable risk of disproportionate liability, that is not to say that the device is forbidden. To the exact contrary, Congress has made its will explicit and the courts must defer. Disproportionate liability, a technique which promotes early settlements and deters litigation for litigation's sake, is an integral part of the statutory plan.

In a related vein, appellants assail the district court's dismissal of their cross-claims for contribution as against all settling PRPs. They contend, in essence, that the district court failed to appreciate that they would potentially bear a greater proportional liability than will be shouldered by any of the settling parties. They claim this result to be both unfair and inconsistent with the statutory plan.

... Congress plainly intended non-settlors to have no contribution rights against settlors regarding matters addressed in settlement. Thus, the cross-claims were properly dismissed; Congress purposed that all who choose not to settle confront the same sticky wicket of which appellants complain.

The statute, of course, not only bars contribution claims against settling parties, but also provides that, while a settlement will not discharge other PRPs, "it reduces the potential liability of the others by the amount of settlement." 42 U.S.C. § 9613(f)(2)(1987). The law's plain language admits of no construction other than a dollar-for-dollar reduction of the aggregate liability.... This clear and unequivocal statutory mandate overrides appellants' quixotic imprecation that their liability should be reduced not by the amount of settlement but by the equitable shares of the settling parties. In a very real sense, the appellants' arguments are with Congress, not with the district court.[6]

On a similar note, appellants bemoan the dismissal of their cross-claims for indemnity against the settling PRPs. We are unmoved. Although CERCLA is silent regarding indemnification, we refuse to read into the statute a right to indemnification that would eviscerate § 9613(f)(2) and allow non-settlors to make an end run around the statutory scheme.

Appellants allege no contractual basis for indemnification. Their noncontractual indemnity claim, by definition and extrapolation, "is in effect only a more extreme form of [a claim for] contribution." *Drake v.*

shall not be liable for claims for contribution regarding matters addressed in the settlement. Such settlement does not discharge any of the other potentially liable persons unless its terms so provide, but it reduces the potential liability of the others by the amount of the settlement.
42 U.S.C. § 9613(f)(2)(1987).

6. The veiled constitutional argument sponsored principally by Kingston–Warren does not withstand scrutiny. There is no federal common law right to contribution, *Texas Indus., Inc. v. Radcliff Materials, Inc.*, 451 U.S. 630, 641–42 (1981); *Northwest Airlines, Inc. v. Transport Workers Union*, 451 U.S. 77, 90–91 (1981), and hence, no deprivation of any constitutionally protected interest.

Raymark Industries, Inc., 772 F.2d 1007, 1011 n. 2 (1st Cir.1985), *cert. denied*, 476 U.S. 1126 (1986). Clearly, if appellants' claims for partial contribution can validly be barred in the course of implementing a CERCLA settlement, their claims for total contribution, i.e., indemnity, can likewise be foreclosed.

The appellants also contend that the government's negotiating strategy must be an open book. We disagree. Congress did not send the EPA into the toxic waste ring with one arm tied behind its collective back. Although the EPA may not mislead any of the parties, discriminate unfairly, or engage in deceptive practices, neither must the agency spoon feed PRPs. In the CERCLA context, the government is under no obligation to telegraph its settlement offers, divulge its negotiating strategy in advance, or surrender the normal prerogatives of strategic flexibility which any negotiator cherishes. In short, contrary to the objectors' thesis, the EPA need not tell de minimis PRPs in advance whether they will, or will not, be eligible to join ensuing major party settlements.

Notes and Comments

1. As mentioned, the premium payment in the first *de mimimis* settlement in *Cannons* was 60%, resulting in a multiplier of 1.6 over that amount which the *de minimis* generators would have paid in the absence of such a premium. Do you think this is an appropriate amount? How do you think it was determined?

2. Should the government be under an obligation to "telegraph its settlement offers" or "divulge its negotiating strategy in advance?" Should it be able to penalize non-settlors in the way that the *Cannons* court appears to bless? In *Cannons*, one of the *de minimis* nonsettlors—Olin Hunt—was able to show that, while its base volumetric share of the overall liability would have been $370,000 (without any premiums), it was now facing liabilities in excess of $2 million because its share comprised 20 percent of the total volumetric share of non-settling defendants. Thus, EPA's tactics had increased Olin Hunt's overall exposure to more than three times what it would have paid had it accepted EPA's first settlement offer ($592,000 versus $2,000,000). Does this seem appropriate? How did the court address the constitutional arguments raised by Kingston–Warren? What are the lessons of this case for those involved in CERCLA negotiations?

3. Did you agree with the court's treatment of the appellants' indemnity claims? Presuming this claim was based on a state-law theory, should Congress be able to take such rights away? Does § 113(f)(2) clearly do so? On the other hand, would the effect of this section be nullified if state law contribution or indemnity claims were allowed to survive?

III. PRIVATE PARTY COST—RECOVERY AND CONTRIBUTION

As previously mentioned, CERCLA's cost recovery authority is not limited to governmental entities. While § 107(a)(4)(A) creates a right of cost-recovery in the Federal Government, the states, and Indian Tribes, § 107(a)(4)(B) creates a substantially similar right in private parties, albeit with one additional requirement. Unlike the sovereigns, private parties bear the burden of demonstrating that any costs incurred were consistent with the NCP. Additionally, § 113(f)(1) and (f)(3)(B) supplement § 107(a)(4)(B) by authorizing contribution actions for PRPs under specified circumstances.

These provisions have the effect of dramatically expanding the scope of the CERCLA program. Over the years, an ever-increasing percentage of the judicial opinions addressing liability issues have been issued in the context of private-party actions. Moreover, private-party CERCLA actions are significant not only for the numbers of cases they generate, but also for the nature of the problems addressed in those cases. As we already have seen, EPA's primary emphasis under CERCLA is on sites qualifying for the NPL; indeed, EPA may perform "remedial" activities only at NPL sites. While states and Indian tribes are not so limited, as sovereigns they face the ever-present need to focus their attention on their highest-priority sites. Those with potential private-party claims, by contrast, may be limited only by the minimal statutory elements, the bounds of their reason, and their ability to locate PRPs.

At first blush, Sections 107(a)(4), 113(f)(1) and 113(f)(3)(B) appear to establish a clear dichotomy pursuant to which one who cleans up a site on her own initiative would have a claim under § 107(a)(4), whereas one who does so in response to governmental prodding (or who reimburses the government for a government-lead cleanup) would have a claim under one of the subparts of § 113(f). Upon closer examination, however, the statutory waters are seen to be muddier than they first appear. One question is whether those who themselves may be liable may bring cost-recovery claims under § 107(a)(4) against other PRPs. This question can come up in a host of different circumstances. In some cases, the plaintiff's liability may be obvious (e.g., where it admits to having played a role in causing the contamination); in others, it may be less so (e.g., in situations in which it owns the relevant property but may have an argument as to whether it qualifies for either the innocent landowner or prospective purchaser defense). Should this make a difference? The pre-complaint legal dynamics may also vary. In some cases, for example, the plaintiff may have cleaned up the site without any governmental edict requiring it to do so (a so-called "voluntary" cleanup). In others, it may have done pursuant to an EPA-induced consent decree or an EPA-issued administrative order. In still others, the State may have compelled it to clean up a site pursuant to State law. Take a close look at the language of § 107(a)(4) and § 113(f)(1) and (f)(3)(B). Do these provisions clearly resolve the circumstances under which a plaintiff has a claim under either each provision? Are there circumstances in which it may have a claim under more than one of them, or none of them? Even if we assume that one who cleans up a site should generally have a claim under at least one of these provisions (which, as we will see, may or may not be a safe assumption), what effect, if any, would the source of the claim have on the nature of the recovery that the PRP might be able to obtain?

Consider these issues as you read the following decisions from the Supreme Court and the Eighth Circuit:

COOPER INDUSTRIES, INC. v. AVIALL SERVICES, INC.

Supreme Court of the United States, 2004.
543 U.S. 157, 125 S.Ct. 577, 160 L.Ed.2d 548.

Justice THOMAS delivered the opinion of the Court.

Section 113(f)(1) of [CERCLA] allows persons who have undertaken efforts to clean up properties contaminated by hazardous substances to seek contribution from other parties liable under CERCLA. Section 113(f)(1) specifies that a party may obtain contribution "during or following any civil action" under CERCLA § 106 or § 107(a). The issue we must decide is whether a private party who has not been sued under § 106 or § 107(a) may nevertheless obtain contribution under § 113(f)(1) from other liable parties. We hold that it may not.

After CERCLA's enactment in 1980, litigation arose over whether § 107, in addition to allowing the Government and certain private parties to recover costs from PRPs, also allowed a PRP that had incurred response costs to recover costs from other PRPs. More specifically, the question was whether a private party that had incurred response costs, but that had done so voluntarily and was not itself subject to suit, had a cause of action for cost recovery against other PRPs. Various courts held that § 107(a)(4)(B) . . . authorized such a cause of action.

After CERCLA's passage, litigation also ensued over the separate question whether a private entity that had been sued in a cost recovery action (by the Government or by another PRP) could obtain contribution from other PRPs. As originally enacted in 1980, CERCLA contained no provision expressly providing for a right of action for contribution. A number of District Courts nonetheless held that, although CERCLA did not mention the word "contribution," such a right arose either impliedly from provisions of the statute, or as a matter of federal common law. That conclusion was debatable in light of two decisions of this Court that refused to recognize implied or common-law rights to contribution in other federal statutes. See *Texas Industries, Inc. v. Radcliff Materials, Inc.,* 451 U.S. 630, 638–647 (1981); *Northwest Airlines, Inc. v. Transport Workers,* 451 U.S. 77, 90–99 (1981).

Congress subsequently amended CERCLA in [SARA] to provide an express cause of action for contribution, codified as CERCLA § 113(f)(1):

> Any person may seek contribution from any other person who is liable or potentially liable under section 9607(a) of this title, during or following any civil action under section 9606 of this title or under section 9607(a) of this title. Such claims shall be brought in accordance with this section and the Federal Rules of Civil Procedure, and shall be governed by Federal law. In resolving contribution claims, the court may allocate response costs among liable parties

using such equitable factors as the court determines are appropriate. Nothing in this subsection shall diminish the right of any person to bring an action for contribution in the absence of a civil action under section 9606 of this title or section 9607 of this title. *Id., at* 1647, as codified in 42 U.S.C. § 9613(f)(1).

SARA also created a separate express right of contribution, § 113(f)(3)(B), for "[a] person who has resolved its liability to the United States or a State for some or all of a response action or for some or all of the costs of such action in an administrative or judicially approved settlement." In short, after SARA, CERCLA provided for a right to cost recovery in certain circumstances, § 107(a), and separate rights to contribution in other circumstances, §§ 113(f)(1), 113(f)(3)(B).[3]

This case concerns four contaminated aircraft engine maintenance sites in Texas. Cooper Industries, Inc., owned and operated those sites until 1981, when it sold them to Aviall Services, Inc. Aviall operated the four sites for a number of years. Ultimately, Aviall discovered that both it and Cooper had contaminated the facilities when petroleum and other hazardous substances leaked into the ground and ground water through underground storage tanks and spills.

Aviall notified the Texas Natural Resource Conservation Commission (Commission) of the contamination. The Commission informed Aviall that it was violating state environmental laws, directed Aviall to clean up the site, and threatened to pursue an enforcement action if Aviall failed to undertake remediation. Neither the Commission nor the EPA, however, took judicial or administrative measures to compel cleanup.

Aviall cleaned up the properties under the State's supervision, beginning in 1984. Aviall sold the properties to a third party in 1995 and 1996, but remains contractually responsible for the cleanup. Aviall has incurred approximately $5 million in cleanup costs; the total costs may be even greater. In August 1997, Aviall filed this action against Cooper in the United States District Court for the Northern District of Texas, seeking to recover cleanup costs. The original complaint asserted a claim for cost recovery under CERCLA § 107(a), a separate claim for contribution under CERCLA § 113(f)(1), and state-law claims. Aviall later amended the complaint, combining its two CERCLA claims into a single, joint CERCLA claim. That claim alleged that, pursuant to § 113(f)(1), Aviall was entitled to seek contribution from Cooper, as a PRP under § 107(a), for response costs and other liability Aviall incurred in connection with the Texas facilities. Aviall continued to assert state-law claims as well.

3. In *Key Tronic Corp. v. United States,* 511 U.S. 809 (1994), we observed that § 107 and § 113 created "similar and somewhat overlapping" remedies. *Id.* at 816. The cost recovery remedy of § 107(a)(4)(B) and the contribution remedy of § 113(f)(1) are similar at a general level in that they both allow private parties to recoup costs from other private parties. But the two remedies are clearly distinct.

[The District Court granted Cooper's motion for summary judgment, determining that Aviall had abandoned its § 107 claim and did not have a valid contribution claim under § 113(f)(1) because it had not been sued under CERCLA § 106 or § 107. Having dismissed Aviall's federal claim, the court declined to exercise jurisdiction over the state-law claims. After a divided panel of the Fifth Circuit affirmed, an en banc panel of the Fifth Circuit reversed, again by a divided vote. The en banc panel concluded that § 113(f)(1) allows a PRP to obtain contribution from other PRPs regardless of whether the PRP has been sued under § 106 or § 107. 312 F.3d 677 (2002).] The court held that "[s]ection 113(f)(1) authorizes suits against PRPs in both its first and last sentence[,] which states without qualification that 'nothing' in the section shall 'diminish' any person's right to bring a contribution action in the absence of a section 106 or section 107(a) action." *Id.*, at 681. The court reasoned in part that "may" in § 113(f)(1) did not mean "may only." *Id.*, at 686–687. . . .

III

A

Section 113(f)(1) does not authorize Aviall's suit. The first sentence, the enabling clause that establishes the right of contribution, provides: "Any person *may* seek contribution . . . *during or following* any civil action under section 9606 of this title or under section 9607(a) of this title," 42 U.S.C. § 9613(f)(1) (emphasis added). The natural meaning of this sentence is that contribution may only be sought subject to the specified conditions, namely, "during or following" a specified civil action.

Aviall answers that "may" should be read permissively, such that "during or following" a civil action is one, but not the exclusive, instance in which a person may seek contribution. We disagree. First, as just noted, the natural meaning of "may" in the context of the enabling clause is that it authorizes certain contribution actions—ones that satisfy the subsequent specified condition—and no others.

Second, and relatedly, if § 113(f)(1) were read to authorize contribution actions at any time, regardless of the existence of a § 106 or § 107(a) civil action, then Congress need not have included the explicit "during or following" condition. In other words, Aviall's reading would render part of the statute entirely superfluous, something we are loath to do. Likewise, if § 113(f)(1) authorizes contribution actions at any time, § 113(f)(3)(B), which permits contribution actions after settlement, is equally superfluous. There is no reason why Congress would bother to specify conditions under which a person may bring a contribution claim, and at the same time allow contribution actions absent those conditions.

The last sentence of § 113(f)(1), the saving clause, does not change our conclusion. That sentence provides: "Nothing in this subsection shall diminish the right of any person to bring an action for contribution in the absence of a civil action under section 9606 of this title or section

9607 of this title." 42 U.S.C. § 9613(f)(1). The sole function of the sentence is to clarify that § 113(f)(1) does nothing to "diminish" any cause(s) of action for contribution that may exist independently of § 113(f)(1). In other words, the sentence rebuts any presumption that the express right of contribution provided by the enabling clause is the exclusive cause of action for contribution available to a PRP. The sentence, however, does not itself establish a cause of action; nor does it expand § 113(f)(1) to authorize contribution actions not brought "during or following" a § 106 or § 107(a) civil action; nor does it specify what causes of action for contribution, if any, exist outside § 113(f)(1). Reading the saving clause to authorize § 113(f)(1) contribution actions not just "during or following" a civil action, but also before such an action, would again violate the settled rule that we must, if possible, construe a statute to give every word some operative effect.

Our conclusion follows not simply from § 113(f)(1) itself, but also from the whole of § 113. As noted above, § 113 provides two express avenues for contribution: § 113(f)(1) ("during or following" specified civil actions) and § 113(f)(3)(B) (after an administrative or judicially approved settlement that resolves liability to the United States or a State). Section 113(g)(3) then provides two corresponding 3–year limitations periods for contribution actions, one beginning at the date of judgment, § 113(g)(3)(A), and one beginning at the date of settlement, § 113(g)(3)(B). Notably absent from § 113(g)(3) is any provision for starting the limitations period if a judgment or settlement never occurs, as is the case with a purely voluntary cleanup. The lack of such a provision supports the conclusion that, to assert a contribution claim under § 113(f), a party must satisfy the conditions of either § 113(f)(1) or § 113(f)(3)(B).

Each side insists that the purpose of CERCLA bolsters its reading of § 113(f)(1). Given the clear meaning of the text, there is no need to resolve this dispute or to consult the purpose of CERCLA at all. As we have said: "[I]t is ultimately the provisions of our laws rather than the principal concerns of our legislators by which we are governed." *Oncale v. Sundowner Offshore Services, Inc.,* 523 U.S. 75, 79 (1998). Section 113(f)(1) authorizes contribution claims only "during or following" a civil action under § 106 or § 107(a), and it is undisputed that Aviall has never been subject to such an action.[5] Aviall therefore has no § 113(f)(1) claim.

B

Aviall [contends] that, in the alternative to an action for contribution under § 113(f)(1), Aviall may recover costs under § 107(a)(4)(B) even though it is a PRP. The dissent would have us so hold. We decline to address the issue. Neither the District Court, nor the Fifth Circuit panel, nor the Fifth Circuit sitting en banc considered Aviall's § 107

---

5. Neither has Aviall been subject to an administrative order under § 106; thus, we need not decide whether such an order would qualify as a "civil action under section 9606 ... or under section 9607(a)" of CERCLA. 42 U.S.C. § 9613(f)(1).

claim. In fact, as noted above, Aviall included separate § 107 and § 113 claims in its original complaint, but then asserted a "combined" § 107/§ 113 claim in its amended complaint. The District Court took this consolidated claim to mean that Aviall was relying on § 107 "not as an independent cause of action," but only "to the extent necessary to maintain a viable § 113(f)(1) contribution claim." Consequently the court saw no need to address any freestanding § 107 claim. [Likewise, at the Fifth Circuit level neither the three-judge panel nor the en banc panel addressed this claim.]

"We ordinarily do not decide in the first instance issues not decided below." *Adarand Constructors, Inc. v. Mineta*, 534 U.S. 103, 109 (2001). Although we have deviated from this rule in exceptional circumstances, the circumstances here cut *against* resolving the § 107 claim. Both the question whether Aviall has waived this claim and the underlying § 107 question (if it is not waived) may depend in part on the relationship between §§ 107 and 113. That relationship is a significant issue in its own right. It is also well beyond the scope of the briefing and, indeed, the question presented, which asks simply whether a private party "may bring an action seeking contribution pursuant to CERCLA Section 113(f)(1)." The § 107 claim and the preliminary waiver question merit full consideration by the courts below.

Furthermore, the parties cite numerous decisions of the Courts of Appeals as holding that a private party that is itself a PRP may not pursue a § 107(a) action against other PRPs for joint and several liability. To hold here that Aviall may pursue a § 107 action, we would have to consider whether these decisions are correct, an issue that Aviall has flagged but not briefed. And we might have to consider other issues, also not briefed, such as whether Aviall, which seeks to recover the share of its cleanup costs fairly chargeable to Cooper, may pursue a § 107 cost recovery action for some form of liability other than joint and several. We think it more prudent to withhold judgment on these matters.

In view of the importance of the § 107 issue and the absence of briefing and decisions by the courts below, we are not prepared—as the dissent would have it—to resolve the § 107 question solely on the basis of dictum in *Key Tronic*. We held there that certain attorney's fees were not "necessary costs of response" within the meaning of § 107(a)(4)(B). 511 U.S., at 818–821. But we did not address the relevance, if any, of Key Tronic's status as a PRP or confront the relationship between §§ 107 and 113. . . . Aviall itself recognizes the need for fuller examination of the § 107 claim; it has simply requested that we remand for consideration of that claim, not that we resolve the claim in the first instance.

C

In addition to leaving open whether Aviall may seek cost recovery under § 107, we decline to decide whether Aviall has an implied right to contribution under § 107. Portions of the Fifth Circuit's opinion below might be taken to endorse the latter cause of action, 312 F.3d, at 687; others appear to reserve the question whether such a cause of action exists, *id.,* at 685, n. 15. To the extent that Aviall chooses to frame its § 107 claim on remand as an implied right of contribution (as opposed to a right of cost recovery), we note that this Court has visited the subject of implied rights of contribution before. See *Texas Industries,* 451 U.S., at 638–647; *Northwest Airlines,* 451 U.S., at 90–99. We also note that, in enacting § 113(f)(1), Congress explicitly recognized a particular set (claims "during or following" the specified civil actions) of the contribution rights previously implied by courts from provisions of CERCLA and the common law. Nonetheless, we need not and do not decide today whether any judicially implied right of contribution survived the passage of SARA . .

* * *

We hold only that § 113(f)(1) does not support Aviall's suit. We therefore reverse the judgment of the Fifth Circuit and remand the case for further proceedings consistent with this opinion . .

Justice GINSBURG, with whom Justice STEVENS joins, dissenting.

In [*Key Tronic,* 511 U.S. at 818], all Members of this Court agreed that § 107 . . . "unquestionably provides a cause of action for [potentially responsible persons (PRPs)] to seek recovery of cleanup costs." The Court rested that determination squarely and solely on § 107(a)(4)(B), which allows *any* person who has incurred costs for cleaning up a hazardous waste site to recover all or a portion of those costs from any other person liable under CERCLA.

The *Key Tronic* Court divided, however, on the question whether the right to contribution is implicit in § 107(a)'s text, as the majority determined, or whether § 107(a) expressly confers the right, as the dissenters urged. The majority stated: Section 107 "*implies*—but does not expressly *command*—that [a PRP] may have a claim for contribution against those treated as joint tortfeasors." 511 U.S., at 818, and n. 11 (emphasis added). The dissent maintained: "Section 107(a)(4)(B) states, as clearly as can be, that '[c]overed persons . . . shall be liable for . . . necessary costs of response incurred by any other person.' Surely to say that A shall be liable to B is the *express* creation of a right of action." *Id.,* at 822. But no Justice expressed the slightest doubt that § 107 indeed did enable a PRP to sue other covered persons for reimbursement, in whole or part, of cleanup costs the PRP legitimately incurred.

In the Fifth Circuit's view, § 107 supplied the right of action for Aviall's claim, and § 113(f)(1) prescribed the procedural framework. 312 F.3d 677, 683, and n. 10 (2002) (stating that § 107 "impliedly authorizes a cause of action for contribution" and § 113(f) "govern[s] and regulate[s]" the action). Notably, Aviall expressly urged in the Court of Appeals that, were the court to conclude that § 113(f)(1)'s "during or following" language excluded application of that section to this case, Aviall's suit should be adjudicated independently under § 107(a).

I see no cause for protracting this litigation by requiring the Fifth Circuit to revisit a determination it has essentially made already: Federal courts, prior to the enactment of § 113(f)(1), had correctly held that PRPs could "recover [under § 107] a proportionate share of their costs in actions for contribution against other PRPs," 312 F.3d, at 687;[2] nothing in § 113 retracts that right. Accordingly, I would not defer a definitive ruling by this Court on the question whether Aviall may pursue a § 107 claim for relief against Cooper.

ATLANTIC RESEARCH CORP. v. UNITED STATES

United States Court of Appeals, Eighth Circuit, 2006.
459 F.3d 827.

ROSENBAUM, District Judge.

Atlantic Research Corp. ("Atlantic") seeks partial reimbursement from the United States for costs incurred in an environmental cleanup.... The issue for consideration is whether CERCLA forbids a party such as Atlantic, which has voluntarily cleaned up a site for which it was only partly responsible, to recover part of its cleanup costs from another liable party....

I. BACKGROUND

Atlantic retrofitted rocket motors for the United States from 1981 through 1986. It performed this service at its Camden, Arkansas, facility. The work included using high-pressure water spray to remove rocket propellant. Once removed, the propellant was burned. Residue from burnt rocket fuel contaminated the Arkansas site's soil and groundwater.

Atlantic voluntarily investigated and cleaned up the contamination, incurring costs in the process. It sought to recover a portion of these costs from the United States by invoking CERCLA §§ 107(a) and 113(f). Atlantic and the government began to negotiate in an effort to resolve these financial matters.

The negotiations ended with the [Supreme Court's] decision in *Cooper Industries, Inc. v. Aviall Services, Inc.,* 543 U.S. 157 (2004) ("*Aviall* "). In *Aviall,* the court found a party could only attempt to obtain § 113(f) contribution "during or following" a §§ 106 or 107(a) CERCLA civil action. As no action had been commenced against Atlantic under either §§ 106 or 107(a), the *Aviall* decision barred its § 113(f) contribution claim.

With its § 113(f) claim *Aviall*-foreclosed, Atlantic amended its complaint. The amended complaint relied solely on § 107(a).... [T]he

---

2. The cases to which the Court refers, *Texas Industries, Inc. v. Radcliff Materials, Inc.,* 451 U.S. 630 (1981), and *Northwest Airlines, Inc. v. Transport Workers,* 451 U.S. 77 (1981), do not address the implication of a right of action for contribution under CERCLA. *Texas Industries* concerned the Sherman and Clayton Acts; *Northwest Airlines,* the Equal Pay Act and Title VII. A determination suitable in one statutory context does not necessarily carry over to a different statutory setting.

government moved to dismiss under [FRCP] 12(b)(6), arguing this Court's pre-*Aviall* decision in *Dico. Inc. v. Amoco Oil Co.,* 340 F.3d 525 (8th Cir.2003) (*"Dico"*) foreclosed Atlantic's § 107 claim. The district court agreed....

As will be discussed in more detail below, *Dico* held that a liable party could not bring an action under § 107. We recognize the generally preclusive effect of a previous panel's ruling. But this rule is not inflexible. Where the prior decision can be distinguished, or its rationale has been undermined, a subsequent decision can depart from the prior path.[4] We are convinced *Dico* is such a case; it is clearly distinguishable from the case at bar, and its analytic is undermined by *Aviall*.

II. ANALYSIS

... To resolve the question before us, we must briefly review the intertwined history of CERCLA §§ 107 and 113, and then analyze this history in light of *Aviall*.

A. CERCLA Cost Recovery and Contribution—Pre-Aviall

When the federal or a state government conducts [a] cleanup, CERCLA permits the sovereign to recover its costs from whomever is liable for the contamination. § 107(a)(4)(A). CERCLA also provides three methods by which private parties may recover cleanup costs. The first is found at § 107(a)(4)(B), a part of the original statute in 1980. Congress added the others, §§ 113(f)(1) and 113(f)(3)(B), as part of SARA.

Sections 107(a) and 113(f)(1) are central to our analysis. The Eighth, and many of its sister Circuits, have previously held that liable parties seeking reimbursement must use § 113(f)(1), and may not use § 107 for that purpose. Today, we consider whether this ruling remains viable in the post-*Aviall* world.

CERCLA's § 107(a) provides that "covered persons," which we will call "liable parties," are liable for, among other things:

> (A) all costs of removal or remedial action incurred by the United States Government or a State or an Indian tribe not inconsistent with the national contingency plan;
>
> (B) any other necessary costs of response incurred by any other person consistent with the national contingency plan[.]

§ 107(a)(4)(A),(B). Courts have found in CERCLA's reference to "any other necessary costs of response" and "any other person," authority to allow private suits under § 107(a)(4)(B).

---

4. "[I]t is well settled that a panel may depart from circuit precedent based on an intervening opinion of the Supreme Court that undermines the prior precedent." *T.L. v. United States,* 443 F.3d 956, 960 (8th Cir.2006). As will be seen, while *Aviall* has undermined *Dico*'s reasoning for parties in Atlantic's position, its holding remains viable for those parties which still have recourse to relief under § 113. Accordingly, *Dico* can be reconciled with our present holding and we need not ultimately answer whether *Aviall* compels reconsideration of *Dico*.

Section 113 contains a subsection entitled "Contribution," the first part of which states:

Any person may seek contribution from any other person who is liable or potentially liable under [§ 107(a)], during or following any civil action under [§§ 106 or 107(a)]. Such claims shall be brought in accordance with this section and the Federal Rules of Civil Procedure, and shall be governed by Federal law. In resolving contribution claims, the court may allocate response costs among liable parties using such equitable factors as the court determines are appropriate. Nothing in this subsection shall diminish the right of any person to bring an action for contribution in the absence of a civil action under [§§ 106 or 107].

§ 113(f)(1).

There is some similarity in the remedial responsibilities borne by liable parties under §§ 107(a) and 113(f). The Supreme Court has termed these sections' remedies "similar and somewhat overlapping," yet "clearly distinct." *Compare Key Tronic Corp. v. United States,* 511 U.S. 809, 816 (1994) *with Aviall,* 543 U.S. at 163 n. 3. Each requires proof of the same elements. They differ, however, in procedure and scope.

Section 107(a) has a six-year statute of limitations, and allows a plaintiff to recover 100% of its response costs from all liable parties, including those which have settled their CERCLA liability with the government. §§ 113(g)(2), 107(a). Prior to SARA's enactment, some courts implied a right to contribution from § 107, see *Mardan Corp. v. C.G.C. Music, Ltd.,* 804 F.2d 1454, 1457 n. 3 (9th Cir.1986) (collecting cases), or as a matter of federal common law. *United States v. New Castle County,* 642 F.Supp. 1258, 1265–66 (D.Del.1986). The right initially was thought to be uncertain in light of the Supreme Court's traditional reluctance to imply rights of action in the context of other statutes.

Congress resolved the uncertainty when enacting SARA in 1986 by adding § 113 to "clarif[y] and confirm" a right to CERCLA contribution. *United Technologies Corp. v. Browning–Ferris Indus., Inc.,* 33 F.3d 96, 100 (1st Cir.1994), citing S.Rep. No. 11, 99th Cong., 1st Sess. 44 (1985). Section 113's explicit right to contribution is more restricted than that afforded by § 107. Section 113's right is subject to a three-year statute of limitations; plaintiffs can recover only costs in excess of their equitable share, and may not recover from previously-settling parties. § 113(f)(1), (f)(2), (g)(3).

Congress's addition of § 113 posed a dilemma. Courts saw that CERCLA, as amended, created a situation where litigants might "quickly abandon section 113 in favor of the substantially more generous provisions of section 107," thus rendering § 113 a nullity. *New Castle County v. Halliburton NUS Corp.,* 111 F.3d 1116, 1123 (3d Cir.1997).

To prevent § 107 from swallowing § 113, courts began directing traffic between the sections. *See id.; United Techns.,* 33 F.3d at 101;

Bedford Affiliates v. Sills, 156 F.3d 416, 424 (2d Cir.1998). As a result, regardless of which CERCLA section a plaintiff invoked, courts typically analyzed §§ 107 and 113 together, aiming to distinguish one from the other.

Traffic-directing dramatically narrowed § 107 by judicial fiat. On its face, § 107(a)(4)(B) is available to "any . . . person" other than the sovereigns listed in § 107(a)(4)(A). In practice, however, courts gradually steered liable parties away from § 107 and required them to use § 113; § 107 was reserved for "innocent" plaintiffs who could assert one of the statutory defenses to liability. See *Bedford Affiliates,* 156 F.3d at 424; [*Pinal Creek Group v. Newmont Mining Corp.,* 118 F.3d 1298, 1301 (9th Cir.1997)]; *New Castle County,* 111 F.3d at 1124; [*Redwing Carriers,* 94 F.3d 1489, 1496 (11th Cir.1996)]; [*Centerior Serv. Co. v. Acme Scrap Iron & Metal Corp.,* 153 F.3d 344, 349 (6th Cir.1998)]; *United Techns.,* 33 F.3d at 100; [*Akzo Coatings, Inc. v. Aigner Corp.,* 30 F.3d 761, 764–65 (7th Cir.1994)]. This cramped reading of § 107 prevented liable parties from using it to evade § 113's Congressionally-mandated constraints, thus preserving the vitality of § 113. *See New Castle County,* 111 F.3d at 1121; [*United States v. Colorado & Eastern R.R. Co.,* 50 F.3d 1530, 1538 (10th Cir. 1995)]; *United Techns.,* 33 F.3d at 98.

In the pre-*Aviall* analysis, § 113 was presumed to be available to all liable parties, including those which had not faced a CERCLA action. See *Akzo Coatings,* 30 F.3d at 763 n. 4; *Pinal Creek,* 118 F.3d at 1306 (liable party's claim for costs voluntarily incurred governed by both §§ 107 and 113). Accordingly, most courts concluded liable parties could not use § 107. *See* [*Pneumo Abex Corp. v. High Point, Thomasville & Denton R.R. Co.,* 142 F.3d 769, 776 (4th Cir.1998)] (collecting cases); *but see Pinal Creek,* 118 F.3d at 1302 (holding liable parties could not seek direct recovery under § 107, but that "§ 107 implicitly incorporates a claim for contribution" which remains available to liable parties through combined operation of both sections); *United Techns.,* 33 F.3d at 99 n. 8 (suggesting, in dicta, that a liable party may bring contribution action under § 107).

Our opinion in *Dico* was the last in this pre-*Aviall* line. [EPA] had forced Dico, Inc., and another party to clean up an Iowa site which both had contaminated. Dico sued the other party, seeking direct recovery of 100% of its costs under § 107 and for contribution under § 113. The other party settled with the EPA and moved for summary judgment in Dico's lawsuit. The district court granted the motion. It found Dico's § 113 claims were barred by the settlement and, as a liable party, Dico had no right to recover its full cleanup cost under § 107.

Dico appealed the dismissal of its § 107 claim, arguing the Supreme Court's opinion in *Key Tronic* allowed liable parties a claim in direct recovery. We disagreed, noting *Key Tronic* dealt with a pre-SARA implied right to § 107 contribution. *Dico,* 340 F.3d at 531. When we affirmed the dismissal, we joined other Circuits in narrowly construing § 107, and holding a liable party may only assert a contribution claim under § 113.

Id. at 530. We now see that *Aviall* undermines *Dico,* and the judge-created analytic upon which it relies.

B.   The Effect of Aviall

[In *Aviall,*] Justice Thomas, writing for a seven member majority, construed § 113's "during or following" language. He said, "[t]he natural meaning of this sentence is that contribution may only be sought subject to the specified conditions, namely, 'during or following' a specified civil action." *Aviall,* 543 U.S. at 165–66. The Court found the words "during or following" established a condition precedent to a § 113(f) claim. As such, a court which allowed a § 113 contribution claim, absent the prior §§ 106 or 107 action, would render § 113' s precondition a nullity.

Having made this determination, the Court turned to its previous *Key Tronic* reference to CERCLA's "similar and somewhat overlapping" remedies. The Court explained that §§ 107's and 113's remedies were only "similar" in that "both allow private parties to recoup costs from other private parties." *Id.* at 163 n. 3. The Court carefully noted, however, that "the two remedies are clearly distinct." *Id.*

Dissenting Justices Ginsburg and Stevens analyzed *Key Tronic* differently. They said the *Key Tronic* court had not questioned whether § 107 afforded liable parties a cause of action against other liable parties. It simply disagreed whether the right was implied or explicit. Justices Ginsburg and Stevens did not agree that Aviall's amended complaint abandoned a § 107 claim, which they would have allowed to proceed. The majority explicitly avoided this question, reserving it for another day.

C.   The Matter At Hand

That day has arrived. We now ask: Can one liable party recover costs advanced, beyond its equitable share, from another liable party in direct recovery, or by § 107 contribution, or as a matter of federal common law?

The Second Circuit is the only Court which has considered this question since *Aviall.* That Court revisited its pre-*Aviall* precedent, much as we have done here, and concluded that § 107 allowed one liable party to recover voluntarily incurred response costs from another. *Consolidated Edison Co. v. UGI Utilities, Inc.,* 423 F.3d 90, 100 (2d Cir. 2005). In reaching this conclusion, the court distinguished its holding in *Bedford Affiliates,* which—like *Dico*—had rejected a liable party's direct recovery claim under § 107. *Id.* at 102.

In light of *Aviall's* holding that §§ 107 and 113's remedies are distinct, the Second Circuit held "it no longer makes sense" to view section 113(f)(1) as the exclusive route by which liable parties may recover cleanup costs. *See Consolidated Edison Co.,* 423 F.3d at 99. The court looked to Section 107(a)(4)(B)'s "any other person" language, and found "no basis for reading into this language a distinction between so-called 'innocent' parties and parties which, if sued, would be held liable under section 107(a)." *Id.* at 99. So saying, the Second Circuit reopened § 107 cost recovery to liable parties.

Our Court now stands at the same crossroad. We agree with our sister Circuit, and hold that it no longer makes sense to view § 113 as a liable party's exclusive remedy. This distinction may have made sense for parties such as Dico, which was allowed to seek contribution under § 113. But here, Atlantic is foreclosed from using § 113. This path is barred because Atlantic—like Aviall—commenced suit before, rather than "during or following," a CERCLA enforcement action. Atlantic has opted to rely upon § 107 to try to recover its cleanup costs exceeding its own equitable share. We conclude it may do so.

The Supreme Court emphasized that §§ 107 and 113 are "distinct." Accordingly, it is no longer appropriate to view § 107's remedies exclusively through a § 113 prism, as we did in *Dico,* and as the government requests. We reject an approach which categorically deprives a liable party of a § 107 remedy. Like the Second Circuit, we return to the text of CERCLA, and find no such limitation in Congress's words.

We have held that "any other person" means any person other than the statutorily enumerated "United States Government or a State or an Indian tribe." *Control Data Corporation,* 53 F.3d at 936 n. 9. Atlantic is such a "person," *see* CERCLA § 101(G)(21); no one disputes its having incurred "necessary costs of response." On its face § 107 applies.

As the Second Circuit stated, "[e]ach of those sections, 107(a) and 113(f)(1), embodies a mechanism for cost recovery available to persons in different procedural circumstances." *Consolidated Edison,* 423 F.3d at 99. Thus, a liable party may, under appropriate procedural circumstances, bring a cost recovery action under § 107. This right is available to parties who have incurred necessary costs of response, but have neither been sued nor settled their liability under §§ 106 or 107.

We recognize that § 107 allows 100% cost recovery. Some pre-*Aviall* cases justified denying liable parties access to § 107, reasoning Congress would not have intended them to recover 100% of their costs and effectively escape liability. *See, e.g., United Techns.,* 33 F.3d at 100 ("it is sensible to assume that Congress intended only innocent parties—not parties who were themselves liable—to be permitted to recoup the whole of their expenditures.") We agree, and reaffirm *Dico's* holding that a liable party may not use § 107 to recover its full response cost.

But § 107 is not limited to parties seeking to recover 100% of their costs. To the contrary, the text of § 107(a)(4)(B) permits recovery of "any other necessary costs of response ... consistent with the national contingency plan." While these words may "suggest full recovery," *United Techns.,* 33 F.3d at 100, they do not compel it. CERCLA, itself, checks overreaching liable parties: If a plaintiff attempted to use § 107 to recover more than its fair share of reimbursement, a defendant would be free to counterclaim for contribution under § 113(f). *Consolidated Edison,* 423 F.3d at 100, n. 9; *Redwing Carriers,* 94 F.3d at 1495.

Accordingly, we find that allowing Atlantic's claim for direct recovery under § 107 is entirely consistent with the text and purpose of CERCLA.

Alternatively, we are satisfied that a right to contribution may be fairly implied from the text of § 107(a)(4)(B). Unlike some other statutes, CERCLA reflects Congress's unmistakable intent to create a private right of contribution. *See Northwest Airlines, Inc. v. Transp. Workers Union of Am.,* 451 U.S. 77, 91 (1981) ("the ultimate question . . . is whether Congress intended to create the private remedy . . . that the plaintiff seeks to invoke"). We discern Congress's intent by looking to CERCLA's language, its legislative history, its underlying purpose and structure, and the likelihood that Congress intended to supersede or to supplement existing state remedies.

Contribution is crucial to CERCLA's regulatory scheme. As the Supreme Court recognized in *Key Tronic,* "CERCLA is designed to encourage private parties to assume the financial responsibility of cleanup by allowing them to seek recovery from others." *Key Tronic,* 511 U.S. at 819, n. 13. At first, Congress left some CERCLA liability issues, such as joint-and-several liability and contribution, to be developed by the federal courts under "traditional and evolving principles of common law." *United States v. Chem–Dyne Corp.,* 572 F.Supp. 802, 806–07 (S.D.Ohio 1983). Courts, thereafter, held § 107 and federal common law supported a right of contribution. *Mardan Corp.,* 804 F.2d at 1457 n. 3. But when Congress revisited CERCLA in 1986, it enacted an explicit right to contribution in § 113. This reflects Congress's unambiguous intent to allow private parties to recover in contribution.

We must next ask whether, in enacting § 113, Congress intended to eliminate the preexisting right to contribution it had allowed for court development under § 107. We conclude it did not. The plain text of § 113 reflects no intent to eliminate other rights to contribution; rather, § 113's saving clause provides that "[n]othing in this subsection shall diminish the right of any person to bring an action for contribution in the absence of a civil action" under §§ 106 or 107. § 113(f)(1). This view is further supported by examining § 113's legislative history reflecting Congress's intention to clarify and confirm, not to supplant or extinguish, the existing right to contribution. S.Rep. No. 11, 99th Cong., 1st Sess. 44 (1985). We conclude therefore that if Congress intended § 113 to completely replace § 107 in all circumstances, even where a plaintiff was not eligible to use § 113, it would have done so explicitly. Accordingly, we consider the plain language of CERCLA to be consistent with an implied right to contribution for parties such as Atlantic.

We conclude that the broad language of § 107 supports not only a right of cost recovery but also an implied right to contribution. *See Pinal Creek,* 118 F.3d at 1302 (" § 107 implicitly incorporates a claim for contribution"); *United Techns.,* 33 F.3d at 99 n. 8 ("It is possible that, although falling outside the statutory parameters for an express cause of action for contribution [under § 113(f)(1)], a [volunteer remediator] who spontaneously initiates a cleanup without governmental prodding might be able to pursue an implied right of action for contribution under § 107(c)"). We discern nothing in CERCLA's words, suggesting Congress intended to establish a comprehensive contribution and cost recovery scheme encouraging private cleanup of contaminated sites, while simultaneously excepting—indeed, penalizing—those who voluntarily assume such duties.

The government argues that if we allow Atlantic a § 107 remedy, we will render § 113 meaningless. This argument fails; liable parties which have been subject to §§ 106 or 107 enforcement actions are still required to use § 113, thereby ensuring its continued vitality. But parties such as Atlantic, which have not faced a CERCLA action, and are thereby barred from § 113, retain their access to § 107. This resolution gives life to each of CERCLA's sections, and is consistent with CERCLA's goal of encouraging prompt and voluntary cleanup of contaminated sites. *Key Tronic,* 511 U.S. at 819, n. 13.

A contrary ruling, barring Atlantic from recovering a portion of its costs, is not only contrary to CERCLA's purpose, but results in an absurd and unjust outcome. Consider: in this, of all cases, the United States is a liable party (who else has rocket motors to clean?). It is, simultaneously, CERCLA's primary enforcer at this, among other Superfund sites.

If we adopted the Government's reading of § 107, the government could insulate itself from responsibility for its own pollution by simply declining to bring a CERCLA cleanup action or refusing a liable party's offer to settle. This bizarre outcome would eviscerate CERCLA whenever the government, itself, was partially responsible for a site's contamination.

Congress understood the United States' dual role. When it enacted SARA, it explicitly waived sovereign immunity. CERCLA § 120(a). This waiver is part and parcel of CERCLA's regulatory scheme. It shows Congress had no intention of making private parties shoulder the government's share of liability.

Here, Atlantic assisted the United States by helping modernize its defenses. Atlantic, recognizing the deleterious environmental consequences, remediated the environment without compulsion. Its choice to do so, especially where the ultimate compulsory authority lay with the United States-corporate, will not be held to its detriment. The United States, under CERCLA, is liable for its share of the burden.

The Court, then, concludes Congress resolved the question of the United States' liability 20 years ago. It did not create a loophole by which the Republic could escape its own CERCLA liability by perversely abandoning its CERCLA enforcement power. Congress put the public's right to a clean and safe environment ahead of the sovereign's traditional immunities.

We hold that a private party which voluntarily undertakes a cleanup for which it may be held liable, thus barring it from contribution under

CERCLA's § 113, may pursue an action for direct recovery or contribution under § 107, against another liable party.

Notes and Comments

1. What did you think of the Supreme Court's analysis in *Aviall*? Do you agree that § 113(f) provides no basis for contribution claims filed by those who have voluntarily cleaned up contaminated sites? In finding that § 113(f) provides for such a claim, the en banc panel of the Fifth Circuit relied on combined effect of the "may seek contribution" language in § 113(f)'s enabling clause together with the breadth of its savings clause. *Aviall Services, Inc. v. Cooper Indus., Inc.* 312 F.3d 677, 681 and 686–687 (5th Cir. 2002) (en banc). Is this approach tenable? Did it attract any votes at the Supreme Court level?

2. As indicated in both *Aviall* and *Atlantic*, before *Aviall* the Courts of Appeals were virtually unanimous in holding that PRPs cannot bring "pure" § 107 actions (seeking to impose joint and several liability) against other PRPs. In *Atlantic*, the Eighth Circuit identified two rationales upon which many of these courts have relied in reaching this conclusion: (1) that otherwise the plaintiff would be able to recover 100% of its costs under a theory of joint and several liability; and (2) that a contrary ruling would render § 113(f)(1) a nullity because such plaintiffs would always choose "the substantially more generous provisions of § 107." In order to put the first of these rationales into perspective, imagine a site to which four parties have sent equal amounts of the exact same pollutant, all of which are commingled in the release. Imagine further that these are the only four PRPs, that they are equally culpable, and that two of them are insolvent. Assume that if all four of these parties were before the court in an EPA-lead action, and that if insolvency were not an issue, the court would be likely to allocate responsibility equally among the parties, with each paying 25% of the cleanup costs. Cf. CERCLA § 113(f)(1). If we assume that the cleanup costs are $20,000,000, each party would wind up paying $5,000,000. What would happen, though, if one of the two solvent parties spent the $20,000,000 cleaning up the site on a voluntary basis and then sued the other? One possibility, of course, is that the plaintiff would have no CERCLA claim whatsoever, a point to which we will return below. If we were to assume that the plaintiff would be entitled to at least some form of partial recovery, however, there would presumably be four possibilities as to how the cleanup costs could be divvied up between the two solvent parties: (1) we could hold the defendant jointly and severally responsible for all of the response costs, resulting in a 100% recovery for the plaintiff; (2) we could require the defendant to bear the burden of the so-called "orphan shares" (that is, the equitable shares of the two insolvent parties), resulting in its ultimately bearing 75% of the cleanup costs; (3) we could compel the plaintiff to bear those shares, resulting in its ultimately absorbing 75% of the cleanup costs; or (4) we could require them to each bear responsibility for half of the orphan shares (in addition to their own shares), resulting in each party's having to bear 50% of the cleanup costs. The Circuits articulating this first rationale appear to have assumed that allowing the plaintiff to proceed under § 107(a)(4) would compel the first of these outcomes. How did the *Atlantic* court respond to this concern? Is its response persuasive?

3.   In *Pinal Creek* (cited in *Atlantic*), the plaintiffs ("the Pinal Group") had engaged in a voluntary cleanup. As a result, they argued that they had § 107 claims against the defendants, while at the same time acknowledging that the defendant might have viable § 113(f)(1) contribution counterclaims against them. 118 F.3d at 1298. In setting up their argument this way, they urged that, even if the court ultimately deemed them liable (a point which they appeared to concede), the defendants should be required to bear the orphan shares, as in the second example in note 2, above. Id. In rejecting this approach, the Ninth Circuit identified both procedural and substantive concerns. On the procedural front, the court determined that the Pinal Group's approach "would guarantee inefficiency, potential duplication, and prolongation of the litigation process." Id. at 1303. Do you agree? Is there any reason why the defendants would have been unable to assert their contribution claims in the same action, presumably by way of an affirmative defense under FRCP 8(c)? Substantively, the court appeared convinced that if it treated the claims in the manner advocated by the plaintiffs (i.e., cost-recovery claims buffered by the possibility of contribution counterclaims), the result would be that the defendants would bear all of the orphan shares. Are you convinced that this would be the case?

4.   The Pinal Group may have compromised its cost-recovery claim by conceding its members' liability. What if there had been a real dispute as to whether they were liable? Even absent a serious question as to whether a particular CERCLA plaintiff is liable, shouldn't the court presume that it is not, and that it therefore has a right to file a pure § 107 claim, until the plaintiff either concedes its own liability or the defendant demonstrates it? This, of course, raises issues regarding the burdens of both pleading and proof. In tort law, the defendant generally bears the burden of both pleading and proof with respect to defenses such as contributory and comparative negligence. Dobbs, The Law of Torts, § 198, p. 493 (West, 2000). Should this same principle apply under CERCLA? If the plaintiff should generally be presumed to be blameless until the defendant shows otherwise, what does this suggest regarding the nature of the plaintiff's claim?

5.   Turning to the second rationale mentioned in the note 1, above, many courts, such as Third Circuit in the *New Castle County* case cited in *Atlantic*, have expressed the concern that allowing PRP plaintiffs to frame their claims under § 107(a)(4) would render § 113(f)(1) a nullity. How effectively did the *Atlantic* court respond to this concern?

6.   Other courts, such as the Second Circuit in *Bedford Affiliates*, have identified a third rationale for denying PRPs cost-recovery claims: that any claim between PRPs is a "quintessential claim for contribution." *Bedford Affiliates v. Sills*, 156 F.3d 416, 424 (2d Cir. 1998). Black's Law Dictionary defines the term "contribution" as the "[r]ight of one who has discharged a common liability to recover of another also liable, the aliquot portion of which he ought to pay or bear." Black's Law Dictionary 328 (6th Ed. 1990). Given that Bedford had entered into a series of consent orders with New York's environmental agency, it is easy to see how the court may have regarded this as a "quintessential" claim of contribution. Indeed, although the court did not focus on it, Section 113(f)(3)(B) appears to give parties such as Bedford an express statutory right of contribution where they have entered into administrative settlements with States. What if Bedford had

voluntarily cleaned up the site on its own, without any governmental order, decree or agreement (again, a so-called "voluntary" cleanup)? Would this still be such a "quintessential" claim? Cf. Restatement (Second) Torts § 886(a), cmt. b. (contribution "applies in favor of a tortfeasor who has paid more than his equitable share of the common liability in settlement, without any judgment or even suit against him"). Even if it might be (which is quite debatable), should that control over the express language of § 107(a)(4)?

7. The last rationale other courts have identified for restricting PRPs to contribution claims is that, at least in circumstances where some of the defendants may have resolved their liability to the government, allowing plaintiffs to frame their claims in cost-recovery might allow them to avoid the contribution protection provisions in § 113(f)(2). See, e.g., *United Technologies*, 33 F.3d at 102–103. Is this a concern? Should it be dispositive? Should it affect the analysis in situations in which the government has had no involvement at the site?

8. If PRPs cannot bring § 107 actions, what non-governmental entities can? The very existence of § 107(a)(4) indicates that Congress intended for some private parties to have cost-recovery claims. Although there does not appear to be any significant case law to date, one obvious candidate for this category would be the truly innocent purchaser; i.e., the landowner that has a valid defense under § 107(b)(3) of the statute (or for that matter, under any portion of § 107(b)). Others might include cleanup contractors whose contracting entities have gone bankrupt, or good samaritans who choose to clean up sites that they do not own. Compare *OHM Remediation Services v. Evans Cooperage Co., Inc.*, 116 F.3d 1574, 1579–1580 (5th Cir. 1997) (indicating that cleanup contractors may pursue a § 107(a)(4) claim despite the lack of any "protectable interest" in the property) with *Pennsylvania Urban Development Corp. v. Golen*, 708 F.Supp. 669 (E.D.Pa.1989) (holding that a subsequent purchaser did not have such a claim for cost associated with its pre-purchase investigations due to the absence of any protectable interest). More controversially, the Seventh Circuit appears to have determined that some "blameless" landowners (in which category it appeared to include any that did not actively contribute to contamination) can pursue claims under § 107(a)(4) even if they do not meet the requirements of the innocent purchaser defense (or any other statutory defense). See, e.g., *Rumpke of Ind., Inc. v. Cummins Engine Co., Inc.*, 107 F.3d 1235, 1240–1241 (7th Cir. 1987). Moreover, the *Rumpke* court appeared to contemplate that such landowners might be entitled to allowed to make full use of joint and several liability in appropriate circumstances. 107 F.3d at 1240; but see *Bedford Affiliates*, 156 F.3d at 424–425, and *Western Properties Service Corp. v. Shell Oil Co.*, 358 F.3d 678, 689–690 (9th Cir. 2004) (both declining to follow *Rumpke* on this point). Assuming that all of these parties can bring claims under § 107(a)(4), does it seem likely that this is the entire universe of potential plaintiffs that Congress intended to empower under that section?

9. Prior to the Supreme Court's decision in *Aviall*, a number of Circuits had embraced "hybrid" claims under some combination of §§ 107 and 113 in situations in which PRP claims did not fall squarely within the meaning of § 113(f)'s enabling clause. While not all of these decisions were clear regarding precisely how the courts viewed these provisions as working together, the better-articulated decisions appeared to treat the claims as

implied claims for contribution originating under § 107, with § 113(f) governing the mechanics of how the liability was to be allocated among the various PRPs. See, e.g., *Pinal Creek*, 118 F.3d at 1301–1306, *New Castle County v. Halliburton NUS Corp.*, 111 F.3d 1116, 1122 (3d Cir. 1997), and *Sun Co., Inc. v. Browning–Ferris, Inc.*, 124 F.3d 1187, 1191–1192 (10th Cir. 1997). Were you persuaded by the *Atlantic* court's discussion on this front?

10. Read § 113(f)(3)(B). What are the implications of *Aviall*, if any, for claims under that subsection in situations in which the plaintiffs have entered into administrative agreements with State officials? In *Consolidated Edison Co. v. UGI Utilities, Inc.*, 423 F.3d 90, 95–96 (2d Cir. 2005), the Second Circuit determined that this provision only applies to those settlements that specifically reference that they are intended to resolve CERCLA claims. Should it also apply to State settlements resolving claims under State cleanup laws, or to State agreements that purport to recognize "voluntary" cleanups?

11. Would the recipient of a unilateral order under § 106 have a contribution claim under either § 113(f)(1) or (f)(3)(B)? See footnote 5 in *Aviall*; see also § 113(f)(1) and (f)(3)(B). If not, should this bear on the question of whether such a party would have a claim under § 107?

12. As discussed in *Atlantic*, in the wake of *Aviall* the Second Circuit also backed away from its prior absolutist position that PRPs cannot use § 107. *Consolidated Edison Co. v. UGI Utilities, Inc.*, 423 F.3d 90, 100 (2d Cir. 2005). Recently, the Seventh Circuit weighed in, finding that one who engaged in a voluntary cleanup had an implied right of contribution under § 107 (without specifically either revisiting or declining to revisit its prior precedent that PRPs can never have "pure" cost-recovery claims). *Metropolitan Water Reclamation District of Greater Chicago v. North American Galvanizing & Coatings, Inc.*, 473 F.3d 824 (7th Cir. 2007). At the same time, however, the Third Circuit recently both reaffirmed its holding that PRPs cannot bring cost-recovery claims and found that § 107 provides no implied right of contribution. *E.I. DuPont De Nemours and Co. v. U.S.*, 460 F.3d 515 (3d Cir. 2006) ("*DuPont*"). As this edition was going to press, the Supreme Court granted certiorari in *Atlantic*. How do you think the Court is likely to address the two issues in the case? Note that under the *DuPont* approach, the vast majority of private parties who engage in voluntary cleanups will have no claim under CERCLA. Is it likely that this is an end that Congress sought to accomplish in enacting SARA in 1986?

13. Finally, it is worth noting that three Circuits have determined that CERCLA preempts state law contribution claims in at least some situations. See *Bedford Affiliates*, 156 F.3d, at 427; *In re Reading Co.*, 115 F.3d 1111, 1117 (3d Cir. 1997); and *PMC v. Sherwin–Williams Co.*, 151 F.3d 610, 617–618 (7th Cir. 1998). Do these decisions survive *Aviall*?

14. If we assume that *Aviall* and the Supreme Court's ultimate resolution in *Atlantic* do not result in the death of private party actions under § 107(a)(4) (and they certainly will not with respect to non-PRP plaintiffs), it is worth considering some of the other dynamics presented thereunder. Unlike governmental entities, private-party plaintiffs bear the burden of demonstrating that their costs were consistent with the NCP. See § 107(a)(4). As we have seen, the NCP imposes both procedural and substan-

tive requirements that guide the remedy-selection process. The burden of establishing consistency with its terms poses two significant concerns for would-be private-party plaintiffs. First, they must determine whether the game is worth the candle; that is, they must determine whether the prospect of recovering some or all of their response costs justifies assuming the significant procedural burdens imposed by the NCP. In situations where the total cleanup costs are likely to be moderate, or where the prospects for significant recovery are dim, potential plaintiffs may determine that the advantages of any potential claims are offset by the burdens of compiling an RI/FS or going through a public comment process. Second, in many instances the NCP is vague concerning the ultimate question of "how clean is clean;" that is, what degree of cleanup will be deemed to be sufficiently protective of human health and the environment while still comporting with competing concerns such as the need to ensure some degree of cost-effectiveness. Private parties bear a significant burden as a result of this uncertainty. Although there has not been much litigation in this area to date, it is easy to foresee controversy concerning whether a particular plaintiff could have achieved a similar level of protection at less cost through the implementation of alternative remedies that may be permissible under the NCP, such as institutional remedies (e.g., precluding access to the site or imposing deed restrictions) and/or natural attenuation. The mere prospect of such controversy is likely to impose a throttle on the degree of cleanup achieved in these private-party cases. The rational potential plaintiff may realize that, in a cost-recovery case, it is unlikely to ever be challenged for not having gone far enough.

15. In promulgating the revised NCP in 1990, EPA sought to afford some relief on the points discussed in the prior note by indicating that "substantial compliance" with the NCP suffices with respect to its procedural and public participation requirements. EPA still requires a strict showing that the end result was a "CERCLA–quality cleanup." See 40 C.F.R. § 300.700(c)(3)(I). While the NCP does not define what constitutes "substantial compliance" on the procedural front, the preamble to the final rule provides the following elaboration on the rationale underlying the new standard:

> EPA's decision to require only "substantial" compliance with potentially applicable requirements is based . . . on the recognition that providing a list of rigid requirements may serve to defeat cost recovery for meritorious cleanup actions based upon a mere technical failure by the private party that has taken the response action.

55 Fed.Reg. at 8793 (March 8, 1990). The preamble goes on to provide two examples of situations where technical failure to fully comply with the listed requirements should not be deemed to preclude recovery: (1) where the private party affords ample opportunity for public comment but does not provide a public hearing; and (2) where it may have been difficult to judge which NCP requirements apply (e.g., determining whether a "focused" feasibility study makes more sense that a full analysis of alternative remedial options). On the substantive side, the NCP also fails to define the term "CERCLA–quality cleanup." Again, however, the preamble provides more specificity:

In order to achieve a "CERCLA–quality cleanup," the action must satisfy the three basic remedy selection requirements of CERCLA section 121(b)(1)—i.e., the remedial action must be "protective of human health and the environment," utilize "permanent solutions and alternative treatment technologies or resource recovery technologies to the maximum extent practicable," and be "cost-effective"—attain applicable and relevant and appropriate requirements (ARARs)(CERCLA section 121(d)(4)), and provide for meaningful public participation (section 117).

55 Fed.Reg. at 8793 (March 8, 1990). Should EPA's view regarding what constitutes compliance with the NCP be binding in the context of wholly-private actions? Does the statute provide clear authority for this sort of legislative rule? See CERCLA §§ 105 and 115; see also Executive Order 12,580, 52 Fed.Reg. 2923 (January 29, 1987)(delegation from President to EPA under § 115); and 55 Fed.Reg. at 8795 (March 8, 1990)(expressing EPA's view that it has the authority to write such a rule). Would EPA have the authority to establish a "substantial compliance" test with regard to its own procedural compliance with the NCP? If so, why has it not done so? Assuming that EPA has the authority to address these issues, do you agree with the balance it has struck? Why should private parties receive a more relaxed standard than EPA? On the other hand, is it really necessary to insist that private parties provide for "meaningful public participation" in selecting remedies at sites that EPA has determined do not warrant federal attention?

Chapter 8

PROTECTION OF PARTICULAR NATURAL RESOURCES

In some of the previous chapters, we have covered pollution prevention. By preventing or reducing pollution, we protect the natural resources of the air, water, and land. In this chapter we deal with federal laws protecting particular natural resources: endangered species, wetlands, and areas affected by surface coal mining.

I. THE ENDANGERED SPECIES ACT OF 1973

The Endangered Species Act (ESA), 16 U.S.C. §§ 1531 *et seq.*, has frequently been called the pit bull of environmental law. Under the ESA, the Supreme Court held that in order to safeguard the endangered snail darter, a three-inch fish with no known economic or ecological value, indistinguishable from 130–odd other species of darters except to the trained ichthyologist, the government could not close the gates to impound water behind a dam on which $150 million had already been spent.[1] *TVA v. Hill*, 437 U.S. 153, 98 S.Ct. 2279, 57 L.Ed.2d 117 (1978). Largely without regard to its economic consequences, Congress passed the ESA as an affirmation of the importance of preserving species. In retrospect it is difficult to imagine how such a radical law could pass by a unanimous vote in the Senate and near unanimous vote in the House and be signed by President Richard Nixon. While those legislators may have voted for the law to protect wolves, grizzly bears, whales, and eagles, its effect has been to protect not only those mega fauna, but also flower loving flies, blind salamanders, cave cockroaches, and a wide variety of other exotic plant and animal species certainly unknown to members of Congress.

For whatever reason, people usually do not demand some instrumental basis for preserving bears, whales, eagles, and similar species. We marvel at them, probably most often on television or in the movies, but

----

1. Not that it was well spent. As the lawyer for the snail darter has taken pains to explain, the dam was an economic mistake and environmental disaster even without regard to the snail darter. *See, e.g.,*

Zygmunt Plater, *Law and the Fourth Estate: Endangered Nature, the Press, and the Dicey Game of Democratic Governance*, 32 ENV. L. 1, 4 *et seq.* (2002).

nevertheless we feel they are unquestionably important to us. Beetles, spiders, flies, and similar species do not have the same cachet. It is often difficult to explain why it is important to preserve such species. The ESA itself states that species are to be protected because of their esthetic, ecological, educational, historical, recreational, and scientific value to the Nation. 16 U.S.C. § 1531(a)(3). But for many of these species it is not clear which, if any, of these values they represent. Nevertheless, the Endangered Species Act remains popular with people. At the same time, experience with its administration has left both environmentalists and persons adversely affected by species' protection with many complaints. With thirty years of experience, it would probably be impossible to pass the ESA today, but it would be equally impossible to repeal it. For better or for worse, for many species it remains the last legal hope against extinction.

A. Outline of the Act

The Endangered Species Act is, of course, designed to protect endangered species, so the first objective of the Act is to establish the procedure and standards for determining which species should be protected and how much of their habitat needs to be protected in order to protect the species. Section 4, 16 U.S.C. § 1533, performs this function. Once the appropriate species and habitat for protection are determined, the ESA operates to protect the affected species in two separate ways. Section 7 of the Act, 16 U.S.C. § 1536, imposes both procedural and substantive duties on federal agencies whose actions may jeopardize the protected species or adversely affect their habitat. It was Section 7 that stopped the Tellico Dam to protect the snail darter. Section 9 of the Act, 16 U.S.C. § 1538, prohibits anyone from engaging in certain actions that might harm threatened or endangered species. Section 10, 16 U.S.C. § 1539, provides a mechanism for persons to avoid the absolute prohibitions of Section 9, and Section 11, 16 U.S.C. § 1540, specifies the civil and criminal penalties to which a person is subject if they violate Section 9, and it provides a citizen suit provision for enforcing the Act.

B. Section 4

Depts. of Int. & Commerce

The Endangered Species Act is unusual in that it assigns responsibility for implementing the Act generally to two different agencies–the Department of Interior and the Department of Commerce. Interior is responsible for terrestrial species; Commerce is responsible for marine species. Exclusively fresh water fish are considered terrestrial species, but fish species that live in both fresh and salt water, such as salmon, are generally considered marine species. Marine mammals, such as sea lions, are marine species. The Secretary of Interior has delegated Interior's duties to the United States Fish and Wildlife Service, and the Secretary of Commerce has delegated Commerce's duties to the National Marine Fisheries Service (NMFS), a subunit of the National Oceanic and Atmospheric Administration in Commerce, sometimes known as NOAA Fisheries.

1. Listing

a. Endangered or Threatened

The respective secretaries are to list a "species" as endangered if it is "in danger of extinction throughout all or a significant portion of its range." 16 U.S.C. § 1532(6). An exception is made for insects constituting a pest whose protection would present great risk to humans. *Id.* A "species" is to be listed as threatened if it is "likely to become an endangered species within the foreseeable future throughout all or a significant portion of its range." 16 U.S.C. § 1532(20). Under the Act, the listing is only supposed to occur if the threat or endangerment is caused by one or more of five listed factors: impacts on the species' habitat; overuse of the species, such as by hunting or fishing; disease or predation; the inadequacy of existing regulations; or any other factor affecting its continued existence. 16 U.S.C. § 1533(a)(1). As a practical matter, these factors would seem to be all inclusive, so any endangerment or threat thereof would seem to require listing.

Today, human caused impacts on species' habitat are overwhelmingly the largest threat to species' existence. This can occur through urban development and the conversion of undeveloped land to agricultural use. For example, the threatened destruction of vernal pools (small seasonal ponds largely in California) that are the unique habitat of three species of fairy shrimp and a vernal pool tadpole shrimp led to the listing of the fairy shrimp as endangered and the tadpole shrimp as threatened. Or the habitat can be altered through timber cutting, which led to the listing of the Northern Spotted Owl as threatened. Or a combination of factors can together degrade the habitat of a species, placing it under significant strain. This is the situation for most listed salmon species, where the combination of dams impeding their migration to and from the ocean and timber and grazing practices at headwaters resulting in increased water temperature and sediment are believed to be the most significant factors causing reduced numbers of wild salmon.

Gathering the scientific evidence of the current status of a species, as well as the stresses under which it is laboring, is a substantial undertaking, and if the Fish & Wildlife Service or NMFS fails to do a good job, there is a high degree of likelihood that either concerned environmentalists or concerned development, agricultural, logging, or grazing interests will sue to overturn the decision. Judicial review of a listing decision (either for or against) will be under the Administrative Procedure Act, and unless the listing agency violates some procedural requirement, *see, e.g., Alabama–Tombigbee Rivers Coalition v. Department of Interior*, 26 F.3d 1103 (11th Cir. 1994)(enjoining the FWS from using information obtained in violation of the Federal Advisory Committee Act's procedural requirements), the review is likely to be under the APA's "arbitrary and capricious" standard. This standard, while deferential to the agency, especially when the agency is operating on the edges of scientific knowledge, requires a "thorough, probing in-depth review" of the agency action. *See, e.g., Alsea Valley Alliance v. Evans,*

161 F.Supp.2d 1154 (D. Or. 2001)(finding NMFS listing of west coast coho salmon arbitrary and capricious); *Northern Spotted Owl v. Hodel*, 716 F.Supp. 479 (W.D. Wash. 1988)(finding FWS decision not to list the owl arbitrary and capricious).

Notes and Comments

1. The determination of whether a species is endangered or threatened is a classic case of risk assessment, which is supposed to be performed by objective scientists, and the Endangered Species Act reflects that in its requirement that a species listing of endangered or threatened is to be based "solely on the basis of the best scientific and commercial data available."[2] 16 U.S.C. § 1533(b)(1)(A). However, neither the Act nor the agencies' regulations provide any further guidance on what might constitute endangerment of extinction or its threat. The risk of extinction necessarily involves at least two variables: time and probability. Probability, of course, refers to the likelihood of extinction. Is a species in "danger of extinction" if there is merely some chance of extinction, perhaps 5%? Or does it take some higher degree of likelihood? More probable than not? Nothing in the agencies' policies answers these questions. There is also the question of time. That is, we are all going to be extinct at some point, perhaps when the sun burns out, maybe earlier. On the other hand, even species under significant pressures are rarely likely to become extinct within only a few years. If there is virtually no danger of extinction within ten years, but a 60% probability within 100 years, is that in "danger of extinction"? Again, the agencies' documents provide no clue. The requirement for "threatened species" is that "in the foreseeable future" the species will become in danger of extinction. What is the foreseeable future? We see into the future with different levels of certainty. That is, we can predict a species' status next year with a high degree of certainty, but its status a hundred years from now, much less 500 years, while certainly foreseeable to some degree, involves a high degree of uncertainty. *Cf. Nuclear Energy Institute, Inc. v. E.P.A.*, 373 F.3d 1251 (D.C.Cir. 2004) (invalidating EPA limitation to 10,000 years of considering risk from repository of high level nuclear waste). Again, the agencies' regulations do not help us (or them) in answering these questions.

2. Obviously, the answers to these questions cannot be answered by science. Rather, the answers are value-laden determinations that may be made by scientists in the course of their supposedly neutral scientific determination of endangerment or may be made by policymakers reviewing the scientists' work. In essence, they reflect the degree of protectiveness desired. That is, if you want to be "protective," then a 40% chance of extinction in 100 years may be unacceptable, but if you do not want to be protective, then a 40% chance of extinction in 100 years simply is not "in danger" of extinction. In any case, the determinations are non-transparent, based upon considerations undisclosed and unknown to the public. *See, e.g.,* Daniel J. Rohlf, *Section 4 of the Endangered Species Act: Top Ten Issues for the* Next *Thirty Years*, 34 Envtl. L. 483, 501–507 (2004).

2. The reference to "commercial data" means that where the threat to the species is from commercial use of the species, then the extent of that commercial use should be determined by the best available commercial data. It does not suggest any consideration of the economic impact of the listing of a species.

3. Interestingly, the issue of these underlying questions has not come up in litigation, which, when it focuses on the validity of a listing (or failure to list), usually involves questions of fact, such as the remaining numbers of the species, the rate of decline, the cause of the decline, the extent of existing habitat, etc. If closing the gates of the Tellico dam will within 3 months totally eliminate the habitat of the snail darter, there may be little question as to its "danger of extinction," but if the indefinite continuation of existing (but unsustainable) timber practices on public lands would lead to a 0.7% annual decline in the Northern Spotted Owl population, the "danger of extinction" is much less clear.

4. There is also the question of the reliability of the data used by scientists. Attempts to count the number of members of a species which naturally tries to hide from humans is difficult to say the least. Computer models that make predictions from data may provide a false sense of certainty. But, as the adage goes, garbage in, garbage out. "One model of Steller sea lion population dynamics, for example, predicted a 100 percent probability of extinction within 100 years when applied to data collected from 1985 to 1994, but only a 10 percent probability of extinction if the data were limited to the period from 1989 to 1994." Holly Doremus, *Listing Decisions Under the Endangered Species Act: Why Better Science Isn't Always Better Policy*, 75 Wash. U.L.Q. 1029, 1120 (1997). Who's to say which years to use?

5. An important issue in deciding whether a species is in danger of extinction, or likely to become so, is how to assess possible future conservation efforts. For example, if a state, seeking to avoid having a species listed, states that it will take various actions to protect the habitat of the species, should FWS or NMFS accept that at face value, assess the probability that the state will indeed do what it says, or ignore it. If taken at face value, the proposed state actions might well end the perceived decline in the species, but will the state really follow through? Even if it follows through, will its actions be successful? Perhaps its proposed actions are to organize a voluntary program by landowners to set aside habitat for the species. Will the landowners actually participate? In several cases the listing agencies have accepted state (and federal) plans, cooperative agreements, memoranda of agreement, and the like as a basis for predicting that a population decline will be arrested. And in 2003, FWS and NMFS adopted their PECE policy, Policy for Evaluation of Conservation Efforts When Making Listing Decisions, 68 Fed. Reg. 15,100 (Mar. 28, 2003). Generally, however, courts have been skeptical. "Courts have specifically and repeatedly interpreted this provision to mean that an agency may not rely upon future actions to justify a decision not to list a species as threatened or endangered." *Center for Biological Diversity v. Badgley*, 2001 WL 844399 (D.Or. 2001)(citing *Oregon Natural Resources Council v. Daley*, 6 F.Supp.2d 1139, 1153–54 (D.Or. 1998)); *Friends of Wild Swan, Inc. v. United States Fish and Wildlife Serv.*, 945 F.Supp. 1388, 1399 (D.Or.1996); *Biodiversity Legal Found. v. Babbitt*, 943 F.Supp. 23, 26 (D.D.C.1996); *Southwest Center for Biological Diversity v. Babbitt*, 939 F.Supp. 49, 52 (D.D.C.1996). Similarly, most courts have held that actions that are voluntary should not be considered. *See, e.g., ONRC v. Daley*, 6 F.Supp.2d 1139 (D.Or. 1998). But the results are not unanimous. *See, e.g., Defenders of Wildlife v. Babbitt*, 1999 WL 33537981 (S.D.Cal. 1999).

Generally, courts have upheld listing agencies' reliance on legally binding regulations requiring conservation efforts. *See, e.g., id.* Recall that Section 4 specifically includes as one of the five factors to be considered in a listing decision "the inadequacy of existing regulatory mechanisms." 16 U.S.C. § 1533(a)(1)(D). This certainly suggests that "existing" (i.e., not future, anticipated) "regulatory" (i.e., not voluntary) mechanisms *might* be adequate to protect species. Section 4 also states that a listing determination is to be made "after taking into account those efforts, if any, being made by any State, or foreign nation, or any political subdivision of a State or foreign nation, to protect such species." 16 U.S.C. § 1533(b)(1)(A). This too seems to focus on the present activities, but it is not stated so as to exclude voluntary activities. If determinations as to endangerment or its threat is all about predicting the future, why should agencies be precluded from considering predictable future activities by states or other federal agencies?

b. "A Significant Portion of its Range"

Contrary to what most lay people consider to be extinction, the ESA refers to "extinction" of a species (or the foreseeable threat thereof) "throughout all or a significant portion of its range." Precisely what this means is unclear.

DEFENDERS OF WILDLIFE v. NORTON
United States Court of Appeals, Ninth Circuit, 2001.
258 F.3d 1136.

BERZON, Circuit Judge:

[After proposing to list the Flat–Tailed Horned Lizard as a threatened species, the Secretary of Interior's final decision was to withdraw the proposed rule on the basis that although the lizard was subject to substantial habitat loss on private lands, "[b]ecause of the large amount of flat-tailed horned lizard habitat located on public lands within the United States and the reduction of threats on these lands . . . , threats due to habitat modification and loss do not warrant listing of the species at this time." This decision was challenged by the Defenders of Wildlife, arguing that the species needed to be listed because the destruction of its habitat on private lands would likely result in its extinction in the foreseeable future throughout a significant portion of its range.]

* * *

Standing alone, the phrase "in danger of extinction throughout . . . a significant portion of its range" is puzzling. According to the Oxford English Dictionary, "extinct" means "has died out or come to an end. . . . Of a family, class of persons, a race of species of animals or plants: Having no living representative." Thus, the phrase "extinc[t] throughout . . . a significant portion of its range" is something of an oxymoron. . . .

1. THE SECRETARY'S EXPLANATION

The Secretary's explanation of this odd phraseology is of no assistance in puzzling out the meaning of the phrase, since her interpretation simply cannot be squared with the statute's language and structure. The Secretary in her brief interprets the enigmatic phrase to mean that a species is eligible for protection under the ESA if it "faces threats in enough key portions of its range that the *entire species* is in danger of extinction, or will be within the foreseeable future." She therefore assumes that a species is in danger of extinction in "a significant portion of its range" only if it is in danger of extinction everywhere....

[handwritten margin note: Sec. explanation]

2. DEFENDERS' EXPLANATION

Defenders' interpretation of the phrase "extinction throughout ... a significant portion of its range" is similarly unsatisfactory. Defenders takes a more quantitative approach to the phrase, arguing that the projected loss of 82% of the lizard's habitat in this case constitutes "a substantial portion of its range." Appellants then cite to other cases in which courts found listing of species warranted after the loss of even smaller amounts of habitat. *Federation of Fly Fishers v. Daley*, Civ. No. 99–981–SI (N.D.Cal. Oct. 25, 2000), Slip Op. at 17–18 (finding listing of the steelhead trout warranted despite protections covering 64% of its range); *ONRC v. Daley*, 6 F.Supp.2d 1139, 1157 (D.Or.1998) (finding the coho salmon in danger of extinction despite federal forest land protections extending over 35% of its range); 45 Fed.Reg. 63,812, 63,817–18 (Sept. 25, 1980) (listing the Coachella Valley fringe-toed lizard as a threatened species although 50% of its historical habitat remained).

[handwritten margin note: Def. argument]

There are two problems with Defenders' quantitative approach. First, it simply does not make sense to assume that the loss of a predetermined percentage of habitat or range would necessarily qualify a species for listing. A species with an exceptionally large historical range may continue to enjoy healthy population levels despite the loss of a substantial amount of suitable habitat. Similarly, a species with an exceptionally small historical range may quickly become endangered after the loss of even a very small percentage of suitable habitat....

[handwritten margin note: Ct. says should not assume loss of predetermined % of habitat = listg]

In the absence of a fixed percentage, Defenders' suggested interpretation of the phrase begins to look a lot like the faulty definition offered by the Secretary, i.e., "a substantial portion of its range" means an amount of habitat loss such that total extinction is likely in the near future. As noted above, this reading does not comport with the other terms of the statute.

3. INSIGHT FROM THE LEGISLATIVE HISTORY

The legislative history of the ESA suggests an entirely different meaning of the inherently ambiguous phrase "extinction throughout ... a significant portion of its range." ...

It appears that Congress added this new language in order to encourage greater cooperation between federal and state agencies and to allow the Secretary more flexibility in her approach to wildlife management. The case of the American alligator, which was frequently cited during the Senate debate, illustrates this likely intent:

In 1973, the range of the alligator stretched from the Mississippi Delta in Louisiana to the Everglades of Florida. Its distribution over that range, however, varied widely. While habitat loss had pushed the species to the verge of extinction in Florida, conservation efforts had resulted in an overabundance of alligators in Louisiana, such that harvesting was required to keep the alligators from overrunning the human population. In order to address problems such as this, the Act allows the Secretary to "list an animal as 'endangered' through all or a portion of its range." Senator Tunney explained:

> An animal might be "endangered" in most States but overpopulated in some. In a State in which a species is overpopulated, the Secretary would have the discretion to list that animal as merely threatened or to remove it from the endangered species listing entirely while still providing protection in areas where it was threatened with extinction. In that portion of its range where it was not threatened with extinction, the States would have full authority to use their management skills to insure the proper conservation of the species.

Id. In describing this provision as "perhaps the most important section of this bill," *id.*, Senator Tunney also noted that

> The plan for Federal–State cooperation provides for much more extensive discretionary action on the part of the Secretary and the State agencies. Under existing law [(namely, the Endangered Species Conservation Act of 1969)], a species must be declared "endangered" even if in a certain portion of its range, the species has experienced a population boom, or is otherwise threatening to destroy the life support capacity of its habitat. Such a broad listing prevents local authorities from taking steps to insure healthy population levels.

Id.

The historical application of the Act is consistent with this interpretation of the statute, not with the interpretation suggested by the Secretary in her briefs in this case. Grizzly bears, for example, are listed as threatened species within the contiguous 48 states, but not in Alaska. Similarly, only the California, Oregon and Washington populations of the marbled murrelet, whose range in North America extends from the Aleutian Archipelago in Alaska to Central California, are listed as threatened. . . .

We conclude, consistently with the Secretary's historical practice, that a species can be extinct "throughout . . . a significant portion of its range" if there are major geographical areas in which it is no longer viable but once was. Those areas need not coincide with national or state political boundaries, although they can. The Secretary necessarily has a wide degree of discretion in delineating "a significant portion of its range," since the term is not defined in the statute. But where, as here, it is on the record apparent that the area in which the lizard is expected to survive is much smaller than its historical range, the Secretary must at least explain her conclusion that the area in which the species can no longer live is not a "significant portion of its range."

* * *

Notes and Comments

1. Can you decipher what the difference is between the three different interpretations of "extinction throughout a significant portion of its range"? The Secretary seems to be saying that the whole species is to be listed if the species will be extinct in enough of its range to be in danger of extinction everywhere, and here there is no need to list the species because there is enough protected public land remaining to preserve the species. The Defenders of Wildlife seem to be saying much the same thing, except that it wants to establish by a percentage of the whole range the amount of range which, if the species were to become extinct there, would require listing of the whole species. Here, it is arguing that because 82% of the lizard's range is on private property, where it is likely to go extinct, that is enough to require listing of the whole species. The court, however, distinguishes between the whole species and that portion of the species that exists (or did exist) on the significant portion of its range. It is this portion of the species that the court suggests should be listed. Do you think the court is right? If it is, how does this relate to the definition of species to include a "distinct population segment," which is discussed below?

c.   "Species" Includes "Subspecies"

Even when one understands what is endangerment or its threat, one must still understand what constitutes a "species." It is only when a "species" is endangered or threatened that it becomes listed and protected. Under the Act, the term is defined to include not only "species" but also "any subspecies of fish or wildlife or plants, and any distinct population segment of any species of vertebrate fish or wildlife which interbreeds when mature."

For those whose biology is rusty, the general taxonomic classifications are:

*   Phylum (e.g., Chordata or vertebrates)
*   Class (e.g., Mammalia or mammals)
*   Order (e.g., Carnivora or carnivores)
*   Family (e.g., Ursidae or bears, including pandas, sloth bears, black bears, brown bears, etc.)
*   Genus (e.g., Ursus or brown, black, polar, and Asiatie black bears)
*   Species (e.g., Ursus Arctos or Brown Bear)
*   Subspecies (e.g., Ursus Arctos Horribilis or Grizzly Bear)

The general rule is that members of the same species can interbreed in the wild and produce fertile offspring, so Grizzly bears and Kodiak bears (Ursus Arctos Middendorfi), different subspecies of the species

Ursus Arctos, can interbreed, but Grizzly bears and Polar bears (Ursus Maritimus), different species, do not.

These classifications and which plants and animals fit into them where, however, are a continuing issue among scientists. For example, during the controversial listing of the Northern Spotted Owl, interests opposed to the listing argued that the Northern Spotted Owl and the California Spotted Owl were not different subspecies of the species Spotted Owl, but merely "clinal" variations of the same subspecies. That is, the subtle differences in appearance between the two owls were really a difference in appearance related to where they lived, rather than to any taxonomic or genetic differentiation. They supported this argument with an early twentieth century study reaching that conclusion and the fact that genetic testing did not reveal any difference between the two types of owls. At the same time, the 1957 edition of the Checklist of North American Birds, published by the American Ornithological Union, the oldest and largest private organization in the New World devoted to the scientific study of birds, listed the two types of owls as separate subspecies, and the AOU's Committee on Classification and Nomenclature decided in 1989 not to reclassify the owls on the basis of the testing showing no genetic difference, because "present techniques for exposing genetic variation examine only a tiny fraction of the genome." The FWS and NMFS joint regulations state that the agencies will "rely on standard taxonomic distinctions and the biological expertise of the Department and the scientific community concerning the relevant taxonomic group." 50 CFR § 424.11(a). Accordingly, the FWS followed the AOU's direction and concluded that they were different subspecies. *See* Determination of Threatened Status for the Northern Spotted Owl, 55 Fed. Reg. 26114, 26130 (June 26, 1990).

These debates are not just academic. Those opposed to listing the Northern Spotted Owl wanted it combined with the Califonia Spotted Owl as all one species, because then the population and dispersal of the Northern/California Spotted Owl would be sufficiently large to suggest that it need not be listed at all. Indeed, in a later decision, the FWS decided that listing the California Spotted Owl was not warranted. *See* 12 Month Finding for a Petition to List the California Spotted Owl, 68 Fed. Reg. 7580 (Feb. 14, 2003). The exercise involved in this example is played out in numerous controversies over whether to list a species as threatened or endangered, with those who desire listing attempting to define the "species" as restrictively as possible, to minimize its range and population and therefore its ability to survive indefinitely, while those who oppose listing attempting to define the species as broadly as possible, to maximize its range and population and therefore its ability to survive indefinitely.

d. "Species" Includes Distinct Population Segments

The concept of "distinct population segment" is easy to understand at one level. Above, in the *Defenders of Wildlife v. Norton* case, the court noted that grizzly bears are listed as threatened species in the lower 48 states, but not in Alaska, where you can legally hunt them for sport. However, the grizzlies in Yellowstone National Park, for example, cannot interbreed with those in Alaska; they are totally isolated from those grizzlies. The Endangered Species Act, especially with its authors' focus on mega-fauna, was intended to protect such isolated populations of fish and vertebrate wildlife. Grizzlies may be easy, but what about some other species? Here the FWS and NMFS have adopted guidance to give further clarification. However, that clarification still leaves a lot of questions.

NATIONAL ASSOCIATION OF HOME BUILDERS v. NORTON

United States Court of Appeals, Ninth Circuit, 2003.
340 F.3d 835.

The National Association of Home Builders, the Southern Arizona Home Builders Association, and the Home Builders Association of Central Arizona (collectively, "Home Builders") appeal the district court's decision upholding the designation of a population of cactus ferruginous pygmy-owls in Arizona as a distinct population segment ("DPS") pursuant to the Fish and Wildlife Service's ("FWS") *Policy Regarding the Recognition of Distinct Vertebrate Population Segments Under the Endangered Species Act,* 61 Fed.Reg. 4722 (Feb. 7, 1996) ("*DPS Policy*").....

The cactus ferruginous pygmy-owl (*Glaucidium brasilianum cactorum*) is a small bird, about 6.75 inches in length, that can be reddish-brown or gray. *Determination of Endangered Status for the Cactus Ferruginous Pygmy Owl in Arizona,* 62 Fed.Reg. 10,730, 10,730 (Mar. 10, 1997) (codified at 50 C.F.R. § 17.11(h)) ("Listing Rule"). It is one of four subspecies of the ferruginous pygmy-owl. *Id.* The range of the cactus ferruginous pygmy-owl ("pygmy-owl") extends "from lowland central Arizona south through western Mexico, to the States of Colima and Michoacan, and from southern Texas south through the Mexican States of Tamaulipas and Nuevo Leon." The pygmy-owls in Arizona represent the northernmost edge of the subspecies' range.

... By the FWS' estimates, pygmy-owls were once common to Arizona prior to the mid–1900s, but only between 20 and 40 pygmy-owls remain in Arizona.

... After a notice and comment period, the FWS issued a final rule listing the Arizona pygmy-owls as endangered (but not listing the Texas pygmy-owls as threatened).

In the Listing Rule, the FWS designated the Arizona pygmy-owls as a DPS. The ESA permits the FWS to designate a population of a species as a DPS and to list it as an endangered species. To designate a DPS under the *DPS Policy,* the FWS must find that a population is discrete "in relation to the remainder of the species to which it belongs" and significant "to the species to which it belongs." 61 Fed.Reg. at 4725. In making this designation in the Listing Rule, the FWS first found that the pygmy-owl populations in the east (southeast Texas south through northeastern Mexico) and west (central Arizona south through northwestern Mexico) are (1) discrete "based on geographic isolation, distribution and status of habitat, and potential morphological and genetic distinctness," and (2) significant because the loss of either population would create a significant gap in the range of the subspecies.

Next, the FWS further subdivided the western pygmy-owl DPS into an Arizona population and a northwestern Mexico population. According to the Listing Rule, the Arizona pygmy-owls are discrete from the northwestern Mexico pygmy-owls because they are "delimited by international boundaries" and "the status of the species in Arizona is different from that in Sonora [Mexico], with records currently indicating a higher number of individuals in Sonora." . . .

Home Builders sued to vacate the Listing Rule and the designation of critical habitat. The district court granted summary judgment to the FWS. . . .

On appeal, Home Builders argue that the FWS violated the *DPS Policy* by designating the Arizona pygmy-owls as a DPS.

. . . Home Builders do not contest the designation of the eastern and western pygmy-owls as DPSs, only the subdivision of the western pygmy-owls into the Arizona DPS and the northwestern Mexico population. Thus, the question we must decide is whether the FWS violated its *DPS Policy* by finding that the Arizona pygmy-owls are a discrete and significant population.

. . . Since the ESA does not define the term "distinct population segment,"[8] the FWS and the National Marine Fisheries Service jointly promulgated the *DPS Policy* to ensure consistency in their respective DPS designations. Under the *DPS* Policy, a DPS must be discrete "in relation to the remainder of the species to which it belongs" and significant "to the species to which it belongs." 61 Fed.Reg. at 4725. A DPS must be both discrete and significant, because "[t]he interests of conserving genetic diversity would not be well served by efforts directed at either well-defined but insignificant units or entities believed to be significant but around which boundaries cannot be recognized." *Id.* at 4724.

A. *The FWS Did Not Arbitrarily and Capriciously Find That the Arizona Pygmy–Owl Population is Discrete*

The purpose of the discreteness standard is to ensure that a DPS is "adequately defined and described," allowing for the effective administration of the ESA. *DPS Policy,* 61 Fed.Reg. at 4724. . . . A population is discrete if (1) "[i]t is markedly separated from other populations of the same taxon as a consequence of physical, physiological, ecological, or behavioral factors"; or (2) "[i]t is delimited by international governmen-

---

8. The term "distinct population segment" is "not commonly used in scientific discourse." DPS Policy, 61 Fed.Reg. at 4722.

tal boundaries within which differences in control of exploitation, management of habitat, conservation status, or regulatory mechanisms exist that are significant in light of section 4(a)(1)(D) of the Act." *Id.* at 4725. Although the use of international borders "may introduce an artificial and non-biological element" into the discreteness standard, "it appears to be reasonable for national legislation ... to recognize units delimited by international boundaries when these coincide with differences in the management, status, or exploitation of a species." *Id.* at 4723.

[margin note: can use int'l borders to ÷ species.]

In the Listing Rule, the FWS found that the Arizona pygmy-owls are discrete from the northwestern Mexico pygmy-owls because the international border divides the two populations and significant differences in conservation status exist between those populations. . . .

[margin note: owls ÷ by int'l {U.S./Mexico treat owls differently.]

Comparing the "conservation status" of pygmy-owls across the border, the FWS found that pygmy-owls were abundant in parts of northwestern Mexico but were rare and declining in Arizona. Home Builders challenge the FWS' assertion that pygmy-owls were once common in Arizona but have been declining in number since the mid 1900s due to habitat modification and destruction. Home Builders contend that the pygmy-owls were never numerous in Arizona, because their numbers have always fluctuated as a peripheral population at the edge of the subspecies' range. . . .

[margin note: HB says the. Owl pop never big]

This case presents exactly the type of informed agency discretion to which we must defer. After examining all the evidence, including the comments and studies cited by Home Builders, the FWS found that the declining numbers of Arizona pygmy-owls were due to habitat destruction and modification, not fluctuations in a peripheral population. . . . The FWS' finding that pygmy-owls were "extremely limited in distribution" in Arizona but existed in greater numbers in northwestern Mexico was an adequate exercise of agency expertise. Thus, we hold that the FWS did not arbitrarily find that the differences in the conservation status of pygmy-owls across the border satisfied the discreteness element of the *DPS Policy*.

B. *The FWS Has Not Demonstrated a Rational Basis in the Listing Rule For its Finding That the Arizona Pygmy Owl Population is Significant to its Taxon*

If a population is discrete, the FWS then considers the "biological and ecological significance" of the population to the taxon to which it belongs. *DPS Policy,* 61 Fed.Reg. at 4724, 4725. The purpose of the significance element is "to carry out the expressed congressional intent that this authority [to list DPSs] be exercised sparingly as well as to concentrate conservation efforts undertaken under the Act on avoiding important losses of genetic diversity." *Id.* at 4724; *see also* S.Rep. No. 96–151, at 7 ("[T]he committee is aware of the great potential for abuse of this authority [to list DPSs] and expects the FWS to use the ability to list populations sparingly and only when the biological evidence indicates that such action is warranted."). The FWS determines the significance of a discrete population by considering the following non-exclusive factors:

[margin note: purpose of significance element]

1. Persistence of the discrete population segment in an ecological setting unusual or unique for the taxon,

2. Evidence that loss of the discrete population segment would result in a significant gap in the range of a taxon,

3. Evidence that the discrete population segment represents the only surviving natural occurrence of a taxon that may be more abundant elsewhere as an introduced population outside its historic range, or

4. Evidence that the discrete population segment differs markedly from other populations of the species in its genetic characteristics.

DPS Policy, 61 Fed.Reg. at 4725.

In the Listing Rule, the FWS found that the discrete population of Arizona pygmy-owls is significant because

[s]hould the loss of either the Arizona or Texas populations occur, the remaining population would not fill the resulting gap as the remaining population would not be genetically or morphologically identical, and would require different habitat parameters. The loss of either population also would decrease the genetic variability of the taxon and would result in a significant gap in the range.

The FWS argues that it found the Arizona pygmy-owl population to be significant to its taxon in the Listing Rule based on the second and fourth significance factors.

1. *The Second Significance Factor*

In the Listing Rule, the FWS concluded that the loss of the Arizona pygmy-owls "would result in a significant gap in the range" of their taxon. The question, then, is whether the FWS arbitrarily determined that the loss of the discrete Arizona pygmy-owl population would cause a gap in the range of its taxon and that such a gap would be significant.

a. *Whether the Loss of the Arizona Pygmy Owl Population Would Cause a Gap in the Range of the Taxon*

The FWS noted in the Listing Rule that the Arizona pygmy-owls "represent the northernmost portion of the pygmy-owl's range." The parties disagree over whether the loss of a peripheral population (*i.e.,* a population at the edge of a species' range) could create a gap in the range of a taxon. . . .

We defer to the FWS' interpretation of a "gap at the end of the fence" because it is not plainly erroneous. Even the loss of a peripheral population, however small, would create an empty geographic space in the range of the taxon. . . .

b. *Whether the Gap Would be Significant*

Since the loss of the Arizona pygmy-owls would create a gap in the range of the taxon, we now consider whether that gap is significant. The *DPS Policy* intended the term "significant" to have its "commonly understood" meaning, which is "important." . . .

In the Listing Rule, the FWS did not clearly explain why the gap that would be caused by the extirpation of the Arizona pygmy-owls is significant. . . .

The FWS argues that it found the gap to be significant in the Listing Rule because the loss of the Arizona pygmy-owls would (1) decrease the genetic variability of the taxon; (2) reduce the current range of the taxon; (3) reduce the historic range of the taxon; and (4) extirpate the western pygmy-owls from the United States. . . .

(1) Decrease the Genetic Variability of the Taxon

In the Listing Rule, the FWS found that the loss of the Arizona pygmy-owl population would "decrease the genetic variability of the taxon." On appeal, the FWS contends that peripheral populations like the Arizona pygmy-owls "may have more genetic divergence than central populations, making them more important to the survival of the species, particularly in response to adaption to environmental change." Thus, since the peripheral Arizona pygmy-owl population might be genetically distinct from the central population of pygmy-owls in northwestern Mexico, the loss of the Arizona population could impair the survival of the northwestern Mexico population in a crisis. . . .

Nowhere in the Listing Rule, however, does the FWS mention the existence of any genetic differences between the pygmy-owls in Arizona and northwestern Mexico, nor does the record provide any evidence to that effect. . . . We cannot defer to the FWS' argument on appeal that the Arizona pygmy-owls are genetically distinct from and important to the central population of northwestern Mexico pygmy-owls because the FWS did not make such a finding in the Listing Rule. Since the Listing Rule does not contain evidence of genetic variability between the Arizona and northwestern Mexico pygmy-owls, the argument that the loss of the Arizona population is significant because it would "decrease the genetic variability of the taxon" appears to be a *post hoc* rationalization. While the FWS can draw conclusions based on less than conclusive scientific evidence, it cannot base its conclusions on no evidence. *See Bennett v. Spear,* 520 U.S. 154, 176, 117 S.Ct. 1154, 137 L.Ed.2d 281 (1997) ("The obvious purpose of the requirement that each agency 'use the best scientific and commercial evidence available' is to ensure that the ESA not be implemented haphazardly, on the basis of speculation or surmise.").

(2) Reduce the Current Range of the Taxon

The FWS argues that the gap would be significant because the loss of the Arizona pygmy-owls would reduce the current range of its taxon. In other listing rules, the FWS has found two ways in which the loss of a discrete population could reduce the current range of its taxon.

First, the loss of a discrete population could reduce the geographic size of the taxon's range. [Citations to listing rules where this was true are omitted] These listing rules suggest that finding a gap significant based on the curtailment of a taxon's current range requires the loss of a geographic area that amounts to a substantial reduction of a taxon's range. The FWS found in the Listing Rule, however, that the Arizona pygmy-owls represented only "a small percentage" of the total range of the western pygmy-owls. It did not find that the loss of this "small percentage" of the western pygmy-owls' current range would substantially curtail that range.

Second, the loss of a discrete population that is numerous and constitutes a large percentage of the total number of taxon members could be considered a significant curtailment of a taxon's current range. Here, the FWS found that the Arizona pygmy-owls number between 20 and 40 individuals. The FWS did not find, however, that the loss of these 20 to 40 individuals would significantly curtail the western pygmy-owls' current range, which consists mostly of the more-numerous northwestern Mexico pygmy-owl population.

(3) Reduce the Historic Range of the Taxon

The FWS argues that the gap would be significant because the loss of the Arizona pygmy-owls would reduce the historical range of its taxon. Other listing rules have found a gap to be significant on these grounds.

The issue here is whether the FWS provided a rational basis in the Listing Rule for its conclusion that the loss of the Arizona pygmy-owl population would significantly reduce the historical range of its taxon. . . . Although "the 'significant gap in the range' analysis required for a DPS" is not the same as "the 'significant portion of the range' analysis required for a listing decision for the entire species," the two analyses are similar. . . . By analogy, the historical range of a taxon would be reduced "if there are major geographical areas in which it is no longer viable but once was."

While the loss of pygmy-owls in Arizona would mean that western pygmy-owls were no longer viable where they once were, the question arises as to whether Arizona is a "major geographic area" in the historical range of the western pygmy-owls. . . .

While the Arizona range might possibly be significant to its taxon's historic range despite its existence as a stable population at the periphery of that range, the FWS did not articulate a reasoned basis in the Listing Rule as to why that is so. . . .

(4) Extirpation of the Western Pygmy Owl from the United States

Finally, the FWS argues that the gap would be significant because it would deprive the United States of its portion of the western pygmy-owl's range. . . .

This argument misconstrues the second significance factor. In designating a DPS under the *DPS Policy,* the FWS must find that a discrete population is significant to its taxon as a whole, not to the United States. *See* 61 Fed.Reg. at 4725. Extirpation of the western pygmy-owl from the United States is certainly significant to the United States, but that does not mean that the loss of the Arizona pygmy-owl population is significant to its taxon. . . .

In other listing rules, the FWS has found a gap to be significant due to the loss of the United States range of a population only where some additional significance to the taxon as a whole also existed. In the case at bench, it is true that the loss of the Arizona pygmy-owls would move the western pygmy-owl range beyond the borders of the United States. Yet, apart from the significance of that loss to the United States, the FWS did not give any additional reason in the Listing Rule why the gap caused by the loss of the Arizona population would also be significant to its taxon as a whole.

In sum, we conclude that the FWS did not articulate a reasoned basis in the Listing Rule for finding that the gap created by the loss of the discrete Arizona pygmy-owl population would be significant to the taxon as a whole.

2. *The Fourth Significance Factor*

A discrete population can be significant to its taxon based on evidence that it "differs markedly from other populations of the species in its genetic characteristics." *DPS Policy,* 61 Fed.Reg. at 4725. . . .

In the Listing Rule, the FWS divided the Arizona pygmy-owls and the northwestern Mexico pygmy-owls into separate populations. Therefore, under the plain language of the fourth significance factor, the FWS needed to show that the Arizona pygmy-owls differed markedly in their genetic characteristics from the northwestern Mexico pygmy-owls. Yet neither the Listing Rule nor the record presented any evidence of marked genetic differences between the pygmy-owls in Arizona and northwestern Mexico. . . .

The FWS promulgated the *DPS Policy* consistently to designate DPSs "in light of Congressional guidance . . . that the authority to list DPS's [sic] be used ' . . . sparingly' while encouraging the conservation of genetic diversity." 61 Fed.Reg. at 4725. . . . As such, to meet this fourth significance factor, the FWS must find significance to the taxon as a whole, not just to the United States. It did not do so in this case.

We conclude, therefore, that the FWS did not articulate a rational basis in the Listing Rule for its finding that the discrete Arizona pygmy-owl population is significant to its taxon as a whole under either the second or fourth significance factor.

. . . The judgment of the district court is reversed and the case is remanded to the district court for further proceedings consistent with this opinion.

Notes and Comments

1.   The court remands the case to the district court for further proceedings consistent with this opinion. What further proceedings might there be? Must the district court set aside the agency rule? Could it remand the rule to the agency without setting aside the rule, to enable the agency to better articulate its explanation of why the discrete population was significant? In some circumstances courts do that. *See, e.g.,* Ronald Levin, *"Vacation" at*

Sea: Judicial Remedies and Equitable Discretion in Administrative Law, 53 Duke L.J. 291 (2003). Even if the court sets the rule aside, can the FWS merely reinstate it by better articulating its rationale? Or, do you think that its conclusion that the Arizona ferruginous pygmy-owl is a distinct population segment cannot be justified?

2. How does the justification for a distinct population segment differ from a determination that a species may become extinct throughout a significant portion of its range? In *NAHB* the FWS argued that the Arizona owl was a distinct population segment because, if it became extinct, there would be a significant reduction in its historic range. The court analogized this argument to the requirement in *Defenders of Wildlife*, excerpted earlier, that in order to say that a species was in risk of becoming extinct throughout a significant portion of its range, the affected range must involve a "major geographic area." Because the FWS had not shown that the range of the Arizona owl was a major geographic area, the court held that the FWS had not shown that the effect of the Arizona owl's extinction would be significant.

3. Why does the court think it is not sufficient to establish that this discrete population, if made extinct, would deprive the United States of this subspecies altogether? The court states that the important issue is the impact on the entire taxon. What leads the court to believe this is the critical issue? Is there anything in the findings, purposes, or policy of the Endangered Species Act that the FWS could refer to support its case that eliminating the owls from the United States should be sufficient in itself to justify listing? Consider 16 U.S.C. § 1531(a). More broadly, why do you think we *should* protect species? What purpose should the ESA serve?

4. A particular problem with regard to distinct population segments involves anadromous fish. These are fish that are born in the headwaters of rivers, but then they migrate downstream to the ocean, where they live their adult life until they return to the headwaters where they were born in order to spawn and then die. Because the fish from the headwaters of one river do not generally interbreed with the fish from adjacent headwaters, each of these different stocks of fish might be considered a distinct population segment. Prior to the FWS and NMFS joint adoption of the DPS Policy in 1996, however, NMFS had on its own adopted a particular distinct population segment policy regarding Pacific Salmon to address this issue. Policy on Applying the Definition of Species Under the Endangered Species Act to Pacific Salmon, 56 Fed. Reg. 58,612 (1991). This policy used the term, Evolutionarily Significant Unit, to describe the distinct population segments for Pacific Salmon, and hence has come to be known as the ESU Policy. Under the ESU Policy, in order for a Salmon stock to be an ESU, (1) it must be substantially reproductively isolated from other conspecific population units, and (2) it must represent an important component in the evolutionary legacy of the species. The first criterion can be measured by movements of tagged fish, recolonization rates of other populations, and the efficacy of natural barriers. The second criteria is concerned with "ecological/genetic diversity" of the species as a whole, so NMFS looks to see if the population is genetically distinct from other conspecific populations, occupies an unusual or distinctive habitat, or shows evidence of unusual or distinctive adaptation to its environment. How, if at all, is this different from the criteria for DPS?

5. Recall that listing is supposed to be a scientific determination. Is determining the significance of a particular population segment a scientific determination, or is it one of those embedded value determinations hidden within the scientific process? What would you say the *Home Builders* case suggests?

6. An interesting problem involves invasive aliens or exotics, in other words, species that humans have intentionally or unintentionally introduced outside their natural range and that lacking natural predators have mushroomed in population. Such species include the kudzu vine, zebra mussels, and the starling. We would like to extirpate some of these species because of the harm they do, but does the ESA stand in the way? Nothing in the ESA limits its protections to species in their "natural" habitats. For the most part, this question is largely academic, because despite our best efforts, these invasive aliens are not in danger of being eradicated. Indeed, Congress has passed certain laws intended to help counter alien invasives. *See* Nonindigenous Aquatic Nuisance Prevention and Control Act of 1990, as amended, 16 U.S.C. 4701 *et seq.*; Federal Noxious Weed Act of 1974, as amended, 7 U.S.C. 2801 *et seq. See also* Invasive Species, E.O. 13112, 64 Fed. Reg. 6183 (Feb. 3, 1999). There are, however, some situations in which the question is real. For example, in the Olympic Mountains in the Olympic National Park there is a population of mountain goats, a beautiful and majestic creature (but is that relevant?). Because these mountain goats harm the rare (but not listed) alpine and sub-alpine plants, the National Park Service has proposed to extirpate the goat population by hiring professional hunters in helicopters to shoot all the goats. The NPS believes that these goats are not native to the Olympic Mountains but were introduced in the 1920s for sport hunting purposes. Others, however, believe that the goats are endemic to the Olympic Mountains, citing reports of early expeditions and Native American artifacts in the area made from mountain goat wool and horns. This population of mountain goats would certainly seem to be a distinct population segment, isolated as it is from other populations. What difference should it make under the Endangered Species Act whether the mountain goat has been in the Olympic Mountains for 80 years, 280 years, or 800 years?

2. Critical Habitat

Section 4 generally requires FWS or NMFS, when they list a species as endangered or threatened, concurrently to designate "critical habitat" for the species. 16 U.S.C. § 1533(a)(3)(A). Critical habitat is a defined term. It includes those areas occupied by the species at the time of listing that provide "those physical or biological features (I) essential to the conservation of the species and (II) which may require special management considerations or protection." 16 U.S.C. § 1532(5)(A)(i). In addition, it includes those areas outside area occupied by the species at the time of listing that the FWS or NMFS determines are essential for the conservation of the species. 16 U.S.C. § 1532(5)(A)(ii). Thus, only areas "essential to [or for] the conservation of the species" can be critical habitat. "Conservation" is also a defined term. It means to do what is necessary "to bring any endangered species or threatened species to the point at which the [protections of the ESA] are no longer necessary." 16 U.S.C § 1532(3). In other words, to conserve the species means not just to preserve the species from extinction but to bring it to the point at which it is no longer likely to become endangered in the foreseeable future absent the protections of the Act.

Like the listing determinations, the FWS and NMFS are supposed to make the determination of whether areas are necessary for conservation of the species "on the basis of the best scientific data available." 16 U.S.C. § 1533(b)(2). However, unlike the listing determinations, that is only the first step. After determining what areas are necessary for conservation of the species, the FWS and NMFS are also to consider "the economic impact, the impact on national security, and any other relevant impact, of specifying any particular area as critical habitat." *Id.* Then those agencies may exclude areas from critical habitat if the benefits of exclusion outweigh the benefits of inclusion, so long as the exclusion will not result in the extinction of the species. *Id.* This exclusion power, for example, was used to exclude approximately one-third of the habitat of the Northern Spotted Owl that otherwise would have been deemed critical, and it has been used to exclude area within military training areas.

To qualify for critical habitat, an area must be necessary for conservation of the species and may also require special management considerations or protection. That is, if an area does not need special management, then it does not qualify for critical habitat designation. Presumably, the concept behind this requirement is that if the habitat in its natural and unregulated state is adequately providing the necessary habitat for the species, there is no need for critical habitat designation. This is unlikely to be the case when the threat to the species comes from habitat destruction or degradation, the source of most risks to threatened and endangered species. The FWS, however, has interpreted this requirement also to exclude areas that are already under management to protect the habitat. For example, the FWS excluded tribal lands of two Native American tribes from the critical habitat designation of the Mexican Spotted Owl because those lands were subject to owl management plans. This exclusion was challenged, however, and the reviewing court found this exclusion "nonsensical." In its view, the fact that there was already an owl management plan in place was proof that the area might need special management. *See Center for Biological Diversity v. Norton*, 240 F.Supp.2d 1090, 1098 (D. Az. 2003).

As might be imagined, the designation of critical habitat is a difficult determination both scientifically and practically. Listing is difficult enough, but at least that decision is polar; that is, the services either list or not. Either the evidence supports the listing or not. Critical habitat designation is more open-ended. Lines must be drawn on a map, and where those lines are drawn must be supportable. Moreover, Section 4 makes clear that the listing decision is to be made without regard to the economic or social impacts listing might have. This at least theoretically insulates the services from much outside pressure from those impacted by the listing. The explicit need to consider such impacts in designating critical habitat, however, means the services must deal with those pressures and respond to them in a coherent manner. As a result of all these difficulties, the resources necessary for critical habitat designation are generally much greater than those necessary for listing a species. At the same time, critical habitat designation is not as vital to a species protection as its listing. That is, even absent a critical habitat designation, a listed species cannot be "jeopardized" by government action and endangered fish and wildlife species cannot be "taken" by anyone. The critical habitat designation only provides additional protection for listed species when government action may adversely affect that habitat. This combination of the need for increased resources to make the designation and its perception that the designation's additional protections were not significant led the FWS over the years to attempt to avoid having to make critical habitat designations to the extent possible.

Section 4 requires a designation of critical habitat "to the maximum extent prudent and determinable." 16 U.S.C. § 1533(a)(3)(A). Difficulty in the determinability of critical habitat provides a basis for delaying its designation for a year, but not a basis for avoiding it altogether. *See* 16 U.S.C. § 1533(b)(6)(C)(ii). However, if it is not "prudent" to designate critical habitat, then the services are excused from designating it altogether. "Prudent" is not a defined term, and the legislative history indicates that it was a narrow concept. For example, it might not be beneficial to designate critical habitat, if, as might be the case for parrots or certain kinds of medicinal plants, their very rarity made them valuable, because such designation would identify on publicly available maps where the species could be found, thereby increasing the risk of predation. However, the services have not so limited their definition of the term. In their regulations, they include the original concept but then also include a more general concept: any time designation of critical habitat "would not be beneficial to the species." 50 CFR § 424.12(a)(1)(ii).

Relying on this provision, the FWS, in particular, has refused to designate critical habitat in a number of cases, arguing that designating critical habitat simply would not increase any protection of the species that does not automatically accrue from its being a listed species. Assessing the merits of this claim requires an understanding of what protections the ESA provides for critical habitat, protections that are specified in Section 7 of the Act, and then comparing them to the protections afforded listed species, protections afforded by both Section 7 and Section 9. As described in the introductory paragraph outlining the ESA, Section 7 only protects against federal government action, not private or state action that might harm endangered species or their habitat. Accordingly, FWS maintains, designating critical habitat on private land would be meaningless because it would have little to no effect other than upset the landowners, who might actually be moved to destroy the habitat—an action that the critical habitat designation would not preclude. On federal land, FWS argues, critical habitat designation does not benefit the species either, because federal actions that harm the species, whether through habitat destruction or otherwise, are prohibited by Section 7. We will postpone a full discussion of these claims and the counterarguments until the discussion of Section 7, but at this point it should be noted that the basis for these claims has been uniformly rejected by the courts. *See, e.g., New Mexico Cattle Growers Ass'n v. USFWS*, 248 F.3d 1277 (10th Cir. 2001); *Sierra Club v. USFWS*, 245 F.3d 434 (5th Cir. 2001); *NRDC v. USDOI*, 113 F.3d 1121 (9th Cir. 1997).

3. Recovery

In addition to requiring FWS or NMFS to list endangered and threatened species and to designate their critical habitat, Section 4 also requires the services to "develop and implement" recovery plans for the conservation of the listed species, unless such a plan would not promote the conservation of the species. 16 U.S.C. § 1533(f). Recall that the term "conservation" means to bring the species to the point that it need not be listed anymore. Thus, recovery plans are intended not only to keep the species from extinction but to recover it to a point that it can be delisted. These plans are supposed to be specific, describing site-specific management actions, objective, measurable criteria, which if met, would enable delisting, and timetables and budgets for achieving recovery. 16 U.S.C. § 1533(f)(1)(B).

Although there is no requirement for when recovery plans must be developed, the FWS adopted a policy of adopting plans within 2½ years of a listing decision. Attempts by environmental groups to force the development of recovery plans through litigation have been generally unsuccessful, as courts have held that decisions as to when to adopt recovery plans is at the discretion of the agency, so long as it does not abandon the attempt altogether. *See, e.g., ONRC v. Turner*, 863 F.Supp. 1277 (D. Or. 1997).

A major issue with respect to recovery plans is their legal status; that is, do they require agencies to comply with their terms, or are they merely "guidance"? The position of FWS is that they are merely guidance, or, as it has sometimes characterized them, they are like a menu from which agencies are free to choose. The lack of enforceability as well as underfunding by Congress has led commentators to conclude that the recovery process does not come close to achieving its objectives. *See, e.g.,* Federico Cheever, *The Road to Recovery: A New Way of Thinking About the Endangered Species Act*, 23 Ecology L.Q. 1 (1996).

4. The Procedures

Section 4 spells out a detailed procedure by which species can become listed or delisted. While a species can be considered for listing or delisting on the initiative of one of the services, Section 4 also provides that an interested person can petition for a species to be listed or delisted. 16 U.S.C. § 1533(b)(3)(A). Increasingly, this has become the method by which new species have been considered for listing. Section 4 requires the service receiving the petition to decide whether the petition presents "substantial scientific or commercial information" indicating that listing "may be warranted." This decision is to be made "to the extent practicable, within 90 days after receiving the petition." *Id.* If the service finds the petition is meritorious, the species is denominated a "candidate species," a denomination that affords no protection to the species, but which triggers the next procedural requirement.

"Within 12 months of receiving a [meritorious] petition," the service is to make a finding whether in fact the petitioned action is warranted or not and promptly to publish its finding. 16 U.S.C. § 1533(b)(3)(B). If the decision is that the petitioned action is warranted, the published finding must either include a notice of proposed rulemaking proposing the species for listing or a determination that such a notice is precluded at this time because of other pending proposals and "expeditious progress" is being made with respect to adding and deleting species to the lists. *Id.* If a proposal is currently precluded, the service has an additional year within which to make the finding again. 16 U.S.C. § 1533(b)(3)(C)(i). However, at the end of that year, the service may again make the "warranted but precluded" determination and thereby recycle these petitions on a year-to-year basis, never proposing the species for listing. In this way the services can devote their rulemaking resources to those species with the greatest need for listing. Indeed, the FWS has developed a priority system to decide which species should be considered first. *See* Endangered and Threatened Wildlife and Plants; Final Listing Priority Guidance for Fiscal Year 2000, 64 Fed. Reg. 57114 (October 22, 1999).

The rulemaking generally follows the procedures for notice-and-comment rulemaking in the Administrative Procedure Act, but within one year the service must adopt the rule listing the species, make a finding that there is insufficient evidence to justify listing, or that there is substantial controversy over the evidence and additional time is required to gather more evidence. 16 U.S.C. § 1533(b)(6)(A). In the last case, the service may extend the one-year period for not longer than six months. 16 U.S.C. § 1533(b)(6)(B)(i).

As described earlier, critical habitat designations are to be made in the same rulemaking as the listing determination, unless the critical habitat is not then determinable, in which case the service can take not more than one additional year in order to designate the critical habitat. 16 U.S.C. § 1533(b)(6)(C)(ii). Given the FWS priorities, the FWS almost never designates critical habitat concurrently with a listing.

Since its original passage, the FWS has had difficulty making listing decisions, critical habitat designations, and recovery plans in a reasonable period of time. For the most part this has been due to inadequate appropriations combined with the inherent difficulty in making the requisite determinations. The current detailed and prescriptive time periods were a response to this earlier failure to list species and designate critical habitat in a timely fashion under earlier provisions of the ESA. This response, however, was not an effective solution. Inadequate funding, reflecting congressional ambivalence with the ESA, and the one-year ban on spending any funds to list a species as threatened or endangered or to designate critical habitat, *see* Emergency Supplemental Appropriations and Rescissions for the Department of Defense to Preserve and Enhance Military Readiness Act of 1995, Pub. L. No. 104–6, 109 Stat. 73 (1995), reflecting congressional hostility to the Act, have stymied any real attempt to make listing and critical habitat determinations on a current and timely basis. Consequently, the FWS took the position that it simply need not respond to petitions for listing, because the 90–day requirement was limited by the phrase "to the extent practicable," and that the 12–month period to decide whether to undertake a rulemaking only began to run after the petition had been acted upon. These arguments have apparently now been rejected by the courts. *See, e.g., Biodiversity Legal Found. v. Badgley*, 309 F.3d 1166 (9th Cir. 2002). As a result, these statutory time periods have provided a handle whereby environmental groups can sue the services to force decisions. Thus, currently, most listing decisions seem to be driven by litigation brought by environmental groups seeking listings for their particular purposes.

This, however, hardly solves the basic problem of too much to do with too little resources. Thus, today, after thirty years, the services have listed 1008 endangered species and 291 threatened species in the United States. While in the decade of the 90's, the services were averaging about 67 listings a year, in the past five years, the average has dropped down to about 15 per year. In 2007, there were currently 10 species proposed for listing, but there were also 280 candidate species. Thus, at current rates, there is already a twenty-year backlog of listing decisions, even if no new petitions for listing were filed.

The services assign priorities to the candidate species and the "warranted but precluded" species, so that at least in theory the most endangered species can be put at the front of the line and the least threatened at the back. In addition, the Act does provide an emergency procedure, if a service finds there is "any emergency posing a significant risk to the well-being of any species." 16 U.S.C. § 1533(b)(7). This procedure allows a service to avoid all the aforementioned procedural requirements, as well as the requirements of the APA, and immediately list a species or designate critical habitat, if it explains the reasons why the immediate action is necessary. This emergency regulation, however, can only be effective for 240 days. *Id.* The idea is that during that period the service could undertake a rulemaking using the normal procedures to supplant the emergency rule.

Notes and Comments

1.   The listing process, including the designation of critical habitat, has been fraught with difficulties since the inception of the ESA. While the technicalities of the law have at least temporarily provided avenues for delay for administrations so inclined, the system is widely perceived as dysfunctional. The problem is that there is no consensus on the nature of the problem, much less how to fix it. To some, the current ESA is viewed as

misguided in its attempt to save all species without regard to their role in the ecosystem or the value to humankind. To others, the process of listing and critical habitat designation unnecessarily strives for amassing overwhelming evidence in support of determinations, rather than following a precautionary principle, resulting in delay in listings and inadequate critical habitat designations. Obviously, the solutions proposed by those with these different views would be very different. What do you think is the problem? How would you fix it?

2. There has been a question as to what role NEPA should play in the listing and critical habitat decisions. The services have always maintained that these decisions are not subject to NEPA. Although it is usually environmental groups arguing for greater use of NEPA, with respect to the ESA environmentalists have opposed applying NEPA to ESA decisionmaking. They perceive, rightly, that requiring EA's or EIS's would slow the process even more, which is precisely why property owners and development interests here favor a greater use of NEPA. The courts have generally sided with environmentalists on this issue, holding uniformly that listing decisions are not subject to NEPA, *see, e.g., Pacific Legal Found. v. Andrus*, 657 F.2d 829 (6th Cir. 1981), and the circuits have split on whether NEPA applies to critical habitat designations. *Compare Catron County Bd. of Commissioners v. USFWS*, 75 F.3d 1429 (10th Cir. 1996)(NEPA applies) *with Douglas County v. Babbitt*, 48 F.3d 1495 (9th Cir. 1995), *cert. denied*, 516 U.S. 1042, 116 S.Ct. 698, 133 L.Ed.2d 655 (1996)(NEPA does not apply).

3. The requirement for the services to create recovery plans, plans designed not just to keep the species from the brink of extinction but to enable them to become a healthy species no longer needing the protections of the ESA, is a potentially powerful tool. In practice, however, they have not been very successful. Thus, while over 1000 of the listed species are covered by recovery plans, only 15 have been "recovered" so that they could be delisted. Is this a failure that can be remedied, such as by providing for judicial enforcement, or is this the inevitable consequence of expanded population and economic growth?

4. The statistics on the number of species listed differ dramatically between the Clinton administration and the George W. Bush administration, just as they had between the Carter administration and the first four years of the Reagan administration. Why would Democratic administrations be more likely to list species than Republican administrations?

C. Section 7

Section 7 of the ESA imposes three different sets of obligations on federal agencies. The first obligation is to "utilize their authorities in furtherance of the purposes of this chapter by carrying out programs for the conservation of [listed] species...." 16 U.S.C. § 1536(a)(1). Their second obligation is to consult with the FWS or NMFS if their actions are likely to affect listed species. 16 U.S.C. § 1536(a)(2). Their final obligation is to insure that their actions are not "likely to jeopardize the continued existence of any endangered species or threatened species or result in the destruction or adverse modification of [critical] habitat...." 16 U.S.C. § 1536(a)(2).

1. The Affirmative Obligation

By its terms, Section 7(a)(1) imposes an affirmative obligation on all agencies to carry out programs for the conservation of listed species by utilizing their existing authorities in furtherance of the ESA. Recall that the term "conservation" means to recover a species to the point that it no longer needs to be listed. 16 U.S.C. § 1532(3). The FWS and NMFS in particular are required to utilize all the programs they administer to further the purposes of the ESA. 16 U.S.C. § 1536(a)(1). What this means to agencies in their everyday activities, however, is open to question. For example, is the United States Forest Service to abandon all its timber harvesting and recreational authorities and manage its forests to recover species at the expense of all of its other goals? Are the military departments to manage their ranges and practice areas for the benefit of species without regard to their mission to prepare and train military personnel?

In practice, agencies have all but ignored Section 7(a)(1)'s mandate. They have argued that they need to conserve species only to the extent consistent with the accomplishment of their primary goals. In other words, if an action to conserve species would interfere at all with their primary goals, they need not take the action to conserve a species. Lawsuits brought to try to enforce a more rigorous requirement have been generally unsuccessful. Courts have recognized the statutory obligation, but in light of its general language the courts have held that how agencies fulfill that mandate is subject to their discretion, which is subject only to arbitrary and capricious review. There is apparently only one court of appeals case that actually directed an agency to take any action under Section 7(a)(1). *See Sierra Club v. Glickman*, 156 F.3d 606 (5th Cir. 1998). And in that case the court only directed the Department of Agriculture to adopt a plan, not to take a specific action. More common is the outcome in *Pyramid Lake Paiute Tribe of Indians v. U.S.D.O.N.*, 898 F.2d 1410 (9th Cir. 1990), where the court recognized the mandate to conserve but interpreted Section 7(a)(1) to give discretion to the agency in determining how to fulfill that mandate in light of its other statutory obligations.

Perhaps the most cited case under Section 7(a)(1) is *Carson-Truckee Water Conservancy Dist. v. Clark*, 741 F.2d 257 (9th Cir. 1984). There, the Bureau of Reclamation withheld water in its dammed reservoir, that it ordinarily would have sold for irrigation purposes, in order to conserve the endangered cui-ui fish. The irrigation district desiring the withheld water sued to require the Bureau to release the water, but the court upheld the Bureau's action, relying on Section 7(a)(1)'s mandate to conserve listed species. This mandate, the court said, authorized the agency to give preference to the ESA over its ordinary contractual obligations to release the water to the irrigation district.

These cases have led commentators to characterize Section 7(a)(1) in practice as an agency shield, rather than an environmentalist's sword, because they appear to suggest that Section 7(a)(1) provides a legal authority to the agency to protect endangered species even when providing such protection would be inconsistent with other legal requirements. The issue whether the ESA trumps other legal requirements by imposing a duty that supersedes other legal requirements is an issue that is before the Supreme Court as this edition goes to press, although it arises not under Section 7(a)(1) but under Section 7(a)(2)'s jeopardy prohibition, which is discussed below.

2. The Procedural Requirements

Section 7(a)(2)-(4) requires agencies to engage in certain inquiries and consultations when they take actions that may affect listed species. As under NEPA, the trigger in Section 7(a)(2) is agency action, which includes not only direct agency action but also agency funding of someone else's action or agency permitting of someone else's action. For example, if the Federal Highway Administration pays for a portion of an interstate highway to be built by a state, that would be a federal agency action, which, if the road were to affect a listed species, would require consultation with the FWS. Similarly, if the Corps of Engineers permits a person to fill a wetland under Section 404 of the Clean Water Act, and the fill would affect a listed species, then the Corps would have to consult with the FWS.

The overall purpose of the procedural requirement to consult is to provide sufficient information to the action agency to assure that it will not violate the substantive command of Section 7 that federal agencies not jeopardize a listed species or adversely affect critical habitat. The process to assure this is somewhat complicated.

- First the agency must decide whether its action is "likely to affect" a listed species or designated critical habitat.

  - In order to make that decision, the agency must determine whether a listed species is present in the area to be affected by the action. The agency may know this on its own, in which case it provides this information to the applicable service for confirmation; otherwise it must request information from the services in order to make that determination. *See* 16 U.S.C. § 1536(c)(1).

    - If no such species or critical habitat is in the area, then that is end of the matter.

  - If a species or critical habitat is in the area, and the action would have physical impacts on the environment sufficient to require an Environmental Impact Statement (EIS) under the National Environmental Policy Act (NEPA), then the agency must make a "biological assessment." *See* 50 CFR § 402.12 and § 402.02 (definition of "major construction activity"). The BA is to assess whether the agency action will likely affect the listed species.

    - If the agency concludes in the BA that its action will not likely have an adverse effect on the species or critical habitat, and the service agrees, that is the end of the matter.

- If a BA is not required, the agency may engage in "informal consultation," which is designed to determine whether "formal consultation" is required.

  - As under the BA, if at the conclusion of "informal consultation" the agency determines and the service concurs that the agency's action will not likely have an adverse effect on the species or critical habitat, that is the end of the matter.

- If, however, there is no negative finding at the conclusion of either the BA or the informal consultation, then the agency must engage in formal consultation with the appropriate service. Formal consultation requires the agency to supply the appropriate service with a full description of the proposed action, the best scientific information available concerning the possible effects on the species and habitat, and any other relevant data to enable the service to determine the extent of the effect on the species or habitat.

- The conclusion of the formal consultation results in a "biological opinion" from the relevant service to the action agency.

  - The BO can have one of three possible conclusions:

  - the proposed agency action will jeopardize the species or result in the adverse modification of critical habitat, but these effects can be avoided through "reasonable and prudent alternatives,"

  - the proposed agency action will jeopardize the species or result in adverse modification to critical habitat, and these effects cannot be avoided, or

  - the proposed agency action will not jeopardize the species or result in the adverse modification of critical habitat.

- As part of the BO, the service can approve the "incidental take" of certain of the listed species, subject to conditions in the BO. The purpose of the incidental take statement is to provide an exemption from Section 9 of the ESA which makes the "take" of any endangered (and in some cases threatened) fish or wildlife species unlawful. But for the incidental take statement, the action agency (or the person using the federal funds or acting under the federal permit) would be acting unlawfully if even a single member of the species was harmed.

- The agency then determines for itself, informed by the BO, whether its action will jeopardize the species or have an adverse effect on critical habitat.

- During the period of consultation, neither the agency nor any permit applicant may make "any irreversible or irretrievable commitment of resources ... which has the effect of foreclosing ... any reasonable and prudent alternative measures." The purpose of this limitation is to assure that agencies or applicants will not commit resources to try to influence the jeopardy outcome by making the cost of a jeopardy finding very great.

Under Section 7(a)(4), 16 U.S.C. § 1536(a)(4), species proposed for listing, but not yet listed, receive a similar procedural protection, although it is called "conferring" rather than "consulting." No biological assessment is required, however, and even if a proposed species or proposed critical habitat is present in the action area, a conference is only required if the agency action is "likely to jeopardize the continued existence" of the species or "result in the destruction or adverse modification of critical habitat proposed to be designated." Under the services' regulation all that is required in the conference is "informal discussions" of ways to minimize the impact on the species or habitat, but if the proposed listing becomes final before the agency action is completed, the agency will need to engage in the formal consultation process. Agencies may request the services actually to make a biological opinion as part of the conference, which then become the formal biological opinion if the listing becomes final. There is no prohibition on the commitment of resources during the conference period.

Section 7(a)(3), 16 U.S.C. § 1536(a)(3), provides the basis for what the services call "early consultation." *See* 50 CFR § 402.11 (2003). The purpose of this procedure is to enable applicants for government permits or licenses to discover before they actually apply for their permits or licenses whether the ESA will stand in their way. In essence, the formal consultation takes place as above except that its results are called "preliminary" determinations. These preliminary determinations can become final determinations after the applicant actually files his application.

As may be seen, these procedural requirements for consultation constitute hurdles that must overcome before an agency takes an action that may adversely affect listed (or even proposed) species. Failure to comply with these procedures, if someone challenges the proposed action in court, may result in the agency action being blocked until the agency has complied with the requisite requirements. There are essentially two ways in which compliance may be lacking: the required consultation may not take place at all (perhaps because the agency or service thinks it is not applicable for one or more reasons), or the consultation that did take place is deemed inadequate and therefore not in compliance with the ESA.

The following cases provide examples.

THOMAS v. PETERSON

United States Court of Appeals, Ninth Circuit, 1985.
753 F.2d 754.

SNEED, Circuit Judge:

Plaintiffs sought to enjoin construction of a timber road in a former National Forest roadless area. The District Court granted summary judgment in favor of defendant R. Max Peterson, Chief of the Forest Service, and plaintiffs appealed....

We conclude that: ... The Endangered Species Act (ESA) requires the Forest Service to prepare a biological assessment to determine whether the road and the timber sales that the road is designed to facilitate are likely to affect the endangered Rocky Mountain Gray Wolf, and construction of the road should be enjoined pending compliance with the ESA.

I.

STATEMENT OF THE CASE

... Plaintiffs—landowners, ranchers, outfitters, miners, hunters, fishermen, recreational users, and conservation and recreation organizations—challenge actions of the United States Forest Service in planning and approving a timber road in the Jersey Jack area of the Nezperce National Forest in Idaho. The area is adjacent to the Salmon River, a congressionally-designated Wild and Scenic River, and is bounded on the west by the designated Gospel Hump Wilderness and on the east by the River of No Return Wilderness. The area lies in a "recovery corridor" identified by the U.S. Fish & Wildlife Service for the Rocky Mountain Gray Wolf, an endangered species....

The plaintiffs filed this action, challenging the Chief's decision, on June 30, 1982. Their three principal allegations are:

(1) NEPA, and regulations issued by the Council on Environmental Quality (CEQ), require the Forest Service to prepare an EIS that analyzes the combined effects of the proposed road and the timber sales that the road is designed to facilitate.

(2) The decision to build the road is inconsistent with the National Forest Management Act, 16 U.S.C. §§ 1600–1614, because the cost of the road will exceed the value of the timber that it will access.

(3) The road is likely to affect the Rocky Mountain Gray Wolf, an endangered species, and the Forest Service has failed to follow procedures mandated by the Endangered Species Act, 16 U.S.C. §§ 1531–1543.

II.

THE NEPA CLAIM

[The court found that NEPA did not allow the Forest Service to engage in this action having only prepared an Environmental Assessment. It agreed with the plaintiffs that an EIS was required.]

III.

THE NATIONAL FOREST MANAGEMENT ACT CLAIM

[The court upheld the decision of the Forest Service under the National Forest Management Act, rejecting the plaintiffs' claim.]

IV.

The Endangered Species Act Claim

The plaintiffs' third claim concerns the Forest Service's alleged failure to comply with the Endangered Species Act (ESA) in considering the effects of the road and timber sales on the endangered Rocky Mountain Gray Wolf.

The ESA contains both substantive and procedural provisions. Substantively, the Act prohibits the taking or importation of endangered species, *see* 16 U.S.C. § 1538, and requires federal agencies to ensure that their actions are not "likely to jeopardize the continued existence of any endangered species or threatened species or result in the destruction or adverse modification" of critical habitat of such species, *see* 16 U.S.C. § 1536(a)(2).

The Act prescribes a three-step process to ensure compliance with its substantive provisions by federal agencies. Each of the first two steps serves a screening function to determine if the successive steps are required. The steps are:

(1) An agency proposing to take an action must inquire of the Fish & Wildlife Service (F & WS) whether any threatened or endangered species "may be present" in the area of the proposed action. *See* 16 U.S.C. § 1536(c)(1).

(2) If the answer is affirmative, the agency must prepare a "biological assessment" to determine whether such species "is likely to be affected" by the action. *Id.* The biological assessment may be part of an environmental impact statement or environmental assessment. *Id.*

(3) If the assessment determines that a threatened or endangered species "is likely to be affected," the agency must formally consult with the F & WS. *Id.* § 1536(a)(2). The formal consultation results in a "biological opinion" issued by the F & WS. *See id.* § 1536(b). If the biological opinion concludes that the proposed action would jeopardize the species or destroy or adversely modify critical habitat, *see id.* § 1536(a)(2), then the action may not go forward unless the F & WS can suggest an alternative that avoids such jeopardization, destruction, or adverse modification. *Id.* § 1536(b)(3)(A). If the opinion concludes that the action will not violate the Act, the F & WS may still require measures to minimize its impact. *Id.* § 1536(b)(4)(ii)-(iii).

Plaintiffs first allege that, with respect to the Jersey Jack road, the Forest Service did not undertake step (1), a formal request to the F & WS. The district court found that to be the case, but concluded that the procedural violation was insignificant because the Forest Service was already aware that wolves may be present in the area. The court therefore refused to enjoin the construction of the road. Plaintiffs insist, based on *TVA v. Hill,* 437 U.S. 153, 98 S.Ct. 2279, 57 L.Ed.2d 117 (1978), that an injunction is mandatory once any ESA violation is found. . . .

We need not reach this issue. The Forest Service's failure goes beyond the technical violation cited by the district court, and is not *de minimis*.

Once an agency is aware that an endangered species may be present in the area of its proposed action, the ESA requires it to prepare a biological assessment to determine whether the proposed action "is likely to affect" the species and therefore requires formal consultation with the F & WS. *See supra.* The Forest Service did not prepare such an assessment prior to its decision to build the Jersey Jack road. Without a biological assessment, it cannot be determined whether the proposed project will result in a violation of the ESA's substantive provisions. A failure to prepare a biological assessment for a project in an area in which it has been determined that an endangered species may be present cannot be considered a *de minimis* violation of the ESA.

The district court found that the Forest Service had "undertaken sufficient study and action to further the purposes of the ESA," Memorandum Decision at 1149, E.R. 103. Its finding was based on affidavits submitted by the Forest Service for the litigation.[7] *See* Memorandum Decision at 1148, E.R. 99. These do not constitute a substitute for the preparation of the biological assessment required by the ESA.

Given a substantial procedural violation of the ESA in connection with a federal project, the remedy must be an injunction of the project pending compliance with the ESA. . . .

Our cases repeatedly have held that, absent "unusual circumstances," an injunction is the appropriate remedy for a violation of NEPA's procedural requirements. . . . We see no reason that the same principle should not apply to procedural violations of the ESA.

The Forest Service argues that the procedural requirements of the ESA should be enforced less stringently than those of NEPA because, unlike NEPA, the ESA also contains substantive provisions. We acknowledge that the ESA's substantive provisions distinguish it from NEPA, but the distinction acts the other way. If anything, the strict substantive provisions of the ESA justify *more* stringent enforcement of its procedural requirements, because the procedural requirements are designed to ensure compliance with the substantive provisions. The ESA's procedural requirements call for a systematic determination of the effects of a federal project on endangered species. If a project is allowed to proceed without substantial compliance with those procedural requirements, there can be no assurance that a violation of the ESA's substantive provisions will not result. The latter, of course, is impermissible.

---

7. The district court relied on the Forest Service's assertion that it had worked in "close cooperation" with the F & WS, but that assertion is undermined by letters in the record from the F & WS indicating that the Forest Service had not consulted with the F & WS on the impact of the road and the timber sales on the gray wolf, and that the F & WS felt that the Forest Service was not giving the wolf adequate consideration. See E.R. 55–58.

The district court, citing *Palila v. Hawaii Dept. of Land and Natural Resources,* 639 F.2d 495 (9th Cir.1981), held that "[a] party asserting a violation of the Endangered Species Act has the burden of showing the proposed action would have some prohibited effect on an endangered species or its critical habitat," and found that the plaintiffs in this case had not met that burden. This is a misapplication of *Palila.* That case concerned the ESA's prohibition of the "taking" of an endangered species, 16 U.S.C. § 1538(a)(1)(B), not the ESA's procedural requirements. Quite naturally, the court in *Palila* found that a plaintiff, in order to establish a violation of the "taking" provision, must show that such a "taking" has occurred. The holding does not apply to violations of the ESA's procedural requirements. A plaintiffs' burden in establishing a procedural violation is to show that the circumstances triggering the procedural requirement exist, and that the required procedures have not been followed. The plaintiffs in this case have clearly met that burden.

The Forest Service would require the district court, absent proof by the plaintiffs to the contrary, to make a finding that the Jersey Jack road is not likely to affect the Rocky Mountain Gray Wolf, and that therefore any failure to comply with ESA procedures is harmless. This is not a finding appropriate to the district court at the present time. Congress has assigned to the agencies and to the Fish & Wildlife Service the responsibility for evaluation of the impact of agency actions on endangered species, and has prescribed procedures for such evaluation. Only by following the procedures can proper evaluations be made. It is not the responsibility of the plaintiffs to prove, nor the function of the courts to judge, the effect of a proposed action on an endangered species when proper procedures have not been followed.

We therefore hold that the district court erred in declining to enjoin construction of the Jersey Jack road pending compliance with the ESA. . . .

LANE COUNTY AUDUBON SOCIETY v. JAMISON

United States Court of Appeals, Ninth Circuit, 1992.
958 F.2d 290.

SCHROEDER, Circuit Judge:

In June of 1989, the United States Fish & Wildlife Service (FWS) proposed listing the northern spotted owl as a threatened species under the Endangered Species Act, 16 U.S.C. §§ 1531 et seq. (ESA). In addition, in October of 1989, the Interagency Scientific Committee to Address the Conservation of the Northern Spotted Owl (the ISC) was formed to "develop a scientifically credible conservation strategy for the northern spotted owl." In May of 1990, the ISC issued its Final Report, concluding that the lack of a consistent planning strategy has resulted in a high risk of extinction for the owl. In June of 1990, the FWS listed the northern spotted owl as a threatened species pursuant to the ESA. The FWS based its decision to list the owl on its finding that "[e]xisting regulatory mechanisms are insufficient to protect either the northern spotted owl or its habitat."

In response to these events, the Bureau of Land Management (BLM), which manages approximately 1,149,954 acres of the remaining old growth forests suitable for spotted owl habitat in western Oregon, promulgated a document entitled "Management Guidelines for the Conservation of the Northern Spotted Owl, FY 1991 through FY 1992", commonly known as the "Jamison Strategy" ("the Strategy"). In this Strategy, the BLM essentially sets forth the criteria for selection of land for logging in the millions of acres administered by the BLM in Washington, Oregon and California. The BLM described the Jamison Strategy as "a four-phase plan ... which will direct BLM management of western forest lands into FY 1994 and beyond." The Strategy contains management guidelines for fiscal years 1991 and 1992, including a program to offer 750 million board feet of timber for sale each year. The Strategy was designed to be implemented immediately.

On December 4, 1990, Lane County Audubon Society and various environmental groups (Lane County), filed the requisite 60–day notice of their intention to file an ESA citizen suit to challenge the BLM's failure to consult with the FWS on the Strategy pursuant to 16 U.S.C. § 1536 ("Section 7") of the ESA. *See* 16 U.S.C. § 1540(g)(2)(A)(i). In January of 1991, the BLM submitted about 174 proposed timber sales to be conducted in fiscal 1991 to the FWS for consultation pursuant to section 7 of the ESA, but did not submit the Jamison Strategy itself.

Lane County then filed this action in United States District Court for the District of Oregon seeking an injunction barring the conduct of any sales until the Jamison Strategy had undergone the consultation process. The district court agreed with Lane County that the Jamison Strategy is an "action" within the meaning of section 7 of the ESA and held that the BLM had violated that section by failing to consult with the FWS to obtain that agency's biological opinion regarding the effects of the Strategy on the northern spotted owl before implementing the Strategy. The district court on April 4, 1991, enjoined the BLM from implementing the Strategy pending compliance with section 7, but stated in its order that the 1991 sales were not affected by its order. At the time of the district court's order, the FWS had reviewed 174 of the proposed 1991 sales and had declared that 122 of these would not be likely to jeopardize the owls' habitat, provided the remaining 52, the so called "jeopardy sales," would take place only within the strict limitations provided for in the FWS' biological opinion. In reviewing the 1991 sales, FWS had before it the Jamison Strategy and found its criteria insufficient to protect owl habitat. It applied instead the criteria recommended in the ISC Final Report.

Lane County now appeals the district court's refusal to enjoin the 1991 timber sales. It seeks an injunction, pending completion of consultation on the Jamison Strategy, prohibiting all future sales on BLM lands in the affected area, including the 1992 sales and the remaining 1991 sales that have not yet been awarded.

The BLM cross-appeals the district court's order holding that the Jamison Strategy is "agency action" and requiring the BLM to submit the Strategy for consultation. The BLM contends that the Jamison Strategy is not an "action" requiring consultation and that it is merely a voluntarily created "policy statement." Moreover, the BLM contends that it has in fact substantially complied with the ESA by submitting the individual 1991 sales for section 7 consultation, and so, an injunction is unwarranted.

We hold that the district court correctly declared the Jamison Strategy itself to be an agency action and correctly enjoined its implementation pending consultation. We further hold that all future sales the BLM proposes to conduct are also "agency actions" and should not go forward until consultation is satisfactorily completed on the sales and on the Jamison Strategy itself or on another functionally similar plan establishing the governing criteria for sale site selections on BLM land. We enjoin, pending completion of such consultation, the award of any sales that may be announced in the future. The status of the remaining announced, but not yet awarded, 1991 sales is somewhat different, since those sales have already been submitted to the FWS. We remand to the district court for reconsideration of whether the award of those sales should also be enjoined based upon our holding today.

I

We turn first to the Jamison Strategy itself. It is intended to establish interim timber management standards to replace standards set forth in the old Timber Management Plans (TMPs) pending issuance of new TMPs.... The TMPs are 10–year plans that "designate commercial forest land under BLM management in [each] district for one of several uses." *Id.* at 1234. TMPs do not designate specific timber-sale boundaries, or require that any particular area be harvested. *Id.* at 1235. Rather, they decide land-use allocation and set the "annual allowable harvest" for each district. *See id.*

The BLM itself described its Jamison Strategy as an "interim strategy" to be carried out while new management plans are prepared. The Strategy outlines in detail the various criteria that will be used to develop the 1991 and 1992 timber sales. It develops a "detailed management strategy" to be carried out in four phases to cover fiscal years 1990 through 1994 "and beyond." Like the TMPs, it establishes total annual allowable harvests. The impact of each individual sale on owl habitat cannot be measured without reference to the management criteria established in the TMPs and the Jamison Strategy.

Section 7(a)(2) of the ESA requires the Secretary of the Interior to ensure that an action of a federal agency is not likely to jeopardize the continued existence of any threatened or endangered species. To this end, section 7(b) sets out a process of consultation whereby the agency with jurisdiction over the protected species issues to the Secretary a "biological opinion" evaluating the nature and extent of jeopardy posed to that species by the agency action. 16 U.S.C. § 1536(b). In order to maintain the status quo, section 7(d) forbids "irreversible or irretrievable commitment of resources" during the consultation period. *Id.* § 1536(d).

Section 7 specifically provides that a federal agency (the "action" agency) *shall* "in consultation with ... the Secretary [of the Interior], insure that any action authorized, funded, or carried out by such agency ... is not likely to jeopardize the continued existence of any endangered species or threatened species.... " *Id.* § 1536(a)(2) (emphasis added).

Procedural guidelines for complying with this consultation requirement are codified at 50 C.F.R. Part 402. The FWS implementing regulations under the ESA require agencies to review their action "at the earliest possible time to determine whether any action may affect listed species." *Id.* § 402.14(a). The FWS defines agency "action" broadly to include "all activities or programs of any kind authorized, funded, or carried out, in whole or in part, by Federal agencies.... " *Id.* § 402.02. Examples include but are not limited to:

(a) actions intended to conserve listed species or their habitat;

* * * * *

(d) actions directly or indirectly causing modifications to the land, water, or air.

Id.

This court also interprets the term "agency action" broadly. *Conner v. Burford,* 848 F.2d 1441, 1452 (9th Cir.1988), *cert. denied sub nom Sun Exploration & Prod. Co. v. Lujan,* 489 U.S. 1012, 109 S.Ct. 1121, 103 L.Ed.2d 184 (1989) (citing *TVA v. Hill,* 437 U.S. 153, 173 & n. 18, 98 S.Ct. 2279, 2291 & n. 18, 57 L.Ed.2d 117 (1978) (Supreme Court held that Congress had explicitly foreclosed the exercise of discretion by courts faced with a violation of section 7 of the ESA)).

We agree with the district court that "without a doubt," the Jamison Strategy as announced was to be an agency action "authorized, funded or carried out by the BLM." Moreover, the Jamison Strategy is action that "may affect" the spotted owl, since it sets forth criteria for harvesting owl habitat. It falls squarely within the definition of agency action set forth in 50 C.F.R. § 402.02. Accordingly, the BLM must submit the Jamison Strategy to the FWS for consultation before the Jamison Strategy can be implemented through the adoption of individual sale programs. In implementing the Jamison Strategy before consultation with the FWS, the BLM has violated the ESA. The district court properly enjoined implementation of the Strategy.

II

This brings us to Lane County's appeal regarding sales. Lane County asks that all sales be enjoined pending consultation on the

Jamison Strategy. The government acknowledges that sales are "actions" under section 7 and require ESA consultation. The government contends, however, that despite the district court's injunction against implementation of the Jamison Strategy, individual sales may nevertheless go forward under the TMPs promulgated between 1979 and 1983 rather than the Jamison Strategy. The TMPs were, of course, not submitted for consultation at the time they were promulgated, because the owl was not listed as a threatened species until 1990. The government argues that the sales may go forward because Lane County has not challenged the TMPs under the ESA.

This is not a tenable position, for if the Jamison Strategy is an "action" requiring consultation, then clearly the BLM's reinstatement of the TMPs would also constitute such action. The two documents serve the same function with respect to sales. Moreover, in adopting the Jamison Strategy in the first place, the government recognized that a new, interim underlying strategy was necessary after the owls were listed pursuant to the ESA, because the old TMPs were inadequate to meet the requirements of that Act....

In sum, neither the underlying TMPs nor the Jamison "interim management strategy" has ever been submitted to FWS for consultation pursuant to the mandate of the ESA. Accordingly, the individual sales cannot go forward until the consultation process is complete on the underlying plans which BLM uses to drive their development.

The district court's order, however, did not make it clear that pending the completion of the consultation process, the BLM should be enjoined from conducting any new sales. Such an injunction is necessary because until consultation is satisfactorily concluded with respect to the Jamison Strategy, or indeed any other conservation strategy intended to establish the criteria under which sites for sales are to be selected, the sales cannot lawfully go forward. The ESA prohibits the "irreversible or irretrievable commitment of resources" during the consultation period. 16 U.S.C. § 1536(d). The sales are such commitments.

NEWTON COUNTY WILDLIFE ASSOCIATION
v. ROGERS

United States Court of Appeals, Eighth Circuit, 1998.
141 F.3d 803.

LOKEN, Circuit Judge.

Newton County Wildlife Association, the Sierra Club, and certain individuals (collectively "the Wildlife Association") sued the United States Forest Service and four of its employees (collectively the "Forest Service") to enjoin or set aside four timber sales in the Ozark National Forest....

I. BACKGROUND.

... In the early 1990's, the Forest Service proposed four timber sales in "general" areas of the Buffalo Ranger District (areas administered under the Plan to yield a high level of timber). The proposed sales—Sand Gap, Round Hill, Junction, and Sandy Springs—involve timber harvesting on a total of 3,011 acres of forest and require 13.64 miles of logging road reconstruction and 5.08 miles of new road. For each proposed sale, the Forest Service mailed notices to affected and interested members of the public, including the Wildlife Association, describing the proposal and soliciting comments. After receiving responses, the Forest Service studied site-specific environmental effects and developed Environmental Assessments ("EAs") evaluating the environmental impacts of various sale alternatives, including the "no action" alternative. Biological evaluations were prepared analyzing likely effects on species known to inhabit the Forest. The District Ranger circulated the EAs with requests for public comment prior to issuing Decision Notices.

The Forest Service issued Decision Notices for Sand Gap and Round Hill on May 27, 1994. Administrative appeals were rejected by September 1994, and the sales took place that fall. Purchasers commenced road construction and logging in the spring of 1995. The Forest Service issued Decision Notices for Junction and Sandy Springs on June 19 and May 22, 1995, and rejected administrative appeals in the fall of 1995. The Wildlife Association filed this lawsuit on December 20, 1995. The second amended complaint alleges that plaintiffs "seek judicial review of final agency action in approving" the four timber sales. Counsel for the Forest Service advised at oral argument that approximately three-fourths of road work and timber harvesting in the four sale areas is now completed. . . .

F. Endangered Species Act. The Endangered Species Act requires federal agencies to consult with the appropriate federal fish and wildlife agency when their actions "may affect" an endangered or threatened species. *See* 16 U.S.C. § 1536(a)(2); 50 C.F.R. § 402.14(a). The Wildlife Association argues the Forest Service was arbitrary and capricious in approving the sales before the United States Fish and Wildlife Service determined whether the logging might significantly affect any listed species. The Forest Service prepared a detailed biological "evaluation" for each sale and found there was no effect on any listed or endangered species. A finding of no effect obviates the need for consultation with the Fish and Wildlife Service. *See* 50 C.F.R. § 402.14. The Wildlife Association argues the Forest Service was required to prepare biological "assessments" to decide whether to consult with the Fish and Wildlife Service. *See* 16 U.S.C. § 1536(c). However, a biological assessment is only required for "major construction activities." 50 C.F.R. § 402.12. Finally, the Wildlife Association argues the Forest Service failed to make an adequate assessment of whether the sales would affect the bald eagle. However, the biological evaluations and the EAs specifically considered impacts on the bald eagle and its habitat and determined that the sales would have no effect. Accordingly, nothing in the administrative record establishes that the Forest Service was arbitrary or capricious in carrying out its ESA obligations regarding these sales.

We have carefully considered all other arguments made by the Wildlife Association and conclude they are without merit.

Questions and Comments

1. What are the differences that lead the courts in *Thomas v. Peterson* and *Newton County* to come out so differently? Why did the court believe a biological assessment was necessary in *Thomas* but not in *Newton County*? Note that in *Thomas* there was no need for the plaintiff to show any adverse effect on the wolf in order to obtain an injunction.

2. In *Thomas* the court says that the ESA's substantive provisions call for more stringent enforcement of the ESA's procedural requirements. Why is that? Why if the substantive provisions are themselves enforceable is there any need to enforce the procedural requirements?

3. In *Lane County* what was the BLM's error? How does the Jamison strategy affect the owls separate from the timber sales? That is, if the timber sales themselves are concededly subject to consultation requirements, what benefit is there is to subjecting the Jamison strategy to consultation as well?

4. Why in *Lane County*, if the BLM has already consulted on the individual 1991 timber sales and the Fish and Wildlife Service has either declared them not to jeopardize the owl or has specified conditions in its Biological Opinion to prevent jeopardy, does the court enjoin those sales as well as those for which there has been no consultation?

5. In *Lane County* the court stresses the broad understanding of what can constitute an agency "action." There are a number of courts and cases making the same point. One of the more dramatic cases involved a determination that EPA's registrations of pesticides under the Federal Insecticide, Fungicide and Rodenticide Act was an action requiring consultation because the application of pesticides has been shown to affect listed salmon. *See Washington Toxic Coalition v. EPA*, No. 01–132C (W.D. Wash. July 2, 2002).

6. As appears in both *Thomas* and *Newton County*, there is often a relationship between and agency's responsibilities under the National Environmental Policy Act and under the ESA. This is often the case and is not surprising in that the responsibilities of each is triggered by agency action. In *Thomas* the agency is found to have failed both those responsibilities, and in *Newton County* the court finds the agency satisfied both responsibilities. The ESA itself specifies that a biological assessment may be undertaken as part of the agency's NEPA compliance. *See* 16 U.S.C. § 1536(c)(1). Thus, even if an agency does not identify an analysis as a biological assessment, if it performs the same functions as part of an Environmental Impact Statement, this can satisfy the ESA requirement. *See Sierra Club v. U.S.A.C.O.E.*, 295 F.3d 1209, 1219 (11th Cir. 2002).

7. Just as there is a requirement for supplemental EIS's under NEPA, the services' regulations require reinitiation of consultation if the incidental take limits are exceeded, if a new species is listed or critical habitat designated that might be affected by the action, if new information develops relevant to the effect on the species or critical habitat, or the action is subsequently modified in a way that would result in an effect not already considered. 50 CFR § 402.16. *See Sierra Club v. Marsh*, 816 F.2d 1376 (9th

Cir. 1987)(Corps violated requirement to reinitiate consultation because mitigation efforts were delayed and might not take place at all).

8. Also similar to NEPA implementation, consultation can be on a programmatic basis, rather than limited to a particular action. Consultation on the Jamison strategy, for example, would likely be deemed programmatic consultation. Still following the NEPA model, these programmatic consultations can be "tiered" when site-specific effects cannot yet be adequately determined. This kind of programmatic BO would not include incidental take authorizations. Only when later site-specific BOs are prepared would any incidental take be authorized.

9. Recently the services have adopted two so-called "counterpart" regulations. Counterpart regulations are regulations that substitute for the normal consultation regulations with respect to particular matters. 50 CFR § 402.04. One was adopted in 2003 and relates to implementing the National Fire Plan, an executive plan for managing wildfires on national lands. 50 CFR Part 402, Subpart C. The other was adopted in 2004 and relates to EPA's implementation of the consultation requirements in registering pesticides. 50 CFR Part 402, Subpart D. Both are intended to streamline the consultation process while maintaining the same overall degree of protection for species, but precisely because they do streamline the process, they raise concerns among environmental groups. Challenges to counterpart regulations have had a mixed result. *Compare Washington Toxics Coalition v. U.S. Dept. of Interior*, 457 F.Supp.2d 1158 (W.D.Wash. 2006)(regulations invalidated) *with Defenders of Wildlife v. Kempthorne*, 2006 WL 2844232 (D.D.C. 2006)(regulations upheld).

3. The Substantive Requirements

Separate from, but obviously connected to, the procedural requirement to engage in consultation, Section 7 also imposes substantive requirements. Specifically, Section 7(a)(2) prohibits federal agencies from taking any action if it is "likely to jeopardize the continued existence of any [listed species] or result in the destruction of or adverse modification of [critical habitat]." The Act does not define "jeopardize the continued existence," but the services' regulations do:

> "Jeopardize the continued existence of" means to engage in an action that reasonably would be expected, directly or indirectly, to reduce appreciably the likelihood of both the survival and recovery of a listed species in the wild by reducing the reproduction, numbers, or distribution of that species.

50 CFR § 402.02 (2004). By requiring an action to adversely affect *both* the survival *and* the recovery of the species the regulation would appear to add a requirement not contained in the statute. However, it is difficult to imagine a circumstance in which, if the survival of a species is put at risk, its recovery will not likewise be put at risk. Thus, while the regulation literally requires the likelihood of both to be reduced, as a practical matter only the effect on survival is relevant.

Because the action agency normally relies on the biological opinion that results from consultation, much of the litigation challenging an action agency's decision is actually an attack on adequacy of the biological opinion. Often the litigation regarding jeopardy to a species involves challenges to the methodology of the biological opinion. For example, in *Gifford Pinchot Task Force v. U.S. Fish & Wildlife Service*, 378 F.3d 1059 (9th Cir. 2004), the environmental plaintiffs challenged the use of impacts on the species' habitat as a proxy for impacts on the species itself. The court rejected the challenge, calling it a close case, concluding that "the habitat models used here reasonably ensure that owl population projections from the habitat proxy are accurate." In *Pacific Coast Federation of Fishermen's Ass'n v. National Marine Fisheries Service*, 265 F.3d 1028 (9th Cir. 2001), the court found the no-jeopardy determination arbitrary and capricious because NMFS failed to consider the short-term effects of logging measurable at smaller than watershed level. In *National Wildlife Federation v. Coleman*, 529 F.2d 359 (5th Cir. 1976), the court held that, while the Department of Transportation adequately considered the effects on the Mississippi Sand Hill crane of the actual loss of habitat occasioned by the right-of-way for a highway, it failed to consider the indirect effects resulting from construction impacts and the commercial and residential development expected to result from the highway construction.

The other half of the substantive requirement—that the agency action not "result in the destruction of or adverse modification of [critical habitat]"—also is not amplified in the statute, but the services' regulations define "destruction or adverse modification" to mean:

> a direct or indirect alteration that appreciably diminishes the value of critical habitat for both the survival and recovery of a listed species. Such alterations include, but are not limited to, alterations adversely modifying any of those physical or biological features that were the basis for determining the habitat to be critical.

50 CFR § 402.02 (2004). This definition has been a source of some contention.

GIFFORD PINCHOT TASK FORCE v. UNITED STATES FISH & WILDLIFE SERVICE

United States Court of Appeals, Ninth Circuit, 2004.
378 F.3d 1059.

GOULD, Circuit Judge:

This is a record review case in which the Appellants, an assortment of environmental organizations, challenge six biological opinions (BiOps) issued by the United States Fish and Wildlife Service (USFWS or FWS) pursuant to the Endangered Species Act (ESA). The BiOps in question allowed for timber harvests in specified Northwest forests and also authorized incidental "takes" of the Northern spotted owl (spotted owl), a threatened species under the ESA. . . .

I

A

We begin by explaining the legal regime created by the ESA. For any federal action that may affect a threatened or endangered species (or its habitat), the agency contemplating the action (the action agency) must consult with the consulting agency to ensure that the federal action is not likely to jeopardize "the continued existence of" an endangered or threatened species and that the federal action will not result in the "destruction or adverse modification" of the designated critical habitat of the listed species. These consultations are known as "Section 7" consultations. The action agency typically makes a written request to the consulting agency, and, after formal consultation, the process concludes with the consulting agency issuing a biological opinion. The BiOp should address both the jeopardy and critical habitat prongs of Section 7 by considering the current status of the species, the environmental baseline, the effects of the proposed action, and the cumulative effects of the proposed action.

If the BiOp concludes that jeopardy is not likely and that there will not be adverse modification of critical habitat, or that there is a "reasonable and prudent alternative" to the agency action that avoids jeopardy and adverse modification, the FWS can issue an Incidental Take Statement (ITS) which, if followed, exempts the action agency from the prohibition on takings found in Section 9 of the ESA. . . .

III

The Appellants challenge the six BiOps on both the jeopardy analysis and the critical habitat requirements of a Section 7 consultation. . . .

A

[The court rejected the challenge to the jeopardy analysis.]

B

We next turn to the critical habitat portion of the challenged BiOps. It is here that the picture is complicated by error and, on our analysis, becomes less rosy for the FWS.

1

Appellants first argue that the FWS's interpretation of "adverse modification," 50 C.F.R. § 402.02, is unlawful. ESA Section 7 consultations require that in every biological opinion, the consulting agency (here the FWS) ensure that the proposed action "is not likely to jeopardize the continued existence of" an endangered or threatened species and that the federal action will not result in the "destruction or adverse modification" of the designated "critical habitat" of the listed species.

The FWS, in turn, defined "destruction or adverse modification" as:

[A] direct or indirect alteration that appreciably diminishes the value of critical habitat for both the survival and recovery of a listed species. Such alterations include, but are not limited to, alterations adversely modifying any of those physical or biological features that were the basis for determining the habitat to be critical.

50 C.F.R. § 402.02. This regulation requires a close reading to grasp its import. Appellants argue that the regulatory definition sets the bar too high because the adverse modification threshold is not triggered by a proposed action until there is an appreciable diminishment of the value of critical habitat for both survival and recovery.[6]

We agree. Here, the FWS has interpreted "destruction or adverse modification" as changes to the critical habitat "that appreciably diminish[ ] the value of critical habitat for *both* the survival *and* recovery of a listed species." This regulatory definition explicitly requires appreciable diminishment of the critical habitat necessary for survival before the "destruction or adverse modification" standard could ever be met. Because it is logical and inevitable that a species requires more critical habitat for recovery than is necessary for the species survival, the regulation's singular focus becomes "survival." Given this literal understanding of the regulation's express definition of "adverse modification," we consider whether that definition is a permissible interpretation of the ESA.

To answer that question, there is no need to go beyond *Chevron's* first step in analyzing the permissibility of the regulation; the regulatory definition of "adverse modification" contradicts Congress's express command. As the Fifth and Tenth Circuits have already recognized, the regulatory definition reads the "recovery" goal out of the adverse modification inquiry; a proposed action "adversely modifies" critical habitat if, and only if, the value of the critical habitat for *survival* is appreciably diminished. *See N.M. Cattle Growers Ass'n v. United States Fish and Wildlife Serv.,* 248 F.3d 1277, 1283 & n. 2 (10th Cir.2001); *Sierra Club v. United States Fish and Wildlife Serv.,* 245 F.3d 434, 441–42 (5th Cir.2001). The FWS could authorize the complete elimination of critical habitat necessary only for recovery, and so long as the smaller amount of critical habitat necessary for survival is not appreciably diminished, then no "destruction or adverse modification," as defined by the regulation, has taken place. This cannot be right. If the FWS follows its own regulation, then it is obligated to be indifferent to, if not to ignore, the recovery goal of critical habitat.

The agency's controlling regulation on critical habitat thus offends the ESA because the ESA was enacted not merely to forestall the extinction of species (i.e., promote a species survival), but to allow a species to recover to the point where it may be delisted. *See* 16 U.S.C. § 1532(3) (defining conservation as all methods that can be employed to

6. This claim, which challenges the FWS regulation, is reviewed under the familiar Chevron U.S.A., Inc. v. Natural Re-sources Defense Council, Inc., 467 U.S. 837, 104 S.Ct. 2778 (1984), framework.

"bring any endangered species or threatened species to the point at which the measures provided pursuant to this [Act] are no longer necessary"). The ESA also defines critical habitat as including "the specific areas ... occupied by the species ... which are ... essential to the *conservation* of the species" and the "specific areas outside the geographical area occupied by the species ... that ... are essential for the *conservation* of the species...." By these definitions, it is clear that Congress intended that conservation and survival be two different (though complementary) goals of the ESA. *See* 16 U.S.C. § 1533(f)(1) ("The Secretary shall develop and implement plans ... for the *conservation* and *survival* of endangered species and threatened species.") (emphasis added). Clearly, then, the purpose of establishing "critical habitat" is for the government to carve out territory that is not only necessary for the species' survival but also essential for the species' recovery.

Congress, by its own language, viewed conservation and survival as distinct, though complementary, goals, and the requirement to preserve critical habitat is designed to promote both conservation and survival. Congress said that "destruction or adverse modification" could occur when sufficient critical habitat is lost so as to threaten a species' recovery even if there remains sufficient critical habitat for the species' survival. The regulation, by contrast, finds that adverse modification to critical habitat can only occur when there is so much critical habitat lost that a species' very survival is threatened. The agency's interpretation would drastically narrow the scope of protection commanded by Congress under the ESA. To define "destruction or adverse modification" of critical habitat to occur only when there is appreciable diminishment of the value of the critical habitat for both survival *and* conservation fails to provide protection of habitat when necessary only for species' recovery. The narrowing construction implemented by the regulation is regrettably, but blatantly, contradictory to Congress' express command. Where Congress in its statutory language required "or," the agency in its regulatory definition substituted "and." This is not merely a technical glitch, but rather a failure of the regulation to implement Congressional will.

The Fifth Circuit reached this same conclusion in *Sierra Club....* The court bolstered its conclusion from the legislative history where Congress had considered an earlier critical habitat regulation that required effects on both recovery and survival and had rejected such an interpretation. We agree with the Fifth Circuit, and with the Tenth Circuit's analogous reasoning, and hold that the regulatory definition of "adverse modification" gives too little protection to designated critical habitat....

Notes and Comments

1. Earlier, in the discussion of Section 4's requirement for designating critical habitat, we noted the services' reluctance to undertake critical habitat designations, finding instead that designation was not "prudent,"

because designation would not increase protections for the species beyond the protection afforded by listing alone. Given the services' definition of "destruction or adverse modification," one might understand how the services made those findings.

2. The Ninth Circuit notes that both the Fifth and Tenth Circuits had earlier found the services' definition improper. Nevertheless, despite three different circuits' rulings, the services' regulation remains on the books and there is no acknowledged intent to change it. Why do you suppose that is?

3. Another issue in the *Gifford Pinchot Task Force* case was a claim by the FWS that, because there was substantial suitable habitat for the owls outside the designated critical habitat, the proposed timber sales would not have any significant adverse effect on the owls' overall habitat. The court rejected the FWS argument, holding that the statute refers only to the adverse modification of critical habitat. If there is other, suitable habitat available to the owls, the agency could by rule modify the critical habitat designation, the court said, and then perhaps the proposed timber sale's effect on the redesignated critical habitat might not be meaningful.

4. To avoid jeopardy determinations, the services have often tried to rely on various agreements or undertakings from action agencies that would mitigate the effects of the action agency's proposed action, or the action agencies have tried to rely on agreements or undertakings from third persons to mitigate the effects of the agencies' actions . This is not unlike action agencies attempting to mitigate out of significance for purposes of NEPA. Litigation challenging these mitigation agreements also has tended to reflect the same considerations as the NEPA litigation. *See, e.g., Selkirk Conservation Alliance v. Forsgren*, 336 F.3d 944 (9th Cir. 2003)(FWS could rely upon legally enforceable conservation agreement between Forest Service and private timber company to lower threats to grizzly bears); *National Wildlife Federation v. NMFS*, 254 F.Supp.2d 1196 (D. Or. 2003)(NMFS no jeopardy determination deemed unlawful because it relied on mitigation measures for which there was no funding, for which the agencies lacked authority, and which were not reasonably certain to occur because of the lack of binding agreements); *Center for Biological Diversity v. Rumsfeld*, 198 F.Supp.2d 1139 (D.Ariz. 2002)(Dept. of Army MOA with FWS inadequate to assure no jeopardy).

5. A question arises when a statute appears to establish the criteria for an agency action, and none of those criteria arguably includes consideration of threatened and endangered species. If the agency's consultation with the FWS results in a jeopardy determination (or in the identification of reasonable and prudent alternatives to avoid jeopardy), is the agency authorized to withhold the action (or condition it on the adoption of the reasonable and prudent alternatives)? This issue arose in the case of *Defenders of Wildlife v. EPA*, 420 F.3d 946 (9th Cir. 2005), *cert. granted sub nom. National Ass'n of Home Builders v. Defenders of Wildlife*, 127 S.Ct. 852, 166 L.Ed.2d 681 (2007). There EPA delegated CWA permitting authority to the state of Arizona notwithstanding a determination by the FWS that such a delegation would have a negative impact on several threatened and endangered species as a result, not of degradation of water quality, but of habitat destruction associated with development that would be subject to NPDES permitting

requirements. EPA argued that the CWA establishes specific criteria governing when states may obtain delegated permitting authority, and the ESA should not be read to add on to those criteria. The Ninth Circuit disagreed in a split opinion, and the Supreme Court is likely to resolve this issue.

4. Exemptions

When the Tellico Dam was halted by the snail darter, the ESA contained no exemptions from the prohibition on agency actions that jeopardize a listed species. The Supreme Court's enforcement of the literal terms of the ESA in those circumstances led to Congress enacting an exemption process in 1979. 16 U.S.C. § 1536(e)-(o).

This process begins with application for exemption when a service has rendered a biological opinion concluding that the agency action would likely jeopardize a listed species or destroy or adversely modify critical habitat. The application may be made by the action agency, the permit or license applicant when the action in question would be granting that license or permit, or the governor of the state in which the action would occur. 16 U.S.C. § 1536(g)(1). The application is made to the Secretary of the Interior, who makes a determination whether the action agency and applicant have engaged in the required Section 7 assessments and consultations in good faith, have made a responsible effort to adopt modifications or alternatives that would not violate the ESA, and have not made any irreversible or irretrievable commitment of resources after initiating consultations. 16 U.S.C. § 1536(g)(3). If the Secretary makes a positive determination, the Secretary is to undertake a formal adjudication under the Administrative Procedure Act in order to prepare a report to be submitted to the Endangered Species Committee, which has the authority to grant the exemption. 16 U.S.C. § 1536(g)(4).

The Endangered Species Committee is a unique entity and its composition and operation are not designed to facilitate granting exemptions. The committee, popularly entitled the God Squad, because of its ability to decide to jeopardize a species, is comprised of at least seven members: the Secretary of the Interior, who chairs the committee; the Secretary of Agriculture; the Secretary of the Army; the Chair of the Council of Economic Advisors; the Administrator of EPA; the Administrator of NOAA; and a person appointed by the President from each affected state after receiving recommendations from the governors of the affected states. 16 U.S.C. § 1536(e). The committee also is supposed to be governed in its consideration of the application by the formal adjudication provisions of the APA, and it takes at least five members (or their representatives) to constitute a quorum. 16 U.S.C. § 1536(g)(5) & (6). When it comes to voting, however, the members are not allowed to have representatives; they must be present and vote themselves. To grant an application, at least five members must vote in person to grant the exemption upon a finding based on the record that: there are no reasonable and prudent alternatives; the benefits of the action with its adverse effects on the species clearly outweigh the benefits that would be available from an action without such adverse effects; the action is of regional or national significance; and there were no irretrievable or irreversible commitment of resources made after initiation of consultation. 16 U.S.C. § 1536(h)(1)(A). If the committee grants the exemption, it must establish mitigation and enhancement measures to minimize the adverse effects on the species. 16 U.S.C. § 1536(h)(1)(B). No exemption can be granted if the Secretary of State informs the committee that to do so would violate a United States treaty or other international obligation. 16 U.S.C. § 1536(i). However, if the Secretary of Defense finds an exemption is necessary for national security purposes, the committee is required to grant the exemption. 16 U.S.C. § 1536(j). If the exemption is granted, Section 9's prohibition on taking endangered species does not apply to actions pursuant to the exemption. 16 U.S.C. § 1536(o).

Despite the relative lax standard for filing an application and for its referral to the Endangered Species Committee, only three applications have made it to the committee. The first two were specifically mentioned in the legislation creating the exemption. One involved the Tellico Dam, but the committee denied the exemption in that case, finding the dam not cost effective even without considering the snail darter. The other involved the Greylocks Dam on the Platte River, which had been found to jeopardize whooping cranes. In this case the committee granted the exemption, but subject to such mitigation and enhancement measures that the result was supported by environmental groups. The third application was not until 1992, when the Secretary of Interior (on behalf of the Bureau of Land Management) sought exemptions for a number of timber sales in Oregon. While the committee by a vote of 5–2 approved a limited number of the requested exemptions, subject to significant mitigation and enhancement requirements, before the approval could take place, the new Secretary of the Interior (in the new administration) withdrew the application.

Notes and Comments

1. Although the Endangered Species Committee refused an exemption for the Tellico Dam, Congress took the matter into its own hands and passed a rider to an appropriations act in 1979 directing that notwithstanding the Endangered Species Act the dam should be completed and operated. The completion of the dam and the filling of the reservoir destroyed the entire habitat of the only known location of the snail darter. However, subsequently other small populations of snail darters were found in the Tennessee River watershed, resulting in the snail darter's being reclassified as threatened, rather than endangered. Is there any lesson to be learned from this?

2. Consider the composition of the Endangered Species Committee. Why do you suppose these specific officers were chosen to be members? And why do you suppose the legislation required these busy, high level officials personally to be present for any vote?

3. The Endangered Species Act has generated significant controversy precisely because in various situations plants or animals of seemingly little

worth have appeared to frustrate significant economic undertakings. *See, e.g.*, David Klinghoffer, What Suckers!, National Review Online, September 10, 2001, www.nationalreview.com/comment/comment-klinghoffer091001.shtml, last visited on 3/10/2007 (describing as "idiotic verging on sadistic" the logic of the ESA saving suckers by depriving farmers of needed water). Why is it then that so few applications for exemptions have been filed, when any applicant for a permit, any governor of an affected state, or any action agency can file an application for an exemption? And why is it that obtaining an exemption is viewed as very difficult when the committee essentially can grant an application simply if the benefits greatly outweigh the benefits of the alternatives, so long as the action has at least regional significance? That is, if the economic benefits of a particular action purportedly stymied by the ESA are so great, why is the exemption process not a solution?

Problem

The Corps of Engineers administers a federal dam that impounds water for flood control in Georgia. The resulting lake is a center for water oriented recreation, especially fishing. Recently, however, an alien invasive plant has begun to grow in the lake, covering much of shoreline and many of the best fishing areas. Moreover, by crowding out the native water plants, the invasive is changing the nature of the lake's ecosystem. Attempts to cut the plant back have been unsuccessful, so the Corps is considering poisoning the plant. Necessarily, this will mean poison in the lake, killing non-invasive plants and perhaps some fish and amphibians. Complicating the matters is the fact that a threatened species of frog lives in the lake, which is designated critical habitat for the frog. Assess the procedural steps and substantive limitations on the Corps' plan to poison the invasive plants.

D.   Section 9

Whereas Section 7 of the ESA only applies when there is federal government action, as in NEPA, Section 9 has no such limitation. It applies to any person, including federal and state actors. It prohibits the sale, delivery, or transport in interstate or foreign commerce, including the importation into or the export from the United States, of any *endangered* species. 16 U.S.C. § 1538(a)(1)(A), (E), (F) & (2)(A), (C), (D). It also makes unlawful the "take" of any *endangered* species of fish or wildlife. *Endangered* species of plants are only protected under Section 9 if they are in areas under Federal jurisdiction or if the person harming them does it in violation of a state trespass law or in knowing violation of any other state law or regulation. Finally, *threatened* species only receive protection to the extent provided by regulations adopted by the Secretary of Interior or the Secretary of Commerce.

While Section 7 speaks of jeopardizing a listed species or harming habitat needed by listed species, Section 9 does not directly speak about habitat, and its most frequently operative term is to "take" a species. "Take" is a defined term, meaning: "to harass, harm, pursue, hunt, shoot, wound, kill, trap, capture, or collect, or attempt to engage in such conduct." The question this definition raises is whether destruction of habitat upon which an endangered species relies is included within the prohibited acts. By regulation, the services have interpreted the word "harm" to include certain significant habitat destruction. In a noteworthy case, the Supreme Court assessed the validity of this regulation.

BABBITT v. SWEET HOME CHAPTER OF COMMUNITIES FOR A GREAT OREGON

Supreme Court of the United States, 1995.
515 U.S. 687, 115 S.Ct. 2407, 132 L.Ed.2d 597.

Justice STEVENS delivered the opinion of the Court.

The Endangered Species Act of 1973 (ESA or Act) contains a variety of protections designed to save from extinction species that the Secretary of the Interior designates as endangered or threatened. Section 9 of the Act makes it unlawful for any person to "take" any endangered or threatened species. The Secretary has promulgated a regulation that defines the statute's prohibition on takings to include "significant habitat modification or degradation where it actually kills or injures wildlife." This case presents the question whether the Secretary exceeded his authority under the Act by promulgating that regulation.

I

Section 9(a)(1) of the Act provides the following protection for endangered species:

> Except as provided in sections 1535(g)(2) and 1539 of this title, with respect to any endangered species of fish or wildlife listed pursuant to section 1533 of this title it is unlawful for any person subject to the jurisdiction of the United States to— ...

> (B) take any such species within the United States or the territorial sea of the United States.

Section 3(19) of the Act defines the statutory term "take": "The term 'take' means to harass, harm, pursue, hunt, shoot, wound, kill, trap, capture, or collect, or to attempt to engage in any such conduct."

The Act does not further define the terms it uses to define "take." The Interior Department regulations that implement the statute, however, define the statutory term "harm":

> "*Harm* in the definition of 'take' in the Act means an act which actually kills or injures wildlife. Such act may include significant habitat modification or degradation where it actually kills or injures wildlife by significantly impairing essential behavioral patterns, including breeding, feeding, or sheltering."

This regulation has been in place since 1975.

A limitation on the § 9 "take" prohibition appears in § 10(a)(1)(B) of the Act, which Congress added by amendment in 1982. That section authorizes the Secretary to grant a permit for any taking otherwise prohibited by § 9(a)(1)(B) "if such taking is incidental to, and not the purpose of, the carrying out of an otherwise lawful activity." . . .

Respondents in this action are small landowners, logging companies, and families dependent on the forest products industries in the Pacific Northwest and in the Southeast, and organizations that represent their interests. They brought this declaratory judgment action against petitioners, the Secretary of the Interior and the Director of the Fish and Wildlife Service, in the United States District Court for the District of Columbia to challenge the statutory validity of the Secretary's regulation defining "harm," particularly the inclusion of habitat modification and degradation in the definition. . . .

Respondents advanced three arguments to support their submission that Congress did not intend the word "take" in § 9 to include habitat modification, as the Secretary's "harm" regulation provides. First, they correctly noted that language in the Senate's original version of the ESA would have defined "take" to include "destruction, modification, or curtailment of [the] habitat or range" of fish or wildlife, but the Senate deleted that language from the bill before enacting it. Second, respondents argued that Congress intended the Act's express authorization for the Federal Government to buy private land in order to prevent habitat degradation in § 5 to be the exclusive check against habitat modification on private property. Third, because the Senate added the term "harm" to the definition of "take" in a floor amendment without debate, respondents argued that the court should not interpret the term so expansively as to include habitat modification. . . .

[The court of appeals found for the respondents.] Although acknowledging that "[t]he potential breadth of the word 'harm' is indisputable," *id.*, at 1464, the majority concluded that the immediate statutory context in which "harm" appeared counseled against a broad reading; like the other words in the definition of "take," the word "harm" should be read as applying only to "the perpetrator's direct application of force against the animal taken. . . . The forbidden acts fit, in ordinary language, the basic model 'A hit B.'" The majority based its reasoning on a canon of statutory construction called *noscitur a sociis,* which holds that a word is known by the company it keeps. . . .

The Court of Appeals' decision created a square conflict with a 1988 decision of the Ninth Circuit that had upheld the Secretary's definition of "harm." See *Palila v. Hawaii Dept. of Land and Natural Resources,* 852 F.2d 1106 (1988) (*Palila II*). . . . We granted certiorari to resolve the conflict. Our consideration of the text and structure of the Act, its legislative history, and the significance of the 1982 amendment persuades us that the Court of Appeals' judgment should be reversed.

II

Because this case was decided on motions for summary judgment, we may appropriately make certain factual assumptions in order to frame the legal issue. First, we assume respondents have no desire to harm either the red-cockaded woodpecker or the spotted owl; they merely wish to continue logging activities that would be entirely proper if not prohibited by the ESA. On the other hand, we must assume, *arguendo,* that those activities will have the effect, even though unintended, of detrimentally changing the natural habitat of both listed species and that, as a consequence, members of those species will be killed or injured. . . .

The text of the Act provides three reasons for concluding that the Secretary's interpretation is reasonable. First, an ordinary understanding of the word "harm" supports it. The dictionary definition of the verb form of "harm" is "to cause hurt or damage to: injure." In the context of the ESA, that definition naturally encompasses habitat modification that results in actual injury or death to members of an endangered or threatened species.

Respondents argue that the Secretary should have limited the purview of "harm" to direct applications of force against protected species, but the dictionary definition does not include the word "directly" or suggest in any way that only direct or willful action that leads to injury constitutes "harm."[10] Moreover, unless the statutory term "harm" encompasses indirect as well as direct injuries, the word has no meaning that does not duplicate the meaning of other words that § 3 uses to define "take." A reluctance to treat statutory terms as surplusage supports the reasonableness of the Secretary's interpretation.[11]

Second, the broad purpose of the ESA supports the Secretary's decision to extend protection against activities that cause the precise harms Congress enacted the statute to avoid. In *TVA v. Hill,* we described the Act as "the most comprehensive legislation for the preser-

---

10. Respondents and the dissent emphasize what they portray as the "established" meaning of "take" in the sense of a "wildlife take," a meaning respondents argue extends only to "the effort to exercise dominion over some creature, and the concrete effect of [sic] that creature." This limitation ill serves the statutory text, which forbids not taking "some creature" but "tak[ing] any [endangered] species"—a formidable task for even the most rapacious feudal lord. More importantly, Congress explicitly defined the operative term "take" in the ESA, no matter how much the dissent wishes otherwise, thereby obviating the need for us to probe its meaning as we must probe the meaning of the undefined subsidiary term "harm." Finally, Congress' definition of "take" includes several words—most obviously "harass," "pursue," and "wound," in addition to "harm" itself—that fit respondents' and the dissent's definition of "take" no better than does "significant habitat modification or degradation."

11. In contrast, if the statutory term "harm" encompasses such indirect means of killing and injuring wildlife as habitat modification, the other terms listed in § 3—"harass," "pursue," "hunt," "shoot," "wound," "kill," "trap," "capture," and "collect"—generally retain independent meanings. Most of those terms refer to deliberate actions more frequently than does "harm," and they therefore do not duplicate the sense of indirect causation that "harm" adds to the statute. In addition, most of the other words in the definition describe either actions from which habitat modification does not usually result (e.g., "pursue," "harass") or effects to which activities that modify habitat do not usually lead (e.g., "trap," "collect"). To the extent the Secretary's definition of "harm" may have applications that overlap with other words in the definition, that overlap reflects the broad purpose of the Act.

vation of endangered species ever enacted by any nation." Whereas predecessor statutes enacted in 1966 and 1969 had not contained any sweeping prohibition against the taking of endangered species except on federal lands, the 1973 Act applied to all land in the United States and to the Nation's territorial seas. As stated in § 2 of the Act, among its central purposes is "to provide a means whereby the ecosystems upon which endangered species and threatened species depend may be conserved.... "

In *Hill,* we construed § 7 as precluding the completion of the Tellico Dam because of its predicted impact on the survival of the snail darter. Both our holding and the language in our opinion stressed the importance of the statutory policy. "The plain intent of Congress in enacting this statute," we recognized, "was to halt and reverse the trend toward species extinction, whatever the cost. This is reflected not only in the stated policies of the Act, but in literally every section of the statute." Although the § 9 "take" prohibition was not at issue in *Hill,* we took note of that prohibition, placing particular emphasis on the Secretary's inclusion of habitat modification in his definition of "harm." In light of that provision for habitat protection, we could "not understand how TVA intends to operate Tellico Dam without 'harming' the snail darter." Congress' intent to provide comprehensive protection for endangered and threatened species supports the permissibility of the Secretary's "harm" regulation.

Respondents advance strong arguments that activities that cause minimal or unforeseeable harm will not violate the Act as construed in the "harm" regulation. Respondents, however, present a facial challenge to the regulation. Thus, they ask us to invalidate the Secretary's understanding of "harm" in every circumstance, even when an actor knows that an activity, such as draining a pond, would actually result in the extinction of a listed species by destroying its habitat. Given Congress' clear expression of the ESA's broad purpose to protect endangered and threatened wildlife, the Secretary's definition of "harm" is reasonable.[13]

Third, the fact that Congress in 1982 authorized the Secretary to issue permits for takings that § 9(a)(1)(B) would otherwise prohibit, "if such taking is incidental to, and not the purpose of, the carrying out of an otherwise lawful activity," strongly suggests that Congress understood § 9(a)(1)(B) to prohibit indirect as well as deliberate takings. The permit process requires the applicant to prepare a "conservation plan"

---

13. The dissent incorrectly asserts that the Secretary's regulation (1) "dispenses with the foreseeability of harm" and (2) "fail[s] to require injury to particular animals." As to the first assertion, the regulation merely implements the statute, and it is therefore subject to the statute's "knowingly violates" language, and ordinary requirements of proximate causation and foreseeability. Nothing in the regulation purports to weaken those requirements. To the contrary, the word "actually" in the regulation should be construed to limit the liability about which the dissent appears most concerned, liability under the statute's "otherwise violates" provision. The Secretary did not need to include "actually" to connote "but for" causation, which the other words in the definition obviously require. As to the dissent's second assertion, every term in the regulation's definition of "harm" is subservient to the phrase "an act which actually kills or injures wildlife."

that specifies how he intends to "minimize and mitigate" the "impact" of his activity on endangered and threatened species, making clear that Congress had in mind foreseeable rather than merely accidental effects on listed species. No one could seriously request an "incidental" take permit to avert § 9 liability for direct, deliberate action against a member of an endangered or threatened species, but respondents would read "harm" so narrowly that the permit procedure would have little more than that absurd purpose.... Congress' addition of the § 10 permit provision supports the Secretary's conclusion that activities not intended to harm an endangered species, such as habitat modification, may constitute unlawful takings under the ESA unless the Secretary permits them....

We need not decide whether the statutory definition of "take" compels the Secretary's interpretation of "harm," because our conclusions that Congress did not unambiguously manifest its intent to adopt respondents' view and that the Secretary's interpretation is reasonable suffice to decide this case. See generally *Chevron U.S.A. Inc. v. Natural Resources Defense Council, Inc*....

III

Our conclusion that the Secretary's definition of "harm" rests on a permissible construction of the ESA gains further support from the legislative history of the statute. The Committee Reports accompanying the bills that became the ESA do not specifically discuss the meaning of "harm," but they make clear that Congress intended "take" to apply broadly to cover indirect as well as purposeful actions....

Two endangered species bills, S. 1592 and S. 1983, were introduced in the Senate and referred to the Commerce Committee. Neither bill included the word "harm" in its definition of "take," although the definitions otherwise closely resembled the one that appeared in the bill as ultimately enacted. Senator Tunney, the floor manager of the bill in the Senate, subsequently introduced a floor amendment that added "harm" to the definition, noting that this and accompanying amendments would "help to achieve the purposes of the bill." Respondents argue that the lack of debate about the amendment that added "harm" counsels in favor of a narrow interpretation. We disagree. An obviously broad word that the Senate went out of its way to add to an important statutory definition is precisely the sort of provision that deserves a respectful reading.

The definition of "take" that originally appeared in S. 1983 differed from the definition as ultimately enacted in one other significant respect: It included "the destruction, modification, or curtailment of [the] habitat or range" of fish and wildlife. Respondents make much of the fact that the Commerce Committee removed this phrase from the "take" definition before S. 1983 went to the floor. We do not find that fact especially significant. The legislative materials contain no indication why the habitat protection provision was deleted. That provision differed greatly from the regulation at issue today. Most notably, the habitat protection provision in S. 1983 would have applied far more broadly than the regulation does because it made adverse habitat modification a categorical violation of the "take" prohibition, unbounded by the regulation's limitation to habitat modifications that actually kill or injure wildlife. The S. 1983 language also failed to qualify "modification" with the regulation's limiting adjective "significant." We do not believe the Senate's unelaborated disavowal of the provision in S. 1983 undermines the reasonableness of the more moderate habitat protection in the Secretary's "harm" regulation.[19]

The history of the 1982 amendment that gave the Secretary authority to grant permits for "incidental" takings provides further support for his reading of the Act.... Indeed, Congress had habitat modification directly in mind: Both the Senate Report and the House Conference Report identified as the model for the permit process a cooperative state-federal response to a case in California where a development project threatened incidental harm to a species of endangered butterfly by modification of its habitat. Thus, Congress in 1982 focused squarely on the aspect of the "harm" regulation at issue in this litigation. Congress' implementation of a permit program is consistent with the Secretary's interpretation of the term "harm."

19. Respondents place heavy reliance for their argument that Congress intended the § 5 land acquisition provision and not § 9 to be the ESA's remedy for habitat modification on a floor statement by Senator Tunney:

"Many species have been inadvertently exterminated by a negligent destruction of their habitat. Their habitats have been cut in size, polluted, or otherwise altered so that they are unsuitable environments for natural populations of fish and wildlife. Under this bill, we can take steps to make amends for our negligent encroachment. The Secretary would be empowered to use the land acquisition authority granted to him in certain existing legislation to acquire land for the use of the endangered species programs.... Through these land acquisition provisions, we will be able to conserve habitats necessary to protect fish and wildlife from further destruction.

"Although most endangered species are threatened primarily by the destruction of their natural habitats, a significant portion of these animals are subject to predation by man for commercial, sport, consumption, or other purposes. The provisions in S. 1983 would prohibit the commerce in or the importation, exportation, or taking of endangered species...."

Similarly, respondents emphasize a floor statement by Representative Sullivan, the House floor manager for the ESA:

"For the most part, the principal threat to animals stems from destruction of their habitat.... H.R. 37 will meet this problem by providing funds for acquisition of critical habitat.... It will also enable the Department of Agriculture to cooperate with willing landowners who desire to assist in the protection of endangered species, but who are understandably unwilling to do so at excessive cost to themselves.

"Another hazard to endangered species arises from those who would capture or kill them for pleasure or profit. There is no way that Congress can make it less pleasurable for a person to take an animal, but we can certainly make it less profitable for them to do so."

Each of these statements merely explained features of the bills that Congress eventually enacted in § 5 of the ESA and went on to discuss elements enacted in § 9. Neither statement even suggested that § 5 would be the Act's exclusive remedy for habitat modification by private landowners or that habitat modification by private landowners stood outside the ambit of § 9. Respondents' suggestion that these statements identified § 5 as the ESA's only response to habitat modification contradicts their emphasis elsewhere on the habitat protections in § 7.

IV

When it enacted the ESA, Congress delegated broad administrative and interpretive power to the Secretary.... The proper interpretation of a term such as "harm" involves a complex policy choice. When Congress has entrusted the Secretary with broad discretion, we are especially reluctant to substitute our views of wise policy for his....

Justice O'CONNOR, concurring.

My agreement with the Court is founded on two understandings. First, the challenged regulation is limited to significant habitat modification that causes actual, as opposed to hypothetical or speculative, death or injury to identifiable protected animals. Second, even setting aside difficult questions of scienter, the regulation's application is limited by ordinary principles of proximate causation, which introduce notions of foreseeability. These limitations, in my view, call into question *Palila v. Hawaii Dept. of Land and Natural Resources,* 852 F.2d 1106 (CA9 1988) (*Palila II*), and with it, many of the applications derided by the dissent. Because there is no need to strike a regulation on a facial challenge out of concern that it is susceptible of erroneous application, however, and because there are many habitat-related circumstances in which the regulation might validly apply, I join the opinion of the Court.

In my view, the regulation is limited by its terms to actions that actually kill or injure individual animals. Justice SCALIA disagrees, arguing that the harm regulation "encompasses injury inflicted, not only upon individual animals, but upon populations of the protected species." At one level, I could not reasonably quarrel with this observation; death to an individual animal always reduces the size of the population in which it lives, and in that sense, "injures" that population. But by its insight, the dissent means something else. Building upon the regulation's use of the word "breeding," Justice SCALIA suggests that the regulation facially bars significant habitat modification that actually kills or injures *hypothetical* animals (or, perhaps more aptly, causes potential additions to the population not to come into being). Because "[i]mpairment of breeding does not 'injure' living creatures," Justice SCALIA reasons, the regulation *must* contemplate application to "*a population* of animals which would otherwise have maintained or increased its numbers."

I disagree. As an initial matter, I do not find it as easy as Justice SCALIA does to dismiss the notion that significant impairment of breeding injures living creatures. To raze the last remaining ground on which the piping plover currently breeds, thereby making it impossible for any piping plovers to reproduce, would obviously injure the population (causing the species' extinction in a generation). But by completely preventing breeding, it would also injure the individual living bird, in the same way that sterilizing the creature injures the individual living bird. To "injure" is, among other things, "to impair." Webster's Ninth New Collegiate Dictionary 623 (1983). One need not subscribe to theories of "psychic harm," to recognize that to make it impossible for an animal to reproduce is to impair its most essential physical functions and to render that animal, and its genetic material, biologically obsolete. This, in my view, is actual injury.

In any event, even if impairing an animal's ability to breed were not, *in and of itself,* an injury to that animal, interference with breeding can cause an animal to suffer other, perhaps more obvious, kinds of injury. The regulation has clear application, for example, to significant habitat modification that kills or physically injures animals which, because they are in a vulnerable breeding state, do not or cannot flee or defend themselves, or to environmental pollutants that cause an animal to suffer physical complications during gestation. Breeding, feeding, and sheltering are what animals do. If significant habitat modification, by interfering with these essential behaviors, actually kills or injures an animal protected by the Act, it causes "harm" within the meaning of the regulation. In contrast to Justice SCALIA, I do not read the regulation's "breeding" reference to vitiate or somehow to qualify the clear actual death or injury requirement, or to suggest that the regulation contemplates extension to nonexistent animals.

There is no inconsistency, I should add, between this interpretation and the commentary that accompanied the amendment of the regulation to include the actual death or injury requirement. Quite the contrary. It is true, as Justice SCALIA observes, that the Fish and Wildlife Service states at one point that "harm" is not limited to "direct physical injury to an individual member of the wildlife species." But one could just as easily emphasize the word "direct" in this sentence as the word "individual." Elsewhere in the commentary, the Service makes clear that "section 9's threshold does focus on individual members of a protected species." Moreover, the Service says that the regulation has no application to speculative harm, explaining that its insertion of the word "actually" was intended "to bulwark the need for proven injury to a species due to a party's actions." That a protected animal could have eaten the leaves of a fallen tree or could, perhaps, have fruitfully multiplied in its branches is not sufficient under the regulation. Instead, as the commentary reflects, the regulation requires demonstrable effect (*i.e.,* actual injury or death) on actual, individual members of the protected species.

By the dissent's reckoning, the regulation at issue here, in conjunction with 16 U.S.C. § 1540(a)(1), imposes liability for any habitat-modifying conduct that ultimately results in the death of a protected animal, "regardless of whether that result is intended or even foreseeable, and no matter how long the chain of causality between modification and injury." Even if § 1540(a)(1) does create a strict liability regime (a question we need not decide at this juncture), I see no indication that Congress, in enacting that section, intended to dispense with ordinary principles of proximate causation. Strict liability means liability without regard to fault; it does not normally mean liability for every consequence, however remote, of one's conduct. I would not lightly assume that Congress, in enacting a strict liability statute that is silent on the causation question, has dispensed with this well-entrenched principle. In the absence of congressional abrogation of traditional principles of causation, then, private parties should be held liable under § 1540(a)(1) only if their habitat-modifying actions proximately cause death or injury to protected animals. . . .

Proximate causation is not a concept susceptible of precise definition. It is easy enough, of course, to identify the extremes. The farmer whose fertilizer is lifted by a tornado from tilled fields and deposited miles away in a wildlife refuge cannot, by any stretch of the term, be considered the proximate cause of death or injury to protected species occasioned thereby. At the same time, the landowner who drains a pond on his property, killing endangered fish in the process, would likely satisfy any formulation of the principle. . . . Proximate causation depends to a great extent on considerations of the fairness to impose liability for remote consequences. . . .

In my view, then, the "harm" regulation applies where significant habitat modification, by impairing essential behaviors, proximately (foreseeably) causes actual death or injury to identifiable animals that are protected under the Endangered Species Act. Pursuant to my interpretation, *Palila II*—under which the Court of Appeals held that a state agency committed a "taking" by permitting mouflon sheep to eat mamane-naio seedlings that, when full grown, might have fed and sheltered endangered palila—was wrongly decided according to the regulation's own terms. Destruction of the seedlings did not proximately cause actual death or injury to identifiable birds; it merely prevented the regeneration of forest land not currently sustaining actual birds. . . .

Justice SCALIA, with whom THE CHIEF JUSTICE and Justice THOMAS join, dissenting.

I think it unmistakably clear that the legislation at issue here (1) forbade the hunting and killing of endangered animals, and (2) provided federal lands and federal funds *for the acquisition of private lands,* to preserve the habitat of endangered animals. The Court's holding that the hunting and killing prohibition incidentally preserves habitat on private lands imposes unfairness to the point of financial ruin—not just upon the rich, but upon the simplest farmer who finds his land conscripted to national zoological use. I respectfully dissent.

I

[T]he regulation has three features which, for reasons I shall discuss at length below, do not comport with the statute. First, it interprets the statute to prohibit habitat modification that is no more than the cause-in-fact of death or injury to wildlife. *Any* "significant habitat modification" that in fact produces that result by "impairing essential behavioral patterns" is made unlawful, regardless of whether that result is intended or even foreseeable, and no matter how long the chain of causality between modification and injury.

Second, the regulation does not require an "act": The Secretary's officially stated position is that an *omission* will do....

The third and most important unlawful feature of the regulation is that it encompasses injury inflicted, not only upon individual animals, but upon populations of the protected species. "Injury" in the regulation includes "significantly impairing essential behavioral patterns, including breeding." Impairment of breeding does not "injure" living creatures; it prevents them from propagating, thus "injuring" *a population* of animals which would otherwise have maintained or increased its numbers....

None of these three features of the regulation can be found in the statutory provisions supposed to authorize it. The term "harm" in § 1532(19) has no legal force of its own. An indictment or civil complaint that charged the defendant with "harming" an animal protected under the Act would be dismissed as defective, for the only *operative* term in the statute is to "take." If "take" were not elsewhere defined in the Act, none could dispute what it means, for the term is as old as the law itself. To "take," when applied to wild animals, means to reduce those animals, by killing or capturing, to human control. This is just the sense in which "take" is used elsewhere in federal legislation and treaty. And that meaning fits neatly with the rest of § 1538(a)(1), which makes it unlawful not only to take protected species, but also to import or export them; to possess, sell, deliver, carry, transport, or ship any taken species; and to transport, sell, or offer to sell them in interstate or foreign commerce. The taking prohibition, in other words, is only part of the regulatory plan of § 1538(a)(1), which covers all the stages of the process by which protected wildlife is reduced to man's dominion and made the object of profit. It is obvious that "take" in this sense—a term of art deeply embedded in the statutory and common law concerning wildlife—describes a class of acts (not omissions) done directly and intentionally (not indirectly and by accident) to particular animals (not populations of animals).

The Act's definition of "take" does expand the word slightly (and not unusually), so as to make clear that it includes not just a completed taking, but the process of taking, and all of the acts that are customarily identified with or accompany that process ("to harass, harm, pursue, hunt, shoot, wound, kill, trap, capture, or collect"); and so as to include attempts. § 1532(19). The tempting fallacy—which the Court commits with abandon, see *ante,* at 2413, n. 10—is to assume that *once defined,* "take" loses any significance, and it is only the definition that matters. The Court treats the statute as though Congress had directly enacted the § 1532(19) definition as a self-executing prohibition, and had not enacted § 1538(a)(1)(B) at all. But § 1538(a)(1)(B) *is* there, and if the terms contained in the definitional section are susceptible of two readings, one of which comports with the standard meaning of "take" as used in application to wildlife, and one of which does not, an agency regulation that adopts the latter reading is necessarily unreasonable, for it reads the defined term "take"—the only operative term—out of the statute altogether.

That is what has occurred here. The verb "harm" has a *range* of meaning: "to cause injury" at its broadest, "to do hurt or damage" in a narrower and more direct sense.... To define "harm" as an act or omission that, however remotely, "actually kills or injures" a population of wildlife through habitat modification is to choose a meaning that makes nonsense of the word that "harm" defines—requiring us to accept that a farmer who tills his field and causes erosion that makes silt run into a nearby river which depletes oxygen and thereby "impairs [the] breeding" of protected fish has "taken" or "attempted to take" the fish. It should take the strongest evidence to make us believe that Congress has defined a term in a manner repugnant to its ordinary and traditional sense.

Here the evidence shows the opposite. "Harm" is merely one of 10 prohibitory words in § 1532(19), and the other 9 fit the ordinary meaning of "take" perfectly. To "harass, pursue, hunt, shoot, wound, kill, trap, capture, or collect" are all affirmative acts (the provision itself describes them as "conduct," see § 1532(19)) which are directed immediately and intentionally against a particular animal—not acts or omissions that indirectly and accidentally cause injury to a population of animals.... What the nine other words in § 1532(19) have in common—and share with the narrower meaning of "harm" described above, but not with the Secretary's ruthless dilation of the word—is the sense of affirmative conduct intentionally directed against a particular animal or animals.

I am not the first to notice this fact, or to draw the conclusion that it compels. In 1981 the Solicitor of the Fish and Wildlife Service delivered a legal opinion on § 1532(19) that is in complete agreement with my reading:

> "The Act's definition of 'take' contains a list of actions that illustrate the intended scope of the term.... With the possible exception of 'harm,' these terms all represent forms of conduct that are directed against and likely to injure or kill *individual* wildlife. Under the principle of statutory construction, *ejusdem generis,* ... the term 'harm' should be interpreted to include only those actions that are directed against, and likely to injure or kill, individual wildlife." Memorandum of Apr. 17, reprinted in 46 Fed.Reg. 29490, 29491 (1981) (emphasis in original)....

So far I have discussed only the immediate statutory text bearing on the regulation. But the definition of "take" in § 1532(19) applies "[f]or the purposes of this chapter," that is, it governs the meaning of the word *as used everywhere in the Act.* Thus, the Secretary's interpretation of "harm" is wrong if it does not fit with the use of "take" throughout the Act. And it does not. In § 1540(e)(4)(B), for example, Congress provided for the forfeiture of "[a]ll guns, traps, nets, and other equipment ... used to aid the taking, possessing, selling, [etc.]" of protected animals.

This listing plainly relates to "taking" in the ordinary sense. If environmental modification were part (and necessarily a major part) of taking, as the Secretary maintains, one would have expected the list to include "plows, bulldozers, and backhoes." As another example, § 1539(e)(1) exempts "the taking of any endangered species" by Alaskan Indians and Eskimos "if such taking is primarily for subsistence purposes"; and provides that "[n]on-edible byproducts of species taken pursuant to this section may be sold ... when made into authentic native articles of handicrafts and clothing." ...

III

[One] point the Court stresses in its response [to this dissent] seems to me a belated mending of its holding. It apparently *concedes* that the statute requires injury *to particular animals* rather than merely to populations of animals. The Court then rejects my contention that the regulation ignores this requirement, since, it says, "every term in the regulation's definition of 'harm' is subservient to the phrase 'an act which actually kills or injures wildlife.' "[T]his reading is incompatible with the regulation's specification of impairment of "breeding" as one of the *modes* of "kill[ing] or injur[ing] wildlife."[5]

But since the Court is reading the regulation and the statute incorrectly in other respects, it may as well introduce this novelty as well—law à la carte. As I understand the regulation that the Court has created and held consistent with the statute that it has also created, habitat modification can constitute a "taking," but only if it results in the killing or harming of *individual animals,* and only if that consequence is the direct result of the modification. This means that the destruction of privately owned habitat that is essential, not for the feeding or nesting, but for the *breeding,* of butterflies, would not violate the Act, since it would not harm or kill any living butterfly. I, too, think it would not violate the Act—not for the utterly unsupported reason that habitat modifications fall outside the regulation if they happen not to kill or injure a living animal, but for the textual reason that only action directed at living animals constitutes a "take."

* * *

The Endangered Species Act is a carefully considered piece of legislation that forbids all persons to hunt or harm endangered animals, but places upon the public at large, rather than upon fortuitously

---

5. Justice O'Connor supposes that an "impairment of breeding" intrinsically injures an animal because "to make it impossible for an animal to reproduce is to impair its most essential physical functions and to render that animal, and its genetic material, biologically obsolete." This imaginative construction does achieve the result of extending "impairment of breeding" to individual animals; but only at the expense of also expanding "injury" to include elements beyond physical harm to individual animals. For surely the only harm to the individual animal from impairment of that "essential function" is not the failure of issue (which harms only the issue), but the psychic harm of perceiving that it will leave this world with no issue (assuming, of course, that the animal in question, perhaps an endangered species of slug, is capable of such painful sentiments). ...

accountable individual landowners, the cost of preserving the habitat of endangered species. There is neither textual support for, nor even evidence of congressional consideration of, the radically different disposition contained in the regulation that the Court sustains. For these reasons, I respectfully dissent.

Notes and Questions

1. After *Sweet Home*, it is clear that the services' regulation is valid on its face, but is it clear how it can be applied? In the *Palila* case, described in *Sweet Home*, the Ninth Circuit had found a violation of Section 9 in the destruction of habitat that was necessary for the *recovery* of a species, but not for its survival. Justice O'Connor says that the *Sweet Home* decision is inconsistent with *Palila*. What do you think? The regulation says that significant habitat modification qualifies as "harm," if "it actually kills or injures wildlife by significantly impairing essential behavioral patterns, including breeding, feeding, or sheltering." Does this mean that *any* significant impairment of "essential behavioral patterns" necessarily kills or injures wildlife, or does it mean that *when* significant impairment of "essential behavioral patterns" actually kills or injures wildlife, only then does habitat modification become "harm"? If the latter, how do you determine the causal connection between the impairment and actual harm? Draining the pond so that all the endangered fish die is an easy case. A more likely scenario is the cutting of trees which are habitat to endangered birds. There is other habitat available to them, but their total habitat has been reduced, putting them under greater stress. Do you need to find a dead bird? How about expert testimony by wildlife biologists that such habitat destruction would "injure or kill wildlife"? *See, e.g., Marbled Murrelet v. Babbitt*, 83 F.3d 1060 (9th Cir. 1996)(significant impairment of breeding and sheltering is a take). How should the FWS interpret its regulation? Under a Republican President? Under a Democratic President?

2. Whatever the intentions of the original drafters of Section 9, it is fairly clear that the amendments in 1982 to Section 10, providing for the Secretary to grant an incidental take permit to private persons who obtain an approved conservation plan, understood that Section 9 "takes" could include results of habitat modification. This, of course, is not surprising, because the FWS regulations had always so provided, and there were some development projects blocked by assertions of the FWS that they would result in habitat modification violating Section 9. These assertions gained some publicity and were an important cause of the amendments providing for permits. How should that later congressional understanding affect the interpretation of the original language?

3. The introductory material on Section 9 noted that its prohibitions are broader with respect to fish and wildlife than to plants. Thus, any "take" of endangered fish and wildlife is prohibited, but harm to endangered plants is prohibited only if the plants are on federal property or the activity would violate state law. Why do you suppose the ESA provides such limited protection to plants compared to fish and wildlife, especially because most hopes for new drugs identify plants as possible sources? Would the explanation for this different treatment support the dissent's view of the meaning of "take" in *Sweet Home*?

4. The introductory material on Section 9 also emphasized that the statute itself only provides Section 9 protections to *endangered* species. However, Section 4(d) requires the Secretary to adopt "such regulations as he deems necessary and advisable to provide for the conservation of [threatened] species," and Section 9 prohibits any person from violating those regulations. While the original conception behind Section 4(d) was probably to tailor protections to the particular needs of a newly listed threatened species, traditionally the FWS has by general regulation extended all the protections afforded endangered species to threatened species. NMFS, on the other hand, has adopted species specific Section 4(d) protections. In recent years there has been increasing interest in using the threat of extending Section 4(d) regulations to newly listed threatened species as an incentive to obtain state and private conservation measures, that if undertaken, would justify the services to find that it is not necessary to adopt the full range of Section 4(d) protections to the species.

5. Section 9 clearly prohibits government action that itself takes an endangered fish or wildlife species, and courts have also routinely held that government action that authorizes private action, which in turn would take an endangered fish or wildlife species, likewise is prohibited by Section 9. *See, e.g., Defenders of Wildlife v. EPA*, 882 F.2d 1294 (8th Cir. 1989)(finding EPA's registration of certain pesticides violated Section 9 because those pesticides were causing the death of endangered species). Courts have not distinguished between federal and state actors in this regard, *see, e.g., Loggerhead Turtle v. County Council of Volusia County*, 148 F.3d 1231 (11th Cir. 1998)(failure of county to ban beach driving and beachfront lighting during loggerhead sea turtle mating season constituted take). There may, however, be a problem in the latter regard. Recall from Chapter 1 that the Supreme Court has interpreted the Tenth Amendment to prohibit the federal government from in effect requiring states to administer federal laws, or as the Court put it, from commandeering state governments. By interpreting the ESA in the *Loggerhead Turtle* case to require the county to regulate beachfront lighting to protect the turtles, however, the Eleventh Circuit, which did not discuss the issue, would seem to be running afoul of that constitutional limitation. *See also Strahan v. Coxe*, 127 F.3d 155 (1st Cir. 1997)(Massachusetts permitting of lobster pot and gillnet fishing violated Section 9 with respect to northern right whales). The irony in *Strahan* is that if Massachusetts abandoned its issuance of permits for lobster pot and gillnet fishing, which it regulates to protect lobster and certain fish species, it would not be engaged in the permitting of the activities that cause the harm to the endangered species. In other words, extending Section 9 liability to states and counties for permitting activities that may harm endangered species might lead states and counties simply to abandon their permitting schemes, which would not increase protection for endangered species, but which could undermine other environmental protection. In Oregon, for example, there was a lawsuit against the state board of forestry under Section 9 for issuing permits for steep slope timber cutting, which allegedly increases siltation of streams, adversely affecting listed salmonids. This permit scheme was adopted to protect against logging that results in dangerous landslides, but in response to the lawsuit, the board rescinded its

regulation requiring a permit, thereby allowing steep slope timber cutting without any permit.

E.   Section 10

Section 10 of the ESA, 16 U.S.C. § 1539, provides exceptions to the prohibitions of Section 9. We have already seen two exceptions to Section 9 arising out of Section 7: incidental take statements contained in Biological Opinions and takings pursuant to an exception granted by the Endangered Species Committee. Section 10 contains several additional exceptions. The first provides for the Secretary to permit takes for scientific purposes or to enhance the species. 16 U.S.C. § 1539(a)(1)(A). Thus, for example, the Secretary can adopt regulations providing for the capture of endangered species for research or breeding purposes. Another provides an exemption for persons that entered into a contract with respect to a species before it was listed, if they would suffer "substantial economic hardship" as a result. 16 U.S.C. § 1539(b). There is also a general exemption for Alaskan natives and residents in Alaskan native villages who take species for subsistence purposes. 16 U.S.C. § 1539(e). The Secretary, however, may adopt specific regulations governing and limiting such subsistence takings. *Id.*

The most significant exception was added in the 1982 amendments and allows the Secretary to grant an incidental take permit when a person obtains approval of a habitat conservation plan (HCP). 16 U.S.C. § 1539(a)(2). Like the incidental takes authorized in biological opinions under Section 7 when there is a federal action, Section 10 provides a procedure whereby private persons may also obtain an exemption from Section 9 for takes incidental to other economic activity, e.g., development projects and timber harvesting. In order to obtain approval of an HCP, a person files an application that identifies what the impacts of the project will be, what steps the applicant will take to minimize and mitigate those impacts, what alternatives the applicant considered that would have less impacts and why those alternatives are not feasible, and such other information as the Secretary requires. Because granting the permit is a federal action, consideration of the proposed HCP requires consultation under Section 7 of the ESA and NEPA analysis. In addition, the process includes public involvement and comment on the proposed HCP. In short, the process is extensive and expensive for the applicant. Approval is granted if the Secretary finds that the HCP will be carried out, including the minimization and mitigation of incidental takes and the inclusion of any measures required by the Secretary, and that as implemented the take will "not appreciably reduce the likelihood of the survival and recovery of the species in the wild." 16 U.S.C. § 1539(a)(2)(B).

The substantial commitment of time and resources to the development and approval of an HCP has been a major disincentive for private persons to seek these permits, especially for limited projects. Indeed, by 1992, only 14 HCPs had been approved, and most of these involved large undertakings, sometimes initiated by state or local planning agencies.

Nevertheless, environmentalists have insisted upon the full process in light of the potential effects of an HCP, which may run as long as 50 to 100 years. Suits have been brought by environmental groups challenging the approval of HCPs, and courts have been vigilant in their reviews. *See, e.g., Gerber v. Norton,* 294 F.3d 173 (D.C. Cir. 2002)(HCP for housing subdivision affecting an endangered squirrel overturned).

The Clinton administration made a number of efforts to facilitate the HCP process and most controversially to create additional incentives for persons to seek them. It adopted what it called the "No Surprises" rule, which in essence provided that, so long as the permittee complied with the HCP, the federal government would not impose additional financial requirements or additional land use restrictions on the permittee, *even if new information was developed indicating the insufficiency of the original HCP.* Instead, the government would undertake the financial commitments necessary to overcome any insufficiency in the HCP. This policy had an immediate effect, resulting in hundreds of new HCPs.

Environmental groups sued, alleging that this policy had been enacted without following the proper procedures and that it violated the ESA. A district court in the District of Columbia agreed that the proper procedures had not been followed and enjoined the "no surprises" rule until the government went through a new notice-and-comment procedure. *Spirit of Sage Council v. Norton,* 294 F.Supp.2d 67 (D.D.C. 2003). The government concluded that process in 2004 and repromulgated the rule effective in January 2005. *See* 69 Fed. Reg. 71723 (2004).

Section 10 also contains a provision governing the treatment of experimental populations introduced into areas beyond the current range of the species. 16 U.S.C. § 1539(j). This has been most notable and controversial with respect to the reintroduction of wolves into areas they historically occupied but from which they have been extirpated. The Secretary is authorized to release populations of endangered or threatened species into areas outside their current range if the Secretary finds that such release will further the conservation of the species. Before making the release, the Secretary must determine whether the population to be released is "essential to the continued existence" of the species. 16 U.S.C. § 1539(j)(2)(B). Experimental populations have been controversial both from an environmental and ranching perspective. Environmentalists have concerns about experimental populations, because members of these populations are not entitled to all the protections afforded members of the same species that are not members of an experimental population. For example, all experimental populations are treated as threatened, even though the species might be endangered. 16 U.S.C. § 1539(j)(2)(C). In addition, in order to make experimental populations politically acceptable, further allowances may be granted, such as allowing the harassment of wolves found on private land and even killing of wolves injuring or killing livestock. At the same time, ranchers are concerned about wolves attacking their livestock, and while they are allowed to kill wolves injuring or killing livestock, the regulations require the rancher to be able to provide proof in the form of an injured animal to justify such takes.

One of the requirements for the introduction of an experimental population is that it be "wholly separate geographically from nonexperimental populations of the same species." 16 U.S.C. § 1539(j)(1). The purpose of this requirement was to ensure that members of the species naturally in an area would not effectively have their protection diminished because they would be intermingled with and indistinguishable from the experimental population. This requirement led to claims from those opposing introductions that there were members of the species already present in the area. The FWS regulation, however, interpreted the term "population" to mean a self-sustaining group in common spatial arrangement, not just individual interlopers. Both the Tenth and Ninth Circuits have found that interpretation reasonable. *See Wyoming Farm Bureau Federation v. Babbitt*, 199 F.3d 1224 (10th Cir. 2000); *United States v. McKittrick*, 142 F.3d 1170 (9th Cir. 1998).

F.   Section 11

Section 11 of the ESA provides the penalties and enforcement mechanisms for violations of the Act. While environmental enforcement issues are dealt with separately in Chapter 6, it is worth noting here that the ESA has a full panoply of enforcement mechanisms, ranging from injunctive relief and administratively imposed civil penalties to criminal penalties. In addition, the ESA has one of the broadest ranging citizen suit provisions, allowing "any person" to bring suit against "any person" alleged to be in violation "of any provision" of the ESA. 16 U.S.C. § 1540(g). Section 11 even has a provision authorizing the payment of rewards to persons to provide information leading to an arrest, conviction, or civil penalty. 16 U.S.C. § 1540(d).

A recurring issue in the enforcement of the ESA is what knowledge the person violating Section 9 must have. The statute refers to a person "who knowingly violates" the statute or regulations. 16 U.S.C. § 1540(a)(1) & (b)(1). The original statute used the phrase "willfully violates." As a result, the courts have uniformly interpreted the "knowingly" requirement to mean only that the person knows he or she is killing or harming an animal; the person need not know that killing the animal is unlawful or that the animal is a member of a listed species.

Problem

A rancher in Montana would like to subdivide some of his 7000 acre ranch into "ranchette" parcels with log cabin McMansions and sell them to wannabe cowboys from the East and California. A surveyor he hires discovers a number of isolated Spaldings Catchfly, a threatened species of plant, on the properties surveyed for ranchettes. A county official mentions to the rancher that the Canada Lynx, a threatened wildlife species, famous for its unwillingness to share habitat with humans, has been sighted in the area. The rancher has heard horror stories about the Endangered Species Act, including that another Montana rancher was convicted and sentenced to six months in prison for killing a wolf. He contacts you in a panic, wondering if his retirement plans have been scuttled by "them damn burricats in Washington DC!"

Assess what further information you need, what the impacts will be on his plans depending upon that information, and what alternatives he might have.

II. PROTECTING WETLANDS

It is only relatively recently that we have come to believe that there is a need to protect wetlands. Throughout much of our history wetlands were viewed at best as worthless. For example, in argument to the Supreme Court in 1829 a wetland was described as "one of those sluggish reptile streams, that do not run but creep, and which, wherever it passes, spreads its venom, and destroys the health of all those who inhabit its marshes." *See* Willson v. Black–Bird Creek Marsh Co., 27 U.S. (2 Pet.) 245, 7 L.Ed. 412 (1829). Moreover, because wetlands are particularly fertile, being one of the most productive ecosystems in the world, when they are drained they make wonderful farmland. Thus, it is not surprising that until recently government policy at all levels encouraged the draining of wetlands. Of the approximately 221 million acres of wetlands that existed in the 1780s in what is now the lower 48 states, today there are only about 105 million acres, 95% of which are freshwater wetlands. In the beginning years of federal regulation there were an average of 260,000 acres a year more lost, almost all of them from freshwater wetlands. Today the estimated losses are down to about 60,000 acres a year, which is significant improvement, but still short of the "no net loss" of wetlands pledged by the first President Bush in 1989.

We now recognize the important role that wetlands play in the environment. As stated by EPA:

> Wetlands play an integral role in the ecology of the watershed. The combination of shallow water, high levels of nutrients, and primary productivity is ideal for the development of organisms that form the base of the food web and feed many species of fish, amphibians, shellfish, and insects. Many species of birds and mammals rely on wetlands for food, water, and shelter, especially during migration and breeding. Wetlands' microbes, plants, and wildlife are part of global cycles for water, nitrogen, and sulfur. Furthermore, scientists are beginning to realize that atmospheric maintenance may be an additional wetlands function. Wetlands store carbon within their plant communities and soil instead of releasing it to the atmosphere as carbon dioxide. Thus wetlands help to moderate global climate conditions.

http://www.epa.gov/owow/wetlands/vital/nature.html (visited on 3/10/ 2007). More than one-third of the United States' threatened and endangered species live only in wetlands, and nearly half use wetlands at some point in their lives. http://www.epa.gov/owow/wetlands/fish.html (visited on 3/10/2007). In addition, wetlands can act as buffers against flooding, because they slow the velocity of the water heading toward rivers during spring thaws or after heavy rains, and against shoreline erosion caused by wave action. Wetlands also act as filters for runoff, capturing pollutants and sediment that otherwise would end up in rivers, lakes, and the ocean. A 1990 study reported by EPA indicated that the Congaree Bottomland Hardwood Swamp in South Carolina performed filtering functions equivalent to a $5 million waste water treatment plant. Many of the species that live in or are dependent on wetlands are significant economic resources. For example, muskrats live in wetlands, and the nation's harvest of muskrat pelts alone is worth over $70 million annually. Wetlands are also an important site for recreation, especially for fishers, birdwatchers, and hunters.

Beginning in the 1970s and with greater emphasis added in the 1980s, the federal government began to regulate the destruction of wetlands. Two laws in particular are involved: Section 404 of the Clean Water Act and the Swampbuster provisions of the Food Security Act of 1985. The first and most important is Section 404. 33 U.S.C. § 1344.

A.   Section 404 of the Clean Water Act

Recall from the portion on the Clean Water Act from Chapter 3 that that Act prohibits the discharge of any pollutant by any person without a permit. There we discussed the NPDES program under Section 402, whereby persons can obtain a permit from EPA (or an authorized state) to discharge pollutants under certain restrictions and standards. Section 404 provides a different permit for a specified subset of pollutants–"dredged or fill material." That is, if the pollutant involved is either dredged or fill material, the discharger needs a permit under Section 404 rather than under Section 402. The 404 permit is granted by the Corps of Engineers (or an authorized state). The differing treatment of dredged and fill material under the Act reflected the Corps' long history both with respect to dredging and the permitting of obstructions to navigation under Sections 9 and 10 of the Rivers and Harbors Act of 1899. 33 U.S.C. §§ 403 and 407.

While the CWA does not define either "dredged material" or "fill material," the Corps of Engineers in its regulations have defined "dredged material" as "material that is excavated or dredged from waters of the United States," 33 CFR § 323.2(c), and "fill material" as "material placed in waters of the United States where the material has the effect of: (i) Replacing any portion of a water of the United States with dry land; or (ii) Changing the bottom elevation of any portion of a water of the United States," but not including trash or garbage. 33 CFR § 323.2(e).[3] While one might imagine that the purpose of Section 404 in

3. Earlier the regulation had excluded "waste" from fill material, rather than "trash or garbage." This led to environmentalists challenging the Corps' ability to permit the discharge of mining overburden from mountaintop removal mining into valleys and headwaters of various streams. The intent of the litigation was to require EPA to be the permitting agency under the NPDES program, rather than the Corps

light of its history together with these definitions was to continue to assure the navigability of the Nation's waters by restricting the placement of dredge spoil (the material taken from the bed of a water as a result of dredging) or any other material that might affect the depth or width of a body of water, Section 404 has become the primary regulatory protection of the nation's wetlands.

1. What Waters are Covered?

Earlier, in the chapter on pollution prevention under the Clean Water Act, we found that the coverage of the Act depends upon whether something is a "navigable water," because only discharges into "navigable waters" are regulated by the Act. The term "navigable waters" actually has quite a history. It was used at least as long ago as 1899 in the Rivers and Harbors Act, which historically was the forerunner to the Clean Water Act. In that Act, for example, persons could not deposit refuse in any navigable water of the United States without the permission of the Secretary of the Army (as the head of the Corps of Engineers, the agency responsible for maintaining the navigability of waters). 33 U.S.C. § 407. The Corps and judicial interpretation had evolved a working definition of navigable waters as "those waters of the United States which are subject to the ebb and flow of the tide, and/or are presently, or have been in the past, or may be in the future susceptible for use for purposes of interstate or foreign commerce."

In enacting the CWA, however, Congress was less than precise in describing the extent of that Act's jurisdiction. Earlier versions of the bill that became the Act defined the term "navigable waters" as "navigable waters of the United States," precisely the term used by the Corps under the Rivers and Harbors Act, but the legislative history is clear that Congress wanted the CWA's jurisdiction to reach waters that the Corps had not historically regulated under the Rivers and Harbors Act. After all, the CWA was not about navigation; it was about water quality. Thus, the final bill that became law simply dropped the word "navigable" from the definition, leaving the definition of "navigable waters" as "the waters of the United States." 33 U.S.C. § 1362(7). The Corps did not distinguish this definition from its historical term, and its initial regulation under the CWA simply imported its historical definition from the Rivers and Harbors Act to the CWA. EPA, however, read the statute differently and adopted a broader definition to which the Corps acceded in 1975. Their regulations then both defined "navigable waters" to include not only waters navigable in fact but also tributaries of such waters, interstate waters and their tributaries, nonnavigable intrastate waters whose use or misuse could affect interstate commerce, and wetlands adjacent to the above waters. The extension of jurisdiction to

under the 404 program, because of a perception that EPA would be more environmentally protective. The Corps' interpretation of "waste" as limited to garbage and trash and not including "mining waste" was upheld in *Kentuckians for Common-* *wealth, Inc. v. Rivenburgh,* 317 F.3d 425 (4th Cir. 2003). In any case, the Corps and EPA amended their regulations to specify the exception was limited to trash and garbage. Thus, the Corps is the permitting agency for such valley fills.

wetlands was controversial, especially because it interfered with the traditional practice of filling wetlands for both industrial, commercial, and residential development as well as for expanding acreage for farming.

As a result, there were attempts by some in Congress to amend the CWA to limit coverage of wetlands in the Act. That attempt failed, and instead in 1977 Congress amended the Act to exempt certain activities (such as "normal farming, silviculture, and ranching activities"), rather than certain areas. Nevertheless, the controversy did not go away, and in 1985 the issue reached the Supreme Court.

UNITED STATES v. RIVERSIDE BAYVIEW HOMES, INC.

Supreme Court of the United States, 1985.
474 U.S. 121, 106 S.Ct. 455, 88 L.Ed.2d 419.

Justice WHITE delivered the opinion of the Court.

This case presents the question whether the Clean Water Act (CWA), together with certain regulations promulgated under its authority by the Army Corps of Engineers, authorizes the Corps to require landowners to obtain permits from the Corps before discharging fill material into wetlands adjacent to navigable bodies of water and their tributaries.

I

... After initially construing the Act to cover only waters navigable in fact, in 1975 the Corps issued interim final regulations redefining "the waters of the United States" to include not only actually navigable waters but also tributaries of such waters, interstate waters and their tributaries, and nonnavigable intrastate waters whose use or misuse could affect interstate commerce. More importantly for present purposes, the Corps construed the Act to cover all "freshwater wetlands" that were adjacent to other covered waters. A "freshwater wetland" [is] defined ... as follows: "The term 'wetlands' means those areas that are inundated or saturated by surface or ground water at a frequency and duration sufficient to support, and that under normal circumstances do support, a prevalence of vegetation typically adapted for life in saturated soil.... "[2]

Respondent Riverside Bayview Homes, Inc. (hereafter respondent), owns 80 acres of low-lying, marshy land near the shores of Lake St. Clair in Macomb County, Michigan. In 1976, respondent began to place fill materials on its property as part of its preparations for construction of a housing development. The Corps of Engineers, believing that the property was an "adjacent wetland" under the 1975 regulation defining "waters of the United States," filed suit in the United States District Court

---

2. The regulations also cover certain wetlands not necessarily adjacent to other waters. These provisions are not now before us.

for the Eastern District of Michigan, seeking to enjoin respondent from filling the property without the permission of the Corps.

[The District Court enjoined the filling, but the Court of Appeals reversed.] The court construed the Corps' regulation to exclude from the category of adjacent wetlands—and hence from that of "waters of the United States"—wetlands that were not subject to flooding by adjacent navigable waters at a frequency sufficient to support the growth of aquatic vegetation. . . . The court also expressed its doubt that Congress, in granting the Corps jurisdiction to regulate the filling of "navigable waters," intended to allow regulation of wetlands that were not the result of flooding by navigable waters. Under the court's reading of the regulation, respondent's property was not within the Corps' jurisdiction, because its semiaquatic characteristics were not the result of frequent flooding by the nearby navigable waters. Respondent was therefore free to fill the property without obtaining a permit.

We granted certiorari to consider the proper interpretation of the Corps' regulation defining "waters of the United States" and the scope of the Corps' jurisdiction under the Clean Water Act, both of which were called into question by the Sixth Circuit's ruling. We now reverse.

II

The question whether the Corps of Engineers may demand that respondent obtain a permit before placing fill material on its property is primarily one of regulatory and statutory interpretation: we must determine whether respondent's property is an "adjacent wetland" within the meaning of the applicable regulation, and, if so, whether the Corps' jurisdiction over "navigable waters" gives it statutory authority to regulate discharges of fill material into such a wetland. [On the question of regulatory interpretation, the Court concluded that the Corps' interpretation of its regulation was correct, and there was no need under the regulation for the water in the wetland to come from flooding as opposed to saturation. Accordingly,] if the regulation itself is valid as a construction of the term "waters of the United States" as used in the Clean Water Act, a question which we now address, the property falls within the scope of the Corps' jurisdiction over "navigable waters" under § 404 of the Act.

IV

A

An agency's construction of a statute it is charged with enforcing is entitled to deference if it is reasonable and not in conflict with the expressed intent of Congress. Accordingly, our review is limited to the question whether it is reasonable, in light of the language, policies, and legislative history of the Act for the Corps to exercise jurisdiction over wetlands adjacent to but not regularly flooded by rivers, streams, and other hydrographic features more conventionally identifiable as "waters."[8]

On a purely linguistic level, it may appear unreasonable to classify "lands," wet or otherwise, as "waters." Such a simplistic response, however, does justice neither to the problem faced by the Corps in defining the scope of its authority under § 404(a) nor to the realities of the problem of water pollution that the Clean Water Act was intended to combat. In determining the limits of its power to regulate discharges under the Act, the Corps must necessarily choose some point at which water ends and land begins. Our common experience tells us that this is often no easy task: the transition from water to solid ground is not necessarily or even typically an abrupt one. Rather, between open waters and dry land may lie shallows, marshes, mudflats, swamps, bogs—in short, a huge array of areas that are not wholly aquatic but nevertheless fall far short of being dry land. Where on this continuum to find the limit of "waters" is far from obvious.

Faced with such a problem of defining the bounds of its regulatory authority, an agency may appropriately look to the legislative history and underlying policies of its statutory grants of authority. Neither of these sources provides unambiguous guidance for the Corps in this case, but together they do support the reasonableness of the Corps' approach of defining adjacent wetlands as "waters" within the meaning of § 404(a). Section 404 originated as part of the Federal Water Pollution Control Act Amendments of 1972, which constituted a comprehensive legislative attempt "to restore and maintain the chemical, physical, and biological integrity of the Nation's waters...." This objective incorporated a broad, systemic view of the goal of maintaining and improving water quality: as the House Report on the legislation put it, "the word 'integrity' ... refers to a condition in which the natural structure and function of ecosystems is [are] maintained." Protection of aquatic ecosystems, Congress recognized, demanded broad federal authority to control pollution, for "[w]ater moves in hydrologic cycles and it is essential that discharge of pollutants be controlled at the source."

In keeping with these views, Congress chose to define the waters covered by the Act broadly. Although the Act prohibits discharges into "navigable waters," the Act's definition of "navigable waters" as "the waters of the United States" makes it clear that the term "navigable" as used in the Act is of limited import. In adopting this definition of "navigable waters," Congress evidently intended to repudiate limits that had been placed on federal regulation by earlier water pollution control statutes and to exercise its powers under the Commerce Clause to regulate at least some waters that would not be deemed "navigable" under the classical understanding of that term.

8. We are not called upon to address the question of the authority of the Corps to regulate discharges of fill material into wetlands that are not adjacent to bodies of open water, and we do not express any opinion on that question.

Of course, it is one thing to recognize that Congress intended to allow regulation of waters that might not satisfy traditional tests of navigability; it is another to assert that Congress intended to abandon traditional notions of "waters" and include in that term "wetlands" as well. Nonetheless, the evident breadth of congressional concern for protection of water quality and aquatic ecosystems suggests that it is reasonable for the Corps to interpret the term "waters" to encompass wetlands adjacent to waters as more conventionally defined. Following the lead of the Environmental Protection Agency, the Corps has determined that wetlands adjacent to navigable waters do as a general matter play a key role in protecting and enhancing water quality:

> The regulation of activities that cause water pollution cannot rely on ... artificial lines ... but must focus on all waters that together form the entire aquatic system. Water moves in hydrologic cycles, and the pollution of this part of the aquatic system, regardless of whether it is above or below an ordinary high water mark, or mean high tide line, will affect the water quality of the other waters within that aquatic system.

> For this reason, the landward limit of Federal jurisdiction under Section 404 must include any adjacent wetlands that form the border of or are in reasonable proximity to other waters of the United States, as these wetlands are part of this aquatic system.

We cannot say that the Corps' conclusion that adjacent wetlands are inseparably bound up with the "waters" of the United States—based as it is on the Corps' and EPA's technical expertise—is unreasonable. In view of the breadth of federal regulatory authority contemplated by the Act itself and the inherent difficulties of defining precise bounds to regulable waters, the Corps' ecological judgment about the relationship between waters and their adjacent wetlands provides an adequate basis for a legal judgment that adjacent wetlands may be defined as waters under the Act.

This holds true even for wetlands that are not the result of flooding or permeation by water having its source in adjacent bodies of open water. The Corps has concluded that wetlands may affect the water quality of adjacent lakes, rivers, and streams even when the waters of those bodies do not actually inundate the wetlands. For example, wetlands that are not flooded by adjacent waters may still tend to drain into those waters. In such circumstances, the Corps has concluded that wetlands may serve to filter and purify water draining into adjacent bodies of water, and to slow the flow of surface runoff into lakes, rivers, and streams and thus prevent flooding and erosion. In addition, adjacent wetlands may "serve significant natural biological functions, including food chain production, general habitat, and nesting, spawning, rearing and resting sites for aquatic ... species." In short, the Corps has concluded that wetlands adjacent to lakes, rivers, streams, and other bodies of water may function as integral parts of the aquatic environment even when the moisture creating the wetlands does not find its source in the adjacent bodies of water. Again, we cannot say that the Corps' judgment on these matters is unreasonable, and we therefore conclude that a definition of "waters of the United States" encompassing all wetlands adjacent to other bodies of water over which the Corps has jurisdiction is a permissible interpretation of the Act. Because respondent's property is part of a wetland that actually abuts on a navigable waterway, respondent was required to have a permit in this case.[9]

Notes and Comments

1. *Riverside Bayview* settled the question whether wetlands could be "waters" of the United States, and it upheld the Corps' interpretation that adjacent wetlands could be covered by the Act. Nevertheless, the decision left a number of questions unsettled.

2. For example, in *Riverside Bayview Homes*, the Court mentions that the Corps and EPA regulations defining "waters of the United States" included "isolated wetlands and lakes, intermittent streams, prairie potholes, and other waters that are not part of a tributary system to interstate waters or to navigable waters of the United States, the degradation or destruction of which could affect interstate commerce." The regulations gave three examples of such waters, which, if harmed, could affect interstate commerce: those which are or could be used by interstate or foreign travelers for recreational or other purposes, those from which fish or shellfish are or could be taken and sold in interstate or foreign commerce, and those which are used or could be used for industrial purposes by industries in interstate commerce. In 1986, the Corps issued a notice interpreting its regulation, which provided four additional examples of isolated, nonnavigable waters whose harm could affect interstate commerce. This notice, popularly known as the Migratory Bird Rule, was challenged in a number of cases, in all but one of which the courts eventually ruled in favor of the validity of the Rule, but in 2000 the Supreme Court granted certiorari in one of the cases. Its decision follows.

SOLID WASTE AGENCY OF NORTHERN COOK COUNTY v. UNITED STATES ARMY CORPS OF ENGINEERS

Supreme Court of the United States, 2001.
531 U.S. 159, 121 S.Ct. 675, 148 L.Ed.2d 576.

Chief Justice REHNQUIST delivered the opinion of the Court.

Section 404(a) of the Clean Water Act (CWA or Act) regulates the discharge of dredged or fill material into "navigable waters." The United

---

9. Of course, it may well be that not every adjacent wetland is of great importance to the environment of adjoining bodies of water. But the existence of such cases does not seriously undermine the Corps' decision to define all adjacent wetlands as "waters." If it is reasonable for the Corps to conclude that in the majority of cases, adjacent wetlands have significant effects on water quality and the aquatic ecosystem, its definition can stand. That the definition may include some wetlands that are not significantly intertwined with the ecosystem of adjacent waterways is of little moment, for where it appears that a wetland covered by the Corps' definition is in fact lacking in importance to the aquatic environment—or where its importance is outweighed by other values—the Corps may always allow development of the wetland for other uses simply by issuing a permit.

States Army Corps of Engineers (Corps) has interpreted § 404(a) to confer federal authority over an abandoned sand and gravel pit in northern Illinois which provides habitat for migratory birds. We are asked to decide whether the provisions of § 404(a) may be fairly extended to these waters, and, if so, whether Congress could exercise such authority consistent with the Commerce Clause. We answer the first question in the negative and therefore do not reach the second.

Petitioner, the Solid Waste Agency of Northern Cook County (SWANCC), is a consortium of 23 suburban Chicago cities and villages that united in an effort to locate and develop a disposal site for baled nonhazardous solid waste. The Chicago Gravel Company informed the municipalities of the availability of a 533–acre parcel, bestriding the Illinois counties Cook and Kane, which had been the site of a sand and gravel pit mining operation for three decades up until about 1960. Long since abandoned, the old mining site eventually gave way to a successional stage forest, with its remnant excavation trenches evolving into a scattering of permanent and seasonal ponds of varying size (from under one-tenth of an acre to several acres) and depth (from several inches to several feet).

The municipalities decided to purchase the site for disposal of their baled nonhazardous solid waste. [B]ecause the operation called for the filling of some of the permanent and seasonal ponds, SWANCC contacted federal respondents (hereinafter respondents), including the Corps, to determine if a federal landfill permit was required under § 404(a) of the CWA.

Section 404(a) grants the Corps authority to issue permits "for the discharge of dredged or fill material into the navigable waters at specified disposal sites." The term "navigable waters" is defined under the Act as "the waters of the United States, including the territorial seas." The Corps has issued regulations defining the term "waters of the United States" to include

> "waters such as intrastate lakes, rivers, streams (including intermittent streams), mudflats, sandflats, wetlands, sloughs, prairie potholes, wet meadows, playa lakes, or natural ponds, the use, degradation or destruction of which could affect interstate or foreign commerce.... " 33 CFR § 328.3(a)(3) (1999).

In 1986, in an attempt to "clarify" the reach of its jurisdiction, the Corps stated that § 404(a) extends to intrastate waters:

> "a. Which are or would be used as habitat by birds protected by Migratory Bird Treaties; or

> "b. Which are or would be used as habitat by other migratory birds which cross state lines; or

> "c. Which are or would be used as habitat for endangered species; or

> "d. Used to irrigate crops sold in interstate commerce."

This last promulgation has been dubbed the "Migratory Bird Rule."

[A]fter the Illinois Nature Preserves Commission informed the Corps that a number of migratory bird species had been observed at the site, the Corps ... asserted jurisdiction over the balefill site pursuant to subpart (b) of the "Migratory Bird Rule." The Corps found that approximately 121 bird species had been observed at the site, including several known to depend upon aquatic environments for a significant portion of their life requirements. Thus, on November 16, 1987, the Corps formally "determined that the seasonally ponded, abandoned gravel mining depressions located on the project site, while not wetlands, did qualify as 'waters of the United States' ... based upon the following criteria: (1) the proposed site had been abandoned as a gravel mining operation; (2) the water areas and spoil piles had developed a natural character; and (3) the water areas are used as habitat by migratory bird [sic] which cross state lines." ...

Petitioner filed suit under the Administrative Procedure Act in the Northern District of Illinois challenging both the Corps' jurisdiction over the site and the merits of its denial of the § 404(a) permit. [Both the district court and the Seventh Circuit affirmed the Corps' determination, and the petitioner sought certiorari.]

We granted certiorari and now reverse.

Congress passed the CWA for the stated purpose of "restor[ing] and maintain[ing] the chemical, physical, and biological integrity of the Nation's waters." In so doing, Congress chose to "recognize, preserve, and protect the primary responsibilities and rights of States to prevent, reduce, and eliminate pollution, to plan the development and use (including restoration, preservation, and enhancement) of land and water resources, and to consult with the Administrator in the exercise of his authority under this chapter." Relevant here, § 404(a) authorizes respondents to regulate the discharge of fill material into "navigable waters," which the statute defines as "the waters of the United States, including the territorial seas." Respondents have interpreted these words to cover the abandoned gravel pit at issue here because it is used as habitat for migratory birds. We conclude that the "Migratory Bird Rule" is not fairly supported by the CWA.

This is not the first time we have been called upon to evaluate the meaning of § 404(a). In *United States v. Riverside Bayview Homes, Inc.*, we held that the Corps had § 404(a) jurisdiction over wetlands that actually abutted on a navigable waterway. In so doing, we noted that the term "navigable" is of "limited import" and that Congress evidenced its intent to "regulate at least some waters that would not be deemed 'navigable' under the classical understanding of that term." But our holding was based in large measure upon Congress' unequivocal acquiescence to, and approval of, the Corps' regulations interpreting the CWA to cover wetlands adjacent to navigable waters. We found that Congress' concern for the protection of water quality and aquatic ecosystems indicated its intent to regulate wetlands "inseparably bound up with the 'waters' of the United States."

It was the significant nexus between the wetlands and "navigable waters" that informed our reading of the CWA in *Riverside Bayview Homes*. Indeed, we did not "express any opinion" on the "question of the authority of the Corps to regulate discharges of fill material into wetlands that are not adjacent to bodies of open water.... " In order to rule for respondents here, we would have to hold that the jurisdiction of the Corps extends to ponds that are *not* adjacent to open water. But we conclude that the text of the statute will not allow this.

Indeed, the Corps' *original* interpretation of the CWA, promulgated two years after its enactment, is inconsistent with that which it espouses here. Its 1974 regulations defined § 404(a)'s "navigable waters" to mean "those waters of the United States which are subject to the ebb and flow of the tide, and/or are presently, or have been in the past, or may be in the future susceptible for use for purposes of interstate or foreign commerce." The Corps emphasized that "[i]t is the water body's capability of use by the public for purposes of transportation or commerce which is the determinative factor." Respondents put forward no persuasive evidence that the Corps mistook Congress' intent in 1974.[3]

Respondents next contend that whatever its original aim in 1972, Congress charted a new course five years later when it approved the more expansive definition of "navigable waters" found in the Corps' 1977 regulations.... Respondents argue that Congress was aware of this more expansive interpretation during its 1977 amendments to the CWA. Specifically, respondents point to a failed House bill, H.R. 3199, that would have defined "navigable waters" as "all waters which are presently used, or are susceptible to use in their natural condition or by reasonable improvement as a means to transport interstate or foreign commerce." ... The failure to pass legislation that would have overturned the Corps' 1977 regulations and the extension of jurisdiction in § 404(g) to waters "other than" traditional "navigable waters," respondents submit, indicate that Congress recognized and accepted a broad definition of "navigable waters" that includes nonnavigable, isolated, intrastate waters.

Although we have recognized congressional acquiescence to administrative interpretations of a statute in some situations, we have done so with extreme care.... Because "subsequent history is less illuminating than the contemporaneous evidence," respondents face a difficult task in overcoming the plain text and import of § 404(a).

---

3. Respondents refer us to portions of the legislative history that they believe indicate Congress' intent to expand the definition of "navigable waters." Although the Conference Report includes the statement that the conferees "intend that the term 'navigable waters' be given the broadest possible constitutional interpretation," nei- ther this, nor anything else in the legislative history to which respondents point, signifies that Congress intended to exert anything more than its commerce power over navigation. Indeed, respondents admit that the legislative history is somewhat ambiguous.

We conclude that respondents have failed to make the necessary showing that the failure of the 1977 House bill demonstrates Congress' acquiescence to the Corps' regulations or the "Migratory Bird Rule," which, of course, did not first appear until 1986....

We thus decline respondents' invitation to take what they see as the next ineluctable step after *Riverside Bayview Homes:* holding that isolated ponds, some only seasonal, wholly located within two Illinois counties, fall under § 404(a)'s definition of "navigable waters" because they serve as habitat for migratory birds. As counsel for respondents conceded at oral argument, such a ruling would assume that "the use of the word navigable in the statute ... does not have any independent significance." We cannot agree that Congress' separate definitional use of the phrase "waters of the United States" constitutes a basis for reading the term "navigable waters" out of the statute. We said in *Riverside Bayview Homes* that the word "navigable" in the statute was of "limited import" and went on to hold that § 404(a) extended to nonnavigable wetlands adjacent to open waters. But it is one thing to give a word limited effect and quite another to give it no effect whatever. The term "navigable" has at least the import of showing us what Congress had in mind as its authority for enacting the CWA: its traditional jurisdiction over waters that were or had been navigable in fact or which could reasonably be so made.

Respondents—relying upon all of the arguments addressed above—contend that, at the very least, it must be said that Congress did not address the precise question of § 404(a)'s scope with regard to nonnavigable, isolated, intrastate waters, and that, therefore, we should give deference to the "Migratory Bird Rule." We find § 404(a) to be clear, but even were we to agree with respondents, we would not extend ... deference here.

Where an administrative interpretation of a statute invokes the outer limits of Congress' power, we expect a clear indication that Congress intended that result. This requirement stems from our prudential desire not to needlessly reach constitutional issues and our assumption that Congress does not casually authorize administrative agencies to interpret a statute to push the limit of congressional authority. This concern is heightened where the administrative interpretation alters the federal-state framework by permitting federal encroachment upon a traditional state power. Thus, "where an otherwise acceptable construction of a statute would raise serious constitutional problems, the Court will construe the statute to avoid such problems unless such construction is plainly contrary to the intent of Congress."

Twice in the past six years we have reaffirmed the proposition that the grant of authority to Congress under the Commerce Clause, though broad, is not unlimited. Respondents argue that the "Migratory Bird Rule" falls within Congress' power to regulate intrastate activities that "substantially affect" interstate commerce. They note that the protection of migratory birds is a "national interest of very nearly the first magnitude," *Missouri v. Holland,* 252 U.S. 416, 435, 40 S.Ct. 382 (1920), and that, as the Court of Appeals found, millions of people spend over a billion dollars annually on recreational pursuits relating to migratory birds. These arguments raise significant constitutional questions. For example, we would have to evaluate the precise object or activity that, in the aggregate, substantially affects interstate commerce. This is not clear, for although the Corps has claimed jurisdiction over petitioner's land because it contains water areas used as habitat by migratory birds, respondents now, *post litem motam,* focus upon the fact that the regulated activity is petitioner's municipal landfill, which is "plainly of a commercial nature." But this is a far cry, indeed, from the "navigable waters" and "waters of the United States" to which the statute by its terms extends.

These are significant constitutional questions raised by respondents' application of their regulations, and yet we find nothing approaching a clear statement from Congress that it intended § 404(a) to reach an abandoned sand and gravel pit such as we have here. Permitting respondents to claim federal jurisdiction over ponds and mudflats falling within the "Migratory Bird Rule" would result in a significant impingement of the States' traditional and primary power over land and water use. Rather than expressing a desire to readjust the federal-state balance in this manner, Congress chose to "recognize, preserve, and protect the primary responsibilities and rights of States . . . to plan the development and use . . . of land and water resources. . . . " 33 U.S.C. § 1251(b). We thus read the statute as written to avoid the significant constitutional and federalism questions raised by respondents' interpretation, and therefore reject the request for administrative deference.

We hold that 33 CFR § 328.3(a)(3) (1999), as clarified and applied to petitioner's balefill site pursuant to the "Migratory Bird Rule" exceeds the authority granted to respondents under § 404(a) of the CWA. The judgment of the Court of Appeals for the Seventh Circuit is therefore

Reversed.

Justice STEVENS, with whom Justice SOUTER, Justice GINSBURG, and Justice BREYER join, dissenting.

In 1969, the Cuyahoga River in Cleveland, Ohio, coated with a slick of industrial waste, caught fire. Congress responded to that dramatic event, and to others like it, by enacting the Federal Water Pollution Control Act (FWPCA) Amendments of 1972, commonly known as the Clean Water Act (Clean Water Act, CWA, or Act). The Act proclaimed the ambitious goal of ending water pollution by 1985. The Court's past interpretations of the CWA have been fully consistent with that goal. Although Congress' vision of zero pollution remains unfulfilled, its pursuit has unquestionably retarded the destruction of the aquatic environment. Our Nation's waters no longer burn. Today, however, the Court takes an unfortunate step that needlessly weakens our principal safeguard against toxic water.

It is fair to characterize the Clean Water Act as "watershed" legislation. The statute endorsed fundamental changes in both the purpose and the scope of federal regulation of the Nation's waters. In § 13 of the Rivers and Harbors Appropriation Act of 1899 (RHA), Congress had assigned to the Army Corps of Engineers (Corps) the mission of regulating discharges into certain waters in order to protect their use as highways for the transportation of interstate and foreign commerce; the scope of the Corps' jurisdiction under the RHA accordingly extended only to waters that were "navigable." In the CWA, however, Congress broadened the Corps' mission to include the purpose of protecting the quality of our Nation's waters for esthetic, health, recreational, and environmental uses. The scope of its jurisdiction was therefore redefined to encompass all of "the waters of the United States, including the territorial seas." That definition requires neither actual nor potential navigability.

The Court has previously held that the Corps' broadened jurisdiction under the CWA properly included an 80–acre parcel of low-lying marshy land that was not itself navigable, directly adjacent to navigable water, or even hydrologically connected to navigable water, but which was part of a larger area, characterized by poor drainage, that ultimately abutted a navigable creek. *United States v. Riverside Bayview Homes, Inc.* Our broad finding in *Riverside Bayview* that the 1977 Congress had acquiesced in the Corps' understanding of its jurisdiction applies equally to the 410–acre parcel at issue here. Moreover, once Congress crossed the legal watershed that separates navigable streams of commerce from marshes and inland lakes, there is no principled reason for limiting the statute's protection to those waters or wetlands that happen to lie near a navigable stream.

In its decision today, the Court draws a new jurisdictional line, one that invalidates the 1986 migratory bird regulation as well as the Corps' assertion of jurisdiction over all waters except for actually navigable waters, their tributaries, and wetlands adjacent to each. Its holding rests on two equally untenable premises: (1) that when Congress passed the 1972 CWA, it did not intend "to exert anything more than its commerce power over navigation"; and (2) that in 1972 Congress drew the boundary defining the Corps' jurisdiction at the odd line on which the Court today settles.

[T]he text of the 1972 amendments affords no support for the Court's holding, and amendments Congress adopted in 1977 do support the Corps' present interpretation of its mission as extending to so-called "isolated" waters. Indeed, simple common sense cuts against the particular definition of the Corps' jurisdiction favored by the majority.

Notes and Comments

1.   The next to last sentence of the Court's opinion in *SWANCC* concludes that paragraph (3) of Section 328.3(a) of the Corps' regulations (the paragraph that includes isolated waters within the definition of "waters of the United States" if an adverse effect on them could affect interstate

commerce) "as clarified and applied" according to the Migratory Bird Rule exceeds the Corps authority. What precisely does this mean? If you were in the Corps of Engineers General Counsel's office after the *SWANCC* decision, how would you advise the various Corps offices across the nation with respect to the Corps' jurisdiction? Are all four examples of covered waters included in the Migratory Bird Rule (waters used as habitat by birds protected by Migratory Bird Treaties, waters used as habitat by other migratory birds which cross state lines, waters used as habitat for endangered species, and waters used to irrigate crops sold in interstate commerce) beyond the Corps' jurisdiction, or only those involving migratory birds? How about the examples of covered isolated waters in paragraph (3) itself (those which are or could be used by interstate or foreign travelers for recreational or other purposes, those from which fish or shellfish are or could be taken and sold in interstate or foreign commerce, and those which are used or could be used for industrial purposes by industries in interstate commerce) that are unrelated to the Migratory Bird Rule? If otherwise isolated waters are connected hydrologically through underground aquifers to navigable waters, do they have a sufficient nexus to navigable waters to be within the CWA's jurisdiction? Or are all isolated nonnavigable waters beyond the Corps' jurisdiction? And if so, what about nonnavigable tributaries of navigable waters?

2. Following *SWANCC*, the Corps and EPA issued an Advance Notice of Proposed Rulemaking, 68 Fed. Reg. 1991 (Jan. 15, 2003), for the purpose of asking for public comment on possible approaches to redefining "waters of the United States" in light of *SWANCC* and to give notice of their interim guidance to agency field offices. The Corps and EPA apparently abandoned that rulemaking, but their interim guidance remained in effect. That guidance concluded that no field office should attempt to exercise jurisdiction over any isolated nonnavigable water on the basis of any of the factors included in the Migratory Bird Rule. Moreover, in the Fourth Circuit, no field office should assert jurisdiction over any isolated, nonnavigable water, because that circuit had earlier ruled that the Corps' regulation asserting jurisdiction over such waters was beyond its authority, *see United States v. Wilson*, 133 F.3d 251 (4th Cir. 1997). Finally, in all the other circuits, because of the questions raised by *SWANCC* with respect to isolated, nonnavigable waters, the guidance directs field offices to "seek formal project-specific Headquarters approval prior to asserting jurisdiction over such waters." Do you agree with this guidance? As an already overworked staff member in a field office, do you think that the need to seek formal headquarters approval for the exercise of jurisdiction over a nonnavigable isolated water on the basis of, say, its potential effect on recreational use by interstate travellers, while requiring no such approval for a denial of jurisdiction, is likely to affect your decision?

3. Both the majority and dissent in *SWANCC* limit their discussion of the reach of "waters of the United States" to the Corps and Section 404, but the term they are interpreting, "navigable waters," as defined by Section 502, 33 U.S.C. § 1362(7), to mean "waters of the United States, including the territorial seas," applies to the whole CWA, not just Section 404. Accordingly, any limitation on the Corps' jurisdiction by reason of the definition of waters will equally restrict EPA's jurisdiction under the

NPDES program and states' jurisdiction under Section 401 to check federal permitting that may affect states' water quality. Moreover, because the Oil Pollution Act, 33 U.S.C. 2701, *et seq.*, has the same jurisdictional reach as the CWA, the ability of EPA and the Coast Guard to obtain cleanups of oil spills and to pursue enforcement against those who spill oil would also be affected.

4. It is often difficult to measure the effects of court decisions, but commentators have suggested that *SWANCC* likely has devastating effects on a wide range of isolated wetlands that provide habitat for various species. Some states have amended their laws to cover such wetlands, but most states have not, including some states likely to be most affected.

5. Prior to *SWANCC*, it was not very important to determine if a wetland was adjacent to a navigable water or not, because there was almost invariably evidence of use of the wetland by migratory fowl. With the invalidation of the Migratory Bird Rule, however, and the suspicion that all isolated waters might likewise be beyond the CWA's jurisdiction, there is a premium on finding a wetland to be "adjacent." The Corps' regulation defines "adjacent" as "bordering, contiguous, or neighboring. Wetlands separated from other waters of the United States by man-made dikes or barriers, natural river berms, beach dunes and the like are 'adjacent wetlands.' " Bordering and contiguous seem pretty clear, but neighboring might be construed to be a little broader, such as "in the neighborhood." Even if we understand what "adjacent" means, the question then becomes: adjacent to what? In *SWANCC* Chief Justice Rehnquist's opinion for the Court characterizes *Riverside Bayview* at one point as upholding jurisdiction over a wetland that "actually abutted on a navigable waterway" and at another point as upholding jurisdiction over a wetland adjacent to "open water." And it is true that both these phrases occur in *Riverside Bayview*. Such a reading would seem to limit adjacent wetlands to those directly adjacent to actually navigable waters. Nevertheless, it is possible to read *Riverside Bayview* more liberally, for example, to approve CWA jurisdiction over wetlands adjacent to any other water within the Corps' definition of waters of the United States, including tributaries that ultimately feed into actually navigable waters. The lower courts that faced this question split on the issue. In some of these cases the government has put more effort into characterizing the wetland not as adjacent to navigable waters but as itself a tributary, because of a hydrological connection whereby water drains from the wetland through ditches and/or creeks ultimately into an actually navigable water. In this regard the government has stressed the language in *SWANCC* suggesting that CWA jurisdiction extends to waters that have a "significant nexus" with an actually navigable water. Both of these issues came before the Supreme Court in the following case.

RAPANOS v. UNITED STATES

Supreme Court of the United States, 2006.
___ U.S. ___, 126 S.Ct. 2208, 165 L.Ed.2d 159.

Justice SCALIA announced the judgment of the Court, and delivered an opinion, in which THE CHIEF JUSTICE, Justice THOMAS, and Justice ALITO join.

In April 1989, petitioner John A. Rapanos backfilled wetlands on a parcel of land in Michigan that he owned and sought to develop. This parcel included 54 acres of land with sometimes-saturated soil conditions. The nearest body of navigable water was 11 to 20 miles away. Regulators had informed Mr. Rapanos that his saturated fields were "waters of the United States," 33 U.S.C. § 1362(7), that could not be filled without a permit. Twelve years of criminal and civil litigation ensued.

The burden of federal regulation on those who would deposit fill material in locations denominated "waters of the United States" is not trivial. In deciding whether to grant or deny a permit, the [Corps] exercises the discretion of an enlightened despot, relying on such factors as "economics," "aesthetics," "recreation," and "in general, the needs and welfare of the people," 33 CFR § 320.4(a) (2004). The average applicant for an individual permit spends 788 days and $271,596 in completing the process, and the average applicant for a nationwide permit spends 313 days and $28,915–not counting costs of mitigation or design changes. "[O]ver $1.7 billion is spent each year by the private and public sectors obtaining wetlands permits." [T]he Clean Water Act "impose[s] criminal liability," as well as steep civil fines, "on a broad range of ordinary industrial and commercial activities." In this litigation, for example, for backfilling his own wet fields, Mr. Rapanos faced 63 months in prison and hundreds of thousands of dollars in criminal and civil fines.

The enforcement proceedings against Mr. Rapanos are a small part of the immense expansion of federal regulation of land use that has occurred under the Clean Water Act—without any change in the governing statute—during the past five Presidential administrations. In the last three decades, the Corps and Environmental Protection Agency have interpreted their jurisdiction over "the waters of the United States" to cover 270–to–300 million acres of swampy lands in the United States— including half of Alaska and an area the size of California in the lower 48 States. And that was just the beginning. The Corps has also asserted jurisdiction over virtually any parcel of land containing a channel or conduit—whether man-made or natural, broad or narrow, permanent or ephemeral-through which rainwater or drainage may occasionally or intermittently flow. On this view, the federally regulated "waters of the United States" include storm drains, roadside ditches, ripples of sand in the desert that may contain water once a year, and lands that are covered by floodwaters once every 100 years. Because they include the land containing storm sewers and desert washes, the statutory "waters of the United States" engulf entire cities and immense arid wastelands. In fact, the entire land area of the United States lies in some drainage basin, and an endless network of visible channels furrows the entire surface, containing water ephemerally wherever the rain falls. Any plot of land containing such a channel may potentially be regulated as a "water of the United States."

I

... We first addressed the proper interpretation of 33 U.S.C. § 1362(7)'s phrase "the waters of the United States" in [*Riverside Bayview*]. That case concerned a wetland that "was adjacent to a body of navigable water," because "the area characterized by saturated soil conditions and wetland vegetation extended beyond the boundary of respondent's property to ... a navigable waterway." Noting that "the transition from water to solid ground is not necessarily or even typically an abrupt one," and that "the Corps must necessarily choose some point at which water ends and land begins," we upheld the Corps' interpretation of "the waters of the United States" to include wetlands that "actually abut[ted] on" traditional navigable waters.

Following our decision in *Riverside Bayview*, the Corps adopted increasingly broad interpretations of its own regulations under the Act. For example, in 1986, to "clarify" the reach of its jurisdiction, the Corps announced the so-called "Migratory Bird Rule," which purported to extend its jurisdiction to any intrastate waters "[w]hich are or would be used as habitat" by migratory birds. In addition, the Corps interpreted its own regulations to include "ephemeral streams" and "drainage ditches" as "tributaries" that are part of the "waters of the United States," see 33 CFR § 328.3(a)(5), provided that they have a perceptible "ordinary high water mark" as defined in § 328.3(e). This interpretation extended "the waters of the United States" to virtually any land feature over which rainwater or drainage passes and leaves a visible mark–even if only "the presence of litter and debris." . . . .

In *SWANCC*, we considered the application of the Corps' "Migratory Bird Rule" to "an abandoned sand and gravel pit in northern Illinois." Observing that "[i]t was the *significant nexus* between the wetlands and 'navigable waters' that informed our reading of the CWA in *Riverside Bayview*," (emphasis added), we held that *Riverside Bayview* did not establish "that the jurisdiction of the Corps extends to ponds that are not adjacent to open water." On the contrary, we held that "nonnavigable, isolated, intrastate waters,"—which, unlike the wetlands at issue in *Riverside Bayview*, did not "actually abu[t] on a navigable waterway,"—were not included as "waters of the United States."

Following our decision in *SWANCC*, the Corps did not significantly revise its theory of federal jurisdiction under § 1344(a). The Corps provided notice of a proposed rulemaking in light of *SWANCC*, but ultimately did not amend its published regulations. . . .

Even after *SWANCC*, the lower courts have continued to uphold the Corps' sweeping assertions of jurisdiction over ephemeral channels and drains as "tributaries." . . .

In addition to "tributaries," the Corps and the lower courts have also continued to define "adjacent" wetlands broadly after *SWANCC*. . . . And the Corps has successfully defended such theories of "adjacency" in the courts, even after *SWANCC* 's excision of "isolated" waters and wetlands from the Act's coverage. . . .

II

In these consolidated cases, we consider whether four Michigan wetlands, which lie near ditches or man-made drains that eventually empty into traditional navigable waters, constitute "waters of the United States" within the meaning of the Act. [T]he Rapanos and their affiliated businesses deposited fill material without a permit into wetlands on three sites near Midland, Michigan: the "Salzburg site," the "Hines Road site," and the "Pine River site." The wetlands at the Salzburg site are connected to a man-made drain, which drains into Hoppler Creek, which flows into the Kawkawlin River, which empties into Saginaw Bay and Lake Huron. The wetlands at the Hines Road site are connected to something called the "Rose Drain," which has a surface connection to the Tittabawassee River. And the wetlands at the Pine River site have a surface connection to the Pine River, which flows into Lake Huron. . . .

[T]he Carabells were denied a permit to deposit fill material in a wetland located on a triangular parcel of land about one mile from Lake St. Clair. A man-made drainage ditch runs along one side of the wetland, separated from it by a 4–foot-wide man-made berm. The berm is largely or entirely impermeable to water and blocks drainage from the wetland, though it may permit occasional overflow to the ditch. The ditch empties into another ditch or a drain, which connects to Auvase Creek, which empties into Lake St. Clair. . . .

We granted certiorari and consolidated the cases to decide whether these wetlands constitute "waters of the United States" under the Act, and if so, whether the Act is constitutional.

III

[W]e need not decide the precise extent to which the qualifiers "navigable" and "of the United States" restrict the coverage of the Act. Whatever the scope of these qualifiers, the CWA authorizes federal jurisdiction only over "waters." The only natural definition of the term "waters," our prior and subsequent judicial constructions of it, clear evidence from other provisions of the statute, and this Court's canons of construction all confirm that "the waters of the United States" . . . cannot bear the expansive meaning that the Corps would give it.

The Corps' expansive approach might be arguable if the CSA [sic] defined "navigable waters" as "water of the United States." But "the waters of the United States" is something else. The use of the definite article ("the") and the plural number ("waters") show plainly that § 1362(7) does not refer to water in general. In this form, "the waters" refers more narrowly to water "[a]s found in streams and bodies forming geographical features such as oceans, rivers, [and] lakes," or "the flowing or moving masses, as of waves or floods, making up such streams or bodies." Webster's New International Dictionary 2882 (2d ed.1954) (hereinafter Webster's Second). On this definition, "the waters of the United States" include only relatively permanent, standing or flowing bodies of water.[5] The definition refers to water as found in "streams," "oceans," "rivers," "lakes," and "bodies" of water "forming geographical features." All of these terms connote continuously present, fixed bodies of water, as opposed to ordinarily dry channels through which water occasionally or intermittently flows. Even the least substantial of the definition's terms, namely "streams," connotes a continuous flow of water in a permanent channel—especially when used in company with other terms such as "rivers," "lakes," and "oceans." None of these terms encompasses transitory puddles or ephemeral flows of water.

[I]n addition, the Act's use of the traditional phrase "navigable waters" (the defined term) further confirms that it confers jurisdiction only over relatively *permanent* bodies of water. The Act adopted that traditional term from its predecessor statutes. On the traditional understanding, "navigable waters" included only discrete *bodies* of water.... Plainly, because such "waters" had to be navigable in fact or susceptible of being rendered so, the term did not include ephemeral flows. As we noted in *SWANCC,* the traditional term "navigable waters"—even though defined as "the waters of the United States"—carries *some* of its original substance: "[I]t is one thing to give a word limited effect and quite another to give it no effect whatever." That limited effect includes, at bare minimum, the ordinary presence of water.

Our subsequent interpretation of the phrase "the waters of the United States" in the CWA likewise confirms this limitation of its scope. In *Riverside Bayview,* we stated that the phrase in the Act referred primarily to "rivers, streams, and other *hydrographic features more conventionally identifiable as 'waters'* " than the wetlands adjacent to such features. We thus echoed the dictionary definition of "waters" as referring to "streams and bodies *forming geographical features* such as oceans, rivers, [and] lakes." Webster's Second 2882 (emphasis added). Though we upheld in that case the inclusion of wetlands abutting such a "hydrographic featur[e]"—principally due to the difficulty of drawing any clear boundary between the two—nowhere did we suggest that "the waters of the United States" should be expanded to include, in their own right, entities other than "hydrographic features more conventionally identifiable as 'waters.' " Likewise, in both *Riverside Bayview* and *SWANCC,* we repeatedly described the "navigable waters" covered by

---

5. By describing "waters" as "relatively permanent," we do not necessarily exclude streams, rivers, or lakes that might dry up in extraordinary circumstances, such as drought. We also do not necessarily exclude *seasonal* rivers, which contain continuous flow during some months of the year but no flow during dry months-such as the 290-day, continuously flowing stream postulated by Justice STEVENS' dissent (hereinafter the dissent). Common sense and common usage distinguish between a wash and seasonal river.

Though scientifically precise distinctions between "perennial" and "intermittent"

flows are no doubt available, we have no occasion in this litigation to decide exactly when the drying-up of a stream bed is continuous and frequent enough to disqualify the channel as a "wate[r]" of the United States." It suffices for present purposes that channels containing permanent flow are plainly within the definition, and that the dissent's "intermittent" and "ephemeral" streams—that is, streams whose flow is "[c]oming and going at intervals ... [b]roken, fitful," Webster's Second 1296, or "existing only, or no longer than, a day; diurnal ... short-lived"—are not.

the Act as "open water" and "open waters." Under no rational interpretation are typically dry channels described as "*open* waters."

Most significant of all, the CWA itself categorizes the channels and conduits that typically carry intermittent flows of water separately from "navigable waters," by including them in the definition of " 'point source.' " The Act defines " 'point source' " as "any discernible, confined and discrete conveyance, including but not limited to any pipe, ditch, channel, tunnel, conduit, well, discrete fissure, container, rolling stock, concentrated animal feeding operation, or vessel or other floating craft, from which pollutants are or may be discharged." 33 U.S.C. § 1362(14). It also defines " 'discharge of a pollutant' " as "any addition of any pollutant *to* navigable waters *from* any point source." § 1362(12)(A) (emphases added). The definitions thus conceive of "point sources" and "navigable waters" as separate and distinct categories. The definition of "discharge" would make little sense if the two categories were significantly overlapping. The separate classification of "ditch[es], channel[s], and conduit[s]"—which are terms ordinarily used to describe the watercourses through which *intermittent* waters typically flow—shows that these are, by and large, *not* "waters of the United States."

[E]ven if the phrase "the waters of the United States" were ambiguous as applied to intermittent flows, our own canons of construction would establish that the Corps' interpretation of the statute is impermissible. As we noted in *SWANCC,* the Government's expansive interpretation would "result in a significant impingement of the States' traditional and primary power over land and water use." Regulation of land use, as through the issuance of the development permits sought by petitioners in both of these cases, is a quintessential state and local power. The extensive federal jurisdiction urged by the Government would authorize the Corps to function as a *de facto* regulator of immense stretches of intrastate land–an authority the agency has shown its willingness to exercise with the scope of discretion that would befit a local zoning board. We ordinarily expect a "clear and manifest" statement from Congress to authorize an unprecedented intrusion into traditional state authority. The phrase "the waters of the United States" hardly qualifies.

Likewise, just as we noted in *SWANCC,* the Corps' interpretation stretches the outer limits of Congress's commerce power and raises difficult questions about the ultimate scope of that power. Even if the term "the waters of the United States" were ambiguous as applied to channels that sometimes host ephemeral flows of water (which it is not), we would expect a clearer statement from Congress to authorize an agency theory of jurisdiction that presses the envelope of constitutional validity.

In sum, on its only plausible interpretation, the phrase "the waters of the United States" includes only those relatively permanent, standing or continuously flowing bodies of water "forming geographic features" that are described in ordinary parlance as "streams[,] . . . oceans, rivers, [and] lakes." See Webster's Second 2882. The phrase does not include channels through which water flows intermittently or ephemerally, or channels that periodically provide drainage for rainfall. The Corps' expansive interpretation of the "the waters of the United States" is thus not "based on a permissible construction of the statute." *Chevron U.S.A., Inc. v. Natural Resources Defense Council, Inc.,* 467 U.S. 837, 843 (1984).

IV

[I]n *Rapanos,* the Sixth Circuit held that the nearby ditches were "tributaries" under § 328(a)(5). But *Rapanos* also stated that, even if the ditches were not "waters of the United States," the wetlands were "adjacent" to *remote* traditional navigable waters in virtue of the wetlands' "hydrological connection" to them. We therefore address in this Part whether a wetland may be considered "adjacent to" remote "waters of the United States," because of a mere hydrologic connection to them.

In *Riverside Bayview,* we noted the textual difficulty in including "wetlands" as a subset of "waters": "On a purely linguistic level, it may appear unreasonable to classify 'lands,' wet or otherwise, as 'waters.' " We acknowledged, however, that there was an inherent ambiguity in drawing the boundaries of any "waters". . . .

Because of this inherent ambiguity, we deferred to the agency's inclusion of wetlands "actually abut[ting]" traditional navigable waters: "Faced with such a problem of defining the bounds of its regulatory authority," we held, the agency could reasonably conclude that a wetland that "adjoin[ed]" waters of the United States is itself a part of those waters. The difficulty of delineating the boundary between water and land was central to our reasoning in the case: "In view of the breadth of federal regulatory authority contemplated by the Act itself and *the inherent difficulties of defining precise bounds to regulable waters,* the Corps' ecological judgment about the relationship between waters and their adjacent wetlands provides an adequate basis for a legal judgment that adjacent wetlands may be defined as waters under the Act."

When we characterized the holding of *Riverside Bayview* in *SWANCC,* we referred to the close connection between waters and the wetlands that they gradually blend into: "It was the *significant nexus* between the wetlands and 'navigable waters' that informed our reading of the CWA in *Riverside Bayview Homes.*" . . . It thus confirmed that *Riverside Bayview* rested upon the inherent ambiguity in defining where water ends and abutting ("adjacent") wetlands begin, permitting the Corps' reliance on ecological considerations *only to resolve that ambiguity* in favor of treating all abutting wetlands as waters. Isolated ponds were not "waters of the United States" in their own right, and presented no boundary-drawing problem that would have justified the invocation of ecological factors to treat them as such.

Therefore, *only* those wetlands with a continuous surface connection to bodies that are "waters of the United States" in their own right, so that there is no clear demarcation between "waters" and wetlands, are "adjacent to" such waters and covered by the Act. Wetlands with only an intermittent, physically remote hydrologic connection to "waters of the United States" do not implicate the boundary-drawing problem of *Riverside Bayview,* and thus lack the necessary connection to covered waters that we described as a "significant nexus" in *SWANCC.* Thus, establishing that wetlands such as those at the Rapanos and Carabell sites are covered by the Act requires two findings: First, that the adjacent channel contains a "wate[r] of the United States," (*i.e.,* a relatively permanent body of water connected to traditional interstate navigable waters); and second, that the wetland has a continuous surface connection with that water, making it difficult to determine where the "water" ends and the "wetland" begins. . . .

VI

* * *

The dissent contends that "[b]ecause there is ambiguity in the phrase 'waters of the United States' and because interpreting it broadly to cover such ditches and streams advances the purpose of the Act, the Corps' approach should command our deference." Two defects in a single sentence: "[W]aters of the United States" is in *some* respects ambiguous. The *scope* of that ambiguity, however, does not conceivably extend to whether storm drains and dry ditches are "waters," and hence does not support the Corps' interpretation. And as for advancing "the purpose of the Act": We have often criticized that last resort of extravagant interpretation, noting that no law pursues its purpose at all costs, and that the textual limitations upon a law's scope are no less a part of its "purpose" than its substantive authorizations. . . .

We vacate the judgments of the Sixth Circuit in both No. 04–1034 and No. 04–1384, and remand both cases for further proceedings.

Chief Justice ROBERTS, concurring.

Five years ago, this Court rejected the position of the [Corps] on the scope of its authority to regulate wetlands under the [CWA]. . . .

In response to the *SWANCC* decision, the Corps and [EPA] initiated a rulemaking to consider "issues associated with the scope of waters that are subject to the Clean Water Act (CWA), in light of the U.S. Supreme Court decision in *[SWANCC].*" . . .

The proposed rulemaking went nowhere. Rather than refining its view of its authority in light of our decision in *SWANCC,* and providing guidance meriting deference under our generous standards, the Corps chose to adhere to its essentially boundless view of the scope of its power. The upshot today is another defeat for the agency.

It is unfortunate that no opinion commands a majority of the Court on precisely how to read Congress' limits on the reach of the Clean Water Act. Lower courts and regulated entities will now have to feel their way on a case-by-case basis. This situation is certainly not unprecedented. See *Grutter v. Bollinger,* 539 U.S. 306, 325 (2003) (discussing *Marks v. United States,* 430 U.S. 188 (1977)). What is unusual in this instance, perhaps, is how readily the situation could have been avoided.

Justice KENNEDY, concurring in the judgment.

* * *

II

* * *

Riverside Bayview and *SWANCC* establish the framework for the inquiry in the cases now before the Court: Do the Corps' regulations, as applied to the wetlands in *Carabell* and the three wetlands parcels in *Rapanos,* constitute a reasonable interpretation of "navigable waters" as in *Riverside Bayview* or an invalid construction as in *SWANCC?* Taken together these cases establish that in some instances, as exemplified by *Riverside Bayview,* the connection between a nonnavigable water or wetland and a navigable water may be so close, or potentially so close, that the Corps may deem the water or wetland a "navigable water" under the Act. In other instances, as exemplified by *SWANCC,* there may be little or no connection. Absent a significant nexus, jurisdiction under the Act is lacking. Because neither the plurality nor the dissent addresses the nexus requirement, this separate opinion, in my respectful view, is necessary.

A

The plurality's opinion begins from a correct premise. As the plurality points out, and as *Riverside Bayview* holds, in enacting the [CWA] Congress intended to regulate at least some waters that are not navigable in the traditional sense. This conclusion is supported by "the evident breadth of congressional concern for protection of water quality and aquatic ecosystems." It is further compelled by [§ 1344(g)(1)], for the text is explicit in extending the coverage of the Act to some nonnavigable waters. . . .

From this reasonable beginning the plurality proceeds to impose two limitations on the Act; but these limitations, it is here submitted, are without support in the language and purposes of the Act or in our cases interpreting it. . . .

The plurality's first requirement—permanent standing water or continuous flow, at least for a period of "some months," makes little practical sense in a statute concerned with downstream water quality. The merest trickle, if continuous, would count as a "water" subject to federal regulation, while torrents thundering at irregular intervals through otherwise dry channels would not. Though the plurality seems to presume that such irregular flows are too insignificant to be of concern in a statute focused on "waters," that may not always be true. Areas in the western parts of the Nation provide some examples. The Los Angeles River, for instance, ordinarily carries only a trickle of water and often looks more like a dry roadway than a river. Yet it periodically releases water-volumes so powerful and destructive that it has been encased in concrete and steel over a length of some 50 miles. Though this particular waterway might satisfy the plurality's test, it is illustrative of what often-dry watercourses can become when rain waters flow.

To be sure, Congress could draw a line to exclude irregular waterways, but nothing in the statute suggests it has done so. Quite the opposite, a full reading of the dictionary definition precludes the plurality's emphasis on permanence: The term "waters" may mean "flood or inundation," Webster's Second 2882, events that are impermanent by definition.... In any event, ... the dissent is correct to observe that an intermittent flow can constitute a stream, in the sense of " 'a current or course of water or other fluid, flowing on the earth,' " while it is flowing. It follows that the Corps can reasonably interpret the Act to cover the paths of such impermanent streams.

Apart from the dictionary, the plurality invokes *Riverside Bayview* to support its interpretation that the term "waters" is so confined, but this reliance is misplaced. To be sure, the Court there compared wetlands to "rivers, streams, and other hydrographic features more conventionally identifiable as 'waters.' " It is quite a stretch to claim, however, that this mention of hydrographic features "echoe[s]" the dictionary's reference to " '*geographical features* such as oceans, rivers, [and] lakes.' " In fact the *Riverside Bayview* opinion does not cite the dictionary definition on which the plurality relies, and the phrase "hydrographic features" could just as well refer to intermittent streams carrying substantial flow to navigable waters....

The plurality's second limitation—exclusion of wetlands lacking a continuous surface connection to other jurisdictional waters—is also unpersuasive. To begin with, the plurality is wrong to suggest that wetlands are *"indistinguishable"* from waters to which they bear a surface connection. Even if the precise boundary may be imprecise, a bog or swamp is different from a river. The question is what circumstances permit a bog, swamp, or other nonnavigable wetland to constitute a "navigable water" under the Act—as § 1344(g)(1), if nothing else, indicates is sometimes possible. *Riverside Bayview* addressed that question and its answer is inconsistent with the plurality's theory. There, in upholding the Corps' authority to regulate "wetlands adjacent to other bodies of water over which the Corps has jurisdiction," the Court deemed it irrelevant whether "the moisture creating the wetlands ... find[s] its source in the adjacent bodies of water." The Court further observed that adjacency could serve as a valid basis for regulation even as to "wetlands that are not significantly intertwined with the ecosystem of adjacent waterways." "If it is reasonable," the Court explained, "for the Corps to conclude that in the majority of cases, adjacent wetlands have significant effects on water quality and the aquatic ecosystem, its definition can stand.".....

As *Riverside Bayview* recognizes, the Corps' adjacency standard is reasonable in some of its applications. Indeed, the Corps' view draws support from the structure of the Act, while the plurality's surface-water-connection requirement does not. . . .

In sum the plurality's opinion is inconsistent with the Act's text, structure, and purpose. As a fallback the plurality suggests that avoidance canons would compel its reading even if the text were unclear. In *SWANCC,* as one reason for rejecting the Corps' assertion of jurisdiction over the isolated ponds at issue there, the Court observed that this "application of [the Corps'] regulations" would raise significant questions of Commerce Clause authority and encroach on traditional state land-use regulation. . . .

Finally, it should go without saying that because the plurality presents its interpretation of the Act as the only permissible reading of the plain text, the Corps would lack discretion, under the plurality's theory, to adopt contrary regulations. The Chief Justice suggests that if the Corps and EPA had issued new regulations after *SWANCC* they would have "enjoyed plenty of room to operate in developing *some* notion of an outer bound to the reach of their authority" and thus could have avoided litigation of the issues we address today. That would not necessarily be true under the opinion The Chief Justice has joined. New rulemaking could have averted the disagreement here only if the Corps had anticipated the unprecedented reading of the Act that the plurality advances.

B

While the plurality reads nonexistent requirements into the Act, the dissent reads a central requirement out–namely, the requirement that the word "navigable" in "navigable waters" be given some importance. . . .

Congress' choice of words creates difficulties, for the Act contemplates regulation of certain "navigable waters" that are not in fact navigable. Nevertheless, the word "navigable" in the Act must be given some effect. Thus, in *SWANCC* the Court rejected the Corps' assertion of jurisdiction over isolated ponds and mudflats bearing no evident connection to navigable-in-fact waters. And in *Riverside Bayview,* while the Court indicated that "the term 'navigable' as used in the Act is of limited import," it relied, in upholding jurisdiction, on the Corps' judgment that "wetlands adjacent to lakes, rivers, streams, and other bodies of water may function as integral parts of the aquatic environment even when the moisture creating the wetlands does not find its source in the adjacent bodies of water." The implication, of course, was that wetlands' status as "integral parts of the aquatic environment"—that is, their significant nexus with navigable waters—was what established the Corps' jurisdiction over them as waters of the United States.

Consistent with *SWANCC* and *Riverside Bayview* and with the need to give the term "navigable" some meaning, the Corps' jurisdiction over wetlands depends upon the existence of a significant nexus between the wetlands in question and navigable waters in the traditional sense. The required nexus must be assessed in terms of the statute's goals and purposes. Congress enacted the law to "restore and maintain the chemical, physical, and biological integrity of the Nation's waters," and it pursued that objective by restricting dumping and filling in "navigable waters." With respect to wetlands, the rationale for [CWA] regulation is, as the Corps has recognized, that wetlands can perform critical functions related to the integrity of other waters—functions such as pollutant trapping, flood control, and runoff storage. Accordingly, wetlands possess the requisite nexus, and thus come within the statutory phrase "navigable waters," if the wetlands, either alone or in combination with similarly situated lands in the region, significantly affect the chemical, physical, and biological integrity of other covered waters more readily understood as "navigable." When, in contrast, wetlands' effects on water quality are speculative or insubstantial, they fall outside the zone fairly encompassed by the statutory term "navigable waters." . . .

As applied to wetlands adjacent to navigable-in-fact waters, the Corps' conclusive standard for jurisdiction rests upon a reasonable inference of ecologic interconnection, and the assertion of jurisdiction for those wetlands is sustainable under the Act by showing adjacency alone. That is the holding of *Riverside Bayview*. Furthermore, although the *Riverside Bayview* Court reserved the question of the Corps' authority over "wetlands that are not adjacent to bodies of open water," and in any event addressed no factual situation other than wetlands adjacent to navigable-in-fact waters, it may well be the case that *Riverside Bayview*'s reasoning—supporting jurisdiction without any inquiry beyond adjacency—could apply equally to wetlands adjacent to certain major tributaries. Through regulations or adjudication, the Corps may choose to identify categories of tributaries that, due to their volume of flow (either annually or on average), their proximity to navigable waters, or other relevant considerations, are significant enough that wetlands adjacent to them are likely, in the majority of cases, to perform important functions for an aquatic system incorporating navigable waters.

The Corps' existing standard for tributaries, however, provides no such assurance. As noted earlier, the Corps deems a water a tributary if it feeds into a traditional navigable water (or a tributary thereof) and possesses an ordinary high-water mark, defined as a "line on the shore established by the fluctuations of water and indicated by [certain] physical characteristics," § 328.3(e). This standard presumably provides a rough measure of the volume and regularity of flow. Assuming it is subject to reasonably consistent application, it may well provide a reasonable measure of whether specific minor tributaries bear a sufficient nexus with other regulated waters to constitute "navigable waters" under the Act. Yet the breadth of this standard—which seems to leave wide room for regulation of drains, ditches, and streams remote from any navigable-in-fact water and carrying only minor water-volumes towards it—precludes its adoption as the determinative measure of whether adjacent wetlands are likely to play an important role in the integrity of an aquatic system comprising navigable waters as traditionally understood. Indeed, in many cases wetlands adjacent to tributaries covered by this standard might appear little more related to navigable-in-fact waters than were the isolated ponds held to fall beyond the Act's scope in *SWANCC*.

When the Corps seeks to regulate wetlands adjacent to navigable-in-fact waters, it may rely on adjacency to establish its jurisdiction. Absent more specific regulations, however, the Corps must establish a significant nexus on a case-by-case basis when it seeks to regulate wetlands based on adjacency to nonnavigable tributaries. Given the potential overbreadth of the Corps' regulations, this showing is necessary to avoid unreasonable applications of the statute. Where an adequate nexus is established for a particular wetland, it may be permissible, as a matter of administrative convenience or necessity, to presume covered status for other comparable wetlands in the region. That issue, however, is neither raised by these facts nor addressed by any agency regulation that accommodates the nexus requirement outlined here.

This interpretation of the Act does not raise federalism or Commerce Clause concerns sufficient to support a presumption against its adoption. To be sure, the significant nexus requirement may not align perfectly with the traditional extent of federal authority. Yet in most cases regulation of wetlands that are adjacent to tributaries and possess a significant nexus with navigable waters will raise no serious constitutional or federalism difficulty. As explained earlier, moreover, and as exemplified by *SWANCC,* the significant-nexus test itself prevents problematic applications of the statute. The possibility of legitimate Commerce Clause and federalism concerns in some circumstances does not require the adoption of an interpretation that departs in all cases from the Act's text and structure.

III

In both the consolidated cases before the Court the record contains evidence suggesting the possible existence of a significant nexus according to the principles outlined above. Thus the end result in these cases and many others to be considered by the Corps may be the same as that suggested by the dissent, namely, that the Corps' assertion of jurisdiction is valid. Given, however, that neither the agency nor the reviewing courts properly considered the issue, a remand is appropriate, in my view, for application of the controlling legal standard. . . .

Justice STEVENS, with whom Justice SOUTER, Justice GINSBURG, and Justice BREYER join, dissenting.

* * *

The narrow question presented in No. 04–1034 is whether wetlands adjacent to tributaries of traditionally navigable waters are ''waters of the United States'' subject to the jurisdiction of the Army Corps; the question in No. 04–1384 is whether a manmade berm separating a wetland from the adjacent tributary makes a difference. The broader question is whether regulations that have protected the quality of our waters for decades, that were implicitly approved by Congress, and that have been repeatedly enforced in case after case, must now be revised in light of the creative criticisms voiced by the plurality and Justice Kennedy today. Rejecting more than 30 years of practice by the Army Corps, the plurality disregards the nature of the congressional delegation to the agency and the technical and complex character of the issues at stake. Justice Kennedy similarly fails to defer sufficiently to the Corps, though his approach is far more faithful to our precedents and to principles of statutory interpretation than is the plurality's.

In my view, the proper analysis is straightforward. The [Corps] has determined that wetlands adjacent to tributaries of traditionally navigable waters preserve the quality of our Nation's waters by, among other things, providing habitat for aquatic animals, keeping excessive sediment and toxic pollutants out of adjacent waters, and reducing downstream flooding by absorbing water at times of high flow. The Corps' resulting decision to treat these wetlands as encompassed within the term "waters of the United States" is a quintessential example of the Executive's reasonable interpretation of a statutory provision. . . .

II

Our unanimous opinion in *Riverside Bayview* squarely controls these cases. There, we evaluated the validity of the very same regulations at issue today. These regulations interpret "waters of the United States" to cover all traditionally navigable waters; tributaries of these waters; and wetlands adjacent to traditionally navigable waters or their tributaries. Although the particular wetland at issue in *Riverside Bayview* abutted a navigable creek, we framed the question presented as whether the [CWA] "authorizes the Corps to require landowners to obtain permits from the Corps before discharging fill material into wetlands adjacent to navigable bodies of water *and their tributaries*."

We held that, pursuant to our decision in *Chevron*,

"our review is limited to the question whether it is reasonable, in light of the language, policies, and legislative history of the Act for the Corps to exercise jurisdiction over wetlands adjacent to but not regularly flooded by rivers, streams, and other hydrographic features more conventionally identifiable as 'waters.' "

Applying this standard, we held that the Corps' decision to interpret "waters of the United States" as encompassing such wetlands was permissible. We recognized the practical difficulties in drawing clean lines between land and water, and deferred to the Corps' judgment that treating adjacent wetlands as "waters" would advance the "congressional concern for protection of water quality and aquatic ecosystems."

Contrary to the plurality's revisionist reading today, *Riverside Bayview* nowhere implied that our approval of "adjacent" wetlands was contingent upon an understanding that "adjacent" means having a "continuous surface connection" between the wetland and its neighboring creek. Instead, we acknowledged that the Corps defined "adjacent" as including wetlands " 'that form the border of or are in reasonable proximity to other waters' " and found that the Corps reasonably concluded that adjacent wetlands are part of the waters of the United States. Indeed, we explicitly acknowledged that the Corps' jurisdictional determination was reasonable even though

> "not every adjacent wetland is of great importance to the environment of adjoining bodies of water.... If it is reasonable for the Corps to conclude that in the majority of cases, adjacent wetlands have significant effects on water quality and the ecosystem, its definition can stand. That the definition may include some wetlands that are not significantly intertwined with the ecosystem of adjacent waterways is of little moment, for where it appears that a wetland covered by the Corps' definition is in fact lacking in importance to the aquatic environment ... the Corps may always allow development of the wetland for other uses simply by issuing a permit."

In closing, we emphasized that the scope of the Corps' asserted jurisdiction over wetlands had been specifically brought to Congress' attention in 1977, that Congress had rejected an amendment that would have narrowed that jurisdiction, and that even proponents of the amendment would not have removed wetlands altogether from the definition of "waters of the United States."

Disregarding the importance of *Riverside Bayview,* the plurality relies heavily on the Court's subsequent opinion in [*SWANCC,*]. In stark contrast to *Riverside Bayview,* however, *SWANCC* had nothing to say about wetlands, let alone about wetlands adjacent to traditionally navigable waters or their tributaries. Instead, *SWANCC* dealt with a question specifically reserved by *Riverside Bayview,* namely, the Corps' jurisdiction over isolated waters—" 'waters that are *not* part of a tributary system to interstate waters or to navigable waters of the United States, the degradation or destruction of which could affect interstate commerce.' "....

Unlike *SWANCC* and like *Riverside Bayview,* the cases before us today concern wetlands that are adjacent to "navigable bodies of water [or] their tributaries." Specifically, these wetlands abut tributaries of traditionally navigable waters....

V

... I close ... by noting an unusual feature of the Court's judgments in these cases. It has been our practice in a case coming to us from a lower federal court to enter a judgment commanding that court to conduct any further proceedings pursuant to a specific mandate. That prior practice has, on occasion, made it necessary for Justices to join a judgment that did not conform to their own views. In these cases, however, while both the plurality and Justice Kennedy agree that there must be a remand for further proceedings, their respective opinions define different tests to be applied on remand. Given that all four Justices who have joined this opinion would uphold the Corps' jurisdiction in both of these cases—and in all other cases in which either the plurality's or Justice Kennedy's test is satisfied—on remand each of the judgments should be reinstated if *either* of those tests is met.

Justice BREYER, dissenting.

In my view, the authority of the [Corps] under the [CWA] extends to the limits of congressional power to regulate interstate commerce. I therefore have no difficulty finding that the wetlands at issue in these cases are within the Corps' jurisdiction, and I join Justice Stevens' dissenting opinion.

My view of the statute rests in part upon the nature of the problem. The statute seeks to "restore and maintain the chemical, physical, and biological integrity of the Nation's waters." 33 U.S.C. § 1251(a). Those waters are so various and so intricately interconnected that Congress might well have decided the only way to achieve this goal is to write a statute that defines "waters" broadly and to leave the enforcing agency with the task of restricting the scope of that definition, either wholesale through regulation or retail through development permissions. That is why I believe that Congress, in using the term "waters of the United States," § 1362(7), intended fully to exercise its relevant Commerce Clause powers.

I mention this because the Court, contrary to my view, has written a "nexus" requirement into the statute. But it has left the administrative powers of the [Corps] untouched. That agency may write regulations defining the term—something that it has not yet done. And the courts must give those regulations appropriate deference.

If one thing is clear, it is that Congress intended the [Corps] to make the complex technical judgments that lie at the heart of the present cases (subject to deferential judicial review). In the absence of updated regulations, courts will have to make ad hoc determinations that run the risk of transforming scientific questions into matters of law. That is not the system Congress intended. Hence I believe that today's opinions, taken together, call for the Army Corps of Engineers to write new regulations, and speedily so.

Notes and Comments

1. As Chief Justice Roberts' concurrence and Justice Steven's final paragraph suggest, there is some question about how lower courts should apply *Rapanos* in light of the lack of a majority opinion. The rule, when a majority of the Supreme Court agrees only on the outcome of a case and not on the ground for that outcome, is that lower-court judges are to follow the narrowest ground to which a majority of the Justices would have assented if forced to choose. *See Marks v. United States,* 430 U.S. 188, 97 S.Ct. 990, 51 L.Ed.2d 260 (1977). What the narrowest ground in *Rapanos* is, however, is not necessarily clear, and the lower courts have not all agreed. The Seventh Circuit said that it was Justice Kennedy's opinion. *See United States v. Gerke*

Excavating, Inc., 464 F.3d 723 (7th Cir. 2006). *Accord Northern California River Watch v. City of Healdsburg*, 457 F.3d 1023 (9th Cir. 2006). On the other hand, the First Circuit in *United States v. Johnson*, 467 F.3d 56 (1st Cir. 2006), specified that the government should win if it were able to satisfy either the plurality's test or Justice Kennedy's test. The First Circuit noted that it is at least possible for a wetland to meet the plurality's and the dissent's tests, but not Justice Kennedy's—where there is a non-significant but adjacent, surface hydrological connection to a non-navigable but perennial water. *Accord United States v. Evans*, 2006 WL 2221629 (M.D. Fla. 2006). A district court in the Fifth Circuit, however, in light of the lack of a majority opinion, decided to rely on prior circuit precedent, which looked much like the *Rapanos* plurality's approach. *See United States v. Chevron Pipe Line Co.*, 437 F.Supp.2d 605 (N.D. Tex. 2006).

2. While *SWANCC* requires us to ask which wetlands are covered by the CWA, there is also a question as to what is a "wetland." It is not a term generally used in the CWA. Its one appearance is in Section 404(g)(1), which exempts wetlands adjacent to traditional navigable waters from state administration pursuant to an EPA delegation. Since 1977 the Corps and EPA have defined "wetlands" in their regulations as: "those areas that are inundated or saturated by surface or ground water at a frequency and duration sufficient to support, and that under normal circumstances do support, a prevalence of vegetation typically adapted for life in saturated soil conditions. Wetlands generally include swamps, marshes, bogs, and similar areas." 33 CFR 328.3(b); 40 CFR § 230.3(t). The devil, however, is in the details. In order to provide guidance to its field offices and hopefully to achieve some consistency in administration, the Corps in 1987 adopted a Wetlands Delineation Manual, essentially describing how one went about establishing the elements of a wetland so that wetlands could be identified and their boundaries established. EPA, however, was not satisfied with the Manual, and there were two other agencies identifying wetlands on the ground that each had their own method—the Department of Agriculture's Natural Resources Conservation Service is responsible for enforcing the Swampbuster law described later in this chapter, and the Department of Interior's Fish and Wildlife Service is charged with mapping the nation's wetlands. An interagency task force in 1989 came up with a new Manual, the effect of which was to reduce the number of criteria needed to find an area to be a wetland. In other words, the new manual effectively enlarged the areas subject to wetlands regulation by a more inclusive form of identifying wetlands. This effect resulted in substantial opposition from the usual suspects—farmers and developers generally—in part because the new manual had been adopted without public notice and comment. As consequence, a new interagency task force under the leadership of then-Vice President Dan Quayle was created. In August 1991, the new task force published a proposed manual for public notice and comment. The comment was devastating. Whatever enlargement of regulated wetlands was the effect of the 1989 manual, the 1991 proposed manual would have undone, and wetlands jurisdiction would have been so difficult to establish that it appeared that the Florida Everglades would no longer be protected. At this point, Congress stepped in and directed that the 1987 manual be the basis for Section 404 jurisdiction until such time as the National Academy of Sciences could make

a study of the issue, which could then form the basis for any further action. The Academy issued its report in 1995, generally confirming the validity of the methods used in both the 1987 and 1989 manuals, but recommending that one manual be used by all agencies. The 1987 manual is still in use today by the Corps. Even if the same manual were used, however, different agencies might still reach different results in terms of the boundaries of a wetland because of the inevitable exercise of judgment the manual requires. For persons subject to regulation by more than one agency, such disparate results did not engender confidence. To improve matters, during the Clinton administration, the Natural Resources Conservation Service was made the lead agency for identifying and delineating wetlands in "agricultural areas," although it would continue to use its delineation manual rather than the Corps',and the Corps was made the lead agency for identifying and delineating wetlands in all other areas. Thus, only one agency would generally be making the delineation, so conflicts between agencies should occur less frequently.

2. What Activities are Covered?

Just as the CWA only protects "navigable waters," defined as "waters of the United States, including the territorial seas," it only protects those waters from a "discharge of any pollutant," and "a discharge of a pollutant" is defined as "the addition of any pollutant from a point source." 33 U.S.C. § 1352(12). In the discussion of the NPDES program, we discovered that there could be some problems in interpreting what the "addition" of a pollutant means. For example, the recent case of *South Florida Water Management Dist. v. Miccosukee Tribe of Indians*, 541 U.S. 95, 124 S.Ct. 1537, 158 L.Ed.2d 264 (2004), concluded that the taking of waters from one water body and returning them unaltered to the same water body could not be the "addition of any pollutant." Section 404's application has also raised questions about the meaning of "addition."

Recall that Section 404 provides for a permit for the addition of two types of pollutants—fill material and dredged material. Clearly, if a dump truck full of dirt backs up to a covered wetland and dumps the dirt into the water, there has been an "addition of any pollutant from a point source," either fill material or dredged material, if the material had earlier been taken out of waters. On the other hand, if someone sinks a well near to the wetland and pumps ground water out of the ground, resulting in a covered wetland's water disappearing, it seems difficult to find any "addition" of anything, even though the wetland has been destroyed just as if dry fill had been trucked in and dumped into the wetland. *See Save Our Community v. U.S. EPA*, 971 F.2d 1155 (5th Cir. 1992). Between those two extremes, however, there is a vast gray area.

A relatively early case, *Avoyelles Sportsmen's League v. Marsh*, 715 F.2d 897 (5th Cir. 1983), held that mechanized landclearing and leveling that involved bulldozing of high spots into low spots of a wetland constituted a redeposit of soil and, therefore, an addition of a pollutant. Developers and farmers retaliated by digging channels or ditches in wetlands to drain wetlands, but "sidecasting," in which the material dug out of the ditch in the wetland is placed alongside the ditch, was then also considered the redeposit of soil, or the addition of a pollutant. While this approach was generally accepted by other courts, some questioned whether the mere redeposit or moving of soil from one place in a wetland to another constituted an "addition" of a pollutant. *See, e.g., United States v. Wilson,* 133 F.3d 251, 258–260 (4th Cir. 1997)(Opinion of Niemeyer for himself).

Nevertheless, if developers or farmers took the expense of trucking away the material dug out of the ditch, the Corps initially believed that they escaped regulation. In response to a suit by environmentalists, however, the Corps reconsidered its position and adopted a regulation, known as the Tulloch Rule, after the name of the case that inspired it. This regulation effectively subjected all mechanical digging or earth movement in a wetland to be the addition of a pollutant, which led to the following case.

NATIONAL MINING ASSOCIATION v. U.S. ARMY CORPS OF ENGINEERS

United States Court of Appeals, District of Columbia Circuit, 1998.
145 F.3d 1399.

STEPHEN F. WILLIAMS, Circuit Judge:

[I]n 1986 the Corps issued a regulation defining the term "discharge of dredged material," as used in § 404, to mean "any addition of dredged material into the waters of the United States," but expressly excluding "*de minimis,* incidental soil movement occurring during normal dredging operations." In 1993, responding to litigation, the Corps issued a new rule removing the *de minimis* exception and expanding the definition of discharge to cover "any addition of dredged material into, *including any redeposit of dredged material within,* the waters of the United States." (emphasis added). Redeposit occurs when material removed from the water is returned to it; when redeposit takes place in substantially the same spot as the initial removal, the parties refer to it as "fallback." In effect the new rule subjects to federal regulation virtually all excavation and dredging performed in wetlands.

The plaintiffs, various trade associations whose members engage in dredging and excavation, mounted a facial challenge to the 1993 regulation, claiming that it exceeded the scope of the Corps's regulatory authority under the Act by regulating fallback. The district court agreed and granted summary judgment for the plaintiffs ... We affirm....

The 1993 rulemaking under challenge here was prompted by a lawsuit, *North Carolina Wildlife Federation v. Tulloch* (E.D. N.C.1992), concerning a developer who sought to drain and clear 700 acres of wetlands in North Carolina. Because the developer's efforts involved only minimal incidental releases of soil and other dredged material, the Corps's field office personnel determined that, under the terms of the

1986 regulation, § 404's permit requirements did not apply. Environmental groups, concerned by what they viewed as the adverse effects of the developer's activities on the wetland, filed an action seeking enforcement of the § 404 permit requirement. As part of the settlement of the *Tulloch* case (a settlement to which the developer was not a party), the two administering agencies agreed to propose stiffer rules governing the permit requirements for landclearing and excavation activities. The result—the regulation at issue here—has come to be called the "*Tulloch* Rule."

As mentioned above, the *Tulloch* Rule alters the preexisting regulatory framework primarily by removing the *de minimis* exception and by adding coverage of incidental fallback. Specifically, the rule defines "discharge of dredged material" to include "[a]ny addition, *including any redeposit,* of dredged material, including excavated material, into waters of the United States which is incidental to any activity, including mechanized landclearing, ditching, channelization, or other excavation."

The *Tulloch* Rule does have its own *de minimis* exception, but it is framed in terms of the Act's overall goals. A permit is not required for "any incidental addition, including redeposit, of dredged material associated with any activity that does not have or would not have the effect of destroying or degrading an area of waters of the United States." Persons engaging in "mechanized landclearing, ditching, channelization and other excavation activity," however, bear the burden of proving to the Corps that their activities would not have destructive or degrading effects. Degradation is defined as any effect on the waters of the United States that is more than *de minimis* or inconsequential. Thus, whereas the 1986 rule exempted *de minimis* soil movement, the *Tulloch* Rule covers all discharges, however minuscule, unless the Corps is convinced that the *activities with which they are associated* have only minimal adverse effects. In promulgating the new rule the Corps "emphasize[d] that the threshold of adverse effects for the *de minimis* exception is a very low one."

It is undisputed that by requiring a permit for "*any* redeposit" (emphasis added), the *Tulloch* Rule covers incidental fallback. According to the agencies, incidental fallback occurs, for example, during dredging, "when a bucket used to excavate material from the bottom of a river, stream, or wetland is raised and soils or sediments fall from the bucket back into the water." (There is no indication that the rule would not also reach soils or sediments falling out of the bucket even *before* it emerged from the water.) Fallback and other redeposits also occur during mechanized landclearing, when bulldozers and loaders scrape or displace wetland soil, as well as during ditching and channelization, when draglines or backhoes are dragged through soils and sediments. Indeed, fallback is a practically inescapable by-product of all these activities. In the preamble to the *Tulloch* Rule the Corps noted that "it is virtually impossible to conduct mechanized landclearing, ditching, channelization or excavation in waters of the United States without causing incidental redeposition of dredged material (however small or temporary) in the process." As a result, the *Tulloch* Rule effectively requires a permit for all those activities, subject to a limited exception for ones that the Corps in its discretion deems to produce no adverse effects on waters of the United States.

The plaintiffs claim that the *Tulloch* Rule exceeds the Corps's statutory jurisdiction under § 404, which, as we have noted, extends only to "discharge," defined as the "addition of any pollutant to navigable waters." It [*sic*] argues that fallback, which returns dredged material virtually to the spot from which it came, cannot be said to constitute an *addition* of anything. Therefore, the plaintiffs contend, the *Tulloch* Rule conflicts with the statute's unambiguous terms and cannot survive even the deferential scrutiny called for by *Chevron U.S.A., Inc. v. NRDC.* . . .

The agencies argue that the terms of the Act in fact demonstrate that fallback may be classified as a discharge. The Act defines a discharge as the addition of any pollutant to navigable waters, and defines "pollutant" to include "dredged spoil," as well as "rock," "sand," and "cellar dirt." The Corps in turn defines "dredged material" as "material that is excavated or dredged from waters of the United States," a definition that is not challenged here. Thus, according to the agencies, wetland soil, sediment, debris or other material in the waters of the United States undergoes a legal metamorphosis during the dredging process, becoming a "pollutant" for purposes of the Act. If a portion of the material being dredged then falls back into the water, there has been an addition of a pollutant to the waters of the United States. Indeed, according to appellants National Wildlife Federation *et al.* ("NWF"), who intervened as defendants below, this reasoning demonstrates that regulation of redeposit is actually *required* by the Act.

We agree with the plaintiffs, and with the district court, that the straightforward statutory term "addition" cannot reasonably be said to encompass the situation in which material is removed from the waters of the United States and a small portion of it happens to fall back. Because incidental fallback represents a net withdrawal, not an addition, of material, it cannot be a discharge. . . . The agencies' primary counterargument—that fallback constitutes an "addition of any pollutant" because material becomes a pollutant only upon being dredged—is ingenious but unconvincing. Regardless of any legal metamorphosis that may occur at the moment of dredging, we fail to see how there can be an addition of *dredged material* when there is no addition of *material*. Although the Act includes "dredged spoil" in its list of pollutants, Congress could not have contemplated that the attempted removal of 100 tons of that substance could constitute an addition simply because only 99 tons of it were actually taken away. . . .

NWF complains that our understanding of "addition" reads the regulation of dredged material out of the statute. They correctly note that since dredged material comes from the waters of the United States, any discharge of such material into those waters could technically be described as a "redeposit," at least on a broad construction of that term.

The Fifth Circuit made a similar observation fifteen years ago: " '[D]redged' material is by definition material that comes from the water itself. A requirement that all pollutants must come from outside sources would effectively remove the dredge-and-fill provision from the statute." *Avoyelles Sportsmen's League v. Marsh.* But we do not hold that the Corps may not legally regulate some forms of redeposit under its § 404 permitting authority. We hold only that by asserting jurisdiction over *"any* redeposit," including incidental fallback, the *Tulloch* Rule outruns the Corps's statutory authority. Since the Act sets out no bright line between incidental fallback on the one hand and regulable redeposits on the other, a reasoned attempt by the agencies to draw such a line would merit considerable deference. But the *Tulloch* Rule makes no effort to draw such a line, and indeed its overriding purpose appears to be to expand the Corps's permitting authority to encompass incidental fallback and, as a result, a wide range of activities that cannot remotely be said to "add" anything to the waters of the United States....

Perhaps the strongest authority for the agencies' position is *Rybachek v. EPA,* 904 F.2d 1276 (9th Cir.1990). There the Ninth Circuit found that the Act permitted EPA to regulate placer mining, a process in which miners excavate dirt and gravel in and around waterways, and, after extracting the gold, discharge the leftover material back into the water. *Rybachek* held that the material separated from gold and released into the stream constituted a pollutant, and, to the extent that "the material discharged originally comes from the streambed itself, [its] resuspension [in the stream] may be interpreted to be an addition of a pollutant under the Act." *Rybachek* would help the agencies if the court had held that imperfect extraction, i.e., extraction accompanied by incidental fallback of dirt and gravel, constituted "addition of a pollutant," but instead it identified the regulable discharge as the discrete act of dumping leftover material into the stream after it had been processed....

In a press release accompanying the adoption of the *Tulloch* Rule, the White House announced: "Congress should amend the Clean Water Act to make it consistent with the agencies' rulemaking." While remarkable in its candor, the announcement contained a kernel of truth. If the agencies and NWF believe that the Clean Water Act inadequately protects wetlands and other natural resources by insisting upon the presence of an "addition" to trigger permit requirements, the appropriate body to turn to is Congress. Without such an amendment, the Act simply will not accommodate the *Tulloch* Rule. The judgment of the district court is *Affirmed.*

Notes and Comments

1. The court says it is not holding that the Corps and EPA cannot regulate *some* redeposits as additions, just that they cannot regulate all redeposits, including incidental fallback. What redeposits do you think the Corps and EPA can still regulate?

2. After the *National Mining* case, the Corps and EPA undertook a rulemaking to address the court's injunction against enforcing the Tulloch Rule. The outcome of that rulemaking was to exempt incidental fallback from the definition of "discharge of dredged material," but to add a new paragraph to the definition as follows: "The Corps and EPA regard the use of mechanized earth-moving equipment to conduct landclearing, ditching, channelization, in-stream mining or other earth-moving activity in waters of the United States as resulting in a discharge of dredged material unless project-specific evidence shows that the activity results in only incidental fallback." 33 CFR § 323.2 (d)(2)(i). How is this different from the Tulloch Rule in its coverage? This new rule was immediately challenged by the same interests that challenged the Tulloch Rule, but that case has not yet been decided.

3. Although the court in *National Mining* does not raise the issue, is there any problem with the fact that, even if the incidental fallback could be considered an "addition of a pollutant," the fallback or redeposit of dredged material is not what causes the damage to the wetland? Rather, it is the ditch that drains the water out. Compare that to the facts in the *Rybachek* case, where it was the discharge of the left over material taken out of the water for mining purposes that affected the quality of the water. Should Section 404 regulate redeposits of dredged material when the redeposit does not cause harm to the wetlands but the associated activity (ditching and draining) does? By its terms, the CWA requires permits (either NPDES or 404) whenever there is a discharge of a pollutant, whether or not the discharge adversely affects the waters. Indeed, if the discharge does not adversely affect the waters, that would be a basis for granting the permit.

4. *National Mining* was not the last word on the "addition" question by any means. In 2000, the Fourth Circuit confirmed that the Corps could regulate sidecasting in the case of *United States v. Deaton*, 209 F.3d 331, 335–36 (4th Cir. 2000), saying:

> The Deatons seize on the word "addition" in the phrase "addition of any pollutant" in the statutory definition of discharge. They argue that the "ordinary and natural meaning of 'addition' means something added, i.e., the addition of something not previously present." Thus, according to the Deatons, no pollutant is discharged unless there is an "introduction of new material into the area, or an increase in the amount of a type of material which is already present." Wilson, 133 F.3d at 259 (op. of Niemeyer, J.). Because sidecasting results in no net increase in the amount of material present in the wetland, the Deatons argue, it does not involve the "addition" (or discharge) of a pollutant. See National Mining Ass'n v. U.S. Army Corps of Engineers, 145 F.3d 1399, 1404 (D.C.Cir.1998) ("[W]e fail to see how there can be an addition of dredged material when there is no addition of material."). We are not convinced by this argument.
>
> Contrary to what the Deatons suggest, the statute does not prohibit the addition of material; it prohibits "the addition of any pollutant." The idea that there could be an addition of a pollutant without an addition of material seems to us entirely unremarkable, at least when an activity transforms some material from a nonpollutant into a pollutant, as

occurred here. In the course of digging a ditch across the Deaton property, the contractor removed earth and vegetable matter from the wetland. Once it was removed, that material became "dredged spoil," a statutory pollutant and a type of material that up until then was not present on the Deaton property. It is of no consequence that what is now dredged spoil was previously present on the same property in the less threatening form of dirt and vegetation in an undisturbed state. What is important is that once that material was excavated from the wetland, its redeposit in that same wetland added a pollutant where none had been before. Thus, even under the definition of "addition" (that is, "something added") offered by the Deatons, sidecasting adds a pollutant that was not present before.

Can *Deaton* be reconciled with *National Mining*, or does this represent a split in the circuits?

5. The Ninth Circuit, in *Borden Ranch Partnership v. U.S. Army Corps of Engineers*, 261 F.3d 810 (9th Cir. 2001), a split decision, followed the logic of *Deaton* with regard to a practice known as "deep ripping." The dissent would have followed and extended *National Mining*. In *Borden Ranch* the Partnership wanted to destroy the wetlands on its ranch to make the land suitable for vineyards. The wetlands existed because of a restrictive layer of soil, which prevented the surface water from penetrating deeply into the soil. Deep ripping involves the dragging of four-to seven-foot long metal prongs through the soil behind a tractor or a bulldozer. The ripper gouges through the restrictive layer, disgorging soil that is then dragged behind the ripper. This then allows the surface water to drain away into the ground. The court said:

> In this case, the Corps alleges that Tsakopoulos has essentially poked a hole in the bottom of protected wetlands. That is, by ripping up the bottom layer of soil, the water that was trapped can now drain out. While it is true, that in so doing, no new material has been "added," a "pollutant" has certainly been "added." Prior to the deep ripping, the protective layer of soil was intact, holding the wetland in place. Afterwards, that soil was wrenched up, moved around, and redeposited somewhere else. We can see no meaningful distinction between this activity and the activities at issue in Rybachek and Deaton.

261 F.3d at 815. The court then added a footnote:

> National Mining Assoc. v. U.S. Army Corps of Eng'rs, upon which [the Partnership] heavily relies, does not persuade us to the contrary. That case distinguished "regulable redeposits" from "incidental fallback." Here, the deep ripping does not involve mere incidental fallback, but constitutes environmental damage sufficient to constitute a regulable redeposit.

Do you think "deep ripping" is like "sidecasting"?

6. That was not the end of the story, however. The Supreme Court granted certiorari in the case and then affirmed by an equally divided Court, when Justice Kennedy recused himself. Why do you think the Court granted certiorari? When the Court affirms by a split vote, it has no precedential value; no opinion is written; and no notation is made as to how the Justices

voted. Court watchers feel confident that the Chief Justice and Justices O'Connor, Scalia, and Thomas voted to reverse, with Justices Stevens, Souter, Breyer, and Ginsburg voting to affirm. One must wonder whether *Borden Ranch* is a harbinger of things to come in a case where Justice Kennedy will cast a deciding vote.

7. An issue that has not received the same attention as the "addition" requirement is what constitutes a "point source." It is, after all, only additions of a pollutant "from any point source" that trigger a permit requirement under either the NPDES program or the 404 program. Recall that "point source" is a defined term in the CWA, 33 U.S.C. § 1362(14), that means: "any discernible, confined and discrete conveyance, including but not limited to any pipe, ditch, channel, tunnel, conduit, well, discrete fissure, container, rolling stock, concentrated animal feeding operation, or vessel or other floating craft, from which pollutants are or may be discharged." The list of items are said to be "included" within the meaning of a "discernible, confined and discreet conveyance"—the basic definition of "point source." Most of the listed items do not seem applicable to the discharge of dredged and fill material. Obviously, the dump truck emptying its load is a discernible, confined, and discrete conveyance, even if it is not clearly a listed item. However, most of the pieces of heavy equipment used for moving earth to destroy wetlands, such as bulldozers, backhoes, and deep ripping machines, are not so obviously "conveyances" at all. However, it might be said that heavy equipment is a "conveyance" to the extent that it moves (conveys) the earth from one place to another. Neither EPA nor the Corps has attempted a regulatory definition that goes beyond the statutory definition.

3. Exceptions from the Permit Requirement

Section 404(f), 33 U.S.C. § 1344(f), specifically exempts some activities from Section 404, even though they may involve the addition of dredged or fill material to jurisdictional waters. The most controversial exceptions are for: "normal farming, silviculture, and ranching activities such as plowing, seeding, cultivating, minor drainage, harvesting for the production of food, fiber, and forest products." 33 U.S.C. § 1344(f)(1)(A). On its face, this language might suggest that one could destroy wetlands so long as one was engaged in "normal farming." Indeed, the Partnership in *Borden Ranch* made that argument in its case. Paragraph (2) of the same subsection, however, known as the "recapture provision," limits the "normal farming" exception by stating that:

> Any discharge of dredged or fill material into the navigable waters incidental to any activity having as its purpose bringing an area of the navigable waters into a use to which it was not previously subject, where the flow or circulation of navigable waters may be impaired or the reach of such waters be reduced, shall be required to have a permit under this section.

To destroy wetlands (at least wetlands that are within the statutory requirement of being waters of the United States) necessarily reduces the reach of those waters, so to destroy wetlands for the purpose of expanding one's farming (or silvicultural or ranching) activities does not obtain the benefit of the exception. In *Borden Ranch*, the Partnership wanted to change the wetlands, which had been used as pasture, into a vineyard, and this it could not do under the exception.

4. The 404 Permit

Under Section 404 the Corps can either issue individual permits for individual discharges of dredged or fill material, or it can issue general permits covering a category of discharges. Individual permits are issued by one of the 38 Corps districts. General permits are issued by Corps headquarters, by Corps divisions, or by Corps districts, depending on their nature. The Corps is required to provide "notice and opportunity for public hearings" before issuing either type of permit, 33 U.S.C. § 1344(a) & (e)(1), but by regulation the Corps has stated that normally there will be no public hearing unless the Corps believes that a hearing is "needed for making a decision." 33 CFR § 327.4 (a). Persons desiring a public hearing must convince the Corps that the hearing is needed.

Because the Corps issuance of a permit is a federal agency action, the Corps must perform the analysis required by NEPA, and if an endangered species may be present, the biological assessment required by the ESA. In addition, if the activity takes place in a coastal area, the Corps must receive a determination from the state that the action is consistent with the state's Coastal Zone Management Plan under the Coastal Zone Management Act, 16 U.S.C. § 1456, and if the activity might affect a historical site, the Corps must coordinate with the State Historic Preservation Office pursuant to the National Historic Preservation Act, 16 U.S.C. § 470f. Because the Corps' action is likely to affect the quality of waters, the Corps must also engage in consultation with the Fish & Wildlife Service under the Fish and Wildlife Coordination Act, 16 U.S.C. §§ 661–666c, and obtain a Section 401 certification from the state that the activity will not impair the state's water quality, 33 U.S.C. § 1341(a). Federal agencies that disagree with the Corps' proposed decision may request that the decision be "elevated" from the District level to the Assistant Secretary of the Army for Civil Works.

The issuance of permits depends on meeting two different substantive standards: the 404(b)(1) Guidelines developed by EPA and the "public interest" evaluation imposed by the Corps on itself. Section 404(b)(1), 33 U.S.C. § 1344(b)(1), requires that proposed permits should be assessed by the Corps according to guidelines developed by EPA in conjunction with the Corps. These guidelines were to be based on similar criteria to those used in setting guidelines for the disposal of pollutants in the ocean, *see* 33 U.S.C. § 1343(c). The ocean discharge criteria listed in the statute generally require the application of an alternatives analysis, and this is the essence of the 404(b)(1) Guidelines, *see* 40 CFR. § 230.10.

Finally, before the Corps may issue a 404 permit, EPA must have the opportunity to review it. Under Section 404(c), 33 U.S.C. § 1344(c), EPA has the authority to veto any permit issuance if EPA finds that it would have "an unacceptable adverse effect on municipal water supplies, shellfish beds and fishery areas (including spawning and breeding areas), wildlife, or recreational areas." Courts have interpreted this veto power broadly and have rejected attempts to require EPA to determine the unacceptability of the adverse effects by balancing them against the social and economic benefits of granting the permit. *See, e.g., James City County, Va. v. EPA*, 12 F.3d 1330 (4th Cir. 1993). EPA rarely needs to exercise this authority, however, because its potential use provides EPA with significant influence on the Corps' decision.

Section 404 does provide for a limited version of "cooperative federalism," *see* 33 U.S.C. § 1344(g). If a state provides assurances to EPA that under its state law it can administer a program in accordance with the requirements of Section 404, EPA authorizes the state to issue individual and general permits in lieu of the Corps. However, only two states, New Jersey and Michigan, have applied and been authorized to issue 404 permits in lieu of the Corps. There are two primary reasons for the lack of state interest. First, the state authorization is very limited. States cannot displace the Corps' authority to issue the 404 permits with respect to traditional navigable waters and their adjacent wetlands. Even before *SWANCC*, this did not leave many waters subject to state permitting; after *SWANCC* it would seem to leave only nonnavigable tributaries. Even with respect to those waters, EPA retains a veto authority over the state's permits. Second, unlike the NPDES program, states do not receive federal funds if they become authorized states. Whereas EPA does not have the infrastructure actually to administer in the states either the Clean Air Act or the NPDES program under the Clean Water Act, the Corps does have the infrastructure to administer Section 404, because of its historic and continuing permitting responsibility under the Rivers and Harbors Act and its residual permitting authority under Section 404 for traditionally navigable waters. That is, under the NPDES program, EPA needs states to administer the program; under the 404 Program, the Corps does not have that need. As with other pollution control statutes, Section 404 does not preclude states from providing protection beyond that in federal law. Many states have enacted laws to protect their wetlands, and the Court's decision in *SWANCC* provided an incentive for more to do so.

a.   The 404(b)(1) Guidelines and the Public Interest Review

The substantive standards governing the decision whether a 404 permit should be issued are to be found in the 404(b)(1) Guidelines and the Corps' Public Interest review standards. The basic requirement of the Guidelines is that: "no discharge of dredged or fill material shall be permitted if there is a practicable alternative to the proposed discharge which would have less adverse impact on the aquatic ecosystem, so long as the alternative does not have other significant adverse environmental consequences." 40 CFR § 230.10(a). If the activity is not "water dependent," a practicable alternative to siting the activity in a special aquatic area (e.g., a wetland) is presumed to exist, but the permit applicant can rebut the presumption. That is, if the activity does not *need* to be near or on water, then it is presumed that there is alternative to filling a wetland or waters for the activity. Moreover, if there is a practicable alternative not located in a special aquatic area, its environmental effects are presumed to be less adverse than the its effects would be in the special aquatic area. Thus, for example, if a developer already owns a parcel that includes a wetlands, and he wishes to develop it for a strip mall and associated parking lot, there will be a presumption that there is an available alternative and practicable site not involving a wetlands, because the development is not wetlands dependent, and that such alternative would be less harmful to the environment.

Under the Guidelines, an alternative is "practicable" if "it is available and capable of being done after taking into consideration cost, existing technology, and logistics in light of overall project purposes." 40 CFR § 230.10(a)(2). Thus, cost and feasibility are factored into whether the discharge should be allowed. In our strip mall example, for instance, the developer may rebut the presumption that there is a non-wetlands alternative by showing that given the market area he proposes to serve and which would support stores that would locate in the strip mall, there is no other feasible location, perhaps because other locations are either too small or too expensive to make his project feasible. If he establishes these facts, then he will have satisfied the Guidelines requirement. The fact that he already owns the proposed site does not foreclose consideration of other possible sites, but the additional cost of purchasing one of those sites might make the alternative impracticable. If the developer came to the area with the intent to develop a strip mall and bought the property in question that contains the wetlands, while passing up the other sites, EPA maintains that the alternatives analysis should proceed from the time he entered the market, not the time he seeks the 404 permit. In other words, the analysis would assume he did not own any property and would consider whether the non-wetlands alternatives were practicable from that perspective. In the case of *Bersani v. U.S. EPA*, 850 F.2d 36 (2d Cir. 1988), the court upheld EPA's position.

As was the case with NEPA analyses, the applicant's project purposes must be respected, but they cannot be framed in too narrow a manner. For example, in our strip mall hypothetical, if the applicant had stated that his purpose was to create a strip mall with 37 stores and 370 parking places, this might be too restrictive. The proper analysis would be whether a profitable strip mall could be developed at an alternative site. If this only required 34 stores and 340 parking places, then a practicable alternative would be presumed to exist unless the developer demonstrated that there was no available site that would accommodate such a strip mall. On the other hand, the Corps' acceptance of a developer's claim, that in order to create a successful alpine destination resort (for skiing in the winter) it was necessary to have an associated 18–hole golf course (for the summer), was upheld in *Sylvester v. U.S. Army Corps of Engineers*, 882 F.2d 407 (9th Cir. 1989). This is an area in which the Corps' judgment, if reasonably explained, is likely to be upheld.

In any case, under the alternatives analysis, it is possible that a permit applicant could show that there was no practicable alternative to filling a wetland to build a strip mall and associated parking lot, but the Guidelines have a safety net: "no discharge of dredged or fill material shall be permitted which will cause or contribute to significant degradation of the waters of the United States." 40 CFR § 230.10(c). What constitutes a "significant degradation," nevertheless, is a matter of judgment, and there is little case law clarifying the concept. Again, this is an area where the Corps' judgment, if reasonably explained, is likely to be upheld.

Under the 404(b)(1) Guidelines, whenever a permit is granted, the permittee must provide for compensatory mitigation for any destruction to wetlands. In practice, this means that, for example, if an acre of wetlands were to be destroyed by the discharge, the permittee would have to restore or create more than an acre of similar wetlands in the area. For a period, it was not clear whether a permit applicant could avoid the alternatives analysis by promising compensatory mitigation, as one can avoid a "significant impact" decision under NEPA by compensatory mitigation actions. However, in 1980, the Corps and EPA entered a Memorandum of Agreement on the the so-called sequence of mitigation. First, the applicant must attempt to avoid impacts on wetlands to the extent practicable (the alternatives analysis); second, the applicant must minimize the impacts on wetlands; and only then, for whatever effects on wetlands remain, the applicant must provide compensatory mitigation.

For the past ten years there has been an attempt to encourage the creation of "mitigation banks," wetlands restored and recreated as an investment, which could then be used as a market from which developers could purchase mitigation credits to satisfy their compensatory mitigation requirements. The idea was to create a financial incentive for creating new or restoring formerly destroyed wetlands in light of an anticipated market demand for needed compensatory mitigation. While the jury is still out on the idea, it certainly did not achieve the success that was hoped for. First, creating and restoring wetlands has turned out to be harder than thought, and initial attempts that failed set a bad precedent. Second, in order for compensatory mitigation to compensate for losses, the new or restored wetlands must serve the same functions as the destroyed wetlands. Usually, although not always, this requires the compensation to be at least near the site of the destroyed wetlands, which severely limits the the potential market for wetlands banks.

The second substantive standard governing the Corps' issuance of 404 Permits is its "public interest" review. *See* 33 CFR § 320.4(a). This review only comes into play after consideration of the 404(b)(1) Guidelines, so that if a permit is to be denied under the Guidelines, there would be no public interest review. The Corps' "public interest" review traces its history to the Corps' administration of the Rivers and Harbors Act, where the statute had provided no meaningful standard for decision and the Corps invented the "public interest" review as the basis for decisions whether to issue permits under that statute. Because Section 404, through the mandated 404(b)(1) Guidelines, does provide a standard for decision, the legal basis for a separate, distinct review is unclear. Nevertheless, the Corps regulation provides one public interest review applicable to all Corps permit actions, whether under Section 404 or the Rivers and Harbors Act. It provides that:

> The decision whether to issue a permit will be based on an evaluation of the probable impacts, including cumulative impacts, of the proposed activity and its intended use on the public interest. Evaluation of the probable impact which the proposed activity may have on the public interest requires a careful weighing of all those factors which become relevant in each particular case. The benefits which reasonably may be expected to accrue from the proposal must be balanced against its reasonably foreseeable detriments.

33 CFR § 320.4(a)(1). The regulation then provides a list of more than 20 factors that should go into the balancing process. At least one lower court has held that the Corps does not have the authority under Section 404 to consider economic costs and benefits unrelated to the activity's effect on the environment. *Mall Properties, Inc. v. Marsh*, 672 F.Supp. 561 (D.Mass. 1987), *appeal dismissed*, 841 F.2d 440 (1st Cir. 1988). For most practical purposes, however, the factors stress environmental protection as in the public interest and the destruction of wetlands as contrary to the public interest, so the public interest review rarely adds much to the 404(b)(1) Guidelines analysis.

The following is a typical case applying the Guidelines.

FUND FOR ANIMALS, INC. v. RICE

United States Court of Appeals, Eleventh Circuit, 1996.
85 F.3d 535.

DUBINA, Circuit Judge:

The Plaintiffs–Appellants ("the Plaintiffs"), seek to prevent the construction of a municipal landfill on a site in Sarasota County, Florida.... The Plaintiffs bring this case before us to challenge the district court's grant of summary judgment in favor of the Defendants–Appellees ("the Defendants"). The district court's challenged judgment has thus far allowed Sarasota County to proceed with construction of the landfill. For the reasons stated below, we affirm the district court's judgment.

I. BACKGROUND

* * *

B. The Landfill

On November 22, 1989, the United States Army Corps of Engineers ("the Corps") received an application from Sarasota County, Florida ("Sarasota County" or "the County") for a permit under Section 404 of the Clean Water Act ("CWA"). The proposed project for which Sarasota County sought a permit consists of constructing an 895–acre landfill and required ancillary structures on a 6,150–acre site known as the "Walton Tract." The Walton Tract is located in west central Sarasota County, north of the Caloosahatchee River, west of the Myakka River, and just southwest of the Myakka River State Park. According to current projections, the fill material for the landfill will impact approximately seventy-four acres of isolated wetlands. The project also includes construction of a roadway extension ("the Knights Trail Road extension"), consisting of approximately 2.5 miles of new road and impacting 0.47 acres of wetlands.

During June of 1990, the Corps dispersed notice of Sarasota County's application to government agencies, private organizations, and other interested persons. The notice invited public comment on the landfill proposal. [T]he Environmental Protection Agency ("the E.P.A.") recommended denial of the permit under Section 404(b)(1) of the guidelines promulgated pursuant to the Clean Water Act. At that time, Sarasota County projected that the landfill would affect 120 acres of wetlands.

The following year, Sarasota County submitted an alternative analysis, which included modifications of the project calculated to reduce the prospective effect on wetlands. Four sites, labeled D, E, F (the Walton Tract), and G, were proposed for the landfill. During September of 1993, Sarasota County submitted a revised plan that would reduce the landfill's effect on wetlands from 120 acres to approximately seventy-four acres. In February of 1994, the E.P.A. notified the Corps that it no longer objected to the issuance of the permit.

At the end of May 1994, the Corps completed an Environmental Assessment and Statement of Findings, determining that no environmental impact statement was required. In addition, the Corps announced that a public hearing would not benefit the decision-making process. After nearly five years of administrative review, the Corps approved the requested permit on June 3, 1994. On August 10, 1994, the Corps verified the applicability of Nationwide Permit No. 26 to Sarasota County's proposal to fill 0.47 acre of wetlands as part of the Knight's Trail Road extension project.

On June 17, 1994, the Plaintiffs submitted a sixty-day notice of intent to sue. The Plaintiffs alleged violations of the Clean Water Act and the Endangered Species Act ("ESA"). Two months later, the F.W.S. requested resumption of § 7 consultation under the ESA to allow consideration of any potential effect on the Florida Panther and the Eastern Indigo Snake. In October of 1994, the F.W.S. issued its first Biological Opinion addressing concerns regarding the Florida Panther and the Eastern Indigo Snake. The Opinion concluded that the project was unlikely to jeopardize further the existence of either the Florida Panther or the Eastern Indigo Snake. However, it did include an "incidental take" statement for the Eastern Indigo Snake and recommendations for Florida Panther conservation, wetland preservation, and a monitoring program. The Corps incorporated the F.W.S.'s recommendations and modified Sarasota County's permit on November 14, 1994. Two weeks later, the Plaintiffs commenced an action in federal district court against the Corps, the F.W.S., the E.P.A., and the Sarasota County Administrator.

In response to the suit, the F.W.S. requested that the Corps resume § 7 consultation on the permit. The Corps suspended Sarasota County's permit the next day, and on February 7, 1995, the Corps also suspended its verification of coverage for discharge of fill associated with the Knight's Trail Road extension project. In April of 1995, the F.W.S. issued to the Corps its second Biological Opinion addressing concerns regarding the Florida Panther and the Eastern Indigo Snake. The Opinion included both an "incidental take" statement for the Eastern Indigo Snake and conservation recommendations for the Florida Panther. This Opinion, which superseded the F.W.S.'s previous Biological Opinion, again concluded that the proposed project was unlikely to jeopardize the continued existence of either the Florida Panther or the Eastern Indigo Snake.

On April 12, 1995, the Plaintiffs submitted comments to the Corps on the F.W.S.'s new Biological Opinion. The next day, the Corps determined, based on the F.W.S.'s Biological Opinion and the Corps' independent environmental assessment, that reinstatement of the permit to dredge and fill seventy-four acres of wetlands with additional modifications was in the public interest. Thus, the modified permit was reinstated on April 13, 1995.

Following final issuance of the permit, the Plaintiffs filed their Second Amended Complaint, which raised claims under the Clean Water Act, the Endangered Species Act, and the National Environmental Policy Act ("NEPA"). The complaint requested declaratory and injunctive relief. . . .

On October 12, 1995, the district court granted summary judgment in favor of Sarasota County and denied the Plaintiffs' contingent request for discovery. The Plaintiffs filed a notice of appeal and asked this court to grant an emergency injunction prohibiting Sarasota County from commencing construction of the new facility until resolution of the appeal. This court denied the Plaintiffs' emergency motion for an injunction pending appeal in an order dated October 26, 1995, and set an expedited briefing schedule.

II. Statement of the Issues

(1) Whether the district court erred in finding that the Corps did not act arbitrarily or capriciously in making the following . . . decision[]:

A.   to grant a permit to fill seventy-four acres of wetland on the Walton Tract for a county landfill. . . .

B.   not to hold its own public hearing on the project.

III. Standards of Review

The standard of review applicable to the main issues in this case is provided by the Administrative Procedure Act ("APA"), 5 U.S.C. § 706, which states that a court may set aside agency action that is "arbitrary, capricious, an abuse of discretion, or otherwise not in accordance with law." . . .

IV. Discussion

* * *

A. *Challenges Under The Clean Water Act.*

The CWA prohibits the discharge of pollutants, including dredged spoil, into the waters of the United States, except in compliance with various sections of the CWA, including Section 404. Section 404(a) authorizes the Secretary of the Army, acting through the Corps, to issue permits for the discharge of dredge or fill material into waters of the United States. The Corps may issue individual permits on a case-by-case basis, or it may issue general permits on a state, regional, or nationwide basis.

The Plaintiffs allege that the Corps violated the substantive and procedural requirements of the CWA in three ways: (1) by not choosing an alternative site where the landfill would have a less adverse impact on wetlands; (2) by not considering the cumulative impact of the permitting decision; and (3) by not giving notice and an opportunity for a public hearing on the permit. We consider each of these contentions in turn.

1. *Alternative Sites*

The Plaintiffs' primary argument is that the Corps ignored alternative sites where the landfill would have had less of an impact on the aquatic ecosystem. Under applicable Section 404 guidelines, a discharge of dredge or fill will not be permitted if, among other things, there is a "practicable alternative" to the proposed discharge that would have a less adverse impact on the aquatic ecosystem. 40 C.F.R. § 230.10(a). An alternative is considered practicable if "it is available and capable of being done after taking into consideration cost, existing technology and logistics in light of overall project purposes." 40 C.F.R. § 230.10(a)(2). The guidelines create a rebuttable presumption that practicable alternatives are available where the activity associated with a proposed discharge would occur on a wetland and is not water dependent. 40 C.F.R. § 230.10(a)(3). If the Corps finds that the permit complies with the Section 404(b)(1) guidelines, the permit "will be granted unless the district engineer determines that it would be contrary to the public interest." 33 C.F.R. § 320.4(a)(1). The public interest review evaluates "the probable impacts, including cumulative impacts, of the proposed activity and its intended use on the public interest." *Id.*

According to the Plaintiffs, Sarasota County itself identified three such practicable alternatives, and use of any of these sites would result in less harm to the environment than use of the Walton Tract. The

Plaintiffs rely heavily on a particular section of a 1991 study performed by Sarasota County in which the County considered alternatives to the Walton Tract. As part of this study, Sarasota County assigned a numerical "environmental score" to each of the four potential sites. The scoring system was designed to give higher scores to those sites most suited for a landfill. As the following point totals illustrate, the Walton Tract received the lowest numerical score of the four tracts in the analysis: Site D—39 points; Site E—39 points; Site F (the Walton Tract)—34 points; and Site G—41 points.

Nonetheless, the Plaintiffs' argument that an alternative to the Walton Tract should have been chosen is meritless for two reasons. First, the ranking was done by Sarasota County and not the Corps, and the Corps is not bound by an applicant's ranking system. In fact, the Corps conducts its own independent evaluation, and its practicable alternative analysis is not susceptible to numerical precision, but instead requires a balancing of the applicant's needs and environmental concerns.

Second, the Corps and Sarasota County point to numerous reasons to explain why, although the Walton Tract received the lowest environmental score, it was nonetheless the most suited for placement of a landfill. Specifically, our review of the record persuades us that the Corps did not act contrary to, but instead adhered to, the sequencing preference expressed in the CWA regulations: (1) avoidance, (2) minimization, and (3) compensatory mitigation. See 33 C.F.R. § 320.4(r); 40 C.F.R. § 230.10.

As its first task, the Corps determined that there was no alternative site available that would avoid any impact on wetlands. Had a suitable upland site existed, such a site would have been entitled to a presumption that it was a practical alternative. See 40 C.F.R. § 230.10(a)(3). Each of the four highest ranking sites contain scattered, isolated wetlands: Site D is 19% wetlands, Site E is 22% wetlands, Site G is 13% wetlands, and the Walton Tract is 22% wetlands. A landfill of 895 acres in Sarasota County would involve impacts on aquatic ecosystems (i.e., filling of wetlands) and raise the same Section 404 permitting concerns no matter which of the four sites was chosen. Since the Plaintiffs have not identified an 895–acre parcel of contiguous uplands in all of Sarasota County, it is not clear that the presumption established by 40 C.F.R. § 230.10(a)(3) would ever apply in this case.

The absence of a suitable upland site required the Corps to analyze all suitable alternatives. In this case, each of the alternative sites poses its own environmental problems which led the Corps to determine that it was less suitable for the landfill than the Walton Tract. Site D contains wetlands across its southern boundary, including the headwaters for a stream know as South Creek. The site contains ninety-two acres of wetlands, which is eighteen more acres of wetlands than would be filled by the project if done on the Walton Tract. Most notably, Site D is confirmed to be a nesting site for the Bald Eagle (Haliaeetus leucocephalus). Site E borders the Myakka River State Park and contains two large wetland systems that drain to both the Myakka River and a waterway called the Cow Pen Slough. Site E contains sixty-one acres of wetlands. Presence of a state listed species, the Florida Sandhill Crane (Grus canadensis), was confirmed on the site. Moreover, any landfill located on Site G would have been within the Myakka River watershed. The Corps noted the probable presence of the Eastern Indigo Snake on Site G, and Site G was also designated a "Priority 1 Florida Panther habitat."

By contrast, the Walton Tract possesses characteristics that the Corps considered to be significant environmental advantages. Each of the other sites is considerably smaller than the Walton Tract: Site D is 2,130 acres, Site E is 3,360 acres, and Site G is 2,100 acres. The Walton Tract is 6,150 acres. Thus, the site is large enough to provide a broad natural vegetative buffer around all sides of the landfill. The large size of the tract also allows a substantial buffer between the landfill and adjoining areas. Sarasota County has zoned approximately 2,971 acres on the site as a conservation area, which includes the most valuable areas of upland wetland habitat on the Walton Tract and adjoins other preserve areas off-site. These preserved lands combine with adjacent properties to form a continuous unit of potentially suitable Florida Panther habitat and serve as a barrier between the Myakka River ecosystem and further development from the west.

Where, as here, filling of wetlands cannot be avoided, then "appropriate and practicable steps" must be taken to minimize the potential adverse impacts of the discharge on wetlands. 40 C.F.R. § 230.10(d). While the original design of the landfill would have impacted approximately 120 acres, Sarasota County subsequently scaled down the project so that wetland impacts would be reduced to approximately seventy-four acres. Furthermore, although the project will eliminate approximately seventy-four acres of isolated wetlands, the large size of the Walton Tract allows on-site mitigation. Sarasota County is replacing the lost acreage with approximately seventy acres of wet prairie habitat in the northeast corner of the tract and enhancing and restoring an additional 262 acres of wetlands. While wetlands will be lost, a greater acreage of higher quality wetlands will be restored and enhanced, resulting in no net loss of wetland resources.

In discussing the alternatives analysis, the district court did not suggest, nor do we, that practicable alternatives may be ignored because of the mitigation potential of a site, as the Plaintiffs claim. To the contrary, the district court recognized, as do we, that the Corps had taken into account all the considerations which factor into the alternatives analysis. There is no substantial question as to whether Sarasota County needs a new landfill, because the County's current landfill must close in 1999. Sarasota County, the Corps, the F.W.S., and the E.P.A. all scrutinized the project for over five years, and all agree that the Walton Tract is the most suitable site for the new landfill. Accordingly, insofar as the CWA practicable alternatives analysis is concerned, we hold that the Plaintiffs failed to demonstrate that the Corps acted arbitrarily and capriciously in granting a permit to fill seventy-four acres of wetlands on the Walton Tract. . . .

3. *Public Hearings*

The Plaintiffs' third argument under the CWA is that the Corps violated requirements by failing to provide the public "any hearings" on the landfill project and by failing to provide the public with information regarding possible effects of the project on the Florida Panther and the Eastern Indigo Snake. The CWA mandates an "opportunity for public hearings." However, the statute does not state that the Corps itself must hold its own public hearings regardless of how many other hearings have been held on a project. The applicable regulations provide the Corps discretion to hold hearings on permit applications on an "as needed" basis. 33 C.F.R. § 327.4. If the Corps determines that it has the information necessary to reach a decision and that there is "no valid interest to be served by a hearing," the Corps has the discretion not to hold one. Id. § 327.4(b).

Here, the Corps recognized that two public hearings on the project had already been conducted under the state process. Given the information generated from these hearings and the voluminous written information submitted to the Corps by opponents of the project, including the Plaintiffs, the Corps concluded that holding its own additional public hearing was unlikely to generate any new information that was not already in the Corps' possession. Moreover, the Plaintiffs point to no such information. Under these circumstances, we are persuaded that the Corps did not act arbitrarily or abuse its discretion in deciding to forego further public hearings on the matter. . . .

AFFIRMED.

Notes and Comments

1. Edited from this case is the challenge to the permit based upon the Endangered Species Act, in which the Fund for Animals alleged that the Fish and Wildlife Service's Biological Opinion was arbitrary and capricious in finding the landfill would not jeopardize the very rare and endangered Florida Panther ("one of the most endangered large mammals in the world") and the threatened Eastern Indigo Snake ("Measuring up to 8 1/2 feet, this docile, nonpoisonous snake is the longest found in North America"). The plaintiffs lost on that issue as well, but first their threat to bring a lawsuit and then their filing of the lawsuit resulted in the Fish and Wildlife Service taking a closer look and imposing conservation requirements regarding the Panther and an incidental take statement for the snake that would not otherwise have been included. Considering the alternative possible locations for the landfill, do you think the plaintiffs were really concerned about the wetlands or about the significant acreage involved at the Walton site?

2. The court refers to the Walton Tract as involving "isolated wetlands." This case, of course is pre-*SWANCC*. After *SWANCC*, would Sarasota County even have needed to involve any of the Federal agencies before using the Walton Tract as a landfill?

3.   How did the County rebut the presumption that a nonwater dependent activity has a practicable alternative?

4.   What about the Corps' denial of a public hearing on its permit? Do you think Congress intended that a county's public hearing regarding the siting of a landfill would satisfy the "opportunity for a public hearing" requirement in Section 404? Does it not seem likely that the public hearing opportunity called for in Section 404 was intended to address Section 404 issues, which probably would not be the focus of a county hearing? On the other hand, if the plaintiffs cannot show any harm from being denied the hearing, what would be the point. Perhaps the court's best response would have been to have found the denial of a public hearing to be harmless error in the circumstances. *See* 5 U.S.C. § 706. Nevertheless, the court's analysis is typical of what other courts have held. *See, e.g., Friends of the Payette v. Horseshoe Bend Hydroelectric Co.*, 988 F.2d 989, 996–97 (9th Cir. 1993). If a hearing were to be held, what kind of hearing should it be? The Corps, when it provides a hearing, always provides a legislative-type hearing, not a trial-type hearing.

5.   In the course of the opinion, the court affirms the Corps' use of a nationwide permit to authorize the filling of .47 acres for road access to the land fill. The use of nationwide permits is discussed below.

b.   General Permits and Alternative Procedures

While most of the focus of litigation has been on individual permits, most discharges actually take place under General Permits of one form or another. In FY 2002, for example, there were roughly 4000 individual 404 permits issued, but there were roughly 75,000 activities occurring under General Permits. General Permits are adopted after notice and comment and are good for up to five years. According to Section 404, a General Permit can be issued only if "the activities in such category are similar in nature, will cause only minimal adverse environmental effects when performed separately, and will have only minimal cumulative adverse effect on the environment." 33 U.S.C. § 1344(e)(1). The Corps by regulation seems to have expanded the statutory standard by adding an additional definition of "general permit" that eliminates the requirement that the activities subject to the permit be "similar in nature" but adds the requirement that the general permit would result in avoiding unnecessary duplication of regulatory control exercised by another Federal, state, or local agency. 33 CFR 323.2(h). There are three General Permits and one "alternative procedure" worth mentioning: Nationwide Permits, Regional Permits, State Programmatic General Permits, and Letters of Permission.

i.   *Nationwide Permits*

Nationwide Permits (NWPs), issued by Corps headquarters, are probably the most important form of General Permit. *See generally* 33 CFR Part 330. In FY 2002, approximately 35,000 activities were authorized under NWPs. The current list of NWPs was adopted in 2002 and contains 44 NWPs. Until 2002 NWPs were published in the Code of

Federal Regulations, but the Corps maintains that NWPs are permits, not rules, so it has ceased their publication in the CFR. They are available online. www.usace.army.mil/inet/functions/cw/cecwo/reg/ nationwide_permits.htm. Despite the Corps' insistence that the NWPs are not rules, the Corps adopts them after notice-and-comment, and the NWPs act in the nature of rules. That is, the NWPs establish on a generic basis that certain types of activities, if carried out in accordance with the terms in the NWPs, are permitted. Moreover, these NWPs are subject to general conditions. For example, persons must assure that state water quality certifications under Section 401, if required, have been obtained before the NWP is effective as to their activity. For discharges likely to have any effect on wetlands or water quality, the Corps requires Preconstruction Notification (PCN) to the District Engineer. This enables the District Engineer to review the particular proposed activity, including the proposed mitigation, to determine whether it raises environmental questions—in particular, whether the activity would have a significant adverse effect on waters or wetlands. The District Engineer is authorized to suspend, modify, or revoke any NWP if he determines that concerns for the environment make the NWP inappropriate in a particular case. If the NWP is revoked for a particular case, the person may still seek an individual 404 permit.

Some NWPs are uncontroversial. For example, NWP 36 authorizes the discharge of dredged and fill material for the creation of boat ramps, so long as the discharge does not exceed 50 cubic yards of an approved material and no discharge occurs in a wetland. NWP 29 authorizes natural persons to fill up to one-quarter acre of non-tidal waters for a single family residence.

There are several, however, that are controversial. Historically, NWP 26 generally authorized discharges to wetlands associated with isolated waters or headwaters so long as the discharge did not adversely affect more than a certain area. Originally, the area was 10 acres, which was reduced to 3 acres in 1996. Because the Corps required Preconstruction Notification (PCN) for discharges affecting greater than 1 acre originally and one-third acre in 1996, which notification could provide a basis for the Corps to remove the activity from the NWP and require an individual permit, the Corps believed the NWP was sufficiently protective. Nonetheless, environmentalists believed this NWP was a significant loophole, and the Corps promised to and did delete it in 2002. However, it replaced it with five new NWPs (NWPs 39, 41–44) that are activity specific: Residential, Commercial, and Institutional Developments; Reshaping Existing Drainage Ditches; Recreational Facilities; Stormwater Management Facilities; and Mining Activities. Because these new NWPs, especially the first, in essence recreate in most respects NWP 26 with slightly different area limitations, this change was opposed by environmentalists. At the same time, developers were not particularly pleased with the change either, because it did not loosen restrictions and in some ways tightened them. For example, developers cannot adversely affect more than one-half acre of non-tidal waters (including wetlands) or more than 300 linear feet of a stream and must provide a PCN if the activity affects more than one-tenth of an acre of non-tidal waters or causes the loss of any open waters.

Another NWP that is controversial is NWP 21, Surface Coal Mining Activities. This NWP originally authorized discharges associated with surface coal mining, so long as the coal mining was authorized by the Department of Interior or an approved state under the Surface Mining Control and Reclamation Act (SMCRA). This NWP has been the authorization for filling valleys with mining overburden associated with mountain-top removal mining. That is, the mining company literally removes the top of a mountain to obtain open access to the coal seam, and the mountain top is dumped into the adjoining valley, invariably covering streams and watersheds. This led to law suits challenging the Corps' authority to permit such activities, which concluded with a settlement agreement in 1998 that in West Virginia the NWP would not authorize valley fills burying a stream draining more than 250 acres and that the Corps and other federal agencies would undertake a Programmatic Environmental Impact Statement regarding mountain-top and valley-fill mining, an analysis that had not previously been done, and, at least of the date of this writing, yet to be completed. One can imagine why environmentalists were and are concerned.

The Corps has defended the concept of its NWP on the grounds that it is unnecessary bureaucratic duplication for it to review what has been reviewed and approved by a federal or state agency under SMCRA. Its latest NWP 21, however, issued in 2002, reflects an increased sensitivity to the issue. First, the NWP requires preconstruction notification to the District Engineer in all cases, and it further requires the District Engineer to determine that the adverse environmental effects of the activity are minimal both individually and cumulatively and must notify the project sponsor of this determination in writing before the activity may commence. Finally, the District Engineer must determine on a case-by-case basis the necessary mitigation to assure that effects to aquatic systems are minimal. In short, according to its NWP and implementing guidance, the Corps seems to engage in virtually the same review under NWP 21 as it would if it were an application for an individual permit.

Even were this so, it would not quell the fears of environmentalists. This is due to the procedural differences between an individual permit action and Corps review pursuant to a preconstruction notification under a NWP. The former requires notice and an opportunity for a public hearing, as well as triggering NEPA and other federal statutory provisions because the action is "federal agency action." The latter, however, does not involve public notice or comment. The issuance of the NWP itself was subject to notice, comment, and a public hearing. Because the "permit" has been issued, the Corps believes no further public participation is required in its review pursuant to the NWP. Moreover, the Corps maintains that its review after a preconstruction notification is not "federal agency action," triggering NEPA and other statutory requirements. Thus, in a sense, the Corps can have its cake and eat it too.

That is, it can retain the ability to review actions to determine whether they should receive intensive review (i.e., individual permit treatment) without all the procedural requirements attendant to individual permit actions. If the Corps believes the action has no significant effect, the Corps can let it go forward with little resource demand on the Corps. When the Corps' review is only as to whether the activity should qualify for treatment under a NWP or should be handled as an individual permit action, the theory that this is not a separate agency action might be well founded. However, when the Corps is making substantive determinations, such as the requisite mitigation to require, its theory becomes more tenuous.

ii. Other General Permits and Letters of Permission

Nationwide Permits are not the only form of General Permit. Another form of General Permit is the Regional Permit, which is issued by Division or District Engineers. *See* 33 CFR § 325(e)(2). These are like NWPs except they are tailored for activities that are more regional or localized in nature. The concept, however, is the same; the Regional Permit authorizes a class of activities, and if an activity is within the terms of the Regional permit and complies with any condition placed on it, the activity may go forward without an individual permit. In FY 2002, there were approximately 38,000 activities authorized by Regional Permits.

Still another form of General Permit is the State Programmatic General Permit (SPGP). This is the Corps' preferred alternative to authorizing states to issue 404 Permits under Section 404(g). This permit relies on the additional definition of a General Permit in the Corps regulations because it is justified by a state having a regulatory program in place that makes the Corps permitting process an unnecessary duplication of regulatory control. If a state establishes to the Corps' satisfaction that its regulatory program operates in a fashion duplicative of the Corps' program, then the Corps can grant a SPGP covering all or some of the activities regulated by the state.

In theory at least, the Corps could in essence delegate its entire Section 404 authority to a state if it was convinced that the state would assure that no permit would individually or cumulatively have more than a minimal adverse effect on the environment. Because of the legal questions this would raise—in particular, the apparent evasion of the statutory procedure and limitation on state authorization to issue 404 permits and the difficulty of justifying the SPGP under the statutory requirement that general permits be for activities "similar in nature"— the Corps in practice has limited its SPGPs to activities of very limited effect. For example, in Vermont, one of the relatively few states with an SPGP, fills of under 1 acre are generally authorized if they comply with the state regulatory procedure. Many, if not most, of these activities are subject to PCNs to the Corps, however, and fills in certain specified waters or wetlands are only authorized if less than 5000 square feet are affected.

"Letters of Permission" (LOP) are in the Corps' terminology an alternative procedure for receiving an individual permit through abbreviated procedures and not involving publication of notice of the particular activity, but including coordination with appropriate federal and state agencies. *See* 33 CFR § 325.2(e)(1). In FY 2002, approximately 3000 LOPs were issued. Despite the Corps' characterization, which would raise serious questions under Section 404, which provides no authorization for such an alternative procedure, the Corps' practice makes LOPs look more like a form of general permit. That is, in order for a District Engineer to issue an LOP, the District Engineer must first, in coordination with federal and state wildlife agencies, develop a list of categories of activities proposed for authorization by LOP. The District Engineer must then publish that list and provide an opportunity for a public hearing and comment. An LOP can only be issued for an activity after the state has given any required 401 certification and CZMA consistency determination. On the face of the regulation there is no requirement that the adverse effect of the activity will be minimal, but before LOPs were authorized for Section 404, the Corps had issued them under Section 10 of the Rivers and Harbors Act, and the implementing regulations there specify that LOPs under Section 10 are authorized only when, in the opinion of the district engineer, the proposed work would be minor, would not have significant or cumulative impacts on environmental values, and should encounter no appreciable opposition. 33 CFR § 325.2(e)(1)(i). Why the same requirement is not made for Section 404 LOPs is unknown, but one might imagine that the Corps treats the two LOPs similarly.

Notes and Comments

1. As may be seen, the Corps approach to its Section 404 responsibilities has in many respects been informed (or distorted) by its experience under the Rivers and Harbors Act as well as the frequent overlap between Section 404 permits involving discharges of dredged and fill material and Section 10 Permits under the Rivers and Harbors Act involving obstructions to navigation. The geographic jurisdiction and the focus of the regulatory review is different between the two provisions, but there has perhaps been a tendency to treat them alike. In particular, the extension of the Corps' public interest review and the use of LOPs for Section 404 permitting, both developed under the Rivers and Harbors Act, are examples of such a tendency.

2. A recurrent theme in the Corps' handling of its permitting responsibilities is the attempt to streamline the procedural requirements while maintaining overall control of the process. The use of general permits of one sort or another combined with PCN requirements enables the Corps to deal with what it believes are routine and minor activities in a summary manner, even as it retains the discretionary authority to impose particular conditions or even to require individual permitting in individual cases the Corps deems appropriate. Because these summary procedures generally shortcut certain analyses and public procedures, environmentalists view them with signifi-

cant skepticism, worrying that the Corps has been captured by agricultural or development interests.

3. Persons who have been denied permits (or offered permits upon conditions they find unacceptable or believe are unlawful) or who dispute a Corps determination that it has regulatory jurisdiction over a water body or wetland may file an administrative appeal with the Corps. *See* 33 CFR Part 331. Interested third persons, such as environmental groups or neighboring land owners, cannot administratively appeal any Corps determination. This is a relatively new procedure, adopted in 2000, after a five year rulemaking proceeding. Unlike most intra-agency review procedures, the review is not de novo. The reviewing official is to overturn the original decision only if on some relevant matter it was arbitrary, capricious, an abuse of discretion, not supported by substantial evidence in the administrative record, or plainly contrary to a requirement of law, regulation, an Executive Order, or officially promulgated Corps policy guidance. 33 CFR § 331.9(b). The reviewing official is one level higher than the deciding official, but the reviewing official is not an independent administrative law judge. An issue that may be administratively appealed must be administratively appealed before the person may seek judicial review.

4. Enforcement of Section 404 generally occurs under the same provisions as enforcement of the NPDES program, including citizens suits, and is dealt with in the chapter on enforcement. There are a couple of idiosyncracies involved with respect to Section 404 enforcement, however, that deserve mention here. First, under the CWA the Administrator of EPA is given the authority for taking actions against persons who unlawfully discharge without a permit, whether the discharge involves dredged or fill material or any other pollutant. *See* 33 U.S.C. § 1319. The Corps (actually the Secretary of the Army, under the statute) is only responsible for enforcement against persons who violate the terms of the permit they receive under Section 404. *See* 33 U.S.C. § 1344(s). In 1989, the Corps and EPA entered into a Memorandum of Agreement relating to the division of enforcement responsibilities for Section 404. While it reflects the statutory division of responsibilities, by making EPA the lead agency for unpermitted discharges and the Corps the lead agency for permit violations, it recognizes the Corps' greater field resources and accordingly generally gives the Corps the lead responsibility for investigating possible unpermitted discharges and making initial determinations whether a permit was required. In addition, the MOA purports to allow EPA to enforce against permit violations when the Corps declines and the Corps to enforce against unpermitted discharges in more minor cases. Second, the citizen suit provision of the CWA allows for suits against persons who violate "an effluent standard or limitation" or an order by the Administrator or a state with respect to such a standard or limitation. 33 U.S.C. § 1365(a)(1). There is no mention of an order by the Secretary of the Army (or the Corps). "Effluent standard or limitation" is a defined term in the citizen suit provision, and it expressly includes a permit or condition thereof under Section 402 (the NPDES program) but does not include permits or conditions thereof under Section 404. *See* 33 U.S.C. § 1365(f). This perhaps suggests that citizens suits cannot be brought to enforce against Section 404 permit violations (as opposed to failures to get permits), but there is no case discussing the issue.

B. The Swampbuster Program

As indicated earlier, it was long the policy of the United States Government to encourage the filling of wetlands to increase agricultural acreage. Indeed, even after passage of the CWA in 1972, the Department of Agriculture was still encouraging the draining of wetlands for agricultural purposes. In 1985, however, Congress passed the Food Security Act of 1985, Pub. L. No. 99–198, 99 Stat.1504 (1985), which included a number of provisions intended to stop the conversion of wetlands to agricultural land. Primary among these was a portion of the Act known as the Swampbuster program. 16 U.S.C. §§ 3801, 3821–3824.

The Swampbuster program denies to farmers certain agricultural subsidies if they produce agricultural commodities on converted wetland. 16 U.S.C. § 3821. Because the agricultural subsidies are often critical to financial survival of farms, the possibility of withholding such subsidies can be as threatening as a potentially large civil penalty.

Until recently, there has not been much attention given to the Swampbuster program by environmentalists. However, because Swampbuster is subject neither to the jurisdictional limitation of "navigable waters" nor to the limitation that only "discharges" are prohibited, Swampbuster is becoming increasingly important as a protection for wetlands. At the same time, as government farm policy has turned toward restricting, if not eliminating, price supports for commodity crops, the government's leverage to induce protection of wetlands by farmers will be reduced.

Swampbuster is administered by two separate agencies in the Department of Agriculture. The Natural Resources Conservation Service (NRCS), formerly the Soil Conservation Service, is responsible for making wetland delineations after consultation with the Fish and Wildlife Service. As a result of a Memorandum of Agreement in 1994 between NRCS, the Corps, EPA, and the Fish and Wildlife Service, the NRCS's wetlands delineations in agricultural areas also govern Section 404 determinations. In making these delineations, the NRCS uses its own delineation manual, rather than the Corps 1987 Manual. In addition, the NRCS is responsible for other biological or geological determinations in administering Swampbuster. The Farm Service Agency (FSA), formerly the Agricultural Stabilization and Conservation Service (ASCS), acting through local committees, enforces Swampbuster by determining when a person has engaged in an act that violates Swampbuster. *See generally* 7 CFR Part 12, Subpart A.

Swampbuster does have its own limitations. First, it only applies to farmers producing an "agricultural commodity," which is defined as sugarcane or a commodity planted and produced by annual tilling of the soil. 16 U.S.C. § 3801(a)(1). While this probably covers most farm acreage, it does not include all of it by any means. The Department of Agriculture reports that only 30% of all farms produce traditional commodity crops. Second, it only applies to "converted wetlands," which is defined as wetlands that have been impaired for the purpose or having the effect of agricultural commodity production, if the land could not have been farmed but for the conversion. 16 U.S.C. § 3801(a)(6). Thus, wetlands that are able to be farmed without any action by the farmer to impair the wetlands are not considered to be converted. This is, in a sense, consistent with the "normal farming" exception from Section 404's permit requirement, but unlike that exception there is no prohibition in Swampbuster to bringing new areas into production so long as the farmer merely farms the wetland, rather than manipulates the wetland in order to farm it. Nevertheless, bringing such wetlands into new production would still violate Section 404. *See United States v. Brace*, 41 F.3d 117 (3d Cir. 1994)(farmers activities that did not violate Swampbuster violated Section 404 by bringing new areas into production).

Moreover, there are a number of exemptions from the prohibition. The most important exemption is that Swampbuster does not apply to any conversion that was commenced before December 23, 1985. 16 U.S.C. § 3822(b)(1)(A). While for a number of years there were disputes as to what constituted "commencing," which spawned a number of court cases, the mere passage of time and an amendment in 1990 barring new conversions, *see* 16 U.S.C. § 3821(c), have effectively ended that litigation. Lands actually converted before December 23, 1985, known as "prior converted croplands," and lands converted after December 23, 1985 (and before 1995), but the conversion of which commenced before that date, known as "commenced conversion croplands," are both exempt from Swampbuster; they are distinguished from "farmed wetlands," those wetlands not subject to Swampbuster because they have not been "converted" at all. Farmers are entitled to have their land certified as prior converted or commenced conversion croplands.

For years the exemption of prior converted and commenced conversion croplands from Swampbuster but not from Section 404 caused confusion to farmers. The Corps regulations were amended in 1993 in an attempt to reduce conflicts by excluding "prior converted croplands" from the definition of "waters of the United States," and hence the jurisdiction of the Corps. 33 CFR § 328.3(a)(8). The Corps' rationale was that normally the conversion destroyed the wetlands characteristics of the land in question and therefore protection of that land was unnecessary. However, the regulatory change does not eliminate all confusion over what is excluded from both Swampbuster and Section 404. First, the Corps uses the term "prior converted cropland" and does not reference "commenced conversion cropland," while both are excluded from Swampbuster. Second, the regulation explicitly states that other agencies' determinations of an area being prior converted croplands do not necessarily govern, because for purposes of the CWA, the final authority resides with EPA. This reservation of EPA authority also exists in the MOA between NRCS, EPA, the Corps, and F & WS as to delineations on agricultural land. As a practical matter, EPA rarely, if ever, exercises this retained authority, but the mere insistence of the retention does not provide confidence to farmers that a NRCS delineation will be respected by EPA.

Unlike Section 404, Swampbuster has a number of "farmer friendly," or some might say "fairness," provisions, mitigating potential harshness. For example, as a result of amendments, a violation of Swampbuster does not automatically mean a total loss of crop subsidies. Rather, the amount of the penalty is to be "proportionate to the severity of the violation." 16 U.S.C. § 3821(a)(2). In addition, there is both a de minimis and a good faith exemption from loss of subsidies, see 16 U.S.C. § 3822(f)(1) & (h). Moreover, if a farmer fully restores the wetlands characteristics destroyed or otherwise mitigates for the harm, then in subsequent years his subsidies can be restored. See 16 U.S.C. § 3822(i). There is also an exception for converting wetlands that were voluntarily created or restored by the farmer after having originally converted them prior to December 23, 1985. See 16 U.S.C. § 3822(b)(1)(H). And perhaps most importantly, if a farmer who commenced his conversion before December 23, 1985, neglects to maintain the drainage or manage the land, so the land returns to a wetland, he may again convert the wetland without violating Swampbuster. See 16 U.S.C. § 3822(b)(1)(G).

In light of these various provisions, many of which were passed in 1996, the environmental protection afforded by Swampbuster has perhaps been diminished, but its overall directive that farmers not destroy wetlands for agricultural commodity production remains intact.

III. THE SURFACE MINING CONTROL AND RECLAMATION ACT OF 1977

The Surface Mining Control and Reclamation Act of 1977 (SMCRA), 30 U.S.C. § 1201 et seq., was another of the many environmental laws passed in the 1970s in response to a widely perceived need for federal regulation to protect the environment. It regulates the surface mining of coal, as well as some of the surface disturbances caused by underground coal mining. Today, almost 60% of all coal produced in the United States comes from surface mining. Because SMCRA, like the other statutes covered in this chapter, regulate the use of land, it also has been highly controversial, at least in coal mining states, and it has led to a large number of court cases, including several cases claiming compensation for regulatory takings under the Fifth Amendment and the only Supreme Court cases addressing the constitutionality of an environmental law. SMCRA shares some of the characteristics of the other 1970 laws, in particular the presence of a citizen suit provision and the reliance on a cooperative federalism model for administration of the Act.

A. Background

Surface mining of coal involves removing overlying soil and rock in order to expose the coal, which typically is 30–90 feet underground. Compared to underground coal mining, surface mining generally costs less, is safer for miners, and usually results in more complete recovery of the coal. However, it also results in much more extensive disturbance of the land.

Surface mining, often called strip mining, is either of two types. One, called area surface mining, occurs on rather flat land, in which case the land is excavated to reach the coal seam and a very large hole results. This occurs generally in the west. The other, called contour mining, occurs in hilly or mountainous areas, generally in Appalachia. First, a cut is made in the hillside above a coal seam and the coal is further exposed as the overburden is removed. The mine is then enlarged by successive cuts that follow the coal seam around the side of the hill. The mining extends into the hill to the point where the overburden is too thick to make further exposure of the coal economic. Auger mining often is used at this stage to maximize coal recovery.[4] In either case, the overburden, the soil and rock removed to reach the coal, must be disposed of in some way.

Historically, when the coal seam was played out in area mining, a giant pit of exposed rock and one or more huge piles of overburden were left . *See* Figure 1. In contour mining, the overburden was simply pushed down the mountain, and when the mining was completed, cliff-like excavated faces of exposed rock, known as a highwall, were left on the hillside. *See* Figure 2.

Surface mining became more widespread in the 1930s, and some states passed laws to deal with its effects, but the laws were uneven, not very rigorous, and not strictly enforced. As a result, as described by the Office of Surface Mining in its 25th Anniversary of SMCRA Report:

> Mining pits were not backfilled. Dangerous highwalls were left exposed. Trees and other vegetation were buried by waste material that was simply dumped down the slopes below mines. Topsoil was buried or allowed to wash away. Landslides formed on unstable hillsides. Slopes eroded rapidly because of the lack of vegetation. Polluted water collected in mine pits. Streams became clogged with sediment. Streams and rivers were frequently polluted by acid mine drainage.

The 1970s, with the energy crisis associated with the OPEC petroleum embargo, saw another significant expansion of surface mining, at the same time as there was a growing awareness of and concern for the environment.

---

4. Auger mining is a method of surface mining whereby a large mechanical screw penetrates a coal seam and turns to extract the coal.

Figure 1

Area Surface Mining Before SMCRA

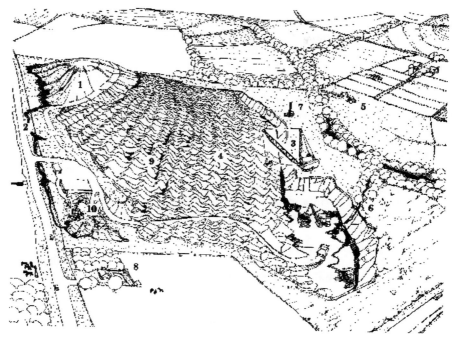

Key

1. Overburden from the initial mining is dumped in a heap at the edge of the operation. Top soil has been buried beneath the heap or mixed in with the rock overburden. Without topsoil grasses and trees do not grow and the overburden pile is exposed to natural elements. The wind blows dust throughout the surrounding area and each rain storm causes the steep sides of the pile to erode.

2. Sediment that is running off the overburden pile has clogged roadside ditches and culverts and is polluting nearby streams. Before the Surface Mining Law was passed, this off site impact was not the responsibility of the mine operator.

3. The dragline removes both the topsoil and overburden from the coal seam in one operation. If acid-forming rock is encountered it is mixed with the overburden and will cause acid mine drainage in the future.

4. Overburden cast by the dragline forms a hill and dale character that will be left when the mining operation is completed. This rough topography eliminates future use of the land.

5. A backhoe digs a diversion that will reroute the stream that is in the way of the mining operation. This keeps the water out of the pit during mining; but, will result in long term bank erosion, downstream flooding, and water pollution. The stream will not be reclaimed.

6. A tributary stream is already being mine through, resulting in some back flow into the pit. As the mine progresses this stream tributary will be permanently eliminated.

7. A drill rig is preparing holes for explosives used to blast the overburden loose. With uncontrolled blasting rock is cast long distances causing damage and potential safety hazards. In addition, extensive blasting has disrupted the groundwater flow and nearby springs and farm wells have become unreliable.

8. This resident living next to the mining operation has had his house hit by large rocks from the blasting, lost his long time natural source of water and has been awaken in the middle of the night by blasting very close to his house. He is afraid to sit in his backyard since he does not know when the blasting will occur and without reclamation of the land his property value will be reduced.

9. In areas where the overburden contains acid forming rock, pools of acid mine drainage begin to collect. In addition, this unrestored land results in permanent loss of farmland and will continue to erode and be a source of sediment and acid drainage to nearby streams for years after the mining is completed.

10. The maintenance yard and refuse dump will be left after the mining operation. This will cause an eyesore and a safety nuisance to both the neighbors and anyone driving along the road.

Figure 2

Contour Mining Before SMCRA

Key

1.   Bulldozers push trees, shrubs, topsoil, subsoil, and overburden over the down-slope with no intention of reclaiming the land. Mixing the trees, soil, and rock together eliminate the chance for plants to grow and create a highly erodible condition that will last for many years in the future.

2.   This corn field has been greatly impacted by a landslide caused by the mining. Large streams of water now rush down across the field carrying rock and sediment from the mine. This common problem associated with contour mines before the Surface Mining Law will continue to damage the farmers land and he will eventually have to abandoned the field.

3.   A drilling rig bores blast holes and blasts consolidated overburden. Without any blasting regulations the mine operator scatters rock for long distances any time day or night. The nearby farmhouse has been damaged by flying rock and the resident is afraid to let his children play outside.

4.   This farm has been using a spring for its water supply for over 100 years. The mining above the house has destroyed the spring and left the resident without water for his family and livestock.

5.   A bulldozer works together with a shovel removing the remainder of the overburden and exposing the coal. Rock spoil is pushed over the slope and crashes down the hillside. When mining is complete the cliff-like highwall behind the mine and the eroded overburden will remain. This exposed material will continue to erode and cause streams in the valley to clog and be polluted.

6.   A front-end loader digs coal and loads trucks which use a haul road located on a previously mined bench. Rainfall accumulating on the bench runs off and cuts deep gullies in the slope as it pours down the hillside.

7.   Auger mining is in progress removing additional coal from the exposed outcrop. Without reclamation acid mine drainage will pour from these holes and run into nearby streams killing all plant and animal life in the water.

B. SMCRA's Provisions

The D.C. Circuit has had a lot of experience with SMCRA, because challenges to SMCRA regulations, as well as certain other types of SMCRA cases, must be brought in the District Court for the District of Columbia, *see* 30 U.S.C. § 1276. In one of those cases the court provided a good summary of the law.

> In brief, the Act is intended to protect the environment from the adverse effects of surface coal mining while ensuring an adequate supply of coal to meet the nation's energy requirements. 30 U.S.C. § 1202(a), (f). Section 501(b) directs the Secretary to promulgate regulations establishing regulatory procedures and performance standards "conforming to the provisions of" the Act (30 U.S.C. § 1251(b)). Section 515 contains detailed "environmental protection performance standards" applicable to "all surface coal mining and reclamation operations." 30 U.S.C. § 1265. Through the Office of Surface Mining Reclamation and Enforcement ("OSMRE"), the

Secretary is to take steps "necessary to insure compliance with" the Act. 30 U.S.C. § 1211(a), (c)(1). The states too have a significant role to play. After an interim period of federal regulation, states had the option of proposing plans for implementing the Act consistent with federal standards on non-federal lands. When the Secretary approved the programs submitted by the states, those states became primarily responsible for regulating surface coal mining and reclamation in the non-federal areas within their borders. 30 U.S.C. § 1253. In states not having an approved program, the Secretary implemented a federal program. 30 U.S.C. § 1254(a), (b). The "permanent program" regulations issued under section 501(b) set standards for federally-approved state programs and for the federal program that takes effect when a State fails to "implement, enforce, or maintain" its program. 30 U.S.C. § 1254(a). Enforcement is carried out by the "regulatory authority," that is, the state agency administering the federally-approved program, the Secretary administering a federal program, or OSMRE conducting oversight of state programs. *See* 30 C.F.R. § 700.5.

The primary means of ensuring compliance is the permit system established in sections 506 through 514 and section 515(a). 30 U.S.C. §§ 1256–1264, 1265(a). [Generally, a] permit is required for "any surface coal mining operations." 30 U.S.C. § 1256. Summaries of applications for permits must be published, and objections may be submitted by local agencies or by "any person having an interest which . . . may be adversely affected" by a proposed operation. 30 U.S.C. § 1263. Each application must include a reclamation plan. Section 507(d), 30 U.S.C. § 1257(d). A reclamation plan describes the present use of the land, proposed and possible post-mining uses of the land, and what steps the operator will take to ensure the viability of the latter. Among other things, the plan must show how the operator will achieve soil reconstruction and revegetation of the mined area.[4] Section 508, 30 U.S.C. § 1258. A permit application can only be approved if it demonstrates that "all requirements" of the Act have been satisfied and that "reclamation as required by [the Act] . . . can be accomplished." 30 U.S.C. § 1260.

Section 509 requires the operator to post a performance bond in an amount sufficient to secure completion of reclamation. The operator and the surety remain liable under the bond for the duration of the surface mining and reclamation operation and until the end of the "revegetation period" (5 or 10 years) prescribed by section 515(b)(20). 30 U.S.C. § 1259(b). At that time, the operator may petition the regulatory authority for release of the bond. The petition must be published, and is subject to the same opportunities for

---

4. The revegetation standards require that an operator establish "a diverse, effective and permanent vegetative cover" over the area after mining has ceased. 30 U.S.C. § 1265(b)(19). By the terms of the Act, the operator "assume[s] the responsibility" for success of the revegetation program for 5 years (10 years in the arid Western states) after the revegetation standard is first met. 30 U.S.C. § 1265(b)(20).

comment and hearing as the permit application. 30 C.F.R. § 800.40(a)(2), (b)(2). Further, "[n]o bond shall be fully released ... until reclamation requirements of the Act and the permit are fully met." *Id.* § 800.40(c)(3).

National Wildlife Fed. v. Lujan, 950 F.2d 765 (D.C. Cir. 1991).

Notes and Comments

1. After the initial federal program period, virtually all the states with active coal mining did apply for and obtain authorization (termed "primacy") to regulate surface mining in their states in lieu of the federal program. Today, of the 36 states with some coal resource, 25 states have active coal production. Twenty-four of these have approved state programs. Tennessee, which previously had an approved program, repealed its program in 1984. There are federal programs not only for Tennessee and the eleven other states with coal resources but no active mining program, but also for four Indian tribes that produce coal on their reservations, as well as for coal production on federal lands.

2. The "environmental protection performance standards" of 30 U.S.C. § 1265 provide detailed requirements both for how the surface mining shall take place and for reclamation after the mining has terminated. Generally, reclamation is required to re-establish the "approximate original contours" (AOC) of the land, 30 U.S.C. § 1265(b)(3); to restore topsoil, 30 U.S.C. § 1265 (b)(6); to establish native plant communities, 30 U.S.C. § 1265(b)(19); all to restore to the extent possible the land to its original uses, 30 U.S.C. § 1265(b)(2). There are special requirements for mining on "prime farm lands," which are promulgated by the Secretary of Agriculture, 30 U.S.C. § 1265(b)(7), and there are special requirements for mining on steep slopes, 30 U.S.C. § 1265(d). Surface mining is prohibited on certain types of lands, such as National Parks and other federal lands where surface mining would be incompatible with their primary uses, within 100 feet of a public right-of-way, and within 300 feet of an occupied dwelling. 30 U.S.C. 1272(e). State plans are required to identify equivalent prohibited areas of state concern and provide a system by which persons may petition for additional prohibited areas to be added. 30 U.S.C. § 1272(a) & (c).

3. In addition to regulating new and existing coal mines, SMCRA also contains provisions relating to the reclamation of coal mines abandoned before passage of SMCRA. *See* 30 U.S.C. §§ 1231–1243. To pay for this reclamation, fees are levied on currently mined coal. If the state has an approved state reclamation program, half the fees go to the state from which the fees originate.

4. Despite its title, SMCRA is not limited to the regulation of surface mining. Section 516, 30 U.S.C. § 1266, specifically requires the Secretary of the Interior to promulgate rules "directed toward the surface effects of underground coal mining operations," and it makes the provisions of the Act "relating to State and Federal programs, permits, bonds, inspections and enforcement, public review, and administrative and judicial review" applicable to surface operations and surface impacts incident to underground

mining.[5] The Secretary's rules, however, are to take account of the "distinct difference" between underground and surface mining. Section 516 also requires "each permit [issued pursuant to a state or federal program under SMCRA] and relating to underground coal mining" to include various specific requirements to protect the environment. Underground coal mining actually can cause many of the same adverse environmental effects as surface mining, such as the placement of overburden and acid or toxic drainage from mines. The one unique potential adverse effect of underground coal mining is subsidence, whereby the land over the underground mine literally sinks to fill in the mined out area. As a result, the federal regulations governing minimum state program requirements are largely identical for both underground and surface mining, except that there are special and detailed requirements for underground mining to avoid subsidence to the extent feasible and to reclaim land that does subside, to the extent feasible.

C. Issues

1. Federalism Issues

While the CWA, the CAA, and RCRA, like SMCRA, all follow a cooperative federalism model for administration of the statute, SMCRA uses a unique word to characterize the state's jurisdiction if it qualifies for authorization—"exclusive" jurisdiction. 30 U.S.C. § 1253(a). In addition, the Congressional findings outlined in SMCRA reinforce the concept of exclusive jurisdiction:

> [B]ecause of the diversity in terrain, climate, biologic, chemical, and other physical conditions in areas subject to mining operations, the primary governmental responsibility for developing, authorizing, issuing, and enforcing regulations for surface mining and reclamation operations subject to this chapter should rest with the States.

30 U.S.C. § 1201(f). Moreover, unlike EPA's authority under the CWA and CAA to review and object to state permitting decisions, SMCRA has no such provision. Consequently, it may not be surprising that the relationship between a state with primacy and the federal government has been described by one court as follows:

> The Surface Mining Control and Reclamation Act of 1977 ("SMCRA") was enacted to strike a balance between the nation's interests in protecting the environment from the adverse effects of surface coal mining and in assuring the coal supply essential to the nation's energy requirements. See 30 U.S.C. § 1202(a), (d), (f); see also *Hodel v. Va. Mining & Reclamation Ass'n*, 452 U.S. 264, 268–69, 101 S.Ct. 2352, 69 L.Ed.2d 1 (1981). The Act accomplishes these purposes through a "cooperative federalism," in which responsibility for the regulation of surface coal mining in the United States is

---

5. The D.C. Circuit, however, upheld an interpretive rule that excluded underground mining from the prohibitions in 30 U.S.C. § 1272(e), banning surface coal mining operations from various places, including within 300 feet of an occupied dwelling, terming the interpretation reasonable and not precluded by the statute. *See* Citizens Coal Council v. Norton, 330 F.3d 478 (D.C.Cir. 2003).

shared between the U.S. Secretary of the Interior and State regulatory authorities. Under this scheme, Congress established in SMCRA "minimum national standards" for regulating surface coal mining and encouraged the States, through an offer of exclusive regulatory jurisdiction, to enact their own laws incorporating these minimum standards, as well as any more stringent, but not inconsistent, standards that they might choose. 30 U.S.C. § 1255(b).

To implement this cooperative federalism, SMCRA directs the U.S. Secretary of the Interior to develop a "federal program" of regulation that embodies the minimum national standards and to consider for approval any "State programs" that are submitted to it for approval. To obtain approval of its program, a State must pass a law that provides for the minimum national standards established as "requirements" in SMCRA and must also demonstrate that it has the capability of enforcing its law. *See* 30 U.S.C. § 1253(a). Once the Secretary is satisfied that a State program meets these requirements and approves the program, the State's laws and regulations implementing the program become operative for the regulation of surface coal mining, and the State officials administer the program, *see id.* § 1252(e), giving the State "exclusive jurisdiction over the regulation of surface coal mining" within its borders, *id.* § 1253(a). If, however, a State fails to submit a program for approval, or a program that it submits is not approved, or approval of a State's program is withdrawn because of ineffective enforcement, then the federal program becomes applicable for the State, and the Secretary becomes vested with "exclusive jurisdiction for the regulation and control of surface coal mining and reclamation operations taking place [in the] State." *Id.* § 1254(a).

Thus, SMCRA provides for either State regulation of surface coal mining within its borders or federal regulation, but not both. The Act expressly provides that one or the other is exclusive, see 30 U.S.C. §§ 1253(a), 1254(a), with the exception that an approved State program is always subject to revocation when a State fails to enforce it, see *id.* §§ 1253(a); 1271(b). Federal oversight of an approved State program is provided by the Secretary's obligation to inspect and monitor the operations of State programs. *See id.* §§ 1267, 1271. Only if an approved State program is revoked, as provided in § 1271, however, does the federal program become the operative regulation for surface coal mining in any State that has previously had its program approved. *See id.* §§ 1254(a), 1271....

As we have noted, under SMCRA Congress intended to divide responsibility for the regulation of surface coal mining between the federal government and the States. But characterizing the regulatory structure of SMCRA as "cooperative" federalism is not entirely accurate, as the statute does not provide for shared regulation of coal mining. Rather, the Act provides for enforcement of either a federal program or a State program, but not both. Thus, in contrast to other "cooperative federalism" statutes, SMCRA exhibits extraordinary deference to the States. The statutory federalism of SMCRA is quite unlike the cooperative regime under the Clean Water Act.... Under SMCRA, in contrast, Congress designed a scheme of mutually exclusive regulation by either the U.S. Secretary of the Interior or the State regulatory authority, depending on whether the State elects to regulate itself or to submit to federal regulation....

Bragg v. West Virginia Coal Assn., 248 F.3d 275, 288–89, 293 (4th Cir. 2001).

This description, however, may be somewhat misleading. As early as 1979, Interior issued a rule providing that OSMRE could issue Notices of Violation (NOV) to mine operators acting in violation of the Act, the state program requirements, or their permit conditions, notwithstanding that the alleged violation occurred in a primacy state and Interior had not instituted proceedings to withdraw or declare the state program administration inadequate. This rule was challenged by the coal industry in 1988, when Interior refused its petition for rulemaking to rescind the rule authorizing the NOVs. The coal industry maintained that once a state had primacy, OSMRE could only issue NOVs incident to withdrawal of a state's authorization or upon a determination that a state was not enforcing part of its program. According to the industry, the agency's issuance of NOVs in primacy states effectively placed OSMRE in the position of enforcing its view of the state-issued permit requirements in opposition to the state agency charged with enforcing the permit conditions. This was said to create confusion in the industry and conflict between federal and state agencies.

The D.C. Circuit upheld the rule, but only on the grounds that the industry could not challenge a SMCRA rule after the 60–day period provided in the statute, *see* 30 U.S.C. § 1276(a)(1). *National Min. Ass'n v. U.S. Dept. of Interior*, 70 F.3d 1345 (D.C.Cir. 1995). Nevertheless, the lower court's opinion, which decided the merits against the industry, and aspects of the D.C. Circuit's opinion strongly suggested that Interior did have the authority directly to enforce the Act, the state programs, and individual permit conditions.

The characterization of primacy states having exclusive jurisdiction has also caused problems under SMCRA's citizen suit provision, 30 U.S.C. § 1270. Compare the following two cases.

HAYDO v. AMERIKOHL MINING, INC.

United States Court of Appeals, Third Circuit, 1987.
830 F.2d 494.

MANSMANN, Circuit Judge.

This appeal presents the question of whether there is subject matter jurisdiction in the federal district court to hear a claim for damages arising from an alleged violation by an operator of the Surface Mining Control and Reclamation Act ("SMCRA"), where a state has submitted and the Secretary of the Interior has approved a program for state regulation as contemplated by the Act. We find that there is no federal jurisdiction, and we will affirm the district court's dismissal of the action.

I.

Donald and Patricia Haydo brought this action for damages for the loss of a water well allegedly due to the coal exploration program of the defendant, Amerikohl Mining, Inc. . . .

II.

The Haydos complained that the defendant's exploratory drilling adversely affected their water supply and violated the environmental protection standards prescribed by Section 515 of the SMCRA, 30 U.S.C. § 1265. The complaint alleged that the Commonwealth of Pennsylvania, administering the SMCRA under a program approved by the Secretary of the Interior, promulgated regulations pursuant to Section 515 of the SMCRA, 30 U.S.C. § 1265, concerning the reclamation of the prevailing hydrologic balance. The plaintiffs alleged that the defendant's operations contravened both the state regulations and the SMCRA. . . .

V.

We turn now to the question of whether the district court had jurisdiction over the subject matter of this action. The complaint alleged violations of the Pennsylvania regulatory plan and of the SMCRA itself and asserted subject matter jurisdiction in the district court under . . . Section 520 of the SMCRA.

A.

[S]ection 520 of the SMCRA, in pertinent part, confers jurisdiction on the federal district courts to hear citizen suits to compel compliance with the SMCRA against the United States or any other governmental instrumentality or agency for violations both of the SMCRA and of any rule, regulation, order or permit issued pursuant thereto. 30 U.S.C. § 1270(a)(1). Section 520 also permits a citizen enforcement action against "any other person who is alleged to be in violation of *any rule, regulation, order or permit issued pursuant to this subchapter.*" *Id.* (emphasis added). The act also permits a damage action by "[a]ny person who is injured in his person or property through the violation by any operation *of any rule, regulation, order, or permit issued pursuant to this chapter.*" 30 U.S.C. § 1270(f) (emphasis added).

While citizen suits against state and federal governmental defendants may be predicated directly upon violations of the provisions of the SMCRA, Section 520 does not provide for an action against individual defendants for violations of the act itself. The principal purpose of the citizen suit provision was to provide "a practical and legitimate method of assuring the *regulatory authority's* compliance with the requirements of the act."

The jurisdictional basis for a citizen suit against a nongovernmental defendant, either to compel compliance or for damages, is an alleged violation of "any rule, regulation, order or permit issued pursuant to this subchapter." The defendant argues that the district court lacked subject matter jurisdiction in this case because the complaint alleged only violations of the SMCRA itself and of the *state* regulatory plan and Section 520 confers federal jurisdiction only over alleged violations of *federal* regulations.

The defendant argues that Section 520 must be read in conjunction with Section 503 of the SMCRA which provides that a regulatory plan may be submitted for approval by "[e]ach state.... which wishes to assume *exclusive jurisdiction* over the regulation of surface coal mining and reclamation operations," 30 U.S.C. § 1253 (emphasis added). The defendant argues that because Pennsylvania's regulatory plan has been approved by the Secretary, jurisdiction over the alleged violations of the state statute and regulations lies exclusively in the courts of Pennsylvania. We agree.

The plaintiffs urge us to interpret Section 520 to include state rules, regulations, orders or permits as among those "issued pursuant to this subchapter," at least where the state regulation is one required by the SMCRA. 30 U.S.C. § 1270(a)(1), (f). However, Section 520* offers "exclusive" jurisdiction to states obtaining approval of a regulatory plan. The obvious and usual meaning of the word "exclusive" is plain enough, and the plaintiffs suggest no other meaning for this language. The plaintiffs cite us to numerous cases involving citizen suits filed under similar jurisdictional provisions in other environmental protection statutes. However, the issues in all of those cases involve questions of the *primacy* of the jurisdiction of administrative agencies or state courts. The plaintiffs have cited us to no other statute where, as in the SMCRA, the state is expressly offered "exclusive" jurisdiction to enforce its regulatory program. We have encountered nothing in the statute or the legislative history which leads us to believe that anything other than the ordinary meaning of "exclusive" was intended by the enactors of the SMCRA.

Congress found that "effective and reasonable regulation of surface coal mining operations by the States and by the Federal Government in accordance with the requirements of this chapter is an effective and necessary means to minimize so far as practicable the adverse social, economic, and environmental effects of such mining operations." 30 U.S.C. § 1201(e). However, the statute does not provide for concurrent jurisdiction in the states and federal government. When a state fails to submit, implement, enforce or maintain an acceptable state regulatory program, the Secretary is required to prepare, promulgate and implement a federal program for the state. 30 U.S.C. § 1254(a). Promulgation and implementation of a federal program for a state preempts and supersedes any inconsistent state law and "vests the Secretary with

---

* So in the original. It should probably say "Section 503." [editor's note].

exclusive jurisdiction for the regulation and control of surface coal mining and reclamation operations" taking place within the state. *Id.*

Congress found the imposition of minimum nationwide environmental protection standards necessary to prevent a state from allowing competitive advantage to its own operators through possible production cost savings due to inadequate environmental protection standards. However, Congress recognized that "because of the diversity in terrain, climate, biologic, chemical, and other physical conditions in areas subject to mining operations, primary governmental responsibility for developing, authorizing, issuing, and enforcing regulations for surface mining and reclamation operations subject to this chapter should rest with the States." 30 U.S.C. § 1201(f). In order to allow the individual states to retain this primary responsibility, the statute provided for state jurisdiction over its own operators to be exclusive once the state plan has been approved.

Interpreting Section 520 to afford federal jurisdiction in this case would render meaningless the Congressional offer in Section 503 of "exclusive" jurisdiction to states obtaining approval of a regulatory plan. Therefore we find that there is no federal jurisdiction under the SMCRA over suits such as this against operators who are alleged to be in violation of an approved state plan.

MOLINARY v. POWELL MOUNTAIN COAL COMPANY

United States Court of Appeals, Fourth Circuit, 1997.
125 F.3d 231.

HAMILTON, Circuit Judge:

In this appeal, we consider whether § 520(f) of the Surface Mining Control and Reclamation Act of 1977 (SMCRA), 30 U.S.C. § 1270(f), provides a federal cause of action for the recovery of damages resulting from violation of state regulations that are a part of the state's surface coal mining and reclamation regulatory program approved by the United States Secretary of the Interior pursuant to § 503 of SMCRA, 30 U.S.C. § 1253. We hold that it does.

I.

In this suit, Jo D. Molinary represents a class of persons, known as the "Pruitt heirs" (Pruitt Heirs), who own more than a 99% undivided interest in the surface estate of a fifty-acre tract of land located in Lee County, Virginia (the Pruitt Tract).... Prior to Congress' enactment of SMCRA in 1977, a three-acre portion of the Pruitt Tract (the Three Acre Tract) was strip mined for coal by parties unrelated to [The Powell Mountain Coal Company (Powell Mountain)]....

In February 1990, Powell Mountain submitted a permit application to the Division of Mined Land Reclamation for the Commonwealth of Virginia (the DMLR), seeking permission to auger mine the Three Acre

Tract for coal that still remained. In its permit application, Powell Mountain listed itself and the "Pruitt Heirs" as cosurface owners, but did not list each heir by name.... Without further submissions from Powell Mountain, the DMLR issued the permit. Powell Mountain then extracted 4423.51 tons of coal from the Three Acre Tract by the auger mining method....

After receiving complaints about the permit's issuance, the DMLR determined that Powell Mountain's permit application did not comply with certain state permitting regulations.... As a result, the DMLR revoked Powell Mountain's permit, issued a cessation order, and ordered Powell Mountain to reclaim the Three Acre Tract.

Subsequently, this class action was filed in the United States District Court for the Western District of Virginia under SMCRA's citizen suit provision, § 520(f) of SMCRA. *See* 30 U.S.C. § 1270(f). Section 520(f) of SMCRA provides that "[a]ny person who is injured in his person or property through the violation by any operator of any rule, regulation, order, or permit issued pursuant to [SMCRA] may bring an action for damages (including reasonable attorney and expert witness fees).... " *Id.* ...

Powell Mountain moved to dismiss the complaint for lack of subject matter jurisdiction. In its motion to dismiss, Powell Mountain argued that federal courts lack subject matter jurisdiction over citizen suits in states whose regulatory and enforcement programs have been approved by the Secretary of the Interior (the Secretary) pursuant to § 503 of SMCRA. Rejecting this argument as inconsistent with the plain language of § 520(f) of SMCRA, the district court denied the motion....

Powell Mountain noted a timely appeal. On appeal, Powell Mountain challenges: (1) the district court's denial of its motion to dismiss for lack of subject matter jurisdiction....

II.

Before we address Powell Mountain's challenge to the district court's denial of its motion to dismiss for lack of subject matter jurisdiction, we briefly set forth some background information about SMCRA and Virginia's federally approved version of SMCRA. Congress enacted SMCRA in 1977 to "establish a nationwide program to protect society and the environment from the adverse effects of surface coal mining operations." 30 U.S.C. § 1202(a). Section 201 of SMCRA, 30 U.S.C. § 1211, "creates the Office of Surface Mining Reclamation and Enforcement (OSM), within the Department of the Interior, and the Secretary of the Interior (Secretary) acting through OSM, is charged with primary responsibility for administering and implementing [SMCRA] by promulgating regulations and enforcing its provisions."

To achieve its goals, SMCRA relies on "a program of cooperative federalism that allows States, within limits established by federal minimum standards, to enact and administer their own regulatory programs, structured to meet their own particular needs." Any state "wish[ing] to assume exclusive jurisdiction over the regulation of surface coal mining and reclamation operations" on nonfederal lands within its borders must submit a proposed program to the Secretary for approval. 30 U.S.C. § 1253(a). A state program must include a permitting system that incorporates SMCRA's environmental protection standards and is in accordance with SMCRA's enforcement and procedural requirements. . . .

[Since December 1981] Virginia has had "exclusive jurisdiction over the regulation" of surface coal mining and reclamation within its borders. . . .

III.

. . . As previously stated, the Pruitt Heirs brought this action in the United States District Court for the Western District of Virginia pursuant to SMCRA's citizen suit provision, § 520(f) of SMCRA. Section 520(f) of SMCRA provides:

Any person who is injured in his person or property through the violation by any operator of any rule, regulation, order, or permit issued pursuant to [SMCRA] may bring an action for damages (including reasonable attorney and expert witness fees) only in the judicial district in which the surface coal mining operation complained of is located. Nothing in this subsection shall affect the rights established by or limits imposed under State Workmen's Compensation laws.

30 U.S.C. § 1270(f). This provision creates a federal cause of action for the recovery of damages resulting from the violation of "any rule, regulation, order, or permit issued pursuant to [SMCRA]." *Id.* The dispute here centers on whether the statutory phrase "issued pursuant to [SMCRA]," includes state-promulgated regulations that comprise a federally approved state surface mining and reclamation program. More precisely for purposes of this case, the issue is whether the Virginia regulations allegedly violated by Powell Mountain were issued "pursuant to" SMCRA, such that the district court had subject matter jurisdiction over the complaint under § 520(f). Powell Mountain contends that the Virginia regulations were not issued pursuant to SMCRA, while the Pruitt Heirs contend that they were. The Secretary, who has submitted an amicus brief in this case, espouses the same interpretation as the Pruitt Heirs.

Congress has not directly spoken on this precise issue through a provision in SMCRA or its legislative history. Because Congress has not "directly spoken to the precise question at issue," we must sustain the Secretary's interpretation so long as it is "based on a permissible construction of the statute." *Chevron U.S.A., Inc. v. Natural Resources Defense Council, Inc.,* 467 U.S. 837 (1984). . . . For the following reasons, we conclude that the interpretation espoused by the Secretary is a permissible construction of § 520(f) of SMCRA.

First, the language at issue is certainly broad enough to support the Secretary's interpretation. It may reasonably be said that once the

Secretary approves a state surface coal mining and reclamation program, the rules, regulations, orders, and permits issued under that program are "issued," in the language of § 520(f), "pursuant to" SMCRA.

Second, creating a federal cause of action so that citizens may redress violations of state surface coal mining and reclamation regulations in federal court is consistent with Congress' goal of establishing "a nationwide program to protect society and the environment from the adverse effects of surface coal mining operations." 30 U.S.C. § 1202(a).

Third, as the Secretary points out in its *amicus* brief, when Congress referred to permits issued by either state or federal regulatory authorities elsewhere in SMCRA, it used the phrase, "permit issued pursuant to this chapter." *See, e.g.,* 30 U.S.C. §§ 1256(d)(1), 1261(b), 1272(a)(6). By contrast, when Congress intended to limit the application of a provision to permits or orders issued pursuant to a federal program, it did so expressly. *See, e.g.,* 30 U.S.C. §§ 1268(e)-(f) ("permit issued pursuant to a Federal program"); 1273(b) ("permit . . . issued by the Secretary"); 1275(a)(1) & (c) ("notice or order" issued "pursuant to Federal Program").

Fourth and finally, as the Secretary also points out, its interpretation is consistent with the operation of § 520(a)(1) of SMCRA, which provides for citizen suits to ensure compliance with the "provisions of [SMCRA] or of any rule, regulation, order or permit issued pursuant thereto," 30 U.S.C. § 1270(a)(1), in conjunction with the operation of § 520(b) of SMCRA, which places limits on the initiation of such suits. Section § 520(b)(1)(B) of SMCRA states that a suit may not be commenced under § 520(a)(1) if "the Secretary or the State" is already "diligently prosecuting a civil action . . . to require compliance." 30 U.S.C. § 1270(b)(1)(B). Because a state would only prosecute a compliance action if it were a primacy state, the language of these subsections shows that Congress contemplated that federal citizen suits for compliance would be brought in primacy states. Considering that the key language in § 520(a)(1) of SMCRA is virtually identical to the key language in § 520(f) of SMCRA, it follows that Congress intended § 520(f) of SMCRA to provide for federal citizen suits for damages in primacy states.

The Secretary's interpretation does not conflict, as Powell Mountain suggests, with the federal grant of "exclusive regulatory jurisdiction over the regulation of surface coal mining and reclamation operations" in § 520(f) of SMCRA to states with federally approved surface coal mining and reclamation programs. *See* 30 U.S.C. § 1253(a). Exclusive regulatory jurisdiction simply does not encompass exclusive adjudicatory jurisdiction. Common sense dictates that a government's acts in regulating a subject are distinctly different than its acts in adjudicating a party's rights related to the subject.[5]

---

5. In Haydo v. Amerikohl Mining, Inc., 830 F.2d 494 (3d Cir.1987), the Third Circuit refused to make this distinction. In that case, the court concluded that reading the language of § 503(a) of SMCRA in conjunction with § 520(f) of SMCRA compelled

Because Congress has not specifically assigned jurisdiction over § 520(f) suits elsewhere, we conclude the district court possessed subject matter jurisdiction. . . .

Notes and Comments

1. What do you think about the contrary arguments between the *Haydo* and *Molinary* courts? These are apparently the only two cases dealing with the question whether the SMCRA citizen suit provision authorizes suits against persons who violate state rules, regulations, or permits in primacy states. Note that the extended selection from *Bragg v. West Virginia Coal Assn.*, that began this Federalism issue, was also from the Fourth Circuit, subsequent to the *Molinary* decision. Some courts have read *Bragg* to have abrogated or cast in doubt the *Molinary* decision. *See Pennsylvania Federation of Sportsmen's Clubs, Inc. v. Hess*, 297 F.3d 310, 318 n.7 (3d Cir. 2002). Of course, the Third Circuit is the *Haydo* circuit. The *Bragg* court itself, however, cited positively to *Molinary*: "It is now settled that 30 U.S.C. § 1270 confers on federal district courts subject matter jurisdiction over at least some sorts of claims. *See Molinary v. Powell Mtn. Coal Co.*, 125 F.3d 231, 235–37 (4th Cir.1997)." The Fourth Circuit includes two major coal producing states with primacy—Virginia and West Virginia, whereas the Third Circuit includes only Pennsylvania.

2. The citizen suit provision explicitly limits suits against states to those permitted by the Eleventh Amendment. This would preclude actions for damages (and attorneys fees) in the normal course. Under the doctrine of *Ex parte Young*, 209 U.S. 123, 28 S.Ct. 441, 52 L.Ed. 714 (1908), it would not normally preclude actions against a state officer for prospective injunctive relief, where the claim is based upon a continuing violation of federal law. *See, e.g., NRDC v. California Dept. of Transportation*, 96 F.3d 420 (9th Cir. 1996)(citizen suit under the CWA). However, given SMCRA's unique character, the Eleventh Amendment can preclude citizen suit actions to compel state compliance in primacy states. In *Bragg v. West Virginia Coal Assn.*, quoted and discussed above, the court barred a citizen suit seeking to prohibit the Director of the West Virginia Division of Environmental Protection (WVDEP) from issuing permits for mountaintop-removal mining, alleging that such permits violated SMCRA. The court, relying on its conclusion that in primacy states the applicable law to be enforced was state law, not federal law, found that the *Ex parte Young* exception to the Eleventh Amendment did not apply. Can the conclusion that in primacy states regulated entities are only subject to state, not federal law, be squared with the same court's holding in *Molinary* or the D.C. Circuit's dicta in *National Min. Ass'n v. U.S. Dept. of Interior*, 70 F.3d 1345 (D.C.Cir. 1995)?

2. Mountaintop-removal/Valley Fill Mining

In the section of this chapter dealing with Section 404, we discussed the Corps' Nationwide Permit 21 authorizing valley fills with mining

the conclusion that a state regulation connected to a federally approved regulatory program was not "issued pursuant to [SMCRA]," in the language of § 520(f) of SMCRA. As the district court in the present case correctly recognized, the holding in Haydo ignores the fact that the word "ex-clusive" in § 503(a) modifies the phrase "regulatory jurisdiction," and nothing more. The Third Circuit is the only federal appellate court that has addressed the scope of the phrase "issued pursuant to [SMCRA]," as found in § 520(f) of SMCRA.

overburden associated with mountaintop removal mining. Mountaintop removal mining is an extreme form of contour mining. As described in OSMRE regulations, "Mountaintop removal mining means surface mining activities, where the mining operation removes an entire coal seam or seams running through the upper fraction of a mountain, ridge, or hill ... by removing substantially all of the overburden off the bench and creating a level plateau or a gently rolling contour...." 30 CFR § 785.14(b). "Valley fills are constructed from and used to dispose of the spoil or coal mine waste material generated during mining operations." *West Virginia Coal Ass'n v. Reilly*, 728 F.Supp. 1276, 1280 (S.D.W.Va. 1989), *aff'd.* 932 F.2d 964 (4th Cir.1991) (unpublished). In other words, the rubble from the top of the mountain is placed in the adjacent valley. "When valley fills are permitted in intermittent and perennial streams, they destroy those stream segments. The normal flow and gradient of the stream is now buried under millions of cubic yards of excess spoil waste material, an extremely adverse effect. If there are fish, they cannot migrate. If there is any life form that cannot acclimate to life deep in a rubble pile, it is eliminated. No effect on related environmental values is more adverse than obliteration. Under a valley fill, the water quantity of the stream becomes zero. Because there is no stream, there is no water quality." *Bragg v. Robertson*, 72 F.Supp.2d 642 (S.D.W.Va. 1999), *rev'd sub nom. Bragg v. West Virginia Coal Ass'n*, 248 F.3d 275 (4th Cir. 2001). Recall that the Corps tried to justify its Nationwide Permit on the grounds that, if the mining process had been approved by a regulatory authority under SMCRA, for the Corps then to engage in individual permitting actions would be duplicative and confusing.

It is fairly clear that mountaintop removal mining is not prohibited by SMCRA. It is specifically included as an example of "surface coal mining operations" in the definition of that term. *See* 30 U.S.C. § 1291(28)(A). It is not as clear that valley fills are permitted. After all, among other things, the environmental protection performance standards required to be included in state or federal programs include requirements that excess spoil not be placed in natural water courses, 30 U.S.C. § 1265(b)(22)(D), and that waivers from the Approximate Original Contours requirement not allow any damage to natural watercourses. *But see Kentuckians for Commonwealth, Inc. v. Rivenburgh*, 317 F.3d 425, 442 (4th Cir. 2003)("It is apparent that SMCRA anticipates the possibility that excess spoil material could and would be placed in waters of the United States").

Two major law suits have been brought by environmental groups challenging the practice of mountaintop removal/valley fill mining, especially prevalent in West Virginia. The first, *Bragg v. Robertson*, was brought against the Director of West Virginia's Department of Environmental Protection, alleging that he had approved mountaintop removal/valley fill mining permits in violation of both SMCRA and the state program approved under SMCRA, and against the Corps of Engineers, alleging it had violated the Clean Water Act, NEPA, and the Administrative Procedure Act.

In the trial court, all but two counts of the complaint were settled through a consent decree that required the Corps and the WVDEP, as well as EPA, OSMRE, and the Fish and Wildlife Service, none of whom had been parties to the suit, to prepare a programmatic EIS on mountop-removal/valley fill mining. *See Bragg v. Robertson*, 83 F.Supp.2d 713 (S.D.W.Va. 2000), *aff'd sub nom. Bragg v. West Virginia Coal Ass'n*, 248 F.3d 275 (4th Cir. 2001). As of this writing, the federal agencies have published a draft EIS but have not published a final EIS. In addition, the Corps agreed to require individual permits for any fill in West Virginia that would result in more than a minimal adverse effect on waters of the United States, with any fill of waters draining a watershed of greater than 250 acres conclusively presumed to have a greater than minimal adverse effect. *Id.*

The two counts that were not settled related to a West Virginia regulation, intended to conform with a federal regulation, known as the Stream Buffer Zone rule (SBZ), that established 100–foot buffer zones around perennial and intermittent streams. The district court held that the state had been violating those requirements and enjoined the state from placing any excess spoil in such streams. *Bragg v. Robertson*, 72 F.Supp.2d 642 (S.D.W.Va. 1999). On appeal, the Fourth Circuit reversed, finding that the Eleventh Amendment precluded the suit against the Director of the WVDEP. *Bragg v. West Virginia Coal Ass'n*, 248 F.3d 275 (4th Cir. 2001). Nevertheless, in 1999, as a result of the lawsuit, EPA, the Corps, OSMRE, and the WVDEP entered into a Memorandum of Understanding (MOU) to clarify the meaning of the SBZ rule.

The second law suit challenging mountaintop/valley fill removal mining was *Kentuckians for Commonwealth Inc. v. Rivenburgh*, 317 F.3d 425 (4th Cir. 2003). In that case, an environmental group sued the Corps, asserting that valley fill disposal of excess spoil in streams was not the discharge of "fill" within the meaning of Section 404. If correct, this would mean that EPA would be the permitting authority under Section 402 and the NPDES program, rather than the Corps. Although the district court agreed with the plaintiffs, the Fourth Circuit reversed, holding that the Corps' (and EPA's) interpretation was reasonable. Accordingly, the Corps remains the permitting authority under Section 404 for valley fill disposal of excess spoil.

Neither of the cases were against OSMRE. Indeed, in *Bragg* the plaintiffs relied on OSMRE's SBZ rule to attack West Virginia's permitting actions, and the Department of Justice, representing the Corps, indicated agreement with the plaintiffs' interpretation of the SBZ rule. However, OSMRE essentially agreed with West Virginia and not with the Department of Justice as to the meaning of its rule. It was this lack of agreement and coordination that created the need for the MOU to clarify the meaning of the rule. The MOU concluded that, if a valley fill was not inconsistent with the 404(b)(1) Guidelines under Section 404, the fill would not be deemed to violate the SBZ rule. This MOU, however, was held by the district court in *Bragg* to be inconsistent with

SMCRA, but this aspect of the district court's decision was overruled on jurisdictional grounds under the Eleventh Amendment.

In *Rivenburgh*, although the suit was against the Corps, asserting it did not have permitting authority for valley fills under the CWA, both the district court and appellate decisions expressed interpretations of SMCRA and the SBZ rule.

As a result of all these actions, OSMRE undertook to clarify the SBZ Rule and SMCRA's treatment of valley fills in a new rulemaking. *See* 69 Fed. Reg. 1036 (January 7, 2004)(Proposed Rule). [As of this writing, the agency has not promulgated a final rule.] The current, unamended SBZ rule applicable to state programs states:

(a) No land within 100 feet of a perennial stream or an intermittent stream shall be disturbed by surface mining activities, unless the regulatory authority specifically authorizes surface mining activities closer to, or through, such a stream. The regulatory authority may authorize such activities only upon finding that—

(1) Surface mining activities will not cause or contribute to the violation of applicable State or Federal water quality standards, and will not adversely affect the water quantity and quality or other environmental resources of the stream; and

(2) If there will be a temporary or permanent stream-channel diversion, it will comply with § 816.43.

(b) The area not to be disturbed shall be designated as a buffer zone, and the operator shall mark it as specified in § 816.11.

30 CFR 816.57. On its face, this would seem to prohibit valley fills, because, as the district court in *Bragg* noted, filling a stream with excess spoil adversely affects the stream by destroying it. However, intermittent streams are defined generally as streams that drain a watershed of at least one square mile, *see* 30 CFR 701.5. Streams draining smaller watersheds, OSMRE maintains, are simply not protected by the SBZ Rule, 69 Fed. Reg. 1036, 1042 (2004), even though perennial streams are not defined by the size of their drainage but simply as streams that flow continuously throughout the year. Thus, this provision allows fill to totally destroy a stream that does not drain at least a one square mile watershed, although OSMRE recognizes that many of these non-qualifying streams "support biological communities or serve as fish spawning areas." *Id*. Moreover, OSMRE indicates that it has always interpreted the SBZ Rule not to actually prohibit stream fills in the mining area, because waivers could be granted to fill streams so long as there were no adverse effects within 100 feet downstream of the fill. *See* 69 Fed. Reg. 1036, 1041 (2004). Under this interpretation, even large streams may be destroyed if they are within the mining area, so long as 100 feet from the mining area the stream is not adversely affected.

Its proposed rule, OSMRE says, is intended to make this idea more clear. It would provide:

(a) No land within 100 feet of a perennial stream or an intermittent stream shall be disturbed by surface mining activities, unless the regulatory authority specifically authorizes such activities closer to or through the stream. The regulatory authority may authorize such activities only upon finding that the activities will, to the extent possible, using the best technology currently available—

(1) Prevent additional contributions of suspended solids to the stream section within 100 feet downstream of the surface mining activities, and outside of the area affected by surface mining activities; and

(2) Minimize disturbances and adverse impacts on fish, wildlife, and other related environmental values of the stream.

Notes and Comments

1. One of the changes in the proposed rule is to require the prevention of additional contributions of suspended solids (silt) and the minimization of disturbance and adverse impacts only "to the extent possible, using the best technology available." The preamble to the proposed rule does not indicate what the best technology available might be, or to what extent it is possible to avoid the adverse effects identified in paragraphs (1) and (2). Indeed, the preamble says that "It is virtually impossible to conduct mining activities within 100 feet of an intermittent or perennial stream without causing some adverse impacts." 69 Fed. Reg. 1036, 1043 (2004).

2. The preamble states that "[w]e believe SMCRA recognizes that an absolute standard of 'no adverse impacts' is unattainable. This is reflected in the fact that SMCRA in most cases requires the mining operation to minimize, rather than completely prevent, adverse environmental impacts." *Id.* For example, 30 U.S.C. § 1265(b)(24) mandates that state and federal programs require mining operations to "minimize disturbances and adverse impacts on fish, wildlife, and related environmental values. . . . " "to the extent possible using the best technology currently available." However, there is no attempt to relate the SBZ Rule to 30 U.S.C. § 1265(b)(22)(D), that requires state and federal programs to flatly prohibit placement of excess spoil material in an area containing "springs, natural water courses or wet weather weeps unless lateral drains are constructed. . . . " Thus, even if the proposed rule more accurately captures OSMRE's interpretation of the original SBZ Rule, does it then square with the requirements of SMCRA?

3. Enforcement Issues

SMCRA was deemed necessary because coal mining states were unable, in the face of both coal industry (think Republican) and union (think Democratic) pressures, to muster sufficient political will to regulate mining themselves. SMCRA, however, still offers states "exclusive jurisdiction" if they have approved state programs. Because a state program, reflecting the state's laws and regulations, will have been approved by OSMRE in a public process with the input of EPA, Agriculture, and other federal agencies, the state's laws and regulations are usually not the problem. The problem is state administration and enforcement. Here, largely out of the view of the public, the same political pressures that historically affected coal regulation in major coal states continue to have substantial effects. In *Bragg* the plaintiffs alleged that the WVDEP routinely issued permits in violation of its own regulations, and in *Molinary* there was testimony from the permitting officer of the Virginia Division of Mined Land Reclamation that he routinely approved permit applications without requiring that all the regulatory requirements were met.

The statute provides for the withdrawal of a state's primacy, in whole or in part, for failing to enforce its laws effectively. *See* 30 U.S.C. § 1271(b). *See also* 30 U.S.C. § 1254(b) (allowing OSMRE, when a state is not enforcing "any part" of its program, to "provide for the federal enforcement, under [§ 1271], of that part of the State program"). And OSMRE has been willing to utilize this authority. In 1984 it instituted direct federal enforcement of the inspection provisions of Oklahoma's and Tennessee's programs. And in 2003 it instituted direct federal enforcement of inspection, enforcement, permitting, and bonding activities in Missouri. While this authority, which EPA has under the CWA, the CAA, and RCRA, may be adequate for OSMRE to ensure general adequacy of a state program, it provides no safety net of enforcement for individual, even serious, violations of state laws or regulations.

SMCRA does provide some safety net, but its extent depends on how some of its provisions are interpreted. First, if, "on the basis of any Federal inspection," conditions or practices are found to exist that cause an imminent danger to health or safety of the public, OSMRE may issue orders to cease mining operations and to take other actions necessary to abate the danger. 30 U.S.C. § 1271(a)(2). This provision, however, only comes into play if the violation is found incident to a federal inspection, and in primacy states federal inspections under SMCRA are only explicitly authorized in two situations. One is "to evaluate the administration of approved programs," not to discover violations or imminent danger conditions, 30 U.S.C. § 1267(a), although if conditions causing imminent danger are then found, the order provision comes into play. The other situation in which a federal inspection is authorized is when, "on the basis of any information available to him, including receipt of information from any person," OSMRE believes that any person is "in violation of any requirement of [SMCRA] or any permit condition required by [SMCRA]." 30 U.S.C. § 1271(a)(1). When the information provided to OSMRE is "adequate proof" that an imminent danger of significant environmental harm exists and that the state has failed to take appropriate action, the inspection may take place immediately. *Id.* Otherwise, before the inspection may take place in a primacy state, OSMRE must give the state regulatory authority 10–days notice, during which time the state regulatory authority may avoid the federal inspection by taking appropriate action or showing good cause why it has not. *Id.* There is an argument, based on the characterization of the violation as a "violation of any requirement of [SMCRA] or any permit condition required by [SMCRA]," that in primacy states an operator is simply incapable of violating SMCRA or a permit condition required by SMCRA, because in primacy states the operative regulatory law is state law, not SMCRA. The language in *Bragg* and the rationale in *Haydo* probably might support this argument. However, OSMRE does not accept this interpretation and its regulations explicitly authorize inspections upon receiving information regarding violations of state program requirements and state-issued permits. *See* 30 CFR § 842.11.

In the absence of an imminent danger, SMCRA may also provide some federal safety net. OSMRE adopted a regulation providing that, if a federal inspection in a primacy state reveals a violation of a state program requirement or permit condition that does not amount to an imminent danger, OSMRE may issue a notice of violation to the violator, requiring it to come into compliance within a reasonable time. 30 CFR § 843.12. If the inspection was not pursuant to enforcing a state program because the failure of a state to enforce that part of its program, *see* 30 U.S.C. 1254(b), OSMRE provides notice of the violation first to the state regulatory authority and allows it 10 days in which to take appropriate action or show good cause why it has not. 30 CFR § 843.12(a)(2). The coal industry challenged this regulation as beyond OSMRE's statutory authority, but its challenge was dismissed as barred by SMCRA's time limit of 60 days in which to challenge a regulation, 30 US.C. 1276(a)(1). *See National Min. Ass'n v. U.S. Dept. of Interior*, 70 F.3d 1345 (D.C.Cir. 1995).

The above discussion has focused on OSMRE being the safety net for enforcing requirements stemming from SMCRA not being adequately enforced by primacy states. Is OSMRE itself reliable? The Department of Interior traditionally has been more "political" than EPA, with its Secretaries reflecting the ideologies of their Presidents, and OSMRE has been affected by those politics. Its rulemakings expand or contract the protections provided by SMCRA depending upon the party in power. What about its enforcement actions? There is little empirical evidence upon which to base a conclusion, but its willingness on a few occasions to institute direct federal enforcement in place of the state regulatory authority, the number of contested enforcement actions reported in cases, and the number of Fifth Amendment takings cases from prohibitions against mining in certain areas, all suggest that OSMRE is a credible enforcement branch.

Perhaps the final safety net is the citizen suit by a person adversely affected to compel compliance with SMCRA. Some of the particular federalism problems as they affect SMCRA citizen suits were addressed earlier. Otherwise, the SMCRA citizen suit provision shares many similarities with other citizen suit provisions in environmental laws, which are discussed at length in the chapter on enforcement. There are two unique aspects to SMCRA's citizen suit provision. First, there is no provision for the citizen suit to result in civil penalties for the violator. Second, perhaps in place of civil penalties, there is provision for a damages action by any person injured in his person or property through the violation by any operator of "any rule, regulation, order, or permit issued pursuant to [SMCRA]." It was this part of the citizen suit provision that was in issue in both *Haydo* and *Molinary*.

Chapter 9

INTERNATIONAL ENVIRONMENTAL LAW

I. INTRODUCTION

International environmental law is, of course, a subject worthy of an entire course in itself, and there are several casebooks devoted exclusively to international environmental law. Necessarily, therefore, this chapter can only provide a most meager introduction. After a brief overview of international law generally, the chapter begins with a section on climate change and international law, in particular the Kyoto Protocol. The purpose of this section is to provide an example of international decisionmaking, warts and all, in an environmental context that just happens to be the most important environmental problem the international community faces. The chapter then provides a selection on trade and the environment. Globalization of the world's economy has been facilitated by the progressive elimination of barriers to trade between nations, which most economists believe raises global standards of living, just as the creation of the United States and much later the European Union as common markets without internal trade barriers raised the standard of living in those areas. At the same time, however, the rules of the General Agreement on Tariffs and Trade and later the World Trade Organization, by limiting the sovereign power of the members, can come in conflict with domestic laws intended to protect the environment. This section of the chapter provides some examples of such conflicts.

II. AN OVERVIEW OF INTERNATIONAL LAW

Whereas domestic law generally regulates individuals, corporations, and government actors, among others, international law applies primarily to States[1] themselves and does not separately recognize State citizens. States are not only traditionally the sole subjects of international law, but also the sole creators, implementers, and enforcers. Given that States control the international law that binds them, international law tends to grant deference to States. Most international laws only bind

---

1. "State" refers to set of governing institutions with sovereignty over a definite territory. The name of a particular State is generally the same as the name of a nation.

consenting States and much of international law confirms State sovereignty and the authority of States to govern.

However, with the rise of international organizations, such as multilateral development institutions and various branches of the United Nations (UN), along with the proliferation of international non-governmental organizations (NGOs), and multinational corporations, the international law landscape is evolving. Even though States are still the primary architects of international law, its development increasingly involves actors other than States. International organizations propose and draft potential binding agreements and issue non-binding but influential directives. NGOs monitor the implementation of existing agreements and influence international decision-making by providing information to policy makers and the public. Multinational corporations lobby decision-makers and participate directly in some international organizations. These examples provide just a sampling of the many non-State actors and their varied functions that influence the formulation and execution of present-day international law.

Increased participation by non-State actors in international law development has catalyzed changes in the character of international law, such as the emergence of international "soft law." Soft law is non-binding and often emanates from instruments like declarations, guidelines, and codes of conduct that may be drafted by non-State actors. We begin now with a look at traditional international law or "hard law" before moving to a further discussion of soft law.

A. Hard Law

Treaties, international custom, and general principles of law recognized by civilized nations constitute hard law. Hard law obligations usually only bind States that have explicitly or implicitly consented and are theoretically enforceable against non-compliant States. While treaties, custom, and general principles—each of which is discussed below—make up the body of international hard law, two additional sources inform interpretations of hard law. First, judicial decisions, which are not precedential in international law, advise formulations of hard law. Second, "the teachings of the most highly qualified publicists of the various nations" may also contribute to an understanding of hard law. *International Court of Justice Statute*, Article 38(1).

1. Treaties

A treaty is a contract between States and places legal obligations on the States that ratify it. Ratification occurs when a State authoritatively declares to the international community that it considers itself bound by the obligations set forth in the treaty. If a treaty permits, or if Parties to a treaty agree, a ratifying State may limit its consent or make reservations from specific treaty obligations, effectively opting out of certain aspects of the agreement. For example, Article 23 of the *Convention on International Trade in Endangered Species of Wild Flora and Fauna* (CITES) allows Parties to make reservations with respect to any particular species. Singapore made such a reservation regarding the spectacled caiman, and thus avoided the requirements the Convention imposes on Parties in the course of trading the reptiles.

A treaty enters into force—meaning it becomes binding on ratifying States—when conditions specified in the treaty, such as a minimum number of ratifications, have been met. For example, Article 16 of the *Convention on Long–Range Transboundary Air Pollution* specified: "The present Convention shall enter into force on the ninetieth day after the date of deposit of the twenty-fourth instrument of ratification, acceptance, approval or accession." Some treaties become automatically binding at the national level or "self execute" as soon as they enter into force. Whether a treaty is self-executing in a particular State depends on the domestic law of that state and the language of the treaty. If a treaty requires passage of domestic legislation to implement its requirements nationally, the treaty would be non self-executing. Some provisions of a treaty may be self-executing, while others are non-self-executing provisions. In the United States self-executing treaties and provisions have the same authority as federal laws.

Some treaties call for the creation of bodies to administer the treaty. A Conference of the Parties (COP), consisting of representatives of each Party to the treaty, is one such administrative body. A COP may meet annually or biennially to revise and make additions to the treaty, to monitor implementation, and to initiate enforcement measures. Another potential body, a secretariat, typically undertakes the routine operations involved in treaty implementation like communicating between and gathering information from Parties, maintaining records, identifying areas of non-compliance and preparing COP meetings. A secretariat may be an entirely new organization or be incorporated into an existing institution such as the United Nations Environment Programme (UNEP), which administers several international environmental treaties. Finally, a treaty may establish, or empower a COP to establish subsidiary bodies and committees to address specific issues raised by the treaty. The *Convention on Biological Diversity*, for example, establishes a Subsidiary Body on Scientific, Technical and Technological Advice (SBSTTA) that meets annually to develop proposals for presentation to the COP.

The Vienna Convention on the Law of Treaties governs the creation and interpretation of treaties. This Convention codifies customary international law so that even those States that are non-Parties, nonetheless adhere to the practices it outlines.

2. Customary International Law

Prior to the proliferation of multilateral treaties that began at the end of the 19th century, custom was the primary source of international law. Customary international law consists of rules that States routinely abide by in practice out of a sense of legal obligation known as *opinio juris*. Customary law consists of existing norms, such as the practice of granting immunity to foreign diplomats. Customary international environmental law is currently developing. For example, States and international law instruments now generally recognize as customary law the "precautionary principle" that countries should err on the side of caution in addressing scientifically uncertain environmental problems. The 1992 *Rio Declaration on Environment and Development* advances this concept in Principle 15: "Where there are threats of serious or irreversible damage, lack of scientific certainty shall not be used as a reason for postponing cost-effective measures to prevent environmental degradation."

Customary law is binding hard law but in some instances a country may opt out of customary law obligations by "persistently objecting" or consistently refusing to recognize a custom as law. However, certain customary law obligations, such as the prohibition on genocide, are compulsory and no State may violate them. Such norms are termed *jus cogens* norms.

3. General Principles of Law Recognized by Civilized Nations

When the domestic law of most States adheres to a principle, that principle constitutes a general principle of international law. General principles often embody typical rules of procedure, evidence, and jurisdiction or natural-law-like concepts that are common in the domestic laws of States, such as equity. General principles make international law workable by filling the gaps left by treaties and custom.

Article 59 of the *United Nations Convention on the Law of the Sea* (UNCLOS) for example, stipulates that equity resolve certain conflicts in exclusive economic zones—an area of the sea that extends up to 200 nautical miles off the coast of a State where the State exercises sovereign rights and exclusive fishery management. Article 59 provides:

> In cases where this Convention does not attribute rights or jurisdiction to the coastal State or to other States within the exclusive economic zone, and a conflict arises between the interests of the coastal State and any other State or States, the conflict should be resolved on the basis of equity and in the light of all the relevant circumstances, taking into account the respective importance of the interests involved to the Parties as well as to the international community as a whole.

B. Soft Law

Soft law is a contemporary innovation in international lawmaking that allows for the international community, including non-State actors, to build consensus around a principle. Non-binding instruments such as UN promulgations and directives of multilateral development institutions like the World Bank are examples of soft law sources. A binding instrument that suggests duties but lacks precise obligations may also be a source of soft law. In contrast to hard law that proscribes present particular obligations, soft law provides goals and guidelines that seek to lay the groundwork for future developments in hard law. Although non-binding in and of themselves, soft law norms help define standards of good behavior for States, and influence interpretations of international law made by national legislatures and international arbitrators.

Soft law evolves when States and international institutions such as UNEP or the UN General Assembly consistently promote certain principles. As more institutions and instruments advocate the same principles a common international understanding emerges. The repetition and widespread acceptance of a principle may result in the eventual codification of the principle in a binding instrument or the acceptance of the principle into customary law. For instance, the principle that States undertaking activities that could harm the environments of neighboring States should provide their neighbors with prior notification and an opportunity to consult turns up in enough soft law instruments that it has arguably become a customary norm and now appears in proposed codifications of general international environmental law. NGOs and multinational corporations among other non-State actors also influence the development of soft law by participating in the negotiations of international institutions or even by independently passing resolutions. Whereas international hard law remains the formal domain of States, international soft law provides a highly participatory and flexible forum for advancing new principles of international law.

C. Enforcement of International Law

Enforcement of international law occurs primarily through mechanisms and standards provided by treaties. Even customary law principles and general principles of law are enforced largely through treaty mechanisms as many of those principles have been incorporated into treaties. In lieu of penalties for non-compliance, some treaties employ positive enforcement mechanisms and reward compliance efforts by providing benefits like access to financial or technological assistance to facilitate treaty implementation. Treaties may require States to make reports on implementation efforts to the treaty secretariat. This obligation, coupled with the fact that NGOs regularly monitor and publicize the details of State treaty compliance, may motivate States to work towards effective implementation. The desire to maintain good standing in the international community may also provide a compliance incentive.

Regardless of intent, the ability to comply with a treaty varies from State to State. Treaties frequently recognize the disparities between States and may set forth varied requirements that depend on compliance capacity. To increase the capacity of less compliance-ready States, which are typically developing nations, treaties may require developed nations to contribute funds, technology, personnel training and so on. NGOs and international organizations are also instrumental in providing such assistance to undercapacitated nations.

In cases of non-compliance, penalties outlined in a treaty, such as trade sanctions and disqualification from the benefits of treaty membership, or the threat of such consequences may motivate a State to change its ways. The so-called "non-compliance procedure" is a more recent non-compliance mechanism included in some treaties. *The Montreal Protocol on Substances that Deplete the Ozone Layer* introduced this proactive mechanism that allows for a State, struggling with compliance, to seek assistance by self-reporting. A response tailored to the State's particular needs follows, in an effort to bring the State into compliance.

States may also enforce international law obligations against other States by bringing an action in an international court or tribunal. In order for a State Party to bring such an action it must have standing. A State has standing if the defendant State caused injury to a right of the complaining State as established by treaty, binding decision of an international organization, customary law, or judgment of an international court of tribunal. A Party to a treaty automatically has standing to bring a complaint against another Party that violates treaty-imposed obligations to the international community (*erga omnes* obligations), regardless of whether the violation caused direct harm to the complaining State. States may have standing to bring an action on behalf of the international community for violation of customary international law committed in the global commons (*action popularis*), such as Antarctica, the moon, or outer space, but no State has ever brought such an action without having also suffered damage in its own territory.

Notes and Questions

1. In 1945, in the wake of World War II, fifty-one countries, hoping to foster security and prevent future conflicts, founded the United Nations by signing the United Nations Charter. Today, the UN includes nearly all independent States and consists of many bodies that serve functions ranging from advancing worldwide health to promoting universal human rights. The various UN bodies indirectly influence the development of international law by, for example, facilitating research and hosting negotiations. The UN also directly contributes to the evolution of international law and in 1999 devised a strategy for the current "era of application of international law." In recent years the UN has begun extending "invitations" to prompt States to join existing treaties that reflect core values of the UN, advocating the teaching of international law in institutions worldwide, and expanding its capacity to provide technical assistance to States. The UN also makes extensive international law resources, such as a complete list of the hundreds of multilateral treaties registered with the UN Secretariat, available on the internet. See untreaty.un.org. For more information on the UN's efforts to promote the international rule of law see the UN website on international law at http://www.un.org/law/.

2. The term non-governmental organization (NGO), often referred to as "civil society" in UN parlance, encompasses a wide range of organizations of varying sizes and missions. All NGOs are similar to one another, however, in that they pursue public rather than private interests and are neither founded nor operated by government. International NGOs, such as the human rights-focused Human Rights Watch, or the conservation-oriented World Wildlife Fund, (WWF) often lend expertise, localized contacts, and innovation to States. States are thus increasingly accepting NGOs as contributors to the development, implementation, and enforcement of international law. Article 8(3) of the Convention Concerning the Protection of the World Cultural and Natural Heritage, for example, allows NGOs to attend in an

advisory capacity the meetings of the Committee that oversees the Convention. Similarly, Article 5(d) of the Convention to Combat Desertification (CCD) instructs parties to seek assistance from NGOs to "promote awareness and facilitate the participation of local populations." These examples demonstrate that States and international law instruments increasingly recognize the role of NGOs in international law. Meanwhile the sheer number of NGOs worldwide is rapidly expanding. Between 1993 and 2003 there was a worldwide 43% growth in the number of NGOs focusing on international issues. Global communication technology, and the internet in particular, has helped prompt this growth by simplifying information exchange and coordination efforts among NGOs, while also providing a forum for NGOs to publicize issues.

3.   Various fora exist for the litigation of international law but many of them limit their jurisdiction to particular types of issues. The International Criminal Court, for example, specifically prosecutes individuals for war crimes, crimes against humanity and genocide. Three fora accommodate the litigation of international environmental law issues: the International Court of Justice (ICJ), ad hoc international tribunals, and domestic courts. The International Court of Justice is the principal judicial organ of the United Nations. Established in 1945 by the Charter of the United Nations, and based in the Hague, Netherlands, the ICJ serves to adjudicate legal disputes submitted by States and to give advisory opinions on legal questions posed by authorized international organizations. To date, the ICJ has produced relatively few decisions and virtually no decisions relating to international environmental issues. Use of the Court has, however, increased since the 1980s, especially among developing countries. For a list of cases brought before the ICJ see http://www.icj-cij.org/icjwww/idecisions.htm. States may also litigate international environmental disputes in ad hoc tribunals, which enable States to select the law and procedures that will apply, along with the hearing judges. Such tribunals, however, also require States to consent to jurisdiction. Finally, international environmental litigation may occur in the domestic courts of involved States but State sovereignty, standing, and the principle of forum non-conveniens all restrict the hearing of international environmental disputes in domestic courts.

4.   International law depends upon domestic law for maximum effectiveness. States establish horizontal agreements between one another in international law, but many of the obligations established under those agreements require vertical State efforts and implementation at the domestic level. For example, in order for the Convention on International Trade in Endangered Species (CITES) to effectively restrict export and import of some animal and plant species, each party must adopt domestic laws and infrastructure to monitor trade. States must thus individually take domestic action in order for many international laws to take full effect. Domestic courts in turn enforce international law by enforcing domestic laws that support international laws. Domestic courts are an especially essential enforcement mechanism of international environmental law because unlike international law, domestic law assumes control over individuals and corporations, which are frequently the perpetrators of environmental harms.

III. THE EMERGENCE OF INTERNATIONAL ENVIRONMENTAL LAW

A. Transboundary Air Pollution

Because the atmosphere does not heed political borders, air pollution has been a concern of international law for longer than many other international environmental issues. The 1941 *Trail Smelter Arbitration* represents one of most famous disputes to come out of international environmental law. The dispute involved the sulfur dioxide (SO_2) emissions of an ore smelter located in Trail, British Columbia, in Canada, a few miles North of Washington State. In 1927, Washington apple growers unable to bring suit themselves in either Canada or the United States, requested that the U.S. government intervene. In this unique scenario the Canadian and American governments became Parties to the nuisance claim of American citizens against a private Canadian corporation. The dispute resulted in lengthy negotiations and arbitration that concluded on March 11, 1941, thirteen years after the initial United States intervention. The arbitrating tribunal tailored its final decision to the particular situation, granting damages to the United States and imposing controls on the Canadian smelter. However, the tribunal's conclusion that a State should prohibit activities in its jurisdiction or control that cause damage to the environments of other States or territories outside of national jurisdiction reflects custom and has continued to be persuasive in international environmental law.

The Trail smelter dispute exposes some of the potential procedural difficulties and legal uncertainties involved in resolving international disputes, especially international environmental disputes. The U.S. and Canadian governments first attempted to settle the matter of the Trail smelter pollution through diplomatic negotiations but a mutually satisfactory solution eluded the two nations. The governments then submitted the issue to the International Joint Commission (IJC), a body consisting of three representatives of each nation, established under the Boundary Waters Treaty of 1909 between Canada and the United States. Treaty Relating to Boundary Waters Between the United States and Canada, Jan. 11, 1909, U.S.-Gr. Brit., 36 Stat. 2448. Under Article 9 of the treaty the IJC could investigate and make a report on questions submitted by either nation involving "the rights, obligations, or interests of either in relation to the other or to the inhabitants of the other, along the common frontier." Following the ICJ's report, the two governments entered into an agreement awarding some damages to the United States and establishing a three-member tribunal to determine additional damages and potentially set emissions levels for the Smelter. Convention for Settlement of Difficulties Arising from Operation of Smelter at Trail, British Columbia, U.S.-Can., Apr. 15, 1935, 1935 U.N.T.S. 74, reprinted in 1 Int'l Envtl L. Rep. 244. The panel convened and spent several years investigating before issuing its decision in the final Trail Smelter Arbitration. Trail Smelter (U.S. v. Canada), 3 R.I.A.A. 1938, 1964–65 (Trail Smelter Arb. Trib 1941).

Transboundary pollution from the Trail smelter has once again given rise to an international dispute between the United States and Canada. For decades the Trail smelter discharged tons and tons of heavy metals, such as mercury, into the Columbia River that flows into Lake Roosevelt in Washington State. In December of 2003, The United States Environmental Protection Agency (EPA) issued a unilateral administrative order demanding that the operators of the Trail Smelter clean up contamination concentrated in the Lake Roosevelt area under the Comprehensive Environmental Response and Compensation Act (CERCLA). EPA Region 10, Upper Columbia River Site Unilateral Administrative Order for Remedial Investigation/Feasibility Study, CERCLA–10–2004–0018 (Dec. 11, 2003). The Smelter's operators refused to submit to EPA's jurisdiction and members of the Colville Confederated Tribes living in the Lake Roosevelt area subsequently brought suit to enforce EPA's order in federal district court. A Washington district court found for the tribal members, and the Ninth Circuit affirmed. Pakootas v. Teck Cominco Metals, Ltd., 452 F.3d 1066 (9th Cir. 2006). The attempt by EPA and by individual citizens to apply U.S. domestic environmental law internationally is highly controversial and, in particular, raises issues of sovereignty and the extraterritorial application of domestic law.

B. UN Conference on the Human Environment—The "Stockholm Conference"

Addressing environmental problems by treaty is relatively new to international law. While a few environmental treaties emerged early in the 20th century, such as the 1916 *Convention for the Protection of Migratory Birds* between the United States and Great Britain (for Canada), it was not until the 1960s that international environmental law began substantially to develop, as scientific evidence of international environmental problems advanced, and public and political awareness of environmental issues increased.

As environmental consciousness grew, developed countries including Canada, European nations, the United States, Japan, Australia, New Zealand, and the former Soviet Union—sometimes termed the "North"—began to share concern about the environment. Meanwhile developing countries—conversely termed the "South"—were much less concerned because due to its lack of development the South did not face the same environmental problems as the North. To some extent, developing countries objected to environmental considerations because of the potential for environmentally protective measures to interfere with desired development.

Many industrialized countries, such as the United States, acted on their environmental concerns by passing domestic environmental legislation. Debate over environmental protections at the international level also ensued, but the conflicting interests of the North and South inhibited consensus. To build international consensus, the UN General Assembly organized an international Conference on the Human Environment in Stockholm, Sweden, in 1972. This "Stockholm Conference" represented the global community's first major endeavor to address the relationship between development and the environment. It resulted in three influential contributions to international environmental law and policy: the *Stockholm Action Plan to Protect the Global Environment*, the *Stockholm Declaration on the Human Environment*, and the United Nations Environment Programme (UNEP).

The *Stockholm Action Plan* highlighted issues requiring international attention and created a worldwide environmental assessment program to continue to identify areas of international environmental concern. The plan also urged a number of actions that the international community subsequently took, such as a ten-year moratorium on commercial whaling. The plan thus provided a framework for undertaking the first generation of global environmental action.

Reflecting both northern and southern concerns, the *Stockholm Declaration on the Human Environment* (Stockholm Declaration) placed the primary responsibility for environmental protection on national and local governments, affirmed States' sovereignty over their own natural resources, and laid the groundwork for global acceptance of the sustainable development concept. In the months leading up to the Stockholm Conference developing countries had sought to secure their right to development by banding together to form the G–77—a group initially consisting of seventy-seven developing nations—and pushing multiple resolutions through the UN General Assembly. Many of the principles in these pre-Stockholm resolutions reappeared as central principles of the *Stockholm Declaration.*

The United Nations Environment Programme (UNEP) is a subsidiary of the UN General Assembly that catalyzes cooperation within the UN system to address environmental issues. UNEP's governing council consists of representatives of fifty-eight States. The UN General Assembly elects States for participation in UNEP for four-year terms. Staggered elections occur every two years, and like many UN elections geographical distribution factors into the decision of which States serve. Following the Stockholm Conference, global and regional environmental treaties proliferated, many of which were negotiated under the guidance of UNEP, including the *Basel Convention on the Transboundary Movement of Hazardous Wastes* and the *Vienna Convention for the Protection of the Ozone Layer*.

C. Between Stockholm and Rio

Following the Stockholm Conference, tension between northern concern over the global environment and southern interests in development continued to influence environmental negotiations. The UN General Assembly convened a World Commission on Environment and Development (WCED) to address both northern and southern priorities by forming sustainable development strategies. In 1987, the WCED issued its report, *Our Common Future*, often termed the *Brundtland Report* after the WCED's chair Gro Harlem Brundtland, which became an important milestone in the evolution of international environmental relations and law. The *Brundtland Report* eased contemporary political tensions by advocating economic growth as a means of both protecting the environment and alleviating poverty. The report also popularized the concept of sustainable development, defined as "development that meets the needs of the present without compromising the ability of future generations to meet their own needs." U.N.G.A. A/42/427 4 Aug. 1987. To highlight the urgent need for sustainable development the report catalogued global environmental problems interrelated with the global economy and suggested a meeting of governments to assess how best to achieve sustainable development. This led to the 1992 United Nations Conference on Environment and Development in Rio de Janeiro, Brazil.

D.   UN Conference on Environment and Development—"Rio Earth Summit"

The Conference on Environment and Development in Rio de Janeiro, Brazil, sought to elaborate a plan of action to achieve the sustainable development aims set forth in the *Brundtland Report*. The differing priorities of the North and South forged the agenda and outcomes of the "Rio Earth Summit." The South advocated issues like food and fresh water security, debt relief, access to northern markets, curbing consumption, and funding southern cooperation, while the North preferred to address matters like deforestation, loss of biodiversity, climate change and population growth.

Despite political differences the twelve-day conference produced tangible results. Both the *Convention on Biological Diversity* and the *Framework Convention on Climate Change* emerged from the summit, as did an influential *Statement of Principles for the Sustainable Management of Forests*. Over the course of the summit States also finalized *Agenda 21*, an 800–page guidebook for sustainable development. Finally, The Rio Earth Summit produced the *Rio Declaration on Environment and Development* (Rio Declaration), a non-binding declaration reflecting the compromises between North and South on twenty-seven environmental and sustainable development principles. To monitor the implementation of the *Rio Declaration* and *Agenda 21,* the States at the Rio Earth Summit also created a Commission on Sustainable Development.

Notes and Questions

1.   Since the Stockholm Conference, differences between northern and southern States have continued to shape international environmental negotiations, but States have worked to arrive at compromises. Initially many southern States perceived the North's insistence on universal environmental protection as a new form of colonialism and a scheme for northern States to retain access to resources in developing States by preventing local economic growth. Southern states have also viewed environmental protection as a luxury and instead prioritized issues like poverty, health, and education. Further, from the southern standpoint, the majority of international damage flows from the consumptive activities of the developed world. Northern

States have conversely criticized overpopulation and rapid growth in the South. To address both northern and southern concerns, negotiating States have adopted the practice of treating States differentially. Agreements and instruments of international environmental law frequently recognize different States' varying degrees of responsibility and capacity. Further, many agreements now include provisions providing funding mechanisms for southern States. These accommodations have helped draw southern States into international environmental law agreements. Southern states have also become more invested in international environmental law issues because developing States are increasingly feeling the negative fallout of many global environmental problems. Small island states, for example, are deeply concerned about potential sea level rise as a consequence of global climate change. Despite increasing cooperation between the North and South, the extent of responsibility of different states nonetheless continues to enflame debate, as the climate change negotiations discussed *infra* reveal.

E. Global Climate Change

1. Climate Change Overview (excerpted from Climate Change Information Kit published by UNEP and UNFCCC 2002)

Greenhouse gases (GHGs) control energy flows in the atmosphere by absorbing infra-red radiation emitted by the earth. They act like a blanket to keep the earth's surface some 20°C warmer than it would be if the atmosphere contained only oxygen and nitrogen. The trace gases that cause this natural greenhouse effect comprise less than 1% of the atmosphere. Their levels are determined by a balance between "sources" and "sinks." Sources are processes that generate greenhouse gases; sinks are processes that destroy or remove them. Apart from industrial chemicals like CFCs [Chlorofluorocarbons] and HFCs [Hydrofluorocarbons], greenhouse gases have been present naturally in the atmosphere for millions of years. Humans, however, are affecting greenhouse gas levels by introducing new sources or by interfering with natural sinks.

The largest contributor to the natural greenhouse effect is water vapour. Its presence in the atmosphere is not directly affected by human activity. Nevertheless, water vapour matters for climate change because of an important "positive feedback." Warmer air can hold more moisture, and models predict that a small global warming would lead to a rise in global water vapour levels, further adding to the enhanced greenhouse effect. Because modeling climate processes involving clouds and rainfall is particularly difficult, the exact size of this crucial feedback remains uncertain.

Carbon dioxide is currently responsible for over 60% of the "enhanced" greenhouse effect. This gas occurs naturally in the atmosphere, but burning coal, oil, and natural gas is releasing the carbon stored in these "fossil fuels" at an unprecedented rate. Likewise, deforestation releases carbon stored in trees. Current annual emissions amount to over 23 billion metric tons of carbon dioxide, or almost 1% of the total mass of carbon dioxide in the atmosphere.

Carbon dioxide produced by human activity enters the natural carbon cycle. Many billions of tonnes of carbon are exchanged naturally each year between the atmosphere, the oceans, and land vegetation. The exchanges in this massive and complex natural system are precisely balanced; carbon dioxide levels appear to have varied by less than 10% during the 10,000 years before industrialization. In the 200 years since 1800, however, levels have risen by over 30%. Even with half of humanity's carbon dioxide emissions being absorbed by the oceans and land vegetation, atmospheric levels continue to rise by over 10% every 20 years.

A second important human influence on climate is aerosols. These clouds of microscopic particles are not a greenhouse gas. In addition to various natural sources, they are produced from sulphur dioxide emitted mainly by power stations, and by the smoke from deforestation and the burning of crop wastes. Aerosols settle out of the air after only a few days, but they are emitted in such massive quantities that they have a substantial impact on climate.

Most aerosols cool the climate locally by scattering sunlight back into space and by affecting clouds. Aerosol particles can block sunlight directly and also provide "seeds" for clouds to form, and often these clouds also have a cooling effect. Over heavily industrialized regions, aerosol cooling may counteract nearly all of the warming effect of greenhouse gas increases to date.

Methane levels have already increased by a factor of two and a half during the industrial era. The main "new" sources of this powerful greenhouse gas are agricultural, notably flooded rice paddies and expanding herds of cattle. Emissions from waste dumps and leaks from coal mining and natural gas production also contribute. Methane is removed from the atmosphere by chemical reactions in the atmosphere that are very difficult to model and predict.

Methane from past emissions currently contributes 20% of the enhanced greenhouse effect. The rapid rise in methane started more recently than the rise in carbon dioxide, but methane's contribution has been catching up fast. However, methane has an effective atmospheric lifetime of only 12 years, whereas carbon dioxide survives much longer.

Nitrous oxide, a number of industrial gases, and ozone contribute the remaining 20% of the enhanced greenhouse effect. Nitrous oxide levels have risen by 16%, mainly due to more intensive agriculture. While chlorofluorocarbons (CFCs) are stabilizing due to emission controls introduced under the Montreal Protocol to protect the stratospheric ozone layer, levels of long-lived gases such as HFCs, PFCs and sulphur hexafluoride are increasing. Ozone levels are rising in some regions in the lower atmosphere due to air pollution, even as they decline in the stratosphere. . . .

Measurement records indicate a warming increase of $0.6 \pm 0.2°C$ in global average temperature since the late 19th century. These observations are in line with model projections of the size of warming to date, particularly when the cooling effect of aerosols is included. Most of the warming occurred from 1910 to 1940 and from 1976 to the present. In the northern Hemisphere (where there are sufficient data to make such analyses), it is likely that the rate and duration of 20th century warming has been greater than any other time during the last 1,000 years. In addition, the 1990s are likely to have been the warmest decade of the millennium in the northern Hemisphere, and 1998 is likely to have been the warmest year.

Mean sea level has risen by 10 to 20 cm. As the upper layers of the oceans warm, water expands and sea level rises. Models suggest that a 0.6°C warming should indeed result in the sea-level rise to date. But other, harder-to-predict, changes also affect the real and apparent sea level, notably snowfall and ice-melt in Greenland and Antarctica and the slow "rebound" of northern continents freed from the weight of ice age glaciers.

Snow cover has declined by some 10% since the late 1960s in the mid-and high latitudes of the northern Hemisphere. It is also very likely that the annual duration of lake and river ice cover has shortened by about two weeks over the course of the 20th century. Almost all recorded mountain glaciers in non-polar regions have retreated during this time as well. In recent decades, the extent of Arctic sea-ice in the spring and summer has decreased by about 10–15%, and the ice Arctic sea-ice has likely thinned by 40% during late summer and early autumn.

There is more precipitation in many regions of the world. An increase of 0.5–1% per decade has been measured over most mid-and high latitude areas of the northern Hemisphere continents, accompanied by a 2% expansion in cloud cover. Precipitation over the tropical land areas (10°N–10°S) seems to have increased by 0.2–0.3% per decade. On the other hand, declines have been observed over northern Hemisphere sub-tropical land areas (10–30°N) during the 20th century, by about 0.3% per decade. In parts of Africa and Asia the frequency and intensity of droughts seem to have worsened.

2.   Climate Change and International Environmental Law

Between 1979 and 1990 States convened a series of international conferences to recognize and begin to address climate change as a global environmental problem. The World Meteorological Organization (WMO) and UNEP, observing the need for consensus on climate change, established the Intergovernmental Panel on Climate Change (IPCC) in 1988 to assess the science and the environmental, economic, and social impacts of climate change. The IPCC consists of three working groups, the science-focused Working Group I, the impact-and-policy-focused Working Group II and the economics-and-sociology-focused Working Group III. The IPCC does not conduct its own inquiries but reviews qualified research from around the world to establish apolitical expert consensus on climate change issues, which it presents in both special and periodic multidisciplinary reports.

Despite consensus building efforts, the varying interests of States have slowed and complicated climate change negotiations. The Association of Small Island States (AOSIS), fearing the consequences of sea level rise, has advocated immediate measures. The Organization of the Petroleum Exporting Countries (OPEC) has urged compensation options for future oil market losses. Nations with large forest economies have opposed controls on forestry practices as a CO_2 mitigation tactic. The United States, the world's largest emitter of CO_2, as well as others, have hesitated to accept specific emission reduction targets and timelines. All of these special concerns and many more have steered the course of international political action on climate change, beginning with the United Nations Framework Convention on Climate Change.

a.   The United Nations Framework Convention on Climate Change

The United Nations Framework Convention on Climate Change (UNFCCC), a product of the 1992 Rio Earth Summit, entered into force in 1994 and has since served as the foundation of global legal and political efforts to combat human-induced climate change. The stated objective of the UNFCCC is the "stabilization of greenhouse gas concentrations in the atmosphere at a level that would prevent dangerous anthropogenic interference with the climate system. Such a level should be achieved within a time-frame sufficient to allow ecosystems to adapt naturally to climate change, to ensure that food production is not threatened and to enable economic development to proceed in a sustainable manner." UNFCCC 1992 Article 2.

Given all of the conflicting interests of States in the climate change debate, the UNFCCC negotiations did not produce a detailed scheme of substantive obligations for States. The UNFCCC, is instead, a "framework agreement," acknowledging the existence of a problem and committing Parties to cooperation and continued efforts towards reaching a consensus on specific obligations. The Convention also created the necessary infrastructure for elaborating obligations in the form of amendments and Protocols to the treaty. This infrastructure includes a Conference of the Parties (COP), which is the "supreme body of the Convention"; a secretariat, which is the administrative entity; and two subsidiary bodies—the Subsidiary Body for Scientific and Technological Advice (SBSTA) and Subsidiary Body for Implementation (SBI)—which provide the COP with expert information and proposals on science, technology, and treaty implementation.

b.   Obligations under the UNFCCC

The UNFCCC divides member States into three categories, all member States, all industrialized member States (Annex I States), and all industrialized member States except those with economies in transition—namely the former Soviet Bloc—(Annex II States). All member States face some obligations, and Annex I States and Annex II States bear additional responsibilities.

First, under the Convention, all Parties submit "national communications," inventorying their national GHG emissions and their emissions' sources. These reports also catalog national "sinks," which are areas such as forests that absorb and sequester carbon at rates higher than they release it, thus reducing overall levels of carbon in the atmosphere and thus canceling a proportional quantity of emissions. The UNFCCC also instructs all Parties to adopt national climate change mitigation programs, promote technology, conservation, and sustainability and consider climate change in policy-making.

The UNFCCC further charged Annex I countries with the voluntary duty to collectively cut GHG emissions from the industrialized world to a level equivalent to 1990 levels by the year 2000. The Kyoto Protocol, discussed below, subsequently changed the timeline and established more specific and binding emissions reductions requirements for individual Annex I countries. Finally, in addition to all other obligations, Annex II countries must provide funding for developing States to carry out their obligations under the Convention.

After the UNFCCC entered into force, debate over the elaboration of more specific obligations ensued. Developing countries advocated especially for quantifiable emission limitation and reduction objectives (QELROs) for the developed world, while many developed States resisted QELROs that did not apply equally to the developing world. The United States Senate, for example, unanimously passed the *Byrd-Hagel Resolution* urging President Clinton not to agree to any convention that lacked binding targets for developing countries. However, as the Parties began to realize that they were not going to stabilize emissions at 1990 levels by 2000, and as the 1995 IPCC *Second Assessment Report* called attention to the validity of climate change science and the gravity of the foreseeable effects of climate change, the Parties undertook drafting a protocol with specific and binding requirements.

c.   The Kyoto Protocol

Despite continued disagreement among the UNFCCC Parties, the 1997 third meeting of the COP produced the Kyoto Protocol. Due to a lack of consensus on many issues, however, the Protocol contains numerous ambiguities. Thus, for over three years following the Protocol's adoption, the UNFCCC Parties negotiated the necessary details to make the Protocol operational. States disagreed on many aspects of the Protocol's various mechanisms, described below, from the methodologies for measuring the carbon sequestration capacity of sinks to which Parties could trade emissions amongst themselves. The United States, which was initially among the leading participants in negotiations, withdrew support and abandoned the Protocol in 2001 after the Senate repeatedly raised concerns about the protocol's lack of obligations for developing States, and President George W. Bush entered office and deemed the Protocol "fatally flawed."

The United States' withdrawal struck a blow to the already fraught Protocol negotiations, but Europe was able to rally sufficient support among other States to keep negotiations moving. With the United States gone, Russia and Japan, two other historical emitters, became central players. Negotiating States ultimately finalized the Protocol's operational systems in July 2001 and recorded them later that year in the *Marrakech Accords* at the seventh meeting of the COP in Marrakech, Morocco. Among other functional aspects of the Protocol, the *Marrakech Accords* outline an emissions trading scheme, a Clean Development Mechanism, a Joint Implementation Mechanism, rules for counting emissions reductions from carbon "sinks," and financial and technological support mechanisms to help developing countries contribute.

Even though the Kyoto Protocol was theoretically ready for implementation in 2001 it did not enter force until February 16, 2005. The Protocol provided that it could not enter force until ninety days after at least fifty-five countries, and countries responsible for at least 55% of the industrialized world's 1990 CO_2 emissions, had consented to be bound by it. The balance-tipping ratification occurred when Russia signed on to the Protocol in the autumn of 2004. In reading the excerpted text of the Kyoto Protocol below notice the ambiguities that raise implementation questions.

KYOTO PROTOCOL TO THE UNITED NATIONS FRAMEWORK CONVENTION ON CLIMATE CHANGE

Article 2

1. Each Party included in Annex I, in achieving its quantified emission limitation and reduction commitments under Article 3, in order to promote sustainable development, shall:

> (a) Implement and/or further elaborate policies and measures in accordance with its national circumstances, such as:

> > (i) Enhancement of energy efficiency in relevant sectors of the national economy;

> > (ii) Protection and enhancement of sinks and reservoirs of greenhouse gases not controlled by the Montreal Protocol, taking into account its commitments under relevant international environmental agreements; promotion of sustainable forest management practices, afforestation and reforestation;

> > (iii) Promotion of sustainable forms of agriculture in light of climate change considerations;

> > (iv) Research on, and promotion, development and increased use of, new and renewable forms of energy, of carbon dioxide sequestration technologies and of advanced and innovative environmentally sound technologies;

> > (v) Progressive reduction or phasing out of market imperfections, fiscal incentives, tax and duty exemptions and subsidies in all greenhouse gas emitting sectors that run counter to the

objective of the Convention and application of market instruments;

(vi) Encouragement of appropriate reforms in relevant sectors aimed at promoting policies and measures which limit or reduce emissions of greenhouse gases not controlled by the Montreal Protocol;

(vii) Measures to limit and/or reduce emissions of greenhouse gases not controlled by the Montreal Protocol in the transport sector;

(viii) Limitation and/or reduction of methane emissions through recovery and use in waste management, as well as in the production, transport and distribution of energy;

(b) Cooperate with other such Parties to enhance the individual and combined effectiveness of their policies and measures adopted under this Article, pursuant to Article 4, paragraph 2(e)(i), of the Convention. To this end, these Parties shall take steps to share their experience and exchange information on such policies and measures, including developing ways of improving their comparability, transparency and effectiveness. The Conference of the Parties serving as the meeting of the Parties to this Protocol shall, at its first session or as soon as practicable thereafter, consider ways to facilitate such cooperation, taking into account all relevant information.

2.　The Parties included in Annex I shall pursue limitation or reduction of emissions of greenhouse gases not controlled by the Montreal Protocol from aviation and marine bunker fuels, working through the International Civil Aviation Organization and the International Maritime Organization, respectively.

3.　The Parties included in Annex I shall strive to implement policies and measures under this Article in such a way as to minimize adverse effects, including the adverse effects of climate change, effects on international trade, and social, environmental and economic impacts on other Parties, especially developing country Parties and in particular those identified in Article 4, paragraphs 8 and 9, of the Convention, taking into account Article 3 of the Convention. The Conference of the Parties serving as the meeting of the Parties to this Protocol may take further action, as appropriate, to promote the implementation of the provisions of this paragraph.

4.　The Conference of the Parties serving as the meeting of the Parties to this Protocol, if it decides that it would be beneficial to coordinate any of the policies and measures in paragraph 1(a) above, taking into account different national circumstances and potential effects, shall consider ways and means to elaborate the coordination of such policies and measures.

Article 3

1.　The Parties included in Annex I shall, individually or jointly, ensure that their aggregate anthropogenic carbon dioxide equivalent emissions of the greenhouse gases listed in Annex A do not exceed their assigned amounts, calculated pursuant to their quantified emission limitation and reduction commitments inscribed in Annex B and in accordance with the provisions of this Article, with a view to reducing their overall emissions of such gases by at least 5 per cent below 1990 levels in the commitment period 2008 to 2012.

2.   Each Party included in Annex I shall, by 2005, have made demonstrable progress in achieving its commitments under this Protocol.

3.   The net changes in greenhouse gas emissions by sources and removals by sinks resulting from direct human-induced land-use change and forestry activities, limited to afforestation, reforestation and deforestation since 1990, measured as verifiable changes in carbon stocks in each commitment period, shall be used to meet the commitments under this Article of each Party included in Annex I. The greenhouse gas emissions by sources and removals by sinks associated with those activities shall be reported in a transparent and verifiable manner and reviewed in accordance with Articles 7 and 8.

4.   Prior to the first session of the Conference of the Parties serving as the meeting of the Parties to this Protocol, each Party included in Annex I shall provide, for consideration by the Subsidiary Body for Scientific and Technological Advice, data to establish its level of carbon stocks in 1990 and to enable an estimate to be made of its changes in carbon stocks in subsequent years. The Conference of the Parties serving as the meeting of the Parties to this Protocol shall, at its first session or as soon as practicable thereafter, decide upon modalities, rules and guidelines as to how, and which, additional human-induced activities related to changes in greenhouse gas emissions by sources and removals by sinks in the agricultural soils and the land-use change and forestry categories shall be added to, or subtracted from, the assigned amounts for Parties included in Annex I, taking into account uncertainties, transparency in reporting, verifiability, the methodological work of the Intergovernmental Panel on Climate Change, the advice provided by the Subsidiary Body for Scientific and Technological Advice in accordance with Article 5 and the decisions of the Conference of the Parties. Such a decision shall apply in the second and subsequent commitment periods. A Party may choose to apply such a decision on these additional human-induced activities for its first commitment period, provided that these activities have taken place since 1990.

5.   The Parties included in Annex I undergoing the process of transition to a market economy whose base year or period was established pursuant to decision 9/CP.2 of the Conference of the Parties at its second session shall use that base year or period for the implementation of their commitments under this Article. Any other Party included in Annex I undergoing the process of transition to a market economy which has not yet submitted its first national communication under Article 12 of the Convention may also notify the Conference of the Parties serving as the meeting of the Parties to this Protocol that it intends to use an historical

base year or period other than 1990 for the implementation of its commitments under this Article. The Conference of the Parties serving as the meeting of the Parties to this Protocol shall decide on the acceptance of such notification.

6.   Taking into account Article 4, paragraph 6, of the Convention, in the implementation of their commitments under this Protocol other than those under this Article, a certain degree of flexibility shall be allowed by the Conference of the Parties serving as the meeting of the Parties to this Protocol to the Parties included in Annex I undergoing the process of transition to a market economy.

7.   In the first quantified emission limitation and reduction commitment period, from 2008 to 2012, the assigned amount for each Party included in Annex I shall be equal to the percentage inscribed for it in Annex B of its aggregate anthropogenic carbon dioxide equivalent emissions of the greenhouse gases listed in Annex A in 1990, or the base year or period determined in accordance with paragraph 5 above, multiplied by five. Those Parties included in Annex I for whom land-use change and forestry constituted a net source of greenhouse gas emissions in 1990 shall include in their 1990 emissions base year or period the aggregate anthropogenic carbon dioxide equivalent emissions by sources minus removals by sinks in 1990 from land-use change for the purposes of calculating their assigned amount.

8.   Any Party included in Annex I may use 1995 as its base year for hydrofluorocarbons, perfluorocarbons and sulphur hexafluoride, for the purposes of the calculation referred to in paragraph 7 above.

9.   Commitments for subsequent periods for Parties included in Annex I shall be established in amendments to Annex B to this Protocol, which shall be adopted in accordance with the provisions of Article 21, paragraph 7. The Conference of the Parties serving as the meeting of the Parties to this Protocol shall initiate the consideration of such commitments at least seven years before the end of the first commitment period referred to in paragraph 1 above.

10.   Any emission reduction units, or any part of an assigned amount, which a Party acquires from another Party in accordance with the provisions of Article 6 or of Article 17 shall be added to the assigned amount for the acquiring Party.

11.   Any emission reduction units, or any part of an assigned amount, which a Party transfers to another Party in accordance with the provisions of Article 6 or of Article 17 shall be subtracted from the assigned amount for the transferring Party.

12.   Any certified emission reductions which a Party acquires from another Party in accordance with the provisions of Article 12 shall be added to the assigned amount for the acquiring Party.

13.   If the emissions of a Party included in Annex I in a commitment period are less than its assigned amount under this Article, this differ-

ence shall, on request of that Party, be added to the assigned amount for that Party for subsequent commitment periods.

14. Each Party included in Annex I shall strive to implement the commitments mentioned in paragraph 1 above in such a way as to minimize adverse social, environmental and economic impacts on developing country Parties, particularly those identified in Article 4, paragraphs 8 and 9, of the Convention. In line with relevant decisions of the Conference of the Parties on the implementation of those paragraphs, the Conference of the Parties serving as the meeting of the Parties to this Protocol shall, at its first session, consider what actions are necessary to minimize the adverse effects of climate change and/or the impacts of response measures on Parties referred to in those paragraphs. Among the issues to be considered shall be the establishment of funding, insurance and transfer of technology.

Article 6

1. For the purpose of meeting its commitments under Article 3, any Party included in Annex I may transfer to, or acquire from, any other such Party emission reduction units resulting from projects aimed at reducing anthropogenic emissions by sources or enhancing anthropogenic removals by sinks of greenhouse gases in any sector of the economy, provided that:

> (a) Any such project has the approval of the Parties involved;

> (b) Any such project provides a reduction in emissions by sources, or an enhancement of removals by sinks, that is additional to any that would otherwise occur;

> (c) It does not acquire any emission reduction units if it is not in compliance with its obligations under Articles 5 and 7; and

> (d) The acquisition of emission reduction units shall be supplemental to domestic actions for the purposes of meeting commitments under Article 3.

2. The Conference of the Parties serving as the meeting of the Parties to this Protocol may, at its first session or as soon as practicable thereafter, further elaborate guidelines for the implementation of this Article, including for verification and reporting.

3. A Party included in Annex I may authorize legal entities to participate, under its responsibility, in actions leading to the generation, transfer or acquisition under this Article of emission reduction units.

4. If a question of implementation by a Party included in Annex I of the requirements referred to in this Article is identified in accordance with the relevant provisions of Article 8, transfers and acquisitions of emission reduction units may continue to be made after the question has been identified, provided that any such units may not be used by a Party to meet its commitments under Article 3 until any issue of compliance is resolved.

Article 10

All Parties, taking into account their common but differentiated responsibilities and their specific national and regional development priorities, objectives and circumstances, without introducing any new commitments for Parties not included in Annex I, but reaffirming existing commitments under Article 4, paragraph 1, of the Convention, and continuing to advance the implementation of these commitments in order to achieve sustainable development, taking into account Article 4, paragraphs 3, 5 and 7, of the Convention, shall:

(a) Formulate, where relevant and to the extent possible, cost-effective national and, where appropriate, regional programmes to improve the quality of local emission factors, activity data and/or models which reflect the socio-economic conditions of each Party for the preparation and periodic updating of national inventories of anthropogenic emissions by sources and removals by sinks of all greenhouse gases not controlled by the Montreal Protocol, using comparable methodologies to be agreed upon by the Conference of the Parties, and consistent with the guidelines for the preparation of national communications adopted by the Conference of the Parties;

(b) Formulate, implement, publish and regularly update national and, where appropriate, regional programmes containing measures to mitigate climate change and measures to facilitate adequate adaptation to climate change:

(i) Such programmes would, *inter alia*, concern the energy, transport and industry sectors as well as agriculture, forestry and waste management. Furthermore, adaptation technologies and methods for improving spatial planning would improve adaptation to climate change; and

(ii) Parties included in Annex I shall submit information on action under this Protocol, including national programmes, in accordance with Article 7; and other Parties shall seek to include in their national communications, as appropriate, information on programmes which contain measures that the Party believes contribute to addressing climate change and its adverse impacts, including the abatement of increases in greenhouse gas emissions, and enhancement of and removals by sinks, capacity building and adaptation measures;

(c) Cooperate in the promotion of effective modalities for the development, application and diffusion of, and take all practicable steps to promote, facilitate and finance, as appropriate, the transfer of, or access to, environmentally sound technologies, know-how, practices and processes pertinent to climate change, in particular to developing countries, including the formulation of policies and programmes for the effective transfer of environmentally sound technologies that are publicly owned or in the public domain and the creation of an enabling environment for the private sector, to promote and enhance the transfer of, and access to, environmentally sound technologies;

(d) Cooperate in scientific and technical research and promote the maintenance and the development of systematic observation systems and development of data archives to reduce uncertainties related to the climate system, the adverse impacts of climate change and the economic and social consequences of various response strategies, and promote the development and strengthening of endogenous capacities and capabilities to participate in international and intergovernmental efforts, programmes and networks on research and systematic observation, taking into account Article 5 of the Convention;

(e) Cooperate in and promote at the international level, and, where appropriate, using existing bodies, the development and implementation of education and training programmes, including the strengthening of national capacity building, in particular human and institutional capacities and the exchange or secondment of personnel to train experts in this field, in particular for developing countries, and facilitate at the national level public awareness of, and public access to information on, climate change. Suitable modalities should be developed to implement these activities through the relevant bodies of the Convention, taking into account Article 6 of the Convention;

(f) Include in their national communications information on programmes and activities undertaken pursuant to this Article in accordance with relevant decisions of the Conference of the Parties; and

(g) Give full consideration, in implementing the commitments under this Article, to Article 4, paragraph 8, of the Convention.

Article 11

1.   In the implementation of Article 10, Parties shall take into account the provisions of Article 4, paragraphs 4, 5, 7, 8 and 9, of the Convention.

2.   In the context of the implementation of Article 4, paragraph 1, of the Convention, in accordance with the provisions of Article 4, paragraph 3, and Article 11 of the Convention, and through the entity or entities entrusted with the operation of the financial mechanism of the Convention, the developed country Parties and other developed Parties included in Annex II to the Convention shall:

(a) Provide new and additional financial resources to meet the agreed full costs incurred by developing country Parties in advancing the implementation of existing commitments under Article 4, paragraph 1(a), of the Convention that are covered in Article 10, subparagraph (a); and

(b) Also provide such financial resources, including for the transfer of technology, needed by the developing country Parties to meet the agreed full incremental costs of advancing the implementation of existing commitments under Article 4, paragraph 1, of the Convention that are covered by Article 10 and that are agreed between a developing country Party and the international entity or entities referred to in Article 11 of the Convention, in accordance with that Article.

The implementation of these existing commitments shall take into account the need for adequacy and predictability in the flow of funds and the importance of appropriate burden sharing among developed country Parties. The guidance to the entity or entities entrusted with the operation of the financial mechanism of the Convention in relevant decisions of the Conference of the Parties, including those agreed before the adoption of this Protocol, shall apply *mutatis mutandis* to the provisions of this paragraph.

3.   The developed country Parties and other developed Parties in Annex II to the Convention may also provide, and developing country Parties avail themselves of, financial resources for the implementation of Article 10, through bilateral, regional and other multilateral channels.

Article 12

1.   A clean development mechanism is hereby defined.

2.   The purpose of the clean development mechanism shall be to assist Parties not included in Annex I in achieving sustainable development and in contributing to the ultimate objective of the Convention, and to assist Parties included in Annex I in achieving compliance with their quantified emission limitation and reduction commitments under Article 3.

3.   Under the clean development mechanism:

(a) Parties not included in Annex I will benefit from project activities resulting in certified emission reductions; and

(b) Parties included in Annex I may use the certified emission reductions accruing from such project activities to contribute to compliance with part of their quantified emission limitation and reduction commitments under Article 3, as determined by the Conference of the Parties serving as the meeting of the Parties to this Protocol.

4.   The clean development mechanism shall be subject to the authority and guidance of the Conference of the Parties serving as the meeting of the Parties to this Protocol and be supervised by an executive board of the clean development mechanism.

5.   Emission reductions resulting from each project activity shall be certified by operational entities to be designated by the Conference of the Parties serving as the meeting of the Parties to this Protocol, on the basis of:

(a) Voluntary participation approved by each Party involved;

(b) Real, measurable, and long-term benefits related to the mitigation of climate change; and

(c) Reductions in emissions that are additional to any that would occur in the absence of the certified project activity.

6. The clean development mechanism shall assist in arranging funding of certified project activities as necessary.

7. The Conference of the Parties serving as the meeting of the Parties to this Protocol shall, at its first session, elaborate modalities and procedures with the objective of ensuring transparency, efficiency and accountability through independent auditing and verification of project activities.

8. The Conference of the Parties serving as the meeting of the Parties to this Protocol shall ensure that a share of the proceeds from certified project activities is used to cover administrative expenses as well as to assist developing country Parties that are particularly vulnerable to the adverse effects of climate change to meet the costs of adaptation.

9. Participation under the clean development mechanism, including in activities mentioned in paragraph 3(a) above and in the acquisition of certified emission reductions, may involve private and/or public entities, and is to be subject to whatever guidance may be provided by the executive board of the clean development mechanism.

10. Certified emission reductions obtained during the period from the year 2000 up to the beginning of the first commitment period can be used to assist in achieving compliance in the first commitment period.

d. Obligations Under the Kyoto Protocol

The Kyoto Protocol lays out binding emissions targets for developed States (Annex I States under the UNFCCC), requiring them to collectively reduce the industrialized world's emissions of six GHGs[2] to 5% below 1990 levels. To achieve this reduction, individual Annex I States must, between 2008 and 2012, meet individual emissions targets, calculated relative to their 1990 emissions levels. The Protocol groups the six regulated GHGs together in a "basket," and translates all emissions into CO_2 equivalents so that no specific reductions requirements exist for individual gasses. This leaves States with control over which gasses they actually regulate.

Switzerland must reduce its 1990 emissions levels by 8%, as must most Central and East European States. The European Union similarly has an 8% reduction obligation but may meet this obligation by distributing different reduction rates among its member States. The United States reduction requirement is 7% but the United States is not a Party to the Protocol and has not consented to this obligation. Canada, Hungary, Japan, and Poland all face 6% reductions, while Croatia's is 5%. Russia, New Zealand, and Ukraine had sufficiently low-level emis-

---

2. The six regulated gases are:
· Carbon dioxide (CO_2);
· Methane (CH_4);
· Nitrous oxide (N_2O);

· Hydrofluorocarbons (HFCs);

· Perfluorocarbons (PFCs); and

· Sulphur hexafluoride (SF_6)

sions in 1990 that those States need only stabilize their emissions at 1990 levels. Norway, Iceland and Australia (upon becoming Party to the Protocol) may actually increase their 1990 level emissions by 1%, 10%, and 8% respectively. The Kyoto Protocol does not set limits on the GHG emissions of the developing world.

The COP of the UNFCCC doubles as the Meeting of the Parties (MOP) for the Protocol. Parties to the UNFCCC that are not Parties to Protocol, such as the United States and Australia, may only observe during Protocol proceedings. The MOP has already begun talks on commitments for the post–2012 period.

e. Kyoto Protocol Compliance Mechanisms

It was expected that Annex I Parties would try to reduce emissions by, for example, reforming the energy and transportation sectors, and phasing out inappropriate market incentives. States that cannot meet their emissions targets by cutting domestic emissions may compensate for excess emissions by creating or enhancing national sinks under the Land Use, Land–Use Change and Forestry program. To supplement national emission reduction and sink development efforts, States also may participate in three different "flexibility mechanisms": emissions trading, clean development in developing States, and projects to reduce emissions in other industrialized countries. These different flexibility mechanisms work to ensure that, even if a Party's net national emissions exceed its targets, the Party reduces emissions elsewhere in the world to offset its excessive emissions, and the overall emissions levels of the industrialized world are decreased.

In order for each of these mechanisms to operate, the total quantity of permissible emissions for all Annex I Parties is translated into "assigned amount units" (AAUs). Each unit is equal to one metric ton of CO_2 equivalent emissions. Pursuant to Articles 3.7 and 3.8, each Annex I Party receives a portion of the total available AAUs in correlation with its individual emissions targets. These units have unique serial numbers that recipients of AAUs record in individual electronic databases known as national registries. Through the various mechanisms a Party may generate new units or acquire units from another Party. Parties log their unit transactions in an international transaction log and adjust their national registries accordingly. The mechanisms thus provide Parties with a transparent means for reallocating units amongst themselves and creating additional units so that all Parties may effectively reach their emissions targets.

i. Land Use, Land–Use Change, and Forestry

Under Articles 3.3 and 3.4 of the Kyoto Protocol Parties may offset national emissions by augmenting sinks through certain land use and forestry practices in their territory. States that augment sinks under what has become the Land Use, Land–Use Change and Forestry (LU-LUCF) program receive "removal units" (RMUs), equivalent in size to AAUs, to add to their registries and measure against their emissions.

Because LULUCF activities may provide reductions, States must conversely count emissions from LULUCF practices in their UNFCCC emissions inventories.

Article 3.3 provides that during the initial 2008–2012 commitment period, States may account for emissions and reductions resulting directly from human-induced afforestation, reforestation, and deforestation that has occurred since 1990, while Article 3.4 permits consideration of further unspecified LULUCF practices. In negotiations subsequent to the elaboration of the Kyoto Protocol the Parties developed definitions of important concepts along with methodologies that would make Articles 3.3 and 3.4 operable. The Parties, for example, adopted definitions for the terms "forest," "reforestation," "afforestation" and "deforestation," and decided that for the first commitment period Article 3.4 would incorporate cropland management, forest management, re-vegetation, and grazing land management into the LULUCF program. However, States must individually elect to include any or all of these Article 3.4 practices in their accounting and may only include them to a limited extent. For instance, the Parties placed State-by-State caps on emissions reductions generated through forest management[3] activities under Article 3.4.

Throughout negotiations the LULUCF scheme has been politically problematic. Many States oppose the system altogether for fear that accounting for sinks alleviates necessary pressure to reduce emissions associated with fossil fuel and other industrial GHG emissions. The details of the LULUCF program have proven equally contentious. States worry that too much leniency will contravene the purposes of the Kyoto Protocol or create incentives that undermine other environmental principles. Harvesting old forests and replacing them with young monocrop forests, for example, may potentially increase acre-for-acre carbon sequestration while sacrificing other environmental values like biodiversity. States attempted to preempt destructive side effects of the LULUCF program by pronouncing a number of environmental principles, such as preservation of biodiversity, that States must adhere to in carrying out LULUCF activities.

Scientific accuracy and methodological consistency have also been major concerns in the LULUCF scheme. The scientific uncertainty inherent in attempting to separate reductions that result directly from human-generated sinks from reductions that would otherwise occur naturally, has prompted Parties to refer to the scientific expertise of other bodies such as the IPCC to develop strict accounting methodologies. Many scientific uncertainties persist, however, and the future of the LULUCF program continues to be a source of confusion and contention

---

3. " 'Forest management' is a system of practices for stewardship and use of forest land aimed at fulfilling relevant ecological (including biological diversity), economic and social functions of the forest in a sustainable manner." *Marrakech Accords*, FCCC/CP/2001/13 Annex A (1)(f) (Jan 21, 2002). To avoid double accounting forest management practices for the purpose of Article 3.4 do not include afforestation, reforestation and deforestation addressed in Article 3.3.

for Parties. The present agreement on sinks only applies to the first commitment period from 2008–2012 and deliberations on the next stages of the scheme have already begun among the Parties.

ii.   Clean Development Mechanism

The first flexibility mechanism, the Clean Development Mechanism (CDM), established by Article 12 of the Protocol, enables industrialized Parties to generate additional emission units for themselves by implementing projects in the developing world that promote sustainable development. Most of these projects involve constructing industrial facilities that employ clean technology or overhauling old facilities. Afforestation and reforestation projects may also qualify as CDM projects but Annex I States may only obtain a minimal amount of reduction units for such projects.

Eligible CDM projects generate new emissions units for the sponsoring nation. These units are equivalent in size to AAUs but are known as "certified emissions reductions" (CERs). Since the Kyoto Protocol does not impose emissions limitations on developing States the number of available CERs is limitless in comparison to the finite quantity of AAUs shared among Annex I States. To ensure accuracy and accountability States track CERs not only in their national registries but also in a CDM specific registry.

The CDM appeals not only to Annex I States seeking emissions reductions units, and to developing States pursuing sustainable development, but also to private investors. CDM projects typically begin under the initiative of private firms that make proposals to the governments of sponsoring and host States. If all involved Parties approve the project, and the project demonstrates a long-term capacity to achieve emissions reductions greater than would otherwise occur, the Executive Board, which oversees the CDM and controls the CERs, may grant CERs to the sponsoring State. To assess the quantity of CERs generated by a CDM project, the Executive Board must first approve a baseline emissions level that approximates what the emissions levels would be on the project site absent the CDM project. Through extensive debate the Parties developed specific rules and methodologies for establishing these project specific baselines.

iii.   Joint Implementation

A second mechanism, known as Joint Implementation (JI), outlined in Article 6 of the Protocol, grants "emission reduction units" (ERUs) to Annex I States that sponsor projects to reduce emissions in other Annex I States. Joint implementation allows industrialized States to upgrade outdated technology in other industrialized States and consequently reduce emissions at lower cost than would be necessary to upgrade their own more advanced technology. In practice Eastern European and former Soviet Bloc States host JI projects. JI projects are similar to CDM projects in that private firms may initiate projects.

A State hosting a JI project may grant ERUs, which are also equal in size to AAUs, directly to the sponsoring State if the host State meets certain qualifications such as demonstrating capacity to take accurate inventories of all GHG emissions, and ability to ensure that projects have an accurate baseline from which to measure the exact quantity of reductions. If a host State does not meet all the eligibility requirements, an international supervisory committee must step in to approve a grant of ERUs. When an Annex I country sponsoring a project acquires ERUs, the Annex I State hosting the project must deduct AAUs from its registry so that the overall allowable emissions within the industrialized world does not increase but is simply reconfigured. Qualified JI projects begun after January 1, 2002, generate ERUs beginning in 2008.

iv. Emissions Trading

The emissions trading scheme, established in Article 17 of the Kyoto Protocol, allows Parties to purchase AAUs, ERUs, CERs, and RMUs from other States holding surplus units. In other words, States may sell units assigned to them, units gained through projects under the CDM or under Joint Implementation, and units acquired through afforestation and reforestation efforts. To prevent Parties from selling too many units and consequently retaining insufficient units to account for their own emissions, States must reserve a certain quantity of units. States may also bank AAUs and use them in subsequent years. Restricted banking of CERs and ERUs is also permissible but RMUs are unbankable.

Emissions trading, although straightforward in principle has proven to be relatively complicated in practice, involving detailed transaction logs, registries, and expert review teams that police compliance. Further, all registry, transaction, and compliance information that is not designated as confidential must be made publicly available to promote transparency.

f. Kyoto Protocol Enforcement

A Compliance Committee oversees State compliance with the Kyoto Protocol. The committee consists of two branches, a facilitative branch and a judicial-like enforcement branch. Each branch is made up of ten State representatives: one small island developing State, two Annex I States, two non-Annex I States and one State from each of five regions: Africa, Asia, Latin America and the Caribbean, Central and Eastern Europe, and finally, Western Europe and others. The facilitative branch advises Parties on how to comply, while the enforcement branch determines consequences for Parties who fail to fulfill obligations. Both branches may consider information submitted by competent intergovernmental and non-governmental organizations in carrying out their functions.

The facilitative branch ensures that States' involvement in the CDM, joint implementation, and emissions trading remains supplemental rather than in lieu of domestic action. The facilitative branch also attempts to identify Parties that are in danger of failing to comply before actual failure, at which point the branch may make recommendations to the Party and even arrange financial and technical assistance. A Party may actively seek assistance from the facilitative branch by raising concerns about its own or another Party's ability to comply.

The enforcement branch determines which Annex I Parties fail to comply with emission targets and reporting requirements and which countries satisfy the requirements for participation in the flexibility mechanisms. To participate in the mechanisms Annex I Parties must have ratified the Kyoto Protocol, calculated their assigned amount in tons of CO_2 equivalent emissions, established a national system for estimating emissions and removals, established a national registry, and report information on emissions and removals to the secretariat.

Upon annual review, Annex I Parties that have not reached their emissions targets, have 100 days to correct the problem by acquiring units through emissions trading. A Party that fails to meet its target even after 100 days must, in the following year, make up the difference multiplied by 1.3. The State also loses its privilege to sell units under emissions trading and, must develop a compliance action plan within three months. Any Party that fails to comply with reporting requirements must similarly develop an action plan. In all instances of non-compliance the enforcement body publicizes information regarding both the non-compliance and the consequences.

To regain eligibility to participate in the mechanisms a Party may make a request, either through an expert review team or directly to the enforcement branch, if it has rectified the relevant problem. Generally, in cases of non-compliance a Party may make formal written submissions and request a hearing before the full Compliance Committee. A Party may appeal to the MOP only if the Party believes it has been denied due process in being charged with failure to meet emission targets.

Notes and Questions

1.   The relationship between the UNFCCC parties and the IPCC illustrates the influential interactions between scientists and policy makers in the context of international environmental law. The IPCC aims to present information to the UNFCCC COP that is relevant to policy but that does not prescribe particular policies. To accomplish this, the IPCC's panel of expert authors prepares reports according to strict procedures. IPCC reports then undergo review twice, first by more experts and second by governments and even more experts. Reports are not finalized until a plenary session of the IPCC approves them. The IPCC is best known for its regular comprehensive "Assessment Reports" (of which there have been three with a fourth scheduled for release in 2007), but the panel also publishes Special Reports or Technical Reports upon request of the UNFCCC COP or other international convention bodies. The IPCC has incidentally helped to create research and analytical capacity around the world through its deliberate efforts to draw in scientific expertise that represents a geographical balance.

2. Consistent with the tone of previous negotiations on climate change, the Kyoto protocol negotiations teemed with disagreement. To list a few of the points of disagreement: the United States persistently opposed both targets and timetables and adoption of mandatory "policies and measures" for reducing GHG emissions; the EU sought to limit emissions trading among States because it planned to trade emissions internally and would thus gain a competitive advantage if other States could not freely trade emissions; States also disagreed on the extent to which the protocol should require actual national emissions reductions, rather than allowing supplemental measures to offset emissions. One of the biggest points of contention that still remains at the forefront of the climate change negotiations is the current lack of binding reduction targets for developing States. The substantial developing nation bloc continues to hold that binding reduction targets are not feasible while other States, and the United States in particular, argue that the lack of such binding targets cripples meaningful action on climate change. Indeed, this last disagreement is the United States stated primary reason for withdrawing from the protocol.

3. In lieu of adopting obligations under the Kyoto Protocol, both the United States and Australia have undertaken independent programs to address climate change. In February of 2002, the United States announced a strategy aimed at reducing emissions per unit of economic activity by eighteen percent over ten years. The strategy entails various voluntary, regulatory, and incentive-based programs that address energy efficiency, agricultural practices, and emissions reductions, such as a Voluntary Greenhouse Gas Reporting Program and tax incentives for installing energy efficient technologies. For a comprehensive list of the United States' various programs see the United States Department of State Climate Change Fact Sheet available at http://www.state.gov/g/oes/rls/fs/46741.htm. Australia similarly developed a "no-regrets" policy involving voluntary initiatives as well as the establishment of the first government agency dedicated to cutting greenhouse gas emissions, the Australian Greenhouse Office. http://www.greenhouse.gov.au/. In July of 2002, the two non-parties to the Kyoto Protocol formulated the Australia–United States Climate Action Partnership and then in January of 2006 Australia and the United States along with China, India, Japan, and the Republic of Korea launched the Asia–Pacific Partnership on Clean Development and Climate. The outcome of most of these relatively new initiatives remains to be seen. Do such voluntary measures potentially offer any advantages over obligatory measures?

4. Developing States that are parties to the Kyoto Protocol but do not face binding emissions limitations under the Kyoto Protocol have, for the most part, upheld their responsibilities under the UNFCCC to submit national communications. As of 2005, 129 of the 148 non-Annex I Parties had completed an initial national communication, and some had submitted a second communication. Nearly all of the reports provided information on GHG mitigation measures the States had undertaken. Many parties agree, however, that these efforts are insufficient and that developing nations, which account for almost eighty percent of the world's population and collectively produce nearly fifty percent of the world's emissions, must begin to participate in emissions reductions especially considering the rapid rate of development in many such States. But, given the lack of infrastructure and

finances in many developing States, implementing the current Kyoto Protocol style emissions cap on developing States may not be feasible. Parties are thus working to develop alternative emissions limitations but progress is slow and attempts to apply emissions limitations to some developing States have met with opposition from other developing States. For example, Kazakhstan asked to become a UNFCCC Annex I party but other developing States prevented the change in status because they feared setting a precedent for developing State accession to Annex I. Similarly, Argentina sought to adopt a flexible sort of emissions target without changing its status under the UNFCCC of the Kyoto Protocol and again other developing States' concern over precedent stifled Argentina's efforts.

5. The mechanisms of the Kyoto Protocol reflect the increasing role of non-state actors in international law and policy. Both Joint Implementation and the Clean Development Mechanism look to private firms to maximize their utility. Without private investment JI and the CDM would be much less active areas since private investment brings more money and more innovation into projects and reduces bureaucracy. Governments thus have an interest in promoting the programs to private investors and do so by providing incentives such as tax and regulatory relief. Additionally, private firms may capitalize on the good will generated by their participation in such projects.

6. The Kyoto Protocol obligations are currently "politically binding" but not "legally binding." That is, the Kyoto Protocol lacks legally binding consequences of non-compliance and decisions by the protocol's enforcement body really only apply political pressure. The United States supported legally binding consequences to non-compliance, but other States such as Japan, and Australia advocated a politically binding compliance regime. The practical distinction between legally binding and politically binding requirements under the protocol is arguably subtle because although States may regard legally binding enforcement decisions more seriously, enforcement of legally binding obligations could still be impracticable. On the other hand, legally binding requirements could produce significant results by, for example, prompting some States to implement domestic legislation.

F. Next Steps in International Climate Change Law and Policy

The current arrangement under the Kyoto Protocol is a first step—a short-term guide to climate change policy that expires in 2012. The protocol and surrounding climate change debate, however, will not only lead to future agreements but have also prompted the establishment of programs that will likely become long term, such as regional emissions trading schemes. The European Union, for example, has implemented an Emissions Trading System (EU–ETS), which came into effect in January of 2005. This "cap and trade" scheme limits the total allowable emissions for each EU member State. States in turn draft a plan that is open to public comment, allocating emissions to individual emitters within their territory. Over-emitters both pay a financial penalty and must ultimately compensate for their excess emissions. Similarly, in the United States seven northeastern and mid-Atlantic States have instituted the

Regional Green House Gas Initiative (RGGI), another cap and trade system focusing initially on limiting CO_2 emissions from the energy sector. Many local governments have also undertaken initiatives to reduce their own emissions by doing things as simple as installing energy efficient light bulbs in government buildings, and private companies, particularly in the eco-tourism business, are beginning to market mechanisms for individuals to offset or purchase offsets of their personal emissions.

Regardless of the ongoing regional, local, and private developments in climate change policy, however, a long-term plan for States must eventually follow the Kyoto Protocol. The controversies surrounding first the reality of anthropogenic climate change, then the gravity of the problem, and now the most effective and feasible remedial efforts, have hindered long-term commitments. But as States become acclimated to the imperative of addressing climate change and as time and science reveal more information concerning the consequences of climate change, a long-term scheme will be essential. States have already begun negotiations on commitments for the second commitment period of the Kyoto Protocol beginning after 2012 but the nagging issue of developing country obligations, in particular, promises to inhibit the efficient elaboration of an effective long-term plan. In order to get beyond this issue, future approaches may allow for different types of emissions targets for developing States. Possible targets could take the shape of: "intensity" targets that limit emissions relative to an economic indicator such as gross domestic product (GDP); "no-lose" targets, which would be non-binding but would allow a State to sell any reductions below its targets, thus providing a financial incentive to reduce emissions; or conditional targets that would be binding so long as certain conditions, such as compliance costs, remain consistent.

The future of international climate change law and policy is in the making as not just States, but scientists, experts, NGOs, private firms, academics, local and regional governments, and intergovernmental communities are all undertaking initiatives and brainstorming about future tactics. The major question is whether sufficient action will occur quickly enough to stave off catastrophic warming. States may still not achieve their targets under the Kyoto Protocol and even if they do major effects of climate change appear inevitable. Estimates of impending changes vary. Current models' projections indicate that in the 21st century global temperatures may climb from 1.4 to 5.8 degrees Celsius and that sea levels may rise anywhere from 9 to 88 centimeters. Despite uncertainty about the exact effects of climate change, disruptive consequences are already occurring, and will continue to occur.

IV.   TRADE AND THE ENVIRONMENT

The end of World War II saw a rebirth of internationalism which it was hoped would prevent any further world wars. The world's nation states created the United Nations to bind one another together in a form of world government, while the General Agreement on Tariffs and Trade

(GATT) was entered into initially by developed nations to foster economic ties that would make war between themselves less likely and to forestall the economic protectionism that some believed was at least partially responsible for the worldwide great depression, which itself provided fertile ground for totalitarian regimes. Shortly thereafter, the European Coal and Steel Community was created by France, West Germany, Italy, Belgium, Luxembourg, and the Netherlands, to establish a free common market in coal and steel, which later developed into the European Economic Community (EEC), often known as the "Common Market," and still later into what is now the European Union. The success of the EEC in rebuilding Europe and making it an economic powerhouse rivaling the United States and the success of the GATT in growing international trade spawned a number of other regional common markets, from the Economic Community of West African States (ECOWAS) to the North American Free Trade Agreement (NAFTA) between the United States, Mexico, and Canada, as well as expansion of GATT to encompass virtually all nations within the World Trade Organization (WTO).

Those who support this expansion of free trade and the international organizations that implement the various multilateral agreements cite a number of benefits flowing from free trade. They believe that, in addition to the hoped for geopolitical stability, free trade will create greater wealth through a more efficient use of scarce resources. Moreover, according to the Kuznets curve, there is a correlation between an increase in national wealth and a decrease in pollution (following an initial increase in pollution). The hypothesis is that poorer nations value economic well-being more than a healthy environment, but that once a certain economic well-being is achieved, the people begin to demand greater protection of the environment. This relationship has been found in developed economies with respect to certain pollutants.

Not all observers favor "globalization." These critics see the growth of international free trade as a form of corporate imperialism, maximizing profits for corporations but not necessarily advancing the interests of people or the environment. Many of these commentators equate free trade with a demand for constant and environmentally destructive growth, which they view as inconsistent with sustainable development. In particular, some see globalization as exploitation of developing nations by developed nations. On the other hand, other critics of globalization see it as exporting jobs to nations where there are fewer environmental and worker protections. In any case, globalization may be considered a threat to the social preferences of individual nations. The threat can be rather obvious when there is pressure on a nation to alter its laws to attract new industry or when an industry with historic and cultural ties to the nation, as agriculture often has been, cannot compete on an equal basis with foreign products. The threat can be even more insidious when, for example, a Western consumer-culture is sold through the media to the people of a more traditional culture.

It is beyond the scope of this section to assess the relative merits of this debate, but whether one likes globalization or not, it is happening. Trade and the environment is itself worthy of an entire course, and there is at least one casebook devoted to the subject. *See* Wold, Gaines & Block, Trade and the Environment (2005). Here our goal is only to introduce you to the legal conflicts that may arise between international legal regimes for maintaining free trade and domestic environmental laws.

A. The World Trade Organization

The World Trade Organization (WTO) was created by international agreement in 1995, incorporating the prior existing General Agreement on Tariffs and Trade (GATT), but now including as well the Agreement on Technical Barriers to Trade (TBT), the Agreement on the Application of Sanitary and Phytosanitary Measures (SPS), and other international agreements. The WTO maintains a website that contains all the various agreements as well as other valuable information about the WTO. *See* www.wto.org/english/thewto_e/thewto_e.htm.

The GATT contains the core principles of free trade—the Most Favored Nation requirement, the National Treatment requirement, and the Ban on Quantitative Restrictions requirement. The Most Favored Nation requirement obliges a party to the GATT to treat all other parties equally with respect to imports and exports. In other words, it forbids a party from discriminating between parties with respect to imports and exports of "like products." For example, it would forbid the United States from allowing imports of televisions from China but banning them (or requiring them to pay a higher duty) if they are from Japan. The National Treatment requirement forbids a party from discriminating against foreign products in favor of like domestic products. For example, it would forbid the United States from restricting imports of MP3 players in favor of domestic MP3 players. The Ban on Quantitative Restrictions bars a party from establishing any numerical restriction, such as a quota, on imports from or exports to another party.

The TBT Agreement (*see* www.wto.org/english/docs_e/legal_e/17–tbt. pdf) incorporates the first two of these GATT principles with respect to technical regulations, and in addition requires that a party's technical standards and regulations not pose an unnecessary obstacle to trade. In addition, this agreement calls on members to improve transparency in setting standards and involve interested parties in standard setting. The United States complies with this through the use of the Administrative Procedure Act's rulemaking process for setting standards. However, another provision of the TBT Agreement, which requires parties to make reasonable efforts at the international harmonization of standards, creates problems for public participation in rulemaking, because often the standards have effectively been pre-determined at international meetings aimed at harmonization. The American Bar Association recognized this problem and called upon the President to encourage agencies to involve the public early in the harmonization process.

The SPS Agreement (*see* www.wto.org/English/tratop_e/sps_e/ spsagr_e.htm#fnt1) relates to regulations protecting a member's human, animal, or plant health from risks arising from diseases and pests and from toxins, additives, and contaminants in foods, beverages, and food-stuffs. It specifically allows such regulations but "only to the extent necessary to protect human, animal or plant life or health" and only if "based on scientific principles." Article 2. However, the agreement does allow for "provisional" SPS measures "where relevant scientific evidence is insufficient," but the member must then "seek to obtain the additional information necessary for a more objective assessment of risk and review the sanitary or phytosanitary measure accordingly within a reasonable period of time." Article 5, ¶ 7. Measures which comply with international standards are presumed to comply with the Agreement.

1. The WTO Dispute System

If a party to the WTO believes that another party is violating one or more of the agreements under the WTO, that party initially is required to consult with the alleged violator to attempt to resolve the dispute. If that attempt fails, the complainant can ask the WTO Dispute Settlement Body (DSB) to appoint a panel to hear the dispute. A panel can consist of three to five experts who are chosen by the parties to the dispute, unless they cannot agree, in which case the WTO Director General appoints them. Other parties to the WTO can participate in the case if they declare themselves to be interested.

The procedure begins with an initial case presentation by both the complainant and the defendant, which involves written submissions and an oral argument. In this sense, it is more like an appellate hearing than a trial-type proceeding, even though the panel may well have to decide disputed facts. There is a second hearing for written rebuttals and oral argument to the initial presentations. The panel may consult experts or appoint an expert advisory group to assist it, and it frequently has in environmental disputes. The panel then issues a draft report limited to describing the facts and arguments without indicating findings and conclusions and provides the parties an opportunity to comment on it. This is followed by issuance of an interim report that includes the panel's findings and conclusions. The parties then have the opportunity to request a "review" of the report by the panel, after which the panel adopts a final report. The report automatically becomes a ruling of the WTO after 60 days, unless a consensus of the entire WTO reject it (which has never happened). Either side may appeal the ruling to the Appellate Body. The appeal, which can only raise legal issues, is heard by a panel of three members of the Appellate Body. The entire appellate procedure is supposed to be concluded within 90 days.

If the ruling is that a party has violated a WTO agreement, the ruling requires the party to adjust its behavior to comply with the agreement. The party must state its intention to comply within 30 days. If it does not in fact adjust its behavior within a reasonable period of time, it must enter into negotiations with the injured party to determine appropriate compensation. If no satisfactory compensation is agreed upon, the injured party may request the Dispute Settlement Body for permission to impose trade sanctions against the other party.

The following is a case study provided by the WTO that involved requirements under the Clean Air Act for reformulated gasoline in order to reduce air pollution:

On 23 January 1995, Venezuela complained to the Dispute Settlement Body that the United States was applying rules that discriminated against gasoline imports, and formally requested consultations with the United States. The case arose because the United States applied stricter rules on the chemical characteristics of imported gasoline than it did for domestically-refined gasoline. Venezuela said this was unfair because US gasoline did not have to meet the same standards—it violated the "national treatment" principle and could not be justified under exceptions to normal WTO rules for health and environmental conservation measures. Just over a year later (on 29 January 1996) the dispute panel completed its final report. (By then, Brazil had joined the case, lodging its own complaint in April 1996. The same panel considered both complaints.) The dispute panel agreed with Venezuela and Brazil. The appeal report upheld the panel's conclusions (making some changes to the panel's legal interpretation), and the Dispute Settlement Body adopted the report on 20 May 1996, one year and four months after the complaint was first lodged. The United States and Venezuela then took six and a half months to agree on what the United States should do. The United States agreed with Venezuela that it would amend its regulations within 15 months, and on 26 August 1997 it reported to the Dispute Settlement Body that a new regulation had been signed on 19 August.

Historically, the model for GATT dispute resolution was arbitration rather than judicial proceedings. Following arbitration practice, the cases were not public, but private, and decisions were not supposed to be precedential. Over time and with the adoption of the WTO, the nature of the dispute resolution has slowly been evolving toward a more public framework and a wider reliance on prior cases for guidance, although the system still more closely resembles arbitration. For example, the transparency of the process has been substantially increased, with all decisions made public on the WTO website, at least the U.S. Government's submissions made public, and the ability of NGOs to have briefs considered by panels or the Appellate Body at least when appended to a party's submission and sometimes on their own, although this remains controversial within the WTO. With respect to precedent, the formal position of the WTO is that common-law notions of stare decisis do not apply, but the WTO itself states that:

If the reasoning developed in the previous report in support of the interpretation given to a WTO rule is persuasive from the perspective of the panel or the Appellate Body in the subsequent case, it is very likely that the panel or the Appellate Body will repeat and follow it. This is also in line with a key objective of the dispute settlement system which is to enhance the security and predictability of the multilateral trading system (Article 3.2 of the DSU). In the words of the Appellate Body, these GATT and WTO panel reports—and equally adopted Appellate Body reports—"create legitimate expectations among WTO Members, and, therefore, should be taken into account where they are relevant to any dispute."

www.wto.org/english/tratop_e/dispu_e/disp_settlement_cbt_e/c7s2p1_e. htm#fnt1(last visited 1/13/2007).

2. "Like Products"

Under both the GATT and the TBT agreement many of the prohibitions are against discriminating against "like products." The question thus arises: what are "like products"? For example, when the U.S. imposed a "gas guzzler" tax as a penalty to making and selling cars with particularly bad fuel economy, the European Communities argued that automobiles were automobiles—they were all "like products"—so that discrimination against gas guzzlers discriminated against like products. The GATT panel denied that claim, finding automobiles with good fuel economy not to be "like products" with respect to automobiles with bad fuel economy.

The issue arises in particular with regulation of products on the basis of how they are made, as opposed to what the products are or do. For example, tuna in cans would not be distinguishable on the basis of whether the tuna was caught using dolphin-safe technology or not. Thus, if the United States wished to bar tuna caught using non-dolphin-safe technology from import into the United States, it would appear to be discriminating against foreign "like products." This was the conclusion of the *Tuna/Dolphin* panel discussed below. Environmentalists and labor unions would like to distinguish products on the basis of their processes and production methods (PPMs). In this way, nations could discriminate against products made by unsustainable methods or under labor conditions that they found intolerable. On the other hand, other nations, in particular less developed nations, might see a comparative advantage in their lower labor and natural resource costs, so they might not want products to be compared on the basis of PPMs, but on the basis of the finished product's characteristics.

Environmentalists found some comfort in a more recent WTO decision in which Canada challenged France's ban on the sale of products containing chrysotile asbestos. Canada argued that the asbestos was a like product to many other fiber products that had the same end uses and competed with each other in the market place; the WTO panel agreed. The WTO Appellate Body, however, disagreed, finding the asbestos fiber not a like product. After laying out the traditional test for likeness, the Appellate Body went on to state that these criteria are "simply tools to assist in the task of sorting and examining the relevant evidence." In its further examination, the Appellate Body considered the health effects of asbestos compared to the health effects of other fibers. Because asbestos was carcinogenic, while the other fibers were not, the Appellate Body found the "carcinogenicity, or toxicity, . . . a defining aspect of the physical properties of the chrysotile asbestos fibres. . . . We do not see how this highly significant physical difference *cannot* be a consideration in examining the physical properties of a product as part of a determination of 'likeness'. . . . " European Communities—Measures Affecting Asbestos and Asbestos–Containing Products, Report of the Appellate Body, WT/DS135/AB/R (Mar. 12, 2001), ¶ 114. While this decision accepted that health and environmental concerns regarding the physical properties of a product could avoid "likeness," it certainly gave no suggestion that PPMs were relevant to a "likeness" determination.

One description of how to determine "likeness" was made some years ago:

> The interpretation of the term [like product] should be examined on a case-by-case basis. This would allow a fair assessment in each case of the different elements that constitute a "similar" product. Some criteria were suggested for determining, on a case-by-case basis, whether a product is "similar": the product's end-uses in a given market; consumers' tastes and habits, which change from country to country; the product's properties, nature and quality.

Report on the Working Party on Border Tax Adjustments, Dec. 2, 1970, GATT Doc. L/3464, BISD 18th Supp. 97, para. 18 (1972). In the gas guzzler case, however, the panel simply focused on whether the "aim and effect" of the tax was discriminatory.

Notes and Questions

1. In light of the above, do you think that a nation could impose different import requirements on paper from recycled sources than from virgin pulp, or on conventionally grown tomatoes than on genetically modified (GM) tomatoes, assuming domestic paper or tomatoes were similarly treated?

3. Health, Safety, and Environmental Exceptions to GATT Requirements

Even when a party discriminates against like products from abroad or between different nations, it is not a violation of GATT if the discrimination falls within one of the exceptions to GATT's requirements. In the environmental field, there are two particular provisions of the original GATT that are most significant.

Article XX

General Exceptions

Subject to the requirement that such measures are not applied in a manner which would constitute a means of arbitrary or unjustifiable discrimination between countries where the same conditions prevail, or a disguised restriction on international trade, nothing in this Agreement shall be construed to prevent the adoption or enforcement by any contracting party of measures:

* * * * *

(b) necessary to protect human, animal or plant life or health;

* * * * *

(g) relating to the conservation of exhaustible natural resources if such measures are made effective in conjunction with restrictions on domestic production or consumption....

These provisions have been invoked in several cases in which the United States has been a party defendant. The first was the Tuna/Dolphin controversy. This is how the WTO describes the case:

UNITED STATES—TUNA (Mexico)

United States—Restrictions on Imports of Tuna, circulated on 3 September 1991, unadopted, DS 21/R.

A.   Parties

Complainant: Mexico.

Respondent: United States.

Third Parties: Australia; Canada; Chile; Colombia; Costa Rica; the European Communities; India; Indonesia; Japan; Korea; New Zealand; Nicaragua; Norway; Peru; the Philippines; Senegal; Singapore; Tanzania; Thailand; Tunisia and Venezuela.

B.   Timeline of Dispute

Panel requested: 25 January 1991.

Panel established: 6 February 1991.

Panel composed: 12 March 1991.

Panel Report circulated: 3 September 1991.

Panel Report not adopted.

C.   Main Facts

1.   Tuna are commonly caught in commercial fisheries using large "purse seine" nets. In the Eastern Tropical Pacific Ocean (ETP), dolphins are known to swim above schools of tuna. Tuna fishermen in the ETP commonly use dolphins to locate schools of tuna, and encircle them intentionally with purse seine nets on the expectation that tuna will be found below the dolphins. It was claimed that this technique might lead to incidental taking of dolphins during fishing operations.

2.   The US Marine Mammal Protection Act (MMPA) of 1972, as revised, required a general prohibition of "taking" (harassment, hunting, capture, killing or attempt thereof) and importation into the United States of marine mammals, except with explicit authorization. It governed in

particular the taking of marine mammals incidental to harvesting yellowfin tuna in the ETP.

3.   Under the MMPA, the importation of commercial fish or products from fish caught with commercial fishing technology, which results in the incidental kill or incidental serious injury of ocean mammals in excess of US standards, was prohibited. In particular, the importation of yellowfin tuna harvested with purse seine nets in the ETP was prohibited (primary nation embargo), unless the competent US authorities established that (i) the government of the harvesting country had a programme regulating takings of marine mammals that was comparable to that of the United States, and (ii) the average rate of incidental taking of marine mammals by vessels of the harvesting nation was comparable to the average rate of such takings by US vessels. To meet this requirement, the exporting country had to prove that the average rate of incidental takings (in terms of dolphins killed each time the purse seine nets are set) was no higher than 1.25 times the average taking rate of US vessels in the same period. In 1991, countries affected by the primary nation embargo were Mexico, Venezuela and Vanuatu. Imports of tuna from countries purchasing tuna from a country subject to the primary nation embargo were also prohibited (intermediary nation embargo). In 1991, countries affected by the intermediary nation embargo were Costa Rica, France, Italy, Japan and Panama.

4.   Mexico claimed that the import prohibition on yellowfin tuna and tuna products was inconsistent with Articles XI, XIII and III. The United States requested the panel to find that the direct embargo was consistent with Article III and, in the alternative, was covered by Articles XX(b) and XX(g). The United States also argued that the intermediary nation embargo was consistent with Article III and, in the alternative, was justified by Article XX, paragraphs (b), (d) and (g).

D.   Summary of Findings on Article XX

1.   The panel found that the import prohibition under the direct and the intermediary embargoes did not constitute internal regulations within the meaning of Article III, was inconsistent with Article XI:1 and was not justified by Article XX paragraphs (b) and (g). Moreover, the intermediary embargo was not justified under either Article XX (b), (d) or (g).

2.   The panel found, on the basis of the drafting history, that Article XX(b) did not extend to measures protecting human, animal or plant life outside of the jurisdiction of the country taking the measure. Moreover, the panel considered that if the broad interpretation of Article XX(b) suggested by the United States were accepted, each contracting party could unilaterally determine the life or health protection policies from which other contracting parties could not deviate without jeopardizing their rights under the GATT. The panel also rejected an extrajurisdictional application of Article XX(g) as well.

3.   The panel further noted that even if Article XX paragraphs (b) and (g) were interpreted to apply extrajurisdictionally, the US measures would not meet the requirements set out in these two provisions. In the

panel's view, the US measure could not be considered to be necessary within the meaning of Article XX(b) as the United States had failed to demonstrate that it had exhausted all options reasonably available to it to pursue its dolphin protection objectives through measures consistent with the GATT, in particular through the negotiation of international cooperative arrangements, which would seem to be desirable in view of the fact that dolphins roam the waters of many states and the high seas. Concerning Article XX(g), the panel recalled that the United States linked the maximum incidental dolphin-taking rate which Mexico had to meet to the taking rate actually recorded for United States fishermen. The panel considered that a limitation on trade based on such unpredictable conditions could not be regarded as being primarily aimed at the conservation of dolphins in terms of Article XX(g).

Notes and Questions

1. It is noted in the timeline of the dispute that the report was not adopted. Under the present WTO system, if WTO members (meeting as the Dispute Settlement Body) do not by consensus *reject* a panel report after 60 days, it is automatically accepted ("adopted"). That was not the case under the old GATT. Mexico decided not to pursue the case and the panel report was never adopted even though some of the "intermediary" countries pressed for its adoption. Mexico and the United States held their own bilateral consultations aimed at reaching agreement outside GATT. Indeed, agreement was reached, essentially providing for Mexico to comply with equivalent dolphin safety standards in return for technical and financial assistance from the United States.

2. Note that the panel made two findings in the alternative as to why the United States' primary embargo failed to meet the exceptions of Article XX, one based on extraterritoriality and one based on a lack of necessity.

3. The panel was also asked to judge the US policy of requiring tuna products to be labelled "dolphin-safe" (leaving to consumers the choice of whether to buy the product). It concluded that this did not violate GATT rules because it was designed to prevent deceptive advertising practices on all tuna products, whether imported or domestically produced.

4. Partially as a result of the Mexico/US dispute not having a report adopted, the European Commission filed its own complaint against the United States with respect to the intermediary nation import restriction. Again, this is how the WTO describes the case.

UNITED STATES—TUNA (EEC)

United States—Restrictions on Imports of Tuna, circulated on 16 June 1994, not adopted, DS29/R.

A. Parties

Complainant: The European Economic Community (EEC) and the Netherlands.

Respondent: United States.

Third Parties: Australia; Canada; Colombia; Costa Rica; El Salvador; Japan; New Zealand; Thailand and Venezuela.

B.   Timeline of Dispute

Panel requested: 5 June 1992.

Panel established: 14 July 1992.

Panel composed: 25 August 1992.

Panel Report circulated: 16 June 1994.

Panel Report not adopted.

C.   Main Facts

1.   The facts of this case are similar to the ones described above in the US—Tuna (Mexico) case. The MMPA provided that any nation (intermediary nation) exporting yellowfin tuna or yellowfin tuna products to the US had to certify and provide reasonable proof that it had not imported products subject to the direct prohibition within the preceding sixth months. After the adoption of a new definition of intermediary nation, France, the Netherlands Antilles and the United Kingdom were withdrawn from the list of intermediary nations. In October 1992, Costa Rica, Italy, Japan and Spain were still covered by the intermediary nation embargo.

2.   The EEC and the Netherlands (on behalf of the Netherlands Antilles) complained that both the primary and the intermediary nation embargoes, enforced pursuant to the MMPA, did not fall under Article III, were inconsistent with Article XI:1 and were not covered by any of the exceptions of Article XX. The United States argued that the intermediary nation embargo was consistent with the GATT since it was covered by Article XX, paragraphs (g), (b) and (d), and that the primary nation embargo did not nullify or impair any benefits accruing to the EEC or the Netherlands since it did not apply to these countries.

D.   Summary of Findings on Article XX

1.   The panel found that the primary and the intermediary nation embargo did not fall under Article III and were contrary to Article XI:1. It found further that the US measures were not covered by the exceptions in Article XX (b), (d) or (g). On Article XX (b) and (g), the panel found that there was no basis for the contention that Article XX applied only to policies related to the protection of human, animal or plant life and health or to the conservation of natural resources located within the territory of the contracting party, and concluded that the policy pursued within the jurisdiction over its nationals and vessels, fell within the range of policies covered by Article XX(b) and (g).

2.   However, the panel found that measures taken so as to force other countries to change their policies could not be considered "necessary" for the protection of animal life or health in the sense of Article XX(b), or primarily aimed at the conservation of exhaustible natural resources, or at rendering effective restrictions on domestic production or consumption, in the meaning of Article XX(g).

Notes and Questions

1.   Note that this report was not adopted as well. Although the European Union and other countries pressed for the report to be adopted, the United States told a series of meetings of the GATT Council and the final

meeting of GATT contracting parties (i.e., members) that it had not had time to complete its studies of the report. There was therefore no consensus to adopt the report, a requirement under the old GATT system.

2. What did this panel say about extraterritoriality? What guidance does this give to the United States or other nations as to the coverage of Article XX (b) and (g)?

3. A more recent case brought under the current WTO dispute procedures follows as described by the WTO:

UNITED STATES—SHRIMP

United States—Import Prohibition of Certain Shrimp and Shrimp Products, Appellate Body Report and Panel Report adopted on 6 November 1998, WT/DS58.

A.   Parties

1.   Panel

Complainant: India, Malaysia, Pakistan and Thailand.

Respondent: United States.

Third Parties: Australia; Colombia; Costa Rica; Ecuador; El Salvador; the European Communities; Guatemala; Hong Kong; Japan; Mexico; Nigeria; the Philippines; Senegal; Singapore; Sri Lanka and Venezuela.

2.   Appellate Body

Appellant: United States.

Appellees: India; Malaysia; Pakistan and Thailand.

Third Participants: Australia; Ecuador; the European Communities; Hong Kong, China; Mexico and Nigeria.

B.   Timeline of Dispute

Panel requested: 9 January 1997 (Malaysia and Thailand); 30 January 1997 (Pakistan) and 25 February 1997 (India).

Panel established: 25 February 1997 and 10 April 1997 (for India).

Panel composed: 15 April 1997.

Panel Report circulated: 15 May 1997.

Notice of appeal: 13 July 1998.

Appellate Body Report circulated: 12 October 1998.

Adoption: 6 November 1998.

C.   Main Facts

1.   Sea turtles at issue are characterized as highly migratory species, spending their lives at sea, migrating between their foraging and their nesting grounds. They have been adversely affected by human activity, either directly (exploitation of their meat, shells and eggs), or indirectly (incidental capture in fisheries, destruction of their habitats, pollution of the oceans). In 1998, all species of sea turtles were included in Appendix I of the 1973 Convention on International Trade in Endangered Species ("CITES").

2. The US Endangered Species Act of 1973 ("ESA") lists as endangered or threatened the five species of sea turtles occurring in US waters and prohibits their take within the United States, within the US territorial sea and the high seas. Pursuant to the ESA, the United States required that shrimp trawlers used "turtle excluder devices" (TEDs)[4] in their nets when fishing in areas where there was a significant likelihood of encountering sea turtles.

3. Section 609 of Public Law 101–162 (hereafter "Section 609"), enacted in 1989 by the United States, intended to, inter alia, develop bilateral or multilateral agreements for the protection and conservation of sea turtles. Section 609 prohibited that shrimp harvested with technology that might adversely affect certain sea turtles be imported into the United States, unless the harvesting nation was certified to have a regulatory programme for the conservation of sea turtles and an incidental take rate comparable to that of the United States, or that the particular fishing environment of the harvesting nation did not pose a threat to sea turtles. In practice, countries having any of the five species of sea turtles within their jurisdiction and harvesting shrimp with mechanical means had to impose on their fishermen requirements comparable to those borne by US shrimpers, essentially the use of TEDs at all times, if they wished to be certified and export shrimp products to the United States. The United States issued regulatory guidelines in 1991, 1993 and 1996 for the implementation of Section 609 detailing how to assess the comparability of foreign regulatory programmes with the US programme, as well as the criteria for certification. The United States effectively banned shrimp imports from countries that were not certified as having comparable conservation policies for endangered sea turtles or as coming from shrimp boats equipped with TEDs.

4. The complainants argued that the import prohibition on shrimp and shrimp products was inconsistent with Article XI:1, with Article I:1, and with Article XIII:1 as it restricted the importation of shrimp and shrimp products from countries which had not been certified, while like products from other countries which had been certified could be imported freely into the US. The US claimed that the measures at issue were justified under Article XX(b) and (g) given that these provisions did not contain jurisdictional limitations, nor limitations on the location of the animals or natural resources to be protected and conserved. The complainants argued to the contrary that Article XX(b) and (g) could not be invoked to justify a measure applying to animals outside the jurisdiction of the Member enacting the measure.

5. On appeal, the US raised, inter alia, the issue of whether the panel erred in finding that the measure at issue constituted unjustifiable discrimination between countries where the same conditions prevail and, thus, was not within the scope of measures permitted under Article XX of the GATT 1994.

D. Summary of Findings on Article XX

1. The panel ruled that it was equally appropriate to analyse first the introductory provision of Article XX, and only thereafter the specific require-

---

4. A TED is a trap door installed inside a trawling net which allows shrimp to pass to the back of the net while directing sea turtles and other unintentionally caught large objects out of the net.

ments contained in the paragraphs. This ruling was rejected by the Appellate Body. It indicated that the sequence of steps followed in the US–Gasoline case (first, characterization of the measure under Article XX(g); second, further appraisal of the same measure under the introductory clauses of Article XX) reflected not inadvertence or random choice, but rather the fundamental structure and logic of Article XX.

2. The panel had found that the ban imposed by the United States was inconsistent with Article XI. It had concluded that the US ban could not be justified under Article XX as it constituted "unjustifiable" discrimination between countries where the same conditions prevail and thus was not within the scope of measures permitted under Article XX. It had reasoned that allowing such a ban would undermine Members' autonomy to determine their own policies. Since the panel had found that the US measure at issue was not within the scope of measures permitted under the chapeau of Article XX, it did not find it necessary to examine whether the US measure was covered by paragraphs (b) and (g) of Article XX.

3. The Appellate Body further ruled that the measure at stake qualified for provisional justification under Article XX(g), but failed to meet the requirements of the chapeau of Article XX, and, therefore, was not justified under Article XX. The Appellate Body found that the sea turtles involved constituted "exhaustible natural resources" for purposes of Article XX(g), and that Section 609 was a measure "relating to" the conservation of an exhaustible natural resource. It ruled, however, with regard to the chapeau, that discrimination resulted not only when countries in which the same conditions prevail were treated differently, but also when the application of the measure at issue did not allow for any inquiry into the appropriateness of the regulatory programme for the conditions prevailing in the exporting countries. Thereby, the failure of the United States to engage the appellees, as well as other Members exporting shrimp to the United States, in serious, across-the-board negotiations with the objective of concluding bilateral or multilateral agreements for the protection and conservation of sea turtles, before unilaterally enforcing the import prohibition against the shrimp exports of those Members, was also taken into account.

4. This is part of what the Appellate Body said:

> In reaching these conclusions, we wish to underscore what we have not decided in this appeal. We have not decided that the protection and preservation of the environment is of no significance to the Members of the WTO. Clearly, it is. We have not decided that the sovereign nations that are Members of the WTO cannot adopt effective measures to protect endangered species, such as sea turtles. Clearly, they can and should. And we have not decided that sovereign states should not act together bilaterally, plurilaterally or multilaterally, either within the WTO or in other international fora, to protect endangered species or to otherwise protect the environment. Clearly, they should and do.
>
> What we have decided in this appeal is simply this: although the measure of the United States in dispute in this appeal serves an environmental objective that is recognized as legitimate under paragraph (g) of Article XX [i.e., 20] of the GATT 1994, this measure has been applied by the United States in a manner which constitutes

arbitrary and unjustifiable discrimination between Members of the WTO, contrary to the requirements of the chapeau of Article XX. For all of the specific reasons outlined in this Report, this measure does not qualify for the exemption that Article XX of the GATT 1994 affords to measures which serve certain recognized, legitimate environmental purposes but which, at the same time, are not applied in a manner that constitutes a means of arbitrary or unjustifiable discrimination between countries where the same conditions prevail or a disguised restriction on international trade. As we emphasized in United States—Gasoline [adopted 20 May 1996, WT/DS2/AB/R, p. 30], WTO Members are free to adopt their own policies aimed at protecting the environment as long as, in so doing, they fulfill their obligations and respect the rights of other Members under the WTO Agreement.

Notes and Questions

1.   As a relatively recent case that reached the Appellate Body, this decision would seem to have more weight than the initial cases. What does it say about extraterritoriality?

2.   The chapeau is the introductory language to an article. What was it about the chapeau that doomed the United States? How is this different from the necessity requirement that the second Tuna decision had imposed?

3.   The WTO's description of the case does not make much of it, but many commentators think an important part of the Appellate Body's opinion involved its discussion of the procedure that the United States used for certifying nations as compliant. The Appellate Body noted that the certification process was largely ex parte, with no formal opportunity for a nation to be heard or to respond to arguments that might have made against it. There was no formal written, reasoned decision, and nations that were denied certification were not so notified and were given no procedure for appeal or rehearing. The Appellate Body concluded: "It appears to us that, effectively, exporting Members applying for certification whose applications are rejected are denied basic fairness and due process, and are discriminated against, vis-a-vis those Members which are granted certification."

4.   In addition, the Appellate Body found fault with the United States's requirement that other nations use "essentially the same" method of turtle protection as the United States without regard to the local conditions or situation. The Appellate Body observed that the statute did not impose that requirement but instead could be read only to require that the other nation's protection was "comparable in effectiveness." The latter standard would provide substantial flexibility, yet achieve essentially the same result. Failure to provide that flexibility was unjustifiable discrimination.

5.   This was not the last word on the Shrimp/Turtle front. After the Appellate Body's report, the United States changed its procedures for certification to respond to report's criticism, adopted a "comparable effectiveness" standard, and attempted to negotiate with the complainant nations to achieve an agreed upon means of protecting the turtles in the course of shrimp fishing. The negotiations, however, ultimately failed, and the United States reimposed its embargo on those nations' shrimp. They, in turn, filed a

new complaint with the WTO, alleging that the United States was violating the earlier report. Here is the WTO's description of that case.

UNITED STATES—SHRIMP (Article 21.5)

United States—Import Prohibition of Certain Shrimp and Shrimp Products. Recourse to article 21.5 by Malaysia, Appellate Body Report and Panel Report, adopted on 21 November 2001, WT/DS58/AB/RW.

A. Parties

1. Panel

Complainant: Malaysia.

Respondent: United States.

Third Parties: Australia; Canada; Ecuador; Hong Kong, China; the European Communities; India; Japan; Mexico; Pakistan and Thailand.

2. Appellate Body

Appellant: Malaysia.

Appellee: United States.

Third Participants: Australia; the European Communities; Hong Kong, China; India; Japan; Mexico and Thailand.

B. Timeline of Dispute

Panel requested: 12 October 2000.

Panel established: 23 October 2000.

Panel composed: 23 October 2000.

Panel Report circulated: 15 June 2001.

Notice of appeal: 23 July 2001.

Appellate Body Report circulated: 22 October 2001.

Panel Report adopted: 21 November 2001.

C. Main Facts

1. In accordance with Article 21.5 of the DSU,[5] Malaysia requested that the Dispute Settlement Body (DSB) refer to a panel its complaint with respect to whether the United States had complied with the recommendations and rulings of the DSB in United States—Import Prohibition of Certain Shrimp and Shrimp Products, adopted on 6 November 1998 (see Part VIII above). The DSB referred the matter to the original panel.

2. In order to implement the recommendations and rulings of the DSB, the United States issued the Revised Guidelines for the Implementation of Section 609 of Public Law 101–162 Relating to the Protection of Sea Turtles in Shrimp Trawl Fishing Operations (the "Revised Guidelines"). These

---

5. Article 21.5 of the DSU reads as follows: "Where there is disagreement as to the existence or consistency with a covered agreement of measures taken to comply with the recommendations and rulings such dispute shall be decided through recourse to these dispute settlement procedures, including wherever possible resort to the original panel. The panel shall circulate its report within 90 days after the date of referral of the matter to it. When the panel considers that it cannot provide its report within this time frame, it shall inform the DSB in writing of the reasons for the delay together with an estimate of the period within which it will submit its report."

Revised Guidelines replaced the guidelines issued in April 1996 that were part of the original measure at stake. The Revised Guidelines set forth criteria for certification.

3. Malaysia claimed that Section 609, as currently applied continued to violate Article XI:1 and that the United States was not entitled to impose any prohibition in the absence of an international agreement allowing it to do so. The United States did not contend that the implementing measure was compatible with Article XI:1 but that it was justified under Article XX(g). The United States argued that the Revised Guidelines responded to its obligation to remedy all the inconsistencies identified by the Appellate Body under the chapeau of Article XX.

D.   Summary of Findings on Article XX

1. The panel was called upon to examine the compatibility of the implementing measure with Article XX(g). It noted that in US—Shrimp, the Appellate Body concluded that Section 609 was provisionally justified under Article XX(g). Therefore, since the implementing measure before the panel was identical to the measure examined by the Appellate Body in relation to paragraph (g), the panel held that the implementing measure was provisionally justifiable under Article XX(g).

2. The panel then recalled the Appellate Body's finding in US—Shrimp concerning the nature of the chapeau of Article XX:

> "the task of interpreting and applying the chapeau is (. . .) essentially the delicate one of locating and marking out a line of equilibrium between the right of a Member to invoke an exception under Article XX and the rights of the other Members under varying substantive provisions (. . .) of the GATT 1994."

3. The panel concluded that the recognition that the protection of migratory species was best achieved through international cooperation significantly moved the line of equilibrium towards a bilaterally or multilaterally negotiated solution, thus rendering recourse to unilateral measures less acceptable. On this basis, the panel proceeded to determine whether the line of equilibrium in the field of sea turtle conservation and protection was such as to require the conclusion of an international agreement or only efforts to negotiate. It concluded that the obligation of the United States was an obligation to negotiate, as opposed to an obligation to conclude an international agreement. It also concluded that the US had made serious good faith efforts to negotiate an international agreement.

4. On appeal, Malaysia claimed that the panel erred in finding that the new measure at issue was applied in a manner that no longer constituted a means of "arbitrary or unjustifiable discrimination" under Article XX. Malaysia first asserted that the United States should have negotiated and concluded an international agreement on the protection and conservation of sea turtles before imposing an import prohibition. The Appellate Body upheld the panel's finding and rejected Malaysia's contention that avoiding "arbitrary and unjustifiable discrimination" under the chapeau of Article XX required the conclusion of an international agreement on the protection and conservation of sea turtles[, although good faith efforts to negotiate an agreement are required]. Malaysia also argued that the measure at issue

resulted in "arbitrary or unjustifiable discrimination" because of the lack of flexibility of the US measure. The Appellate Body upheld again the panel's finding and agreed with the reasoning of the panel that conditioning market access on the adoption of a programme comparable in effectiveness, allowed for sufficient flexibility in the application of the measure so as to avoid "arbitrary or unjustifiable discrimination."

Notes and Questions

1. The United States finally wins a case! Can you find a common thread to these cases that provides guidance to nations? If so, what kind of barrier does the WTO place in the way of environmental regulations?

4. The Effect of International Environmental Agreements on WTO Requirements

As the decisions in the shrimp/turtle case suggest, the presence of international environmental agreements may have some effect on the permissibility of a trade restriction under Article XX of the GATT. Exactly what that effect is, however, is not clear. One of the recent innovations of the WTO in an attempt to respond to criticisms of environmental NGOs was to create a Committee on Trade and the Environment (CTE). Its role is to study relationships between trade and the environment and to make recommendations to the WTO. The following is a product of the WTO, *see* http://www.wto.org/english/thewto_e/whatis_e/tif_e/bey2_e.htm.

How do the WTO trading system and "green" trade measures relate to each other? What is the relationship between the WTO agreements and various international environmental agreements and conventions?

There are about 200 international agreements (outside the WTO) dealing with various environmental issues currently in force. They are called multilateral environmental agreements (MEAs).

About 20 of these include provisions that can affect trade: for example, they ban trade in certain products, or allow countries to restrict trade in certain circumstances. Among them are the Montreal Protocol for the protection of the ozone layer, the Basel Convention on the trade or transportation of hazardous waste across international borders, and the Convention on International Trade in Endangered Species (CITES).

Briefly, the WTO's committee says the basic WTO principles of non-discrimination and transparency do not conflict with trade measures needed to protect the environment, including actions taken under the environmental agreements. It also notes that clauses in the agreements on goods, services and intellectual property allow governments to give priority to their domestic environmental policies.

The WTO's committee says the most effective way to deal with international environmental problems is through the environmental agreements. It says this approach complements the WTO's work in seeking internationally agreed solutions for trade problems. In other words, using the provisions of an international environmental agreement is better than one country trying on its own to change other countries' environmental policies (see shrimp-turtle and dolphin-tuna case studies).

The committee notes that actions taken to protect the environment and having an impact on trade can play an important role in some environmental agreements, particularly when trade is a direct cause of the environmental problems. But it also points out that trade restrictions are not the only actions that can be taken, and they are not necessarily the most effective. Alternatives include: helping countries acquire environmentally-friendly technology, giving them financial assistance, providing training, etc.

The problem should not be exaggerated. So far, no action affecting trade and taken under an international environmental agreement has been challenged in the GATT–WTO system. There is also a widely held view that actions taken under an environmental agreement are unlikely to become a problem in the WTO if the countries concerned have signed the environmental agreement, although the question is not settled completely. The Trade and Environment Committee is more concerned about what happens when one country invokes an environmental agreement to take action against another country that has not signed the environmental agreement.

Here the situation is unclear and the subject of debate. Some environmental agreements say countries that have signed the agreement should apply the agreement even to goods and services from countries that have not. Whether this would break the WTO agreements remains untested because, so far, no dispute of this kind has been brought to the WTO. One proposed way to clarify the situation would be to rewrite the rules to make clear that countries can, in some circumstances, cite an environmental agreement when they take action affecting the trade of a country that has not signed. Critics say this would allow some countries to force their environmental standards on others.

Suppose a trade dispute arises because a country has taken action on trade (for example, imposed a tax or restricted imports) under an environmental agreement outside the WTO and another country objects. Should the dispute be handled under the WTO or under the other agreement? The Trade and Environment Committee says that if a dispute arises over a trade action taken under an environmental agreement, and if both sides to the dispute have signed that agreement, then they should try to use the environmental agreement to settle the dispute. But if one side in the dispute has not signed the environment agreement, then the WTO would provide the only possible forum for settling the dispute. The preference for handling disputes under the environmental agreements does not mean environmental issues would be ignored in WTO disputes. The WTO agreements allow panels examining a dispute to seek expert advice on environmental issues.

5. The SPS and TBT Agreements

Included under the WTO umbrella but in addition to the GATT are two other agreements that are particularly relevant to environmental concerns. The following is a WTO explanation of those agreements. *See* www.wto.org/english/thewto_e/whatis_e/tif_e/utw_chap2_e.pdf.

The Agreement on the Application of Sanitary and Phytosanitary Measures (SPS) sets out the basic rules regarding food safety and animal and plant health standards. The Agreement on Technical Barriers to Trade (TBT) tries to ensure that technical regulations, standards, testing and certification procedures do not create unnecessary obstacles.

In general, the SPS allows countries to set their own standards, but it also says regulations must be based on a scientific risk assessment. They should be applied only to the extent necessary to protect human, animal or plant life or health, and they should not arbitrarily or unjustifiably discriminate between countries where identical or similar conditions prevail.

Member countries are required to use international standards, guidelines and recommendations as the basis for their own SPS standards, where they exist. However, members may use measures which result in higher standards if there is scientific justification. They can also set higher standards based on appropriate assessment of risks so long as the approach is consistent, not arbitrary. And they can to some extent apply the "precautionary principle," a kind of "safety first" approach to deal with scientific uncertainty. Article 5.7 of the SPS Agreement allows temporary "precautionary" measures.

The agreement still allows countries to use different standards and different methods of inspecting products. So how can an exporting country be sure the practices it applies to its products are acceptable in an importing country? If an exporting country can demonstrate that the measures it applies to its exports achieve the same level of health protection as in the importing country, then the importing country is expected to accept the exporting country's standards and methods.

The agreement includes provisions on control, inspection and approval procedures. Governments must provide advance notice of new or changed sanitary and phytosanitary regulations, and establish a national enquiry point to provide information. The agreement complements that on technical barriers to trade.

The TBT agreement recognizes countries' rights to adopt the standards they consider appropriate—for example, for human, animal or plant life or health, for the protection of the environment, or to meet other consumer interests. Moreover, members are not prevented from taking measures necessary to ensure their standards are met. In order to prevent too much diversity, the agreement encourages countries to use international standards where these are appropriate, but it does not require them to change their levels of protection as a result.

The agreement sets out a code of good practice for the preparation, adoption and application of standards by central government bodies. It also includes provisions describing how local government and non-governmental bodies should apply their own regulations—normally they should use the same principles as apply to central governments.

The agreement says the procedures used to decide whether a product conforms with national standards have to be fair and equitable. It discourages any methods that would give domestically produced goods an unfair advantage. The agreement also encourages countries to recognize each other's testing procedures. That way, a product can be assessed to see if it meets the importing country's standards through testing in the country where it is made.

Manufacturers and exporters need to know what the latest standards are in their prospective markets. To help ensure that this information is made available conveniently, all WTO member governments are required to establish national enquiry points.

The scope of the two agreements is different. The SPS Agreement covers all measures whose purpose is to protect:

- human or animal health from food-borne risks;
- human health from animal-or plant-carried diseases;
- animals and plants from pests or diseases;

whether or not these are technical requirements.

The TBT Agreement covers all technical regulations, voluntary standards and the procedures to ensure that these are met, except when these are sanitary or phytosanitary measures as defined by the SPS Agreement. It is thus the type of measure which determines whether it is covered by the TBT Agreement, but the purpose of the measure which is relevant in determining whether a measure is subject to the SPS Agreement.

TBT measures could cover any subject, from car safety to energy-saving devices, to the shape of food cartons. To give some examples pertaining to human health, TBT measures could include pharmaceutical restrictions, or the labelling of cigarettes. Most measures related to human disease control are under the TBT Agreement, unless they concern diseases which are carried by plants or animals (such as rabies). In terms of food, labelling requirements, nutrition claims and concerns, quality and packaging regulations are generally not considered to be sanitary or phytosanitary measures and hence are normally subject to the TBT Agreement.

On the other hand, by definition, regulations which address microbiological contamination of food, or set allowable levels of pesticide or veterinary drug residues, or identify permitted food additives, fall under the SPS Agreement. Some packaging and labelling requirements, if directly related to the safety of the food, are also subject to the SPS Agreement.

The two agreements have some common elements, including basic obligations for non-discrimination and similar requirements for the advance notification of proposed measures and the creation of information offices ("Enquiry Points"). However, many of the substantive rules are different. For example, both agreements encourage the use of international standards. However, under the SPS Agreement the only justification for not using such standards for food safety and animal/plant health protection are scientific arguments resulting from an assessment of the potential health risks. In contrast, under the TBT Agreement governments may decide that international standards are not appropriate for other reasons, including fundamental technological problems or geographical factors.

Also, sanitary and phytosanitary measures may be imposed only to the extent necessary to protect human, animal or plant health, on the basis of scientific information. Governments may, however, introduce TBT regulations when necessary to meet a number of objectives, such as national security or the prevention of deceptive practices. Because the obligations that governments have accepted are different under the two agreements, it is important to know whether a measure is a sanitary or phytosanitary measure, or a measure subject to the TBT Agreement.

To flesh out some of these general considerations, let us consider a case, indeed the first case, that arose under the SPS Agreement, the EC–Measures Concerning Meat and Meat Products. The European Communities had adopted a directive banning the importation of meat or meat products from cattle which had been fed certain natural hormones or synthetic hormones for growth promotion purposes. The United States and Canada challenged this directive as violating the SPS Agreement. The applicable provisions of the Agreement follows:

Agreement on the Application of Sanitary and Phytosanitary Measures

* * *

Article 2

Basic Rights and Obligations

1. Members have the right to take sanitary and phytosanitary measures necessary for the protection of human, animal or plant life or health, provided that such measures are not inconsistent with the provisions of this Agreement.

2. Members shall ensure that any sanitary or phytosanitary measure is applied only to the extent necessary to protect human, animal or plant life or health, is based on scientific principles and is not maintained without sufficient scientific evidence, except as provided for in paragraph 7 of Article 5.

3. Members shall ensure that their sanitary and phytosanitary measures do not arbitrarily or unjustifiably discriminate between Members

where identical or similar conditions prevail, including between their own territory and that of other Members. Sanitary and phytosanitary measures shall not be applied in a manner which would constitute a disguised restriction on international trade.

4. Sanitary or phytosanitary measures which conform to the relevant provisions of this Agreement shall be presumed to be in accordance with the obligations of the Members under the provisions of GATT 1994 which relate to the use of sanitary or phytosanitary measures, in particular the provisions of Article XX(b).

Article 3

Harmonization

1. To harmonize sanitary and phytosanitary measures on as wide a basis as possible, Members shall base their sanitary or phytosanitary measures on international standards, guidelines or recommendations, where they exist, except as otherwise provided for in this Agreement, and in particular in paragraph 3.

2. Sanitary or phytosanitary measures which conform to international standards, guidelines or recommendations shall be deemed to be necessary to protect human, animal or plant life or health, and presumed to be consistent with the relevant provisions of this Agreement and of GATT 1994.

3. Members may introduce or maintain sanitary or phytosanitary measures which result in a higher level of sanitary or phytosanitary protection than would be achieved by measures based on the relevant international standards, guidelines or recommendations, if there is a scientific justification, or as a consequence of the level of sanitary or phytosanitary protection a Member determines to be appropriate in accordance with the relevant provisions of paragraphs 1 through 8 of Article 5.[2] Notwithstanding the above, all measures which result in a level of sanitary or phytosanitary protection different from that which would be achieved by measures based on international standards, guidelines or recommendations shall not be inconsistent with any other provision of this Agreement. . . .

Article 5

Assessment of Risk and Determination of the Appropriate Level of Sanitary or Phytosanitary Protection

1. Members shall ensure that their sanitary or phytosanitary measures are based on an assessment, as appropriate to the circumstances, of the risks to human, animal or plant life or health, taking into account risk

---

2. For the purposes of paragraph 3 of Article 3, there is a scientific justification if, on the basis of an examination and evaluation of available scientific information in conformity with the relevant provisions of this Agreement, a Member determines that the relevant international standards, guidelines or recommendations are not sufficient to achieve its appropriate level of sanitary or phytosanitary protection.

assessment techniques developed by the relevant international organizations.

2.   In the assessment of risks, Members shall take into account available scientific evidence; relevant processes and production methods; relevant inspection, sampling and testing methods; prevalence of specific diseases or pests; existence of pest-or disease-free areas; relevant ecological and environmental conditions; and quarantine or other treatment....

4.   Members should, when determining the appropriate level of sanitary or phytosanitary protection, take into account the objective of minimizing negative trade effects.

5.   With the objective of achieving consistency in the application of the concept of appropriate level of sanitary or phytosanitary protection against risks to human life or health, or to animal and plant life or health, each Member shall avoid arbitrary or unjustifiable distinctions in the levels it considers to be appropriate in different situations, if such distinctions result in discrimination or a disguised restriction on international trade....

6.   Without prejudice to paragraph 2 of Article 3, when establishing or maintaining sanitary or phytosanitary measures to achieve the appropriate level of sanitary or phytosanitary protection, Members shall ensure that such measures are not more trade-restrictive than required to achieve their appropriate level of sanitary or phytosanitary protection, taking into account technical and economic feasibility.[3]

7.   In cases where relevant scientific evidence is insufficient, a Member may provisionally adopt sanitary or phytosanitary measures on the basis of available pertinent information, including that from the relevant international organizations as well as from sanitary or phytosanitary measures applied by other Members. In such circumstances, Members shall seek to obtain the additional information necessary for a more objective assessment of risk and review the sanitary or phytosanitary measure accordingly within a reasonable period of time....

The definitions are in Annex A of the SPS Agreement.

ANNEX A

DEFINITIONS[1]

1.   *Sanitary or phytosanitary measure*—Any measure applied:

(a) to protect animal or plant life or health within the territory of the Member from risks arising from the entry, establishment or spread

---

3. For purposes of paragraph 6 of Article 5, a measure is not more trade-restrictive than required unless there is another measure, reasonably available taking into account technical and economic feasibility, that achieves the appropriate level of sanitary or phytosanitary protection and is significantly less restrictive to trade.

1. For the purpose of these definitions, "animal" includes fish and wild fauna; "plant" includes forests and wild flora; "pests" include weeds; and "contaminants" include pesticide and veterinary drug residues and extraneous matter.

of pests, diseases, disease-carrying organisms or disease-causing organisms;

(b) to protect human or animal life or health within the territory of the Member from risks arising from additives, contaminants, toxins or disease-causing organisms in foods, beverages or feedstuffs;

(c) to protect human life or health within the territory of the Member from risks arising from diseases carried by animals, plants or products thereof, or from the entry, establishment or spread of pests; or

(d) to prevent or limit other damage within the territory of the Member from the entry, establishment or spread of pests.

Sanitary or phytosanitary measures include all relevant laws, decrees, regulations, requirements and procedures including, inter alia, end product criteria; processes and production methods; testing, inspection, certification and approval procedures; quarantine treatments including relevant requirements associated with the transport of animals or plants, or with the materials necessary for their survival during transport; provisions on relevant statistical methods, sampling procedures and methods of risk assessment; and packaging and labelling requirements directly related to food safety. . . .

4. *Risk assessment*—The evaluation of the likelihood of entry, establishment or spread of a pest or disease within the territory of an importing Member according to the sanitary or phytosanitary measures which might be applied, and of the associated potential biological and economic consequences; or the evaluation of the potential for adverse effects on human or animal health arising from the presence of additives, contaminants, toxins or disease-causing organisms in food, beverages or feedstuffs.

5. *Appropriate level of sanitary or phytosanitary protection*—The level of protection deemed appropriate by the Member establishing a sanitary or phytosanitary measure to protect human, animal or plant life or health within its territory.

NOTE: Many Members otherwise refer to this concept as the "acceptable level of risk."

The Case

Technically two panels were created to hear the two cases, but the same persons constituted the panels in both cases, so they are usually referred to as "the panel." The panel concluded that the EC had violated the SPS Agreement in several ways. Simplifying somewhat, first, the panel found that the EC ban on the importation of meat and meat products from cattle which had been fed certain natural or synthetic hormones for growth hormone purposes was not "based" on an international standard, and the EC had not carried the burden of proof under Article 3.3 for a standard not based on an international standard. Second, the panel found that the EC had violated Article 5.1 by adopting a measure that was not based on a risk assessment. Moreover, the panel rejected the EC's claim that its measure was justified under Article 5.7 as an exercise of the precautionary principle. The EC appealed to the Appellate Body.

On the first issue, the panel had concluded that to "base" a measure on an international standard, as required in Article 3.1, meant the same as having a measure "conform" to an international standard as required in Article 3.2 in order to be deemed necessary and consistent with the SPS Agreement. Under this analysis, Article 3.3 was an exception to the requirement that otherwise all measures had to conform to—be the same as—an international standard. As an exception, the person invoking the exception would have the burden of proving compliance with it. The Appellate Body rejected this interpretation. It read Articles 3.1, 3.2, and 3.3 as all having independent significance. A measure could be based on an international standard without being the same as an international standard. If it was the same as an international standard, there was a rebuttable presumption that it was necessary and consistent with the SPS Agreement. If it was not based on an international standard, then the measure would have to meet the requirements of Article 3.3, but there was no shift in the burden of proof.

On the second issue, however, the Appellate Body upheld the ultimate conclusion of the panel, that the EC had violated Article 5.1, although it did not accept all the intermediate conclusions of the panel. To provide an exposure to an actual DSB report, the following is an edited version of the Appellate Body's discussion of the issue.

XI.   The Reading of Articles 5.1 and 5.2 of the SPS Agreement: Basing SPS Measures on a Risk Assessment

178.   We turn to the appeal of European Communities from the Panel's conclusion that, by maintaining SPS measures which are not based on a risk assessment, the European Communities acted inconsistently with the requirements contained in Article 5.1 of the SPS Agreement.

179.   Article 5.1 of the SPS Agreement provides:

> Members shall ensure that their sanitary or phytosanitary measures are based on an assessment, as appropriate to the circumstances, of the risks to human, animal or plant life or health, taking into account risk assessment techniques developed by the relevant international organizations. (underlining added)

A.   The Interpretation of "Risk Assessment"

180.   At the outset, two preliminary considerations need to be brought out. The first is that the Panel considered that Article 5.1 may be viewed as a specific application of the basic obligations contained in Article 2.2 of the SPS Agreement, which reads as follows:

> Members shall ensure that any sanitary or phytosanitary measure is applied only to the extent necessary to protect human, animal or plant life or health, is based on scientific principles and is not maintained without sufficient scientific evidence, except as provided for in paragraph 7 of Article 5. (underlining added)

We agree with this general consideration and would also stress that Articles 2.2 and 5.1 should constantly be read together. Article 2.2 informs Article 5.1: the elements that define the basic obligation set out in Article 2.2 impart meaning to Article 5.1.

181.   The second preliminary consideration relates to the Panel's effort to distinguish between "risk assessment" and "risk management." The Panel observed that an assessment of risk is, at least with respect to risks to human life and health, a "scientific" examination of data and factual studies; it is not, in the view of the Panel, a "policy" exercise involving social value judgments made by political bodies. The Panel describes the latter as "non-scientific" and as pertaining to "risk management" rather than to "risk assessment." We must stress, in this connection, that Article 5 and Annex A of the SPS Agreement speak of "risk assessment" only and that the term "risk management" is not to be found either in Article 5 or in any other provision of the SPS Agreement. Thus, the Panel's distinction, which it apparently employs to achieve or support what appears to be a restrictive notion of risk assessment, has no textual basis. The fundamental rule of treaty interpretation requires a treaty interpreter to read and interpret the words actually used by the agreement under examination, and not words which the interpreter may feel should have been used.

   1.   *Risk Assessment and the Notion of "Risk"*

182.   Paragraph 4 of Annex A of the SPS Agreement sets out the treaty definition of risk assessment: This definition, to the extent pertinent to the present appeal, speaks of:

> . . . the evaluation of the <u>potential for adverse effects on human</u> or animal <u>health</u> arising from the presence of additives, contaminants, toxins or disease-causing organisms in food, beverages or feedstuffs. (underlining added)

183.   Interpreting the above definition, the Panel elaborates risk assessment as a two-step process that "should (i) *identify the adverse effects* on human health (if any) arising from the presence of the hormones at issue when used as growth promoters *in meat* . . . , and (ii) if any such adverse effects exist, *evaluate* the *potential* or probability of occurrence of such effects."

184.   The European Communities appeals from the above interpretation as involving an erroneous notion of risk and risk assessment. Although the utility of a two-step analysis may be debated, it does not appear to us to be substantially wrong. What needs to be pointed out at this stage is that the Panel's use of "probability" as an alternative term for "potential" creates a significant concern. The ordinary meaning of "potential" relates to "possibility" and is different from the ordinary meaning of "probability." "Probability" implies a higher degree or a threshold of potentiality or possibility. It thus appears that here the Panel introduces a quantitative dimension to the notion of risk.

185.   In its discussion on a statement made by Dr. Lucier at the joint meeting with the experts in February 1997, the Panel states the risk referred to by this expert is an estimate which " ... only represents a statistical range of 0 to 1 in a million, not a scientifically identified risk." The European Communities protests vigorously that, by doing so, the Panel is in effect requiring a Member carrying out a risk assessment to quantify the potential for adverse effects on human health.

186.   It is not clear in what sense the Panel uses the term "scientifically identified risk." The Panel also frequently uses the term "identifiable risk," and does not define this term either. The Panel might arguably have used the terms "scientifically identified risk" and "identifiable risk" simply to refer to an ascertainable risk: if a risk is not ascertainable, how does a Member ever know or demonstrate that it exists? In one part of its Reports, the Panel opposes a requirement of an "identifiable risk" to the uncertainty that theoretically always remains since science can never provide absolute certainty that a given substance will not ever have adverse health effects. We agree with the Panel that this theoretical uncertainty is not the kind of risk which, under Article 5.1, is to be assessed. In another part of its Reports, however, the Panel appeared to be using the term "scientifically identified risk" to prescribe implicitly that a certain magnitude or threshold level of risk be demonstrated in a risk assessment if an SPS measure based thereon is to be regarded as consistent with Article 5.1. To the extent that the Panel purported to require a risk assessment to establish a minimum magnitude of risk, we must note that imposition of such a quantitative requirement finds no basis in the SPS Agreement. A panel is authorized only to determine whether a given SPS measure is "based on" a risk assessment. As will be elaborated below, this means that a panel has to determine whether an SPS measure is sufficiently supported or reasonably warranted by the risk assessment.

2.   Factors to be Considered in Carrying Out a Risk Assessment

187.   Article 5.2 of the SPS Agreement provides an indication of the factors that should be taken into account in the assessment of risk. Article 5.2 states that:

> In the assessment of risks, Members shall take into account available scientific evidence; relevant processes and production methods; relevant inspection, sampling and testing methods; prevalence of specific diseases or pests; existence of pest-or disease-free areas; relevant ecological and environmental conditions; and quarantine or other treatment.

The listing in Article 5.2 begins with "available scientific evidence"; this, however, is only the beginning. We note in this connection that the Panel states that, for purposes of the EC measures in dispute, a risk assessment required by Article 5.1 is "a scientific process aimed at establishing the scientific basis for the sanitary measure a Member intends to take." To the extent that the Panel intended to refer to a process characterized by systematic, disciplined and objective enquiry and analysis, that is, a mode of studying and sorting out facts and opinions, the Panel's statement is unexceptionable. However, to the extent that the Panel purports to exclude from the scope of a risk assessment in the sense of Article 5.1, all matters not susceptible of quantitative analysis by the empirical or experimental laboratory methods commonly associated with the physical sciences, we believe that the Panel is in error. Some of the kinds of factors listed in Article 5.2 such as "relevant processes and production methods" and "relevant inspection, sampling and testing methods" are not necessarily or wholly susceptible of investigation according to laboratory methods of, for example, biochemistry or pharmacology. Furthermore, there is nothing to indicate that the listing of factors that may be taken into account in a risk assessment of Article 5.2 was intended to be a closed list. It is essential to bear in mind that the risk that is to be evaluated in a risk assessment under Article 5.1 is not only risk ascertainable in a science laboratory operating under strictly controlled conditions, but also risk in human societies as they actually exist, in other words, the actual potential for adverse effects on human health in the real world where people live and work and die.

B. The Interpretation of "Based On"

1. A "Minimum Procedural Requirement" in Article 5.1?

188. Although it expressly recognizes that Article 5.1 does not contain any specific procedural requirements for a Member to base its sanitary measures on a risk assessment, the Panel nevertheless proceeds to declare that "there is a minimum procedural requirement contained in Article 5.1." That requirement is that "the Member imposing a sanitary measure needs to submit evidence that at least it actually *took into account* a risk assessment when it enacted or maintained its sanitary measure in order for that measure to be considered as based on a risk assessment." The Panel goes on to state that the European Communities did not provide any evidence that the studies it referred to or the scientific conclusions reached therein *"have actually been taken into account by the competent EC institutions* either when it *enacted* those measures (in 1981 and 1988) or *at any later point in time."* (emphasis added) Thereupon, the Panel holds that such studies could not be considered as part of a risk assessment on which the European Communities based its measures in dispute. Concluding that the European Communities had not met its burden of proving that it had satisfied the "minimum procedural requirement" it had found in Article 5.1, the Panel holds the EC measures as inconsistent with the requirements of Article 5.1.

189. We are bound to note that, as the Panel itself acknowledges, no textual basis exists in Article 5 of the SPS Agreement for such a "minimum procedural requirement." The term "based on," when applied as a "minimum procedural requirement" by the Panel, may be seen to refer to a human action, such as particular human individuals "taking into account" a document described as a risk assessment. Thus,

"take into account" is apparently used by the Panel to refer to some subjectivity which, at some time, may be present in particular individuals but that, in the end, may be totally rejected by those individuals. We believe that "based on" is appropriately taken to refer to a certain objective relationship between two elements, that is to say, to an objective situation that persists and is observable between an SPS measure and a risk assessment. Such a reference is certainly embraced in the ordinary meaning of the words "based on" and, when considered in context and in the light of the object and purpose of Article 5.1 of the SPS Agreement, may be seen to be more appropriate than "taking into account." We do not share the Panel's interpretative construction and believe it is unnecessary and an error of law as well. . . .

    2. Substantive Requirement of Article 5.1—Rational Relationship Between an SPS Measure and a Risk Assessment

192. Having posited a "minimum procedural requirement" of Article 5.1, the Panel turns to the "substantive requirements" of Article 5.1 to determine whether the EC measures at issue are "based on" a risk assessment. In the Panel's view, those "substantive requirements" involve two kinds of operations: first, identifying the scientific conclusions reached in the risk assessment and the scientific conclusions implicit in the SPS measures; and secondly, examining those scientific conclusions to determine whether or not one set of conclusions matches, i.e. conforms with, the second set of conclusions. Applying the "substantive requirements" it finds in Article 5.1, the Panel holds that the scientific conclusions implicit in the EC measures do not conform with any of the scientific conclusions reached in the scientific studies the European Communities had submitted as evidence.

193. We consider that, in principle, the Panel's approach of examining the scientific conclusions implicit in the SPS measure under consideration and the scientific conclusion yielded by a risk assessment is a useful approach. The relationship between those two sets of conclusions is certainly relevant; they cannot, however, be assigned relevance to the exclusion of everything else. We believe that Article 5.1, when contextually read as it should be, in conjunction with and as informed by Article 2.2 of the SPS Agreement, requires that the results of the risk assessment must sufficiently warrant—that is to say, reasonably support—the SPS measure at stake. The requirement that an SPS measure be "based on" a risk assessment is a substantive requirement that there be a rational relationship between the measure and the risk assessment. . . .

195. We turn now to the application by the Panel of the substantive requirements of Article 5.1 to the EC measures at stake in the present case. . . .

196. Several of the . . . scientific reports appeared to the Panel to meet the minimum requirements of a risk assessment. . . . The Panel assumes accordingly that the European Communities had demonstrated the existence of a risk assessment carried out in accordance with Article 5 of the SPS Agreement. At the same time, the Panel finds that the conclusion of

these scientific reports is that the use of the hormones at issue (except MGA) for growth promotion purposes is "safe." The Panel states:

> ... none of the scientific evidence referred to by the European Communities which specifically addresses the safety of some or all of the hormones in dispute when used for growth promotion, indicates that an identifiable risk arises for human health from such use of these hormones if good practice is followed. All of the scientific studies outlined above came to the conclusion that the use of the hormones at issue (all but MGA, for which no evidence was submitted) for growth promotion purposes is safe; most of these studies adding that this conclusion assumes that good practice is followed.

197. Prescinding from the difficulty raised by the Panel's use of the term "identifiable risk," we agree that the scientific reports listed above do not rationally support the EC import prohibition.

198. With regard to the scientific opinion expressed by Dr. Lucier at the joint meeting with the experts, ... we should note that this opinion by Dr. Lucier does not purport to be the result of scientific studies carried out by him or under his supervision focusing specifically on residues of hormones in meat from cattle fattened with such hormones. Accordingly, it appears that the single divergent opinion expressed by Dr. Lucier is not reasonably sufficient to overturn the contrary conclusions reached in the scientific studies referred to by the European Communities that related specifically to residues of the hormones in meat from cattle to which hormones had been administered for growth promotion.

199. The European Communities laid particular emphasis on the 1987 IARC Monographs and the articles and opinions of individual scientists referred to above. The Panel notes, however, that the scientific evidence set out in these Monographs and these articles and opinions relates to the carcinogenic potential of entire categories of hormones, or of the hormones at issue in general. The Monographs and the articles and opinions are, in other words, in the nature of general studies of or statements on the carcinogenic potential of the named hormones. The Monographs and the articles and opinions of individual scientists have not evaluated the carcinogenic potential of those hormones when used specifically *for growth promotion purposes*. Moreover, they do not evaluate the specific potential for carcinogenic effects arising from the presence in *"food,"* more specifically, "meat or meat products" of residues of the hormones in dispute. The Panel also notes that, according to the scientific experts advising the Panel, the data and studies set out in these 1987 Monographs have been taken into account in the 1988 and 1989 JECFA Reports and that the conclusions reached by the 1987 IARC Monographs are complementary to, rather than contradictory of, the conclusions of the JECFA Reports. The Panel concludes that these Monographs and these articles and opinions are insufficient to support the EC measures at issue in this case.

200. We believe that the above findings of the Panel are justified. The 1987 IARC Monographs and the articles and opinions of individual scientists submitted by the European Communities constitute general studies which do indeed show the existence of a general risk of cancer; but they do not focus on and do not address the particular kind of risk here at stake—the carcinogenic or genotoxic potential of the residues of those hormones found in meat derived from cattle to which the hormones had been administered for growth promotion purposes—as is required by paragraph 4 of Annex A of the SPS Agreement. Those general studies, are in other words, relevant but do not appear to be sufficiently specific to the case at hand. . . .

209. Since we have concluded above that an SPS measure, to be consistent with Article 3.3, has to comply with, inter alia, the requirements contained in Article 5.1, it follows that the EC measures at issue, by failing to comply with Article 5.1, are also inconsistent with Article 3.3 of the SPS Agreement.

On the third issue, the applicability of Article 5.7 and the precautionary principle, the Appellate Body had this to say:

VI. The Relevance of the Precautionary Principle in the Interpretation of the SPS Agreement

120. We are asked by the European Communities to reverse the finding of the Panel relating to the precautionary principle. The Panel's finding and its supporting statements are set out in the Panel Reports in the following terms:

> The European Communities also invokes the precautionary principle in support of its claim that its measures in dispute are based on a risk assessment. To the extent that this principle could be considered as part of customary international law and be used to interpret Articles 5.1 and 5.2 on the assessment of risks as a customary rule of interpretation of public international law (as that phrase is used in Article 3.2 of the DSU), we consider that this principle would not override the explicit wording of Articles 5.1 and 5.2 outlined above, in particular since the precautionary principle has been incorporated and given a specific meaning in Article 5.7 of the SPS Agreement. We note, however, that the European Communities has explicitly stated in this case that it is not invoking Article 5.7.

> We thus find that the precautionary principle cannot override our findings made above, namely that the EC import ban of meat and meat products from animals treated with any of the five hormones at issue for growth promotion purposes, in so far as it also applies to meat and meat products from animals treated with any of these hormones in accordance with good practice, is, from a substantive point of view, not based on a risk assessment. (underlining added)

121. The basic submission of the European Communities is that the precautionary principle is, or has become, "a general customary rule of international law" or at least "a general principle of law." Referring more specifically to Articles 5.1 and 5.2 of the SPS Agreement, applying the precautionary principle means, in the view of the European Communities, that it is not necessary for all scientists around the world to agree on the "possibility and magnitude" of the risk, nor for all or most of the WTO Members to perceive and evaluate the risk in the same way. It is also stressed that Articles 5.1 and 5.2 do not prescribe a particular type of risk assessment and do not prevent Members from being cautious in their risk assessment exercise. The European Communities goes on to state that its measures here at stake were precautionary in nature and satisfied the requirements of Articles 2.2 and 2.3, as well as of Articles 5.1, 5.2, 5.4, 5.5 and 5.6 of the SPS Agreement.

122. The United States does not consider that the "precautionary principle" represents customary international law and suggests it is more an "approach" than a "principle." Canada, too, takes the view that the precautionary principle has not yet been incorporated into the corpus of public international law; however, it concedes that the "precautionary approach" or "concept" is "an emerging principle of law" which may in the future crystallize into one of the "general principles of law recognized by civilized nations" within the meaning of Article 38(1)(c) of the Statute of the International Court of Justice.

123. The status of the precautionary principle in international law continues to be the subject of debate among academics, law practitioners, regulators and judges. The precautionary principle is regarded by some as having crystallized into a general principle of customary international environmental law. Whether it has been widely accepted by Members as a principle of general or customary international law appears less than clear. We consider, however, that it is unnecessary, and probably imprudent, for the Appellate Body in this appeal to take a position on this important, but abstract, question. We note that the Panel itself did not make any definitive finding with regard to the status of the precautionary principle in international law and that the precautionary principle, at least outside the field of international environmental law, still awaits authoritative formulation.

124. It appears to us important, nevertheless, to note some aspects of the relationship of the precautionary principle to the SPS Agreement. First, the principle has not been written into the SPS Agreement as a ground for justifying SPS measures that are otherwise inconsistent with the obligations of Members set out in particular provisions of that Agreement. Secondly, the precautionary principle indeed finds reflection in Article 5.7 of the SPS Agreement. We agree, at the same time, with the European Communities, that there is no need to assume that Article 5.7 exhausts the relevance of a precautionary principle. It is reflected also in the sixth paragraph of the preamble and in Article 3.3. These explicitly recognize the right of Members to establish their own appropriate level of sanitary protection, which level may be higher (i.e., more

cautious) than that implied in existing international standards, guidelines and recommendations. Thirdly, a panel charged with determining, for instance, whether "sufficient scientific evidence" exists to warrant the maintenance by a Member of a particular SPS measure may, of course, and should, bear in mind that responsible, representative governments commonly act from perspectives of prudence and precaution where risks of irreversible, e.g. life-terminating, damage to human health are concerned. Lastly, however, the precautionary principle does not, by itself, and without a clear textual directive to that effect, relieve a panel from the duty of applying the normal (i.e. customary international law) principles of treaty interpretation in reading the provisions of the SPS Agreement.

125. We accordingly agree with the finding of the Panel that the precautionary principle does not override the provisions of Articles 5.1 and 5.2 of the SPS Agreement.

Notes and Questions

1.　The Panel required a risk assessment to be the basis of a measure, in the sense that the member actually considered the risk assessment in deciding to impose the measure. The Appellate Body rejects this requirement. Why? Does this mean that a member might impose a measure on no basis at all but then when challenged sustain the measure if it can then dig up sufficient support for it?

2.　What exactly was the problem with the EC's data in terms of a risk assessment?

3.　If the precautionary principle "indeed finds reflection in Article 5.7," how is it that the EC loses on its claim that its ban is based on the precautionary principle?

4.　As related above, the United States and Canada prevailed in its challenge to the EC's ban on meat from cattle receiving growth hormones. But what happened? As described by the WTO:

> On 8 April, 1998, the EC requested that the "reasonable period of time" for implementation of the recommendations and rulings of the DSB be determined by binding arbitration, pursuant to Article 21.3(c) of the DSU. The Arbitrator found the reasonable period of time for implementation to be 15 months from the date of adoption (i.e. 15 months from 13 February 1998). The report of the Arbitrator was circulated to Members on 29 May 1998.

> The period for implementation . . . expired on 13 May 1999. The EC undertook to comply with the recommendations of the DSB within the implementation period. At the DSB meeting on 28 April 1999, the EC informed the DSB that it would consider offering compensation in view of the likelihood that it may not be able to comply with the recommendations and rulings of the DSB by the deadline of 13 May 1999.

> On 3 June 1999, the United States and Canada, pursuant to Article 22.2 of the DSU, requested authorization from the DSB for the suspension of concessions to the EC in the amount of US$202 million and

Can.$75 million, respectively. The EC, pursuant to Article 22.6 of the DSU, requested arbitration on the level of suspension of concessions requested by the United States and Canada. The DSB referred the issue of the level of suspension to the original panel for arbitration.

The arbitrators determined the level of nullification suffered by the United States to be equal to US$116.8 million, and the level of nullification suffered by Canada to be equal to CDN$11.3 million. The report of the arbitrators was circulated to Members on 12 July 1999. At its meeting on 26 July 1999, the DSB authorized the suspension of concessions to the EC by the United States and Canada in the respective amounts determined by the arbitrators as being equivalent to the level of nullification suffered by them.

At the DSB meeting on 7 November 2003, the EC stated that following the entering into force of its new Directive (2003/74/EC) regarding the prohibition on the use in stockfarming of certain hormones, there was no legal basis for the continued imposition of retaliatory measures by Canada and the US; one of the reasons cited by the Appellate Body in its ruling against the EC was its failure to carry out a risk assessment within the meaning of Articles 5.1 and 5.2 of the SPS Agreement; and, having commissioned such an assessment to be undertaken on its behalf by an independent scientific committee whose findings indicated that the hormones in question posed a risk for consumers, the EC had fulfilled its WTO obligations and was entitled to demand the immediate lifting of the sanctions imposed by Canada and the US in accordance with the provisions of Article 22.8 of the DSU. The US stated that they had carefully reviewed the new EC Directive and did not share the view that it implemented the recommendations and rulings of the DSB. The new measure lacked any scientific basis and as such could not be justified under the SPS Agreement. Contrary to the EC's claim, a number of studies had found that there was no increased health risk from the consumption of meat from animals treated with growth-promoting hormones. In the circumstances, the US was not in a position to accede to the request by the EC. Canada said that while his country was prepared to discuss this matter further with the EC, it doubted whether the new studies presented any new scientific basis for the ban of hormone-treated beef, and was also not in a position to accede to the request of the EC. The EC responded that on the basis of the negative position expressed by the US and Canada, it would reflect on the appropriate actions that would be necessary in order to preserve its rights under the WTO agreements.

At the DSB meeting on 1 December 2003, the EC stated that: in light of the disagreement between the parties to the dispute with regard to the EC's compliance with the DSB's recommendations, the matter should be referred to the WTO for a multilateral decision; this situation was similar to other cases, which had been resolved in the past through recourse to Article 21.5 of the DSU; Canada and the US should initiate multilateral procedures to determine whether or not the EC was in compliance; the EC stood ready to discuss this matter with Canada and the United States. Canada stated that, although at the 7 November DSB meeting, Canada had put forward a suggestion for bilateral discussions concerning the justification for the EC's position regarding its compliance with the WTO ruling, the EC had not responded to this suggestion; it was up to the EC to establish that it had complied with the WTO ruling; Canada continued to be open to discussions with the EC regarding its justification for its position; at this stage, Canada did not see any basis for removal of its retaliatory measures nor wished to take any other action. The US stated that: the US failed to see how the revised EC measure could be considered to implement the DSB's recommendations; with regard to the EC's suggestion that multilateral proceedings be established to determine whether or not the EC was in compliance with the WTO rulings, the US was ready to discuss this matter along with other outstanding issues in relation to the EC's ban on US beef.

On 8 November 2004, the European Communities filed a request for consultations with the United States asserting that the United States should have removed its retaliatory measures since the EC has removed the measures found to be WTO-inconsistent in the EC—Hormones case.

The issues which the EC intends to raise in the consultations include, but are not limited to:

* the failure by the United States to remove the retaliatory measures despite the EC's removal of the WTO-inconsistent measures;

* the unilateral determinations by the United States that the new EC legislation is a continued WTO violation; and

* the failure of the United States to follow DSU Article 21.5 dispute settlement procedures to adjudicate the matter.

The EC considers that the continued use by the United States and of retaliatory measures in this case, in the current circumstances, are violations of Articles I and II of GATT 1994, and Articles 21.5, 22.8, 23.1 and 23.2 (a) and (c) of the DSU.

On 17 November 2004, Canada requested to join the consultations. On 19 November 2004, Australia and Mexico requested to join the consultations. On 16 December 2004, the United States informed the DSB that it had accepted the request of Canada to join the consultations.

On 13 January 2005, the European Communities requested the establishment of a panel. At its meeting on 25 January 2005, the DSB deferred the establishment of a panel. At its meeting on 17 February 2005, the DSB established a panel. Australia, Canada, China, Mexico and Chinese Taipei reserved their third-party rights. On 23 February 2005, Norway reserved its third party rights. On 25 February 2005, Brazil reserved its third party rights. On 28 February 2005, India and New Zealand reserved their third party rights. On 27 May 2005, the European Communities requested the Director General to compose the panel. On 6 June 2005, the Director–General composed the panel. The first substantive meeting of the Panel with the parties took place on 12–15 September 2005, which was open for observation by the public.

On 20 January 2006, the Chairman of the Panel informed the DSB that due to the complexity of the dispute, and the administrative and procedural matters involved, the panel would not be able to complete its work in six months. Based on the current assessment of the process, the panel expects to issue its final report to the parties in the course of October 2006.

As of this writing, the panel has not issued its final report, which, of course, when it is rendered will be appealed. In other words, the EC continues its ban more than ten years after the United States' first complaint, and the controversy continues. Remember what ultimately happened with respect to the United States' loss in the tuna/dolphin and shrimp/turtle cases. Does this suggest some slippage between the theory and practice of free trade under the WTO?

Glossary of Acronyms

AAPCC: American Association of Poison Control Centers
AAU: Assigned Amount Units
ADA: Americans with Disabilities Act
AEC: Atomic Energy Commission
ADEC: Alaska Department of Environmental Conservation
AID: Agency for Internal Development
ALJ: Administrative Law Judge
AMC: American Mining Congress
AOSIS: Association of Small Island States
AOU: American Ornithological Union
APA: Administrative Procedure Act
API: American Petroleum Institute
ARAR: Applicable or Relevant and Appropriate Requirement
ASCS: Agricultural Stabilization and Conservation Service
ASTM: American Society for Testing and Materials

BA: Biological Assessment
BACT: Best Available Control Technology
BADT: Best Available Demonstrated Control Technology
BART: Best Available Retrofit Technology
BAT: Best Available Control Technology that is Economically Achievable
BDAT: Best Demonstrated Available Technology
BEN: Economic Benefit
BiOp: Biological Opinion
BLM: Bureau of Land Management
BMP: Best Management Practice
BO: Biological Opinion
BOD: Biochemical Oxygen Demand
BPJ: Best Professional Judgment
BPT: Best Practicable Control Technology
BTU: British Thermal Unit

CAA: Clean Air Act
CAFO: Concentrated Animal Feeding Operation
CAIR: Clean Air Interstate Rule
CBE: Citizens for a Better Environment
CCD: Convention to Combat Desertification
CDM: Clean Development Mechanism
CEGs: Conditionally-Exempt Generators
CEQ: Council on Environmental Quality
CEQA: California Environmental Quality Act
CER: Certified Emissions Reduction

CERCLA:	Comprehensive Environmental Response, Compensation, and Liability Act
CFC:	Chlorofluorocarbon
CITES:	Convention on International Trade in Endangered Species of Wild Flora and Fauna
CJO:	Chief Judicial Officer
CMA:	Chemical Manufacturers Association
CO:	Carbon Monoxide
CO_2:	Carbon Dioxide
COP:	Conference of the Parties
CSO:	Combined Sewer Overflow
CTE:	Committee on Trade and the Environment
CWA:	Clean Water Act
CZMA:	Coastal Zone Management Act
DEIS:	Draft Environmental Impact Statement
DOH:	Department of Health
DMC:	*de minimis* classification
DMLR:	Division of Mined Land Reclamation
DMR:	Discharge Monitoring Report
DPS:	Distinct Population Segment
DSB:	Dispute Settlement Body
DSU:	Dispute Settlement Understanding
EA:	Environmental Assessment
EC:	European Community
ECHO:	Expanded Characteristic Option
ECOWAS:	Economic Community of West African States
EDF:	Environmental Defense Fund
EEC:	European Economic Community
EGU:	Electric Generating Unit
EIS:	Environmenta Impact Statement
ELR:	Environmental Law Reporter
EMS:	Environmental Management Systems
EPA:	Environmental Protection Agency
EPCRA:	Emergency Planning and Community Right-to-know Act
EPD:	Environmental Protection Division
ERP:	Equipment Replacement Provision
ERU:	Emission Reduction Units
ESA:	Endangered Species Act
ESECA:	Energy Supply and Environmental Coordination Act
ESU:	Evolutionary Significant Unit
ETP:	Eastern Tropical Pacific Ocean
EU:	European Union
EU-ETS:	European Union—Emissions Trading System
FAA:	Federal Aviation Administration
FDF:	Fundamentally Different Factors

FEC: Federal Election Commission
FEIS: Final Environmental Impact Statement
FERC: Federal Energy Regulatory Commission
FESOPP: Federally Enforceable State Operating Permit Program
FHAA: Fair Housing amendments Act
FHWA: Federal Highway Administration
FIFRA: Federal Insecticide, Fungicide, and Rodenticide Act
FIP: Federal Implementation Plan
FLPMA: Federal Land Policy and Management Act
FONSI: Finding of no Significant Impact
FPC: Federal Power Commission
FR: Federal Register
FSA: Farm Service Agency
FWPCA: Federal Water Pollution Control Act
FWS: Fish and Wildlife Service
FY: Fiscal Year

GACT: Generally Available Control Technologies
GAO: General Accounting Office
GATT: General Agreement on Tariffs and Trade
GDP: Gross Domestic Product
GHG: Greenhouse Gas
GPM: Grams Per Mile
GVWR: Gross Vehicle Weight Rating

HAP: Hazardous Air Pollutant
HC: Hydrocarbons
HCP: Habitat Conservation Plan
HDE: Heavy-Duty Engines
HFC: Hydrofluorocarbon
HNO_3:   Nitric Acid
HRS: Hazard Ranking System
HSWA: Hazardous and Solid Waste Amendments

ICJ: International Court of Justice
IG: Inspector General
IJC: International Joint Commission
I/M: Inspection and Maintenance
IPCC: Intergovernmental Panel on Climate Change
IPM: Integrated Planning Model
IRC: Internal Revenue Code
ISC: Interagency Scientific Committee
ITS: Incidental Take Statement

JI: Joint Implementation

LAER: Lowest Achievable Emission Rate
LDT: Light-Duty Trucks

LDV:	Light-Duty Vehicles
LLC:	Limited Liability Company
LOP:	Letters of Permission
LULUCF:	Land Use, Land–Use Change and Forestry
LULUs:	Locally Unwanted Land Uses
LVW:	Loaded Vehicle Weight
MACT:	Maximum Achievable Control Technology
MEA:	Multilateral Environmental Agreements
MIR:	Maximum Individual Risk
MMBtu:	Pounds of NO_x emitted per million BTU burned
MMPA:	Marine Mammal Protection Act of 1972
MMT:	Million Metric Tons
MOA:	Memorandum of Agreement
MOP:	Meeting of the Parties
MOU:	Memorandum of Understanding
MP:	Major Party
MPG:	Miles Per Gallon
MY:	Model Year
N:	Nitrogen
NAAQS:	National Ambient Air Quality Standards
NAFTA:	North American Free Trade Agreement
NAHB:	National Association of Home Builders
NAMF:	National Association of Metal Fisheries
NAPAP:	National Acid Precipitation Assessment Program
NBAR:	Nonbinding Preliminary Allocation of Responsibility
NCP:	National Contingency Plan
NEPA:	National Environmental Policy Act
NESPHAPs:	National Emission Standards for Hazardous Air Pollutants
NGO:	Non-Governmental Organization
NIMBY:	Not In My Back Yard
NMA:	National Mining Association
NMFS:	National Marine Fisheries Service
NNSR:	Nonattainment New Source Review
NO_2:	Nitrogen Dioxide
NO_x:	Nitrogen Oxide
NOAA:	National Oceanic and Atmospheric Administration
NOAEL:	No Observable Adverse Effect Level
NOD:	Notice Of Deficiency
NOEL:	No Observable Effect Level
NOV:	Notices of Violation
NPDES:	National Pollution Discharge Elimination System
NPL:	National Priorities List
NPPD:	Nebraska Public Power District
NPS:	Nonpoint Source
NRCS:	National Resources Conservation Service

NRDC: National Resources Defense Council
NSPS: New Source Performance Standard
NSR: New Source Review
NWF: National Wildlife Federation
NWP: Nationwide Permit

O_3:   Ozone
OIG: Office of Inspector General
OIRA: Office of Information and Regulatory Affairs
OMB: Office of Management and Budget
ONDA: Oregon National Desert Association
OPEC: Organization of the Petroleum Exporting Countries
OSM: Office of Surface Mining
OSMRE: Office of Surface Mining Reclamation and Enforcement

PA/SI: Preliminary Assessment and Site Investigation
PCB: Polychlorinated Biphenyl
PCN: Preconstruction Notification
PECE: Policy for Evaluation of Conservation Efforts
PFC: Perfluorocarbons
pH: Measure of the acidity of a solution in terms of activity of hydrogen
PIRG: Public Interest Research Group
PM: Particle Matter
POTW: Publicly Owned Treatment Work
PPA: Prospective Purchaser Agreement
PPM: Parts Per Million
PPM: Processes And Production Methods
PRP: Potentially Responsible Party
PSD: Prevention of Significant Deterioration
PUD: Public Utility District
PWO: Public Welfare Offense

QELRO: Quantifiable Emission Limitation and Reduction Objectives

RACT: Reasonably Available Control Technology
RCRA: Resource Conservation Recovery Act
RD/RA: Remedial Design/Remedial Action
RGGI: Regional Green House Gas Initiative
RHA: Rivers and Harbors Appropriation Act
RI/FS: Remedial Investigation and Feasibility Study
RMRR: Routine Maintenance, Repair, and Replacement
RMU: Removal Unit
RPM: Engine Speed, in Revolutions Per Minute
RRAM: Routine Repair and Maintenance

SARA: Superfund Amendments and Reauthorization Act
SBI: Subsidiary Body for Implementation

SBSTA:	Subsidiary Body for Scientific and Technological Advice
SBSTTA:	Subsidiary Body on Scientific, Technical and Technological Advice
SBZ:	Stream Buffer Zone
SCR:	Selective Catalytic Reduction
SEIS:	Supplementary Environmental Impact Statement
SEP:	Supplemental Environmental Project
SEQRA:	State Environmental Quality Review Act
SIC:	Standard Industrial Classification
SIPs:	State Implementation Plans
SMCRA:	Surface Mining and Reclamation Act
SO_2:	Sulfur Dioxide
SO_x:	Sulfur Oxide
SPGP:	State Programmatic General Permit
SPS:	Sanitary and Phytosanitary Measures
SQG:	Small Quantity Generator
SRLPTF:	Small Refiner Lead Phase-down Task Force
SUV:	Sport Utility Vehicle
SWANCC:	Solid Waste Agency of Northern Cook County
TBT:	Technical Barriers to Trade
TCE:	Trichloroethylene
TED:	Turtle Excluder Device
TKN:	Total Kjeldahl Nitrogen
TLCP:	Toxicity Characteristic Leachate Procedure
TMDL:	Total Maximum Daily Load
TMP:	Timber Management Plan
TPY:	Tons Per Year
TRI:	Toxic Release Inventory
TSCA:	Toxic Substances Control Act
TSD:	Treatment, Storage and Disposal Facility
TSS:	Total Suspended Solids
UAA:	Use Attainability Analysis
UN:	United Nations
UNCED:	United Nations Conference on Environment and Development
UNCLOS:	United Nations Convention on the Law of the Sea
UNEP:	United Nations Environment Programme
UNFCCC:	United Nations Framework Convention on Climate Change
USFWS:	United States Fish and Wildlife Service
USDOT:	United States Department of Transportation
UST:	Underground Storage Tank
VMT:	Vehicle Miles Traveled
VOC:	Volatile Organic Compound

WAS:	Waste Activated Sludge
WCED:	World Commission on Environment and Development
WEPCO:	Wisconsin Electric Power Company
WHITEX:	Winter Haze Intensive Tracer Experiment
WHO:	World Health Organization
WMO:	World Meteorological Organization
WQS:	Water Quality Standard
WTO:	World Trade Organization
WVDEP:	West Virginia Department of Environmental Protection
WWF:	World Wildlife Fund
XL:	EPA's Project Excel

*

Index

404(b)(1) Guidelines, Clean Water Act, 707–717

A

Ability to Pay, Penalty Calculations, 458
Acid Rain Control, Clean Air Act, 388–391
Addition of a Pollutant, Clean Water Act, 140–147, 698–705
Adler, Robert, 211–212
Administrative Adjudication, Generally, 80–81
Administrative Enforcement, 428, 443–459
Administrative Hearings, 458
Administrative Orders, 443–448, 526
Administrative Penalties, 448–459, 505, 508
Agreement on Technical Barriers to Trade, 782, 785, 799, 800–801
Agreement on the Application of Sanitary and Phytosanitary Measures, 799–816
Alternatives Analysis, NEPA, 129–130
Ambient Air Quality Criteria, 243–266
Antidegradation Policy, Clean Water Act, 189–190, 191–192, 194, 200–201, 202, 206
ARARs, CERCLA, 566, 567–568
Article II, U.S. Constitution, 499, 500–503, 504
ASTM Standards, 558–563
Attorney Fees, 508–521
Authorization, RCRA, 471
Authorization Requirements, Clean Water Act, 159–171, 475
Authorization Status, Clean Water Act, 159

B

Best Available Control Technology, Clean Air Act, 288, 336–337
Best Available Control Technology, Clean Water Act, 172, 176, 181, 182–183, 184–185, 432
Best Available Demonstrated Control Technology, Clean Water Act, 172, 183, 185

Best Available Retrofit Technology, Clean Air Act, 351–358
Best Practicable Control Technology, Clean Water Act, 172–182, 183–185, 432
Best Professional Judgment, Clean Water Act, 167–171
Brownfields, 559, 563–564
Brownfields Amendments, the, 522, 530, 558–561, 563–564
Bubble Policy, Clean Air Act, 304–313
Bush Administration, 136

C

California Environmental Quality Act, 133–134
California Mobile Source Standards, 379, 388
Cap and Trade Regulations, 7–8, 388–392
Catalyst Theory, 511–521
Categorical Exclusions, NEPA, 94–98
Causation, CERCLA, 528, 529
Causation, Standing, 484, 486–487
Characteristic Waste, RCRA, 408–410
Chevron Deference, 80–90, 141, 150, 151, 181, 203, 208, 220, 399, 400, 402–403, 540
Citizen Suits, 162, 475–521, 665, 722, 747
Civil Enforcement in Court, 429–442
Civil Penalties, 436–442, 490
Clapton, Eric, 504–505
Climate Change, 69–79, 243–252, 759–780
Closed–Loop Exception, RCRA, 398, 402
Closure Requirements, RCRA, 421–425
Command and Control Regulations, 6, 522
Commerce Clause, U.S. Constitution, 37–48
Common Law, State, 3–5
"Comparison Factors," Clean Water Act, 176–177, 181
Conditionally–Exempt Generators, RCRA, 412
Conservationism, 2–3
"Consideration Factors," Clean Water Act, 176–177, 181
Consultation, Endangered Species Act, 627–640
Contribution, CERCLA 523, 552, 579–600

Contribution Protection, CERCLA, 569, 571, 578–579
Convention on Biological Diversity, 750
Convention on International Trade in Endangered Species of Wild Flora and Fauna, 749–750, 754, 797
Convention on Long–Range Transboundary Air Pollution, 750
Cooperative Federalism, see Federal/State Relationship
Cost–Benefit Analysis, 15–20, 173–175, 567–568
Cost–Benefit Regulations, 6
Council of Environmental Quality, 92
Covenants Not to Sue, CERCLA, 569, 571
Criminal Enforcement, 428–429, 459–469, 665
Criteria Pollutants, Clean Air Act, 243–252
Critical Habitat, Endangered Species Act, 619–622

D

De Minimis Settlements, CERCLA, 552, 569–570, 572–579
Defenses, CERCLA, 528, 530, 556–563
Derived From Rule, RCRA, 410, 411
Design Standards, 7
Designated Uses, Clean Water Act, 187–189, 204–206, 208–209, 211
Diligent Prosecution, 505–508
Discharge, Clean Water Act, 203, 207, 209–210
Discharge Monitoring Reports, 427
Discharge of a Pollutant, Clean Water Act, 139–159, 429–430, 698–705
Distinct Population Segments, Endangered Species Act, 610–619
Donora, Pennsylvania, 222–240
Dormant Commerce Clause, U.S. Constitution, 56–58

E

Economic Benefit, Penalty Calculations, 436–442, 455–456
Effluent Limitation Guidelines, Clean Water Act, 172
Ehrlich, Paul, 25
Eleventh Amendment, U.S. Constitution, 49–50
Emission Controls, Automobiles, Clean Air Act, 379–388
Endangered Species Committee (God Squad), 646–648
Environmental Assessments, NEPA, 98
Environmental Audit Policy, 459
Environmental Impact Statements, NEPA, 92–93, 98–99, 120–134
Environmental Justice, 32–35, 559
Environmental Management Systems, 9
EPA Review of State–Issued Permits, Clean Water Act, 166–171
EPA Review of State Water Quality Standards, Clean Water Act, 188–190

Equitable Discretion, 429–436
Ethics, Environmental, 30–32
Exhaustion, 86–87
Existing Uses, Clean Water Act, 188, 191
Expanded Characteristic Option, RCRA, 411

F

Facility, CERCLA, 525
Federal/State Relationship, 9–10, 159–171, 201, 210–211, 211–212, 36–378, 469–475, 707, 720–721, 732–741
Federal Implementation Plans, Clean Air Act, 269, 270, 285
FERC Licenses, Applicability of Water Quality Certification Requirements, 209, 210
Finality, 84–86
Financial Responsibility Requirements, RCRA, 425
Fishable/swimmable Goal, Clean Water Act, 138, 187–188
Free Market Environmentalism, 5, 14
Fundamentally Different Factors Variance, Clean Water Act, 184

G

General Agreement on Tariffs and Trade, 780–781, 782–816
General Mining Act of 1872, 2, 13
General Permits, Clean Water Act, 717–722
Generator Liability, CERCLA, 541–547
Generator Requirements, RCRA, 412–416
Global Warming, 69–79, 243–252, 388, 759–780
Governmental Preclusion of Citizen Suits, see Preclusion
Greenhouse Gases, 69, 72–73, 76–78, 243–253, 388, 759–780
Groundwater Monitoring Requirements, RCRA, 417–421, 425
Gwaltney Doctrine, 476, 487–505

H

Habitat Conservation Plans, Endangered Species Act, 663–665
Hazard Ranking System, CERCLA, 565
Hazardous Air Pollutants, Clean Air Act, 339–351
Hazardous Substance, CERCLA, 523–525
Hazardous Waste, RCRA, 393–394, 408–411
Houck, Oliver, 138–139, 180, 187
Household Waste, RCRA, 410
How Clean is Clean, CERCLA, 565–568

HSWA, 393, 425

I

Imminent and Substantial Endangerments, 490, 523, 526
Incidental Takes, Endangered Species Act, 628, 663
Injunctive Relief, 429–436, 490–491
Injury in Fact, 61–79, 478–486
Innocent Landowner Defense, CERCLA, 530, 557–563
Interference, Clean Water Act, 187
Intergovernmental Panel on Climate Change, 761, 777
Interim Owners, CERCLA, 530
Interim Status, RCRA, 417
Interstate Transport, Clean Air Act, 269–285
Investigations, 426–427

J

Jeopardy, Endangered Species Act, 640–646
Joint and Several Liability, CERCLA, 547–556
Judicial Review, Generally, 82–90
Judicial Review of Administrative Orders, 443–448, 526
Judicial Review of Administrative Penalties, 458
Judicial Review of Consent Decrees, 573–579
Judicial Review of Permits, 171
Judicial Review of Rules, 402, 405
Jurisdiction, CERCLA, 523–525
Jurisdiction, Clean Water Act, 139–159, 667–705
Jurisdiction, RCRA, 393–411

K

Kyoto Protocol, 763–780

L

Land Ban, RCRA, 413, 425
Layla, Derek and the Dominos, 504–505
Lender Liability, CERCLA, 541
Lenity, the Rule of, 154, 156–157, 158
Leopold, Aldo, 30–32
Letters of Permission, Clean Water Act, 720–721
Liable Parties, CERCLA, 526–547
"Like Products," 785–786
Listed Waste, RCRA, 408–410
Listing, Endangered Species Act, 603–619, 622–625
Lomborg, Bjorn, 25–26

Love Canal, 522
Lowest Achievable Emission Rate, Clean Air Act, 289, 336

M

Major Federal Actions, NEPA, 110–113
Minnesota Environmental Protection Act, 134
Mitigation Under NEPA, 130–133
Mixing Zones, Clean Water Act, 198
Mixture Rule, RCRA, 410, 411
Mobile Sources, Clean Air Act, 379–388
Montreal Protocol on Substances that Deplete the Ozone Layer, 752–753
Mootness, 493, 495, 497–504
Mountaintop-removal/Valley-fill Mining, 741–745
Muir, John, 2

N

Narrative Permit Conditions, Enforceability Thereof, Clean Water Act, 193, 198–200
National Ambient Air Quality Standards, 243–266
National Contingency Plan, CERCLA, 525–526, 564–568, 580, 599–600
National Pollutant Discharge Elimination System, 138–201
National Priorities List, CERCLA, 523, 565, 580
Nationwide Permits, 717–720
Navigable Waters, Clean Water Act, 147–151, 668–698
Necessary and Proper Clause, U.S. Constitution, 37
New Source Performance Standards, Clean Air Act, 287, 288, 290–303
New Source Performance Standards, Clean Water Act, see Best Available Demonstrated Control Technology
New Source Review, Clean Air Act, 303–339
New York State Environmental Quality Review Act, 134
Nonbinding Preliminary Allocation of Liability, CERCLA, 571
Nonpoint Pollution, Clean Water Act, 151, 211–212, 214–221
Normal Farming Exemption, Clean Water Act, 705–706
Notice Letters, CERCLA, 568, 570–571
Notice Requirements, Citizen Suits, 477, 491, 493–494

O

Office of Information and Regulatory Affairs, 15, 81–82

Office of Management and Budget, 15, 17, 19–20, 81–82
Operator Liability, CERCLA, 531–541
Overfiling, 469–475
Ownership Liability, CERCLA, 527–530

P

Parent Corporations, Liability thereof Under CERCLA, 531–541
Pass Through, Clean Water Act, 187
Pedersen, William, 180–181
Permit Shield Doctrine, 167
Permitting Requirements, RCRA, 417
Personnel Training, RCRA, 415–416
Petroleum Exclusion, CERCLA, 524–525
Piercing the Corporate Veil, CERCLA, 531–541
Pinchot, Gifford, 2
Point Source, Clean Water Act, 151–159
Pollutant, Clean Water Act, 140, 143–147
Polluter Pays Principle, 24
Potentially Responsible Parties, CERCLA, see Liable Parties
Precautionary Principle, 26–30
Preclusion, 491–492, 493–494, 505–508
Preenforcement Review, 443–448, 526
Preliminary Investigation and Site Assessment, CERCLA, 564–565
Premium Payments, CERCLA, 569–570
Preservationism, 2
Presidential Oversight, 81–82
Pretreatment, Clean Water Act, 172, 186–187
Prevention of Significant Deterioration, Clean Air Act, 288, 303–336, 336–339
Private Party Cleanup and Cost Recovery, CERCLA, 523, 579–600
Privatization, 13–15
Project XL, 8–9
Property Clause, U.S. Constitution, 36
Prospective Purchaser Exclusion, CERCLA, 530, 559–561
Protectiveness, CERCLA, 567–568
Public Goods, 11–15
Public Welfare Offense Doctrine, 462–469
Publicly Owned Treatment Works, Clean Water Act, 172, 185–186

R

RCRA Civil Penalty Policy, 449–458
Recovery, Endangered Species Act, 622, 626
Reasonably Available Control Technology, Clean Air Act, 285, 289
Redressability, 496–497, 497–503
Release, CERCLA, 525
Remedial Action, CERCLA, 523, 565–568, 580
Remedial Investigation and Feasibility Study, CERCLA, 565–568, 570–571
Remedial Purpose Canon, 529

Removal Action, CERCLA, 523, 565, 580
Removal Credits, Clean Water Act, 187
Res Judicata, 475
Retroactivity, CERCLA, 529–530
Rio Declaration on Environment and Development, 751, 758
Ripeness, 88
Risk Analysis, 20–24
Rulemaking, 79–80

S

Sanctions for Failure to Produce an Adequate SIP, Clean Air Act, 285–287
Seminole Rock Deference, 90, 150–151, 220
Settlement, CERCLA, 526, 568–579
Skidmore Deference, 89–90, 141, 220
Small Handles Problem, NEPA, 110
Small Quantity Generators, RCRA, 412
Solid Waste, RCRA, 394–408
Speculative Accumulation, RCRA, 397
Spending Clause, U.S. Constitution, 36
Standing to Sue, 58–79, 477–487
State Environmental Policy Acts, 133–134
State Implementation Plans, Clean Air Act, 266–285
Statute of Limitations, 442, 458, 589
Stockholm Conference, The, 756–757, 758–759
Strict Liability, CERCLA, 527–529
Superfund, the, CERCLA, 522–523
Supplemental Environmental Projects, 458–459
Sustainable Development, 24–26
Swampbuster Program, 723–725

T

Takings, Endangered Species Act, 648–663
Takings Clause, U.S. Constitution, 50–54
Technology–Based Standards, Clean Water Act, 171–187
Tenth Amendment, U.S. Constitution, 48–49
Third–Party Defense, CERCLA, 557
Thoreau, Henry, 2
Threatened Release, CERCLA, 525
Title V Permit Program, Clean Air Act, 358–378
Total Maximum Daily Loads, Clean Water Act, 192, 196, 212–221
Toxicity Characteristic, RCRA, 409–410
Toxicity Characteristic Leachate Procedure, 409–410
Trading, Clean Air Act, 388–392
Tragedy of the Commons, 11–15
Trail Smelter Arbitration, 755
Treatment, Storage and Disposal Facilities, RCRA, 416–425

U

Unilateral Orders, see Administrative Orders

Unitary Waters Theory, Clean Water Act, 146

United Nations Convention on the Law of the Sea, 751

United Nations Environment Programme, 750, 752, 757

United Nations Framework Convention on Climate Change, 762–763, 777–779

Used Oil, RCRA, 403

V

Visibility Protection, Clean Air Act, 351–358

Voluntary Cleanup, CERCLA, 580–600

W

Waste Determination Requirement, RCRA, 413

Water Quality–Based Permit Conditions, Clean Water Act, 171, 192–201

Water Quality Certification, Clean Water Act, 201–211

Water Quality Criteria, Clean Water Act, 187, 188–189, 190, 205

Water Quality Standards, Clean Water Act, 187–192

Waters of the United States, Clean Water Act, see Navigable Waters

Wetland Delineation, Clean Water Act, 697–698

World Trade Organization, 781, 782–816

Z

Zone of Interests, 83–84

†